REFORMED
DOGMATICS

Herman Bavinck (1854–1921)
Graphite sketch by Erik G. Lubbers

REFORMED DOGMATICS

VOLUME 1: PROLEGOMENA

HERMAN BAVINCK

JOHN BOLT, GENERAL EDITOR
JOHN VRIEND, TRANSLATOR

Baker Academic

A Division of Baker Book House Co
Grand Rapids, Michigan 49516

© 2003 by the Dutch Reformed Translation Society
P.O. Box 7083, Grand Rapids, MI 49510

Published by Baker Academic
a division of Baker Book House Company
P.O. Box 6287, Grand Rapids, MI 49516-6287
www.bakeracademic.com

Second printing, July 2004

Printed in the United States of America

Library of Congress Cataloging-in-Publication Data
Bavinck, Herman, 1854–1921.
    [Gereformeerde dogmatiek. English]
    Reformed dogmatics / Herman Bavinck ; John Bolt, general editor ; John Vriend, translator.
       p. cm.
    Contents: v. 1. Prolegomena
    Includes bibliographical references and indexes.
    ISBN 0-8010-2632-6 (cloth : v. 1)
       1. Christelijke Gereformeerde Kerk (Netherlands)—Doctrines. 2. Reformed Church—Doctrines.
    3. Theology, Doctrinal. I. Bolt, John, 1947– II. Vriend, John, d. 2002. III. Title.
    BX9474.3.B38 2003
    230′.42—dc21   2003001037

Sketch of Herman Bavinck ©1996 by Erik G. Lubbers

CONTENTS

5

Dutch Reformed
Translation Society

"The Heritage of the Ages for Today"
P.O. Box 7083
Grand Rapids, MI 49510

BOARD OF DIRECTORS

PREFACE

The Dutch Reformed Translation Society (DRTS) was formed in 1994 by a group of businesspeople and professionals, pastors, and seminary professors, representing five different Reformed denominations, to sponsor the translation and facilitate the publication in English of classic Reformed theological and religious literature published in the Dutch language. It is incorporated as a nonprofit corporation in the State of Michigan and governed by a board of directors.

Believing that the Dutch Reformed tradition has many valuable works that deserve wider distribution than the limited accessibility of the Dutch language allows, society members seek to spread and strengthen the Reformed faith. The first project of the DRTS is the definitive translation of Herman Bavinck's complete four-volume *Gereformeerde Dogmatiek* (*Reformed Dogmatics*). The society invites those who share its commitment to and vision for spreading the Reformed faith to write for additional information.

ACKNOWLEDGMENTS

The editor here gratefully acknowledges the helpful suggestions of several board members of the Dutch Reformed Translation Society and particularly the contribution of Dr. M. Eugene Osterhaven, emeritus Albertus C. Van Raalte Professor of Systematic Theology at Western Theological Seminary, Holland, Michigan. Dr. Osterhaven carefully read a number of chapters and made many helpful translation and stylistic suggestions as well as critical corrections. Calvin Theological Seminary Ph.D. student Rev. J. Mark Beach put in many hours checking bibliographic information, and CTS students Patricia Vesely and Courtney Hoekstra provided superb support in producing the final bibliography during the long summer of 2002. Finally, the efforts of each of these assistants were immeasurably helped by the theological librarians at Calvin College's Hekman Library, Paul Fields and Lugene Schemper. To all, a heartfelt thanks.

The satisfaction of seeing this volume finally in print is mixed with sadness because John Vriend, whose initiative led to the formation of the Dutch Reformed Translation Society and who ably served as the translator of all four volumes of the *Reformed Dogmatics,* was unable to see this fruit of his labors. John Vriend went to be with his Lord on February 7, 2002.

John Bolt

Editor's Introduction

With the publication of this first full volume of Herman Bavinck's *Reformed Dogmatics,* the Dutch Reformed Translation Society has reached a significant milestone in its decade-long project to publish the complete English translation from Dutch of Bavinck's classic four-volume work. Prior to this, two half-volume works, one on the eschatology unit[1] and the other on the creation unit[2] had been published. The present volume is a translation of the entire first volume of Herman Bavinck's magisterial work, material never before translated into English. A word or two on Bavinck the man and the theologian are in order at this point. Who was Herman Bavinck, and why is this work of theology so important?

Herman Bavinck's *Gereformeerde Dogmatiek,* first published one hundred years ago, represents the concluding high point of some four centuries of remarkably productive Dutch Reformed theological reflection. From Bavinck's numerous citations of key Dutch Reformed theologians such as Voetius, De Moor, Vitringa, van Mastricht, Witsius, and Walaeus as well as of the important Leiden *Synopsis purioris theologiae,*[3] it is clear he knew that tradition well and claimed it as his own. At the same time it also needs to be noted that Bavinck was not simply a chronicler of his own church's past teaching. He seriously engaged other theological traditions, notably the Roman Catholic and the modern liberal Protestant ones, effectively mined the church fathers

---

1. Herman Bavinck, *The Last Things: Hope for This World and the Next,* ed. John Bolt and trans. John Vriend (Grand Rapids: Baker, 1996). This volume represented the second half of volume 4 of the *Gereformeerde Dogmatiek.*

2. Herman Bavinck, *In the Beginning: Foundations of Creation Theology,* ed. John Bolt and trans. John Vriend (Grand Rapids: Baker, 1999). This volume represented the second half of volume 2 of the *Gereformeerde Dogmatiek.*

3. The Leiden *Synopsis,* first published in 1625, is a large manual of Reformed doctrine as it was defined by the Synod of Dordt. It served as a standard reference textbook for the study of Reformed theology well into the twentieth century. (It is even cited by Karl Barth in his *Church Dogmatics.*) As an original-source reference work of classic Dutch Reformed theology, it is comparable to Heinrich Heppe's nineteenth-century, more broadly continental anthology *Reformed Dogmatics* (London: Allen & Unwin, 1950). While serving as the minister of a Christian Reformed church in Franeker, Friesland, Bavinck edited the sixth and final edition of this handbook, which was published in 1881.

and great medieval thinkers, and placed his own distinct neo-Calvinist stamp on the Reformed Dogmatics.

KAMPEN AND LEIDEN

To understand the distinct Bavinck flavor, a brief historical orientation is necessary. Herman Bavinck was born on December 13, 1854. His father was an influential minister in the Dutch Christian Reformed Church (Christelijke Gereformeerde Kerk) that had seceded from the National Reformed Church in the Netherlands twenty years earlier.[4] The secession of 1834 was in the first place a protest against the state control of the Dutch Reformed Church; it also tapped into a long and rich tradition of ecclesiastical dissent on matters of doctrine, liturgy, and spirituality as well as polity. In particular, mention needs to be made here of the Dutch equivalent to English Puritanism, the so-called Second Reformation[5] (*Nadere Reformatie*), the influential seventeenth- and early-eighteenth-century movement of experiential Reformed theology and spirituality,[6] as well as an early-nineteenth-century international, aristocratic, evangelical revival movement known as the *Réveil*.[7] Bavinck's church, his family, and his own spirituality were thus definitively shaped by strong patterns of deep pietistic Reformed spirituality. It is also important to note that though the earlier phases of Dutch pietism affirmed orthodox Reformed theology and were also nonseparatist in their ecclesiology, by the mid–nineteenth century the Seceder group had become significantly separatist and sectarian in outlook.[8]

The second major influence on Bavinck's thought comes from the period of his theological training at the University of Leiden. The Christian Reformed Church had its own theological seminary, the Kampen Theological

---

4. For a brief description of the background and character of the Secession church, see James D. Bratt, *Dutch Calvinism in Modern America* (Grand Rapids: Eerdmans, 1984), chap. 1, "Secession and Its Tangents."

5. See Joel R. Beeke, "The Dutch Second Reformation (*Nadere Reformatie*)," *Calvin Theological Journal* 28 (1993): 298–327.

6. The crowning theological achievement of the *Nadere Reformatie* is the devout and theologically rich work of Wilhelmus à Brakel, *Redelijke Godsdienst,* first published in 1700 and frequently thereafter (including twenty Dutch editions in the eighteenth century alone!). This work is now available in English translation: *The Christian's Reasonable Service,* trans. Bartel Elshout, 4 vols. (Ligonier, Pa.: Soli Deo Gloria, 1992–95).

7. The standard work on the *Réveil* is M. Elizabeth Kluit, *Het Protestantse Réveil in Nederland en Daarbuiten, 1815–1865* (Amsterdam: Paris, 1970). Bratt also gives a brief summary in *Dutch Calvinism in Modern America,* 10–13.

8. Bavinck himself called attention to this in his Kampen rectoral oration of 1888 when he complained that the Seceder emigration to America was a spiritual withdrawal and abandonment of "the Fatherland as lost to unbelief" ("The Catholicity of Christianity and the Church," trans. John Bolt, *Calvin Theological Journal* 27 [1992]: 246). Recent historical scholarship, however, suggests that this note of separatism and cultural alienation must not be exaggerated. Though clearly a marginalized community in the Netherlands, the Seceders were not indifferent to educational, social, and political responsibilities. See John Bolt, "Nineteenth- and Twentieth-Century Dutch Reformed Church and Theology: A Review Article," *Calvin Theological Journal* 28 (1993): 434–42.

School, established in 1854. Bavinck, after studying at Kampen for one year (1873–74), indicated his desire to study with the University of Leiden's theological faculty, a faculty renowned for its aggressively modernist, "scientific" approach to theology.[9] His church community, including his parents, was stunned by this decision, which Bavinck explained as a desire "to become acquainted with the modern theology firsthand" and to receive "a more scientific training than the Theological School is presently able to provide."[10] The Leiden experience gave rise to what Bavinck perceived as the tension in his life between his commitment to orthodox theology and spirituality and his desire to understand and appreciate what he could about the modern world, including its worldview and culture. A telling and poignant entry in his personal journal at the beginning of his study period at Leiden (September 23, 1874) indicates his concern about being faithful to the faith he had publicly professed in the Christian Reformed church of Zwolle in March of that same year: "Will I remain standing [in the faith]? God grant it."[11] Upon completion of his doctoral work at Leiden in 1880, Bavinck candidly acknowledged the spiritual impoverishment that Leiden had cost him: "Leiden has benefited me in many ways: I hope always to acknowledge that gratefully. But it has also greatly impoverished me, robbed me, not only of much ballast (for which I am happy), but also of much that I recently, especially when I preach, recognize as vital for my own spiritual life."[12]

It is thus not unfair to characterize Bavinck as a man between two worlds. One of his contemporaries once described Bavinck as "a Secession preacher and a representative of modern culture," concluding: "That was a striking characteristic. In that duality is found Bavinck's significance. That duality is also a reflection of the tension—at times crisis—in Bavinck's life. In many respects it is a simple matter to be a preacher in the Secession Church, and, in a certain sense, it is also not that difficult to be a modern person. But in no way is it a simple matter to be the one as well as the other."[13] However, it is not necessary to rely only on the testimony of others. Bavinck summarizes

9. For an overview of the major schools of Dutch Reformed theology in the nineteenth century, see James Hutton MacKay, *Religious Thought in Holland during the Nineteenth Century* (London: Hodder & Stoughton, 1911). For more detailed discussion of the "modernist" school, see K. H. Roessingh, *De Moderne Theologie in Nederland: Hare Voorbereiding en Eerste Periode* (Groningen: Van der Kamp, 1915); Eldred C. Vanderlaan, *Protestant Modernism in Holland* (London and New York: Oxford University Press, 1924).

10. R. H. Bremmer, *Herman Bavinck en Zijn Tijdgenoten* (Kampen: Kok, 1966), 20; cf. V. Hepp, *Dr. Herman Bavinck* (Amsterdam: W. Ten Have, 1921), 30.

11. Bremmer, *Herman Bavinck en Zijn Tijdgenoten*, 19.

12. Hepp, *Dr. Herman Bavinck*, 84.

13. Cited by Jan Veenhof, *Revelatie en Inspiratie* (Amsterdam: Buijten & Schipperheijn, 1968), 108. The contemporary cited is the Reformed jurist A. Anema, who was a colleague of Bavinck at the Free University of Amsterdam. A similar assessment of Bavinck as a man between two poles is given by F. H. von Meyenfeldt, "Prof. Dr. Herman Bavinck: 1854–1954, 'Christus en de Cultuur,'" *Polemios* 9 (October 15, 1954); and G. W. Brillenburg-Wurth, "Bavincks Levensstrijd," *Gereformeerde Weekblad* 10.25 (December 17, 1954).

this tension in his own thought clearly in an essay on the great nineteenth-century liberal Protestant theologian Albrecht Ritschl:

> Therefore, whereas salvation in Christ was formerly considered primarily a means to separate man from sin and the world, to prepare him for heavenly blessedness and to cause him to enjoy undisturbed fellowship with God there, Ritschl posits the very opposite relationship: the purpose of salvation is precisely to enable a person, once he is freed from the oppressive feeling of sin and lives in the awareness of being a child of God, to exercise his earthly vocation and fulfill his moral purpose in this world. The antithesis, therefore, is fairly sharp: on the one side, a Christian life that considers the highest goal, now and hereafter, to be the contemplation of God and fellowship with him, and for that reason (always being more or less hostile to the riches of an earthly life) is in danger of falling into monasticism and asceticism, pietism and mysticism; but on the side of Ritschl, a Christian life that considers its highest goal to be the kingdom of God, that is, the moral obligation of mankind, and for that reason (always being more or less adverse to the withdrawal into solitude and quiet communion with God), is in danger of degenerating into a cold Pelagianism and an unfeeling moralism. Personally, I do not yet see any way of combining the two points of view, but I do know that there is much that is excellent in both, and that both contain undeniable truth.[14]

A certain tension in Bavinck's thought between the claims of modernity, particularly its this-worldly, scientific orientation, and Reformed pietist orthodoxy's tendency to stand aloof from modern culture, continues to play a role even in his mature theology expressed in the *Reformed Dogmatics*. In his eschatology, for example, Bavinck in a highly nuanced way still continues to speak favorably of certain emphases in a Ritschlian this-worldly perspective.[15]

In Bavinck's creation theology we see the tension repeatedly in his relentless efforts to understand and, where he finds appropriate, either to affirm, correct, or repudiate modern scientific claims in light of scriptural and Christian teaching.[16] Bavinck takes modern philosophy (Kant, Schelling, Hegel), Darwin, and the claims of geological and biological science seriously but never uncritically. His willingness as a theologian to engage modern thought and science seriously is a hallmark of his exemplary work. It goes without saying that though Bavinck's theological framework remains a valu-

---

14. H. Bavinck, "De Theologie van Albrecht Ritschl," *Theologische Studiën* 6 (1888): 397. Cited by Veenhof, *Revelatie en Inspiratie,* 346–47, emphasis added by Veenhof. Kenneth Kirk contends that this tension, which he characterizes as one between "rigorism" and "humanism," is a fundamental conflict in the history of Christian ethics from the outset. See K. Kirk, *The Vision of God* (London: Longmans, Green, 1931), 7–8.

15. Bavinck, *The Last Things,* 161 (*Reformed Dogmatics,* #578). According to Bavinck, Ritschl's this-worldliness "stands for an important truth" over against what he calls the "abstract supernatualism of the Greek Orthodox and Roman Catholic Church."

16. Bavinck, *In the Beginning,* passim (*Reformed Dogmatics,* ##250–306).

able guide for contemporary readers, many of the specific scientific issues he addresses in this volume are dated by his own late nineteenth-century context. As Bavinck's own work illustrates so well, today's Reformed theologians and scientists learn not by repristination but by fresh address to new and contemporary challenges.

GRACE AND NATURE

It is therefore too simple merely to characterize Bavinck as a man trapped between two apparently incommensurate tugs at his soul, that of otherworldly pietism and this-worldly modernism. His heart and mind sought a trinitarian synthesis of Christianity and culture, a Christian worldview that incorporated what was best and true in both pietism and modernism, while above all honoring the theological and confessional richness of the Reformed tradition dating from Calvin. After commenting on the breakdown of the great medieval synthesis and the need for contemporary Christians to acquiesce in that breakdown, Bavinck expressed his hope for a new and better synthesis: "In this situation, the hope is not unfounded that a synthesis is possible between Christianity and culture, however antagonistic they may presently stand over against each other. If God has truly come to us in Christ, and is, in this age too, the Preserver and Ruler of all things, such a synthesis is not only possible but also necessary and shall surely be effected in its own time."[17] Bavinck found the vehicle for such an attempted synthesis in the trinitarian worldview of Dutch neo-Calvinism and became, along with neo-Calvinism's visionary pioneer Abraham Kuyper,[18] one of its chief and most respected spokespersons as well as its premier theologian.

Unlike Bavinck, Abraham Kuyper grew up in the National Reformed Church of the Netherlands in a congenially moderate-modernist context. Kuyper's student years, also at Leiden, confirmed him in his modernist orientation until a series of experiences, especially during his years as a parish minister, brought about a dramatic conversion to Reformed, Calvinist orthodoxy.[19] From that time Kuyper became a vigorous opponent of the mod-

17. H. Bavinck, *Het Christendom*, in the series *Groote Godsdiensten*, vol. 2, no. 7 (Baarn: Hollandia, 1912), 60.

18. For a brief overview, see J. Bratt, *Dutch Calvinism in Modern America*, chap. 2, "Abraham Kuyper and Neo-Calvinism."

19. Kuyper chronicles these experiences in a revealing autobiographical work entitled *Confidentie* (Amsterdam: Höveker, 1873). A rich portrait of the young Abraham Kuyper is given by G. Puchinger, *Abraham Kuyper: De Jonge Kuyper (1837–1867)* (Franeker: T. Wever, 1987). See also the somewhat hagiographic biography of Kuyper by Frank Vandenberg (Grand Rapids: Eerdmans, 1960) and the more theologically and historically substantive one by Louis Praamsma, *Let Christ Be King: Reflection on the Times and Life of Abraham Kuyper* (Jordan Station, Ont.: Paideia, 1985). Brief accounts can also be found in Benjamin B. Warfield's introduction to A. Kuyper, *Encyclopedia of Sacred Theology: Its Principles*, trans. J. H. De Vries (New York: Charles Scribner's, 1898), and the translator's biographical note in A. Kuyper, *To Be Near to God*, trans. J. H. De Vries (Grand Rapids: Eerdmans, 1925).

ern spirit in church and society[20]—which he characterized by the siren call of the French Revolution, "Ni Dieu! Ni maitre!"[21]—seeking every avenue to oppose it with an alternative worldview, or as he called it, the "life-system" of Calvinism:

> From the first, therefore, I have always said to myself, "if the battle is to be fought with honor and with a hope of victory, then principle must be arrayed against principle; then it must be felt that in Modernism the vast energy of an all-embracing life-system assails us, then also it must be understood that we have to take our stand in a life-system of equally comprehensive and far-reaching power. . . . When thus taken, I found and confessed and I still hold, that this manifestation of the Christian principle is given us in Calvinism. In Calvinism my heart has found rest. From Calvinism have I drawn the inspiration firmly and resolutely to take my stand in the thick of this great conflict of principles.["][22]

Kuyper's aggressive, this-worldly form of Calvinism was rooted in a trinitarian theological vision. The "dominating principle" of Calvinism, he contended, "was not soteriologically, justification by faith, but in the widest sense cosmologically, the Sovereignty of the Triune God over the whole Cosmos, in all its spheres and kingdoms, visible and invisible."[23]

For Kuyper, this fundamental principle of divine sovereignty led to four important derivatory and related doctrines or principles: common grace, antithesis, sphere sovereignty, and the distinction between the church as institute and the church as organism. The doctrine of common grace[24] is based on the conviction that prior to and, to a certain extent, independent of the particular sovereignty of divine grace in redemption there is a universal divine sovereignty in creation and providence, restraining the effects of sin and bestowing general gifts on all people, thus making human society and culture possible even among the unredeemed. Cultural life is rooted in creation and common grace and thus has a life of its own apart from the church.

---

20. See especially his famous address, *Het Modernisme, een Fata Morgana op Christelijke Gebied* (Amsterdam: De Hoogh, 1871). On page 52 of this work he acknowledges that he, too, once dreamed the dreams of modernism. This important essay is now available in English translation: J. Bratt, ed., *Abraham Kuyper: A Centennial Reader* (Grand Rapids: Eerdmans, 1998), 87–124.

21. A. Kuyper, *Lectures on Calvinism* (Grand Rapids: Eerdmans, 1931), 10.

22. Ibid., 11–12.

23. Ibid., 79.

24. Kuyper's own position is developed in his *De Gemeene Gratie*, 3 vols. (Amsterdam and Pretoria: Höveker & Wormser, 1902). A thorough examination of Kuyper's views can be found in S. U. Zuidema, "Common Grace and Christian Action in Abraham Kuyper," in *Communication and Confrontation* (Toronto: Wedge, 1971), 52–105. Cf. J. Ridderbos, *De Theologische Cultuurbeschouwing van Abraham Kuyper* (Kampen: Kok, 1947). The doctrine of common grace has been much debated among conservative Dutch Reformed folk in the Netherlands and the United States, tragically leading to church divisions. For an overview of the doctrine in the Reformed tradition, see H. Kuiper, *Calvin on Common Grace* (Goes: Oostebaan & Le Cointre, 1928).

This same insight is expressed more directly via the notion of sphere sovereignty. Kuyper was opposed to all Anabaptist and ascetic Christian versions of world-flight but was also equally opposed to the medieval Roman Catholic synthesis of culture and church. The various spheres of human activity—family, education, business, science, art—do not derive their raison d'être and the shape of their life from redemption or from the church, but from the law of God the Creator. They are thus relatively autonomous—also from the interference of the state—and are directly responsible to God.[25] In this regard Kuyper clearly distinguished two different understandings of the church—the church as institute gathered around the Word and sacraments and the church as organism diversely spread out in the manifold vocations of life. It is not explicitly as members of the institutional church but as members of the body of Christ, organized in Christian communal activity (schools, political parties, labor unions, institutions of mercy) that believers live out their earthly vocations. Though aggressively this-worldly, Kuyper was an avowed and articulate opponent of the *volkskerk* tradition, which tended to merge national sociocultural identity with that of a theocratic church ideal.[26]

Though Kuyper is best known for his social and political role in Dutch life—as a journalist, founder of a university (*The Free University of Amsterdam*), founder and long-time leader of a Christian political party (The Antirevolutionary Party), and finally as Dutch prime minister from 1901–5— it must not be forgotten that he was first a church reformer. His first publications and initial political activity were calls for reform of the national church, reforms that would make it a more orthodox Reformed church committed to its confessions and also to its polity.[27] Dutch neo-Calvinism contended for the heart and the mind of the Dutch people, and Bavinck's theology did so as well. Dutch neo-Calvinism was closely allied with the orthodox party in the Dutch Reformed community; however, its vision was not limited to the church but embraced the entire world of thought, the arts, the professions, education, culture, society, and politics. The *Reformed Dogmatics* is indeed churchly and confessional in tone and character, but it is not sectarian or aloof from the difficult questions of the modern era. Like Kuyper, Bavinck is appreciative of much in the modern world but not uncritically so.

25. "In this independent character a special *higher authority* is of necessity involved and this highest authority we intentionally call—*sovereignty in the individual social sphere,* in order that it may be sharply and decidedly expressed that these different developments of social life have *nothing above themselves but God,* and that the state cannot intrude here, and has nothing to command in their domain" (Kuyper, *Lectures on Calvinism,* 91).

26. On Kuyper's ecclesiology, see H. Zwaanstra, "Abraham Kuyper's Conception of the Church," *Calvin Theological Journal* 9 (1974): 149–81; on his attitude toward the *volkskerk* tradition, see H. J. Langman, *Kuyper en de Volkskerk* (Kampen: Kok, 1950).

27. The literature on Kuyper's view of the church, including a discussion of Kuyper's own treatises, can be found in Zwaanstra, "Abraham Kuyper's Conception of the Church."

To state this differently: Kuyper's emphasis on common grace, used polemically to motivate pious, orthodox Dutch Reformed Christians to Christian social, political, and cultural activity, must never be seen in isolation
from his equally strong emphasis on the spiritual antithesis. The regenerat-
ing work of the Holy Spirit breaks humanity in two and creates, according
to Kuyper, "two kinds of consciousness, that of the regenerate and the unregenerate; and these two cannot be identical." Furthermore, these "two kinds
of people" will develop "two kinds of science." The conflict in the scientific
enterprise is not between science and faith but between "two scientific systems . . . each having its own faith."[28]

It is here in this trinitarian, world-affirming, but nonetheless resolutely
antithetical Calvinism that Bavinck found the resources to bring some unity
to his thought.[29] "The thoughtful person," he notes, "places the doctrine of
the Trinity in the very center of the full-orbed life of nature and mankind. . . . The mind of the Christian is not satisfied until every form of existence has been referred to the Triune God and until the confession of the
Trinity has received the place of prominence in all our life and thought."[30]
Repeatedly in his writings Bavinck defines the essence of the Christian religion in a trinitarian, creation-affirming way. A typical formulation: "The essence of the Christian religion consists in the reality that the creation of the
Father, ruined by sin, is restored in the death of the Son of God and re-
created by the grace of the Holy Spirit into a kingdom of God."[31] Put more
simply, the fundamental theme that shapes Bavinck's entire theology is the
trinitarian idea that grace restores nature.[32]

The evidence for "grace restores nature" being the fundamental defining
and shaping theme of Bavinck's theology is not hard to find. In an important address on common grace, given in 1888 at the Kampen Theological
School, Bavinck sought to impress on his Christian Reformed audience the
importance of Christian sociocultural activity. He appealed to the doctrine
of creation, insisting that its diversity is not removed by redemption but
cleansed. "Grace does not remain outside or above or beside nature but
rather permeates and wholly renews it. And thus nature, reborn by grace,

28. Kuyper, *Lectures on Calvinism,* 133; cf. *Encyclopedia of Sacred Theology,* 150–82. A helpful discussion of Kuyper's view of science is given by Del Ratzsch, "Abraham Kuyper's Philosophy of Science,"
Calvin Theological Journal 27 (1992): 277–303.

29. The relation between Bavinck and Kuyper, including differences as well as commonalities, is dis-
cussed in greater detail in John Bolt, "The Imitation of Christ Theme in the Cultural-Ethical Ideal of
Herman Bavinck" (Ph.D. diss., University of St. Michael's College, Toronto, 1982), especially chap. 3:
"Herman Bavinck as a Neo-Calvinist Thinker."

30. H. Bavinck, *The Doctrine of God,* trans. W. Hendriksen (Grand Rapids: Eerdmans, 1951), 329
(*Reformed Dogmatics,* #231).

31. See below, p. 112.

32. This is the conclusion of Veenhof, *Revelatie en Inspiratie,* 346; and Eugene Heideman, *The Relation of Revelation and Reason in E. Brunner and H. Bavinck* (Assen: Van Gorcum, 1959), 191, 195. See
Bavinck, *The Last Things,* 200 n. 4 (*Reformed Dogmatics,* #572).

will be brought to its highest revelation. That situation will again return in which we serve God freely and happily, without compulsion or fear, simply out of love, and in harmony with our true nature. That is the genuine *religio naturalis.*" In other words: "Christianity does not introduce a single substantial foreign element into the creation. It creates no new cosmos but rather makes the cosmos new. It restores what was corrupted by sin. It atones the guilty and cures what is sick; the wounded it heals."[33]

PROLEGOMENA

This entire first volume—one quarter of Bavinck's full exposition—deals with the introductory matters of definition and method, commonly called "theological prolegomena." We have chosen to retain the title "Reformed Dogmatics" because it underscores Bavinck's firm commitment to Reformed orthodoxy. Above all this is rooted in a high view of Scripture as divine revelation. Dogmatics, according to Bavinck, is the knowledge that God has revealed in his Word to his church concerning himself and all creatures as they stand in relation to him. Though modern thought tends to devalue all dogma, Bavinck observes that is not a general objection to dogma as such but rather a rejection of certain dogmas and an affirmation of others.

Standing commitedly in a particular tradition of Christian orthodoxy did not hinder Bavinck from a thorough and honest engagement with modern thought. In particular, Bavinck again and again addresses the Kantian claim that God cannot be known and the subsequent effort to maintain the study of theology as a form of human religious experience. This issue was an important practical-existential issue for the nineteenth-century Dutch Reformed church as well as an interesting philosophical and theological question. Bavinck indicates his thorough acquaintance with post-Kantian thought in his discussion of the *principia* (fundamentals of thought) in chapters 7 and 8 and especially in the detailed discussion of theological method in chapter 15. Yet, the ecclesiastical and academic context in which these questions lived and moved and had their being was the 1876 Law Concerning Higher Education, which effectively turned university theology faculties into departments of religious studies.[34] Rather than a confessionally normative dogmatic theology, a neutral, phenomenological approach to religion was mandated by law. The response of the more pietist Reformed community in the Netherlands was to create specific, confessionally oriented theological schools such as the one at Kampen. Though Bavinck taught at the Kampen seminary for some twenty years, his ideal of a scientific theology required a university setting. Thus, when the attempted unification of

33. H. Bavinck, "Common Grace," trans. Raymond Van Leeuwen, *Calvin Theological Journal* 24 (1989): 59–60, 61.

34. On the 1876 law and its role in bringing about the Free University of Amsterdam, see A. J. Rasker, *De Nederlandse Hervormde Kerk vanaf 1795,* 2d ed. (Kampen: Kok, 1981), 179ff.

theological education in the newly formed union church (*Gereformeerde Kerk in Nederland;* formed in 1892 from a union of the Secession church and Abraham Kuyper's *Doleantie* group) failed, Bavinck left Kampen and took a post at Kuyper's Free University of Amsterdam. The tension in Bavinck's mind and heart were also played out in his life.

Bavinck follows the traditional organization of orthodox Reformed theology into six loci: doctrine of God, humanity, Christ, salvation, the church, last things. What makes this prolegomena distinctive is the extent to which Bavinck confronts the profound epistemological crisis of post-Enlightenment modernity. Not only the Kantian denial of true god-knowledge but also the varied attempts to construct alternatives that simply accept the divorce of religion and knowledge (theology and science) are dealt with in detail. Bavinck is familiar with such new efforts of the history of religions school (e.g., Troeltsch) and provides able critique. At the same time he also makes use of insights gained from a more phenomenological approach to religion, particularly acknowledging, even insisting, that all religious conviction is born in concrete, historical religions, in the narratives of communities of faith. Though Christianity is the true narrative, it does not have a special, spiritual access to God apart from the mediation of the church and its proclamation, apart from the discipleship exercised by the community of faith.

What may be Bavinck's most incisive contribution to theological prolegomena is his discussion of certainty in chapter 2 and in chapter 16. Whereas modernity sought certainty only in the confidence of sense perception and that which can be deduced by autonomous reason, Bavinck insists that believing is itself a form of certainty. All religion is based on authority and thus on revelation. Christian dogmatics depends on the truth of Scripture as the revelation of God himself. While we are all, Christians included, influenced by our environment and upbringing, the Christian claim is that we are able to some degree to distance ourselves from our immediate limitations because God has not only addressed us in Scripture but become incarnate among us. As John writes, "We have seen . . ." (1 John 1:1–3).

Yet this does not lead Bavinck to approve of a strictly "biblical theology." In fact, he contends that this is impossible. Even efforts to be purely "biblical" reflect the ecclesiastical and social environment in which they arise. A proper theological method thus must take Scripture, Christian tradition, and Christian consciousness seriously as resources. Hence, the term "dogmatic theology" is appropriate since it reflects the normative reality that theology arises from faith and seeks to serve the community of faith.

While theology is rooted in faith and serves the community of faith, not all reflection on faith is theology, properly speaking. Dogmatic theology is a science; it is a disciplined, rigorous, systematic study of the knowledge of God. Strictly speaking not every believer is or needs to be a theologian. The long history of theology parallels the life-history of the church but is not identical with it. In that connection, Bavinck's lengthy discussion of the history of dogmatics (chapters 3–6) has few parallels in any single volume published more recently.[35] The four chapters (9–12) on revelation are also of special relevance to the debate about revelation, perhaps the single most discussed theological issue of the twentieth century.[36] What I am suggesting here is that, though it is a century old, Bavinck's *Reformed Dogmatics* continues to be relevant to many issues still discussed in theology today.

In sum, Bavinck's *Reformed Dogmatics* is biblically and confessionally faithful, pastorally sensitive, challenging, and still relevant. Bavinck's life and thought reflect a serious effort to be pious, orthodox, and thoroughly contemporary. To pietists fearful of the modern world on the one hand and to critics of orthodoxy skeptical about its continuing relevance on the other, Bavinck's example suggests a model answer: an engaging trinitarian vision of Christian discipleship in God's world.

In conclusion, a few words are needed about the editing decisions that govern this translated volume, which is based on the second, expanded edition of the *Gereformeerde Dogmatiek*.[37] The seventeen chapters of this volume correspond to twenty-three in the original (called "paragraphs" in the Dutch edition), the major difference being the division of Bavinck's original chapter 5 (with its six subdivisions) into four distinct chapters (chapters 3–6 of the English edition) and the combination of several shorter chapters into one. This volume also has five parts instead of the original four. Bavinck's original chapter 5, which was in the first part, is now its own part, "The History and Literature of Dogmatics." The headings subdividing each chapter are new. These, along with the chapter synopses, which are also not in the original, have been supplied by the editor. All Bavinck's original footnotes have been retained and brought up to contemporary bibliographic standards. Additional notes added by the editor are clearly marked. All works from the nineteenth century to the present are noted with full bibliographic information given in the first note of each chapter and with subsequent references abbreviated. Classic works produced prior to the nineteenth century (the church fathers, Aquinas's *Summa,* Calvin's *Institutes,* post-Reformation Protestant and Catholic works) for which there are often numerous editions are cited only by author, title, and standard notation of sections. More complete information for the original or an accessible edition for each is given in the bibliography appended at the end of this volume. Where English transla-

---

35. The one exception here is Otto Weber's treatment in volume 1 of *Foundations of Dogmatics,* trans. Darrell L. Guder (Grand Rapids: Eerdmans, 1981), I, chaps. III–VI.

36. An excellent overview of the various options set forth on the doctrine of revelation is Avery Dulles, *Models of Revelation* (Garden City, N.Y.: Image Books, 1983). For a more recent discussion from a more philosophical perspective, see Nicholas Wolterstorff, *Divine Discourse: Philosophical Reflections on the Claim That God Speaks* (New York and Cambridge: Cambridge University Press, 1995).

37. The four volumes of the first edition of *Gereformeerde Dogmatiek* were published in the years 1895 through 1901. The second revised and expanded edition appeared between 1906 and 1911; the third edition, unaltered from the second, in 1918; the fourth, unaltered except for different pagination, in 1928.

tions of foreign titles were available and could be consulted, they have been used rather than the original. Unless indicated in the note by direct reference to a specific translation, translations of Latin, Greek, German, and French material are those of the translator taken directly from Bavinck's original text. References in the notes and bibliography that are incomplete or could not be confirmed are marked with an asterisk (*). To facilitate comparison with the Dutch original, this English edition retains the subparagraph numbers (##1–160 in square brackets) used in the second and subsequent Dutch editions. Internal cross-references cite the page number; cross-references to other volumes of the *Reformed Dogmatics* cite the subparagraph number.

PART I

INTRODUCTION TO DOGMATICS

1

THE SCIENCE
OF DOGMATIC THEOLOGY

The orderly study of the truths of the Christian faith has been described by many different terms. The designator "dogmatics" has the advantage of anchoring such study in the normative teachings or dogmas of the church. Dogmas are only those truths properly set forth in Scripture as things to be believed. A truth confessed by the church is not a dogma because the church recognizes it but solely because it rests on God's authority. Still, religious dogma is always a combination of divine authority and churchly confession. Dogmas are truths acknowledged by a particular group. Though the church's dogmas have authority only if they are truly God's truths, church teaching is never identical with divine truth itself. At the same time, it is a mistake to devalue most dogma as impermanent aberrations from the pure essence of a nondogmatic gospel, as some modern theologians do. Opposition to dogma is not a general objection to dogma as such but a rejection of specific dogmas judged unacceptable by some. Thus, theology after Kant denies dogmas rooted in a science of God because of the modern dogma that God is unknowable. Dogmas rooted in morality or religious experience are then substituted in their place. However, from the viewpoint of Christian orthodoxy, dogmatics is the knowledge that God has revealed in his Word to his church concerning himself and all creatures as they stand in relation to him. Though objections to this definition in the name of faith often miss the mark, it must never be forgotten that the knowledge of God, which is the true object of dogmatic theology, is only obtained by faith. God cannot be known by us apart from revelation received in faith. Dogmatics seeks nothing other than to be true to the faith-knowledge given in this revelation. Dogmatics is thus not the science of faith or of religion but the science about God. The task of the dogmatician is to think God's thoughts after him and to trace their unity. This is a task that must be done in the confidence that God has spoken, in humble submission to the church's teaching tradition, and for communicating the gospel's message to the world.

The proper place of dogmatics in the larger encyclopedia of theological study is not a matter of great debate. The main issue here has to do with the relation between dogmatic theology and philosophy. Neither the subjection of dogmatics to philosophical presuppositions nor the dualistic separation of confessional theology from the scientific study of religion is acceptable. Such a split fractures the *lives of theology professors and pastors alike. Efforts to "rescue" religious studies from the acids of modernistic philosophy are a favor the church cannot afford to accept. All knowledge is rooted in faith and all faith includes an important element of knowing. The task of dogmatic theology, in the final analysis, is nothing other than a scientific exposition of religious truth grounded in sacred Scripture. Apologetic defense of this truth and ethical applications to Christian conduct both are based in and **proceed from** divine revelation and faith; they do not **ground** or shape faith. Dogmatics and ethics are a unity, though they may be treated as distinct disciplines. Dogmatics describes God's deeds for and in us; ethics describes what renewed human beings now do on the basis of and in the strength of these deeds.*

TERMINOLOGY

[1] The term *dogmatics* is of relatively recent date. In the past numerous other designations were in use. Origen entitled his main dogmatic work *On First Principles* (Περι Ἀρχων). Theognostus, one of Origen's successors at the school in Alexandria, chose for his work—since lost—the title *Outlines,* and Lactantius spoke of *The Divine Institutes.* Augustine expanded the title of his *Little Handbook* or *Enchiridion* with the words *On Faith, Hope and Love.* John of Damascus published an *Exact Treatise on the Orthodox Faith.* First surfacing in the work of Isodore of Seville (c. 560–636), the term *Sentences* in the thirteenth century gave way to *Summa Theologiae.* Melanchthon spoke of *Common Places* (*Loci Communes*). The term *loci* was borrowed from Cicero and served to translate the Greek word τοποι. By τοποι Aristotle meant the general rules of dialectic that were known "of themselves" and "established" and could therefore serve as "elements of proofs."[1] Transferring this theory of the τοποι from dialectics to rhetoric, Cicero used the term for the general rules or places where a rhetorician could find the arguments he needed when treating any given topic. He defined the *loci* as "bases from which arguments are adduced, i.e., reasons which give credence to matters of doubt," and referred to such sources as the idea, the definition, the division, the basic meaning of words and synonyms, and so forth.[2] For centuries these topical *loci,* which made available to public speakers the means by which they could find the necessary material and proofs for their chosen topics, continued to be important in rhetoric. When these *sedes argumentorum* (debating databases!) bore a general character so that they could serve in relation to all subjects, they were called *common loci;* by contrast, the name *proper loci* served to designate the proof texts that could only be applied to a certain subject.

Melanchthon's *loci communes* owe their existence to two lines of work he was pursuing in the same period: a series of critical comments on Lombard's

---

1. Aristotle, *Rhetoric,* II.22.13; *Metaphysics,* IV.3.3.
2. Cicero, *De inventione. De optimo genere oratorum, Topica,* trans. H. M. Hubbell (Cambridge: Harvard University Press, 1949), II.2.

Sentences and a commentary on Paul's *Letter to the Romans*. In 1520, as a result of this twofold activity, he conceived the plan to write *Locos Communes* concerning "law, sin, grace, sacraments as well as other mysteries." In other words, he sought to summarize and discuss under a number of general concepts—in the manner of rubrics, following the instruction of the rhetoricians—the scriptural material he derived from his study of the *Letter to the Romans*. These general rubrics or *loci* he borrowed from Lombard but filled them with content, derived not from scholasticism but from Scripture, specifically from Paul's letter to the Romans. In Melanchthon, therefore, the term *loci communes* thus did not yet refer to fundamental truths but to the formal rubrics or schemata under which the truths of Scripture could appropriately be subsumed and discussed. Nor did the treatment of these *loci* aim at any scholarly goal but served only to introduce the unlearned to the knowledge of Holy Scripture. In terms of completeness and organization, the work therefore left much to be desired and was considerably expanded only in a later edition. Because Melanchthon himself characterized his *loci communes* by the phrase "theological outlines" and later even spoke of *loci praecipui* (*principal loci*), the formal meaning of the name, gradually and unnoticed, passed into a material one, and *loci communes* became the name for the principal truths of the Christian faith. Accordingly, Spalatin's German translation of Melanchthon's work perfectly reproduced the title in terms of content: "The main articles and chief points of Holy Scripture in its entirety."[3]

This new name for the treatment of the truths of the faith, with rare exceptions, gained little acceptance among Roman Catholic theologians. While they use the expression *loci*, they do not employ it in the sense it had gradually acquired thanks to Melanchthon, but in the sense it had had from the days of Aristotle and Cicero. For them it refers not to the articles of the faith (*articuli fidei*) but to the principles or sources of theology.[4] Melchior Canus's famous work, which was published in 1563 under the title of *Loci Theologici*, does not deal with dogmatics itself but with its sources, of which there are ten: Scripture, tradition, pope, councils, church, church fathers, scholastics, reason, philosophy, history. On the other hand, numerous Lutheran and Reformed theologians, like Chemnitz, Hutter, Gerhard, Calovius, Martyr, Musculus, Hyperius, Ursinus, Maccovius, Chamier, and others, did adopt Melanchthon's term *loci communes*.

3. Philipp Melanchthon, *Hauptartikel und fürnehmste Punkte der ganzen Heiligen Schrift*, trans. Georg Spalatin (Strassbourg: Joh. Knobloch, 1522).

4. Pierre Dens, *A Synopsis of the Moral Theory of Peter Dens; as Prepared for the Use of Romish Seminaries and Students of Theology* [*Theologia ad usum seminariorum et sacrae theologiae alumnorum*], trans. from the Latin of the Mechlin edition of 1838 by Joseph F. Berg, 4th ed. (Philadelphia: Lippincott, Grambo, 1855 [1790]); Charles Rene Billuart, *Summae S. Thomae: sive Compendium Theologiae* (Wirceburn: Joan, Jacob Stahel, 1765–66), I, 47 [Ed. note: Bavinck's subtitle is *sive Cursus Theologiae*, 1747]; Carolus Gislenus Daelman, *Theologia, seu, Observationes Theologicae in Summa D. Thomae divisae in duos tomos* (Antverpiae: Apud Jacobum Bernardum Jouret, 1735), I, 18 [Ed. note: Bavinck's publication date is 1759].

Still, in time, as the need for a more systematic treatment of the truths of faith increasingly made itself felt, the name could not maintain itself. From the beginning of the Reformation, other names had already been in use as well. Zwingli had published dogmatic writings under the title of *Commentary on True and False Religion: A Brief and Lucid Exposition of the Christian Faith.*[5] Calvin preferred the name *Institutes of the Christian Religion.*[6] And later theologians of the Lutheran and Reformed churches returned to the ancient name of "theologia." To distinguish it from other theological disciplines, which gradually increased in number and importance, this name "theologia" had to be qualified. To that end the adjectives "didactic," "systematic," "theoretical," or "positive" were added, and since L. Reinhart (*Synopsis theologiae dogmaticae,* 1659) also that of "dogmatic." This description made obvious sense since the truths of the faith had for a long time already been designated "dogmata" and the separation of dogmatics and ethics begun with the work of Danaeus and Calixtus required a distinct name for each of the two disciplines. Since then the addition "dogmatic" gained such dominance that, having banished the main term "theology," it took over, found acceptance among theologians of various confessional stripes, and could not be ousted by the later names "doctrine of the faith," "doctrine of salvation," or "Christian doctrine."

DOGMA, DOGMATICS, AND THEOLOGY

[2] The word *dogma,* from Gr. *dokein* ("to be of the opinion"), denotes that which is definite, that which has been decided, and is therefore fixed.[7] In Scripture (LXX) it is employed to refer to government decrees (Esther 3:9; Dan. 2:13, 6:8; Luke 2:1; Acts 17:7); the statutes of the Old Covenant (Eph. 2:15; Col. 2:14); and the decisions of the Council at Jerusalem (Acts 15:28; 16:4). In the classic writers it has the meaning of a decision or decree, and in philosophy that of truths established by axiom or by proofs.[8] The word in these senses was also adopted in theology. Josephus[9] says that from childhood on Jews view the books of the Old Covenant as divinely given *dogmata.* In the same sense the church fathers speak of the Christian religion or doctrine as *the divine dogma,* of Christ's incarnation as *the dogma of theology,* of the truths of the faith that are authoritative in and for the church as the *dogmata of the church,* and so forth. The word continues to have the same meaning in the Latin writers, like Vincent of Lerins in his *Commoni-*

5. Ulrich Zwingli, *Commentary on True and False Religion,* ed. Samuel Macauley Jackson and Clarence Nevin Heller (Durham, N.C.: Labyrinth Press, 1981).

6. John Calvin, *Institutes of the Christian Religion* (1559 ed.), ed. John T. McNeill and trans. Ford Lewis Battles, 2 vols. (Philadelphia: Westminster, 1960).

7. A fixity reflected in the words used: το δεδογμενον, *statutum, decretum, placitum.*

8. Plato, *The Republic,* VII.16; Aristotle, *Physics,* 4.2; Cicero, *On the Limits of Good and Evil,* 2.32; *Academica,* trans. James S. Reid (London: Macmillan and Company, 1880), 2.9 §27; Seneca, *Letters,* 94, 95.

9. Josephus, *Against Apio,* I.8.

tory[10] and among Protestant theologians like Sohnius, Ursinus, Hyperius, Tolanus, and others.[11]

The use of the word *dogma* teaches us, in the first place, that a wide range of commands, decisions, truths, propositions and rules for living can be denoted by it. Nonetheless, the element that they all have in common is that *dogma* consistently stands for something that is established and not subject to doubt. Cicero, therefore, correctly characterizes it[12] as something stable, fixed, reasoned and that no argument can shake. Still, there is nothing in the word itself that explains why something is a *dogma* and deserves credence. The authority or ground from which a dogma derives its firmness differs in accordance with the type of dogma it is. Political dogma rests on the authority of the civil government, while philosophical dogmas derive their power from self-evidence or argumentation. By contrast, religious or theological dogmas owe their authority solely to a divine testimony, whether this is perceived, as among pagans, from an oracle, or, among Protestant Christians, from Scripture or, among Roman Catholics, from the magisterium of the church. Some say, incorrectly, that dogma rests on personal authority or coincides with the theological construction of a devout scholar.[13] Etymologically and historically there has always been a sharp distinction between δογμα and δοξα, between a doctrine based on a given authority and authoritative for a specific circle and in a specific area on the one hand, and the private opinion of a person, however renowned, on the other. Accordingly, no one would think of labeling, say, the ideas of Swedenborg on the spirit-world as "dogmas." Nor is it correct to say, as Lobstein does, that in its historical sense a dogma is nothing other than "a conceptually apprehended statement of belief officially formulated by the proper authority." Lobstein specifies this authority as "the church in collaboration with the state." Dogma would then be "briefly, an obligatory statement of belief drawn up by the infallible church and sanctioned by the absolute power of the state."[14] This is incorrect since, in the first place, the authority of the state is not the

10. Vincent of Lerins, *Letter of Instructions* [*Commonitorium*], trans. Reginald Stewart Moxon (Cambridge: Cambridge University Press, 1915), chap. 29.

11. Georg Sohnius, *Opera Sacrae Theologiae*, 2 vols. (Herborn: C. Corvin, 1609), I, 32; Zacharias Ursinus, *Tract-Theol.*, 1584, 22. Ed. note: The reference in Bavinck's footnote reads *Pract. theol.*, clearly a typographical error; see note 18 below. Andreas Hyperius, *Methodi theologiae, sive praecip. Christ. relig. locurum communium* (Basel, 1567), 34 [Ed. note: Bavinck's publication date is 1574]; Amandus Polanus, *Syntagma Theologiae Christianae*, 5th ed. (Hanover: Aubry, 1625), 133.

12. *Academica*, II.9.

13. Friedrich August Kahnis, *Die Luthersche Dogmatik, historisch-genetisch dargestellt* (Leipzig: Dörfling & Francke, 1874), I, 4; Groenewegen, "De Theologie aan de Universiteit," *Theologisch Tijdschrift* (May 1905): 193–224.

However, by personal authority Kahnis does not mean that any person can establish a dogma but that a dogma is always based on a pronouncement, either of God, a government, or church. But even then that conception of dogma is too limited. For example, philosophical dogmas are not based on any specific official pronouncement but on internal self-evidence or the power of proofs.

14. P. Lobstein, *Einleitung in die Evangelische Dogmatik* (Freiburg, 1897), 23.

sole basis on which the so-called political dogmas rest. Even the Roman Catholic Church professes and maintains its dogmas independently of and, if necessary, over against all state authority. Nor, in the second place, does the authority of a dogma rest on a pronouncement and determination of the church, as Schleiermacher and many others after him have taught us.[15] Rome can teach this because it attributes infallibility to the church. But the Reformation recognizes no truth other than that which is given on the authority of God in holy Scripture. "The Word of God grounds the articles of faith and beyond that no one, not even an angel."[16] Dogmas, articles of faith, are only those truths "which are properly set forth in Scripture as things to be believed."[17] It is only those "propositions [*sententiae*] which must be believed on account of a mandate from God."[18] Among Reformed theologians, therefore, the following proposition returns again and again: "the principle into which all theological dogmas are distilled is: God has said it."

In the second place, usage informs us that the concept of dogma contains a social element. From the character of authority that belongs to it, it naturally follows that as such a dogma is recognized in a certain circle. However well-established a truth may be, unless it is recognized, it is nothing more—in the eyes of people outside that circle—than the opinion of some teacher, and therefore a private opinion. The notion of dogma implies that the authority it possesses is able to command recognition and thus to maintain itself. A distinction has to be made, therefore, between dogma as it has to do with itself (*quoad se*) and dogma as it has to do with us (*quoad nos*). A given proposition is a dogma in itself, apart from any recognition, if it rests on the authority of God. Nonetheless, it is intended, and has an inherent tendency, to be recognized by us as such. Truth always seeks to be honored as truth and can never be at peace with error and deception. It is, moreover, of the greatest importance for every believer, particularly for the dogmatician, to know which Scriptural truths, under the guidance of the Holy Spirit, have been brought to universal recognition in the church of Christ. By this process, after all, the church is kept from immediately mistaking a private opinion for the truth of God. Accordingly, the church's confession can be called the dogma *quoad nos* (for us), that is, the truth of God as it has been incorporated in the consciousness of the church and confessed by it in its own language.

This means that the church of Christ therefore has a certain task to fulfill with respect to dogma. To preserve, explain, understand, and defend the

---

15. Friedrich Schleiermacher, *Die Christliche Sitte nach dem Grundsazen der evangelischen Kirche dargestellt* (Berlin: G. Reimer, 1884), 5 [*Introduction to Christian Ethics*, trans. John Shelley (Nashville: Abingdon, 1989)]; Richard Rothe, *Zur Dogmatik* (Gotha: Perthes, 1869), 10; Alexander Schweizer, *Die Glaubenslehre der evangelisch-reformirten Kirche* (Zurich: Orell, Fussli, 1847), I, 23.

16. *The Smalcald Articles*, II.2.

17. Hyperius, *Methodi theologicae*, 34–35.

18. Zacharias Ursinus, *Volumen Tractationum Theologicarum* (Neustadii Palatinorum: Mathes Harnisch, 1584), 22.

truth of God entrusted to her, the church is called to appropriate it mentally, to assimilate it internally, and to profess it in the midst of the world as the truth of God. It is most definitely not the authority of the church that makes a dogma into dogma in a material sense, elevates it beyond all doubt, and enables it to function with authority. The dogmas of the church have, and may have, this status only if and to the degree they are the dogmas of God (δογματα του θεου). The power of the church to lay down dogmas is not sovereign and legislative but ministerial and declarative. Still, this authority has been granted by God to his church, and it is this power that enables and authorizes her to confess the truth of God and to formulate it in speech and writing. In this connection it must also be kept in mind that the dogmas have never been fully incorporated in the church's creedal statements and ecclesiastically fixed. The life and faith that the church possesses is much richer than what comes to expression in its creedal statements. The church's confession is far from formulating the entire content of the Christian faith. To begin with, a confession generally comes into being in response to specific historical events and arranges its positive and antithetical content accordingly. Furthermore, a confession does not make clear the inner coherence that exists among the various dogmas nor does it ever fully articulate the truth which God has revealed in his Word. The task of the dogmatician differs therefore from that of the student of the church's creedal statements. The latter satisfies himself with the status of the dogmatic content of the creeds, but the former has to examine how the dogma arose genetically from Scripture and how, in accordance with that same Scripture, it ought to be expanded and enriched. Therefore, just as wood does not burn because it smokes but smoke nonetheless signals the presence of fire, so a truth confessed by the church is not a dogma because the church recognizes it but solely because it rests on God's authority.[19] Still, having made this point, we must add that the confession of the church supplies us with an excellent—though not infallible—means to find our way amid many and varied errors to the truth of God laid down in his Word.

[3] In the third place, usage teaches us that religious or theological dogma is always a combination of two elements: divine authority and churchly confession. In case a dogma is not based on divine authority, it is wrong to call it by that name, and it should not have a place in the faith of the church. Conversely, in case there is a truth concealed in Scripture that has not yet been assimilated by the church, it may be called a dogma *quoad se* (as it has to do with itself), though it is not yet a dogma *quoad nos* (as it has to do with us) and still awaits its future development. Now one of the greatest difficulties inherent in the dogmatician's task lies in determining the relation between divine truth and the church's confession. No one claims that content and expression, essence and form, are in complete correspondence and coincide.

19. J. Kleutgen, *Die Theologie der Vorzeit*, 2d ed., 5 vols. (Münster: Theissing, 1867–74), I, 97.

The dogma that the church confesses and the dogmatician develops is not identical with the absolute truth of God itself. Not even the Roman Catholic Church dares to make that claim. For though it confesses the infallibility of the pope, it makes an essential distinction between papal infallibility and apostolic inspiration; it stands by the matters themselves but not the exact words and therefore does not literally elevate dogma to the level of the Word of God.[20] In Catholic theology there is thus room left for the question of how far the truth of God has found fully adequate expression in the church's dogma. On the basis of Protestant assumptions, however, this is much more the case, for here the guidance of the Holy Spirit promised to the church does not exclude the possibility of human error. On the one hand, there is Hegel who elevated history in general and that of the church and dogma in particular to the level of a necessary, logical unfolding of the absolute idea and claimed that all that is real is therefore rational. But in Hegelian philosophy with its dialectical method, this statement only meant that at any given moment reality was precisely that which it had to be. There was absolutely no implication here that reality coincided with truth. On the contrary, in Hegel's system truth was forever unattainable, for there was no unchangeable being, only an eternal becoming. All reality was therefore at the same time and in the same sense irrational if it was destined to make way for another reality.

In the development of idealistic philosophy, this revolutionary principle, which was basic to it but lay hidden under the appearance of conservatism, clearly came to the fore. In the field of the history of dogma, this revolutionary principle manifested itself in the teaching that Christian dogma, along with its entire history, was one enormous aberration, one colossal error. Following Ritschl, who regarded the development of Protestantism in complete disagreement with the principle originally advanced by Luther, Harnack in his *History of Dogma* developed the thought that Christian dogma was a product of the Greek spirit working on the substratum of the gospel. And in general, since Kant distinguished between statutory religion and the religion of reason, Hegel between sight and concept, and Schleiermacher between piety and belief, it is to some extent acknowledged by all that there is in dogma both a permanent and a variable element. In France, August Sabatier in particular attempted to show that Christian dogma is composed of three elements: the piety of the heart, intellectual reflection, and ecclesiastical authority.[21] On the components of a dogma and their mutual relationship, there is a wide range of opinion, a subject to which we must return later.

20. J. B. Heinrich and C. Gutberlet, *Dogmatische Theologie*, 2d ed., 10 vols. (Mainz: Kirchheim, 1881–1900), II, 220–45; G. M. Jansen, *Praelectiones Theologie Fundamentalis* (Utrecht: 1875–77), I, 616.

21. A. Sabatier, *Esquisse d'une philosophie de la religion,* 7th ed. (Paris: Fischbacher, 1903), 264. Ed. note: An English translation of this work is also available: *Outlines of a Philosophy of Religion* (New York: Harper, 1957). Idem, *Die Christliche Dogmen, ihr Wesen und ihre Entwicklung,* trans. M. Schwabb (Leipzig: Otto Wigand, 1890).

Here it is enough to point out that ultimately no one can deny to dogma an invariable, permanent element. People may regard the genuine core of a dogma as being ever so small and sharply restrict the element of truth concealed in it (say, to the religion of the Sermon on the Mount, to the personal faith of Jesus, to the "essence of Christianity" distilled into a number of abstract generalities, or to religious feeling or religious experience), but one who clings to the truth of religion cannot do without dogma and will always recognize in it an unchanging and permanent element. A religion without dogma, however vague and general it may be, without, say, faith in a divine power, does not exist, and a nondogmatic Christianity, in the strict sense of the word, is an illusion and devoid of meaning.[22] Whereas Harnack sends dogma off through the front door, he smuggles it back in through the back door;[23] and the very moment that Kaftan says the old dogma has changed, he calls for a new dogma. Similarly, the nondogmatic Christianity of Otto Dreyer has not been rendered free of all doctrine but only of that which the preacher himself finds inconvenient.[24] Finally, in the same article in which Groenewegen polemicizes against a dogmatically bound theology, he energetically calls for the restoration of dogmatics in the department of theology. Granted, by this he only means a system of theological constructs fashioned by a devoutly religious philosopher, a scientific exposition, and a defense of the intellectual content of his faith-life. Nevertheless, this does assume that in the faith-life of the individual a transcendent reality, i.e., God, is being manifested. Without faith in the existence, the revelation, and the knowability of God, no religion is possible.[25] Opposition to dogma is not resistance to dogma as such, for "unbelief has at all times been most dogmatic" (Kant), but to certain specific dogmas with which people can no longer agree.

Finally, in the fourth place, the use of the word *dogma* teaches us that it is sometimes employed in a broader, and then again in a more restricted, sense. Sometimes it denotes the Christian religion as a whole, and St. Basil the Great[26] could mean by δογματα (in contrast with the κηρυγματα: the articles of faith drawn from Scripture) the rites and ceremonies of the church. Elsewhere Polanus says that dogma in the broad sense encompasses everything contained in Holy Scripture, not only the doctrines of gospel and law, but all the discourses and sacred stories as well.[27] As a rule, however, the word was used in a more restricted sense for the doctrine of gospel and law, for "the judgments which have to be believed and obeyed because of a mandate from God." It therefore embraced not only doctrinal but also ethical truth. Later, however, the word was further delimited because the doctrine of the

---

22. J. Kaftan, *Dogmatik* (Tübingen: Mohr, 1901), 81.
23. Stange, *Das Dogma und seine Beurteilung in der neueren Dogmengeschichte* (Berlin, 1898), 70ff.
24. Dreyer, *Zur undogmatischen Glaubenslehre* (Berlin: C. A Swetschke, 1901).
25. H. Bavinck, *Christelijke Wetenschap* (Kampen: Kok, 1904), 73ff.
26. Basil, *On the Holy Spirit*, chap. 27.
27. A. Polanus, *Syn. Theol.*

law was distinguished and separated from the doctrine of the gospel. Then only judgments that one must believe and obey because of a mandate from God qualified as "dogmata." Proceeding further on this road, Polanus also distinguished between the dogmas and the principles of theology. So *dogma* came to denote the articles of faith that were based on the Word of God and therefore obligated everyone to faith. Dogmatics, then, is the system of the articles of faith.

THE CONTENT OF THEOLOGY

[4] Still, with all this we have only defined the concept of dogmatics in a formal sense. A definition of dogmatics as the science of dogmas is of little use as long as we do not know the material content of the dogmas. In order now to determine the material concept of dogmatics, we must remember that originally *dogmatics* was an adjective used to describe the main concept of theology. In earlier times, in keeping with this concept, dogmatics was usually taken to be the "doctrine of God, primarily, and of creatures according to the respect in which they are related to God as to their source and end."[28] Others, however, objected to making God the main concept of dogmatics and preferred to call its object by another name. Lombard[29] followed Augustine who says "all doctrine is either of things or of signs," and assigned to theology two areas: *things,* i.e., God, world, and man; and *signs,* i.e., sacraments.[30] But this incomplete designation was soon abandoned and improved by the commentators. Alexander of Hales and Bonaventure,[31] describing the material and content of theology or dogmatics, referred to Christ and his mystical body, the church; Hugo St. Victor,[32] the work of reparation. Sometimes Lutheran and Reformed theologians also defined the content of dogmatics in this fashion. Calovius, for example, opposes in the strongest terms the idea that God is the real object of theology. Etymology, he contends, settles nothing here; theology on earth where we do strive for the knowledge of God but do not

28. Thomas Aquinas, *Summa Theologiae,* I, Q.1, art. 3, 7; Albertus Magnus, *Sententiae,* I.1, §2; Dionysius Petavius, *Opus de theologicis Dogmatibus,* 8 vols. (Paris: Vives, 1865–67) cap. 1; Gerhard, *Loci Comm., prooemim de natura theologiae;* Karl von Hase, *Hutterus Redivivus, oder, Dogmatik der Evangelischen-lutherischen Kirche: ein dogmatisches Repertorium für Studierende* (Leipzig: J. Sühring, 1829), §11; H. Schmid, *Doctrinal Theology of the Evangelical Churches,* trans. Charles A. Hay and Henry E. Jacobs (Philadelphia: United Lutheran Publication House, 1899), §2. Also see Franciscus Junius, *Opuscula Theologica Selecta,* ed. Abraham Kuyper (Amsterdam: F. Muller, 1882), I fol., 1375–1424; A. Polanus, *Syn. Theol.,* I, 1–4; Franciscus Gomarus, *Disput. Theolog.,* thesis 1; John Owen, *Theologumena pantodapa, sive, De natura, ortu progressu, et studio verae theologiae, libri sex quibus etiamorigines & processus veri & falsi cultus religiosi, casus & instaurationes ecclesiae illustiores abipsis rerum primordiis, enarrantur* (Oxen, 1661), lib. 1, cap. 1–4; Gisbertus Voetius, *Diatribe de Theologia* (Ultraj., 1668); Johannes Coccejus, *Summa Theologiae ex Scripturis Repetita* (Amsterdam: J. Ravenstein, 1665), cap. 1.

29. P. Lombard, *Sententiae,* I, 1.

30. Augustine, *De Doctrinae Christianae,* I, chap. 2.

31. Bonaventure, *Prolegomena,* Q. 1 in *Sententiae* 1 and *Breviloquium,* I, 1.

32. Hugo of St. Victor, *De Sacr.,* I, 2.

attain it is something very different from theology in heaven. In his opinion, to make God the object of theology is as wrong as to make a prince instead of the commonwealth the object of the study of politics.[33] The real object of theology is man "insofar as he is to be brought to salvation," or the religion prescribed by God in his Word.[34] Similarly, some Reformed theologians described "living for God through Christ, religion, the worship of God," as the content of dogmatics.[35] Thus, step by step, the subjective practical notion of theology began increasingly to find acceptance.

This tendency was strongly promoted by the philosophy of Immanuel Kant. In his critical examination of the human faculty of cognition this philosopher came to the conclusion that the supernatural is unattainable for us human beings, since our capacity for knowledge is bound to its innate forms and therefore limited to the circle of experience. But next to this form of knowing there is room for a faith that, based on moral freedom and under warrant of the categorical imperative, postulates the existence of God, and the soul and its immortality. However, these postulates are not scientific theses capable of rigorous proof but rest on personal, practical motives. Accordingly, believing and knowing are separated in principle, each having its own domain. In the sensuous world, science is possible; with respect to the supersensuous, we have to be satisfied with faith. So in Kant dogma was given the status of a personal conviction of faith grounded in moral motives. On the basis of other considerations, Schleiermacher arrived at a similar conclusion. It is true that he opposed Kant when he defined religion not as knowing or doing but as a certain kind of feeling. Nevertheless, precisely for that reason dogmas became for him accounts of subjective mental states, formulations of religious emotion, reflections in the mind of subjective piety.[36] Others pursued this line of thought even further.

Schleiermacher, it must be noted, still tried in his dogmatic work to give an account, not of religion in general, but of the Christian religion, of Christian piety in particular. This piety, in his view, was marked by the fact that everything in it was related to the person of Christ the Redeemer. The mystical element was anchored in history and thus safeguarded from many ex-

---

33. Calovius, *Isagoge ad theologiam* (1662), 283ff, 291ff.

34. Ibid., 252, 280, 299, 324.

35. W. Ames, *The Marrow of Theology*, ed. John D. Eusden (Grand Rapids: Baker, 1997 [1968]), I, 1 (pp. 77–79 [ed. note: Bavinck mistakenly cites I, 5]); Peter van Mastricht, *Theoretico-practica theologia* (Utrecht, 1714), I, 1, 47; Johannes a Marck, *Het merch der christene got-geleertheit*, 4th ed. (Rotterdam: Nicolaes en Paulus Topyn, 1741), I, 34; Bernhard de Moor, "Commentarius Perpetuus," in *Johannes Marckii Compendium Theologiae Christianae Didactico-elencticum*, 6 vols. (Leiden: J. Hasebroek, 1761–71), I, 112; Fransicus Burmannus, *Synopsis Theologiae & Speciatim Oeconomiae Foederum Dei: Ab Initio Saeculorum Usque ad Consummationem Eorum*, 2 vols. in 1 (Amsterdam: Joannem Wolters, 1699), I, 2, 30. Cf., also, Phillip van Limborch, *Theologia Christiana ad praxin pietatis ac promotionem pacis christianae unice directa* (Amsterdam: Wetstein, 1735), I, 1.

36. F. Schleiermacher, *The Christian Faith*, ed. and trans. H. R. MacIntosh and J. S. Steward (Edinburgh: T. & T. Clark, 1928), §15–16.

cesses. His followers, though maintaining the subjective starting point in dogmatics, therefore made every effort to push forward from the subjective to the objective in religion. Even Ritschl and his school proceeded from an a priori, viz., from the absolute character of Christianity. He took his position not outside but within the faith of the church and so, according to the more recent positivistic view of science, was highly prejudiced. Younger scholars in the field therefore turned their backs on him and went their own way. Following the example of Lagarde and Overbeck, Bernoulli and Troeltsch demanded that the scientific theologian had to abandon all so-called prejudices, also those favoring Christianity. Otherwise, so they contend, dogmatics will be too much isolated from other disciplines, it will come to rest on an unprovable foundation, and cannot be a science in the true sense of the word. Therefore, if theology, and specifically dogmatics, wants to become a genuine science, it must put aside all prejudices and proceed only on the basis of the indisputable fact—which is an established certainty for all—that religions exist. These religions are the object of theology; and if it studies them historically, psychologically, and comparatively, it may foster the hope that it will in the end break through to the essence of religion. And this, then, it has to set forth, to justify, and to apply as criterion of the value and place of the different religions, in the discipline of dogmatics. In the Netherlands this is the direction that has been taken by modern theologians for many years already and is embodied in the Higher Education Act of 1876.[37] On this position the content of dogma is not Scripture, confession, Christian piety, and the faith of the church but only the "essence" of religion, something to be uncovered by totally unbiased research.

[5] Thomas in his time, addressing those who offered a different definition of theology, already commented that they arrived at it because they were "preoccupied with the things treated of by sacred doctrine rather than with the formal interest engaged."[38] In theology and hence in dogmatics much more is considered than only the things pertaining to God; angels and human beings, heaven and earth, indeed all creatures are considered there. But the question is: From what viewpoint and with what aim are they treated in theology? After all, all these things are treated also in other disciplines. The unique feature of their treatment in theology consists in the fact that they are viewed in their relation to God as to their source and end. Furthermore, the definition of dogmatics as the science of the Christian religion was not wrong as such when, as in an earlier period, this meant the religion objectively laid down in Scripture. But after Kant and Schleiermacher this definition acquired another meaning, and dogmatics became the account of the historic phenomenon that is called the Christian religion and manifests

37. Ed. note: In 1876, by a decree of the Dutch Parliament, the theology faculties at all state universities were effectively turned into religious studies departments when they were separated from confessional moorings.

38. Aquinas, *Summa Theol.*, I, qu. 1, art. 7.

itself in a unique faith and doctrine. Now when dogmatics is understood in this sense, it ceases to be dogmatics and simply becomes the account of what in a certain specific circle is held to be true in the sphere of religion.

But science aims at truth. If dogmatics aims to be real science, it cannot be content with the description of what is but must demonstrate what has to be considered truth. It must set forth not the *that* (ὅτι) but the *wherefore* (δι-ότι), not reality but truth, not the real but the ideal, the logical, the necessary. In recent years this is being recognized by an increasing number of people. On the one hand, a group to the left is marching ever further down the road of positivism. It turns its collective back on all metaphysics, dogma, and dogmatics and permits religion—now considered to be the same everywhere—to be lost in subjective moods of the mind, in ecstasy and ascesis. Furthermore, denying the specific character of Christianity, it seeks fraternization with all religions, especially with that of Buddha and Mohammed. Precisely against this process, a reaction has surfaced among others for whom this is going too far. They are beginning to recognize that in religion feeling and mood are not really everything, that all religion necessarily includes ideas and that as such these are subject to the test of truth. Accordingly, these people again devote themselves more or less assiduously to the preservation or restoration of departments of theology, to metaphysics in religion, to the reincorporation of dogmatics among the theological disciplines. But this, then, has to be a dogmatics that, like all theology, is completely free, is bound a priori to no dogma whatever, and is nothing other than an account and justification of the content of religion as it has been brought to light by the historical and psychological examination of existing religions. It is a dogmatics, therefore, that contains no dogma but consists only in a system of theological constructs drawn up by a devoutly religious philosopher.[39]

Although this reaction against an extreme radicalism is to be warmly welcomed, it is doomed to fruitlessness from the start if it does not undertake a fundamental revision of the present-day concept of science. A choice has to be made: either there is room in science for metaphysics and then positivism is in principle false, or positivism is the true view of science and metaphysics must be radically banished from its entire domain. One who specifically devotes his energies to the restoration of metaphysics in the science of religion has in principle broken with the basic idea from which the science of religion took its rise and is, again in principle, returning to the old view of theology. For anyone who makes a religion or Christianity in particular into the object of a unique science is no longer proceeding from the fact of the *existence* of that religion or of Christianity, but from a particular appreciation of that fact.[40] Theology as a

---

39. Groenewegen, *De Metaphysica in de Wijsbegeerte van de Godsdienst* (Amsterdam, 1903); idem, "De Theologie aan de Universiteit"; Bruinig, "Over de Methode van onze Dogmatiek," *Teylers Theologische Tijdschrift* (1903): 153–85.

40. J. H. Gunning and P. D. de la Saussaye Jr., *Het Ethische Beginsel der Theologie* (Groningen, 1877), 67.

particular science assumes that God has unmistakably revealed himself; in other words, it assumes the existence, the self-revelation, and the knowability of God and therefore proceeds from a highly significant dogma. A dogmatically free theology, or dogmatics, is a self-contradiction. If religion is not just a psychological and historical fact, like belief in ghosts or witches, for example, but rests on truth and has an absolute value, then a thinker who views and studies religion in that sense will always end up with God. The truth and value of religion depend on the existence, the revelation, and the knowability of God. Also the science of religion that incorporates metaphysics is in principle theology, and proceeds from the existence and knowability of God. If God is not knowable, did not reveal himself, or does not even exist, not only dogmatics or theology but religion itself collapses, for it is built on the knowledge of God. Thus dogmatics is, and can only exist as, the scientific system of the knowledge of God. More precisely and from a Christian viewpoint, dogmatics is the knowledge that God has revealed in his Word to the church concerning himself and all creatures as they stand in relation to him.

IS THEOLOGY A SCIENCE?

[6] However, numerous objections are being advanced against this definition of dogmatics. All of these objections come down to saying that the object of dogmatics is not the knowledge of God but the content of faith, that dogmatics is not a science, and that it can never be made into a system. It is particularly the Berlin professor Julius Kaftan who has brought these objections to the fore; and in his mouth they are the more weighty because in his view of the task of dogmatics he agrees to a large extent with the position sketched above.[41] Kaftan acknowledges that dogmatics presumes a divine revelation and has to accept it as its principle and origin; there is no religious knowledge without revelation, without God. The external, i.e., historical, revelation is the epistemological principle of the Christian faith. For that reason he does not hesitate as a dogmatician to position himself on the standpoint of authority, because to him the authority principle is the natural and necessary principle of dogmatics. In Kaftan's thinking, accordingly, dogmatics is not just an account of devout states of consciousness, nor speculation about the data of religious experience, nor even a religious worldview built up solely out of value judgments, but it is a normative science that, on the basis of the authority of revelation, speaks in an absolute tone of voice and has to set forth what we *must* believe. And in Kaftan all this flows from the insight that religious faith is not merely a feeling, a mental experience, but in fact real knowledge and definitely includes knowledge of God.

Still, he does not simply want to stop at the old view of dogma and dogmatics. His opinion is that while faith includes knowledge, this knowledge

41. J. Kaftan, *Dogmatik;* idem, "Zur Dogmatik, Sieben Abhandlungen," *ZthK* 13 (1903): 96–149, 214–66, 457–519; 14 (1904): 148–92, 273–357.

has again been correctly understood by the Reformation as a recognition of its own peculiar nature (*ein Erkennen seiner Art*). Earlier, before the Reformation, and again in Protestant orthodoxy the prevailing view of faith, dogma, and dogmatics was intellectualistic. Religious truth was viewed as doctrine, or a scientific system, which had to be accepted in the same intellectual fashion as a result of science or a fact in history. But the Reformation discovered the enormous difference between the two and replaced intellectualism with the voluntarism of the evangelical faith. On the basis of this principle, the whole of theology, and dogma and dogmatics in particular, must be reviewed and renewed. The old dogma has had its time; today we need a new dogma. Our task today is to frame the whole of Christian knowledge in accordance with the manner in which it develops out of the evangelical faith. If today we undertake this reform, the implication is that revelation is viewed as antecedent to faith but dogma is not. Revelation is said to bear a religious-ethical character and is appropriated, not intellectualistically by the mind but voluntaristically by the will. Religion is about practical experiences, about demands on the will. Knowing is not, as among the Greeks, the highest goal of the human mind. Kant is correctly called the philosopher of Protestantism insofar as he saw that it is the moral will, without which the highest good cannot be conceived, through whose activation alone the road leads to God and to knowing God. The supreme place in the life of the mind belongs to the moral will; it is the part in us that is akin to God and therefore also the way to knowing God. Knowledge is limited to experience and does not extend to the world that lies behind it, just as swimming stops where there is no water and flying where there is no air. What carries us further is not knowledge but the whole of our personal life; that is a value judgment, a judgment on the question wherein the human spirit (*Geist*) thinks it ought to experience itself above all as spirit. Faith, then, is practically grounded; the highest activities, the life of the spirit, also as knowledge, rests and is rooted in the will.

The second implication of Kaftan's view is that dogma is not the object but the expression of faith and therefore, in virtue of its origin, necessarily bears a religious-moral character, not an intellectualistic, scientific one. Dogma is not to be accepted intellectually as though it were an ordinary scientific truth, for then faith would again become a mere holding-as-true and dogmatics a kind of metaphysics. On the contrary, while faith is rooted in a personal relationship to God and has his revelation for its object, the sole aim of dogmatics is to mediate to faith its own true object: God in his living self-revelation. Dogmatics does not develop doctrine that we then have to accept with our intellect but shows people how the Word of God has to be proclaimed in order to arouse the listeners to a true faith and educate them to an interior knowledge of faith that corresponds to the truth. Accordingly, the sequence is: Revelation (Scripture), faith, dogma; faith stands between the Bible and dogmatics. Finally, the new principle generates the view that dogmatics is not the science of God, nor a scientific system of the knowledge of God.

So, while faith is knowledge and definitely also knowledge of God, this knowledge is of a particular kind; it is not scientific and demonstrable but gained through personal experience by the activity of the moral will. There is therefore a world of difference between faith knowledge and the knowledge we acquire in the domain of science. Scientific knowledge arises from the compelling evidence of facts, but religious knowledge is gained through moral experience by an act of the will and hence is ethically conditioned.

Against this background the difference between the two kinds of knowledge becomes evident. For the content of our knowledge of God depends on the epistemological road taken. In the case of the knowledge of God, this road is totally different from that taken in the case of the visible world. And for that reason there is no science of God. There is faith in God, and there is faith-knowledge of God. God is the object of faith, not the object of knowledge. Therefore, if dogmatics aspires to be a science, it must give up aspiring to know God and limit itself to the development of the knowledge that comes with faith. It must not seek to be a science of God but of faith in God and must always set forth the knowledge of faith as such, i.e., in its relations to the inner life. Otherwise dogmatics inevitably relapses into the old intellectualistic view that its task is to develop a kind of philosophy and a comprehensive worldview. Christian knowledge of God and scientific knowledge of the world are two very different things and ought, in the interest of both, to be kept rigorously separate. The knowledge of God must remain the knowledge of faith. For us to pursue something other than this is to aspire to know God in the way we know some sector of the world over which we are called to exercise control or in which to integrate ourselves as members on an equal footing—an obviously impossible undertaking. And when dogmatics develops the content of this faith-knowledge, its task is not to reconstruct in human thought the objective unity of all reality—existing in and for itself—but confine itself to demonstrating the connectedness that arises from the unity of faith or—since faith orients itself to revelation—from revelation. Since in any case dogmatics will never understand the objective connectedness of God and the world, it should confine itself to making clear the subjective connectedness that to our minds exists between the two.

THEOLOGY AND FAITH

[7] Kaftan's vigorous defense of the unique character of religious knowledge, knowledge that becomes our mental and spiritual possession only in the way of faith, deserves our appreciation. It is indeed the case that religious knowledge comes into being in a particular way and thus bears its own unique character. Similarly praiseworthy is that he again, at least in part, conceives faith as a kind of cognition and ventures to speak of a knowledge of faith, the object of which is God as he has revealed himself. And finally he can count on our agreement when he bases faith on revelation and seeks to

maintain its authority also for dogmatics. Formally all this is so right that at first blush it surprises us that orthodoxy did not accord this dogmatics a more favorable welcome than in fact it did. Kaftan himself, complaining about this, interprets this lack of appreciation from the fact that orthodoxy itself abandoned the old authority-standpoint and changed into pietism. In part this observation is correct; many theologians who agree materially with the old confession, formally adopt Schleiermacher's subjective stance and attempt rationally to infer the objective dogmas from religious experience, from the faith of the church. Still, this is not the only or even the main reason why orthodoxy withheld its assent from Kaftan's dogmatics. This reason is much more that Kaftan, in applying his principle, became unfaithful to it and himself later undermined and even tore down the authority of revelation and Holy Scripture he postulated earlier. We will demonstrate this in greater detail later on. With a view to the subject under discussion in this chapter, we will confine ourselves to the following comments.[42]

It is completely true that saving faith does not originate as a result of the compelling evidence of the facts in the same way knowledge originates in the field of arithmetic or natural science. Believing is a free act; no one believes unless he wants to. Accordingly, there is a yielding of the will and an illumination of the mind that precedes faith. But believing is nevertheless itself an act of the intellect; even if it were in the first place an act of trust—which, however, is not the case either—according to Kaftan himself it is still a way of knowing whose content is divine revelation. Now if faith is not the source but the organ of knowledge—as Kaftan argues in his comments against the subjectivists—if religious experience is indeed an indispensable means of knowing but not the guiding principle of knowledge, then it is self-evident that the content of the knowledge of faith is antecedent to faith itself and an element of revelation. Now Kaftan indeed opposes the idea that revelation consists in a communication of doctrine and does not come to us with external authority. But this does not detract from the fact that, if faith is not the source but the organ of knowledge, revelation must also—even if not exclusively—consist in the making known of truth, in communicating the thoughts of God; it is not only manifestation but also inspiration, not only deed-revelation but also word-revelation. Kaftan is thus wrong when in his starting point he denies this. The knowledge of God that Kaftan ascribes to faith is genuine and reliable only if God has revealed himself in such a way that from this revelation we can learn to know him by faith.

But then that knowledge of God also lies spread out before us objectively in his revelation and can be absorbed and thought through by us in faith. When Groenewegen comments that the knowledge of God is not the object

42. Cf. L. Ihmels, "Blicke in die neure dogmatische Arbeit II: Die Dogmatik von Kaftan," *Neue Kirchliche Zeitschrift* 7 (1905): 273–311; J. Riemens, "Principia in de Dogmatiek," *Theologische Studien* 21 (1903): 379–97; Traub, "Zur dogmatischen Methodenlehre," *Theologische Studien und Kritiken* (1905): 425–52.

but the goal of dogmatics he is mistaken.[43] Kaftan very correctly says that God cannot, like the phenomena of nature and the facts of history, be made the object of scientific investigation. For God to be knowable he must have revealed himself not only in deeds but also in words. Contained in that revelation is the knowledge of God in the objective sense, and as such it is the object of theology, more specifically of dogmatics. To say that dogmatics is the system of the knowledge of God serves to cut off all autonomous speculation; it is to say that God cannot be known by us apart from his revelation and that the knowledge of him we aim at in dogmatics can only be a transcript of the knowledge God has revealed concerning himself in his Word.

However, if the revelation contains such a knowledge of God, it can also be thought through scientifically and gathered up in a system. In that activity the dogmatician remains bound to the revelation from beginning to end and cannot bring forth new truth; in his activity as thinker he can only reproduce the truth God has granted. And because revelation is of such a nature that it can only be truly accepted and appropriated by a saving faith, it is absolutely imperative that the dogmatician be active as believer not only in the beginning but also in the continuation and at the end of his work. The theologian can never arrive at knowledge that is higher than the faith. Faith (religion, the knowledge of faith) and theology are not related as *pistis* and *gnosis* but differ only in degrees. In a later chapter we will deal intentionally with the relationship between faith and theology, but here it only needs to be pointed out that Kaftan, as a result of an incorrect view of science, places dogmatics outside the realm of faith. To maintain the scientific character of dogmatics, he assigns to it as its content not the knowledge of God but the knowledge of faith. When Kaftan judges that though there is no science of God a knowledge of faith does exist, he himself lapses into the error of which he accuses Schleiermacher. For Kaftan, too, dogmatics becomes an account of the knowledge of faith, i.e., of the religious experience of the subject. Admittedly, Kaftan distinguishes himself favorably from the subjectivists by viewing faith also as a kind of knowledge and even as knowledge of God. But instead of taking advantage of this position for the benefit of dogmatics, he stops halfway and says that though there is knowledge of God there is no science of God. That conclusion is a result, as he himself admits, of Kaftan's neo-Kantianism and his empiricistic view of science. He agrees with Kant that the supersensuous is unknowable and that science in the strict sense can rest only on experience. Consequently, he sees no way he can maintain dogmatics as a science except by positing an undeniable fact of experience, i.e., the knowledge of faith, as its object. On the other hand, Kaftan very well understands the objections to the assumption of the subjective position and thus strongly disapproves of Schleiermacher's theology of experience. So now he opts for a middle way and thinks he has found it by ac-

43. Groenewegen, "De Theologie aan de Universiteit," 196ff.

cepting a kind of faith-knowledge of God but not a science. This, however, is a dead-end road. For if strictly speaking there is no science of God, then neither can there be a faith-knowledge of God. Conversely, if indeed there exists a true and trustworthy knowledge of God, even though it is acquired in a special way that corresponds to the nature of its object, then one can certainly speak properly of a science of God. Correctly assuming a faith-knowledge of God, therefore, Kaftan should have pushed consistently forward along that line, broken with Kant's dualism, reviewed the modern concept of science, and made a simple and decisive assertion: Precisely because a true faith-knowledge of God exists, dogmatics has the knowledge of God as part of its content and can rightly claim to be a science.

All the more reason for this exists because Kant's dualism and the empiricist view of science are in fact inherently untenable as such. For although the faith-knowledge of God—and therefore also the whole domain of dogmatics and theology—bears a distinct character, in this respect it is absolutely not alone in the world of the sciences. Like every other departmental discipline, theology too has its own object and principle, method and aim. At the same time, theology also possesses a range of characteristics in common with the other sciences. For it is impossible, just to mention an example, to base the sciences in general—with the possible exception of the science of mathematics and a number of subdivisions of natural science—on facts that are accepted as certain by all without distinction. It is precisely the facts about which there is immediately a difference of opinion; everyone observes them through his own eyes and his own pair of lenses. To the degree that the sciences lie closer to the center and cease to be merely formal, the subjectivity and personality of the scientific investigator play a larger role. It is totally futile to silence this subjectivity, to deny to faith, to religious and moral convictions, to metaphysics and philosophy their influence on scientific study. One may attempt it but will never succeed because the scholar can never be separated from the human being. And therefore it is much better to see to it that the scientific investigator can be as much as possible a normal human being, that he not bring false presuppositions into his work but be a man of God completely equipped for every good work. To that end the knowledge that God has revealed of himself in his Word is serviceable; it does not hinder but rather advances scientific study and research. Whatever misuse has been and can be made of it, the saying remains true: "Godliness is of value in every way" (1 Tim. 4:8).

THE SCIENCE OF GOD

[8] In that sense one can speak with complete justice of dogmatics as a science about God, and there is no objection whatever to gathering this knowledge of God in a system. Kaftan declares himself to be very strongly opposed to this view and insists that the dogmatician present the truth of faith only in

a certain clear order.[44] But he attaches to the idea of system and systematic construction a view that does not necessarily belong to it. It is completely true that in the sciences in general and in philosophy and theology in particular, systematic construction has done much harm. As a result content has frequently been sacrificed to form, reality to idea, and capacity to will. When a theologian or philosopher attempts dialectically to construct reality from an a priori principle, when for the sake of system a hiatus is arbitrarily filled or a troublesome fact eliminated, there is every reason to join Kaftan in warning against the Moloch of system and to recall the words of Liebmann: "The fact that authentic philosophy does *not need* to appear in the form of a system has been demonstrated by Plato, by Bacon and Leibnitz; is demonstrated by the pronounced horror expressed by so many eminent philosophers at all exclusive system-building."[45] But the misuse that has often been made of system does not justify our positing an either-or and saying with Kaftan: "Either systematic construction and then no dogmas or, [alternatively], dogmas and precisely then no system." In any case, everything in dogmatics depends on what one means by system and systematic construction. There is no room in dogmatics for a system in which an attempt is made to deduce the truths of faith from an a priori principle, say, from the essence of religion, from the essence of Christianity, from the fact of regeneration, or from the experience of the devout. For dogmatics is a positive science, gets all its material from revelation, and does not have the right to modify or expand that content by speculation apart from that revelation. When because of its weakness or limitations it is faced with the choice either of simply letting the truths of faith stand alongside of one another or, in the interest of maintaining the systematic form, of failing to do justice to one of them, dogmatics must absolutely opt for the former and resist the desire for a well-integrated system. On the other hand, one must maintain the position that such a dilemma can occur only as a result of the limitations of our insight. For if the knowledge of God has been revealed by himself in his Word, it cannot contain contradictory elements or be in conflict with what is known of God from nature and history. God's thoughts cannot be opposed to one another and thus necessarily from an organic unity.

The imperative task of the dogmatician is to think God's thoughts after him and to trace their unity. His work is not finished until he has mentally absorbed this unity and set it forth in a dogmatics. Accordingly, he does not come to God's revelation with a ready-made system in order, as best he can, to force its content into it. On the contrary, even in his system a theologian's sole responsibility is to think God's thoughts after him and to reproduce the unity that is objectively present in the thoughts of God and has been recorded for the eye of faith in Scripture. That such a unity exists in the

44. Kaftan, *Dogmatik,* §12; idem, "Zur Dogmatik," 5ff. Cf., A. F. C. Vilmar, *Dogmatik,* 2 vols. (Gütersloh: C. Bertelsmann, 1874), I, 68.
45. Liebmann, *Zur Analysis der Wirklichkeit,* 3d ed. (Strassburg: K. J. Trübner, 1900), 9.

knowledge of God contained in revelation is not open to doubt; to refuse to acknowledge it would be to fall into skepticism, into a denial of the unity of God. Kaftan, too, acknowledges that it is the responsibility of dogmatics to present a clear and simple overview of the material it treats and that this material must constitute an internal unity, for "the faith and the knowledge we possess in the faith is an internal unity, a faith-world that is coherently ordered and devoid of contradictions." But if that is the case, there can be no objection to our attempts, in dogmatics as in any other science, at achieving a system that is not imposed on the truths of faith but rationally inferred from them. And the objection against this is even less weighty since dogmatics is not a kind of biblical theology that stops at the words of Scripture. Rather, according to Scripture itself, dogmatics has the right to rationally absorb its content and, guided by Scripture, to rationally process it and also to acknowledge as truth that which can be deduced from it by lawful inference. In the case of Kaftan, his opposition to all system in dogmatics is certainly in large part explicable from the misuse that theologians and philosophers have often made of systematic construction. In addition, it is also rooted in part in the belief that theological reflection on the content of revelation is neither necessary nor permissible. He states for example: "Every dogma which asserts an insight of faith must be directly derived from faith itself, for otherwise it would not be a dogma but a theological reflection on the faith." According to Kaftan, the unity of the truths of faith, which, as was stated earlier, he acknowledges, rests therefore on the fact that they all stem from the same root and not on the idea that, like connected and interdependent parts, they together form a whole. Questionable in these statements is not only that it is faith and not the revelation received in faith that seems to supply the content of dogmatics, but even more that the dogmatician must abstain from all theological reflection on the content of revelation. Without such theological reflection, however, not only no system, but no dogmatic labor at all is possible. The task of dogmatics is precisely to rationally reproduce the content of revelation that relates to the knowledge of God.

Naturally, in this reproduction of the content of revelation, a danger exists on many levels of making mistakes and falling into error. This fact should predispose the dogmatician, like every practitioner of science, to modesty. The confession of the church and in even greater measure the dogmatics of an individual person, is fallible, subject to Scripture, and never to be put on a level with it. It does not coincide with the truth but is a human, hence a fallible, transcript of the truth laid down in Scripture. Faith, or, better, the faithful intellect, occupies an intermediate position between Scripture and dogmatics. Still, by comparison with the other practitioners of science, the dogmatician is favorably situated. He may and can, as Kaftan puts it, to some extent speak in an absolute tone of voice.[46] A

46. Kaftan, "Zur Dogmatik," 21ff.

dogma is a faith-proposition that claims to be true and demands universal recognition, and dogmatics is a normative science that prescribes what we must believe. But dogma and dogmatics cannot on their own authority and in their own name strike that absolute tone of voice but only because and insofar as they rest on the authority of God and can appeal to a "God has said it." The weakness of dogmatics consists precisely in the fact that this discipline itself has so little faith in this "God has spoken." According to Kaftan, this is completely correct: The contempt in which dogmatics is held today is rooted in the fact that it has forgotten its own task and given up its own unique character. And therefore he also, correctly, believes that precisely as science and in order to regain its honor as a science, dogmatics cannot do better than again become what it ought to be. It must again become a normative science, bravely and boldly avow the authority principle, and speak in an absolute tone of voice. Provided this tone of voice is solely derived from the content of the revelation that it is the dogmatician's aim to interpret and is struck only insofar as he explicates this content, it is not in conflict with the demands of modesty. For both the absolute tone of voice and the modesty find their unity in the faith that must guide and animate the dogmatician from beginning to end in all his labor. By that faith he subjects himself to the revelation of God and is organically connected with the church of all believers. Whereas today, with the help of a little psychology and some philosophy of religion, everyone establishes his own dogma, it is a privilege and an honor for the Christian dogmatician to position himself in the faith and by doing this to articulate his submission to the Word of God and his participation in the fellowship of the church of all ages. For that reason the definition of dogmatics given above also contains the idea that it sets forth the knowledge of God that is laid down in his Word *to the church*. This is not to say that Holy Scripture is only intended for the institutional church. On the contrary, it is a book for the whole of humankind and has meaning for all of human life. But the "natural man" has no idea what to do with Holy Scripture as such. Furthermore, the individual believer who puts his mind to the pursuit of dogmatic studies will only produce lasting benefit from his labors if he does not isolate himself, either in the past or from his surroundings, but instead takes his place both historically and contemporarily in the full communion of the saints.[47] It is part of the calling of the ἐκκλησια to learn to know the love of Christ that surpasses all knowledge and also to make known within the world of science "the manifold wisdom of God" in order that the final end of theology, as of all things, may be that the name of the Lord is glorified. Theology and dogmatics, too, exist for the Lord's sake.

47. A. Kuyper, *Encyclopaedie der Heilige Godgeleerdheid*, 2d ed., 3 vols. (Amsterdam: J. A. Wormser, 1894), III, 353, 409.

THE ENCYCLOPEDIC PLACE OF DOGMATIC THEOLOGY

From Revelation to Religion

[9] Among theologians there is little difference of opinion about the place of dogmatics in the encyclopedia of theology. Most include it under systematic, dogmatic, or dogmatological theology, i.e., in the group of disciplines that pursue the study of dogma. In addition to dogmatics, the disciplines of ethics, symbolics, the history of dogma, and apologetics belong to this group as well. Only Schleiermacher subsumed dogmatics under historical theology because it is the science of "patterns of doctrine current in the Church at a given time." He was followed in this by Rothe and even, recently, by Dorner. Schleiermacher arrived at this singular view because his aim was to separate dogmatics as rigorously as possible from apologetics. Whereas the latter, as a subdivision of philosophical theology, must demonstrate what Christian truth is, the responsibility of the former is only to describe that which is held to be truth in one Christian church or another. Still, in saying this, Schleiermacher by no means meant to ascribe a merely descriptive character to dogmatics. In fact, he definitely assigns a critical task to it and demands that it be systematic, that it convey a conviction of its own, and that it describe what is current now, not what was current in the past. But given this definition of its character and task, it is already more than mere historical description. The Christian church cannot be satisfied with an objective account of the content of its faith but wishes that its faith be unfolded and set forth also as truth. Nor does the dogmatician take a neutral position outside of and opposed to the faith of the church, as he does, say, vis-à-vis the religious doctrine of Islam or Buddhism. On the contrary, he belongs to that church and therefore also describes what counts, and has to count, as truth for himself. And finally there is an essential distinction between works like those of Hase, Schmid, Schweizer, and Heppe, which present an objective account of Lutheran and Reformed doctrine, and the dogmatics that seeks to demonstrate and present the truth of religious convictions. If in calling dogmatics a historical discipline, Schleiermacher only meant that it is a thetic, positive science that is not in search of but has found its object and now describes it, his intention can be appreciated, but the adjective "historical" is still incorrect. If, however, he held that the task of dogmatics was merely to give an account of a set of historical data and made no claim to articulating normative truth, his view was certainly incorrect and is therefore generally rejected today.

There was still another reason, however, why Schleiermacher assigned to dogmatics a place in historical theology. The philosophical viewpoint he assumed, as is evident from his *Dialektik*,[48] prevented him from conceiving theology as a "science concerning God" (*scientia de Deo*) and naturally had to lead him into asserting a rigorous separation between theology and phi-

---

48. Ed. note: Bavinck is referring to F. Schleiermacher, *Dialektik* (Hamburg: Meiner, 1986 [1811]).

losophy (a science). God, as the unity of the ideal and the real, is still unknowable to the intellect (which always thinks in terms of opposites) and
can be experienced only in the heart; religion, therefore, is not cognition or
action but a certain emotional state. Accordingly, for Schleiermacher Scripture and confession could no longer carry authority on the ground that they
contained divine revelation but were entitled to a measure of authority only
insofar as they were more or less accurate accounts of religious experience or
of Christian piety. Theology and dogmatics could therefore retain a kind of
scientific authority only if they found their content in a given object, viz.,
the church, and their purpose in serving the leadership of that church. Both
disciplines were thus given a subjective starting point and a practical aim.
Specifically, dogmatics was given the task to describe, for the benefit of the
leadership of the church, the features that characterized this Christian piety,
what elements it contained and to what components in the New Testament
and Christian dogma they corresponded. Its task was not and could not be
to mark this Christian piety as the only true and correct one but was limited
to the obligation of making this Christian piety known in its essential elements. Therefore, according to Schleiermacher, the scientific nature of dogmatics lay solely in the didactic character of its language and in its systematic
arrangement, i.e., in something purely formal. And this is precisely what
Schleiermacher intended with his rigorous separation of dogmatics and apologetics, of theology and philosophy. The question of whether Christianity
was the true religion lay outside the reach of dogmatics; its sole task was to
set forth positively the elements of Christian piety.

But Schleiermacher himself did not uphold this principle in its application. In the first place, he in fact attempted in his dogmatics, by reflection
on Christian piety, to arrive at a genuinely objective knowledge of God and
man, of Christ and the world. Further, at the very outset he already brought
philosophy into his dogmatics by deriving his concept of the church from
ethics and his concept of religion from the philosophy of religion. As a result
dogmatics not only formally but also materially fell completely under the
sway of philosophy. And this dependence of theology on philosophy in
Schleiermacher surfaced even more pronouncedly in the fact that he prefaced his historical and practical theology with a philosophic part, the design
of which, in his apologetics, was to set forth the truth of Christianity. So the
separation Schleiermacher intended ended in a complete fusion. Although
this example could have served as a warning to others, many theologians
later followed it. Generally speaking, this manifests itself in the fact that
dogmas, in order to avoid conflict with science, are limited as much as possible to their religious-ethical content. In many schools of theology, there is a
tendency to replace all transcendent-metaphysical statements about God, his
essence and attributes, his words and works, with descriptions of Christian
experience and its content. In the past, as Harnack and Kaftan tell the story,
dogma had been construed as knowledge of God-and-the-world (*Gott-Welt-*

erkenntnis), which discussed a wide variety of theoretical problems and believed it had solved them. But, so they say, the Reformation has taught us to view dogma as an expression of religious faith alone, and that is how we must also understand and process it in dogmatics today. Soon, however, it became clear that one cannot stop there. For dogma, despite all the trimming and shrinking it was subjected to, still contained a variety of elements that could be attacked and were in fact attacked from the side of modern science. More fundamentally it was significant that, however cleansed of theoretical components, dogma still always proved to be predicated on an a priori and to rest on metaphysical assumptions. These assumptions could not be reconciled with a "presuppositionless" positive science. Consequently, others finally arose who wanted to put an end to all "mediations in the spirit of Schleiermacher and neo-Kantianism" and to dissolve the whole of theology in a completely secularized science of religion.[49]

The result of this development, however, was a collision with the practical demands of church life: ministers were needed, and they had to be trained. Practically, therefore, a compromise had to be made. Various approaches were taken. As early as 1876 Lagarde[50] advocated a completely free science of religion practiced at the university and, alongside of it, an ecclesiastical theology taught in a seminary. Overbeck considered science and religion, Christianity and culture, completely incompatible, regarded the idea of a Christian theology impossible, and thought that science and the church would be able to live peacefully side by side if in the lives of students and pastors a sharp distinction was made between their personal and their official, their private and public, convictions. Bernoulli demanded that in the exegetical and historical disciplines the scientific method should be rigorously applied but that, alongside of this, in dogmatics and the practical disciplines the ecclesiastical method should prevail, a method that took account of the confession of the church and the requirements of worship. Gross expressed the wish that alongside of rigorously academic lectures, there would be nonscientific, practical, devout discussions in which a personal witness could be heard and expression given to things that can be utilized in preaching and Christian fellowship. In the Netherlands, in 1876, following the ideas of Tiele and Rauwenhoff, a division was instituted at state universities between the science of religion, which would be taught by the university, and the dogmatic and practical disciplines, which would be taught under the auspices of the church. Later, also De la Saussaye Jr. and

---

49. Ed. note: Bavinck is referring here to a movement in nineteenth-century German theology known as "mediating theology" (*Vermittelungstheologie*). This theology, inspired by Schleiermacher, proceeded from the subjectivity of faith and attempted to join Christian faith with the modern scientific worldview of its "cultured despisers." Important representatives of this school were I. Dorner, J. Neander, H. Martenson, K. Nitsch, and J. Müller.

50. Ed. note: Bavinck is referring to Paul Lagarde (1827–91), an early representative of the "philosophy of religions" school (*Religionswissenschaftschule*).

Valeton[51] proposed that the science of religion be kept at the university but that theology be taught at a seminary under church auspices.[52]

Theology or Religious Studies?

[10] Against this division there are so many theoretical and practical objections that it should be viewed as profoundly inadvisable. From a practical point of view, if the so-called "unbiased" science of religion is taught at the university and theology is pursued at the seminary, one can imagine that either the lectures at both institutions will be attended by all students in theology or that lectures at the university will be attended by one group and those at the seminary by another. In the latter case, one would see emerging among ministers of the Word a distinction in rank between those who had a "scientific" education and those who had a practical training. This inequality would have a most pernicious effect on the ministerial office as well as the ministry itself, and indeed on the whole life of the church. If, however, both kinds of lectures were attended by all theological students, the result would be that the conflict that had been avoided on the institutional level would rage in full force in the minds of the students. Students, and following them the churches, would become the dupes of this full-blown scientific dualism. In this connection it would not help at all to console them with the notion of making a distinction between their own personal and their official, ministerial convictions. Certainly, despite this well-intended advice, the two sets of convictions would be at war in the minds of students and ministers and not let up before one of them had fully subjugated and driven out the other. The human mind is not amenable to such double-entry bookkeeping, such a dual conception of truth. The human conscience is even less disposed to be silenced by this dualism than by the Hegelian type. According to Hegel, it is the essence of religion to confess the truth of faith in the mode of pictorial language (*vorstellungsmässig*), and so the dogmatician or philosopher who has transposed this truth into pure concepts (*Begriffe*) does not cease and cannot cease as a believing Christian to live in the world of pictorial thought rather than in that of pure concepts. Similarly, a chemist does not cease to eat like an ordinary human being, though as a scientific man he analyzes food chemically and has very different thoughts about it than the unlearned person. Kaftan, commenting on this point, correctly remarks that while eating and chemically analyzing food are not disparate functions in relation to the same object and can very well go together, it is impossible to believingly

51. Ed. note: Franz C. Overbeck (1837–1905) was a professor of theology in Basel, Switzerland; Cornelis P. Tiele (1830–1902) was a Remonstrant theologian at Leiden University; L. W. E. Rauwenhoff (1829–99) taught theology at Leiden University; Pierre Daniel Chantepie de la Saussaye (1848–1920) was a leader of the "ethical" school of theology and taught at the State University of Amsterdam and Leiden University; J. J. P. Valeton (1848–1912) taught Old Testament at the University of Utrecht.

52. P. D. Chantepie de la Saussaye, *Stemmen Voor Waarheid en Vrede* (May 1896); J. Valeton, "Het Theologisch Hooger Onderwijs," *Onze Eeuw* (1905).

represent God as personal and as philosopher to say that such a representation is incorrect and that God is impersonal.[53]

The proposed split would be no less damaging for the character and work of the professors. A university, after all, has a dual purpose: the pursuit of science and training students for a position in society. Although these two goals sometimes clash and are sometimes hard to keep in mind simultaneously, it can be said in general that not only individually but especially in combination they are of great utility and can protect the universities and their educational programs from one-sidedness. Here, too, theory and practice have proven that they complement one another and need each other for correction. However, when the science of religion and theology are placed side by side, one in the department of theology and the other in a seminary, this link between science and life is radically broken, to the detriment of both. Professors in the science of religion may then easily imagine that they need not concern themselves with life, practice, or the church. They are at their liberty, without in any way thinking about the consequences, to "sell" the most foolish theories as the latest wisdom, since responsibility for the training of their students has been completely lifted from their shoulders and laid on those of the ecclesiastical professors. And the latter, oppressed by a sense of their inferiority, can hardly feel enthusiasm for a task based on nothing but an arrangement that is untrue to life and must despair of engendering in the minds of their students, beside the personal, an ecclesiastical conviction as well.

The theoretical objections are, if possible, even more serious. The proposed split, after all, is predicated on the idea that positivism is the only true conception of science. This hypothesis, however, is premature, for what thinker in the past ever believed in the possibility that, the moment he stepped into his study, a scholar like himself could silence his deepest religious, moral, and philosophical convictions? It is also diametrically in conflict with the theory of those who launched it, for the recognition that positivism represents the true understanding of science is a presupposition that in advance robs scientific investigation of its claim to be presuppositionless. Especially the science of religion cannot be pursued apart from a spectrum of metaphysical premises. The science of religion, whether it is studied in a department of its own or as a independent cluster of disciplines in the literary department, always bases itself on the premise that not only are the religions of the world a historical fact but they also are worthy of intentional study. Such study also presupposes that religions are interrelated, that they all possess a common component, and that in an ascending order they produce and develop "religion" proper. Fundamental is the conviction that religion is not an illusion but a reality—in a word, the premise that in religion God makes himself known and enters into fellowship with human beings. All these are weighty suppositions that place beyond all doubt the fact that

53. Kaftan, "Zur Dogmatik," 142.

people are not opposing dogmas in theology from purely scientific motives simply because they are dogmas but because they themselves entertain dogmas with which they wish to replace the others. The theology that is based on a Christian footing has to yield to a science of religion based on a positivistic footing. However the two differ, they have in common the fact that they do not hang in the air but rest on faith.

We conclude, therefore, that when in the interest of church practice the modern science of religion concedes to dogmatics an ecclesiastical method and to the practical disciplines an ecclesiastical seminary, it is thereby doing the church a "favor" that Christian theology cannot accept. If it did, it would thereby be admitting that materialistic or pantheistic unbelief bears a scientific character and at the same time that Christian faith does not belong in the domain of science. As a special favor, space may be cleared for it in an annex of the temple, in an ecclesiastical seminary! And by some this dishonor done to Christian theology is regarded, of all things, as an honor! Knowledge, it is then argued by some (e.g., Kaftan[54]), is not the highest aim of the human mind. The original gospel, the principle of the Reformation, and especially Kant, "the philosopher of Protestantism," have taught us that it is only the moral will whose activity unlocks the way to God and the knowledge of him. The intellect, after all, is confined to the world of the senses and does not extend to the origin, essence, and end of things. However, the assumption of a worldview that brings the world, as science causes us to know it, into harmony with our moral life is an act of the will and is rooted in a value judgment about our spirit. The heart has its own reasons, reasons that reason does not know. For that reason the gospel is also addressed to our will. The purpose of revelation is practical; it is not intended to serve the increase of our knowledge but the advancement of our salvation. Believing is not an activity of the intellect but an act of the will. And theology is not a speculative but a practical science.[55]

However much good there is in this argumentation, as a whole it is nevertheless unacceptable. The idea that faith assumes a certain quality or disposition of the will is nothing new and was even better understood in the past than it is today. But believing is not for that reason an act of caprice; we cannot believe whatever and whenever we please. A worldview is not a product of the will that can be said to function completely arbitrarily and to accept what it pleases. If one were to teach this, one would lapse into complete indifferentism and skepticism in the sphere of religion and theology and do violence to the nature of the faith as well. For all faith, as Kaftan correctly holds

---

54. Ibid., 129–39. Cf., also William James, *The Will to Believe and Other Essays in Popular Philosophy* (Cambridge, Mass.: Harvard University Press, 1979 [1897]); Th. Lorenz, *Essays Deutsch* (Stuttgart, 1899).

55. Essentially this is the teaching of medieval thinkers such as Duns Scotus and Durandus; cf. A. Stöckl, *Geschichte der Philosophie des Mittelalters*, 3 vols. (Mainz: F. Kirchheim, 1864–66), II, 78ff.; Schanz, *Ist die Theologie eine Wissenschaft?* (Stuttgart, 1900).

in opposition to Schleiermacher, includes a certain kind of knowing. And this knowledge is not produced but accepted by faith. Faith always comes from what is heard, and what is heard comes through the word of God (Rom. 10:17). If then the content of faith comes through revelation, faith itself, too, is in a sense generated by the "compelling evidence of the facts." It is true by virtue of its nature that the word of God impacts the human subject differently than, say, a report of purely historical events; it also addresses the will and cannot generate faith apart from the will. But though believing does not occur apart from the will, it is not the product of the will. Therefore, the word of God has stood and still stands independently of our will and acceptance. The word of God has an objective content that was established before, and persists apart from, our faith, just as much as the world of colors and sounds exists independently of the blind and the deaf. In that case, however, knowledge of the objective content of revelation has significance of and for itself. This is true of all science. All science has inherent value and purpose, apart from whether it has practical utility or yields benefits for life.

Misuse has often been made of the slogans "art for art's sake" and "science for the sake of science," but they contain the truth nevertheless that the true, the good, and the beautiful are invaluable, not merely as means by which each benefits the other but also individually by themselves. The intellect, accordingly, is not subordinate to, or merely a resource for, the will. Voluntarism is as one-sided as the intellectualism that defines human beings exhaustively in terms of their intellect. But both intellect and will, the true and the good, have their own legitimacy and place. On the basis of positivism, which knows neither a final ground nor a final purpose of things, people alternately have to make the intellect subordinate to the will or the will to the intellect. Psychologically, positivist thought swings back and forth between the two, just as in the socioeconomic sector it is unable to find a way of reconciling the individual and society. But theism, here as elsewhere, furnishes the true solution. For in an absolute sense, neither the intellect nor the will, the true or the good, can be an end in itself (*Selbstzweck*); were this the case, they would be elevated to the level of the divine, and we would relapse into paganism. A "creature" can never be an end in itself, neither individual nor society nor the state, and neither can abstractions like the true, the good, and the beautiful be ends in themselves. For every creature as such exists by and, hence, for God. Science exists also for God's sake and finds its final goal in his glory. Specifically, this then is true of theology; in a special sense it is from God and by God, and hence for God as well. But precisely because its final purpose does not lie in any creature, not in practice, or in piety, or in the church, amidst all the [other] sciences it maintains its own character and nature. Truth as such has value. Knowledge as such is a good. To know God in the face of Christ—by faith here on earth, by sight in the hereafter—not only *results* in blessedness but *is* as such blessedness and eternal life. It is this knowledge dogmatics strives for in order that God may see his own image reflected and his own name recorded in the human consciousness. And for that reason theology and dogmatics do not belong, by the grace of a positivistic science, in a church seminary, but in the university of the sciences (*universitas scientiarum*). Furthermore, in the circle of the sciences, theology is entitled to the place of honor, not because of the persons who pursue this science, but in virtue of the object it pursues; it is and remains—provided this expression is correctly understood—the queen of sciences.[56]

Dogmatics, Apologetics, Ethics

[11] If dogmatics, then, finds its rightful place in the third division of theological science, the task still remaining is to distinguish it from a number of other disciplines that belong to this third division as well.[57] All the disciplines of this group have to do with dogma, i.e., with the truth as God has revealed it in his Word, but each in its own way. It can be heard in the way the church clearly and forcefully confesses it in its written and unwritten creeds, and then symbolics, the science of symbolic theology, results. It can be conveyed in simple, comprehensible form (the "milk" of 1 Pet. 2:2) to the youthful members, the children of the church, and then we are dealing with catechetic theology, which is to be distinguished from catechetics, the art of doing this in church education. It can be defended and maintained in its truthfulness and legitimacy against its opponents, and that is the task of apologetics (or elenctic theology). It can also be set forth thetically and positively, and at the same scientifically, in a systematic form, and then we are speaking of the practice of dogmatics. All these disciplines have in common the fact that they put on display the treasures of the sacred Scriptures, but each in its own way. Dogmatics does this, as it was described in the past, in a scholastic or scholarly way, i.e., in the manner in which it ought to be done in schools of higher learning. Much, if not everything, depends of course on the position adopted by the dogmatician. If, along with Pietists and "biblical theologians," he assumes a sharp contrast between Scripture and church doctrine, he will adhere as closely as possible, in language, expressions, and other ways, to Scripture and make a minimal attempt to process the discovered material rationally. If he views the confession of the church, the history of dogma, not as corruption but as development of the truth of Scripture, his dogmatics will have an ecclesiastical and confessional character. If he takes a rationalist position over against both Scripture and the church, the religious convictions he advances will be largely negative. All

56. On this expression, *regina scientiarum,* see H. Denzinger, *Vier Bücher von der religiose Erkenntniss* (Würzburg, 1857), II, 564.

57. Ed. note: Bavinck's terminology reflects the division found in Abraham Kuyper's *Encyclopaedie,* where the first grouping of dogmatics is "The Bibliographical Group," the second "The Ecclesiological Group," and the third "The Dogmatological Group"; see A. Kuyper, *Encyclopaedie der Heilige Godgeleerheid,* vol. III. In Kuyper's encyclopedic division, included in the dogmatological group, in addition to dogmatics proper, are symbolics, history of dogma, ethics, elenctics, and apologetics.

this relates to a difference in method and will be discussed later. But for this very reason it is not a good idea, with J. I. Doedes,[58] to distinguish three kinds of dogmatics: New Testament, ecclesiastical, and critical dogmatics. By doing this, one ascribes to all three equal status and legitimacy, and the confusion in the field of dogmatics, already considerable, becomes even greater. New Testament dogmatics as the preeminently Christian kind will inevitably come to stand over against the two others. Furthermore, the first two species of dogmatics may be practiced apart from one's own convictions, and critical dogmatics becomes solely that of one's own independent views. The task of dogmatics, however, is always the same. It is and can, from its very nature, be nothing other than a scientific exposition of religious truth, a detailed exposition and interpretation of the Word of God. It is a laying out of the treasures of sacred Scripture, a commitment to the standard of teaching (Gr. παραδοσις εἰς τυπον διδαχης, Rom. 6:17), so that in it we possess a form and image of the heavenly doctrine (*forma ac imago doctrinae coelestis*). Accordingly, dogmatics is not itself the Word of God. Dogmatics is never more than a faint image and a weak likeness of the Word of God; it is a fallible human attempt, in one's own independent way, to think and say after God what he in many and various ways spoke of old by the prophets and in these last days has spoken to us by the Son.[59]

The question of how dogmatics can best fulfill this task is a question of method and will be answered in the following chapter. Here we only still need—because of the importance of the matter—to discuss the relation of dogmatics to apologetics and ethics. Up until the present day, there has been difference of opinion about the definition and task, the method and the place, of apologetics. It has been variously classified with every group of theological disciplines. Sometimes it has been put at the top of the entire theological enterprise and then again barely tolerated, as a practical field of little importance, in the last division of theology or even completely banished from its domain. There is no valid reason for either such overvaluation or such disdain. Its very name, like that of polemics and elenctics, already shows that it is not a heuristic science whose aim—either under that name or as the doctrine of principles, fundamental dogmatics, philosophical dogmatics, etc.—is to discover the essence of Christianity and to apply the outcome of that search to the whole of theology as its standard. For theology, as an independent scientific enterprise, has its own first principles and does not borrow them from philosophy. Placing apologetics at the head of all the other theological disciplines, as this occurs in Schleiermacher and others, is explicable only from the fact that these theologians no longer recognized theology's own principles and were forced to look elsewhere for a foundation on which the building of theology could rest. If, however, theology is de-

58. J. I. Doedes, *Encyclopedie der Christelijke Theologie* (Utrecht: Kemink, 1876), §48.

59. A. Polanus, *Syn. Theol.*, 539; Johann Heinrich Heidegger, *Corpus Theologiae Christianae*, 2 vols. (Zurich: J. H. Bodmer, 1700), I, §58.

duced from its own source, i.e., from revelation, it has its own certainty and does not need the corroboration of philosophical reasoning. Accordingly, apologetics cannot and may not precede dogmatics but presupposes dogma and now gets the modest but still splendid task of maintaining and defending this dogma against all opposition. It now attempts to do this, not in response to some specific challenge, but fundamentally in terms of the opposition that dogmas as the truth of God encounter at all times, be it in ever changing forms, from the side of the "natural man." Hence, it gradually advanced from the level of *apologia* to that of apologetics and assumed an increasingly more scientific character. Such a scientific defense of the dogma, i.e., of the entire content of revelation and of Christianity as a whole, is possible for the reason that nature and grace, creation and redemption, coming as they do from one and the same God, are not and cannot be in conflict. Only sin, which consists not only in a perverse disposition of the heart but also in the darkening of the mind, has brought opposition and conflict between the two. However, because redemption serves precisely to eradicate that sin, root and branch, and to restore creation to its original state, the patient investigator will always find his discoveries confirming a saying by J. Görres: "Only dig a little deeper, and everywhere you will stumble upon Catholic (or rather, Christian, theistic) ground." "Perhaps small sips taken in philosophy lead a person to atheism, but fuller draughts will bring him back to religion."[60]

[12] Dogmatics is most closely related to ethics. In ancient times the word *dogma* embraced both the articles of the faith and the precepts of the decalogue, the dogmas of the faith and the dogmas of conduct. Ethics was either incorporated in dogmatics (in Lombard, Aquinas, Melanchthon, Calvin, Martyr, Musculus, Sohnius, etc.), or treated in a second part after dogmatics (in Polanus, Amesius, Heidegger, Wollebius, Wendelinus, Mastricht, Brakel, etc.), or discussed separately from dogmatics (as in Danaeus[61] in his *Ethices Christ.* [1577], bk. III, as well as in Keckermann, Walaeus, Polyander, Amyraldus, Pictet, Driessen, Hoornbeek, Heidegger, Osterwald, J. A. Turretin, Stapfer, Beck, Wyttenbach, Endemann).[62] Although this separate treatment is not wrong per se, still, in conjunction with the influence of Aristotle, which already made itself felt in Melanchthon's *Philosophia moralis* (1539), and in conjunction also with the growing interest of recent philosophy in moral issues, it had the effect of increasingly depriving ethics of its

60. Latin: Leves gustus in philosophia movent fortasse ad atheismum, sed pleniores haustus ad religionem reducunt. Ed. note: Joseph Görres (1776–1848) was a renowned apologist for the Roman Catholic Church in Münich, Germany.

61. Danaeus, *Ethices Christianae* (1577), book III.

62. Cf., A. Schweizer, "Die Entweckung des Moralsystems in Reformirte Kirche," *Studien und Kritiken* 1 (1850); W. Gass, *Geschichte des Christlichen Ethik*, 2 vols. in 3 (Berlin: Reimer, 1881–87), II, 131ff.; Christoph Ernst Luthardt, *Geschichte der Christlichen Ethik* (Leipzig: Dorfflung und Franke, 1893); W. Geesink, *De Ethiek in de Gereformeerde Theologie* (Amsterdam: Kirchener, 1897).

theological and Christian character. Kant made human beings not only epistemologically but also morally autonomous; in listening to the moral law, human beings obey their higher natures and are thus led automatically to faith in God and to religion. Morality and religion are not materially different but nevertheless formally distinct; religion causes us to conceive the moral law as divine commandment and so facilitates its accomplishment; it is not the foundation of, but an aid to, morality.

Many theologians since then have represented the religion-morality relation in the same way. In Schleiermacher, and especially in Rothe, ethics is not deduced from Christianity, but Christianity is still in fact incorporated in ethics. And among the more recent moralists like Krarup and Herrmann, the Christian religion is not the foundation of morality but only supplies us with the power better to fulfill the commandments of the moral law, which are self-existent. Troeltsch decisively rejects all attempts at grounding ethics in dogmatics and conceives dogmatics as the doctrine of the final ends of human life and as an account of the moral goods, for the realization of which human beings ought to live in the family, the state, society, etc. Proceeding from this foundation, a leftward development occurred in the direction of a morality independent of all religion, a naturalistic ethics grounded in biology and sociology and even in a transvaluation (*Umwertung*) of all that had hitherto had moral value.[63] Over against this development others, like Dorner, Wuttke, Palmer, Luthardt, H. Weiss, Köstlin, Scharling, Frank, Kähler, and Kübel, sought greater connectedness for the science of ethics with the Christian religion. But, generally speaking, this still did not take place to the full extent, for not only did these theologians assume a mediating position between theology and philosophy, but as a rule they did not sharply define the relation between Scripture and confession either. The result of this was that the boundary lines between dogmatics and ethics almost never became really clean. This is the case when the distinction between them is characterized as that between knowing and doing, the doctrine of salvation and living, the life of Christ in the church and that in the individual, the doctrine of God and the doctrine of man.[64]

63. Bruno Bauch, "Ethik," in *Die Philosophie im Beginn des Zwanzigsten Jahrhunderts: Festschrift für Kuno Fischer,* ed. W. Windelband (Heidelberg: C. Winter, 1901), I, 54–103.

64. I. A. Dorner, *A System of Christian Doctrine,* trans. Alfred Cave and J. S. Banks, rev. ed., 4 vols. (Edinburgh: T. & T. Clark, 1888), I, 26; idem, *A System of Christian Ethics,* trans. C. M. Mead and R. T. Cunningham (New York: Scribner & Welford, 1887), 17ff.; A. Wuttke, *Christian Ethics,* trans. John Power (New York: Nelson & Phillips; Cincinnati: Hitchcock & Walden, 1874), I, 21; Palmer, *Moral des Christentums,* 24; J. I. Doedes, *Encyclopaedie,* §59, 4; J. J. Van Oosterzee, *Christian Dogmatics,* trans. John Watson and Maurice J. Evans, 2 vols. (New York: Scribner, Armstrong & Co., 1874), §4, 4; Gunning and Saussaye, *Het Ethische Beginsel der Theologie,* 12; F. E. Daubanton, "De Inrichting der wijsgeerige Godgeleerdheid," *Theologische Studiën* 3 (1878): 114ff. Cf. O. Ritschl, "Die Ethik der Gegenwart in der Deutschen Theologie," *Theologische Rundschau* (1903): 399–414, 445–61, 491–505; idem, *Wissenschaftliche Ethik im moralische Gezetzgebung* (Tübingen: Mohr, 1903).

All these distinctions suffer from the same defect: they all seek a fundamental difference between dogmatics and ethics. Such a fundamental difference is nonexistent. Theological ethics, which is in the nature of the case to be distinguished from philosophical ethics, is totally rooted in dogmatics. The lines of separation described above create a dualism between God and man, individual and community, salvation and life, rest and movement, intellect and will, and pave the way for ethics to go, by way of a speculative philosophy, in search of a principle of its own. The result is—as in the work of Rothe—that ethics loses its theological character, and from its speculative heights looks down with disdain upon historical, positive dogmatics. If dogmatics and ethics are to be treated as distinct disciplines—which for various reasons is desirable but still opposed by many[65]—the distinction between the two can only consist in the fact that human beings, however always and utterly dependent on God, are nevertheless also free and independent agents. Regenerated and renewed by the grace of the Holy Spirit, sinful human beings again receive the desire and strength to live in accordance with God's commandments. Dogmatics describes the deeds of God done for, to, and in human beings; ethics describes what renewed human beings now do on the basis of and in the strength of those divine deeds. In dogmatics human beings are passive; they receive and believe; in ethics they are themselves active agents. In dogmatics, the articles of the faith are treated; in ethics, the precepts of the decalogue. In the former, that which concerns faith is dealt with; in the latter, that which concerns love, obedience, and good works. Dogmatics sets forth what God is and does for human beings and causes them to know God as their Creator, Redeemer, and Sanctifier; ethics sets forth what human beings are and do for God now; how, with everything they are and have, with intellect and will and all their strength, they devote themselves to God out of gratitude and love. Dogmatics is the system of the knowledge of God; ethics is that of the service of God. The two disciplines, far from facing each other as two independent entities, together form a single system; they are related members of a single organism.

65. Karl Sartorius, *Die Leichenverbrennung innerhalb der christlichen Kirche* (Basel: C. Detloff, 1886); Friedrich Nitzsch, *Lehrbuch der Evangelischen Dogmatik*, prepared by Horst Stephan, 3d ed. (Tübingen: J. C. B. Mohr, 1902); J. T. Beck, *Einleitung in das System der Christlichen Lehre*, 2d ed. (Stuttgart: J. F. Steinkopf, 1870). A. Dorner, "Über das Verhältnis der Dogmatik und Ethik," *Theologische Jahrbuch für Protestantische Theologie* 15, no. 4 (October 1889): 481–552; J. C. C. von Hofman, *Der Schriftbeweis*, 3 vols. (Nördlingen: Beck, 1857–60), I, 14; H. H. Wendt, *Die Aufgabe der Systematische Theologie* (1894), 12.

2

THE METHOD
AND ORGANIZATION
OF DOGMATIC THEOLOGY

The material for constructing a dogmatic theology comes from Holy Scripture, church teaching, and Christian experience. From the beginning, Scripture served as the rule of faith and the foundation of all theology. As the church spread into and engaged the broader world, it became necessary to clarify and firm up the rule of faith against false teaching. This led to the rise of a strong episcopal teaching authority and an increased dependence on authoritative church tradition. Over time the weight of tradition increased while Scripture's role receded. The Reformation sought to renew the church's moorings in Scripture and, in time, gave rise to an antischolastic "biblical theology." The philosophical reversal in philosophy, represented by Kant, Schleiermacher, and Hegel, produced yet another theological method—the subjective. Experience replaced knowledge as the foundation of theology, which was itself separated from science and metaphysics. Taking the starting point in Christian consciousness, attempts were made to ground theology in morality, the feeling of absolute dependence, or the unfolding of the universal Spirit. The concern about normativity and objectivity eventually led to an emphasis on the scientific study of religion, its history, and psychology. Christianity was to be studied critically, just as the other religions of the world.

*Neither scientific objectivity nor complete subjectivity are possible. All knowledge is rooted in faith, and for faith to be real it must have an object that is knowable. This requires a divine revelation that is more than a fulfillment of subjective desire. Religion must be true and provide its own distinct path to knowledge and certainty. Christian theologians must place themselves within the circle of faith and, while using church tradition and experience, take their stand in the reality of revelation. Though dogmaticians are bound to divine revelation and must take seriously the confessions of the church, their work is also personal and contextual. Religious feeling cannot serve as the epistemic source of religious truth; divine revelation is needed. At the same time, this truth must be personally appropriated by faith. The liberty that this provides has not been adequately understood and practiced by Roman Catholicism. There are times when heroic figures such as Martin Luther **needed** to stand up to false teaching and misconduct in the church. We must obey God rather than men.*

*The concern for revelation-based normativity in dogmatics must not be construed to serve as a reason to overlook or deny the importance of confessional and cultural factors in dogmatic treatises. No one is free from the biases of church upbringing and particular environmental contexts. We are always products of our background, including our ecclesiastical upbringing. Awareness of this reality led some to attempt divesting themselves of their confessional identities and returning to the more confused and "pure gospel" situation of the New Testament and the early church. So-called "biblical theology" is then opposed to "scholastic theology," as though the latter were not at all biblical. But setting Scripture over against church teaching is as wrong as separating heart and mind, feeling and knowing. The sole aim of dogmatics is to set forth the thoughts of God that he has laid down in Holy Scripture. A good dogmatic method must take into account church teaching and Christian experience as well as Scripture. Dogmatic theology is possible only for one who lives in the fellowship of a Christian church. While Scripture is logically the only foundation of church and theology, pedagogically the church is prior to Scripture. Dogmatics is not, however, the same as symbolics. The latter describes and explains the church's confession, while dogmatics sets forth what **ought** to count as truth even if it differs from a church's current confession. Symbolics and dogmatics do, nevertheless, mutually influence and assist each other.*

Virtually every dogmatics begins with the doctrine of Scripture as the sole foundation of theology. The knowledge of God given in revelation is not abstract and impersonal but the vital and personal knowledge of faith. The objective revelation in Scripture must be completed in subjective illumination, which is the gift of the Holy Spirit. The best-equipped theologian carries out the task by living in the full communion of faith with the church of Christ. The best method for doing theology is thus the synthetic-genetic method, which replicates the manner in which Christian dogma has arisen organically from Scripture as a whole. The experimental method of Charles Hodge, on the other hand, by gathering facts and then framing a testable hypothesis to explain these facts, separates fact and word and fails to do justice to the unity of Scripture's teaching.

Once the preferable method for dogmatic theology has been chosen, we face the problem of ordering the material. How should the content of dogmatics be organized? The church's first theologians provided some order in their treatment but often lacked a clear principle of organization. Among the earliest arrangements were those that followed the basic trinitarian order of the Apostle's Creed. It is worth noting that from the beginning ethical implications of certain doctrines were included in theological overviews. The material of theology became much more organized in the Middle Ages, thanks to the work of such men as Bonaventure, Peter Lombard, and Thomas Aquinas. A critical development during this period was the acceptance of the distinction between "mixed" and "pure" articles of faith. Articles of faith derived from revelation and theology alone were pure; those derived from philosophy (and theology) were mixed. This distinction led to a greater emphasis on and role for philosophical prolegomena to theology. The foundations for theology were regarded as "natural theology," and thus to be derived from philosophy and by reason apart from revelation. This part of theology grew significantly in relation to the doctrinal content itself.

Reformation theologians initially ignored these questions of prolegomena, choosing to concentrate on biblical content. As Protestant theologians followed the path of medieval Roman Catholics, their final products became more "scholastic," triggering once again a reaction that favored "biblical" and "practical" teaching and preaching. Focusing on practical issues has both advantages and disadvantages. The analytic method, which is dominated by practical concerns of how to obtain salvation, as well as Cocceius's covenantal theology are problematic because their theological starting point is not God but humanity's need for covenantal fellowship, for salvation. The impact of modern philosophy changed the face of dogmatics by diminishing the content and enlarging the formal discussion about method. Since Kant declared God to be unknowable, reason and natural theology were substituted for divine revelation. Morality and religious feeling became the starting point and subject matter of theology; the prolegomena of religious philosophy grew in size and influence in comparison with the content of theology.

Properly speaking, the content of dogmatics is the knowledge of God as he has revealed himself in Christ through his Word. Dogmatics is neither a philosophical system nor a subjective description of personal faith. Instead, it is an explication of the content of Christian faith as that is objectively given by God in revelation and received by believers in faith through the power of the Holy Spirit. In terms of order, while a trinitarian order, divided in terms of the economy of divine works (Father and Creation, Son and Redemption, Holy Spirit and Sanctification) is to be commended for its thoroughly theological character, the historical-genetic method is much to be preferred. In the trinitarian order, there is too much overlap in content, and the history of theology and philosophy makes clear that it too easily ends up in theogonic speculation. Much better is the method that proceeds from God and then descends to his works in creation and redemption in order through them to bring creation back to God. The essence of the Christian religion consists in the reality that the creation of the Father, ruined by sin, is restored in the death of the Son of God, and re-created by the grace of the Holy Spirit into a kingdom of God. Theology is about God and should reflect a doxological tone that glorifies him.

[13] By the method of dogmatics, broadly speaking, one must understand the manner in which the dogmatic material is acquired and treated. Three factors come into play in this acquisition: Holy Scripture, the church's confession, and Christian consciousness. Depending on whether or not any one of these factors is used, overestimated or underestimated, and how it is positioned in a modified relation to the remaining two, the starting point of dogmatics as well as its development and content will differ.

In the earliest period of the Christian church, it lived by the word of the gospel proclaimed to it by the apostles, which was clarified and expanded in the Epistles and the Gospels. There was no difference between the word received in preaching and the word passed down in writing. The whole of it was based on the Old Testament, which was, at once and without resistance, accepted and recognized by the Christian churches as the Word of God. From the beginning the Old Testament was, for Christians, the book of revelation augmented and completed in these last days by the word of the gospel through the oral and written preaching of apostles. Accordingly, from the very beginning both the Old Testament and the apostolic writings held authority in the churches of Christ and were viewed as sources of knowledge. From them people drew their knowledge of God and the world, of angels and human beings, of Christ and Satan, of church and sacrament. From the most ancient times on, it was customary to demonstrate the truth of the faith, the confession of the church, by means of Holy Scripture, the Scriptures of the prophets and apostles. Dogma was that which Christ and the apostles had taught, not that which had been conceived by philosophy. Scripture was the rule of faith (*regula fidei*); confession and church were subordinate to it. The most ancient and, from ancient times, the most important proof for the dogma was the proof from Scripture.[1]

APOSTLES, BISHOPS, AND THE RETURN TO SCRIPTURE

But, in the nature of the case, in that beginning period the boundary lines between apostolic and nonapostolic writings were not always sharply drawn. Just as the prophetic and the apostolic writings were not equally well known in the different churches, by all and in every place, so also certain nonapostolic writings were highly valued in some churches and publicly read in their worship services. Even though, materially speaking, a large group of apostolic writings enjoyed canonical authority, the canon, in a formal sense, was not established till much later. Also, at a very early stage the baptismal formula developed into a short creed that was gradually expanded into the Apostles' Creed. Seeberg even believes that various New Testament expressions, such as διδαχη (teaching), ὁδος (way), λογος (word, reason), and particularly τυπος διδαχης (the form of teaching), that the apostles proclaimed and to which the churches had to adhere (Rom. 6:17; 16:17; 1 Cor. 4:17)

1. Adolf von Harnack, *History of Dogma*, trans. Neil Buchanan, J. Miller, E. B. Speirs, and W. McGilchrist and ed. A. B. Bruce, 7 vols. (London: Williams & Norgate, 1896–99), I, 13, 145–49; idem, *The Mission and Expansion of Christianity in the First Three Centuries* (New York: Harper, 1962 [1908]), 219ff., 279ff.; Rudolf Knopf, *Das nachapostolische Zeitalter: Geschichte der christlichen Gemeinden vom Beginn der Flavierdynastie bis zum Ende Hadrians* (Tübingen: J. C. B. Mohr [P. Siebeck], 1905), 348, 393ff.; Reinhold Seeberg, *Textbook of the History of Doctrine*, trans. Charles A. Hay, 2 vols. in 1 (Philadelphia: Lutheran Publication Society, 1905), 46, 135. Johannes Knuze, *Glaubensregel, Heilige Schrift und Taufbekenntnis Untersuchungen über die dogmatische Autorität, ihr Werden und ihre Geschichte, vornehmlich in der alten Kirche* (Leipzig: Dörffling & Franke, 1899), 493; Th. Zahn, "Glaubensregel," *PRE³*, VI, 682–88.

already suggest the existence of a small dogmatic and ethical catechism.[2] Although we should probably not assume that these expressions point to an established, fixed creed, there is no doubt that elements of the Apostles' Creed go back to the end of the first century.[3] And although in the earliest period the authority of Scripture was decisive for the doctrine of the church, gradually the tradition developing alongside of it gained independent status as a source of knowledge. Soon, with the rise of the episcopacy and over against a wide range of sects and heresies, the idea surfaced that the bishops were the lawful successors of the apostles and the bearers of truth. Consequently, in virtue of the "grace of truth" (*charisma veritatis*) given them, they were entitled to decide what was the pure, apostolic Christian truth. Through this process, the teaching of the bishops became the "rule of truth" (*regula veritatis*), and the authority of Scripture increasingly receded into the shadows. Tradition became a force alongside of, and, not long afterwards, superior to, Holy Scripture. Finally, when tradition even received its own infallible organ in the person of the pope, it also, in fact, took the place of the Word of God, for "the *auctoritas interpretiva* is invariably the supreme and the true authority."[4]

[14] Already in the Middle Ages, and later especially during the Reformation, many movements rose up in opposition to this devaluation and neglect of Scripture. The Reformation again squarely took its position in the original gospel, just as Jesus returned from the tradition of the elders to the law and the prophets and restored to Scripture the place of honor due to it. And later, each time tradition in the Protestant churches again threatened to become a freedom-suppressing force, a movement arose that, turning its back on scholasticism, sought its moorings in Holy Scripture. Erasmus already advocated a simple, practical, biblical Christianity,[5] a position shared by many Renaissance men, as well as by Socinians, Remonstrants, and numerous sects that later played a role inside as well as outside the churches of the Reformation. This movement even gained support from theologians like Calixtus and Cocceius and in the eighteenth century became increasingly more significant. Then, partly under the influence of rationalism and pietism, it assumed a decidedly hostile attitude to the confession of the church and opposed it in the name of Holy Scripture.[6]

2. Alfred Seeberg, *Der Katechismus der Urchristenheit,* Mit einer Einführung von Ferdinand Hahn, Unveränderter Nachdruck der Ausg. von 1903 (München: Kaiser, 1966); idem, *Das Evangelium Christi* (Leipzig, 1905).

3. Adolf von Harnack, "Apostolisches Symbolum," *PRE³,* I, 741.

4. Harnack, *Mission and Expansion of Christianity,* 233; Seeberg, *History of Dogma,* 137.

5. Friedrich Lezius, *Zur Charakteristik des Religiösen Standpunktes des Erasmus* (Gütersloh: C. Bertelsmann, 1895).

6. Cf., e.g., *Anton Friderich Büsching, *Epitome Theol. Christ.* (1756); *Gedanken von der Beschaffenheit und dem Vorzüge der biblischen dogmatischen Theologie vor der scholastischen* (1755). Ed. note: Bavinck does not indicate the author of *Gedanken* and gives 1755 as year of publication rather than 1756 for *Epitome.*

Later, others, while also advocating biblical dogmatics, as a rule had a deeper understanding of it than was possible under the sway of an unhistorical supernaturalism. It was especially F. C. Oetinger[7] who, dissatisfied with the abstract concepts of the prevailing eighteenth-century theology and philosophy, returned to the concrete, substantial, and living ideas he found in Scripture. In his dogmatics,[8] which was published only many years after his death, he strove not to remain with the words of Scripture but, through the words, to penetrate to reality and to grasp the things indicated in the words. In this respect he was deeply indebted to Bengel,[9] but in another way he owed much to the influence of Jacob Böhme. He did not allow the things he found in the words to stand side by side in isolation from each other but conceived them as a system. In his mind God and the world, matter and spirit, nature and grace became a vital unity, an organic system of truths, in which the idea of life animated all the parts and every particular was viewed in the light of the whole. J. T. Beck,[10] while avoiding the theosophic elements Oetinger derived from Böhme, took over his conception of biblical dogmatics. Against those who viewed the Christian consciousness as the epistemic source of truth, Beck maintained that Holy Scripture and it alone is the proper source of dogmatics. The content of faith, after all, lies outside of us and only becomes our possession by faith. The intellect is not productive but receptive and is made receptive, sanctified, and renewed by the truth that comes to us from without, from Scripture. However, since the content of faith, i.e., the divine truth, exists independently of us and apart from us (and as such can be accepted only by faith), it has its own principle, its own method, and its own system. Scripture contains the full divine truth in its entirety, i.e., the truth that was hidden in God before all times, indeed, as the foundation for the creation of the world and God's continuing care for it. Even now after the fall, sin notwithstanding, God's truth is made known in the world by its own inner divine power. It is therefore the task of dogmatics to reproduce this truth in its objective existence, in the reality of its organic relations. This means setting aside all special theological and philosophical knowledge (*gnosis*) in that reproduction. The theologian must pursue no other method than

---

7. Ed. note: Friedrich Christoph von Oetinger (1702–82) was a Lutheran theologian and pastor who grew up in a pietist religious tradition and was influenced greatly by the theosophical thought of Jacob Böhme (1572–1624).

8. F. C. Oetinger, *Theologia ex idea vitae deducta,* republished by Konrad von Ohly, 2 vols. (Berlin and New York: W. De Gruyter, 1979).

9. Ed. note: Johannes Albrecht Bengel (1687–1752) was a Lutheran New Testament scholar and textual critic. His text of the NT and critical apparatus (1734) represent the beginning of modern textual criticism.

10. Ed. note: Johann Tobias Beck (1804–78) taught theology and ethics in Basel and later in Tübingen. His theology was characterized by a decidedly biblical method (setting aside philosophy and church dogma) focusing on the idea of the kingdom of heaven.

the genetic, i.e., the method that sets forth the truth in terms of its own course of development in a manner in which all its parts stand in their organic relation to each other.[11]

Although J. C. K. von Hoffmann[12] does not belong to this school of thought, he nonetheless became prominent through his emphasis that dogmatics should be characterized by a strictly biblical pattern and proof. Animated from his youth on by a great love of history, he was deeply struck at a later age by the unity that fact and word, history and doctrine, content and form, together constitute in Holy Scripture. From this vantage point, he saw the whole of the Old and New Testament as a history of salvation (*heilsgeschidenis*) that was coherent in all its parts. In this history of the redemption of humanity, both word and fact consistently go together and both point and lead to Christ, to the church, and to the new heaven and the new earth. In keeping with this reality, Hoffmann now also determined the character of the scriptural proof needed in dogmatics. It is not the case that isolated dogmas should be demonstrated with the aid of isolated texts, but the whole system of truth must be proven with the whole of Scripture. Accordingly, Scripture in its entirety, word combined with deed and history with doctrine, is the foundation of dogmatics, and the dogmatic system must have the same material content as Holy Scripture. According to Hoffmann, then, dogmatics is not an account of pious states of consciousness, nor an exposition of the doctrine of Scripture or the church, nor a system deduced from a supreme principle. Instead, it is the scientific unfolding of that which makes the Christian a Christian, the self-knowledge and self-declaration of the believer. For that reason scriptural proof for a dogmatic system itself must correspond with Holy Scripture in all its parts, in content, articulation, and order.[13] With this determination of "the essence and law of Scriptural proof," Hoffmann exerted enormous influence on a broad and diverse number of theologians such as Kähler, Cremer, and Schlatter, as well as others.[14]

---

11. J. T. Beck, *Einleitung in das System der christlichen Lehre* (Stuttgart: J. F. Steinkopf, 1870), 255–81; idem, *Die Christlich Lehrwissenshaft* (Stuttgart: J. F. Steinkopf, 1875), 15–45; idem, *Vorlesungen über christliche Glaubenslehre*, herausgegeben von J. Lindenmeyer (Gütersloh: C. Bertelsmann, 1886–87), I, 530–48.

12. Ed. note: Johann Christian Konrad von Hoffman (1810–77) was a Lutheran theologian who taught at Erlangen and is known for his pioneering biblical theology work on the idea of salvation history (*heilsgeschichte*).

13. J. C. K. von Hoffmann, *Weissagung und Erfüllung im Alten und im Neuen Testamente: Ein theologischer Versuch* (Nördlingen: C. H. Beck, 1841–44), 1ff.; idem, *Der Schriftbeweis: Ein theologischer Versuch* (Nördlingen: C. H. Beck, [1853]) I, 1–32.

14. M. Kähler, *Die Wissenshaft der Christlichen Lehre*, 3d ed. (Leipzig: A. Deichert, 1905); Herman Cremer in Otto Zöckler's, *Handbuch der theologischen Wissenschaften*, 3d ed., 5 vols. (Nördlingen and Münich: C. H. Beck, 1889–90), III, 59–84, esp. 81–84; Franz Reiff, *Die christliche Glaubenslehre* (Basel, 1884); R. Kübel, *Das christlichen Lehrsystem nach der Heiligen Schrift* (1873); Eduard Böhl, *Dogmatik: Darstellung der christlichen Glaubenslehre auf reformirt-kirchlicher Grundlage* (Amsterdam: Von Scheffer, 1887), xiiiff.

THE TURN TO THE SUBJECT

[15] As a result of the great reversal that occurred in recent decades in philosophy, there has come into vogue yet another method in addition to the traditionalistic and biblical method. This method does not start out from the doctrine of the church or from the teaching of Scripture but from the believing subject, from the Christian consciousness. Kant, Schleiermacher, and Hegel were in agreement in no longer regarding religious truth as objectively given in Scripture or confession, and all three believed that it could be found in and derived from the religious subject. While their ideas about the origin and essence of religion diverged widely, each of them still took a different road to arrive at the knowledge of God and divine things. Kant based theology on morality and on the basis of the moral freedom of man postulated the existence of God and immortality. For Schleiermacher the essence of religion lay in a feeling of absolute dependence, and he thus viewed dogmatics as an account of the pious states of consciousness encompassed in that feeling. And finally, Hegel attributed primacy in religion to religious representations (pictorial images) and believed that by dialectical reasoning from these representations he could arrive at true and pure concepts. All these three methods have been taken over in dogmatics by theologians of various schools. Those who are more intellectual and speculative by nature link themselves most closely with Hegel and with respect to their dogmatic method have in common the following basic ideas: (1) Humans have no distinct organ, no special faculty, for religious knowledge; they can acquire knowledge, of whatever kind, only through their intellect and power of reasoning. (2) To speak correctly about religious knowledge requires an assumption that the supersensuous is knowable. Consequently, one must be able to advance proofs that are more or less compelling for the existence of God, of the soul, and of immortality, or for the reality of the facts of salvation as held to by Christians. (3) From this it follows that there cannot be two worldviews existing side by side, one religious and the other scientific. Instead, there can be only one worldview, a worldview that is simultaneously religious and scientific. Faith and knowledge, in other words, are not incompatible. (4) Nevertheless, should a distinction between religious and philosophical truth arise, this could only consist in the form or mode of expressions. Even though religion articulates in the form of representations what philosophy expresses in the form of concepts, materially they have the same content. Mediating theologians like Rothe and Dorner, and especially modern theologians like Strauss, Biedermann, Pfleiderer, and Scholten, readily accepted this method, and it also is favored by some Dutch theologians today.

But after speculative philosophy lost its fascination and yielded its place to exact natural science, other theologians, both of the more conservative and the more progressive schools of thought, sought refuge in the method of Schleiermacher and Kant. In this respect they agree on the following formal points: (1) The source and organ of religious knowledge is not the intellect and reason but the human conscience, the heart, the feelings, and will. Religion is rooted in the interior spiritual nature of man, in his moral needs and experiences. (2) To those who follow Kant's method, these moral experiences, while not themselves immediately religious in nature, are nevertheless the starting point for religion. From this base one can make further progress and by reasoning and postulation conclude the existence of a reality that corresponds to the religious representations. To those, however, who favor Schleiermacher's method, these internal spiritual experiences themselves already bear a religious character. The feeling of absolute dependence is by nature a religious feeling, and religion is an original and essential element in human nature. Consequently, dogmatics has no other task than to describe these devout states of consciousness, and by way of this description it already gains the religious knowledge attainable by human beings. (3) This religious knowledge, gained one way or the other, is essentially distinct from that which science seeks to acquire. Religion and science, believing and knowing, though occurring side by side, are totally distinct from each other. Each has its own field of interest, and the two have nothing to do with each other. As a human being the philosopher has the same picture of God as anyone else, though as a philosopher he may be a deist or a pantheist. At most, as Lipsius and Rauwenhoff think,[15] it may in the end be possible to bring about some measure of agreement between the religious and the scientific worldviews.

[16] Up until a few years ago, this subjective method—whether of a more ethical or a more mystical cast—held virtually uncontested sway in the field of dogmatics. No essential change was made in this regard even by Ritschl. It is true that in his second period he began seriously to resist not only the concept-philosophy of the Hegelian school but also the method of Schleiermacher and Hoffmann who chose the religious consciousness as their starting point. Under the influence of the fresh appreciation for the human personality that he had gained from his historical studies, he even returned, in dogmatics, to the revelation of God in the person of Christ. He conceived this revelation, however, in a manner peculiar to him and in a very restricted sense. Revelation contained no metaphysical teaching about the origin, essence, and end of things but only the gracious disclosure of God's will to establish his kingdom on earth. Accordingly, for Ritschl, the content of religion was limited to "value judgments"; dogmas implied no theoretical or philosophical worldviews but only that which corresponds to the religious need of the church. Thus dogmatics was not a pure but a practical science, limited to a doctrine of faith and salvation. It is restricted to what can be utilized in preaching and the relations of Christians among themselves. In order to treat the subject, it is therefore necessary for the dogmatician to position himself within, not outside of, the church of Christ. He must gain the

15. I. J. De Bussy, "De Ontwikkelingsgang der Moderne Richting," *De Gids* 7, no. 3 (October 1889): 91–135. Ed. note: This essay is a review of L. N. C. Rauwenhoff, *Wijsbegeerte van den Godsdienst*, vol. 1. (Leiden, 1887).

same religious-ethical experience that in the case of the church constitutes the basis for its faith. Only then can he understand the religious significance of Jesus and appreciate the gift of God's gracious love in his person. Although Ritschl was fond of appealing to Luther and Melanchthon for this method, he forgot to designate the criterion by which the content of the Christian religion could be judged. This resulted in great difficulty for his followers and caused them to split up in various directions.

To the left Hermann sought as much as possible to detach faith from all knowledge (*notitia*) and to think of it purely as trust (*fiducia*). This faith, conceived as practical assurance, is not based on any authority but arises by way of a moral experience, by the deep impression that the personality of Jesus makes on every mind in search of God. For the historical Jesus who rises before our minds in the Gospels, while he humbles us by his moral purity on the one hand, on the other again lights us up by his friendliness and love of sinners and generates trust in him in our hearts and so in God. This picture of Jesus, his "inner life," apart from his miracles, is the final and most basic ground of our faith. To the degree our moral experience grows richer, the content of our faith increases. This faith content, however, does not consist in "empirically apprehensible entities" but in religious-ethical experiences that always remain personal and cannot be summed up in a system.[16] By this process of reasoning Hermann shifted completely to the stance of the theology of experience. Christian consciousness, moral experience, is the source of knowledge for dogmatics since the content of faith grows out of the faith itself. It is true that Hermann does distinguish between the ground and the content of faith, but the ground of faith, which is the "inner life" of Jesus, is so vague that not much can be done with it and it disappears completely to the degree that faith is detached from all knowledge (*notitia*). Still, many students of Ritschl followed Hermann in this direction, although some of them acknowledge that faith is not always, as Hermann believes, generated by the direct impact of Jesus' image on the human mind but also indirectly by preaching and one's upbringing.[17] Nevertheless all agree that faith with its content is the product of personal moral experience (an *Erlebnis*).[18] The ideas of Kant (religion is based

16. W. Hermann, *Die Verkehr das Christen mit Gott*, 4th ed. (Stuttgart: Cotta, 1903), 82ff. Ed. note: English translation: *The Communion of the Christian with God*, ed. Robert T. Voelkel (Philadelphia: Fortress, 1971). Cf. M. Peters, "Zur Frage nach dem Glauben," *Neue Kirchliche Zeitschrift* (1903).

17. E.g., O. Ritschl, "Der geschichtlich Christus, der christliche Glaube und die theologische Wissenschaft," *ZthK* 3 (1893): 384ff.; J. Weiss, *Die Nachfolge Christi und die Predigt der Gegenwart* (Göttingen: Vandenhoeck & Ruprecht, 1894), 134ff.

18. Gottschick, *Die Kirchlichkeit der sogenannte kirchliche Theologie* (Freiburg, 1890), 11ff.; Reischle "Der Streit über die Begründung des Glaubens auf den geschichtlichen Jesus Christus," *ZthK* 7 (1897): 171–264; A. Von Harnack, *Zur gegenwartige Lage des Protestantismus* (Leipzig, 1896); idem, *What Is Christianity?* trans. Thomas Bailey Saunders (New York and Evanston: Harper and Row, 1957 [1900]); Sabatier, *Esquisse d'une philosophie de la religion d'aprés la psychologie et l'histoire*, 7th ed. (Paris: Fischbacher, 1903), 359ff. Ed. note: This volume is also available in English translation: *Outlines of a Philosophy of Religion based on Psychology and History* (London: Hodder and Stoughton, 1897).

on morality; the human spirit first asserts itself in the moral sphere and then ascends to the noumenal or supersensuous) are still operative here. But just as in Kant, so here dogmatics and science end up far apart from each other. According to Otto Ritschl, science is concerned only with the finite. However, people are also religious beings who besides their science have faith—i.e., moral experience of God—in their hearts and from that vantage point they interpret all things religiously. The worldview is the same for believer and unbeliever, but the believer assesses everything differently. The believer subordinates all things to God as the Holy and Loving One and renders an account of this in his dogmatics. Consequently, such a dogmatics is the consistently changing formulation of the life of faith and is thoroughly personal.[19]

But in the school of Ritschl a right turn was taken by theologians like Kaftan, Wobbermin, Kattenbusch, Traub, and others, who made a serious attempt to escape the subjectivism of the theology of consciousness and to take a more objective position. So, while Kaftan recognizes that faith is rooted in one's personal life and arises in the way of moral experience, he nevertheless again realizes that it is not merely trust but also knowledge. Thus dogmatics must be a normative science. It needs an authority on which to base itself and must speak in an absolute tone of voice. Hence in Kaftan's work, revelation and Scripture become more prominent and achieve greater significance for dogmatics. Wobbermin, analogously, contends that the content of our religious-moral consciousness is traceable to an objective authority present outside of it, an authority that appears before us in the person of Christ. Christ has authority for us because he lived in unbroken fellowship with the Father and in the exercise of that fellowship was never disturbed by any sin. We know this Jesus only from history, however. Our devout consciousness and religious experience cannot be the source of the truth of faith since we can know the latter only from the apostolic witness. This apostolic witness, however, must not be considered as inspired Scripture but as the historic source of the authority given us in the way of revelation for the religious-moral life. In this way dogmatics again acquires an objective source and norm and so also accepts the task of presenting and explaining the Christian religion as *truth*. Dogmatic theology, therefore, cannot be dualistically separated from science or be utterly detached from metaphysics. On the contrary it has a twofold duty: (1) to demonstrate that it is reasonable and even necessary with respect to the ultimate questions of knowledge to adopt the position of the Christian faith; (2) to indicate what kind of knowledge, relative to these questions, the Christian faith addresses; and (3) to demonstrate that the doctrines of faith do not contradict the recognized findings of science. However much the attempt of Kaftan and Wobbermin to escape subjectivism deserves our appreciation, they nevertheless do not succeed in finding a firm basis for dogmatics. They do not accept rev-

19. O. Ritschl, "Theologische Wissenschaft und religiöse Spekulation," *ZThK* 12 (1902): 202–48.

elation and Scripture as these present themselves to us, but, in terms of content and scope, make them dependent on the judgment of the dogmatician. The fact is, Kaftan says, that in our use of Scripture we must let ourselves be guided by the practical ideas of religion, specifically by those of the kingdom of God and of reconciliation. Wobbermin does say that the ultimate authority for a truth of faith lies in the religious-moral consciousness of Jesus, but what the content of that consciousness is is something we must first seek to discover. This discovery must be obtained by following the historical-psychological method, proceeding from Scripture as a purely historical source and document of revelation. The maxim "according to Scripture" is subordinated to the rule "according to the faith." In that way authority is finally located in the religious subject. Hence we must conclude that the right wing of Ritschl's school also fails to rise above consciousness-theology.[20]

THE SEARCH FOR A SCIENTIFIC, OBJECTIVE THEOLOGY

[17] In recent years this has been felt and expressed by younger theologians as well. In their opinion Ritschl was still inconsistent, stopping halfway as he did. His real intention, after all, was no other than—following in Kant's footsteps—to make a complete separation between religion and science. But he failed to make the separation complete. In religion he continued to incorporate theoretical elements, bound it to history, adopted a biased viewpoint in favor of Christianity, made exegesis and the history of dogma subservient to a system, and fundamentally remained a dogmatician. But, so it is argued, this remnant of dogmatism also must be discarded. On the one hand, consistently applying the separation principle, we must view religion as purely practical. With Schleiermacher we must see religion as subjective piety, as the mysticism of the heart. On the other hand, we must emancipate the whole of theology from all subjective bias. Scripture and church, exegesis and the history of dogma must be studied scientifically, and the whole of Christianity must be classified among the universal human phenomena of religion. Accordingly, a few years back the so-called history-of-religion method was applied in the study of the Old and New Testaments by Wellhausen, Duhm, Smend, Delitzsch, Zimmern, Winckler, Gunkel, Bousset, Deismann, Wrede, Wernle, and Heitmuller, among others. That method was applied to the history of dogma, among others, by Krüger, von Schubert, Sell, and Weinel and in dogmatics especially by Ernst Troeltsch of Heidelberg.

20. J. Kaftan, "Was ist Schriftgemäss?" *ZThK* 3 (1893): 93ff.; idem, "Zur Dogmatik," *ZthK* 13 (1903): 114; Wobbermin, *Grundprobleme der Systematische Theologie* (Berlin, 1899); idem, *Theologie und Metaphysik* (Berlin: 1901); F. Traub, "Die Religionsgeschichtliche Methode und die Systematische Theologie," *ZthK* 11 (1901): 323ff.; Häring, "Zur Verständigung in der Systematische Theologie," *ZthK* 9 (1899): 97ff.; Kattenbusch, "Die Lage der Systematische Theologie in de Gregenwart," *ZthK* 15 (1905): 103–46; F. Traub, "Zur dogmatischen Methodenlehre," *Theologische Studien und Kritiken* 78 (1905): 425–52; J. Bovon, *Dogmatique Chrétienne*, 2 vols. (Laussane: Georges Bridel, 1895–96), I, 63–96. Cf. Ecke, *Die Theologische Schule Albrecht Ritschls und die evangelische Kirche der Gegenwart* (Berlin, 1897).

According to Troeltsch, the unity that used to exist between religion (Christianity) and science has been definitely broken up since the rise of eighteenth-century rationalism. This breakup was caused by the change that occurred both in the view of science and in that of religion. Science laid aside all apriorism, became positive, and banished metaphysics. Today it exists solely as mathematical-mechanical, natural science and as the critical-comparative study of history. In both respects it is opposed to the old view of religion and theology. And so the latter gradually changed in the sense that theologians no longer want anything to do with an external authority, as much as possible reduce or abandon the supernatural elements—like prophecy, miracle, and inspiration—that occur in authority-based religion, fully accept the historical criticism of Scripture, and regard dogmas purely as expressions of personal faith. Accordingly, there no longer exists a method by which Christianity could still be upheld as absolute religion. The historical-apologetic and speculative method, as well as the method of religious experience, attempted this in vain. Theology, therefore, has no alternative but to radically break with every dogmatic method and apply with honesty and consistency the history-of-religions method. Christianity must be freed, objectively as well as subjectively, from its isolation and incorporated into the context of history as a whole as a part of the general history of religions. It must be studied in terms of the history-of-religions method, which will not prove Christianity to be the absolute religion, because history makes all things relative. An advantage, however, is that one can study Christianity as a genuinely historical phenomenon without fear of criticism. In addition, one can judge Christianity by a criterion provided by history and the comparative examination of religions and thus still recognize and honor it in its enormous historical value as the highest religion.[21]

While, as was to be expected, this history-of-religions method did not meet with much approval among Ritschlians,[22] it does deserve credit for its consistency. For if one accepts the positivistic concept of science and seeks refuge for religion in separation from science, there will be no peace until religion has re-

---

21. E. Troeltsch, "Die Selbständigkert der Religion," *ZthK* 6 (1896): 177; idem, "Geschichte und Metaphysik," *ZthK* 8 (1898): 1ff.; idem, *Die Wissenschaftliche Lage und ihre Anforderungen an die Theologie* (Tübingen: J. C. B. Mohr, 1900); idem, "Ueber historische und dogmatische Methode in der Theologie, in *Gesammelte Schriffen von Ernst Troeltsch*, 10 vols. (Tubingen: J. C. B. Mohr [Paul Siebeck], 1913), II, 729–53; idem, *The Absoluteness of Christianity and the History of Religions*, trans. David Reid (Richmond, Va.: John Knox, 1971 [1902]); idem, *Psychologie und Erkenntnistheorie in der Religionsgeschichte* (Tübingen: J. C. B. Mohr, 1905); Cf. Rade, "Zum Streit um die rechte Methode der christlichen Glaubenslehre," *ZthK* 11 (1901): 429–34.

22. Hegler, "Kirchengeschichte oder Christliche Religionsgeschichte," *ZthK* 13 (1903): 1–38; Traub, "Kirchliche und unkirchliche Theologie," *ZthK* 13 (1903): 39–76; Gottschick, "Die Entstehung der Losung der Unkirchlichkeit," *ZthK* 13 (1903): 77–94; Reischle, "Historische und dogmatische Methode der Theologie" *Theologische Rundschau* (1901): 261–75, 305–24; Traub, "Die religionsgeschichtliche Methode und die Systematische Theologie," *ZthK* 11 (1901): 301–40; W. Hermann, Review of "E. Troeltsch, *Die Absolutheit des Christenthums und die Religionsgeschichte*," *Theologische Literaturzeitung* 27 (1902): 330; A. von Harnack, *Die Aufgabe der Theologischen Fakultäten und die Algemeine Religionsgeschichte* (Berlin: G. Schade: 1901).

linquished all theoretical elements to science and itself has nothing left but a vague mystical feeling. But it seems that modern science cannot leave religion alone even in this hidden corner of the human heart. For not even the historical method is regarded as fully scientific. Many scholars do maintain the independence of the science of history alongside that of nature,[23] but it is very significant that nowadays this independence has to be vigorously defended. It is a goal of modern science to make the human sciences positive and exact by applying the methods of natural science as much as possible to their domain as well. For a considerable period of time, this has already been done in psychology—with some results. In the same way, for a number of years now, the experimental method has been applied to religious phenomena. Before one can begin to speculate, one must first, as objectively as possible, study the phenomena and establish the facts. Religious people must be observed and examined in the same exact way as sick people, neuropaths, and mental patients. Their spiritual life must become the object of scientific study by the same method that is used when the psychic life of animals, children, and adult men and women is observed and studied. Of course, in this connection the "interesting cases" are first in line for attention. Just as art can best be studied by the masterpieces that have been created in this area, so one can best discover the essence of religion by studying those people who were totally absorbed in it. Prophets, seers, ecstatics, visionaries, enthusiasts, miracle-working saints, heretics, and schismatics best display religion in its personal, individual, original, and creative power. The content of religion is immaterial; everything depends on the characteristic form. These religious phenomena, then, must first be observed objectively without predetermined judgment or evaluation. "The exclusion of transcendence," as Flournoy calls it, is the first necessary requirement in the application of the scientific method to religious phenomena. In the second place, one must add, as heuristic principle, "the biological interpretation of religious phenomena," i.e., viewing religious phenomena "as the manifestation of a vital process." Religion must be examined in its psychophysical nature, its growth and development, in its connection with the other functions of the soul, and in its importance for the individual and society. Once all this has been done, one has a solid foundation for possible speculation and can, perhaps, draw a number of metaphysical conclusions. The historical-comparative and experimental-psychological study of religion, then, finally culminates in a philosophy of religion, a philosophical dogmatics.[24]

23. H. Bavinck, *Christelijke Wetenschap* (Kampen: Kok, 1904); 65ff.

24. Th. Flournoy, *Les principes de la psychologie religieuse* (Geneva: H. Kündig, 1903); Georges Berguer, *L'application de la Méthode Scientifique à la Theologie* (Geneva, 1903); Murisier, *Les Maladies du sentiment religieux*, 2d ed. (Pans: Félix Alcan, 1903); William James, *The Varieties of Religious Experience* (Cambridge: Harvard University Press, 1985 [1904]); B. Duhm, *Das Geheimnis in der Religion* (Tübingen: J. C. B. Mohr, 1927 [1896]); G. Verbrodt, *Psychologie in Theologie und Kirche* (Leipzig, 1893); idem, *Psychologie des Glaubens* (Göttingen, 1895); idem, *Beiträge zur religiosische Psychologie* (Leipzig, 1904); S. Cramer, *De Godsvrucht Voorwerp van Christliche historische Onderzoek* (Amsterdam, 1903); cf. C. Hylkema, review of Cramer in *Theologische Tijdschrift* 34 (1900): 385–98.

[18] On the method of dogmatics, as we have seen, there are large differences of opinion. These differences, however, can be immediately cut down to size by saying that for the study of dogmatics the history-of-religions and the psychological method do not really qualify. This is not to say, of course, that these two methods have no right to exist and that their application cannot bear any fruit at all for the study of dogmatics. Rather, the contrary is the case. Religion is always and everywhere a most important phenomenon, one that is fully deserving of examination and study. This is true not only for historical but also for psychological studies. Religion is a matter of the whole person, affects him as no other power in the world, is connected with all the functions of his psychic life, and expresses itself in mental images, emotions, and actions. It is therefore of the greatest importance psychologically as well. It is fascinating, not to mention fruitful, to look at religious phenomena like conversion, faith, prayer, devotion, ecstasy, contemplation, and so forth from a psychological angle. But for all that, the history-of-religions and psychological method cannot be the method of dogmatics. The reasons are as follows.

The experimental method is applicable only to a very limited degree even in psychology and therefore less so in the case of psychic-religious phenomena. In addition, one cannot, in a historic and psychological sense, understand the religious life, thought, and feelings of others if one is not personally religious, has no idea of religion, and cannot evaluate religious phenomena by a specific criterion. Total "presuppositionlessness" (*Voraussetzungslosigkeit*) renders study and research impossible. But if nevertheless presuppositionlessness is one's aim and one takes a positivistic position with respect to religion, the inevitable result is a "theology of 'mood' in place of concepts, a system of paradoxes in place of sober truth, the 'art' of being enthused about everything in place of the conviction which looks for a fixed standard of things."[25] In this area the purely empirical method results in surrender to the relativism of the historical process or event and the loss of one's ability to judge the truth-content of a religion. It also results in the tendency to judge religious phenomena purely esthetically in terms of their "beauty." Then, as Nietzsche did with Nero and Cesar Borgia, one goes into raptures over ecstatics and fanatics as the religious showpieces of humanity.

It also must be said that such consistent relativism, which is synonymous with total indifferentism, is certainly not the intent of the advocates of the history-of-religions and psychological method. It is precisely their aim, by the use of this method, to arrive at a dogmatics based not on abstract ideas but on facts. But it is not hard to demonstrate that the path chosen does not and cannot lead to this goal. Let scholars show historically and psychologically—something they are not now and probably will never be able to do—how religion originates, grows, develops, and falls into decay. Let them also,

25. Hegler, "Kirchengeschichte oder Religionsgeschichte," 18ff.

if need be, prove statistically that religion is a cultural power of the first rank and will probably remain so in the future. How can they ever deduce from all this that religion is based on truth, that an invisible reality underlies it? Anyone who has not acquired this conviction by another route will certainly not get it by way of the history-of-religions and psychological method. One arrives at metaphysics, at a philosophy of religion, only if from another source one has gained the certainty that religion is not just an interesting phenomenon—comparable to belief in witches and ghosts—but truth, the truth that God exists, reveals himself, and is knowable. One who believes in a philosophy of religion may assume the appearance of being totally unbiased in his study of religions, but that appearance is false. He does not proceed from a fact that is recognized as certain by all but from a certain valuation of that fact. He assumes a priori—without investigation—that religion is a normal, not a pathological, phenomenon, and that it has its warrant in the existence and self-revelation of God. This fundamentally deprives these philosophers of religion of every right to look down disparagingly from the heights of their scientific impartiality on those who proceed from the premise that Christianity is the true religion and that it should serve as the standard in the study of the different religions. These philosophers of religion proceed, no less certainly than the latter, from an unproven presupposition that they have accepted a priori in faith, namely the telling presupposition that God exists, that he can be known, and consequently that religion is based on truth. Over against the consistent empiricists and positivists, they have as much right to defend this premise as those who proceed from the truth of Christianity. Their supposition is more vague and general than that of the latter, but it bears the same character and is of the same kind.

In addition, whereas the modernist and the Christian premise exhibit the same character when viewed from the perspective of positivistic science, and both are equally unproven a priori suppositions of faith, still, in terms of plausibility, the first is by no means on a level with the second. For the premise from which modern psychologists and philosophers of religion proceed, namely that religion is truth, itself again presupposes a concept of religion that was not obtained by careful research but imported into theology by the romanticism of Schleiermacher. According to that concept, what counts in religion is solely states of consciousness, not mental images and actions. But this view is untenable. To say that religion consists in states of consciousness will not do. Not every state of consciousness and feeling can be called religious but only a certain feeling, a distinct quality of feeling, hence a feeling triggered in a certain way by a specific force. Consequently, religious feeling is not ultimate but points back to God, who arouses that feeling and accords a uniquely religious quality to it. A logical implication, then, is that religious feeling depends on, and is determined by, the idea a given person has of God. Religious feeling will differ depending on whether God is conceived pantheistically or deistically, monotheistically or polytheistically. This is proven by psychology and history. Ideas in religion have never been viewed as indifferent but are always considered of the greatest importance. Faith always and everywhere includes knowledge (*notitia*) and, in accordance with this knowledge, arouses a certain kind and degree of trust. This again arises from the fact that God not only reveals himself in the human heart but also in the human intellect and conscience and, outside of humanity, in nature and history as well. Neither the concept of religion with which the modern philosophy of religion operates nor its concept of revelation have been obtained by careful research but have rather been supplied to it by romantic philosophy. The notion that God works only and exclusively in the human heart and has everywhere else retreated from his creation is simply untenable. We have to make a choice here. We can consider the world in its entirety and in all its parts as the work of God's hands and in that case also as a revelation of his attributes. The other possibility is that it originated and exists apart from God, but then there is no reason why we should believe in a revelation of God in the human heart either.

In fact, no one actually relates to the religions of the world as objectively as he might pretend in theory. Those who assume this position are the indifferent ones who have broken with all religion but are for that reason, precisely because of their profound partiality, unfit for the study of religion. Those, however, who value religion and acknowledge it as truth, always, in their studies, bring a certain kind of religion along with them and cannot rid themselves of it in the pursuit of those studies. A human being cannot keep silent about that which is most precious to him or her in life and death. A Christian cannot keep his faith, his most profound religious convictions, outside the door of his study nor view his own religion as objectively as he would that of a practitioner of some primitive religion. No one, therefore, in the pursuit of his studies, consistently applies the idea of the equivalence of all religions.

It is Troeltsch's aim, not to move from Christianity to the history of religions, but to ascend from the latter to the Christian faith as the highest religion. And that is, in fact, a serious aspiration on his part. He does not really wish to deny that Christianity is the highest, indeed the absolute, religion. He even acknowledges that Christianity publicly asserts that claim and that this claim is not untrue simply because it cannot be scientifically proven. But to his mind this is a matter of faith that cannot be allowed to have a voice in the scientific study of religions. The science of religion must pursue its work objectively and impartially. Nevertheless, he expects that in the end this science will demonstrate that Christianity is the highest, if not the absolute, religion in the world.[26] As we remarked above, such study, undertaken with this aim in mind, very definitely proceeds from a religious premise, namely that religion is truth. Underlying such historical investigation as well is the

---

26. E. Troeltsch, "Selbstandigkeit," 212f.; idem, "Geschichte und Metaphysik," 54ff.

premise that the history of religions constitutes a single whole, that in this history a progressive revelation of God takes place, and that in the development of the religions Christianity occupies the highest rank. Troeltsch is persuaded of all this, not as a result of purely empirical research, but in virtue of a personal appreciation, by another route therefore than that by which, in theory, he looks for certainty. In the end he even hopes to achieve a summation of Christian truth uncovered by historical research, including the results of the special sciences, and in so doing again believes that religion and science cannot be in conflict—that truth, that the world, that God is one. All this is convincing evidence that the history-of-religions method and the psychological method are more appearance than reality, that in fact they quite definitely proceed from a certain metaphysics, from personal appreciation, from certain faith premises. This means, therefore, that they are in principle equally dogmatic as the method of a positively Christian dogmatics. The difference is that the theorists in question hold as true a dogma other than what Scripture has taught us. Furthermore, in the name of science, by way of the history-of-religions method and the psychological method, they promote this dogma, which to them is axiomatic. Practically, the application of this method produces a serious conflict between faith and theology, church and school, and Scripture and science, a conflict they then seek in vain to resolve with the distinction between an exoteric and an esoteric theology.[27]

THE CERTAINTY OF THEOLOGICAL KNOWLEDGE

[19] As is evident from what has been said so far, the method of dogmatics is totally dominated by the question of whether in religion, and specifically in Christianity, there is a way to arrive at certainty other than that which is usually taken in science. If that is not the case, religion in general and Christianity in particular, including Christian dogmatics, lose all independence. Christian dogmatics would then constitute an area that should—the sooner, the better—be surrendered to other sciences whose object is either nature or history. But if there exists a unique religious certainty, it should be made plain both in its distinction from and its connection with other kinds of certainty.[28] Later when we deal with the external and internal principles of theology (revelation and faith), we will do this at length. Among other things we will then argue specifically that the historical-apologetic, the speculative, and the ethical-practical methods cannot lead us to absolute certainty in the realm of religion. But here we will confine ourselves to the following remarks.

27. In his essay "Geschichte und Metaphysik" Troeltsch gives us cause to suspect that he agrees with this distinction.

28. Ed. note: Bavinck provides a more extensive discussion of faith's certainty in his book-length treatment *The Certainty of Faith,* trans. H. der Nederlanden (Jordan Station, Ont.: Paideia, 1980). The original Dutch version, *De Zekerheid des Geloofs* was first published in 1901.

Even within the circle of the nontheological sciences, there are varying kinds and degrees of certainty. There is a certainty that is acquired by personal observation; we are absolutely certain of that which we see with our eyes and hear with our ears and touch with our hands. There is an intuitive kind of certainty, moreover, which, in virtue of the peculiar organization of our mind, arises automatically and spontaneously without any compulsion and prior to all rational reflection. In this manner we accept the so-called eternal verities (*veritates aeternae*) that constitute the bases and premises of the various sciences. For example, we intuitively and without proof accept that a straight line is the shortest distance between two points, that sense perception does not deceive us, that the world outside of us really exists, that the laws of logic are reliable, that there is a difference between true and false, good and evil, right and wrong, beautiful and ugly, and so forth. Beyond this there is a certainty that is based on the witness of credible persons, a certainty that in our daily lives and in the study of history is of the greatest significance and substantially expands our knowledge. Finally, there is still another form of certainty that is acquired by reasoning and supported by proofs. Depending on whether one kind of certainty or another is attainable in the various sciences, the compelling character of their results will differ. There is no single kind of certainty that is equally strong in all the sciences, but the certainty obtainable in mathematical science differs from that in natural science, and the latter again differs from that in history, morality, law, philosophy, and so forth.

Since religion[29] is an independent phenomenon in a class by itself, we may expect that the certainty attainable in this area has a character of its own and is acquired in a way peculiar to it. The first kind of certainty mentioned above is specifically excluded because religion has to do with invisible matters not susceptible to sense perception. Excluded as well is the certainty acquired by reasoning, for religion is not a science but innate to all human beings and a need of all of them. Since humanity's entire weal and woe depends on religion, only that certainty will do that is absolute and obtainable by all, even the simplest of people. If religion is to be what it is said to be, viz., the service of God, the love of God with all one's mind, heart, and strength, then it must be grounded in revelation, in a word from God that comes with his authority. Divine authority is the foundation of religion and therefore the source and basis of theology as well. All this is naturally implied in the concept and essence of religion.

Christianity meets these criteria. In the first place, viewed now from the objective angle, it claims that God reveals himself in nature and history and particularly and centrally in Christ. So while incorporating general revelation, it still offers a special revelation. It relates itself to the entire world and

---

29. Ed. note: The Dutch word here is *Godsdienst*, which can also be translated as "worship" or "devotion."

to all of history and nevertheless claims a distinct place for itself in this setting. And viewed from the subjective side, it makes an appeal to, and connects with, humanity, which was created in the image of God and even in its fallen state cannot forget or erase its divine origin, nature, and destiny. At the same time, it says that this natural man who cannot understand the things of the Spirit of God (1 Cor. 2:14) must be born again and renewed to understand the revelation of God and to submit to the authority of his Word. Only those who are heartily disposed to do the will of God will confess that Jesus' teaching is from God (John 7:17).

The Christian theologian who sets forth the content of his faith in his dogmatics, because and insofar as he is a Christian, can only take his position within the Christian faith itself. All the questions about what Christianity is, about the manner, measure, and limits of revelation, can still be disregarded here. The issue before us is simple: A theologian can believe that there is no revelation, no greater and higher revelation, in Christianity (in the person of Christ, in the prophets and apostles, in Scripture) than can be observed elsewhere in nature or history. Anyone who so judges is then no longer a Christian and is not qualified or able to write a Christian dogmatics. Or a theologian can believe that there is a higher or greater revelation in Christianity. Someone who believes this cannot reject the greater light given him and must then look at all of nature and history, as well as the religions of non-Christian nations and people, by that light. We can set aside for now the question of where revelation is be found (in the church, in Scripture, in the person of Christ). Wherever the revelation that is foundational to Christianity is to be found, the Christian dogmatician has to take his stance there. This is where he stands as a Christian, and this is where he must still take his stand as a dogmatician, for with it his dogmatics will stand or fall.

[20] If the Christian dogmatician is to take a stand in revelation, we must ask where revelation can be found. At most three factors come up for consideration—Scripture, the church, and the Christian consciousness—and all three in turn, successively or in conjunction, have been used as sources for dogmatics. The Reformation returned to Holy Scripture and, along with the ancient Christian church, acknowledged it as the sole foundation of theology. Rome by degrees elevated tradition to a level above Scripture, while mystics and rationalists alike draw the content of dogmatics from the religious subject. Since for many people authority in religion has totally faded from view and subjective religion was made independent of objective religion, the religious consciousness (conscience, feeling, reason, or whatever one wants to call it) has become the source and standard of religious ideas. Since Schleiermacher the whole of theology has changed, among orthodox as well as modern theologians, into a theology of consciousness. Though in treating the different dogmas Scholten, Schweizer, Biedermann, and Lipsius may still work on the basis of ecclesiastical formulations, what they offer finally is nothing other than their personal faith. Theologians like Martensen,

Dorner, Hofmann, Philippi, Frank, and others also take their point of departure in the consciousness of the believer. Some time ago Schian argued that dogmatics had to take much greater account of human individuality than was currently done, for every dogmatician is subjective and can only articulate his own faith.[30] In the Netherlands, Van Oosterzee included the Christian consciousness among the sources of dogmatics. The poet Des Amorie van der Hoeven Jr., in *The Faith of the Human Heart,* composed the line: "The ineffable word is written in our heart and for it Christ supplied the sounds." Nicholas Beets sang:

> To be objective through and through
> is the demand,
> is a desideratum.
> But can it be?
> Ah, do not fool yourself:
> the systems are either personal—
> or quite inhuman.[31]

Van Manen, in his inaugural oration at Groningen, pointed to the personal character of doctrinal theology. And Doedes, in his *Encyclopaedia of Christian Theology* explained the boundless confusion prevalent in dogmatics in light of its personal character.[32]

In this picture of the state of affairs in dogmatics, there is a mixture of truth and error. The idea that dogmatics is, has always been, and must be, personal, is so self-evident that it does not have to be expressly mentioned or demanded. All works of scholarship, including dogmatics, bear the stamp of their authors. Precisely because a work of dogmatic theology is not a historic account but sets forth what we ought to believe, it cannot escape the influence of individuality. But this is something very different from the notion that the dogmatician is free of all objective ties. Like every science, dogmatics is bound to its own object and has its own source and norm. It is true that all dogmaticians will view and reproduce that object in their own way and their own language. However if they look at and describe the same object, personal differences will contribute to revealing the richness of thought inherent in dogmatics. However, the demand that doctrinal theology be personal may not function so as to consign it to a realm of caprice as though the content of faith, the images and ideas of religion, do not matter. It is God's will that we should love him also with the mind and think of him in a manner worthy of him. To that end he gave his revelation, the revelation to which dogmatics is absolutely bound, just as every other science is bound to the object it studies. If dogmatics should cease to recognize such a revelation, then what is left, as

30. M. Schian, "Glaube und Individualität," *ZthK* 7 (1897): 513ff.; 8 (1898): 170–94.
31. Hildebrand (N. Beets), *Dichtwerken* (Leiden: A. W. Sijthoff, 1885), vol. V, 130.
32. J. I. Doedes, *Encyclopaedie der Christelijke Theologie* (Utrecht: Kemink, 1876), 168ff.

Schian correctly states, is no more than the subjective and hence individual knowledge of that which belongs to the Christian faith.[33] But that would also be the end of dogmatics and of the Christian faith.

Dogmatics can only exist if there is a divine revelation on whose authority it rests and whose content it unfolds. Consciousness theology, which rejects Scripture and confession as sources of knowledge and seeks to derive all religious truth from the subject, is first of all in conflict with a sound theory of knowledge. We are products of our environment also in the area of religion. We receive our religious ideas and impressions from those who raise and nurture us, and we remain at all times bound to the circle in which we live. In no domain of life are the intellect and the heart, reason and conscience, feeling and imagination, the epistemic source of truth but only organs by which we perceive truth and make it our own. Just as physically we are bound to nature and must receive food and drink, shelter and clothing from it, so psychically—in the arts, sciences, religion and morality—we are dependent on the world outside of us. Feeling is especially unfit to serve as the epistemic source of religious truth, for feeling is never a *prius* (a prior thing) but always a *posterius* (something which follows later). Feeling only reacts to what strikes it and then yields a sensation of that which is pleasant or unpleasant, agreeable or disagreeable.[34]

The assertion that the religious and moral human being is autonomous is always linked with either deism or pantheism. Deism makes human beings independent of God and the world, teaches the all-sufficiency of reason, and leads to rationalism. Pantheism, on the other hand, teaches that God discloses himself and comes to self-consciousness in human beings and fosters mysticism. Both destroy objective truth, leave reason and feeling, the intellect and the heart, to themselves, and end up in unbelief or superstition. Reason criticizes all revelation to death, and feeling gives the Roman Catholic as much right to picture Mary as the sinless Queen of Heaven as the Protestant to oppose this belief.[35] It is therefore noteworthy that Holy Scripture never refers human beings to themselves as the epistemic source and standard of religious truth. How, indeed, could it, since it describes the "natural" man as totally darkened and corrupted by sin in his intellect (Ps. 14:3; Rom. 1:21–23; Rom. 8:7; 1 Cor. 1:23; 2:14; 2 Cor. 3:5; Eph. 4:23; Gal. 1:6, 7; 1 Tim. 6:5; 2 Tim. 3:8), in his heart (Gen. 6:5; 8:21; Jer. 17:9; Ezek. 36:26; Mark 7:21), in his will (John 8:34; Rom. 7:14; 8:7; Eph. 2:3), as well as in his conscience (Jer. 17:9; 1 Cor. 8:7, 10, 12; 10:28; 1 Tim. 4:2; Titus 1:15)?

33. M. Schian, "Glaube und Individualität," 176.

34. Tholuck, "Gefühl," *PRE¹*, IV, 704–9; Bender, *Jahrbuch für deutsche Theologie* (1872): 659ff.; F. Philippi, *Kirchliche Glaubenslehre*, 6 vols. (Gütersloh: Bertelsmann, 1902), I, 60ff.; C. Hodge, *Systematic Theology*, 3 vols. (New York: Charles Scribner's Sons, 1888), I, 65ff.; S. Hoekstra, *Godgeleerde Bydragen* (1864), I, 43; idem, *Wijsgerige Godsdienstleer* (1894), 59ff., 213ff.; H. Bavinck, *Beginselen der Psychologie*, 2d ed. (Kampen: Kok, 1923).

35. A. Schweizer, *Die Glaubenslehre der evangelisch-reformirte Kirche* (Zurich: Orell, Fussli, 1847), I, 94.

For the knowledge of truth Scripture always refers us to objective revelation, to the word and instruction that proceeded from God (Deut. 4:1; Isa. 8:20; John 5:39; 2 Tim. 3:15; 2 Pet. 1:19; etc.). And where the objective truth is personally appropriated by us by faith, that faith still is never like a fountain that from itself brings forth the living water but like a channel that conducts the water to us from another source.

[21] Rome, understanding perfectly well this impossibility of religious and moral autonomy, bound human beings to the infallible church on pain of losing the salvation of their souls. For Roman Catholic Christians the infallible church, and so in the final analysis the infallible pope, is the foundation of their faith. The words *Papa dixit* (the Pope has spoken) is the end of all back talk. History teaches, however, that this theoretical and practical infallibility of the church has at all times encountered contradiction and opposition, not only in the churches of the Reformation but inside the Roman Catholic Church as well. It is not unbelievers primarily but the devout who have always experienced this power of the hierarchy as a galling bond to their conscience. Throughout the centuries there has not only been scientific, societal, and political resistance but also deeply religious and moral opposition to the hierarchical power of the church. It simply will not do to explain this opposition in terms of unbelief and disobedience and intentionally to misconstrue the religious motives underlying the opposition of various sects and movements. No one has been bold enough to damn all these sects because they were moved to resist the church and its tradition. Even Rome shrinks from this conclusion. The *extra ecclesiam nulla salus* (no salvation outside the church) is a confession that is too harsh for even the most robust believer. Accordingly, the "law" we see at work in every area of life is operative also in religion and morality. On the one hand, there is a revolutionary spirit that seeks to level all that has taken shape historically in order to start rebuilding things from the ground up. There is, however, also a false conservatism that takes pleasure in leaving the existing situation untouched simply because it exists and—in accordance with Calvin's familiar saying—not to attempt to change a well-positioned evil (*malum bene positum non movere*). At the proper time everywhere and in every sphere of life, a certain radicalism is needed to restore balance, to make further development possible, and not let the stream of ongoing life bog down. In art and science, state and society, similarly in religion and morality, there gradually develops a mindless routine that oppresses and does violence to the rights of personality, genius, invention, inspiration, freedom, and conscience. But in due time there always arises a man or woman who cannot bear that pressure, casts off the yoke of bondage and again takes up the cause of human freedom and that of Christian liberty. These are the turning points of history. Thus Christ himself rose up against the tradition of the elders and returned to the law and the prophets. Thus one day the Reformation had the courage, not in the interest of some scientific, social, or political goal, but in the name of Chris-

tian humanity, to protest against Rome's hierarchy. Frequently, even in the case of the sects and movements that later arose in the Protestant churches, that religious and ethical motive is undeniably present. So-called biblical theology also defends an important part of religious truth. When a church and theology prefer peace and quiet over struggle, they themselves trigger the opposition that reminds them of their Christian calling and task. Rome, in the nature of the case, can never approve of such opposition and has to condemn it in advance. The Reformation is itself the product of such opposition and cannot withhold from others what it assumed for itself. And Holy Scripture, though far removed in spirit from all revolutionary resistance, nevertheless, in Peter's regal statement "We must obey God rather than men" (Acts 5:29), legitimates the right to oppose every human decree that is contrary to the Word of God.

BIBLICAL THEOLOGY AND THE CHURCH

[22] Thus it seems the correct method is that followed by the so-called biblical theologians. However, this school suffers from grave one-sidedness as well. While it thinks that it is completely unbiased in relating to Scripture and that it reproduces its content accurately and objectively, it forgets that every believer and every dogmatician first of all receives his religious convictions from his or her church. Accordingly, theologians never come to Scripture from the outside, without any prior knowledge or preconceived opinion, but bring with them from their background a certain understanding of the content of revelation and so look at Scripture with the aid of the glasses that their churches have put on them. All dogmaticians, when they go to work, stand consciously or unconsciously in the tradition of the Christian faith in which they were born and nurtured and come to Scripture as Reformed, or Lutheran, or Roman Catholic Christians. In this respect as well, we cannot simply divest ourselves of our environment; we are always children of our time, the products of our background.[36] The result, therefore, is what one would expect: all the dogmatic handbooks that have been published by members of the school of biblical theology faithfully reflect the personal and ecclesiastical viewpoint of their authors. They cannot, therefore, claim to be more objective than those of explicitly ecclesiastical dogmaticians. The "pure" gospel that Ritschl finds back in Luther and Jesus corresponds perfectly to the conception he himself formed of it. All these so-called biblical schools, accordingly, are continually being judged by history; for a time they serve their purpose and recall a forgotten truth, but they do not change the course of ecclesiastical life and have no durability of their own.

36. *J. J. van Toorenenbergen, *De Christelijke Geloofsleer,* 6; A. Kuyper, *Encyclopaedie der Heilige Godgeleerdherd,* 2d ed., 3 vols. (Kampen: Kok, 1908–9), II, 522; III, 166; C. E. Nitzsch, *System of Christian Doctrine* (Edinburgh: T. & T. Clark, 1849), 8ff.; J. Kaftan, "Zur Dogmatik," *ZthK* 13 (1903): 513–18; J. Bovon, *Dogmatique Chrétienne,* 2 vols. (Laussane: Georges Bridel, 1895–96), I, 46–63.

As a rule they arise from a religious conviction that can no longer find itself in Scripture either. Admittedly, they consistently begin by appealing *from* the confession *to* Scripture but soon move from Scripture to the person of Christ and end by questioning his authority as well. And then history always demonstrates that the Christian faith has been preserved relatively most purely in the confessions of the churches. "In a certain sense modern Bible research has restored to a position of honor the old orthodox theology with its certainty that above all in its dogma it was speaking for the Bible."[37]

But such a conception of "biblical theology," besides being practically impossible, is also theoretically incorrect. Scripture is not a legal document, the articles of which only need to be looked up for a person to find out what its view is in a given case. It is composed of many books written by various authors, dating back to different times and divergent in content. It is a living whole, not abstract but organic. It nowhere contains a sketch of the doctrine of faith; this is something that has to be drawn from the entire organism of Scripture. Scripture is not designed so that we should parrot it but that as free children of God we should think his thoughts after him. But then all so-called presuppositionlessness and objectivity are impossible. So much study and reflection on the subject is bound up with it that no person can possibly do it alone. That takes centuries. To that end the church has been appointed and given the promise of the Spirit's guidance into all truth. Whoever isolates himself from the church, i.e., from Christianity as a whole, from the history of dogma in its entirety, loses the truth of the Christian faith. That person becomes a branch that is torn from the tree and shrivels, an organ that is separated from the body and therefore doomed to die. Only within the communion of the saints can the length and the breadth, the depth and the height, of the love of Christ be comprehended (Eph. 3:18). Add to this that the proponents of this school forget that the Christian faith is universal; it can and must enter into all forms and conditions. They oppose grace to nature in a hostile fashion and do not sufficiently take account of the incarnation of the Word. For just as the Son of God became truly human, so also God's thoughts, incorporated in Scripture, become flesh and blood in the human consciousness. Dogmatics is and ought to be divine thought totally entered into and absorbed in our human consciousness, freely and independently expressed in our language, in its essence the fruit of centuries, in its form contemporary (Da Costa). Accordingly, the contrast often made between biblical theology and dogmatics, as though one reproduced the content of Scripture while the other restated the dogmas of the church, is false. The sole aim of dogmatics is to set forth the thoughts of God that he has laid down in Holy Scripture.[38] But it does this as it ought to, in a scholarly fashion, in a scholarly form, and in ac-

---

37. F. Kattenbusch, "Die Lage der Systematische Theologie," *ZthK* 15 (1905): 145. Ed. note: Bavinck's page reference here is 45, which is clearly incorrect. P. 145 is within the boundaries of the cited article.

38. S. Maresius, *Syst. Theol.* loc. 1 §8.

cordance with a scholarly method. In that sense, Reformed scholars in earlier centuries defended the validity of so-called scholastic theology (*theologia scholastica*). They had no objections whatever to the idea of presenting revealed truth also in a simpler form under the name of positive theology, catechetics, and so forth. But they utterly opposed the notion that the two differed in content; what distinguished them was merely a difference in form and method. By taking this position they, on the one hand, as firmly as possible maintained the unity and bond between faith and theology, church and school. On the other hand, they also held high the scientific character of theology. However high and wonderful the thoughts of God might be, they were not aphorisms but constituted an organic unity, a systematic whole, that could also be thought through and cast in a scientific form. Scripture itself prompts this theological labor when everywhere it lays the strongest emphasis, not on abstract cognition, but on doctrine and truth, knowledge and wisdom.

[23] A good dogmatic method, therefore, needs to take account of all three factors: Scripture, church, and Christian consciousness. Only then can a person be kept from one-sidedness. Still, the relationship between these three must be defined. As a rule we receive our religious convictions from our environment. That is true in all religions, including Christianity. We were all born as members of a church, and we have been incorporated from birth in the covenant of grace. The promises of God are addressed not only to believers but also to their offspring. In critical times like our own, it not infrequently happens that later a painful break occurs between the faith of one's childhood and one's personal conviction. If this break is such that though one has to leave his own church one can still join another historic church, the break is healed relatively soon. Though change indeed occurs, there is no loss of religion itself, of the name "Christian," of the fellowship and confession. A dogma that is established and supplies comfort and support in life still remains. On this basis, then, a dogmatics that describes the truth of God as it is recognized in a particular church remains possible.

But frequently doubt makes much deeper inroads in the religious life. Many people lose all faith and fall into skepticism and agnosticism. Then dogmatics, faith, confession, and fellowship are gone; mere negation is incapable of creating fellowship. Others, however, unable to maintain the faith of their childhood, attempt by earnest effort and struggle to acquire a religious conviction of their own. In this connection, too, the influence of one's environment naturally asserts itself; one never arrives at a religious conviction totally on one's own. In this case the only difference is that what one could no longer find in a church one now seeks in a school of philosophy. In recent times every philosophy has been utilized in turn to generate and maintain certain religious convictions. In this situation, too, there is no longer any question of dogmatics. What remains is only a religious faith, a theory, a philosophy of religion, a philosophical theory of religion.

Accordingly, dogmatics is possible only for one who lives in the fellowship of faith with one Christian church or another. This is implicit in the very nature of religious faith. Religious ideas are distinguishable from scientific concepts, among others, in that the former are not rooted in one's own insight, in the authority of some human being, but only in the authority of God. Implied in this, however, is that these ideas have found credence and recognition in a religious circle, i.e., a church. This is evidence that in a dogma we are not dealing with human opinion but with divine truth. A church does not believe its confession because it appreciates the truth of it scientifically but solely on the basis of the word of God, whether this is expressed exclusively in Scripture or also through ecclesiastical organs. One who seeks his religious conviction in a school of philosophy confuses religion with science and gains nothing but a learned judgment or opinion (*sententia* or *opinio doctoris*), an opinion that is always uncertain and opposed by many. In virtue of its own nature, religious faith, however, is always bound to a religious community and its confession. Here, also, the situation is the same as everywhere else. Abstractions—universals—do not exist in reality. *The* tree, *the* human being, *the* science, *the* language, *the* religion, *the* theology are nowhere to be found. Only particular trees, human beings, sciences, languages, and religions exist. Just as a language is associated with a particular people, and science and philosophy are always pursued in a certain school and ideological context, so religion and theology can be found and nurtured only in a related community of faith.

A church is the natural soil for religion and theology. *The* religion and *the* theology do not now exist, anymore than *the* church. There are only differing churches and similarly differing theologies. This will be the case until in Christ the church has attained its full maturity and all have come to the unity of faith and the knowledge of the Son of God. This unity cannot be reached by force but can best be advanced if each person thinks through the faith of his own church and makes the most accurate presentation of it. It is not apart from the existing churches but through them that Christ prepares for himself a holy, catholic church. Nor is it apart from the different ecclesiastical dogmas but through them that the unity of the knowledge of God is prepared and realized. In the same way the dogmatician will best be able to work fruitfully for the purification and development of the religious life and the confession of his church. Tying in with what exists is the condition for achieving improvement in the future. Concealed in the "now" is what is to come.[39] This significance of the church for theology and dogmatics is grounded in the link that Christ himself forged between the two. He promised his church the Holy Spirit, who would guide it into all truth. This promise sheds a glorious light upon the history of dogma. It is the explica-

---

39. A. D. C. Twesten, *Vorlesungen über die Dogmatik*, 2d ed., 2 vols. (Hamburg: F. Perth, 1826–37), I, 46.

tion of Scripture,[40] the exposition that the Holy Spirit has given, in the church, of the treasures of the Word. Accordingly, the task of the dogmatician is not to draw the material for his dogmatics exclusively from the written confession of his own church but to view it in the total context of the unique faith and life of his church, and then again in the context of the history of the whole church of Christ. He therefore stands on the shoulders of previous generations. He knows he is surrounded by a cloud of witnesses and lets his witness merge with the voice of these many waters. Every dogmatics ought to be in full accord with and a part of the doxology sung to God by the church of all ages.

[24] This is not to elevate the history of dogma and the confession of the church to a position of infallible authority. There is a difference between the way in which the dogmatician is shaped and the primary principle from which dogmatics receives its material. In every branch of learning, the practitioner begins by living from the tradition. He always gains his first acquaintance of his field from an authority. He must first absorb the history of his discipline and attain a knowledge of the present state of his field; then he can go to work independently and acquire his own insights into the object of his research. But no one in his right mind will, for that reason, view the tradition, which was pedagogically so important to him, as the source of his discipline. It is no different for the dogmatician. Pedagogically the church is prior to Scripture. But in the logical order Scripture is the sole foundation (*principium unicum*) of church and theology. In case of conflict between them, the possibility of which can never be denied on a Reformational view, church and confession must yield to Scripture.

Not the church but Scripture is self-authenticating (αὐτόπιστος), the judge of controversies (*iudex controversiarum*), and its own interpreter (*sui ipsius interpres*). Nothing may be put on a level with Scripture. Church, confession, tradition—all must be ordered and adjusted by it and submit themselves to it. The Remonstrants charged that the Reformed, by their use of the confession, failed to do justice to the authority, sufficiency, and perfection of Holy Scripture. But the Reformed, though deeming a confession a necessity in this dispensation of the church in order to explain the Word of God, to turn aside heresies, and to maintain the unity of the faith, denied with the utmost emphasis that the confession had any authority apart from Scripture. Scripture alone is the norm and rule of faith and life (*norma et regula fidei et vitae*). The confession deserves credence only because and insofar as it agrees with Scripture and, as the fallible work of human hands, remains open to revision and examination by the standard of Scripture. Accordingly, the confession is at most a secondary standard, and even then not of truth but of the doctrine embraced in a particular church (*norma secundaria, non*

40. J. P. Lange, *Christliche Dogmatik*, 3 vols. (Heidelberg: K. Winter, 1852), I, 3; L. Schöberlein, *Prinzip und System der Dogmatik* (Heidelberg: C. Winter, 1881), 26.

veritatis sed doctrinae in aliqua ecclesia receptae) and therefore binding for all who wish to live in fellowship with that church. Within the church the confession has authority as "an agreement of fellowship," as the expression of the faith of the church, but it believes and maintains that confession only on the basis of Scripture.[41] All Christian churches are united in the confession that Holy Scripture is the foundation of theology, and the Reformation unanimously recognized it as the only foundation (*principium unicum*). The Belgic Confession states this in article 5, and all Lutheran and Reformed theologians are in agreement with it.[42]

Admittedly, article 2 of the Belgic Confession states that God is known by two means—nature and Scripture—and natural theology is upheld in its truth and value by all Reformed theologians. But in that first period, before rationalism infected Reformed theology, it was clearly seen that nature and Scripture are not detached and independent entities, any more than natural and revealed theology are. Calvin incorporated natural theology into the body of Christian dogmatics, saying that Scripture was the spectacles by which believers see God more distinctly also in the works of nature.[43] Originally natural theology was by no means intended to pave the way, step by laborious step, for revealed theology. In adopting it, one was not assuming the provisional stance of reason in order next, by reasoning and proof, to mount to the higher level of faith. But from the very outset the dogmatician took a stand on the ground of faith and, as a Christian and believer, now also looked at nature. Then, with his Christian eyes, armed by Holy Scripture, he also discovered in nature the footprints of the God whom he had come to know—in Christ and by Scripture—as Father. From a subjective point of view, in dogmatics it was not therefore natural reason that first took the floor, after which faith in the Word had its say. On the contrary, it was always the believing Christian who, in catechism, confession, and in dogmatics, gave voice to his faith. And in the same way, speaking objectively, nature did not stand on its own as an independent principle alongside of Holy Scripture, each of them supplying a set of truths of their own. Rather, nature was viewed in the light of Scripture, and Scripture not only contained revealed truth (in the strict sense) but also the truths that a believer can discover in nature. Thus Alsted did indeed acknowledge the existence of a natural theology in the unregenerate, but a confused and obscure natural

41. G. Voetius, *Pol. Eccl. IV*, 1–74; F. Turrentin, *Elenctic Theology*, loc. 18, 30; A. Comrie, *Examen van het Ontwerp van Tolerantie*, vol. 8, 50; Moor, *Comm. in Marcki Comp.*, VI, 353ff. A general defense of the right, the value, and the authority of confessions can be found in the preface to William Dunlop's *A Collection of Confessions of Faith, Catechisms, Directories, Books of Disciplinne, etc. of Publick Authority in the Church of Scotland*, 2 vols. (Edinburgh: James Watson, 1719), v–cxliv.

42. Schmid, *Dogmatik der evangelische Lutherische Kirche*, chap. 4; H. Heppe, *Reformed Dogmatics*, trans. G. T. Thomson (Grand Rapids: Baker, 1978 [1950]), chap. 2.

43. J. Calvin, *Institutes*, I.vi.1.

theology. By contrast, for the believer the principles and conclusions of natural theology are replicated clearly and distinctly in Scripture.[44]

So, though one can speak of a knowledge of God derived from nature, dogmatics still has but one external foundation (*principium externum*), i.e., Holy Scripture, and similarly only one internal foundation (*principium internum*), i.e., believing reason. And it is not simply the case that Holy Scripture is only the norm and not the source of dogmatics, but it is specifically the foundation (*principium*) of theology. Between earlier theologians and those of today there is a major difference. Since Schleiermacher retrogressed from the object to the subject, a large number of theologians have begun to view the church and its confession as the source of dogmatic truth. They have not only—correctly—acknowledged and articulated the confessional and ecclesiastical character of dogmatics, but they have also made the church's confession into an epistemic source by demoting Scripture to norm,[45] or by placing the confession alongside of Scripture as an epistemic source.[46] And J. H. Gunning, in the work cited, even asserted that the teaching of Scripture as source rather than norm is not a Reformed position but actually Remonstrant. But this notion is based on a mistaken view of the relation between church and Scripture. In the earliest period of the Christian church, there could yet be such a thing as a pure tradition running parallel to the apostolic writings. But the two streams have long since merged. Today we no longer have any knowledge of Christian truth except that which comes to us from Holy Scripture. Even though the religious life of the church tends to nurture itself more from devotional works than from Scripture, as also Ritschl observes,[47] they are still but channels by which the truth of Holy Scripture is brought to believers in a more understandable form. Furthermore, dogmatics is a very different thing than symbolics. The latter describes and explains the confession of the church. But dogmatic theology dogmatizes, i.e., it sets forth, not what is currently held to be truth in the domain of religion, but what ought to count as truth. Though it should have its connections with the confession, as it does with the school and the church, dogmatics is an independent discipline alongside of the church's confession and explains the truth of God in its own way. Scripture has been given to the church but also to the school and hence to science, and both read and research, explicate and describe, its content. In that connection, confession and dogmatics mutually af-

44. J. Alsted, *Praecognita Theologia* (1623), 115; C. Hodge, *Systematic Theology*, I, 11–15; W. G. T. Shedd, *Dogmatic Theology*, 3d ed., 3 vols. (New York: Scribner, 1894), I, 68.

45. F. Schleiermacher, *The Christian Faith*, §19; R. Rothe, *Zur Dogmatik* (Gotha: F. A. Perthes, 1863), 27; L. Schoeberlein, *Prinzip und System*, 23; J. H. Gunning and D. Chantepie de la Sausaye, *Het Ethische Beginsel der Theologie* (Groningen, 1877), 12; *I. Van Dyk, *Begrip en Methode der Dogmatiek*, 14; *F. E. Daubanton, *Confessie en Dogmatiek*, 29.

46. J. P. Lange, *Dogmatiek*, II, 3; J. J. Van Oosterzee, *Christian Dogmatics*, trans. J. Watson and M. Evans, 2 vols. (New York: Scribner, Armstrong, 1874), §9; H. Von der Goltz, *Die Christlichen Grundwahrheiten* (Gotha: Perthes, 1873), §18.

47. A. Ritschl, *Die Christliche Lehre von der Rechtfertigung und Versöhnung*, II, 12.

fect each other. The church's confession is in turn as much dependent on dogmatics as the latter is on the former. Dogmas were produced by the church but not apart from the labor of theologians; dogmas are in part the fruit of theology. First the apologists did their work, then came Nicea. First the Reformers appeared on the scene, then the Protestant confessions followed.[48] Finally, the doctrine of Holy Scripture as the sole foundation (*unicum principium*) of theology is truly reformational and Reformed. Articles 2 and 7 of the Belgic Confession expressly teach that the knowledge of God and of serving him can only be drawn from Scripture. Therefore Scripture is definitely a source and not only a norm. Calvin in his *Institutes,* Melanchthon in the preface of his *Loci,* and all dogmaticians assert that clear and complete knowledge of God can only be obtained from Scripture.

Virtually every dogmatics begins with the doctrine of Scripture as the sole foundation of theology. The attributes of authority, sufficiency, and perfection, which Protestants in their struggle with Rome attributed to Holy Scripture, demonstrate the same thing. The fact that in this connection they prefer to speak of foundation (*principium*) rather than source (*fons*) does not weaken the utterly unique significance of Scripture for the field of dogmatics. The term *principium* is, in fact, to be preferred over that of *fons*. The latter describes the relation between Scripture and theology as a mechanical one, as though dogmas could be drawn from Holy Scripture like water from a well.[49] But "first principle" suggests an organic connection. In a formal sense, there are no dogmas in Scripture, but the material for them is all to be found in it. Hence dogmatics can be defined as the truth of Scripture, absorbed and reproduced by the thinking consciousness of the Christian theologian.

THE ROLE OF FAITH

[25] This, however, is not to deny the personal character of doctrinal theology. This cannot and may not be the case, since dogmatics is not a historical report but a description of what in religion ought to count as truth. This personal character does not flow from our cutting all ties with its object and allowing every theologian to say and write what he pleases. For then dogmatics ceases to be a science and is no more than private opinion. If—following Van Manen[50]—dogmatics must abandon the illusion that there exists

48. A. von Harnack, *History of Dogma,* I, 10ff.; H. Bavinck, "Confessie en Dogmatiek," *Theologische Studiën* 9 (1891): 258–75.

49. Ed. note: Bavinck's theological method distances itself at this point from the Princeton tradition represented by Charles Hodge, who advocates an empirical-inductive method that sees the Bible as a "storehouse of facts." The task of the theologian is then "to ascertain, collect, and combine all the facts" in an orderly system, guided by the same rules as the man of Science" (C. Hodge, *Systematic Theology,* I, 10–11).

50. Ed. note: Willem Christiaan Van Manen (1842–1905) was a Reformed professor of theology at the University of Groningen (1884–85), and then professor of biblical theology at the University of Leiden (1885–1903).

a body of objective truth given us from without, then dogmatics has ceased to exist. Then all we are left with is a body of subjective opinions in which one is as good as another. Every science that can claim the name and status of a science must have its own object that exists in the real world. There is, furthermore, an assumption that such an object is knowable, and that the science is, accordingly, bound to that object as rigorously as possible. For dogmatics the requirements are identical: it must have its own object; the object must be knowable; and it is strictly bound to that object. The denial that dogmatics has such a knowable object of its own may never be vindicated with an appeal to the personal character of doctrinal theology. This confuses two totally different matters. It is only possible to speak of a dogmatics having a personal character if beforehand it is fully accepted that dogmatic theology has its own object.

Dr. Groenewegen[51] is therefore wrong in saying that positing a knowable object for dogmatics is in conflict with the demand that it be personal. According to him, the earlier description of dogmatics as a systematic statement of the knowledge of God, an exposition of the Word of God, is countered by the demand made here that dogmatics has to bear a personal character, since it is not a historical report but an exposition of what has to count as truth in the domain of religion. After all—he reasons—if there is a revelation that gives us knowledge of God, it remains authoritative whether or not the dogmatician agrees with it. On this view the dogmatician has no other task than to report, and in reporting he at the same time provides what has to count as truth.[52]

In reply it needs to be said, first, that the denial that dogmatics is a historical report was primarily advanced against Schleiermacher and others insofar as they believed that the sole task of dogmatics was to set forth what at a given time counted as religious truth in a particular church. This, as we explained at length in the previous chapter, cannot be the task of dogmatics. The case is different when it is said that the sole task of dogmatics is to furnish a historical report on the content of revelation. This, in a sense, is the position adopted by the "biblical theologians." The truth in this position—which Groenewegen correctly affirms—is that if there is a revelation furnishing knowledge of God, it has and will continue to have authority whether or not the dogmatician personally agrees with it. This is not peculiar to dogmatics, however, but something it has in common with all sciences. Every science is bound to its object, and that object, with its authority and normative power, remains above the corresponding science. Nature, for example, is the source and norm for the natural sciences, and these sciences must continually return to it and submit the scientific results achieved to it for verification.

---

51. Ed. note: Herman I. Groenewegen (1862–1930) was a Remonstrant theologian who taught at the University of Leiden (1902–16) and the University of Amsterdam (1916–30). His major contribution was in the field of philosophy of religion.

52. *Herman Groenewegen, *De Theologie en hare Wijsbegeerte*, 104–6.

This is not to deny that there is a difference between dogmatics and many other sciences. In the latter case, however, personal assent as a rule matters less: human sympathies and antipathies are not at all or not heavily invested in it. In dogmatics this is by no means the case. In dogmatic theology personality plays an important role, not because, unfortunately, it is unavoidable, but because it ought to play an important role. The revelation in which God communicates knowledge of himself intends to foster religion; it is *designed* to generate faith in our hearts, to place us in a proper relation to God. Revelation is designed to give us knowledge—not merely abstract theoretical knowledge, as in the other sciences, but vital personal knowledge; in a word, the knowledge of faith. Therefore, in dogmatics, whoever aims to give no more than a historical report of revelation would misconstrue the character and intent of that revelation and certainly fail in practice. However objectively he sets out to do his work, he would in the end prove to have been, in many ways, subject to the influence of his own faith-convictions. This has been clearly demonstrated by the history of "biblical theology." Hence for dogmatic work personal faith is imperative. In that respect the statement that every dogmatics is a confession of one's own faith is perfectly true. But this is something very different from what, since Schleiermacher, has been understood by the theology of consciousness. For this theology denies that in nature or in Scripture there is a revelation that provides knowledge of God. It thus severs theology, and particularly dogmatics, from all its objective connections, robs it of its own object, and then tries nevertheless to build up a kind of dogmatics from the material of one's own consciousness (mind, feelings, heart, conscience) without this being bound to anything objective. In the realm of theology, this is to do what rationalists or mystics would do if they sought to derive knowledge of nature and history from their own thoughts or experience instead of from objective reality.[53] An appeal to the disagreement that exists among dogmaticians—who, though proceeding from the same Scripture as a revelation of God, nevertheless arrive at very different conclusions—cannot justify the subjectivism of consciousness theology. This parallels the failure of legitimizing the rationalistic or mystical method in the domain of nature and history by the vast differences existing with respect to a variety of phenomena and facts among the practitioners of sciences in these areas.

Upon further reflection this should be obvious. If a given science has no object and no epistemic source of its own, then neither does it have any right to exist. So if there really is some religious knowledge among us—no matter what its scope and extent, and regardless of whether a system of such knowledge can be credited with the name "science"—there has to be a source from which it is drawn. Now there are many people who say that na-

---

53. Ed. note: Bavinck here anticipates and counters what at the end of the twentieth century has come to be known as "postmodern" thought.

ture and Scripture cannot be considered such a source and that religious knowledge can be derived only from one's own inner self. If we take this assertion seriously, it implies the idea that though God reveals himself nowhere else, he still makes himself known in the hearts, minds, consciousness, or feelings of human beings. In that case the inner self of human beings possesses a specific quality and needs to be considered as the object and source of the discipline of dogmatics since God reveals himself there. Anyone who only wished to describe the religious experiences of the inner self objectively, in a historical report, would perhaps give us an important religious psychology but not a dogmatics. Dogmatics presupposes that there is a source of religious knowledge and that from it we can derive this knowledge, not by a neutral intellect, but by a personal faith. So, despite themselves, the proponents of consciousness theology also prove that for dogmatics to be a body of truth it must have its own source, object, and authority and also that in order to recognize and use them one must have personal faith.

Every science, for that matter, be it the science of nature, history, law, morality, or whatever, has an object that is present in the real world. Nonetheless, each science still bears a personal character, one certainly less than another; to mention an example, mathematics is much less personal than history. But to the degree that the sciences are less formal and lie closer to the human center, to that degree the influence of human personality increases. A person can no more divest himself of self in the pursuit of science than anywhere else. Every scientist brings along with him his early upbringing, his life view, his heart and conscience, his sympathies and antipathies, and these automatically exert their influence on his research and reflections. By itself there is nothing wrong with this. The dualism that divides a person into two halves and, in the pursuit of the sciences, reduces him or her to a naked intellect is practically impossible and theoretically false. The only requirement, as we remarked earlier, is that a person, always and everywhere, also when he or she is engaged in scientific work, be a good person, proficient, equipped for every good work (2 Tim. 3:17). This is not different in the field of dogmatics. If anything, all this is even more true here. For dogmatics has to do above all with the deepest religious convictions of human beings and with the center of all science. Here, above all, it is imperative that a person be a good person, that he or she stand in a true relationship to God, whom to know is eternal life.

Consequently, it is also the teaching of Scripture that objective revelation be completed in subjective illumination. The Reformed doctrine of Scripture is most intimately tied in with that of the testimony of the Holy Spirit. The external word does not remain outside of us but, through faith, becomes an internal word. The Holy Spirit who gave us Scripture also bears witness to that Scripture in the heart of believers. Scripture itself attends to its own acceptance in the consciousness of the church of Christ. Believers, in consequence, feel that with their whole soul they are bound to Scripture.

They are inducted into it by the Holy Spirit, the church's supreme Teacher (*Doctor ecclesiae*). And the whole intent of believers is to take the thoughts of God laid down in Scripture into their consciousness and to understand them rationally. But in all this they remain human beings with disposition, upbringing, and insights all their own. Faith itself does not originate in the same way in every person, nor does it have the same strength in all. Individual powers of reasoning differ in sharpness, depth, and clarity since the influence of sin also remains operative in the human consciousness and intellect. As a result of all these influences, doctrinal theology continues to bear a personal character.

As it is in every other science, so that is the case here. Even prophets and apostles saw the same truth from different perspectives. Unity of faith has no more been realized than unity of knowledge. But precisely through this diversity, God leads his church toward unity. Once that unity of faith and knowledge has been reached, dogmatics too will have accomplished its task. Until then, however, it is entrusted with the calling, in the domain of science, to interpret the thoughts that God has laid down for us in Holy Scripture.

[26] The dogmatician will be most fully equipped to carry out this task if he lives in communion of faith with the church of Christ and confesses Scripture as the only and sufficient basis (*principium*) of the knowledge of God. Accordingly, the dogmatician receives the content of his faith from the hands of the church. Pedagogically he comes to Scripture through the church. But no more than any other believer can he stop there. He is called to analyze the very fiber of the dogmas he has come to know from the church and to examine how they are rooted in Holy Scripture. Thus his task is sometimes said to consist in first objectively reproducing the dogmas and then tracing them to Holy Scripture—a method called historical-analytical. For a few dogmas as such this method may be highly commendable, and it may be true that theologians undervalue it. Nonetheless, the objection to it is that by using this method one cannot achieve a scientific system. The dogmatician therefore will do better taking a different road. Instead of proceeding from the river to the source, it is preferable to travel from the source to the river. Without shortchanging the truth that in a pedagogical sense the church precedes Scripture, a theologian can nevertheless be positioned in Scripture itself as the foundation of theology (*principium theologiae*) and from there develop dogmas. What a theologian does in that case is replicate, as it were, the intellectual labor of the church. We are shown how dogmas have arisen organically from Scripture—that the firm and broad foundation on which the edifice of dogmatics rises is not a single text in its isolation but Scripture as a whole.[54]

This synthetic-genetic method must not be confused with the empirical or experimental method, as this happens in Charles Hodge and R. Mc. Ch.

---

54. J. Kleutgen, *Die Theologie der Vorzeit*, 2d ed., 5 vols. (Münster: Theissing, 1867–74), V, 77ff.

Edgar of Dublin.[55] According to the latter, Bacon's experimental method is characterized by three things: (1) it collects the facts; (2) it frames a hypothesis to explain them; (3) it tests this provisional hypothesis by experiment. Correspondingly, he says, the first task of Christian dogmatics is to gather the facts, say, the facts of the moral world order, sin, the person of Jesus, holy Scripture, etc. The second task is to attempt to explain these facts by the presuppositions of creation, fall, the deity of Christ, the inspiration of Scripture. And, finally, the theologian must verify them by what Scripture teaches concerning these presuppositions.

When examined, this method fails to stand up. In divine revelation, word and fact are always connected; it does not merely convey facts that we have to explain, but itself clearly illumines those facts. Scripture does not show us some facts that we then summarize under the rubric of sin, but it tells us itself what the essence of sin is. It not only tells us what Jesus has done but also who he was. Without this explanation we would not understand the facts at all and would give them a totally wrong interpretation. Accordingly, the term *hypotheses* is completely inappropriate here. In the first place, the doctrine of the origin and essence of sin, to cite an example, or the doctrine of the deity of Christ, is not a hypothesis we have conceived but part of the witness of Holy Scripture. Furthermore, that doctrine, based as it is on this witness, is not a human hypothesis but a word of God that as such demands faith. Hodge, accordingly, speaks of truth alongside of facts, and Edgar substitutes the term *doctrine* for that of *hypothesis*. With that the entire theory collapses. Finally, if God has spoken in his Word, there is no longer any room for "experiment." Subsequent to the witness of Scripture, verification is in the nature of the case impossible in this area.

The above-mentioned synthetic method, on the other hand, receives from revelation both fact and word, word and fact, and the two in conjunction with each other. The fact, for that matter, is made known to us in Scripture precisely by means of the word and is for that very reason inseparable from it. Of the person of Jesus, for example, we have no knowledge other than what we gain from the witness of the apostles. As the history of Gnosticism and of recent idealism has made very clear, one who rejects this witness no longer has the facts of revelation either. The synthetic-genetic method also gives the dogmatician the advantage that he can show the unity and organic interconnectedness of dogmatics. The different dogmas are not isolated propositions but constitute a unity. Actually there is only one dogma, one that is rooted in Scripture and that has branched out and divided in a wide range of particular dogmas. Consequently, the method of the dogmatician cannot and may not be other than systematic. Finally, he is also called,

55. C. Hodge, *Systematic Theology* I, 1. On Hodge, see further, A. Kuyper, *Encyclopaedie*, II, 268 (ed. note: see the English translation in A. Kuyper, *Principles of Sacred Theology*, trans. J. H. De Vries [Grand Rapids: Eerdmans, 1965 (1898)], 318–19); Robert McCheyne Edgar, "Christianity and the Experimental Method," *Presbyterian and Reformed Review* 6, no. 22 (April 1895): 201–23.

in this genetic and systematic unfolding of the dogmas, to point out possible deviations, to fill possible gaps, and so to work at the development of dogmas in the future. That is the critical task to which the dogmatician is called but which is already and automatically implied in the systematic nature of the work he does on the dogmatic material. In that way he attempts in dogmatics to furnish an exposition of the treasures of wisdom and knowledge that are hidden in Christ and exhibited in Scripture.

THE PROBLEM OF ORDER

[27] From the time the pursuit of dogmatics began, it needed a way of organizing the material treated. At the beginning, the division of material was extremely simple. The three main works of Clement of Alexandria, viz., his *Hortatory Address to the Greeks* (Προτρεπτικος προς Ἑλληνας), *The Instructor* (Παιδαγωγος), and *Miscellanies* (Στρωματα), though united by the theme of the Logos instructing the human race, do not actually contain an orderly structure. Furthermore, though the last-mentioned work unfolds the true philosophy of Christianity over against paganism and Judaism, Clement himself says (at the beginning of the sixth book and at the end of the seventh)[56] that there he only wrote down what came to his mind and that the readers should not be surprised at the lack of order. Origen's work on *First Principles* (Περι Ἀρχων) attempts to introduce some order in the material and, accordingly, has four headings: God, the world, freedom, and revelation. The first book deals with God, the Trinity, and the angels; the second with the world, the God of the Old Testament, good and evil, the incarnation, and the resurrection; the third with freedom of the will and its relation to grace, the temptations, and the end of the world; and the fourth with Holy Scripture, its inspiration, and interpretation. Already making their appearance here are the various topics (*loci*) concerning God, the angels, humanity, Christ, and so forth. However, they do not appear in a proper order, are not properly delimited, and are still incomplete. For example, the doctrine of the sacraments is lacking, that of Scripture comes trailing behind, and there is as yet no clear principle of organization. Origen's structure is adopted in amended and improved form by Theodoret of Cyrrhus in the fifth book of his *Compendium of Heretical Tales* (Αἱρετικης κακομοθιας ἐπιτομη), which contains a sketch of the orthodox faith. This sketch deals, successively, with God, the world, angels and humanity, Christ, Scripture and sacraments, resurrection and judgment, while at the end there are a few additional chapters of an ethical kind on vir-

---

56. Ed. note: Clement uses botanical metaphors to make his point: "The form of the *Miscellanies* is promiscuously variegated like [flowers in] a meadow (*Miscellanies*, vi, 1); "Now the *Miscellanies* are not like parts laid out, planted in regular order for the delight of the eye, but rather like an umbrageous and shaggy hill, planted with laurel, and ivy, and apples, and olives, and figs; the planting being purposely a mixture of fruit-bearing and fruitless trees." (*Miscellanies* viii, 18). Clement has a specific reason for writing in what he calls "summarily in a fragmentary way," inserting "here and there germs of true knowledge, so that the discovery of the sacred traditions may not be easy to any one of the uninitiated" (ibid.).

ginity, penitence, and fasting. The same scheme also underlies the *Exact Treatise on the Orthodox Faith* by John of Damascus. The division of this work into four books did not occur until the Middle Ages, when in 1194, on instructions from Pope Eugene III, it was translated into Latin by the jurist John of Burgundy of Pisa after Peter Lombard had set a precedent by dividing his Sentences (*Sententiae*) into four books. John of Damascus starts with the doctrine of God, Trinity, and attributes (book I), then speaks of the world, creation, angels, humanity, and providence (book II), after which he treats the person and work of Christ (books III and IV, chaps. 1–9), and ends with chapters on soteriology (faith, baptism, etc.), ethics (law, sabbath, etc.), and eschatology (book IV, chaps. 10–28).

The seven books of Lactantius's *Divine Institutes* similarly resemble this order of treatment. The first three are purely apologetic and refute pagan religion and philosophy. But in the fourth, Lactantius, beginning a discussion on Christianity, first explains that here wisdom and religion are most intimately united because the knowledge of the one true God and of Jesus Christ his Son is the true wisdom. God, after all, is knowable in the Son who, toward the end of the ages, became man in order to bring humanity back to righteousness. That righteousness is then described in the fifth book. It is taught by Christ, has its origin in godliness, and manifests itself in *aequitas,* the recognition of the equality of all people. The sixth book further sets forth the duties of this righteousness, and the seventh, concerning the life of blessedness, treats the blessed life of the hereafter as the reward of the true knowledge and worship of God.

Alongside of this, the Apostles' Creed, following the baptismal formula, at an early stage offered a somewhat different arrangement of the material of dogmatics. *The Commentary on the Apostles' Creed (Expositio Symboli)* by Rufinus and Augustine's *On Faith and the Symbol (De fide et symbolo)* furnished commentary on the Apostles' Creed. In their treatment of the main points of the Christian faith, they followed the trinitarian scheme that underlies the apostolic symbol. Augustine was a model for many others not only in this division, but in his *Enchiridion,* where he treated—though in a very uneven way—the subjects of dogmatics and ethics under the headings of the three Christian virtues faith, hope, and love. Following his introduction (paragraphs 1–8) he sets forth what has to be believed in paragraphs 9 to 113, in the main following the outline of the apostolic symbol, but then devotes only three paragraphs (114–16) to hope, following the Lord's Prayer as his guideline, and the remaining paragraphs 117–22 to love.[57] Accordingly, faith, prayer, and commandment here furnish the outline of dogmatics, one that was often taken over in later times, especially in catechisms. Similarly, Isodore of Seville, in the first book of his *Sentences or Treatise con-*

---

57. Ed. note: Augustine's *Enchiridion* is divided into 32 main chapters, which are further subdivided into 122 paragraphs.

cerning the Supreme Good in Three Books, mainly follows the order of the apostolic symbol and in thirty chapters deals with God, creation, world, angels and human beings, Christ, the Holy Spirit, the church, Scripture and sacraments, the resurrection, and the last things. He then treats ethics exclusively in the second and third books.

[28] The division that Lombard chose in the Middle Ages again recalls that of Origen, Theodoret, and John of Damascus. His *Sentences* are divided into four books. The first three deal with things (*res*), the last with signs (*signa*). The entire content of revelation, to his mind, consists of these two: *things* and *signs.* The things are again subdivided: some can only be enjoyed, as, for instance, the divine Trinity; others, like created things, can only be used; still others can be enjoyed as well as used, as, for example, the virtues. In accordance with this order, the first book of the *Sentences* deals with the mystery of the Trinity and the second with the creation and formation of physical and spiritual things: creation, angels, the six-day period of creation, humanity, fall, sin. The third book deals with the incarnation of the Word: the person and work of Christ; faith, hope, and love; the four principal virtues; and other ethical topics. Finally, the fourth book, concerning the sacraments, contains the doctrine of the seven sacraments, the resurrection, the judgment, heaven, and hell.

There is discernible progress here. Not only is there better grouping and delimitation of the topics, but the whole is divided into four parts, each with its own distinct object. The ethical material has not been appended to the end, as in Theodoret, but incorporated in the dogmatics itself. The sacraments, formerly only touched upon, are treated at length. On the other hand, the order still leaves much to be desired, and several subjects, like Scripture, the church, and particularly soteriology, are left virtually undiscussed. Most scholastic theologians, following in Lombard's footsteps, wrote commentaries on his *Sentences,* some of them introducing significant improvements in the order of the material. Thomas, for example, in the Prologue to his commentary on the *Sentences* shows beautifully how first God and then his works (creation, restoration, and completion) constitute the subjects of the four books. But a place of honor, especially from a formal viewpoint, is held by Bonaventure's *Breviloquium.*[58] In the first place, Bonaventure prefaces his work with a prologue and in its seven sections offers a splendid survey of the doctrine of Scripture, especially of its content, which he briefly unfolds in its length, breadth, depth, and height. Next, in seven parts, he sketches the content of true faith: part 1 discusses the Trinity, part 2 the creation of the world, part 3 the corruption of sin, part 4 the incarnation of the Word, part 5 the grace of the Holy Spirit, part 6 the sacramental remedy, and part 7 the last stage, the final judgment. We find here a firmly methodical approach, complete mastery of the material, a clean de-

---

58. Hallenberg, "Bonaventura als Dogmaticus," *Theologische Studien und Kritik* (1868).

limitation of the topics, and a purposefully chosen principle of division. This is apparent when in part I, chapter 1, Bonaventure states that though theology comprises all seven topics it is nevertheless a single science, for "God is not only the efficient and exemplary Cause of things in creation, but also their renewing (*refectivum*) Principle in redemption, and their perfective Principle in restoration."[59]

Thomas's division in his *Summa* is quite different. This work contains three parts; the parts are divided into questions, and these again into articles. Part I deals in 119 questions with God and his creation before and apart from sin: God as first principle and exemplary cause of all things. Part II speaks of man as his image and again is divided into a *prima* and a *secunda*. The *prima* contains 114 questions, begins with man's final end, i.e., eternal bliss, and with an eye to this goal develops the doctrine of the will (questions 6–17), the good and sinful quality of human acts, passions, and habits (18–54), the virtues in general (55–70), sins divided as to location,[60] cause, and consequences (71–89). It concludes with the external and internal motives that spur human beings on to the good: law, gospel, grace, and merit (90–114). Then the *secunda* of the second part, in 189 questions, deals with sins and virtues in particular, especially in accordance with the three theological and four cardinal virtues. After the final end of man has thus been established and his virtues and sins exposited, part III describes the way by which we human beings can attain to the blessedness of eternal life, i.e., Christ and the sacraments. The person and work of Christ and then the concept of sacrament, baptism, confirmation, eucharist, and penitence are described in 90 questions. Here ends the work of Thomas; at his death he left it behind unfinished. The supplement, composed of material from his other writings, contains 99 questions, continues his teachings on the sacraments, and in questions 69–99 treats the state of human souls after death, the resurrection, judgment, blessedness, and damnation. An appendix composed of three questions discusses purgatory.

Thomas's division not only differs from that of Bonaventure but is in many respects inferior to it. While in part I, qu. 1, there is a lengthy discussion of the essence of theology, the doctrine of Scripture is not discussed at all. Furthermore, at the beginning of part II, Thomas leaps abruptly to the final end of human life and is, consequently, frequently forced to anticipate issues that can only be treated later. The Christian virtues, the gospel, the law, and grace, which Thomas takes up in this second part, presuppose the person and work of Christ treated in part III. Thomas's division is already linked deeply with the Catholic doctrine of the supernatural order to which human beings must be elevated. After the first part has dealt with the doctrine of God, the second discusses man, who is destined for supernatural

---

59. Cited from *The Works of Bonaventure*, vol. 2, *The Breviloquium* (New York: St. Anthony Guild Press, 1963), 33.

60. Ed. note: Bavinck's Dutch terms are *verdeeling, zetel, oorzaak*, and *gevolgen*.

grace but cannot attain it, and the third then points to the person of Christ and to the sacraments as the way by which man can reach his destiny. Accordingly, the topics of the three parts are God, man, and Christ.[61] Finally, the question-and-reply form of his teaching is not unobjectionable.[62] Thomas frames every tenet of faith in the form of a question and raises all the objections advanced against it by opponents. Then, with an appeal to authority (Scripture, church fathers, or Aristotle) he demonstrates the truth of the thing questioned and draws the conclusion. This is then further explained and finally defended against the objections raised.

[29] As a rule these divisions were taken over by later Roman Catholic theologians, not only in the many commentaries they wrote on the *Sententiae* and the *Summa,* but also in independent dogmatic works. Thus Thomas's division was adopted by M. Becanus in his *Theologia scholastica* (1619), and the loci-method of Theodoret, John of Damascus, and Lombard by Petavius (*Opus de theol. dogm.* [Paris 1644], proleg. chap. I, §4). But scholasticism affected the division of the material in still another way. Bonaventure had already included the doctrine of Scripture in his prologue, while Thomas treated the essence of theology first. Scholasticism's development led to the distinction between *mixed* and *pure articles*[63] and to the doctrine of the preamble of faith and the motivations toward belief (*motiva credibilitatis*). In the process the material for the prolegomena became more and more extensive. And when the Reformation before long appeared on the scene with the exclusive authority of Scripture, it became imperative for Roman Catholic theologians to give an account also of the foundations of theology (*principia*). Especially Melchior Canus, in his *Loci theologici* (1563), developed the doctrine of the *loci,* i.e., the sources of theology. This work is not a dogmatics but a *topica* [a collection of standard topics] in Cicero's sense of the word. In twelve books he treats ten sources of theology (Scripture, tradition, pope, council, church, church fathers, scholastics, reason, philosophy, and history), the first seven of which can be reduced to two (Scripture and tradition). The last three are theological only in an ancillary sense.

61. Werner, *Die Heilige Thomas von Aquino* (Regensburg, 1858), I, 801ff.; J. Kleutgen, *Theologie der Vorzeit,* V, 60–70; Kling, *Descriptio Summae theologiae Thomas Aquino* (Bonn, 1846).

62. Allard Pierson, *Studien over Johannes Calvijn (1527–36)* (Amsterdam: P. N. Van Kampen & Zoon, 1881), I, 228. Ed. note: Bavinck cites Pierson's study of Calvin here but fails to indicate the specific objection to Thomas's question-and-answer method. Pierson judges that Thomas is more investigative in his method while Calvin is more dogmatic. Pierson does not judge Thomas as negatively as Bavinck suggests. In fact, according to Pierson, Thomas is often more critical of ecclesiastical authority than is Calvin. He also contends that Thomas's pioneering work in a skeptical age settled many questions that were unnecessarily taken for granted by Calvin's time. Thomas's *Summa* thus made it possible for Calvin to write the *Institutes* in the clear dogmatic-assertive form that he did.

63. Ed. note: "articuli puri/mixti: *pure/mixed articles;* articles of doctrine distinguished as to their derivation from the disciplines of theology and philosophy—those deriving from one discipline alone are 'pure,' and those deriving from both are 'mixed.' The existence of mixed articles, e.g., the existence and idea of God, demands that theology answer the question of its relation to philosophy" (Richard A. Muller, *Dictionary of Latin and Greek Theological Terms* [Grand Rapids: Baker, 1985], 46).

In this way a broad introduction became necessary prior to the actual dogmatics, an introduction that grew into a large, sharp dogmatics in part because of the fundamental criticism of theology from the side of philosophy. Accordingly, most Roman Catholic dogmatic theologies in a first part discussed the essence or concept of theology. This includes the preamble of faith (natural theology); the motivations for, or grounds of, belief (*motiva credibilitatis:* religion, revelation, prophecy, miracles, the miraculous expansion of Christianity, the martyrs, etc.); sources of faith (Scripture and church), theology, and philosophy (faith and reason); and the concept of dogmatics. This is the case in Klee, Heinrich, Scheeben, Liebermann, Perrone, Pesch, Jansen, Mannens, Van Noort, and others. Perrone's work, for example, deals in vol. I with the true religion and in the final two volumes (VIII and IX) with the theological *loci.* The latter two were, admittedly, published later, after the actual dogmatics, but, according to the author's own statement (vol. VIII, preface), should materially follow the first volume. In these *loci* Perrone, in distinction from Canus, intentionally gives priority to the church over Scripture. And in most Roman Catholic dogmaticians of recent decades, the order is the same. The church increasingly comes into the foreground as the fundamental principle of faith (*principium fidei*). The development of dogmatics then as a rule occurs in terms of the *loci*-method. The authors begin with God regarded in himself as unique and triune and then proceed to deal with God in relation to his creatures: first as Creator, then as Redeemer, next as Sanctifier, and finally as Consummator.

ORDER IN REFORMATION DOGMATICS

[30] Dogmatics, in the case of the Reformers, was originally anti-scholastic and first presented in a very simple and practical form. Melanchthon's *Loci Communes,* published in 1521, have their roots in lectures on Paul's *Letter to the Romans.* They are practical through and through in that they only treat anthropological and soteriological topics, especially those of sin and grace and law and gospel, while leaving completely undiscussed the objective dogmas of God, Trinity, creation, incarnation, and satisfaction. The 1535 edition, greatly expanded by Melanchthon, introduced the second period of the *Loci.* The preface was dedicated to King Henry VIII. The *Loci* began with five new chapters on God, unity, Trinity, creation, and the cause of sin. The middle was enriched with a few chapters, and Melanchthon expanded the last three ethical chapters to ten on ethics, ecclesiology, and eschatology. Altogether the expanded *Loci* came to 39 chapters or articles. In 1543 the *Loci* entered their third period. A preface to the pious reader was added, and the number of *loci* went down, as a result of simplification, from 39 to 24. However, the content was considerably expanded. The final edition, prepared by Melanchthon himself, is that of 1559. The successive editions exhibit an ever-growing approxima-

tion to the synthetic division, which begins with God and from there descends to his works in nature and grace. It must be noted here that the prolegomena are completely lacking and that the Christology is deficient because Christ's person and work are not treated separately. Finally, the dogmatic and ethical materials remain intimately bound up with each other, and the entire work is concluded not with eschatological dogmas but with a number of ethical topics.[64]

Zwingli's *Commentary on True and False Religion,* as well as his *Exposition of the Christian Faith,* while also treating a number of dogmatic *loci,* were soon overshadowed by Calvin's *Institutes of the Christian Religion.* The first edition, which was written in Latin and published at Basel in March 1536, contained a preface dated August 23, 1535, which was addressed to King Francis I, and six chapters on the law, faith, prayer, the sacraments, the Catholic sacraments, and liberty. Three times it was expanded (1539, 1543, 1559). The last edition was about five times as large as the first and, though substantially expanded, contained no [doctrinal] change. While Melanchthon, in the later editions of his *Loci,* had become synergistic and crypto-Calvinistic, Calvin remained the same. Melanchthon's *Loci,* though becoming more synthetic in form, kept its character as a series of *loci,* while Calvin's *Institutes* increasingly assumed a more systematic form. The 1559 edition contained four books, covering the knowledge of God as Creator, Redeemer, and Sanctifier in the first three and dealing with the external means of grace in a final book. Accordingly, the division is not strictly trinitarian but derived from the apostolic creed, which is the reason why the fourth book comes trailing behind and deals primarily with the church and the sacraments. The first book offers far more than its title promises, treating as it does also the sources of the knowledge of God and the doctrine of the Trinity. Cosmology and anthropology are distributed over the first and second books. The third book contains, aside from soteriological, also many ethical chapters, as well as the doctrines of election and resurrection. The starting point of the *Institutes* is theological, but Calvin does not proceed from an abstract concept of God but from God as he is known by humanity from nature and Scripture.[65]

Initially Lutheran and Reformed theologians almost universally adopted Melanchthon's and Calvin's synthetic division. For a variety of reasons, it was

64. P. Melanchthon, *Loci Theol.,* ed. Augusti (1821), 167ff.; *Die Loci Communes des Ph. Melancthon in ihrer Urgestalt nach G. L. Plitt,* prepared by Th. Kolde, 2d ed. (Erlangen: Deichert, 1890); Herrlinger, "Philippus Melanchton," *PRE²,* IX, 503; Zöckler, *Handbuch der theologischen Wissenschaft,* II, 622ff.; also see the edition of the *Loci Communes* in the *Corpus Reformatorum.*

65. J. Kostlin, "Calvin's *Institutio* nach Form und Inhalt in ihrer geschichtliche Entwicklung," *Theologische Studien und Kritiken* 33 (1861): 7–62, 410–86; idem, *Godgeleerde Bijdragen* (1868): 861ff.; (1869): 483ff.; Gass, *Geschichte der protestantische Dogmatik,* I, 99ff.; A. Pierson, *Studien over Johannes Calvijn,* I, 127ff.; *Corpus Reformatorum* XXXIX, ixff.; E. Doumergue, *Jean Calvin* I, 589–95; Brunctiére, "L'oeuvre literairre de Calvin," *Revue de deux Mondes* (October 15, 1900); B. B. Warfield, "The Literary History of Calvin's *Institutio,*" *Presbyterian and Reformed Review* 10 (April 1899): 193–220.

considered best. Not just Reformed[66] but also Lutheran scholars[67] preferred the synthetic method, since in it, as Hyperius says, "there is continuous progress from the very first beginnings through a series of forms and differences all the way to the end." This division was preferred for a number of reasons: (1) it followed the historical course that God prefigured in his revelation; (2) it provided a minimum of occasion for a priori speculation and best preserved the positive character of theology; and (3) it was analogous to the method followed in the other sciences, sciences that also began with the most simple elements or principles and then progressed to the complex. Accordingly, this division continued to hold sway up until Calixtus; one finds it, in the main, in Strigel, Selneccur, Heerbrand, Chemnitz, Hutter, Gerhard, and others. In Reformed theology it was followed up until Cocceius by Sohnius, Musculus, Hyperius, Ursinus, Martyr, Wollebius, Polanus, Amesius, and others.

Still, in some respects there was significant change. At an early stage already an introduction was inserted prior to the actual dogmatics, one in which the concept of theology, the doctrine of Scripture, and occasionally, as in Amesius and Mastricht, also the essence of faith was treated. Dogmatics was thus divided into two parts: the foundations of theology and the articles of faith.[68] In the body of dogmatics itself, one discerns a better distinction and delimitation, as well as a more systematic ordering, of the *loci*. Election, treated by Calvin in the third book, was moved forward to the doctrine of the decrees, and the world, humanity, Christ, etc. were all given a place of their own. Also, the conclusion was no longer preempted by ethical topics but by the consummation of the world. Ethical issues were either discussed in soteriology or treated in a second part (on works) in distinction from the first (on faith), or, as in Danaeus and Calixtus, totally separated from dogmatics. In the course of the seventeenth century, the treatment of the separate *loci* became increasingly more scholastic, and their connectedness with the life of faith became less apparent as it was experienced less.

[31] Reaction to this scholasticism was bound to come eventually. In the Lutheran Church it started with Calixtus, in the Reformed with Cocceius. Calixtus viewed theology as a practical science and in his *Epitome theologiae* (1619) followed an analytical arrangement. This was not altogether new since Thomas, following his doctrine of God, also proceeded in the second part to the destiny of man and in the third described the way that—in Christ—leads to it. But Calixtus immediately plunges into human destiny. Part I deals with the end, i.e., the immortality of the soul, resurrection, and final judgment.

---

66. Hyperius, *Meth. Theol.* (1574), 11–16; J. Alsted, *Theol. Schol.* (praefatio); Z. Ursinus, *Opera* (1612), I, 417; H. Alting, *Oratio inauguralis de methodo loci communes* (Heidelberg, 1613), Leydekker, *De verit. Relig. Christ.* (1690), 77.

67. M. Flacius, *Clavis scripturae sacrae*, II, tract I, p. 54. "Declaratio tabulae trium methodorum theologiae," in Gass, *Geschichte*, I, 46.

68. A. Polanus, *Synt. Theol.*, 133.

Part II speaks of the subject, i.e., God, angels, man, sin. Part III treats the means, i.e., predestination, incarnation, Christ, justification, word, sacrament, and so forth. These three divisions constitute the common part, which concerns all believers; but then follows a special part, which deals primarily with the church and is important particularly for the office bearers.

Although there was considerable advantage—compared with the scholastic treatment of theology—in stressing its practical character, this division is nevertheless burdened by numerous objections. Apart now from the fact that the doctrine of the church treated in the special part concerns a truth that is important to all believers, it is strange to begin dogmatics with the end, the immortality of the soul. The second part was designed to treat the subject of theology, humanity, but also contains the entire doctrine of God. The third part accords best with its title but shortchanges the doctrine of the Redeemer in the context of soteriology.[69] Still, this analytic method was followed by the later Lutheran theologians: Calovius, Quenstedt, König, Baier, and Scherzer.

It also found acceptance among some Reformed theologians. In 1603, even before Calixtus, Bartholomaus Keckermann at Danzig had published a *Systema Summa Theologiae,* which appeals to Ursinus's *Catechesis* in describing theology, not as a contemplative science but as a practical discipline, or, better still, as religious wisdom for arriving at salvation (ch. 1). This is why he opts decisively for the analytic method, because, while the synthetic method is characteristic for the sciences, the analytic fits the practical disciplines. Accordingly, he divides his theology into three parts. In the first, he discusses the foundations (*principia*) of theology, viz., God, the essential foundation (*principium essendi*), and his Word, the cognitive foundation (*principium cognoscendi*). From these two foundations, we learn only the end and the means that lead to it. In the second part he simply says that the end of theology is life (*vita*), eternal salvation (*salvus aeterna*), just as Ursinus makes this primary in his Catechism, question 1. The means for reaching this end are twofold: knowledge of and redemption from our misery (bk. III, chap. 1). So book II deals with man and his sin, and book III with the means of salvation, election, Christ, church, justification, and the sacraments. Noteworthy, further, is that Keckermann has a penchant for comparing theology to medical science and even derives from it the names for the various divisions of his theology, as Bonaventure did before him (in his *Breviloquium,* part I, chap. 1).[70] Following Bonaventure and others, Keckermann speaks of a "pathological," a "therapeutic," and a "dietetic" part of theology.[71]

In a similar way Cocceius exchanged the theological for an anthropological viewpoint. What was new in his *Doctrine of the Covenant and Testament of God* (1648) was not the covenant concept as such, for that occurs already

69. Gass, *Geschichte,* I, 304.

70. *Breviloquium,* I, 1.

71. B. Keckerman, *Systema sacrosanctae theologiae,* pp. 214, 295; cf. A. Kuyper, *Encyclopaedie,* I, 42–43; von Oettingen, *Dogmatik,* I, 62.

in Zwingli and Calvin and had been developed by Bullinger, Olevianus, and Cloppenburg. Cocceius's novelty lay rather in the fact that he was the first to divide all the material of dogmatics in terms of the covenant idea and planned in this way to offer a more biblical-theological and antischolastic dogmatics. Furthermore, in the arrangement of the material, he followed the historical order of the dispensations of the covenant and distinguished these dispensations so sharply that their unity was lost and could be preserved only by arbitrary typological exegesis. In addition, finally, he viewed the entire history of the covenant of grace from beginning to end as an abolition of the covenant of works. Sin, Christ, the new covenant, physical death, and resurrection are to him the five turning points by which the covenant of works is successively robbed of its power and effect.

This division is objectionable for a number of reasons. Its theological starting point is not God but the covenant between God and man. Given this position, he can treat the doctrines of God and man only in an introduction by way of presupposition. By its historical movement his perspective erases the boundary between the history of revelation and dogmatics and thereby undermines the latter. This approach is highly repetitious and tends automatically to exaggerate the analogies on the one hand and the distinctions between the various dispensations of the covenant on the other. Still, it was imitated in the work of many theologians, such as Momma, Heydanus, Vitringa, Braun, Witsius, and also in that of Lutherans, as in W. Jäger (1702). Even Leydecker, a disciple of Voetius and opponent of Cocceius, attempted to combine the trinitarian division with the federalist in such a way that the successive economies of grace were related to the three Persons and the threefold activity within the Trinity.[72]

THE IMPACT OF PHILOSOPHY

[32] The shape of dogmatics was changed even more, however, by the influence of philosophy. This is evidenced especially by the fact that the genuinely material part of dogmatics became increasingly more impoverished while the formal part grew in scope and extent. Up until this time, this had been very different. The prolegomena had been totally lacking or were narrow in scope and at most treated theology and Scripture. Instead, available energy went into the elaboration and defense of the particular dogmas. The foundation was so stable and solid that it was not examined at all; all the work was expended on the building erected on it. This changed under the influence of philosophy as the prerogatives of reason were gradually and increasingly asserted over against revelation. Reason was no longer content with the modest role of servant and demanded a controlling voice. The material result was that the scholastic elaboration of dogmas was avoided as much as possible. Theologians moved from the church's confession back to

72. A. Schweizer, *Glaubenslehre*, I, 115.

Scripture and assiduously followed the historical-biblical method. Dogmas were simplified and smoothed down, losing their characteristic angularity. Deeper reflection on the dogmas became taboo as simplicity turned into shallowness.

The influence of philosophy was even greater on the formal part of dogmatics. Here the reformational position and its starting point in faith was abandoned and replaced by a return to that of Roman Catholic theology. The conviction took hold that human reason, even apart from faith, could of itself produce all the truths of natural theology. Thus, natural theology, as the preamble of faith, became antecedent to revealed theology, and reason was emancipated from faith and revelation. Revelation and reason became independent entities standing side by side. S. van Til treated them separately in his *Compendium of Theology, Both Natural and Revealed* (1706).[73] Reason not only received its own domain alongside of revelation but eventually extended its powers over that of revelation itself. Reason was given the prerogative of investigating the truth of revelation. Natural theology was believed to provide a solid ground on which to stand, a purely scientific foundation, and revelation too was examined this way. Only when reason, by an assortment of rational and historical evidences, like so many grounds for belief (*motiva credibilitatis*), had demonstrated the truth of revelation, was it judged reasonable to believe this revelation and to submit to it.

In this manner the prolegomena to theology consistently grew in scope. Religion as distinct from theology was discussed first, followed by natural theology or the truths of nature and reason. The possibility, necessity, and reality of revelation were demonstrated at length before Scripture itself was considered, and Scripture's truth was substantiated with an assortment of historical, critical, and rational proofs. Only after traveling this long road, did theologians get to the actual content of dogmatics, which they presented as plainly and simply as possible. The entire viewpoint has changed; not faith but reason is the starting point. It is not surprising, then, that in deism and rationalism reason rejected revelation altogether since revelation offers nothing new and is entirely superfluous. This order of treatment is essentially characteristic of scholastic and Roman Catholic theology. The Socinians never rose above this rationalistic viewpoint[74] and the Remonstrants again returned to it. Limborch, in his *Christian Theology*,[75] speaks in chapter 1 of theology and religion; in chapter 2 of the existence of God; and finally in chapter 3 of Holy Scripture. Simon Episcopius, in his *Institutes of Theology*, expands this introductory material. He even speaks first of the requirements for a theologian and then about the practical character of theology, natural theology, religion, revelation, and Holy Scripture. Gradually this ex-

---

73. S. Van Til, *Theologiae utriusque compendium cum naturalis tum revelatae* (Leiden, 1704).

74. O. Fock, *Der Socinianismus* (Keil: C. Schröder, 1847), 291ff.

75. Ed. note: For fuller bibliographic information on the following theologians mentioned by Bavinck, see the bibliography at the end of this volume.

pansion of the prolegomena also filtered through into orthodox dogmatics. The division of dogmatics into two parts (faith and works) leads W. Amesius and P. van Mastricht in their introductions to discuss the nature of faith after theology and Scripture. Joh. Marck and B. De Moor speak in the third chapter on religion, and W. Brakel begins with a chapter on natural theology. There is therefore much difference of opinion and confusion about what belongs in the introduction. But gradually, in the eighteenth century, a series of topics—theology, the natural knowledge of God, revelation, Scripture—became fixed features. We see this in the works of J. A. Turretin, Werenfels, Osterwald, Buurt, and all the theologians of the rationalist and supernaturalist stripe.

[33] This rationalistic foundation of dogmatics was, however, undermined by Kant, and then Schleiermacher did indeed attempt to save faith and the doctrine of faith by restricting them to feeling and the description of feeling respectively. But in actual fact no change occurred in this order of dogmatics. Attacks on the Christian religion in the nineteenth century were primarily directed against the foundations themselves. In earlier centuries faith was more robust, and the question Why do I believe? rarely came up. The foundations seemed so secure that to examine them was totally unnecessary; all available energy was devoted to the erection of the edifice itself. But today it is, above all, the philosophical underpinnings of dogmatics that are under fire; not some isolated doctrine but the very possibility of dogmatics is being questioned.[76] The human ability to know is restricted to the visible world, and revelation is considered impossible. In addition, Holy Scripture is being robbed of its divine authority by historical criticism and even the warrant for and value of religion is being seriously disputed. Consequently, and partly caused by all this, religious life today is dramatically less vigorous than before. It must be granted that there is much movement in the domain of religion, but there is little genuinely religious life. Faith is no longer sure of itself; even among believers there is much doubt and uncertainty. The childlike and simultaneously heroic statement "I believe" is seldom heard and has given way to the doubts of criticism. People perhaps still believe their confessions, but they no longer confess their faith (Schweizer).

When religious life is vital, people speak "as those having authority," not "as the scribes," and the words "I know whom I believe" trip from the lips of believers. In a critical time like our own, however, there is uncertainty, above all, about the foundations, about the source of knowledge, method, and evidence of faith. For that reason the formal part is still regarded as the most important division of dogmatics. An entire apologetics tends to precede the dogmatics proper.[77] Schleiermacher indeed made dogmatics a positive, historical science and tried to liberate it from all apologetics. How-

---

76. A. Pierson, *Ter Uitvaart* (1876).
77. S. Hoekstra, *Godgeleerde Bijdragen* (1864), 2.

ever, he prefaced historical theology, to which dogmatics belongs, with a philosophical theology. This philosophical theology took its starting point in community religious consciousness in general and from there critically determined the essence of Christianity. In this way Schleiermacher did not liberate theology from philosophy but instead made it dependent on it to the highest degree possible. This is apparent, for example, from the fact that he prefaces *The Christian Faith* with a general introduction containing a wide assortment of propositions borrowed from ethics, the philosophy of religion, and apologetics. Now it is true that Schleiermacher's model—giving encyclopedic priority to philosophical theology over the historical—has been followed by relatively few theologians. Nonetheless, following his example, it has become customary to start dogmatics with an apologetic section. Thus Voigt wrote a fundamental dogmatics and Lange a philosophical dogmatics, both of which preceded the positive. Similarly, Van Oosterzee's dogmatic foundation is apologetics; in Dorner and Biedermann a fundamental part, or apologetics, occupies first place, and in Lipsius and Nitzsch a doctrine of fundamental principles, and so forth. Liebner's advice to dogmaticians was to limit introductions to a discussion of the concept of dogmatics, since otherwise one gets an entire dogmatics before dogmatics proper.[78] Furthermore, the ideas of religion and revelation already presuppose the doctrines of God and humanity. His suggestion, however, has found little resonance. The topics treated in these introductory foundations are not the same everywhere, but they do include the following ideas: the nature of our religious knowledge, religion, revelation, Holy Scripture, and church. The chapter on "theology," often included in earlier times, has been moved to the "encyclopedia."

The ordering of the material part of dogmatics differs widely. Many theologians, like Vilmar, Böhl, Hodge, and Shedd, continue the usual order: theology, anthropology, Christology, etc. Others, however, such as Marheinecke, Martensen, Lange, Kahnis, Ebrard, and Schweizer prefer the trinitarian division or take as their principle of organization one particular attribute of God, like love (Schoeberlein), or life (Oetinger, Reiff). A greater change in organizing the dogmatic material has been brought about by the exclusively soteriological conception of Christianity. Those who view the salvation presented by the Christian religion more objectively proceed from Christology and in their dogmatics treat the presuppositions, the person and work of Christ (thus Liebner, Thomasius, Lange, von Oettingen, Lobstein). Others view salvation more from the side of the subject and think of it as one or more of the benefits that we owe directly or indirectly to Christ and that thus constitute the central idea of dogmatics. Schleiermacher and Rothe made the contrast between sin and grace basic to the division of the material. Hofmann, Philippi, Luthardt, Schnedermann, and

78. *Liebner, *Jahrbuch für die Theologie* (1856), 106ff.

Ihmels took as their starting point the concept of covenant, i.e., fellowship with God. They successively treat the origin, disturbance, and the objective restoration as well as the subjective realization and completion of that fellowship. Some—for example, Schenkel, Lipsius, Gretillat—make salvation in general the center of their dogmatics; others centralize it in a single benefit and elevate it to the level of a principle governing the whole of the dogmatic material. Following Kant, Ritschl saw the essence of Christianity as consisting in the kingdom of God established by Christ. Van Oosterzee also adopted this concept as his principle of division. Kähler regarded justification by faith the soul of Christianity. Schultz, uniting the two, spoke of the kingdom of God or justification by faith as the religious standard for the dogmatic evaluation of Christianity. Bouvier, in picturing the salvation embraced in the Christian religion, saw it above all as the new life given by Christ. Biedermann claimed that our status as children of God was the great benefit that needed to be given prominence in dogmatics.

THE FOUNDATION AND TASK OF PROLEGOMENA

[34] The organization of dogmatics in general and in particular not only became necessary in the face of fundamental opposition to the dogmatic enterprise but is in itself useful and good. Already at an early stage in Reformed theology, it was deemed necessary to describe the essence of theology and its foundations before treating the actual dogmas. Polanus (1561–1610) already made a distinction between the foundations (*principia*) and the articles of faith (*articuli fidei*). In time it became an urgent necessity for believers to know not only what they believed but also why. The first and general part of dogmatics was thus confined to a consideration of the reasons for believing. This first part does not have to deal with an assortment of encyclopedic questions, such as the essence, the history, and the division of theology, as Gretillat does. In the past this was done because theology was equated with dogmatics and theological encyclopedia was not yet practiced as a distinct discipline. Today, however, the development of the essence of theology has to be left to the domain of theological encyclopedia.[79] The task of dogmatics is restricted to the exposition of the designation, concept, method, division, and history of dogmatics itself, as this is furnished in the introduction. In still another way, however, the foundational part of dogmatics has to be limited. The method that arose already with scholasticism and later found acceptance also among Protestants, viz., of first treating the natural knowledge of God (the preamble of faith) and then all the historical and rational proofs (*motiva credibilitatis*) supporting revelation, must be rejected. At the very outset and in principle it abandons the viewpoint of faith, denies the positive character of dogmatics, moves onto

79. Ed. note: See, for example, Abraham Kuyper, *Encyclopaedie der Heilige Godgeleerdheid*, 2d ed., 3 vols. (Kampen: J. H. Kok, 1908).

the opponent's ground, and is therefore in fact rationalistic, and makes dogmatics dependent on philosophy.[80]

This dependency is clearly seen in the efforts of Schweizer and Scholten to equate natural theology or religion with the covenant of works. They then treat this natural religion as preparation for revealed religion, which is materially identical with the covenant of grace.[81] Both of them construe natural religion (the covenant of works, the state of integrity), the religion of the law (the covenant of grace before and under the law), and redemptive religion (the covenant of grace after the law) as three stages in the religious process. By this approach not only is revelation robbed of its supernatural character, but use is made of the Reformed division in a way that is contrary to its intent. The covenant of works before the fall is not a preparation for, but a contrast to, the covenant of grace, which arises in history only after the violation of the covenant of works by sin. The distinction between natural theology and revealed theology, on the other hand, is a very different one, not a historical distinction of periods but one that still and always exists and continues to be applicable in theology. Over against such a rationalization of religion and theology, one has to maintain (along with Schleiermacher, Rothe, Frank, Ritschl, etc.) the positive character of dogmatics. The foundations of faith (*principia fidei*) are themselves articles of faith (*articuli fidei*), based not on human arguments and proofs but on divine authority. The recognition of revelation, of Scripture as the Word of God, is an act of faith as well as its fruit. Dogmatics is from start to finish the work of a believer who is confessing and giving an account of the ground and content of his faith. This is no less true for the foundation issues as it is for the articles of faith (doctrine) themselves. In the introductory section of dogmatics, therefore, only the foundations of faith are set forth and developed. Just as the objective and subjective aspects of religion must be distinguished, so the foundations of faith are twofold: the external and internal, the objective and the formal, revelation and faith.[82] The entire first part of dogmatics properly deals only with these two foundations.

In structuring dogmatic content, the material second part, the trinitarian scheme is not altogether satisfactory for a number of reasons. First, it cannot accommodate the treatment of the Trinity itself because it does not naturally fit in any of the three economies and so has to be discussed by way of hypothesis in a prior chapter. Furthermore, in following this division one runs the risk that the outward or external works of God (*opera Dei ad extra*) are conceived too much as the works of the three Persons (*opera Dei personalia*) and

---

80. Ed. note: Bavinck makes a crucial distinction between a scientific theology to be practiced in a university and the discipline of dogmatics, which has as its task the unfolding of Christian truth as taught in Scripture and confessed in the church's creeds.

81. A. Schweizer, *Glaubenslehre*, I, 107–15, II, 1ff.; J. H. Scholten, *De Leer der Hervormde Kerk*, 2d ed., 2 vols. (Leiden: P. Engels, 1850–51), I, 304; I. Van Dijk, *Studien* VI (1880): I, 11ff.

82. G. Voetius, *Disp.* I, 2; Alting, *Theol. Schol. Didact.*, 10.

not enough as essential works of the one God (*opera Dei essentialia*), i.e., the common works of the divine Person. The other risk is that though unity is preserved, the Trinity is viewed only economically and its ontological character not recognized. A final disadvantage of this order is that, subsumed under the Persons of the Trinity, the *loci* on creation, angels, humanity, sin, church, etc., cannot come into their own. However, the christological organizing principle is subject to even more objections. However attractive it may seem at first sight, it is still unusable. It often rests on the false assumption that rather than Scripture the person of Christ specifically is the foundation and epistemic source of dogmatics. However, we know of Christ only from and through Scripture. In addition, though Christ is quite certainly the central focus and main content of Holy Scripture, precisely because he is the midpoint of Scripture, he cannot be its starting point. Christ presupposes the existence of God and humanity. He did not make his historical appearance immediately at the time of the promise [in Eden] but many centuries later. It is, moreover, undoubtedly true that Christ revealed the Father to us, but this revelation of God through the Son does not nullify the many and varied ways he spoke through the prophets. Not the New Testament alone, nor only the words of Jesus, but Scripture as a whole is a Word of God that comes to us through Christ. It is clear, finally, that the christological division only permits the development of the *loci* on God, creation, world, and humanity by way of assumptions and postulates and therefore not in the fullness of their rich significance.[83] Other organizations of dogmatics, such as those modeled on the three virtues (faith, hope, and love), on the scheme of faith, prayer, and commandment, on the final end and destiny of humanity, on the covenant or the fellowship between God and man, on the kingdom of God, on the concepts of life, love, spirit, etc., are also inadequate. Though they may have many practical advantages and be perfectly appropriate in a catechism, for a dogmatics, which is a system of the knowledge of God, they are not suitable because they are not central and comprehensive enough. Accordingly, either they have been introduced from the outside and do not govern the system, as in the case of Van Oosterzee, or they are strictly adhered to as principle of organization but fail to do justice to the different *loci*.

[35] The content of dogmatics is the knowledge of God as he has revealed it in Christ through his Word. The knowledge of believers is unique in that they view the whole of life religiously, theologically, and see everything in God's light, from the perspective of eternity (*sub specie aeternitatis*). That is the difference between their worldview and a philosophical or scientific worldview. In dogmatics it is always believers, Christians, who are speaking. They do not speculate about God; they do not proceed from an abstract philosophical concept of God, nor do they arrive at revealed theology by way of natural theology. They do not reason about God as he is in himself,

83. Cf. J. Kaftan, "Zur Dogmatik," 31–47.

for this knowledge is completely unattainable. They only describe the knowledge of God, which has been revealed to them in Christ. Accordingly, when in the first part of dogmatics they treat the subjects of God, his attributes, and the Trinity, they speak and think as believers, as Christians, as theologians, and not as philosophers. In every dogma, therefore, throbs the heartbeat of religion. Dogmatics is not a philosophical system but theology. But precisely for that reason dogmaticians do not tell us in their system of the knowledge of God how they came to faith and through that faith subjectively and successively gained insight into the various truths of faith. That would be an analytic method, which would be perfectly suitable in a catechism but not in a dogmatics. Instead, dogmatic theologians explicate the content of their faith as that is objectively exhibited by God himself before their believing eyes in revelation. They derive the principle of organization and the arrangement of the material, not from their own faith-life, but from the selfsame object that it is their task to describe in their dogmatics. They are not governed by the believing subject but by the object of faith.[84] So, although we most heartily agree that in dogmatics it is believers who always and everywhere, from beginning to end, think and speak, this is something very different from the idea that they should also derive the way they structure the material of dogmatics from their own experience. If this were the case, the character of dogmatics would be misconstrued, would change into anthropology, and cease to be theological. It remains theological only if the system of dogmatics is derived from its own material and content.

If this starting point is correct, then there are two methods of division that commend themselves.[85] The basic outline of the dogmatic system, after all, lies objectively before us: in Scripture, in the confession of the church, in the faith of the Christian community. The content of the Christian faith is the knowledge of God in his being and in his works. There exists a difference only in that some confessions, like the Apostles' Creed, in each instance mention the divine Persons first in connection with the works particularly attributed to that Person in an economic sense, while other confessions first fully treat the dogma of God, including the Trinity, and only then proceed to God's works. Hence the first-mentioned trinitarian method is not in itself objectionable. There is actually much that is appealing, and for that reason it has time after time found considerable acceptance and exerted great influence, also in philosophy. It commends itself by its purely theological character: God is beginning and end, alpha and omega. Nature and history are both subsumed under him. All things are from God and unto God. The trinitarian scheme guards against a barren uniformity and guarantees life, development, process. However, even apart from the objections raised above, this very description of it signals its danger. It can easily be speculatively mis-

---

84. Ibid., 36ff.
85. Simar, *Dogmatik* (1893), 67; Kaftan, *Dogmatik,* §12.

used, and in that case tends to sacrifice history to the system, incorporates cosmogony into the trinitarian life of God and so turns into theogony. The philosophies of Erigena, Böhme, Baader, Schelling, and Hegel supply proof of this.

Accordingly, the order that is theological and at the same time historical-genetic in character deserves preference. It, too, takes its point of departure in God and views all creatures only in relation to him. But proceeding from God, it descends to his works, in order through them again to ascend to and end in him. So in this method as well, God is beginning, middle, and end. From him, through him, and to him are all things (Rom. 11:36). But God is not drawn down into the process of history here, and history itself is treated more justly. God and his works are clearly distinguished. In his works God acts as Creator, Redeemer, and Perfecter. He is "the efficient and exemplary Cause of things through creation, their renewing Principle through redemption, and their perfective Principle in restoration" (Bonaventure). Dogmatics is the system of the knowledge of God as he has revealed himself in Christ; it is the system of the Christian religion. And the essence of the Christian religion consists in the reality that the creation of the Father, ruined by sin, is restored in the death of the Son of God and re-created by the grace of the Holy Spirit into a kingdom of God. Dogmatics shows us how God, who is all-sufficient in himself, nevertheless glorifies himself in his creation, which, even when it is torn apart by sin, is gathered up again in Christ (Eph. 1:10). It describes for us God, always God, from beginning to end—God in his being, God in his creation, God against sin, God in Christ, God breaking down all resistance through the Holy Spirit and guiding the whole of creation back to the objective he decreed for it: the glory of his name. Dogmatics, therefore, is not a dull and arid science. It is a theodicy, a doxology to all God's virtues and perfections, a hymn of adoration and thanksgiving, a "glory to God in the highest" (Luke 2:14).

PART II
THE HISTORY AND LITERATURE OF DOGMATIC THEOLOGY

3

The Formation of Dogma: East and West

Dogmatics arises from reflection on the truth of Scripture. This is not the task of individuals but the whole church. Contra Harnack, dogma is not the product of Hellenization and thus one grand error. Harnack simply has a different view than the historic church does of the essence of Christianity: If Harnack is too negative about the history of dogma, Roman Catholicism makes the opposite error, giving tradition a status nearly equivalent to Scripture. The Reformation neither underestimated nor overestimated tradition but distinguished between true and corrupted tradition and insisted on the need for Holy Spirit-led discernment. The Reformation tradition does respect the development of dogma in the church's history.

The early church articulated its dogmas in epistolary writings and simple creeds. During the time of the apologists in the second century, the opposition faced by Christians pressed the church into deeper reflection upon and a more sophisticated defense of the faith. Most of the perennial arguments against Christianity were already advanced in the second century. Learned Christians such as Justin Martyr and, later, Irenaeus used the tools of their intellectual training to defend the faith against such movements as Gnosticism and helped to create a Christian vocabulary and worldview. Some, such as Tertullian, were antithetically opposed to the Greek philosophic tradition, while the Alexandria school embraced its language. For Clement and Origen the Christian faith was a form of gnosis and Christ the great pedagogue. Here Christianity came to be understood primarily as a set of ideas. Primarily motivated by apologetic and polemic concerns, the foundations of Christian theology were in place by the end of the third century. However, the third and fourth centuries were times of great controversy about doctrines such as the unity of God and the deity of Christ.

With the Edict of Toleration (A.D. 313), external pressure was replaced by the internal pressure of heresy in the church. The major dogmatic developments, especially in Christology, took place in the East. Though christological debates dominate the fourth to the eighth centuries, the demands of catechesis led to numerous treatises on a broad range of topics—God, cosmology, anthropology, and moral issues such as virginity. The most important dogmatic works during this period were the writing of Pseudo-Dionysius and the orthodox summary works

of John of Damascus. The Damascene was also a strong defender of the venera-
tion of images, a key and controversial element of Eastern Orthodox Christianity.

Western theology focused on different themes. While for the East the dominant
emphasis was on humanity's liberation from the corruption of sin to be made par-
takers of the divine nature, the West emphasized legal themes such obedience,
guilt, and forgiveness. Christ's death, rather than his incarnation, was the point
of gravity. This gave to the Western church as aggressive, world-conquery impulse.
For all the differences, the Western church's dogmas relied heavily on the pioneer-
ing work done earlier in the East.

It is in the magisterial work of Augustine that the dogmatic work of East and
West finds its culmination. In particular, Augustine's emphasis on grace and his
view of the church left an indelible imprint. A sign of Augustine's importance to
the church is that every reformation returns to him and to Paul. The other great
figure of this period is the great pastoral theologian Gregory I. As we move toward
the end of the first millennium, mention must be made of the importance of
monasteries and schools in maintaining orthodoxy. After the darkness of the
tenth century, reformed monastic life helped create the conditions for the great
scholastic theologians such as Albertus Magnus, Thomas Aquinas, and Bonaven-
ture. Scholastic theology was the attempt, with the aid of philosophy, to gain sci-
entific knowledge of revealed truth. Scholasticism also provoked dissent in theo-
logians such as Duns Scotus and the rise of nominalism. The important role of
Pseudo-Dionysius also led to a mystical form of scholastic theology.

[36] Holy Scripture is no dogmatics. It contains all the knowledge of God
we need but not in the form of dogmatic formulations. The truth has been
deposited in Scripture as the fruit of revelation and inspiration, in a language
that is the immediate expression of life and therefore always remains fresh
and original. But it has not yet become the object of reflection and has not
yet gone through the thinking consciousness of the believer. Here and there,
for example in the letter to the Romans, there may be a beginning of dogmatic development, but it is no more than a beginning. The period of revelation had to be closed before that of dogmatic reproduction could start.
Scripture is a gold mine; it is the church that extracts the gold, puts its stamp
on it, and converts it into general currency.[1]

THE DEFINITION AND CHARACTER OF DOGMA

Processing the content of Scripture dogmatically, however, is not just the
work of one individual theologian, or of a particular church or school, but of
the entire church throughout the ages, of the whole new humanity regenerated by Christ. The history of dogma and dogmatics is therefore to be regarded as a mighty attempt to appropriate the truth of God revealed in

---

1. A. Ritschl, *Die Christliche Lehre von der Rechfertigung und Versöhnung,* 4th ed., 3 vols. (Bonn:
A. Marcus, 1895–1903), II, 20ff.

Christ and to fully understand the essence of Christianity. In evaluating that agelong dogmatic labor, people have erred both to the left and to the right and in turn been guilty both of overestimation and underestimation. The history of church and dogma has been disdained by all schools of thought that in the name of Scripture opposed all creeds, by Socinians and Remonstrants, by rationalistic and supernaturalistic, mystical and "biblical" theologians. Specifically, the first group already attributed the corruption of theology to the influence of Platonic philosophy.[2] In more recent times this view has been advanced by Harnack.[3] His *History of Dogma* is a work of great importance. Not only has it enriched our knowledge of the history of dogma and opened many fresh viewpoints, but above all it has been successful because it broke with the *loci*-method, traced the origin and development of dogma genetically, viewed particular dogmas as parts of the total outlook of Christianity, and saw the latter in its connection with the entire cultural milieu in which the Christian religion arose and propagated itself. However, these great merits are overshadowed by his one-sided and mistaken definition of dogma. According to Harnack, "dogma in its conception and development is a work of the Greek spirit on the soil of the Gospel,"[4] hence a mixture of Christian religion and Hellenic culture. This view of dogma is wrong, first of all, because from the outset the Christian church was very much on its guard against a mingling of Christian religion and pagan philosophy and later decisively condemned such a mingling in the case of Origen.[5] But this view also resulted in reducing the whole history of dogma to one grand error, a progressive corruption of the simple gospel of Jesus, a false interpretation of the original essence of Christianity.

According to Harnack, this essence consists solely in the experience of the individual soul that God is his Father, in the experience of God's powerful love as the power of his kingdom within us, which comes into being by the operation of Jesus' image within.[6] Now, according to Harnack, this process of the corruption of the original gospel did not really take off until the second century. Under the influence of Ritschl, Harnack tried to exempt the New Testament from this corruption, assigning it to a place by itself. But this is, of course, an inconsistency that the later proponents of the history-of-religions method recognized and abandoned. For if the Trinity, the "logos" doctrine, the preexistence of Christ, the incarnation, satisfaction, etc., are all elements foreign to the original gospel of Jesus, the process of cor-

2. O. Fock, *Der Socinianismus nach seiner Stellung in der Gesammtentwicklung des christlichen Geistes, Nach Seinem Historischen Verlauf und Nach Seinem Lehrbegriff* (Kiel: C. Schröder, 1847), 548.

3. Cf. Auguste Sabatier, *Esquisse d'une philosophie de la religion d'après la psychologie et l'historie* (Paris: Fischbacker, 1898), 208ff., 232ff.

4. Adolf von Harnack, *History of Dogma,* trans. N. Buchanan, J. Millar, E. B. Speirs, and W. McGilchrist and ed. A. B. Bruce, 7 vols. (London: Williams & Norgate, 1896–99), I, 17.

5. Cf., e.g., Joseph Mausbach, *Christentum und Weltmoral* (Münster i. W.: Aschendorffschen, 1905).

6. Adolf Harnack, *What Is Christianity?* trans. Thomas Bailey Saunders, with an introduction by Rudolf Bultmann (New York: Harper & Brothers Publishers, 1957).

ruption must already have started much earlier. It must have started in the circle of the apostles and in the first Christian community; specifically, the apostle Paul is the man who, by his Christology and his doctrine of satisfaction and the sacraments, corrupted the original Christianity of Jesus. This is openly acknowledged by Wernle, Wrede, Bousset, Weinel, and others; materially they agree with Nietzsche, for whom Paul was tantamount to the Antichrist.[7] Obviously, on this position the thing for Christian theology to do is to get rid of the whole history of dogma and all dogma and to return, decisively and radically, to the original gospel of Jesus, which is to be found primarily in the Sermon on the Mount. This, in fact, in Harnack's view, was fundamentally the significance and intent of the Reformation. Whereas in Roman Catholicism the formation of dogmas, that is, the corruption of Christianity, still continues, in the churches of Protestantism the history of dogmas has been the history of their dissolution. Here there is no longer any room for the history of dogma, for dogma, and for dogmatics; only the doctrine of faith remains. Of course, the Holy Scripture and dogmatics, or, if you will, original Christianity and our understanding of that original Christianity, are, in the nature of the case, not identical but distinct. Therefore, the gist of all of Harnack's views on dogma is simply that for the view of original Christianity that the church distilled in its dogma he substitutes his own personal dissenting view. He does not clear the field of dogma; he merely offers an interpretation of the essence of Christianity other than that which the Christian church has at all times presented. He only replaces the church's dogma by his own. Apart from everything else, it is more likely that Harnack errs in his view of the essence of Christianity than the church of all ages.[8]

[37] Diametrically opposed to the underestimation the history of dogma and dogma suffer at the hands of Harnack is the overestimation they are accorded from the side of Roman Catholicism. In the case of Catholicism, the material content of dogma, that is, revealed truth, is not even completely embodied in Scripture and tradition. In addition, interpretation of dogma formally promulgated by the church, or rather *ex cathedra* by the pope, is also crowned with infallible authority. The Catholic Church has not yet progressed to the point where it dares to equate ecclesiastical interpretation with divine truth. A twofold distinction still remains. In the first place, the church receives no new revelations. The pope possesses only interpretive power; he can and may proclaim as dogma only that which was, at all times, materially implicit in Scripture and tradition. And, in the second place, in proclaiming the church's dogmas the pope is not, like the prophets and apos-

7. Friedrich W. Nietzsche, *The Anti-Christ*, trans. and with an introduction by H. L. Menchen (Tucson: See Sharp Press, 1999).

8. Cf. Loofs, "Dogmengeschichte" *PRE³*, IV, 752–64; W. Bousset, *Theologische Rundschau* (July 1904): 266; J. Kaftan, *Zur Dogmatik sieben Abhandlungen aus der "Zeitschrift für Theologie und Kirche"* (Tübingen: J. C. B. Mohr [Paul Siebeck], 1904), 56ff.; and my article [1906], H. Bavinck, "Het Wezen des Christendoms," republished in *Verzamelde Opstellen* (Kampen: Kok: 1921), 17–34.

tles, the recipient of the *inspiration* but only of the special *assistance* of the Holy Spirit. Consequently, the dogma proclaimed is not literally the word of God but only contains it in essence.[9]

Nonetheless, the infallibility of the pope rivals that of Scripture and tradition—rivalry that can only end with the former crowding the latter into a corner or allowing it to exist in name only. The pope not only declares *what* is, but also decides *that* something is, the content of revelation. And then believers are denied all right to question or judge his decision. This fosters a passivity unworthy of Christians and imperceptibly fuels the urge to downgrade Scripture in favor of the church. In Roman Catholic theology, as it has developed since the Reformation, this tendency manifests itself over and over. The approval that modern criticism meets in the work of many Catholic theologians bears eloquent testimony to this fact, the strongest proof of which has recently been furnished by Alfred Loisy.[10] This abbot has made skillful use of the infallibility of the church for the purpose of uniting the modern view of the teaching of Jesus with Roman Catholic orthodoxy. His understanding of the original gospel virtually coincides with that of Harnack. But in the work of Loisy, that original Christianity, which consisted in a few simple elements, is a seed that found its normal development in the Catholic Church and specifically in Catholic dogma. In other words, it is a principle embodied in its purity in the church and a text on which the church has furnished infallible commentary. But this view undermines both Scripture and dogma. For if Jesus is not truly God, was not conceived by the Holy Spirit, did not rise from the dead and ascend to heaven, if—in other words—the dogma was not materially implicit in the original gospel, no church has the authority or right to proclaim and recommend it to the consciences of people as divine truth. There is a history of dogma and a dogma only if there is a revelation that furnishes the material for it. The verdict pronounced upon Loisy and his writings by the French episcopacy proves that Rome, too, still maintains this position today. Nevertheless it continues to face the dilemma of whether to subordinate Scripture to dogma or dogma to Scripture.

From the beginning the Reformation was on its guard against this underestimation and overestimation of history. It is true that in its public pronouncements it spoke harsh words against Aristotelian philosophy and medieval philosophy. But in principle, it was opposed not to all but only to a false and corrupted tradition. It accepted the Apostles' Creed and the creedal statements of the first four councils. It also took advantage of the theology of the church fathers, especially Augustine. However, in its evaluation of tradition, the Reformation returned to Holy Scripture. It recognized no tradition except that

9. *Documents of Vatican Council I, 1869–1870,* selected and trans. John F. Broderick (Collegeville, Minn.: Liturgical, 1971), I, IV c. 3. 4; J. Schwane, *Dogmengeschichte,* 4 vols. (Freiburg im Breisgau: Herder, 1882–95), I, §1–3.

10. A. Loisy, *Evangelium und Kirche* (München: Kirchheim, 1904); idem, *Autour d'un petit livre* (Paris: A. Picard, 1903).

which flowed from Scripture and continued to be subject to its norms. The Holy Spirit's leading of believers and the entire Christian church is essentially distinct from that in which the apostles participated (Rom. 8:14; cf. John 16:13). It lacks the character of infallibility and possesses as its permanent norm the word of the apostles, for the Holy Spirit will take everything from Christ and little by little apply his wisdom, righteousness, and holiness in the church. What takes place in theology also takes place *mutatis mutandis,* in the other sciences. Though their object is given in nature or history, the ultimate object of all sciences is to understand the infallible thoughts of God embodied in the works of his hands. Similarly the material and content for theology, specifically dogmatics, are given in Holy Scripture. And the church is led by the Holy Spirit in such a way that it gradually absorbs this content into its consciousness and reproduces it in its own language. The interpretation, formulation, and systematization of divine revelation therefore advances slowly and not without much aberration to the right and to the left. But it does go forward. The Holy Spirit's leading is the guarantee that it will; he does not rest until he has caused the fullness of Christ—which includes the fullness of his truth and wisdom—to dwell in the church and has filled that church with all the fullness of God (Eph. 3:19). Therefore, just as there is unity and continuity in the development of every science, so is this true in theology and dogmatics. These, too, have a history—not only in the sense that their material content was gradually revealed by God over many centuries and not even only in the sense that the different truths were formulated with increasing clarity by the church and applied in human life. History is reflected also in the sense that scientific consciousness gained increasingly clearer insight into the organism and system of revealed truth. The scientific character of theology and dogmatics has passed through a history as well. A distinction must also be made, therefore, between the history of dogma and the history of dogmatics. Even though in these historical chapters the distinction is not, for practical reasons, strictly observed, it does exist and ought to be recognized as such.

DOGMA IN THE EARLY CHURCH

The Biblical Theology of the Apostolic Fathers

[38] The first period, which extends from the second to the fourth century, was that of the formation of dogma, and it exhibits dogmatics in its earliest beginnings. In the case of the Apostolic Fathers[11] there is as yet no such thing as dogma or dogmatics. They still completely operate on the basis of a

---

11. See *Patrum apostolicorum opera,* ed. O. Gebhardt, A. Harnack, and T. Zahn, 3 vols. (Leipzig: J. C. Hinrichs, 1876–78); Adolf Hilgenfeld, *Novum Testamentum extra canonem receptum* (Leipzig: T. O. Weigel, 1866); the Dutch translation of A. C. Duker and W. C. van Manen, *Oud Christelijke Letterkunde: De Geschriften der Apostolische Vaders,* 2 vols. (Amsterdam: C. L. Brinkman, 1869–71); F. X. Funk, *Die apostolischen Väter* (Tübingen: J. B. C. Mohr, 1901); J. B. Lightfoot, *The Apostolic Fathers: A Revised Text with Introductions, Notes, Dissertations, and Translations,* 2d ed. (London; New York: Macmillan, 1889–90).

naïve, childlike faith. Christianity was not the product of human research and reflection but of revelation and in the first place, therefore, demanded faith. They tried as well as they could to take in and to reproduce the oral and written teaching of the apostles. They took over the biblical concepts of God, of Christ as Lord, of his death and resurrection, of the Holy Spirit, of faith, repentance, church, baptism, communion, offices, prayer, watching, fasting, alms, resurrection life, immortality, etc. However, they did not think through, analyze, and relate them to each other. After all, Christianity found acceptance mostly, though not exclusively,[12] among the simple and unlearned. Its entire focus was therefore all the more to convert Christian truth into life and, practically, to bring the worship, life, and organization of the church under its sway. The accent, thus, was not on *gnosis* but on a holy life, on the practice of the Christian virtues of love, meekness, humility, obedience, chastity, peace, unity, etc. The circle of ideas in which people operated was therefore still small; many biblical concepts were completely missing; others were modified, weakened, or confused and combined with ideas of Jewish and pagan origin. Generally speaking, the real essence of Christianity, in distinction from Judaism and paganism, was not yet clearly recognized and in any case better understood ethically than dogmatically. Despite the epistolary form that the Apostolic Fathers, like the apostles, usually employed, and though in part they addressed the same churches, the difference and the distance between the two, both in content and form, is striking. "Indeed, the earliest Christian writings are something special, clearly distinct in language and spirit from the later literature. It is, above all, comparison that teaches us to appreciate the distance correctly."[13] The consciousness nurtured in a pagan milieu could not absorb Christian ideas so fast.[14]

The Apologists against Paganism

However, theology could not stop at this simple repetition and practical application of the truth of Scripture. The opposition that Christianity gradually came to experience from the side of pagan culture forced Christians into reflection and defense. In the earliest period pagan authorities limited themselves to persecution, or to hatred and mockery, as expressed by Tacitus and Lucian in his *Peregrinus Proteus*.[15] But in time the pagan world had to take account of Christianity and began to attack it scientifically. Heinrich

12. James Orr, *Neglected Factors in the Study of the Progress of Christianity* (London: Hodder and Stoughton, 1899).

13. Ernst von Dobschütz, *Probleme des apostolische Zeitalters* (Leipzig: J. C. Hinrichs, 1904), 121.

14. Lübkert, "Die Theologie de apostolischen Väter," *Niedners Zeitschrift für historische Theologie* 1 (1854); J. Sprinzl, *Die Theologie der apostolischen Väter: Eine dogmengeschichtliche Monographie* (Wien: W. Braumüller, 1880); Brehm, "Das Christlichen Gesetzthum der apostolischen Väter," *Zeitschrift für Kirchliche Wissenschaft und kirchliches Leben* 7 (1886). Also see the works cited above by Lechler, Harnack, Bardenhewer, Lightfoot, etc.

15. Ed. note: Bavinck's reference to Tacitus is likely to his famous description of Christian persecution in his *Annals*, xv.44.; Lucian, *Peregrinus Proteus*.

Kellner, in his *Hellenismus und Christenthum*,[16] describing the intellectual reaction of ancient paganism to Christianity, points out its kinship with
present-day opposition to Christianity. The main scientific opponents were
Celsus, Porphyry, Fronto the friend of Aurelius, and later Julian [the "Apos-
tate"] who, as is evident from Cyril's refutation entitled *Against Julian*, wrote
a book against Christians. All the arguments later advanced against Christianity can already be found in these writers—arguments, for example,
against the authenticity and truth of many Bible books (the Pentateuch,
Daniel, and the Gospels) and against revelation and miracles in general; arguments against an assortment of dogmas such as the incarnation, satisfaction, forgiveness, the resurrection, and eternal punishment; arguments also
against norms of morality such as asceticism, contempt of the world, and
lack of refinement; and, finally, slanderous accusations of worshiping an ass's
head, and of committing child murder, adultery, and all sorts of immorality.

This scientific polemic, however, did not succeed in overcoming Christianity either. And pagans saw themselves forced either to revive the old religion, as neopythagoreanism and neoplatonism attempted, and especially the
Mithras religion[17] aspired to do, or to mix and combine Christianity with
paganism, as this was happening in Gnosticism and Manichaeism. Gnosticism was a particularly powerful attempt to absorb Christianity (and so deprive it of its absolute character) in its combination and fusion of a range of
pagan elements: neoplatonic philosophy, Syrian and Phoenician mythology,
Chaldean astrology, Persian dualism, etc. In this connection the main question was how the human spirit had fallen into the bonds of matter and could
now be delivered from these bonds. In Gnosticism God, as a rule, is abstract
undifferentiated oneness. Matter, the cause of evil, cannot be explained as
coming from him. It is derived from a lower deity, the demiurge, who stands
between the supreme God and the world of the senses and is equated with
the God of the Old Testament. Proceeding from God—for the purpose of
liberating spirits in bondage to matter—are various aeons, which represent
the different religions and culminate in the aeon Christ. Accordingly, Christianity is not the only religion but the highest. Christ, however, is understood docetically. What counts is not the fact or history [of Christ] but the
idea. For that reason the highest bliss consists in knowledge; what saves a
person is knowledge combined with ascesis. *Pistis* (theology) may be fine for
the unlearned, but *gnosis* (philosophy) is supreme and the possession of the
truly spiritual (πνευματικοι). These ideas were harmonized with Scripture by
allegorical exegesis and presented in forms and images derived from mythology and adorned by fanciful imagination. They changed Christianity into a
kind of philosophy of religion, a speculative philosophy, which has exerted

16. K. A. Kellner, *Hellenismus und Christenthum* (Köln: M. DuMont-Schauberg, 1866), 431ff.

17. Franz Cumont, *Die Mysterien des Mithra: Ein Beitrag zur Religionsgeschichte der römischen Kaiserzeit* (Leipzig: Teubner, 1903); Julius Grill, *Die persische Mysterienreligion im römischen Reiche und das
Christentum* (Tübingen: Mohr, 1903).

its influence throughout the centuries right down to the systems of Hegel and Schelling.

To counter these various attacks, defense was needed. Christians were forced to reflect on the content of revelation and to posit a true Christian *gnosis* against the false. Accordingly, revealed truth now became the object of methodical scientific thought. Theology arose, not from within and for the church and for the purpose of training its ministers, but prompted by and in opposition to the attacks aimed at Christianity. Naturally, knowledge of pagan philosophy was needed for such rational activity. Actually theology originated with the help of and in alliance with philosophy. This had already been attempted by the Gnostics as well, but there was an essential difference in the way the Gnostics and the apologists sought such synthesis. That difference does not lie, as Harnack thinks, in the fact that the former undertook an acute and the latter a gradual Hellenization of Christianity.[18] The truth is that in the case of the Gnostics the positive and absolute content of the Christian religion was lost, while in the case of the apologists it was preserved. For the former the use of philosophy was material while for the latter it was mainly formal. Therefore the former were disowned by the church and the latter recognized. While the Gnostics presented the different philosophies as a religious process in which Christianity was included, the latter tried to show that the Christian religion, which they recognized and accepted as the supreme truth, is the true philosophy that unites within itself all elements of truth that come from without.

This last point even constitutes the fundamental idea of the apologists. They developed it as follows: God is one, inexpressible, spiritual, etc., but through the Logos he is also the Creator of the world, the final cause of all that is and the first principle of everything that is morally good. Gnostic dualism is overcome here since the world everywhere bears the stamp of the divine Logos and matter is good and created by God as well. Humanity was originally created good, received reason and freedom, and was destined for immortality (ἀθανασία); this it had to and could attain in the way of free obedience. But humanity allowed itself to be seduced by demons, came under the sway of sensuality, and fell into error and death. At this point as well dualism is avoided, and the cause of sin is located in the human will. New means are therefore required to bring human beings back from the way of deception and death and to lead them to immortality. From the most ancient times, God revealed himself by the Logos, imparting the knowledge of the truth even to some pagans but especially to the prophets of Israel and finally in his Son Jesus Christ. In him all earlier truth is confirmed and perfected. Through Christ, as the teacher of truth, humanity is again brought to its destination. Accordingly, though the apologists are intellectualistic as well as moralistic, still there is present, as for example in Justin Martyr, an effort

18. Harnack, *History of Dogma*, I, 227ff.; II, 169ff.

to understand Christ also as Reconciler and Redeemer by whose blood we receive the forgiveness of sin.[19]

Christian Theology and/or Philosophy: Two Ways

[39] The beginnings of theology in the apologists were not only weak but also marred in many respects by one-sidedness and error. The problems that presented themselves were numerous and immense. Questions like the relationship between theology and philosophy, the doctrine of the Logos in its relation to God, the significance of Christ and his death, etc., were much too deep for rapid and correct resolution. Differences in understanding were frequent. The moment theology came into being, divergence in trends and schools arose as well. Soon two dogmatic trends became distinguishable. On the one hand is that represented by Tertullian, Cyprian, Lactantius, as well as Irenaeus, from whom only his great work *Against Heresies*[20] has been preserved. Here we also include Irenaeus's pupil Hippolytus of Rome, the likely author of *Refutation of All Heresies,* initially attributed to Origen.[21] All these men are sharply opposed to philosophy. Irenaeus issued strong warnings against it, and Tertullian banished it totally and in the sharpest possible

---

19. The writings of the apologists are printed in J. P. Migne, *Patrologiae Graeca*, vol. 6, and in Gebhardt and Harnack, *Texte und Untersuchungen zur Geschichte der altchristliche Literatur* (Leipzig: Hinrichs, 1882).

For the theology of the apologists, see Karl Werner, *Geschichte der apologetischen und polemischen literatur der christlichen Theologie*, 5 vols. (Schaffhausen: Hurter'sche Buchhandlung, 1861–88); Gregor Schmitt, *Die Apologie der drei ersten Jahrhunderte in historisch-systematischer Darstellung* (Mainz: Rupferberg, 1890).

The most significant of the apologists by far was Justin Martyr. See: J. G. Semisch, *Justin Martyr: His Life, Writings, and Opinions,* trans. J. E. Ryland, 2 vols. (Edinburgh: Thomas Clark, 1843); Weiszäcker, "Die Theologie des Justin Märtyrer," *Jahrbuch für die Theologie* (1867); Heinrich Veil, *Justinus des Philosophen und Märtyrers Rechtfertigung des Christentums: Apologie I, u. II* (Strassburg: Heitz, 1894); Bonwetsch, "Justin der Märtyrer," *PRE³*, IX, 641–50.

20. Irenaeus, *Against Heresies,* II, 25–28, *ANF,* I, pp. 396–401.

21. Here follows an abbreviated list of some works about the church fathers, ecclesiastical writers, councils, etc. The acts of the councils are collected in Jean Hardouin, *Acta conciliorum et epistolae decretales* (Paris, 1714–15) 11 vols. in 12 (through 1714); Giovan Domenico Mansi, *Sacrorum conciliorum nova et amplissima collectio,* 31 vols. (Flor, 1759–98); a more recent edition, 53 vols. in 60 (Graz: Akademische Druck, 1901; reprinted, 1960). *Acta et decreta Sacrorum Conciliorum recentorium,* Collectio Lacensis, 7 vols. (Freiburg: Herder, 1870–92) contains the conciliar acts from 1682 through 1870. The most important documents of councils and popes have been collected by H. Denzinger, *Enchiridion symbolorum: Definition um et declarationum de rebus fidei et morum,* 36th rev. ed. (Westminster, Mich.: Herder, 1976); the history of the councils is most thoroughly covered by Karl Joseph von Hefele, 5 vols. (Edinburgh: T. & T. Clark, 1883–96); Andreas Gallandi, *Biblotheca veterum patrum antiquorumque scriptorum ecclesiasticorum, postrema Lugdunesi longe locupletior atque accuratior* (Venetiis: J. B. Hieron fil., 1765–81); J. P. Migne, *Patrologia Graecorum,* 473 vols. (Paris, 1844). Key editions of the works of individual church fathers include Tertullian by Oehler (Leipzig, 1853); Tertullian, Cyprian, Lactantius, each by Ephraim G. Gersdorf, in *Bibliotheca patrum ecclesiasticorum latinorum selecta,* 13 vols. (Leipzig: sumptibus B. Tauchnitz jun., 1838–47); Irenaeus by Stieren (Leipzig, 1853); Origen by Delarue (Paris, 1733); Chrysostom by Montfaucon (1718); Augustine by Delfau, e.g., (1679–1702); and finally the excellent edition of the Latin church fathers, published in Vienna under the Auspices of the Imperial Academy of

terms in his familiar saying: "What fellowship is there between Athens and Jerusalem, the academy and the church, Christians and heretics?"[22] Still, they all make the most naïve use of it. Tertullian's great importance for theology lies in the fact that he introduced a number of terms crucial to trinitarian and christological dogma, such as *trias, trinitas, satisfacere, meritum, sacramentum, una substantia* and *tres personae, duae substantiae in una persona,* etc., none of which occurs in Scripture. But as these men do this, they nevertheless position themselves in the faith of the church; they are historical, positive, realistic, and do not make a qualitative—at most a quantitative— distinction between faith and theology, πιστις and γνωσις.[23]

It must be granted that in the case of these men we cannot yet speak of a dogmatic system. In their work the various dogmas stand, unconnected, side by side; one looks in vain for a specific organizing principle. Even more, Tertullian and Hippolytus have not yet succeeded in completely overcoming Gnosticism in Christology. Still, their theology, particularly that of Irenaeus, was that of the succeeding centuries. All the later dogmas can be found in him. The unity of God, the essential unity of Father and Son, the unity of

---

Science: Corpus etc. (Vienna, 1866–); and the even more carefully prepared edition of the Greek church fathers by the Royal Prussian Academy of Science (Church Fathers Commission) in which the one work that has appeared is Otto Stählin's work on Clement of Alexandria (Leipzig: J. C. Hinrichs, 1905).

Ed. note: With the publication of Augustine's *De Genesi contra Manichaeos* in 1998, the *Corpus Scriptorium Ecclesiasticorum Latinorum* put out its ninety-first volume in this series. Bavinck continues his lengthy footnote by calling attention to other works, including translations.

A German translation of the most important texts from the church fathers appeared in the 80 volumes of the *Bibliothek der Kirchenvätter* (Kempten: Kösel, 1869–88). See further, Bellarmine, *De Scriptoribus ecclesiasticis* (Rome, 1673); El. du Pin, *Nouvelle bibliothèque des auteurs ecclèsiastiques,* 47 vols. (Paris: Chez André Pralard, 1686–1714); W. Cave, *Scriptorum ecclesiasticorum historia literaria,* 2 vols. (London, 1689; Basel, 1741); Johann Georg Walch, *Bibliotheca theologica selecta litterariis adnotationibus instructa,* 4 vols. (Ienae, 1757–); Heinrich Ritter, "Geschichte der Christlichen Philosophie," vols. 5–12 in his *Geschichte der Philosophie,* 12 vols. (Hamburg: Perthes, 1829–53), F. Ueberweg, *Grundress der Geschichte der Philosophie,* 5 vols. (Berlin: E. S. Mittler & Sohn, 1923–28).

The following are useful tools for ecclesiastical Greek: J. C. Suicerus, *Thesaurus ecclesiasticus,* 2 vols. (Amsterdam: J. H. Westen, 1682); 2d and longer edition (Amsterdam, 1728). For Medieval Greek: C. Du Fresne Du Cange, *Glossarium ad scriptores mediae et infimae graecitatis,* 3 vols. (Paris, 1678). For Medieval Latin: idem, *Glossarium ad scriptores mediae et infimae latinitatis,* 3 vols. (Paris, 1678). Also see E. Forcellini, *Totius latinitatis lexicon,* 4 vols. (Padua: J. Manfie, 1771); for an English edition, see F. P. Leverett, ed., *A New and Copious Lexicon of the Latin Language; compiled chiefly from the Magnum totius latinitatis lexicon of Facciolati and Forcellini, and the German works of Scheller and Luenemann,* 2 vols. in 1 (Boston: Wilkins, Carter, and Co., 1845).

For place names: Johann Wilhelm Muller, *Lexicon manuale, geographiam antiquam et mediam cum Latine tum Germanice illustrans* (Leipzig: Impensis Hartmanni, 1831); and J. G. Th. Graesse, *Orbis Latinus; oder, Verzeichniss der lateinischen benennungen der bekanntesten städe, meere, seen, berge und flüsse in allen theilen der erde, nebst einem deutsch-lateinischen register derselben* (Dresden: G. Schonfeld, 1861).

Ed. note: For the various lexical tools Bavinck cites in the last paragraph, he also lists a number of editions and translations of various works that are not provided in this lengthy note.

22. Irenaeus, *Against Heresies,* II, 25–28, *ANF,* I, pp. 350–53; Tertullian, *The Prescription against Heretics,* chap. 7, *ANF,* III, p. 246.

23. Irenaeus, *Against Heresies,* II, 25–28, *ANF,* I, pp. 350–53.

the God of creation and redemption, the unity of the God of the Old Testament and the God of the New Testament, the creation of the world out of nothing, the unity of the human race, the origin of sin in the freedom of the will, the two natures of Christ, the absolute revelation of God in Christ, the resurrection of all human beings, etc., are all clearly stated and maintained by Irenaeus over against Gnosticism. In the work of Irenaeus, Christianity for the first time unfolded its own independent theological science.[24]

The attitude adopted toward philosophy and Gnosticism by the Alexandrian theologians was quite different. Toward the end of the second century and in the beginning of the third, at various places, but especially in Alexandria, the ambition arose to articulate the truth of Christianity scientifically and to thus convey it to contemporary consciousness. The origin and establishment of the Catechetical School in Alexandria are not known to us, but it existed already about A.D. 190 and rapidly rose in status and influence.[25] The first teacher who is known to us from writings that still survive is Clement of Alexandria. But he is overshadowed by Origen, the most influential theologian of the early centuries. It was their aim to convert the church's doctrine into a speculative science. They did, to be sure, uphold the faith and, by contrast with the Gnostics, based themselves on the positive doctrine of the church. Clement even called the faith a γνῶσις σύντομος (concise science) and valued it more highly than pagan wisdom. Christianity is a way to salvation for all human beings and can be appropriated only by faith. The content of that faith has been summarized by the church in its creed, and the sole epistemic source of truth is revelation, Holy Scripture. All this is held by Clement and Origen as firmly as by Irenaeus and Tertullian.

The difference begins with the fact that the Alexandrians assumed a qualitative distinction between faith and science. Faith may be wholesome and necessary for the unlearned; for the learned it is not enough. Theology must aim to develop the content of faith into a science that does not rest on authority but finds its certainty and validity within itself. *Pistis* (faith) must be raised to the level of *gnosis* (knowledge). Here *gnosis* is no longer a means with which a theologian resists and fights against heresy but becomes its own goal. *Pistis* merely produces a χριστιανισμός σωματικός ("somatic" Christianity), but the task of theology is to develop from Scripture a χριστιανισμός πνευματικός ("pneumatic" Christianity). What Philo attempted to do for the Jews, Clement and Origen undertook for Christians: they continued the work of Justin Martyr. To reach this goal they of course had to be familiar with and make use of philosophy. Not that they adopted a specific system, but they did employ the whole of Greek philosophy from Socrates on, especially that of Plato and the Stoa. And with the aid of these philosophies, Origen produced a system that, though it undoubtedly evinces a genial vision

24. Harnack, *History of Dogma*, II, 230–318.

25. Fritz Lehmann, *Die Katechetenschule zu Alexandria* (Leipzig: A. Lorentz, 1896); A. Harnack, "Alexandrinische Katechetenschule und Schule," *PRE*[3], I, 356–59.

and profound cognitive strengths, also again and again runs the danger of collapsing theology into philosophy. The subordination of the Son, the eternity of creation, the preexistence of souls, a dualism of spirit and matter, earthly purification, the restoration of all things—all these are elements in Origen's system that brought it into conflict with the faith of the church and later brought about his condemnation. A pneumatic, allegorical exegesis served to harmonize it all with Scripture, but actually, in this theology of Origen, the Christian religion was dissolved into ideas. It sought to make a deal between the church and the world, faith and science, theology and philosophy, a compromise between the foolishness of the cross and the wisdom of the world. In that way, Origen's is the most impressive and richest specimen of the mediating theology (*Vermittelungstheologie*) that surfaces in the church again and again.[26]

By the beginning of the third century, the foundations of Christian theology had been laid. Against paganism and Judaism, Gnosticism and Ebionitism, the church had deliberately assumed a firm position and rescued the independence of Christianity. In the third century, however, a variety of internal disputes arose. The great controversy of this century concerned the relation of the Logos (and the Spirit) to the Father, and the heresy that had to be combated was Monarchianism in its two forms: dynamic and modalistic Monarchianism. In the East, from 260 on, the "dynamic" party (the Alogi, Theodotus and his group, Artemas *cum suis,* and especially Paul of Samosata, bishop of Antioch) sought to maintain the oneness of God by regarding the Son and the Spirit, not as persons but as [divine] attributes, and denied Jesus' deity. Jesus, they said, was a human being especially equipped by the divine Logos and anointed with God's Spirit. Modalistic Monarchians, on the other hand, taught that the deity himself had become flesh in Christ. They therefore recognized the deity of Christ but identified the Father with the Son and thus arrived at patripassianism. In the third century this opinion was very widespread and enjoyed much adherence. It was defended and advocated by Noetus, Epigonus, Cleomenes, Aeschines, Praxeas, Victorinus, Zephyrinus, Callistus, and especially Sabellius. It was also vigorously combated by Hippolytus, Tertullian, Dionysius of Alexandria, Eusebius, etc. By the end of the third century, the dogma of Christ's deity and his distinctness from the Father was firmly established. Three hypostases, Father, Son, and Spirit, existed in the divine being. This was accepted doctrine both in the East and in the West. The concepts that would engage theological thought in the following century, such as μονας, τριας, ουσια, υποστασις, προσωπον, etc., already existed but would not acquire their specific character and firm value until later. The foundation had been laid, and the boundaries within which Christian speculation was to test its strength had been marked off.

---

26. Charles Bigg, *The Christian Platonists of Alexandria* (Oxford: Clarendon Press; New York: Macmillan, 1886).

The dogmatic writings that saw the light of day in this first period all served the cause of apologetics and polemics and generally restricted themselves to an explanation of points of doctrine in dispute. Accordingly, a large number of treatises were published that dealt with particular dogmatic and ethical subjects—the unity of God, the reality of Christ's incarnation, the resurrection, baptism, etc. As specimens of a dogmatic system in that period, only Origen's *First Principles*—discussed earlier already—and Lactantius's *Divine Institutions* can be considered.

DOGMA AND THEOLOGY IN THE EAST

[40] As the fourth century began, a great change occurred. The Edict of Toleration of A.D. 313 brought peace and quiet to the church, a peace and quiet that was soon followed by prestige and honor. Free from external pressure, the development of theology could be more vigorous; in fact, all parts of theology were now cultivated fruitfully. The moment the enemies from without had been vanquished, however, those from within began to assert themselves. When dogma assumes specific shape, heresy in many forms raises its head. The characteristic feature of the period that now follows is the development, fixation, and defense of dogma, something that took place particularly in the East. Here the period of the fourth to the eighth century was almost completely taken up by christological controversies. The dogma *par excellence* was the *homoousia* of the Son, who is incarnate in Christ, with the Father. The religious issue at stake here is that God himself had to become man so that humanity would be freed from death, led to immortality and the vision of God, and made partakers in the divine nature. The deity of Christ is the essence of Christianity. No one understood this better than Athanasius. His history is that of his century. For him what Christianity essentially comes down to is redemption to eternal life by the true Son of God. In holding this he is upholding the specific character of Christian religion, rendering the teaching of the Trinity free from cosmological speculations such as still adhere to it in Origen and Tertullian, and saving it from secularization.[27] Athanasius was a Christologist who felt deeply the religious significance of the deity of Christ. Christ has to be God to be our Savior. As a result of this wholly unique significance of christological dogma, no actual dogmatic systems emerged. Seeing the light of day, in fact, were a number of important dogmatic treatises by Alexander, Athanasius, Basil, Gregory of Nazianzus, Gregory of Nyssa, Didymus, etc., on the deity of Christ, the incarnation, the personality and deity of the Holy Spirit, the Trinity—all of them straightforwardly or obliquely directed against the Arians and Macedonians.

When in A.D. 381 this controversy was settled in favor of orthodoxy at the Synod of Constantinople, another point of dispute surfaced. In the midst of

27. A. Harnack, *History of Dogma*, III, 139–44; IV, 26–38.

the controversy about the *homoousia* of the Son, the question concerning the nature of the union of the human with the divine nature in Christ had already come up. While recognizing that the Redeemer had to be God, Apollinaris asserted that the Redeemer could not be fully human, for then two beings and two persons were united who did not make up a true unity. Accordingly, in his view the Logos assumed "animated" flesh (σαρξ), himself constituting its *pneuma,* the self, the principle of self-consciousness and self-determination. But he was opposed by Athanasius and the two Gregorys and condemned at the Synod of Rome in 377 and at Constantinople in 381. The moment the two natures were established, a difference arose about the nature of their union. It is not substantial and essential, said Nestorius, but moral and relative; in Christ there are two ὑποστασεις (hypostases), two persons. But he had a strong opponent in the person of Cyril of Alexandria and was condemned at the Synod of Ephesus in 431. The diametrically opposite sentiments of Eutyches were contested by Theodoret of Cyrus in his work *Eranistes* and by Leo the Great in his *Letter to Flavian* and were condemned by the Council of Chalcedon in 451.

The Chalcedonian formula, however, failed to bring peace. Since the monophysitism of the East was strong, a confused situation became even more confused. Leontius of Byzantium (485–543), whom Harnack calls the first "scholastic," was a strong defender of monophysitism, and it was also recognized at the fifth Synod of Constantinople in 551. But the Monophysites were not persuaded, not even by the interventions of Justinian I. The monergistic and monotheletic conflicts that arose in the seventh century ended at the sixth synod at Constantinople (680) with the dogmatic fixation of the two wills in Christ. And in Syria to this very day there are monophysite Christians who believe there is but one nature in Christ (*ex* not *in* two natures), reject Chalcedon and recognize the so-called Robber Council of Ephesus. They also eat leavened bread at communion, make the cross with one finger, have taken the veneration of images and saints over from the Greek and Roman Catholic Church, and are subject to the "Patriarch of Antioch" (who, however, usually lives in Diarbekr). There are also Monophysites in Egypt called Copts, under a patriarch who lives in Cairo; in Ethiopia, under an Abbuna appointed by the patriarch in Cairo and residing in Gondar; and in Armenia, under a "Catholicos" in Etschmiadsin, a monastery near Erivan.[28]

However, from a dogmatic viewpoint, not only the christological writings need to be considered but other treatises as well. The doctrine of God, his

---

28. E. Nestle, "Jacobiten," *PRE³*, VIII, 565–71; H. G. Kleyn, *Jacobus Baradaeüs: de stichter Syrische Monophysietische Kerk* (Leiden: Brill, 1882); Rudolf Hugo Hofmann, *Symboliek of stelselmatige uiteenzetting van het onderscheidene christelijke Kerkgenootschappen en voornaamste sekten* (Utrecht: Kemink en Zoon, 1861), §62–68; Kattenbusch, *Lehrbuch der vergleichenden Confessionskunde,* vol. 1 (Freiburg i.B.: J. C. B. Mohr [Paul Siebeck], 1894), 205–34. The creed of Jacob Baradeus can be found in Kleyn, 110f. Ed. note: Jacob Baradeus (c. 500–78) was a Monophysite cleric who inspired the nickname "Jacobite" for the Syrian Orthodox Church.

names, attributes, and providence, were treated in line with the apologists, who had maintained the Christian view of God against Gnosticism. As a rule the starting point was the natural knowledge of God as a simple unchanging Being whose existence could be proven psychologically, cosmologically, and teleologically. Though God is unknowable in his essence, he was revealed in Scripture as the Triune God.[29] Cosmology and anthropology were primarily treated in connection with Genesis 1–3 and in a way that avoided Origenism. God created the world by the Logos on the model of a superterrestrial spiritual world; sin arose as a result of free will and is counterbalanced by punishment and redemption.[30] In addition, numerous treatises were written about virginity, monasticism, perfection, the priesthood, resurrection, etc., like those by Ephraem Syrus, the two Gregories, and Chrysostom, alongside of many apologies against Jews, pagans, and heretics. More important for the history of dogmatics are the *Theological Institutes* of Theognostus, which are no longer extant but of which, according to Photius, the first three books treat God the Father and the Creator, the Son, and the Spirit; the fourth, angels and demons; the fifth and sixth, the incarnation; and the seventh, creation.[31] In this list as well belong Cyril of Jerusalem's *Catechesis,* eighteen lectures for the "enlightened" on the truths of faith and five for the "newly enlightened" on the mysteries, on baptism, confirmation, and the Eucharist. The work of Gregory of Nyssa, the *Catechetical Oration,* in forty chapters, contains a philosophical argumentation for the main truths of Christianity, God's existence, essence, Trinity, creation and fall, redemption, sacraments (especially penance and the Eucharist), and eschatology. Chrysostom's *Two Catecheses* are in the main moral addresses to catechumens. Theodoret offered a compendium of the Christian faith in the fifth book of his *Compendium of Heretical Tales.* Maximus Confessor dealt with

29. Chrysostom, *On the Incomprehensible Nature of God,* trans. Paul W. Harkins (Washington, D.C.: Catholic University Press, 1984); also see *John Chrysostom's On Providence,* translation and theological interpretation by Christopher Alan Hall (Ph.D. diss., Drew University, 1991), book III; Pseudo-Dionysius, *The Divine Names and Mystical Theology,* translation, with an introductory study by John D. Jones (Milwaukee: Marquette University Press, 1980); Theodoret, Bishop of Cyrrhus, *Divine Providence,* trans. Thomas Halton (New York: Neman, 1988), oration X; Harnack, *History of Dogma,* III, 241–47; Wilhelm Münscher, *Dr. Wilhelm Münschers Lehrbuch der christlichen Dogmengeschichte,* ed. Daniel von Coelln, 3d ed. (Cassel: J. C. Krieger, 1832–38), I, 124ff.

30. Basil, The *Hexaemoron,* homily IX, in *NPNF (2),* VIII, pp. 101–7; Gregory of Nyssa, *Explicatio apologetica in hexaemoron en hominis opificio* [*On the Making of Man,* in *NPNF (2),* 387–427]; St. Ambrose, *Hexameron, Paradise, and Cain and Abel,* book VI, in *The Fathers of the Church;* Augustine, *On Genesis against the Manichaeans.* Ed. note: no English translation of this work is available; see *De Genesi contra Manichaeos,* book II, in *PL; De Genesi ad litteram liber imperfectus* [*The Literal Meaning of Genesis,* Ancient Christian Writers, vol. 41.]; Johannes Philoponus, *De aeternitate mundi c. Proclum, en de mundi creatione,* 1. VII; Anastasius of Sinai, *Anagogicae contemplationes in hexaemeron,* book XII; cf. Harnack, *History of Dogma,* III, 247–54; W. Münscher, *Dr. Wilhelm Münschers Lehrbuch der christlichen Dogmengeschichte,* I, 141ff.; Joseph Schwane, *Dogmengeschichte,* 4 vols. (Freiburg i.B.: Herder, 1882–95), II.

31. Otto Bardenhewer, *Patrologie* (Freiburg i.B.: Herder, 1894), 166. The same title is in English; see *Patrology: The Lives and Works of the Fathers of the Church,* trans. T. J. Shahan (St. Louis: Herder, 1908).

the church's doctrines in brief chapters called *Theological Topics* (*Capita theologica*), two hundred of which treat the doctrine of God, three hundred the incarnation and sin, and five hundred love.[32]

However, the most important dogmatic works in this period were the five writings for a long time attributed to Dionysius the Areopagite, which appeared in the fifth century: *The Divine Names, The Celestial Hierarchy, The Ecclesiastical Hierarchy,* and *The Mystical Theology,* as well as ten *Letters.*[33] They used neoplatonic philosophy and pantheistic mysticism to explain and elaborate Christian doctrine and were highly rated at an early date, commented on by Maximus Confessor, Pachymeres, and others and used diligently and almost put on a level with Scripture especially in the Middle Ages by theologians, mystics, and ascetics alike.[34] In the end all the elements of dogmatic development were summarized and united by John of Damascus in his *Source of Knowledge,* a work composed of three parts. In part 1, *philosophical topics,* he offers a sketch of philosophy as maidservant and instrument of theology, specifically of logic, in accordance with Aristotle and Porphyry. Part 2 is historical ("On Heresies") and presents an overview of the heresies up to Mohammed. Part 3 ("A Brief Exposition of the Orthodox Faith") is the actual dogmatic part in one hundred chapters. In these pages John of Damascus acknowledges he offers nothing but what the fathers have taught and therefore cites the Greek fathers and Pope Leo again and again.[35]

[41] A history of theology and dogmatics in the Eastern church after John of Damascus does not yet exist. The patristic period, in which the formation of the great dogmas took place, ended approximately with Justinian I (527–565) or perhaps with Photius (c. 860). This entire period from the sixth to the ninth century is a time of transition. In this period the characteristic event is the iconoclast controversy (726–842).[36] Already before the fifth century relics and images were in use as well, but christological dogma came to support them. The peculiar nature of Christianity seemed to consist in the fact that it made the divine sensorily and physically present. From being a symbol, an image soon became a bearer and organ of the holy. Paganism returned in the Christian church. But the defense of images was above all asso-

---

32. Cf. Maximus Confessor, *Selected Writings,* Classics of Western Spirituality (New York: Paulist Press, 1985).

33. Pseudo-Dionysius, *The Complete Works,* Classics of Western Spirituality (New York: Paulist Press, 1987).

34. Cf. Bonwetsch, "Dionysius Areopagita," *PRE³,* IV, 687–96; Hugo Koch, *Pseudodionysius Areopagita in seinen Beziehungen zum Neuplatonismus und Mysterienwesen eine litterarhistorische Untersuchung* (Maniz: F. Kirchheim, 1900).

35. Joseph Langen, *Johannes von Damaskus: Eine patristische Monographie* (Gotha: F. A. Perthes, 1879); Frederik H. J. Grundlehner, *Johannes Damascenus* (Utrecht: Kemink & Zoon, 1876); Kattenbusch, "Johannes von Damaskus," *PRE³,* IX, 286–300.

36. Harnack, *History of Dogma,* IV, 317ff.; Karl Schwarzlose, *Der Bilderstreit, ein Kampf der Griechische Kirche um ihre eigenart und um ihre Freiheit* (Gotha: Perthes, 1890); Bonwetsch, "Bilderverehrung und Bilderstreitigkeiten," *PRE³,* III, 221–26.

ciated with that of the freedom of the church and with the religious interests at stake at the time. Over against this view stood the imperial party, which opposed the images but in so doing also sought to subject the church to the state, to leave to the emperor the determination of ecclesiastical dogma, and by its opposition to images to meet the objections of Jews and Muslims. Orthodoxy, on the other hand, concentrated itself totally in the veneration of icons. Believers sought to possess and enjoy the divine through the senses. John of Damascus, in his *Three Apologies on the Divine Images,* emerged as one of the most forceful defenders of the veneration of images.[37] He related images as intimately as possible to the incarnation of God in Christ, regarding opposition to them as Judaism and Manichaeism. The dogmatic justification of the veneration of images was the last labor of the church in the East.

Now began the Byzantine period, extending from the ninth century to the capture of Constantinople by the Turks in 1453. It was a time of quiescence, of powerlessness in production. The Greek church is the church of orthodoxy; it only preserves, and christological dogma is the dogma *par excellence.* Still, up until 1453 there was vigorous scientific activity. In the *Cursus patrologiae graecae* of Migne, the writings of the Byzantine theologians, from John of Damascus to those who personally experienced the capture of Constantinople, form volumes 94–161.[38] From the Byzantine period, following John of Damascus whose dogmatics is still the standard today, we need to mention especially Photius, patriarch of Constantinople (891), whose main work, Μυριοβιβλος (or *Bibliotheca*), contains learned excerpts from a variety of authors and who wrote his *The Mystagogy of the Holy Spirit* as a dogmatician.[39] Then there is Euthymius Zigabenus in the twelfth century, who on orders from Emperor Alexius I wrote the *Dogmatic Panoply of the Orthodox Faith,* or *The Armory of Dogmas,* and Nicetas Choniates (c. 1220), who supplemented the work of Euthymius in his *Thesaurus of Orthodoxy.*[40] Next is the work of Nicolas Cabasilas, *The Life in Christ,* in seven books,[41] and a treatise of Demetrius Cydones on *The Contempt of Death.*[42]

Following the capture of Constantinople by the Turks, the Greek church of the East would have been totally destroyed or reduced to the level of a sect had it not found support in Russia, a country that was Christianized in the

37. St. John of Damascus, "On the Divine Images," in *Three Apologies against Those Who Attack the Divine Images* (Crestwood, N.Y.: St. Vladimir's Seminary Press, 1980).

38. Migne, *PG.*

39. See Photius's *Liber de Spiritus Sancti my stagogia,* ed. Joseph Hergenröther (Ratisbonae: G. J. Manz, 1857); cf. F. Kattenbusch, "Photius," *PRE³,* XV, 374–93.

40. C. Ullman, "Über die dogmatische Entwickelung der griechischen Kirchen im zwölften Jahrhundert," section 1: "Geistiger Zustland der griechischen Kirchen im zwölften Jahrhundert"; section 2: "Euthymius Zigabenus und Nicetas Choniates"; section 3: "Nicolaus von Methone," *Theologische Studien und Kritiken* 7, no. 3 (1833): 647–743.

41. Published by Gass in 1849.

42. Published by Kühnol in Leipzig, 1786.

tenth century and had adopted the Greek Orthodox faith in its entirety and without criticism. Of the theological literature after that time, we know even less than of that of the preceding period. Migne's edition ends here, leaving us in the lurch. An overview of names and works occurs in *Neo-Hellenic Philology*, a treatise by Constantine Satha.[43] Attempts at union with Rome at the councils of Lyon (1274) and Florence (1439) are known to us from the Acts of these councils. Correspondence between the Tübingen theologians (1576) and the patriarch Jeremias II was published at Wittenberg in 1584.[44] One cannot encapsulate the history of this literature in a single word: petrification, orthodoxism, or the like.

The Greek church's center of gravity has been transferred to Russia, and Russia is still young. As yet it has no past and is just emerging. Its literary and scientific life has only just taken off. In the eighteenth century we note Theophanes Prokopovitch, who is considered the father of Russian systematic theology. More recently it seems especially three men have made a name in dogmatics. The first is Philaret (d. 1866), who, aside from a *History of the Russian Church,* also produced an *Orthodox Dogmatic Theology.*[45] The second is Makari, Metropolitan of Moscow (d. 1882), the author of an *Orthodox Dogmatic Theology* in five volumes.[46] Through 1893 this work was reprinted five times. An extract made by the author himself was published in German (*Manual for the Study of Christian Orthodox Dogmatic Theology*).[47] The third is Sylvester, rector of the academy at Kiev and author of an *Essay in Orthodox Dogmatic Theology.*[48] The Russian church, state, and society, as also Russian science and theology, are caught up in a critical process that is becoming all the more serious to the degree they come into contact with Western civilization. It is a process the end of which no one can foresee.[49]

43. Νεοελληνικη φιλολογια, συγγραμμα Κωνσταντινου Σαφα, published in Athens, 1868.

44. Wilhelm Gass, *Symbolik der Griechischen Kirche* (Berlin: Georg Reimer, 1872), 45ff. For material on Joseph Bryennias, see Ph. Meyer, "Joseph Bryennios als Theolog," *Theologisch Studien und Kritiken* (1896): 282–319; on Cyril Lucaris [1570–1638], who corresponded with many Protestant theologians, likewise see Meyer's article "Lukaris," *PRE³,* XI, 682–90; Kattenbusch, *Lehrbuch der vergleichenden Confessionskunde,* I, 141f.; and D. C. Hesseling, "Een Protestantsche patriarch," *Theologische Tijdschrift* 36 (May 1902): 218–54.

45. Third printing, 1882; German title: *Rechtgläubig-dogmatische Gottesgelehrtheit.*

46. Published in St. Petersburg, 1849–53.

47. German title: *Handleitung zum Erlernen der Christlichen rechtgläubig-dogmatische Gottesgelehrtheit,* trans. Blumenthal (1875). Ed. note: This extract was reprinted in a collection edited by Karl Konrad Grass, *Geschichte der Dogmatik in russischer Darstellung* (Gütersloh: C. Bertelsmann, 1902).

48. A work in five volumes, published 1884 and following. Cf. Kattenbusch, *Theologische Literaturzeitung* (1903), col. 183–86. Ed. note: An extract of this work was also printed in Grass, *Geschichte der Dogmatik.*

49. Cf. Viktor Frank, *Russische Selbstzeugnisse,* vol. I, *Russisches Christenthum* (Paderborn: Russ. Christ., 1889); Hermann von Dalton, *Die russische Kirche* (Leipzig: Duncker & Humbolt, 1892); Nicholas Bjerring, "Religious Thought in the Russian Empire," *Presbyterian and Reformed Review* 3 (January 1892): 103–22; A. Leroy-Beaulieu, *Das Reich des Czaren und der Russen,* 3 vols. (Sonderhausen: L. Pezold und J. Müller, 1887–90); in English: *The Empire of the Tsars and the Russians,* trans. from the 3d

DOGMA AND THEOLOGY IN THE WEST

Contrasts between East and West

[42] From the beginning the church and theology in the West bore a character of their own. In the work of Tertullian, Cyprian, and Irenaeus, this is already clearly evident. In the East, the dominant theme in dogmatics was that humanity was subjected by sin to corruption ($\phi\theta o\rho\alpha$) and in Christ is now liberated from death by God himself and made partakers of life, immortality, the divine nature. In the foreground are the ideas of *substance, essence, nature,* ideas that foster stagnation and quiescence in doctrine as in life. In the West, on the other hand, the human relationship to God is stressed. And this relationship is that of a guilty being before a just God whose commandments he has violated. However, Christ by his work obtained the grace of God, the forgiveness of sins, the power to obey the law. And this pushes a person to live an active life, toward obedience and submission. In the East people resonate especially to the apostle John, in the West to Paul.[50] In the former the point of gravity lies in Christ's incarnation; for the latter his death. In the former the person of Christ is primary; in the latter the work of Christ. In the East the primary focus is the divine-human nature, the unity of the two natures in Christ. In the West, on the other hand, what counts is the distinction between the two natures, the mediatorial place occupied by Christ between God and humanity. There the mystical-liturgical element predominates; here the juridical-political element.[51] Since this

---

French edition, with annotations by Zénaïde A. Ragozin, 3 vols. (New York and London: G. P. Putnam's Son, 1893–96). Hermann Dalton, *Evangelische Strömungen in der russischen Kirche der Gegenwart,* 3 vols. (Heilbronn: Henninger, 1881); C. Nicolaus von Gerbel-Embach, *Russische Sectirer* (Heilbronn: Gebr. Henninger, 1833), which are, respectively, vols. VI and VIII in *Zeitfragen des Christlichen Volkslebens,* 20 vols. (Stuttgart: C. Belser, 1876). On the Stundists and other sects, see John Brown, *The Stundists: The Story of a Great Religious Revolt* (London: James Clarke, 1893); F. Knie, *Die Russisch-schismatische Kirche: Ihr Lehre und ihr Cult* (Graz: Verlagsbuchhandlung Styria, 1894); Kattenbusch, 234f., 542f.; J. Gehring, *Die Sekten der russischen Kirche (1003–1897): Nach Ursprunge und inneren Zusammenhange* (Leipzig: F. Richter, 1898).

50. Ed. note: See Krister Stendahl, "The Apostle Paul and the Introspective Conscience of the West," *Harvard Theological Review* 55 (July 1963): 199–215.

51. Kattenbusch, *Lehrbuch der vergleichenden Confessionskunde,* vol. 1, 103f.; also cf. R. Sohm, *Kirchenrecht,* 2dl. (Leipzig: Duncker & Humbolt, 1892), 428f. This difference between the theology of the East and that of the West is grossly exaggerated and misrepresented by Ritschl and especially by Harnack. According to Harnack divinization is the last and highest notion of Greek theology. He understands this deification in the sense that Christ in his death delivers humanity from temporal existence itself and is elevated to an immortality that is characteristic of God himself. According to Harnack this is not a Christian but a pagan notion that dominated all reflection during the period of dogma formation. The soteriological doctrines that developed in the church during the third century, according to Harnack, are to be explained from this pagan influence, from the egotistical wish of pagans to become immortal. Furthermore, he claims that it is this pagan soteriology that in its turn is responsible for the development of the doctrine of the Trinity and the deity of Christ. This entire representation has rightly been repudiated by K. B. Bornhäuser, *Die Vergottungslehre des Athanasius und Johannes Damasenus* (Gütersloh: C. Bertelsmann, 1903). Harnack's defense in response was very weak; see *Theologische Literaturzeitung* (August 15, 1903). Also see S. Greijdanus, *Menschwording en vernedering* (Wageningen: Vada, 1903), 158ff.

difference was present from the beginning, the schism was only a matter of time. With the rise of Constantinople an open struggle began. Constantinople, which could not claim apostolic origin, derived all its importance from the imperial court, from politics, and sought to be a second Rome. According to the Council of 381 (can. 3), the bishop of Constantinople acquired "seniority of honor" after Rome on account of its being the new Rome. With this status, a place alongside of Rome, it was content. The East wanted one church, indeed, but in two halves, with two emperors, two capitals, and two bishops of equal rank. The Greek church calls itself "orthodox," considers itself to be in full possession of the truth, at rest and happy. It also calls itself "Anatolian,"[52] thus binding itself to a specific geographic area, and is content with that. With Rome matters stood very differently. It maintained and asserted itself, not as a political city alongside of Constantinople, but itself as apostolic seat (*sedes apostolica*) on a level much higher than Constantinople. Rome represented and defended a religious interest. At an early stage it based its claims and rights on Matthew 16:18 and demanded a universal (or *catholic*) place. There is, thus, in the Western church an aggressive, world-conquering impulse. This dual tendency drove the East and the West apart. When, in addition, differences in usages, rites, and especially with respect to the *filioque* emerged, the two moved ever closer toward a schism which became a reality in 1054.

Still in many respects the West was dependent on the East. Here, after all, the church had been established first. Here the Apostolic Fathers and the apologists did their work, and the immense struggle against Gnosticism and Manichaeism occurred. Here, at the councils, the theological and christological dogmas were formulated and fixed. Synods first originated in the second century in Asia Minor. From 325 to the middle of the ninth century, all the ecumenical councils were held in the East, in Asia Minor or Constantinople, and up until the Council of 879 were recognized by the West as well. The objective foundations of the doctrine of the church are the same in the East and the West. From the latter half of the second century on, Eastern theology also penetrated the West. Marius Victorinus, professor of rhetoric, Hilary, Ambrose, Jerome, Rufinus, Marius Mercator, and John Cassian brought the theological thought world of the East to the West. Old Testament exegesis, Platonic theology, monasticism, and the ideal of virginity made their debut in the West and were there wedded to the Western mind. Ambrose (d. 397) studied the works of Clemens, Origen, Didymus, and especially Basil and imported to the West Old Testament exegesis,[53] the ideal of virginity in the sense of the soul's mystical marriage to Christ,[54] as well as the trinitarian doctrine and the Christology of the Cappadocians.[55] Hilary of Poitiers

---

52. Ed. note: "Anatolian" is an older name for the region roughly coextensive with Asia Minor.

53. *Hexaemeron, de Paradisio, de Cain et Abel,* etc., following Basil.

54. *Concerning Virgins (de virginatete), liber de Isaac et anima.*

55. *Libri V de fide, Libri III de Spiritu Sanctu, liber de incarnationis dominical sacramento.*

(d. 368), who spent the years of his exile (356–359) in Asia Minor, in his work *On the Councils, or the Faith of the Easterners*[56] informed the bishops of Gaul about the christological conflict in the East. He defended this doctrine in his *De Trinitate* in twelve books, and in his exegetical works on Matthew and a few of the Psalms he made ample use of typological and allegorical exegesis. Marius Victorinus, who was highly praised by Augustine in his *Confessions* (bk. VIII, chap. 2), in a number of works[57] introduced neoplatonic philosophy into theology and as a result exerted the greatest influence on Augustine. Rufinus of Aquileia (d. 410) spent many years in Egypt and Palestine, associating with hermits, with Jerome, with Didymus in Alexandria, and with John in Jerusalem. His significance is due especially to the fact that he rendered many Greek works of Josephus, Eusebius, Origen, Basil, Gregory of Nazianzus, etc., into Latin. In addition, he wrote a *History of Monks,* biographies of thirty-three "desert saints," as well as *Travels to Holy Places,* various commentaries on books of the Old Testament, and finally a *Commentary on the Apostles' Creed,* whose value is greater for students of history than it is for dogmatics. Particularly Jerome (d. 420) needs to be mentioned here. Though brought up in Rome, he spent his life mainly in Syria and Palestine. He deserves credit especially for his numerous scriptural studies. In theology he shows little independence and is highly sensitive about his orthodoxy. In his exegesis he often employs the allegorical method of Philo and the Alexandrian theologians. He is above all the panegyrist of asceticism. He defended the virginity of Mary against Helvidius, the merits of fasting and celibacy against Jovinian, and the veneration of martyrs and their relics against Vigilantius. According to a saying by Luther in his Table Talk, Jerome always spoke of fasting, food, and virginity and hardly ever of faith, hope, and love.

East and West Meet in Augustine

[43] This entire dogmatic development in East and West culminated in Augustine. The doctrine of the Trinity and Christology of the Eastern theologians—the doctrine of humanity, sin, grace, faith, satisfaction, and merit, in the work of Tertullian and Ambrose; the neoplatonism of Victorinus; Cyprian's doctrine of church and sacrament; Jerome and Hilary's monastic ideal—all this was absorbed and, over a lifetime of rich experience, internally appropriated by Augustine. He did not produce a theological dogmatic system. The material that flowed toward him from every direction—from Scripture, tradition, and philosophy—and that he expanded and increased with his richly endowed personality, was not such that one could readily gain a comprehensive view of it and organize it. The main work Augustine produced along this line is his *Handbook on Faith, Hope, and Love,* an interpretation of the principal truths of faith that follows the Apostles' Creed. But con-

---

56. De Synodes seu de fide Orientalium.

57. Marius Victorinus, *Liber ad Justinum Manichaeum, contra duo principia Manichaeorum et de vera carne-Christi; liber de generatione divina; Adversus Arium Libri IV.*

tradictions are not lacking in his teaching, especially those between his doctrine of the church and his doctrine of grace. Reuter has demonstrated that these contradictions are not resolvable and that Augustine's ideas cannot be summed up in a system. Still, there has been no church father who entered into all the problems of theology more deeply than Augustine and who strove so hard to arrive at unity as he did. He was the first person who attempted clearly to account for all the theological issues that would later be treated in the prolegomena of dogmatics and who penetrated the ultimate psychological and noetic problems [which arise in the pursuit of theology].

Augustine's firm point of departure was the human being, his self-consciousness, his ineradicable yearning and need for truth, happiness, and goodness, all of which are one. This starting point is certain and reliable (against the skeptics), since doubt itself still assumes belief in truth and self-consciousness is the final ground of truth. Augustine himself was consumed by this burning love of truth. Admittedly, Augustine accepted two cognitive organs, sense and intellect. But the knowledge gained by the latter goes far beyond that of the former. The sensible is not the truth itself but only an image of it. Eternal, immutable truth can only be found by the activity of the mind. Augustine does not deny that we can also rise up to the invisible through the visible, but as a rule he looked for the way to truth, not outside of ourselves through nature, but through the activity of the human spirit. There, in reason, his own and that of everyone, he finds eternal, immutable truths that themselves again refer back to and converge in God, who is the supreme truth, the only good, eternal reason, the origin of all things. Therefore, because God is himself the whole truth, being itself, the good and the beautiful, there is rest for human beings thinking and striving in him alone. The knowledge of self and the knowledge of God are the two poles between which all human thought oscillates. Though knowledge of nature is not despised, it is made subordinate. "I desire to know God and the soul! O that I may know myself! O that I may know You!" God is the sun of spirits. We neither see nor know truth except in and by his light.

Still, philosophy is not sufficient, not only as a result of the inability of reason to find the way to truth but also and especially because it is blocked by pride (*superbia*). Humility alone is the way to life. Hence there is another way to the truth, the way of authority, the way of faith. On the one hand, faith assumes a measure of knowledge, but, on the other, it seeks to know, strives after knowledge. Augustine attempted to prove from nature, and especially from human nature, not only the existence of God and the immortality of the soul but also the Trinity. But for him God is not abstract, unqualified being but the living One, the supreme truth and the highest good, the greatest bliss and therefore the only being fully able to satisfy the human heart. All of Augustine's thought is religious, theological; he views everything in the light of God. In that light he also views the world. On the one hand, it is nonbeing, an image, and therefore perishable. On the other, as God's creation, it is a work of art created in accordance with the ideas in the mind of God, little by little, step by step, realizing those ideas and forming a universe that contains the richest diversity within itself. Things individually differ from each other in the measure of being and thus also of the truth and goodness each possesses. Creation is a cosmos, based on idea, number, order, and measure and held together by one will, one intellect. Creation is a most spacious, immeasurable commonwealth in which miracles are events only against that which is known of nature, in which sin is merely a privation compensated for by punishment and a cocontributor to the beauty and harmony of the whole.

In the most beautiful song of creation, this antithesis is also needed. Sin is like the contrasts in a speech, like barbarisms in a language, like shadows in a painting. Augustine thus attempts to fit evil into the order of the whole. But he does not thereby excuse sin. The truth is, he does not locate the end of things in the ethically good but in the fact that Creation is, and will increasingly be, a harmonious revelation of all God's attributes and perfections. And to that end, by the will of God, sin is subordinated as well. Also, we know how deeply and seriously Augustine viewed sin: "You have not yet considered what a great burden sin is."[58] Augustine saw it all around him and felt it: human beings seek God and need him while at the same time they cannot and will not come to him. What is good in humanity is only the fact that they exist. Humanity as a whole is a "mass of perdition." Sin is, above all, haughtiness—pride (*superbia*) in the soul and lust (*concupiscentia*) in the body. In Adam we all sinned, and thus sin became the fate of us all. It is a lack of God (*carentia dei*), a privation of the good (*privatio boni*), not just an act but a condition; it is vitiated nature, a defect, a lack, a corruption, an inability not to sin. Salvation from this condition exists only by grace, which has its origin in predestination and is objectively revealed in the person and work of Christ. Objective grace is the sure and proper foundation of the Catholic faith but must also come into us subjectively as internal grace to infuse faith and love.

But in Augustine that grace only works within the boundaries of the visible church. The church, to Augustine, is an institution of salvation, a dispenser of grace, the seat of authority, the guarantor of Scripture, the dwelling place of love, a creation of the Spirit, indeed, the kingdom of God himself. Augustine sensed deeply the importance of community to religion; the church is the mother of believers. The doctrine of predestination and of grace cannot be harmonized with this concept of church and sacrament. "Many who seem to be outside are inside, and many who are inside seem to be outside."[59] There are sheep outside the sheepfold and wolves inside it. Also, though Augustine taught the perseverance of the saints, he dared not risk the subjective certainty

---

58. Ed. note: This specific slogan is also found in Anselm, *Cur Deus Homo*, chap. 21.
59. "Multi qui foris videntur intus sunt et multi qui intus videntur foris sunt."

of it. And precisely because of this view of the church and the sacrament, faith and forgiveness could not come into their own in the theology of Augustine. Faith and love, forgiveness and sanctification, are not clearly distinguished in his work. It is as if faith and forgiveness are only temporary and provisional; from them Augustine immediately proceeds to love, sanctification, and good works. Consequently, communion with God, religion, becomes the result of a process, gradually brought about by faith, love and good works, etc. Salvation, eternal life, the vision and enjoyment of God—despite all that was said earlier—again become a fruit of meritorious living, and asceticism is one of the means by which human beings reach this goal.

Thus Augustine became a theologian of the greatest importance for later dogmatics, one who dominated the following centuries. Every reformation returns to him and to Paul. For every dogma he found a formula that was taken over and repeated by everyone else. His influence extends to all churches, schools of theology, and sects. Rome appeals to him for its doctrine of the church, the sacrament, and authority, while the Reformation felt kinship with him in the doctrine of predestination and grace. Scholasticism, in constructing its conceptual framework, took advantage of his sharp observation, the acuteness of his intellect, the power of his speculation—Thomas, in fact, was called the best interpreter of St. Augustine. Mysticism, in turn, found inspiration in his neoplatonism and religious enthusiasm. Both Catholic and Protestant piety buoy themselves up on his writings; asceticism and pietism find nourishment and support in his work. Augustine, therefore, does not belong to one church but to all churches together. He is the universal teacher (*Doctor universalis*). Even philosophy neglects him to its own detriment. And because of his elegant and fascinating style, his refined, precise, highly individual and nevertheless universally human way of expressing himself, he, more than any other church father, can still be appreciated today. He is the most Christian as well as the most modern of all the fathers; of all of them he is closest to us. He replaced the aesthetic worldview with an ethical one, the classical with the Christian. In dogmatics we owe our best, our deepest, our richest thoughts to him. Augustine has been and is *the* dogmatician of the Christian church.

Augustine's Legacy

[44] For more than a century Augustinianism was the object of a intense struggle that kept the passions of men at loggerheads. It was opposed not only by Pelagius, Coelestius, Julian—the real Pelagians—but also by many monks in Gaul. Among them especially the following deserve mention: John Cassian, Vincent of Lerins (who in his *Commonitorium* not only lists the marks of tradition but also, at the end, registers his opposition to a rigorous Augustinianism), Eucherius of Lyon, Hilary of Arles, Salvian of Massilia, Faustus of Rhegium, and Gennadius of Massilia.[60] Standing on the side of

---

60. Author of *De fide seu de dogmatibus ecclesiasticis* in eighty-eight chapters.

Augustine, aside from Possidius of Colama in Numidia, Orosius of Bracara in Spain, Marius Mercator in Constantinople, and others, were in particular Prosper Aquitanus, Vigil of Tapsus in Numidia, Fulgentius of Ruspa (author of a brief sketch of the main truths of the faith),[61] Caesarius of Arles, Avitus of Vienna, and others. In this struggle the Synod of Orange (529) took some decisions favoring Augustine but did not prevent the spread of semi-Pelagian ideas. It accepted prevenient grace but did not decisively adopt irresistible grace and particular predestination. In the years following, not much Augustinianism was left intact.

Pope Gregory the Great (d. 604), sometimes called the fourth great teacher of the church (alongside of Augustine, Jerome, and Ambrose), produced nothing new but appropriated and in various ways applied the ideas of earlier church teachers to life. His bent was both practical and mystical-allegorical. He never built a system but simply preserved the gains of the past, clarifying the dogmas for the benefit of clergy and laity alike. Above all, he diagrammed the various mediators and means (angels, saints, Christ, alms, masses for the soul, purgatory, the sacrament of penance) that make it possible for the weakened human will to be delivered from the punishments of sin. In all these efforts he labored faithfully at the nurture of new nations and the formation of the clergy. It was he who sanctioned the external legal religion of the Roman Catholic Church and conferred on medieval Catholicism its actual character. He is the capstone of the ancient world, the foundation stone of the new. Through his liturgical writings and his church music, he introduced the Roman Catholic form of worship to the Germanic peoples of the north. By popularizing the dogmas of the church fathers, he made church doctrine practically useful for uncivilized pagan Germanic peoples and also promoted superstition, asceticism, and works righteousness. Along with Boethius and Cassidorius, he exerted great influence on education and the rise of science among the Germanic peoples. Cassidorius (d. approx. 565) wrote a book on *The Liberal Arts and Disciplines,* discussing the seven liberal arts, and in his work *De Institutione Divinarum Litterarum* furnished a methodology for theological study. By means of his translations and expositions of Aristotle's logic as well as the *Isagoge* of Porphyry,[62] Boethius introduced the knowledge and use of Greek philosophy to the Germanic nations. And in the church Gregory brought them theology.

In that early period, in view of the lack of culture and the unrest associated with mass migration, scientific endeavor did not have a chance among the Germanic peoples. The first traces of it are to be found in the Bible translation and Arian confession of Ulfilas (d. 383). Ostrogoths, Visigoths, Vandals, Suevi, Burgundians, Herulers, Longobards, etc., had all been Chris-

---

61. Entitled *De fide de regular verae fidei ad Petrum.*

62. Ed. note: Porphyry (c. A.D. 232–300), born in Tyre, studied in Athens and then joined the School of Plotinus in Rome. Porphyry is one of the founders of neoplatonism; he published Plotinus's lectures and defended and developed Plotinus's ideas in his own writings.

tianized by the end of the fifth century along Arian lines. But it was Clovis (481–511), along with his kingdom of France, who adopted the Christianity of Rome. Patrick (d. 465), author of *Confessions,* was the apostle to the Irish, while Scotland was Christianized by Columba (d. 597). Anglo-Saxons were converted by Augustine and his forty monks sent to Britain by Pope Gregory I in 596. Fridolinus and Columbanus (d. 615), as well as others, worked in France and Italy. The latter left behind important letters as well as a monastic rule. Alamannia, Bavaria, Thuringia, Frisia, etc. were Christianized in the sixth and seventh century. In the eighth century, Boniface (d. 755) was the apostle to the Frisians. The Saxons were the last to be brought into the fold under Charlemagne by wars conducted from 772–804, and the North especially by Ansgar (d. 865).

One of the first dogmaticians is Isidore of Seville (d. 636). His writings, which encompass everything there was to be known at the time, are grammatical, historical, archeological, dogmatic, moral, and ascetic in nature. He brought classical and patristic learning to his people, offering extracts from pagan and Christian works but nothing original. In his *Etymologies* (in twenty books)[63] he speaks in book 6 of Scripture; in book 7 about God, angels, prophets, apostles, clergy, and believers; in book 8 of the church; and in book 9 about the nations. His *Three Books of Sentences concerning the Supreme Good*[64] are excerpted especially from Augustine and Gregory and was a model for medieval collectors of sentences. Book I treats God, creation, time, world, sin, angel, humanity, soul, Christ, Holy Spirit, church, heresy, law, Scripture, Old and New Covenant, prayer, baptism, martyrdom, miracles, Antichrist, and the end of the world. Books II and III are ethical in content. Isidore's work is a compendium that delivered the theological capital of previous centuries to the Germanic people. But an independent treatment of this legacy was not achieved.

Admittedly, Charlemagne did attempt to introduce by force the culture of antiquity into the kingdom of France. And, indeed there was no lack of men of great learning in the Carolingian period. Still, diligent gathering and slavish reproduction remain the characteristic features of the period, which starts with the seventh century and ends only with the crusades. *The* authorities were Augustine and Gregory. Among Carolingian theologians the most important was Alcuin (d. 804), who resisted the adoptionism of Elipandus of Toledo and Felix of Urgel.[65] In all the works listed here (n. 65), Alcuin demonstrates his familiarity with the works of the church fathers, refuting adoptionist errors with the same arguments that were advanced against Nestorianism, say, by Cyril in an earlier age.

---

63. *Originum—Sive etynologiarum libri XX.*

64. *Libri III Sententiarum s. de summo bono.*

65. The titles are *Liber contra haeresin Felicis, Libri VII contra Felicem en Libri IV adv. Elipandum; De fide sanctae et individuae Trinitatis Libri III, de Trinitate ad Fredegisum quastiones en Libellus de processione Sp. Si.*

In the ninth century the study of Augustine led Gottschalk to confess double predestination. Though he found support in Prudentius of Troyes, Remigius of Lyon, Ratramnus, Lupus of Ferrières, and others, he was at the same time fiercely opposed by Rhabanus, Hinkmar, and Erigena. The filioque formula entered the kingdom of France from Spain and was incorporated in the Creed. Already at the Synod of Gentilly (767) people were convinced that it was creedal. It was skillfully defended by Charlemagne's theologians, Alcuin and Theodulf of Orleans. The Synod of Aachen (809) decided that the filioque formula belonged in the Creed. The veneration of images was opposed in the kingdom of France. The seventh ecumenical council, which called for the cult (*servitium*) and adoration (*adoratio*) of images, was not recognized, but after the ninth century the opposition gradually grew silent. Finally the Carolingian period saw the further development of the mass, especially by Radbert Paschasius (*De corpore et sanguine domini,* 831), who was opposed by Rhabanus and Ratrammus. Radbert is also known as the author of the compendium *On Faith, Hope, and Love* (*De fide, spe et caritate*), which sums up the truths of faith in a somewhat organized whole. Especially deserving of mention in this period is John Scotus Erigena (d. approx. 891), although he belongs to philosophy more than theology. He is not the father of scholasticism but of speculative theology. He linked himself up with the gnosis of Origen and the mysticism of Pseudo-Dionysius. His fundamental principle is the neoplatonic doctrine of emanation. In his work *De divisione naturae,* he first states that theology and philosophy are really one. Right reason (*recta ratio*) and true authority (*vera auctoritas*) are not in conflict. Faith locates its truth as *affirmative* theology in Scripture and tradition, but reason, as *negative* theology, strips this truth of its wrappings and seeks out the idea of it. Thus he changes dogmatic truth into the philosophical doctrine of a cosmic and theogonic process. He subsumes all that exists under one heading, viz., *nature,* which in four stages of being manifests itself through the Logos in the world of phenomena and then returns to God.

4

ROMAN CATHOLIC DOGMATICS

After the tenth century, thanks in good measure to the monastic reforms and crusades, new life stirred the Western church. The birth of the universities led to a scientific theology using the scholastic method. Though scholasticism brought significant gains to the study of theology, it also developed a character that brought it into disrepute. Negatively, scholasticism neglected the study of Scripture and other original sources; positively, it was too closely linked to Aristotle's philosophic methodology. Losing its connection to the living faith of the church, dogmatics became a system of philosophy.

Scholastic theology passed through three phases, beginning with Anselm's sincere desire to deepen the understanding given in faith. Anselm's form was more in keeping with Plato's dialogues than with the Aristotelian scholastic method. In the work of Peter Lombard and Alexander of Hales, theology moved beyond individual treatises to systematic handbooks on dogmatics and ethics. In spite of opposition from some Platonists, the Aristotelian method, in the hands of Albertus Magnus, Thomas Aquinas, and Bonaventure, became the accepted manner of defending church doctrine. Scholasticism did not maintain this high level, but in the work of Duns Scotus, and especially in nominalism, theology lost its certainty. As a result skepticism, as well as the mysticism of Eugena, Eckhart, and Böhme, flourished in spite of ecclesiastical condemnation.

Under the influence particularly of the officially approved neoplatonism of Pseudo-Dionysius, mysticism linked up with monastic efforts to reach God through contemplation, and theological knowledge was often disparaged.

The Middle Ages also gave birth to significant protest movements, including the Cathars, the Waldensians, and "Protestant" precursors such as John Wycliffe and John Huss. Even though the conciliar movement in the church itself appealed to many, little actual reform was achieved. The Roman Catholic Church resisted reform and did so at the time of the sixteenth-century Protestant Reformation as well. The post-Tridentine Roman Catholic Church was again shaped by Thomas, with the key difference being the diligent study of Scripture and tradition by neoscholastics such as Suarez. Engaged as the neoscholastics were in polemics with Reformation theologians, scholastic theology became simpler in form, method, language, and articulation.

Neoscholastic theology arose and flourished in Spain by such (primarily Dominican) practitioners as Francis de Vithona, Melchior Canus, and Peter de

143

*Soto. But it was especially the Jesuits, such as Bellarmine, Peter Canisius, and Fr. Suarez, who contributed to its revival and fluorescence. Thanks to their Pelagianism, the Jesuits diverged from Thomas in the doctrine of sin, free will, and grace. The work of Dominican Augustinians such as Baius of Louvain and, later, Cornelius Jansen, bishop of Ypres, finally was condemned, by the often-reaffirmed bull **Unigenitus** (1713). Pelagianism triumphed in dogmatics, probabilism in ethics, and papal curialism in the church.*

Neoscholasticism came under severe attack by the modern rationalism of Bacon and Descartes. Historical and critical studies pushed theology to the side, and scholasticism withdrew into the schools. Deism and naturalism rose up and influenced or sidelined Roman Catholic theology. In 1773 the Jesuit order was suppressed by Pope Clement XIV himself. Conflicts with Protestant theologians were pushed into the background, and a struggle was joined against freethinkers and unbelievers. With philosophers such as Jacobi, Schelling, and Hegel revisioning Christian doctrine and theology in the terms of speculative philosophy, some were led to a conciliatory and mediating position, bringing the two together.

*However, these efforts failed to satisfy, and the nineteenth century witnessed a rebirth of neoscholasticism. The Jesuit order was restored in 1814, and papal authority was enhanced by the 1854 proclamation of the dogma concerning the immaculate conception of Mary, the publication of the Syllabus of Errors in 1864, and finally by Vatican I's approval of papal infallibility in 1870. In 1879 Pope Leo XIII in his encyclical **Aeterni Patus** acclaimed Thomas as the teaching doctor of the church, and Thomism regained momentum in Roman Catholic theology. Restricted as it is to scholarly life, Thomism does not have the capacity to nurture or renew Roman Catholic piety. It is more likely that Reform Catholicism or Roman Catholic Americanism, with its acceptance of much that is good in modern life, will lead the Roman church to serious self-evaluation.*

SCHOLASTICISM

[45] After the tenth century, the dark age (*saeculum obscuram*), new life awakens everywhere. Starting in the monastery of Cluny, a religious reformation took off that continued in the mendicant orders of the twelfth century. Piety was conceived as an imitation and literal copying[1] of the life of Jesus, especially in his seven days of passion. The Crusades brought home new ideas and expanded people's horizons. The power of the popes increased and aimed at nothing less than the ideal of world rule. In the universities science was given its own "nursery" and manifested itself in theology in the form of scholasticism.

Scholastic theology, in distinction from positive theology, which presents dogmas in a simple propositional form, means that the material of dogmas is processed in accordance with a scientific method, the method followed in the schools. By itself scholasticism is nothing other than scientific theology. It be-

---

1. Ed. note: Bavinck's terms are *navolgen* and *nabootsen*.

gins where positive theology leaves off. The latter is content when it has stated
and proven the dogmas. But scholastic theology proceeds from these dogmas
as its first principles[2] and tries by reasoning to trace their interconnectedness,
to penetrate more deeply into the knowledge of revealed truth, and to defend
them against all opposition. In the Middle Ages, however, as a result of various
circumstances, scholasticism gained a certain character that brought it into disrepute. In the first place, the study of original sources was sorely neglected.
Though in theory observation as the first principle of knowledge was not denied, in practice the tradition was simply and passively accepted in the belief
that earlier generations had adequately observed and had already completely
recorded the results in books. Physics, medicine, psychology, etc.—everything
was studied from books. In theology the essential material lay ready-made and
complete before one's eyes in Scripture and especially in tradition, in the
church fathers, the councils, etc. Scholasticism did not view this mass of material critically and skeptically but in childlike faith. Faith was the starting point
of scholasticism. Theologians sought the dogmatic material in Scripture and
tradition and accepted it uncritically. However, since Hebrew and Greek were
unknown, not much was done with Scripture. Grammatical and historical
sense were almost totally lacking. The material for theology was drawn mainly
from the church fathers, from Augustine, Hilary, Ambrose, Jerome, Gregory,
Isidore, Pseudo-Dionysius, John of Damascus, and Boethius.

In the second place, scholasticism was discredited because it depended
methodologically on Aristotle's logic to process the dogmatic material dialectically and systematically. At first, only Aristotle's two books on logic in Latin
translation (*On Categories* and *On Interpretation*) were known, besides Porphyry's *Introduction to the Categories* and various commentaries, especially of
Boethius. Of Plato's writings only a part of the *Timaeus* in translation and
some quotations in Augustine, Pseudo-Dionysius, and others, were available.
Outside of theology scientific work was divided into the *trivium* and *quadri-
vium* and embodied in the encyclopedic work of Cassiodorus. Aristotle's *Orga-
non* was not completely known until the middle of the twelfth century, and it
was not before the beginning of the thirteenth century that his other works—
on metaphysics, physics, psychology, and ethics—became available as well.
From this philosophy scholars derived the dialectical method, but also a range
of problems and questions about the relation between faith and reason, theology and philosophy, about the reality of universals, about the attributes of
God, miracles, creation from eternity, the soul, etc. In the things of nature, Aristotle became the precursor of Christ, just as in the things of grace John the
Baptist was. Consequently, a great variety of cosmological, (natural-) scientific,
psychological, and philosophical material was incorporated in dogmatics. No
longer the doctrine of faith, dogmatics became a system of philosophy, an en-

2. Thomas Aquinas, *Summa Theol.* I, qu. 2 and 8.

cyclopedia of scientific knowledge, in which all sorts of philosophical material was taken up but in which religion often failed to get its due.

Finally, this entire scholastic system was presented in a form that increasingly occasioned serious misgivings. The material was often presented so dialectically, so minutely picked apart, and treated so juridically, that the connection with the church's religious life was completely broken—to say nothing of the various contrived questions about angels and devils, heaven and hell, etc., which theologians fancied. In addition, the question-and-answer form in which all the material was cast fostered doubt, often permitting authority and reason to go in totally different directions and to end up in opposition. Frequently the point of a given dogma would seem completely lost, but a simple appeal to a text, or to a church father, would again redeem everything. The impression that remained, however, was that from a scientific viewpoint the case of dogma was irredeemable. In time, the language employed, along with the content of the system, proved unsatisfactory. According to a remark made by Paulsen, though the barbarous Latin that people wrote was a sign that they thought independently and freely shaped the words needed to convey their ideas, it would fail to satisfy them the moment they somewhat regained a sense of the simple beauty of classic Latin.

[46] Scholasticism passed through three periods: the old, middle, and new. It begins with Anselm, who still operated in the naïve confidence that faith could be elevated to the level of knowledge. For the existence of God, he attempts to demonstrate this in his *Monologium;* for the incarnation and atonement, in his *Cur Deus homo.* He does not yet do this in the Aristotelian scholastic form but rather in the form of Plato's dialogues. Still, scholastic speculation starts with him. Lombard, in his *Sentences* (four books), did not, like Anselm, offer single treatises but a complete handbook on dogmatics and ethics. He produced the text for scholastic theology, and he himself made ample use of philosophy for the purpose of clarifying and defending the truth. Alexander of Hales wrote a *Summa* of universal theology, actually an early commentary on the work of Lombard. However, whereas the latter takes a topic and reasons to the end of it in a single movement, Hales casts his ideas in a rigorously dialectical and syllogistic form. With that the scholastic method was established once and for all. This did not, however, occur without conflict. Many objected to the use of Aristotle in theology. And then there were always Platonists, who considered Plato to be much more in harmony with church doctrine. John of Salisbury, Gerhoch, Walter of St. Victor, Peter Cantor, Alanus de Insulis, William of Auvergne, and others, all pointed out the dangers of philosophy, of which Abelard seemed a frightening example.

Still, the scholastic method, sanctioned by famous names, gained acceptance. Soon Aristotle's philosophy, though modified here and there, was considered the best defense of the church's doctrine. Dogmatics was most completely practiced by this method by Albertus Magnus (d. 1280), Thomas Aquinas (d. 1274), and Bonaventure (d. 1274). Each of them wrote a commentary on the work of Lombard and were later followed in this by many others. Claude Fleury (1640–1723) in his day already counted 244 of them. In addition, Albertus wrote a *Summa of theology* (incomplete) as well as a *Summa concerning creatures;* Thomas a *Summa of theology* (incomplete) as well as a *Summa concerning the truth of the Catholic faith against Gentiles;* Bonaventure a *Breviloquium.* All three earned universal acclaim for scholasticism, secured for theology a place of honor among the sciences, and treated the most profound problems with extraordinary intelligence.

But scholasticism was not able to maintain itself at that level. In the work of Duns Scotus (d. 1308) confidence in it is already greatly diminished. Though he rejects nominalism, he opposes Thomas wherever he dares to and can. The Franciscan scholar de Rada (d. 1608), in his *Theological Controversies between Thomas and Scotus* (Cologne, 1620), later counted no fewer than eighty-six points of dispute between them. Of these the most important were those concerning the knowability of God, the distinction between the divine attributes, original sin, the merits of Christ, etc., and particularly the immaculate conception of Mary as well. Though Scotus is still a realist, he is also skeptical and puts theology and philosophy side by side. Philosophy does not reach God, while theology only rests on authority, revelation.

But it was above all nominalism that contributed to the decline of scholasticism. It already surfaced in Roscellin and Berengarius but gained ground especially in the fourteenth and fifteenth century. Peter Aureolus (d. 1321), the author of a commentary on Lombard and of *Quodlibeta* (Miscellany), stated that universals do not objectively exist in things and are no more than ideas—the real is always individual. William Durand of St. Porciano (d. 1332) denied the existence of universals as well as the scientific character of theology. It is not a coherent whole, he argued, nor can it demonstrate the truth of dogmas or refute the arguments against it. William of Occam (d. 1349)—who, denying that the pope had any power over secular rulers, supported the latter in their resistance to the pope but also in turn asked him for protection—attacked both the school of Thomas and that of Scotus. He delighted in demonstrating the uncertainty of theology. According to Occam, the existence, unity, and omnipotence of God, the finiteness of the world, the immateriality of the soul, the necessity of revelation, etc., are all unprovable. Everything is solely as it is because God wills it. There are no truths of reason. God could become a man, but he could also become a stone. Platonism and Augustinianism disappeared from theology. Everything becomes arbitrary. Theology dissolved in skepticism. Although realism continued to dominate in the schools, it no longer had creative vitality; the form became more rigid, the language more barbarous, the method more sophisticated; subtlety replaced thoroughness, ostentation took the place of scientific seriousness, and dogmatics degenerated into endless argumentation. Occam's nominalism also gained adherents: Adam Goddam, Armand de Beauvoir, Robert Holkot (who was said to have originated the saying that something can be true in theology and simultaneously false in philosophy), John Buridan, Peter of Alliaco, and Gabriel Biel (d. 1495), the last scholastic.

Mysticism was a special form of scholasticism. At an earlier time mysticism was viewed by some [scholars] as hostile to scholasticism, but it is now better understood. The mystics never opposed scholastic theology. Men like Hugo and Richard of St. Victor treated various parts of theology with the same method as Lombard had done. Conversely, scholastics like Alexander of Hales, Albertus Magnus, Aquinas, and Bonaventure left behind a legacy of mystical writings as well. Mysticism is even incorporated in scholastic theology.[3] So there is no question of conflict and antagonism between them. Furthermore, the church and theology have at all times distinguished between true and false mysticism. Neoplatonism, Gnosticism, Erigena, Almarich, Eckhart, Molinos, Böhme, etc., have been consistently condemned, but the writings of Pseudo-Dionysius, Albert, Bonaventure, etc., have always been praised and approved by the Roman Catholic Church.

We are thus led to a distinction between orthodox and pantheistic mysticism. The former, it must be said, though not opposed to scholasticism, was, however, distinct from it—in the first place, in *method*. Following Aristotle's analytic method, scholasticism attempted by reasoning to ascend from finite things to God. Mysticism followed the synthetic method of Plato and attempted to gain insight into the truths of faith from the perspective of the higher view that the soul attained by grace. Second, there was a distinction in *origin*. Above all, scholasticism originated from Aristotle's writings becoming known and had Lombard's *Sentences* as its object. Mysticism, on the other hand, originated especially as the works of Pseudo-Dionysius—which in the West were read in Erigena's translation—found acceptance. Finally, there was a difference in *essence*. Scholasticism is the attempt, with the help of philosophy, to gain scientific knowledge of revealed truth. The object of mystical theology, however, is the mystical communion with God granted by special grace to a small number of privileged persons. Mysticism describes how and by what way the soul could attain to such communion with God and what light could be shed on the truths of faith from that vantage point. In that sense mysticism has always had its representatives in the Christian church and occurs in greater or lesser measure in all the church fathers. It is most intimately bound up with the monastic ideal and proceeds from the assumption that there is a twofold knowledge of God, that of the mind and that of the heart's experience and communion with God. In the Middle Ages mysticism linked up especially with Augustine, who, as the first to do so, examined the depths of the life of the soul and conveyed his findings in inimitable language. It also utilized Pseudo-Dionysius, who had outlined the steps and mileposts by which the soul could climb up from finite existence to the infinite God. By practical exercises such as those of asceticism, purification,

---

3. Aquinas, *Summa Theologica*, II, 2 qu., 179ff.

self-torture, world flight, etc., or by theoretical [θεωρια, a viewing contemplation] reflection, such as listening [for the voice of God] reading [Scripture], prayer, logical thought, contemplation, and meditation,[4] the soul on earth could already enter a state of beholding or enjoying God. This is how mysticism is conceived and described in the various works of Bernard of Clairvaux, Hugo and Richard of St. Victor, Bonaventure, Aquinas, Gerson, and Thomas à Kempis. But it was natural, given mysticism's accent on contemplation, that it would disparage knowledge. In the enjoyment of the heart, clarity of mind and the value of knowledge were lost. Often mysticism fell under the influence of neoplatonism and, in the case of Eckhart (d. 1327) and others, acquired a pantheistic flavor.

PROTEST AND RESPONSE

[47] The direction in which church and theology were headed, as was sketched in the previous discussion, was not universally accepted. The Middle Ages were not lacking in protests against it. Various sects arose—Cathars, Albigensians, the followers of Amalrik of Bena, David of Dinant, Ortlieb, the sect of the free Spirit, etc.—and renewed the ancient Manichean and Gnostic errors.[5] The Waldensians ran into conflict with Rome over their teaching of the freedom to preach. In many circles there was a return to Augustine and Paul. Thomas Bradwardine (d. 1349), in a writing called *The Case of God against Pelagius* (*De causa Dei contra Pelagium*), emerged as a courageous defender of the grace of God. John Wycliffe (d. 1384) was dependent on him as Huss (d. 1451) in turn was on Wycliffe. Wycliffe's teaching can best be learned from his *Summa* in twelve books, condensed and summarized in his *Trialogus,* as well as from his treatise *Christ and his Adversary the Antichrist,* his *On the Church,* and his *The Truth of Sacred Scripture.* The fact that Huss was totally dependent on Wycliffe has been demonstrated by Loserth.[6] Even within the church many people arose who desired a "root-and-branch" reformation. Peter d'Ailly (d. 1425), Gerson (d. 1429), Nicholas of Clémanges, Nicolaus Cusa (d. 1464), and others, all championed an episcopal system; and the reform-minded councils of Pisa (1409),

4. Ed. note: Latin: *auditio, lectio, oratio, cogitatio, consideratio, meditatio.*
5. H. Reuter, *Geschichte der religiösen Aufklärung im Mittelalter,* 2 vols. in 1 (Berlin: W. Hertz 1875–77); C. U. Hahn, *Geschichte der Ketzer im Mittelalter,* (Stuttgart: J. F. Steinkopf, 1845); J. H. Kurtz, *Lehrbuch der Kirchliche Geschichte,* 2 vols. (Leipzig: F. A. Brockhaus, 1885), §108; translated into English as *Text-book of Church History,* 2 vols. in 1 (Philadelphia: Lippincott, 1886–90); J. J. I. Döllinger, *Beiträge zur Sektengeschichte des Mittelalters,* 2 vols. (Münich: Beck, 1890).
6. Johann Loserth, *Hus and Wiclif,* trans. M. J. Evans (London: Hodder and Stoughton, 1884; reprinted as *Wiclif and Hus* (New York: AMS Press, 1980).
Ed. note: Bavinck specifies the following publishers for Wycliffe's writings: Wycliffe's works by the Wycliffe Society of London; *Trialogus* by Lechler; *De Christo et suo adversario Antichristo* by Buddensieg; *Die ecclesia* by Loserth; *De veritate Sacrae Scripturae* in 3 vols. by Buddensieg and printed in Leipzig by Dietrich (1904).

Constance (1414), and Basel (1431) pronounced themselves as being in favor of it as well. The Council of Constance stated, in its fourth and fifth session, that an ecumenical council derived its authority immediately from Christ and that the pope was subject to this authority as well. But all these reformations had but little success. They constituted criticism of the status quo on the basis of a principle identical with that of the status quo.[7]

And when in the sixteenth century the Protestant Reformation arose, it was not long before the Roman Catholic Church took a stand against it as well. Supporting the Council of Trent were the most prominent theologians: Cajetan (d. 1534), John Eck (d. 1543), Cochlaus (d. 1552), Sadoletos (d. 1547), and others. They distinguished themselves also by the fact that they frankly admitted the failings of the church but for the rest sharply polemicized against the Reformers. The most remarkable document is John Eck's *Enchiridion of commonplaces against Luther and other enemies of the church,* 1525, reprinted forty-six times up until 1576.[8] Theology—especially as a result of humanist ridicule—was discredited. Scholars looked back upon the Middle Ages as a period of Gothic barbarism, and the devout also longed for more simplicity and truth, for more practical Christianity. It took both courage and time for Catholic theologians to come to their senses and to pick up again the thread of scholasticism. Though Trent took several decisions to reform the church, it positioned itself as firmly as possible against the Reformation. The dogmas on which it differed with the Reformation, such as the doctrine of tradition, sin, free will, justification, and the sacraments, were defined clearly and radically in Roman Catholic terms, but internal differences were left alone. The issues of the authority of the pope versus that of the council, of Thomism versus Scotism, etc., were either not discussed or treated as circumspectly as possible.[9] During a discussion at Trent about giving lectures on Holy Scripture in all the monasteries, a Benedictine abbot proposed to add to this a prohibition of scholasticism. But the Dominican de Soto took the floor, refuted the objections, extolled the usefulness of scholasticism, and won general agreement.[10]

Gradually scholasticism regained its position of honor but with some modifications. Melchior Canus (d. 1560), in his work *de locis theologicis,* devoted an entire book (bk. VIII) to the defense of scholasticism ("The authority of scholastic teachers"). While admitting that many scholastics made mistakes and censuring these defects, Canus vigorously defended the scholastic method. It was simplified and stripped of exaggeration but otherwise preserved. A second change was

7. Adolf von Harnack, *History of Dogma,* trans. Neil Buchanan, J. Miller, E. B. Speirs, and W. McGilchrist and ed. A. B. Bruce, 7 vols. (London: Williams & Norgate, 1896–99), VI, 136–37; VII, 10ff.

8. Hugo Lämmer, *Die vortridentinisch-katholische Theologie des Reformations-Zeitalters* (Berlin: Schlawitz, 1858).

Ed. note: English translation of Eck's *Enchiridion* by Ford Lewis Battles (Grand Rapids: Baker, 1979).

9. Harnack, *History of Dogma,* VII, 35ff.; Paul Tschadert, "Trienter Konzil," *PRE²,* XVI, 4 and the literature cited there.

10. J. Kleutgen, *Die Theologie der Vorzeit,* 2d ed., 5 vols. (Munster: Theissing, 1867–74), IV, 80.

that Lombard increasingly had to yield to Thomas. In the Middle Ages, Lombard's *Sentences* had been *the* dogmatic handbook, and even after the Reformation de Soto (d. 1560), Maldonatus (d. 1583), Estius (d. 1608), and others, still wrote commentaries on it. But the renowned Cajetan produced a commentary on the *Summa* of Thomas. And Frances Vittoria (d. 1566), Jerome Perez (d. 1556), Bartholomew of Torres (d. 1558), and others, followed his example. Toward the end of the sixteenth century, Lombard had been replaced by Thomas in most of the schools; the latter was more sound, more extensive, more methodical, and more profound in his penetration of the dogmas than Lombard. Another difference between the old scholasticism and the new was that the latter tied in more closely with positive theology. In the Middle Ages positive dogmatics, i.e., proving the truth of dogma from Scripture and tradition, had been almost totally neglected; but now this branch of theology was incorporated in dogmatics itself and practiced with great erudition. Canus wrote a work of his own on the sources of proof, which he called *loci theologici*. All the neoscholastics—Gregory of Valentia, Suarez, Bañez, Diego Ruyz, etc.—diligently pursue the study of Scripture and tradition. Exegesis, church history, patristics, archeology, etc., are given the status of independent disciplines. Theology is considered something other and bigger than dogmatics. And finally, because the new scholastics did not have the leisure enjoyed by the theologians of the Middle Ages but were attacked from all directions and had to defend Catholic doctrine at all points, there was not much time or room left for subtle issues and contrived distinctions. The form, method, language, and articulation of scholastic theology became simpler. The works of Canisius, Canus, Petavius, Bellarmine, etc., are written in pure Latin and a pleasing style and are distinctly superior in this respect to the works of medieval theologians. But whatever was changed and improved, the spirit remained the same; Rome had not denied its own character or learned anything from the Reformation. The real character of Catholic doctrine has even emerged more clearly since, and as a result of, the Reformation. After the Council of Trent, Pelagianism and curialism were further developed and gained a complete victory.

COUNTER-REFORMATION AND NEOSCHOLASTICISM

[48] Neoscholastic theology arose in Spain and was practiced especially at the universities of Salamanca, Alcala (Complutum), and Coimbra. Francis de Vittoria (1480–1566), a native of Vittoria in Cantabria, a Dominican, was sent by his order to Paris to study theology. There he concentrated on the study of Thomas. Upon returning to Spain, he became professor at Salamanca, where he propagated the teaching of Thomas, on whose *Summa* he wrote a commentary. Among his students were the most renowned theologians of Spain: Melchior Canus (d. 1560; *Loci theolog.*, 1563); Domingo de Soto (d. 1560; *Comm. in 4 librum Sent.* [1557–60] and *De natura et gratia* [1547], libri II, against the Scotist Catharinus); Bartholomew Medina (*Expositio in 1, 2 Thomae*, 1576). Thomistic

theology was pursued especially by the Dominicans, to whom, in addition to the above, also belonged: Peter de Soto, professor at Dillingen (d. 1563, *Institutiones christ.*, 1548; *Methodus confessionis*, 1553; *Compendium doctrinae cathol.*, 1556; *Defensio cathol. Confessionis*, 1557 against Brenz); Dom. Bannez (*Comm. In I Thomae*, 2 tomi 1584, 88); Didacus Alvarez (*de auxiliis gratiae div. Et humani arbitrii viribus et libertate*, Lud. 1611); *de incarn. Verbi div.*, Lugd., 1614); Vincentius Contenson (*Theologia mentis et cordis*, 2 tom. Colon., 1687); J. Baptista Gonetus (d. 1681, *Clypeus theol. Thomist.*, 1659–69; *diss. Theol. De probabilitate casuistarum*); Natalis Alexander (*Theol. Dogm. Et mor. Sec. Ordinem catech. Conc. Trid.*, Paris, 1703); Billuart (d. 1757, *Summa S. Thomae hodiernis academiarum moribus accommodata*, 19 tom. Leodii 1747–59, new edition, Paris, in 8 vol.); further Fr. De Sylvestris, Joh. Viguerius, Joh. Gonsalez, Martin Ledesma, Joh. Vincentius, Balt. Navarretus, Raphael Ripa, Francis and Dominicus Perez, Gazzaniga (d. 1799, *Praelect. Theol.*, Bononiae 1790). Joining the Dominicans were the Carmelites, who authored the famous *Salmanticensis collegii Carmelitarum discalceatorum cursus theol. In D. Thomam* (10 vol. Lugd. 1679ff.). But Scotist theology in that period still had its supporters and defenders as well: Ambrosius Catharinus (d. 1553), Fr. Lychetus (*Comm. In I II III librum Sent. Scoti*, Venet. 1589); Frassenius (d. 1711, *Scotus Academicus*, 4 tom. Paris 1662–77); Dupasquier (d. 1718, *Summa theol. Scotisticae*); Barth. Durandus (*Clypeus Scoticae doctrinae*), Thomas of Charmes (*Theol. universa*); Brancatus, Mastrius, Faber (d. 1630), Bonaventura Bellutus (d. 1676), Lukas Wadding (d. 1657), publisher of Scotus works at Lyons 1639ff., and others. The Franciscan de Rada, bishop of Trani (d. 1608), in the work cited above, produced a survey of the controversies between Thomists and Scotists.

However, scholastic theology was practiced above all by the Jesuits, who more than any other order contributed to its revival and florescence. Methodically, and with extraordinary talent, they initiated and promoted the Counter-Reformation. Among them, as polemicists against Protestant doctrine, were the following: Possevinus (d. 1611); Bellarmine (d. 1621, *Disput. De controv. Christ. Fidei adv. Hujus temporis haereticos*, Ingolstadt 1581); Gretser (*Opera omnia* in 17 tomi, Regensburg 1734f.); Becnaus *(Manuale controversiarum)*. The most famous Jesuit theologians are: Peter Canisius (d. 1597, *Summa doctrinae et institutionis christ.* 1554, reprinted 400 times in 130 years; and a smaller catechism: *Institutiones christ. Pietatis*, 1566); Franc. Toletus (d. 1596, *In Summam S. Thomae*. tom. 4, again issued in Rome 1869); John Maldonatus, pupil of Toletus and de Soto at Salamanca (d. 1583), famous exegete and author of numerous dogmatic treatises (*de sacramentis, de libero arbitrio, de gratia*, etc.); Leonh. Lessius, prof. at Leuven (d. 1623, *Disput. de gratia decretis divinis, libertate arbitrii et praescientia Dei conditionata*, Antw., 1610; *De perfectionibus divinis libri* 14, Antw. 1620; *Theologia*, 1651, etc.); Lud. Molina, prof. at Evora, later at Madrid (d. 1600, *Liberi arbitrii cum gratiae donis, divina praescientia, provid. Praedest. et reprob concordia*, 1588; *de justitiaet jure*, and a commentary on the first part of Thomas); Greg. De Valentia, prof. at Dillingen, Ingolstadt,

Rome (d. 1603, *Analysis fidei cathol.* 1585; *Theol. Comment. in Summam S. Thomae* [1602], tomi IV); Mart. Becanus, prof. at Mainz (d. 1624; *Theol. Scholastica*, 3 parts [1612–22]); Roderich Arriaga, professor at Valladolid, Salamanca, Praag (d. 1667; *Disputationes theol.*, 8 tomi, [1643 sq.]); Franz. Suarez (d. 1617; *Commentaria et disputationes in Thomam*, tomi V, and numerous treaties such as *De gratia*, etc.); a brief excerpt of his theology is *Theologiae R. P. Fr. Suarez S. J., Summa seu Compendium auctore* T. Noel, S. J. Tomi II (Paris: Migne, 1858); Gabr. Vasquez (d. 1604, *Comm. in Summam S. Thomae*, Ingolstadt, 7 vol. 1609ff.); Didacus Ruyz de Montoya (d. 1632, *Comment.* on various loci of Thomas; *Theol. Scholastica* 1630; *Clavis Theol.*, 1634); Antoine (*Theologia universa speculativa et dogmatica*, Paris, 1713); Dion. Petavius (d. 1652, *De theol. dogmatibus*, 5 tomi, incomplete Paris 1644); further, Melch. de Castro, Lusitanus, Zunniga, Tannez, Hurtado, Ripalda (d. 1648), Mendoza, Lugo (d. 1660), Arriago, Gotti (d. 1742), Zacccaria (d. 1795), and others. Worthy of separate mention is *Theologia Wirceburgensis, dogmatica polemica scholastica et moralis* 14 vol. Wirceburgensi, 1766–71; new edition in 10 vol. Paris 1880, authored by the Jesuit professors of Wurzburg.

Generally the Jesuits followed Thomas, but on account of their Pelagianism diverged from him in the doctrine of sin, free will, and grace. This fact occasioned a long-lasting struggle, which began with Baius, professor at Louvain (d. 1589), who advocated Augustine's doctrine of sin and the bondage of the will and rejected the immaculate conception of Mary. Various propositions of Baius were rejected by the Sorbonne as early as 1560, and Pope Pius V condemned seventy-nine propositions of Baius in the bull *Ex omnibus afflictionibus* (1567). Baius recanted. But this did not end the conflict. It flared up again in 1588 as the result of Molina's work *Concordia liberi arbitrii cum gratiae donis . . . concordia.* The Thomists, most of them Dominicans, attacked it, especially through the voice of one of their most renowned representatives, Domingo Báñez (d. 1604), who taught a natural predetermination. For years, Thomists (Báñez, Sylvester, Alvarez, Lesmos, Reginaldi, etc.), Augustinians (Noris [d. 1704], Laur. Berti [d. 1766], Bertieri), and Jesuits (Molinists, or Congruists [Bellarmine]) opposed each other. A mass of pamphlets on sin, free will, and grace were published.[11] A commission appointed in Rome was dissolved in 1607 without making a decision. The pope stated he would make a pronouncement later and until that time neither party should brand the other as heretical. In 1640, when the work *Augustine* by Cornelius Jansen, bishop of Ypres, made its appearance, fresh fuel was thrown on the fire, prolonging the conflict into the eighteenth century. The men of Port Royal sided with Jansen, Arnauld (d. 1694), Pascal (d. 1662), Nicole (d. 1695), Sacy (d. 1684), Tillemont (d. 1698), and Quesnell (d. 1719). But learning and eloquence did not avail. In a series of bulls (1653, 1656, 1664, 1705, 1713) Jansenism, and by implication Augustine and even Paul, were

---

11. J. G. Walch, *Bibliotheca Theologia selecta,* 4 vols. (Jenae: vid. Croeckerianal, 1757–65), I, 179ff.

condemned, the bull *Unigenitus* (1713) being later reaffirmed many times. Just as Pelagianism triumphed in dogmatics, so did probabilism in ethics, and curialism, or the papal system, in matters ecclesiastical.

ROMAN CATHOLICISM AND MODERNITY

[49] By the beginning of the eighteenth century, the time in which neoscholasticism flourished was past. In all of Europe a rationalistic spirit sprang up. The philosophy of Bacon and Descartes displaced that of Aristotle. Even theologians who accepted the premises of scholasticism believed in the necessity of other methods. Among them were Bossuet (d. 1704), the famous defender of the Gallican system and opponent of Protestants, who wrote *Exposition de la doctrine de l'église cath. sur les matières de controverse* (1671), *Histoire des variations des églises protest.,* 2 vols. (Paris, 1688); Fénélon (1715); and Thomassinus (d. 1695, *Dogmata theol.*). The historical and critical studies pursued especially in France forced actual theology into the background. Many learned Maurists and Oratorians even lapsed into unbelief. In the schools, admittedly, scholasticism continued to hold sway until well into the eighteenth century. Continuing to exist side by side were the various schools: Thomists (e.g., Peri, *Quaest. Theol.,* 5 vol., 1715–32); Scotists (e.g., Krisper, *Theol. scolae scotisticae,* 4 tom., 1728–48); Molinists (e.g., Anton Erber, *Theol. specul. tractatus octo,* 1787); and Augustinians (e.g., Amort, *Theol. eclestica moralis et scholastica,* 23 tomi, Augsburg, 1752). Still, scholasticism increasingly withdrew into the schools. Other parties— deistic, naturalistic—rose up, achieved vocal superiority, and influenced Roman Catholic theology. In France scholastic theology was sidelined by Descartes; in Germany by Leibniz and Wolff. In Austria peripatetic doctrine was prohibited in 1752, and in 1759 leadership in theological and philosophical studies was taken away from the Jesuits. In 1773 the order was suppressed by [pope] Clement XIV. In 1763 the Gallican system was defended by Nic. of Hontheim, suffragan bishop of Trier, in a work entitled *de statu ecclesiae et legitima potestate Romani Pontificio* and introduced as ecclesiastical law by [Holy Roman Emperor] Joseph II in 1781. Confessional differences were forgotten; in the place of conflict with the Protestants came the struggle against freethinkers, unbelievers, and the like, in the work of Klüpfel, Fahrman, Stattler, Storchenau, Burkhauser. Theology fell completely under the sway of the shifting philosophy. The Enlightenment had its representative in the person of Ad. Wieshaupt, professor at Ingolstadt, founder of the order of the Illuminati. Kant's influence is noticeable in the work of Ildefons Schwarz, Peutinger, and Zimmer. Jacobi's philosophy found support in the work of J. Salat and Cajetan Weiller. Thanner was subject to Schelling's influence. The most important theologian, one who in the eighteenth century held his ground against all errors, was Alphonsus Liguori (d. 1787), included by Pope Pius IX in 1871 among the doctors of the Church.

Even in the nineteenth century, rationalism initially continued to predominate in Catholic circles. In Germany there was a large group of people who sought to bring the organization and teaching of the Catholic Church into harmony with the demands of the time: Dalberg (d. 1817), Wessenberg (d. 1860), Werkmeister, and others. Georg. Hermes, professor at Bonn (d. 1831) and author of *Einleitung in die Christkatholische Theologie* (1819, 1829), and *Christkatholische Dogm.* (1834, 1836), attempted to ground revelation and authority in reason. In evaluating the question of what revelation is, he gave to reason the same rights as Wolffian philosophy had attributed to it. At first Hermes had many adherents (Achterfeldt, who published his dogmatics, Braun, von Droste-Hulfshof, professor of law in Bonn, Spiegel, archbishop of Cologne), but after Hermesianism had been condemned by Pope Gregory XVI (September 26, 1835), his influence waned. Anton Günther (d. 1863) in Vienna, author of *Vorschule zur specul. Theol.* (1828); *Peregrius Gastmahl* (1830), etc., adopted Hegel's thesis that philosophy and speculative theology are really one and the same. There are no two kinds of truth and certainty. But the act of believing is the beginning and premise of all knowledge, and all belief, also belief in revelation, can pass into knowledge and be elevated to the level of evidence. Günther also had many adherents (Pabst, Merten, Veith, Gangauf, Baltzer, Knoodt); but he was condemned in 1857. Franz von Baader (d. 1841), author of *Vorlesungen über speculatieve Dogmatik, Sammtliche Schriften,* 15 vols. (Leipzig, 1850–57), sought refuge, under the influence of Böhme and Schelling, not in a return to but in the development of the ancient truths, in the renewal of the ancient dogmas, and sought to elevate belief into knowledge by way of theosophy. His adherents were Schaden, Lutterbek, Hoffmann, Hamberger, Sengler, Schlüter, but Baader was censured on account of his opposition to papal primacy. J. Frohschammer, author of *Einleitung in die Philosophy and Grundriss der Metaphysik* (1858) and other works, rejected scholastic and idealistic philosophy and attempted to build metaphysics, or theology, not on a foundation of abstract reason but on the concrete, universal, historical fact of the God-consciousness present in humanity. Accordingly, for him theology and philosophy coincide in content; they only differ in method; the natural and the supernatural cannot be rigorously distinguished. In a letter to the archbishop of München, dated December 11, 1862, Pope Pius IX condemned this philosophy. His works were put on the *Index,* and he himself was suspended in 1863. Frohschammer did not submit, however, and in numerous writings continued the battle, advocating academic freedom and opposing the claims of the pope. Thus, on the one hand, Rome combated the independence of science and, on the other, recognized its relative freedom.

Traditionalism—the teaching that the higher metaphysical truths cannot be discovered by reason but can only be obtained from revelation, a revelation that from the first human being on was transmitted by tradition and preserved in language—surfaced in France following the French Revolution. This theory was skillfully defended by de Bonald, author of *Recherches philosophiques sur les premiers objects des connaissances morales* (Paris, 1817); Lamennais, *Essai sur l'indifférence en matière de religion*, 2 vols. (Paris: Le Clère, 1817); and Bautain, *de l'enseignement de la philosophie en France au 19e siècle* (1833), *Philosophie du Christianisme* (1835). But it found no favor in the eyes of Rome. In 1840 Bautain signed six propositions submitted to him, thereby retracting his teaching. The ontologism of Gerdil (d. 1802), Gioberti (d. 1852), Rosmini (d. 1855), Gratry (d. 1872), Ubaghs, and others, an ontologism rooted in the idealism of Malebranche, which derived all higher truth from immediate intuition of God and the ideas, was similarly condemned.

All these condemnations prove that following the rationalism of the previous century, Rome became increasingly self-conscious and wide-awake. After the [French] revolution both the Catholic Church and Catholic theology experienced renewal. Romanticism, which benefited Catholicism, made many converts: Winckelmann, Stolberg, Schlegel, Ad. Müller, Z. Werner, Schlosser, Haller, etc. In France a reaction against the revolution and unbelief set in as a result of the work of Chateaubriand, author of *Génie du Christianisme*, Joseph de Maistre (d. 1821), de Bonald, and Lamennais. Puseyism, or Tractarianism, which started in 1833 at Oxford under Pusey and Newman, led many people into the Catholic Church and strengthened the high church ritualizing and Romanizing movement in the Anglican (Episcopalian) Church. Faith-driven Catholic theology, which came up in Germany, in many respects first linked up with Schleiermacher. His doctrine of Scripture, rebirth, justification, and the church contained many elements Catholics could use to their advantage. Accordingly, this was done with skill and energy by Görres, Baader, Philips, Döllinger in Munich; by Klee in Bonn; by Möhler, Hirscher, and Drey in Münich and Tübingen; by Staudenmaier and Kuhn in Giessen, etc. Admittedly, the men who chose this path were not yet fully pleasing to Rome and to the Jesuits. They all still pursued mediation and sought the conciliation of faith and knowledge. By a speculative method they attempted to prove the dogmas, were much too liberal vis-à-vis Protestants, and from time to time made important concessions [in their direction]. But they were superb spokesmen for Catholic theology and contributed much to its revival.

Still, in time this conciliating and mediating trend failed to satisfy. Gradually the neoscholastic movement arose. In 1814 the Jesuit order was restored and its influence on the papacy increased with mounting vigor. Its power expanded in all countries. It fought "academic freedom" with all the means at its disposal. All the above-cited condemnations culminated in the famous encyclical of December 8, 1864,[12] and in the Vatican Council of 1870, at which papal infallibility was promulgated. Especially advocating this neoscholastic trend in Italy were the philosopher Sanseverino, *Philosophia christiana*, 7 vol. (1878), and

---

12. Ed. note: Bavinck is referring here to Pope Pius IX's "Syllabus of Errors," which condemned, *inter alia*, pantheism, naturalism, rationalism, socialism, secret societies, and Latitudinarianism.

the theologian J. Perrone, *Praelectiones theologiae*, 9 vol. (1838–43); in Germany, J. Kleutgen, *Theologie der Vorzeit* (Münster, 1867) and *Philosophie der Vorzeit* (Innsbrück, 1878), and A. Stöckl in various works. Pope Leo XIII, on August 4, 1879, set his seal on this trend by recommending the study of Thomas Aquinas in his encyclical *Aeterni Patris*. And since that time there has been a powerful universal effort to restore Thomas's authority in every area of science. Political and legal science, psychology and ethics, theology and philosophy are all being studied from a Thomist mind-set.[13] Dogmatics has been treated in the same perspective by Franzelin, Scheeben, Heinrich, Bautz, Ottiger, Hunter, Pesch, Janssens, Pohle, etc.; in the Netherlands by M. Jansen, professor at Rijsenburg, *Praelect. theol. fundam.* (Ultraj. 1875–76); *Theol. dogm. spec.* (1877–79); Mannens, professor at Roermond (*Theol. Dogm. Institutiones*, 3 vols., 1901–3); G. van Noort, professor at Warmond, who published various treaties (*De vera religione de ecclesia Christi, De Deo Cretaore, De Deo Redemptore, De Sacramentis*).[14]

Nevertheless the recommendation to study Thomas has not brought about the desired unity in the Catholic Church and Catholic theology. On the one hand, it becomes evident again and again that Thomism remains restricted to a circle of scholarly men, to centers of study and works of erudition, and does not control the religious life of Roman Catholic believers. Although established doctrine is still being recognized, it does not nurture and animate Catholic piety. The latter, at least in large part, is not born of dogma but called into being and maintained by sacraments and good works, rosaries and relics, pilgrimages and miracles, amulets and scapulars. Depending on time, place, and circumstances, Catholic devotion consistently creates new forms and currently focuses in increasing measure on the veneration of saints, devotion to Mary, and the adoration of the physical heart of Jesus. Superstition and idolatry, which are increasing alarmingly among Catholics,[15] are not countered by the clergy but rather even favored and encouraged by popes like Pius IX and Leo XIII. With a view to this ongoing corruption of original Christianity, one is not surprised by the rise of a trend like Americanism or Reform Catholicism. This movement is in general characterized by the fact that, contrary to the syllabus of 1864, it recognizes much that is good in modern culture, science, philosophy, art, and literature in the currents and movements of modern times. It also demands that the church reconcile herself with this fact by a series of concessions in doctrine and life, in organization and practice.

13. Friedrich Nippold, *Die jesuitischen Schriftsteller der Gegenwart in Deutschland* (Leipzig: F. Jansa, 1895).

14. Published by van Langenhuyzen in Amsterdam. Additional literature can be found in H. Kihn, *Encyklopädie und Methodologie der Theologie* (Freiburg im B.: Herder, 1892), 412ff.

15. Notably the tragic "Taxil affair" of 1897 provides evidence of this. See P. Bräunlich, *Der neueste Teufelsschwindel in der römisch-katholischen Kirche* (Leipzig: Braun, 1897).

Ed. note: Bavinck is referring to Leo Taxil, a con artist who claimed to know Masonic secrets and was encouraged by Leo XIII to publicly expose them. Taxil later revealed publicly that his exposé was a hoax intended to mock Roman Catholic piety. For a more recent study, see Eugene Eugen Joseph Weber, *Satan franc-maçon la mystification de Léo Taxil* (Paris: René Julliard, 1964).

Positive Protestantism ought not to base great expectations on this movement, any more than on those of old Catholicism. It does not proceed from a deeply religious-moral principle like the Reformation and lacks a firm standard by which to assess truth and error in the doctrine and life of Catholic Christianity. It cannot give a clear account of the basis, character, and limit of the reforms proposed by it, and its kinship with Febronianism and Josephinism[16] makes it likely that, like these other movements, it will be a passing phenomenon and prove powerless to give a different direction to the development of the Catholic Church and Catholic theology.

Still, Reform Catholicism is a movement that has a message for Rome and summons it to self-evaluation and revision. In America, England, France, Germany, Austria, and Italy, it is spreading with great force, manages to win the loyalty of large numbers of people, and propagates its ideas in brochures, books, and periodicals. It thus voices and reinforces in large circles—especially that of the clergy—the deep dissatisfaction felt in the Catholic Church at its own condition, organization, and development. Even the condemnation of Americanism by the pope in a communication to Cardinal Gibbons dated January 22, 1899, has not stopped its progress.[17] The seriousness of the free-from-Rome movement does not consist in the number of converts it adds to the rolls of positive or negative Protestantism but in the profound conflict that it makes patently visible within the Catholic Church between the ancient faith and modern consciousness.[18]

16. Ed. note: Febronianism and Josephinism were late-eighteenth-century reform movements in Germany and by Joseph II, Holy Roman Emperor from 1765 to 1790, respectively. Their principles included religious toleration and a restriction of the papacy's temporal power.

17. Ed. note: Cf. "Americanism," in *New Catholic Encyclopedia*, I, 443.

18. I. T. Hecker, *The Church and the Age: An Exposition of the Catholic Church in View of the Needs and Aspirations of the Present Age* (New York: Catholic World, 1887); Herman Schell, *Theologie und Universität* (Würzburg: A. Göbel, 1896); idem, *Der Katholizismus als Princip des Fortschritts* (Würzburg: A. Göbel, 1899); idem, *Die neue Zeit und der Alte Glaube* (Würzburg: A. Göbel, 1898); Georg Hertling, *Das Princip des Katholizismus und die Wissenschaft,* 4th ed. (Freiburg im Breisgau; St. Louis: Herder, 1899); Josef Müller, *Der Reformkatholizismus,* 2d ed. (Zurich: C. Schmidt, 1899); idem, *Reformkatholizismus im Mittelalter und zur Zeit der Glaubensspaltung* (Strassburg i. E.: C. Bongard, 1901); Albert Erhard, *Der Katholizismus und das Jahrhundert im Lichte der kirchliche Entwicklung der Neuzeit* (Stuttgart and Vienna: J. Roth, 1902); J. E. Alaux, *La religion progressive,* 2d ed. (Paris: G. Baillère, 1872); Albert Houtin, *L'Americanisme* (Paris: E. Nourry, 1904); Anton Vogrinec, *Nostra maxima culpa* (Vienna: C. Fromme, 1904). Among those writing in opposition: P. Einig, *Katholischer "Reformer"* (Trier: Paulinusdruckerei, 1902); Carl Braun, *Amerikanismus* (Würzburg: Göbel & Scherer, 1904); Albert M. Weisz, *Die religiöse Gefahr* (Freiburg im B.: Herder, 1904), 246ff.

5

LUTHERAN DOGMATICS

*Martin Luther was not really the first Lutheran dogmatician; that honor belongs to Philipp Melanchthon and his Loci Communes (1521). After decades of debate about the Lord's Supper, the law, and Christ's descent into hell, among other things, Lutheran orthodoxy achieved its definitive form in the Formula of Concord (1577–80). The seventeenth century witnessed a refinement of Lutheran scholasticism as well as a reaction to its objectivism. In the eighteenth century the human subject asserted itself in different forms. Pietism and rationalism, each in its own way, undermined the authority of Lutheran orthodoxy by shifting the center of gravity to the human subject. The Enlightenment enthroned autonomous reason to a place of dominance over the objective truth of Scripture. Kant's critique of reason shifted the focus of theology toward morality; religion became a means of achieving virtue. Romanticism provided another alternative to rationalism and deism; the immediate experience of human feeling is seen as the locus of the divine in each person. This trend found its culmination in the theology of Schleiermacher. The turn to the subject also found expression in Hegel's idealism. The history of religion is the history of ideas; the incarnation is important because it expresses the **idea** of the union of God and man. By divorcing Christianity from its particular historical base, the Hegelian emphasis repudiated orthodox Christianity. Dissatisfaction with these trends gave rise to a revival of interest in classic Lutheran theology in the late nineteenth century as theologians such as Kaftan and Seeberg attempted a "mediating theology" that sought to join orthodoxy and modernism in some kind of synthesis. At the same time a resistance to the mingling of theology and philosophy led to a "return to Kant" movement. Theology, according to Ritschl, is thus about value judgments; the kingdom of God is a moral community. Ritschlian social gospel theology had a profound influence beyond Germany itself. Though Ritschl separated theology and philosophy, science and religion, into two distinct domains, objections arose against his aprioristic commitment to the isolation of Christianity away from all scientific inquiry. As the nineteenth century came to a conclusion, the a priori superiority of Christianity was set aside by many scholars, and Christian theology was abandoned for a universal history of religions that includes the Christian faith. This history of religions approach, of which Ernst Troeltsch is the best example, means the end of Christian dogmatics. It is impossible for the Christian theologian, or anyone else for that matter, to set aside a commitment to the faith and treat all religions objectively and neutrally.*

THE BEGINNING OF LUTHERAN THEOLOGY

[50] Luther was not the systematic type; he did not leave behind a dogmatics. But he *was*—all the more—an original and creative thinker. He rediscovered the Christianity of Paul and Augustine. He again grasped the gospel as a glorious message of grace and forgiveness and brought religion back into religion. As a result he has proven fruitful for the whole theological and dogmatic enterprise. Incorporating even the old dogmas in his thinking, he infused them with new religious life.[1] Before the Lutheran Reformation had a confession of its own, it already had a dogmatics: Melanchthon's *Loci* (1521). This work, which originated in an interpretation of the Letter to the Romans, was practical, simple, soteriological, devoid of scholasticism, and actually more of a confession than a dogmatics. For a long time the German reformation found its unity in this work. But already in 1526 Melanchthon changed his mind somewhat with respect to a rigorous view of predestination and before long he also began to diverge from Luther at other points, particularly in the doctrine of the Lord's Supper. This dissent from Luther first clearly surfaced in the new editions of the *Loci* of 1535 and 1543, then in the revision of the Augsburg Confession (1540 and 1542), and finally in the Leipzig Interim and the Adiaphoristic controversy it triggered.[2] Two opposing parties emerged from this struggle. On the one side were the followers of Melanchthon, the Philippists, found especially at the academies of Wittenberg and Leipzig, such as G. Major, Paul Eber, John Pfeffinger, Victor Strigel (d. 1569), whose *Loci Theologici,* originated in lectures on Melanchthon's *Loci* and was published by Pezel in four volumes (1582–85); Chr. Pezel (d. 1604), author of *Argumenta et objectiones de praecipuis articutis doctrinae Christianae* (1580–89); Sohnius, *Opera,* (1609); and others. On the other side were the Gnesio-Lutherans, especially in Weimar and Jena, such as Nich. von Amsdorf (d. 1505); Matt. Flacius (d. 1575), author of the *Solida confutatio et condemnatio praecipurum sectarum* and numerous other polemical writings; John Wigand (d. 1587); John Marbach (d. 1581); Joachim Westphal (d. 1574), who particularly opposed Calvin's doctrine of the Lord's Supper; Tileman Heshusius (d. 1588); etc. The multifarious dogmatic disputes that arose among Lutheran theologians in this first period (over the law with Osiander; over justification with Agricola; over Christ's descent into hell with Aepinus; over the active obedience of Christ with Parsimonius; over adiaphora, synergism, and crypto-Calvinism with Melanchthon and like-minded contemporaries;

1. Th. Harnack, *Luthers Theologie,* 2 vols. (Erlangen: T. Blaesing, 1862–66; reprinted, Amsterdam: Editions Rodopi, 1969); J. Köstlin, *Theology of Luther,* trans. Charles E. Hay, 2 vols. (Philadelphia: Lutheran Publication Society, 1897); S. Lommatzsch, *Luthers Lehre vom ethische-religiöse Standpunkt* (Berlin: L. Schleiermacher, 1879); J. Köstlin, "Luther," *PRE³*, XI, 720–56.

2. Ed. note: The Leipzig Interim (1548) was a more rigorously Protestant doctrinal formula than the Augsburg Interim of the same year. The Leipzig Interim led to the Adiaphorist controversy about the degree to which Lutheran Protestants could concede to certain Roman Catholic practices without violating Protestant doctrine. The controversy was concluded by the Formula of Concord (1577).

over good works with Major; over original sin with Flacius) finally led to and were settled in the *Formula Concordiae* of [1577–] 1580.[3] It was the work especially of Jacob Andreae (d. 1590) and of Martin Chemnitz (d. 1586), the most prominent Lutheran theologian of this century, author of *Examen Concilii Tridentini,* four tomes (1565–73), a treatise *de duabus naturis in Christo* (1571), and *Loci Theologici,* published posthumously in 1592.

Lutheran dogma, having thus been given definitive form, was discussed and developed scholastically in the seventeenth century. Making a start with this were Heerbrand (d. 1600, *Compendium theologiae,* 1573, significantly enlarged in 1578) and Hafenreffer, *Loci Theologica certa methodo ac ratione in libros tres tributi* (1603). This scholastic treatment was continued by Leonard Hutter (d. 1616, *Compendium locorum theol. ex Scriptura sara et libro Concordiae collectum,* 1610) and Joh. Gerhard (d. 1637, *Loci Communes theologici,* 9 tomes, 1610–22; the best edition being that of Cotta, 1762–87, reprinted Berlin-Leipzig, 1864–75) and culminated in Dannhauer (d. 1666, *Hodosophia christiana*), Hülsemann (d. 1635, *Breviarium theologiae,* 1640), Calovius (d. 1686, *Systema loc. theol.,* 1655–77), Quenstedt (d. 1688, *Theologia didact-polem.,* 1685), Hollaz (d. 1713, *Examen theol. acroamaticum,* 1707), and König (d. 1664, *Theol. positiva acroamatica,* 1664). The power of this dogmatics lay in its objectivity. The dogmas were ready-made and the human subject submitted to them without criticism. They were only developed and applied exegetically, dogma-historically, polemically, scholastically, and practically. But already in the seventeenth century a reaction arose against this method. Philippism had not been overcome by the Formula of Concord; it continued to have its exponents, particularly in the persons of Altdorf and Helmstadt. Georg Calixtus, professor at Helmstadt (d. 1656), as a result of his study of Aristotle, his acquaintance with Catholic as well as Reformed theologians, and his aversion to scholastic orthodoxy, developed a moderate and irenic theology. In his works *de praecipuis religionis christianae captibus* (1613), *epitome theologiae* (1619), and *de immortalitate anime et resurrectio mortis* (1627), he advocated a sharper separation of philosophy and theology. He also returned to the original Christianity of the first four centuries in order to find a basis for union among Lutherans, Reformed, and Catholics in that which all Christian confessions have in common.

Pietism and Rationalism

Naturally Calixtus with his syncretism encountered much opposition. But the age of objectivity had passed. In the eighteenth century the human subject asserted itself, reclaiming its rights and resisting the power of the objective. In the Pietism of the period between 1700 and 1730, subjective piety was adopted as the starting point, the point of gravity being transferred from

---

3. Franz H. R. Frank, *Die Theologie der Conkordienformel,* 4 vols. (Erlangen: T. Blaesing, 1858–65). Ed. note: The Formula of Concord was achieved in 1577 and the *Book of Concord* published in 1580.

the object to the subject. Spener, the father of Pietism (1635–1705), exerted enormous influence by his personality and works (*Pia desideria,* 1678; *Allgemeine Gottesgelahrtheit aller gläubigen Christen und rechtschaffenen Theologen,* 1680; *Tabulae Catecheticae,* 1683; and *Theolog. Bedenken,* 1712). In Halle the most prominent Pietists were Francke (d. 1727), Breithaupt (d. 1732), Freylinghausen (d. 1739), Joachim Lange (d. 1744), and Rambach (d. 1735). In Wurtemberg, in the works of Hedinger (d. 1704), Bengel (d. 1752), and Oetinger (d. 1782), Pietism united with a kind of biblical realism and apocalyptic expectations. Orthodoxy as represented, for example, by Löscher in Dresden (d. 1749) naturally took a very hostile position against this Pietism. But orthodoxy had had its day. In the years 1730–60, in the persons of Buddeus (d. 1729), *Institutiones theologiae dogmaticis et moralis,* Weismann (d. 1760), Crusius (d. 1775), J. G. Walch, *Einleitung in die dogmatischen Gottesgelahrheit* (1749), and his son Ch. W. F. Walch, *Breviarium theol. dogm.* (1775), orthodoxy united with Pietism. Orthodoxy moved in the direction of a warm piety, stressed the practice of faith, was averse to scholastic subtlety, moderate in its polemics, and devoted its energies especially to learned historical inquiries. Akin to Pietism is Herrnhuttism [Moravianism], similarly a reaction of feeling against an intellectual brand of orthodoxy. Nicholas von Zinzendorf's father was a Spenerian. But whereas Pietism sought to lead people to conversion by way of a penitential crisis, Moravianism attempted to achieve conversion by preaching a sweet Savior. It wanted no part of law, only gospel. Grace, here, so totally crowds out nature that Jesus even replaces the Father: Jesus is the Creator, Ruler, Father, the Yahweh of the Old Testament. Under Catholic influence, Zinzendorf conceived Jesus' person and suffering with such pathos that, especially in the first romantic period (1743–50), the kinship between mysticism and sensibility clearly came out into the open.

Running along parallel lines with Pietism was rationalism. Both—each in its own way—undermined the authority of orthodoxy, by transferring the point of gravity to the human subject. Rationalism was spawned by the philosophy of Descartes (d. 1650), Spinoza (d. 1677), Leibnitz (d. 1716), and Wolff (d. 1754). They made clarity—mathematical clarity—the standard of truth. Jacob Carpov, professor of mathematics at Weimar, in his *Theologia revelata, dogmatica scientifica adornata* (1737–65), attempted mathematically to demonstrate church doctrine. Belonging to this Wolffian school were Canz, Reusch, Schubert, Reinbeck, especially S. J. Baumgarten at Halle (d. 1757), author of *Evangelische Glaubenslehre* (1759–60), and J. L. von Mosheim at Göttingen (d. 1755). In the main, these men were orthodox, but they no longer felt the religious importance of truth and turned church doctrine into an object of historical erudition and intellectual demonstration. It is no wonder that other Wolffians, such as Töllner (*Syst. der dogm. Theol.*), Heilmann (*Compendium theol. dogm.,* 1761), J. P. Miller (*Instit. theol. dogm.* 1761), and Seiler (*Theol. dogm. polem.,* 1774), already adopted a freer attitude to the doctrine of the church.

Following 1760, when this rationalistic trend was further fed and reinforced from without by British deism and French unbelief, the Enlightenment (*Aufklärung*) arose in Germany, a movement that sought to bring the commonsense intellect of the individual to a position of dominance over all objective truth. On every front the positive, the traditional, that which has come into being historically, had to yield to the rational, the clearly intelligible. Wolff and his followers still found revelation rational. The Enlightenment, however, was deistic and rationalistic. Frederick the Great was its king, Berlin its center, the journal *Allgemeine Deutsche Bibliothek* (1765–1805) its means of communication. Dogmatics was done from within this rationalistic mind-set by W. A. Teller, *Lehrbuch des Christliche Glaubens* (1764), *Religion der Vollkommneren* (1792); Henke, *Lineamenta instit. fidei christ.* (1793); Eckermann, *Compend. theol.* (1791); and especially by Wegscheider, *Institutiones theologiae Christianae dogmaticae* (1815, 8th ed. 1844). Against this rationalism, orthodoxy assumed the weakened form of supranaturalism. It no longer had the courage—positively and assertively—to take its position in the faith but shared with its adversaries the foundation of reason. From that base it still attempted to arrive at revelation, whose necessity, possibility, and reality it defended; but in its outlook its content gradually shrank in scope. Dogmas were as much as possible shorn of their offensive features and made fit for reason by so-called biblical representation. This position was held by Doederlein, *Instit. theol.* (1780); Morus, *Epitome Theol. Christ.* (1789); Knapp, *Vorlesungen über die Christliche Glaubenslehre* (1827); and especially Reinhard, *Vorles über die Dogmatik* (1801); and Storr, *Doctrinae Christ. pars theoret.* (1793); among others. An attempt at reconciling rationalism and supranaturalism was made by Tzschirner, von Ammon, Schott, and especially C. G. Bretschneider, *Dogmatik der evangelischlutheranischen Kirche,* 1814.

THE TRIUMPH OF PHILOSOPHY

[51] In the nineteenth century Lutheran dogmatics was characterized by the fact that it had almost completely fallen under the influence of philosophy.[4] As a result of rationalism, it had almost altogether lost its own starting point, method, and content. It had become a compendium of rational ideas about God, virtue, and immortality. Immanuel Kant was the first who, by his sharp

---

4. The following should be consulted for the history of Lutheran dogmatics. Ed. note: In the interest of space, only names and titles of the works in Bavinck's lengthy bibliography will be listed here. For full data see the bibliography at the back of this volume. Unlike in Bavinck's original, items will be separated here into books and articles, and include the items listed at the head of par. 5.E in the *Gereformeerde Dogmatiek,* 4th ed., p. 134. Items already indicated in previous footnotes of this chapter are not included here.

Books: I. A. Dorner, *Geschichte der protestantischen Theologie besonders in Deutschland;* G. Ecke, *Die theologische Schule Albrecht Ritschl und die evangelische Kirche der Gegenwart;* idem, *Die evangelische Kirchen Landeskirchen Deutschlands im neunzehnten Jahrhundert;* Otto Flügel, *Die spekulative theologie der Gegenwart;* F. H. R. Frank, *Geschichte der protest. Theologie; idem, Geschichte und Kritik der neueren Theologie; G. Goyau, *L'Allemagne religieuse, vol. 1, Le Protestantisme; vol. 2, Le Catholicisme;* W. Gass, *Geschichte der*

critique of pure reason, totally undermined this rational basis of dogmatics. His criticism was discouraging, even devastating, for the rationalism and eudaemonism of the Enlightenment. But in his critique of practical reason, he sought to regain what he lost as a result of pure reason. The categorical imperative— our moral consciousness—gives us the right to postulate the existence of God, freedom, and immortality. Dogmatics is built on a foundation of morality; religion becomes a means of achieving virtue, and God an emergency relief worker for human beings. The content of religion and dogmatics, as Kant develops it in his *Religion within the Limits of Reason Alone*,[5] is purely rationalistic. Kant is still situated completely in the eighteenth century. The historical and positive has no value for him, and he isolates human beings from all [external] influences. For Kant, only the religion of autonomous reason is the true religion. But by his critique of reason, by his appeal to the moral consciousness, his rigorous view of morality—a view that even made him speak of radical evil in human beings and of the necessity of a kind of rebirth—he has had great influence on theology. Not only the moral destiny of man but also the inability of reason to reach the supersensible became an argument for the necessity of revelation, faith, and authority. Dogmatics was treated from this Kantian perspective by J. H. Tieftrunk in his *Dilucidationes ad theoreticam religionis christ. partem,* (1793), as well as by Stäudlin, J. E. C. Schmidt, Ammon, etc.

A different reaction against the Enlightenment came from the side of feeling. Sentimentality was a characteristic trait of the second half of the eighteenth cen-

---

protestantischen Dogmatik, 4 vols.; K. R. Hagenbach, *Über die sogennante Vermittelungstheologie;* Harnack, *History of Dogma* (vol. VII); E. von Hartmann, *Die Krisis des Christenthums in der modernen Theologie;* H. Heppe, *Dogmatik des deutschen Protestantismus in sechzehnten Jahrhundert;* K. F. Kahnis, *Der innere Gang des deutschen Protestantismus;* E. Kalb, *Kirchen und Sekten der Gegenwart;* Kattenbusch, *Von Schleiermacher zu Ritschl;* L. Lemme, *Die Vertreter der systematischen Theologie;* F. A. Lichtenberger, *Historie des idées religieuses en Allemagne depuis le milieu du XVIIIe sièle jus gu'a nos jours,* 3 vols.; A. Mücke, *Die Dogmatik des neunzehnten Jahrhunderts;* C. M. Pfaff, *Introductio in historiam theologiae literariam notis amplissinis. . . ,* 3 vols.; Otto Pfleiderer, *Die Entwicklung der protestantischen Theologie in Deutschland seit Kant und in Grossbritannien seit 1825* (in English, *The Development of Theology in Germany since Kant, and Its Progress in Great Britain since 1825*); A. Ritschl, *Geschichte des Pietismus,* 3 vols.; R. Seeberg, *Die Kirche Deutschlands im neunzehnten Jahrhundert;* Carl Schwarz, *Zur geschichte der neuesten Theologie;* C. A. Thilo, *Die Wissenschaftlichkeit der modernen speculativen Theologie in ihren Principien;* A. Tholuck, *Vorgeschichte des Rationalismus,* 4 vols. in 2: vol. 1, *Das akademische Leben des siebzehnten Jahrhunderts;* vol. 2, *Das kirchliche Leben des siebzehnten Jahrhunderts;* idem, *Geschichte des Rationalismus;* idem, *Der Geist der lutherischen Theologen Wittenbergs im Verlaufe des 17 Jahrhunderts;* T. Ziegler, *Die geistigen und socialen Strömungen des neunzehnten Jahrhunderts;* for Denmark, see Jessen, *Die hauptströmungen des religiösen lebens der jetztzeit in Dänemark.*

Articles: O. Ritschl, "Studien zur Geschichte der Protestantischen Theologie im 19. Jahrhundert," 5 *ZThK* (1895): 486–529; Zöckler, *Handbuch der theologischen Wissenschaften in enzyklopadischer Darstellung,* 5 vols. (Nordlingen: C. H. Beck, 1889–90), suppl. volume, 144ff.; For Scandinavia, see Conrad E. Lindberg, "Recent Dogmatic Thought in Scandinavia," *Presbyterian and Reformed Review* 4 (October 1893): 562ff.

5. Immanuel Kant, *Religion within the Limits of Reason Alone,* trans. Theodore M. Greene and Hoyt H. Hudson (La Salle, Ill.: Open Court Publishing Co., 1934; reprinted, New York: Harper & Brothers, 1960).

tury. Just as in England Shaftesbury countered Hume, and Rousseau countered Voltaire in France, so in Germany, in men like Hamann, Claudius, Lavater, Stilling, Herder, and Jacobi, feeling asserted its rights against a cold rationalism. The premise from which all of them proceed is immediate experience, the power and inwardness of the emotions. According to these men, emotion is the most essential part, the seat of humanity, where lies the root of religion, where faith originates, where man perceives the divine. And from this center he sees and discovers the divine all around him—in nature, in history, above all in Christ, the most human of all human beings. Faith's content greatly differed in the case of each of these men—the more so since they were all averse to system—but for all of them the ground of faith was the same. Feeling, faith, reason, inspiration, enthusiasm, experience—whatever one calls it—is the ground and norm of truth in all of them. Over against the advancing criticism, Jacobi pointed to the immediate sense in which another, higher objectivity holds true. Thus he arrived at a consistent dualism of head and heart, of philosophy and faith, of the sensible and the spiritual world. In dogmatics this dualism was applied by de Wette, *Bibl. Dogmatik,* 3d ed., 1831, *Dogm. der prot. Kirche,* 3d ed., 1840, *Ueber Religion und Theol,* 2d ed., 1821, *Das Wesen des Christl. Glaubens vom Standpunkt des Glaubens;* 1840; and after him by Hase, *Evang. Dogm.,* 1826, 6th ed., 1870. Common to all is the separation of faith and knowledge, of the aesthetic (ethical, religious) and the intellectual (empirical) worldview, of the ideal and the sensible world. Truth, demanded by the religious consciousness or feeling, is inviolable to the intellect because it belongs to another, a nonperceptible world.

The theology of Schleiermacher is closely related to this trend. In his *Speeches on Religion* (1799) and *Monologues* (1800), he is totally under the influence of romanticism. Religion is feeling, feeling for the universal, a sense of the infinite, an emotional focus on eternity, like Spinoza's intuitive knowledge of God (*cognito Dei intuitiva*). Hence Schleiermacher also took his starting point in the subject, only not in intellect or will, but in feeling. For him God is the unity of the world, not an object of thought (for thinking always moves between opposites), to be enjoyed in feeling. And religion is the enjoyment of God in one's feelings. Schleiermacher, however, immediately connects this with the idea of community. From the heart of religion springs the desire for community, the yearning to exchange that which has been enjoyed. Religions differ as the infinite determines feeling differently and shapes the community differently. In his *The Christian Faith* the basic philosophical ideas are the same, but here feeling is further defined as absolute dependence, God is conceived as absolute causality, and Christianity is described as an ethical religion in which everything is related to redemption through Christ. Dogmas, therefore, are and remain descriptions of subjective states of consciousness, still of such subjective states as are determined by the Christian community and thus by the person of Christ. With these three ideas—the immediate consciousness of the self as the source of religion, the community as the necessary form of its existence, and the per-

son of Christ as the center of Christianity—Schleiermacher has exerted incalculable influence. All subsequent theology is dependent on him. Though no one
took over his dogmatics, he has made his influence felt on all theological orien-
tations—liberal, mediating, and confessional—and in all churches—Catholic,
Lutheran, and Reformed. Most closely akin to him are the so-called mediating
theologians: Nitzsche, Twesten, Neander, J. Müller, Rothe, Dorner, Martensen,
Schenkel, etc. What distinguishes all these men and what they all have in common is the subjective starting point. They all proceed, not from an external authority but from the feelings, from the religious consciousness. Initially they accept the truth as the content of subjective Christian experience. But they do not
stop there; they want to go beyond Schleiermacher, and to that end they combine Schleiermacher's subjective religious starting point with Hegelian speculation. The agnostic elements in Schleiermacher, which he shared with Kant,
were replaced by the Hegelian theory of the knowability of the absolute. Truth,
initially accepted as the content of religious experience, must then be understood in the way of speculation as conceptually necessary and legitimated before
the bar of philosophy. Thus, according to these theologians, faith and science,
the natural and the positive, church and culture, the authority of Scripture and
criticism, the ancient and the modern worldview, are reconciled and each of
these two alternatives is satisfied.

This had also been Hegel's goal. Hegel is the superlatively consistent idealist: in him the Cartesian premise finds its ultimate expression. Thinking
produces being; all being, accordingly, is logical, rational. But he unites this
idea with that of becoming, of evolution. The realization of the idea in being
occurs step by step, gradually. That kind of thinking achieves consciousness
in human beings first. But at the lowest stage, as natural, finite mind, man
feels separated from God. In religion, especially the Christian religion, that
separation is overcome: God and man are one. This unity of God and man,
though it is the essence of all religion, is not expressed in religion with perfect adequacy but is veiled in forms of pictorial representation and feeling.
Only in philosophy does the idea find commensurate expression in conceptual form and become absolute knowledge, humanity's knowledge of God,
God's knowledge of himself. Hegel attempted to explain all Christian dogmas (Trinity, incarnation, atonement, etc.) in terms of these philosophical
ideas. Many scholars believed in Hegel's reconciliation of theology and philosophy. The so-called right wing (Marheinecke, Daub, Göschel, Rosen-
kranz), while treating the dogmas along Hegelian lines, attempted to unite
Hegelian speculation with orthodox theology. But in time the danger lurk-
ing in Hegelian philosophy to the dogmas of Christianity became clear.
Feuerbach, Strauss, Vatke, and Bruno Bauer drew out the implications,
abandoning representation—the cloak of religion—and retaining only the
abstract idea. Strauss viewed the Gospel narratives as unconscious symbolic
condensations of ideal truth and held that the infinite pours itself out in the
finite, not, however, in the individual person but in humanity as a whole.

Humanity is the true son of God, the ideal Christ. In his *Glaubenslehre* (1840) he attempted to show that the history of every dogma is simultaneously its critique and dissolution. Since religion and philosophy differ in form, they also differ in content; philosophy replaces religion. Although the neo-Hegelians (Biedermann, Pfleiderer, etc.) became more cautious, they did take over from Hegel the theory that thinking is of a higher order than the religious consciousness and is therefore duty-bound to strip religious representation of its temporal sensuous husk, to represent its ideal essence, and to bring this essence into harmony with our entire worldview. One senses the same aim in the lectures held at Hamburg by the Protestant Society in 1902 and later published.[6]

While Hegel's philosophy thus led to the repudiation of Christianity, it became known—especially in the years following 1830—that Schelling gradually abandoned Hegel's system of identity [between philosophy and theology] and had developed a positive philosophy in which not necessity but freedom held sway and in which the will and the act took the place of the logical process. Just as a century earlier Hamann, Lavater, and others had done, so now Schelling gradually came to the conviction that there is another, deeper way of being and living than that of the logical intellect, viz., that of the will, of the deed, of freedom. But all living is becoming, an interplay of opposites. This is how it is in God and so it is in the world. At first there is in God only the dark ground of nature, then the intellect, and from these two the will is born. In the world there is first chaos, then spirit, thereupon the cosmos. Similarly, in religion there is first natural instinct in paganism, then the Word or the light in Christ, and finally God's being in all. With these ideas, under the influence of Böhme and Oetinger, Schelling combined an assortment of theosophical notions. Theosophy always occupies itself with two problems: the connection between God and the world and that between soul and body. The first problem is solved by seeking the ground of the world in the nature of God and by the idea that theogony, the trinitarian process in God, is more or less equated with or at least paralleled by cosmogony. God himself comes to the full development of his being only in and through the cosmic process. The second problem is similarly solved by the idea of spiritual corporeality. The spiritual—God, the soul—is not strictly incorporeal—though admittedly immaterial—but rather transmaterial, and so the Spirit's task in turn is to etherealize and spiritualize the body and the world, whose coarse materiality is the result of sin. This theosophic speculation of Schelling also found acceptance in theology: Baader, Görres, Windischmann, J. F. von Meyer, Steffens, Wagner, Stahlf, Rothe, Hamberger, Fr. Hoffmann, Koerl, Osiander, Lange, Delitzsch, Bähr, Kurtz, and Splittgerber have all to some degree been influenced by him.

6. *Christliche Glaubenslehren im Lichte der liberalen Theologie*, vorträge von J. W. Hintze usw. mit einer Einleitung von Curt Stage (Hamburg: 1903).

RESISTANCE AND REVISION OF LUTHERAN ORTHODOXY

[52] From the side of a churchly orthodoxy, there naturally arose resistance against these various minglings of theology and philosophy. After the theology of mediation, a theology of separation was bound to follow. The study of the church's confessions and the historical dogmatics of de Wette, Bretschneider, Hase, Schmid, and Schneckenburger, strengthened confessional consciousness. Old Lutherans, like Guericke and Rudelbach; neo-Lutherans, like Harms, Hengstenberg, Keil, Philippi, Vilmar, Kliefoth, Höfling, Thomasius, and Hofmann; and men of the positive Union, such as Kahnis, Luthardt, Zöckler, H. Schmidt, Frank, Grau, etc., all labored to restore the old Lutheran theology. Still, they too were children of their time. There is an afterglow of Pietism in men like Hengstenberg and Tholuck. Vilmar, Löhe, Münchmeyer, and others, were not free from Roman Catholic exaggeration in their view of church sacrament and office. South German theologians in Erlangen and Thomasius, as well as present-day positive theologians, adopted a more relaxed view of the confession and in important points—Christology, satisfaction, and Scripture—departed from the old Lutheran dogmatics. Even a Lutheran as orthodox as Philippi based his theology, like Hofmann and Frank, on the subjective religious consciousness and hence derived his starting point from Schleiermacher. The influence of the new ideas emerged even more conspicuously in the work of von Oettingen. In his *Lutherische Dogmatik* (2 vol., München, 1897–1902) he offers much that is excellent, fundamentally opposes the theology of Ritschl, and, rather than dualistically putting religious and scientific knowledge side by side, he connects the two very closely. Nevertheless, he regards faith—the Christ within us—as the noetic source of dogmatics, adopts a soteriological standpoint so that he regards all the *loci*—also that of God and the world—exclusively from this viewpoint, and allows his whole system, especially Christology, to be controlled by the idea of the self-limitation of God.

In recent years a mediating endeavor can be observed in a number of theologians. Although Schnedermann is a student of Frank, he nevertheless clearly shows leanings in the direction of the school of Ritschl.[7] He is driven by the desire to make the ancient evangelical truth fruitful for the requirements of the present. For that reason he heavily stresses the time-conditioned character of the New Testament, attempts to separate the gospel from its historical background, and pursues the aim of producing a "Germanized version of the Gospel." Similarly, Theodor Kaftan, superintendent of Schleswig, is attempting to construct a "modern theology of the ancient faith," and Reinhold Seeberg, supported in this especially by R. H. Grütz-

---

7. Georg Schnedermann, *Der Christliche Glaube im Sinne der gegenwärtigen evangelischen lutherischen Kirche*, 3 vols. (Leipzig: A. Deichert, 1899–1902). At present only three volumes have appeared: *Introduction, Doctrine of God, Doctrine of the World* and *Humanity.* Cf. his *Von dem Bestande unserer Gemeinschaft mit Gott durch Jesum Christum* (Leipzig: F. C. Hinrichs, 1888).

macher, is in search of a "modern positive Theology." What they are above all seeking is a reconciliation of two basic principles, principles that now stand in sharp conflict with each other in the terms *revelation* and *development*.[8] However, the lectures Seeberg gave to students on "the principal truths of the Christian religion" in the winter of 1901–2 were not too favorably received from the side of orthodoxy,[9] and it remains to be seen whether this "mediation" attempt will fare better than earlier ones. Of late W. Rohnert may be considered the purest representative of the old Lutheran dogmatic tradition. He is averse to any compromise with modern ideas and places himself squarely on the basis of the confession of the church.[10] Positioning themselves alongside of this moderately or rigorously confessional school of theology are the "biblical" theologians (Beck, K. J. Nitzsch, Kübel, Reiff, Gess, and in part Kähler), who wished to derive the truths of faith, not from the believing consciousness, nor from the confession of the church, but solely from Scripture itself. But Beck, the most prominent representative of this school, conceived Scripture in terms of the mystical theosophy practiced in Zwaben since the days of Oetinger and Michael Hahn. He saw Scripture as a system of heavenly truths, truths that were expressions of heavenly forces, which by the working of the Holy Spirit instilled them in the souls of men. As a result he often arrived at rather arbitrary exegesis and produced a system that, though profound and original, was not free of a one-sided asceticism and individualism.

Opposition to the mingling of philosophy and theology arose from still another side. In philosophy Liebmann, through his work *Kant und die Epigonen* (Stuttgart, 1865), and F. A. Lange in his *Geschichte des Materialismus* (1866), issued the slogan: "Back to Kant." The speculation of Hegel and Schelling had come to nothing. The intellect must again come to a realization of its own finitude and limitations and not presume to have knowledge of the supersensible. Alongside of it room must be reserved for faith or imagination. Reason is restricted to the sphere of sense perception. In dogmatics this neo-Kantianism was adopted by Lipsius and Ritschl—with an important difference between them. Lipsius acknowledges, while Ritschl denies, the mystical element in religion. Lipsius views religion as an independent power by itself, whereas Ritschl allows it to be virtually swallowed up by ethics. Lipsius regards religion as

---

8. Th. Kaftan, *Vier Kapitel von der Landeskirche* (Schleswig: J. Bergas, 1907); idem, *Moderne Theologie des alten Glaubens* (Schleswig: J. Bergas, 1905); R. Seeberg, *Grundwahrheiten der christliche Religion* (Leipzig: A. Deichert [Georg Böhme], 1903), translated into English as *The Fundamental Truths of the Christian Religion,* trans. G. E. Thomson and Clara Wallentin from the 4th rev. ed. (New York: G. P. Putnam's Sons, 1908); R. H. Grützmacher, *Studien zur systematische Theologie,* 3 vols. (Leipzig: A. Deichert, 1905–9); idem, *Modern-Positive Vorträge* (Leipzig: A. Deichert, 1906).

9. A. H. Cremer, *Die Grundwahrheiten der christlichen Religion nach Dr. R. Seeberg* (Gütersloh: Bertelsmann, 1903). Cf. similar judgments in the journal *Die Studierstube* (1905).

10. W. Rohnert, *Die Dogmatik der evangelischen lutherischen Kirche* (Braunschweig: H. Wollermann, 1902).

primarily a matter for the individual; Ritschl for the community. Lipsius still attempts in every case to reconcile religious notions with the results of science; Ritschl totally separates the domains of theology and science. For Lipsius the grace of God-in-Christ is the main content of revelation, but to Ritschl it is the kingdom established by Christ; and so forth. Both of them, however, concur with Kant's aversion to metaphysics and with his doctrine of the limits of the cognitive capacities of humanity. For that reason Ritschl seeks a complete separation between metaphysics (philosophy, science) and religion (theology). Religion and theology pronounce, not ontological, but value judgments. Religion does not say anything about the unknowable essence of things but only expresses the value and meaning they have to us. By a separation of this kind, Ritschl attempts to ensure for religion and theology a place that is inviolable by science. Religion is not supported by science but based on a unique *principle* of its own: the moral nature of humankind. It has a *content* of its own, viz., value judgments, i.e., purely religious-ethical statements, not ontological judgments. It has a *purpose* of its own, viz., to make human beings ethically independent of the world.

For a long time Ritschl's theology exerted much influence, not only in Germany but also far beyond its borders. This popularity had various causes. The apparent reconciliation of faith and knowledge, the religious-ethical view of religion, its alignment with the revelation of God-in-Christ, Holy Scripture, and the theology of Luther and Melanchthon, the rejection of all natural theology and scholastic dogmatics, etc., all contributed to the unexpected expansion and extraordinary vogue of this theology. Associating themselves with it were a large number of men, Herrmann, Kaftan, Häring, Harnack, Schürer, Gottschick, Kattenbusch, Stade, Wendt, Schultz, Lobstein, Reischle, O. Ritschl, Rade, etc., who applied its principles over the entire range of theological scholarship. Still, Ritschl's theory of the human capacity for knowing, the complete separation of theology and metaphysics, the moralistic view of religion, the restriction of religion to making value judgments, and so forth, is unsatisfactory. In the long run this school, too, failed to satisfy either the human intellect or heart.[11]

[53] In the school itself there gradually grew a split between a right wing and a left wing.[12] Ritschl's legacy was not a well-rounded system. It neglected to pronounce itself on many subjects and was not always equally clear in defining the relation between theology and metaphysics. As a result Ritschl's basic principle and method, though widely endorsed, permitted all kinds of differences about sin, the person and work of Christ, the Holy Spirit and his operations, prayer, mysticism, etc. So some of his followers took a more conservative tack, and others aligned themselves ever more closely with the theol-

---

11. Cf. H. Bavinck, "De Theologie van Albrecht Ritschl," *Theologische Studiën* 6 (1888): 369–403.

12. Cf. Gustav Ecke, *Die theologische Schule Albrecht Ritschl und die evangelische Kirche der Gegenwart,* 2 vols. (Berlin: Reuther & Reichard, 1897–1904).

ogy of the Protestant Society.[13] A difference arose specifically about the connection between theology and metaphysics. Herrmann sought to maintain to the end the separation between ontological and value judgments, between theoretical judgments and practical convictions, and was followed in this by Harnack, O. Ritschl, Reischel, Rade, and others.[14] Kaftan, on the other hand, saw with increasing clarity the impossibility of this separation and, at least formally, again sought points of contact in orthodox dogmatics and gained support for this from Kattenbusch, Häring, Wobbermin, and others.[15]

But this was not the end. In recent years an ever growing number of theologians turned their backs on Ritschl's intellectual orientation and school. Like Schleiermacher and Hegel, Ritschl still held to the *sui generis* character of religion and to the absoluteness of Christianity and even more firmly than Schleiermacher placed theology at the service of the church. Hence, generally speaking, he did not abandon the ecclesiastical, confessional, and reformational foundation of dogmatics. Schleiermacher, Hegel, and also Ritschl knew, of course, that at many points they departed from the church's confession and even from Scripture. Still, they all shared the singular characteristic that—in the name of a better understanding of the confession and Scripture, in the name of the authentic Luther, in the name of the pure original principles of the Reformation—they opposed the doctrine and practice then generally in vogue. Accordingly, they were all reformationally minded, holding broadly to the position of the mediating theology (*Vermittelungstheologie*) and sought to restore the original gospel as well as relating it to the entire culture. Ritschl, too, was caught up in this endeavor, though he tried to reach his goal in a different way than the old mediating theologians. The latter strove to reconcile faith and science by speculatively raising faith to the level of knowledge. But Ritschl, living under the impact of the exact sciences, which were supremely powerful in his day, and profoundly averse to all speculation and philosophy, sought refuge, with the aid of Kant and Comte, not in mediation, but in separation. If science and religion each strictly limited itself to its own domain, there could be no question of conflict.

But this separation of metaphysics and theology became the very first point of attack. Increasingly people began to see that such a separation was

13. Ed. note: The so-called *Protestantenverein* (founded in 1863) largely represented the liberal wing of the Lutheran Church and its aim to reconcile the church with modern ideas and to win back its estranged members.

14. W. Herrmann, *The Communion of the Christian with God,* trans. J. S. Stanyon, 2d ed., rev. R. Wallace Stewart (New York: G. P. Putnam's Sons, 1906); A. Harnack, *What Is Christianity?* (New York: G. P. Putnam's Sons, 1901; reprinted, Philadelphia: Fortress Press, 1986); Max Reischle, *Werturteile und Glaubensurteile* (Halle: Max Niemeyer, 1900).

15. Julius Kaftan, *Dogmatik* (Freiburg i.B.: J. C. B. Mohr, 1897); idem, *Zur Dogmatik* (Tübingen: J. C. B. Mohr [Paul Siebeck], 1904); Th. Häring, "Zur Verständigung in der systematischen Theologie," *ZThK* 9 (1899): 97–135; Georg Wobbermin, *Zwei akademische vorlesungen über grundprobleme der systematische Theologie* (Berlin: A. Duncker, 1899); idem, *Theologie und Metaphysik* (Berlin: A. Duncker, 1901).

not possible: ontological and value judgments (*Seins- und Werthurtheile*) cannot be dualistically put side by side.[16] Added to this was a second and more serious objection. The isolation in which Christianity (the person of Christ, special revelation, the faith of the church) had been placed by Ritschl had an arbitrary aprioristic character. Many younger theologians began to see that theology was in this way too isolated and reared upon an unstable and undemonstrable foundation. Proof for the unique place and absolute character of Christianity was solely derived from religious experience and hence subjective through and through. The most recent trend in theology therefore wishes to abandon this aprioristic standpoint, and it aspires to lay aside all prejudice in favor of Christianity. It then seeks to incorporate Christianity in the universal history of religion, treat it in accordance with the same method as all other religions, and accord to theology a rigorously scientific character by converting it into the science of religion.

These younger theologians, in pursuing this goal, increasingly appeal to Ritschl himself. What, after all, was the basic idea of his theology? It was, remember, that religion and science are two totally different things, which have nothing in common. Now then, this principle must be applied with greater consistency than was done by Ritschl himself. He, remember, stopped halfway, did not extend the lines of separation far enough, kept incorporating theoretical and scientific elements in religion, and therefore did not limit religion strictly enough to what it really is. For that reason Ritschl, too, was still partial and prejudiced. He still made exegesis and the history of dogma subservient to his system. He was still a dogmatician, and this dogmatism must be completely discarded. On the one hand, religion must be exclusively viewed for what it is—purely subjective piety, the inner experience of the soul—as Harnack has done in his *What is Christianity?* On the other hand, the whole theological enterprise (exegesis, history of dogma, dogmatics, etc.) must be made strictly scientific, freed from all prejudice, whether it is based on scriptural authority, ecclesiastical authority, or religious experience. This can only be to the advantage of religion. Actually Ritschl had too shallow a view of religion; he allowed it to be almost completely swallowed up by morality. But the essence of religion is mysticism, enthusiasm, something personal, mysterious, and intimate that lies hidden behind all forms of religion and emerges most clearly in prophets, visionar-

16. *Luthardt, *Zeitschrift für kirchliche Wissenschaft und kirchliche Leben* (1881): 621; Ludwig von Haug, *Darstellung und Beurtheilung der Ritschl'schen Theologie* (Stuttgart: D. G. Bundert, 1895), 75; Leonhard Stählin, *Kant, Lotze, Albrecht Ritschl* (Leipzig: Dörffling & Franke, 1884), 224; same title in English, *Kant, Lotze, and Ritschl: A Critical Examination* (Edinburgh: T. & T. Clarke, 1889); R. Wegener, "Kurze Darstellung und Kritik der philosophischen Grundlage der Ritschl-Herrmann'schen Theologie," *Jahrbuch für Prot. Theologie* 11/2 (1884): 221; Otto Pfleiderer, "Die Theologie Ritschl's," *Jahrbuch für Prot. Theologie* 16/1 (1889): 42–83 (ed. note: Bavinck's reference is to pp. 180ff.); A. L. Biedermann, *Christliche Dogmatik*, 2 vols. (Berlin: G. Reimer, 1884–85), I, 54; Theobald Ziegler, *Die geistigen und socialen Strömungen des neunzehnten Jahrhunderts* (Berlin: G. Bond, 1901), 482ff.; F. J. Schmidt, *Der Niedergang des Protestantismus* (Berlin: 1904), esp. 18–23.

ies, enthusiasts, and fanatics. Ritschl has done Schleiermacher an injustice, and this injustice needs to be corrected: the latter's concept of religion is much to be preferred over that of Ritschl.

If people could again view religion as Schleiermacher had done, it would reside securely in the depths of the human heart. It would then have nothing to fear from science. Theology, that is, the science of religion, would examine all religions freely and without prejudice, make a radical break with the dogmatic method, and in all its branches apply the method of the history of religions [German: *Religionsgeschichte;* Dutch: *godsdienstwetenschap*]. It would attempt, finally, by means of comparative criticism, to determine the place to which Christianity is entitled in the history of religions. Accordingly, Scripture may not as in the past be studied and used solely with a view to dogmatics but must be viewed historically and explained in terms of the milieu in which it originated.

The religion of Israel must be seen in the context of the religions of the surrounding nations, Babylonia, Assyria, Egypt, and Persia, etc. (Wellhausen, Duhm, Smend, Gunkel, Fr. Delitzsch, Zimmern, Wincler, Schürer, etc.). The New Testament, too, does not exist in isolation but forms a constituent part of ancient Christian literature (Krüger), nor is it distinguished, as Cremer asserted, by a language of its own (Deissmann). To understand the religion of Jesus, of the primitive church, of the apostles, especially that of Paul and John, the entire cultural history of the time has to be studied—not only the conceptions that occur in the official literature of Jews and pagans, but particularly the religious life, the religious moods, experiences, fantasies, visions, etc., as they are found among the people. If this method is followed, we will find that all the ideas in the New Testament on the person of Christ, his supernatural conception, his messiahship, his divine nature, his miracles, his resurrection, his ascension, and so forth (Bousset, Pfleiderer), on the kingdom of God (Weiss), on angelology and demonology (Everling), on the Holy Spirit and his operations (Gunkel, Weinel), on sin (Wrede), on baptism (Heikmüller), on communion, (Eichhorn), on redemption (Brüchner), on spirit and life (Sokolovski), on the Antichrist (Bousset), on the revelation of John (Gunkel, Vischer), etc., arose out of all sorts of Jewish and pagan elements. Then Christianity in its entirety is nothing other than "a syncretistic religion" (Gunkel).[17]

In the history of dogma, Harnack already began with the practice of relating the development of the Christian religion to the development of culture and to explain Christian dogma in terms of the Hellenization of Christianity. Scholars following his example now attempt to explain the development of church and

---

17. In addition to the works by the above-mentioned authors, which deal with specialized topics, the following can be consulted for a general acquaintance of the history-of-religions approach: Paul Wernle, *Die Anfänge unserer Religion,* 2d ed. (Tubingen: J. C. B. Mohr [Paul Siebeck], 1904), translated into English as *The Beginnings of Christianity* (New York: G. P. Putnam, 1903); Hermann Gunkel, *Zum religionsgeschichtlichen Verständnis des Neuen Testaments* (Göttingen: Vandenhoeck & Ruprecht, 1903); J. Weiss, "Heitmüller, 'Im Namen Jesu,'" *Theologische Rundschau* 6 (May 1904): 186ff.; Bousset, "Die Religionsgeschichte und das Neue Testament Theologie," *Theologische Rundschau* 6 (May 1904): 265–77, 311–18, 353–65.

dogma in terms of a wide range of pre- and post-Christian influences and to transform this development into an extended history of the Christian religion, which preceded and underlies the organized church and formulated dogma (Tischhäuser, Paul Drews, Jüngst, Schian, Sell, etc.). They are proposing to treat dogmatics in accordance with the same history-of-religions method. While no dogmatic handbook of this stripe has as yet seen the light of day, Ernst Troeltsch in Heidelberg has demonstrated with sufficient clarity the consequences to which the application of the history-of-religions method leads. It is therefore not surprising that theologians of every stripe have rejected this method and try to maintain the independence of religion as well as the absolute character of Christianity.[18] Not only are we deluded if we expect that Christianity can be deduced from all kinds of strange Jewish and pagan elements and understood as a syncretistic religion, but the history-of-religions method also entails the danger of wanting to see analogies everywhere, of placing them in some historical context, of constructing history in terms of preconceived evolutionistic ideas, and thus overlooking the particular and unique in every religion and in religious phenomena. This history-of-religions method is even less applicable in dogmatics. Certainly, the dogmatician has an obligation to be acquainted with and to take advantage of the illumination furnished by the history of religions. But this is something totally different from what the proponents of the history-of-religions method have in mind. They, after all, intend that the essence of religion and of Christianity, the place every religion occupies and the value to be accorded to it, should be determined and established solely by comparative historical research. This is a demand that cannot be realized. No one can or ought to rid himself of his faith, and this approach theoretically causes one to assume a highly partisan position with regard to Christianity because it decrees in advance that the Christian religion, contrary to its own witness, is one among many religions and constitutes a passing phase in the religious process of humankind. Accordingly, for dogmatics no other outcome can be expected from this method than that it will either terminate its existence or reduce it to a number of vague generalities, which do not benefit anyone.

18. Cf. Max Reischle, *Theologie und Religionsgeschichte* (Tübingen: J. C. B. Mohr [Paul Siebeck], 1904); Lemme, *Religionsgeschichtliche Entwicklung oder göttliche Offenbarung* (Karlsruhe, 1904); E. von Dobschütz, *Probleme des Apostolischen Zeitalters* (Leipzig: J. C. Hinrich's, 1904), pp. 126ff. Ed. note: See also E. von Dobschütz, *The Apostolic Age*, trans. F. L. Pogson (London: P. Green, 1909); Carl Clemen, *Die religionsgeschichtliche Methode in der Theologie* (Giessen: J. Ricker, 1904); Karl Girgensohn, *Die moderne historische Denkweise und die christliche Theologie* (Leipzig: A. Deichert, 1904); C. F. Georg Heinrici, *Dürfen wir noch Christen bleiben?* (Leipzig: Dürr, 1901); idem, *Theologie und Religionswissenschaft* (Leipzig: Dürr, 1902); L. Ihmels, *Die Selbständigkeit der Dogmatik gegenüber der Religionsphilosophie* (Erlangen: Deichert, 1901); idem, "Blicke in die neuere dogmatische Arbeit," *Neue Kirchl. Zeitschrift* 13 (July 1905): 505–22; Karl Beth, *Das Wesen des Christentums und die moderne historische Denkweise* (Leipzig: Deichert, 1904); F. W. Nösgen, "Die Religionsgeschichte und das Neue Testament," *Neue Kirchl. Zeitschrift* 12 (1904): 923–55; F. Kattenbusch, "Die Lage der systematischen Theologie in der Gegenwart," *ZThK* 15 (March 1905): 103–46; P. Biesterveld, *De jongste methode voor de verklaring van het Nieuwe Testament* (Kampen: Bos, 1905).

6

Reformed Dogmatics

*Though agreeing in many areas, Lutherans and Calvinists from the outset had important differences between them—geographically as well as theologically. At the heart of the theological difference was a difference in ultimate emphasis. The primary question asked by Lutherans was **anthropological:** "How can I be saved?" Works-righteousness was seen as the great departure from gospel truth. The Reformed, by contrast, sought to explore the foundations of salvation in the electing counsel of God and asked the **theological** question: "How is the glory of God advanced?" Avoiding idolatry is the major concern for the Reformed. Doctrines such as election, justification, regeneration, and sacraments were richer and more multifaceted among the various Reformed churches than in the Lutheran.*

Reformed theology begins with Zwingli, whose starting point in the radical dependence of humanity on a sovereign and gracious God was marred by vestiges of humanistic philosophical ideas. Calvin was a more systematic thinker, as well as a thoroughly biblical and practical theologian. Thanks to Calvin's influence, the Reformed faith spread from Switzerland to France, Germany, the Low Countries, and the British Isles. Though the English Reformation initially had a strong Reformed tone into the seventeenth century, Anglican lukewarmness led to the Puritan movement. It was in Scotland under the leadership of John Knox that Calvinism flourished. Though the Reformed theology of the palatinate (Heidelberg) did develop somewhat independently of Calvin himself, it is a mistake to accent theological differences with the Swiss Reformation.

In the seventeenth century, Reformed theologians such as Junius Zanchius and Polanus move away from Calvin's "biblical theology" to a more scholastic one paralleling the development of the Middle Ages. Reformed theology of this sort reached a terminus in such confessional statements as the Canons of Dordt (1618–19), the Westminster Confession and Catechism (1646), and the Helvetic Consensus (1675). However, direct challenges to the Reformed faith also developed. Rationalism, mysticism, subjectivism, Anabaptism, Socinianism, Arminianism, and Cartesianism reared their heads. An ally of the last-mentioned was the federalist theology of Johannes Cocceius (1603–69). In the Netherlands the scholastic theology of men such as G. Voetius was eclipsed by Cartesian and Cocceian theology. Departures from the Reformed faith were particularly striking at the French Academy at Saumur, where Moïse Amyraut introduced rationalist universalism into the church. The confusion over English

Puritans during the Civil War contributed to the growth of Baptist groups as well as deism. During the middle of the eighteenth century, Reformed theology everywhere declined as rationalism gained ground.

As we move into the nineteenth century, an evangelical renewal movement (the Réveil) competed with modernist theology for the soul of Reformed churches. Attempts such as that of the Parisian School represented by August Sabatier attempted to wed orthodoxy and rationalism. Here the influence of Wesleyan Methodism also deserves mention, as well as the Oxford Movement, which brought a number of Anglicans to the church of Rome. In all of this a high level of tolerance and a strong desire for church union was a serious challenge to nineteenth-century Calvinism. The same must be said for the growing influx of Darwinian evolution. Reformed theology was introduced to North America from many directions, including England, Scotland, France, Holland, and Germany. A distinction needs to be made here between the Puritan Calvinism, which took root in New England, and the Scottish Presbyterian Calvinism, which was imported into the southern and central states. Divergent streams include the Princeton "Old School" Presbyterians (Archibald Alexander, Charles Hodge, A. A. Hodge, Benjamin Warfield). In addition, a revivalist stream, continuing the spirit of the Great Awakening, as well as a modernist trend can be observed. Reformed Christianity is in crisis in America. There is no rosy future for Calvinism in America.

LUTHERANS AND CALVINISTS

[54] For all the agreement between them—extending even to the confession of predestination—there was from the very beginning an important difference between the German and the Swiss Reformation. The differences in country and people where Luther and Zwingli played out their respective roles, the differences between the two in origin, upbringing, character, and experience all contributed to a parting of their ways. It did not take long before it became evident that the two Reformers were of different minds. In 1529, at Marburg, an agreement had been made—but only on paper. And when Zwingli passed away and Calvin, despite his high regard for and conciliatory approach to Luther in the doctrine of the Lord's Supper, basically sided with Zwingli, the split between Lutheran and Reformed Protestantism deepened and became a fact that could no longer be undone. Historical researches into the characteristic difference between the two in recent years have clearly demonstrated that underlying the split is a difference of principle. In earlier times scholars tended simply to sum up the dogmatic differences without reducing them to a common principle.[1] Max Goebel, by contrast, was the first to produce a historical and fundamental explanation of the difference between the two.[2] Since then various people—Ullmann,

---

1. For example, Johannis Hoornbeek, *Summa Controversiarum Religionis* (Utrecht, 1653), 618.

2. Max Goebel, *Die religiöse Eigenthümlichkeit der lutherischen und der reformirten Kirche* (Bonn: Adoph Marcus, 1837).

Semisch, Hagenbach, Ebrard, Herzog, Schweizer, Baur, Schneckenburger, Guder, Schenkel, Schoeberlein, Stahl, Hundeshagen, to mention some— have continued that research.[3] The difference seems to be conveyed best by saying that the Reformed Christian thinks theologically, the Lutheran anthropologically. The Reformed person is not content with an exclusively historical stance but raises his sights to the idea, the eternal decree of God. By contrast the Lutheran takes his position in the midst of the history of redemption and feels no need to enter more deeply into the counsel of God. For the Reformed, therefore, election is the heart of the church; for Lutherans, justification is the article by which the church stands or falls. Among the former the primary question is: How is the glory of God advanced? Among the latter it is: How does a human get saved? The struggle of the former is above all against paganism—idolatry; that of the latter against Judaism—works-righteousness. The Reformed person does not rest until he has traced all things retrospectively to the divine decree, tracking down the "wherefore" of things, and has prospectively made all things subservient to the glory of God; the Lutheran is content with the "that" and enjoys the salvation in which he is, by faith, a participant. From this difference in principle, the dogmatic controversies between them (with respect to the image of God, original sin, the person of Christ, the order of salvation, the sacraments, church government, ethics, etc.) can be easily explained.

THE BEGINNINGS OF REFORMED THEOLOGY

It is much more difficult to describe the history of Reformed theology than that of Lutheran theology. The Reformed church is not limited to one country and nation but has expanded into various countries and nations. That which is typically Reformed has not been laid down in a single confession but found expression in numerous creeds. Dogmatic development, say, in the doctrine of election, justification, regeneration, the sacraments, etc., has been much richer and more multifaceted in the Reformed churches than in the Lutheran. And, finally, the history of Reformed theology has been much less studied than that of the other churches. A field of study still lies fallow here.

Reformed theology starts with Zwingli. In his work the basic ideas are already present—the theological starting point, the absolute dependence of humanity, predestination, the human nature of Christ, the spiritual conception of the church and sacraments, the ethical and political import of the Reformation. But there are still many lacunae in Zwingli's theology. As a re-

3. The works of these theologians are critically discussed by Heinrich Voigt, *Fundamentaldogmatik* (Gotha, F. A. Perthes, 1874), 307–480; cf. J. H. Scholten, *De Leer der Hervormde Kerk in hare Grondbeginselen,* 2d ed., 2 vols. (Leiden: P. Engels, 1861, 1862), II, 309ff.; Paul Lobstein, "Zum evangelischen Lebensideal in seiner lutherischen und reformierten Ausprägung," in *Collected Works: A Corpus of the Monographic Publications of Paul Lobstein (1850–1922),* 2 reels (Chicago: University of Chicago, 1977), reel 2; H. Hastie, *The Theology of the Reformed Church in Its Fundamental Principles* (Edinburgh: T. & T. Clark, 1904), 32–44, 129–77; F. Kattenbusch, "Protestantenverein," *PRE³,* XVI, 156.

sult of his humanism, he fails to plumb the depths of sin and the atonement; as a result of his spiritualism, he abstractly and dualistically construes God and man, divine and human justice, the sign and the thing signified in the sacrament, as opposites. Zwingli's clarity and lucidity of thought cannot compensate for the lack of depth. He never arrived at a somewhat well-rounded and coherent system. Zwingli laid down only the general contours within which various strains in the Reformed churches later unfolded. It took Calvin's organizational genius and systematic mind to give to the Swiss Reformation its clearly defined doctrine and stable organization. Calvin's theology had already assumed firm shape in the first edition of his *Institutes* (1536). There is expansion and development but no change. Calvin differs from Zwingli in that he banishes all philosophical and humanistic ideas and adheres as rigorously as possible to Scripture. Further, more successfully than Zwingli, he maintains the objectivity of the Christian religion, of the covenant of God, of the person and work of Christ, of Scripture, church, and sacrament, and is therefore in a stronger position to resist the Anabaptists. Moreover, he overcomes both Luther's antithesis between the spiritual and the secular and Zwingli's antithesis between flesh and spirit and therefore, though rigorist, is in no way an ascetic. Finally, he introduced unity and system in his thinking—something neither Luther nor Zwingli succeeded in doing—and nevertheless consistently maintained the connection with the Christian life. In time Calvin managed to win all of Switzerland for his views—even in the doctrine of the Lord's Supper (*Consensus Tigurinus,* 1549) and predestination (*Consensus Genev.,* 1552, *Second Helvetic Confession,* 1564).[4] Soon Calvin's *Institutes* were studied everywhere. Later the Bernese appealed to Calvin as much as the men of Geneva, Zürich, Basel, and Schaffhausen. In sixteenth-century Switzerland, theology was pursued completely along the lines of Calvin by Beza, *Tractationes theol.* (1570), Petrus Martyr Vermigli, *Loci Communes* (1576), Musculus, *Loci Comm.* (1560, 1567) and Aretius, *Theol. problemata* (1579).

From Switzerland Calvin's theology spread to France. With a long preface he dedicated his *Institutes* to King Francis I in 1536 and became the soul of the French Reformation. His teachings were generally accepted and his works translated into French and distributed far and wide. People sought advice and comfort from him, and many went to Geneva to be trained for the ministry of the Word. The most prominent theologians in France in this century were: Chandieu (d. 1591), who under the pseudonyms Sadeel and Zameriel wrote a number of theological treatises, *de verbo Dei de Christi sacerdotio, de remissione peccatorum,* etc.; Marlorat (d. 1562), author of *Thesaurus S. Scripturae in locos comm. rerum et dogmatum,* published in 1574 by Feugueraeus; and du Plessis Mornay (d. 1623), known for his *Traité de l'Eg-*

---

4. Karl B. Hundeshagen, *Die Conflikte des Zwinglianismus, Lutherthums und Calvinismus in der bernischen Landeskirche von 1532–1558* (Bern: C. A. Jenni, Sohn, 1842).

lise 1578, *Traité de la vérité de la religion chrétienne* (1581), and particularly for his *Le mystère d'iniquité c'est à dire l'histoire de la papauté* (1611) (egregiously inaccurate in its quotations).

By way of refugees to Ost Friesland, the Palatinate, Kleefsland, and Geneva, and through the personal influence of Calvin himself, Calvinism penetrated the Netherlands long before the second half of the sixteenth century.[5] Already in 1560 Calvin's *Institutes* was translated into Dutch. Peter Dathenus, Guy de Brès, Moded, Marnix, Caspar Heydanus, and others, were strict Calvinists. Many of them pursued their training in Geneva and Heidelberg. But as early as 1575 the academy at Leiden was founded, followed by that of Franeker in 1585. At Leiden Feugueraeus, Danaeus, Saravia, Trelcatius Sr., Bastingius, and Junius and at Franeker Lubbertus, Lydius, and Nerdenus were the most famous professors in this century. Theological activity consisted primarily in polemics against Rome and the Anabaptists. Still, even then a number of dogmatic handbooks saw the light of day: Gellius Snecanus, *Methodica descriptio et fundamentum trium locorum communium S. Scr.* (1584), Bastingius, the first Exposition of the *Catechism* (1590), Feugueraeus *Propheticae et apostolicae, i.e. totius divinae et canonicae Scripturae thesaurus* 1574, Trelcatius Sr. *Loci Communes* (1587), Junius, *Theses Theologiace* (*Opera Omnia* I, 1592ff.).

Calvinism also found acceptance in England and Scotland. There it became involved not only in conflict with Roman Catholicism but also with the reformation undertaken from the top by King Henry VIII and Queen Elizabeth. Reformation-minded men, who under the reign of Queen Mary fled to the continent, here encountered the teachings of Calvin (Bullinger, Beza, Martyr, etc.) and upon their return were troubled by the half-heartedness of the English Reformation. The dispute first concerned the ecclesiastical ceremonies. In doctrine Puritans and Anglicans were originally in agreement. Up until the beginning of the seventeenth century, English theology was decidedly Calvinistic. Calvin's *Institutes* was taught at the universities. Even episcopacy was defended by Cranmer, Jewel, Hooker, and others, not as the only true form of church government but solely in the interest of the well-being of the church.[6] But when during and after 1567 the Nonconformists seceded, among whom Pilkington, Whittingham, Thomas Sampson, and Humphrey of Oxford were the most important, the conflict concerning the whole polity of the church spread. The most vigorous advocate of the Presbyterian form of church organization was Thomas Cartwright, professor at Cambridge (deposed 1570, died 1603). Added to this toward the end of the century was the controversy over doctrine. William Perkins (d. 1602) and William Whitaker (d. 1595), professors at Cambridge, still attempted to maintain predestination in the nine Lambeth articles.[7] They pro-

5. F. L. Rutgers, *Calvijns invloed op de Reformatie in de Nederlanden, voor zooveel die door hemzelven is uitgeoefend* (Leiden: D. Donner, 1899).

6. Philip Schaff, *Creeds of Christendom*, 3 vols. (New York: Harper, 1881), I, 602ff.

7. Schaff, *Creeds of Christendom*, I, 658; III, 523.

posed this to Elizabeth's councillor Whitgift, but High Church and Pelagian sentiments increasingly gained the upperhand. In Scotland, however, Calvinism was introduced with vigor by John Knox (d. 1572) and John Craig (d. 1600) and finally recognized also by the king in 1581.

In Germany the Reformed church and Reformed theology were less dependent on Calvin. In many respects the Heidelberg Catechism, the theology of Pareus, Ursinus, Olevianus, Hyperius, and Boquinus, as well as that of à Lasco, exhibits a character of its own. Hofstede De Groot, Ebrard, and Heppe have explained this peculiarity in terms of Melanchthon's influence, but this notion is unhistorical and has been adequately refuted. Professor Gooszen, in his two studies on the *Heidelberg Catechism* (1890 and 1893), and Dr. Van't Hooft, in his *De Theologie van Heinrich Bullinger* (1888), have more persuasively explained it in terms of Zwingli's successor in Zürich. Still, between the theology of Calvin and that of Bullinger there is not a single material difference, only a formal and methodological one. It is the difference between supralapsarianism and infralapsarianism, between a strictly theological and a federalist starting point, a difference that has always existed in the Reformed churches and been recognized by both sides as Reformed. People mistakenly oppose to each other the positions that have always existed side by side and become antithetical only by very one-sided overstatement.[8] Accordingly, in Heidelberg the strict Calvinist Zanchius worked alongside of Ursinus and Olevianus.

REFORMED SCHOLASTICISM

[55] The scholastic method already surfaced in Reformed theology toward the end of the sixteenth century. In time people lost interest in the simple treatment of dogma as we find it in Calvin, Hyperius, and Sohnius. In Martyr, Sadeel, and Junius we already encounter familiarity with the questions treated in the Middle Ages by the scholastics. Especially Zanchius (d. 1590), in his works *De tribus Elohim, de natura Dei, de operibus Dei, de incarnatione* (*Opera Omnia* in 8 tomes, Geneva, 1619), and Polanus a Polansdorf (d. 1610) in his *Syntagma Theologiae*, prove to be very well acquainted with the theology of the church fathers and the scholastics. After that, dogmatics was treated scholastically in the Reformed churches in this century—in the Netherlands by Trelcatius Jr., *Scholastica et methodica locorum omnium S. Scr. institutio* (1604), Nerdenus, *Systema theol.* (1611), Maccovius, *Collegia theologica* (1623, ed. 3a 1641), *Loci Comm. Theol.* (1626), Fr. Gomarus, *Opera theol. omnia* (Amstel. 1664), Gisb. Voetius, *Disputationes sel.* 5 parts (Utrecht, 1648–59), and elsewhere especially by H. J. Alsted, professor at Herborn and Weissenburg (d. 1638), in his *Theol. scholastica didactica, exhibens locos communes theol. methodo scholastica* (1618). The scholastic method was far from

---

8. Rutgers, *Calvijns invloed,* 32; cf. H. Bavinck, "Calvinistisch en Gereformeerd," *Vrije Kerk* 19 (February 1893): 49–71, and the reply by Prof. Gooszen in *Geloof en Vrijheid* (December 1894).

being endorsed by everybody, however. At the Synod of Dordt, Maccovius was expressly admonished to consult with the Holy Spirit, not with Bellarmine or Suarez.[9] Maccovius's dispute with Lubbertus and Ames,[10] and that of Maresius with Voetius, was rooted in the same scholastic method. Maresius called Voetius a "theologian of paradoxes," counting no fewer than 600 paradoxes in his theology, and accused him in particular of "diverting the filthy lake of the scholastics into the [pure] fountain of Siloam."[11] But even in places where people were on their guard against philosophical terminology, scholastic distinctions, and futile academic questions and presented the truth in a simpler form, the seventeenth century was still the century of objectivity. The material was ready-made and needed only to be ordered. Tradition became a force to be reckoned with. Not only Scripture, but also the creed, indeed even the dogmatic treatment of dogma, acquired an aura of inviolable authority, causing Camero to utter the lament that in doctrine one could not disagree with those who "were reputed to be pillars"[12] (Gal. 2:9) without being persecuted. The most important theologians in the Netherlands were Polyander, Walaeus, Thysius and Rivet (the authors of the *Synopsis Purioris theologiae*), Trigland, Hoornbeek at Leiden; Maccovius, Acronius, Ames, Schotanus, Bogerman, Cloppenburg, Arnold at Franeker; Ravensperger, Gomarus, H. Alting, Maresius at Groningen; Voetius, Essenius, Mastricht, Leydecker at Utrecht; further Bucanus at Lausanne; Wollebius at Basel; Danaeus, Francis Turretin, B. Pictet at Geneva; J. H. Heidegger and J. H. Hottinger at Zürich; Chamier, Bérault, Garissoles at Montauban; Tilenus, Dumoulin, Beaulieu at Sedan; also Benj. Basnage, David Blondel, Sam. Bochartus, Jean Mestrezat, Charles Drelincourt, Jean Daillé, and especially the theologians at Saumur: Camero, Amyraldus, Cappellus, and Placaeus.

In England, the High Church and Arminian strains gained influence in the seventeenth century. They received support from the Stuarts, the archbishops, and the nobility, and were promoted by Bancroft (Whitgift's successor as archbishop of Canterbury [1604–10], who in a sermon preached in 1589 defended the episcopacy as necessary), as well as by Buckingham (1625–28), Archbishop Laud (1628–45), and Lord Clarendom (d. 1674). Opposed to them were still many theologians in the Church of England who, while defending episcopalianism, nevertheless remained faithful to Calvinism. This was true of Whitgift, archbishop of Canterbury (1583–1604) and counsellor to queen Elizabeth; Archbishop Abbot (1604–33, who in 1622 fell into disfavor); the delegates to

9. J. Heringa, "De twistzaak van Johannes Maccovius," *Archief voor kerkelijke geschiedenis* 3 (1831): 505–664; A. Kuyper Jr., *Johannes Maccovius* (Leiden: D. Donner, 1899), 82ff.

10. Heringa, "De twistzaak van Maccovius," 643; H. E. Van der Tuuk, *Johannes Bogerman* (Groningen: Wolters, 1868), 229ff.; H. Visscher, *Guilielmus Amesius: Zijn leven en werken* (Haarlem: J. M. Stap, 1894), 125ff.; A. Kuyper, Jr., *Johannes Maccovius*, 315ff.

11. S. Maresius, *Theologus paradoxus retectus et refutatus* (1649); cf. G. Voetius's reply, *Selectarum Disputationum theologicarum Pars. I–V* (Utrecht, 1648–69), V, 572–716.

12. Alexander Schweizer, *Die protestantischen Centraldogmen in ihrer entwicklung innerhalb der reformirten kirche,* 2 vols. (Zürich: Orell, Fuessli, 1854, 1856), II, 237.

the Synod of Dordt: Carleton, Hall, and Davenant (professor at Cambridge, later bishop of Salisbury and the author of *Determinationes quaestionum quarundam theologicarum* [Cambridge, 1634]). Others include Ward, Goad, Balcanqual, Burton, Warton, Prynne, Rouse, Preston, Usher (*Corpus theologiae*[13] [Dublin, 1638]), Morton, Joh. Prideaux (*Lectiones theologicae, Scholasticae theologiae syntagma* [1651]), Saunderson, Hammond, Westfield, Stillingfleet (1709), Tillotson (archbishop of Canterbury), John Pearson (*Exposition of the Creed* [1659], *Lectiones de Deo et ejus attributis*), Burnet (d. 1715, professor at Glasgow, later bishop of Salisbury, *An Exposition of the 39 Articles*), Roger Boyle (*Summa theologiae christ.* [Dublin, 1687]), J. Forbesius a Corse (professor at Aberdeen, *Instructiones histor. theol. de doctrina christ.* [1699]), Thomas Pierce (*Pacificatorium orthodoxae ecclesiae corpusculum* [1685]), Foggius (*Theol. speculativae schema* [1712]), W. Beveridge (*Thesaurus theo. or a Complete System of Divinity* [London, 1710–11]), Th. Bennet (*Instructions for Studying [1] A General System or Body of Divinity, [2] The 39 Articles of Religion* [London, 1715]). Puritans of this period who gained strong recognition were Bradshaw, Baynolds, Baynes, Byfield, Rogers, Hooker, White, Archer, Hildersham, Davenport, Lightfoot, Seldenus, Twissus, Calamy, Gataker, Baxter, Bates, Mead, Owen, etc.

Arminianism had great influence in England among dissenters as well as Anglicans. Alongside of it, brought over to England from France, was Amyraldianism. The two strains often flowed together and found common ground in the neonomian theory, which occasioned important and longlasting conflict. The neonomian located the ground of justification in faith, as did, for example, the Arminian John Goodwin, Milton's friend, in his *The Banner of Justification Displayed, Imputatio fidei,* (1642); Richard Baxter, *Justifying Righteousness;* Dr. Dan. Williams, *Works* (1750); and Benjamin Woodbridge, *The Method of Grace in the Justification of Sinners* (1656). In the opposing camp were others—incorrectly called antinomians; they actually should have been named antineonomians—who located the ground of justification exclusively in the imputed righteousness of Christ. These included such as Dr. Crisp; Dr. Tully, *Justificatio paulina sine operibus* (1677); Isaac Chauncy, *Neonomianism unmasked* (1692), *Alexipharmacon, a Fresh Antidote against Neonomian Bane* (1700); John Eaton, *The Honeycombe of Free Justification by Christ Alone* (1642); William Eyre, *Vindiciae justificationis gratuitae* (1654); and others.[14] In general, however, the center of gravity in English theology lay, not in dogmatic, but in biblical, church-historical, patristic, archeological, and practical studies, studies to which the political and ecclesiastical situation naturally gave rise.[15]

13. Dutch translation by Ruytingius, *'t Lichaam der Goddelyke Leer* (Amsterdam, 1656).

14. Cf. H. Witsius, *Misc. Sacra,* II, 753ff.; James Buchanan, *The Doctrine of Justification* (Edinburgh: Clark, 1867), 176, 464; W. Gass, *Geschichte der protestanischen Dogmatik,* 4 vols. (Berlin: G. Reimer, 1854–67), II, 324; III, 311.

15. Gass, *Geschichte,* III, 297ff.; *A. Ypey, *Beknopte letterk gesch der syst Godgeleerdheid* (1793–98), II, 268f. In general about this period see further: Hermann Weingarten, *Die Revolutionskirchen Englands*

The dogmatic life in Scotland, by comparison, was richer and more vigorous. Here Calvinism had found receptive soil and was further developed along rigorous, positive lines. The most prominent theologians in this period were: Rollock, principal of the university of Edinburgh from 1583 on, author of commentaries on the letters of Paul, the Psalms, and Daniel, and—especially— of a treatise on the effectual calling; John Welsh of Ayr, who wrote gainst Romanism; John Sharp, who published a harmony of the prophets and apostles; the brothers Simpson: Patrick, who wrote a history of the church, and William, who wrote on Hebrew stress marks, and Archibald, who furnished an exposition of the seven penitential psalms. The following also need to be mentioned: Boyd of Trochrigg, professor at Saumur, principal of the university of Glasgow, famous for his commentary on the letter to the Ephesians, which is not only an interpretation but a veritable thesaurus containing numerous dogmatic and theological excursus on the Trinity, predestination, incarnation, sin, baptism, etc.; David Calderwood, who spent time in the Netherlands and wrote his *Altare damascenum* against the Anglican episcopacy; Samuel Rutherford, professor at Saint Andrews, famous not only for his letters but also for many other works, *Exercitationes apol. pro divina gratia* (1637), *de Providentia, Examen Arminianismi, The Spiritual Antichrist,* etc.; George Gillispie, author of *Nihil respondes, Male audis, Aaron's Rod blossoming, Miscellanies;* and further Baillie, Dickson, Durham, Dr. Strang, James Wood, Patrick Gillespie, and Hugh Binning.[16] This positive development of Reformed dogmatics in a sense reached its zenith and at the same time its terminus in the Canons of Dordt (1618–19), in the Westminster Confession and Catechism (1646), in the Consensus Helveticus (1675), and in the Walcherse Articles (1693).

CHALLENGES: RATIONALISM AND MYSTICISM

[56] Already in the seventeenth century, however, the principles were present that undermined Reformed theology and brought about its decline. In the century of the Reformation, there was not only a Lutheran and Calvin-

---

(Leipzig: Breitkopf und Härtel, 1868); Daniel Neal, *The History of the Puritans or Protestant Non-conformists* (London: J. Buckland, 1754); J. B. Marsden, *The History of the Early Puritans: From the Reformation to the Opening of the Civil War in 1642* (London: Hamilton, Adams & Co., 1853); idem, *The History of the Later Puritans: From the Opening of the Civil War in 1642, to the Ejection of the Non-conforming Clergy in 1662* (London: Hamilton, Adams & Co., 1854); J. Gregory, *Puritanism in the Old World and in the New* (London: J. Clarke, 1895); E. H. Byington, *The Puritan in England and New England,* with an introduction by A. McKenzie (London: Sampson Low, Marston, 1896); John Stoughton, *History of Religion in England from the Opening of the Long Parliament to 1850,* 8 vols. (London, Hodder and Stoughton: 1881–84); John Tulloch, *Rational Theology and Christian Philosophy in England in the Seventeenth Century,* 2 vols. (Edinburgh: W. Blackwood, 1872); F. Kattenbusch, "Anglikanische Kirche," *PRE³,* I, 525–47; idem, "Puritaner," *PRE³,* XVI, 323–48.

16. Cf. James Walker, *The Theology and Theologians of Scotland* (Edinburgh: Clark, 1872); Henry T. Buckle, *History of Civilization in England,* 2 vols. (New York: D. Appleton & Co., 1861, 1862), II, chaps. 17–20.

istic version of it but, alongside of these, other parties. The humanists opposed the Church of Rome and its theology, not from a religious-ethical perspective but solely from an intellectual and aesthetic starting point. For that reason the humanists viewed the revival of Greek and Roman culture as a means to the harmonius development of humanity. In addition, two other parties made their appearance: the Anabaptists and the Socinians, who at all times exerted great influence especially in the Reformed churches and Reformed theology in Switzerland, the Netherlands, England, and America. They represent the mystical and the rational element in religion and theology. Socianism remains caught up in the Catholic separation of nature and grace and develops it into an antithesis in which nature in the end completely banishes grace. From all eternity matter stands alongside of and over against God. Man, being of the earth, and therefore earthly, has nothing in common with God except dominion, power, and free will, but not knowledge, righteousness, or life. He is by nature mortal. Accordingly, Christ, who received extraordinary revelations by being caught up into heaven, was solely a prophet who sealed his teaching by his death and by his resurrection acquired immortality. As king and priest, which he became only as a result of his ascension into heaven, he bestows this immortality on all who serve him in faith, trust, and obedience, while the others at some time cease to exist.[17] Anabaptism proceeds from the same basic idea: the natural and the supernatural, the human and the divine, stand irreconcilably side by side. But whereas Socinianism abandons grace in favor of nature, Anabaptism sacrifices nature to grace. Adam was "of the earth earthly" (1 Cor. 15:47); creation and all of nature is of a lower order: material, physical, carnal, impure. Christ, however, brings with him from heaven another, higher human nature. In regeneration he infuses a new substance into human beings and thereby makes them into different people who are no longer allowed to maintain any fellowship with unbelievers, the world, the state, and so forth.[18] Both of these strains tend to foster subjectivism, a break with authority, and human autonomy. In the Nether-

17. *Catechismus Racoviensis* (1609); *Bibliotheca fratrum Polonarum,* 6 vols. (Irenopoli: 1656); F. Trechsel, *Die protestantischen Antitrinitarier vor Faustus Socin,* 2 vols. (Heidelberg, K. Winter, 1839, 1844); O. Fock, *Der Socinianismus* (Kiel: C. Schröder, 1847); idem, with J. J. Herzog, "Socin und der Socinianismus," *PRE²,* XIV, 376–401; A. Harnack, *History of Dogma,* III, 137–67; M. Schneckenburger, *Vorlesungen über die Lehrbegriffe der kleineren protestantischen Kirchenparteien* (Frankfurt: H. L. Brönner, 1863).

18. For early literature on Anabaptism, see J. G. Walch, *Bibliotheca theologica selecta litterariis adnotationibus instructa* (Ienae, 1757), II, 13–29; more recently see J. Scholten, *De leer der Hervormde Kerk,* II, 271ff. The literature on Anabaptism continues to grow significantly: Max Goebel, *Geschichte des christlichen Lebens in der rheinisch-westphälischen Evangelischen Kirche,* 3 vols. (Coblenz: K. Bädeker, 1849–60), I, 134ff.; A. Ritschl, *Geschichte des Pietismus,* 3 vols. (Bonn: A. Marcus, 1880–86), I, 22ff.; L. Keller, *Geschichte der Wiedertäufer und ihres Reichs zu Münster* (Münster: Coppenrath, 1880); idem, *Die Reformation und die älteren Reformparteien in ihrem Zusammenhange* (Leipzig: S. Hirzel, 1885); C. Sepp, *Geschiedkundige nasporingen* (Leiden, De Breuk & Smits, 1872–75); idem, *Kerkhistorische studiën* (Leiden: E. J. Brill, 1885); J. H. Maronier, *Het inwendig woord* (Amsterdam: Tj. van Holkema, 1890); Rudulph Hofman, "Baptisten," *PRE³,* II, 285–93; S. Cramer, "Menno Simons," *PRE³,* XII, 586–94; idem, "Mennoniteten," *PRE³,* XII, 594–616.

lands this first clearly manifested itself in Arminianism, which had its sixteenth-century precursors in Coolhaes, Coornhert, Wiggers and others. It was akin to Socinianism and in the early seventeenth century systematically opposed the confession of God's absolute sovereignty at five points: predestination, atonement, human depravity, conversion, and perseverance.[19]

In the domain of philosophy, this intellectual trend expressed itself in Cartesianism. In principle Cartesianism was a complete emancipation from all authority and objectivity and an attempt, epistemologically, to build the entire cosmos from within the subject, out of his thinking: "I think, therefore I am; therefore the world exists; therefore God is." The repudiation of all tradition and the seeming certainty of the mathematical method, by means of which Descartes concluded to the existence of the world, of God, and of the mind, was pleasing to many people. He won many adherents, also among theologians. Renerius and Regius in Utrecht, Raey, Heerebord, A. Heydanus in Leiden, as well as Roell, Bekker, John Van de Waeyen, Hautecour, and Andala all adopted Cartesianism and introduced rationalism into the church. The relation between reason and revelation now became the most crucial issue. Reason emancipated itself from revelation and attempted to regain its independence. Added to this was the theology of Johannes Cocceius (1603–69), which in method was in fact akin to Cartesianism. Cocceianism was also a reaction against traditional theology and at an early date—toward the end of the century—entered into an alliance with Cartesianism. The new feature in Cocceius as is generally recognized today was not his covenant doctrine, for this already occurs in Zwingli, Bullinger, Olevianus, etc., and in the Netherlands in Snecanus, Gomarus, Trelcatius, Cloppenburg, and others. What was different was his federalist method. Cocceius's *Summa doctrinae de foedere et testamento* (1648) was a dogmatics along biblical-historical lines. It made Scripture not only the primary principle and norm but also the object of dogmatics and thus advanced a theology of Scripture against the theology that had been handed down, the covenant (*foedus*) against the decree, history against the idea, the anthropological against the theological method. The danger of this method consisted in the fact that it drew that which is eternal and immutable (*substantia foederis*) down into the stream of the temporal and historical (*oeconomia foederis*) and thus transferred the notion of becoming to God himself.

Nevertheless, many theologians—Heydanus, Wittichius Momma, Burman, Braun, Van der Waeyen, Witsius, Camp, Vitringa, S. van Til, John d'Outrain, F. A. Lampe, and others—followed the Coccceian method.[20] The controversy between the followers of Voetius and Cocceius, and later that

---

19. Arminian teaching can be gathered from the following: the *Remontrance* of 1610, submitted to the States; the Acts of the *Collatio Hagensis* (1611); the *Confessio* and the *Apologia pro Confessione* drafted by Episcopius (*Opera*, II, 69ff., 95ff.). It can also be gathered from the *Works* of Arminius, *Opera Theologica Francof* (1631); J. Uytenbogaert, *Onderwijzing in de Christelijke Religie* (1640); Episcopius, *Inst.-theol.* (*Opera*, I, 11ff.); Limborch, *Theol. Christ.*, ed. 5a (1730); Curcellaeus *Opera theol.* (Amsterdam, 1675).

20. Diestel, "Studien zur Foederal Theologie," *Jahrbuch für deutsche Theologie* (1865), part II.

between the green and the dry, the flexible and the rigid Cocceians, lasted till deep into the eighteenth century.[21] Actually it ended with a victory for Cocceianism and Cartesianism. Scholasticism had had its day; the time when Aristotelian philosophy flourished was past. Most academic chairs were now occupied by Cocceians. The arrival of Lampe at Utrecht (1720) was a victory for the Cocceians. The dogmatic handbooks that now came out were mostly Cocceian in outlook: Melchior, *Systema* (1685); C. Virtringa, *Korte Grandstellingen der Godgeberdheid* [*The Basics of Theology Briefly Stated*] (1688); S. Van Til (1704); T. H. VandeHonert, *Waeragtige Wegen Gods* [*The True Ways of God*] (1706); Ravestein (1716); J. Van de Honert (1735); etc. In the main they are still orthodox, avoid all scholastics, and diverge at many points from the old view. Doubt now arises concerning a particular atonement, election, the generation of the Son (Roell), the Trinity (P. Maty), the covenant of works (Alting, Vlak, Bekker, etc.), reason and revelation (Roell). Voetians were increasingly forced to retreat and withdrew into silence. Marck's *Merch* [*Marrow*] (1686), and Brakel's *Redelijke Godsdienst* [*Reasonable Religion*] (1700) were the last dogmatics to be written along Voetian lines but were already devoid of the vigor of the earlier ones. Owing to the influence of men like Lodenstein, Labadie, Koelman, Lampe, Verschoor, Schortinghuis, Eswijler, Antoinette de Bourignon, etc., Pietist, Labadist, and antinomian ideas penetrated into their circles as well.

In all Reformed churches the development of theology was similar. In France the academy at Saumur became the center of a range of startling theses. John Cameron (d. 1625) not only joined Piscator in Herborn in denying the imputation of Christ's active obedience but also taught that the will always follows the intellect and therefore that the bending of the will in regeneration is not a physical act but an ethical one.[22] Amyrald (d. 1664), author of *Traite de la Predestination,* turned the common doctrine of the revealed will of God (*voluntas signi*), the sincere and well-meant offer of grace, into a separate decree that precedes that of election. In doing this he laid a Remonstrant foundation under the Calvinist building and ran the danger of weakening man's powerlessness to believe into a moral one. In his work *The Mystery of Punctuation Revealed* (*Arcanum punctuationis revelatum*), anonymously published at Leiden by Erpenius, Louis Cappel (d. 1658) asserted that with respect to their configuration (*quoad figuram*) Hebrew vowel pointings had

---

21. Ed. note: Gisbert Voetius (1589–1676) was the noted defender of Reformed orthodoxy (and piety) against Arminian and Cocceian theology, both of which he and his followers regarded as too anthropocentric and insufficiently theocentric. A major battle ensued in the Dutch Reformed Church between the two groups concerning the appointment of professors to the Dutch University theology faculties. Voetians tend to favor the philosophical tradition of Aristotle; the Cocceians the philosophy of Descartes.

22. Gaston Bonet-Maury, "Jean Cameron," in *Etudes de théologie et d'histoire,* by the Protestant theological faculty of Paris honoring the theological faculty of Montaubon on the occasion of the tricentennial of its founding (Paris: Fischbacher, 1901), 79–117.

been invented later and inserted into the text by Jewish scholars, a view that evoked contradiction from Buxtorf (1648). In his *Critica sacra* (1650) Cappel taught that the Hebrew text was not corrupted, and in his *Diatribe de veris et antiquis Hebraeorum literis* (1645) that the Samaritan script was older than the block script of the Hebrews. In *The State of fallen Man before Grace* (*de statu hominio lapsi ante gratiam* [1640]), Placaeus denied the immediate imputation of Adam's sin. Claude Pajon (d. 1685) denied the necessity of internal grace and was opposed by Jurieu in his treatise on *Nature and Grace* (*Traité de la nature et de la grace* [1687]). In France, therefore, the theological struggle especially concerned the nature of subjective grace.[23] Cameron restricted it to the illumination of the intellect, Amyrald made objective grace universal, and Pajon taught that special subjective grace was superfluous. All this prepared the way for deism and rationalism.

In England there was great diversity among the Nonconformists. After the Westminster Assembly, Presbyterians shrank in numbers and declined in influence and had to make way for the Independentism that was embraced already in the sixteenth century by Robert Browne, Johnson, Ainsworth, and John Robinson (d. 1625).[24] Independentism increased in power and prestige during the Civil War. At the Westminster Assembly, Presbyterians still had the majority and Independents commanded only a few voices: Thomas Goodwin (d. 1680), Philip Nye (d. 1672), Jeremias Burroughs (d. 1646), William Bridge (d. 1670), William Carter (d. 1658), Sydrach Simpson (d. 1658), Joseph Caryll (d. 1673), and others. But already present at a meeting in London held October 12, 1658, there were representatives from more than a hundred independent churches. There the *Savoy Declaration* was drawn up; it was translated into Latin by Hoornbeek in 1659 and printed in the back of his *Epistola ad Duraeum de Independentismo*.[25] Their most prominent theologian was John Owen (1616–83), of whose works an edition was published in London (1826) in 21 volumes. Milton's *Treatise on Christian Doctrine* was published at Cambridge in 1825.[26]

Baptist belief occurred sporadically in England as early as the sixteenth century but did not establish its own congregations till 1633. In 1644 Baptists numbered seven congregations inside London and forty-seven outside that city. In 1677 Baptists issued a *Confession of Faith* that differed from the Westminster Confession and the Savoy Declaration only in church government and baptism. On the basis of this confession William Collins, in 1693, drew up a catechism that found general acceptance. The General, Arminian,

23. Cf. A. Schweizer, *Die protestantischen centraldogmen*, II.

24. Cf. concerning Robinson, *Nederlands Archief van Kerkelyke Geschiedenis* 8 (1848): 369–407.

25. P. Schaff, *Creeds of Christendom*, 6th ed., 3 vols. (New York: Harper, 1931; reprinted, Grand Rapids: Baker, 1983), I, 820–40; III, 707, 729.

26. Cf. R. Libach, "John Milton als Theologe," *Theologische Studien und Kritiken* 51 (1879): 705–32; also see J. Fletcher, *The History of the Revival and Progress of Independency in England*, 4 vols. (London: John Snow, 1847–49); see Schaff, *Creeds of Christendom*, I, 820 for further literature.

or Free-Will Baptists are distinguished from Calvinist Baptists. In later years Baptist belief was propagated especially in America by Roger Williams (d. 1683). It did not do much for dogmatics but in the persons of John Bunyan (d. 1688), Robert Hall, John Foster, etc., it produced powerful preachers.[27]

In the area of religion and theology, the period of the Civil War was a time of immense confusion in England. All kinds of ideas and trends whirled about and through each other. Earlier the different groupings would have been called "sects," but along with Weingarten[28] it is better to view them as variously shaded formations within the one great coalition of "Holy People." Arminian, Baptist, millenarian, antinomian and even libertine views and sentiments found acceptance. Religious individualism held sway, reaching its zenith in Quakerism. Emancipation from tradition, from the creeds, and from ecclesiastical organization culminated in a situation in which every believer was on his own, detached from Scripture, possessing within himself—his mind, the inner light—the source of his religious life and knowledge. All that which is objective—Scripture, Christ, church, office, sacrament—was set aside. Believers lived by their own principles, distinguishing themselves in society as well by their own mores, customs, clothing, and so forth. George Fox (1624–90), author of *Works* (3 volumes, London, [1694–1706]), was the founder of this sect; Robert Barclay (1648–90), author of *Apology for the True Christian Divinity*, its theologian; and William Penn (1644–1718) its statesman.[29]

All these individualistic currents paved the way for deism. The realism of the popular character of the English, the nominalism of Roger Bacon and William of Occam, and the empiricist philosophy of Francis Bacon (d. 1626) had laid the groundwork for it. And when in the seventeenth century there was added to this the confusion in religious convictions and all of England had been divided into parties and sects, it occurred to many people that the essence of religion could only consist in that which they all had in common. Latitudinarianism found acceptance and issued in deism. The procession of deists started with Herbert of Cherbury (d. 1648), who in his *De veritate* (1624) and *De religione gentilium* (1645) reduced the essence of religion to five truths: the existence of God, the worship of God, virtue, repentance, and retribution. This original, true and pure religion, he said, has been falsified in

---

27. Schaff, *Creeds*, I, 845–59, III, 738–56. J. M. Cramp, *Baptist History: From the Foundation of the Christian Church to the Close of the Eighteenth Century* (London: Elliot Stock, 1868); R. Hofmann, "Baptisten," *PRE³*, II, 385–93.

28. Ed. note: see next note.

29. William Sewel, *History of the Rise, Increase, and Progress of the Christian People Called Quakers*, written originally in Low-Dutch and also translated into English (London: J. Sowle, 1725); Thomas Evans, *An Exposition of the Faith of the Religious Society of Friends* (Philadelphia: Kimber & Sharpless, 1828); M. Schneckenburger, *Vorlesungen über die Lehrbegriffe der kleineren protestantischen Kirchenparteien* (Frankfurt a. M.: H. L. Brönner, 1863), 69ff.; H. Weingarten, *Die Revolutionskirchen Englands* (Leipzig: Breitkopf und Hartel, 1868), 364ff.; Möhler, *Symbolik* (Regensburg: G. J. Manz, 1873), 492ff.; P. Schaff, *Creeds*, I, 859–78; R. Buddensieg, "Quäker," *PRE³*, XVI, 357–80.

a variety of ways by the priests. This was the program of the deists. From this base various thinkers then undertook the battle against revelation. John Locke (d. 1704), author of *The Reasonableness of Christianity* (1695), assigned to reason the decision concerning revelation. John Toland (d. 1722), author of *Christianity not Mysterious* (1696), stated that Christianity not only contained nothing *against* reason but also nothing *above* reason. Anton Collins (d. 1729), author of *Discourse on Freethinking* (1713), recommended *free*, i.e., unbelieving, thinking. Thomas Woolston (d. 1731) wrote his *Discourses on the Miracles of Our Saviour* (1727–30) and attempted to explain them by allegory. M. Tindal (d. 1733), author of *Christianity as Old as Creation* (1730), set aside all revelation. Deism ended in skepticism in Henry Dodwell, author of *Christianity Not Founded on Argument* (1742). And in philosophy this skepticism was perfected by David Hume (d. 1776).[30]

DECLINE OF REFORMED THEOLOGY

[57] Around 1750 Reformed theology everywhere fell into decay. The elements responsible for this decomposition, already present in the previous century, continued to have their effect, undermining dogmatics. After Cocceianism in the Netherlands had emerged victorious came the Era of Tolerance (1740–70). The power of truth was denied; people retreated from the church's confessions to Scripture and abandoned doctrines characteristic for the Reformed faith, such as original sin, the covenant of works, limited atonement, etc. In beautiful dress and the name of being biblical, a variety of Remonstrant and Socinian errors rose to the surface. At best, those who professed the Reformed religion accepted the theology they had "in stock," but they no longer had their hearts in it, nor did they any longer speak out of its content. The old dogmatics [simply] became an object of historical study. Professor Bernh. de Moor wrote a *Commentarius perpetuus in Marckii Compendium,* 6 vols. (Leiden, 1761–71); and Martin Vitringa commented on the *Doctrina Christ. religionis* of his father Campegius, under the title *Doctrina Christ. religionis per aphorismos summatim descripta,* 9 vols. (Amsterdam, 1761).[31] Foremost among the few people who still clung heart and soul to the old Reformed doctrine, defending and developing it with talent were Alex. Comrie (d. 1774), *A. B. C. des geloofs* (1739), *Eigenschappen des zaligmakende geloofs* (1744), *Verklaring van den Catechismus* (1753), *Brief over de Rechtvaardigmaking* (1761); Nic. Holtius (d. 1773), *Verhandeling over de Rechtvaardigmaking door het geloof* (1750); and J. J. Brahé, *Aanmerkingen*

---

30. G. V. Lechler, *Geschichte des englischen Deismus* (Stuttgart: J. G. Cotta, 1841); E. Troeltsch, "Deismus," *PRE*[3], IV, 532–59.

31. Ed. note: The full title of Vitringa's work is *Doctrina Doctrina christianae religionis, per aphorismos summatim descripta: Editio sexta. Cui nunc accedit ὑποτύπωσις [hypotypōsis] theologiae elencticae in usum scholarum domesticarum Campegii Vitringae, curante* Martino Vitriniga, *qui praefationem, prolegomena et adnotationes adjecit, nec non analysin v. cl.* Theodori Scheltingae.

Wegens de vijf Walch. art. (1758). Comrie and Holtius, in their *Examination of the Tolerance Project,* in 10 lectures (Amsterdam, 1753–59), joined battle against the "Tolerant," among whom especially the professors J. Van den Honert, J. J. Schultens, and Alberti had to bear the brunt. Deserving of mention as well is J. C. Appel, known especially for his struggle over the Lord's Supper: *Zedig en Vrijmoedig Onderzoek* (1763); *Over het avondmaal* (1764); *Aanmerkingen over het Rechte Gebruik van het Evangelie; Vervolg van de Aanmerkingen;* and *De Hervormde Leer* (1769).

But from 1770 on, the so-called *neology* increasingly gained influence. English deism, French unbelief, and German rationalism found fertile soil in the Netherlands. The revolution meant a total conceptual turnaround. Orthodoxy, in the form of a nonrationalist but rational, moderate, biblical supranaturalism, was carried into the nineteenth century and was represented by P. Chevallier, *Schema Institutionum theol.* (1773–75); Br. Broes, *Institu. Theol. theor.* (1788); J. van Nuys Klinkenberg, *Onderwijs in den godsdienst* 12 vols. (1780); Samuel van Emdre, *Katechismus der Heilige Godgeleerdherd* (1780); W. E. de Perponcher, *Beschouw. Godg.* (1790); and above all by H. Muntinghe, *Pars theologiae Christ. theoretica* (1800).

The same thing occurred in other countries. In the eighteenth century France no longer had a Reformed theology of its own. The revocation of the Edict of Nantes (1685) banished the best minds from the land. In the eighteenth century Paul Rabaut (d. 1794) and Antoine Court (d. 1760) gained renown as the "restorers" of the Reformed church in France. French preachers as a rule received their training in Lausanne, where a seminary of their own had been started for French students along the lines proposed by Antoine Court. In Switzerland the *Consensus Helveticus* (1675) proved unable to stem the tide of rationalism. J. R. Wettstein and his son in Basel, J. C. Suicerus and his son Henri in Zurich, and Mestrezat and Louis Tronchin in Geneva already levelled their objections against this confession.[32] As early as 1685 attempts were made to set it aside, attempts that were crowned with success in the eighteenth century in Geneva, Basel, Appenzell, Zurich, and Bern, among others. In the person of J. F. Osterwald, preacher at Neuchatel (d. 1747), we witness the transition from seventeenth-century orthodoxy to eighteenth-century rationalism. In his *Traite des sources de la corruption, qui regne aujourdhui parmi les Chretiens* (1700), his *Catechisme* (1702), and his *Compendium theol. Christ.* (1739), he complains about dead orthodoxy and the finely spun-out dogmas, remains silent on many points of doctrine (e.g., election), and seeks the renewal of morality. Together with Osterwald, J. A. Turrentin (d. 1737), author of *Opera*, 3 vol., and S. Werenfels (d. 1740), author of *Opuscula*, 2d ed. (1739), formed the Swiss triumvirate. The moderate orthodoxy they represented virtually led to assertive heterodoxy in J. J. Zimmerman (d. 1757), author of *Opuscula* (1751–59); J. J. Lavater (d. 1759), au-

---

32. A. Schweizer, *Die protestantischen Centraldogmen,* II, 663ff.

thor of the article on *Geneva* in the *Dictionnaire Encyclopaedie* edited by Diderot and d'Alembert; and J. Vernet, author of *Instruction Chretienne* (1754). Wolf's mathematical method was applied to theology by D. Wyttenbach, *Tentamen theol. dogm. methodo scientifica pertractat,* 3 vols. (1747); J. F. Stapfer, *Institut. theol . . . ordine scientifico dispositae,* 5 vols. (1743) and *Grundlegung zur wahren Religion* (Zürich, 1751–52); and Bernsau (later professor at Franeker), *Theol. dogmatica, methodo scientifica pertractata* (1745–47). German applications of Wolf include Ferdinand Stosch (d. 1780), *Summa paedagogiae scholasticae ad praelectiones academicas in theologiam revel. dogm.* (1770); Sam. Endemann (prof. at Marburg), *Instit. theol. dogm.* (1777); and Sam. Mursinna (professor at Halle), *Compendium theol. dogm.* (1777).

In England dogmatics was almost totally occupied with questions brought up by deism concerning predictive prophecy, miracles, and revelation. Although apologetics often had a rationalist slant, it nevertheless had numerous—among them some outstanding—representatives: Samuel Clarke (d. 1729), Nathan Lardner (d. 1768), Joseph Butler (d. 1752), Richard Bentley, William Whiston, Arthur Ashley Sykes, Thomas Sherlock (d. 1761), Daniel Waterland (d. 1752), John Coneybeare, John Leland, James Foster, William Warburton (d. 1779), Richard Watson (1816), William Paley (d. 1805), *Evidences of Christianity* (1794), *Natural Theology* (1802), etc. Among the dogmatic works published in this period, the most important are those of Hutchinson, of which an extract is given in *A Letter to a Bishop concerning Some Important Discoveries in Philosophy and Theology* (1735); Stackhouse (d. 1752), *A Complete Body of Speculative and Practical Divinity* (1709); Philip Doddridge (d. 1751); and Isaac Watts (d. 1748), who was known not only for his hymns and his logic but also for his *Catechism* (1728) and *Rise and Progress of Religion in the Soul* (1745).

Prominent among Scottish theologians in the eighteenth century were Thomas Boston (d. 1732), *A Complete Body of Divinity,* 3 vols. (1773), *Human Nature in its Fourfold State, A View of the covenant of grace;* Adam Gib, and the first five Seceders, Fisher, Wilson, Moncrieff, and the brothers Ralph and Ebenezer Erskine. Of importance was the so-called "Marrow controversy," which began in 1717 and was prompted by a work of the Independent Edward Fisher called *The Marrow of Modern Divinity,* which first appeared in 1646, was reissued by Boston in 1700, and again, with a preface by Mr. Hog of Carnock, in 1718. As a result the neonomian battle, which had been fought in England the century before, was now transplanted to Scotland. The book was attacked by Principal Hadow of St. Andrews in a sermon preached at the opening of the Synod of Fife, April 7, 1719, and later published under the title *The Antinomianism of the Marrow Detected,* 1721. The "Marrow Divines," among whom Boston was the most prominent, were accused of antinomianism, but opponents themselves were not free of neonomianism. The General Assembly of 1720 condemned as erroneous some propositions in the *Marrow,* which in part prompted the Erskines—

who along with twelve others, Hog, Bonar, Williamson, Kid, Wilson, Wardlaw, etc., had sided with Boston—to secede. Neonomianism was a stepping-stone to the rationalism that also penetrated the theology and church of Scotland and already clearly manifested itself in men like Simpson, McLaurin, and others.[33]

NINETEENTH-CENTURY STREAMS

[58] In the beginning of the nineteenth century, Reformed theology was almost everywhere in a sad state of decline. In the form of supranaturalism, theology in the Netherlands was pursued by Van der Palm, Van Voorst, Borger, Clarisse, Kist, van Hengel at Leiden; by Abresch, Chevallier, Muntinghe, Ypey at Groningen; Heringa, Royaards, Bouman, Vinke at Utrecht; by many able and prominent preachers like Dermout, Broes, Donker, Curtius, van Senden, Egeling, etc.; by many participants in the Stolpian legacy (1756), the Teyler's Society (1778), and the Hague Society (1787). This supranaturalistic school aspired to be rational but not rationalistic in the way of Wegschneider, Röhr, and Paulus. It maintained revelation, asserting its necessity, possibility, and validity on a variety of rational and historical grounds. It sought to be biblical but was anticonfessional, antiphilosophical, and anti-Calvinistic. It produced a dogmatics that was deistic in its doctrine of God (theology proper), Pelagian in anthropology, moralistic in Christology, collegialist in ecclesiology, and eudaemonist in eschatology. Around 1835, in the northern provinces of the country, it was replaced by Groninger theology. Following in the footsteps of the Socratic philosophy of Van Heusde (d. 1839), this theological movement replaced the idea of revelation and doctrine with that of education, thus incorporating an ethical component in the relation between God and man. In this school of theology, God was not primarily the Teacher but the great Nurturer who—through nature and history, the person and the church of Christ—brought up people as his children to become wise and devout Christians, so to achieve godlikeness. The opposition it encountered from the side of the orthodox, and a little later from that of the modernists as well, and its own inner development into an evangelical current, resulted around 1850 in its having to make way for modernist theology.

Modernist theology first made its appearance with C. W. Opzoomer, who in 1845 became professor at Utrecht, applied the empiricist philosophy of John Stuart Mill and August Comte to religion, thus arriving at an anti-supranaturalist position. Finally, J. H. Scholten, in his *Leer der Hervormde*

---

33. James Walker, *The Theology and Theologians of Scotland: Chiefly of the Seventeenth and Eighteenth centuries* (Edinburgh: T. & T. Clark, 1888), 25ff., 39ff., 53ff.; James Buchanan, *The Doctrine of Justification* (Edinburgh: T. & T. Clark, 1867), 182–88; Merle d'Aubigné, *Duitschland, Engeland en Schotland* (Rotterdam: Van der Meer & Verbruggen, 1849). Also see my foreword to the new release of a Dutch translation of selected writings of the Erskines published by J. C. van Schenk Brill of Doesburg.

Kerk [*Doctrine of the Reformed Church*], presented a modernist dogmatics under Reformed colors. In the field of Old Testament studies, A. Kuenen emerged as a proponent of evolution. In theology, therefore, there was a gradual development in the direction of unbelief; modern theology no longer has a dogmatics. It is true that in the case of many modern theologians in recent years there has arisen a felt need for a dogmatics, even for a confession and an ecclesiastical organization. This was expressed by the Rev. Fleischer at the meeting of modern theologians held in April 1902. J. van den Bergh, at a meeting in 1903, also argued for the organization of all liberal Protestants in a new denomination. In addition, L. Knappert raised his voice in favor of a modern confession and Groenewegen championed the rights of metaphysics in the philosophy of religion and the development of a philosophical dogmatics. Finally, Bruining wrote a study on the method of a modern dogmatics and furnished proofs for the existence of God and the immortality of the soul. It does not, however, look as if this desire for a modern dogmatics will soon be fulfilled. For not only is there the remaining difference, in modified form, between the intellectualists and "ethicals" among modern liberals, but opinions among them are vastly divergent on all dogmatic issues, including the doctrine of God, of man, his origin and immortality, of sin, of the person of Christ, of redemption, and so forth. Even before, and still more clearly at the Congress of Liberal Protestants held in Amsterdam in 1903, it was evident that many younger members had entered the phase of syncretism and abandoned a specifically Christian position in exchange for that of a universal-religious one. At the congress in 1903, however, Professor Cannegieter brilliantly managed to console himself over the lack of a modern dogmatics: it was caused not by poverty of thought but by wealth; only the destitute know what they possess! In opposition to these negative trends, however, we have seen the rise, in this century and our country, of the positive movements of the Réveil and the Secession, of the Utrecht School, the ethical-irenic school, and, finally, of Calvinism, which seeks to win a position of its own also in the domain of theology.[34]

In Germany Reformed theology increasingly deteriorated. In that country the Reformed church originally achieved dominance over a wide territory. Its theology was cultivated in Heidelberg, Duisburg, Marburg, Frankfurt-am-O., Herborn, Bremen, and Halle. This was the situation up until the middle of the eighteenth century. But then came the Enlightenment, the Union (1718), the influence of Kant's philosophy and of Schleiermacher, and so forth, and all these factors served to bring about the total decline of the Reformed church and Reformed theology in Germany. Admittedly, in the beginning of this century, there occurred a kind of awakening of the Re-

---

34. See, further, my essay on "Recent Dogmatic Thought in The Nederlands," *Presbyterian and Reformed Review* 3 (April 1892): 209–28, and "Theologische Richtingen in Nederlands," *Tijdschrift voor Gereformeerde theologie* 1 (June–July 1894): 161–88, and the literature listed there. Ed. note: The Dutch article is an abridged version of the English one.

formed consciousness in the case of Krafft in Erlangen, G. D. Krummacher in Elberfeld, Geibel in Lubeck, Mallet in Bremen, and so forth. Still, this awakening was not strong enough. Even men like Ebrard (d. 1888) in Erlangen and Heppe (d. 1879) in Marburg, as a result of their Melanchthonianism, inflicted grave injury on the Reformed cause. Only Wichelhaus (d. 1858) in Halle, Karl Südhoff (d. 1865) in Frankfurt-am-M., Böhl in Vienna, A. Zahn in Stuttgart, O. Thelemann in Detmold, Kohlbrugge (d. 1875) in Elberfeld, and others positioned themselves firmly on the Reformed confession. Today, in Germany, there is not a single theological university or school left that stands on the basis of the Reformed confession.[35]

Switzerland and France experienced renewal as a result of the *Réveil* transplanted there from Scotland.[36] The *Réveil* was a powerful spiritual movement but in its origins unecclesiastical and anticonfessional. Its foundation was generally Christian and further distinguished by its individualistic, aristocratic, methodistic, and philanthropic character. In Switzerland especially, two dogmas—election (Cesar Malan [d. 1864]) and inspiration (Merle d'Aubigné [d. 1872], Gaussen [d. 1863])—were central. But Alexander Vinet (1797–1847), who in 1822–23 came under the influence of the *Réveil,* took a different tack theologically. The vital principle of his faith and theology was the harmony between Christianity and conscience, the full satisfaction with which revelation meets man's religious and moral needs, the genuine "naturalness" of the gospel. Accordingly, he stressed as strongly as possible the bond between dogma and morality, i.e., the ethical side of truth. As a result he was led as well to ground Christian truth on Christian experience, the witness of conscience; to repudiate election; to advocate synergism; and in general to move the center of gravity from the object to the subject. Vinet continued to the very end, however, to cling to the main truths of Christianity.[37] His pupil E. Scherer, who was originally strictly orthodox but gradually broke with his past, went much further and ended his life in total unbelief. From that time on there arose in France and Switzerland a liberal Protestantism whose primary organ of publication was the Strasbourg *Revue de théologie et de philosophie Chrétienne* and whose interpreters were men like Ed. Reuss, Albert Réville Pécaut, and Colani. Thus, based on Scherer's initiative in 1849, two opposing schools of thought, a liberal and an orthodox one, confronted each other. But in the latter, Vinet's principles, and later on

35. Adolf Zahn, *Die Ursachen des Niederganges der reformirten Kirche in Deutschland* (Barmen: H. Klein, 1881); idem, *Abriss einer Geschichte der evangelischen Kirche auf dem europäischen Festlande im neunzehnten Jahrhundert*, 3d ed. (Stuttgart: J. B. Metzler, 1893), chap. 12.

36. L. H. Wagenaar, *Het Réveil en de Afscheiding* (Heerenveen: J. Hepkema, 1880); see p. 40 for literature; H. F. von der Goltz, *Die Reformirte Kirche Genf's im neunzehnten Jahrhundert* (Basel: H. Georg, 1862); Léon Maury, *la réveil religieux dans l'église réformée a Genève et en France*, 2 vols. (Paris: Fischbacher, 1892); W. van Oosterwijk Bruyn, *Het Réveil in Nederland* (Utrecht: C. H. E. Breijer, 1890); A. Pierson, *Oudere tijdgenooten* (Amsterdam: Kampen, 1888).

37. J. Cramer, *Alexander Vinet als Christliche Moralist en Apologeet Geteekend en Gewaardeerd* (Leiden: Brill, 1883); see literature cited on p. 6.

also the influence of Kant and Ritschl, continued to have impact. Its adherents consequently gradually split apart in a mediating and a moderate orthodox faction. The former was supported by men like de Pressensé, Astié, Sécrétan, Sabatier, Leopold Monad, Chapuis, Dandiran, and Lobstein; the interpreters of the latter were Godot, father and son, Porret, Berthoud, Martin, Doumergue, Bertrand, H. Bois, and Grétillat. The struggle between the two schools primarily concerned two questions. The first concerned the issue of authority in religion, viz., whether it lies in Scripture, or the person of Christ, or in human reason and conscience. The other question concerned the person of Christ: was he truly God, even though some held he had emptied himself through kenosis; or was he solely a human being, albeit a human being who lived perfectly and undisturbedly in fellowship with God?[38]

But the march of ideas did not stop. Various phenomena indicated that a new theology was on its way. In 1897, heralded by several smaller writings indicating its drift, August Sabatier, professor in theology at Paris, published his *Outlines of a Philosophy of Religion Based on Psychology and History*.[39] In this work actually only the following two themes were developed: (1) The essence of religion, which has its source in a feeling of uneasiness or distress, consists in faith, trust, surrender of the heart, inner piety. This is the core of all religion and the essence of Christianity and of the Reformation as well. This idea was specifically developed by his colleague Ménégoz into the thesis that faith by itself, apart from its beliefs (*la foi indépendamment des croyances*), was the essence of religion, Christianity and Protestantism, and as such bestowed forgiveness and eternal life. (2) This faith expresses, objectivizes, and interprets itself in pictorial representations, in dogmas that therefore contain two factors: a mystical, religious, and practical element on the one hand, and, on the other, an intellectual, theoretical, philosophical element. The latter is changeable, conditioned by circumstantial factors of refinement, education, and environment. It always has to contend, moreover, with the inadequacy of human cognition, which is restricted to the finite and can express the infinite only in images, symbolically.

Consequently, dogmas are not only changeable and transient in the sense that today we can no longer be fully at ease with the religious notions of Jesus, the apostles, the Reformers, and the old orthodoxy, but even when today we try as carefully as we can to define the piety of our hearts, the dogmas remain imperfect, subjective, inadequate, and symbolic. These two ideas earned the theology of the Parisian school the name "symbolic fideism." Though these ideas were not new, Sabatier's work was astonishingly well re-

---

38. Cf. A. Grétillat, "Movements of Theological Thought among French-Speaking Protestants from the Revival of 1820 to the End of 1891," *Presbyterian and Reformed Review* 3 (July 1892): 421–47; idem, "Theological Thought among the French Protestants in 1892," *Presbyterian and Reformed Review* 4 (July 1893): 390–417.

39. French edition: *Esquisse d'une philosophie de la religion d'après la psychologie et l'histoire* (Paris: Fischbacher, 1897); English edition, trans. T. A. Seed, published in New York by James Pott, 1902.

ceived and highly praised by Ménégoz, Emery, Chapuis, Lobstein, and others. But although Sabatier had specifically intended by means of his new theology to reconcile rationalism and orthodoxy, science and religion, this attempt was by no means successful. A large group of theologians declared their dissatisfaction with this attempt at reconciliation. Pillon, Frommel, Godet, H. Bois, Bovon, and Berthoud, among others, lodged a wide array of more or less weighty objections against it and continued their faithfulness to a mediating or moderate orthodox position.[40] The first was especially held by the *Dogmatique Chrétienne* of Jules Bovon (Lausanne, 1895); the second by the *Theologie Systématique* of Grétillat, 4 vols. (Paris, 1885ff.). The *Dogmatique Chrétienne* of Bouvier (Paris, 1903), is even further to the left than Bovon; it does not say a word about the church, Scripture, baptism, or the Lord's Supper but develops the idea of life in God, Christ, the church, and as a result occasioned the charge of being pantheistic.

[59] It is Methodism that put its stamp on religious England as we know it today.[41] John Wesley (1703–91), though not a scientific theologian, was a

40. Sabatier earlier had written two works, *De la vie intime des dogmes et de leur puissance d'évolution* (Paris: Librairie Fischbacher, 1890), English translation, *The Vitality of Christian Dogmas and Their Power of Evolution*, trans. E. Christen (London: Adam & Charles Black, 1898), and a *Théorie critique de la connaissance religieuse*, both of which were taken up in revised form in the *Outlines of a Philosophy of Religion*. After his death in 1901, the following of his writings were published: *La doctrine de l'expiation et son évolution historique* (Paris: Fischbacher, 1903); English translation, *The Doctrine of the Atonement and Its Historical Evolution*, trans. V. Leuliette (New York: London: G. P. Putnam; Williams and Norgate, 1904); and *Les religions d'autorité et la religion dell'esprit* (Paris: Fischbacher, 1904); English translation, *Religions of Authority and the Religion of the Spirit*, trans. Louise Seymour Houghton (New York: McClure, Phillips, 1904). Several of Prof. E. Ménégoz's earlier writings were published together in a single volume, *Publications diverses sur le fidéisme et son application à l'enseignement chrétien traditionnel* (Paris: Fischbacher, 1900); cf. further, G. Keizer, "De Parijsche School," *Tijdschrift voor gereformeerde theologie* 6 (1899): 19–42; *Riemens Jr., *Het Symbolo-Fideisme* (Rotterdam, 1900); G. A. Lasch, *Die Theologie der Pariser Schule: Charakteristik und Kritik des Symbolo-Fideismus* (Berlin: C. A. Schwetschke, 1901); J. Michalcescu, *Darlegung und Kritik der Religionsphilosophie Sabatiers* (Bern: Scheitlin, Spring & Cie., 1903).

41. Otto Pfleiderer, *Die Entwicklung der protestantischen Theologie in Deutschland seit Kant und in Grossbritannien seit 1825* (Freiburg i.B.: J. C. B. Mohr, 1891), 386ff.; Adolph Zahn, *Abriss einer Geschichte der Evangelischen Kirche im britischen Weltreich im neunzehnten Jahrhundert* (Stuttgart: J. F. Steinkopf, 1891); C. Clemen, "Der gegenwärtige Stand des religiösen Denkens in Grossbritannien," *Theologische Studien und Kritiken* 65 (1892): 513–48; *G. Elliott, *Bilder aus dem kirchlichen Leben Englands* (Leipzig: Akademische Buchhandlung); G. d'Alviella, *L'évolution religieuse comtemporaine chez les Anglais, les Américains et les Hindous* (Paris, New York, G. Bailliere et Cie: F. W. Christern, 1884); N. L. Walker, "Present Theological Drifts in Scotland," *Presbyterian and Reformed Review* 4 (January 1893): 25–48; J. Guinness Rogers, *The Church Systems of England in the Nineteenth Century,* 2d ed. (London: Congregational Union of England and Wales, 1891); idem, *Present-Day Religion and Theology Including a Review of the Down-Grade Controversy* (London, 1888); John Hunt, *Religious Thought in England in the Nineteenth Century* (London: Gibbings, 1896); Newton H. Marshall, *Die gegenwärtigen Richtungen der Religionsphilosophie in England und ihre erkenntnistheoretischen Grundlagen* (Berlin: Reuther & Reichard, 1902); Burchhardt, "Aus der Modernen Systematischen Theologie Grossbrittanniens," *Festschrift für Theologie und Kirche* (1899): 421–39, 441–71; F. Kattenbusch, "Anglikanische Kirche," *PRE³*, I, 525–47; Ueberweg-Heinze, *Friedrich Ueberwegs Grundriss der Geschichte der Philosophie seit Beginn des neunzehnter Jahrhunderts,* 10th ed., 4 vols. (Berlin: Ernst Siegfried Mittler & Sohn, 1906), III, chap. 2, 56ff.

mighty preacher who individualized the gospel and made it into a question of life and death for everyone. Methodism, which arose as a result of the work of John [and Charles] Wesley and George Whitefield (1714–71), did not primarily consist in departure from one or the other of the Thirty-nine Articles but concentrated the entire truth of the Christian religion around two points: first, the sudden conscious experience of sin and grace, i.e., a personal conversion; second, around the revelation of that new life in an entirely new form, which consisted in seeking the conversion of others, showing oneself to be a different person by abstention from a number of adiaphora, and considering Christian perfection as already attainable in this life. This one-sided focus gradually led to a situation where various dogmas were opposed, modified, or deemed of secondary importance.[42] The influence that Methodism has had on Anglicans and Presbyterians, Independents and Baptists, is incalculable. Wesley has been the reshaper of English and American Protestantism, the mediate producer of revivals that ever since his emergence on the scene have been recurrent in Protestant churches, the "Archbishop of the Slums," the father of "home missions," the founder of Christian socialism.

In the main, however, Methodism was restricted to the common people. In higher ranks in politics, philosophy, and letters, a cold liberalism continued to hold sway. Reaction to it came from romanticism (W. Scott, Southey, S. T. Coleridge [d. 1834]), which in the sphere of church and theology emerged in the Oxford Movement. This movement considerably strengthened the ranks of the High Church party, which had already existed from the sixteenth century on, and vigorously promoted Catholic doctrine and ritual in the Anglican church.[43] In his work *England and the Holy See,*[44] Spencer Jones openly urged the union of the Anglican with the Catholic Church. The writers of *Lux Mundi,* 1890 (Canon Holland, Moore, Illingsworth, Talbot, C. Gore, and others) attempted to renew Puseyism and at the

42. Julia Wedgwood, *John Wesley and the Evangelical Reaction of the Eighteenth Century* (London: Macmillan, 1870); Robert Southey, *The Life of John Wesley,* abridged (London: Hutchinson, 1903.); C. Schoell, "Methodismus," *PRE²,* IX, 681–719; Loofs, "Methodismus," *PRE³,* XII, 747–801; W. E. H. Lecky, *Entstehungsgechiste und Characktersistik des Methodismus aus dem England* (Leipzig, Heidelberg, C. F. Winter, 1880); D. F. Chantepie de la Saussaye, *De godsdienstige bewegingen van dezen tijd in haren oorsprong geschetst* (Rotterdam: E. H. Tassemeijer, 1863), 109f.; J. A. Möhler, *Symbolik* (Regensburg: G. J. Manz, 1873), chaps. 75–76; Schnechenburger, *Vorlesungen,* 103–51; T. Kolde, *Der Methodismus und seine Bekämpfung* (Erlangen: A. Deichert, 1886); idem, *Die Heilsarmee (The Salvation Army): Ihre Geschichte und ihr Wesen* (Erlangen: A. Deichert, 1899); idem, "Heilsarmee," *PRE³,* VII, 578–93; idem, "Die Engelsche Kirchenarmee," *Neue Kirchliche Zeitschrift* (February 1899): 101–38; Hardeland, *Die Heilsarmee nach Geschichte, Wesen und Wert* (Stuttgart: Belser, 1898); J. D. du Toit, *Het Methodisme* (Amsterdam: Höveker & Wormser, 1903).

43. R. Buddensieg, "Tractarianismus," *PRE³,* XX, 18–53; F. Kattenbusch, "Anglikanische Kirche," *PRE³,* I, 525–47; Blötzen, "Der Anglikanismus auf dem Wegen nach Rome," *Stimmen aus Maria Laach* (1904): 125ff.

44. Spencer Jones, *England and the Holy See,* with a foreword by the Right Honorable Viscount Halifax (London: Longmans, Green, & Co., 1902).

same time to make Christian dogmas plausible by placing them in the light of modern times.

Alongside the High Church party there was the Broad-Church faction, whose roots lay in the latitudinarianism of the seventeenth and eighteenth centuries. In the nineteenth century this group gained outstanding representatives in Thomas Arnold (d. 1842), Hampden (d. 1868), F. D. Maurice (d. 1872), Charles Kingsley (d. 1874), Whately (d. 1863), F. W. Robertson (d. 1853), and A. P. Stanley (d. 1881). Averse to the Methodism of the Low Church party, they all strove seriously and nobly toward a reconciliation of Christianity and culture. In their conviction, the church should become the moral educator of the nation; religion should reconcile itself with the true, the good, and the beautiful, wherever it is to be found; and it was the task of Christianity to manifest its power above all in the moral renewal of society. Increasingly, this broad and tolerant position found acceptance. The rise and progress of ritualism, the numerous sects and schools of thought, the distress of the underclasses, and particularly higher criticism—which made its entry into the English world with the debut of Bishop Colenso and was propagated by Robert Smith, T. K. Cheyne, and S. R. Driver—gave the Broad-Church party the upper hand. One of its most prominent spokesmen in recent years is F. W. Farrar, dean of Westminster Abbey. But this inclusive position is presently held by many, not only within the state church but also far beyond it. Among the most eminent spokesmen up until recently or still today are the Baptist J. Clifford; the Congregationalists R. W. Dale (1889), Dr. Joseph Parker at London, Dr. Fairbairn of Mansfield College (London, 1893–45); the Presbyterians Professor Henry Drummond, Marcus Dods (Edinburgh, 1905), A. B. Bruce (Edinburgh: Clark, 1892), James Lindsay (Edinburgh: Blackwood, 1892), Rev. J. B. Heard (Edinburgh: Clark), and James Orr (Edinburgh: Elliot, 1893);[45] in addition, Flint, Milligan, Gloag in the Established Church of Scotland; Brown, Rainy, Davidson, Salmond, Laidlaw, G. A. Smith in the Free Church; Cairns, Muir, Thomson, J. Smith in the United Presbyterian Church; and so forth.

Aside from its christological starting point, which centers everything around the incarnation, this movement is marked by its emphasis on church union. Ecclesiastical differences are brushed aside or presented as relatively

45. See further my essay "Eene Belangrijke Apologie van het Christelijke Wereldbeschouwing," *Theologische Studiën* 12 (1894): 142–52.

Ed. note: Bavinck included the following titles in the text; they are given here with fuller bibliographic data. A. M. Fairbairn, *The Place of Christ in Modern Theology* (New York: Scribner, 1893); idem, *Philosophy of Christian Religion* (New York: Macmillan, 1902); Henry Drummond, *The Natural Law in the Spiritual World* (London: Hodder and Stoughton, 1905); idem, *The Greatest Thing in the World* (New York: J. Pott & Co., 1897); Marcus Dods, *The Bible, Its Origin and Nature* (New York: Scribner, 1905); A. B. Bruce, *Apologetics or Christianity Defensively Stated* (Edinburgh: Clark, 1892); James Lindsay, *The Progressiveness of Modern Christian Thought* (Edinburgh: Blackwood, 1892); J. B. Heard, *Alexandrian and Carthaginian Theology* (Edinburgh: T. & T. Clark, 1893); James Orr, *The Christian View of God and the World, As Centering in the Incarnation* (Edinburgh: Elliott, 1893).

unimportant. Practically, its proponents work together with men of all sorts of churches and schools of thought; and theoretically many even strive for the union of all Protestant churches, as, e.g., J. Clifford. Certainly W. T. Stead takes this line the farthest when he hopes for a "church of the future" that will lead the whole field of social reform, incorporate within itself the whole domain of culture, even including the theaters, and encompass all human beings. Often coupled with these aims is the hope of a restoration of all things on the other side of the grave.[46] Strict Calvinism is daily losing ground. It is still maintained here and there, in the Scottish Highlands, in Wales and the like, but the scientific study and defense of it no longer exists. The work of Professor Hastie in Glasgow on the basic principles of Reformed theology[47] is certainly important and deserves attentive reading, but it is too heavily influenced by the Leiden professor J. H. Scholten for it to be welcomed as a sign of the revival of Calvinism in theology.

On the other hand, the theory of evolution is gaining ground in England by the day. After deism had already subjected the miracles, predictive prophecy, and revelation to fearsome criticism, this process of religious dissolution further continued under the impact of Darwin's theory of the descent of man, Spencer's agnosticism, Stuart Mill's empiricism, and Tyndale's materialism. The critique of Christian dogmas received unexpected but strong support from Edwin Hatch's *The Organization of the Early Christian Churches* (1881) and *The Influence of Greek Ideas and Usages upon the Christian Church* (Hibbert Lectures, 1888), which explained the dogmas—as Hampden had already done before him in his *The Scholastic Philosophy in Its Relation to Christian Theology* (1832)—from the synthesis of pagan philosophy with original Christianity.[48] Over against these negative trends, Christian theology in England and Scotland generally adopts a conciliatory posture. Many theologians, following Henry Drummond, attempt to combine Christianity with the theory of evolution and advocate a mediating position. One of the most important representatives of this position is Hastings Rashdal, author of *Christus in Ecclesia* (1904).[49] Others, following Hamilton and Mansel, take refuge in agnosticism and along with Balfour (*The Foundations of Belief: Being Notes Introductory to the Study of Religion* [1895])[50] secure a basis for faith and religion in the ignorance of science concerning invisible things.

46. Cf. W. T. Stead, *The Wider Hope,* Essays and Strictures on the Doctrine and Literature of Future Punishment by Numerous Writers, Lay and Clerical (London: Fisher Unwin, 1890).

47. The Croall Lecture for 1892: *The Theology of the Reformed Church in Its Fundamental Principles,* by the late William Hastie, D.D. and ed. William Fulton (Edinburgh: Clark, 1904).

48. Edwin Hatch, *The Organization of the Early Christian Churches* (London: Rivingtons, 1881); idem, *The Influence of Greek Ideas and Usages upon the Christian Church* (London: Williams and Norgate, 1890); R. D. Hampden, *The Scholastic Philosophy Considered in Its Relation to Christian Theology* (London: Simpkin, Marshall, 1832).

49. Hastings Rashdall, *Christus in Ecclesia* (Edinburgh: T. & T. Clark, 1904).

50. A. J. B. Balfour, *The Foundations of Belief: Being Notes Introductory to the Study of Religion* (London: Longmans, Green, & Co., 1895).

Particularly after Coleridge, Carlyle, and Hutchison Stirling (in his book, *The Secret of Hegel,* 1865) had furnished an entry in England for German philosophy, the ambition arose to find in idealism—an idealism based on the objective empirical data of nature and the human mind—a means of reconciling faith and learning. T. H. Green in Oxford (1836–82) started the project, and Edward Caird (*The Evolution of Religion,* Gifford Lectures, 2 vols. [1903]) along with his brother John (*Introduction to the Philosophy of Religion* [1880]) continued his work. Unitarianism, which founded its first church in 1773, acquired a forceful defender of theism in the person of James Martineau (1805–1900), the author of *A study of Religion, its Sources and Contents* (1888) and *The Seat of Authority in Religion,* 5th ed. (London: Longmans, 1905). Then there is the not insignificant number of those who, like G. Eliott, Ch. Bradlaugh, A. Besant, W. St. Ross, and J. C. Morison, entirely broke with Christianity[51] and sought religious fulfillment elsewhere. These include: in Buddhist philosophy (Madame Blavatzky, A. Besant); in morality (Matthew Arnold, *Literature and Dogma* [1873] and *God and the Bible* [1875], which described religion as "morality touched with emotion and God as the eternal power, not ourselves, which makes for righteousness"); in "a society for ethical culture" (founded in America in 1876 and in England in 1886);[52] or even in Islam, for the practice of which a mosque was opened in Liverpool in 1891.

REFORMED THEOLOGY IN NORTH AMERICA

[60] From the outset Reformed theology in North America displayed a variety of very diverse forms.[53] A wide range of churches were successively transplanted from England and the European continent to the United States of America and Canada. The oldest and wealthiest is the Episcopal Church, which goes way back to the immigration to Virginia in 1607. The Dutch Reformed

51. Cf. Ch. Bradlaugh, A. Besant, and Ch. Watts, *The Freethinker's Textbook* (London: Charles Watts, 1876); and W. Copeland Bowie, ed., *Liberal Thought at the Beginning of the 20th Century,* Addresses and Papers at the International Council of Unitarian and other Liberal Religious Thinkers and Workers, held in London, May 1901 (London: P. Green, 1901). The second international congress was held in Amsterdam in 1903. See *Religion and Liberty,* Addresses and Papers at the Second International Council of Unitarian and other Liberal Religious Thinkers and Workers, ed. P. H. Hugenholtz Jr. (Leiden: Brill, 1904).

52. Cf. W. M. Salter, *Die Religion der Moral,* trans. G. von Gizycki (Leipzig: W. Friedrich, 1885); English edition: *Ethical Religion* (Boston: Roberts Brothers, 1889).

53. See P. Schaff and S. M. Jackson, eds., *Encyclopedia of Living Divines and Christian Workers of All Denominations in Europe and America,* being a supplement to the *Schaff-Herzog Encyclopedia of Religious Knowledge* (New York: Funk & Wagnalls, 1887); Adolf Zahn, *Abriss einer Geschichte der evangelische Kirche in Amerika im neunzehnten Jahrhundert* (Stuttgart: Steinkopf, 1889); F. Nippold, *Amerikanische Kirchengeschichte seit der Unabhängigkeitserklärung der Vereinigten Staaten* (Berlin: Wiegandt & Schotte, 1892); L. Brendel and Pannebecker, "Nordamerika," *PRE³,* XVI, 165–74, 784–801. An outline of the history of Presbyterian theology is given by Prof. P. Schaff in his *Theological Propaedeutic* (New York: Scribner, 1893), 374–405, and in *The Independent* (New York), vol. 45, nos. 2321, 2324, 2329, and 2330.

Church was established following the discovery of the Hudson River and Manhattan Island in 1609. The Independents or Congregationalists first landed at Plymouth in 1620. The Quakers were led to Pennsylvania by William Penn in 1680. Baptists gained a firm foothold on Rhode Island under Roger Williams in 1639. Methodists found acceptance in the colonies through the efforts of John Wesley (1735) and George Whitfield (1738). German churches, both Lutheran and Reformed, were started there after the middle of the eighteenth century. Presbyterian churches are divided in a number of distinct groupings. Almost all of these churches and currents in these churches were of Calvinistic origin. Of all religious movements in America, Calvinism has been the most vigorous. It is not limited to one church or other but—in a variety of modifications—constitutes the animating element in Congregational, Baptist, Presbyterian, Dutch Reformed, and German Reformed churches, and so forth.

Calvinism was introduced to North America from many directions: England, Scotland, France, Holland, Germany. During the colonial period (1620–1776), it shaped the character of New England. One must distinguish, however, between the Puritan Calvinism, which came especially from England and found rootage in New England, and the Presbyterian Calvinism, which was imported into the southern, central, and western states from Scotland. Both forms of Calvinism had the Westminster Confession of 1647 as their basis, but before long a conflict between an Old School and a New School broke out in both as well. The first and most important theologian of New England was Jonathan Edwards (1703–58), who combined profound metaphysical mental ability with deep piety.[54] In 1734, still before Wesley's coming to America, a remarkable revival occurred in his congregation at Northampton; and later, with his friend George Whitfield, he himself repeatedly conducted and defended similar revivals. Theologically he especially opposed Arminianism, which came to New England via the writings of Daniel Whitby and John Taylor. By his metaphysical and ethical speculations he attempted to strengthen Calvinism but actually weakened it by the distinction between natural and moral impotence—a distinction that already occurs in John Cameron—and by a peculiar theory concerning freedom of the will, original sin, and virtue. Thus he became the father of the Edwardians, New Theology men, or New Lights as they are called, who, though they maintained the Calvinistic doctrine of God's sovereignty and election, combined it with the rejection of original sin and the universality of atonement, just as the theologians of Saumur had done in France. In the doctrine of the atonement, his son Jonathan Edwards (1745–1801) essentially taught the theory of Hugo Grotius. Samuel Hopkins, a pupil of Edwards (1721–1803), whose works were published in 1852 at Boston by Professor Park of Andover, wrote a system of divinity in which he reproduced Edwards's system and especially developed the unconditional love of God in the manner of Fénélon and Madame Guyon. Nathaniel

54. Stowe, "J. Edwards," *PRE³*, V, 171–75.

Emmons (1745–1840), *Works,* (Boston, 1842), was one of the most able defenders of Hopkinsianism. In the case of Timothy Dwight (1752–1817) and Nathaniel W. Taylor (1786–1858), Edwards's system was modified in a Pelagian direction and acquired the label "New School."

More recently, at the theological school in Andover founded in 1808, under the leadership of Egbert C. Smyth, professor of church history, it led to the defense of a progressive orthodoxy and the theory of a future probation. The Old School in the theology of New England was especially represented by Dr. Bennet Tyler (1783–1858) and Dr. Leonard Woods (1774–1854), who defended the old Calvinism. Puritanism, however, increasingly abandoned the standards of Dordt and Westminster. At the Assembly of Congregationalistic Churches in America at St. Louis (1880), a new confession of twelve articles was drafted from which characteristic Reformed doctrines were omitted. This new *Statement of Doctrine* was written by a commission of twenty-five theologians in 1883. Two famous preachers, W. E. Channing (1780–1842) and Horace Bushnell of Hartford (1802–76) removed themselves still further from Puritanism. Channing became the most prominent representative of Unitarianism in America, and Bushnell refurbished Sabellius's teaching on the Trinity and conceived the atonement exclusively as a moral act.

Theology in the Presbyterian churches in America had a parallel development. Here, too, a break occurred not only among theologians—between Old Lights and New Lights—but also in the churches between the Synod of Philadelphia and that of New York (1741–58). One of the earliest theologians was John Dickinson (1688–1747), whose most important work is a defense of the five articles against the Remonstrants.

The Old School found support above all at the theological seminary of Princeton, a school started in 1812 under the auspices of the General Assembly and represented by Dr. Archibald Alexander (1772–1851), Dr. Charles Hodge (1797–1878), author of *Systematic Theology*,[55] and his son and successor Archibald Alexander Hodge (1823–86), author of *Outlines of Theology,* and *Evangelical Theology*.[56] So-called Princeton theology is in the main a reproduction of the Calvinism of the seventeenth century as it was laid down in the Westminster Confession and the Helvetic Consensus and elaborated especially by F. Turretin in his *Theologia Elenctica.* The same system is represented as well by the Southern theologians James H. Thornwell (1812–62), Robert J. Breckinridge (1800–1871), and Robert L. Dabney. One of the youngest representatives of the Old School is W. G. T. Shedd, emeritus professor since 1890 at Union Seminary, New York, and author of the two-volume *Dogmatic Theology*.[57] However, between Hodge and Shedd there is a remarkable differ-

---

55. Charles Hodge, *Systematic Theology,* 3 vols. (New York: Charles Scribner's Sons, 1888).

56. A. A. Hodge, *Outlines of Theology,* ed. W. H. Goold (London: T. Nelson & Sons, 1867); idem, *Evangelical Theology* (London: T. Nelson, 1890).

57. W. G. T. Shedd, *Dogmatic Theology* (New York: Scribner, 1888). Ed. note: Bavinck refers to the 1888 edition; the 3d ed. (1891–94) is 3 vols.

ence. The former is a federalist and creationist, the latter a realist and traducianist. Both, however, agree in taking a very broad view of election, including in it also all the children who die in infancy.

The New Lights, aside from their differences with the Old School over the authority of the General Assembly, revivals, union with the Congregationalists, etc., also diverged from it in the matter of original sin and limited atonement, to which were later still added the inspiration of Holy Scripture and eschatology. The representatives of this new direction, aside from James Richards (1767–1843) and Baxter Dickinson (1794–1876), were Albert Barnes (1798–1870), Lyman Beecher (1775–1863), and Thomas H. Skinner (1791–1871), none of whom, however, left behind a theological system. Barnes and Beecher were accused of heresy but were acquitted. Nonetheless, a schism occurred in 1837: the Old School gained a majority in the General Assembly with the result that four synods were cut off from the fellowship. However, in 1869 they were reunited, especially through the influence of Union Theological Seminary at New York, founded in 1836. Here dogmatics was taught by Henry B. Smith (1815–77), author of *System of Christian Theology*,[58] who sought to mediate between the Old and the New School from a Christocentric standpoint. One of his pupils, Lewis French Stearns (d. 1892), wrote a work on *Present-day Theology*, published in New York in 1893, already advocating more recent views on inspiration, providence, kenosis, predestination, and salvation. Another professor at Union Seminary, Dr. Charles Briggs, was charged with heterodoxy in 1892 on the ground that he considered reason a source, accepted errors in Scripture, and recognized [the validity of] higher criticism.[59] Briggs was condemned by the General Assembly in 1893. But Union Seminary, which because of its ample endowments could well afford to do without the support of the churches, simply terminated the churches' veto power over professorial appointments—a power voluntarily given to the churches in 1870—and retained the professor. Some time later Arthur C. McGiffert, in the inaugural oration with which he accepted his professorate at Union Seminary and which dealt with *Primitive and Catholic Christianity*, identified himself as an adherent of the school of Ritschl, whose influence is advanced as well by the large number of American students attending German universities.

Against the inroads of the new trends the universities offer no resistance, either because they have no departments of theology at all, or put upon them the secular stamp that characterizes American universities in general. And the theological seminaries are on the whole too weak to resist the influence of these modern ideas, to say nothing of countering that influence. An

58. Henry B. Smith, *System of Christian Theology*, ed. W. S. Karr, 4th ed. (New York: Armstrong, 1890).

59. Cf. C. A. Briggs, *The Bible, the Church, and the Reason: The Three Great Fountains of Divine Authority* (New York: Scribner's, 1892); idem, *Messianic Prophecy*, 2d ed. (New York: Charles Scribner's Sons, 1893); idem, *Inspiration and Inerrancy* (London: J. Clarke, 1891).

illustrious exception to this rule is the seminary of the Presbyterian church at Princeton. It exists entirely independently alongside the university in that city, is bound to the church's confession, has an excellent set of professors (Warfield, Vos, Dick Wilson, Greene, etc.) and upholds the Reformed position with honor in *The Princeton Theological Review.*

Still, the influence of the modern mind is also penetrating the Northern Presbyterian Church. The revision of the Westminster Confession, which was under study for many years, was concluded and put into effect in 1903. In the process only a few changes were made, but the additions and omissions, the two new chapters on the Holy Spirit and the love of God and missions incorporated in it, as well as the Declaratory Statement, which contradicts certain false interpretations of Reformed doctrine, are obviously all intended to strongly highlight—alongside of the particularism taught in the Confession—the universalism of the love of God, of the atonement, of the preaching of the gospel and the offer of grace, of the work of the Holy Spirit, and of the salvation of all children who die in infancy.

Accordingly, the revision made in the Confession was opposed from two directions. A number of Reformed theologians, like R. A. Webb, professor at the Theological School at Clarksville, as well as Arminians, like the Rev. Dr. S. M. Templeton, agreed in the assertion that the universalism of the revision was at odds with the particularism of the Confession.[60] It is remarkable in any case that at the General Assembly of the Presbyterian Church North held in May 1905—hence, two years after the revision had been adopted— that denomination united with the Cumberland Presbyterian Church, which, in 1770, was born out of revivals and in its confession decisively adopts the Arminian position. Thus Reformed churches and theology in America are in serious crisis. The dogmas of the infallibility of Holy Scripture, of the Trinity, of the fall and human impotence, of particular or limited atonement, of election and reprobation, and of everlasting punishment are either secretly denied or openly rejected. There is clearly no rosy future awaiting Calvinism in America.[61]

---

60. B. B. Warfield, *The Confession of Faith as Revised in 1903* (Richmond, Va.: Whittet & Shepperson, 1904).

61. H. Bavinck, "The Future of Calvinism," *Presbyterian and Reformed Review* 5 (January 1894): 1–24; B. B. Warfield, "The Latest Phase of Historical Rationalism," *Presbyterian Quarterly* 9 (1895): 36–67, 185–210; N. M. Steffens, "Calvinism and the Theological Crisis," *Presbyterian and Reformed Review* 12 (April 1901): 211–25.

PART III
FOUNDATIONS OF DOGMATIC THEOLOGY (*PRINCIPIA*)

7

Scientific Foundations

If we consider theology a science, we must inquire into the scientific foundations of its structure. In the modern era this was a task usually given to philosophy, an illusory starting point since then dogmatic theology has no independent scientific status of its own. Normatively, theology should begin with revelation, proceed from faith, and articulate its own first principles (principia).

*By **principia** in general is usually meant the basic cause and ground of reality as well as the means by which we come to know them. Thus Aristotle, for instance, distinguished principles of **being,** of **existence,** and of **knowing.** Theologians also adapted this terminology. By way of revelation God makes himself known to us as the primary efficient cause of all things. Holy Scripture is the external instrumental efficient cause of theology, and divine revelation also requires the internal illumination of the Holy Spirit. We thus identify three fundamental principles for theology: God is the essential foundation (**principium essendi**); Scripture is the external cognitive foundation (**principium cognoscendi externum**); and the Holy Spirit is the internal principle of knowing (**principium cognoscendi internum**). The foundations of theology are thus trinitarian: The Father, through the Son as Logos, imparts himself to his creatures in the Spirit.*

Historically there are basically two schools of scientific thought: rationalism (subject oriented) and empiricism (object oriented). Rationalism is the not unreasonable attempt to impose mental order on the changing world of perceptions and representations. If we have access only to representations and not the things themselves, a form of idealism gains the upper hand in which only the thought is judged to be real. Rationalist idealism, however, violates the natural realism of our ordinary experience in the world. Idealism confuses the organ of knowledge with its source and has as its consequence the notion that our senses always deceive us and give us a false impression of reality.

Empiricism, on the other hand, proceeds from the diametrically opposite view, namely that sense perceptions alone are the source of our knowledge. The mind is a passive blank slate; human consciousness is completely subjected to the world outside of us. This view is also in error in failing to take into account the active role of the human mind, the role of unproven presuppositions in all scientific observation. In addition to its flawed starting point, empiricism denies the term "science" for all but the "exact sciences." The entire range of the "human sciences," including theology, is excluded; the fundamental religious and metaphys-

ical questions faced by all people must be ignored. It is especially here that modern philosophy and science is most disappointing and needs fundamental revision so that we are protected from both materialism and idealism.

The proper starting point for any theory of knowledge is the universal and natural certainty we find spontaneously in our ordinary experience. We trust our senses, which lead us to believe in an objective world external to us, and our mental representations of that world point back to that reality. From this we conclude that scientific demonstrative certainty is neither the basic nor the only kind of human certainty; there is also a universal, metaphysical, intuitive, immediate kind of certainty that is self-evident and which we call the "certainty of faith." Christian thinkers from Augustine on rejected rationalism in favor of a "realism" that acknowledges the primacy of the senses and the constraints placed by reality on the human mind. At the same time, in distinction from empiricist thought, Christian theology also insists that the mind does have its own nature, operates in its own way, and possesses the freedom to soar beyond the senses to the world of the ideal. The human mind is therefore not a blank slate, the representations it forms are faithful interpretations of the real world outside us. The human intellect also has the capacity to abstract general and universal judgments from particular events. Contrary to all forms of nominalism, which by denying the reality of universals in effect makes all science impossible, realism correctly assumes their reality **in the thing itself** *(in re) and therefore also in the human mind subsequent to the thing itself* **(in mente hominis post rem)**. *The theological explanation for this is the conviction that it is the same Logos who created both the reality outside of us and the laws of thought within us. The world is created in such a way that an organic connection and correspondence is possible between our minds and the reality external to us. The world is an embodiment of the thoughts of God. In the words of the Belgic Confession (art. 2), the creation is "a beautiful book in which all creatures, great and small, are as letters to make us ponder the invisible things of God." The created world is the external foundation of human knowledge* **(principium cognoscendi externum)**. *However, so that this knowledge becomes part of our human consciousness, the light of reason enables us to discover and recognize the logos in things. This internal foundation of knowledge* **(principium cognoscendi internum)** *is also a gift of the mind of God. The Father, by the Son, and in the Spirit, conveys the knowledge of truth to us.*

THEOLOGICAL PROLEGOMENA

[61] In theological works of an earlier time, it was customary to preface the actual *loci* with an exposition of the nature of theology. Later, under the influence of rationalism, this space was preempted by natural theology, as well as the proofs for revelation and Holy Scripture. After Kant by his critique deprived these intellectual arguments of their power, Schleiermacher, attempting to provide theology with another foundation, took his stance in religion. Though this differed from the old rationalism in that Schleierma-

cher viewed religion not as a kind of knowing but as a certain kind of feeling, he in fact, by his borrowed propositions (*Lehnsätze*), made dogmatics dependent on philosophy. For a long time under the heading of "prolegomena," "fundamental theology," or "philosophical theology" and the like, following Schleiermacher's footsteps, many theologians prefaced dogmatics with a far-ranging introduction that had an apologetic thrust. Theology lacked a foundation of its own and was not developed from its own first principles; it could only undertake its task after first letting philosophy examine and judge its basis and right to exist. The theologian did not from the outset take his stance within Christianity but took his initial position outside of Christianity, in religion in general, in order from that vantage point to proceed to an exposition of Christian doctrines.

This theological starting point was first—altogether correctly!—abandoned and opposed by Ritschl and Frank and later by numerous others.[1] A religion and a natural theology [in general], as rationalism conceives it, does not exist. For the religion and the natural theology we know was not acquired by us apart from special revelation but became our own from and in the light of Holy Scripture. Accordingly, we never find it among pagans in a pure form but always buried under all kinds of idolatry and mixed with numerous superstitions. The same is true of the concept and nature of religion. If we now have a purer idea of it than the pagans, we did not arrive at it by a comparative study of religions but owe it to Christianity and, thus equipped beforehand, proceeded to study and compare other religions. If Troeltsch wants to make the philosophy of religion foundational for the study of theology, then this is either a mere illusion or we can be sure that at the end of this study no Christian dogmatics will ever emerge. There is indeed no room for a philosophical theory of fundamental principles that must first lay the foundation for the study of theology and has the right to justify this pursuit. If dogmatics or theology in general did not, like other disciplines, have its own fundamental principles (principia),[2] it could not lay claim to the name of being "a science concerning God" (*scientia de Deo*). Holy Scripture, however, teaches us otherwise; it states that all knowledge of God comes to us from his revelation and that we on our own part cannot appropriate its con-

---

1. A. Ritschl, *Die Christliche Lehre von der Rechfertigung und Versöhnung*, 4th ed. (Bonn: A. Marcus), III, 1ff.; F. H. R. Frank, *System der christlichen Gewissheit*, 2 vols. in 1 (Erlangen: Deichert, 1884), I, chaps. 1–7; E. Böhl, *Dogmatik* (Amsterdam: Scheffer, 1887), lviii; H. Cremer in *Zöcklers Handbuch der theologischen Wissenschaften*, 612, 637; A. von Oettingen, *Lutherische Dogmatik*, 2 vols. (München: C. H. Beck, 1897–1902), I, 42; Paul Lobstein, *Einleitung in die evangelische Dogmatik* (Freiburg i.B.: J. C. B. Mohr, 1897), 1ff.; L. Ihmels, *Die Selbständigkeit der Dogmatik gegenüber der Religionsphilosophie* (Erlangen: Deichert, 1901).

2. Ed. note: For a full discussion of the classical use and meaning of *principia* language in theology, see Richard A. Muller, *Dictionary of Latin and Greek Theological Terms* (Grand Rapids: Baker, 1985), s.v. "principia theologiae" (pp. 245–46). We will be translating *principia* as "fundamental principles," "foundations," or "sources."

tent except by a sincere and childlike faith. Only those who are born of water and Spirit can see the kingdom of God.

But this directly leads us to the conviction that there is indeed room in theology for theoretical reflection on fundamental principles in a sense that differs from that often intended. The question is whether the foundations of theology, and particularly dogmatics, are derived from other disciplines or whether theology is an independent discipline advancing its fundamental principles out of its own storehouse. If so, theologians not only have the freedom but also the obligation to place these first principles in the clearest possible light and to treat them at least as extensively as other dogmas. For in doing so they do not take a position outside of Christianity but within it. They do not first, as rationalism does, position themselves on the standpoint of reason in order later to ascend or descend to that of faith. Nor do they treat topics that actually lie outside the territory of dogmatics, belong in other disciplines, and can only come up as "borrowed propositions" in the introduction of dogmatics. But in the discussion of these first principles as well, they immediately adopt the standpoint of faith. After all, the teaching that revelation is the only source of the knowledge of God and that only the spiritual person can know and discern the things that are spiritual is also a dogma in the full sense of the word—a dogma of fundamental significance. For if there is no revelation of God, or no means by which we can make that revelation our own spiritual possession, the entire edifice of theology, however skillfully constructed, collapses like a house of cards.

FOUNDATIONS OF THOUGHT

[62] In order to get to know the first principles that belong to dogmatic theology, it is first of all necessary to take account of what is generally understood by "fundamental principles" (*principia*) in general. According to Simplicius, the neoplatonic commentator on Aristotle, and similarly Hippolytus in his *Refutatio omnium haeresium,* Anaximander was the first to describe the ground of things he found in the ἀπειρον (the unbounded) with the term ἀρχη (beginning, origin, foundation, or source).[3] By doing this, however, he may have meant only that the ἀπειρον was the beginning and first of all things.[4] But in the philosophy of Plato and Aristotle this word acquired the meaning of the ultimate cause of things. Plato already speaks of the principle of motion, of becoming, and of proof,[5] and Aristotle understands ἀρχαι in general to refer to the first things in a series and particularly the first causes

---

3. Heinrich Ritter and Ludwig Preller, *Historia philosophiae Graecae* (Gothae: F. A. Perthes, 1888), 16, 17.

4. Eduard Zeller, *Die Philosophie der Griechen,* 4th ed., 3 vols. (Leipzig: O. R. Reisland, 1879, 1919), I, 203; English translation under the title *Outlines of the History of Greek Philosophy,* 13th ed., rev. Wilhelm Nestle and trans. L. R. Palmer (London: Routledge & Kegan Paul, 1969), 28–29.

5. ἀρχη κινησεως, ἀρχη γενεσεως, and ἀρχη ἀποδειξεως.

that cannot be traced to other causes. He offers the well-known definition: So, then, the first common element of all principles (ἀρχαι) is that whence something either is or becomes or is known.[6] He assumed that such principles existed especially in two areas, that of being and that of consciousness, in metaphysics and in logic. He derived the being of things from four ἀρχαι, namely the material, formal, efficient, and final cause.[7] He similarly assumed that such principles were present in logic. Aristotle commented, namely, that it is far from possible to offer proof for all things; the fact is that of many things we do not have a mediate knowledge by proof but an immediate knowledge by reason. In order not to create an infinite regression, the proofs themselves must proceed from the kind of propositions that, being immediately certain, are not capable of proof or do not need it. And these propositions Aristotle called principles of proof, syllogistic principles, immediate [lacking a middle term] principles, or also, as general assumptions underlying all proof, *axioms*.[8] Of these he says: "I mean those principles in each genus which it is not possible to prove that they are."[9] The Latin word *principium* was used in the same sense. Cicero, for example, speaks of the *principia* of things, *principia* of nature, natural *principia,* the *principium* of philosophy, the *principia* of law. In logic, in keeping with the definition of Aristotle cited above, three types of *principia* were later distinguished: the principle of being, of existence, and of knowing. The distinction depended on whether the being, the becoming, or the knowledge of a thing has to be derived from something else. The term *principium* was distinguished from *causa* in that the latter referred to the former as "something determining by its own inner impulse that which was insufficient for existence by itself"[10] and so as prior *in time* or at least *by nature* than the thing it caused. *Causa* is a particular kind of *principium*. Every *causa* is a *principium,* but not every *principium* is a *causa.*

This terminology was adopted in theology as well. In Scripture ἀρχη not only often has a temporal meaning (Mark 1:1; John 1:1, etc.) but also, a few times, a causative meaning. In the Septuagint the fear of the Lord is called the ἀρχη of wisdom (Prov. 1:7), and in Colossians 1:18 and Revelation 3:14 Christ is called the ἀρχη of creation and of the resurrection. The church fathers frequently spoke of the Father as ἀρχη (origin), πηγη (source), and αἰτιον (cause) of the Son and Spirit, just as Augustine calls the Father "the principle of the whole divinity" (*principium totius divinitatis*).[11] Thus God was the essential foundation (*principium essendi*) or the principle of existence (*principium existendi*) of all that has been created, hence also of science and

---

6. πασων μεν οὖν κοινον των ἀρχων το πρωτον εἰναι ὁθεν ἡ ἐστιν ἡ γιγνεται ἡ γιγνωσκεται .

7. ὑλη, εἰδος, ἀρχη της κινησεως, and τελος.

8. ἀρχαι ἀποδειξεως, ἀρχαι συλλογιστικαι ἀρχαι ἀμεσοι.

9. λεγω δ᾽ ἀρχας ἐν ἑκαστῳ γενει ταυτας, ἁς ὁτι ἐστι μη ἐνδεχεται δειξαι.

10. *Influxo suo determinans aliquid sibi insufficiens ad existendum.*

11. Athanasius, *Orations against Arians,* II; Basil, *Books against Eunomius,* I; John of Damascus, *The Orthodox Faith,* I, 9; Augustine, *On the Trinity,* IV, 20.

specifically again of theology. In this last domain it was always expressly repeated that God was the essential foundation of theology. There was a special reason for this. No knowledge of God is possible except that which proceeds from and by God (Matt. 11:27; 1 Cor. 2:10ff.). Earlier theology had an axiom for it: "What we need to understand about God must be taught by God himself, for this cannot be known except by the author himself."[12] The fact that the creature knows anything of God at all is solely due to God. He is knowable only because and insofar as he himself wants to be known. The human analogy already proves the truth of this statement. A human is to a certain extent the origin (*principium essendi*) of our knowledge concerning his person (1 Cor. 2:11). A man must reveal himself, manifest himself by appearance, word, and act, so that we may somewhat learn to know him. But in the case of human beings this is always relative. We often reveal ourselves in totally arbitrary ways and in spite of ourselves; we often manifest ourselves in character traits and peculiarities that are unknown to us. Sometimes our self-manifestation belies who we are—it is false, untrue, misleading. But none of this is true of God. He is, in the absolute sense of the term, the source, the primary efficient cause[13] of our knowledge of him, for he is absolutely free, self-conscious, and true. His self-knowledge and self-consciousness is the source (*principium essendi*) of our knowledge of him. Without the divine self-consciousness, there is no knowledge of God in his creatures. Pantheism is the death of theology. The relation of God's own self-knowledge to our knowledge of God used to be expressed by saying that the former was archetypal of the latter and the latter ectypal of the former. Our knowledge of God is the imprint of the knowledge God has of himself but always on a creaturely level and in a creaturely way. The knowledge of God present in his creatures is only a weak likeness, a finite, limited sketch, of the absolute self-consciousness of God accommodated to the capacities of the human or creaturely consciousness. But however great the distance is, the source (*principium essendi*) of our knowledge of God is solely God himself, the God who reveals himself freely, self-consciously, and genuinely.

[63] Distinct, now, from this essential foundation (*principium essendi*) is the principle by which we know (*principium cognoscendi*). The fact that theology exists we owe solely to God, to his self-consciousness, to his good pleasure. But the means, the way, by which that knowledge of God reaches us is God's revelation, understood here in an altogether general sense. This is implied in the nature of the thing. Other people only become knowable to us when they reveal themselves to us, i.e., manifest their presence, speak, or act. Appearance, word, and deed are the three revelational forms between one human and another. The same is true in the case of the Lord our God; his knowledge, too, flows to us only through the channel of his revelation. Fur-

---

12. *A deo discendum quid de ipso intelligendum, quia non nisi auctore cognoscitur.*
13. *Principium esssendi, causa efficiens principalis.*

thermore, that revelation, too, can only be his appearance, his word, and his deed. Accordingly, the principle by which we know (*principium cognoscendi*), the principle of theology, is the self-revelation or self-communication of God to his creatures. Whether that self-revelation comes individually to every human or is recorded for all humanity in Scripture or in the church is something we can examine later on. For the present it is enough to say that the self-revelation of God can, in the nature of the case, be the only *principium cognoscendi* of our knowledge of God. We must add to this only that if that self-revelation of God is deposited in Scripture or in the church, that Scripture and that church can have only instrumental—hence, in a sense, incidental, provisional—significance. At best, therefore, Holy Scripture is the instrumental efficient cause[14] of theology.

The aim of theology, after all, can be no other than that the rational creature know God and, knowing him, glorify God (Prov. 16:4; Rom. 11:36; 1 Cor. 8:6; Col. 3:17). It is his good pleasure (εὐδοκια) to be known by human beings (Matt. 11:25, 26). The object of God's self-revelation, accordingly, is to introduce his knowledge into the human consciousness and through it again to set the stage for the glorification of God himself. But that divine self-revelation, then, cannot end outside of, before, or in the proximity of human beings but must reach into human beings themselves. In other words, revelation cannot be external only but must also be internal. For that reason a distinction used to be made between the external and the internal principle of knowing, the external and the internal word, revelation and illumination,[15] the working of God's Word and the working of his Spirit. The internal word (*verbum internum*) is the principal word (*verbum principale*), for it is this which introduces the knowledge of God into human beings, and that is the purpose of all theology, indeed of the whole self-revelation of God. The external word, the revelation recorded in Holy Scripture, in this connection serves as a means. It is the instrumental word (*verbum instrumentale*), necessary perhaps for all kinds of secondary reasons in this dispensation, but still by its nature provisional, temporary, and incidental.

Thus we have discovered three foundations (*principia*): First, God as the essential foundation (*principium essendi*), the source, of theology; next, the external cognitive foundation (*principium cognoscendi externum*), viz., the self-revelation of God, which, insofar as it is recorded in Holy Scripture, bears an instrumental and temporary character; and finally, the internal principle of knowing (*principium cognoscendi internum*), the illumination of human beings by God's Spirit. These three are one in the respect that they have God as author and have as their content one identical knowledge of God. The archetypal knowledge of God in the divine consciousness; the ectypal knowledge of God granted in revelation and recorded in Holy Scrip-

---

14. *Causa efficiens instrumentalis.*

15. *Principium cognoscendi externum et internum, verbum externum et internum, revelatio et illuminatio.*

ture; and the knowledge of God in the subject, insofar as it proceeds from revelation and enters into the human consciousness, are all three of them from God. It is God himself who discloses his self-knowledge, communicates it through revelation, and introduces it into human beings. And materially they are one as well, for it is one identical, pure, and genuine knowledge of God, which he has of himself, communicates in revelation, and introduces into the human consciousness. They may and can, therefore, never be separated and detached from each other. On the other hand, they do need to be distinguished. For the knowledge of God has of himself, is absolute, simple, infinite, and in its absoluteness incommunicable to the finite consciousness. In earlier times, therefore, the archetypal knowledge of God was occasionally restricted to the part of the self-knowledge of God that he had decided to communicate to creatures. But this distinction makes the revelation between archetypal and the ectypal knowledge of God into a mechanical one and ignores the fact that absoluteness consists not only in quantity but also in quality. Still, the distinction contains the true idea that the ectypal knowledge of God that is granted to creatures by revelation is not the absolute self-knowledge of God but the knowledge of God as it has been accommodated to and made fit for the finite consciousness—hence anthropomorphized. This ectypal knowledge of God, which lies objectively before us in revelation, is external but intended to be transferred into the consciousness of rational creatures to become ectypal internal knowledge of God, knowledge of God in the subject. In the process this knowledge again undergoes changes, depending on the nature of the subject. It differs, not in substance and rational order (*re et ratione*), but nevertheless in degree and manner (*gradu et modo*): in Christ (*theologia unionis;* theology of union), in the angels and the blessed (*theologia visionis;* theology of vision), and in human beings on earth (*theologia viatorum, viae, revelationis;* theology of people in pilgrimage, on a journey, of revelation). Among human beings it again differs in prophets and apostles, and in theologians and lay people. It is modified in each person's consciousness, depending on his or her capacity for it. But materially it is and remains identical knowledge, knowledge that proceeds from God and is transplanted by way of revelation to the consciousness of his rational creatures. These three principia, distinct yet essentially one, are rooted in the trinitarian being of God. It is the Father who, through the Son as Logos, imparts himself to his creatures in the Spirit.

RATIONALISM

[64] Science always consists in a logical relation between subject and object. Our view of science depends on the way we relate the two. At all times there have been two basic schools of thought that were diametrically opposed to each other in this respect: rationalism and empiricism.

The two schools surfaced already in Greek philosophy. There already a contrast was construed between αἴσθησις and λόγος, sense perception and thought, and therefore between opinion (δόξα) and knowledge (ἐπιστήμη). The Eleatic school (Parmenides), Plato, and the neoplatonists stood on the side of rationalism, believing that sense perception yields no knowledge because it is focused on changing phenomena. Sense perception only teaches us that something is and is such but not *why* it is such. Furthermore, sense perception often deceives us and gives us false ideas, like the "crooked" stick standing in the water, the "rising" sun, etc., ideas that can be cleansed of their untruth only by thinking. Accordingly, thinking is far superior to sense perception. Only thinking yields knowledge (ἐπιστήμη); scientific knowledge does not come from without; it is a product of the human mind.

In more recent philosophy this rationalistic trend again surfaced in Descartes who, casting all tradition aside, finally found his fixed starting point in thought and from it inferred being: *cogito ergo sum*. With that move logical necessity and coherence, the mathematical order of ground and consequence in the work of Spinoza, became the standard of truth. The world of sense perception is at most the occasion for, not the source of, our knowledge; the human mind is able to produce all knowledge from within itself, with its own means, by means of thought. Said Leibnitz: "Our ideas, even those of perceptible things, come from within ourselves."[16] Kant admittedly did temper this rationalism insofar as he did not derive the content but only the forms of perception from the human mind (transcendental, critical idealism). But Fichte correctly noted that such a distinction is impossible and therefore stated that all the elements of our knowledge, including even perception, are a priori and posited by the ego (absolute idealism). This rationalism was still consistently restricted by these philosophers to the area of knowing and therefore only intended in an epistemological sense. But this subjective rationalism was expanded by Fichte, Schelling, and Hegel into an objective rationalism. Not only knowledge but also being, not only ideas but also the things themselves, issued from thinking. Thinking and being, thus, are one (metaphysical idealism). There is a dynamic at work in this history of rationalism: thinking, not sense perception, yields truth. To this end thinking brings with it from within itself the origins (*principia*), the seeds (*semina*) of all knowledge. Thinking creates the form of our conceptual world (Kant), and also its matter and content (Fichte); indeed, it creates and constructs the entire world, not only the world of thought, but also the being itself.

In whatever different forms this rationalism manifested itself, it was always marked by the same basic idea, namely that the origin of knowledge is to be found in the subject. It is not at all hard to understand how people ar-

16. G. W. Leibnitz, *Nouveaux essais sur l'entendement humain* (Paris: C. H. Delagrave, 1886), bk. I, chap. 1.

rived at this idea. Even apart from the unreliability of sense perception, there is such an essential difference between the representations in us and the things outside of us that the former cannot be explained in terms of the latter. Matter cannot operate on the mind. Mental phenomena, which is what these representations are, can be explained only in terms of the mind; like can only be known by like. From this it follows that the existence and cooperation of matter and mind, of the things outside of us and the representations within us, can *either* be maintained solely by hypotheses like occasionalism (Geulinx), preestablished harmony (Leibnitz), the intuition of the ideas in God (Malebranche), etc., *or* the duality of matter and mind must simply be denied, and thing and representation, being and thinking, are viewed as essentially one. For, says idealism, if a thing and the representation of a thing are two different realities, then we must despair of knowledge of the thing. Since we simply can never test our representation of a thing by the thing itself, we can never step outside of ourselves, of our representational world. "We cannot put ourselves at the window in order [simultaneously] to see ourselves pass in the street" (Scherer).[17] We always remain inside the circle of our representations and never come into contact with the thing itself, only with our representation of the thing. Stated differently, only that which is conscious exists for us; I can only think the thought, not the thing itself. That which is not my thought is inconceivable, unknowable to me; it does not exist for me.

This idealism is further reinforced by what the physiology of the senses now teaches. Democritus already made a distinction between such properties as weight, density, and hardness—properties that are objective and inherent in the things themselves—and other properties such as warmth, coldness, flavor, and color—properties only subjectively present in our perceptions. This distinction between objective and subjective, quantitative and qualitative, properties was adopted by Descartes, Hobbes, and Locke (who was the first to call them primary and secondary properties) and has been worked out in this century especially by Helmholtz. According to this so-called semi-idealism, outside of us only the mechanical movements of atoms exist in the world; matter itself is devoid of quality. Our senses merely receive impressions resulting from the movement and undulation of atoms. Those impressions are qualitatively the same, but out of those uniform movements we produce the infinite diversity of the world of perception in our brains. Light, sound, color, flavor, warmth, coldness—all of them qualitative properties we think we are perceiving in things—do not exist outside of the human mind but originate and exist only in it. The same movement of matter, impinging on our sense of touch, creates an impression of warmth, and impinging on our eye creates in us a perception of light. Not in

---

17. Ed. note: Bavinck may be referring to Edmond Henri Adolphe Scherer (1815–89), professor at the Theological School of Geneva.

its substance but in its form the world is a product of man. Thus idealism has gradually gained more ground in philosophy and even received vigorous support from natural science.

[65] Still, there are serious objections to this idealism. In the first place, it is contrary to all experience. By nature we are all realists, including, in practice, the idealists themselves. Actually idealism is something—an opinion belonging to a school—directly contrary to life and experience. It does not explain how and why every human automatically and spontaneously gets to ascribing objectivity and independent reality to the things perceived, instead of viewing them purely as inner states of consciousness. At the same time we clearly distinguish between internal states and external things, between that which is in us and that which is outside of us, between dream (hallucination) and reality. Add to this that man is never, in any area, autonomous but everywhere and always dependent on the nature surrounding him. By his body he is bound to the earth. Shelter, food, and clothing come to him from the earth; it would be strange if intellectually things were different. Just as with our own hands we prepare food and clothing while nevertheless deriving the materials for them from nature outside of us, so with our intellect we also receive the material from without. Here, too, the intellect is an instrument, not a source. Idealism equates the organ of knowledge with the source of knowledge, as it were making the eye into the source of light, deducing the thought from the process of thinking. However, this is not possible because a thing and the representation of a thing, being and thinking, to be and to perceive, are distinct and cannot be equated. These two, after all, are totally different in kind.

A thing does not arise in me like a dream and does not follow logically from antecedent impressions but often comes to me abruptly from without, breaking down the train of earlier impressions. Such things are not dependent on me but have existence apart from me and possess properties that cannot be attributed to the representation I have of them. The thing we call a stove is warm, say, but the representation of the stove present in my mind does not have that property. If the thing and the representation of it are nevertheless equated with each other, idealism must lead to absolute illusionism. Not only does the world outside of me become an illusion, but I myself also am nothing but a representation, a phenomenon to myself. Everything becomes a dream; there is no longer any reality, or truth. Now idealism may not exert influence on the actions and conduct of its adherents, since often a person's practice is better and stronger than his theory. It is hard to see how religion and morality, say, can still be theoretically defensible if neither of them assumes a real relationship to beings existing outside of me but both are merely representations within me. Accordingly, the dualism of thinking and being from which idealism proceeds in the case of Plato, Descartes, and Kant always, as in the case of Spinoza, Fichte, Schelling, and Hegel, ends up in an identity of the two. Subjective rationalism leads to absolute and objective rationalism.

But abstract, contentless thought, the most universal principle of "substance," the absolute, existence, thought—all of them names for idealism's starting point—is not able to produce being in its fullness and riches. The living world cannot be explained from that sterile abstraction, nor the multiplicity of phenomena from that lifeless "one." The rock on which all pantheism runs aground is multiplicity; there is no discoverable passage from the abstract to the concrete, from the general to the particular. Accordingly, Schelling openly stated, "It is hard to get to reality [from here]." Finally, a distinction like that of Kant between the form that we ourselves bring with us in perception and the matter that comes to us from without or that of semi-idealism between objective (primary) and subjective (secondary) phenomena is untenable for the reason that no boundary between the two can be indicated. The matter of a representation, as Fichte pointed out, belongs as much to that representation as its form. And the primary quantitative properties, indeed the bodies themselves, are just as much perceived phenomena as the qualitative phenomena of tone and color and so forth. There is no reason to accept the witness of one of the senses, the sense of touch, and to reject that of the other four and therefore to make an exception solely for the properties of extension, hardness, etc. We have to make a choice: either the perceptions we gain by way of the senses are all subjective, or they all correspond to an objective reality. It would be extremely odd if, observing, say, a flaming fire, we held the form, the size, and movement of the flames to be objective properties but considered the orange-reddish color and the crackling of the flames to be purely subjective perceptions. Of the two qualities so closely connected in visual perception, viz., color and form, the former would be merely a sign, but the latter a reliable image of reality! The consequence of this view would be that the most important of our senses, that of sight and that of hearing, would always give a false impression of reality and actually always deceive us.

They are therefore wrong who believe that the physiology of the senses prohibits us from maintaining the objectivity of the qualitative properties. One only has to make a distinction between the *conditions* under which (or the *occasion* on which) and the *causes* by which the perceptions originate in our soul. Just as a telegraph transmits a message by means of mechanical vibrations while the message itself is something very different from those vibrations, so the stimuli that proceed from objects to the nerves of our senses are only physical means by which the perceptions are aroused in our soul. These perceptions themselves, however, are of a very different nature. Their qualities, as the theory of psycho-physical parallelism acknowledges today as well, cannot be explained in terms of physical and physiological phenomena alone. Rather, they are merely the conditions under which they originate in the soul. We can only say, therefore, that certain perceptions correspond to certain stimuli. But we have no right to conclude that the latter are actually the cause of the former, neither with respect to the quantitative nor in regard to the qualitative properties. In this respect the two are completely equal. Accordingly, it is not the senses that perceive the phenomena outside of us but it is always one and the same soul that by means of the senses perceives the things and receives the corresponding impressions.

EMPIRICISM

[66] Diametrically opposed to rationalism is empiricism, which among the Greeks already had its precursors in the atomists then emerged in the Middle Ages as nominalism. As a philosophical trend in modern times, empiricism made its debut with Francis Bacon and by way of Locke, Hume, and the French encyclopedists culminated in this century in the positivism of A. Comte, the empirical philosophy of J. Stuart Mill, the agnosticism of H. Spencer, and the materialism of Büchner, Czolbe, Moleschott, etc. Empiricism also appears on the scene in various forms and systems, but its starting point is always the principle that sense perception alone is the source of our knowledge. Whereas in rationalism the objective world lets itself be directed in whole or in part in accordance with the human mind, empiricism totally subjects the human consciousness to the world outside of us. In the pursuit of knowledge, human beings bring with them nothing but the faculty of perception. All intellectual activity has its beginning and source in this faculty. Innate ideas, therefore, do not exist; the scientific investigator must set aside all preconceived opinions. From the temple of truth, which he aspires to construct in his mind, he must remove all idols. No anticipation of the mind but the interpretation of nature—just experience—must lead him (Bacon).

The human mind, therefore, is and must be a *tabula rasa* on which nothing has as yet been written, an entity completely devoid of presupposition. Knowledge is trustworthy only when it is constructed out of the material of perception. "Concepts without sense perception are empty." The further a human removes himself from experience and goes beyond it, the less he is to be trusted in his scientific pursuit. No science of the supersensible (noumena) and the supernatural is therefore possible. Metaphysics, theology, the intellectual disciplines in general, even psychology according to Comte, are not sciences in the real sense of the word. Scientific knowledge is limited to the exact sciences. And even within the circle of perceptible phenomena, our knowledge is limited to the *that* and the *how*; the *what* and the *why* remain hidden. The cause and the end, the origin and the destiny of things, lie outside our reach; only the mutual relation between things, the "invariable relations of succession and of resemblance," are the object of scientific research.[18]

18. Auguste Comte, *Cours de Philosophie Positive*, 6 vols. (Paris: Bachelier, 1830–42), I, 5; in English see *Auguste Comte and Positivism: The Essential Writings,* edited and with an introduction by Gertrud Len-

Whether behind and above the perceptible phenomena there is still something else, whether the soul, God, or the beyond (*Jenseits*) exists, may perhaps be made plausible by some other way, say, by practical reason, faith, imagination, etc., but scientifically all of this is and remains unknown territory. Accordingly, the aim of science can no longer consist in giving an explanation of the world but is merely to obtain a knowledge of reality such that we can arrange our lives by it and draw practical benefit from it. "To know is to foresee; from knowledge comes foresight; from foresight comes action." But this absolute connectedness of the mind to the perceptible world has led others to make the attempt to explain not only the cognitive content of the mind in terms of the world but also consciousness and the mind itself. The result then is that empiricism ends in materialism. Here, too, progression can be noted, a history, a development. First the cognitive content, then the faculty of knowing, and finally the mind itself is derived from the material world.

Now this empiricism, too, though enjoying tremendous support from the fact of man's dependence on the natural world surrounding him, is nevertheless burdened by weighty objections. It is firmly established, first of all, that in its intellectual activity the human mind is never totally passive or even receptive but also always more or less active. It is not the eye that sees or the ear that hears but the person himself who sees through the eye and hears through the ear. Even the most simple perception and representation already presupposes consciousness and hence some activity of the soul. The human mind is never a mere *tabula rasa* on which the external world can write what it pleases; it is the person himself who perceives and connects, compares and judges, the perceptions. But there is more to be added. Kant rightly says: "Experience teaches us, to be sure, that something is constituted thus and so, but not that it could not be otherwise."[19] After all, we possess not only particular and incidental truths but also universal and necessary truths—in logic, mathematics, etc.—which empiricists have tried in vain to deduce from experience. The principle of causality has in truth been called the bulwark of the intuitive school; and all the pains taken to explain this principle and foundation of all science from determination by the will or from custom, etc., have been fruitless.[20] Indeed, all sciences proceed from a series of unproven and unprovable propositions that are accepted *a priori* and serve as

zer (New York: Harper & Row, Publishers, 1975), 72; or *The Essential Comte: Selected from Cours de philosophie positive,* edited, with an introduction by Stanislav Andreski, translated and annotated by Margaret Clarke (London: Croom Helm; New York: Barnes & Noble, 1974), 20.

19. Immanuel Kant, *Critique of Pure Reason,* Cambridge Edition of the Works of Immanuel Kant, trans. and ed. Paul Guyer and Allen W. Wood (Cambridge: Cambridge University Press, 1997), introduction(B) chap. 2, p. 137.

20. G. Heijmans, *Schets eener Kritische Geschiedenis van het Causalititsbegrip in de Nieuwere Wysbegeerte* (Leiden: Brill, 1890); E. Koenig, *Die Entwicklung des Causal problems von Cartesius bis Kant* (Leipzig: Wigand, 1888); C. B. Spruyt, *Proeve van eene Geschiedenus van de Leer der Aangeboren Begrippen* (Leiden: Brill, 1879).

starting point for all argumentation and proof. Aristotle already saw this. There is no infinite regress; precisely in order to have evidential value, proofs must finally rest in a proposition that needs no proof, that rests in itself, and can therefore serve as principle of proof (ἀρχη ἀποδειεως, *principium argumentationis*). A building cannot stand in the air, and a given argumentation can rest only on a foundation that is established by being self-evident and not by proof.

Empiricism's starting point is judged by this, but its view of science is also subject to serious question. Science, after all, is by its very nature interested in knowledge of that which is universal, necessary, eternal, and logical. Knowledge of phenomena, persons, facts, etc., though good, is still only preparatory; analysis comes first but synthesis must follow. Scientific knowledge exists only when we see the cause and essence, the purpose and destiny of things, when we know not only the *that* (ὁτι) but also the *wherefore* (διοτι) and thus discern the causes of things (*rerum dignoscimus causas*). Empiricism, however, is compelled to deny the name of "science" to all sciences except the exact sciences. But this restriction is impossible for two reasons. First, because aside from the purely formal sciences (logic, mathematics, mechanics, astronomy, chemistry), and then only in a certain sense, there can be no science without a philosophical element. In every science, inventiveness, intuition, imagination, in a word, *genius* (and in this connection the scientific hypothesis) play a most important role. And second, because then the name of "science" can finally be reserved only for a few subsidiary disciplines, and precisely the knowledge that is most important to human beings and that in their research is their primary interest is banished from the domain of science. Thomas's maxim, in which he follows Aristotle, remains true: "The slenderest acquaintance we can form with heavenly things is more desirable than a thorough grasp of mundane matters."[21] And Schopenhauer made a similar statement: "People never stop praising the reliability and certainty of mathematics. However, what benefit is there for me in knowing with ever so much certainty and reliability something which I do not in the least care about?"[22]

In addition to this, the world of nonmaterial things, the world of values, of good and evil, law and custom, religion and morality, of all that inspires love and hatred in our hearts, lifts us up and comforts us or crushes and grieves us, that whole magnificent invisible world is as much a reality to us as the "real world" that we perceive with our senses. Its impact on our lives and on the history of humankind is still much greater than that of the visible things about us. Human beings may be freely asked, then, to limit themselves in their research since in this domain no knowledge is possible, but this demand bounces off what Schopenhauer called the metaphysical need of the human spirit. Man is not only an in-

21. Aquinas, *Summa Theol.*, I, qu. 1, art. 5, ad 1.
22. Cited by J. J. Van Oosterzee, *Voor Kerk en Theologie,* 2 vols. (Utrecht: Kemink, 1872–75), I, 101.

tellectual but also a willing and feeling being; he is not a thinking machine but in addition to his head also has a heart, an [inner] world of feelings and passions. He brings these with him in his scientific research. In his activities in study and laboratory, he cannot lock himself out. It cannot rightly be demanded of man that in his scientific labors, that is, in one of the noblest activities of his mind, he silence the voice of his feelings, his heart, the best part of him, and thus cripple himself. Only this may always—and therefore also in the case of the practitioner of science—be demanded: that he be a good, a true man, a man of God, proficient and equipped for every good work, including this work of pursuing scientific knowledge.

If, however, the pursuit of science is both subjectively and objectively restricted, the only outcome will be that people will seek the satisfaction of their metaphysical needs in other ways. Kant took the road of practical reason; Comte introduced the cult of humanity, consecrating himself as its high priest; and Spencer humbly bowed down before "The Unknowable." In one way or another—including even spiritism, magic, and theosophy—they all seek compensation for what science will not give them. And religion, along with all spiritual knowledge, having first been shamefully dismissed through the front door, is again admitted through the back door but now frequently in the form of superstition. "You may expel nature with might and main; it will nevertheless always come bounding back" (Horace). Only, the inevitable result is that science is then left, undefended and unarmed, to materialism. And, in fact, this is what empiricism has led to. If the content and, soon, the intellectual faculty of the soul as well proceed altogether from the external world, why then could not the soul itself be explained in terms of it as well? But over against this still always stand the "seven riddles of the world" as a source of torment and vexation to the materialistic mind. The spiritual still has not yet been explained in terms of the material, any more than rationalism has succeeded in deriving "being" from "thinking." No passage between the two has been found. Here is a gap that neither idealism nor materialism can bridge. It is not too daring even now to say not only "we do not know" (*Ignoramus*) but also "we shall not know" (*Ignorabimus*). But when we see that, despite the great promises made and the still greater expectations entertained, empiricism and rationalism in this century ended up in mere materialism and illusionism, we wonder. Despite the opposition between materialism and illusionism, they still advanced and aided each other—in the case of Feuerbach and Strauss, Hegel's idealism ended in materialism, and in the cases of many natural scientists, materialism is turning into full or semi-idealism. So there is good reason to ask some questions. Does not the whole of modern philosophy, in its Cartesian as well as in its Baconian expression, need revision? Are there not other and better principles of science, principles that protect us from materialism as well as idealism?

REALISM

Natural Certainty

[67] The starting point of the theory of knowledge ought to be ordinary daily experience, the universal and natural certainty of human beings concerning the objectivity and truth of their knowledge. After all, it is not philosophy that creates the cognitive faculty and cognition. Philosophy only finds it and then attempts to explain it. Any solution that does not explain the cognitive faculty but instead destroys it and, failing to understand cognition, turns it into an illusion, is judged by that fact. Only a theory of knowledge such that on the one hand it never leaves the ground of experience and on the other penetrates the very depths of the problem has a chance to succeed. Tertullian rightly says: First there was man, then the philosopher or the poet.[23] One must first live, then philosophize (*Primum vivere, deinde philosophari*). Natural certainty is the indispensable foundation of science. Scientific knowledge is not a destruction but a purification, expansion, and completion of ordinary knowledge.[24] Every human, after all, accepts the reliability of the senses and the existence of the external world, not by a logical inference from the effect, in this case the representation in his consciousness, to the cause outside of himself, nor by reasoning from the resistance his will encounters to an objective reality that generates this resistance. Prior to all reflection and reasoning, everyone is in fact fully assured of the real existence of the world.

This certainty is not born out of a syllogism, nor is it supported by proof; it is immediate, originating spontaneously within us along with perception itself. It is not a product but the foundation and starting point of all other certainty. Every human, even the least knowledgeable, a child already and an animal also, accepts in advance, without any reasoning, the existence of an external world. In the mental representation itself, therefore, there must be an element that points directly back to reality. As representation it includes the essential distinguishing mark indicating that it represents that reality ideally. Idealism therefore errs at the outset by not taking the representation as it presents itself but denies its representative character. Materially, in terms of content, idealism puts the representation on a level with an image from a dream and consequently makes all kinds of futile attempts to move by reasonings and proofs from the subject to the object. Accordingly, in modern times many people have accepted the position of phenomenalism or absolute idealism and consider the world of perceptions and representations the only true world.[25] Realism, by contrast, holds fast to the existence of the world because that world is, in an ideal sense, given in the representation it-

---

23. Tertullian, *De Testimonio Animae*, chap. 5; see *The Soul's Testimony, ANF,* III.

24. Julius Kaftan, *The Truth of the Christian Religion*, trans. George Ferries, 2 vols. (Edinburgh: T. & T. Clark, 1894), II, chap. 1.

25. For a good review, see Rudolf Eisler, *Kritische Einführung in die Philosphie* (Berlin: E. S. Mittler, 1905), 82–119.

self. It does not deny the distinction that exists between the representation and the thing but at the same time maintains the inseparable connection between the two because it takes the representation as it presents itself. We must not, however, fail to distinguish between the certainty immediately given with the actual perception of an object and the certainty that later, when the perception is long past, follows from the memory. We are here talking only about the former, and this certainty is not a conclusion drawn from a process of reasoning but is immediately present in us and given along with the perception itself.[26]

This one fact alone—the natural certainty concerning the reliability of the senses and the reality of the external world—is proof that there exists a certainty other than scientific demonstrative certainty. Empiricists were wrong when they denied this. Experience only teaches us that something is, but not that it has to be; it only teaches us to know the accidental, the changeable, the real. However, we also possess universal necessary truths of which we are certain *a priori*—not by perception and reasoning. Most philosophers, therefore, have also accepted a metaphysical, intuitive, immediate certainty besides a scientific or mediate certainty. We call this the certainty of faith, of self-evidence. Aristotle was the first to see clearly that knowledge (ἐπιστήμη) is in the final analysis built on undemonstrable self-evident truths. Some thinkers, like Plato, Descartes, Leibnitz, and Rosmini, have sought to explain this unchangeable, eternal character of truth by the theory of innate ideas. But this theory is based on an untenable dualism between subject and object, is in principle rationalistic, and leads logically as well as historically to absolute idealism. According to Prof. Spruyt[27] this was the probable reason why the theory of innate ideas was unanimously rejected by scholastic as well as by Reformed theologians.[28] Voetius himself devoted a lengthy disputation to the arguments against Descartes's theory.[29] Reformed theologians even took over the empiricist thesis "there is nothing in the intellect which is not first in the senses" and spoke of man, prior to the act of perceiving, as a blank page on which nothing is written.[30] And they maintained this because, in distinction from angels, man is corporeal, because his body is not a prison but belongs to his very nature and he is bound to the cosmos by that body.[31]

26. Cf. Otto Flügel, *Die Probleme der Philosophie und ihre Lösungen* (Cöthen: O. Schulze, 1888), 104ff.; Engelbert L. Fischer, *Die Grundfragen der Erkenntnisstheorie* (Mainz: F. Kirchheim, 1887), 392ff.; W. Schmid, *Erkenntnislehre*, 2 vols. (Freiburg im Breisgau: Herder, 1890), II, 307ff.; Georg Wobbermin, *Theologie und Metaphysik* (Leipzig: J. C. Hinrich, 1901), 42ff.; J. P. N. Land, *Inleiding tot de wijsbegeerte* (s'Gravenhage, Nijhoff, 1900), 97ff.

27. Spruyt, *Proeve van eene Geschiedenis*, 57–60.

28. Jakob Frohschammer, *Die Philosophie des Thomas von Aquino* (Leipzig: F. A. Brockhaus, 1889), 44ff.; M. Liberatore, *Die Erkenntniss-theorie des heiligen Thomas von Aquino* (Mainz: F. Kirchheim, 1861); 103ff.; Polanus, *Synt. Theol.*, 324; J. Zanchius, *Opera*, III, 636.

29. G. Voetius, *Disput. Sel.*, V, 477–526.

30. Aquinas, *Summa Theol.*, 1a 79, 2; Voetius, *Disput. Sel.*, V, 459, 525.

31. Aquinas, *Summa Theol.*, I, qu. 84, art. 3; qu. 8.5, art. 1; G. Voetius, *Disput. Sel.*, V, 483.

So, on the one hand, they rejected rationalism as firmly as possible, not only in the guise of innate ideas in which it was taught by Plato, Descartes, and Leibnitz, but also in that of the innate forms in which it surfaced in Kant, and in that of the innate idea of being in which it emerged in Rosmini and the ontologists. But, on the other hand, the statements cited above must not be understood in the sense of Locke's empiricism. When Thomas calls the human mind a blank page (*tabula rasa*), it is not at all his intent to deny that understanding itself (*ipse intellectus*) is innate in human beings. To the maxim "there is nothing in the intellect which was not first in the senses," Leibnitz added the restriction: "except understanding itself" (*nisi ipse intellectus*). Thomas expresses himself still more correctly: "The forms of other intelligible things are not innate in it [the mind] but each essence is, so that it does not have to acquire this essence from sense images."[32] And Voetius explains the saying cited above by stating that this does not exclude the notion that in the world perceived by the senses the intellect can discern and know that which is eternal and unchanging. He gives as an example that in the works of nature the intellect can discern and know its author, namely God. And so this is the core notion of their theory of knowledge: the human intellect is not able, and in any case does not have the opportunity, apart from the sensible world, to produce, out of its own resources and with its own means, the knowledge of things, nor the knowledge of eternal principles, of common notions (κοιναι ἐννοιαι).

The intellect is bound to the body and thus to the cosmos and therefore cannot become active except by and on the basis of the senses. From the outset the intellect is pure potentiality, a blank page (*tabula rasa*) without any content, and is only activated, aroused to actuality, by the sensible world. The primary impetus therefore comes from the sensible world; it impinges upon the human mind, arouses it, urges it to action. But the moment the intellect is activated, it immediately and spontaneously works in its own way and according to its own nature. And the nature of the intellect is that it has the power (*vis*), ability (*facultas*), inclination (*inclinatio*), and fitness (*aptitudo*) to form certain basic concepts and principles. It does this by means of perception that is immediate, automatic, involuntary, and without any strain, previous effort, or exercise of reasoning power (*sine ratiocinatione*). Since these concepts that are certain are a priori and precede all reasoning and proof, they deserve to be called eternal truths (*veritates alternae*). Thus the moment the intellect itself proceeds to act, it automatically knows itself bound to the laws of thought. In the activity of thought, the laws of thought inhere and come to expression. Thus experience teaches us what is a part and what is a whole, but the intellect immediately grasps that a whole is greater than a part. Thus, experience teaches us what is good and evil, but the practical intellect immedi-

---

32. Aquinas, qu. de mente, art. 8, ad 1, "species aliorum intelligibilium non sunt ei innatae, sed essentia sua sibi innata est, ut non eam necesse habeat a phantasmatibus acquirere"; cf. Liberatore, *Die Erkenntniss-theorie des heiligen Thomas von Aquino*, 144.

ately knows that the one must be done and the other avoided. This does not mean that every human can give a clear account to himself and to others of these basic concepts and principles. But every human, even the most simple, applies these basic concepts and principles in life without any scientific reflection, unconsciously, and with the utmost certainty.

The difference between this theory of knowledge and that of rationalism and empiricism consists in two points: First, in a special view of the intellect, which has its own nature and, accordingly, operates in its own way; second, that this intellect, thus working in its own way, nevertheless restricts itself to abstracting from the things perceived the logical element naturally inherent in those things as well. Rationalism, as it were, forces things to align themselves with the intellect, presses them into forms of which it does not know whether things fit them, and constructs the world in terms of a set of concepts. Empiricism forces the intellect to align itself with the sensible world, curtails it in its ideal development, and finally explains the intellect itself in terms of matter. But the theory of knowledge that gradually arose in Christian theology and in its basic features was first conceived by Augustine maintains both the freedom and the constraints of the human mind: the freedom to soar to the world of the ideal; the constraints that, in this upward flight, keep it from losing touch with the world of reality.

Priority of the Senses

[68] Hence the starting point of all human knowledge is sense perception. "The mind does not know things apart from sense perception."[33] "All intellectual knowledge proceeds from the senses."[34] "Our intellect understands nothing apart from sense images."[35] And all Christian theologians believed the same thing. The error of scholasticism, in the case of Protestants as well as Catholics, was only that it treated sense perception far too summarily and thought of it as completely digested and recorded, in every branch of science, in the books of Euclid, Aristotle, the church fathers, and the confessions. On that assumption they skipped sense perception and immediately started dealing with the concepts already accumulated. It could therefore almost be called a fresh discovery when Francis Bacon returned to sense perception as the only source of knowledge. Only it was not a new discovery but a necessary rejuvenation of science, for science always has to go back to the sources. Truth must not be drawn from books but from the real world. Observation is the source of all real science. "Observations are the small coins; concepts the paper money," said Schopenhauer.[36]

---

33. Aristotle, *De sensu*, c. 6: Οὐδε νοει ὁ νους τα ἐκτος μετ᾽ αἰσθησεως ὀντα; E. Zeller, *Die Philosophie der Griechen*, III, 198.

34. Aquinas, *Summa Theol.*, I, qu. 84, art. 1 & 7.

35. Aquinas, *Summa contra Gentiles*, III, 41.

36. A. Schopenhauer, *Die Welt als Wille und Vorstellung*, 2 vols. (Leipzig: F. A. Brockhaus, 1859), II, 76–98; in English see *The World as Will and Idea*, 3 vols. (New York: Scribner, 1883).

In sense perception every one of the senses has its own nature and task; each seeks in the phenomena that which relates to it. The sense of touch yields information on the mechanical properties of a thing; taste and smell tell us about its chemical properties; hearing opens up to us the world of sounds and sight that of colors.[37] Each of the senses by itself therefore perceives, not the entire object, but only certain properties pertaining to that object. The perceptual image arising in our consciousness is composed of numerous different impressions, which, having been received by the different senses, are transmitted along the neural paths in our brain, are inexplicably converted there into perceptions and united into a whole. There are no simple perceptions; they are all composites; each object we see, every sound we hear is as such already a complex of perceptions. Accordingly, the human mind is already active in the most simple perceptions. The mind is not a blank page on which the external world merely writes what it pleases, nor a mirror in which objects are simply reflected. But every perceptual image is formed in the consciousness itself from factors that are brought from the object to the mind by the different senses.

The important question, therefore, is: what is the relation between the perceptual image in our consciousness and reality, the object outside of us? Greek philosophy generally proceeded from the idea that like can only be known by like.[38] From this some thinkers concluded that the human soul had to consist of the same elements and atoms as the real world and that in perception material atoms from the objects entered the soul. Aristotle, however, understood this as meaning that the soul consists of all that is thought, not actually but potentially.[39] Objects thus acquire an ideal existence in the soul by way of perception and thought. Scholasticism, adopting this position, said: "The thing known is in the knower by the mode of cognition, not by the mode of the thing known"; i.e., the things themselves do not pass into the soul but only their image or form (εἶδος, *forma, species, similitudo*).[40] So on the one hand there is an essential difference between the thing and its representation, because the thing exists outside of us, has real existence there, while the second exists in us and merely has ideal existence. On the other hand, there is complete correspondence; the representation is an image, a faithful ideal reproduction of the object outside of us.

Modern philosophy, however, noting the activity of human consciousness in the forms of perceptual images, has created an ever-growing gap between

37. Aristotle, see Zeller, *Die Philosophie der Griechen*, III, 533ff.; Aquinas, *Summa Theol.*, I, qu. 78, art. 3; Schopenhauer, *Die Welt als Wille und Vorstellung*, II, 30–36; W. Willem Bilderdijk, *Taal- en dichkundige verscheidenheden*, 4 vols. (Rotterdam: J. Immerzeel Jr., 1820, 1823), II, 39ff.; *idem, Verhandelingen, Ziel- Sede- en Rechtsleer Betreffende* (1821), 12ff.; idem, *Brieven*, 5 vols. (Amsterdam: W. Messchert, 1836, 1837), V, 58; Land, *Inleiding tot de wijsbegeerte*, 63ff.

38. Aristotle, *De anima*, I, 2: φασι γαρ γιγνωσκεσθαι το ὁμοιον τῳ ὁμοιῳ.

39. Aristotle, *De anima*, III, 8: ἡ ψυχη τα ὀντα πως ἐστι παντα.

40. Aquinas, I, qu. 75; I, 2, qu. 5, art. 5; II, 2, qu. 23, art. 6 ad 1; idem, *Summa contra Gentiles*, I, 77; II, 77, 98.

a thing and its representation. According to it, perceptual images are not forms (*species, formae*) but at most still signs, symbols, diagrams of the outside world, formed freely in our mind in response to the modifications effected from without in our brain cells by the senses and the nerves. If this is so, the objective world disappears ever farther from our view; it dissolves, in fact, into illusion. The verification of the perceptual image by reality is simply impossible because we can never get near it: the perceptual image will always slip in between reality and us.

The error underlying this theory seems to be that the actual object of our perception is said to be, not the thing outside of us, but some impression or neural vibration within us. Now it is certainly true that no representation can be formed in our consciousness apart from the transmission to our brain cells of vibrations in the nerves. But neither the image projected on the retina of the eye, nor the modifications in the brain cells resulting from neural vibrations, are the cause of the perceptions and representations in our consciousness. All the psychometric research, however important, has not brought us a step closer to an explanation of this amazing phenomenon. We are confronting here, it seems, an insoluble riddle. The neural vibrations can be tracked down to the center of the brain; their intensity and speed can be calculated; but the representation that subsequently originates in our consciousness is something totally different in kind from those vibrations. It is a psychic mental act, which can never be explained in terms of the physical phenomena, which is what the neural vibrations are. Consequently, the representations cannot be products effected in our consciousness by the neural vibrations without our being conscious of it. Nor can they be conscious creations of our mind prompted by the modifications in our brain cells, for the simple reason that no one knows by perception anything at all of this entire process of neural vibrations since a person gets to know of this process only by intentional physiological research. Coupled with this is that, though the neural vibrations and modifications in the brain cells sometimes—in seeing without noticing, in hearing without understanding—occur in a purely mechanical fashion, they are in actual perception always accompanied nevertheless by a psychic act. It is not the case that the neural vibrations are first transmitted in our brains and that the consciousness is only subsequently aroused and from those modifications in the brain cells then forms the representation. Rather the very perception by the senses is an act of consciousness. It is the human mind that sees through the eye and hears through the ear. Accordingly, the object of perception is not any phenomenon within myself but the thing outside myself. The mind that sees the object is the same mind that forms the representation. Both of these acts are psychic acts. There is therefore no reason to doubt that in the representations we have a faithful, ideal reproduction of the objects outside ourselves. In that connection it is relatively immaterial whether we call the representations εἴδη, species, formae, signs, or symbols. These words too are images drawn largely from visual perception. What needs to be mentioned is that, in their totality and in their parts, the representations are faithful interpretations of the world of reality outside us.

Universals

The human mind, however, does not stop with these representations. Scientific knowledge is not produced by the senses but by the intellect. Not pure observation but serious reflection made Copernicus the father of astronomy and Newton the discoverer of gravity. The observation of phenomena is necessary and good, but it is not the only or the highest activity of the mind. The object of science is not the particular but the universal, the logical, the idea. Greek philosophy already knew this. Socrates was the first human who conceived the idea of intentional knowledge and made it the principle of his philosophy. Science, said he, is knowledge not of the appearance but of the essence of things. Plato distinguished δοξα, the content of which was the ordinary knowledge of experience, from ἐπιστημη, whose content was the true being of things. And Aristotle similarly defined science as knowledge of being, of the whole, of first causes and principles.[41]

Especially Augustine highlighted this intellectual knowledge. Not that he rejected knowledge obtained by the senses. In fact, in a separate writing he defended its validity against the academics and acknowledges that we understand the invisible things of God through the things that have been made.[42] Still, like Plato, he underestimates its value; the sensible merely yields δοξα;[43] it is not the truth itself, only an image of it.[44] The knowledge of nature lacks value.[45] Actually there are only two things that are important to know— God and ourselves: "I desire to know God and the soul. Nothing more? Nothing at all."[46] And man gains this knowledge, not by looking outside but by looking inside himself. Truth dwells in the inward man.[47] We know not by sense perception but by reflection; "it is one thing to feel, another to know."[48] Scholasticism, linking itself more closely to Aristotle, had a better view of the value of sense perception but also fully acknowledged the importance of the intellect for science. Thomas succinctly and lucidly expressed this as follows: "Science is not concerned with individual cases; the intellect concerns itself with universal matters."[49] The object of science is the universal and necessary, so science can only be produced by the intellect. For

41. E. Zeller, *Die Philosophie der Griechen,* III, 161ff.
42. Augustine, *The Literal Meaning of Genesis,* Ancient Christian Writers, vols. 41–42, trans. and annotated by John Hammond Taylor, 2 vols. (New York: Newman Press, 1982), vol. I, bk. IV, chap. 32.
43. Augustine, *Against the Academics,* 3, 26.
44. Augustine, *Soliloquies,* 2, 32.
45. Augustine, *Confessions,* 5, 7; 10, 55; idem, *Enchiridion,* 3, 5.
46. Augustine, *Soliloquies,* 1, 7.
47. Augustine, *Of True Religion,* XXIX, 72.
48. Augustine, *De Ordin.* 2, 5; cf. *Soliloquies,* 2, 33.
49. Aquinas, *Summa Theol.,* Ia, qu. 1, art. 2; *Summa contra Gentiles,* I, 44.

whereas sense perception views things so far as it concerns their exterior accidents, it is the peculiar capacity of the intellect to penetrate to the interior or essence of a thing.[50] Its true object is the quiddity, the real nature, of a material thing.[51] The case is that as the active intellect, i.e., as the capacity for abstraction, as we would say, the intellect isolates from sense perceptions that which is universal; it leaves out the particulars, shines like a light over them, makes them intelligible, makes that which is universal in them knowable, and as the cognitive capacity of the intellect assimilates that universal component and makes it a possession of the mind.[52]

[69] On the position that not sense perception but the intellect is the organ of science there is really no difference yet. Empiricism, too, agreed with this position. Francis Bacon, Hume, and Stuart Mill fully recognize that though sense perception is primary it is not the only thing and that by induction the intellect attempts to infer the general from the particular. It was precisely Francis Bacon's objective to develop a reliable method by which universally valid judgments could be derived from particular observations. But in the case of the concepts that the intellect forms from mental representations, one again faces—but now with even greater urgency—the question raised earlier in the case of the images of perception: What is the relation between these intellectual concepts and the world of reality?

At this point nominalism and realism part company. Both schools of thought are basically already present in Greek philosophy. Plato and Aristotle were both realists, though in different ways. Furthermore, the basic idea of nominalism already occurs, for example, in the cynical philosopher Antithenes, who denied the reality of general concepts and said to Plato: "I indeed see a horse, but I do not see horseness." It occurs as well in the Stoic philosophers who held concepts (ἐννοήματα) to be merely phenomena of thought (φαντάσματα διανοίας).[53] In the Middle Ages this view of the general concepts was resurrected and called nominalism. Roscellin believed that universals were merely verbal (*flatus vocis*), conceptual things, for which there was no corresponding reality. In reality there are no universals, he said, but only particular, individual things. There is, for example, no humanity, only individual human beings. The battle between realism and nominalism continued to the fifteenth century.[54] But even after that the issue did not disappear from philosophy. The controversy between realism and nominalism,

50. Aquinas, *Summa contra Gentiles*, I, 58; III, 56; IV, 11; *Summa Theol.*, II, 2, qu. 8, art. 1.

51. Aquinas, *Summa Theol.*, Ia qu. 85, art. 5 and 3.

52. Aquinas, *Summa Theol.*, Ia, qu. 79, art. 3 and 4; Ia, art. 6; *Summa contra Gentiles*, II, 76, 77; III, 45.

53. E. Zeller, *Die Philosophie der Griechen*, II, 295; IV, 79, 125.

54. Albert Stöckl, *Geschichte der Philosophie des Mittelalters*, 3 vols. (Mainz: F. Kirchheim, 1864–66), I, 135ff.; II, 986ff.; B. Hauréau, *De la philosophie scolastique*, 2 vols. (Paris: Pagnerre, 1850); Joseph Schwane, *Dogmengeschichte der Mittleren Zeit* (Freiburg im Breisgau: Herder, 1882), 4ff.; A. Pierson, *Disquisitio historico-dogmatica de realismo et nominalismo* (Trajecti ad Rhenum, 1854); idem, *Geschiedenis van het Roomsch-katholicisme tot op het Concilie van Trente*, 4 vols. (Haarlem, A. C. Kruseman, 1868–72), III, 1871, 53ff., 87ff., 183ff.; Spruyt, *Proeve van eene Geschiedenis*, 66ff.

after all, is not a matter of dispute of interest only to scholastic hairsplitters but has far-reaching significance. In another form, i.e., as empiricism, nominalism again surfaced in modern philosophy as well.[55]

If nominalism is correct, we can forget about science altogether. We have to make a choice: if we can sum up the corresponding features of a group of things in a concept or word, then either this is done groundlessly and these concepts and words do not represent reality, or things do resemble each other in reality and have common characteristics. But if the latter is true, concepts are not "empty things of thought" but the sum of the essential properties of things and therefore not names (*nomina*) but realities (*res*). Realism, accordingly, was doubtlessly correct in assuming the reality of universal concepts, not in a Platonic or ontological sense prior to the thing itself (*ante rem*), but in an Aristotelian sense in the thing itself (*in re*) and therefore also in the human mind subsequent to the thing itself (*in mente hominis post rem*). The universality we express in a concept does not exist as such, as a universal, apart from us. In every specimen of a genus, particularly individualized and specialized, however, it has its basis in things and is abstracted from it and expressed in a concept by the activity of the intellect.[56] So, in entertaining concepts we are not distancing ourselves from reality but we increasingly approximate it. It may seem that in the process of forming concepts and judgments and conclusions we are increasingly moving away from the solid ground beneath the edifice of our knowledge and are soaring into the stratosphere. It seems strange, even amazing, that, converting mental representations into concepts and processing these again in accordance with the laws of thought, we should obtain results that correspond to reality. Still, one who abandons this conviction is lost.[57] But that conviction can, therefore, rest only in the belief that it is the same Logos who created both the reality outside of us and the laws of thought within us and who produced an organic connection and correspondence between the two. Only in this way is science possible, i.e., knowledge not only of the changing appearances but of the universal, the logical connections inherent in things. To be sure, the being of things as such, their existence, remains outside of us. In a realistic sense things themselves never enter into us. Being itself therefore can never be approached by us; it is a fact that has to be assumed and constitutes the basis of thought. But insofar as things also exist logically, have come forth from thought, and are based in thought (John 1:3; Col. 1:15), they are also apprehensible and conceivable by the human mind.

Plato clarified this scientific process by means of a beautiful and striking image. Just as the sun objectively illumines the object and subjectively the

---

55. Spruyt, *Proeve van eene Geschiedenis*, passim; Hugo Spitzer, *Nominalismus und Realismus in der neuesten deutschen Philosophie, mit Berücksichtigung ihres Verhältnisses zur modernen Naturwissenschaft* (Leipzig, 1876); Paul Janet, *Traité élémentaire de philosophie* (Paris: C. Delagrave, 1887), 162ff.; Land, *Inleiding tot de wijsbegeerte*, 107ff.; Pierson, *Wijsgeerig Onderzoek* (Deventer, 1882), 200ff.

56. Aquinas, *Summa Theol.*, I, qu. 85, art. 2 ad 2; *Summa contra Gentiles*, I, 65.

57. Land, *Inleiding tot de wijsbegeerte*, 250.

human eye, so God, or the idea of the good, is the light by which the truth or essence of things becomes visible and by which at the same time our mind is able to see and recognize that truth.[58] Augustine adopted this image and said, "God is the sun of minds." In the unchangeable light of truth, our mind sees and makes judgments about all things ("in the unchanging truth itself the rational and intellectual mind perceives all things and in the same light it judges all these things").[59] Just as with the physical eye we cannot see anything unless the sun sheds its rays over it, so neither can we see any truth except in the light of God, which is the sun of our knowledge.[60] God is the light of reason in which, by which, and through which all things that shine so as to be intelligible, shine. Thomas repeatedly speaks in the same way and uses the same metaphor.[61] Only he points out that this should not be understood pantheistically as Averroes, under neoplatonic influence, taught his students to do and was later followed in this by Malebranche and the ontologistic school. Says Thomas: just as we look into the natural world, not by being in the sun ourselves, but by the light of the sun that shines on us, so neither do we see things in the divine being but by the light that, originating in God, shines in our own intellect. Reason in us is that divine light; it is not itself the divine logos, but it participates in it. To be (*esse*), to live (*vivere*), and to understand (*intelligere*) is the prerogative of God in respect of his being (*per essentiam*), ours in respect of participation (*per participationem*).[62]

This image of the sun led people to speak in a commonsense way of "the natural light of reason,"[63] by which they merely meant the permanent property or power of the human mind enabling human beings, at the very moment of perceiving things, to form the basic concepts and principles that would guide them further in all perception and reflection. In the first place the light of reason is therefore identical with the active intellect, the faculty of abstraction, which shines its light on objects and brings to light the intelligible components of these objects. In addition, it is also identical with the fund of general concepts, which our mind acquired by that same faculty of abstraction. But in both ways we owe that light to God or, more specifically, to the Logos (Ps. 36:9; John 1:9). It is he who causes this light to arise in us and constantly maintains it. And so, when the truth discloses itself to our mind by the rays of that light, we owe it to God and not to human beings, who are merely the instrument.[64]

58. Hermann Siebeck, *Geschichte der Psychologie*, 2 vols. (Gotha: F. A. Perthes, 1880–84), I, 226; II, 70.

59. Augustine, *The Literal Meaning of Genesis*, VIII, 25.

60. Augustine, *Soliloquies*, I 8, 13; *De Trinitate*, 12, 15.

61. Aquinas, *Summa Theol.*, I, qu. 12, art. 2, ad 3; qu. 79, art. 4; qu. 88, art. 3, ad 1; II, 1, qu. 109, art. 1 and 2; *Summa contra Gentiles*, III, 47.

62. Aquinas, *Summa Theol.*, I, qu. 79, art. 4.

63. Polanus, *Synt. Theol.* 325; Zanchius, *Opera* III, 636.

64. M. Liberatore, *Die Erkenntniss-theorie des heiligen Thomas von Aquino*, 185ff.; Joseph Kleutgen, *Philosophie der Vorzeit*, 2 vols. (Innsbruck: Rausch, 1878), I, 89.

These beautiful images make clear to us the principles from which all science proceeds. Not only in theology, as the preceding discussion showed, but in every science we may discern three fundamental principles. Here, too, God is the first principle of being (*principium essendi*); present in his mind are the ideas of all things; all things are based on thoughts and are created by the word. It is his good pleasure, however, to reproduce in human beings made in his image an ectypal knowledge that reflects this archetypal knowledge (*cognitio archetypa*) in his own divine mind. He does this, not by letting us view the ideas in his being (Malebranche) or by passing them all on to us at birth (Plato, the theory of innate ideas), but by displaying them to the human mind in the works of his hands. The world is an embodiment of the thoughts of God; it is "a beautiful book in which all creatures, great and small, are as letters to make us ponder the invisible things of God" (art. 2, Belgic Confession). It is not a book of blank pages in which, as the idealists would have it, we human beings have to write down the words but a "reader" in which God makes known to us what he has recorded there for us. Accordingly, the created world is the external foundation of knowledge (*principium cognoscendi externum*) for all science.

But that is not enough. We need eyes in order to see. "If our eyes were not filled with sunshine, how could we see the light?" There just has to be correspondence or kinship between object and subject. The Logos who shines in the world must also let his light shine in our consciousness. That is the light of reason, the intellect, which, itself originating in the Logos, discovers and recognizes the Logos in things. It is the internal foundation of knowledge (*principium cognoscendi internum*). Just as knowledge within us is the imprint of things upon our souls, so, in turn, forms do not exist except by a kind of imprint of the divine knowledge in things.[65] So, in the final analysis, it is God alone who from his divine consciousness and by way of his creatures conveys the knowledge of truth to our mind—the Father who by the Son and in the Spirit reveals himself to us. "There are many who say, 'O that we might see some good!' Let the light of your face shine on us, O Lord!" (Ps. 4:6).

---

65. Thomas Aquinas, according to Liberatore, *Die Erkenntniss-theorie des heiligen Thomas von Aquino*, 148.

8

Religious Foundations

The meaning of the Christian religion cannot be determined from the disputed etymology of the word "religion." The Bible provides no general idea of religion but covenantally presents God's revelation as its objective side and the fear of the Lord as the subjective side. God is to be revered and his revelation is to be believed and obeyed. Biblical religion is in the first place a matter of the heart; it is never exhausted by external observance.

According to Thomas Aquinas, religion is not a matter of theological virtues (faith, hope, love), which have God as their direct object, but of the moral virtues (prudence, justice, fortitude, and temperance), in which God is the end. The actual object in religion here is the devotion dutifully offered to God. Religion belongs to the virtue of justice, it is the virtue by which human beings offer to God the devotion and worship that is due to him.

*The Reformation theologians distinguish more clearly piety as the principle and worship as the act of religion. Piety is first of all a state of being, a habit and disposition leading human beings to worship God. Schleiermacher even defined religion in terms of piety, as the "absolute feeling of dependence." While this definition is inadequate, it also contains elements of truth. We human creatures **are** radically dependent on God. Subjectively this is known as faith, faith that leads to service, acts of obedience, and love. True religion consists of absolute trust in God and a sincere desire to live in obedience to him.*

The modern age has given rise to a scientific, historical, or psychological comparative study of all religions. While all religions do have formal similarities (revelation, cult, dogma), no generic religion exists, only concrete ones, all with conflicting claims. Efforts to arrive at the essence of religion in general have led to meager results with vague proposals, and the search must be judged a dead end. There can be no escape from the need to judge the content of specific religions as "true" or "false." Dogmatic judgments cannot be avoided.

Anthropologically, what is the place of religion in the human psyche? Is religion primarily knowledge, morality, or feeling? Much modern thought, notably idealism, has an intellectualistic view of religion. For Hegel, the entire world is an unfolding of mind. Religion is a form of knowledge superseded only by philosophy. The Kantian tradition, however, defines religion voluntaristically as moral conduct and locates its seat in the human will. Others, like Schleiermacher, influenced by Romanticism, consider religion as primarily aesthetic and lo-

cate it in human feeling. While intellect, morality, and feeling do play significant roles in true religion, it should not be reduced to a single faculty. True religion embraces the whole person in relation to God. Religion is central to all human cultural acts and products: science, morality, and art.

Scientific, historical attempts to explain the origin of religion fail. Neither fear, priestly deception, human weakness, the search for happiness, nor ignorance, is a satisfactory explanation. Attempts to account for religion as a "self-assertion of the life of the Spirit" makes God and religion a human creation, invented to satisfy human need. God is humanity's servant.

Finally, the scientific, historical study of religions cannot find the answer to the origin of religion—only revelation can. Religion cannot be understood without God, and to know him he must reveal himself to us. Revelation is religion's external principle of knowing. Revelation and religion are not alien to human nature, however. Rather, as God's image bearers, human beings are by nature religious. Hence religion is a universal reality. We are created for God. Religion exists because God is God and wants to be honored. To that end he reveals himself to us and makes us subjectively fit to know him.

THE ESSENCE OF RELIGION

[70] Just like science, so religion too has its fundamental principles or foundations (*principia*). To get to know them, it is first of all necessary for us to determine the essence of religion, especially as it differs from science, morality, and art. The word *religion* is not very illuminating. Cicero derived the word from *relegere,* to reread, to do over, to observe with care, and thus described religion as the ongoing, diligent observance of all that pertains to the veneration of the gods.[1] Lactantius explained it in terms of the verb *religare* and therefore meant by religion the bond that unites human beings to God.[2] A third derivation, based on the verb *relinquere,* occurs in Gellius and indicates that everything that belongs to religion is set apart, on account of its sanctity, from the secular.[3] Augustine on one occasion relates it to the verb *re-eligere:* in religion we re-elect God, whom we had lost as a result of sin, as the source of our salvation.[4] J. C. Leidenroth, basing himself on the fact that the three verbs *diligere, negligere,* and *intelligere* have a perfect stem form that differs from *lego* and its compounds, assumed a lost stem *ligere,* meaning to see.[5] *Diligere* would then mean to look at with love; *negligere,* to not see; *intelligere,* to have insight into; and from this stem the words *religere,* to look back, and *religio,* to look about with fear (cf. *respec-*

1. Cicero, *On the Nature of the Gods* (*de natura deorum*), II, 28: *qui omnia, quae ad cultum deorum pertinent, diligenter retractarent et quasi relegerent, religiosi sunt dicti;* cf. *de inventione,* II, 22, 53.
2. Lactantius, *Divinia Institutiones,* N, 28.
3. Gellius, *Noctes atticae,* IV, 9.
4. Augustine, *City of God,* X, 4.
5. Sanskrit *lok;* Greek *leussein;* German *lugen;* English *look;* cf. Latin *lucere,* "to shine."

tus) are said to derive.[6] The derivation from *religare, relinquere, re-eligere* is burdened by grammatical difficulties and also fails to explain the unique meanings that *religio* has in Latin. While the difference between Cicero's derivation and that of Leidenroth has not yet been resolved, the two agree materially in that *religio* refers to a disposition of timid fear vis-à-vis the deity and the resulting anxiously scrupulous observance of what the worship of the gods requires. This view is supported by a line of verse taken over by Nigidius Figulus, a contemporary of Cicero, from an ancient poem and preserved in Gellius: "It is right to be devout but wrong to be superstitious" (*religentem esse oportet, religiosum nefas*).[7] The word, accordingly, is absolutely unsuited to convey the full content of the Christian faith. But Lactantius's use and derivation, which found general acceptance, have Christianized the word. The Vulgate introduced it in Acts 26:5 and James 1:27. The word has passed into all European languages and, alongside of piety and godliness, has found and retained acceptance in English as well.[8]

Holy Scripture offers no definition, nor does it possess a general term to denote the phenomenon of religion. It has distinct words for its objective as well as its subjective side. Objective religion is identical with the revelation of God and consists in the covenant (ברית), which God gave to Israel and may therefore be called, in the full sense of the word, a divine establishment (διαθηκη; Exod. 20:1ff.; 34:10ff.; 27ff.; Isa. 54:10 etc.). The ordinances embodied in that covenant, which Israel must keep, together form the content of the תורה (instruction, teaching, law, the book of the law of the Lord) and are designated by very different names. They are called דברים, words (Num. 12:6; Ps. 33:4, etc.); מצוות, commandments (Gen. 26:5; Exod. 15:26, etc.); פקודים, precepts (Ps. 119:4, 5, 15, etc.); חקים, statutes, decrees (Exod. 15:26, Lev. 25:18; Ps. 89:32, MT [89:31 Eng.]; Job 28:26, etc.); משפטים, legal cases and verdicts (Num. 36:13; Ps. 19:10 MT [19:9 Eng.]; etc.); ארחות, דרכים, ways, paths (Deut. 5:33; Job 21:14; Ps. 25:4, etc.); משמרות, laws to be kept (Gen. 26:5; Lev. 18:30 etc.). The many expressions indicate how in Israel's religion the objective side of religion the ordinances of God—is in the foreground.

Corresponding to this objective religion is the subjective, the יראת יהוה, the fear of the Lord. This term expresses the inner disposition of the devout Israelite toward the holy laws that the Lord has instructed him to keep. But this fear is essentially different from the anxious timidity conveyed by the

---

6. *Leidenroth, *Neue Jahrbuch für Philologie und Pädagogik*, ed. Seebode, Jahn, and Klotz (1834), 455.

7. A. Gellius, *Noctis Atticae*, IV, 9. On the derivation of the word, see also H. Voigt, *Fundamentaldogmatik* (Gotha: F. A. Pertes, 1874), 9–30; F. Nitzsch, *Lehrbuch der Evangelischen Dogmatik* (Tubingen: J. C. B. Mohr, 1880), 83; Georg Runze, *Katechismus der Dogmatik* (Leipzig: J. J. Weber, 1898), 38; S. Hoekstra, *Wijsgeerige godsdienstleer*, 2 vols. (Amsterdam: P. N. van Kampen & Zoon, 1894–95), I, 49–57.

8. Ed. note: Bavinck refers explicitly to the Dutch language here and observes that the word *religie* has found wide acceptance along with words such as *godsdienst*, *vroomheid* (from the Gothic *fruma*, Latin *primus*, meaning "taking the foremost place," "virtuous" [*deugdzaam*]).

original Latin word *religio*. This is evident from the fact that this fear of the Lord passes into and is bound up with an assortment of other religious attitudes such as believing (Gen. 15:6; Isa. 7:9; Hab. 2:4), trust (Ps. 26:1; 37:3, 5), taking refuge in (Ps. 5:11; 37:40), leaning on (Isa. 48:2), holding on to (2 Kings 18:6), hoping, expecting, even loving God (Exod. 20:6; Deut. 6:5; Ps. 91:14). The Lord's claims do not remain outside of and above the Israelites as the object of their terror and fear but become the object of their love. They ponder them with their intellect and observe them with their will. They are their delight all day long.

In the New Testament we encounter essentially the same view. Only now God gives his revelation, not in a series of laws, but in the person of Christ. He is the *way* and the *truth* (John 14:6). The *way of the Lord* (Acts 18:25; 19:9, 23; 22:4), the *teaching* (Matt. 7:28; 22:33; John 7:16, 17; Acts 2:42; Rom. 6:17; 1 Tim. 1:10; 4:6, 16; 6:1, 3; 2 Tim. 4:2, 3; Titus 1:9; 2:1, 7, 10); the *gospel* (Mark 1:1, 14, 15, etc.), the *word of God* (Matt. 13:19; Mark 2:2; 4:14f.; 2 Cor. 5:19; etc.) are all concentrated in Christ and are nothing other than an explication of his person and work. Hence the subjective disposition changes accordingly. Ordinary Greek words were not suited to convey the uniqueness of this disposition. Δεισιδαιμονια was used by Festus for the Jewish religion (Acts 25:19) and the corresponding adjective by Paul for the pagan religion (Acts 17:22). Θεοσεβεια occurs only once (1 Tim. 2:10). Εὐσεβεια indicates holy reverence toward God; its meaning is related to that of the Latin *pietas* and hence expresses an attitude such as is present in children toward their parents. The word repeatedly occurs in the New Testament, especially in the Pastoral Letters. But what εὐσεβεια really is and ought to be was first revealed only in the gospel (1 Tim. 3:16). Also fear has not completely vanished from subjective religion in the New Testament (Luke 18:2; Acts 9:31; 2 Cor. 5:11; 7:1; Rom. 3:18; Eph. 5:21; Phil. 2:12; 1 Pet. 1:17; 3:2, 15) but occurs much less frequently as a term for the religious disposition. In most instances it relates to special events, such as a judgment of God, and is elsewhere replaced by love (Rom. 8:15; 1 John 4:18). The usual word for subjective religion in the New Testament is faith (πιστις). Corresponding to the good news of forgiveness and salvation in Christ on the human side is faith, which is a childlike trust in God's grace and hence immediately produces love in our heart. Πιστις and ἀγαπη are the basic attitudes inherent in Christian piety. The words λατρεια (Rom. 9:4, 12:1; Heb. 9:1, 6) and θρησκεια (Acts 26:5; Col. 2:18; James 1:27) refer to the worship and adoration offered to God from the principle of faith.

Objective and Subjective Religion

[71] In keeping with this teaching of Scripture, a distinction was made in earlier times between objective and subjective religion, and religion itself was usually described as "the right manner of knowing and serving the true God" (*recta verum Deum cognoscendi et colendi ratio*). This definition already

occurs in Lactantius,[9] found general acceptance, and is still being used by many people today. In more modern times the objection has been raised that it views religion as something external, which completely passes by the human heart. While it is true that it does not further define the "right manner" (*recta ratio*), which is central in the definition, nor explain the connection between knowing and serving God, and tends to highlight objective religion more than subjective religion, the objection raised is not sufficiently well-grounded. For in the earlier interpretation the law in which God laid down the manner in which he wanted to be served was to be understood not only literally but also spiritually. It controlled not only the words and the actions but also the attitudes, thoughts, and desires of human beings. It claimed the whole person, soul and body, the mind, the heart, and all a person's strengths. It therefore required that human beings serve God not only and not even in the first place with external actions and rituals but above all with a sincere faith, firm hope, and ardent love, with worship in spirit and in truth, with the sacrifices of a broken spirit and a contrite heart. Religion, accordingly, was not exhausted by external observance but consisted above all in internal devotion, a knowing and serving of God from the heart. But also this internal devotion could not, any more than the external observance, be self-willed. Essential in religion is first of all the manner in which God himself wills and determines that people shall know and serve him. Hence in the first place it is also a duty with which God confronts us human beings in the first table of his law, a duty to which subjective religion in human beings must correspond. It is the inner disposition and motivation to know and serve God in the way he has revealed in his Word.[10]

For that reason, religion was discussed in earlier times in the interpretation of the first commandment of the Decalogue, in the doctrine of "the duties and virtues." Thomas, for example, divides the virtues into three kinds. The first two are the intellectual virtues (wisdom, knowledge, understanding, etc.) and the moral virtues (the four cardinal virtues are prudence, justice, fortitude, and temperance.) Both of these two groups were derived from Aristotle. Added to these as a third group were the three supernatural or theological virtues: faith, hope, and love.[11] Religion, here, is not subsumed under the theological but under the moral virtues, for the theological virtues are qualified by the fact that they have God as their direct object: they immediately and directly relate us to God as to its object,[12] but in religion God is not the object but the end. The actual object in religion is the devotion offered to God. Religion, accordingly, is not a theological virtue whose object is God but a moral virtue that belongs among the things that are directed to an end; it relates man to God, not as toward an object but as toward an end.

9. Lactantius, *Divine Institutes*, IV, 4.
10. Cf. H. Bavinck, *Godsdienst en Godgeleerdheid* (Wageningen: Voda, 1902), 14ff.
11. Aquinas, *Summa Theologica*, II, 1, qu. 57, 58, 62.
12. Aquinas, *Summa Theologica*, II, 1, qu. 62, art. 2.

Among the moral virtues it is, however, the primary virtue because it is most closely related to him who is the end of all virtues, viz., God.[13] Thomas further counts religion as belonging to the moral virtue that is called justice, inasmuch as he views religion as the virtue by which human beings offer to God the devotion and reverence that is due to him. Although the act of visiting widows and orphans (James 1:27) is counted as belonging to religion, religion in its true and restricted sense is solely a relation to God and never to human beings. And although all things must be done to the honor of God, the honor brought to God in religion is nevertheless meant in a special sense and, strictly speaking, only includes that which relates to reverencing God. Hence it is identical with *latreia*.[14] While this definition of Thomas was later adopted by many scholars,[15] in modern times it is usually modified and expanded in a manner such that the subjective disposition from which religion as devotion springs comes more into its own.[16] It is a fact that subjective religion is not just an act of worship and adoration but primarily a disposition or mind-set that expresses itself in such devotion. Also, the distinction between moral virtues and theological virtues is too supernaturalistic and dualistic. There is of course some truth in it, the truth that also in a fallen humanity there are still remnants of the image of God, and moral virtues are not—even religion is not—totally eradicated. But the moral virtues and also the religious disposition must be renewed and reborn to be truly good. Thomas therefore recognized that the theological virtues (faith, hope, and love) "bring about the actuality of religion which works certain things in proper order toward God"[17] but which nevertheless are themselves excluded from religion; and whereas the intellectual and moral virtues are according to human nature, the theological virtues are above nature.[18]

Piety and Worship

In the main the Reformation modified this view of religion in two ways. First, the theologians of the Reformation made a better and clearer distinction between piety as the principle and worship as the act of religion. And second, faith, hope, and love are not placed alongside of religion as separate theological virtues but incorporated into religion itself as the primary acts of internal religion. Religion, says Zwingli, embraces the total piety of Chris-

13. Aquinas, *Summa Theologica*, II, 2, qu. 81, art. 5, 6.

14. Aquinas, *Summa Theologica*, II, 2, qu. 81, art. 1–4.

15. C. R. Billuart, *Summa Sancti Thomae: Hodiernis academiarum moribus accomodat*a, 10 vols. (Paris: Lecoffre Filio et sociis, successoribus, 1878), IV, 5ff.; Petrus Dens, *Theologia ad usum seminariorum et sacræ theologiæ alumnorum*, 7 vols. (Mechliniæ: H. Dessain, 1880–82), IV, 9ff.; Pierre Collet, *Institutiones theologiae moralis*, 4 vols. (Lyon: J. M. Bruyset, 1768), III, 401ff.

16. Heinrich Denzinger, *Vier Bücher von der religiösen Erkenntniss*, 2 vols. (Würzburg: Stahel, 1856–57), I, 3; Augustin Lehmkuhl, *Theologia moralis*, 2 vols. (Freiburg im Breisgau: Herder, 1898), I, 208; Anton Koch, *Lehrbuch der Moraltheologie* (Freiburg im Breisgau: Herder, 1905), 322.

17. Aquinas, *Summa Theologica*, II, 2, qu. 81, art. 5, ad. 1.

18. Aquinas, *Summa Theologica*, I, 2, qu. 62, art. 2.

tians—faith, life, laws, rites, and sacraments. It consists in "that linkage by which a human has a firm trust in God—as one might expect—as the highest good and enjoys him in the place of a parent." Finally, "it is the marriage between the soul and God."[19] In Calvin we encounter three key concepts. The first is the knowledge of God, the sense of his attributes. This knowledge, secondly, is the appropriate teacher of piety, which Calvin defines as "reverence joined with love of God which the knowledge of his benefits induces." Finally, religion, in the sense of worship or devotion, is also born from piety.[20] Similarly, Zanchius makes a distinction between the devotion, which denotes the action, either external or internal, by which we worship God, and religion or piety, which is the power (*virtus*) from which this worship (*cultus*) is born.[21] Polanus says that *religio* differs from the worship of God (*cultus Dei*) as the cause from the effect. Religion (*religio*) or piety (*pietas*) is the internal cause of the worship of God (*cultus Dei*).[22] This devotion (*cultus*), the fruit of piety (*pietas*), is then distinguished as in the scholastics, into internal and external, the former being the primary acts: faith, trust, hope, adoration, love, invocation, giving thanks, sacrifice, obedience. External devotion is then categorized either as moral (confession, prayer, etc.) or ceremonial (sacraments, offerings, holy things).[23]

[72] Subjective religion is first of all a state of being ἕξις (*habitus*), a certain predisposition in human beings that, as a result of the influence of objective religion, passes into actions (internal or external worship). Such a predisposition is present in every human; "the seed of religion has been implanted in all humans."[24] But in fallen humanity this predisposition is corrupted and, being fecundated by an untrue and impure objective religion, also produces worship that is "idolatry" or "will-worship" (ἐθελοθρησκεια). Two things are, therefore, necessary for a religion to be true: first, that the objective religion that comes to us from without again makes God

19. Zwingli, *Opera*, ed. Schuler and Schulthess, III, 155, 175, 180.

20. J. Calvin, *Institutes of the Christian Religion*, ed. John T. McNeil and trans. Ford Lewis Battles (Philadelphia: Westminster Press, 1960), I.ii.1.

21. J. Zanchius, *Opera*, iv, 263ff.

22. A. Polanus, *Syntagma theologiae christianae* (1609), 580.

23. J. Zanchius, *Opera*, IV, 410ff.; Z. Ursinus, questions 94–103 of the Heidelberg Catechism as well as his *Commentary* on these questions; see *The Commentary of Dr. Zacharias Ursinus on the Heidelberg Catechism*, trans. G. W. Williard (1852; reprinted, Grand Rapids: Eerdmans, 1954), 489–570; idem, *Volumen tractationum theologicarum*, 2 vols. (1584), I, 283; Polanus, *Syntagma theologiae christianae*, 32; J. Hoornbeek, *Disputatio theologica practica* (1659–61), bk. 9, chaps. 6–8; idem, *Summa controversiarum religionis* (1653), 7ff.; J. Alsted, *Theologica catechectica* (1616), 5ff.; B. de Moor, *Comentarius perpetuus in Joh. Marckii compendium theologiae christianae didactico-elencticum*, 6 vols. (1761–71), I, 44; For the comparison with Lutheranism, see A. Calovius, *Isagoges ad SS. theologiam libri duo* (1652), 301; Heinrich Schmid, *Doctrinal Theology of the Evangelical Lutheran Church*, trans. Charles A. Hay and Henry E. Jacobs (Philadelphia: United Lutheran Publication House, 1899; reprinted, Minneapolis: Augsburg, 1961), 21ff.; Karl von Hase, *Hutterus redivivus; oder, Dogmatik der evangelisch-lutherischen Kirche* (Leipzig: Breitkopf und Hartel, 1848), loc. 1, chap. 2.

24. J. Calvin, *Institutes*, I, iv.1.

known to us as he really is; second, that the corrupted religious predisposition in human beings be regenerated and renewed. Hence in this sense subjective religion is "a virtue infused by the Holy Spirit."[25] But this definition is inadequate. A human being has many virtues both in intellect and will. Hence the peculiar nature of the virtue at work in religion must be further qualified. In earlier times this "virtue" was described as piety, reverence, fear, faith, etc. and similarly today as respect, deference, fear, a feeling of dependency. Still, these terms are not specific enough, for to some degree we have all these feelings in relation to creatures as well. There has to be an essential distinction between religious worship and civil devotion, between λατρεια and δουλεια, between the feelings of fear, respect, deference, etc. as we have them toward God and those feelings as we have them toward creatures. That distinction can consist only in the fact that in religion the *absolute* dignity and power of God and *absolute* subjection on our part comes into play.[26] We are only partially dependent on creatures; as fellow creatures we are on the same level with them. God, however, is a being on whom we depend totally and who decides about our weal and woe in every respect. Among pagans this divine absoluteness is as it were divided over many deities, but in his own territory every one of these deities nonetheless possesses such power that human beings are totally dependent on him for their good fortune or misfortune.

It was especially Schleiermacher who defined religion as the "absolute feeling of dependence."[27] Many objections have been raised against this definition, objections briefly reproduced (*inter alia*) by Hoekstra.[28] This definition in Schleiermacher indeed has a meaning that cannot be allowed to go unchallenged. In his thinking dependence is so pantheistically construed that objectively it relates only to the whole of the universe and is limited, subjectively, to feeling. Nevertheless, there is in Schleiermacher's definition a substantial element of truth. What makes human beings religious beings and drives them toward religion is the realization that they are related to God in a way that specifically differs from all their other relationships. This relationship is so deep and tender, so rich and many-dimensional, that it can only with difficulty be expressed in a single concept. But certainly the concept of *dependence* deserves primary consideration and is best qualified for this purpose. For in religion a human feels related to a personal being who has one's destiny in his hands in every area of life, for time and eternity. For that reason God is not yet exclusively conceived in religion as mere power. As the gracious, merciful, just, and holy One, God nevertheless still always confronts us as Sovereign, as the Absolute, as God. And human beings always

25. Hoornbeek, *Disputatio theologica practica*, II, 207, 213.

26. Hoornbeek, *Disputatio theologica practica*, II, 205ff.

27. F. Schleiermacher, *The Christian Faith*, ed. H. R. MacIntosh and J. S. Steward (Edinburgh: T. & T. Clark, 1928), chap. 4, 2, p. 15.

28. S. Hoekstra, *Wijsgerige Godsdienstleer*, 2 vols., I, 70ff.

relate to God in their capacity as creatures; they so relate to no one and nothing else, but only to God. Accordingly, this creaturely dependence, though it is not the essence of religion, is its foundation. We human beings, however, are not just creatures but rational and moral creatures as well. Our relation to God, therefore, is quite different from that of the angels and animals. By implication this absolute dependence in which human beings stand toward God does not exclude freedom. We are dependent but in a way that differs from that of other creatures. We are dependent in the manner and sense that we simultaneously remain rational and moral creatures who are akin to God, are his offspring and his image. We are absolutely dependent in such a manner that the denial of this dependence never makes us free, while the acknowledgment of it never reduces us to the status of a slave. On the contrary: in the conscious and voluntary acceptance of this dependence, we human beings arrive at our greatest freedom. We become human to the degree that we are children of God.

Holy Scripture does not undertake the study of the essence of subjective religion as it is still found in all human beings and religions. It would also be a hopeless undertaking, for the religious disposition is so diverse in the various religions that one could at most find a very general and vague term to describe it. Scripture does, however, stamp the religious disposition that the *Christian* feels toward God and his revelation with the name *faith*. That is the key term in the subjective religion of the Christian. About the nature of that faith there has at all times been much disagreement in the Christian church. The religious life is so rich and so deep that it can be viewed again and again from different perspectives. But included in that faith nevertheless there are two elements: First, over against God and his revelation, human beings are totally receptive and absolutely dependent on God. Second, precisely by the acknowledgment of this dependence, they become the beneficiaries of forgiveness, adoption as children, and salvation by grace. Certainly, in other religions there are analogies to this subjective religion in Christianity, but only in the Christian religion is the subjective relation of human beings to God completely normal, inasmuch as dependence and freedom are reconciled here. While God's sovereignty is fully maintained, human kinship to God is nevertheless fully recognized as well. A human being is all the more religious and all the more deeply conformed to the image of God to the degree that someone realizes and acknowledges his dependence on God more deeply. While all virtues can therefore be overdone in relation to creatures, no such exaggeration is possible with respect to God. One can never believe him, trust in him, or love him too much; faith can never expect too much.[29]

29. Heinrich Voigt, *Fundamentaldogmatik* (Gotha: F. A. Perthes, 1874), 65ff.; A. Dorner, "Über das Wesen der Religion," *Theologische Studien und Kritiken* 55 (1883): 217–77; F. A. Kahnis, *Die lutherische Dogmatik,* 2d ed., 2 vols. (Leipzig: Dörffling und Francke, 1874–75), I, 81; Abraham des Amorie van der Hoeven Jr., *De Godsdienst het wezen van den mensch* (Leeuwarden: G. T. N. Suringar, 1857), 38ff.

Under the impact of objective religion, subjective religion passes from its habitual state into action. These actions are either internal or external and are differentiated as internal or as external worship. Religion and worship, as we remarked earlier, are related as cause and effect. Still, this does not mean that worship is a free invention or expression of subjective religion. All "will-worship" (ἐθελοθρησκεια) is prohibited (Matt. 15:9; Mark 7:7; Col. 2:23). Both antinomian Anabaptism and nomistic Romanism are to be avoided. God alone determines how he wants to be served. And the rebirth of sin-corrupted subjective religion, of the religious predisposition, consists above all in that believers receive a sincere desire to live in perfection according not only to some but according to all God's commandments.[30] It is their daily food to do the will of the Father. Jesus never said or did anything other than that for which he had received a commandment from the Father. For that reason Scripture places such heavy emphasis on walking in God's commandments and keeping his ordinances. And God regenerates human beings in order to restore in the depths of their being those who are averse to his service to harmony with his will and law as these are laid down in objective religion.

Internal worship embraces acts of faith, trust, fear, love, prayer, thankfulness, etc., and external worship manifests itself in confession, prayer, song, the ministry of the Word and sacraments, making vows, fasting, watching, etc. Hence the latter is in part moral and in part ceremonial and can further be solitary or social. In the latter case, it is either private or public with communal public worship being regulated in the various church orders. In all these religious actions, the sense of absolute dependence is basic and inspiring. Detached from this sense of dependence, it becomes a religion of the letter, lip service, cold and dead formalism. But inspired by it, worship acquires all of its specifically religious character. Creatures, too, are objects of our faith and our love, etc. What makes all these actions typically religious, however, is the fact that they put us in relation to a person on whom we, along with all things, are absolutely dependent and on whom we as human beings are uniquely, i.e., as rational creatures, dependent. Yet the essence of religion cannot consist in anything other than that in it God is glorified and acknowledged precisely as God. Every religion that falls short in this respect falls short of the glory of God and to that degree also ceases to be truly religious. True religion, on the other hand, consists in the kind of human disposition that on the one hand is rooted in a deep sense of one's absolute dependence on God as Creator, Redeemer, Sanctifier, etc., and on the other seeks in sincerity to live according to all God's commandments. Hence, no more beautiful description of religion is conceivable than that offered in the Heidelberg Catechism, question and answer 94: "That I, not wanting to endanger my salvation, avoid and shun all idolatry, magic, superstitious rites, and prayer to saints or to other creatures. That I sincerely acknowledge the

---

30. Ed. note: Bavinck alludes here to Q & A 114 of the Heidelberg Catechism.

only true God, trust him alone, look to him for every good thing humbly and patiently, love him, fear him, and honor him with all my heart. In short, that I give up anything rather than go against his will in any way."

A Science of All Religions?

[73] In modern times this view of religion has given way to a totally different one. From time to time in earlier ages, e.g., in the case of the Muslim philosopher Averroes, someone launched the opinion that religion was meant only for the common people, that the scholar had no need for it, and that all religions were the same. But such ideas were only held privately and were not based on the comparative study of religions. The nineteenth century brought about a great change in this. When after the Reformation the number of churches, creeds, and religious trends continually increased, many scholars retreated from the particular into the universal and found the essence of religion in the Apostles' Creed or in the rationalistic triad, God, virtue, and immortality. Kant and Schleiermacher, going back even further, viewed religion as a form of moral conduct or as a specific quality of feeling. In this manner the point of gravity was shifted from the object to the subject, and subjective religion was completely detached from objective religion. This philosophical view of religion was boosted by the astonishing expansion of historical horizons and by the enormous amount of material produced on languages, morals, and customs, as well as the religion of other peoples. A science was needed that examined, classified, and evaluated these religions, and beginning in 1821 in his lectures on the philosophy of religion, Hegel made a start and gave impetus to it. The intent of this new science was, first in comparative religion (the history of religion), to examine all religions entirely objectively and impartially, without any dogmatic presuppositions. The inductive method was used to study religion as a universal human, psychological, and historical phenomenon and to trace in it the constant and universal elements within the variations and developmental forms. The goal was to acquire knowledge of religion in its life and growth. The second purpose of this philosophy of religion based on the preceding research was to speculatively utilize the results acquired and, following the deductive method, to lay bare the origin and essence, the truth content and value of religion.

In this connection a significant difference concerning the method to be followed immediately asserted itself. Some scholars favored the historical method and wished to try, by comparative historical study of the religious phenomena, to establish the essence of religion.[31] This method runs into the serious objection, however, that a comparative study of all religions is unfeasible. Furthermore, it is, above all, the religious disposition—which is supposed to be the focus of the religion's essence—that is most deeply hidden

---

31. A. Bruining, "Wijsbegeerte van de Godsdienst," *Theologische Tijdschrift* 15 (1881): 365–428.

and virtually eludes all observation. What, for example, do we even know of the attitude and disposition that underlies the religious phenomena in the various modalities and churches within Christianity? Other scholars, therefore, deem it necessary to supplement the historical with the psychological method and attempt to explain the essence of religion psychologically.[32] Hence they also want the practitioner of the science of religion to be a religious person and as such to observe and assess the religious phenomena. This is, in itself, completely unobjectionable. To silence one's own religious consciousness in the study of religions, as Dr. Bruining would have us do, would be the same, as Dr. Hugenholtz correctly observes, as gouging out one's own eyes from a fear of optical illusion. But, in the nature of the case, the psychological method can only inform us as to the psychological side of the religious life, the psychic forms in which it is manifest. However, it tells us nothing about the essence of religion as such, i.e., in the sense that by it also the validity and value of the religion have been established. Still, this is what most of the science-of-religion practitioners aim for. Despite all the "presuppositionlessness" they claim, they nevertheless assume that religion is a normal—not a pathological—manifestation of the life of the human soul and that it gradually achieves a purer development in the various forms of religion. But in that case also the historical-psychological method is inadequate and has to be augmented, in the third place, by the philosophical or metaphysical method, which establishes the validity and value of religion and hence also its ideas and actions (dogma, cult).[33]

In general there is little disagreement about the validity and value of such a science of religion. Also on a positive Christian basis there is a name and a place for this science.[34] But everything depends on the correctness of the assumptions underlying this science and the aim with which it is pursued. Certainly the following comments are then in order. First, as we already explained in our discussion of the religion-historical method in dogmatics, a completely objective attitude in studying the different religions is theoretically unjustifiable and practically unsustainable. Students of religions bring with them a general, vague concept of religion by which they can distinguish religious phenomena from other, say, ethical or aesthetic phenomena. Furthermore, just as all scientific investigation requires a certain congeniality between subject and object, so also in the study of religions it is essential for the investigator to be at least moderately sympathetic toward the object of his re-

32. *Hugenholtz, *Studien op Godsdienstlijke en Zedelijke Gebied*, II, 83ff. L. W. E. Rauwenhoff, *Wijsbegeerte van de Godsdienst* (Leiden: Brill & Van Doeburgh, 1887), 41ff.

33. Hermann Siebeck, *Religionsphilosophie* (Tübingen: J. C. B. Mohr, 1893), 34ff.; Oswald Külpe, *Einleitung in die Philosophie*, 2d ed. (Leipzig: S. Hirzel, 1898), 96; English translation, *Introduction to Philosophy: A Handbook for Students of Psychology, Logic, Ethics, Aesthetics and General Philosophy* (London: S. Sonnenschein & Co.; New York: Macmillan Co., 1901).

34. A. Kuyper, *Encyclopaedie der Heilige Godgeleerdheid*, 3 vols. (Amsterdam: J. A. Wormser, 1894), III, 563–77.

search. Only a religious person is able to study and evaluate religious phenomena in their actual significance. It is not enough after all for the student of the science of religion simply to observe; he or she must introduce order into the chaos of phenomena, determine the place and value of the different religions, trace the life and growth and hence also the degeneration and adulteration of religion, and indicate where religion displays itself in its purest form and richest development. None of this is possible unless the practitioners of the science of religion bring along a standard that they apply to the various religious phenomena. Add to this that students of this science are human beings endowed not only with intellect but also with reason and conscience, a heart and emotions, that they bring along not only a vague concept of religion but also a certain fund of religious and moral convictions, and that in carrying out this research they neither can nor should divest themselves of all these things. In fact, nobody does. "Not even the most sober thinker can nor should detach himself from what there is in his soul in the way of belief, deeper insight and discernment, higher understanding and intimate conviction." "Neutrality in the sense of detachment from and indifference toward one's most sacred convictions is either an absurdity or, perhaps, a sin."[35] These convictions are not working hypotheses that a person must immediately be prepared to surrender the moment the scientific investigation decrees their untenability. For those who hold them, they have the character of incontestable truths, since they are implied in the very object of their research. The nature and quantity of those convictions vary, but for the nature of the issue this makes no difference. No one who recognizes the existence and validity of such religious and moral convictions has the right to accuse another of dogmatism because the latter has different or more convictions of this nature than he himself. Included in the idea, say, of religion is that God exists and that he has revealed himself in some way and is therefore more or less knowable. That conviction is not a working hypothesis for the person who holds it but a truth that stands or falls with the religion itself. This does not mean of course that persons—also in the process of their scientific research—cannot lose such a conviction, but when they do they have not abandoned a scientific hypothesis but lost a treasure, a loss by which their spiritual life is impoverished for as long as they do not find others to replace it.

[74] In the second place, in striving to detach the science of religion from all religious assumptions, people do not achieve what they are aiming at. The purpose of this attempt, after all, is to accord to the science of religion, in the place of or alongside theology, the character of a genuine and pure science. The tacit assumption here is that positivism is the true view of science and that therefore the method of the natural sciences ought to be adopted and applied also in the so-called human sciences. But in making that assumption one faces a dilemma: On the one hand it is possible to rob the human sci-

---

35. H. I. Groenewegen, *De Theologie en hare Wijsbegeerte* (Amsterdam: 1904), 24.

ences of their own character and convert them into purely natural sciences. The other is to maintain them in their independence but then also to state openly that the positivistic notion of science is much too narrow and the methods of natural science are not susceptible of application to the area of the human spirit. The choice one makes between the two in turn depends on the fundamental question of whether there are norms, i.e., whether truth coincides with reality or whether it exists in a realm of its own above reality. This is not the place for a treatment of this philosophical problem,[36] but at least this much is certain: the different religions have always viewed themselves as being subject to the categories of truth and falsehood. The philosophical premise that all religions are essentially the same and only differ in forms is directly contradicted by unbiased historical investigation. The comparison between the study of religions and that of languages is indeed popular, and in many respects there exists a striking resemblance between the two. But this resemblance must not blind us to the difference. In the study of language, we do not speak of heretics, schismatics, and heathens, but in religion we encounter these and similar terms everywhere. And it is contrary to the perspective of unbiased research to dismiss these terms beforehand as immaterial and worthless.[37] Religious indifferentism is, for many reasons, untenable.

All religions, certainly, are formally similar. There are a number of elements that consistently return in every religion. First, in every religion there is a tradition concerning its divine origin; every religion appeals to revelation, an appeal that is the historical, the positive component, the component of tradition. Then, in every religion there is a certain teaching in which God makes known to human beings the knowledge that is indispensable to serving him; in religion this teaching is designated by the term *dogma*. Every religion further contains certain laws that prescribe to human beings what they must do and avoid doing to live in communion with God. That is the moral doctrine that every religion brings with it. And finally, in every religion there is a larger or smaller number of ceremonies, i.e., solemn actions and customs that, when practiced in private or public worship, accompany and reinforce human communion with God and give it an external form. That is the cultic or liturgical component of religion. In the various religions, the relative proportion of these components is very different. In some there is much dogma and little cultic activity; in others the proportions are reversed. In some cases one finds a rich tradition and a small number of moral precepts; in others the opposite is true. But in all religions the above components are present; there is no religion without history, dogma, morality, worship, and communion.[38] Among these components doctrine takes

---

36. See H. Bavinck, *Christelijke Wereldbeschouwing* (Kampen: Kok, 1904).

37. C. P. Tiele, *Elements of the Science of Religion*, 2 vols. (Edinburgh & London: William Blackwood & Sons, 1897–99), I, 9–10.

38. F. A. B. Nitzsch, *Lehrbuch der evangelische Dogmatik* (Tübingen: J. C. B. Mohr, 1889), 101–8; Hermann Siebeck, *Lehrbuch der Religionsphilosophie* (Freiburg i.B.: J. C. B. Mohr, 1893), 263ff.

first place. Even when the disposition in a given religion as well as the moral life are considered of inestimable value, one will have to agree with Tiele that doctrine, whatever its form, is the main source of our knowledge of that religion. It supplies us with the most information about its essence and character. From it alone we know how human beings picture God and their relation to him. Religious actions, the practices of worship, do not teach me anything when I look at them unless I am given some explanation of what they mean.[39]

The Question of Truth

If this is so, if in virtue of its nature all religion includes some kind of cognition and in its doctrine posits the reality of its object, it automatically falls under the heading of truth or untruth. Religion is never the product of feeling or fantasy alone; if that were the case, it would attach only an aesthetic value to its representations. But every religion is convinced of the reality and truth of its representations and cannot exist without this conviction.[40] Accordingly and in fact everyone applies the categories of "true" and "false" to religions. Even the most "presuppositionless" philosopher of religion does not believe in the truth of the gods of the nations, however much he appreciates the religious disposition that comes to expression in it, and speaks, for example, of intellectualism, mythical sentimentalism, moralism, as well as of the pathological phenomena that contrast with sound and vital religion.[41] The religions, accordingly, are far from viewing themselves as indifferent with respect to each other; they do not think they form a graduated series from the lower to the higher, but each in turn presents itself as true over against every other religion as untrue. Frederick the Great may say, and a philosopher of religion may say after him: "In my realm every citizen is free to be saved in his own fashion," but the religions themselves have a very different view of this matter. And they cannot do otherwise: what one religion posits as true is disregarded by another. If Christ is the one sent by the Father, then Mohammed is not. If the Catholic doctrine of the Lord's Supper is correct, that of the Reformation is in error. One who thinks and speaks otherwise and calls all religions equally true or equally false, in principle takes the position of the sophists who saw man as the measure of all things.

In line with this position, objective religion (dogma, morality, cult, etc.) actually occupies a totally different place in the religions than is commonly accorded to it in the philosophy of religion. The latter views it as being merely the different and changing expressions of one and the same life and does not see that the religious life as a rule comes to expression above all under the impact of that objective religion. All human beings find it ready-

---

39. C. P. Tiele, *Elements of the Science of Religion,* I, 22–23.
40. A. Bruining, "De Moderne Richting en de Dogmatiek," *Theologische Tijdschrift* 28 (1894): 563ff., 598ff.
41. C. P. Tiele, *Elements of the Science of Religion,* I, 9.

made at the time of their birth; they grow up in it as they do in the family and society and state. All of these are objective institutions and powers that do not arise arbitrarily from and by the agency of human beings but that incorporate them at the time of birth, shape and nurture them, and even continue to govern them, even against their will, throughout their entire life. In determining the essence of religion, it is contrary to history and psychology for scholars to start from subjective religion and to see in the different religions nothing but the changing forms and indifferent expression of the religious life. In that way one's daily experience is disowned, the power of objective religion denied, and all the relations between object and subject are reversed in revolutionary fashion. Most certainly also objective religion has its origin, an origin that has to be searched out and explained. But all the religions whose origin is somewhat known show us that they emerged in direct connection with existing circumstances and are most intimately bound up with the given historical milieu. There is not a single religion that is purely the creation of someone's religious disposition and can be explained exclusively in terms of it.

Subjective religion indeed modifies existing religious ideas and practices and frequently animates them with new life. But they do not produce the religion itself; on the contrary, it is itself aroused and developed under the influence and impact of an existing religion. Hence founders of religions, strictly speaking, do not exist: objective religion is the nursery of subjective religion.[42] Add to this that all religions wish to be regarded as the fruit of revelation, not as an expression and form of a religious disposition. They derive their origin from God, not from a human. One may or may not regard this appeal to revelation as valid, but the fact itself comes across vigorously that it may not simply be disregarded as an illusion. It is indicative, rather, of the fact that the concept of revelation is inseparably bound up with religion. There is no religion without revelation. Scripture too derives subjective religion from revelation (Heb.1:1). It is, for that matter, perfectly natural that religion and revelation consistently go together and are most intimately connected. For if religion really contains a doctrine of God and of his service, it is self-evident that God alone has the right and ability to say who he is and how he wants to be served. "It is not the part of men to establish and shape the worship of God, but, having been handed down by God, it is for them to receive and maintain."[43] Religious indifferentism assumes that it is immaterial to God how he is served. It deprives him of the right to determine the manner of his service; in any case it postulates that God has not prescribed the manner of his service. This indifferentism in the matter of religion can, of course, go to greater or lesser lengths. Syncretism considers the church creed to be indifferent; deism so considers all positive religion; modern philosophy

42. S. Hoekstra, *Wijsgerige Godsdienstleer*, I, 123; R. Eisler, *Kritische Einführung in die Philosophie* (Berlin: E. S. Mittler, 1905), 420.

43. Helvetic Confession, II, art. 1g.

so regards all objective religion; and the "moral independent" so views all that is religious. Factually and objectively, however, nothing is indifferent, neither in nature, nor in the state, nor in science and art. All things, even the most humble, have their specific place and meaning in the context of the whole. Human beings are indifferent only to what they do not, or do not sufficiently, know; they automatically assess and appreciate what they do know. God, who knows all things, is not indifferent to anything.[44]

[75] In the third place, all the research that has been devoted to the religions has led to very meager results as it pertains to knowledge of the essence of religion. This is absolutely not to say that this study as such is without value or has been unfruitful as a whole. The contrary is true. But it has not, or only to a small degree, achieved one of the most important objects with which this study was undertaken, viz., knowledge of the universal essence of religion. What religion is essentially, says Tiele in the opening lecture of his *Elements of the Science of Religion,* can only be determined at the end of the study as a whole. At the end of this study, we are then given a definition that describes the essence of religion as "the adoration of the superhuman power on which we feel dependent."[45] This result hardly stuns us with its surprising novelty and instinctively prompts the question whether for this outcome we needed such an extensive study of all religions. The same question comes up when we mentally review all the other definitions of the essence of religion. Whether one hears religion described as knowledge of our duties as divine imperatives (Kant), as an absolute feeling of dependence (Schleiermacher), as the sole knowledge of the absolute Spirit (Hegel), as the human perception of the infinite (Max Müller), as adoration of a supreme intellect and will (Martineaux), as belief in a supersensual deity as the ground and guarantee for the realization of the good (Siebeck), as the demonstration and maintenance of the spirituality of our being in its pursuit of infinity, eternity, and freedom (Eucken), as belief in a moral world order (Rauwenhoff), etc., in each case one finds himself thinking that the outcome of all the energies spent in the search for the essence of religion is, all in all, a disappointment.

44. Félicité Robert de Lamennais, *Essai sur l'indifférence en matière de religion,* 9th ed., 4 vols. (Paris: Garnier Frères, 1835); English translation, *Essay on Indifference in Matters of Religion,* trans. Lord Stanley of Alderley (London: John Macqueen, 1895). See especially volume 1, in which the introduction begins with the words, "It is not the age that is passionate for error that is the sickest, but the age that despises the truth."

45. C. P. Tiele, *Elements of the Science of Religion,* II, 198. Ed. note: Bavinck provides here a very loose summary of key ideas in the last chapters of Tiele's work. Tiele's actual definition reads as follows: "Now, whenever I discover piety, as manifested in different stages of religious progress, and particularly as exhibited in full beauty in the highest stage yet attained, I maintain that its essence, and therefore the essence of religion itself, is adoration" (*Aanbidding*). Bavinck's summary is potentially misleading in that it calls to mind Schleiermacher's understanding of religion as "a feeling of absolute dependence." Tiele explicitly indicates his disagreement with Schleiermacher's view since, while it does explain some key elements of religion, it fails to "account for religion as a whole." For this reason, Tiele adds, "It has long been rejected as inadequate by all competent authorities" (ibid., II, 222).

And that is not all, for none of these definitions, however general and vague, covers all religions: one religion is too much degraded by it and another too highly elevated. Tiele defends his definition with a view to the more primitive nature of religions by saying that a religion only manifests its essence in its full beauty when it has reached its maturity.[46] Further, these definitions differ a lot among themselves. The number of views concerning the essence of religion almost equals the number of philosophers and historians who have occupied themselves with these questions. All of these views have clearly been influenced by the convictions these scholars brought with them in doing their research and are much less grounded in the history of religion and the philosophy of religion than in personal experience and feeling. The impression one gets from all these different theories concerning the essence of religion, as Dr. Groenewegen correctly judges, is briefly that in regard to the question at hand the practitioners of the science of religion have virtually arrived at a dead end.[47]

Anyway, the very question concerning the essence of religion, because it is so indefinite, is not susceptible to solution. The religious life is much too deep and too rich for it to find its correct interpretation in a single formula. Nor will the empirical-psychological method, which in recent years has been applied by many scholars in the study of religious phenomena and is also recommended by Dr. Groenewegen, bring about any change in this situation. However much important information such investigation can bring to light concerning the state and activity of the religious life of the soul, in the nature of the case it can no more explain the essence of religion by it than the same method can do this with regard to the norms of thought and of the moral life. But even if it did succeed in giving a definition of the essence of religion that satisfied everyone, it would still be no more than a vague formula that was open to a variety of interpretations and without the least practical utility. This is established by the fact that no one is content with such a "core," "essence," or "spirit" of religion. Tiele may say that doctrine and cult no more belong to the essence of religion than the body belongs to the essence of man, but this comparison already breaks down simply because the body very definitely belongs to the essence of our humanity. Tiele's claim is, moreover, directly contradicted by daily experience. Everyone is looking for a religion with a dogma, a morality, a cult, and a communion. And if the modern philosophy of religion, by its investigation into the essence of religion, has engendered indifference toward the forms of religion, this has merely borne two kinds of fruit. On the one hand, neo-romanticism has begun to look for the original essence and power of religion in various abnormal ascetic and ecstatic

46. C. P. Tiele, *Elements of the Science of Religion*, II, 198, 204.

47. Groenewegen, *De Theologie en haar Wijsbegeerte*, 67–71; Adolf von Harnack, *What Is Christianity?* trans. Thomas Bailey Saunders, 2d ed. (New York: G. P. Putnam's Sons, 1901), 9ff. Ed. note: Herman I. Groenewegen (1862–1930) was a Remonstrant theologian who taught at Leiden and at the City University of Amsterdam. He is best known for his contribution to the philosophy of religions.

phenomena,[48] and to glorify enthusiasts in the same manner as Nietzsche elevated to the status of supermen men like Nero, Cesar Borgia, and Napoleon. On the other hand, members not only of the underclasses of the nation but even of the highest circles in society are attempting to find a surrogate for religion in spiritism, theosophy, the worship of spirits, the service of humanity, hero worship, the formation of ideals, ethical culture, the deification of art, and a spectrum of other forms of—more or less refined—superstition.[49]

And even if people do not lapse into such extremes, life proves over and over to be stronger than theory. Alongside of the science and philosophy of religion—which are then said to meet completely the demands of impartial, open-minded science—people again take in through the back door the previously expelled study of dogmatics, plus the task assigned to it of scientifically describing and maintaining the content of our religious consciousness. Let us grant for the sake of argument that from a scientific viewpoint dogmatics, which describes and vindicates the content of faith, has a less stable foundation. Let us grant that its authority and influence depend much less on its scientific than on its religious caliber and that it is indeed a science but is not as deserving of that name as the science of religion since it is based on the personal life of faith. All this is presently less pertinent to our purpose and in any case contains the good idea that dogmatics, like all theology, is a science with a character of its own, with its own first principle, method, and aim. Dogmatics, in fact, does accept the content of faith as truth; it proceeds from the truth of the religion it confesses and speaks of God, his attributes, his government of the world, and his purpose for humanity. Accepting the axioms of life and attempting to render its "I believe" as "I understand" in the assurance of its faith, it is broader, deeper, and richer than any metaphysics. The content of the faith it accepts appears not just as the most intimate but also as the religious person's highest consciousness of truth. That faith is sure of itself and testifies: "I have the truth," resisting with its "eureka!" where necessary, all science and philosophy.[50]

If all this is so, then in a formal sense the entire old study of dogmatics returns here. In the end, the concessions first made in the science and philosophy of religion to modern positivistic science clearly turn out not to have been meant seriously. If in the end dogmatics and the philosophy of religion should clash, then, for Dr. Groenewegen and for all others, *that* will be con-

---

48. B. Duhm, *Das Geheimnis in der Religion* (Freiburg i.B.: J. C. B. Mohr), 1896; H. S. Chamberlain, *Die Grundlagen des neunzehnten Jahrhundert,* 4th ed., 2 vols. (München: F. Bruckmann, 1903); translated into English as *Foundations of the Nineteenth Century,* trans. John Lees, 2 vols. ([1911]; reprinted, New Orleans: Flander Hall, 1988).

49. Helene von Druskowitz, *Moderne Versuche eines Religionsersatzes* (Heidelberg: G. Weiss, 1886); K. F. Heman, *Über wissenschaftliche Versuche neuer Religionsbildungen* (Basel: C. Detloff, 1884); E. Haack, *Die Modernen Bemühungen um eine Zukunftreligion* (Leipzig, 1903); E. L. Fischer, *Die modernen Ersatzversuche für die aufgegebene Christentum* (Regensburg, 1902); A. M. Weisz, *Die religiöse Gefahr* (Freiburg i.B.: Herdersche Verlagshandlung, 1904).

50. Groenewegen, *De Theologie en haar Wijsbegeerte,* 55ff., 81ff., 89, 97ff.

sidered the more important what *is to him* the more important. For the sake of the assurance of faith he will, if need be, resist science and philosophy and uphold against the science of the day a worldview in which there is room for his religion, for belief in a personal God, in the independence of the human spirit, in the triumph of the good, in a kingdom of God, and a cosmic goal. Materially there will be a large difference between his dogmatics and that of others. But formally he conducts himself like any other dogmatician and any other believer. Only, what Dr. Groenewegen says at the end, the Reformed dogmatician—from conviction and for the sake of honesty—puts at the beginning. The faith that we confess and on which the salvation of our soul depends compels us to ask of modern positivistic science that it amend itself and not deny to religion and Christianity, to theology and to dogmatics, the place that by right belongs to these phenomena and sciences.

THE SEAT OF RELIGION: INTELLECT, WILL, OR HEART?

[76] Now that we have examined the essence of religion, we must indicate the place of religion in the life of the human psyche. In that connection the psychic faculties and functions that are operative in the religious life will emerge, and the way religion relates to science, art, and morality also immediately becomes clear. Scholasticism already raised the question whether religion was an intellectual or a moral virtue, a question Thomas answered by saying it was the latter.[51] But as a result of the change that has come about in the concept of religion, this question has acquired much greater importance in modern times. Now, in the main three views have been put forward about the place of religion in the life of the soul.

Religion as Knowledge

First, there is the intellectualistic view, which locates the essence of religion in knowledge and its seat in the intellect. Gnosticism already said that *gnosis* was redemptive, that knowledge was "the redemption of the inner man."[52] This Gnosticism has at all times found its defenders in the Christian church, but it especially again emerged in modern philosophy. Spinoza considers the intellect and the will as "one and the same" and sees the love of God (*amor Dei*) arising from clear and distinct human self-knowledge and human affects and hence also calls it "intellectual love" (*amor intellectualis*). Inasmuch as our mind is part of the infinite mind of God, the highest virtue our mind can achieve is knowledge of God. And this knowledge of God, which is essentially one with the contemplation of things under the aspect of eternity, is "the highest possible peace of mind."[53] According to

51. Aquinas, *Summa Theologica*, II.2, qu. 81, art. 5.
52. Irenaeus, *Against Heresies,* I, chap. 21.
53. B. Spinoza, *Ethics,* part II, 44, 49; part V; prop. 15, 27, 32; in English, *Ethics,* trans. G. H. R. Parkinson (Oxford and New York: Oxford University Press, 2000).

Schelling in his first period, only an absolute knowledge is possible of the absolute as the identity of the finite and the infinite. Hence religion here completely loses its independence, and belief is an incorrect and impure view of the idea.[54] Especially Hegel developed this intellectualistic definition of the essence of religion. In him the absolute is thought itself entering into the antitheses and from these again returning to identity with itself. The entire world is therefore a development of the mind (*Geist*), a logical unfolding of the content of reason, a process in which the idea first objectivizes itself in nature and from there returns in the spirit to itself. One of the phases through which this process passes is religion. It is in the human mind that the absolute comes to itself and becomes conscious of itself. And this self-consciousness of the absolute mind in the finite mind is religion. Hence religion *is* essentially a knowing, not feeling or acting, but a knowing: knowing God by the finite mind or an objective divine knowing of himself through and in the finite mind. "Man only knows of God insofar as God has knowledge of himself in man; this knowledge is the self-consciousness of God but also a knowledge of the same by man, and this knowledge of God by man is the knowledge of man by God. The mind of man in coming to know God, is just the mind of God itself."[55]

Religion, however, is not the highest knowledge for Hegel; it is only a knowledge of the absolute in the form of sensual historical representations. The highest true knowledge can be attained only in philosophy. Religion, therefore, is temporary, a lower form [of knowledge], suited only to the uneducated. But philosophy separates the idea from the husk of the sensual representations of religion and thus arrives at an absolute, adequate, conceptual knowledge of God.[56] When religion and philosophy were related to each other in that fashion, it was natural for people to elevate the latter above the former and to rob it of all value. This, accordingly, happened soon after Hegel's death and primarily at the hands of Feuerbach. In his thought religion and philosophy were no longer merely a lower and a higher form of knowledge but constituted an antithesis and excluded each other. Faith makes human beings servile; science makes them free. Theology is based on miracle, philosophy on reality; the former is founded on fantasy, the latter on thought. Theology demands faith in dogma, and dogma is nothing but a ban on thought. The task of philosophy is not to justify dogma but to explain the illusion from which it springs. For indeed faith, religion, theology, and dogma are nothing other than a grand illusion. Their only origin is anthropological. They are nothing but an apotheosis of

54. F. W. J. Schelling, *Ausgewählte Werke: Schriften von 1813–1830*, 5 vols. (Darmstadt: Wissenschaftliche Buchgesellschaft, 1967–68), III, 597ff. ("*Philosophie und Religion,*" in *Werke*, I/VI, 11ff.).

55. G. W. F. Hegel, *Sämtliche Werke*, "Jubilee" edition, ed. H. Glockner, 22 vols. (Stuttgart, 1927–30), XVI, 428. ("*Vorlesungen uber die Philosophie der Religion,*" in *Werke*, XII, 428).

56. Hegel, *Sämtliche Werke*, XVI, 15ff. ("*Vorlesungen uber die Philosophie der Religion,*" in *Werke*, XII, 15ff.); D. F. Strauss, *Die Christliche Glaubenslehre*, 2 vols. (Tubingen: C. F. Osiander, 1840–41), I, 12.

man by man himself, the reflection of the human being in his own imagination. Theology is essentially anthropology. Wishful thinking is the origin and essence of religion.

Arguing in the same spirit, Strauss appeared, saying that theology and philosophy, theism and pantheism, are irreconcilable. Although religion and philosophy have in common the idea of the unity of the divine and the human, religion clothed this idea in the form of a conception such that God and man came to stand dualistically side-by-side and could only be brought together again supernaturally by miracles, creation, incarnation, revelation, etc. Thought, however, divests itself of this form of representation, recognizes God as the eternal process that produces the world from within itself, and only comes to self-consciousness, personality, and itself in humanity. All miracles are excluded here: God and man are one; humanity is the true son of God. These two positions held respectively by religion and philosophy, of representation and concept, are incompatible. Religion is the worldview of folk-consciousness, which is dissolved by philosophy in the adequated form of a concept. Both Feuerbach and Strauss ended up in materialism: sensual nature is the only reality; human beings are what they eat. "No religion," said the former, "is my religion," "No philosophy is my philosophy," and, he might have added, "No morality is my morality."[57] As it was by Lamettrie in the eighteenth, so in the middle of the nineteenth century faith in God was regarded by Bruno Bauer, Arnold Ruge, Edgar Bauer, Max Stirner, Büchner, Vogt, and others as the most enormous and pernicious error.[58]

Now Hegel understood very well that religion also includes knowledge and that religion and metaphysics are most intimately connected. This is obvious from the nature of the case. Religion is always a relation of a human to a superior divine power. Religion does not and cannot exist, therefore, without a certain specific idea of God; and this idea in turn includes other ideas concerning the world, humanity, the origin and the destiny of things. To believers these religious ideas have transcendental significance; they are profoundly convinced of their objective reality and truth. The moment we begin to regard these ideas as products of our own imagination, as ideals without reality, or even despair of the knowability of the metaphysical, our religion is done for. Skepticism destroys the object of religion and, in so doing, religion itself. God must also be served with the mind, and when the mind notes that religious notions do not correspond to reality, it ceases to be religious. While a religious and a theoretical worldview, theology and sci-

57. Cf. A. Drews, *Die deutsche Spekulation seit Kant*, 2 vols. (Berlin: P. Maeter, 1893), II, 237ff.

58. Cf., for example, Max Stirner, *Der Einzige und sein Eigenthum* (Leipzig: O. Wigand, 1882); in English, *The Ego and His Own*, trans. Steven T. Byington (New York: B. R. Tucker, 1907); Karl C. Vogt, *Kohlerglaube und Wissenschaft*, 3d ed. (Giessen: J. Ricker, 1855); L. Büchner, *Force and Matter: Or Principles of the Natural Order of the Universe*, 4th ed., trans. from the 15th German edition (New York: P. Eckler, 1891), 392ff.; Karl A. Specht, *Theologie und Wissenschaft*, 3d ed. (Gotha: Stollberg, 1878), 74ff.

ence, are not identical, they cannot possibly be at war with each other. Such a dualism is inevitably in conflict with the unity of the human mind.[59]

But Hegel did err when he opposed religion and philosophy to each other in a relation of "lower" and "higher," as [pictorial] representation and [universal] concept, and therefore viewed them as successive phases in a single process. Hegelians such as Strauss and Biedermann themselves understood this error.[60] Form and content are never so mechanically and externally related that a total change in the one will leave the other unaltered. The conversion of religious "representations" into philosophical "concepts" also affects the religious content itself. The history of Hegelian thought soon brought this reality to light. In it virtually nothing remained of the Christian dogma; "Trinity," "incarnation," "satisfaction," though retaining their orthodox names, were interpreted very differently. The facts of Christianity were regarded as its form and considered worthless. In their place came concepts that no longer had any content. A second error made by Hegel consisted in the fact that he assigned the same content to religion and philosophy but nevertheless considered the former "lower" than the latter. Religion was thereby reduced to a relative good that still had value only for the simple and uneducated. Philosophers were on a level far above it and were content with philosophy.

Now this is based on a total misconstrual of the essence of religion. For though religion and philosophy are related, there is also a world of difference between them. Although they frequently have the same content and object, these objects are viewed in each domain from a very different perspective. The aim of science is knowledge; in religion it is comfort, peace, salvation. Nor are religion and philosophy, like the theological, metaphysical, and positive stages of August Comte, historically successive states of the human mind but different vantage points from which the same matter can be viewed. Even the most profound philosopher, therefore, for all his knowledge does not rise above religion; he can never meet his religious needs by science. Though science may tell him *that* God is and *what* God is, it is only by religion that he knows that that God is also *his* God and *his* Father. Science may teach him that sin and grace exist, but it is only by religion that he takes part in the blessedness of religion and the sonship of God. Even if science could know all things and solve all metaphysical problems, it would still only yield theoretical knowledge and not personal participation in the benefits of salvation. For salvation is bound up with believing, not with knowing. But it is far from true that science and philosophy can attain this benefit. There are still many people, to be sure, who continue to expect all salvation from science and to consider religion superfluous. Ernst Haeckel, in his *The Riddle of the Universe at the Close of the Nineteenth Century,* comes across as a true prophet of the Enlightenment, as an intellectualist who no

59. Eduard von Hartmann, *Die Religion des Geistes,* 2d ed. (Leipzig: W. Friedrich, 1889), 3–27.

60. D. F. Strauss, *Die Christliche Glaubenslehre,* 2 vols. (Tübingen: C. F. Osiander, 1840–41), I, 12ff.; A. E. Biedermann, *Christliche Dogmatik,* 2 vols. (Berlin: G. Reimer, 1884–85), I, 18ff.

longer tolerates any riddle, any mystery or mysticism, and believes that human beings can know or at least will know by the use of ordinary common sense everything there is to know. At a conference of scientists and physicians held at Cassel, September 21, 1903, Ladenburg gave a speech in which he rejected all Christian dogmas and regarded the French Revolution a greater blessing to humankind than Christianity. In November of the same year, at a feast of and for freethinkers, Berthelot gave an oration in which he raved over science, progress, and liberty and took virtually no account of the human heart, conscience, religion, and morality. Nonetheless, a turnabout is in progress. Prominent men of science are beginning to see that science fails to answer the most important questions of life. The expectation Renan had of science in 1848 proved to himself in 1890 to have been an illusion. As early as 1880, Dubois Reymond spoke of the seven riddles of the world. Brunetière, following a visit to the pope, spoke in 1895 of the bankruptcy of science—wrongly so, inasmuch as not science, but the foolish expectations people build on it have suffered bankruptcy. In the natural sciences the mysteries are not diminishing but increasing, and the philosophy of nature is again raising its voice. In literature and art, mysticism has made its debut. The rights of religion and metaphysics are being acknowledged in ever-widening circles. Even among the socialists men are emerging who wish to put aside a hostile attitude to religion. And, further, the numerous manifestations of superstition evident today demonstrate that humankind cannot live by the bread of science alone but need every word that comes from the mouth of God. Indeed, science does not tell us what God is or what humanity is; it leaves us ignorant of the origin, essence, and goal of things. It can therefore never replace religion, nor ever compensate for its loss.[61]

Religion as Morality

[77] Other scholars therefore defined religion as moral conduct and located its seat in the human will. Pelagianism in its various forms—semi-Pelagianism, Socinianism, Remonstrantism, deism, rationalism, etc.—has paved the way for this view insofar as faith, in this approach, is supplemented by or even solely exists in a "new obedience." Doctrine in that case is merely a means and secondary; the main thing is love, living a virtuous moral life. Also in Spinoza, besides the intellectualistic, there occurs this moralistic view. Holy Scripture is God's Word because it contains true religion, the divine law.[62] It has no aim beyond obedience, and this obedience toward God consists in the love of neighbor alone. Philosophy and faith are distinguished in that the former aims at truth, the latter at obedience and piety. The intellectual or pre-

61. Voigt, *Fundamentaldogmatik*, 120ff.; von Hartmann, *Die Religion des Geistes*, 3–27; Herman Siebeck, *Der Religionsphilosophie*, 1–11; F. Nitzsch, *Lehr der Evangelischen Dogmatik*, 3d ed. (Tubingen: J. C. B. Mohr, 1902), 92–96; O. Pfleiderer, *Grundriss der Christlichen Glaubens und Sittenlehre* (Berlin: G. Reimer, 1888), §11.
62. B. Spinoza, *Tractatus Theologica-Politicus*, trans. Samuel Shirley (Leiden: Brill, 1991), chaps. 12ff.

cise knowledge of God is not a gift given to all believers, but obedience is: it is required of everyone. It was especially Kant, however, who gained acceptance for this moralism. Theoretical reason, after all, cannot reach the supersensual: God, freedom, and immortality cannot be scientifically demonstrated. They are only the postulates of practical reason for the fulfillment of the moral law and the attainment of the highest good, i.e., the salvation that is bound up with virtue. Believing, accordingly, is "to hold as true," not on theoretical but on practical grounds, and morality becomes the basis of religion.

Religion, subjectively considered, is the knowledge of all our duties as divine imperatives. Religion here is not directly and immediately grounded in human nature but only by way of morality. It has no material content of its own and is nothing but a further qualification of morality. The distinction between the two does not lie in the object but only in the form. Kant, accordingly, had to admit that no actual religion was ever satisfied with his notion of religion. Aside from a purely rational faith, all religions contained many other dogmas—a doctrinal and historical faith. But he interprets this in terms of a weakness in human nature, which cannot be easily persuaded that moral conduct is all God asks of us. It is our calling increasingly to purify the faith of the church and to turn it into a purely rational faith which actually has no other content than the rationalistic triad: God, virtue, and immortality.

Others went further. J. G. Fichte derived from the moral consciousness no other postulate than that the "ego" view the entire "non-ego," the world, as the "sense-infused material" of his duty. The "ego" must acknowledge the non-ego as so ordered that his moral evolution and conduct is in line with the moral purpose of the whole, in other words, that there exists a moral world order. Here religion has been exhaustively absorbed by morality. This moralism has been deepened into ethicism inasmuch as morality is understood as being not only psychological but metaphysical. In that case the will, the good, and love are the true primal being of the world, the absolute. All else— the Trinity, the world, redemption—must be explained in the light of this absolute. The power of the good is realized in the human world by means of morality. This is the basic idea from which Schelling proceeded in his second period: ultimately and supremely there is no other being than will—will is primal being.[63] In Schelling this will was originally unconscious and hence as such no more than a drive, a desire, a longing. But along with intellect it arises from nature, from the abyss, which is in God, and, uniting with that intellect and appropriating the idea as its content, becomes spirit, personality, conscious will, the will of love. "The abyss is divided into two equally eternal principles, solely in order that the two may become one by love; i.e., it only divides that there may be life and love and personal existence.[64]

63. F. W. J. Schelling, "Über das Wesen der Menschliche Freiheit," in *Erste Abth.*, VII, 331ff.; reprinted in vol. 1 of *F. W. J. Schelling's philosophische Schriften* (Landshut: Bei Philipp Krüll, 1809).

64. Ibid, 406–8.

With these ideas of Kant, Fichte, and Schelling, *voluntarism* made its debut in modern philosophy.[65] It was not long before it also found support in theology. Schleiermacher, for that matter, in the introduction to his dogmatics had already elevated ethics to the status of norm for the development of Christianity. Since dogmatics is a positive science and does not exist in virtue of a scientific idea but only for the sake of a practical purpose (to guide the church), it cannot derive its nature from its own idea but must in its introduction borrow certain propositions from a variety of sciences. Among the sciences from which these borrowings are to be made, ethics ranks foremost. In Schleiermacher, this science (ethics) is "that speculative presentation of Reason, in the whole range of its activity which runs parallel to natural science," the science of the principles of history. Whereas natural science has for its object the real, ethics has to do with the ideal, with human conduct, the action of reason upon nature, by which especially four moral goods—the state, society, school, and church—are produced. Ethics therefore also has to set forth what "pious communities" are, how they arise and develop, and how in their development they continue to answer to their idea. Hence with respect to the church, ethics sets forth what in the development of Christianity must be regarded as a pure expression of its idea and what on the other hand is a deviation from it and consequently must be regarded as a state of disease. In token of that fact, dogmatics becomes dependent on a nontheological science, viz., ethics, and derives from it its principle and norm.[66]

To this must be added that later on in his dogmatics Schleiermacher describes the Christian religion as an ethical religion. Among the monotheistic religions, which compare favorably with polytheistic religions, there is in turn a difference between those that subordinate the moral to the natural and others that subordinate the natural to the moral. Belonging to the former is especially Islam; to the latter, especially Christianity. The latter, after all, is a teleological religion, which urges human beings to fulfill their task in the world and to join in working for the coming of the kingdom.[67] Dogmatics not only has its principle and norm rooted in ethics but now also receives its goal in moral conduct. And Rothe only continued this line of thought when he denied to piety a content of its own, equated it with morality, and finally allowed the church to be absorbed into the state.[68]

In all kinds of schools of thought, the continuing impact of these ideas gave to the ethical principle a powerful significance in modern theology.

65. Rudolf Eisler, *Wörterbuch der philosophische Begriffe*, 2 vols. (Berlin: E. S. Mittler, 1904), s.v. "voluntarisme."

66. F. Schleiermacher, *Christian Faith*, §2; idem, *Brief Outline of Theology as a Field of Study*, trans. Terrence N. Tice (Lewiston, N.Y.: E. Mellen Press, 1988), §§29, 35.

67. F. Schleiermacher, *Christian Faith*, §§8, 9.

68. R. Rothe, *Theologische Ethik*, 2d rev. ed., 5 vols. (Wittenberg: Zimmerman, 1867–71), §§114–26, 440.

Nevertheless, concerning the application and development of this principle, there was wide variety. First, both among the orthodox and mediating theologians (*Vermittelungstheologen*) and among modernists, there were a great many scholars who followed Kant's epistemology and attempted to construct religion on the foundation of the moral nature of humankind. They all agree in saying that the foundation of dogmatics cannot lie in any external authority, nor in intellectual arguments and proofs, but only in the human will, in the self-reliance and independence of the human mind over against nature. Although in many respects human beings are seen as creatures of nature, in their minds and specifically in their moral nature they belong to a different and higher order of things, are citizens of another world than that controlled by natural laws. It is in religion they maintain themselves as such. Lifting themselves up by the supernatural, they leave the natural beneath them. Putting themselves in communion with God, they emancipate themselves from the world. Religion here is a means of self-assertion, the will to live.

Others view morality not merely as a foundation but also as the principle and norm of religion and theology. Following in the footsteps of Schleiermacher and Rothe, they elevate morality—as the triumph of the human mind over nature—to the level of an absolute power and as a result base dogmatics on ethics. In the Netherlands de la Saussaye was the talented representative of this trend and in virtue of this principle posed the demand that Christian dogmas should not be further developed metaphysically but be revised and deepened ethically.[69] The "ethicals" among the modernists even went much further. After Hoekstra had started locating the foundation for religious faith in practical reason or in the will, many others, prompted by his example, started to describe religion as dedication to the moral ideal, as pure morality. Here God was not just reduced to the good, but the good was elevated to the rank of deity so that there was not only talk of an ethical pantheism but also for a time of an atheistic nuance among the modernists.[70] Joining this list then were the adherents of an independent morality,[71] the proponents of a nondogmatic practical Christianity,[72] and particularly also the followers of

69. See further, H. Bavinck, *De Theologie van Prof. Dr. Daniel Chantepie de la Saussaye,* 2d rev. ed. (Leiden: D. Donner, 1903).

70. S. Hoekstra, *Bronnen en grondslogen van het godsdienstig geloof* (Amsterdam: P. N. van Kampen, 1864), 23ff.; *I. Hooykaas, *God in de geschiedenis* (1870); idem, *Vier voorlezingen over den godsdienstig volgens de beginselen der ethische richting onder de modernen* ('s Hertogenbosch: G. H. van de Schuyt, 1876): "Het recht van den godsdienst" by I. Hooykaas; "De godsdienst der ervaring en hare verhouding tot het bidden" by Johs. Hooykaas Herderscheê; "De historische godsdiensten" by H. Oort; "Godsdienstig leven" by A. G. van Hamel.

71. C. Coignet, *La morale indépendante dans son principe et dans son objet* (Paris: G. Baillière, 1863); E. Vacherot, *La religion* (Paris: Chamerot et Lauwereyns, 1869).

72. O. Dreyer, *Undogmatisches Christentum,* 3d ed. (Braunschweig: C. A. Schwetschke und Sohn, 1890); idem, *Zur Undogmatischen Glaubenslehre* (Berlin: C. A. Schwetschke, 1901); C. M. von Egidy, *Ernste Gedanker* (Leipzig, 1890).

the ethical movements,[73] which, according to a saying by Jodl, wanted nothing to do with "cult" (worship) but only still with culture and considered the only religion worthy of human beings to consist in the autonomous development of their own moral personality.

This whole ethical trend in religion and theology deserves our appreciation to the degree that, over against all intellectualistic and mystical underestimation of the moral life, it again pointed out the intimate connection that exists between religion and morality. That connection is immediately evident from the fact that religion itself is a moral relationship. Religion is indeed based on a mystical union between God and humanity; however, it is not itself a substantial but an ethical union between human beings and their God. In the case of God, one cannot speak of religion. It is his indwelling in human beings that from that side fosters the relation to God we call religion.[74] Thus this relation, too, is of an ethical nature; it is regulated by the same moral law that governs the other relations human beings sustain to their fellow creatures. All religious actions performed by human beings are moral duties, and all of religion is a moral mandate. Conversely, the moral life is in turn a service to God. Visiting widows and orphans (James 1:27) is not, strictly speaking, a religious act but can be called religion because religion has to manifest and prove itself in that act. Scholasticism, accordingly, distinguished between acts "called forth" (*actus eliciti*) and acts "demanded" (*actus imperati*) by religion.[75] Faith without works, without love, is dead. Also for us love for God proves itself in love for one's neighbor (Jer. 22:16; Isa. 1:11ff.; 1 John 2:3ff.; James 2:17; etc.). Our entire life is meant to be a service to God. The inscription: "I am the Lord your God" is also written above the commandments of the second table. Love is the one grand principle that fulfills the entire law (Rom. 13:10). The moral law is one great organic whole so that those who break one commandment violate the whole law (James 2:10). One's neighbor must be loved for God's sake, and a sin against a neighbor is indirectly a sin also against God.

Still, this close relation between religion and morality may not lead to a denial of the distinction between the two. Although both are regulated in the same moral law, that law itself is divided into two tables. Religion is always a relation to God; morality a relation to human beings. The principle of religion is faith (πιστις); that of morality is love (ἀγαπη). Religion manifests itself in the religious actions that together form the internal and exter-

73. Salter, *De Godsdienst der Moraal*, trans. Hugenholtz (1889); Stanton Coit, *Die ethische Bewegung in der Religie*, German trans. Georg von Gizychi (Leipzig: Reisland, 1890). F. Adler, *Die ethischen Gesellschaften* (Berlin: Ferd. Dümmlers Verlagsbuchhandlung, 1892); A. Schinz, "Le récent mouvement moral en Amérique et en Europe," *Revue de Theologie et Philosophie* (September 1896): 419–46.

74. H. Denzinger, *Vier Bücher von der religiösen Erkenntniss*, 2 vols. (Würzburg: Verlag der Stahel'schen Buch-und-Kunst-handlung, 1856, 1857), I, 3ff.; S. Hoekstra, *Wijsgerige Godsdienstleer*, 2 vols. (Amsterdam: P. N. van Kampen & Zoon, 1894–95), I, 57ff., 64.

75. Aquinas, *Summa Theol.*, II. 2, qu. 81, art. 1.

nal cult; morality manifests itself in acts of righteousness, mercy, honesty, etc. toward one's neighbor. This distinction between religion and ethos cannot be maintained by pantheism because in it God has no independent existence of his own. A personal relation between God and human beings is therefore impossible in pantheism, and love for God can only express itself in love for one's neighbor. Also, deism, because of its denial of communion between God and humanity, is unable to foster true religion. There is indeed still belief in God but no service of God other than in the fulfillment of the moral commandments. On a theistic position, however, while human beings stand in relation to the world, they also stand in a unique and distinct relation to God as a personal being. Religion, accordingly, is something essentially different from morality and manifests itself in a series of deeds of its own. If this is true, then morality can be neither the foundation nor the principle, or the norm, or the content of religion, but, conversely, religion has to form the basis of morality. The relation to God is then the primary and central relation that governs all other human relations. Historically as well as logically, morality is always grounded in religion. All religions insist on moral duties, and morality seeks religious sanction. In reality, an autonomous morality does not exist anywhere. Everywhere and among all peoples morality finds its final ground and final goal in religion. Morality loses the ground under its foot when it is robbed of divine authority in the human conscience. "Historically all morality has developed from religion; and even though the spiritual propensities of mankind toward morality—which have thus developed—can for a time and thanks to their origin persist independently when separated from their native soil, this capacity for independent existence is temporally very limited and already in the second generation the symptoms of moral decay become clearly perceptible.[76] Materially, of course, hardly all the obligations and actions that people consider moral are in keeping with the will of God. But, formally, that which makes every duty an unconditional duty, that which obligates the human conscience, is rooted in divine authority. Hence there is no morality without metaphysics.

People, customs, morals (etc.) cannot absolutely compel anyone's conscience; only God can. That, too, is the reason why the conscience is sacrosanct and freedom of conscience an inexorable demand and inalienable right. The laws and prohibitions that are not anchored in the human conscience are not perceived as moral. A law that has no foundation in a people's conscience is powerless. Thanks to this connection, religion and morality have a mutual impact on each other. For a time they may go their separate ways in an individual or a nation and even be in conflict, but they cannot be at rest until they are back in harmony and balanced. That which is approved in religion cannot be condemned in morality, and vice versa. Both the relation to God and the relation to human beings must have the same moral character and be

---

76. Eduard von Hartmann, *Die Religion des Geistes* (Leipzig: W. Friedrich, 1880), 59.

regulated in one and the same moral law. Religion and morality, cult and culture, must spring from the same principle. That is the case in Christianity: love is the fulfilling of the law and the bond of perfection.[77]

Religion as Feeling

[78] Finally, there are also still those who give to religion a place in feeling and to that end even postulate a separate faculty in human beings. In an earlier age mysticism and Pietism had already paved the way for this development. But this view only achieved hegemony as a result of the romanticism of the nineteenth century. Romanticism was, generally speaking, a reaction of the free unfettered life of the emotions to objective, all-obligating and all-regulating classicism. Human subjects raised themselves above the laws laid down to prohibit them from spontaneous expression in every area of life. The imagination again asserted its rights over against the intellect. The organic view came in the place of the mechanical. The idea of "becoming" suppressed that of "making." In every sector of life, people opened their eyes to the free, to the natural, and to genius. Becoming, growth, development was the mode in which things came into being. Not the practical but the beautiful, not prose but poetry, not work but play, not manufactured things but art was supremely valuable. The affected mannerisms of an earlier day yielded to a superficial sentimentality.

Such was the movement that in England found its interpreters in Young, Southey, Wordsworth, and S. T. Coleridge. In France it was introduced by Rousseau, who in his "Profession of faith of the vicar of Savoy," in the fourth book of his Emile, constructs his whole deistic dogmatics and morality on a basis of feeling: "Feeling is more than reason and our sensitivity precedes our intelligence." In Germany Winckelmann opened people's eyes to the beauty of Greek art. Lessing contrasted the genius of Shakespeare to the poetry of French classicism. Herder pointed out the revelation and workings of the

---

77. Hermann Schultz, "Religion und Sittlichkeit in ihrem Verhältniss zu einander, religionsgeschichtlich untersucht," *Theologische Studien und Kritiken* 56 (1883): 60–130; J. Köstlin, "Religion und Sittlichkeit," *Theologische Studien und Kritiken* 43 (1870): 50–122; Otto Pfleiderer, *Moral und Religion* (Haarlem: n.p., 1872); R. Rothe, *Theologische Ethik*, §114ff.; H. Martensen, *Die Christliche Ethik*, 3d ed. (Gotha: Besser, 1878); Paul Janet, *La Morale* (Paris: C. Delagrave, 1874), 596ff.; English trans. Mary Chapman, *The Theory of Morals* (New York: Scribner, 1883); S. Hoekstra, "Godsdienst en Zedelijkheid," *Theologisch Tijdschrift* 2 (1868): 117–55; idem, *Godsdienstleer*, I, 251ff.; *Lamers, *Godsdienst en Zedelijkheid* (Amsterdam, 1882); *idem, *De Godsdienst evenmin Moraal als Metaphysica* (1885); P. D. Chantepie De la Saussaye, *Lehrbuch der Religions geschichte*, 2 vols. (Tübingen: J. C. B. Mohr [Paul Siebeck], 1905), I, 166ff.; G. H. Lamers, *De Wetenschap van de Godsdienst*, 5 vols. in 1 (Utrecht: C. H. E. Breijer, 1891, 1893), II, 167ff.; P. H. Hugenholtz, *Studiën op Godsdienstlich en Zedekundig Gebied* (Amsterdam, 1884), I, passim; Eduard von Hartmann, *Religionsphilosophie*, 2d ed., 2 vols. (Bad Sachsa im Harz: Hermann Haacke, 1907), II, 55–64; Hermann Siebeck, *Lehrbuch der Religionsphilosophie* (Freiburg i.B.: J. C. B. Mohr, 1893), 243ff.; Julius Kaftan, *Das Wesen der christliche Religion* (Basel: Bahnmaier's Verlag, 1881), 124ff.; F. Nitzsch, *Lehrbuch der evangelische Dogmatik*, 96ff.; Wilhelm Herrmann, *In Beitrage zur Weiterbildung*, 183ff.; H. Visscher, *Religie en zedelijk leven* (Utrecht: G. R. Ruys, 1904); Otto Pfleiderer, *Religion und Religionen* (München: J. F. Lehmann, 1906), 19ff.

eternal divine nature in history. Hamann, Claudius, Lavater, and Stilling took their starting point in the richness of subjectivity, contrasting it with the flat, mechanical view of the Enlightenment. Kant and Fichte placed the human "I" in the foreground. Everywhere there was a break with objectivity; the subject became the absolute first principle. Under the impact of this influence, Jacobi appealed to feeling as "the immediate perception of the divine." Religion is a feeling for the true, the beautiful, and the good; it is admiration, love, and regard for the divine; and such feeling is inborn as the basic drive of human nature. This aesthetic rationalism of Jacobi was then developed by Fries and de Wette so as to make a sharp split between the empirical-mathematical worldview of the intellect and the ideal aesthetic-religious worldview of feeling.

Schleiermacher's view of religion is to be explained in light of this same romanticism. In the second lecture of his *Speeches on Religion* (1799), he describes religion as the immediate consciousness of the essence of all that is finite in and through the infinite. Religion is neither thinking nor acting, neither metaphysics nor morality, but feeling for the infinite. The object of that feeling is not a personal God with whom a human lives in fellowship but the universe, the world as a whole, conceived as a unity. And the faculty for the perception of that infinite is not the intellect, reason, or will but feeling, the focus of the mind on and capacity for intuiting the infinite. Schleiermacher fails to provide a more refined definition of this feeling. Even more undefined is the answer to the question of when that feeling becomes specifically religious.[78] In the third lecture of his *Speeches,* Schleiermacher answers it using metaphorical language: one must open his faculty of feeling as widely as possible to the world as a whole, view all things in the One and the One in all things, regard all that is particular as a revelation of the infinite, etc. All this does not say very much; finally it seems that every feeling which has been aroused by the totality of the world and reveals to us the highest unity is religious. In any case, religious feeling is not clearly demarcated from the aesthetic. In *The Christian Faith* we basically encounter the same view. Here, too, piety is feeling, a feeling of absolute dependence. Still there is a twofold difference between the two works. In *Speeches* God was the [cosmic] whole; in *The Christian Faith* he is the absolute causality of the world. Correspondingly, feeling in the former was an intuition of the infinite; in the latter it is immediate self-consciousness and absolute dependence. Hence here God tends more to acquire an existence of his own, one that is distinct from the world, and religion therefore also acquires its own content, one that is distinct from the intuition of the world.

We see here that the aesthetic view has yielded more to the ethical. Hence one can discern some degree of rapprochement with theism. Still, the basic

---

78. Ed. note: The Dutch includes a rhyming play on the words *nader* ("precise, refined") and *vager* ("vague, undefined").

idea is the same insofar as God is not conceived as transcendent over but only as immanent in the world and the faculty for the divine is not reason or conscience (etc.) but feeling. This view of religion is not only taken over— be it with some modification—by certain mediation theologians but is found in principle in all those who attempt to construct an aesthetic world-view alongside the mechanical and either incorporate religion in it or equate religion with it. F. A. Lange wrote that the core of religion consists, not in a doctrine about God, (etc.), but in the elevation of the heart above reality and in the creation of a home for human minds. Above the world of facts, the world of being, human beings by their imagination are building a world of values, a world of poetry.[79] Pierson believed in such formation of ideals: the human heart, aroused from without, creates from the images, which the intellect derives from the world of sense perception, religious, ethical, aesthetic ideals, which, though they are not realities existing apart from us, are nevertheless of great value for our life. Opzoomer even assumed the existence of a distinct religious feeling or intuition and saw in it the source of religious representations. Though Rauwenhoff thought the essence of religion consisted in belief in a moral world order, he attributed the form of religion—the worship of a personal God—to the human imagination.[80]

Also in the case of this view, it has to be granted that feeling occupies an important place in religion. Religious ideas or representations as such, and without further qualification, cannot yet be equated with religion. Religion originates only when a human enters into a real personal relation to the object of those representations. And such a personal relation to God cannot but have impact on one's feelings. It does not leave people cold and indifferent but moves them in the depths of their heart. It arouses in them a strong feeling of delight or displeasure and generates a long series of affections: sense of guilt, sorrow, contrition, regret, sadness, joy, trust, peace, rest (etc.). Religion awakens the deepest and most tender affections in the human heart. There is no power that seizes and stirs up people more deeply, more generally, and more powerfully than religion. All these affections, sparked by the religious representations, give to one's religion warmth, inwardness, life and power, feelings that sharply contrast with the deadness of intellectualism and the coldness of moralism. The heart is the center of religion.

But feeling is not for that reason the only religious function, nor the only seat and source of religion. Feeling, here taken not as a separate faculty, which it is not, but as the whole of our passions and affections is, in the nature of

79. Ed. note: Bavinck provides no source for his citation here. He is likely referring to F. A. Lange, *Geschichte des Materialismus und Kritik seiner Bedeutung in den Gegenwart*, 8th ed. (Leipzig: Gaedeker, 1908).

80. Ed. note: Bavinck lists no bibliographic sources here. Among the works he may have been referring to are Allard Pierson, *Bespiegeling, Gezag, en Ervaring* (Utrecht: Kemink, 1885); C. W. Opzoomer, *Wetenschap en Wijsbegeerte* (1857); L. W. E. Rauwenhoff, *Wijsbegeerte van den Godsdienst* (Leiden: Brill en van Doesburgh, 1887).

the case, passive. It reacts only to what is brought into contact with it by the consciousness and then turns into a feeling of delight or displeasure. It possesses nothing of itself and does not produce anything from within itself but judges all things, the representations and images that come from without, solely by whether they are pleasant or unpleasant. By itself every feeling and affection is neither good nor bad, neither true nor untrue. These are categories of the representations, not really of the affections. They can be applied to the affections only as they are aroused by true or false representations and are accompanied by good or bad tendencies of the will. In religion, therefore, it is not feeling but faith, the religious representation, that is primary; that faith, however, then also impacts the feeling. But when, as in Schleiermacher, feeling is detached from faith, from the religious representation, and made into an independent and exclusive source and seat of religion, it loses its own quality and becomes completely independent of the categories of truth and untruth, good and evil. Then every individual feeling is already as such religious, true, good, and beautiful. And that was romanticism's great fault as a whole.

One then, naturally, also slips into the error of confusing and equating religious feeling with sensual and aesthetic feeling. Known to us all from history is the kinship between religious and sensual [erotic] love and the passage from one to the other. But equally dangerous is the confusion of religious and aesthetic feeling, of religion and art. The two are essentially distinct. Religion is life, reality; art is ideal, appearance. Art cannot close the gap between the ideal and reality. Indeed, for a moment it lifts us above reality and induces us to live in the realm of ideals. But this happens only in the imagination. Reality itself does not change on account of it. Though art gives us distant glimpses of the realm of glory, it does not induct us into that realm and make us citizens of it. Art does not atone for our guilt, or wipe away our tears, or comfort us in life and death. It never turns the beyond into the here and now. Only religion does. It is and conveys reality. It bestows life and peace. It poses the ideal as the true reality and makes us participants in it. Aesthetic feeling, accordingly, can never take the place of religious feeling, anymore than art can replace religion. Granted, the two are connected. From the very beginning religion and art went hand in hand. The decline of the one brought with it the decay of the other. The ultimate driving force of art was religion. In recent years this fact is being acknowledged by increasing numbers of people who keenly realize the indispensability of religion to art. In religion, specifically in worship, the imagination has its rightful place and value. "Also the imagination, mind you, is involved in the religious process, not as the generative principle, but only as the principle of experience. The power of the imagination can never do more than shape the already available materials and drives; it is powerless to give birth to religion itself."[81] The stage is by no means cut out to be a moral institution (Schiller). The theater

---

81. F. Nitzsch, *Lehrbuch der evangelische Dogmatik*, 91.

cannot replace the church, nor is Lessing's Nathan a suitable substitute for the Bible (Strauss). The ideals and creations of imagination cannot compensate for the reality that religion offers. Religious feeling, however intimate and deep it may otherwise be, is pure only when it is evoked by true ideas.[82]

The Whole Person

[79] The result, accordingly, is that religion is not limited to one single human faculty but embraces the human being as a whole. The relation to God is total and central. We must love God with all our mind, all our soul, and all our strength. Precisely because God is God he claims us totally, in soul and body, with all our capacities and in all our relations. Admittedly, there is order in this relation of a human being to God. Here, too, every faculty exists and functions in a person according to its own nature. Knowledge is primary. There can be no true service of God without true knowledge: "I do not desire anything I do not know" (*Ignoti nulla cupido*). To be unknown is to be unloved. "Whoever would approach God must believe that he exists and that he rewards those who seeks him" (Heb. 11:6). Faith comes from what is heard (Rom. 10:17). Pagans fell into idolatry and unrighteousness because they did not acknowledge God (Rom. 1:18ff.). But that knowledge of God penetrates the heart and arouses there an assortment of affections, of fear and hope, sadness and joy, guilt feelings and forgiveness, misery and redemption, as these are pictured to us throughout Scripture but especially in the Psalms. And through the heart it in turn affects the will: faith is manifest in works, in love (James 1:27; 1 John 1:5–7; Rom. 2:10, 13; Gal. 5:6; 1 Cor. 13 etc.). Head, heart, and hand are all equally—though each in its own way—claimed by religion; it takes the whole person, soul and body, into its service.

For that reason religion also comes into contact with all the other cultural forces, especially science, morality, and art. Proudhon once stated: "It is astonishing how at the base of all things we find theology." But to that statement Donoso Cortes correctly replied: "The only astonishing thing in this fact is Mr. Proudhon's astonishment." Religion as the relation to God indicates the place in which human beings stand in relation to all other creatures. It embraces dogma, law, and cult and is therefore closely connected with science, morality, and art. It encompasses the whole person in his or her thinking, feeling, and action, in the whole of his or her life, everywhere and at all times. Nothing falls outside of its scope. Religion extends its power over the whole person, over all of humanity, over family and society and

---

82. E. von Hartmann, *Die Religion des Geistes,* 27, 55; F. Nitzsch, *Lehrbuch der evangelische Dogmatik,* 97; Friedrich Paulsen, *System der Ethik* (Berlin: W. Hertz, 1889), 434ff.; Gustav Portig, *Religion und Kunst in ihrem gegeseitigen Verhältnis,* 2 vols. (Iserlohn: J. Bädeker, 1879, 1880); Ernst Linde, *Religion und Kunst* (Tübingen: J. C. B. Mohr, 1905); Sytze Hoekstra, *Godsdienst en Kunst* (Amsterdam: J. C. B. Mohr, 1859); G. H. Lamers, *Wetenschap van de Godsdienst,* II, 164ff.; G. Gross, *Die Bedeutung des Ästhetischen in der evangelischen Religion* (Gütersloh: C. Bertelsmann, 1905); also see H. P. Berlage, *Over de Waarschijnlijke ontwikkeling der architecture* (Delft: J. Waltman Jr., 1905).

state. It is the foundation of the true, the good, and the beautiful. It introduces unity, coherence, and life into the world and its history. From it science, morality, and art derive their origin; to it they return and find rest. "All the higher elements of human life first surfaced in alliance with religion."[83] It is the beginning and the end, the soul of everything, that which is highest and deepest in life. What God is to the world, religion is to humanity.[84]

Nevertheless, religion is distinguished from all the forces of culture and maintains its independence from them all. Religion is central; science, morality, and art are partial. While religion embraces the whole person, science, morality, and art are respectively rooted in the intellect, the will, and the emotions. Religion aims at nothing less than eternal blessedness in fellowship with God; science, morality, and art are limited to creatures and seek to enrich this life with the true, the good, and the beautiful. Religion, accordingly, cannot be equated with anything else. In the life and history of humankind, it occupies an independent place of its own, playing a unique and all-controlling role. Its indispensability can even be demonstrated from the fact that at the very moment people reject religion as an illusion they again turn some creature into their god, thus seeking to compensate for their religious need in some other way.

THE ORIGIN OF RELIGION

[80] We no more have a satisfactory explanation for the origin of religion than we do for the origin of language. Since science, in its search for this origin, journeys into the domain of the prehistorical, it has to be content with hunches and conjectures and therefore trots out one hypothesis after another. In this area the historical method leaves us completely in the lurch, for wherever we witness human beings in action, they are already in possession of religion. Strictly speaking, cultureless peoples do not exist, and "primitive man," the human without religion, morality, reason, or language, is a fiction.[85] The derivation of religion from fear, priestly deception, or ignorance, though still current in some atheistic circles, is no longer being defended by scholars. Darwin located the germ of religion, embryonically, even in animals, for example, in the love that a dog displays toward its owner and that is accompanied by a feeling of subordination and fear.[86] But for various reasons this analogy does not stand up. In the first place, we know very little about the internal psychic life of animals. Moreover, religion is always associated with veneration, ritual worship; and religious conduct like prayer and

---

83. Wilhelm Bousset, *Das Wesen der Religion* (Halle a.S.: Gebauer-Schwetschek, 1903), 3; English trans. F. B. Low, *What Is Religion?* (New York: G. P. Putnam, 1907); C. P. Tiele, *Elements of the Science of Religion,* II, 247.

84. Franz A. Staudenmaier, *Encyklopädie der theologischen Wissenschaften als System der gesammten Theologie* (Mainz: F. Kupferberg; Wien: K. Gerold, 1834), 114f., 146.

85. George T. Ladd, *The Philosophy of Religion,* 2 vols. (New York: Scribner, 1905), I, 135f., 150.

86. Charles Darwin, *The Descent of Man,* rev. ed. (New York: D. Appleton, 1896).

sacrifice does not occur among animals. Further, though in animals there doubtlessly exist certain attributes of faithfulness, attachment (etc.), these attributes by themselves no more constitute religion than the same attributes practiced among people are religion. An actual object of religion, a supersensual power, is entirely unknown to animals. Hence for the time being we must content ourselves with the saying of Lactantius: "Religion is virtually the only thing which distinguishes man from the beasts."[87]

The notion of explaining religion in terms of animism, as E. B. Tylor proposes, from fetishism as Schultze favors, from ancestor worship as Spencer and Lippert advocate, or from magic as J. G. Frazer espouses, proceed from the totally arbitrary assumption that the lowest forms of religion are the primitive and views the accompanying phenomena of religion as its essence. Also the attempt of Max Müller to derive religion from the "feeling for the infinite" has rightly found but little acceptance. Certainly the perception of the infinite in nature does not by itself and without further qualification lead to the concept of the infinite and even less to the adoration of the infinite, i.e., God.[88] Equally unacceptable is the hypothesis of O. Peshel and others, which locates the origin of religion in the human urge to pursue causality, in the need for an explanation of the world and of life. Despite its kinship to metaphysics, religion is essentially different from metaphysics and philosophy and meets a very different set of human needs. And, finally, only a few people exist who, with Cicero, Sextus Empiricus, and the optimistic rationalists of the nineteenth century, derive the origin of religion from childlike poetry, the feeling of gratitude and naïve delight, which were aroused in the innocent human beings of nature's beauty and beneficence and led them to the recognition and adoration of a supernatural being who gave all this. Contemporary science regards this picture of the innocence of the human beings of nature and of the beauty and beneficence of nature as little more than a poetic idyll and instead observes everywhere a hard struggle for life.

Fear

Since one after another of the above conjectures proved inadequate,[89] in later years another explanation for the origin of religion has been proposed, one that found wide acceptance. According to this interpretation, nature is frequently hostile toward human beings. With its hurricanes and thunderstorms, its scorching heat and stinging cold, its furious powers and unruly elements, nature is bent on the destruction of human life and existence. Over against nature, human beings are constantly obligated to protect their lives and to maintain their existence. But they are weak and powerless. And

---

87. Lactantius, *Divine Institutes*, VII, 9.

88. Ladd, *The Philosophy of Religion*, I, 133–57.

89. On this see Otto Zöckler, *Lehre vom Urstand des Menschen* (Gutersloh: C. Bertelsmann, 1879), 188ff.; idem, "Polytheïsmus," *PRE³*, XV, 538–49; C. Gutberlet, *Der Mensch: Sein Ursprung und seine Entwicklung* (Paderhorn: Schöningh, 1903), 513ff.

so, in this fearful conflict between themselves and nature, between self-awareness and a sense of distress, they appeal for help to an invisible power that is above nature and can assist them in the conflict. Human beings want to be happy, but they are not happy and cannot ever achieve happiness in their own strength. So in religion they try to placate all those personal powers, which to their mind are present in the phenomena of nature. This interpretation is marked by the peculiar fact that it sees religion arising, not from theoretical, but specifically from practical motives; not from ideas but from the emotions of fear, dread, a sense of distress, etc. To that extent it is a return to Petronius's view that it was first of all fear that fashioned the gods.

This view is also found in Hume[90] and in Holbach's *Système de la nature* but has especially in recent years been accepted in very wide circles as the best answer to the question concerning the origin of religion. Still it does not occur in everyone in the same form. Some say that religion arose from the human instinct for self-preservation in general. Human beings, that is, seek some benefit in religion, whatever that benefit may be: a fleshly, physical, and self-gratifying benefit or a moral and spiritual benefit. In a word they want a happy life, deliverance from physical as well as ethical evil.[91] Others specifically look for the origin of religion in ethical self-assertion, in the human desire to maintain their moral freedom and value against the necessity and coercion of the physical world. Thus on the basis of the moral nature of humankind, Kant already postulated the existence of a God who could subordinate the world of necessity to that of freedom, natural law to the moral law, nature to ethos. This is also the reasoning of many theologians and philosophers who after 1860 again adopted a Kantian position and are known as neo-Kantians.[92]

Finally there are also people who recognize not only an ethical but also a mystical element in religion and who therefore consider it grounded not more or less in a free act of the human will but in the nature of human beings. According to them, though human beings do seek in religion a basis for ethical self-assertion, they are also looking for something else, something better, viz., fellowship with or life in God and by this means also and especially freedom over against the world. In their view religion is first of all a relation to God and after that a relation to the world.[93] Eucken then again gave a special twist to

90. Cf. J. Köstlin, "Der Ursprung der Religion," *Theologische Studien und Kritiken* 63 (1890): 245.

91. Wilhelm Bender, *Das Wesen der Religion und die Grundgesetze der Kirchenbildung* (Bonn: M. Cohen, 1886); E. Zeller, "Über Ursprung und Wesen der Religion," in *Vorträge und Abhandlungen*, II, 1–83 (Leipzig: Fues, 1877); J. Kaftan, *Das Wesen der christliche Religion*, 38ff.; Siebeck, *Lehrbuch der Religionsphilosophie*, 58ff.

92. A. Ritschl, *Rechtfertigung und Versöhnung*, 2d ed., 3 vols. (Bonn: A. Marcus, 1882, 1883), III, 186; Wilhelm Herrmann, *Die Religion in Verhältniss zum Welterkennen und zur Sittlichkeit* (Halle: M. Niemeyer, 1879), 267ff.; cf. Rauwenhoff, *Wijsbegeerte van de Godsdienst*, 94ff.

93. Otto Pfleiderer, *Religionsphilosophie auf geschichtlicher Grundlage*, 2d ed., 2 vols. (Berlin: G. Reimer, 1883, 1884), II, 28ff.; idem, *Grundriss der christlichen Glaubens und Sittenlehre*, 3d ed. (Berlin: Reimer, 1886), §10; R. A. Lipsius, *Lehrbuch der evangelish-protestantischen Dogmatik*, 2d ed., 2 vols. (Braunschweig: C. A. Schwetschke, 1879), §18; F. Nitzsch, *Lehrbuch der evangelische Dogmatik*, 99ff.

this explanation of the origin as well as the essence of religion. He stressed that in terms of its essence religion is not a means to happiness—to a spectrum of lower human ends—but the "self-assertion of the life of the spirit." Indeed, on a lower level, religion is still a natural life instinct. This life instinct, however, is the first thing that takes human beings onto the road of religion. And, on a higher level, this striving becomes a metaphysical life urge. On that level, people seek to maintain, in religion, that higher life of the spirit, which comes to expression in them in its norms and ideals of truth and goodness, in its yearning for infinity, freedom, equality, and eternity, and shows its superiority in cultural activity on a level far above nature. Of that life of the spirit, religion is the indispensable completion and fulfillment, for manifest in that life of the spirit is a world of a higher order. Present and active in it is an absolute power, which is at the same time a conscious agent that controls both nature and spirit and strives, through humankind, toward the unity of a realm of reason. The recognition of, the belief and trust in, that power is religion; it is the possession of infinite life as the most intimate dimension of our own being. Hence religion is rooted in "the presence of divine life in human beings; it develops in apprehending this life as the life of their own being; hence it consists in the fact that human beings, in the innermost ground of their being, are lifted up into the divine life and thereby become participants in its divinity."[94]

Critique: God as Humanity's Servant?

Yet this explanation of religion, however generally accepted, cannot satisfy us. In the first place, its God-concept remains unexplained here. It is usually said that the undeveloped childlike "natural man" makes no distinction between the personal and impersonal, conceives the powers of nature on the analogy of himself or herself, and thinks of all things as being inhabited by souls or spirits. In that case the underlying foundation of religion is the so-called animistic worldview. But, in the first place, it is most unlikely that the obvious distinction between personal beings and impersonal things was unknown to those first human beings. Second, belief in souls or spirits, which inhabit and work in the phenomena of nature, as such does not yet constitute religion. These souls or spirits become religious objects only when the concept of the divine is attributed to them. A certain sense of the deity must be assumed in human beings before they can make the souls and spirits they deem present in the forces of nature into objects of religious veneration. Admittedly, the psychological method attempts to reverse the order here. According to this method, the "natural man" first assumed a religious posture toward one or another natural force that was thought of as being personal and later abstracted from this entity the idea of the divine.[95]

---

94. Rudolf Eucken, *Der Wahrheitsgehalt der Religion*, 2d ed. (Leipzig: Veit & Comp., 1905), 149ff.: idem, "Wissenschaft und Religion," in *Beiträge zur Weiterentwicklung der christlichen Religion*, ed. Gustav Adolf Deissmann (München: J. F. Lehmann, 1905), 241–81.

95. Von Hartmann, *Religionsphilosophie*, 1, 15.

In reply it must in any case be said that this is not how things occur in the lives of people who appear before us in history. Here they all first, by education and upbringing, receive the concept of deity, accept it inasmuch as it finds support in their own understanding, and on that basis they develop a religious relation. This argument is all the more compelling because in recent years it is generally recognized that both the religions of prehistoric peoples and the religion of the most ancient peoples known to us include belief in one supreme being, one who is himself good and requires of human beings that they conduct themselves well.[96] There is not a shred of evidence that in the case of the earliest human beings things were or could have been any different. A religious relation to some power or other always already presupposes the idea of God, and in the method mentioned above this fact remains unexplained. Add to this that also the origin of religion in a subjective sense remains unintelligible in this psychological analysis. Let it be so that belief in personal beings is given in nature; the question is why, and especially when, does this search for some fleshly or moral benefit from these beings become religion? Religion, after all, originates only when human beings do not just ask for help in general, as people do when they look for help from each other or from art and science, but when in a special way belief, trust, and a feeling of dependence with respect to an invisible power are aroused in their heart. Religion always assumes a certain distinction between God and the world, between the power of a being above nature and subordinate forces in nature. True, that divine power can then be conceived as inhabiting the natural phenomena, but it is never the power of nature itself that is the object of religious veneration but the divine being that manifests itself and works in it.

The most serious objection to the above explanation, however, is the fact that in it God becomes nothing but a helper-in-need, a being whose existence is invented to provide human beings with some kind of benefit. Religion becomes a means to satisfy the fleshly or moral but always selfish needs of human beings. *Egoism* was the source and origin of religion.[97] The first form in which this explanation of the origin of religion was reproduced above expresses this clearly and candidly. In the second form, religion is derived not from material but from moral needs: the deity is not a product of eudaemonistic wishes but a postulate of practical reason. In essence, however, this makes little difference. The subjective egoistic starting point is still supreme: God remains the servant of human beings. The third form attempts to overcome this egoism by recognizing in religion a mystical element, thus making God the direct object of religious veneration. But here, too, this mysticism was a later addition: it was not the first principle and origin of religion.

96. Schroeder in *Beiträge zur Weiterentwicklung der Christliche Religion,* 17; G. Tr. Ladd, *The Philosophy of Religion,* I, 88, 111, 124, 145.
97. Von Hartmann, *Religionsphilosophie,* I, 27.

In the explanation offered above, in whatever form presented, the human being always first occurs as standing in relation to the world. It is out of the conflict with that world that religion and the idea of God are born. The starting point and foundation of religion is the opposition between awareness of self and awareness of need,[98] the dualism between (the life of the) spirit and nature, the tension between self-consciousness and world-consciousness. In this connection it is not at all clear how this "natural" antithesis can lead to an antithesis between ethos and nature, between a moral and a natural order. But what remains especially obscure here is how this antithesis between *ethos* and *physis* can assume the character of a conflict between what human beings ought to be and what those human beings are, between their duty and their pleasure. Furthermore, how can this then produce all those ideas and feelings of guilt, contrition, need for atonement, prayer for forgiveness (etc.), which are all typically religious and cannot be inferred from the above-mentioned antithesis between "spirit" and "nature" but precede them and are actually basic to them. In addition, if religion was thus born from the conflict between human beings and the world, God is left to stand in third place. He becomes a product of human wishes, of human egoism, and an aid in the conflict with nature. The kinship between all these explanations and that of Feuerbach immediately springs to mind.[99] But why, one may ask, are human beings not content with the forces present in nature? Why do they not seek the help they need in the battle with nature in science, art, industry (etc.), i.e., in all the factors of culture? How do we explain the fact that human beings continue to believe in the gods—those creations of their own wishes—even when those gods so often disappoint them and abandon them to their fate? Why is it that human beings offer everything—even the most precious thing they have—to their gods and consider nothing too costly for their veneration? Finally, how is it that they continue to serve their gods even when by other means and ways their dominion over nature is gradually expanding? If the above explanation of the origin of religion is correct, then religion loses its independence vis-à-vis art and science and reaches its end the moment human beings can manage their affairs in some other way.

But, aside from these particular objections, there is also a serious problem with this method of searching for the origin of religion. What does it mean that the origin of religion has to be scientifically established? It cannot mean that the religion of the first human(s) has to be traced historically. For the history of religions leaves us completely in the lurch here: the historical method is useless. As is increasingly recognized, the habit of considering the religious forms of the meanest, most savage peoples to be the original ones is totally without warrant. Hence the method can only be a psychological one,

---

98. Ed. note: The translation here is an attempt to catch Bavinck's own play on words contrasting *zelfgevoel* and *noodgevoel*.

99. C. P. Tiele, *Elements of the Science of Religion,* II, 229, 233.

and the best this method can, in the nature of the case, produce is a hypothesis that seems plausible and may, for lack of a better one, rejoice for a time in general acceptance. But what is the question that this psychological method puts to itself in its search for the origin of religion? Certainly no other than this: from what causes and forces in human beings or humankind did religion arise? The scholars of religion must therefore look for the point "at which non-religious human life forces united themselves into the vital germ of religion."[100] Hence a human has to be hypothetically assumed to exist so primitive and barbarian that there was as yet no trace of religion in that person. On this position one may not even acknowledge the [possible] existence of an original increated "seed of religion." For then this original sense, or whatever one wants to call it, is something that has not been scientifically explained, a kind of mystical revelation, an a priori assumption of what one seeks to explain.[101] Hence the psychological method demands that religion be explained from factors present in human beings, factors that are not themselves religious but that by somehow combining under the impact of natural influences from without cause religion to spring up.

However, such a "religionless" human is a mere construct, as thin and vacuous an abstraction as the "natural man" of Rousseau and the adherents of the social contract. In reality it never existed. Religion itself, like morality in the thought of Darwin, thus becomes completely a product of chance. "Pure chance," says Professor Rauwenhoff, can prompt a person to take some thing in nature and make it into a god for himself.[102] Had there been another chance combination of factors, there never would have been religion. With that approach, religion loses its independent place, its universality and necessity; not even its value or right to exist could then be maintained. For it is not true, as Zeller asserts,[103] that the value of religion is independent of the manner of its origination. If religion's origin is accidental, it loses the firm foundation on which it must rest. And also its right to exist is then seriously threatened. For, if religion is explained in a manner that in no way requires the assumption of the existence of God, then, even if its origin were a psychological necessity, it would still be nothing but a metaphysical absurdity. Indeed, the psychological method attempts to understand religion apart from the existence of God. Human beings are purely natural entities, products of nature. It is the human being himself or herself who, under the impact of a variety of circumstances, is led to religion and produces the idea of God. God does not create human beings; human beings create God. Subjective religion is the source of objective religion. Human beings determine whether and how they will serve God. But by that very token the psycholog-

100. Holsten as cited by Rauwenhoff, *Wijsbegeerte van de Godsdienst*, 50.
101. A. Bruining, "De Theologie in den Kring der Wetenschappen," *De Gids* 47 (June 1884): 449–501.
102. Rauwenhoff, *Wijsbegeerte*, 97; cf. 193, 250, 263.
103. E. Zeller, *Vorträge und Abhandlung*, II, 57ff.

ical method condemns itself. It is fundamentally at war with the essence of religion and destroys the very phenomena it has to explain.[104]

An Alternative Model: Revelation

[81] The conclusion from the above investigation can be no other than that we have to select another starting point and must follow another method. The essence and origin of religion cannot be explained by means of the historical and psychological method; its right to be and its value cannot be maintained with these means. It will not do to [attempt to] understand religion without God. God is the great supposition of religion. His existence and revelation are the foundation on which all human religion rests. Granted, it is considered unscientific, in attempting to explain any given phenomena, to go back to God; and indeed he may not be used as a last resort for our ignorance. Still it is a poor science that may not take account of God and seeks to explain all things aside from and without God. This is true in a double sense in the case of the scientific explanation of religion. For here God is the actual and immediate object. Aside from him religion is an absurdity. We have a choice only between two alternatives: either (1) religion is folly since God does not exist or is in any case strictly unknowable; or (2) it is truth but then demands and presupposes the existence and revelation of God in a rigorously logical and scientific sense. Those who cannot accept the former are compelled to assume the latter and to recognize God as the very principle of being, the essential foundation (*principium essendi*) of all religion. Religion exists solely because God exists and wants to be served by his creatures. Only when the existence of God is certain can we understand the essence and origin, the validity and value of religion.

But religion demands even more. It does not only assume that God exists but also that he in some fashion reveals himself and makes himself known. All religions have this concept of revelation. It is not forced on religion from without but automatically flows forth from its origin and essence. There is no religion without revelation; revelation is the necessary correlative of religion. The essence of religion does not just exist subjectively in a religious disposition, which expresses itself as it sees fit, but also in an objective religion, in dogma, morality, and cult, which have authority for believers only because in the conviction of those believers they contain the will and proper service of God. The origin of religion can neither be historically demon-

---

104. Leonard Stählin, *Kant, Lotze, Albrecht Ritschl* (Leipzig: Dörffling & Franke, 1888), 245ff.; same title in English trans. D. W. Simon (New York: Scribner & Welford, 1889), idem, *Über den Ursprung der Religion* (München: C. H. Beck, 1905); J. Köstlin, "Der Ursprung der Religion," *Theologische Studien und Kritiken* 63 (1890): 213–94; idem, *Die Begründung unserer sittlich-religiösen Überzeugung* (Berlin: Reuther & Reichard, 1893), 54ff.; Karl Girgensohn, *Die Religion, ihre psychischen Formen und ihre Zentralidee* (Leipzig: A. Deichert, 1903); J. Ehni, "Ursprung und Entwicklung der Religion," *Theologische Studien und Kritiken* 71 (1898): 581–648; Karl F. Heman, *Der Ursprung der Religion* (Basel: C. Detloff's Buchhandlung, 1886); Hugo Visscher, *De Oorsprong der Religie* (Utrecht: Kemink, 1904); idem, *De religie en de gemeenschap* (Utrecht: G. J. A. Ruys, 1907).

strated nor psychologically explained but points, from necessity, at revelation as its objective foundation.

The distinction between religion on the one hand and art on the other supplies us with the same concept of revelation. Nature, the world all around us, is the source of our knowledge and the teacher of art. But in religion that same world comes under consideration from still another viewpoint, viz., as the revelation of God, as the disclosure of his eternal power and divinity. In religion humans are concerned with something very different from what their aim is in science and art. In religion they do not seek to increase their knowledge, nor to satisfy their imagination, but aim at eternal life in communion with God, true transformation of their being, liberation from sin and misery. In religion they are concerned about God because they realize that in God alone they can find peace and rest. For that reason religion requires another source than do science and art; it assumes a revelation that causes God himself to come to people and bring them into fellowship with him. In its essence and origin, religion is a product of revelation. Gradually this truth is being recognized. The philosophy of religion, which for a time did not deem the concept of revelation worthy of serious discussion and only subjected it to negative criticism, is now being forced to reckon with it. The understanding of that revelation is still very diverse and sometimes utterly wrong, but it is nevertheless very telling that many scholars are again working with this concept and attempting to credit it with a positive meaning.[105] Holy Scripture proceeds from the existence and revelation of God. God does not leave himself without a witness, and for that reason there is from the side of humans a searching to see if they could perhaps grope for him and find him (Acts 17:27). Revelation, according to Scripture, existed both before and after the fall. Revelation is religion's external principle of knowing (*principium cognoscendi externum*).

If the essence and origin of religion are thus explained from revelation, this must not, however, be understood in a Socinian sense as though religion were not grounded in human nature but originated solely as a result of an external communication of doctrine.[106] In that case Schelling would have been correct in commenting: "If the original human being as such were not already a consciousness of God, if a consciousness of God first had to be conferred on him by a special act; then those who believe this must themselves insist on an original atheism of the human consciousness."[107] In that case religion would be a super-added gift, not essentially a part of human nature. But a human is a human because he is the image of God; a human is at

105. Pfleiderer, *Grundriss*, §13f.; Rauwenhoff, *Wisbegeerte*, 46; Von Hartmann, *Religionsphilosophie*, II, 69ff.; A. E. Biedermann, *Christliche Dogmatik* (Zurich: Füssli, 1869), I, 264; Lipsius, *Dogmatik*, §53; F. Nitzsch, *Lehrbuch der evangelische Dogmatik*, 127; S. Hoekstra, *Wijsgeleerde Godsdienstwetenschap*, I, 136.

106. Otto Fock, *Der Socianismus* (Kiel: C. Schröder, 1847), 291ff.

107. F. W. J. von Schelling, *Philosophie der Mythologie*, 2 vols. (Stuttgart und Augsburg: J. G. Cotta, 1857), I, 141.

once a religious being in virtue of being human. Religion is not "the essence" of a human, as Amorie van der Hoeven Jr. expressed himself somewhat less correctly, for religion is not a substance but a disposition or virtue. Still religion is an essential of human nature so integral to it and inseparably bound up with it that, though sin can devastate it, it cannot eradicate it. For that reason religion is universal and has such immense power in life and history.

Whether one wishes or not, one always finally encounters in humans a certain religious propensity. One can call it by various names: "the seed of religion," "a sense of divinity" (Calvin), religious feeling (Schleiermacher, Opzoomer), belief (Hartmann), a feeling for infinity (Tiele), etc., but there is always in humans a certain capacity for perceiving the divine to which philosophical inquiry into religion has to return and in which it must end.[108] It cannot penetrate things behind it. For one of two things is true: either religion essentially belongs to human nature and is therefore native to it, or humans were originally not religious beings, hence not humans but animals, and gradually evolved into religious beings. In the latter case religion is an accidental and passing stage in the process of evolution. The question with which philosophical inquiry finally ends is this: Were humans human from the beginning, or did they gradually develop into, religious beings? Was culture or was coarse and savage nature the earliest condition of the human race? Is the beginning of humanity absolute or relative?[109]

Those who want to maintain religion in its essence and view, as well as recognize it as an essential property of human nature, take the beginning of humanness to be absolute and see humans as natively akin to God and religiously inclined. Such people can no longer object to the state of integrity in which Scripture shows humanity appearing on the scene. According to Scripture, humans were human beings from the first moment of their existence, created in God's image, hence religious beings from that moment on. Religion was not something added later by a separate creation or a long process of evolution but is automatically implied in the fact of humanity's having been created in the image of God. That original state has been corrupted and devastated by sin, to be sure, but human beings nevertheless remain related to God, God's offspring, and continue to search for God and perhaps grope for God and find him (Acts 17:27).

Corresponding to the objective revelation of God, therefore, there is in human beings a certain faculty or natural aptitude for perceiving the divine.

108. Cf. C. P. Tiele, *Elements* II, 126, 237, 239; Groenewegen, *De Theologie en hare Wijsbegeerte*, 79, 80.

109. F. W. J. Schelling, "Vorlesungen über die Methode des akademischen Studiums," in *Schriften*, 5 vols. (Darmstadt: Wissenschaaftische Buchgesellschaft, 1967–68), 3:441–586. Ed. note: Bavinck cites pages 520ff. In the Dutch edition Bavinck cites Schelling's *Werke* (Stuttgart: Augsburg, J. G. Cotta, 1856, 1861), I/IV, 286ff. This work has been translated into English by E. S. Morgan under the title *On University Studies*, edited and with an introduction by Norbert Guterman (Athens, Ohio: Ohio University Press, 1966), see pp. 82–91.

God does not do half a job. He creates not only the light but also the eye to see it. Corresponding to the external reality there is an internal organ of perception. The ear is designed for the world of sounds. The "logos" implicit in creatures corresponds to the "logos" in human beings and makes science possible. Beauty in nature finds a response in the human sense of beauty. Similarly, there is not only an external and objective but also an internal and subjective revelation. The former is the external principle of the knowledge of religion (*principium cognoscendi externum*); the latter the internal principle of that knowledge (*principium cognoscendi internum*). The two principles are most intimately related, as light is to the human eye and as intelligent design in the world is to human reason. The question—which of the two was first, external or internal revelation—is superfluous. In the selfsame moment in which God revealed himself to human beings by creating them in his image, the latter knew this God and served him, and, vice versa, served and knew him. True and genuine religion can exist only in the complete correspondence of the internal to the external revelation. Those who love God—with all their heart, soul, and strength—as he is and as he makes himself known by revelation, these are the truly religious, images of God, servants and children of God; they are human beings in the full sense.

Just as in science, so in religion there are three principles to be distinguished. Religion exists because God is God and wants to be served as God by his rational creatures. To that end he reveals himself to human beings in word and deed (the external principle of knowledge) and makes them subjectively fit to know and love God by that revelation (the internal principle of knowledge). The forms in which revelation occurs both objectively and subjectively may be altered in accordance with the different states in which human beings find themselves as mutable creatures. They differ in the state of integrity and in the state of corruption; again they are not the same in the state of grace and in the state of glory. But the three principles remain the same. There is no religion apart from God making himself known to human beings both objectively and subjectively. And also in religion these three principles again have their foundation in the trinitarian being of God. It is the Father who reveals himself in the Son and by the Spirit. No one knows the Father except the Son and anyone to whom the Son, by the Spirit, chooses to reveal him (Matt. 11:27; John 16:13, 14; 1 Cor. 2:10).

Part IV

REVELATION

(*PRINCIPIUM EXTERNUM*)

9

THE IDEA OF REVELATION

The concept of revelation is a necessary correlate of all religion. Since belief in revelation can be found in all religions, revelation and religion stand or fall together. Religion is the arena of redemption; saviors can be found everywhere. Disagreements exist concerning the what and how of religion but the question remains: "What must I do to be saved?" The answer to the three major concerns of religion—God, humanity, salvation—require revelation.

The relation between general or natural revelation and special revelation leads to questions about the relation between believing and knowing, theology and philosophy. A dependence on philosophy to provide categories for understanding revelation often leads to abstraction and intellectualism. Deism in particular subordinated revelation to reason, making scriptural revelation unnecessary. Since this rationalism was cold and spiritually, as well as intellectually, unsatisfying, others began to understand revelation as the spark of divinity evidenced in artistic genius and moral perfection. Since Jesus embodies this genius and moral perfection supremely, he becomes the great Revealer, who somehow communicates his divinity and holiness to those in communion with him. The Christian faith came to be understood as a historical process of moral amelioration, building the kingdom of God on earth.

The nineteenth century also produced philosophical understandings of revelation in which God's self-consciousness in humanity is identical to humanity gaining consciousness of God. This consciousness is expressed first symbolically in art, then visually in religion, and finally in its highest form conceptually in philosophy. The history of religions is the history of the absolute coming to himself in human consciousness and achieves its zenith in Christianity, which brings to light the essential unity of God and humanity. This evolutionary pantheism found favor among a number of nineteenth-century theologians. Revelation coincides with course of nature, the true revelation of rational knowledge. All notions of supernatural revelation have vanished here.

The theological discussion of revelation today is very confused and inherently contradictory. On a naturalistic level there cannot be such a reality as revelation; there is no personal communication from God to humanity. However, the term "revelation" remains in use even among naturalist philosophers and theologians. The reality of religion depends on some form of revelation, and the very possibility of revelation as a communication from a personal God requires a theistic, su-

283

pernaturalist worldview. A materialist worldview is diametrically opposed to all ideas of such revelation. The chief error here is a commitment to a religiously neutral scientific method, a goal that is impossible. On the other hand, a scientific investigation rooted in Christian faith yields results that are compatible with Scripture and science. Thus, a true concept of revelation can only be derived from revelation itself.

[82] The study of religion in its essence and origin itself leads us to the subject of revelation, and the history of religions is proof that the concept of revelation is not only integral to Christianity and occurs in Holy Scripture but is a necessary correlate of all religion. A few examples will suffice to illustrate this point.

No Religion without Revelation

Of the gods in the so-called nature religions, C. P. Tiele tells us that they "reveal themselves by their oracles and prophets and by signs and wonders which are observed or are supposed to be observed in nature, especially in the vault of heaven or in any deviation from the ordinary course of events. Yet all these revelations, though they are not entirely abandoned and though later again surface in modified form, are eclipsed by the one great revelation which is regarded as comprising the whole law of God."[1] This is especially the case in what Tiele calls the ethical religions, which all have personal gods and which all say that they have been founded by a mediator through whom the deity has made known the highest revelation to humankind.[2] This is not saying too much. The Indian Vedas, which contain the holy laws, are not of human origin but rest on revelation and are in the strictest sense of the word of divine origin.[3] Zarathrustra received his call to be a prophet in a dream and was often transported by angels into heaven, where he had conversations with Ormazd.[4] Hammurabi wrote down his laws as revelations from the sun god Tamas.[5] Mohammed received his first revelation when he was already forty years old and was later repeatedly blessed with a variety of revelations whose content was recorded in the Koran.[6] Among Greeks and Romans there existed a common belief that the gods were saviors, helpers, and advisors to human beings and that of their own volition they gave revelations or allowed their will to be discovered by special observations or actions, from

1. C. P. Tiele, *Elements of the Science of Religion,* 2 vols. (Edinburgh and London: William Blackwood & Sons, 1897–99), I, 131.

2. Tiele, *Elements,* I, 130.

3. P. D. Chantepie de la Saussaye, *Lehrbuch der Religionsgeschichte,* 2 vols. (Tübingen: J. C. B. Mohr [Paul Siebeck], 1905), II, 8ff.

4. Ibid., II, 171.

5. Ibid., I, 285.

6. Ibid., I, 476; cf., Otto Pautz, *Mohammeds Lehre von der Offenbarung* (Leipzig: J. C. Hinrichs, 1898).

the flight of birds, the entrails of animals, or celestial phenomena (etc.).[7] This is enough to indicate that belief in divine revelations occurs without exception in all religions. Nowadays this is frankly acknowledged by all practitioners of the study of religions. Says Tiele: "The idea of revelation is common to all religions, however differently the term may be interpreted,"[8] and this verdict is confirmed by all who know the field.

This unanimity removes all doubt that with regard to belief in revelation we are not dealing with an incidental or arbitrary phenomenon but with an essential component of religion. Revelation and religion are so closely related, so intimately interwoven, that the one stands or falls with the other. As explained above, religion is essentially distinct from science, art, and morality and is so because it puts human beings in relation, not to the world or their fellow human beings, but to a supernatural, invisible, external power, however it may then conceive that power. It is true that many theorists today attempt to remove this relation to a supernatural power from religion and conceive it as a relation of a human to him- or herself (Feuerbach), to humanity as a whole (Comte), to the universe as a whole (Strauss), to the true, the good, and the beautiful (Haeckel), to the spirits of the dead (spiritism), etc. But in so doing these theorists actually change the character of religion, deliberately convert it into superstition, or dissolve it in illusion. "Belief in one or more supernatural powers, in a God or a divine world, is the foundation on which all religion rests. There is no religion without a god."[9] Nor is Buddhism an exception, for when it first made its appearance, Buddha was its god.[10]

If indeed religion consistently implies a relation to God, it follows that this deity must exist to the mind of the believer, must reveal himself, and hence to some extent be knowable. Religion is either an illusion or it must be based on belief in the existence, revelation, and knowability of God. In every one of its three components, as representation or idea of God, as religious affection, and as religious act, religion implies that we believe in God's existence and consider him knowable from his revelation. Agnosticism is diametrically opposed to the essence of religion and, like skepticism, is built on the truth of what it denies. But the deity to which a given religion connects a human is a supernatural invisible power. It is inaccessible to ordinary human investigation; science leaves us in the lurch here. If we are to know something about

7. Ibid., II, 321ff., 439ff.

8. C. P. Tiele, *Elements*, I, 131. Cf. C. H. Weisse, *Philosophische Dogmatik oder Philosophie des Christenthums*, 3 vols. (Leipzig: S. Hirzel, 1855), I, 76ff.; R. Rothe, *Zur Dogmatik* (Gotha: F. A. Perthes, 1863), 61; H. Gunkel, "Das Alte Testament im Licht der modernen Forschung," in *Beiträge zur Weiterentwicklung der christlichen Religion*, ed. Gustav Adolf Deissmann (Munchen: J. F. Lehmann, 1905), 62; G. Wobbermin, "Das Wesen des Christentums," in *Beiträge zur Weiterentwicklung der christlichen Religion*, 343; see also above, 276–79.

9. C. P. Tiele, *Elements*, II, 73.

10. Ibid., I, 128, II, 74; Chantepie de la Saussaye, *Lehrbuch*, II, 89ff.; G. T. Ladd, *Philosophy of Religion*, 2 vols. (New York: Scribner, 1905), I, 107ff.

God, he must come forward out of his hiddenness, in some way make himself perceivable, and hence reveal himself. Naturalism, at least in a strict sense, and religion are incompatible; and nature religions, as opposed to revelation-based religions, no more exist than so-called peoples of nature, who are devoid of all culture, hence also of language, religion, morality, etc. Even in the lowest nature-religions, according to Tiele, there is already present belief in gods in their transcendence, in humankind's kinship with them.[11] All religion is supernaturalistic in the sense that it is based on the belief in a divine power that is distinct from and elevated above the world and nevertheless somehow descends into it and has communion with it. We must leave undecided for now how and by what means God reveals himself, by nature or history, in the intellect or in the heart, by theophany or prophecy. This much, however, is certain: all religion rests on revelation, on belief in a conscious, voluntary, intentional disclosure of God to human beings.

This is further confirmed by still another consideration. What do human beings look for in religion, and what is at stake for them in religion? Speaking generally and without fear of contradiction, one can say that in religion human beings seek deliverance from evil and the acquisition of what to them is the highest good. Siebeck indeed divides religions into nature religions, morality religions, and redemption religions, but Tiele rightly rejects this division and truthfully states that the idea of redemption in a general sense is characteristic of all religions. All religions are religions of redemption; all religious doctrine is a doctrine of salvation.[12] About the evil from which people desire to be redeemed, and about the good people seek to obtain, all sorts of differences exist; the one as well as the other is viewed either more physically, or more ethically, or more religiously. But in the matter of religion people are always concerned about redemption. The big question in religion is always: what must I do to be saved? In religion, what people pursue is something no lust or sensual pleasure, no science or art, no human or angel, something not even the whole world can give them: unperturbable happiness, eternal life, communion with God. But if this is the case, then again revelation is absolutely necessary; revelation, then, has to be the foundation of religion.

All this becomes even more obvious when we analyze the idea of redemption. All the religious conceptions that constitute the content of dogmatics revolve around three centers: they contain a doctrine of God, a doctrine of humanity in relation to God, and a doctrine concerning the means of restoration and of maintaining communion with God. Humanity's relation to God must also be seen in a twofold sense: (1) as it is in fact, empirically, and (2) as it ought to be, ideally; hence, in brief, a theology, an anthropology, and a soteriology.[13] And, again, in all three areas it is clearly demonstrable that they are inseparably bound up with the concept of revelation. With re-

11. C. P. Tiele, *Elements*, I, 85–87.
12. Ibid., I, 62ff.; II, 75, 117.
13. Ibid., II, 73.–75.

spect to the first, theology, this is already clear: if we are to know God he must reveal himself. But revelation is necessary for the second, anthropology, as well. For this study does not concern itself with the knowledge of "humanness," which can be obtained by scientific research, by anatomy, physiology, and psychology, but deals with human origin and destiny, with our relation to God, our misery due to sin, our need for redemption, our memories of paradise, and hopes for the future.[14] All these things exist in a domain that is not accessible to science but can be uncovered for human beings only by revelation. In even greater measure, this applies to the third part of dogmatics, soteriology, for this part discusses the means of restoration, or more precisely the saviors who restore the broken communion with God and again cause human beings to answer to their destiny. This belief in saviors is also universal[15] and can rest only on revelation. Revelation and grace are closely connected, as are grace and faith.

REVELATION IN THEOLOGY AND PHILOSOPHY

[83] This intimate nexus that exists between religion and revelation summons not only the dogmatician but also the philosopher of religion to give a clear account of the essence and concept of revelation. For Christian dogmatics the revelation that God had granted in his Word was of course certain from the outset, and from the beginning there was therefore little urgency to think through the concept of revelation more deeply. Between Christians and pagans, after all, the possibility of revelation was not in dispute. The controversy between them concerned only the truth of that revelation that was contained in the books of the Old and the New Testament. And on a variety of grounds this truth was defended by the apologists against attacks, launched especially by Celsus and Porphyry. Anyhow, the ideas on revelation came down to the following scheme: God can be known only by God. All knowledge and service of God, accordingly, is rooted in revelation on his part, but the revelation of God in nature and history is insufficient. Needed, for that reason, is a special, supernatural revelation, which begins immediately after the fall and reaches its zenith in Christ.[16]

Later theologians, especially the scholastics, therefore devoted great care to the determination and description of the relation between natural and supernatural revelation and, by implication, between knowing and believing, philosophy and theology, but did not think deeply about the concept of revelation and only mentioned it in passing.[17] Protestant theologians also de-

14. Ibid., II, 75ff., 109ff.
15. Ibid., I, 130, 166; II, 124ff.
16. Adolf von Harnack, *History of Dogma*, trans. N. Buchanan, J. Millar, E. B. Speirs, and W. McGilchrist and ed. A. B. Bruce, 7 vols. (London: Williams & Norgate, 1896–99), II, 177ff., 196ff., 215ff.
17. Aquinas, *Summa Theologica*, I, qu. 57, art. 5, ad. 3; II, 2, qu. 2, art. 6; III, qu. 55, art. 3.

voted too little attention to this concept. They usually described it as the "external divine act by which God made himself known to the human race by his Word so that it might have a saving understanding of him." Hence already very soon they equated revelation with the inspiration of Holy Scripture and therefore did not altogether escape the abstract supernaturalistic and one-sidedly intellectualistic view of it that had gradually taken shape in theology.[18] Socinianism rode this supernatural and intellectual notion of revelation to its limit and was followed in this trend, be it at some distance, by the Remonstrants.[19] In Cartesianism and deism, reason emancipated itself from revelation, initially placed itself alongside of it, soon also over against, and above it. Initially deism did not yet deny the necessity, possibility, and reality of revelation. Herbert, Locke, Toland, Collins, and others were persuaded of the contrary, while Leibniz and Wolff, along with their followers in Germany, sincerely believed that their philosophy was exceptionally well-suited to confirm and defend revelation.[20]

But deism's danger to revelation lay in the following: first it ascribed to reason—which had acquired a place of independence outside of revelation—the right to examine and determine whether something that represented itself as revelation did this with good warrant and in truth. Second, reason gradually gained for itself the power to pronounce on the content of revelation as well. This content could not and might not be inimical to reason and therefore could not contain anything but what was principally and potentially present in reason and could therefore also be judged by it. Materially the gospel could not be anything other than the truth of reason. Third, revelation, accordingly, if it really occurred, had only made known somewhat earlier, with more authority and in a wider circle, that which reason, left to itself, over a longer period of time and with more effort, could eventually have discovered from its own resources. Thus the difference between nature (reason) and revelation was reduced to a matter of time and shrank even more when Herbert, Locke, Hobbes, and others began to make a distinction between "original" and "traditional" revelation. The former was directly addressed to prophets and apostles, but the latter has come to us via Scripture. For us, therefore, the question is not whether revelation took place but only whether the reports on that subject are reliable. And to that question Hume replied in the negative. Though revelation did perhaps occur, we will never have certainty concerning such an occurrence; though revelation may be

18. J. Gerhard, *Loci Theol.*, I, §12; Calovius, *Isagoge ad theol.*, 101ff. 142ff.; A. Polanus, *Syntagma theologiae christianae*, VI, 9; S. Maresius, *Syst. Theol.*, I, §15ff.; J. H. Heidegger, *Corpus Theologiae*, XII, 46.

19. Otto Fock, *Der Socinianismus* (Kiel: C. Schröder, 1847), 296ff., 314ff.; P. van Limborch, *Theologia christiana* (Amsterdam, 1695), II, 9, 18; translated into English by William Jones and edited by John Wilkins under the title *A Complete System, or Body of Divinity* (London, 1713).

20. G. V. Lechler, *Geschichte des englischen Deismus* (Stuttgart: J. G. Cotta, 1841), 49; E. Troeltsch, "Aufklärung," *PRE³*, II, 225–41; and "Deismus," *PRE³*, IV, 532–59; H. Hoffmann, "Die Frömmigkeit der deutschen Aufklärung," *Zeitschrift für Theologie und Kirche* 16 (1906): 234–50.

possible and even necessary, in any case it is unknowable. Consistent rationalism, finally, drew the conclusion that there is no revelation other than
that which occurs by nature and history. In any case, what is the value of a
revelation that only communicates an intellectual truth that reason could
also have discovered by itself?

NINETEENTH-CENTURY "RECOVERY" OF REVELATION

Yet it soon became evident that the theorists had too swiftly dismissed
revelation. Upon deeper historical and philosophical investigation, religion
and revelation evinced a much closer kinship than they had thought under
the sway of rationalism. Thus, in more modern theology and philosophy, the
concept of revelation again regained some respectability, and various attempts at reconstruction were made. The critical philosophy of Kant led
Fichte to undertake an inquiry into all revelation, which, though it modified
the concept, nevertheless maintained its possibility. According to Fichte, humanity's destiny is moral perfection, an ethical kingdom of God. However,
since humanity may for a time fall into a deep moral decay, it then becomes
necessary for God to take extraordinary measures. He does so by raising up
in history a person who with divine authority and power again reminds humankind of its moral destiny, lifts it up out of its decay, and again persuades
it to go forward on the road of virtue. Such a revelation then consists in
something external, in a manifestation, a person who appears on the stage of
history or an event that happens, and makes such a strong impression on
people that they are compelled to learn to understand this manifestation's
moral purpose. The content of revelation may, therefore, still be no different
from what is implied in natural religion and morality but be again brought
to the attention of people in an impressive manner and be inferred by those
people themselves from that revelation. In that way, for example, the person
of Christ was raised up by God in an extraordinary manner to proclaim with
authority the content of natural religion and morality and to instill it in the
hearts of humankind. Hence revelation here became a stratagem in the divine nurture of humankind and was understood in that sense by Lessing and
by the Groningen school of theology in the Netherlands.[21]

By contrast, Hamann, Claudius, Lavater, Herder, Jacobi, and others
placed more stress on the kinship between religion and art and thus associated revelation with the inspiration of genius. They expanded the concept of
revelation to such an extent that almost everything seemed to originate from
revelation: religion, poetry, philosophy, history, and language are all seen as
expressions of the one and same original life: *omnia divina et humana omnia*
(all things divine and all things human). And the person of Christ came to
stand in the center of all those revelations: everything pointed to him, and ev-

21. P. Hofstede De Groot, *De Groninger Godgeleerdheid in hunne Eigenaardigheid* (Groningen: A. L.
Scholtens, 1855).

erything revolved around him.[22] Related to this is the definition Schleiermacher gave of revelation in his *Speeches on Religion:* just as for the religious person everything is a miracle, so for that person also "every original and new communication of the universe and of that person's inmost life" is a revelation.[23] The same view returns in the *Christian Faith.* The uniqueness of a revelation does not consist in its natural or supernatural character but in the newness or originality with which it appears in history, in "the originality of a fact which underlies a religious community." But in the *Christian Faith,* more clearly than in the *Speeches,* it emerged that in Christianity the person of Christ has such original significance. Since Christ fully and uninterruptedly participated in communion with God, he is in a special sense the revelation of God, even though we do not know how and by what process he became that revelation. Further, by the spiritual energies that proceed from Christ, we too are incorporated in the communion of God and participate in a new and holy life that is freed from sin. So while revelation is typically marked by its own inherent originality, its effect and aim consist in the new life it imparts. By these assertions Schleiermacher paved the way for the view of revelation that defined it in terms of the communication not of doctrine but of life.

MEDIATING THEOLOGY

This idea is retained in the mediating theology (*Vermittelungstheologie*),[24] but it is placed in a richer historical context. Rothe increasingly stressed the notion of manifestation as an element of revelation. God-consciousness in human beings, as we know, has been weakened and defiled by sin and therefore needs restoration, a restoration that can be effected only by an inner operation of God, by inspiration. But to the end that such an inspiration does not occur mechanically or magically but is mediated morally, God has to make a detour and first reveal himself externally and supernaturally in the events of nature and history, i.e., in manifestation. In order that human beings may rightly understand such a manifestation, however, it has to be accompanied by inspiration. The two belong together, continually occur side by side in history, and then coincide in Christ. But this Christ in turn assumes for us the place of a manifestation. He is the perfect revelation of God, which we learn to understand by the inspiration of his Spirit and which by its effect in us strengthens our God-consciousness and renews communion with God. Proceeding along this line, the mediating theology

22. F. Ehrenfeuchter, *Christenthum und moderne Weltanschauung* (Göttingen: Vandenhoeck und Ruprecht, 1876), 243ff.

23. F. Schleiermacher, *On Religion, Speeches to Its Cultured Despisers* (New York: Harper & Brothers, 1950), 89.

24. Ed. note: *Vermittelungstheologie* ("mediating theology") was a specific school of nineteenth-century German theology that, influenced by Schleiermacher, sought to synthesize Christianity and modern idealistic philosophy into a rationally and morally defensible religion. Representatives include I. Dorner, J. Neander, H. Martenson, K. Nitzsch, and J. Muller. See above, 49 n. 49.

did more justice than Schleiermacher to the historical continuity of God's revelation in Christ with that revelation in Israel, especially in the prophets. It bathed the originality of the revelation in Christ in a clearer light by returning to the confession of his deity and, in clearer terms than we find in Schleiermacher, attributed the working of Christ in his church to the Spirit of God. For that reason the new ideas on revelation found acceptance, not only in the mediating theology strictly defined,[25] but also among the theologians on the right.[26]

Even Ritschl showed affinity with Schleiermacher when, while rejecting internal revelation in human beings as mysticism and fanaticism, he returned to the person of Christ and called Christ—specifically in his professional life as founder of the kingdom of God—the revealer of God's love, grace, and faithfulness.[27] But since Ritschl left undecided how and by what process Christ became this revealer, his school broke up in to a left wing and a right wing. Harnack, in his *What is Christianity?*[28] for example, firmly rejected all supernatural revelation and miracles and thereby returned to the position of natural religion. Kaftan, on the other hand, in his *Dogmatik*[29] accorded much space to the subject of revelation and recognized both a general and a special revelation, one whose foundation was laid in Israel and which achieved its completion in the person of Christ and the outpouring of the Holy Spirit. When we compare this newer concept of revelation with what was generally accepted before that time, we find that it is distinguished by the following features: (1) Special revelation, which is the basis of Christianity, is more organically conceived and more intimately connected in heart and conscience with general revelation in nature and history; (2) scholars adhering to this newer concept attempt to understand special revelation itself as a historical process, not only in word but also in deed, both in prophecy and miracle, which then culminate in the person of Christ; (3) they view its content as existing exclusively or predominantly in religious-ethical truth, which aims primarily, not at teaching, but at moral amelioration, redemp-

25. C. E. Nitzsch, *System of Christian Doctrine* (Edinburgh: T. & T. Clark, 1849), §22; August Twesten, *Vorlesungen über die Dogmatik der evangelisch-lutherischen Kirche,* 2 vols. (Hamburg: F. Perthes, 1834, 1837), I, 341ff.; L. Martensen, *Christian Dogmatics,* trans. William Urwick (Edinburgh: T. & T. Clark, 1871), §11, 12; J. P. Lange, *Christliche Dogmatik,* 3 vols. (Heidelberg: K. Winter, 1852), I, §56; I. A. Dorner, *A System of Christian Doctrine,* trans. Rev. Alfred Cave and Rev. J. S. Banks, rev. ed., 4 vols. (Edinburgh: T. & T. Clark, 1888), II, 133ff.; H. Bavinck, *De Theologie van Prof. Dr. Daniel Chantepie de la Saussaye,* 2d ed. (Leiden: D. Donner, 1903); *Gunning and de la Saussaye, *Het ethisch beginsel,* 21ff.

26. F. H. R. Frank, *System der Christlichen Wahrheit,* 2 vols. (Erlangen: A. Deichert, 1894), II, 8ff.; Martin Kähler, *Wissenshaft der Christlichen Lehre,* 3d ed., 3 vols. (Leipzig: A. Deichert, 1905), I, 188; A. K. von Oettingen, *Lutherische Dogmatik,* 2 vols. (Munich: C. H. Beck, 1897–1902), I, 83ff.

27. A. Ritschl, *Unterricht in der Christlichen Religion,* 6th ed. (Bonn: A. Marcus, 1903), §20ff.; idem, *Die Christliche Lehre von der Rechfertigung und Versöhnung,* 3d ed., 3 vols. (Bonn: A. Marcus, 1895–1903), III, 190ff., 599ff.

28. A. von Harnack, *What Is Christianity?* trans. Thomas Bailey Saunders and with an introduction by W. R. Matthews, 5th ed. (London: Ernest Benn, 1958), lecture 2.

29. Julius Kaftan, *Dogmatik* (Tübingen: J. C. B. Mohr, 1901).

tion from sin; and (4) they make a sharp distinction between the revelation that gradually took place in history and its documentation or description in Holy Scripture; the latter is not itself the revelation but only a more or less accurate record of it.

NINETEENTH-CENTURY PHILOSOPHIES OF REVELATION

At the beginning of the nineteenth century, philosophy also gave attention to [the concept of] revelation. Both Schelling and Hegel tried—not to rob Christian revelation of its reality by means of a purely intellectual critique but—speculatively to get to know the idea that is basic to it and to all Christian dogmas. Thus they substituted a speculative rationalism for the vulgar rationalism that had held sway up until their time. According to Schelling in his first period, the entire world was the self-revelation of God. Nature is visible spirit; spirit is invisible nature. God's essence becomes known to human beings from the whole of nature, especially from the development of the human mind in art, religion, and science. Hegel similarly taught that God does not reveal himself *to* human beings by a passing event in time but *in* human beings themselves and achieves self-consciousness in them. And this process by which God achieves consciousness in human beings is identical with human beings gaining knowledge of God. Hence revelation and religion are two sides of the same thing: God's self-consciousness in human beings coincides with humanity's consciousness of God. This consciousness first expresses itself symbolically in art, then visually in religion, and finally conceptually in philosophy. So, though nature and history also reveal God, they do so on a much lower level and to a much smaller degree. The highest revelation of God can be seen in the human spirit, where God comes to himself and becomes conscious of himself. But this revelation of God in the human spirit also takes place in the way of a historical process. The history of religions is the history of the absolute coming to himself in human consciousness and achieves its zenith in Christianity, which brings to light the essential oneness of God and humanity.

This pantheistic notion of revelation not only found acceptance in the case of philosophers like Ed. von Hartmann and A. Drews but also exerted great influence on numerous modern theologians.[30] In this connection there

---

30. D. F. Strauss, *Christliche Glaubenslehre*, 2 vols. (Tübingen: C. F. Osiander, 1840–41), §19; A. E. Biedermann, *Christliche Dogmatik*, 2d ed., 2 vols. (Berlin: G. Reimer, 1884–85), I, 264ff.; O. Pfleiderer, *Grundriss der Christlichen Glaubenslehre und Sittenlehre* (Berlin: G. Reimer, 1888), §16; R. A. Lipsius, *Lehrbuch der evangelisch-protestantischen Dogmatik* (Braunschweig: L. C. A. Schwetschke, 1893), §52ff.; Auguste Sabatier, *Esquisse d'une philosophie de la religion d'après la psychologie et l'histoire* (Paris: Fischbacher, 1901), 32ff.; English trans. T. A. Seed, *Outlines of a Philosophy of Religion Based on Psychology and History* (New York: James Pott, 1902); C. W. Opzoomer, *De Godsdienst* (Amsterdam: J. H. Gebhard & Comp., 1861); J. H. Scholten, *Dogmatices Christianae initia*, 2d ed. (Lyons: P. Engels, 1858), 26–39; *I. Hooykaas, *God in de Geschiedenis* (1870); Tiele, *Elements*, I, 35, 243ff.; II, 160ff.; Cannegieter, "De Godsdients in den Mensch en de Mensch in den Godsdients," *Teylers Theologische Tijdschrift* (1904): 178–211.

is indeed some disagreement about whether revelation is to be found primarily in nature, or in history with its array of great men, or in human beings themselves. And then again there is disagreement about whether revelation occurs in the human intellect or especially in the human heart and conscience. Three characteristic features, nevertheless, consistently recur: (1) Revelation and religion are viewed as the two sides of one and the same thing. In the religious equation revelation represents the objective divine component, and religion[31] the subjective human component. The two, accordingly, have the same content. All revelation is psychologically mediated and reaches human beings via their own thinking, feeling, and conduct. (2) Consequently, the developmental history of the religious consciousness in humankind is identical with the history of divine revelation. (3) On this position the distinction between natural and supernatural revelation completely vanishes. All revelation is supernatural in origin, but in the manner in which it comes to human beings and in the content that it imparts to human beings, it is natural through and through. Revelation has reality only and is knowable and intelligible only to the religious person.

That these are the characteristic features of the modern concept of revelation came very clearly to light in Friedrich Delitzsch's lectures on *Babel and Bible*.[32] Already in his first lecture he frankly admitted that he did not believe in any kind of special revelation and placed the concept of revelation found in Babylon and the Bible on the same level. When this was criticized, he explained himself in more detail, saying he was well aware that "nowadays many people assume a humanly-mediated revelation of God which gradually unfolds in a historical process" and that he himself admittedly had no problem believing in a revelation in that sense. At the same time he acknowledged that such a view of revelation was a "dilution" of the same biblical concept of revelation and that of the ancient church.[33] The correctness of this admission can hardly be doubted. Gunkel, for example, says that revelation is indeed the foundation of all religions and that divine revelation is certainly still compatible with our view of history, but then it must not be interpreted in the sense in which a "coarse supernaturalism" views it, for that is "a child's faith."

Nevertheless, Gunkel insists, revelation does exist in the sense that to the historian who surveys the whole, history displays an order and a logic that prompt him to say: all this has not been produced by chance; "a unique spirit" indwells and controls history. The great events in the life of nations, the great personalities who appear especially in the sphere of religion, show us how God himself is and how he wants us to be. Accordingly, the idea of

31. Ed. note: The word *religion* here is a translation of the Dutch *godsdienst*, which has in view the outward expression (worship, cult) of religion.

32. Friedrich Delitzsch, *Babel and Bible*, trans. W. H. Corruth (Chicago: Open Court, 1903); German original: *Babel und Bibel: Ein Rückblick und Ausblick* (Stuttgart: Deutsche Verlags-Anstalt, 1904).

33. Ibid., 166–67.

historical development automatically leads to the idea of revelation; on the other hand, to the historically minded person a revelation apart from history is totally inconceivable.[34] Even in the case of the person of Christ, all that is supernatural vanishes. Says Bousset, "We no longer start with the idea that Jesus is absolutely different from ourselves: he being from above and we from below. We rather tend to say that his identity in all its dimensions is the highest and most complete ever granted to humankind on its long journey from below to above, the crown of our existence, the leader of our life, one without an equal."[35]

The reason why many persons have changed the earlier concept of revelation into this modern one is the opinion that otherwise the content of revelation can never become the spiritual property of human beings but always remains transcendently and supernaturally above them. Gunkel puts it as follows: "Divine truth could never as such be intelligible to humankind but first had to be prepared [for acceptance] in the souls and minds of humankind."[36] This comes down to the idea of Spinoza and Hegel that God cannot reveal himself *to* human beings by words and signs but only *in* human beings by way of their own minds. The revelation of God coincides with the course of nature, with immanent cosmic evolution. Thus, in Haeckel's words, the revelations on which the religions base themselves are merely creations of human fantasy; the truth that the believer finds in it is a human invention, and childlike faith in it is superstition. Nature alone is the true revelation, i.e., the true source of rational knowledge.[37]

Hence we cannot speak of anything like a unanimous opinion on the essence and concept of revelation. Although we can perhaps draw a line between those who accept only a natural kind of revelation and others who additionally accept a supernatural kind, still on both sides of this boundary there is disagreement again about all sorts of details, and also the meaning of the terms *natural* and *supernatural* is far from settled. A host of questions remain. If revelation bears a supernatural character, does this refer to the manner in which it came to us or only to the new and original character of its content (Schleiermacher)? How is such a supernatural revelation different from natural revelation in nature and history, especially from the religious, poetic, and heroic inspiration that is found outside of Christianity as well and that has so often been compared with Christian revelation (Hamann, Herder, Jacobi, Schleiermacher)? Again, where can that supernatural revela-

---

34. Gunkel, "Das Alte Testament im Licht der modernen Forschung," in *Beiträge zur Weiterentwicklung der christlichen Religion,* 62ff.; cf. Wobbermin, "Das Wesen des Christentums," in *Beiträge zur Weiterentwicklung der christlichen Religion,* 360ff.

35. W. Bousset, *Das Wesen der Religion* (Halle: a. S.: Gebauer-Schwetschke, 1903), 250; English trans. F. B. Low, *What Is Religion?* (New York: G. P. Putnam, 1907).

36. Gunkel, "Das Alte Testament im Licht der modernen Forschung," 62ff.

37. E. Haeckel, *The Riddle of the Universe at the Close of the Nineteenth Century,* trans. Joseph McCabe (New York: Harper & Brothers, 1900), 306–7; German original: *Die Welträthsel* (Stuttgart: E. Strauss, 1899), 354.

tion be found—also in pagan religions, or only in Israel, or even exclusively in the person of Christ (Schleiermacher, Ritschl)? How far does revelation extend itself after Christ's appearance? Is it limited to him, or is also the outpouring of the Holy Spirit (Kaftan) and his working in regeneration and conversion to be included under the term *revelation* (Frank)? Is the content of revelation primarily cognitive, so that it enlightens the intellect (Hegel, Biedermann, Scholten), or is it above all mystical or ethical in nature, a sensation in the mind, an arousal of feeling, or reinforcement of the will (Schleiermacher, Lipsius, Sabatier, Opzoomer, the ethical theologians)? In revelation, is the external and objective event, the manifestation, be it in nature (Scholten, Haeckel), in history (Hegel, Schelling, Troeltsch), or in both (Rothe), the main thing, or does the point of gravity lie in the subject, in the self-revelation of God in the human heart, in human reason, or in the human conscience (Biedermann, Lipsius, Sabatier)?

NATURALIST CONFUSION ABOUT REVELATION

[84] There is an immense confusion prevailing in the efforts to determine the essence and concept of revelation. This confusion springs in large part from the fact that there are theologians who still continue to speak of revelation though by virtue of their principle and position have forfeited the right to do so. While this continuation of the old terminology is proof that the concept of revelation represents a value that is also recognized by many persons outside the circle of Christian theology, it nevertheless fosters misunderstanding and confusion. "Revelation" certainly is not a series of sounds without content, not a neutral flag, which can cover all kinds of cargoes, but a word that conveys a specific concept. Generally speaking, revelation is the communication or announcement of something that is still unknown and in the domain of religion includes three elements: (1) The existence of a personal divine being who originates the announcement; (2) a truth, fact, or event that up until the time of its announcement was not yet known; (3) a human being to whom the announcement was made.

If we hold onto these elements, it is self-evident that on a naturalistic basis there can be no revelation. The word *naturalism,* however, is used in various senses. For those who know no other nature than the material world, deny the independent existence of the mind or spirit, and explain all psychic phenomena in terms of the physical, naturalism coincides with materialism. It is not hard to see that this school of thought leaves no room whatever for revelation. While Haeckel may still speak of it, for him the knowledge of nature along with the rational decisions derived from it is the only truth. If God does not exist and if, as Feuerbach has it, "anthropology is the secret of theology," then by that token religion and revelation are automatically condemned and are nothing but the reactions of human fantasy. While the cult of the true, the good, and the beautiful may then be stamped with the name of a new religion, everyone recognizes that in that way the word *religion* is used in a sense that is utterly foreign to it. The same thing applies here to the use of the word *revelation*. No one may or can be prohibited from using this word, but if there is to be such a thing as precise scientific argumentation, words must be matched with concepts.

In the second place, the name "naturalism" can be given to the school of thought that, while it does not recognize a transcendent personal God, still makes a distinction in the world between "matter" and "spirit" and views both as manifestations of an immanent, impersonal, omnipotent, and external power. In this case naturalism is identical with pantheism. Here there is no room for revelation in the strict sense either. Indeed present here is the acknowledgment that the content of being does not coincide with its appearance and that there is a "something" that lies behind the phenomena and is manifest to us in these phenomena, but this is still no revelation in the ordinary sense of the word. For, in the first place, pantheism does not know what that "something" is that lies behind the phenomena and therefore refers to it with an assortment of names like "nature," "substance," "reason," "will," "power," etc., words that can mean everything and nothing. It teaches a revelation that does not reveal anything. In the second place, it can at most speak of a process of becoming and being manifest, of an unconscious and involuntary act. In the case of human beings, one can speak of revelation inasmuch as human beings can make themselves known, say by their speech; but no one will apply the word *revelation* to an animal, a plant, or a stone because their inner being becomes manifest in appearance. Revelation and religion always assume that God and humanity are distinct and nevertheless stand in a certain relation to each other. Religion, as the historical study of all religions teaches us, is a relation between human beings and a personal God and for that reason ceases to exist if God and human beings are essentially one. Similarly, according to that same historical study, revelation is an act of God by which he communicates himself and makes himself known to human beings. For that reason revelation and religion are not, as Hegel, Hartmann, Drews, and others represent them, two sides of the same thing but two distinct relations, which however are closely interrelated and of which the one cannot possibly exist without the other.

In the third place, one can understand by the term *naturalism* that school of thought that is better known as deism, rationalism, or antisupernaturalism. Those who take this position do recognize a personal God and also believe in a general revelation in nature and history, in the intellect and heart of human beings, but they dispute the necessity, possibility, and reality of a special supernatural revelation. Here, indeed, people have a revelation in the true sense, an act of God by which he makes himself known to human beings. But the moment deism, and similarly, modern theism follow through on their recognition of a general revelation, they can no longer maintain their position and must either move forward or back away from it. For if a personal all-knowing and almighty God exists, it follows that he never does anything unconsciously but always acts deliberately and has a purpose for everything. Revelation, in that case, is never an unconscious emanation, an involuntary translucency of God in his works, but always a free, intentional, and active act of making himself known to human beings. The ways and forms in which God reveals himself may vary, just as one human can make himself or herself known to another in different ways. God can reveal himself directly and immediately and in the process use ordinary or extraordinary means. These forms, being instrumental, are in a sense of secondary importance. But revelation, whether it comes to us in an ordinary or an extraordinary manner, is always an act of God.

Now those who interpret revelation as a conscious and voluntary act of God by which he makes himself known to human beings are in principle supernaturalistic, whether or not they accept a special revelation in prophecy and miracle. The question of naturalism versus supernaturalism is not settled only in confrontation with so-called supernatural revelation but is actually decided already at the outset in dealing with the concept of revelation in a general sense. Deism is untenable; the only choice is between theism and pantheism (materialism). In the case of pantheism not even general revelation can be maintained, while in the case of theism there is absolutely no reason to accept a general revelation while opposing a special revelation. Theism is inherently supernaturalistic, not yet immediately in the historic sense of the word but in the sense that it assumes a transcendent personal God and, by implication, recognizes a world beyond this world. This order is above this present nature (*ordo supra hanc naturam*), an order from which proceeds—in whatever way this may occur—an effect upon this world. Religion, revelation, supernaturalism, and theism are inseparably interconnected. They stand and fall together.

But, in addition, theism is supernaturalistic also in the sense that it has forfeited the right, in principle, to oppose a special revelation. For if it remains true to itself and does not lapse into pantheism, it will maintain both creation and providence. But if God has created the world and by his providence still maintains and governs it, the implication is that he is absolutely elevated above the world and can use it in the manner it pleases him. In that case both creation and providence are proof that God *can,* and *wants to,* reveal himself. The world, in that scenario, is not a second god, not an antidivine power that is unwilling or unfit to incorporate divinity into itself, but an instrument, fashioned by God himself, to reveal his glory and by it to make himself known to human beings. Also this last point cannot be denied by theism. If there truly exists a revelation of God, then it also has the purpose—even if it is not the sole purpose—that human beings will learn to know God from it and will love and serve him. Opinions may differ on whether the revelation that comes to us from nature is sufficient for this purpose. The necessity and reality of a special revelation remains in dispute at this point. But, on a theistic position, its possibility cannot be denied.

IMPOSSIBILITY OF SCIENTIFIC NEUTRALITY

Up until now we have merely reasoned on the basis of the concept of revelation as it is concealed in the word as commonly used. Of greater importance, however, is the question of whether such a revelation—in the sense of a conscious and voluntary disclosure by God concerning himself to human beings—exists and how we can get to know that revelation. The different answers given to this question concerning method is a second reason for the vast disagreement that exists in philosophy and theology about the essence and concept of revelation. As was the case in the investigation into the essence of religion, so also with reference to the attempt to find out what revelation is, many theorists recommend the religion-historical method as the only true one. All religions, after all, appeal to revelation. It would be a biased and unscientific a priori to declare oneself in favor of one religion and to reject all others as false. The only properly scientific method is one in which the investigator takes his position (as it were) outside of the religions and outside of their real or alleged revelations. A "scientist" is unbiased, like a judge who as a supporter of no party stands above all the parties in his courtroom, gives them all a chance to speak, and then renders his own independent verdict.

We have already discussed and argued against this method earlier. Now, with reference to the concept of revelation we are to investigate, let it suffice to briefly recall the following. It is indeed a perplexing fact that all religions base themselves on revelation and on that basis present themselves as the true religion. Although we cannot endorse Lessing's views, it is certainly understandable that many theorists join him in retreating to the position of indifferentism and try to console themselves with the idea that it does not matter what one believes provided one lives a good life. But this consolation soon evaporates. Aside from the fact that religion does not simply allow itself to be shouldered aside, the study of ethnology shows that humanity is as divided over morality and justice as it is over religion. And even if the scientific investigator assumes a "neutral" stance, he or she does not thereby make any difference in this awesome reality of the division of humankind over its highest interests and values. All people, including the men and women of science, have to acknowledge this fact; and they can do this only if, along with Paul, they see in this reality an effect of the darkening of the human mind, a cross that sin has forced humanity to bear. No science, however "presuppositionless," is or will ever be able to undo this division and bring about, in the life of all nations and people, unity in the most basic convictions of the heart. If there is ever to be unity, it will have to be achieved in the way of mission; only religious unity will be able to bring about the spiritual and intellectual unity of humankind. As long as disagreement prevails in religion, science too will be unable to achieve the ideal of unity.

If science in our day frequently judges otherwise, it is mistaken in two ways: first, in thinking that religious faith, also belief in a revelation, is based on scientific grounds and could therefore at some future date be uprooted by scientific arguments; second, in cherishing the illusion that it could ever take a position outside of history and in that sense be unbiased and impartial. Like the investigation into the essence of religion, so also inquiry into the concept of revelation will only result in the attainment of a vague abstraction that will be of no use to anyone or in making available a concept that was already firmly established beforehand as the conviction of the investigator.

Actually in that way one plays an unseemly game with the scientific enterprise. It is much more honest and much more scientific to state in advance what convictions have guided us in undertaking the investigation. Without such a conviction one is in any case not going to achieve anything worthwhile in the study of religion and revelation. In order to investigate [the concept of] revelation in the different religions we need a criterion. If we do not bring such a criterion with us (actually an impossibility), we are bound to fall victim to the endless division that the history of religions offers to the viewer, and in the end we will no longer be capable of making a choice. Revelation, however, is not a philosophical but a religious category. Science cannot and may not say in advance what revelation is and which facts conform to that definition. It would thereby exceed its own jurisdiction and be guilty of the grossest partiality vis-à-vis the religions [of the world].

A true concept of revelation can be derived only from revelation itself. If no revelation ever took place, all reflection on the concept is futile. If, however, revelation is a fact, it—and it alone—must furnish us the concept and indicate to us the criterion we have to apply in our study of religions and revelations. The appeal to revelations, which we encounter in all religions, cannot be an argument for Christians to relinquish their conviction with regard to the truth of the Christian religion any more than logically thinking or ethical or esthetic persons will relinquish their convictions concerning the laws of thought, morality, or beauty because there are thousands of people who say that truth, virtue, and beauty are merely relative concepts and find their criterion in the individual human beings themselves. This applies both to the personal lives of Christians as well as their scientific pursuits. Muslims, Buddhists, and others, will of course reason in the same way and in the study of the religions proceed from *their* beliefs. But that remains for them to deal with. In this respect everyone had best be fully persuaded in his or her own mind. Division in life is a fact that we cannot undo and also has a ripple effect in the sphere of science. But a science that—driven by free convictions, of course, and not by coercion—allies itself with the Christian faith will be able to do more and labor more energetically for the spiritual and intellectual unity of humankind. Such unity is guaranteed in the unity of God and is the hope of all religion. By contrast, science, which seeks its salvation in indifferentism, does not know what to do with religion and revelation and abandons both to superstition.

This method, which proceeds from the premise of faith and is actually applied by everyone, at once affords those who take their position in the Christian faith the immense advantage that they do not a priori establish by their own thinking what revelation is. Instead they seek the answer to that question in the words and facts that in Christianity present themselves as constituents of revelation and are recorded in Holy Scripture. They proceed to do their work positively, not speculatively. They do not dictate to God whether and how he may reveal himself but listen to what God himself has to say on that matter. The following chapters, accordingly, have to deal with what Holy Scripture teaches concerning revelation: its subject and object, its essence and content, its manner and intent.

10

GENERAL REVELATION

From the earliest days of the church, Christian theology made a distinction between "natural" and "supernatural" revelation. God makes himself known to all people through his creation—accounting for those elements Christianity and other religions have in common. What is unique and distinctive about Christianity is based on God's special revelation in Scripture. The great theological debates in the church concerned the nature of the relationship between these two.

While the Roman Catholic tradition gave natural theology greater weight than did the major reformers, the extreme wing of the Anabaptist tradition rejected the natural order and attempted in revolutionary fashion to establish a kingdom of heaven on earth. Socinianism also rejected natural theology and inferred all knowledge of God from special revelation. Even Luther was not free from a dualistic view that separated the spiritual and temporal realms.

The result was that in Anabaptism and Socinianism excessive supernaturalism turned into rationalism. Among Lutherans and some Calvinists, reason came to have some authority alongside of faith. Eventually an expanding natural theology was judged by German naturalists and English deists to make revelation unnecessary. By contrast the influence of Immanuel Kant's philosophy led theologians to search for nonrational means of affirming the reality of God.

The Scriptures do not distinguish between "natural" and "supernatural" revelation. Creation revelation is no less supernatural than Scripture; in both, God himself is at work and his providential creating, sustaining, and governing form a single mighty ongoing revelation. Revelation comes already before the fall into sin; the covenant of works is a fruit of supernatural revelation. As image bearers of God, human beings are intrinsically supernaturalists.

Supernatural revelation is not the same as immediate revelation. All revelation is mediate. God makes himself known by theophanies, by word and deed. Sin does not alter matters. God's general revelation still holds for all people at all times. There are, however, periods in which special revelation does not occur. Therefore the distinction between natural and supernatural revelation is not identical with the distinction between general and special revelation. The latter term is preferable to the former.

It is the unanimous conviction of Christian theologians that general revelation is inadequate. Pelagians do assert the sufficiency of natural revelation, and they were followed in the eighteenth century by rationalists and deists. The defect of all general revelation is that it can supply us with no knowledge of Christ and divine grace and forgiveness. In addition, natural knowledge is not without error and its claims highly debated.

General revelation is of great significance for the world of paganism. It is difficult to provide an agreed-upon view of religion's origins. Many have become enamored of an evolutionary view, though this ignores the fact of religion among so-called primitive people and denies the possibility of retrogression. Attempts to explain the origin and essence of religion without reference to God and his knowable revelation are bound to fail. Even paganism holds some truths.

All revelation—general and special—finally finds its fulfillment and meaning in Christ. God's revelation in Scripture and in Christ provides the spectacles of faith that enable us to understand general revelation better, as well as a basis for encounters with non-Christians. In no way should the Christian faith be represented as otherworldly or anti-creation. Rather, grace and nature are united in the Christian faith, and general revelation links the kingdom of heaven and the kingdom of earth—it joins creation and redemption together in one great eschatological cantata of praise. Grace restores nature, a religious life is woven into the very fabric of ordinary human experience. Finally, God is one and the same loving God in creation and redemption; grace restores nature.

[85] It was not long before Christian theology, instructed by Holy Scripture, made an important distinction in the matter of revelation. On the one hand, the connections and agreement between the religion of Christians and the religion of pagans, between theology and philosophy, could not be completely denied. On the other hand, Christianity certainly was a unique and independent religion, essentially different from that of pagans. In the face of this tension, early Christian theologians were led to make a distinction between "natural" revelation (religion, theology) and "supernatural" revelation. Materially this distinction can be found already in the work of the most ancient church fathers. Justin Martyr speaks of a "human teaching" obtained from "the seed of reason (σπερμα του λογου) that is innate in the whole human race" and of "a [spiritual] knowledge (γνωσις) and vision (θεωρια)" that comes to us only through Christ.[1] Tertullian has a separate treatise on the "Testimony of the Soul" and refers to a knowledge of God from the works of creation and of another, more complete, knowledge by the agency of Spirit-filled men, and Irenaeus repeatedly expresses himself along the same lines.[2] Augustine recognizes a revelation of God in nature[3] but alongside of reason posits authority and faith,[4] which alone leads to the true knowledge of God.[5] In the work of John of Damascus,[6] this distinction already

---

1. Irenaeus, *Apology*, II, 8, 10, 13.
2. Tertullian, *Apology*, II, 18; Irenaeus, *Against Heresy*, II, 6, 9, 28; III, 24; IV, 6.
3. Augustine, *The Literal Meaning of Genesis*, IV, 32; *City of God*, VIII, 11; XIX, 1.
4. Augustine, *Against the Academics*, III, 20; *The Profit of Believing*, 11.
5. Augustine, *Confessions*, V, 5; VIII, 26; *City of God*, X, 29.
6. John of Damascus, *Exposition of the Orthodox Faith*, I, chap. 1, V.

has the character of dogma. Also the further differentiation of natural theology into "innate" and "acquired" can be found in the most ancient Christian authors. Tertullian appeals to the internal witness of the soul and the contemplation of the works of God. Augustine expressly states that God can be known from the things that are visible[7] but refers especially to self-consciousness and self-knowledge as the road to eternal truth.[8] John of Damascus already clearly places increated knowledge and acquired knowledge side by side.

"NATURAL" AND "SUPERNATURAL" REVELATION

It took longer, however, to define the boundaries between the two kinds of revelation. For a long time Christian thinkers still attempted to prove Christian dogmas from nature and reason. Thus Augustine (in *The Trinity*) tried a posteriori to prove the doctrine of the Trinity, Anselm (*Cur deus homo?*) the doctrines of the incarnation and satisfaction, and Albert the Great and Thomas the doctrine of creation.[9] The most radical in this respect was Raymund de Sabunde, who in his *Liber natural sive creaturarum*, later mistakenly called *Theologia naturalis*,[10] attempted to construct the whole Christian doctrine of faith from human nature without help from Scripture and tradition and without using the scholastic method. But this rational argumentation was still no more than a form of help that came after the fact. Christian dogmas were established a priori on the basis of revelation. "Belief in invisible things is assisted by the things which are made."[11] Knowledge that could be obtained from nature was, for that matter, restricted to certain "mixed articles," which focused on the three terms *God, virtue,* and *immortality*.[12] In scholasticism, however, the distinction between natural and supernatural theology was progressively made more rigorous and became an absolute contrast. As a result of natural revelation, one could only obtain a certain amount of rigorously scientific knowledge.[13]

Thomas was so sure of this that he raised the question whether, this being the case, the acceptance of these naturally-known truths did not lose all meritoriousness. Believing, after all, is meritorious only if it is not knowing but an act of accepting as true on the basis of authority, an act of the intellect prompted by a motion of the will that is moved by grace. The answer to the question of merit is that knowing indeed diminishes the nature of faith (*ratio fidei*) but that there al-

7. Augustine, *The Literal Meaning of Genesis*, IV, 32.

8. Augustine, *Of True Religion,* 72; *The Teacher,* 38; *On the Trinity,* IV, 1.

9. For Albertus Magnus, see A. Stöckl, *Philosophie des Mittelalters,* 3 vols. (Mainz: Kirchhein, 1864–66), II, 384ff.; Thomas Aquinas, *Summa contra Gentiles,* II, 15ff.

10. Raymond of Sabunde, *Theologia Naturalis seu liber creaturarum* (Stuttgart: Bad Cannstatt, Frommann, 1966); facsimile of J. Sighart edition (Sulzbach,1852); cf. O. Zöckler, *Theologia naturalis* (Frankfurt a.M.: Heyder & Zimmer, 1860), 33.

11. P. Lombard, *Sentences,* I, dist. 3.6; cf 2.1.

12. Aquinas, *Summa contra Gentiles,* bk. 1–3.

13. Aquinas, *Summa Theol.,* II, 2, qu. 1, art. 5; cf. Bellarmine, IV, 277ff., *Controversiis.*

ways remains in the believer the nature of love (*ratio charitatis*), i.e., the disposition, on God's authority, to consistently accept as true that which is known (apart from faith).[14] Furthermore, this disposition to believe the mixed articles on authority always remains necessary for special reasons. Added by supernatural revelation to this knowledge from nature and reason is the knowledge of the mysteries, but this latter knowledge is exclusively based on authority and is and remains from beginning to end a matter of faith. The mysteries of Christianity belong to an order that is not incidentally supernatural (as a result of sin) but is intrinsically and strictly supernatural for every human, also for the sinless human, indeed even for the angels, and can therefore be known only by revelation. This peculiarly Roman Catholic teaching will be discussed further after the chapter on special revelation. But we must already note here that in Catholic theology knowing and believing, reason and authority, natural and supernatural revelation, occur dualistically side by side. Rome, on the one hand, recognizes the claims of rationalism in the sphere of natural revelation and condemns the excessive supernaturalism that also in the mixed articles considers knowledge possible only by revelation. On the other hand, in the sphere of the mysteries it adheres as rigorously as possible to supernaturalism and condemns all rationalism that in the dogmas attempts a priori or a posteriori to evade authority and faith and seeks to convert them into knowledge. It rejects both Tertullian and Origen and condemns the traditionalism of de Bonald as well as the rationalism of Hermes. According to the Vatican Council, the Roman Catholic church confesses that "God . . . can be known with certitude by the natural light of human reason from created things," but that it has pleased God "to reveal himself and the eternal decrees of his will to mankind in another, supernatural manner."[15]

The Reformation took over this distinction between natural and supernatural revelation while nevertheless in principle assigning a very different meaning to it. The Reformers indeed assumed a revelation of God in nature. But the human mind was so darkened by sin that human beings could not rightly know and understand this revelation either. Needed, therefore, were two things: (1) that God again included in special revelation those truths which in themselves are knowable from nature; and (2) that human beings, in order to again perceive God in nature, first had to be illumined by the Spirit of God. Objectively needed by human beings to understand the general revelation of God in nature was the special revelation of God in Holy Scripture, which, accordingly, was compared by Calvin to glasses. Subjectively needed by human beings was the eye of faith to see God also in the works of his hands.

Equally important was the change introduced by the Reformation in the way supernatural revelation was viewed. Supernatural revelation did not, in the first place, mean that it belonged as such to another order and surpassed

---

14. Aquinas, *Summa Theol.*, II, 2 qu. 2, art. 9, 10.

15. Vatican Council I, session III, "Dogmatic Constitution *Dei Filius*, On the Catholic Faith," chap. 2; in *Documents of Vatican Council I (1869–1870)*, trans. John F. Broderick (Collegeville, Minn.: Liturgical Press, 1971), 37–52.

even the intellect of sinless human beings and angels. Rather, this revelation was supernatural primarily because it far exceeded the thoughts and wishes of sinful fallen human beings. Hence in the Reformation, natural theology lost its rational autonomy. It was no longer treated separately but incorporated in the doctrine of the Christian faith.[16] There were several factors, however, that held back the development and complete application of this reformational principle. On the one side there was excess. Anabaptism completely rejected the natural order and attempted in revolutionary fashion to establish a kingdom of heaven on earth. Socinians totally rejected natural theology and inferred all knowledge of God from revelation.[17] Luther, by his opposition to scholastic doctrine ("the things of nature have remained whole") got to the point where he denied to Aristotle, to reason, and to philosophy all right to speak in theological matters and called reason stone-blind in religious matters.[18] The rigorous Lutherans followed the master, and the *Formula Concordiae,* though recognizing that "human reason or the natural intellect of man has retained some faint glimmer of that knowledge, which is of God, and retains some particle of that law," it nevertheless so one-sidedly stresses the darkness and impotence of the natural man in matters of religion that the bond between special and general revelation is broken. In "spiritual matters and as it pertains to conversion and regeneration" a human is no more than a "stone, a trunk, or mud."[19]

Reaction to this was inevitable. In Anabaptism and Socinianism excessive supernaturalism turned into rationalism. Luther, inasmuch as he could not really deny to reason all insight and discernment, was compelled to make a sharp distinction between the spiritual and the secular, the heavenly and the earthly, the eternal and the temporal. Following his example, Lutheran theologians made a distinction between "two hemispheres, one of which was inferior, and the other superior." In earthly things reason is still free and capable of much good; in this domain it is to some extent self-reliant and independent of faith.[20] Calvin too, although because of his theory of common grace he was in a much more favorable position than Luther, did not always succeed in transcending the ancient dualistic dichotomy between natural and supernatural

16. U. Zwingli, *Commentary on True and False Religion,* ed. S. M. Jackson and C. N. Heller (Durham, N.C.: Labyrinth Press, 1981), §3, "God"; J. Calvin, *Institutes of the Christian Religion,* I.i–v; A. Polanus, *Syn. Theol.,* I, 10; P. Vermigli, *Loci. Comm.,* loc. 2.

17. *The Racovian Catechism,* trans. Thomas Rees (London: Longman, Hurst, Rees, Orme and Brown, 1818), 92.46–49; cf. O. Fock, *Der Socinianismus* (Kiel: C. Schröder, 1847), 307ff.

18. Köstlin, *Theology of Luther,* trans. Charles Hays, 2 vols. (Philadelphia: Lutheran Publication Society, 1897), II, 287ff. C. E. Luthardt, *Die Ethik Luthers,* 2d ed. (Leipzig: Dörffling & Franke, 1875), 14ff.; D. F. Strauss, *Die Christliche Glaubenslehre,* 2 vols. (Tübingen: C. F. Osiander, 1840–41), I, 311ff.

19. J. T. Müller, *Die Symbolischen Bücher des Evangelisch-Lutherschen Kirche,* 5th ed. (Gütersloh: Bertelsmann, 1882), 589, 594.

20. J. Köstlin, *Theology of Luther,* II, 244ff.; H. F. F. Schmid, *The Doctrinal Theology of the Evangelical Lutheran Church,* trans. Charles A. Hay and Henry E. Jacobs, 5th ed. (Philadelphia: United Lutheran Publishing House, 1899), 192ff.

revelation.[21] As a result, reason again achieved some measure of authority alongside of faith. It seemed reason did not always have to be guided by faith and was in fact, be it in an ever so small and indifferent area of life, free and independent. With this right being granted to it—at least not seriously contested—reason turned it to its own advantage and gradually expanded its domain. First in civil matters, then in science, soon also in philosophy, reason elevated itself to a position alongside of and over against faith. Alsted, who published an independent "natural theology" (1615), listed as its content seven dogmas: God exists; we must love him above all things; we must live a good life; we must not do to others what we do not want others to do to us; to each must be given his due; no one ought to be injured; more value is invested in the common good than in the private good.[22] Many Reformed theologians followed suit, especially when Cartesian philosophy gained more influence.[23]

As a result of English deism and German rationalism, "natural" or "rational" theology so increased in power and prestige that it rejected revealed religion as totally unnecessary. Herbert of Cherbury (1581–1648) devoted five articles to the content of natural religion: that God is supreme; that he ought to be worshiped; that virtue is the chief part of this worship; that we must grieve on account of our sins and turn from them; that from within the goodness and justice of God reward and punishment is awarded, whether in this life or the next.[24] But after it had banished revealed theology, natural theology was itself judged in turn. Kant asserted in his *Critique of Pure Reason* that the latter is restricted to phenomena of sense perception and can neither penetrate to the supersensible nor to the supernatural. The history of religions demonstrated that a purely natural religion did not exist anywhere and that all religions were positive (concrete). Bible criticism undermined supernatural revelation and erased the boundaries between it and natural revelation. A common conviction arose, therefore, that for us to attain to some knowledge of God, we must find a road other than reason and scientific proof, viz., the road of faith, or of moral experience, or of fantasy. Natural theology and religion, and consequently also natural revelation, lost their value. The proofs for God's existence, the soul, and immortality were abandoned and banished from dogmatics. Pierson even declared that education in natural theology at national universities was a waste of the nation's money.[25] Nevertheless, in the law for higher education,[26] under the heading of the history of the doctrine of God and of the philosophy of religion, the subject was again included. Professor Doedes, who rejected it in his *Encyclo-*

21. J. Calvin, *Institutes*, II, 2, 12, 13.
22. Alsted, *Praecognitia Theol.*, 37–114.
23. Cf. J. I. Doedes, *Inleiding tot de Leer van God* (Utrecht: Kemink, 1880), 200ff.
24. G. V. Lechler, *Geschichte des Englischen Deismus* (Stuttgart: J. G. Cotta, 1841), 42.
25. A. Pierson, *Eene Levensbeschouwing*, 2 vols. (Haarlem: Kruseman & Tjeenk Willink, 1875), 83.
26. Ed. note: Bavinck is referring here to the 1876 Dutch parliamentary law concerning higher education, which established nonconfessional departments of religious studies at all Dutch state universities.

pedia, actually resumed teaching it in his *Introduction to the Doctrine of God* (1880) and *The Doctrine of God* (1871) (Dutch). Everything points to the fact—as will be shown in the locus concerning God—that the proofs for the existence are again rising in value. The sound idea inherent in the old natural theology is gradually gaining more recognition.

ALL REVELATION IS SUPERNATURAL

[86] Scripture, though it knows of an established natural order, in the case of revelation makes no distinction between "natural" and "supernatural" revelation. It uses the same terms for both; it also uses גלה, φανερουν, and ἀποκαλυπτειν for natural revelation, for example (Job 12:22; 33:16; 36:10; Rom. 1:18, 19). Nösgen[27] was therefore mistaken when he objected to giving to the revelation of God in nature the name "revelation." Actually, according to Scripture, all revelation, also that in nature, is supernatural. The word itself says nothing about the manner in which something is revealed but only conveys that something that was hidden comes to light. In the area of religion, it indicates that God has an independent life of his own that is distinct from nature and now, in one way or another, comes forward before the eyes of his rational creatures. Strictly speaking, therefore, only those can speak of revelation who recognize the supernatural, "an order above this natural order"; and everyone who employs the word in this sense is in principle a "supernaturalist," even though he or she only assumes a revelation that occurs "naturally." The distinction between a natural and a supernatural revelation has not been derived from the action of God, who expresses himself both in the one and in the other revelation, but from the manner in which that revelation occurs, viz., "through" or "from beyond" this natural order. In its origin all revelation is supernatural. God is always working (John 5:17).

That work of God outward began with the creation. The creation is the first revelation of God, the beginning and foundation of all subsequent revelation. The biblical concept of revelation is rooted in that of creation.[28] God first appeared outwardly before his creatures in the creation and revealed himself to them. In creating the world by his word and making it come alive by his Spirit, God already delineated the basic contours of all subsequent revelation. But immediately linking up with the event of creation is the action of providence. This, too, is an omnipotent and everywhere-present power and act of God. All that is and happens is, in a real sense, a work of God and to the devout a revelation of his attributes and perfections. That is how Scripture looks at nature and history. Creating, sustaining, and governing together form one single mighty ongoing revelation of God. No nature poetry has surpassed or

27. D. F. Nösgen, "Wezen und Umfang der Offenbarung nach dem Neuen Testament," *Beweis des Glaubens* 26 (1890): 416–17.

28. G. F. Oehler, *Theology of the Old Testament*, trans. Ellen D. Smith and Sophia Taylor (Edinburgh: T. & T. Clark, 1892–93), 21.

even equaled that of Israel.[29] To the devout everything in nature speaks of God. The heavens are telling the glory of God; and the firmament proclaims his handiwork. God's voice is in the great waters. That voice breaks the cedars; it rumbles in the thunder and howls in the hurricane. The light is his garment, the heavens his curtain, the clouds his chariot. His breath creates and renews the earth. He both rains and causes his sun to shine upon the just and the unjust. Herbs and grass, rain and drought, fruitful and barren years, indeed, all things come not by chance but by his fatherly hand. The Bible's view of nature and history is religious and hence also supernatural.

To Scripture, religion and supernatural revelation are even most intimately connected. It tells of such a revelation not only after but even before the fall. The God-human relation in the state of integrity is depicted as one of personal contact and association. God speaks to human beings (Gen. 1:28–30), gives them a command they could not know by nature (Gen. 2:16), and, as by his own hand, brings to the man a woman to be his helper (Gen. 2:22). Also the covenant of works (*foedus operum*) is not a covenant of nature (*foedus naturae*) in the sense that it arises from a natural human proclivity but is a fruit of supernatural revelation. And inasmuch as the covenant of works is nothing other than the form of religion that fits the human beings created in God's image who had not yet achieved their ultimate destiny, we can [safely] say that Scripture cannot conceive of pure religion without supernatural revelation. The supernatural is not at odds with human nature, nor with the nature of creatures; it belongs, so to speak, to humanity's essence. Human beings are images of God and akin to God and by means of religion stand in a direct relation to God. The nature of this relation implies that God can both objectively and subjectively reveal himself to human beings created in his image. There is no religion without tradition, dogma, and cult; and every one of these realities is interwoven with the concept of revelation. All religions, accordingly, are concrete and are based not only on natural but also on (real or supposed) supernatural revelation. And all human beings by nature recognize the supernatural. Naturalism, like atheism, is an invention of philosophy but has no support in human nature. As long as religion is integral to the essence of our humanity, so long will human beings be and remain supernaturalists. All believers, regardless of their particular persuasion, though they may be naturalists in their head, are supernaturalists in their heart.

Those who wish to banish the supernatural from religion, hence from their prayers, from their communion with God, are killing religion itself. For religion presupposes real kinship and communion with God and is supernaturalistic through and through. It is inseparable from the belief that God stands above nature and that he can do with nature what he pleases; that he makes the natural order serviceable to the moral order, the kingdoms of the world to the kingdom of heaven, nature (φυσις) to ethos. It has therefore been correctly

---

29. A. Pierson, *Geestelyke Voorouders*, 5 vols. (Haarlem: H. D. Tjeenk Willink, 1887), I, 389ff.

said that the prayer for a pure heart is as supernaturalistic as the prayer for a healthy body (Pierson). The theist who wants to be truly theistic and nevertheless denies supernatural revelation is by no means finished with this denial. Either he has to go back to deism or pantheism, or he has to go forward and embrace the possibility of supernatural revelation as well. For not a single religion can confine itself to the abstract truths of natural religion. The only true alternative to the recognition of the supernatural, accordingly, is not a rationalistic deism but naturalism, i.e., the belief that there is no other higher power but that which is immanent in the present natural order and reveals itself [there]. But then one loses all warrant for believing in the triumph of the good, the ultimate victory of the kingdom of God, in the power of the moral world order. For the good, the true, the moral world order, and the kingdom of God are matters that have no power to realize themselves on their own. The hope that human beings will bring them to supremacy and yield to the power of truth is daily dashed by disappointments. Their triumph is assured only if God is a personal omnipotent being who, in the face of all opposition, can lead the entire creation to the goal he has in mind for it. Religion, morality, the acknowledgment of a destiny for humankind and for the world, belief in the triumph of the good, a theistic worldview, and belief in a personal God are all inseparably bound up with supernaturalism. In sum: the idea of God and the idea of religion involves that of revelation.[30]

Supernatural revelation may not, however, be equated with immediate revelation. The distinction between mediate and immediate revelation tends in different periods to be taken in a different sense. In the past a revelation was called immediate if it came to the recipient without a go-between, and mediate when it was transmitted to others by angels or human beings.[31] Inasmuch as revelation usually came to prophets and apostles in person but to us only through their writings, the former as immediate revelation could be contrasted with the latter as mediate revelation. In the writings of rationalistic and modern theologians, these terms often acquired a totally different meaning, thus causing increasing confusion in the view of revelation.[32] In a strict sense there is no immediate revelation either in nature or in grace. God always uses a means—whether taken from among creatures or chosen freely—by which he reveals himself to human beings. By signs and symbols he makes his presence felt by them; by acts he proclaims his attributes; by speech and language he makes known to them his will and mind. Even in cases where he reveals himself internally in the human consciousness by his Spirit, this revelation always occurs organically and hence mediately. The

30. A. Pierson, *Gods Wondermacht en ons Geestelijke Leven* (Haarlem: H. D. Tjeenk Willink, 1887), 10ff., 36ff.; James Orr, *The Christian View of God and the World* (Grand Rapids: Kregel, 1989 [3d. ed., 1887]); cf. Rauwenhoff, *Wijsbegeerte van de Godsdienst,* (Leiden: Brill & Van Doesburgh, 1873), 530ff.

31. Witsius, *Miscellaneorum Sacrororum libri quatro* (Herborn: Joh. Nicolai Andreae, 1712), I, 16.

32. R. Rothe, *Zur Dogmatik,* 2d ed. (Gotha: Perthes, 1869), 55ff., 64ff.; F. Nitzsch, *Lehrbuch der Evangelischen Dogmatik,* 3d. ed., prep. by Horst Stephan (Tübingen: J. C. B. Mohr, 1902), 163ff.

distance between the Creator and creature is much too great for human beings to perceive God directly. The finite is not capable of containing the infinite (*finitum non est capax infiniti*).

Whether in the state of glory there will be a vision of God in respect of his being (*visio Dei per essentiam*) is something we can only examine later. But in this dispensation all revelation is mediate. No creature can see or understand God as he is and as he speaks in himself. Revelation therefore is always an act of grace; in it God condescends to meet his creature, a creature made in his image. All revelation is anthropomorphic, a kind of humanization of God. It always occurs in certain forms, in specific modes. In natural revelation his divine and eternal thoughts have been deposited in creatures in a creaturely way so that they could be understood by human thought processes. And in supernatural revelation he binds himself to space and time, adopts human language and speech, and makes use of creaturely means (Gen. 1:28; 2:16f., 21f.; 3:8f.). And by these means human beings understood God just as well and just as clearly as the devout person now perceives the speech of God in all of nature. Just as little as the revelation of God in nature and history is impossible and deceptive to the believer, so also is the supernatural revelation in the course of which God uses extraordinary means but to which he also opens people's eyes in a special way. Hence, in the state of integrity, according to the teaching of Scripture, natural and supernatural revelation go together. They are not opposites but complementary. Both are mediate and bound to certain forms. Both are based on the idea that God in his grace condescends to human beings and conforms himself to them. And the modes of both are that God makes his presence felt, his voice heard, and his works seen. From the beginning, by theophanies, word, and deed, God made himself known to people.

Now it is remarkable that sin, which entered the world by the first human beings, brings about no change in the fact of revelation itself. God continues to reveal himself; he does not withdraw himself. First of all, throughout the Bible we are taught a general revelation. God's revelation began in creation and continues in the maintenance and governance of all things. He reveals himself in nature all around us, displays in it his eternal power and divinity, and in blessings and judgments alternately shows this goodness and wrath (Job 36; 37; Ps. 29; 33:5; 65; 67:7; 90; 104; 107; 145; 147; Isa. 59:17–19; Matt. 5:45; Rom. 1:18; Acts 14:16–17). He reveals himself in the history of nations and persons (Deut. 32:8; Ps. 33:10; 67:4; 115:16; Prov. 8:15, 16; Acts 17:26; Rom. 13:1). He also discloses himself in the heart and conscience of every individual (Job 32:8; 33:4; Prov. 20:27; John 1:3–5, 9, 10; Rom. 2:14, 15; 8:16). This revelation of God is general, perceptible as such, and intelligible to every human. Nature and history are the book of God's omnipotence and wisdom, his goodness and justice. All peoples have to a certain extent recognized this revelation. Even idolatry presupposes that God's "power" and "divinity" manifests itself in creatures. Philosophers, natural scientists, and historians have often spoken in striking words about this revelation of God.[33] This general revelation has at all times been unanimously accepted and defended in Christian theology.[34] It was particularly upheld and highly valued by Reformed theologians.[35]

But, according to Scripture, this general revelation is not purely natural; it also contains supernatural elements. The revelation that occurred immediately after the fall bears a supernatural character (Gen. 3:8ff.) and via tradition becomes the possession of humankind. For a long time the original knowledge and service of God remains intact in a more or less pure state. Cain was granted grace over justice; he even became the father of a line of descendants who gave the impetus to culture (Gen. 4). The covenant that after the flood was made with Noah and in him with the new human race is a covenant of nature, yet no longer natural but the fruit of non-obligatory supernatural grace (Gen. 8:21, 22; 9:1–17). Scripture repeatedly mentions miracles that God performed before the eyes of pagans (in Egypt, Canaan, Babel, etc.), and supernatural revelations that came to non-Israelites (Gen. 20; 31:24; 40; 41; Judg. 7; Dan. 2:4ff.; etc.). Pagan religions, accordingly, do not rest only on the acknowledgment of God's revelation in nature but most certainly also on elements that from the most ancient times were preserved from supernatural revelation by tradition even though that tradition was frequently no longer pure. And even an operation of supernatural forces in the pagan world is not a priori impossible or even improbable. There may be truth in the appeal to revelations, an appeal that is common to all religions. Conversely, not everything that belongs to the area of special grace is, strictly speaking, supernatural. Long periods pass in the history of Israel, many days and years in the life of Jesus, and similarly in the life of the apostles, in which no supernatural revelation occurs and which nevertheless form an important part in the history of revelation. When Jesus preaches the gospel to the poor, this is of no less weight than when he heals the sick and raises the dead. His death, which seems "natural," is not less significant than his supernatural birth. Hence the distinction between natural and supernatural revelation is not identical with the distinction between general and special reve-

---

33. E.g., Xenophon, *Memorabilia*, I 4, 5; Cicero, *The Nature of the Gods*, II 2; idem, *On Divination*, II 72; Cf. for the practitioners of science, O. Zöckler, *Gottes Zeugen im Reich der* Natur (Gütersloh: C. Bertelsmann, 1881); K. A. Kneller, *Das Christenthum und die Vertreter der neueren Naturwissenschaft* (Freiburg im B.; St. Louis, Mo.: Herder, 1903). An English translation by T. M. Kettle, *Christianity and the Leaders of Modern Science* was published in 1911 by B. Herder (London, St. Louis), and reprinted in 1995 by Real-View Books, Fraser, Mich.

34. Irenaeus, *Against Heresies*, II 6; Tertullian, *Against Marcion*, I 10; Augustine, *City of God*, 8, 9ff., 19, 1; *The Trinity*, 4, 20; John of Damascus, *The Orthodox Faith*, I, 1 and 3; Aquinas, *Summa contra Gentiles*, 1–3; idem, *Summa Theol.*, 1, qu. 2; Cf. H. Denzinger, *Vier Bücher von der religiösen Erkenntniss.*, 2 vols. (1856; reprinted, Frankfurt/M.: Minerva-Verlag, 1967), II, 27–45.

35. J. Calvin, *Institutes*, I.iv; cf. A. Schweizer, *Die Glaubenslehre der evangelisch-reformirten Kirche* (Zürich: Orell, Fussli, 1847), I, 241ff.; H. Heppe, *Reformed Dogmatics* rev. and ed. Ernst Bizer and trans. G. T. Thomson (1950; reprinted, Grand Rapids: Baker, 1978), 1ff.; J. H. Scholten, *De Leer der Hervormde Kerk*, 2d. ed., 2 vols. (Leiden: P. Engels, 1850–51), I, 304–26; J. I. Doedes, *Inleiding tot de leer van God* (Utrecht Kemink, 1876), 107–252.

lation. To describe the twofold revelation that underlies pagan religions and the religion of Scripture, the latter distinction is preferable to the former.

GENERAL REVELATION IS INSUFFICIENT

[87] For various reasons, however, this general revelation is not sufficient. On this point, too, Christian theologians are unanimous. Over against the Gnostics, Irenaeus asserts the limited character of human knowledge, while Justin Martyr, Tertullian, Lactantius, Arnobius, and others depict the weakness of reason in very vivid colors.[36] Augustine does not deny that among pagans also there is some truth that can be used profitably by Christians,[37] but for him philosophy is not the true road to salvation. It can only teach the few and these few it can only teach a little.[38] It knows the goal but not the road that leads to it.[39] It often leads people astray and suppresses the truth in unrighteousness (*The Trinity* 13, 24), does not seek it piously (*Conf.* 5, 4), lacks the love that is necessary to the knowledge of the truth (*City of God* 9, 20), and is handicapped by its own pride in acquiring the knowledge of the truth, for only humility is the road to life.[40] Hence another road to truth is needed, viz., that of authority.[41] Thomas asserts the necessity of revelation even for the mixed articles of faith also known to reason.[42] The Roman Catholic church has already asserted the insufficiency of natural theology in the preface of the Roman Catechism and in the Vatican Council [I], session III, chap. 2 on revelation, and canons 2, 2–4. Protestant theologians agreed with Catholics on the insufficiency of general revelation.[43] In earlier times the sufficiency of general revelation and the natural religion based on it was taught only by the Pelagians, who embraced a threefold path to salvation, viz., the law of nature, the law of Moses, and the law of Christ. In the Christian church there have always been a number of theologians as well who held a more favorable view of pagans and even of the possibility of their salvation, such as Justin, Clement of Alexandria, Erasmus, Zwingli, and others.[44] As a rule, however, in their case this belief was based not on the doctrine of the sufficiency of general revelation but on the premise that God was also at work with his special grace among pagans, either in this life or the life

---

36. Justin Martyr in his introduction to his *Dialogue with Trypho;* Tertullian, *A Treatise on the Soul,* 1; Lactantius, *The Divine Institutes,* III 1, IV 1; Arnobius, *Against the Heathen,* I 38, II 6.

37. Augustine, *On Christian Doctrine,* II, 60.

38. Idem, *On the Trinity,* XIII, 12; *City of God,* XII, 20; *The Usefulness of Belief,* X, 24.

39. Idem, *Confessions,* V, 5; VII, 26; *City of God,* X, 29.

40. Idem, *On the Trinity,* XIII, 24; *Confessions,* V, 4; *City of God,* II, 7; IX, 20.

41. Idem, *On True Religion,* chap. 24; *On the Morals of the Catholic Church,* I, 2.

42. Aquinas, *Summa Theol.,* I, qu. (1) art. 1; idem, *Summa contra Gentiles,* I, 4.

43. J. Calvin, *Institutes,* I.v.11, I.vi; Heidegger, *Corpus Theol.* I §9–13; Trigland, *Antapologia,* chap. 17; J. C. Owen, *Theologoumena,* I, chap. 6; Turretin, *Institues of Elenctic Theology,* 1 qu. 4; B. De Moor, *Theol. Christ.,* I, 61ff.

44. Cf. G. J. Vossius, *Historiae de Controversiis: Quas Pelagius* (Amsterdam: Elzevier, 1655), 383ff.

to come. In contrast, the total sufficiency of general revelation and of natural religion was taught in the eighteenth century by deists and rationalists, like Cherbury, Tindal, Collins, Rousseau, Kant, and others.[45]

On the insufficiency of general revelation, however, there can scarcely be any doubt. In the first place, it is evident from the fact that this revelation at most supplies us with knowledge of God's existence and of some of his attributes such as goodness and justice, but it leaves us absolutely unfamiliar with the person of Christ, who alone is the way to the Father (Matt. 11:27; John 14:6; 17:3; Acts 4:12). General revelation, therefore, is insufficient for human beings as sinners; it knows nothing of grace and forgiveness; it is frequently even a revelation of wrath (Rom. 1:18–20). Grace and forgiveness, which for fallen human beings have to be the primary content of religion, are acts of God's good pleasure, not of nature and necessity. General revelation can at best communicate certain truths but conveys no facts, no history, and therefore changes nothing in existence. It somewhat illumines the mind and restrains sin but does not regenerate the nature of human beings and the world. It can instill fear but not trust and love.[46]

In the second place, the knowledge that general revelation can supply is not only meager and inadequate but also uncertain, consistently mingled with error, and for far and away the majority of people unattainable. The history of philosophy has been a history of systems that broke each other down and ended among the Greeks, in skepticism, in the Middle Ages in nominalism, and today among many in agnosticism. The truths most necessary to religion (the existence and essence of God; the origin and destiny of humanity and the world; sin and forgiveness; reward and punishment) have alternately been taught and combated. On all these issues no adequate certainty can be obtained in philosophy. Cicero, therefore, correctly asks the question: "Does not every eminently competent and serious philosopher confess himself to be ignorant of many things and that—even more—there are still many things to be learned by him?"[47] But even if some thinkers arrived at some true and pure knowledge, it came inevitably mixed with error of various kinds. Every philosophical system has lacunae and defects. Plato, whose system according to Augustine[48] is the most closely akin to Christianity, defends the practice of abandoning weak children, pederasty, community of wives, etc. Even in morality there is much disagreement and uncertainty: "Truth on this side of the Pyrenees is error on the other side"(Pascal). "I do not know of anything as absurd as can be said which is not already being said

45. Lechter, *Geschichte des Englischen Deismus* (Stuttgart: J. G. Cotta, 1841); K. G. Bretscheider, *Systematische Entwicklung aller in der Dogmatik Verkommende Begriffe* (Leipzig: J. A. Barth, 1841), 35ff.; J. Clarisse, *Encyclopaediae theologicae epitome* (Lugduni Batavorum: Apud S. et J. Luchtman, 1852), 405ff.; Doedes, *Inleiding*, 197ff.

46. W. G. T. Shedd, *Dogmatic Theology*, 3d. ed., 3 vols. (New York: Scribner, 1891–94), I, 66, 218.

47. Cicero, *Tuscalan Disputations*, I, 5.

48. Augustine, *City of God*, VIII, 5.

by some philosopher."[49] And even if the philosophers had the most splendid and pure doctrine at their disposal, they would still have lacked the authority to gain acceptance for it among the people. In the practice of life they themselves, therefore, often again adapt to popular belief and morals. Either that or with a snide "I hate the common crowd and keep my distance," they loftily retreat from contact with the people. The controversies among themselves and the clash between their teaching and their life weakened their influence. And even if all this had not been the case, the teaching of the philosophers could never have become or remained the religion of the people, because in matters of religion, intellectual clericalism and scientific hierarchy are intolerable. For that reason Thomas was absolutely right when he said that even in those truths that general revelation makes known to us, [special] revelation and authority are needed because that knowledge is suited only to the few, would take too much time to study, and even then remained incomplete and uncertain.[50]

In the third place, the insufficiency of natural revelation is clearly demonstrated by the fact that not a single people has been content with so-called natural religion. The general religion of the deists, Kant's religion of "moral reason," the "piety" and "obedience" of Spinoza are all of them mere abstractions, which have never existed in reality. Even if the five articles of Herbert or the rationalistic trilogy of Kant were completely certain and demonstrable by rigorous scientific standards, they would still be incapable of founding a religion or starting a church. For religion is something that is essentially different from science; it has another source and foundation. The eighteenth century was able to find pleasure in such truths of reason and vain abstractions. The nineteenth century with its sense of history soon saw that such a natural religion neither existed nor can exist anywhere. Today it is generally agreed that all religions are concrete and rest on revelation. [51]

GENERAL REVELATION AND THE UNIVERSALITY OF RELIGION

[88] This is not to say, however, that general revelation has lost its value and importance. In the first place it is of great significance for the world of paganism. It is the stable and permanent foundation of all pagan religions. Holy Scripture pronounces a severe judgment on "ethnicism" and explains its

---

49. Cicero, *On Divination*, II, 58; cf. Montaigne in Stöckl, *Philosophie des Mittelalters*, III, 372.

50. Aquinas, *Summa Theol.*, I qu. 1, art. 1; II. 2 qu. 2, art. 4; idem, *Summa contra Gentiles*, I, 4.

51. F. Schleiermacher, *The Christian Faith*, ed. H. R. MacIntosh and J. S. Steward (Edinburgh: T. & T. Clark, 1928), §10; In addition see A. Ritschl, *Rechfertigung und Versöhnung*, 4th ed., 3 vols. (Bonn: A. Marcus, 1895–1903), III 4, 500); idem, *Unterricht in der Christliche Religion*, 3d. ed. (Bonn: A. Marcus, 1886), 20; F. H. R. Frank, *System der Christlichen Wahrheit*, 2 vols. (Erlangen: A. Deichert, 1878–80), I, 512ff.; J. Doedes *Encyclopaedie der Christelijke Theologie* (Utrecht: Kemink, 1876), 190–91; W. Bender, "Zur Geschichte der Emancipation der natürlichen Theologie," *Jahrbuch für Protestantischen Theologie* (1883): 529–92; R. Rütschi, "Die Lehre von der natürlichen Religion und von Naturrecht," *Jahrbuch für Protestantischen Theologie* (1884): 1–48; S. Hoekstra, *Wijsgerige Godsdienst*, I, 19ff.

origin in terms of apostasy from the pure knowledge of God. That knowledge, which was humanity's original possession, did continue for a long time to exert a leavening influence (Gen. 4:3; 8:20), and the creation revealed God's eternal power and divinity (Rom. 1:20). But people, though knowing God, did not honor him as God or give thanks to him and became futile in their thinking, and their senseless minds were darkened. In addition, the confusion of tongues and the dispersion of the peoples (Gen. 11) were certainly also of great influence for the development of polytheism.[52] The Hebrew word גּוֹי (the mass of people or nation united by origin and language), alongside עַם (the people connected by a unified government), also suggests this. For גּוֹיִם (Gr. ἔθνη) is commonly used to denote Gentile nations and refers not only to peoples but also to pagans. The word has a national but also an ethno-religious meaning, as does the Latin *pagani* and our word "heathen."[53]

At the breakup of the human race into separate peoples, the oneness of God and hence the purity of religion was lost. Every people or nation acquired its own national god. Once the concept of the unity and absoluteness of God had been lost, other powers could gradually be recognized and venerated as gods alongside of that one national god. As the idea of the divine became impure and declined, the various forces of nature came to the fore and increased in importance. The boundary between the divine and the creaturely was erased, and religion could even degenerate into animism and fetishism, sorcery and magic. According to Scripture, therefore, the character of pagan religions consists in idolatry. Heathen gods are idols; they do not exist; they are lies and vanity (Isa. 41:29; 42:17; 46:1f.; Jer. 2:28; Ps. 106:28; Acts 14:15; 19:26; Gal. 4:8; 1 Cor. 8:5). At work in those religions there is even a demonic power (Deut. 32:17; Ps. 106:28; 1 Cor 10:20ff.; Rev. 9:20). The condition in which the pagan world finds itself outside of the revelation to Israel and outside of Christ is described as darkness (Isa. 9:1; 60:2; Luke 1:79; John 1:5; Eph. 4:18), ignorance (Acts 17:30; 1 Pet. 1:14; Rom. 1:10ff.), imaginary and vain wisdom (1 Cor. 1:18f.; 2:6; 3:19f.), as sin and unrighteousness (Rom. 1:24ff.; 3:9f.).

In its origin, character, and destiny, the pagan world is an enormous problem. By itself the solution to this problem that Scripture offers is not only not absurd but even commends itself by its simplicity and naturalness. Nonetheless, both the philosophy of history and the philosophy of religion have not been content with this solution and have put forward another view,

---

52. Origen, *Contra Celsus* V; Augustine, *City of God*, 16:6; F. W. J. Schelling, *Einleitung in die Philosophie der Mythologie*, 2 vols. (Darmstadt: Wissenschaftliche Buchgesellschaft, 1957 [1857]), I, 94. F. Delitzsch, *A New Commentary on Genesis*, trans. Sophia Taylor, 2 vols. (Edinburg: T. & T. Clark, 1899), I, 346–76 (on Gen. 11); C. A. Auberlen, *The Divine Revelation*, trans. A. B. Paton (Edinburgh: T. & T. Clark, 1867), 164ff.; F. Fabri, *Die Entstehung des Heidenthums und die Aufgabe der Heidenmission* (Barmen: W. Langewiesche, 1859).

53. Cf. regarding the meaning of the word *pagan*: Zahn, "Paganus," *Neue Kirchliche Zeitschrift* 10 (1899): 18–44; A. Harnack, *The Mission and Expansion of Christianity* (New York: Harper, 1962), 416–18 (includes n. 1, ed.).

one that is directly antithetical to that of Scripture. Admittedly, the idealization of the childlike state of the peoples, which was in vogue in the eighteenth century, is no longer accepted today. But the theory of evolution, which presently serves as explanation, is equally antithetical to Scripture. Just as the natural sciences attempt to infer the animate from the inanimate, the organic from the inorganic, human beings from the animal world, the conscious from the unconscious, the higher from the lower, so also the science of religion of modern times seeks to explain religion in terms of an earlier areligious state of affairs and pure religion from the primitive forms of fetishism, animism, ancestor worship, etc. Earlier in this volume we have already sufficiently explained and refuted this theory of the origin of religion. But because it bases itself especially on the pagan world and derives from it a strong argument for its correctness, we will now add the following.

In the first place, we may observe with some joy that in the last few years the tone in which many people of science speak has become more modest. A few years ago, when Darwinism and materialism were fashionable, everyone who had the nerve to take a position against them or even dared to express some reservation was immediately ostracized and accused of having a "backwards religion." The animal origin of humanity was then considered, as it is still today by Haeckel, a proven and irrefutable fact. But today there is growing recognition that with all such notions about the origin of human beings, their language, religion, and morality, (etc.), we find ourselves in the area of the prehistorical where no one knows anything with certainty and that, scientifically speaking, we must therefore be content with suspicions and conjectures. Thus Reinke writes that, though he believes that the natural scientist cannot dispense with the [Darwinian] theory of descent as hypothesis, "we must unreservedly acknowledge that not a single fully unobjectionable proof for its correctness is available to us."[54] And as it specifically concerns the origin of religion, Pfleiderer recently testified: "What do we know about the origins of religion? Strictly speaking, nothing! For all the historical documents fail by a long shot to reach back to the first beginnings of religion, as they do to the beginnings of language. To be honest, we know absolutely nothing about the earliest conditions of humankind and will never know anything that is certain about them. We can only put forward our hunches about them, which insofar as they are based on conclusions from what is known may have greater or less probability, but must always in fact be distinguished from certain knowledge. Since none of these hypotheses can be proven, we need not argue about them either."[55]

54. J. Reinke, *Die Entwicklung der Naturwissenschaften* (Kiel: Universitäts Buchhandlung [P. Toeche], 1900), 19, 20.

55. O. Pfleiderer, *Religion und Religionen* (München: J. F. Lehmann, 1906), 53; cf. Hellwald *Kulturgeschichte*, 4 vols. (Leipzig: Friesenhann, 1896), I, 11, 32, 58; L. Stein, *Die Soziale Frage im Lichte der Philosophie*, 2d ed. (Stuttgart: F. Enke, 1903), 38, 63, 105, 107; C. P. Tiele, *Elements*, II, 215; G. T. Ladd, *Philosophy of Religion*, 2 vols. (New York: Scribner, 1905), I, 150.

Second, the appeal to the religions of primitive peoples as proof by analogy for the character of the original religion is, for various reasons, inadmissible. For though scholars may speak of primitive (savage) people, or nature-
peoples, strictly considered such peoples do not exist. All the peoples we
know possess intellect and reason, language and religion, morality and law.
Though they may be culturally poor, they are not without culture. Hence,
on an evolutionary position, original religion is not to be found among
them either; such religion lies far behind them. To have gotten where they
really are now they must, according to this same evolutionary theory, have
experienced a development extending over centuries. For that reason Hellwald comments: "Even the coarsest savages of the present have obviously
reached a higher cultural level than we can attribute to the Ur-humans."[56] If
that is the case, the possibility remains that in the case of these primitive peoples we are dealing, not with evolution, but with a process of devolution. In
any case this is something that cannot be settled a priori; history shows that
frequently also in religion decline rather than progress set in. Even Pfleiderer
cautions us in this regard: "For we cannot say in advance that the religion of
savages is really only the undeveloped beginning of all human religion. The
possibility of retrogression, of a degeneration of higher beginnings, is all the
less to be ignored when in fact symptoms of it occur frequently."[57]

Third, it is a remarkable fact that, when we leave the domain of conjec-
ture and surmise behind and with the help of history try to go back as far as
we can into humanity's past, we encounter among the most ancient peoples
in Babylonia and Assyria in high antiquity a culture that astonishes us. We
also encounter a religion that was originally more pure but later became
corrupted and even from the beginning bore a more or less monotheistic
character. Schelling therefore already in his day expressed the opinion that
the original religion was a relative monotheism. Max Müller assumed a so-
called henotheism as primitive religion.[58] In recent years many scholars
have therefore asserted that basic to all religions—not only the ancient religion of Babylonia but all pagan religions—there was an original monotheism.[59] As a matter of fact, one has to come to some such conclusion if and
as long as one believes in the truth and value of religion. In the religions
one then has to distinguish between a pure and impure development. In

56. Hellwald, *Kulturgeschichte*, I, 11.
57. Pfleiderer, *Religion und Religionen*, 54; Tiele, *Elements*, II, 215.
58. Müller, "Vorlesung über Ursprung und Entwicklung der Religion," *Theologische Rundschau* 2
(September 1898): 292; Rauwenhoff, *Wijsbegeerte van de Godsdienst* (Leiden: Brill & Van Doesburgh,
1887), 95ff., 191ff.; S. Hoekstra, *Wijsgerige Godsdienstleer* (Amsterdam: Van Kampen, 1894, 1895), 146;
Pfleiderer, *Religion und Religionen*, 64.
59. See the following works in the bibliography: Quirmbach; Stahl; Lüken; Fabri; Schelling (Mythologie); Diestel; Tholuck; Zöckler (Urstand, "Polytheismus"); E. L. Fischer; J. N. Sepp; C. Pesch (*Gott und
Götler*); Steude; G. Stosch; Grützmacher; also see J. Calvin, *Institutes*, II.ii.12ff.; J. H. A. Ebrard, *Apologetics*, trans. William Stewart and John MacPherson, 2d ed., 3 vols. (Edinburgh: T. & T. Clark, 1886–87), II,
520ff. Henry Formby and Cornelius Krieg, *Der Monotheismus der Offenbarung und des Heidenthum*

other words a distinction must be made between true and false religion (even if one avoids the terms). Superstition in that case can no more be the primitive form and origin of pure religion than a lie can be the origin of truth or vice the origin of virtue. Certainly the least one then has to acknowledge is that one must judge the essence of a religion, not by its most primitive beginnings, but by its later times of flourishing, just as one can only know the child from the mature adult and an acorn from the oak that grows from it.[60] But then that highest point of development must already have been inherent in the earliest beginning as its leading idea and dynamic. And by analogy one is forced, whether one wants to or not, to posit the idea of God, which is the foundation of all religion, not at the end but at the beginning. Without God, without the acknowledgment of his existence, his revelation and his knowability, one cannot satisfactorily explain the origin and essence of religion.

But, however severely Scripture judges the character of paganism, it is precisely the general revelation it teaches that enables and authorizes us to recognize all the elements of truth that are present also in pagan religions. In the past the study of religions was pursued exclusively in the interest of dogmatics and apologetics. The founders of [non-Christian] religions, like Mohammed, were simply considered impostors, enemies of God, accomplices of the devil.[61] But ever since those religions have become more precisely known, this interpretation has proven to be untenable; it clashed both with history and psychology. Also among pagans, says Scripture, there is a revelation of God, an illumination by the Logos, a working of God's Spirit (Gen. 6:17; 7:15; Ps. 33:6; 104:30; Job 32:8; Eccles. 3:19; Prov. 8:22f.; Mal. 1:11, 14; John 1:9; Rom. 2:14; Gal. 4:1–3; Acts 14:16, 17; 17:22–30). Many church fathers (Justin Martyr, Clement of Alexandria, and others), assumed an operation of the Logos in the pagan world. Although Augustine repeatedly spoke very unfavorably about pagans, he nevertheless recognized that they saw adumbrations of the truth,[62] that the truth was not wholly concealed from them,[63] and, accordingly, that we must take advantage of the truth elements in pagan philosophy and appropriate it.[64] "Still, since God's image has not been so completely erased in the soul of man by the stain of earthly affections, as to have left remaining there not even the merest lineaments of it, whence it might be justly said that man, even in the ungodliness

(Mainz: F. Kirchheim, 1880); *Leopold von Schroeder, in *Beiträge zur Weiterentwicklung der Christliche Religion*, 1–39; A. Jeremias, *Monotheïstische Strömungen innerhalb der babylonischen Religion* (Leipzig: J. C. Hinrichs, 1904); H. Winckler, *Die Weltanschauung des Alten Orients* (Leipzig: E. Pfeiffer,1904).

60. Pfleiderer, *Religion und Religionen*, 5; Tiele, *Elements*, II, 141–42; Ladd, *Philosophy of Religion*, I, 34, 103, 144.

61. Cf. Snouck Hurgronje, "De Islam," *De Gids* 50 (1886): 239–73, 454–98.

62. Augustine, *City of God*, XIX, 1; *On the Trinity*, IV, 20.

63. Augustine, *City of God*, VIII, 11.

64. Augustine, *On Christian Doctrine*, II, 60.

of his life, does or appreciates some things contained in the law."[65] Also many impure people recognize much that is true.[66]

In the Middle Ages Thomas not only asserted that as rational beings human beings can—without supernatural grace—know natural truths but also testifies that it is impossible for there to be "some knowledge which is totally false without any admixture of some truth" and in this connection appeals to the words of Beda and Augustine: "There is no false doctrine which does not at some time mix some truth with falsehoods."[67] The Reformed theologians were even better positioned to recognize this by their doctrine of common grace. By it they were protected, on the one hand, from the Pelagian error, which taught the sufficiency of natural theology and linked salvation to the sufficiency of natural theology, but could, on the other hand, recognize all the truth, beauty, and goodness that is present also in the pagan world. Science, art, moral, domestic, and societal life, etc., were derived from that common grace and acknowledged and commended with gratitude.[68] As a rule this operation of common grace, though perceived in the life of morality and intellect, society and state, was less frequently recognized in the religions of pagans. In the latter context the Reformed only spoke of natural religion, innate and acquired, but the connection between this natural religion and the [pagan] religions was not developed. The religions were traced to deception or demonic influences. However, an operation of God's Spirit and of his common grace is discernible not only in science and art, morality and law, but also in the religions. Calvin rightly spoke of a "seed of religion," a "sense of divinity."[69] Founders of religion, after all, were not impostors or agents of Satan but men who, being religiously inclined, had to fulfill a mission to their time and people and often exerted a beneficial influence on the life of peoples. The various religions, however mixed with error they may have been, to some extent met people's religious needs and brought consolation amidst the pain and sorrow of life. What comes to us from the pagan world are not just cries of despair but also expressions of confidence, hope, resignation, peace, submission, patience, etc. All the elements and forms that are essential to religion (a concept of God, a sense of guilt, a desire for redemption, sacrifice, priesthood, temple, cult, prayer, etc.), though corrupted, nevertheless do also occur in pagan religions. Here and there even unconscious predictions and striking expectations of a better and purer religion are voiced. Hence Chris-

---

65. Augustine, *On the Spirit and the Letter*, chap. 48.

66. Augustine, *Retractions*, I, chap. 4.

67. Aquinas, *Summa Theol.*, I 2 qu. 109 art. 1; II 2 qu. 172 art. 6.

68. J. Calvin, *Institutes*, II.ii.13; J. Zanchius, *Opera*, VIII, 646ff.; P. Wittwrongel, *Oeconomia Christiana ofte Christelicke Huys-houdinghe* (Amsterdam, 1661), 288, 299; H. Witsius, *The Oeconomy of the Covenants*, 3 vols. (New York: Lee & Stokes, 1798), III, 12, 52; idem, *Twist des Heeren met zijn Wijngaart*, (Utrecht: Balthasar Lobe, 1692), chap. 19; F. Turretin, *Institutes of Elenctic Theology*, X, 5; Vossius, *Hist. Pelag.*, III, 3; Pfanner, *Syst. Theol. Gent.*, xxii, 33; Trigland, *Antapologia*, chap. 17; B. de Moor, *Comment*, IV, 826–29.

69. J. Calvin, *Institutes*, I.iii.1–3; I.iv.1; II.ii.18.

tianity is not only positioned antithetically toward paganism; it is also paganism's fulfillment. Christianity is the true religion, therefore also the highest and purest; it is the truth of all religions. What in paganism[70] is the caricature, the living original is here. What is appearance there is essence here. What is sought there can be found here. Christianity is the explanation of "ethnicism." Christ is the Promised One to Israel and the desire of all the Gentiles. Israel and the church are elect for the benefit of humankind. In Abraham's seed all the nations of the earth will be blessed.[71]

GENERAL REVELATION AND CHRISTIAN DISCIPLESHIP

[89] Yet general revelation has meaning not only for the pagan world but also in and for the Christian religion. Its value, however, does not consist in the fact that it has furnished us a natural theology or religion, a faith of moral reason, which by itself would be enough for us and could dispense with all that is concrete in religion. Such a natural religion cannot be found anywhere, nor can it exist. Neither is it the intent of general revelation that Christians should draw from it their first knowledge of God, the world, and humanity in order later to augment this knowledge with the knowledge of Christ. Ritschl and his followers picture the earlier dogmaticians working on the loci of God and humanity as only drawing the materials from general revelation and subsequently drawing the material for the subsequent loci from Scripture. In that scenario dogmaticians would first take their position outside of and prior to the Christian faith and then position themselves in that faith in dealing with the later dogmas.[72] But this was not the method of reformational dogmatics, at least not in the beginning. When Christians confess their faith in God the Father Almighty, Creator of heaven and earth—that is Christian faith in the full sense of the term. And dogmaticians do not first divest themselves of their Christian faith in order to construct a rational doctrine of God and humanity and in order later to supplement it with the revelation in Christ. But they draw their knowledge solely and alone from special revelation, i.e., from Scripture. This is their unique principle.

70. Ed. note: *Paganism* here and later in this paragraph is a translation of Bavinck's Dutch term *ethnicisme*. The primary meaning of the Greek word ἔθνος in the biblical context is "Gentile."

71. See the works of Fabri, Sepp, Tholuck, et al., in n. 59, above, and the bibliography. In addition, see Clement of Alexandria, *Stromata*, 1, 1; 4, 5; 6, 8; idem, *Exhortation to the Heathen*, §6; Origen, *Contra Celsus*, 4, 4; A. Ritschl, *Rechtfertigung und Versöhnung*, 2d. ed., III, 184; F. Philippi, *Kirchliche Glaubenslehre*, 6 vols. (Gütersloh: Bertelsmann, 1902), I, 2; J. T. Beck, *Einleitung in das System der christlichen Lehre*, 2d. ed. (Stuttgart: J. F. Steinkopf, 1870), 45ff.; H. Bavinck, *De Theologie van Prof. Dr. Chantepie de la Saussaye*, 2d. rev. ed. (Leiden: D. Donner, 1903), 31ff., 46ff., 83ff.; *V. von Strauss & Torney, "Das unbewust Weissagende im vorchristliche Heidenthum," in *Zeitschrift des Christliche Volkslebens*, VIII; F. A. Staudenmaier, *Encyklopädie der Theologischen Wissenschaften*, 2d ed. (Mainz: Florian Kupferberg, 1840), §428ff. (reprinted by Minerva: Frankfurt, 1968); Nitzsch, *Lehrbuch der Evangelische Dogmatik*, 134ff.; A. Kuyper, *Encyclopaedie der Heilige Godgeleerdherd*, 2d. ed., 3 vols. (Kampen: Kok, 1908–9), III, 445ff.; 563ff.

72. A. Ritschl, *Rechtfertigung und Versöhnung*, III, 4.

Stated differently, Reformed theology does not restrict this special revelation to the person of Christ as it is delineated in certain sections of Scripture, say, in the Synoptic Gospels or only in the Sermon on the Mount. The whole of revelation, summed up in Scripture, is a special revelation that comes to us in Christ. Christ is the center and content of that whole special revelation, which starts in Paradise and is completed in the Apocalypse. Now special revelation has recognized and valued general revelation, has even taken it over and, as it were, assimilated it. And this is also what the Christian does, as do the theologians. They position themselves in the Christian faith, in special revelation, and from there look out upon nature and history. And now they discover there as well the traces of the God whom they learned to know in Christ as their Father. Precisely as Christians, by faith, they see the revelation of God in nature much better and more clearly than before. The carnal person does not understand God's speech in nature and history. He or she searches the entire universe without finding God. But Christians, equipped with the spectacles of Scripture,[73] see God in everything and everything in God. For that reason we find in Scripture a kind of nature poetry and view of history such as is found nowhere else. With their Christian confession, accordingly, Christians find themselves at home also in the world. They are not strangers there and see the God who rules creation as none other than the one they address as Father in Christ. As a result of this general revelation, they feel at home in the world; it is God's fatherly hand from which they receive all things also in the context of nature.

In that general revelation, moreover, Christians have a firm foundation on which they can meet all non-Christians. They have a common basis with non-Christians. As a result of their Christian faith, they may find themselves in an isolated position; they may not be able to prove their religious convictions to others; still, in general revelation they have a point of contact with all those who bear the name "human." Just as a classic preparatory education forms a common foundation for all people of learning, so general revelation unites all people despite their religious differences. Subjectively, in the life of believers, the knowledge of God from nature comes after the knowledge derived from Scripture. We are all born in a certain concrete religion. Only the eye of faith sees God in his creation. Here too it is true that only the pure of heart see God. Yet objectively nature is antecedent to grace; general revelation precedes special revelation. Grace presupposes nature.[74] To deny that natural religion and natural theology are sufficient and have an autonomous existence of their own is not in any way to do an injustice to the fact that from the creation, from nature and history, from the human heart and conscience, there comes divine speech to every human. No one escapes the power of general revelation. Religion belongs to

73. Raymond de Sabunde, *Theologia Naturalis* (*Prologus*); J. Calvin, *Institutes*, I.vi.1.

74. In keeping with this objective order, the dogmatician should consider general revelation before special revelation, and not the reverse, as Kaftan does: J. Kaftan, *Dogmatik* (Tübingen: Mohr, 1901), 40ff.

the essence of a human. The idea and existence of God, the spiritual independence and eternal destiny of the world, the moral world order and its ultimate triumph—all these are problems that never cease to engage the human mind. Metaphysical need cannot be suppressed. Philosophy perennially seeks to satisfy that need. It is general revelation that keeps that need alive. It keeps human beings from degrading themselves into animals. It binds them to a supersensible world. It maintains in them the awareness that they have been created in God's image and can only find rest in God. General revelation preserves humankind in order that it can be found and healed by Christ and until it is. To that extent natural theology used to be correctly denominated a "preamble of faith," a divine preparation and education for Christianity. General revelation is the foundation on which special revelation builds itself up.

Finally, the rich significance of general revelation comes out in the fact that it keeps nature and grace, creation and re-creation, the world of reality and the world of values, inseparably connected. Without general revelation, special revelation loses its connectedness with the whole cosmic existence and life. The link that unites the kingdom of nature and the kingdom of heaven then disappears. Those who, along with critical philosophy, deny general revelation exert themselves in vain when via the way of practical reason or of the imagination they try to recover what they have lost. They have then lost a support for their faith. In that case the religious life exists in detachment from and alongside of ordinary human existence. The image of God then becomes a "superadded gift" (*donum superadditum*). As in the case of the Socinians, religion becomes alien to human nature. Christianity becomes a sectarian phenomenon and is robbed of its catholicity. In a word, grace is then opposed to nature. In that case it is consistent, along with the ethical moderns, to assume a radical break between the power of the good and the power of nature. Ethos and φύσις are then totally separated. The world of reality and the world of values have nothing to do with each other. In that scenario we at bottom face a revival of Parsism or Manichaeism. By contrast, general revelation maintains the unity of nature and grace, of the world and the kingdom of God, of the natural order and the moral order, of creation and re-creation, of φύσις and ethos, of virtue and happiness, of holiness and blessedness, and in all these things the unity of the divine being. It is one and the same God who in general revelation does not leave himself without a witness to anyone and who in special revelation makes himself known as a God of grace. Hence general and special revelation interact with each other. "God first sent forth nature as a teacher, intending also to send prophecy next, so that you, a disciple of nature, might more easily believe prophecy" (Tertullian). Nature precedes grace; grace perfects nature. Reason is perfected by faith, faith presupposes nature.[75]

75. Cf. P. Hofstede de Groot, *Institutio Theologia Natura*, 4th. ed. (Groningen: W. Zuidema, 1861); J. Scholten, *Leer der Hervormde Kerk*, I, 270ff.; A. Kuyper, "Vruchten der Naturlijke Godskennis," *Uit het Woord* (Amsterdam: Höveker & Wormser, n.d.), III, 216–19; H. Voigt, *Fundamentaldogmatik* (Gotha: F. A. Perthes, 1874), 172ff.

11

SPECIAL REVELATION

Religion cannot survive on general revelation alone; a special divine disclosure or manifestation is needed. All religion can be reduced to three basic means. First, religious belief desires a God who is near so that in almost every religion there are holy places, holy times, and holy images. Second, in all religions one can find the belief that the gods in some way reveal their will to human beings. Finally, there is a universal belief in the special assistance of the gods in times of distress. Belief in manifestation, prediction, and miracle are thus necessary elements in all religions. Biblical religion may share some forms with other religions (sacrifices, temples, priests), but its substance is categorically different. In Scripture God takes the initiative; the Messiah came forth only from Israel.

A frequent mode of biblical revelation is a perceptible divine presence, a theophany (angelophany). These manifestations do not presuppose God's corporeality nor are they emanations of the divine Being. These appearances can be impersonal presence (wind, fire) or via personal beings (angels). Among God's envoys the Messenger of God occupies a special place. This theophany is still incomplete; theophany reaches its climax in Jesus Christ.

Prophecy, or "inspiration," is another mode of revelation; in it God communicates his thoughts to human beings. This address can be an audible voice, a dream, a vision, or a communication by casting lots (Urim and Thummim). Again, in form these are similar to their function in nonbiblical religions, though significant differences remain. Unlike the Greek seers, the biblical recipients of revelation did not experience a suppression of consciousness. Biblical prophetic ecstasy occurred in a state of conscious wakefulness, and most revelations to prophets occurred apart from visionary experience but through the inward illumination of the Holy Spirit. This is confirmed by the New Testament's testimony concerning the Old Testament's prophetic word.

While the Holy Spirit in the Old Testament comes upon a person momentarily, it is not until the New Testament that the supreme and definitive prophet makes his appearance. While some individual believers are still equipped by the Holy Spirit for the office of prophet, it is more important to underscore the universal prophetic task of all believers. Prophecy as a special gift is destined to pass away in the New Jerusalem.

In miracles God reveals himself by his works. Word and deed go together; God's word is an act, and his activity is speech. God's works are first to be ob-

served in creation and providence, which are an ongoing work and a miracle. A distinction must be maintained, however, between the ordinary order of nature and extraordinary deeds of divine power. In a special way, the latter are miracles, God doing something new. Thus the history of salvation is replete with miracles until the consummation. The anticipation of this final glory can be seen in the powerful signs of the kingdom performed by Jesus as acts of healing and restoring creation. When Christianity became established, God began to manifest his power and glory in spiritual miracles. Miracles have ceased until the fullness of Christ's kingdom comes in all its glory.

God's self-revelation to us does not come in bits and pieces; it is an organic whole, a grand narrative from creation to consummation. All nature and history testify to God the Creator; all things return to him. Fallen humanity sees this revelation only in part and with blinded eyes. A special revelation is needed that is provided in grace. In this revelation God makes himself known to us as the Triune God, Father, Son, and Holy Spirit. This revelation is historical and progresses over the course of many centuries, reaching it culmination in Jesus Christ, the Mediator of creation and redemption. From this history we discover that revelation is not exclusively addressed to the human intellect. In Christ, God himself comes to us in saving power. At the same time we must not make the opposite error and deny that revelation communicates truth and doctrine. Revelatory word and deed belong together in God's plan and acts of salvation.

Finally, the purpose and goal of special revelation is God's own trinitarian glory, his delight in himself. The aim of revelation is to re-create humanity after the image of God, to establish the kingdom of God on earth, to redeem the world from the power of sin, and thus to glorify the name of the Lord in all his creatures. In addition to the objective work of Christ in revelation and redemption, the work of the Spirit is needed to enable human beings to acknowledge and accept the divine revelation and thereby become the image of the Son. God redeems and reveals; we know, understand, and believe. Revelation and religion are distinct but not separable. Revelation is possible only if God has a personal existence distinct from the world and possesses the will and power to reveal himself in deeds and words.

[90] History teaches us that not a single religion can survive on general revelation alone. The Christian religion too bases itself on a special revelation, and Scripture is the book of special revelation. The words by which Scripture expresses the concept of revelation are mainly these: גלה, to uncover (niphal: be uncovered, display, appear, be revealed; Gen. 35:7; 1 Sam. 2:27; 3:21; Isa. 53:1; 56:1; Hos. 7:1; etc.); ראה, to see (niphal: be seen, show oneself, appear; Gen. 12:7; 17:1; 18:1; etc.); ידע, to know (niphal, piel, hiphal, hithpael: make known, teach; Num. 12:6); ἐπιφανειν, to appear (Luke 1:79; Titus 2:11); subst. ἐπιφανεια, appearance, especially of Christ's return (2 Thess. 2:8; 1 Tim. 6:14; 2 Tim. 4:1; Titus 2:13; 2 Tim. 1:10 of Christ's first coming); ἐμφανιζειν, to manifest oneself, make oneself visible; passive, show oneself, appear (Matt. 27:53; John 14:21, 22); γνωριζειν, to

make known (Luke 2:15; Rom. 9:22; Eph. 3:3, 5, 10); δηλουν, to make known, disclose, reveal (1 Pet. 1:11; 2 Pet. 1:14); δεικνυναι, to show (John 5:20); λαλειν, to speak (Heb. 1:1; 2:2; 5:5); especially also ἀποκαλυπτειν and φανερουν. These two words are not to be differentiated as subjective, internal illumination versus objective, external display or manifestation, as Scholten thought,[1] inasmuch as ἀποκαλυπτειν is repeatedly used with reference to objective revelation (Luke 17:30; Rom. 1:17, 18; 8:18; Eph. 3:5; 2 Thess. 2:3, 6, 8; 1 Pet. 1:5; 5:1). Neither does the distinction between them consist, as Neander believed,[2] in that φανερουν denotes God's general revelation in nature, while ἀποκαλυπτειν denotes the special revelation of divine grace; for φανερουν is repeatedly used for special revelation (John 17:6; Rom. 16:26; Col. 1:26; 1 Tim. 3:16; 2 Tim. 1:10; etc.); and ἀποκαλυπτειν also occurs (Rom. 1:18) as a word for general revelation. A consistent difference in the use of the two words can hardly be demonstrated from the NT. Etymologically, however, ἀποκαλυπτειν indicates the removal of a cover by which a given object was hidden, and φανερουν denotes making known a matter that was hidden or unknown before. In the former, then, the stress is on the removal of a hindrance that prevented knowledge of what was hidden, on the mysterious nature of what up until then had not been understood, and on the divine deed that removed the cover and caused the mystery to be understood. The latter word generally indicates that something that was hidden and unknown before has now become manifest and public. Ἀποκαλυψις takes away the cause by which something was hidden; φανερωσις makes known the matter itself. Associated with this distinction is that φανερωσις is always used of objective revelation, while ἀποκαλυψις is used both of objective and subjective revelation. Also, φανερωσις repeatedly denotes both general and special revelation, but ἀποκαλυψις almost always refers to special and only rarely to general revelation. And these two words are in turn distinguished from γνωριζειν and δηλουν by the fact that the former two verbs bring things to light and the latter two, in consequence of this, now also make these things into the content of our thinking consciousness.[3]

1. J. H. Scholten, *De Leer der Hervormde Kerk,* 2d ed., 2 vols. (Leiden: P. Engels), I, 163ff., idem, *Dogmatices Christianae,* 2d ed. (Lyons: P. Engels, 1858), I, 26.

2. A. Neander, *Geschichte der Pflanzung und Leitung der christlichen Kirche durch die Apostel,* 5th ed. (Gotha: Friedrich Andreas Perthes, 1862), 131ff.

3. Cf. F. G. B. van Bell, *Disputatio academica de patefactionis Christianae indole e vocabulis "φανερόω et ἀποκρύπτω" in libris N.T. efficienda* (Lugduni-Batavorum: P. Engels, 1849); A. Niermeijer, "Het Wezen der Christelijke Openbaring," *De Gids* 14 (1850): 109–49; *Rauwenhoff, *De Zelfstandigheid van den Christen* (1857); *Cramer, *Jaarboek van Wetenschappelijke Theologie* (1870): 1–70; Hermann Cremer, *Biblisch-theologisches Wörterbuch der neutestamentlichen Gräcität* (Gotha: F. A. Perthes, 1880); in English, *Biblico-Theological Lexicon of New Testament Greek,* trans. William Urwick, 4th ed. (Edinburgh: T. & T. Clark; New York: Scribner, 1892); Heinrich Voigt, *Fundamentaldogmatik* (Gotha: F. A. Perthes, 1874), 201ff.; E. H. Van Leeuwen, *Prolegomena van Bijbelsche Godgeleerheid* (Utrecht: C. H. E. Breijer, 1890), 41ff.

MODES OF REVELATION

The Christian religion, accordingly, is similar to all other historical religions in that it bases itself on revelation. But the similarity does not stop there; it extends also to the forms and modes in which revelation occurs. All the means of revelation can be reduced to three. In the first place, religious belief desires a God who is near and not far away (Acts 17:27); it was at all times convinced, therefore, that gods appeared in one form or another, under one sign or another, and at one place or another. In almost every religion there are holy places, holy times, and holy images. The gods are not like human beings and do not live with them on equal terms. The sphere of the sacred is separate from that of the profane. Still, the gods do live near and among human beings at certain places, in special objects, and impart their blessing at certain times. Idolatry, taken in its broadest sense, is born of the human need for a God who is near.[4] Integral to all religions, secondly, is the belief that the gods in some way make known their thoughts and will, either by human beings as their mediums, such as fortune-tellers, oracles, dreamers, necromancers, occult visionaries, etc., or, artificially and externally, by the stars, the flight of birds, the entrails of sacrificial animals, the play of flames, the lines of the hand, the chance opening of a book, etc., divination. "No man ever became great without some kind of divine inspiration."[5] Present in all religions, finally, is belief in the special intervention and assistance of the gods in times of distress. Widespread everywhere is magic: the art by which, using mysterious means, sacred words and formulas, amulets, liquors, etc., people make the divine power subservient to themselves and produce marvelous effects.[6] Theophany, mantic, and magic are the ways by which all revelation comes to human beings.

This universal religious belief in manifestation, prediction, and miracle is certainly not—in any case not exclusively—to be attributed to deception or demonic effects nor to ignorance of the natural order but is a necessary element in all religion. Religious need seeks satisfaction; and where it is not met in a real revelation from God, it seeks it in the way of "will-worship" (ἐθελοθρησκεία). It takes into its service those mysterious powers inherent in human beings or in nature that can bring that need in rapport with a supernatural world. Superstition is an illegitimate surrogate for true religion and a caricature

4. P. D. Chantepie de la Saussaye, *Lehrbuch der Religionsgeschichte,* 2 vols. (Tübingen: J. C. B. Mohr [Paul Siebeck], 1905), I, 54ff., 114ff.

5. Cicero, *De natura deorum,* II, 66 [modern English edition, *The Nature of the Gods,* trans. P. G. Walsh (New York: Clarendon Press, 1997)]; cf. concerning divination and oracles Auguste Bouché-Leclercq, *Histoire de la divination dans l'antiquité,* 4 vols. (Paris: E. Leroux, 1879–82); de la Saussaye, *Lehrbuch,* I, 93ff.

6. Joseph Ennemoser, *Geschichte der Magie,* 2d ed. (Leipzig: F. A. Brockhaus, 1844); in English translation as *The History of Magic,* trans. William Howitt (London and New York: George Bell & Sons, 1893); Alfred Wiedeman, *Magie und Zauberei im alten Ägypten* (Leipzig: J. C. Hinrichs, 1905); A. G. L. Lehmann, *Aberglaube und Zauberei von den ältesten Zeiten an bis in die Gegenwart* (Stuttgart: F. Enke, 1898); de la Saussaye, *Lehrbuch,* I; Zöckler, "Magier, Magie," *PRE*[3], XII, 55–70.

of [Christian] faith (πιστις). The contemporary phenomena of spiritism, theosophy, telepathy, magnetism, hypnosis, etc. are proof of this. Perhaps they also demonstrate that concealed in the so-called "dark side" of human nature there are forces that can effect a more immediate rapport with a supersensible world and can in any case sufficiently explain belief in such rapport without recourse to the hypothesis of intentional deception. "There are more things in heaven and earth than are dreamt of in your philosophy" (Shakespeare).

Holy Scripture does not seem to deny all reality to such phenomena (Gen. 41:8; Exod. 7:8–12; Deut. 13:1, 2; Matt. 7:22; 24:24; 2 Thess. 2:9; 2 Tim. 3:8; Rev. 13:13–15). But the religion of OT and NT absolutely refuses to have anything in common with all these religious phenomena. It is fundamentally opposed to them. It neither recognizes nor tolerates them, but categorically forbids them (Lev. 19:26, 31; 20:27; Num. 23:23; Deut. 18:10, 11; Acts 8:9; 13:6; 16:16; 19:13f.; Gal. 5:20; Rev. 21:8; 22:15). Prophets and apostles alike are utterly opposed to being put on a par with pagan fortune-tellers and magicians. Sometimes, for example in appearances to the patriarchs, there may be correspondence in form, but there is no such correspondence in substance. Theophany, mantic, and magic, like offerings, temple priesthood, cult, etc., are essential elements in religion. Thus they occur in all religions, also in that of Israel and Christianity. Also the Christian religion has its sacrifice (Eph. 5:2), its priest (Heb. 7), its temple (1 Cor. 3:16f., etc.). The difference between Christianity and the other religions does not consist in that all these necessary elements of religion are lacking there; it consists in that all that occurs in paganism in the form of caricature has become shadow and image in Israel and authentic spiritual reality in Christianity. This may explain why in form, circumcision, sacrifice, tabernacle, priesthood, etc., the religion of Israel bears so much resemblance to pagan religions on the one hand and is fundamentally different from them on the other, so that the Messiah came forth only from Israel. This fundamental distinction arises from the fact that in Scripture the initiative in religion is not taken by human beings but by God. In pagan religions it is human beings who seek God (Acts 17:27). In every way they attempt to bring God down to themselves and into the dust (Rom. 1:23), and by all kinds of methods they try to achieve power over God. But in Scripture it is always God who seeks human beings. He creates them in his image and calls them after the fall. He saves Noah, chooses Abraham, gives his laws to Israel. He calls and equips the prophets. He sends his Son and sets apart the apostles. He will one day judge the living and the dead. The religions of the nations,[7] on the other hand, teach us to know human beings in their restlessness, misery, and discontent but also in their noble aspirations and their everlasting needs—human beings both in their poverty and riches, their weakness and strength. The noblest fruit of these religions

---

7. Ed. note: The phrase "religions of the nations" renders a single Dutch word, *Ethnicisme*. This word appears to have been coined by Bavinck, and the translation provided here is illumined by the context of the larger paragraph.

produces humanism. But Holy Scripture teaches us to know God in his coming to and search for human beings, in his compassion and grace, in his justice and his love. And here, too, theophany, prophecy, and miracle are the means by which God reveals and gives himself to people.[8]

Theophany (Angelophany, Christophany)

[91] In Scripture there are repeated references to divine appearances, sometimes without any circumstantial description (Gen. 12:7; 17:1, 22; 26:24; 35:9; Exod. 6:2; also cf. Gen. 11:5; Exod. 4:24; 12:12, 23; 17:6; Num. 23:4, 16; 1 Sam. 3:21; 2 Sam. 5:24), but elsewhere in a dream (Gen. 20:3; 28:12ff., 31:24; 1 Kings 3:5; 9:2), or in a prophetic vision (1 Kings 22:19ff.; Isa. 6; Ezek. 1:4ff.; 3:12f.; 8:4f.; 10:1f.; 43:2f.; 44:4; Amos 7:7; 9:1; Dan. 7:9f.; Luke 2:9; 2 Pet. 1:17), and even more frequently in clouds of smoke and fire as signs of his presence; thus to Abraham (Gen. 15:17f.), to Moses (Exod. 3:2; 33:18f.), on Sinai (Exod. 19:9, 16f.; 24:16, cf. vv. 9–11; Deut. 5:23; 9:15; Heb. 12:18), to the people (Exod. 13:21f.; 14:19–24; 40:38; Num. 9:21; 14:14; Deut. 1:33; Neh. 9:12, 19; Ps. 78:14), above the tabernacle (Exod. 33:9; 40:34f.; Lev. 9:23; Num. 9:15–23; 11:17, 25; 12:5; 17:7; 20:6; Deut. 31:15; Ps. 99:7; Isa. 4:5), and in the holy of holies (Exod. 25:8, 22; 29:45, 46; Lev. 16:2; 26:11, 12; Num. 7:89); cf. also to Elijah (1 Kings 19:11f.). These appearances do not presuppose God's corporeality (Exod. 20:4; 33:20; Deut. 4:12, 15) but are perceptible signs by which his presence is made known, just as on Pentecost the Holy Spirit made himself known by wind and fire. Nor are we to think in this connection of the emanation of this cloud from the divine Being but of the divine presence revealing itself in creaturely forms. In those signs the divine glory (כבוד, δόξα) is manifested (Exod. 16:10; 24:17; Lev. 9:6, 23, 24; Num. 14:10; 16:19; 20:6), and for that reason that glory is also described as a consuming fire (Exod. 24:17; Lev. 9:23, 24) and as a cloud (1 Kings 8:10, 11; Isa. 6:4).

God does not appear only in impersonal signs, however, but also visits his people in personal beings. Surrounded and served by many thousands of angels (Isa. 6:2, 6), he sends them to the earth in human form to make known his word and will. They already occur in Genesis 18; 19; 28:12; 32:1, 2; Deuteronomy 33:2; Job 33:23; 1 Kings 13:18; and, according to Acts 7:53 and Galatians 3:19, serve at the time of the giving of the law but function as mediators of revelation especially after the exile (Dan. 8:13;

---

8. *G. F. Oehler, *Über Verhältniss der alttestamentische Prophetie zur Heiden* (Mantik: 1861); idem, *Theologie des Alten Testaments*, 2 vols. (Stuttgart: J. F. Steinkopf, 1882), I, 29ff.; in English: *Theology of the Old Testament*, trans. Ellen D. Smith and Sophia Taylor (Edinburgh: T. & T. Clark, 1892–93), §8, II, 28ff.; August Tholuck, *Die Propheten und ihre Weissagungen* (Gotha: F. A. Perthes, 1860), §1; F. A. Staudenmaier, *Encyklopädie der theologischen Wissenschaften als System der gesammten Theologie* (Mainz; Wien: F. Kupferberg; K. Gerold, 1834); §231ff., §271ff. H. Schulz, *Alttestamentliche Theologie*, 4th ed., 2 vols. (Frankfurt a.M: von Heyder & Zimmer, 1889), 226ff.

9:21; 10:5; Zech. 1:7–6:5). They appear even more frequently in the NT. They are present at the birth of Jesus (Matt. 1:20; 2:13, 19; Luke 1:11; 2:9), repeatedly in his life (John 1:51; Matt. 4:6), at the time of his suffering (Matt. 26:53; Luke 22:43), and at the resurrection and ascension (Matt. 28:2, 5; Luke 24:23; John 20:12; Acts 1:10). In the history of the apostles, they repeatedly make appearances (Acts 5:19; 8:26; 10:3; 11:13; 12:7; 23:9; 27:23; Rev. 22:6, 16). Finally, at his return Christ will be accompanied by the angels (Matt. 16:27; 25:31; Mark 8:38; Luke 9:26; 1 Thess. 3:13; etc.).

Among all these envoys of God the Messenger of the Lord (מלאך יהוה) occupies a special place. He appears to Hagar (Gen. 16:6–13; 21:17–20); to Abraham (Gen. 18; 19; 22; 24:7; 40); to Jacob (Gen. 28:13–17; 31:11–13; 32:24–30; cf. Hos. 12:4; Gen. 48:15, 16); to, and at the time of, Moses (Exod. 3:2f.; 13:21; 14:19; 23:20–23; 32:34; 33:2f.; cf. Num. 20:16; Isa. 63:8, 9; and further also Josh. 5:13, 14; Judg. 6:11–24; 13:2–23). This *Malak* YHWH is not an independent symbol nor a created angel but a true personal revelation and appearance of God, distinct from him (Exod. 23:20–23; 33:14f.; Isa. 63:8, 9) and still one with him in name (Gen. 16:13; 31:13; 32:28, 30; 48:15, 16; Exod. 3:2f.; 23:20–23; Judg. 13:3), in power (Gen. 16:10, 11; 21:18; 18:14, 18; Exod. 14:19; Judg. 6:21), in redemption and blessing (Gen. 48:16; Exod. 3:8; 23:20; Isa. 63:8, 9), in adoration and honor (Gen. 18:3; 22:12; Exod. 23:21). Following the redemption from Egypt, the *Malak* YHWH recedes from view; God dwells among his people in the temple (1 Kings 8:10f.; 2 Chron. 7:1f.; Ps. 68:17; 74:2; 132:13f.; 135:21). To that temple the longings of Israel's devout are directed (Ps. 27:4; 42; 43; 48; 50; 63:2; 65; 84; 122; 137). But this theophany is incomplete. God does not dwell in a house made by human hands (1 Kings 8:27; Jer. 7:4; Mic. 3:11; Acts 7:48; 17:24). The high priest was allowed to enter the Holy of Holies only once every year. In the OT theophany does not yet reach its end and its goal. For that reason still another, more glorious coming of God to his people is expected, with a view to both redemption and judgment (Ps. 50:3; 96:13; Isa. 2:21; 30:27, 40f., passim; Mic. 1:3; 4:7; Zeph. 3:8; Joel 3:17; Zech. 2:10f.; 14:9). The angel of the covenant again appears in prophecy (Zech. 1:8–12:3) and will come to his temple (Mal. 3:1). Theophany reaches its climax, however, in Christ who is the ἀγγελος, δοξα, εἰκων, λογος, υἱος του θεου, in whom God is fully revealed and fully given (Matt. 11:27; John 1:14; 14:9; Col. 1:15; 2:19; etc.). By him and by the Spirit whom he sends forth, the dwelling of God in and among his people even now becomes a true spiritual reality (John 14:23; Rom. 8:9, 11; 2 Cor. 6:16). The believing community is [now] the house of God, the temple of the Holy Spirit (Matt. 18:20; 1 Cor. 3:16; 6:19; Eph. 2:21). But even this indwelling of God in the church of Christ is not yet of the final and highest order. It attains its full realization only in the New Jerusalem. Then the tabernacle of God will be with his people; he will dwell among them; they will be his people, and God himself will be with them and be their God. They will see his face, and his name will be on their foreheads (Matt. 5:8; 1 Cor. 15:28; 1 John 3:2; Rev. 21:3; 22:4).[9]

Prophecy

[92] By prophecy we here mean God's communication of his thoughts to human beings. Often the word *inspiration* is used for this and is also more accurate insofar as the concept of prophecy is broader than that of inspiration, including as it does also the announcement of those thoughts to others. But, on the basis of 2 Timothy 3:16, inspiration is especially used with reference to written revelation. In the past the word *prophecy* was repeatedly employed in the sense in which we used it above.[10] It also includes the reception of the thoughts of God, because only that person is a prophet who proclaims God's Word. It brings out better than inspiration the intent of God with which he communicates his thoughts, viz., that human beings themselves should be prophets and proclaimers of his virtues. Now the thoughts of God that are communicated in prophecy may relate to the past, as is the case in the historical books of Scripture, or to the present, or to the future. But prophecy consistently opposes the thoughts of God to the thoughts of human beings, his truth to their lies, his wisdom to their folly.

According to Scripture, this communication of God's thoughts to human beings can take place in various ways. Sometimes God himself speaks audibly with a human voice and in human language (Gen. 2:16; 3:8–19; 4:6–16; 6:13; 9:1, 8f.; 32:26f.; Exod. 19:9f.; Num. 7:89; Deut. 5:4; 1 Sam. 3:3f.; Matt. 3:17; 17:5; John 12:28, 29). In many places, God is introduced as speaking, without any further description of the manner in which that speech occurs, externally or internally, in a dream or a vision, etc. This speech of God is most personal and intimate in the case of Moses, who is not terrified, nor falls to the ground when God speaks to him, but with whom God spoke "mouth to mouth" and associated as friends (Num. 12:6–8; Exod. 33:11; 34:29; Deut. 5:5; 18:15, 18; 2 Cor. 3:7; Gal. 3:19; Heb. 3:5). The Jews later spoke of a Bath-Kol, a heavenly voice, by which God re-

9. Cf. Emil Kautzsch, "Theophanie," *PRE²*, XV, 537–42; Mallet, "Schechia," *PRE²*, XIII, 458–59; Orelli, "Feuer und Wolkensäule," *PRE³*, VI, 60–62; G. B. Winer, "Wolken und Feuersäule," *Biblisches Realwörterbuch*, 2 vols. (Leipzig: C. H. Reclam, 1847–48); C. J. Trip, *Die Theophanien in den Geschichtsbuechern des Alten Testaments* (Leiden: D. Noothoven van Goor, 1858), and the literature cited there; Hermann Schultz, *Alttestamentliche theologie*, 2d ed. (Göttingen: Vandenhoeck & Ruphrecht, 1889), 507ff.; G. F. Oehler, *Theology of the Old Testament*, §58, I, 187ff.; Rudolf Smend, *Lehrbuch der alttestamentlichen Religionsgeschichte* (Freiburg i.B. and Leipzig: J. C. B. Mohr, 1893), 42ff.; F. W. Weber, *System der altsynagogalen palastinischen Theologie* (Leipzig: Dörffling & Franke, 1880), 179ff.; Cremer, *Wörterbuch*, s.v. "doxa"; F. Delitzsch, *Biblische Psychologie* (Leipzig: Dörffling & Franke, 1861), 49; in English: *A System of Biblical Psychology*, trans. Robert E. Wallis, 2d ed. (Edinburgh: T. & T. Clark, 1875), 59–61; P. F. Keerl, *Die Lehre des Neuen Testaments von der Herrlichkeit Gottes* (Basel: Bahnmaier, 1863); Van Leeuwen, *Prolegomena van Bijbelsche Godgeleerheid*, 72ff.

10. Thomas Aquinas, *Summa Theologica*, II, 2, qu. 171, art. 1.

vealed himself, but this "voice" ranked lower than the earlier prophecy and came after the spirit of prophecy had ceased.[11]

In communicating his thoughts, however, God frequently adopted those lower forms by which also among pagans the gods were deemed to make known their will. In those cases there is almost complete correspondence in form. Especially to be mentioned in this connection are the lot, the Urim and Thummim, the dream, and the vision. The lot was used on many occasions: on the great Day of Atonement (Lev. 16:8); in dividing the land (Josh. 13:6; 14:2, etc.; Neh. 11:1), the cities of the Levites (Josh. 21:4), the booty (Joel 3:3; Nah. 3:10; Obad. 11), and garments (Matt. 27:35; John 19:23); in deciding difficult cases (Josh. 7:1ff; 1 Sam. 14:42; Prov. 16:33; 18:18; Jonah 1:7); in elections to office (1 Sam. 10:19; Acts 1:26; 1 Chron. 24:5; Luke 1:9; etc.); also the trial by ordeal (Num. 5:11–31) can be counted in this category.[12] The Urim and Thummim (LXX δηλωσις και αληθεια; Vulg. doctrina et veritas), light and justice, occur seven times (Exod. 28:30; Lev. 8:8; Num. 27:21; Deut. 33:8; 1 Sam. 28:6; Ezra 2:63; Neh. 7:65). They are not, as Josephus thinks and many others after him as well, identical with the twelve precious stones on the high priest's breast-piece, but, according to Exodus 28:30 and Leviticus 8:8, objects secured in the breastpiece. But how they made known God's will—by the glitter of the stones, by a voice, by inspiration, etc.; and in what they consisted—in two stones with the tetragrammaton, or in little images, or in a neck chain made of one of the precious stones, or in stones for casting lots—is entirely unknown. This last opinion has in relatively recent times gained support in the text of 1 Samuel 14:41, as altered by Thenius (1842) in keeping with the LXX. The Urim and Thummim are then said to be lots with "yes" and "no" answers and were also used (Judg. 1:1; 20:18; 1 Sam. 22:10, 15; 23:6, 9–11; 30:7f.; 2 Sam. 2:1; 5:19, 23). But in that light it is hard to explain the answers, not of yes or no, but of elaborate length (Judg. 20:27; 1 Sam. 30:7f.; 2 Sam. 5:23; 21:1; Judg. 1:1; 20:18; 2 Sam. 2:1; esp. 1 Sam. 10:22b; 2 Sam. 5:23; 1 Chron. 14:14). The Urim and Thummim, however, must certainly have been of the same revelatory character as the lot. Instances of their use occur especially in the time of Solomon and then seem to have yielded to real prophecy.[13]

11. F. W. Weber, *System der altsynagogalen palästinischen Theologie* (Leipzig: Dörffling & Franke, 1880), 187; G. Dalman, "Bath Kol (Gottesstimme)," *PRE³*, II, 443.

12. Benzinger, "Los bei den Hebräern," *PRE³*, XI, 642.

13. Emil Kautzsch, "Urim & Thummim," *PRE²*, XVI, 226–33; Winer, "Urim & Thummim," *Realwörterbuch*; Riehm, "Urim & Thummim," *Wörterbuch*; C. F. Keil, *Manual of Biblical Archaeology*, trans. A. Cusin, 2 vols. (Edinburgh: T. & T. Clark, 1887–88), I, §35; W. M. L. De Wette and Julius Räbiger, *Lehrbuch der hebräisch-jüdischen Archäologiei* (Leipzig: F. C. W. Vogel, 1864), 281ff.; G. F. Oehler, *Theology of the Old Testament*, §97, I, 318ff.; Hermann Schultz, *Alttestamentliche Theologie*, 4th ed., 2 vols. (Göttingen: Vandenhoeck & Ruprecht, 1889), 507ff.; Henry E. Dosker, "Urim and Thummim," *Presbyterian and Reformed Review* 3 (October 1892): 717–30; G. Wildeboer, "Urim en Thummim in de Priester wet," *Theologische Studien* 23 (1905): 195–204.

Also dreams occur in Scripture as means of revelation. Throughout antiquity they were considered as such means.[14] Still in our day many people attach great value to dreams.[15] Now it was always known that dreams were also very deceptive. Not only Homer and Aristotle but also Holy Scripture regularly point to the vanity of dreams (Ps. 73:20; Job 20:8; Isa. 29:7; Eccles. 5:3, 6; Sir. 31:1f.; 34:1f.) and frequently ascribe them to false prophets (Jer. 23:25; 29:8; Mic. 3:6; Zech. 10:2). Despite this fact God nevertheless repeatedly uses dreams to make known his will (Num. 12:6; Deut. 13:1–6; 1 Sam. 28:6, 15; Joel 2:28f.); they occur among Israelites but also repeatedly among non-Israelites (Gen. 20; 31; 40; 41; Judg. 7; Dan. 2 and 4), and convey either a word, a communication from God (Gen. 20:3; 31:9, 24; Matt. 1:20; 2:12, 19, 22; 27:19), or a representation of the imagination, which then often requires explanation (Gen. 28; 37:5; 40:5; 41:15; Judg. 7:13; Dan. 2 and 4).[16]

Akin to the dream is the vision (Gen. 15:1, 11; 20:7; Num. 12:6). Just the names (נביא הזה ראה, and perhaps also צפה) by which the prophet is called[17] and the names מראה and חזון for prophetic vision probably indicate that a vision was a not unusual means of revelation. But these words have often lost their original meaning and are also used when no actual vision has occurred (1 Sam. 3:15; Isa. 1:1; Obad. 1; Nah. 1:1; etc.). In Scripture we regularly encounter the reports and descriptions of visions, from Genesis to Revelation (Gen. 15:1; 46:2; Num, 12:6; 22:8–13; 24:3; 1 Kings 22:17–23; Isa. 6; 21:6; Jer. 1:11–14; 24:1; Ezek. 1–3; 8–11; 40; Dan. 1:17; 2:19; 7; 8; 10; Amos 7–9; Zech. 1–6; Matt. 2:13, 19; Luke 1:22; 24:23; Acts 7:55; 9:3; 10:3, 10; 16:9; 22:17; 26:19; 1 Cor. 12–14; 2 Cor. 12:1; Rev. 1:10; etc.). Visions were often accompanied by a kind of ecstatic experience. Music, dance, and ecstasy go together; prophecy and poetry are related (1 Sam. 10:5f.; 19:20–24; 2 Kings 3:15; 1 Chron. 25:1; 2 Chron. 29:30). When the hand of the Lord comes upon the prophets (Isa. 8:11; Ezek. 3:14; 11:5) or the Spirit comes upon them, they frequently enter a state of rapture (Num. 24:3;

---

14. Homer, *Odyssey*, XIX, 560ff., II.I.63; II.22.56; Aristotle, *De Somniis (On Dreams)*, 1–3; Cicero, *On Divination*, I, 29; Philo, *de somniis*.

15. Franz Splittgerber, *Schlaf und Tod*, 2d ed., 2 vols. (Halle: Julius Fricke, 1881), I, 66–205.

16. B. Orelli, "Träume," *PRE²*, XVI, 734; *G. E. W. de Wijs, *De droomen in en buitem de Bijbel* (1858).

17. Abraham Kuenen, *De Profeten en de Profetie onder Israël*, 2 vols. (Leiden: P. Engels, 1875), I, 49, 51ff.; 97; in English as *The Prophets and Prophecy in Israel*, trans. Adam Milroy (London, 1877; reprinted, Amsterdam: Philo, 1969), 41–42, 43ff., 83–84; idem, *De godsdienst van Israel tot den ondergang van den Joodschen Staat*, 2 vols. (Haarlem: A. C. Kruseman, 1869, 1870), I, 212; in English as *The Religion of Israel to the Fall of the Jewish State*, trans. A. H. May, 3 vols. (London: Williams and Norgate, 1874, 1875), I, 213ff.; idem, *Historisch-critisch onderzoek naar het ontstaan en de verzameling van de boken des Ouden Verbonds*, 3 vols. (Leiden: P. Engels en Zoon, 1885, 1893), II2, 5ff.; Eduard König, *Der Offenbarungsbegriff des Alten Testamentes*, 2 vols. (Leipzig: J. C. Hinrichs, 1882), I, 71; F. Delitzsch, *Commentar über die Genesis*, 3d ed. (Leipzig: Dörffling und Franke, 1860), 634; in English: *A New Commentary on Genesis*, trans. S. Taylor, 2 vols. (Edinburgh: T. & T. Clark, 1894, 1888), II, 1ff., 8, 68; Hermann Schulz, *Alttestamentliche Theologie* (Göttingen: Vandenhoeck und Ruprecht, 1896), 239; R. Smend, *Lehrbuch der Alttestamentlichen Religionsgeschichte* (Freiburg: J. C. B. Mohr, 1893), 79ff.

2 Kings 9:11; Jer. 29:26) and fall to the earth (Num. 24:3, 15, 16; 1 Sam. 19:24; Ezek. 1:28; 3:23; 43:3; Dan. 10:8–10; Acts 9:4; Rev. 1:17; 11:16; 22:8). In that state they are given to see and hear the thoughts of God in symbolic form. In images and visions his counsel is revealed to them (Jer. 1:13f.; 24:1f.; Amos 7–9; Zech. 1–6; Rev.; etc.), especially with regard to the future (Num. 23f.; 1 Kings 22:17; 2 Kings 5:26; 8:11f.; Jer. 4:23f.; 14:18; Ezek. 8; Amos 7; etc.). In that state they also hear a variety of voices and sounds (1 Kings 18:41; 2 Kings 6:32; Isa. 6:3, 8; Jer. 21:10; 49:14; Ezek. 1:24, 28; 2:2; 3:12; Rev. 7:4; 9:16; 14:2; 19:1; 21:3; 22:8; etc.) They are even taken up in the spirit and translocated (Ezek. 3:12f.; 8:3; 43:1; Dan. 8:2; Matt. 4:5, 8; Acts 9:10, 11; 22:17; 23:11; 27:23; 2 Cor. 12:2; Rev. 1:9; 12; 14:1; 21:10). After the reception of a vision, Daniel was sick for some days (7:28; 8:27).

Still, the state of ecstasy in which the recipients of revelation frequently found themselves was not one in which their consciousness was totally or partly suppressed. Such was in fact the state in which the Greek seers (μαντεις) uttered their oracles.[18] Philo, Justin Martyr, Athenagoras, Tertullian, and in modern times Hengstenberg[19] so viewed the ecstasy of the prophets. These, however, received visions not in a state of sleep but of wakefulness, not only when they were alone but also in the presence of others (Ezek. 8:1). While receiving the vision they remained conscious of themselves, saw, heard, thought, spoke, raised questions, and gave answers (Exod. 4–6; 32:7f.; Isa. 6; Jer. 1; Ezek. 4–6; etc.) and later remembered everything and gave an accurate report of it.[20] For that reason the psychic state of the prophets when receiving a vision was considered by most theologians to be a process of self-conscious spiritual visioning, an "alienation of the mind from the bodily senses" but not an "alienation from the mind."[21] Only König, in order to maintain the objectivity of a vision, has added to this view the peculiar opinion that all visions were external, physical, and perceptible by the senses. Many appearances, as in Genesis 18, 32; Exodus 3, 19, etc., are indeed, according to the authors' intent, to be considered objective. There is a difference between a theophany and a vision. But the above-mentioned visions (1 Kings 22:17f.; Isa. 6; Jer. 1; Ezek. 1–3; Dan.; Amos 7–9; Zech. 1–6; etc.) are certainly internal and spiritual. Many of them are of a kind that are not perceptible and observable by the senses. König goes too far when he

18. Tholuck, *Die Propheten*, 64ff.; cf. Thomas Achelis, *Die Ekstase in ihrer kulturellen Bedeutung* (Berlin: J. Räde, 1802).

19. In the 1st ed. of his *Christology of the Old Testament*, III, 2, 158ff.

20. König, *Offenbarungsbegriff*, I, 160ff.; Kuenen, *Prophets and Prophecy*, 40–41; Oehler, *Theology of the Old Testament*, §207, II, 318ff.; *Orelli, *PRE²*, XVI, 724.

21. Origen, *On First Principles*, III, 3, 4; Augustine, *Against Simplician* II, qu. 1; Aquinas, *Summa Theologica*, II, 2 qu. 175; H. Witsius, *De Propheten*, I, c. 4; J. F. Buddeus, *Institutiones theologiae dogmaticae* (1724), I, 2, 5. In more recent work, Häverdink, *O.T. Introduction*; Keil, *O.T. Introduction*; Oehler, *Theology of the Old Testament*, §210, II, 330ff.; Tholuck, *De Propheten*, 64ff.; Dr. Küper, *Das Prophetenthum des Alten Bundes* (Leipzig: Dörffling und Franke, 1870), 51ff.; B. Orelli, "Weissagung" *PRE²*, XVI, 724; König, *Offenbarungsbegriff*, II, 132ff.

makes the objectivity and truth of a revelation depend on its external character and cannot conceive of an internal operation of God's Spirit in the mind of human beings except by way of the external senses. He forgets that there also exist hallucinations of seeing and hearing, that the external as such does not exclude the possibility of self-deception, and therefore that the certainty of revelation is not sufficiently established by its external character.[22]

The last form of revelation to be mentioned is interior illumination. Hengstenberg[23] believed that ecstasy was the usual state in which the prophet found himself when receiving a revelation. But many scholars, Riehm and König[24] (among others), have opposed this opinion, and today that rejection is universal; ecstasy, so far from being the rule, is the exception. Also in the OT most revelations to the prophets occurred without any vision, e.g., in the case of Isaiah, Haggai, Malachi, Obadiah, Nahum, Habakkuk, Jeremiah, Ezekiel. Granted, the word "vision" was still frequently used for divine prophecy, but this also occurs where nothing has been seen (Isa. 1:1; 2:1; Amos 1:1; Hab. 1:1; 2:1; 1 Sam. 3:15; Obad. 1; Nah. 1:1; etc.). The revelation then occurs inwardly by the Spirit as the Spirit of revelation. König[25] indeed has stated that the Spirit is not the principle of revelation but only the principle of illumination; i.e., it is YHWH who reveals, and the Spirit only makes people subjectively receptive to that revelation. König came to this position in order to maintain the objectivity and externality of revelation and to bind the subjective Spirit to the objective word of YHWH. But Numbers 11:25–29; Deuteronomy 34:9; 1 Samuel 10:6; 19:20f.; 2 Samuel 23:2; 1 Kings 22:24; 1 Chronicles 12:18; 28:12; 2 Chronicles 15:1; 20:14f.; 24:20; Nehemiah 9:30; Isaiah 11:1; 30:1; 42:1; 48:16; 59:21; 61:1; 63:10f.; Ezekiel 2:2; 3:24; 8:3; 11:5, 24; Micah 3:8; Hosea 9:7; Joel 2:28; and Zechariah 7:12 cannot be understood exclusively in terms of a formal subjective enabling of the Spirit. They clearly teach that the prophets spoke not only by the power of the Holy Spirit but from the Spirit, that the prophecy proceeded from the Spirit that was within them. Certainly there was also an enabling activity of the Spirit that rendered the prophet subjectively able to prophesy, but this is not the sole activity of the Spirit. It cannot be so rigorously separated from the revelatory activity of the Spirit as König does, nor is it even necessary on König's position, a position in which revelation is wholly external.[26] Furthermore, even

22. Orelli, *PRE²*, XVI, 724; Kuenen, *Historische Critische Onderzoek*, II 2, 13; Van Leeuwen, *Bijbelsche Godgeleerdherd*, 62ff.; P. Borchert, "Die Visionen der Propheten," *Theologische Studien und Kritiken* 68 (1895): 217–51.

23. Hengstenberg, *Christology of the Old Testament*, III², 2, 158ff.; cf. Küper, *Das Prophetenthum*, 53ff.

24. Eduard Riehm, *Die messianische weissagung*, 2d ed. (Gotha: F. A. Perthes, 1885), 15ff.; in English: *Messianic Prophecy*, trans. Lewis A. Muirhead (Edinburgh: T. & T. Clark, 1891); König, *Offenbarungsbegriff*, II, 48ff., 132ff.

25. König, *Offenbarungsbegriff*, I, 104ff., 141ff., 155ff.

26. A. Kuenen, *Historisch-Critisch Onderzoek*, II, 14.

the "lying spirit" in 1 Kings 22:22 clearly teaches that the Spirit of God is the source of the word. Jewish theology saw the Spirit as a source not only of illumination but also of revelation and prophecy.[27]

The New Testament with equal clarity asserts that the OT prophets spoke from and by the Spirit of God (Acts 28:25; 1 Pet. 1:11; 2 Pet. 1:21). There is indeed a distinction in the manner in which the Holy Spirit inwardly imparts revelation in the Old and New Testament. In the OT the Holy Spirit comes down from above and momentarily upon a person. He came down upon the prophets (Num. 24:2; 1 Sam. 19:20, 23; 2 Chron. 15:1; 20:14); came mightily upon them (Judg. 14:19; 15:14; 1 Sam. 10:6); fell upon them (Ezek. 11:5); put them on as a garment (Judg. 6:34; 1 Chron. 12:18); the hand, i.e., the power of the Lord, seized them (Isa. 8:11; Ezek. 1:3; 3:22; 8:1; 37:1; 40:1). In the face of this working of the Spirit, accordingly, the prophets are mostly passive; they are silent, fall to the earth, are appalled, and find themselves for a time in an abnormal, ecstatic state. The Spirit of prophecy is not yet the permanent possession of the prophets. There is still some separation and distance between the two; and the class of prophets is still separated from the people as a whole. Prophecy as a whole is still imperfect. It therefore looks forward and expects a prophet on whom the Spirit of the Lord will rest (Deut. 18:18; Isa. 11:2; 61:1); indeed, it predicts the fulfillment of Moses' wish that all the people of the Lord might be prophets (Num. 11:29); and testifies to a future dwelling of God's Spirit in all the Lord's children (Isa. 32:15; 44:3; 59:21; Joel 2:28; Ezek. 11:19; 36:27; 39:29).

In the NT the supreme, the unique and true prophet makes his appearance. As Logos he is the full and complete revelation of God (John 1:1; 18; 14:9; 17:6; Col. 2:9). He does not receive a revelation from above or from outside of himself but is himself the source of prophecy. The Holy Spirit does not come upon him and does not fall upon him but indwells him without measure (John 3:34). From that Spirit he was conceived; by that Spirit he speaks, acts, lives, and dies (Matt. 3:16; 12:28; Luke 1:17; 2:27; 4:1, 14, 18; Rom. 1:4; Heb. 9:14). That Spirit he endows upon his disciples, not only as the Spirit of regeneration and sanctification, but also as the Spirit of revelation and illumination (Mark 13:11; Luke 12:12; John 14:17; 15:26; 16:13; 20:22; Acts 2:4; 6:10; 8:29; 10:19; 11:12; 13:2; 18:5; 21:4; 1 Cor. 2:12f.; 12:7–11). Certain special individuals are still equipped for the office of prophet by that Spirit (Rom. 12:7; 1 Cor. 14:3; Eph. 2:20; 3:5; etc.), nor is true prediction lacking in the NT (Matt 24; Acts 20:23; 21:10; 1 Cor. 15; 2 Thess. 2; Revelation). Still, now all believers have the anointing of the Spirit (1 John 2:20) and are taught by the Lord (Matt. 11:25–27; John 6:45). All are prophets who proclaim the excellencies of the Lord (Acts 2:17f.; 1 Pet. 2:9). Prophecy as a special gift will pass away (1 Cor. 13:8). In

27. Weber, *System der altsynagogalen palastinischen Theologie*, 184–87.

the new Jerusalem, the name of God will be upon everyone's forehead, and falsehood will be completely excluded (Rev. 21:27; 22:4, 15).[28]

Miracles

[93] Just as human beings, aside from their appearance and words, also make themselves known by their deeds, so God not only reveals himself by his words but also by his works. Word and deed are intimately connected. God's Word is an act (Ps. 33:9), and his activity is speech (Ps. 19:2; 29:3; Isa. 28:26). Word and deed accompany each other, both in creation and re-creation. Usually the word comes first, as a promise and a threat, but in principle it already contains within itself a deed. God's Word does not return to him empty, but it accomplishes what he wants (Isa. 55:10, 11). The word demands the deed; miracle accomplishes prophecy; not only consciousness but being itself must be renewed. The words in Scripture by which the deeds or works of God are denoted differ. In terms of their external appearance, they are נִפְלָאוֹת, wonders (Exod. 3:20; 34:10; Ps. 71:17); פֶּלֶא, extraordinary events (Exod. 15:11; Isa. 25:1); and מוֹפְתִים, something splendid (Exod. 4:21; 7:9; Ps. 105:5), the latter two rendered in the Greek by τέρατα, something special, unusual, which differs from ordinary events. They are called גְּבוּרוֹת (Deut. 3:24; Ps. 21:14 MT [21:13 Eng.]; 54:3 MT [54:1 Eng.]; 66:7); δυνάμεις, מַעֲשִׂים (Ps. 8:7; 19:2 MT [19:1 Eng.]; 103:22; Isa. 5:19); or עֲלִילוֹת (Ps. 9:12 MT [9:11 Eng.]; 77:13 MT [77:12 Eng.]), mighty works, ἔργα μεγαλεῖα, on account of the great divine power that is manifest in them. They are also—and especially—called אוֹתוֹת signs (Exod. 3:12; 12:13; etc.) because they are a demonstration and sign of God's presence.

Those works of God are, first of all, to be observed in his creation and providence. All God's words are wonders. Also his works are frequently described in Scripture as wonders (Ps. 77:13; 97:3; 98:1; 107:24; 139:14). From this fact, however, we must not infer, with Scholten,[29] that Scripture makes no distinction between nature and miracle. Certainly the notion that a miracle would be contrary to the laws of nature and therefore impossible does not arise. All of Scripture proceeds rather from the belief that nothing is too wonderful for God (Gen. 18:14; Deut. 8:3f.; Matt. 19:26). This does not imply, however, that Scripture lacks the distinction between the ordinary order of nature and the extraordinary deeds of divine power. The OT knows a stable natural order, ordinances that apply for heaven and earth and are firmly established in the expressed will of the Lord (Gen. 1:26, 28; 8:22; Ps. 104:5, 9;

---

28. Further on prophecy, in addition to the literature already cited, see Carl H. Cornill, *Der Isaelitische Propetismus* (Strassburg: Trübner, 1894); F. Giesebrecht, *Die Berufsbegabung der Alttestamentliche Propheten* (Göttingen: Vandenhoeck & Ruprecht, 1897); Rudolf Kittel, *Profetie und Weissagung* (Leipzig: J. C. Hinrichs, 1899); E. König, *Das Berusungsbewusstsein der alttestamentlichen Propheten* (Barmen: Wupperthaler Traktat Gesellschaft, 1900); A. B. Davidson, *Old Testament Prophecy* (Edinburgh: T. & T. Clark, 1903).

29. J. H. Scholten, *Supranaturalisme in Verband met Bijbel Christendom en Protestantisme* (Leiden, 1867), 9ff.

119:90, 91; 148:6; Eccles. 1:10; Job 38:10f.; Jer. 5:24; 31:35f.; 33:20, 25). And the NT makes an equally clear distinction between the two (Matt. 8:27; 9:5, 24, 33; 13:54; Luke 5:9; 7:16; 8:53; John 3:2; 9:32; etc.). Miracles are a בְּרִיאָה, a creation, something new that has never been seen otherwise (Exod. 34:10; Num. 16:30). The facts reported in Scripture as miracles are still regarded as such by us; on the qualification of those facts there is no difference.[30] Scripture indeed further acknowledges that also outside of divine revelation unusual forces can be at work and unusual things can happen (Exod. 7:11, 22; 8:7, 18; 9:11; Matt. 24:24; Rev. 13:13ff.). A sign or a miracle by itself, therefore, is not enough to seal the reliability of a prophet (Deut. 13:1–3). It is only the God of Israel, however, who does miraculous things (Ps. 72:18; 77:14; 86:10; 136:4). Sometimes he himself directly brings about these miracles; sometimes he employs human beings or angels. But always it is God who does them. It is his power (δυναμις) that is manifest in them (Luke 5:17; 6:19; Mark 7:34; Luke 11:20; John 3:2; 5:19f.; 10:25, 32; Acts 2:22; 4:10). It is the Spirit of the Lord who brings them about (Matt. 12:38; Acts 10:38).

Miracles have their starting point and foundation in the creation and maintenance of all things, which is an ongoing work and miracle of God (Ps. 33:6, 9; John 5:17). All that happens has its final ground in the will and power of God. Nothing can withstand him. He does with the host of heaven what he pleases (Isa. 55:8f.; Ps. 115:3). This power and freedom of God is proclaimed by nature (Jer. 5:22; 10:12; 14:22; 27:5; Isa. 40:12; 50:2, 3; Ps. 33:13–17; 104; Job 5:9f.; 9:4f.; etc.) but emerges especially in the history of his people (Deut. 10:21; 11:3; 26:8; 29:2; 32:12f.; Ps. 66:5f.; 74:13f.; 77:15f.; 78:4f.; 135:8f.; Isa. 51:2, 9; Jer. 32:20f.; Acts 7:2f.). Especially in this history miracles make their appearance. They occur for various reasons, sometimes to punish the wicked (Gen. 6:6f., 11, 19; Exod. 5f.; Lev. 10:1; Num. 11:30f.; 14:21; 16:1f.; 21:6; etc.; Matt. 8:32; 21:19; Acts 13:11; etc.), other times to save and redeem God's people, to bring salvation and healing, like the plagues in Egypt, the passage through the Red Sea, the miracles in the wilderness, the healings of Jesus. Frequently also they have the direct or indirect purpose of confirming the mission of the prophets, the truth of their word, and thus belief in their witness (Exod. 4:1–9; Deut. 13:1f.; Judg. 6:37f.; 1 Sam. 12:6f.; 1 Kings 17:24; 2 Kings 1:10; 20:8; Isa. 7:11; etc.; Matt. 14:33; Luke 5:24; John 2:11; 3:2; 5:36; 6:14; 7:31; 9:16; 10:38; 12:37; Acts 2:22; 10:38; etc.). Prophecy and the gift of miracle go together. All the prophets, and the apostles as well, are aware of their ability to perform miracles. Moses was great also in his miracles (Exod. 5–15; Deut.

---

30. J. Köstlin, "Wunder" *PRE²*, XVII, 360; *A. Pierson, *Gods Wondermacht en ons Geestelijk Leven* (Leiden, 1867), 10ff.; P. Gloatz, "Wunder und Naturgesetz," *Theologische Studien und Kritiken* 59 (1886): 408ff.; W. Bender, *Der Wunderbegriff des Neuen Testaments* (Frankfurt: Verlag von Heyder & Zimmer, 1871), 100ff.; H. Schultz, *Alttestamentliche Theologie*, 577ff.; P. Kleinert, "Naturanschauung des A.T.," *Theologische Studien und Kritiken* 64 (1891): 1ff.; Justus Köberle, *Natur und Geist nach der Auffassung des Alten Testaments* (München: C. H. Beck, 1901), passim, esp. 231ff., 260ff.

34:10–12). His sin on one occasion consisted in doubting God's miraculous power (Num. 20:10f.). Grouped around Elijah and Elisha there is a cycle of miracles (1 Kings 17–2 Kings 13). In the case of the later prophets, the miracles no longer figure so largely. Frequently they employ so-called symbolic actions in order thereby to underscore their prophecy and provisionally to realize them, as it were (1 Kings 11:29–39; 20:35f.; 22:11; Isa. 7:3; 8:1; 20:2f.; 21:6; 30:8; Jer. 13; 16; 18; 19; 25:15; 27; 28:10f.; 32:6f.; 43:8f.; Ezek. 4; 5; 6:11; 7:23; 12:3; 17:1f.; Hos. 1–3; Acts 21:10f.)[31] Still also in connection with them we are told of miracles and they, too, are convinced of their ability to perform them (Isa. 7:11; 16:14; 21:16; 38:7; cf. 2 Kings 20; Jer. 22:12, 30; 28:16; 29:22; 36:20; 37:7f.; Dan. 1–6).

Yet for all their number these OT miracles did not effect an elevation or renewal of [human] nature. They certainly had their effect. They alternately rebuked and blessed humanity, in any case kept it from destroying itself. In Israel they created a special people, redeemed it from Egyptian bondage, kept it from coalescing with pagans, and protected the people of God against the oppressive power of nature. But they were momentary, incidental; they diminished in effect and were forgotten. Life resumed its usual course. Nature seemed to triumph. Then prophecy again raised its voice and proclaimed that Israel could not perish and fade into the naturalistic life of pagans. God would again, and in greater glory, come to his people. God would not forget his covenant; it is an everlasting covenant (Ps. 89:1–5; Isa. 54:10). With that coming of God, the old era passed into the new. That is the turning point in world history. It is the Day of the Lord יֹום יְהוָֹה (יְהוָֹה יֹום) on which he will reveal his glory and display his miraculous power. God will then give miraculous signs in the heavens (Amos 8:8f.; Joel 2:30). All of nature—heaven and earth—will be moved (Amos 9:5; Isa. 13:10, 13; 24:18–20; 34:1–5; Joel 2:2, 10; 3:15; Mic. 1:3f.; Hab. 3:3f.; Nah. 1:4f.; Ezek. 31:15f.; 32:7f.; 38:19f.). The judgment will come upon the ungodly (Isa. 24:16f.) but will also purify and liberate. God will save his people by his miracles (Isa. 9:3; 10:24f.; 11:15f.; 43:16–21; 52:10; 62:8). He does something new on earth (Isa. 43:19), again brings Israel back from death (Ezek. 37:12–14), and causes it to share in a fullness of spiritual and material blessings. Israel will be the recipient of the forgiveness of sins, holiness, a new covenant (Isa. 44:21–23; 43:25; Ezek. 36:25–28; Jer. 31:31f.; Zech. 14:20, 21), but also of peace, security, and prosperity. Even nature will change into a paradise (Hos. 2:17f.; Joel 3:18; Jer. 31:6, 12–14; Isa. 11:6–8; 65:25; Ezek. 34:29; 36:29f.; Zech. 8:12). A new heaven and a new earth is on the way, and the former things will no longer be remembered (Isa. 65:17; 66:22).

This Day of YHWH, this coming aeon, in contrast to the present one, according to Scripture, has dawned in the NT. The coming of Christ is the

---

31. H. Schultz, *Alttestamentliche Theologie*, 250ff.; Smend, *Lehrbuch der Alttestamentlichen Religionsgeschichte*, 88; König, *Offenbarungsbegriff*, II, 111ff.

turning point of the ages. Grouped around his person is a new cycle of miracles. He is himself the absolute miracle, descended from above, and yet the true and complete human. In him, in principle, the creation has been restored, again raised from its fall to its pristine glory. His miracles are the signs (σημεια) of the presence of God, proof of the messianic era (Matt. 11:3–5; 12:28; Luke 13:16), a part of his messianic labor. In Christ there appears a divine power (δυναμις) that is stronger than all the corrupting and destructive power of sin. This latter power he attacks, not only peripherally by healing diseases and performing all kinds of miracles, but centrally, by penetrating the core, breaking and overcoming them. His incarnation and satisfaction, his resurrection and ascension are God's great deeds of redemption. They are in principle the restoration of the kingdom of glory. These facts of salvation are not only means of revelation but are the revelation of God himself. Miracle here becomes history, and history itself is a miracle. The person and work of Christ is the central revelation of God; all other revelation is grouped around this center. But after Jesus' departure, his miraculous power is also continued in the disciples (Matt. 10; Mark 16:18; Luke 8). Many miracles are recounted not only in Acts (2:43; 3:5f.; 5:12–16; 6:8; 8:6, 7, 13; 9:34, 40; 13:11; 14:3; 16:18; 19:11; 20:10; 28:5, 8), but Paul also bears witness to this miracle-working power of the apostles (Rom. 15:18, 19; 1 Cor. 12:9, 10; 2 Cor. 12:12; Gal. 3:5; cf. Heb. 2:4). For a time this power continues to be operative in the church as well. But it *ceased* when Christianity was established and the church became the object in which God glorified the miracles of his grace.[32] It is now spiritual miracles in which God manifests his power and glory.[33] Yet Scripture points to a future in which miracle will again be operative. The coming aeon finally culminates in the new heaven and a new earth in which righteousness dwells. Then miracle will have become "nature." What ought to be and what is will be reconciled. The kingdom of God and the kingdom of the world will then be one (Rev. 21–22).[34]

32. Augustine, *City of God*, XXII, 8; idem, *The Advantage of Believing*, XVI; idem, *On True Religion*, XXV.

33. According to Luther. See J. Köstlin, *The Theology of Luther*, trans. and ed. Charles E. Hay, 2 vols. (Philadelphia: Lutheran Publication Society, 1897), II, 526ff., 571ff.; J. H. Scholten, *De Leer der Hervormde Kerk*, 2d ed., 2 vols. (Leyden: P. Engels, 1850–57), I, 143.

34. On miracles in Scripture, see Neander, *Geschichte der Pflanzung und Leitung der christlichen Kirche* (5th ed.), 49ff., 154ff., 336ff.; August Tholuck, *Vermischte Schriften grösstentheils apologetischen Inhalts*, 2 vols. (Hamburg: F. Perthes, 1839), I, 28ff.; Oehler, *Theology of the Old Testament*, §63, I, 201ff. Schultz, *Alttestamentliche Theologie*, 270ff., 534ff.; Smend, *Lehrbuch*, 88ff.; Wilhelm Bender, *Der Wunderbegriff des Neuen Testaments* (Frankfurt a.M.: Verlag von Heyder & Zimmer, 1871); Philip Schaff, *The Person of Christ: The Miracle of History* (New York: C. Scribner, 1871); Borchert, "Die Wunder der Propheten," *Beweis des Glaubens* 33 (1897): 177–89; Paul Feine, *Das Wunder im Neuen Testament* (Eisenach: M. Wilckens, 1894); Eugene Menegoz, *La notion biblique du miracle* (Paris: Fischbacher, 1894); Richard C. Trench, *Notes on the Miracles of Our Lord* (New York: Appleton, 1870); I. H. Ziese, *Die Gesetz- und Ordnungsgemätzheit der biblischen Wunder* (Schleswig: Johs. Ibbeken, 1903); G. Fulliquet, *Le Miracle dans la Bible* (Paris: Librarie Fischbacher, 1904).

REVELATION AS GOD'S SELF-REVELATION

[94] The revelation that Scripture discloses to us does not just consist in a number of disconnected words and isolated facts but is one single historical and organic whole, a mighty world-controlling and world-renewing system of testimonies and acts of God. The material offered to us is so rich that it is difficult to sum it up in a single term, all the more because Scripture employs not one but many words to describe the action of God by which he makes himself known to human beings. We therefore easily run the danger of neglecting some element or other that actually belongs to revelation or of including another that falls outside of it. Upon detailed consideration and careful arrangement, it is not impossible, however, to present a succinct overview of what Scripture puts forward as and understands by revelation.

In Creation

In the first place, Scripture knows and teaches the type of revelation that theology later designated "natural" or "general" revelation and that was discussed in the previous chapter. The subject also of *this* revelation is the personal, living, and true God. This revelation is still recognized by very many theologians but has been so construed in modern times, under the sway of evolutionary theory, that it runs the risk of losing its objective meaning. If it is nevertheless said that the religious person interprets all things religiously and sees all things in God's hands, these expressions are open to misunderstanding. One may mean by them—and people often do—that as such nature and history do not in an objective sense reveal God but that they are only interpreted by the religious person *as though* they reveal God. This Kantianism, however, is as untenable in theology as it is in philosophy. We have to make a choice: either the religious person thus interprets nature and history correctly and on good grounds, and then there is indeed a revelation of God; or this religious interpretation is without grounds and in that case is pure illusion and a product of the poetic imagination. Holy Scripture, however, teaches us that God very definitely, consciously, and intentionally reveals himself in nature and history, in the heart and conscience of human beings, and adds to this that when people do not acknowledge and understand this revelation, this is due to the darkening of their mind and therefore renders them inexcusable. Hence the conscious, voluntary, acting agent of this general revelation is God alone, the God who is the Creator, maintainer, and ruler of all things; and in the light of Scripture we know it is the Father who by his Word and Spirit also reveals himself in the works of nature and history (Ps. 33:6; 104:30; John 1:3; Col. 1:15; Heb. 1:3).

The means that God employs in this general revelation are the whole of nature and all of history, the history not only of the human race and the various peoples of the earth, but also of the generations, families, and persons; the history of states and societies not only, but also of religions and morals and all of culture. Since nothing has durability except in and through God, nothing is excluded from his revelation. Materially it coincides with God's maintenance of and rule over all things. But not all things are equally revelatory: the finger of God can be more readily perceived in one event than in another. Special persons and events more clearly exhibit God's leading than those that are swallowed up in the stream of time. But ultimately nothing is excluded from general revelation; if our "eyes" were good, we would see God's attributes shine in all that is and all that happens. Accordingly, we best perceive the leading of God in the big and little occurrences of our own life. And while nature and history in this personal sense are the external objective means God employs for this revelation, intellect and reason, conscience and heart are the internal subjective means by which God makes his revelation known to us. Here, too, there is correspondence between the subject and the object. There is revelation of God outside but also in human beings. This revelation of God in human beings, however, is not an independent source of knowledge alongside of nature and history but serves as subjective organ to enable us to receive and understand the revelation of God in nature and history. It is certain that there is an indwelling of God in every person, as much as but more strongly than in nature and history. But the moment we pass from the subconscious to the conscious level and want to learn to know the indwelling of God as a revelation, we as subject are bound to the "object" around us and ascend by way of the creatures to the Creator (Ps. 19:1; Isa. 40:26; Rom. 1:20).

Corresponding to the subject and the means of this revelation are their content and purpose. If God is the author of revelation, it naturally follows that he is also the content of it. All divine revelation is, in the nature of the case, self-revelation; and Scripture further indicates that it is especially the attributes of omnipotence and wisdom, wrath and goodness, that are made known by this revelation (Ps. 90:2; Isa. 40:26; Job 28:25f.; Prov. 8:24f.; Matt. 5:45; Rom. 1:18). It is the deity of God (Rom. 1:20), the existence and essence of an absolutely transcendent divine power, that general revelation makes known to every human being. In a sense we can say that also all knowledge of nature and history as we acquire and apply it in our occupation and business, in commerce and industry, in the arts and sciences, is due to the revelation of God. For all these elements of culture exist only because God has implanted in his creation thoughts and forces that human beings gradually learn to understand under his guidance. Scripture itself testifies of this when it says that it is God who teaches the farmer about the way he has to work the fields (Isa. 28:24–29). But since the creation's existence is distinct from God, and nature and history can also be studied by themselves and for their own sake, knowledge of God and knowledge of his creatures do not coincide, and in the latter case we usually do not speak of revelation as the source of knowledge. But the moment creatures are related to God and considered *sub specie aeternitatis* (under the aspect of eternity), they assume the character of a revelation to us and to some greater or lesser degree make God known to us. The concept of revelation, therefore, is a religious concept; it belongs in the domain of religion. In revelation God becomes knowable. And it is always also the purpose of revelation that human beings should know, serve, and honor God. Revelation indeed has God as its author and content and so also as its final end; God does all things ultimately for his own sake: of him, through him, and to him are all things (Rom. 11:36). But the end of revelation subordinate to this goal is nevertheless always that the rational creature might know and serve God. This also applies, moreover, to general revelation (Acts 14:17; 17:27; Rom. 1:19, 20); there is a real vocation (*vocatio realis*), a calling from God that comes to human beings through nature and history and that, when they do not obey this calling, renders them inexcusable.

To Fallen Humanity

[95] Since this general revelation is insufficient, special revelation is added after the fall. While the two are closely connected, they are nevertheless essentially, and not only in degree, distinguished from each other as well. Since the correct determination of the relation that exists between the two is a matter of such great importance, the following chapter will be devoted to a separate discussion of it. Here I will confine myself to the comment that the distinction between general and special revelation does not consist primarily in the fact that the latter consistently and in all parts bears a strictly supernatural character; the difference is evinced fundamentally and primarily by the fact that special revelation is a revelation of special grace and thus brings into existence the salvific religion known as Christianity. Special revelation is salvific revelation and consequently casts the subject and the means, the content and the purpose of revelation, into another form. First of all, as it concerns the subject, it is certainly the same God who makes himself known to human beings, both in general and in special revelation. But whereas in general revelation God's deity (θειοτης) comes to the fore, in special revelation it is the Triune God who ever more clearly makes himself known in his personal distinctions. This must not be understood to mean that only the work of re-creation—to the exclusion of creation and providence—is a trinitarian work, for all God's outward works (*opera ad extra*) are the essential works of God [*opera Dei essentiala,* the works performed by the Godhead in its oneness]. In the light of Scripture, both creation and providence also exhibit traces of God's threefold existence. But these traces can be seen only by the eye of faith and are significantly distinguished from the clear portrayal that lies before us in Scripture. In the works of nature it is at most only the Father as Creator who speaks to us by the Word (Logos) and the Spirit. But in the works of grace, God comes to us as Father in the entirely unique sense of the Son, and as Father he consequently also reveals himself to us by that Son, more precisely by the Son who became incarnate in Christ and by the Spirit acquired by that Christ. Hence in the subject [agent] of revelation, both the connection and the difference between general and special revelation clearly emerges.

The same is true of the means God employs in special revelation. Those means are theophany, prophecy, and miracle and simultaneously show correspondence to and dissimilarity from what we encounter in the area of general revelation. In the case of general revelation in nature and history, we can already speak analogically of the appearance, speech, and working of God (Ps. 19:2; 29:3; 104:29). But the correspondence comes to light especially when in the area of general revelation we include the different [world] religions in our purview. Not only do these religions exhibit a variety of resemblances to the religion of Israel and Christianity so that together they belong to one genus—for all religions have a dogma, a code of ethics, a cult, a temple and altar, sacrifice and priesthood, etc.—but special revelation also employs the extraordinary means whose analogues occur in the various religions. It employs theophany, prophecy, and miracle and does not even disdain the use of lot, dream, and vision. The divine descends so deeply into the human that the boundaries between special revelation and analogous phenomena are sometimes hard to draw. Divine speech and oracle, prophesy and mantic, miracle and magic, prophetic and apostolic inspiration on the one hand, poetic and heroic inspiration on the other, seem frequently to approximate one another. In a peripheral and atomistic view, it is even difficult in each special case to clearly point out the difference between them. But the person who positions himself squarely in the center of special revelation and surveys the whole scene from that perspective soon discovers that, for all the formal similarity, there exists a large material difference between the prophets of Israel and the fortune-tellers of the Greeks, between the apostles of Christ and the envoys of Mohammed, between biblical miracles and pagan sorceries, between Scripture and the holy books of the peoples of the earth. The religions of the peoples, like their entire culture, show us how much development people can or cannot achieve, indeed not without God, yet without his special grace. But the special grace that comes to us centrally in Christ shows us how deeply God can descend to his fallen creation to save it.

As Triune God

This becomes very clear when we begin to reflect on the content of special revelation. Just as in the case of general revelation, so here too the God who is the author of it is also its content. Special revelation too is God's self-revelation, but now the self-revelation of the God who is not only just and holy but also gracious and merciful, who not only speaks to us through the law but also through the gospel, and who therefore centrally explains to us his name and essence in Christ and becomes known to us as the Triune God, as Father, Son, and Spirit. In the interest of a further unfolding of this content of special revelation, we need to pay attention to three things.

First, Scripture clearly teaches that this revelation bears a historical character and unfolds its content only gradually over the course of many centuries. Modern theology sees and recognizes this fact much more keenly than earlier theology. The "history of revelation" is a discipline of only recent date and deserves to be pursued seriously. It shows us that special revelation is akin to general revelation in nature and history, and especially to general revelation as it is expressed in the religions of the world, yet is essentially different from them and inspired and guided by an idea of its own. That idea is no other than that God in his grace again looks for and restores to his fellowship the people who have left and lost him. Special revelation is God's search for, and God's coming to, human beings. The incarnation of God is the central fact in special revelation, the fact that sheds light upon its whole domain. Already in creation God made himself like human beings when he created them in his image. But in re-creation he became human and entered totally into our nature and situation. In a sense God's becoming human starts already immediately after the fall, inasmuch in his special revelation God reached back deeply into the life of the creation, linked up with the work of his own providence, and so ordered and led persons, situations, and events, indeed the entire history of a people, that he gradually came close to the human race and became ever more clearly knowable to it. But it reaches its culmination only in the person of Christ, who therefore constitutes the central content of the whole of special revelation. He is the Logos who made and sustains all things (John 1:3; Col. 1:15; Heb. 1:3) and may be considered the angel of YHWH who led Israel (Exod. 14:19; 23:20; 32:34; 33:2; Isa. 63:8, 9), and the content of prophecy (John 5:39; 1 Pet. 1:11; Rev. 19:10); and in the fullness of time he became flesh and dwelt among us (John 1:14). Thus Christ is the mediator both of creation and re-creation. "It was his part and his alone, whose ordering of the universe reveals the Father, to renew the same teaching."[35] In creation and in providence (John 1:3–10), and in the leading of Israel (John 1:11), he prepared his own coming in the flesh. Special revelation in the days of the Old Testament is the history of the coming Christ. Theophany, prophecy, and miracle point toward him and reach their fulfillment in him. He is the manifestation, the word, and the servant of God. He shows us the Father, explains to us his name, and does his work. The incarnation of God is the end of Israel's history and the center of all human history. "Up until now, and from that point on, history proceeds on its course" (Joh. von Muller). The incarnation is the central miracle: "It is the wonder of all wonders when the divine enters into direct contact with the human."[36]

Salvation as Focal Point

Second, from this description of the content of special revelation, one can infer that it does not consist exclusively in word and teaching and is absolutely not addressed only to the human intellect. This fact, too, is better understood in present-day theology than in the past. Revelation does not consist only in prophecy but also in theophany and miracle, and Christ, who is

35. Athanasius, *On the Incarnation*, chap. 14; Irenaeus, *On Heresies*, I, IV, 6.
36. L. von Ranke, *Weltgeschichte*, VIII, 72.

the center of revelation, is not only a prophet but also priest and king; not only the Word but also the manifestation and servant of God. In him the divine attributes of truthfulness and wisdom, but also of righteousness and holiness, mercy and grace, become manifest. In Christ, God himself comes to us and imparts himself to us. He grants to us not only truth but also righteousness and life. Whereas earlier theology viewed prophecy especially as prediction and saw in this prediction, and similarly in the miracles, primarily confirmations and evidences of the truth announced by the prophets and apostles, today it is realized that prophecy is much richer and that prediction and miracle are not mere appendices and evidences for but elements and essential constituents in revelation. Certainly, predictions and miracles in Scripture often serve as signs and seals of the truth of the word, but this function does not at all exhaust them. Miracles such as, say, the redemption of Israel from Egypt, the conception and birth, the resurrection and ascension of Christ, have independent significance; they are redemptive acts, which themselves bring about certain outcomes and do not serve exclusively as proofs for a doctrinal statement. Still, for all this, it is not advisable to reduce the content of revelation to manifestation and inspiration (with Rothe) or (with von Oettingen) to incarnation and inspiration.

For in the first place, inspiration is here confused with illumination, i.e., with the illuminating activity of the Holy Spirit by which human beings believingly accept and understand the revelation of God occurring outside of themselves. In the second place, the objective revelation of God occurring outside of human beings absolutely does not consist solely in acts, in the events of nature and history, but certainly also in words, in the communication of truth. The earlier view, which held that revelation consisted only in the communication of doctrine, was one-sided; but no less one-sided is the view that says that it consists only in the communication of power and life. For in Scripture truth and life, word and fact, are most intimately connected. They are not one and the same thing; still they belong together and always go together. Special revelation contains both and is therefore directed toward the whole person, to his or her intellect and heart, his or her conscience and will.

In the third place, it is therefore also completely correct to say that special revelation bears a soteriological character and is salvific. Over against a false intellectualism that attaches salvation to a historical faith, one cannot stress this too emphatically. But while opposing an error to the right, one had better guard against wandering off to the left as well. Certainly, special revelation is soteriological through and through. But this soteriological character must then be understood scripturally, i.e., in the sense that the whole person has been tainted by sin and must therefore also be wholly saved and redeemed by grace in Christ. Error, lies, darkness of intellect are all constituents of sin; hence the revelation of salvation ought not to consist only in a communication of life but also in the announcement of truth. Christ has become for us wisdom and righteousness (1 Cor. 1:30). He is the compete Savior, the Savior of the whole person and the whole world.

Trinitarian Glory as Goal

[96] Clearly emerging from all this, finally, is the purpose of special revelation. The final goal again is God himself, for he can never come to an end in creation but can only rest in himself. God reveals himself for his own sake: to delight in the glorification of his own attributes. But on the journey toward this final end we do after all encounter the creature, particularly the human being, who serves as instrument to bring to manifestation the glory of God's name before the eyes of God. Precisely in order to reach this final goal, the glorification of God's name, special revelation must strive to the end of re-creating the whole person after God's image and likeness and thus to transform that person into a mirror of God's attributes and perfections. Hence the object of revelation cannot only be to teach human beings, to illuminate their intellects (rationalism), or to prompt them to practice virtue (moralism), or to arouse religious sensations in them (mysticism). God's aim in special revelation is both much deeper and reaches much farther. It is none other than to redeem human beings in their totality of body and soul with all their capacities and powers; to redeem not only individual, isolated human beings but humanity as an organic whole. Finally, the goal is to redeem not just humanity apart from all the other creatures but along with humanity to wrest heaven and earth, in a word, the whole world in its organic interconnectedness, from the power of sin and again to cause the glory of God to shine forth from every creature. Sin has spoiled and destroyed everything: the intellect and the will, the ethical and the physical world. Accordingly, it is the whole person and the whole cosmos at whose salvation and restoration God is aiming in his revelation. God's revelation, therefore, is certainly soteriological, but the object of that salvation (σωτηρια) is the cosmos, and not only the ethical or the will to the exclusion of the intellect, and not only the psychological to the exclusion of the somatic and physical, but everything in conjunction. For God has consigned all human beings under sin that he might have mercy upon all (Rom. 5:15f.; 11:32; Gal. 3:22).

When we keep this goal in mind, it will not be hard for us to draw the boundary to which special revelation is extended. Special revelation, according to Scripture, has occurred in the form of a historical process, which culminates in the person and work of Christ. But when Christ has appeared and is again taken up into heaven, special revelation does not immediately cease as a result. Still to come, then, are the outpouring of the Holy Spirit and the extraordinary operation of powers and gifts through and under the guidance of the apostolate. Without doubt, Scripture still counts all this as belonging to the area of special revelation; and the continuation of this revelation in the apostolic age was necessary to give to special revelation, which had culminated in Christ, permanence and stability in the midst of the world, a permanence and stability in the text of Scripture as well as in the existence and life of the church. Truth and life, prophecy and miracle, word and deed, inspiration and regeneration go hand in hand also at the completion of special revelation.

But when in Scripture and in the church the revelation of God that appeared in Christ has become a constituent of the cosmos, a new dispensation begins. Just as up until this time everything had been prepared with a view to Christ, now everything is traced back to him. Then Christ was made to be the head of the church; now the church is made to be the body of Christ. Then Scripture was completed; now it is worked out. No new constitutive elements can any longer be added to special revelation now, because Christ has come, his work is finished, his Word completed. The question of whether the gift of prophecy (prediction) and of miracles has continued after the apostolic age and still continues is, therefore, of secondary importance. The testimonies of the church fathers are so numerous and powerful that for the most ancient times this question can hardly be answered in the negative.[37] But even if those extraordinary gifts and powers have in part remained in the Christian church, the content of this special revelation, which is concentrated in Christ and recorded in Scripture, is not enriched by them; and if, in line with Augustine's view, they have diminished or ceased, special revelation is not impoverished by this fact.[38] The case is different when with Rome people believe in an ongoing progressive revelation in the tradition, or with the "enthusiasts" in a special inspiration of God in the pious individual, or with the evolutionists in the surpassability of Christianity. Scripture clearly teaches that God's full revelation has been given in Christ and that the Holy Spirit who was poured out in the church has come only to glorify Christ and take all things from Christ (John 16:14).

But to that end, accordingly, the activity of the Spirit is continually needed. For the special revelation in Christ is not meant to be restricted to himself but, proceeding from him, to be realized in the church, in humanity, in the world. The aim of revelation, after all, is to re-create humanity after the image of God, to establish the kingdom of God on earth, to redeem the world from the power of sin and, in and through all this, to glorify the name of the Lord in all his creatures. In light of this, however, an objective revelation in Christ is not sufficient, but there needs to be added a working of the Spirit in order that human beings may acknowledge and accept that revela-

37. Aquinas, *Summa Theologica*, II, 2 qu. 178; G. Voetius, *Selectarum Disputationum theologicarum*, II, 1002ff.; J. Gerhard, *Loci Theol.*, loc. XXII, sect. 11; C. Middleton, *A Free Inquiry into the Miraculous Powers Which Are Supposed to Have Subsisted in the Christian Church*, 3d ed. (London: R. Manby and H. S. Cox, 1749); Tholuck, "Über die Wunder der Katholischen Kirche," in *Vermischte Schriften*, I, 22–48; J. H. Newman, *Two Essays on Biblical and on Ecclesiastical Miracles*, 8th ed. (London: Longmans, Green, 1890); E. Müller, *Natur und Wunder* (Freiburg, Breisgau, and St. Louis: Herder, 1892), 182.

38. According to Schaepman, *Menschen en Boeken* (Utrecht, 1900): "Now that the miracle of Christianity has become constitutive of humanity, the few miracles which occur are no longer an urgent necessity for the maintenance of the Christian faith" (18).

tion of God and thereby become the image of the Son. Just as in the sciences the subject must correspond to the object, and in religion subjective religion must answer to objective religion, so external and objective revelation demands an internal revelation in the subject. Many people, accordingly, rightly attach great value to such an internal revelation. But it can come into its own only if it is positioned in relation to the objective revelation granted in Christ. Detached from or elevated above this revelation, it loses its criterion and corrective and opens the door to all sorts of arbitrariness and fanaticism. Even the very concept of subjective revelation is determined and controlled by that of objective revelation. If the objective revelation serves only to clarify and reinforce the God-consciousness in us by the oneness of God and humanity asserted by Christ (Hegel, Biedermann), or consists only in an original way of invigorating pious feeling (Schleiermacher), or tends only to elevate us above the world by the consciousness that God is love and prompt us to collaboration in building the kingdom of God (Ritschl), it is impossible to see and maintain the necessity of an internal illumination by the Holy Spirit. Along with the deity of the Son, that of the Spirit collapses and finally also that of the Father. But if the Creator of heaven and earth revealed in Scripture differs essentially from the idols of pagans; if Christ is not just one founder of religion among many but the fullness of the Godhead dwells in him bodily—hence if Christianity is distinct in kind from all idolatry—then also the Spirit of Christ who indwells the church is a unique, independent, personal divine Spirit, his activity in the church bears a special character, and in virtue of special grace the church of Christ is separate from the world.

Thus in special revelation everything hangs inseparably together. Now the activity of the Holy Spirit, which is subjectively necessary in human beings to bring them to [saving] faith in Christ, can in a broad sense also be called a revelation. Jesus even says to Peter, when the latter recognizes him and confesses him to be the Son of God, "Flesh and blood has not revealed this to you, but my Father who is in heaven" (Matt. 16:17; cf. Gal. 1:15–16). Still Scripture makes a sharp distinction between objective revelation (which includes prophetic and apostolic inspiration by the Holy Spirit) and this subjective revelation. The latter is sometimes indeed called a revelation (ἀποκαλυψις) and can be called that because in fact a new light had dawned in the heart of the believer about himself and about Christ, about God and the world, about sin and grace, about all things in heaven and on earth; but it is not a revelation in the sense that it adds a new element to objective revelation.

Subjective revelation serves only to make this objective revelation known and have it appropriated by the believer. For that reason the activity of the Holy Spirit by which he leads people to Christ is usually mentioned in Scripture by other names, especially by the names "enlightenment" and "regeneration" (φωτισμος and ἀναγεννησις, 2 Cor. 4:6; John 3:5). Inasmuch as objective revelation embraces both word and deed, the activity of the Spirit must focus on the consciousness and being of a person and hence consist simultaneously in the illumination of the mind and the renewal of the heart. Objective revelation aims at the re-creation of the whole person and must, therefore, be accepted and appropriated by the whole person. Accordingly, it reaches its ultimate goal only when the church has been prepared and adorned as the bride of Christ and humanity and the world have been re-created into a kingdom of God.

REVELATION AND RELIGION

[97] If we finally briefly sum up what Scripture teaches about revelation, we first of all have to understand by revelation quite generally that deliberate and free act of God by which he makes himself known to human beings in order that by it they may come to stand in the right relation to him. Corresponding to the revelation of God on the human side is religion, the knowledge and service of God. In Scripture the two are very closely connected: knowledge and service of God are possible only because God reveals himself. Still the two, revelation and religion, are absolutely not identical, nor the two sides of, or two names for, the same thing. This identity can be asserted only on the position of pantheism, according to which God has no existence of his own distinct from the world but only achieves self-consciousness and self-revelation in that world, specifically in humanity. But on this position there is absolutely no room for any revelation of God, at most for a manifestation or unconscious appearance of an unknown and unknowable "something," which cannot even be designated by a name. Though people still love to speak of "revelation," they are playing a frivolous game with the word. This comes out clearly in the idea—mindlessly taken over by many, nevertheless basically pantheistic—that God can reveal himself only by deeds or by a communication of life, not by speech or utterances. For if God has no personal existence, is devoid of self-consciousness and hence cannot think, it needs no further argument that he cannot speak or communicate his thought by the vehicle of words either. But people should be aware that, having denied to God the possibility of revelation by means of words, they cannot assume and maintain a revelation of deeds and communication of life either.

If God has no personal existence distinct from the world, he also lacks the will and power to reveal himself in deeds and also misses a divine life of his own that differs essentially from our sinful, mortal life and could be communicated by him to us. In that case, while one can still speak of "the facts of revelation" and of "the communication of life," one is only mouthing sounds. Pantheistic philosophy dissolves one element after another of what Scripture reveals to us as the facts of revelation into ideas; and what these thinkers have left of divine life and communion with God comes down to a vague feeling, the generally religious character of which does not lend itself to description and which therefore runs together with all kinds of other "feelings" of an aesthetic or even sensual nature. But if God, as both nature and Scripture teach, is a personal being equipped with self-consciousness and self-determination, then revelation in a true sense, as well as revelation in word and deed, comes fully into its own in truth and life. He can then not only take us up into fellowship with him and make us partakers of his divine nature but also by speaking, by his word, communicate his thoughts to us and do it as "unmechanically" as one human to another, a father to his child, a teacher to his or her pupil. In that case, however, revelation and religion are not one and the same thing, for then revelation comes to us objectively from God's side, and we have the obligation to accept that revelation of God, to understand it, and to respond to it with a life consisting in knowing, serving, and loving God with all our mind and heart.

The revelation that thus comes to us objectively from the side of God is to be differentiated into a general and special one. General revelation is that conscious and free act of God by which, by means of nature and history (in the broadest sense, hence including one's own personal life experience), he makes himself known—specifically in his attributes of omnipotence and wisdom, wrath and goodness—to fallen human beings in order that they should turn to him and keep his law or, in the absence of such repentance, be inexcusable.

Special revelation, in distinction from the above, is that conscious and free act of God by which he, in the way of a historical complex of special means (theophany, prophecy, and miracle) that are concentrated in the person of Christ, makes himself known—specifically in the attributes of his justice and grace, in the proclamation of law and gospel—to those human beings who live in the light of this special revelation in order that they may accept the grace of God by faith in Christ or, in case of impenitence, receive a more severe judgment. Both this general and this special revelation are primarily objective; and included in this objective special revelation, accordingly, is the revelation that occurs in the consciousness of prophets and apostles by addressive and interior speech, by divine inspiration in the sense of 2 Timothy 3:16.

Corresponding to this objective revelation, general as well as special, there is a subjective revelation, which in a broad sense can be called revelation but for the sake of clarity can be better described as illumination. Answering to this objective general revelation, there is an illumination of the Logos (John 1:9), or of the Spirit of God, in intellect, conscience, heart, and mind of human beings, such that they can understand God's general revelation in nature and history. Likewise, answering to this objective special revelation, there is an illumination of human beings who live in the light of the gospel, by the Spirit of God, such that they can recognize and know the special revelation that comes to them in Christ and more specifically in Scripture *as* special revelation of God.

This objective general and special revelation always was and is accompanied by the subjective illumination of the Spirit of God and the Spirit of Christ. The distinction between "original" and "traditional" revelation denies this truth and is therefore open to all kinds of misunderstanding. Although special revelation in a sense belongs to the past insofar as it came directly to the prophets and apostles, it is and remains present to us all in Scripture. Just as by general revelation God continually makes himself known to all human beings, so by Scripture he from day to day continues in a special way to reveal himself to all who live under the gospel. Rousseau believed that God could be much better known from his general than from his special revelation, since in the latter case there are so many people standing between God and us. He forgot, however, that he owed to Scripture what he understood of general revelation; and he did not take account of the fact that objective special revelation, in virtue of the ongoing activity of the Holy Spirit, receives witness in every human conscience. Thus objective and subjective revelation, in a general as well as a special sense, are carried forward by the witness of the Spirit throughout the centuries until in the final manifestation of Christ they will have attained their end. The objective special revelation was completed with the first coming of Christ; at his second coming, its full effect in the history of humankind will be completed. The time of sowing will then be concluded in the time of harvest.

12

REVELATION IN NATURE
AND HOLY SCRIPTURE

The doctrine of revelation is misconstrued by naturalism and supernaturalism alike. Since naturalism considers the material and sensible world along with its internal laws to be all that there is, some notion of the supernatural is needed to affirm the reality of God. The term "supernatural" should not be used for the higher capacities of the human spirit such as morality and genius. Nor must the supernatural be confused with the miraculous. Though all miracles are supernatural, not all supernatural events are miraculous. While the distinction is helpful, the great risk here is that special (supernatural) revelation become dualistically detached from creation and nature. Special revelation should never be separated from its organic connection to history, the world, and humanity.

Roman Catholic supernaturalism fails to keep this organic link between nature and grace. The result is a twofold conception of human nature and destiny along with a dualism of spiritual callings; the order of grace is elevated above nature, and all reality becomes sacred or profane depending on whether it has been sacramentally sanctified. Reality becomes holy only by an ecclesiastical act of consecration and is thus incorporated into the service of the church.

The Reformation converted this quantitative antithesis between revelation and nature into a qualitative one. Grace was not opposed to nature but to sin. The reality of the incarnation militates against any nature/grace dualism; the gospel is not hostile to the world as creation but to the world under dominion of sin.

If supernaturalism undervalues nature, naturalism exalts it at the expense of revelation. Rationalists and deists accept the idea of revelation only insofar as it satisfies the bar of reason. The arguments against revelation arise from the conviction that all revelation is at odds with reason and science, which do not need the hypothesis of God or the supernatural. In addition, even if revelation occurred, we would not be able to recognize it. This is not the end of the matter, however, since rationalism must still account for the universality of religion and the accompanying conviction among people that their religion is based on revelation. Shifting and conflicting interpretations indicate the elusiveness of a satisfactory purely scientific explanation.

Scripture, however, resists all naturalistic and rationalist explanations of its origin and attributes it solely to an extraordinary operative presence of God the

Holy Spirit. Scripture does not give us data to interpret; it is itself the interpretation of reality, the shaper of a distinct worldview. This theistic worldview is sharply opposed by monism, which reduces all reality to a single substance, either matter (materialism) or mind (pantheism). Theism, by contrast, honors the distinction between God and the world and the distinct realities of the world. Instead of monistic uniformity, theism aims at unity in diversity, honoring the multiformity of creation itself. This unity is not based on a single metaphysical substance but is rooted in the creative will of the Triune God.

This worldview is fully compatible with the reality of revelation and miracles. Nature is not a machine, as deists claim, nor a finished product but in the process of becoming. Revelation and miracles are not contrary to nature but part of a nature caught up in an ongoing teleological development toward its divine destiny. Miracles are not alien intruders in a fallen creation but are incorporated in the divine design of the world itself and serve God's work of redeeming and perfecting fallen nature. Revelation and miracles are not simply individual acts of God but follow a divinely planned order in a progressive history. In revelation God comes to us to bring us to him to dwell with us forever.

Still, revelation and miracles constitute an order of reality that is essentially distinct from the ordinary order of nature. They are not simply the product of a heightened natural capacity of inspired human beings. Nor should they be linked to such esoteric phenomena as spiritism, hypnotism, and telepathy. The miracles of Scripture are a unique and an indispensable component of a Christian worldview. God's presence and activity is neither restricted to the natural order nor excluded from it. Revelation and miracle are at the same time closely bound to the natural and distinct from it.

Not only is there a close bond between religion and revelation but also one between revelation and scripture. Almost all religions have some texts that include myths, ceremonial rules, liturgical texts, priestly documents, and so forth. Many also have a sacred book or collection of books serving as sacred scripture. These scriptures contain the content of religion, its ideas, doctrine, dogma, which it owes to revelation, expresses in words, passes over from one generation to another, and finally renders permanent in scripture. The written word is the incarnation of the spoken word and renders revelation permanent, universal, everlasting. This must not be understood as Lessing did, namely in opposition to the truths of history. History is itself the realization of God's thoughts, the expression of his divine plan. The truths of history are not "accidental" nor are the "truths of reason" universal in Lessing's sense.

In the Christian tradition truth is incarnational, based on the history of the incarnate Son of God in our space and time. It is a truth both historical and universal and is borne through history incarnationally, through the tradition of the church universal. For divine revelation to fully enter the life of humankind, it assumed the servant form of written language. In this sense Scripture too is an incarnation of God, the product of God's incarnation in Christ. Twin errors are to be rejected. The first is to equate scriptural revelation with inspiration itself, thus separating Scripture from the history of redemption and revelation that stands behind it. It is worth noting that not all inspiration and revelation given by God is recorded in Scripture. The second error is to devalue the "letter" of the written Word in favor of the "spirit." Scripture alone is the one certain revelation we have from God. For the church, revelation is found in the form of Holy Scripture.

Revelation as a whole is not complete until the parousia of Christ. It is divided into two dispensations, the objective revelation of God in Christ (including the Old Testament time of preparation) and the dispensation of the Spirit, in which the objective salvation in Christ is subjectively appropriated by the believer. There is no new objective revelation in the dispensation of the Spirit; the Holy Spirit applies the finished work of Christ, God's full gift and revelation to humanity. The effect of Christ's work continues as history continues to be unfolded according to God's purpose, until God is dwelling with humanity. The Spirit regenerates individual believers, gathers and indwells the church, and affects the consciousness of humanity. The life of the church is a mystery without the light of Scripture, while apart from the church Scripture is an enigma and offense. Until the consummation when revelation ends and Scripture is no longer necessary, church and Scripture are inseparably joined by God the Holy Spirit.

[98] The doctrine of revelation contained in Scripture and elaborated in the previous chapters has been misconstrued in two ways in the Christian church: by supernaturalism as well as by naturalism (rationalism). Accordingly, it has to be further elucidated and maintained against these two deviations.

We first consider supernaturalism, which arose primarily in Catholicism and then influenced various schools of thought within Protestantism. While Scripture does know a distinction between the ordinary course of things and the extraordinary works of God, it does not posit a contrast between "the natural" and "the supernatural." This contrast first surfaces in the works of the church fathers. Special revelation is [there] equated with the supernatural and contrasted to the natural. Clement of Alexandria already speaks of a supernatural vision (ὑπερφυης θεωρια), which a person acquires by faith. Chrysostom describes the miracles as "surpassing nature" (ὑπερ φυσιν) and "greater than nature" (φυσει μειζονα). Ambrose opposes "grace," "miracle," and "mystery" to the "order of nature." John of Damascus repeatedly speaks of miracles such as the conception of Christ, the eucharist, etc., as "surpassing nature," "surpassing reason and thought."[1] Since then the distinction between the "natural" and the "supernatural" has found acceptance and been adopted throughout the whole of Christian theology.

---

1. Clement, *Stromata,* II 2; Chrysostom, *Homilies on Genesis,* 36; Ambrose, *On the Mysteries,* chap. 9; John of Damascus, *Exposition of the Orthodox Faith,* IV 12–15. Cf. H. Denzinger, *Vier Bücher von der religiösen Erkenntniss* (Würzburg: Staehl'schen Buch-und-Kunst-handlung, 1856–57), I, 82f.

"NATURAL" AND "SUPERNATURAL"

This distinction doubtless has validity. While Scripture may not make it explicit, it does recognize an ordinary order of nature as well as the deeds and works that are causally rooted in the omnipotence of God. Revelation in Scripture presupposes that there exists still another, higher and better world than this nature and hence that there is an order of things "surpassing this natural order." For that reason the terms *natural* and *supernatural* need to be clearly defined. Nature, derived from *nasci*, to become, generally denotes that which develops apart from any alien power or influence, solely in terms of its own internal forces and laws.[2] Nature so defined is even contrasted to art, nurture, culture, and history, which do not originate spontaneously on their own but come about by human agency. But in addition the concept of nature is frequently conceived more broadly and expanded to include the entire material and sensible world in distinction from spiritual and invisible things, or even to include the entire cosmos insofar as it moves and develops, not from without but from within, by immanent forces and its own increated laws. "Supernatural," in this latter case, is all that surpasses created things and does not have its cause in creatures but in the omnipotence of God. In Christian theology special revelation was understood in this sense. Taken as a whole, it had its origin in a special act of God, which had not been revealed in the ordinary course of nature but in a distinct order of things of its own. In this connection a further distinction was made between the supernatural in an absolute sense, when something surpasses the power of all creatures, and the supernatural in a relative sense, when it surpasses the power of a specific cause in the given circumstances. A further distinction was also made between the supernatural with respect to substance, when the fact itself is supernatural, e.g., the raising of a dead person, and the supernatural with respect to mode, when only the *modus operandi* is supernatural, e.g., the healing of a sick person without means.[3]

In these distinctions as such there was still no danger. They even have to be defended against a philosophy that denies or weakens the supernatural. In later theology and philosophy, the term *supernatural* has frequently been used in a very modified sense and equated in turn with the "supersensible" (Kant) the "free" (Fichte), the "unknown" (Spinoza, Wegschneider), the "new" and "original" (Schleiermacher), the "religious-ethical" or "spiritual" (Saussaye), etc. But such a modification of the established and clear meaning of a word leads to misunderstanding. If by "supernatural" one only means the "supersensible," the "ethical," etc., it is better to avoid the term. The confusion becomes still greater when the natural and the supernatural are intermixed and someone gives to that fusion the name "spirituo-physical," "di-

---

2. Rudolf Eisler, *Wörterbuch der philosophischen Begriffe*, 2 vols. (Berlin: E. S. Mittler und Sohn, 1904), s.v. "Natur."

3. Thomas Aquinas, *Summa contra Gentiles*, III, 101.

vine-human." The term *nature* encompasses all that is created, not only matter but also soul and spirit; not only the physical but also the psychological, religious, and ethical life insofar as it automatically arises from human nature: not only visible but also invisible supersensible things. The supernatural is not identical with the original, the genial, the free, the religious, or the ethical, etc. but is the plain and established term only for that which cannot be explained in terms of the forces and laws of created things. To that extent the distinction between the natural and the supernatural that arose in Christian theology is completely correct, firm, and clear and cuts off all confusion. Aside from what was said above (p. 311), special revelation in its three forms of theophany, prophecy, and miracle is supernatural in the strict sense of the word.

In Christian theology, however, the concept of the supernatural was gradually restricted even more. It was differentiated on the one hand from the creation and on the other from such spiritual miracles as regeneration, etc. The first distinction was made because the supernatural does not exist for God but only for us [humans] and presupposes the natural order called into being by the act of creation. One can speak of the supernatural only if nature has existed antecedently. On the other hand, while regeneration, forgiveness, sanctification, the mystical union, etc., were indeed held to be direct acts of God, they were not counted as supernatural revelation, inasmuch as they are not uncommon or rare but belong to the common order of things in the church. The church itself, though supernatural, is not a miracle. Again, the supernatural and miracle are differentiated as well. All that is supernatural is not miraculous; conversely, a miracle is always supernatural. Miracles are not only supernatural but in addition unusual and rare events in the realm of nature or grace. They occur not only outside the order of any particular nature but outside the order of every created nature.

In a real sense, therefore, angels and devils cannot do miracles but only such things as seem miraculous to us and occur outside of the order of created nature as we know it.[4] Thomas not only speaks of miracles outside and above but also *contrary* to nature.[5] And Voetius said that, though miracles are indeed not contrary to nature as a whole but above and beyond it, they could nevertheless be contrary to some particular nature.[6] Hence miracles had the following distinguishing marks: they were an "immediate work of God"; "above all nature"; "occured to the senses"; were "rare," and happened

4. Aquinas, *Summa Theol.*, I, qu. 110 art. 4; idem, *Summa contra Gentiles*, I, 6; III, 112; Voetius, *Select. Disp.*, 973f.

5. Ed. note: Bavinck's footnote reads: Aquinas, *Summa Theol.*, "qu. de miraculis," art. 2 ad 3, without indicating the exact work. While there is no specific question in the *Summa Theologiae* on "miracles," Aquinas discusses miraculous acts that are contrary to nature in *Summa Theol.*, I, qu. 105, art. 6. A general discussion on miracles can also be found in *Summa contra Gentiles*, III, 2, chap. 101. Cf. Eugene Müller, *Natur und Wunder* (Freiburg i.B. and St. Louis: Herder, 1892), 145.

6. Voetius, *Select. Disp.*, II, 973. Cf. also Gerhard, *Loci Theol.*, XXII §271f.

"for the confirmation of truth."[7] However much good there may be in these scholastic qualifications and distinctions, they nevertheless brought with them substantial dangers. On the one hand, special revelation was detached from creation and nature. Although it was recognized that supernatural revelation occurred not just after but also already before the fall,[8] and therefore could not as such be contrary to nature, still not enough attention was paid to this position. On the other hand, special revelation was opposed to spiritual miracles, the works of grace, which happen continually in the church of Christ. Hence, on this view, they take place in isolation from re-creation and grace. When this distinction was understood as a separation—which could easily happen—special revelation came altogether to stand by itself, without any connection with nature and history. In that case, its historical and organic character was denied. Special revelation did not enter into the fabric of the world and humanity but floated outside and above it. This was all the more the case when special revelation was treated as a doctrine, a proclamation of uncomprehended and incomprehensible mysteries whose truth was confirmed by the miracles. In that case it was and remained, in a word, a "gift superadded" to the cosmos.

In Roman Catholicism this supernaturalistic and dualistic system has been consistently worked out. In God there are two conceptions of human beings, their nature and destiny. The merely natural human (*in puris naturalibus*), without the image of God, as he or she still is after the fall, may acquire a pure knowledge of God from his works, can serve and fear him, stand in a normal, as such even a good servant-relation to him, practice all the natural virtues, even also a natural love for God, and thus achieve a certain state of happiness in this life and the life to come. If people fail to achieve this state, it is their own fault, a fate that is due to the non-employment or misemployment of the natural powers given them.

It is God's will, however, to give human beings a higher, a supernatural and heavenly, destiny. To that end he had to furnish them the so-called "superadded gifts" both before and after the fall. He must grant them a supernatural grace by which they can know and love God in another, a better and higher way, practice better and higher virtues, and attain a higher destiny. This higher knowledge consists in faith (*fides*) and this higher love in charity (*caritas*). Also, the higher virtues are the theological virtues, faith, hope, and love, which differ essentially from the cardinal (intellectual and moral) virtues. Finally, the higher destiny consists in being children of God, birth from above, the mystical union with God, participation in the divine nature, deification (θέωσις), the vision of God, etc. While the seeds of this doctrine had already been planted in some pronouncements of the church fathers, it was actually first developed by scholasticism, especially by Hales, Bonaventure,

7. Voetius, *Select. Disp.*, II, 965; Gerhard, *Loci Theol.*, XXII §271f.
8. A. Calovius, *Isagoges*, 49.

and Thomas.[9] In the fight against Baius and Jansen, it was officially laid down ecclesiastically and later emphatically repeated[10] by the Vatican Council that "revelation must . . . be called absolutely necessary . . . because God, in his infinite goodness, has destined man for a supernatural goal, namely, to share divine benefits that completely surpass human understanding" with an appeal to 1 Corinthians 2:9.

ROMAN CATHOLIC SUPERNATURALISM

[99] Now one must recognize that the difference in state before and after the fall does not lie in revelation as such. There was supernatural revelation also in Paradise (Gen. 1:28f.; 2:16f.). Revelation was therefore not first made necessary by sin. Even in the state of integrity, there was a revelation of grace, for then also the love relation in which God placed himself to human beings was a demonstration of unrestrained goodness. Hence what sin made necessary was not revelation as such but the specific content of revelation, i.e., special grace, the revelation of God in Christ, the incarnation of God. Divine revelation was necessary also for religion in the state of integrity. But the Christian religion is based on a certain special revelation. This is what Paul had in view when in 1 Corinthians 2:4–16 he speaks of the wisdom of God, which had always been hidden and did not arise in the human heart. Roman Catholicism itself cannot really deny this, unless it accepts the theory that, assuming God wanted to bestow a supernatural end upon human beings, the entire supernatural order that now exists in the incarnation, the church, and the sacraments, would have been necessary also without and aside from sin. On that view, however, the soteriological character of revelation would be entirely lost, the fall would lose its meaning, and sin would scarcely have introduced any change at all. The doctrine of a supernatural end, accordingly, has always encountered much contradiction in the Roman Catholic Church (Baius, Jansen, Hirscher, Hermes, Günther); but it is integral to the entire Catholic system, which is constructed, not on the religious antithesis between sin and grace, but on the graduated scale of the good, on the ranking of creatures and virtues, on hierarchy both in a physical and an ethical sense. The Reformation, by contrast, had but one idea, one conception of human beings, that is, of human beings as the image bearers of God, and this was true for all human beings. When that image in the narrow sense is lost, the whole of human nature is mutilated, and human beings can no longer have a religion and ethos that answer to God's demand and their own idea. Then their religion and virtue, however beautiful they may seem, are tainted to the very roots. A purely natural religion does not exist anywhere. All [natural] reli-

9. Alexander of Hales, *Summa universae theologiae*, II qu. 91 m. 1 a. 3; Bonaventure, *Breviloquium*, V, 1; Thomas Aquinas, *Disputed Questions on Truth*, qu. 27; *Summa Theol.*, I, 2 qu. 62, art. 1.

10. H. J. D. Denzinger, *Enchiridion symbolorum definitionum* (Wirceburgi, 1865), n. 882f.; *Vatican Council* I, sess. III. c. 2, cf. can. II, 3.

gions have become superstitions. For that reason, however, the Christian religion is essentially identical with the true religion in the state of integrity. At one time Reformed theologians took this view so far they said that Adam, too, had knowledge of the Trinity and believed that then the Logos had also been the mediator, not of reconciliation, to be sure, but of union; that then too the Holy Spirit was the author of all virtue and power, etc.

There was truth here in that the will of God is not capricious, now entertaining one idea of human nature and now another; in that the view of "humanness," the nature of the image of God, and hence also of religion, has to be all of a piece. From this, finally, it followed that the revelation was not absolutely but relatively necessary, not with respect to substance, but to its mode. Religion is one, both before and after the fall; but that it is "Christian" is a necessity occasioned by sin. The Christian religion is a means, not an end; Christ is mediator, but the end is that God may be "all things in all" (1 Cor. 15:28).

Further implied in this is that revelation cannot stand absolutely over against nature. In Roman Catholicism there is a quantitative contrast between the two. Natural religion is essentially different from supernatural religion, and the two are conceptually wholly different—two totally distinct systems and orders. The order of grace is elevated high above the order of nature. The whole of existence, accordingly, is divided between a sacred and a profane area. The world is the unconsecrated, profane area where Satan with his unholy minions holds sway. But squarely within that unholy world God planted his holy, infallible church and endowed it with a great treasure of grace. The God-man continues to live, rule, and work here. All that passes from that world to the area of the church has to be consecrated and blessed. Roman Catholics constantly make the sign of the cross—when eating and drinking, when rising and going to bed, on every important occasion—to arm themselves against the assaults of the devil and to call down the blessing of heaven, for at sight of this sign the power of hell trembles and flees. When they go into or out of the church, they sprinkle themselves with holy water, and sometimes also when engaging in certain activities in or outside their homes, in cases of illness and temptation, in order thereby to counter the influences of Satan. Not only persons but also inanimate objects, like salt, bread, churches, altars, clocks, candles, garments, etc., are thus consecrated, when they are separated from the area of the profane and pass over into the area of the sacred. These consecrations are accomplished by prayer, the sign of the cross, holy water, etc. but at solemn events are accompanied also by exorcisms and adjurations of the devil. Thus, Roman Catholicism presses the stamp of the profane, the unconsecrated, the demonic upon all that is natural. Things become holy only by an ecclesiastical act of consecration, and such a consecration is necessary for everyone and everything that is incorporated into the service of the church.[11]

11. Joseph Deharbe, *Verklaring der Katholieke Geloofs- en Zedeleer,* ed. and enlarged by B. Dankelman, 4 vols. (Utrecht: J. R. Van Rossum, 1880–88), I, 170; III, 588f.; IV, 598f.

Ensuing from this worldview are both the world domination for which the Roman Catholic Church always strives and the contempt of the world that it evidences, especially in monasticism. Since nature is of a much lower order than grace, the latter must always have priority over the former and hold sway over it. Furthermore, since what is Christian coincides with the ecclesiastical and does not exist apart from it, the whole world needs to be subordinated to the church. There is no room in Roman Catholicism for the free cultivation of the arts and sciences, for a free state and society, etc. Always the ideal is that the pope as the vicar of Christ possess all power in heaven and on earth. But the same fundamental idea that grace belongs to a higher order than nature can also lead to contempt of the world, as it is manifest in Roman Catholic asceticism. This world contempt is only another form of world domination. While of course it is not impossible to live as a Christian, to secure salvation, and even to achieve perfection also in the world—for otherwise no Christianity would be possible except in a monastery—the shortest and most certain route to perfection runs through the three counsels of poverty, chastity, and obedience. Hence asceticism, according to Rome, though certainly not identical with perfection, is the best road to perfection, the most eminent instrument of perfection,[12] and hence much better as a means than life in the family and in society, than ordinary daily labor in one's vocation.

THE REFORMATIONAL VIEW

The Reformation revolted against this worldview, which toward the end of the Middle Ages ended on the one hand in a lack of freedom and on the other in licentiousness. It converted the quantitative antithesis between revelation and nature into a qualitative antithesis; in place of a physical, it gave to it an ethical character. The revelation that appeared in Christ as such is absolutely not opposed to nature but only to sin, which as an alien element has insinuated itself into the world. Revelation and creation are not opposed to each other, for creation itself is a revelation. Revelation was present before the fall. Even now revelation is present still in all the works of God's hand in nature and history; his external power and deity are perceived and understood from his creatures. And even supernatural revelation as such is so far from being in conflict with nature that every human in the core of his or her being is a supernaturalist and believes in a direct operative presence of God in this world. The inspiration of heroes and artists, the marvelous powers that are sometimes observed, though certainly not identical with the facts of revelation reported in Scripture, do nevertheless point back to another and higher order of things than that which holds sway in the mechanical causality of the natural phenomena perceptible by the senses. Belief in a special revelation is universal in the religions

12. P. Höveler, *Professor A. Harnack und die katholische Ascese* (Düsseldorf: L. Schwann, 1902), 24.

[of the world], and the phenomena of divination and magic, though a caricature, still bear resemblance to, and therefore serve as indirect confirmation of, the true prophecy and real miracles that Scripture discloses to us. We can even much less think of revelation and nature as opposites when we note the content and purpose of the revelation as given in Christ. For it proclaims to us that God loved the world, and that Christ came not to condemn but to save the world (John 3:16, 17), to destroy not the works of the Father but only the works of the devil (1 John 3:8). And just as Christ himself assumed a full human nature, denied the natural life in an ethical sense but did not mutilate and mortify it physically, and in the end again raised his body from the dead, so his disciples, while indeed called to cross-bearing and self-denial and following their Master, are not called to asceticism and world flight.

On the contrary, Jesus prayed to the Father that his disciples would not be taken out of the world but kept in the world from the evil one (John 17:15). In line with this, Christians did not have to go out of the world (1 Cor. 5:10), but to remain in their occupations (1 Cor. 7:17–23); to obey the powers God had ordained (Rom. 13:1); to regard all things their own (1 Cor. 3:21–23); to enjoy every gift of God with thanksgiving (1 Tim. 4:3–5); and to consider godliness as of value in every way, as it holds promise for the present life and also for the life to come (1 Tim. 4:8). And that, too, was what the Reformation wanted: a Christianity that was hostile, not to nature but only to sin. Such a Christianity was not externally imposed in the name of an infallible church but was inwardly assumed in one's conscience by a free personality. Thus, through this personality, it had a reforming and sanctifying effect upon natural life as a whole. We are far from having reached the ideal and will presumably never reach it in this dispensation. Still it is full of fascination and beauty and worthy of being pursued with all our strength. Coming again into its own in the Reformation was the old adage: nature commends grace; grace emends nature.

RATIONALISTIC NATURALISM

[100] Just as supernaturalism denies nature, so naturalism does not permit revelation to come into its own. Fundamental opposition to revelation first began in modern philosophy. Spinoza still held onto the word "revelation" and even considered it necessary but understood by it only that simple believers cannot find the true religion, the word of God, by the light of reason but have to accept it on authority.[13] For the rest Spinoza did not acknowledge revelation in the true sense of the word. All the decrees of God are eternal verities and identical with the laws of nature. Prophecy and miracle are subjected to sharp

---

13. Spinoza, *Tractatus Theologico-Politicus*, XV, 27, 44; IV, 22–37. In English, Spinoza, *Works of Spinoza: A Theologico-Political Treatise* and *A Political Treatise*, trans. and introduced by R. H. M. Elwes (New York: Dover Publications, 1951).

criticism and explained in terms of nature.[14] This criticism was continued by deism and rationalism. But rationalism, like the naturalism discussed earlier, can assume different forms and each time changes its meaning. By "rationalism" is meant, in the first place, the school of thought that, while it assumes a supernatural revelation, assigns the decision concerning the genuineness and meaning of that revelation to reason. To this school belonged numerous Cartesian theologians like Roëll, Wolzogen, G. W. Duker, as well as Leibnitz, Wolff, et al. Secondly, "rationalism" is the term for the view that still in fact deems a supernatural revelation possible but only of such truths that reason by itself could sooner or later have been able to discover as well. In that setting revelation is only temporarily and incidentally necessary. It serves merely as preparation and education for the universal rule of the religion of reason and only furnishes more swiftly and easily what reason would otherwise have reached by way of a longer and more arduous road. Such is the concept of revelation in Lessing, Fichte, and Kant. Known as rationalism, in the third place, is the theology that denies all supernatural revelation but does believe that God, by special dispositions of his providence, has equipped persons who, and paved the roads which, can bring humanity to a better and purer knowledge of religious truth. The most important representative of this school is Wegschneider; others are Röhr, Henke, Gabler, Paulus, Gesenius, etc. Finally, the name "rationalism" is given also to the school that from the middle of the seventeenth century on was called naturalism, known in England as deism as well as atheism and materialism, and that, denying all revelation, considered natural religion completely adequate. Belonging to this "school" were Spinoza, Lud. Meyer, Voltaire, Rousseau, Reimarus, Nicolai, and numerous others.

The arguments advanced by this rationalism against revelation come down to the following: (1) Revelation is impossible on God's part for it would mean God was changeable, that his creation was imperfect and deficient, and therefore needed improvement; and that he himself—otherwise otiose—only worked when he worked in an extraordinary manner. (2) Revelation is also impossible from the side of the world since science has increasingly discovered that the world is always and everywhere controlled by an unbreakable system of laws that leaves no room for a supernatural intervention by God. Science always proceeds from this causal web of things and cannot really act otherwise, for supernaturalism, positing caprice in place of regularity, actually makes science impossible. Accordingly, with every advance of science, all phenomena have lost their supernatural character. There is not even any right, in the face of all experience, to consider a phenomenon supernatural: "the supernatural would be superdivine." (3) A revelation, even if it really happened, would still be unrecognizable and undemonstrable to the recipient himself and still more to those who lived after him. How could one ever decide whether a prophecy or miracle came from God and not from the devil? By what features is a revela-

14. Ibid., I; VI; IV, 37; III, 8; VI, 9.

tion recognizable by the person receiving it or by those who live later? Such criteria cannot be established. Accordingly, those who accept a revelation only believe on human authority and in the most sublime and weighty matters depend on human beings. "What humans could there be between God and me!" (4) Finally, revelation militates against human reason. For whatever one may say, all revelation that is above reason is by that token contrary to reason, suppresses reason, and leads to fanaticism. Furthermore, if revelation communicates something that is above reason, it can never be absorbed and assimilated and continues to hover as an uncomprehended mystery outside of our consciousness. If it does communicate something that reason could have discovered by itself, it is unnecessary. At most it offers sooner and with less effort that which would nevertheless have been discovered otherwise and so unnecessarily robs reason of its strength and energy.

Those, however, who combat the necessity, possibility, and reality of a revelation on these grounds cannot confine themselves to this denial but face the task of explaining belief in and the reports concerning such a revelation historically. No more than religion itself can all this have originated in deception. Belief in revelation is not something arbitrary or accidental, which occurs only here and there under special conditions, but is truly integral to all religion. The question of revelation is not as simple as rationalism pictures it. This is immediately clear from the fact that all attempts made from the side of naturalism to give a "natural" explanation of the biblical miracle stories have thus far failed. If revelation in all its forms—theophany, prophecy, and miracle—is not actually supernatural but derived from God only in the sense that all human activity ultimately has its final cause in him, one is compelled to resort either to the so-called material or the formal interpretation of the miracle stories. That is, on the one hand, one can to some extent leave the facts intact and accept them as truth. In that case one tries to explain these facts in terms of the ignorance of common people concerning the natural causes and from a religious need to attribute everything directly to God.[15] One explains them either physically in terms of unfamiliar forces of nature,[16] or psychologically in terms of a special ability to presage future events[17] and to heal the sick without medical means.[18] Or one explains them

15. Ibid., I; VI; Karl A. von Hase, *Evangelische Dogmatik* (Leipzig: Breitkopf und Härtel, 1860), §19; idem, *Das leben Jesu* (Leipzig: Breitkopf und Härtel, 1853), §15; D. F. Strauss, *Christliche Glaubenslehre*, 2 vols. (Tubingen: C. F. Osiander, 1840–41), I, 280; J. H. Scholten, *Supranaturalisme in Verband met Bijbel, Christendom en Protestantisme* (Leiden, 1867), 8f.

16. I. Kant, *Religion within the Limits of Reason Alone,* trans. Theodore M. Greene and Hoyt H. Hudson (New York: Harper & Row, 1960 [1934]), 81; S. F. N. Morus, *Epitome theologiae christianae* (Lipsiae: E. B. Schwickerti, 1820), 23; Alexander Schweizer, *Die Glaubenslehre der Evangelisch-reformirten Kirche,* 2 vols. (Zürich: Orell, Füssli und Comp., 1844–47), I, 324ff.

17. Karl G. Bretschneider, *Handbuch der Dogmatik der evangelish-lutherische Kirche,* 2 vols (Leipzig: J. A. Barth, 1838), I, 300.

18. C. H. Weisse, *Philosophische Dogmatik oder Philosophie des Christenthums,* 3 vols. (Leipzig: S. Hirzel, 1855–62), I, 115; C. F. von Ammon, *Die Geschichte des Lebens Jesu* (Leipzig: Vogel, 1847), 248.

teleologically in terms of a kind of ordering of physical and psychic powers inherent in nature such that they produce unusual results and prompt people to recognize God's providence and to have faith in the preacher.[19] On the other hand, one can look for a solution in the formal or genetic interpretation, i.e., in a special view of the [biblical] reports about the revelation. In that case, one invokes the Oriental manner of presentation and the accommodation of Jesus and the apostles to popular ideas.[20] Alternatively one can take refuge in the allegorical,[21] the natural,[22] the mythical,[23] the symbolic,[24] or, as happens in our day, the religious-historical[25] interpretation.

THE SCRIPTURAL DIFFERENCE

But up until now none of these attempts has had much success. Granted, they have all made their contribution to a better understanding of Scripture; but the changing nature of the attempts and the taking of ever different roads are proof enough that the right interpretation has so far eluded the scholars. Before and after, the revelation that comes to us in Scripture remains an unsolved riddle. The words and facts recorded in Scripture continue to resist all naturalistic or rationalistic interpretation. Formally, revelation in Scripture indeed shows some resemblance to that on which other religions base themselves. Still, in principle, it is opposed to them and makes a firm distinction between them and itself. It attributes its origin, deliberately and with complete assurance, solely to an extraordinary operative presence of God. Scripture prohibits all fortune-telling and sorcery (Lev. 19:16, 31; 20:6, 27; Deut. 18:10f.; Isa. 8:19; Jer. 27:9; Acts 8:9f.; 13:8f.; 19:13; Rev. 21:8; 22:15). The prophets and apostles want nothing to do with it. They are utterly opposed to it and do not follow cleverly devised fables (2 Pet. 1:16). Prophecy in earlier times never came by the will of human be-

---

19. J. A. L. Wegscheider, *Institutiones theologiae christianae dogmaticae* (Lipsiae: 1844), §48; Bretschneider, *Handbuch der Dogmatik*, I, 314.

20. K. G. Bretschneider, *Systematische Entwickelung aller in der Dogmatik vorkommenden Begriffe* (Leipzig: J. A. Barth, 1841), 135ff.

21. Thomas Woolston, *Six Discourses on the Miracles of Our Saviour and Defences of his Discourses* (1727; reprinted, New York: Garland Pub., 1979).

22. H. E. G. Paulus, *Philogisch-kritischer und historischer commentar über das Neue Testament*, 4 vols. (Lübeck, J. F. Bohn, 1800–1804); idem, *Das leben Jesu* (Heidelberg: C. F. Winter, 1828); idem, *Exegetisches Handbuch über die drei ersten Evangelien*, 3 vols. (Heidelberg: C. F. Winter, 1830–33).

23. D. F. Strauss, *Das leben Jesu*, 2 vols. (Tübingen: C. F. Osiander, 1835–36). Ed. note: Bavinck begins this note with a reference to three authors without indicating titles: Eichhorn, Gabler, G. L. Bauer. Likely he is referring to N. Eichhorn, *Jesus von Nazaret: Ein tragisches Festspiel* (Berlin: G. Bemmster, 1880); G. L. Bauer, *Biblische Theologie des Neuen Testaments* (Leipzig: Weyand, 1800); and G. A. Gabler, *System der theoretischen Philosophie* (Erlangen: Palm, 1827), or possibly *Lehrbuch der philosophischen Propädeutik: Als Einleitung zur Wissenschaft* (Erlangen: Palm, 1827).

24. A. D. Loman, "Symbool en Werkelijkheid in de Evangelische Geschiedenis," *De Gids* 48 (February 1884): 265–304.

25. See above, pp. 70–76, 170–74.

ings, but the Holy Spirit moved the prophets (2 Pet. 1:21; 1 Cor. 2:11, 12), and miracles are a sign (σημειον) of the presence of God. The lucid self-confidence we encounter in the prophets and the utterly clear self-witness that accompanies revelation everywhere in Scripture present an insurmountable obstacle to naturalistic interpretations. The psychological method[26] too is unable to do justice to this self-assurance and self-witness of the prophets and apostles, indeed even of Christ himself. We may gratefully acknowledge that the modern view of revelation has completely ceased to consider the prophets and apostles as deliberate impostors. Still, they cannot escape the conclusion that all these men were wretched dupes and bona fide blunderers inasmuch as they based themselves on supposed revelation and acted on the basis of an imagined divine authority.

The case, after all, is not that revelation only contains certain facts whose interpretation it leaves to our own insights. Revelation, rather, itself casts a peculiar light on these facts; it has, so to speak, its own view and its own theory about those facts. In the revelation of Scripture, word and fact, prophecy and miracle, always go hand in hand. Both are needed so that the human mind as well as being itself are re-created and the entire cosmos is redeemed from sin. "The light needs the reality and the reality needs the light to produce . . . the beautiful creation of his grace. To apply the Kantian phraseology to a higher subject: without God's acts the words would be empty, without his words the acts would be blind."[27] Word and fact are so tightly interwoven in revelation that the one cannot be accepted or rejected without the other. Every attempt to explain the facts of revelation naturalistically has up until now therefore always ended with the acknowledgment that between the supernatural worldview of Scripture and that of naturalists there yawns an enormous gap and that reconciliation between them is impossible. Professor Scholten has produced a striking example of this reality. Initially he still accepted the pronouncements of the Johannine Jesus as truth. Then he attempted to explain these pronouncements in terms of his changed insights and to make the exegesis serviceable to his heterodox dogmatics. Finally, in 1864, he openly acknowledged that the worldview of the fourth evangelist was different from his own.[28]

Every negative school of theology finally acknowledges that the revelation of Scripture is still understood and conveyed most accurately in orthodoxy. Radicalism takes Scripture for what it is and is through with revelation.

26. Strauss, *Die Christliche Glaubenslehre*, I, 77; Abraham Kuenen, *De Profeten en de Profetie onder Israël: Historisch-dogmatische Studie* (Leiden: P. Engels, 1875), I, 106f.; in English: *The Prophets and Prophecy in Israel* (London: Longmans, Green, 1877).

27. G. Vos, *The Idea of Biblical Theology as a Science and a Theological Discipline: Inauguration of the Rev. Geerhardus Vos as Professor of Biblical Theology, Princeton Theological Seminary, May 8, 1894* (New York: A. D. F. Randolph, 1894), 15; reprinted in Richard B. Gaffin Jr., *Redemptive History and Biblical Interpretation: The Shorter Writings of Geerhardus Vos* (Phillipsburg, N.J.: Prebyterian and Reformed, 1980), 3–24. A. Kuyper, *Uit het Woord* (Amsterdam: J. A. Wormser, n.d.), I, 69–160.

28. J. H. Scholten, *Het Evangelie naar Johannes* (Leiden: P. Engels, 1864), III–VI; cf. the statement by Kattenbusch above, p. 83.

With that the issue has been reduced to its most fundamental level. Whether revelation is accepted or not is decided by our whole life-and-worldview. Decisive here is not historical criticism but self-criticism, not science but faith, not the head but the heart. Also obduracy comes out of the heart (cf. Mark 7:22). Our thinking is rooted in our being. "What you do follows from what you are" (*Operari sequitur esse*—Schopenhauer). "Your choice of philosophy depends on the person you are. Our ideology is often only the history of our heart" (Fichte). That the recognition or non-recognition of revelation, in the final analysis, is a matter of faith is sufficiently proven by the fact that neither the supernatural nor the naturalistic view is capable of clearing up all the difficulties or meeting all the objections. The naturalistic view seems to be strong when it focuses on a few isolated miracle stories; but the narrative as a whole, the system of revelation and the person of Christ at the center of it, remain to it an insoluble riddle and a stone of stumbling. Conversely, the supernatural view has not yet succeeded in fitting all the particular facts and words of revelation into the order of the whole. Still, here one finds agreement with revelation in its entirety, insight into its system, the overall conception in its splendid harmony. Now if the recognition of revelation were a philosophical proposition, it would be of relatively little weight. In fact, however, a profound religious interest is at stake here. Religion itself is interconnected with, and dependent on, revelation. Those who abandon revelation also lose the religion based upon it. The revelation of Scripture and the religion of Scripture stand or fall together.

MONISM AND THEISM

[101] The worldview that is opposed to Scripture and must in principle oppose all revelation can best be labeled *monism*. Monism, both in its pantheistic and in its materialistic form, strives to reduce all the forces, materials, and laws perceptible in nature to a single force, material, and law. Materialism only accepts qualitatively identical atoms, which everywhere and always work according to the same mechanical laws, and, by combination and separation, make and break all things and all phenomena. Pantheism only recognizes the existence of a single substance, which is the same in all creatures and which everywhere transmutes and transforms itself in accordance with the same laws of logic. Both materialism and pantheism are driven by the same urge, the urge and drive toward unity, which is characteristic of the human mind. But there is a difference. Materialism attempts to rediscover the unity of matter and law that holds sway in the physical world, in all other historical, psychological, religious, and ethical phenomena as well, and thus to transform all sciences into natural science. Pantheism, on the other hand, attempts to explain all phenomena, including the physical, in terms of the mind and to convert all sciences into the science of the mind. Both are naturalistic insofar as they may perhaps still make room for the su-

persensible, but not in any case for the supernatural, and with respect to science and art, religion and morality, are content with this cosmos and the here-and-now.[29]

The worldview of Scripture and of all of Christian theology is a very different one. Its name is theism, not monism; its orientation is supernatural, not naturalistic. According to this theistic worldview, there is a multiplicity of substances, forces, materials, and laws. It does not strive to erase the distinctions between God and the world, between spirit (mind) and matter, between psychological and physical, ethical and religious phenomena. It seeks rather to discover the harmony that holds all things together and unites them and that is the consequence of the creative thought of God. Not identity or uniformity but unity in diversity is what it aims at. Despite all the pretensions of monism, this theistic worldview has a right and reason to exist. It is a fact, after all, that monism has not succeeded in reducing all the forces and materials and laws to just one element. While materialism stumbles into psychological phenomena, pantheism cannot find a bridge between thought and existence and does not know what to do with multiplicity. Existence itself is a mystery and a miracle. That anything exists at all compels astonishment in the thinking mind, and this astonishment, accordingly, has rightly been called the beginning of philosophy. The more deeply human beings penetrate this existence intellectually, the more astonished they become, for within the sphere of existence, of the cosmos, we see various forces in action: in the mechanical, vegetative, animal, and psychological world, but also in religious and ethical, aesthetic and logical, phenomena.

Creation displays before our eyes an ascending order. Indeed, some interpret and misuse the laws of the sustenation of power, of causality and continuity ("nature does not make leaps") in the interest of monism. Over and over, however, forces arise in nature that cannot be explained from a lower-level form of existence. Causality holds sway in mechanical nature but only in a hypothetical sense. Identical causes have identical effects but only under identical circumstances. In the organic world a force is at work that does not arise from the inorganic. Hegel correctly notes: "An animal is a miracle by comparison with vegetable nature and even more the mind by comparison with life, with merely sensory nature."[30] To a stone it is a miracle that a plant grows; to a plant that an animal moves; to an animal that a human thinks; and to a human that God raises the

---

29. D. F. Strauss, *Der alte und der neue Glaube*, 2d ed. (Leipzig: S. Hirzel, 1872), I, 211ff.; in English: *The Old Faith and the New* (New York: D. M. Bennett, 1879); E. Haeckel, *Der Monismus als Band zwischen Religion und Wissenschaft*, 6th ed. (Bonn: Verlag von Emil Strauss, 1893); idem, *Die Welträthsel* (Bonn: E. Strauss, 1901); in English: *The Riddle of the Universe*, rev. E. R. Lankester, 2 vols. (New York: Appleton, 1883); idem, *Die Lebenswunder* (Stuttgart: A. Kröner, 1904); in English: *The Wonders of Life* (New York: Harper 1904); Benjamin Vetter, *Die moderne Weltanschauung und der Mensch*, 5th ed. (Jena: G. Fischer, 1906). During the year 1906 a society of Monists was founded in Jena with Ernst Haeckel as honorary chairman. The first copy of their publication, *Der Monist*, appeared in May 1906.

30. G. F. W. Hegel, *Vorlesungen über die Philosophie der Religion*, in *Sämtliche Werke* (Stuttgart: Frommanns, 1959), vol 16, p. 256 (= *Werke*, XII, 256 [German ed.])

dead.[31] Operative in life in the intellect, the will, religion, morality, art, science, law, and history there are forces that differ essentially from the mechanical and that up until now resist any and all mechanical explanation. To this very day the intellectual sciences have kept their independence.[32] Since the rise of historical materialism, historical researchers, having reflected more deeply on their discipline, have argued for its independence alongside of natural science.[33] And in recent times even many practitioners of natural science have registered a protest against mechanical monism, again acknowledged the mystery of life, and traded in a rigorous theory of descent for a notion of development that involves [discontinuous] leaps.[34] Professor Land has to admit, be it reluctantly, that for the time being science is compelled to remain dualistic and even pluralistic.[35]

Each of these forces operates according to its own nature, its own law, and in its own way. They all differ, hence also their effects and the way they function. The idea of natural law only emerged gradually. In earlier times the "law of nature" (*lex naturae*) meant an ethical rule that was known "by nature." Later on this term was transferred in a very metaphorical sense to nature, for no one enacted those laws for nature and no one has the power to obey or transgress them. That is the reason why even today there is much disagreement about the concept and meaning of the "laws of nature." "In the seventeenth century God legislated the laws of nature; in the eighteenth, nature itself decreed them; and in the nineteenth century the individual natural scientists furnish them" (Wundt). This much is certain, however: the so-called laws of nature themselves are not forces that govern the phenomena but merely a frequently very deficient and always fallible description of the manner in which the forces inherent in nature work. A natural law only means that certain forces, under the same conditions, work in the same way.[36]

---

31. Martin von Nathusius, *Die Mitarbeit der Kirche an der Lösung der sozialen Frage*, 2d ed. (Leipzig: J. C. Hinrichs, 1897), 238.

32. Wilhelm Dilthey, *Einleitung in die Geisteswissenschaften* (Leipzig: Duncker & Humblot, 1883), I, 3ff.; in English: *Introduction to the Human Sciences* (Princeton, N.J.; Oxford: Princeton University Press, 1991); Henry Drummond, *Das Naturgesetz in der Geisteswelt* (Leipzig: J. C. Hinrichs, 1889), 18ff.; in English: *Natural Law in the Spiritual World* (Chicago: Donohue Brothers, 1881).

33. Cf. Alexander Giesswein, *Deterministiche und metaphysische Schichtsauffassung* (Wien: Mayer, 1905); and H. Bavinck, *Christelijke Wetenschap* (Kampen: Kok, 1904), 65ff.

34. See for example, Johannes Reinke, *Die Welt als Tat* (Berlin: Gebrüder Paetel, 1905).

35. J. P. N. Land, *Inleiding tot de Wijsbegeerte* (s'Gravenhage: Nijhoff, 1900), 328; and compare further against the monism o.a. Konrad Dieterich, *Philosophie und Naturwissenschaft: Ihr neustes Bündniss und die monistische Weltanschauung* (Tübingen: H. Laupp'schen Buchhandlung, 1875; 2d ed., Freiburg, 1885); Tilmann Pesch, *Die grossen Welträthsel*, 2d ed. (Freiburg i.B.: Herder 1892); C. Gutberlet, *Der mechanische Monismus: Eine Kritik der modernen Weltanschauung* (Paderborn: F. Schöningh, 1893); Herman Bavinck, *Christelijke Wetenschap*; idem, *Christelijke Wereldbeschouwing* (Kampen: Kok, 1904).

36. Eduard Zeller, *Vorträge und abhandlungen geschichtlichen inhalts*, 3 vols. (Leipzig: Fues's Verlag [L. W. Reisland], 1865–84), III, 194ff.; Hermann Lotze, *Mikrokosmus: Ideen zur Naturgeschichte & Geschichte der Menschheit*, 4th ed., 3 vols. (Leipzig, 1880–85), I, 31ff.; II, 50ff.; III, 13ff.; in English: *Microcosmus: An Essay concerning Man and His Relation to the World*, 2 vols. (New York: Scribner and Welford, 1885); Wilhelm Wundt, *Psychologische Studien*, 10 vols. (Leipzig: W. Englemann, 1905–18), III, 195ff.; IV, 12ff.; M. Heinze, "Naturgesetz," *PRE³*, XIII, 657–59; Eisler, *Wörterbuch der philosophischen Begriffe*, s.v. "Gesetz."

The regularity of the phenomena, accordingly, is ultimately based on the immutability of the various forces operative in nature and of the most basic elements or substances of which it is composed. The laws differ to the extent that these elements and forces are distinct. Mechanical laws differ from physical laws; the laws of logic in turn differ from ethical and aesthetic laws. In a physical sense giving [money or goods] makes one poorer, but in an ethical sense it makes one richer. Hence the laws of nature, i.e., of the whole cosmos and every creature in it, do not form a cordon around things so that nothing can enter or come out but only a formula for the way in which, according to our perception, every force works in accordance with its nature.

All these elements and forces with their inherent laws, according to the theistic worldview, are from moment to moment upheld by God, who is the final, supreme, intelligent, and free causality of all things. As creatures, they have no stability or durability in themselves. It is God's omnipresent and eternal power that upholds and governs all things. In him, in his plan and also in his rule, originates the unity or harmony that holds together and unites all things over the entire range of their diversity and leads them to a single goal. Consequently, as Augustine keeps saying, there is unity, measure, order, number, mode, degree, and kind of creatures. "To some things he gave more of being and to others less and, in this way, arranged an order of nature in a hierarchy of being."[37] God is present in all things. In him all things live and move and have their being. Nature and history are his work; he works always (John 5:17). All things reveal God to us. Although his finger may be more clearly observable to us in one event than in another, the pure in heart see God in all his works. Hence miracles are absolutely not necessary to make God known to us as the upholder and ruler of the universe. Everything is his deed. Nothing happens apart from his will. He is present with his being in all things. And therefore all things are also a revelation, a word, a work of God.

Supernatural revelation is entirely compatible with such a worldview. In it, after all, nature does not for a moment exist independently of God but lives and moves in him. Every force that asserts itself in it originates from him and works according to the law he has put in it. God does not stand outside of nature and is not excluded from it by a hedge of laws but is present in it and sustains it by the word of his power. He works from within and can generate new forces, which in nature and operation are distinct from the existing ones. And these higher forces, though they do not cancel out the lower ones, occupy a place of their own alongside of and amidst these lower forces. The human spirit attempts at every moment to counter the lower forces in their workings and to subordinate them to its will. All of culture is a power by which human beings hold sway over nature. Art and science are a triumph of the mind over matter. Similarly in revelation, in prophecy and miracle, there appears a new divine force which, though it occupies a place of its own in the cosmos, absolutely

37. Augustine, *The City of God*, XII, 2.

does not conflict with the lower forces and their laws. There is no such thing as the suspension of natural laws by miracles. Nature is not "shot full of holes" by them. Thomas already observed: "When God does anything contrary to the course of nature, the whole order of the universe is not subverted, but the course resulting from the relation between one particular thing and another."[38] Indeed, even the relation between cause and effect is not destroyed: although the fire in the furnace did not burn the three young men, the fiery furnace did retain its relation to burning. Miracles do not bring about a change in the forces inherent in nature nor in the laws according to which they operate. The only thing that happens in a miracle is that the operation of the forces of nature is suspended at a given point as the result of the appearance of another force which works according to a law of its own and produces an effect of its own.

Science, accordingly, has nothing to fear from the supernatural. But every science must remain within the bounds of its own area and not arrogate to itself the right to pose the law to another science. It is the right and duty of natural science to search within its area for the natural causes of phenomena. But it should not attempt to rule over philosophy when the latter investigates the origin and destiny of things. It should also recognize the right and independence of religion and theology and not attempt to undermine the foundation on which they rest. For at stake here are religious motives for belief in a revelation about which natural science as such cannot make any judgment. Also in the different sciences the goal does not lie in uniformity but in harmony. Theology must respect natural science and insist on being treated similarly. For when the different sciences do not respect each other, we get assertions like those of Hume, Voltaire, and Renan, viz., that no miracle has ever been adequately ascertained and that constant experience cannot be overturned by a few testimonies. Renan puts it like this: "We do not say, 'Miracles are impossible.' We say: 'Up to this time a miracle has never been proved.'" He refuses to believe in a miracle as long as no commission composed of an assortment of natural scientists, physiologists, chemists, etc. has examined such an event and after repeated experimentation established it to be a miracle.[39] Given such a condition, miracles are a priori ruled out: for in the case of the miracles of Scripture the opportunity to conduct such tests are given neither to Renan nor to anyone of us. At this point these miracles irrevocably belong to history, and in history a different method has to be applied than in the natural sciences. In the latter, experimentation is in order. But in history we are dealing with the testimonies of witnesses. If, however, the experimental method has to be introduced and applied in history, there is not a single fact that can stand the test. In that case all historiography is done for. Let every science, therefore, remain

38. Thomas Aquinas, *On the Power of God,* trans. Lawrence Shapcote (Westminster, Md.: Newman Press, 1952), qu. 6, art. 1, as cited by Eugen Müller, *Natur und Wunder, ihr Gegensatz und ihre Harmonie* (Freiburg i.B. and St. Louis, Mo.: Herder, 1892), 133.

39. Ernest Renan, *Vie de Jésus* (Paris: C. Lévy, 1897), LI.; in English: *The Life of Jesus,* trans. William G. Hutchinson (New York: A. L. Burt, 1897).

in its own area and there investigate things according to their own nature. One cannot see a thing by means of the ear, or weigh them with a yardstick; neither can one test revelation by means of an experiment.[40]

MIRACLES

[102] Nature, i.e., the cosmos, furthermore, is still far too frequently conceived as a ready-made machine that is now driven by a single force and always moves under the governance of a single law. This inept conception is a legacy of deism. But it is still being unconsciously held by many people and serves as an argument in opposing revelation. But nature, i.e., the cosmos, is not a finished product but φύσις (*natura*) in the true sense of the word; it is always becoming, caught up in an ongoing teleological development. It is guided in successive periods toward a divine destiny. In such a view of nature, miracles are again completely at home. On the last page of his *Kulturgeschichte* ("History of Culture"), Fr. Hellwald says that some day all life on earth will perish in the eternal rest of death and ends with the following dreary words: "Then the earth, robbed of its atmosphere and biosphere, will circle around the sun in moon-like desolation as before. But the *human* race—its culture, its struggles and striving, its creations and ideals—will be *a thing of the past*. To what end?" Of course, in a system that ended with such an unanswered question, revelation and miracles would be a mere absurdity.

Scripture teaches us, however, that revelation serves the end of re-creating the creation, which was corrupted by sin, into a kingdom of God. Here revelation assumes a completely proportionate and teleological place in the world plan God made and realized in the course of the ages. In that sense Augustine already commented: "A portent is not contrary to nature as it is, but contrary to nature as known."[41] The expression has frequently been misinterpreted in the interest of a theology that attempted to understand miracles as the effect of a power naturally present in human beings or in nature or was restored in them by regeneration or faith. This peculiar view, which already occurs in Philo and neoplatonism, resonated repeatedly in the work of various Christian theologians, Erigena, Paracelsus, Cornelius Agrippa, Bohme, and Oetinger,[42] and is found now and then also in the mediating theology (*Vermittelungstheologie*).[43]

40. F. Vigouroux, *Les Livres Saints et la critique rationaliste,* 3d ed., 5 vols. (Paris: A. Roger et F. Chernoviz, 1890–1902), I, 73; II, 294.

41. Augustine, *The City of God,* XXI, 8; *Against Faustus the Manichaean,* XXIX, 6; XXVI, 3.

42. Denzinger, *Vier Bücher,* II, 182ff., 361ff.

43. A. D. C. Twesten, *Vorlesungen über die Dogmatik der Evangelisch-Lutherischen Kirche,* 2 vols. (Hamburg: F. Perth, 1837–38), I, 370ff.; II, 171ff.; H. Martensen, *Christian Dogmatics: A Compendium of the Doctrines of Christianity,* trans. William Urwick (Edinburgh: T. & T. Clark, 1878), §16f.; Schleiermacher, *The Christian Faith,* §13, 1; §129; Karl Sack, *Christliche Apologetik* (Hamburg: Friedrich Perthes, 1841), 137ff.; J. Lange, *Philosophische Dogmatik,* §64; on Saussaye, see H. Bavinck, *De Theologie van Prof. Dr. Daniel Chantepie de la Saussaye: Bijdrage tot de Kennis der Ethische Theologie* (Leiden: D. Donner, 1903), 36ff.; J. H. Gunning, *Blikken in de Openbaring* (Amsterdam: Höveker, 1866–69), II, 37ff.

In that view, revelation, inspiration, and miracle belong to the original capacity of human nature. Although that capacity has been weakened by sin, it still comes to expression in poetic and heroic inspiration, in magnetism, and other related phenomena. This capacity can be renewed and strengthened, however, by way of ethics, by union with God, by ascetic purification, by regeneration, etc. All believers, accordingly, are really inspired and can do miracles. "If human nature had not sinned and had clung without change to Him who had created it, it would certainly be omnipotent."[44] According to Zimmer, miracles are "signs of man in his lordship over nature in which the glory of the first pair of human beings is depicted before the appearance of sin."[45] When the soul is oriented in love toward God, says Böhme, it can do miracles at will. In a similar way, C. Bonnet, in his *Recherches philosophiques sur les preuves du Christianisme* (Geneva, 1771), sees a preformation of prophecy and miracle in nature and consider them realized by the operation of ordinary natural powers. In the eighteenth century some theologians therefore spoke of the "seminal, primordial, and radical ideas" (rationes) of miracles.

But this attempt to explain miracles cannot be accepted. It confuses the natural with the supernatural, the supernatural with the religious/ethical, and erases the boundaries between prophecy and divination, miracle and magic, inspiration and illumination. Neither may the above-mentioned statement by Augustine be interpreted along those lines. By "known" nature he is referring to a nature in our sense of the word. And with a view to it he even says that miracles are contrary to nature, as Thomas and Voetius did later as well. But that same miracle has from the beginning been included by God in nature in the broader sense, i.e., in the divinely determined destiny of things, in the divine world plan.[46] The same idea was later expressed also by Leibnitz.[47] God included miracles in his world plan from the beginning and brings them about in due course. Miracles cannot be explained "by the natures of created things but reasons of an order higher than that of nature induce it to perform them." According to Leibnitz, therefore, miracles are not germinally and potentially present in the powers of nature, as Nitzsch interprets Leibnitz,[48] but are constitutive elements in the world plan of God. To that extent miracles most certainly belong to nature. They do not enter the existing cosmos from without to disturb it but are incorporated in the design of the world itself and serve the completion and perfecting of fallen nature. Indeed, even without sin there would have been room for prophecy and miracle in the world. The supernatural was not first made necessary by

44. John Scotus Erigena, *De Divisione Naturae*, IV, 9.

45. B. Zimmer, *Philosophische Untersuchung über den allegemeinen Verfall des menschlichen Geschlechtes* (Landshut: Weberschen Buchhandlung, 1809), III, n. 90ff.

46. F. Nitzsch, *Augustinus' Lehre vom Wünder* (Berlin: E. S. Mittler, 1865).

47. Leibniz, *Théodicée*, §54, 207.

48. F. Nitzsch, *Lehrbuch der evangelischen Dogmatik* (Freiburg i.B.: J. C. B. Mohr [Paul Siebeck], 1892), 146.

the fall. Not revelation and miracle as such, only the soteriological character that they bear now, has been necessitated by sin. To that extent even miracle is not an alien element that was added to the fallen creation. Revelation and religion, prophecy and miracle are not as such superadded gifts. They are completely natural insofar as they belong to the cosmic design of God and to the world plan, which he, despite all opposition, will implement in time.

Still, revelation constitutes an order of things that is essentially distinct from the ordinary order of nature. Just as, on the one hand, it is necessary to maintain the bond between nature and revelation, so, on the other hand, it is equally necessary to cling to the essential distinction between the two. In the past the discipline of apologetics sometimes attached too much importance to the fact that science had to face inexplicable phenomena or was surprised by the discovery of hitherto unknown forces and laws. It then appealed too eagerly to the many marvelous phenomena that turned up in magnetism and spiritism, hypnotism and telepathy, and sometimes cherished the idea that by all these phenomena the miracles of Scripture could be sufficiently justified and explained. Not that all these discoveries and phenomena were unimportant; they are, in fact, extremely well-suited for the purpose of urging modesty upon science, which arrogantly thinks it can explain everything. But the miracles of Scripture constitute a unique category of their own and cannot be put on a level with such strange phenomena, much less be equated with them. Over against attempts to interpret the biblical miracles as a form of spiritism,[49] we may well take to heart Fechner's statement: "Between the miracles of holy Scripture and spiritist phenomena there is a contrast in character such that it seems blasphemous to bring them together under a single rubric and to wish to support Christianity with the attempt to make Christ into an exceptionally gifted medium. The difference between them is one between night and day."[50]

The advantage of the comparative-historical method is that, after initial astonishment over the formal resemblance between many phenomena in and outside of revelation, it has yielded to a more sober assessment and will now bring out all the more clearly the difference in kind between the two. Now already there is universal recognition that the miracles of Holy Scripture are not susceptible to a naturalistic or rationalistic interpretation. The events that Scripture relates as miracles were not considered miracles because at the time people were not yet familiar with the laws of nature but are still miracles in the full sense for us as well. One can differ about matters of historical truth, but if those events took place they were in a very real sense miracles and absolutely not dependent on a greater or lesser degree of familiarity with the laws of nature. Modern theology recognizes this and simply rejects them because they are miracles and supposedly incompatible with the laws of na-

---

49. Maximilian Perty, *Der jetzige Spiritualismus* (1877), 212ff.; J. Kreyher, *Die mystischen Erscheinungen des Seelenlebens und die biblischen Wunder: Ein apologetischer Versuch* (Stuttgart: J. F. Steinkopf, 1881).

50. With Eduard Weber, *Der moderne Spiritismus* (Heilbronn: Henninger, 1883), 68.

ture. Remarkable, however, is that the interpreters of this point of view are nevertheless unwilling to abandon miracles in every sense of the word. As in every dogma, they think that in belief in miracles two elements are combined: a theoretical and a religious element. The theoretical element they abandon altogether because they judge that it is embedded in an unscientific and untenable worldview. However, they attempt to maintain the religious element, the unlimited confidence in God's leading in human life.[51] They unintentionally prove by this that the idea of "miracle," like that of revelation, contains more value for religion than naturalism and rationalism imagined. Indeed, miracle is as indispensable to religion as revelation. "A faith without miracles is a crippled faith" ("Ein Glaube ohne Wunder ist ein wunder Glaube"—Jos. Muller).

This indispensability of miracles does not lie in that believers can only perceive God's hand in his extraordinary works and not in the ordinary course of nature. For prophets, apostles, and all devout believers, while believing in miracles, have with equal tenacity held to the belief that God's providence encompasses all things. But those who deny "miracle," i.e., those who deny not just one or another specific miracle but the possibility of miracles, box God in and bind him to nature. In principle they assert that God does not have an independent existence of his own, one that is distinct from the world. Consequently they also have to deny—as being miraculous—creation, divine providence, answers to prayer, direct fellowship between God and human beings. Moreover, they lose all grounds for believing in a future victory of the kingdom of God, in a teleology operative in world history, and therefore end in pantheistic or materialistic naturalism. Conversely, those who cannot live with such naturalism and do without all the above-mentioned elements as constituents of religion, themselves live in the wonder of the miraculous and see the door to belief in the miracles of Holy Scripture opened to them. And they accept them the more willingly to the degree that they come to the realization that all the words and deeds of God in Scripture constitute an interconnected whole, which is governed by a single idea.

Revelation is not an individual act of God in time, isolated from nature as a whole,[52] but a world by itself, distinct from nature, to be sure, but still made for it, akin to it, and intended for it. In this system of revelation, which begins in paradise and ends only in the parousia, there is still much that is obscure and unexplained. But the outline of it can be discerned. Both

---

51. Cf. with Auguste Sabatier, *Esquisse d'une philosophie de la religion d'après la psychologie et l'histoire* (Paris: Fischbacher, 1903), 64–95; in English: *Outlines of a Philosophy of Religion Based on Psychology and History* (New York: James Pott, 1902); Eugène Ménégoz, *Publications diverses sur le fidéisme et son application à l'enseignement chrétien traditionnel* (Paris: Fischbacher, 1900), 124–205, 307–16; Adolf von Harnack, *What Is Christianity?* trans. Thomas Bailey Saunders, 2d ed. (New York: G. P. Putnam's sons, 1908), 25ff.; R. A. Lipsius, *Lehrbuch der evangelisch-protestantischen Dogmatik* (Braunschweig: C. A. Schwetschke, 1893), §58–61.

52. Strauss, *Die Christliche Glaubenslehre*, I, 274.

in the history of prophecy and that of miracles there is discernible order and development. Revelation, too, has its own laws and rules. It is the beautiful assignment of the "history of revelation" to track them down and to discover the system that is concealed in its history. There are still many facts in it that cannot be understood in their true significance for, and connection with, the whole; also many words and deeds that cannot be subsumed under a specific rule. This need not surprise us and may by no means be exploited as a ground for unbelief. The philosophy of nature and history is likewise far from being finished with its work. It, too, is confronted at every moment by cruxes that it cannot unravel. Nevertheless, no one questions the unity of nature and the existence of a plan of history. By comparison with it, the situation of revelation is even quite favorable. Its outline is established. Beginning in paradise and ending in the parousia, it forms a grand story line that casts light on all of nature and history and thus, as Augustine puts it, by the ordinary protects the extraordinary from extravagance and ennobles the ordinary by the extraordinary.[53] Without it we walk in darkness and go to the eternal rest of death without an answer to the question: what is the purpose of it all? But with it, we find ourselves in a world that, despite all the power of sin, is led to restoration and perfection. Israel is the preparation, Christ the center, the church the consequence, and the parousia the crown—that is the cord that binds the facts of revelation together.

Accordingly, faith in special revelation is ultimately one with faith in another and better world. If this world with its naturally immanent forces and laws is the only world and the best world, then of course we have to be content with it. Then the laws of nature are identical with the decrees of God; then the world is the Son, the Logos, the true image of God; then the order of nature in which we live is already the full and exhaustive revelation of God's wisdom, power, goodness, and holiness. But then what right do we have to expect that the "there" will one day become the "here," that the ideal will become reality, that the good will triumph over evil, that the "world of values" will one day prevail over the "world of reality"? Evolution will not take us there. Nothing comes out of nothing (*nihil fit ex nihilo*). This world will never turn into a paradise. Nothing can come forth from it that is not in it. If there is no beyond (Jenseits), no God who is above nature, no supernatural order, then sin, darkness, and death have the last word. The revelation of Scripture makes known to us another world, a world of holiness and glory. This other world descends into this fallen world, not just as a doctrine but also as a divine power (δυναμις), as history, as reality, as a harmonious system of words and deeds in conjunction. It is work, no, as *the* work of God by which he lifts this world out of its fall and leads it out of the state of sin, through the state of grace, to the state of glory. Revelation is God's coming to humankind to dwell with it forever.

53. According to Müller, *Natur und Wunder*, 180.

REVELATION, SACRED SCRIPTURES, AND HISTORY

[103] The history of religions not only reveals a close connection between religion and revelation but also one between revelation and scripture. In the domain of religion, magical formulas, liturgical texts, ritual treatises, ceremonial laws, priestly documents, historical and mythological literature, etc., are found among all peoples of culture. But in an even more restricted sense there is reason to speak of holy scriptures in the religions [of the world]. Many peoples also have a book or a collection of books that have divine authority and serve as the standard for doctrine and life. Included are the Shu Ching of the Chinese, the Vedas of the [South East Asian] Indians, the Tripitaka of the Buddhists, the Avesta of the Persians, the Koran of the Muslims, the Hebrew Bible (Tanak) of the Jews, and the Bible of the Christians. Collectively these seven religions are categorized as "book religions."[54] This phenomenon as such already indicates that the connection between revelation and scripture cannot be accidental or arbitrary. The history of the doctrine of the Koran even shows remarkable parallels with that of the dogma of Scripture in the Christian church.[55] This linkage between religion, revelation, word, and scripture is not at all surprising. For the content of religion is first of all ideas, doctrine, dogma, which it owes to revelation, expresses in words, passes on by tradition from one generation to another, and, finally, renders permanent in scripture. Intimately related, first of all, are thought and word, thinking and speaking. Indeed, they are not, as Max Müller thinks,[56] identical, for there is also a kind of thinking, a consciousness, a sense, however unclear, which is non-verbal. "For man is not able to say anything which he cannot also think; he can, however, think that which he is not able to say."[57]

But certainly a word is primarily the fully matured, independent, and therefore lucid thought—an indispensable tool for conscious thinking. Language is the soul of a nation, the custodian of the goods and treasures of humankind, the bond that unites human beings, peoples, and generations, the one great tradition that unites in consciousness the world of humankind, which is one by nature. But just as the thought embodies itself in a word, so words are embodied in scripture. And language itself is no more than a body of signs, audible signs. And the audible sign naturally seeks stability in the visible sign, in writing. The art of writing is actually the art of recording signs and, in this broad sense, while it occurs among all peoples, has gradually developed from pictograms through ideograms to alphabetic script.

54. Max Müller, *Vorlesungen über den Ursprung und die Entwickelung der Religion* (Strassburg: K. J. Trübner, 1880), 149. Idem, *Deutsche Rundschau* (March 1895): 409f.

55. M. Th. Houtsma, *De strijd over het dogma in den Islam tot op el-Ash'ari* (Leiden: S. C. van Doesburgh, 1875), 96f.

56. Max Müller, *Vorlesungen über die Wissenschaft der Sprache,* 3d ed. (Leipzig: J. Klinkhardt, 1875), 459; idem, *Das Denken im Lichte der Sprache* (Leipzig: W. Engelmann, 1888), 70–115.

57. Augustine, *Sermon* 117, c. 5.

However refined and increased in precision, it is inadequate. Our thinking, says Augustine,[58] fails to do justice to the subject, and our speech fails to measure up to our thoughts; so also there is a big gap between the spoken word and the written word. The sounds are always only roughly reproduced in visible signs. Thought is richer than speech, and speech is richer than writing. Still, the written word is of immense value and importance. The written word is the word made permanent, universal, everlasting. It communicates the thought to those who are far from us and live long after us, and makes it the common property of humankind. It depicts the word, thus speaking to the eyes. It gives body and color to the thought and at the same time confers on it permanence and stability. The written word is the incarnation of the [spoken] word.

That is true in general. The traditionalists, de Bonald, Lamennais, and Bautain, certainly went too far when they claimed that language came directly from God, that in language all the treasures of truth were preserved and that human beings now enjoy access to all truth from and through the language enshrined in tradition.[59] Still, there is a valuable idea expressed here, and especially in the domain of religion, word and scripture gain a higher meaning. Revelation in Christianity is a history. It consists in deeds, events, which pass and soon belong to the past. It is a transitory act, temporary and even momentary, and has this transitory character in common with all earthly things. Still, it encompasses eternal thoughts, which not only had meaning for the moment in which their disclosure occurred and for the persons to whom it came, but which are of value for all times and all human beings.

How can we harmonize this seemingly contradictory state of affairs, the strangeness of which has almost always been felt? Deism in England called attention to it. Herbert of Cherbury stated that credence could be given only to a revelation that came directly to us ourselves; revelations received by other people only have for us the status of history and tradition, and in our reading of history we can never get beyond probability.[60] Likewise, Hobbes wrote that a revelation that others had received could not be proven to us. In the same way Locke made a distinction between "original" and "traditional" revelation. From this state of affairs, deism deduced that natural religion was enough and had to be the real content of revelation. It therefore made a dichotomy between fact and idea, the temporal and eternal, the "accidental truths of history" and the "necessary truths of reason." The speculative rationalism of Hegel continued along the same lines: the idea does not pour itself out in a solitary individual.

Now in practice this dichotomy has proven to be impossible. In Christianity, as in every other religion, the detachment of the idea from history has always amounted to the loss of the idea itself. Lessing's thesis in his essay

---

58. Augustine, *On the Trinity,* VII, 4; *Christian Doctrine,* I, 6.
59. Albert Stöckl, *Lehrbuch der Philosophie,* 2 vols. (Mainz: Kirchheim & Co., 1905, 1912), I, 406f.
60. G. V. Lechler, *Geschichte des englischen Deismus* (Stuttgart: J. G. Cotta, 1841), 49.

"On the Proof of the Spirit and of Power," "accidental truths of history can never become the proof of necessary truths of reason,"[61] at the time encountered wide acceptance. But that fact can only be explained in terms of the lack of historical sense and the deification of reason that marked the eighteenth century. The present century [the nineteenth century] has distanced itself from this raving about "the necessary truths of reason" and this contempt for history. It has learned to understand history in its deeper meaning and in its eternal significance. If the facts of history were accidental, history itself would be the aggregate of isolated atomistic cases, without order, connection, and plan. Then history would no longer exist and the study of it would be useless. Implied in this position is that also the history of revelation would lose its value. But on the contrary: history is above all the realization of the thoughts of God, the expression of a divine plan for his creatures; and there is unity, movement, order, and design (logos) in it.

Such a view of history, it must be said, became possible only under the impact of Christianity. It is not found among the Greeks and Romans: they only knew of peoples, not of humanity. Scripture, however, makes known to us the unity of the human race; it teaches us the grand conception of a world history. And in this world history Scripture itself occupies the preeminent and all-dominating place. The "truths of history," accordingly, are not accidental, least of all the truths of the history of revelation. They are necessary to the degree that without them all of history and all of humankind would fall apart. History is the bearer of the thoughts of God, the revelation of God's intent, which over and over filled the apostle Paul with wonder and adoration, the revelation of mystery, without which human beings grope around in the dark. The "truths of reason" of which Lessing spoke, on the other hand, are far from necessary. Kant's critique has shown that to be otherwise. Precisely with respect to the "necessary truths of reason" a doubt-filled skepticism prevails today. Hence the relation is exactly the reverse of what Lessing believed. The historical is now understood in its eternal significance, and the rational has evinced its mutability.

The fact is we inherit all things from previous generations. We bring nothing into the world (1 Tim. 6:7). Physically and psychologically, intellectually and ethically, we are dependent on the world around us. Religiously, things are no different. The revelation that consists in history can come to us only in the way of tradition, tradition understood in the broadest possible sense. The question of why that revelation has not been granted to every human[62] is really not appropriate. It assumes that the Christian revelation contains only doctrine and forgets that it is and has to be history. The center of that revelation is the person of Christ. And Christ is a historical person; his incarnation, his suffering and death, his resurrection and ascension to

---

61. See *Lessing's Theological Writings,* ed. Henry Chadwick (Stanford University Press, 1957), 53.

62. Jean-Jacques Rousseau, *Profession de foi du vicaire savoyard* (Paris: Persan et Cie, 1822); Strauss, *Die Christliche Glaubenslehre,* I, 268f.

heaven are not susceptible of repetition. Indeed it is integral to the incarnation that he enter history and live in the form(s) of time. He would not have been like us in all things had he not subjected himself to time and space, to the law of becoming. Revelation, not as doctrine but as incarnation, can self-evidently be nothing other than history, i.e., occur at a certain time and be bound to a certain place. The incarnation is the unity of being (ἐγω εἰμι, John 8:58) and becoming (σαρξ ἐγενετο, John 1:14). Further, also in his revelation God follows the basic lines he has drawn for the coexistence of human beings. Humankind is not an aggregate of individuals but an organic whole in which all people live interdependently. Revelation follows this law; re-creation is adapted to creation. Just as in every domain of life we participate in the goods of humankind by means of tradition, so also in religion. That, too, belongs to the idea of the incarnation. It is itself an event, which at one time happened in time but which through the tradition becomes the possession and blessing of all human beings. That this revelation is still limited to such a small number of people produces a difficult problem, one that needs to be examined further; but on the part of those who know the revelation, this poignant fact can never be a reason for rejecting it. Many ethnic groups still live in a state of crude barbarism. That, too, happens according to God's will and good pleasure. But it occurs to no one to despise the blessings of civilization for that reason. Rousseau who raved about the "people of nature" continued to live quietly in France.

INCARNATION, LANGUAGE, AND THE BIBLE

[104] The bearer of the ideal goods of humankind is language, and the σαρξ of language is the written word. In making himself known, God also adapts himself to this reality. To be able fully to enter the life of humankind and for it fully to become its possession, revelation assumes the form (μορφη) and fashion (σχημα) of Scripture. Scripture is the servant form of revelation. Indeed, the central fact of revelation, i.e., the incarnation, leads to Scripture. In prophecy and miracle revelation descends so low and so deeply that it does not despise even the lowest forms of human and specifically religious life as a means. The Logos himself does not merely become a human (ἀνθρω-πος) but a servant (δουλος), flesh (σαρξ). And the word of revelation similarly assumes the imperfect and inadequate form of Scripture. But thus alone revelation becomes the good of humankind. The purpose of revelation is not Christ; Christ is the center and the means; the purpose is that God will again dwell in his creatures and reveal his glory in the cosmos: θεος τα παντα εν πασιν ["that God may be all things in everyone," 1 Cor. 15:28]. In a sense this, too, is an incarnation of God. And to achieve this purpose the word of revelation passes into Scripture. Hence Scripture, too, is a means and an instrument, not a goal. It is the product of God's incarnation in Christ and in a sense its continuation, the way by which Christ makes his home in the

church, the preparation of the way to the full indwelling of God. But in this indwelling, accordingly, it has its τελος, its end and goal (1 Cor. 15:28). Like the entire revelation, Scripture, too, is a passing act.

This discussion makes clear the relation in which Scripture stands to revelation. The earlier theology almost completely allowed revelation to coincide with divine inspiration (θεοπνευστια), the gift of Scripture. It only incidentally referred to revelation and conceived of it much too narrowly. It seemed as if there was nothing behind Scripture. As a result Scripture came to stand in complete detachment and isolation and made it seem as if it had suddenly dropped out of heaven. The mighty conception of revelation as a history that began at the fall and ends only in the parousia was—at least to scientific theology—almost totally foreign. This view is untenable. After all, in by far the majority of cases, revelation is antecedent to divine inspiration (θεοπνευστια) and often separated from it for a long time. The revelation of God to the patriarchs, in the history of Israel, in the person of Christ was sometimes not described till centuries and years later, and also the prophets and apostles frequently recorded their revelations only after their reception (e.g., Jer. 25:13; 30:1; 36:2ff.). In this connection not everything was recorded that, when it came, did in fact belong to the circle of revelation (John 20:30; 21:25). In addition there were many persons, such as Elijah, Elisha, Thomas, and Nathanael, etc., organs of revelation, who nevertheless never wrote a book that was included in the canon; others, by contrast, received no revelations and performed no miracles but did record them in writing, as for example the writers of many historical books. Revelation further took place in different forms (dream, vision, etc.) and was intended to make known something that was hidden; θεοπνευστια was always an interior working of God's Spirit in and upon the [human] consciousness and served to guarantee the content of Scripture.

Modern theology therefore rightly made a distinction between divine revelation and Scripture. But this theology often fell into the opposite extreme. It so completely detached revelation from Scripture that it became no more than an accidental appendix, an arbitrary addition, a human record of revelation, which might perhaps still be useful but was in any case not necessary. This theme was acclaimed in all sorts of variations: "Not the letter but the Spirit"; "not Scripture but the person of Christ"; "not the word but the fact is the fundamental principle of Scripture." And Lessing managed to produce the familiar petition: "O Luther, you great and holy man! You have delivered us from the yoke of the pope but who will deliver us from the yoke of the letter, the paper pope?" This view is no less wrong but even more dangerous than the other. For in many cases revelation and divine inspiration (θεοπνευστια) do coincide. Far from everything that is recorded in Scripture was revealed in advance but arose in the authors' consciousness during the writing itself, e.g., the Psalms and the Letters, etc. Those who deny divine inspiration and despise Scripture will also in large part lose the revelation; they will have left nothing but human writings. In addition the revelation, even where in fact or word it preceded its recording, is known to us solely from Holy Scripture. We literally know nothing of the revelations of God in the time of Israel and in Christ except from Holy Scripture. There is no other primary principle. With the fall of Holy Scripture, therefore, all of revelation falls as well, as does the person of Christ. Precisely because revelation is history there is no way to learn something about it other than the ordinary way that applies to all of history, and that is human attestation. To our mind attestation decides about the reality of a fact. We have no fellowship with Christ except through fellowship in the word of the apostles (John 17:20, 21; 1 John 1:3). For us, for the church of all the ages, revelation exists only in the form of Holy Scripture. Finally, divine inspiration, as will be evident later, is an attribute of the Scriptures, a unique and distinct activity of God in connection with the production of Scripture and therefore also itself to be acknowledged and honored to that extent as an act of revelation. Hence contempt for and the rejection of Scripture is not a harmless act with regard to human testimonies concerning revelation but denial of a special revelational act of God.

Hence both schools are one-sided, the one that fails to do justice to revelation for the sake of Scripture as well as the one that fails to do justice to Scripture for the sake of revelation. In the former, divine revelation (φανερωσις), in the latter, divine inspiration (θεοπνευστια) does not come into its own. In the one, people have Scripture without scriptures; in the other, scriptures without Scripture. In the former there is a neglect of history; in the other contempt for the Word. The former lapses into orthodox intellectualism; the latter is in danger of Anabaptistic spiritualism. The right view is one in which Scripture is neither equated with revelation nor detached from it and placed outside of it. Divine inspiration is an element *in* revelation, a last act in which the revelation of God in Christ is concluded for this dispensation. Hence it is in that sense the end, the crown, the making permanent, and the publication of revelation, the means by which immediate revelation is made mediate and recounted in books.[63]

CONTINUING REVELATION

[105] Revelation taken as a whole, after all, will have reached its end and goal only in the parousia of Christ. But it is divided in two great periods, two distinct dispensations. The purpose of the first dispensation was to incorporate the full revelation of God into—and to make it a part of—the history of humankind. That entire economy can be regarded as a coming of God to his people, as a search for a "tabernacle" for Christ. It, accordingly, is predominantly a revelation of God in Christ. It bears an objective character.

---

63. Baumgarten, with A. D. C. Twesten, *Vorlesungen über die Dogmatik der Evangelisch-Lutherischen Kirche*, 2 vols. (Hamburg: F. Perth, 1837, 1838), I, 402.

It is characterized by extraordinary deeds; theophany, prophecy, and miracle are the ways by which God comes to his people. Christ is the content and focal point of it. He is the Logos who shines in the darkness, comes to his own, and becomes flesh in Jesus. As yet the Holy Spirit had not been given because Christ had not yet been glorified [cf. John 7:39]. In this dispensation inscripturation keeps pace with revelation. Both of them grow from century to century. To the degree that revelation advances, Scripture increases in volume. When the full revelation of God has been given in Christ, when theophany, prophecy, and miracle have reached their pinnacle in him and the grace of God in Christ has appeared to all human beings, then the completion of Scripture is there as well. Inasmuch as in his person and work Christ fully revealed the Father to us, that revelation is fully described for us in Scripture.

The dispensation of the Son then makes way for the dispensation of the Spirit. Objective revelation passes into subjective appropriation. In Christ, in the middle of history, God created an organic center; from this center, in an ever widening sphere, God drew the circles within which the light of revelation shines. The sun as it rises covers only a small area of the surface of the earth with its rays, but at its zenith it shines brilliantly over the whole earth. Israel was only an instrument of revelation; it performed its service and disappears when it has brought forth the Christ according to the flesh. Presently the grace of God appears to all human beings. The Holy Spirit takes everything from Christ, adding nothing new to revelation. The latter is complete and therefore no longer susceptible of increase. Christ is the Logos, full of grace and truth; his work is completed; the Father himself rests in the Son's labor. His work cannot be augmented or increased by the good works of the saints, nor his word by tradition, nor his person by the pope. In Christ God both fully revealed and fully gave himself. Consequently also Scripture is complete; it is the perfected Word of God.

But though the revelation has been completed, its effect does not for that reason cease. On the contrary, precisely because it has been completed, it now enters into the whole spectrum of the life and history of humankind. The reason is that its ultimate goal does not lie in itself, nor in Christ who is the mediator, but in the new humanity, in God's dwelling with his people. Consequently it cannot and may not be a fact that once took place and has now disappeared without a trace. By means of Scripture God himself now bears revelation into the world and realizes its content in the life and thought of humankind. The revelation itself came into being by means of theophany, prophecy, and miracle. Corresponding to this triad is the threefold activity of God by which he makes the content of revelation into the possession of humankind. By his Spirit he indwells the church of Christ and is in its midst wherever two or three are gathered in Christ's name. He ever continues to perform miracles, for he renews the church of Christ by regeneration, sanctification, and glorification; the spiritual miracles do not cease, for God works always.

But that is not enough. Not only the world of being must be renewed; also that of human consciousness. In the Logos was not only the life but also the light of human beings; Christ was not only full of grace but also full of truth; revelation consisted not only in miracle but also in prophecy. Word and deed went hand in hand in the first dispensation; they also go hand in hand in the economy of the Holy Spirit. The Holy Spirit not only regenerates but also illumines. Just as the spiritual miracles do not add a new element to the objective facts of revelation but are only the working out of the miracle of God's grace accomplished in Christ, so also the illumination of the Holy Spirit is not a revelation of things previously hidden but the application of the treasures of wisdom and knowledge present in Christ and displayed in his Word. And in this dispensation both of these activities of the Holy Spirit occur in conjunction. Just as prophecy and miracle, word and fact accompany each other in effecting revelation; so also in applying revelation, illumination and regeneration, Scripture and church are linked to each other. Now too revelation is not just doctrine that illumines the mind but at the same time a life that renews the heart. It is both together in unbreakable unity. We must avoid both the one-sidedness of intellectualism and that of mysticism, for they are both a denial of the riches of revelation. Since both head and heart, the whole person in being and consciousness, must be renewed, revelation in this dispensation is continued jointly in Scripture and in the church. In this context the two are most intimately connected. Scripture is the light of the church, the church the life of Scripture. Apart from the church, Scripture is an enigma and an offense. Without rebirth no one can know it. Those who do not participate in its life cannot understand its meaning and point of view. Conversely, the life of the church is a complete mystery unless Scripture sheds its light upon it. Scripture explains the church; the church understands Scripture. In the church Scripture confirms and seals its revelation, and in Scripture the Christian—and the church— learn to understand themselves in their relation to God and the world, in their past, present, and future.

Scripture, accordingly, does not stand by itself. It may not be construed deistically. It is rooted in a centuries-long history and is the fruit of God's revelation among the people of Israel and in Christ. Still it is not a book of times long past, which only links us with persons and events of the past. Holy Scripture is not an arid story or ancient chronicle but the ever-living, eternally youthful Word, which God, now and always, issues to his people. It is the eternally ongoing speech of God to us. It does not just serve to give us historical information; it does not even have the intent to furnish us a historical story by the standard of reliability demanded in other realms of knowledge. Holy Scripture is tendentious: whatever was written in former days was written for our instruction, that by steadfastness and by the encouragement of the Scriptures we might have hope [Rom. 15:4]. Scripture was written by the Holy Spirit that it might serve him in guiding the church, in the perfecting of the saints, in building up the body of Christ. In it God daily comes to his people. In it he speaks to his people, not from afar but from nearby. In it he reveals himself, from day to day, to believers in the fullness of his truth and grace. Through it he works his miracles of compassion and faithfulness. Scripture is the ongoing rapport between heaven and earth, between Christ and his church, between God and his children. It does not just tie us to the past; it binds us to the living Lord in the heavens. It is the living voice of God, the letter of the omnipotent God to his creature. God once created the world by the word, and by that word he also upholds it [Heb. 1:2, 3]; but he also re-creates it by the word and prepares it to be his dwelling. Divine inspiration, accordingly, is a permanent attribute of Holy Scripture. It was not only "God-breathed" at the time it was written; it *is* "God-breathing." "It was divinely inspired, not merely while it was written, God breathing through the writers; but also, whilst it is being read, God breathing through the Scripture, and the Scripture breathing Him [He being their very breath]."[64] Having come forth from revelation, it is kept alive by divine inspiration and made efficacious. It is the Holy Spirit who maintains both prophecy and miracle, Scripture and church, joining them together, thus preparing the parousia. Some day when being and consciousness are completely renewed, revelation will end and Scripture will no longer be necessary. Divine inspiration (θεοπνευστια) will then be the portion of all God's children. They will all be taught by the Lord and serve him in his temple. Prophecy and miracle have then become "nature," for God dwells among his people.

---

64. J. A. Bengel, *Gnomon of the New Testament,* rev. and ed. Andrew R. Fausset, 5 vols. (Edinburgh: T. & T. Clark, 1877), IV, 319 (Commentary on II Timothy 3:16).

13

THE INSPIRATION OF SCRIPTURE

Evidence for the doctrine that Scripture is inspired by God is found already in the Old Testament. The prophets were conscious of being called by God and having a message that was not their own word but God's. The same is true for the written prophetic word. Written prophecy is a later but necessary stage in the history of revelation, a way for the divinely inspired prophetic word to address future generations. The prophets did not, as is claimed by critical scholars, "invent" ethical monotheism. Prophecy presumes the Torah, though it is not simply inferred from it; prophecy is a covenant-renewing new revelation. The historical books of the Old Testament are properly prophetic history, a commentary on the divine acts of salvation history. The poetic books, too, presuppose an earlier, objective revelation from the covenantal God and apply it to the religious-ethical aspects of Israel's life. Eventually, these writings were all received as an authoritative canon.

For Jesus and the apostles, the books of the Old Testament canon had divine authority. This is reflected in the way they refer to the Old Testament as authoritative ("it is written," "Scripture says"). In addition Scripture provides self-testimony of its inspiration in explicit passages such as 2 Timothy 3:16 and 2 Peter 1:19, 21. Not only is the Old Testament frequently cited in the New Testament—commonly in the Greek translation of the LXX—but it is also always acknowledged as authoritative. This is not challenged by the various and diverse manners in which the New Testament authors cite the Old Testament. The New Testament ultimately, also in its use of the Old Testament, seeks in the power of the Holy Spirit to bear witness to the Christ. It is this apostolic testimony that led to the church accepting these writings as canonical. It is Christ himself who is the "Word" to whom Scripture bears testimony.

From its very beginning, the Christian church has always accepted Holy Scripture as the Word of God, beginning with the Old Testament. As this recognition was extended to include the apostolic writings of the New Testament, the conviction that these were "divine writings" was the church's universal belief. Formally speaking, the acknowledgment of Scripture as divine and authoritative revelation enjoyed undisputed sway in the medieval church. The Council of Trent affirmed this trust in the Scriptures, though it also extended inspiration to the church's tradition. In the post-Tridentine era, Roman Catholic theologians developed a variety of views on scriptural inspiration, including differing convictions about the nature and extent of inspiration. Some maintained the more rigorous view that the Spirit of God exerted a positive influence on the authors, extending even to individual words. A less rigorous view rejected the verbal inspiration of Scripture and extended the notion of general inspiration to other writings as well, provided they contained no falsehoods. Yet others held to the view that the Spirit's guidance was only passive or negative, preserving the authors from error. Finally, yet others limited inspiration only to the so-called religious-ethical teachings, allowing for varying degrees of fallibility for the rest.

Modern Roman Catholic thought tends toward a middle way between the rigorous notion of verbal inspiration and ideas of limited inspiration. A growing trend among Roman Catholic theologians is "concessionism," an attempt to affirm biblical inspiration in a general sense while also accepting many of the most radical conclusions of historical criticism.

By contrast, the Reformers fully accepted the God-breathed character of Scripture. They accepted inspiration in its full positive sense and extended it to Scripture in all its parts. However, in the eighteenth century rationalist criticism rose again and separated the "Word of God" from the Bible. The difference between the inspiration of biblical writers and all believers was seen to be only a matter of degree. Scripture, judged in many ways to be fallible and deficient, was still believed in some way to reveal God or at least the person of Christ. A great deal of attention is paid to the doctrine of biblical inspiration in the modern era, though critical hostility to the Bible seems to have increased.

This is an unstable situation, intellectually and spiritually, and occasionally draws some theologians back to a higher view of inspiration and revelation. The situation in the church seems to be better than in the academy. There are still many Christians in whom remains the consciousness of Scripture as God-breathed and authoritative for teaching and practice. Efforts to undermine this confidence continue when modernists elevate the teaching of Jesus over that of the apostles. Others acknowledge a weaker form of inspiration but insist upon accommodating it to the phenomena of Scripture from which they deduce a view of inspiration at odds with Scripture's self-witness. This is improper in that it opposes a theologian's own scientific insight to Scripture's teaching about itself. No doctrine about Scripture can be based on such a method.

Scripture says about itself that it is "divinely inspired" or "God-breathed" (θεοπνευστος, 2 Tim. 3:16). This verbal should be taken in a passive rather than active sense; the Bible is inspired as well as inspiring. Inspiration is possible because the Spirit of God is immanent in creation, though biblical inspiration may not be equated with heroic, poetic, or other religious inspiration. It is not a work of God's general providence but of his saving purpose in special revelation. Prophets and apostles are people "borne by God" (2 Pet. 1:19–21); it is God who speaks in and through them.

Inspiration should not be reduced to mere preservation from error, nor should it be taken in a "dynamic" way as the inspiration of persons. The view that inspiration consists only in actively arousing religious affections in the biblical au-

thors, which were then committed to writing, confuses inspiration with regeneration and puts Scripture on par with devotional literature. At the same time a "mechanical" view of inspiration fails to do justice to the role of the biblical writers as secondary authors. One-sidedly emphasizing the divine, supernatural element in inspiration disregards its connection with the author's gifts, personality, and historical context. God treats human beings, including the biblical writers, not as blocks of wood but as intelligent and moral beings.

Neither a "dynamic" nor a "mechanical" view suffices. The proper view of biblical inspiration is the organic one, which underscores the servant form of Scripture. The Bible is God's word in human language. Organic inspiration is "graphic" inspiration, and it is foolish to distinguish inspired thoughts from words and words from letters. Scripture must not be read atomistically, as though each word or letter by itself has its own divine meaning. Words are included in thoughts and vowels in words. The full humanity of human language is taken seriously in the notion of organic inspiration.

Critical opposition to this view of inspiration remains strong. While objections—e.g., from historical criticism—should not be ignored, we must not overlook the spiritual-ethical hostility to Scripture from the forces of unbelief. While not all questioning of Scripture reveals hostile unbelief, it is important to underscore the duty of every person to be humble before Scripture. Holy Scripture must judge us, not the reverse. The Holy Spirit opens our heart to trust, believe, and obey God's Word in Scripture. Submission remains a struggle, also an intellectual one. We must acknowledge our limitations, the reality of mystery, our weakness of faith, without despairing of all knowledge and truth. Our hope is in Christ, the true man in whom human nature is restored. That is the purpose of Scripture: to make us wise unto salvation (2 Tim. 3:15).

Salvation is in the one who considered nothing human as alien and through his Holy Spirit joins us to himself through a word that is also fully human and wholly true. The Bible is not given to us as a text for scientific investigation of creation, but it does provide principles for knowing and living that guide us all. These principles also guide scientists and are a source of blessing for science and art, society and state. Jesus is Savior, and the reach of his grace extends as far as the effects of sin's corruption.

THE WITNESS OF THE OLD TESTAMENT

[106] For the doctrine of inspiration, the Old Testament supplies the following important components.

a. At a certain time in their life, the prophets knew they were being called by the Lord (Exod. 3; 1 Sam. 3; Jer. 1; Ezek. 1–3; Amos 3:7, 8; 7:15). In many cases the call ran counter to their own wishes and desire (Exod. 3; Jer. 20:7; Amos 3:8), but YHWH was too strong for them. In Israel there was a general conviction that the prophets were emissaries of God (Jer. 26:5; 27:15), raised up and sent by him (Jer. 29:15; Deut. 18:15; Num. 11:29;

2 Chron. 36:15), his servants (2 Kings 17:23; 21:10; 24:2; Ezra 9:11; Ps. 105:15; etc.), standing before his face (1 Kings 17:1; 2 Kings 3:14; 5:16).

b. They are aware that YHWH has spoken to them and that they have received a revelation from him. He tells them what to say (Exod. 4:12; Deut. 18:18), puts the words in their mouth (Num. 22:38; 23:5; Deut. 18:18), speaks to them (Hos. 1:2; Hab. 2:1; Zech. 1:9, 13; 2:2, 8; 4:1, 4, 13, 14; 5:5, 10; 6:4; Num. 12:2, 8; 2 Sam. 23:2; 1 Kings 22:28). A much used formula is: "thus says the Lord," or "the word of the Lord came to me," or word, oracle, **נְאֻם** (pass. part.), the "utterance" of YHWH. The whole OT Scripture is full of this expression, time after time introducing prophetic discourse. Repeatedly YHWH is even introduced in the first person as the one speaking (Josh. 24:2; Isa. 1:1, 2; 8:1, 11; Jer. 1:2, 4, 11; 2:1; 7:1; Ezek. 1:3; 2:1; Hos. 1:1; Joel 1:1; Amos 2:1; etc). Actually it is YHWH speaking through the prophets (2 Sam. 23:1, 2), who speaks through their mouth (Exod. 4:12, 15; Num. 23:5) and ministry (Hag. 1:1; 2 Kings 17:13). Their entire message is covered by YHWH's authority.

c. In the prophets this consciousness is so clear and firm that they even tell us the place where and the time when YHWH spoke to them and distinguish the times when he did and when he did not speak to them (Isa. 16:13, 14; Jer. 3:6; 13:3; 26:1; 27:1; 28:1; 33:1; 34:1; 35:1; 36:1; 49:34; Ezek. 3:16; 8:1; 12:8; Hag. 1:1; Zech. 1:1; etc.). Moreover, that consciousness is so sharply objective that they clearly distinguish themselves from YHWH; he speaks to them (Isa. 8:1; 51:16; 59:21; Jer. 1:9; 3:6; 5:14; Ezek. 3:26; etc.); they listen with their ears and see with their eyes (Isa. 5:9; 6:8; 21:3, 10; 22:14; 28:22; Jer. 23:18; 49:14; Ezek. 2:8; 3:10, 17; 33:7; 40:4; 44:5; Hab. 3:2, 16; 2 Sam. 7:27; Job 33:16; 36:10), and ingest the words of YHWH (Jer. 15:16; Ezek. 3:1–3).

d. The prophets therefore make a sharp distinction between what God has revealed to them and what arises from within their own heart (Num. 16:28; 24:13; 1 Kings 12:33; Neh. 6:8; Ps. 41:6, 7). Their complaint against the false prophets is precisely that they speak from within their own heart (Ezek. 13:2, 3, 17; Jer. 14:14; 23:16, 26; Isa. 59:13), without being sent (Jer. 14:14; 29:9; Ezek. 13:6). They are, therefore, false prophets (Jer. 23:32; Isa. 9:15; Jer. 14:14; 20:6; 23:21, 22, 26, 31, 36; 27:14; Ezek. 13:6f.; Mic. 2:11; Zeph. 3:4; Zech. 10:2) and fortune-tellers, diviners (Isa. 3:2; Mic. 3:5f.; Zech. 10:2; Jer. 27:9; 29:8; Ezek. 13:9, 23; 21:23, 29; Isa. 44:25).

e. Finally, the prophets are conscious, when speaking or writing, of proclaiming not their own word but the word of the Lord. Indeed, the word was not revealed to them for themselves but for others. They were not at liberty to hide it. They had to speak (Jer. 20:7, 9; Exod. 3, 4; Ezek. 3; Amos 3:8; Jonah 1:2) and therefore do not speak to win human favor or out of calculation (Isa. 56:10; Mic. 3:5, 11). Precisely for that reason they are prophets, speakers in YHWH's name and of his word. Therefore, they know that they have to give—no more, no less than—what they have received (Deut. 4:2; 12:32; Jer. 1:7, 17; 26:2; 42:4; Ezek. 3:10).

The writing of the prophets may and must be derived from a similar impulse. The literal texts where a command to write is given are few in number (Exod. 17:14; 24:3, 4; 34:27; Num. 33:2; Deut. 4:2; 12:32; 31:19; Isa. 8:1; 30:8; Jer. 25:13; 30:2; 36:2, 24, 27–32; Ezek. 24:2; Dan. 12:4; Hab. 2:2) and apply to only a small part of OT Scripture. The act of recording prophecies in writing, though a later one, is still a necessary stage in the history of prophetism. Surely, many prophecies were never uttered orally but were meant to be read and pondered. The majority have been carefully, even artfully, crafted and show by their very form that they were intended to be written. Behind the inscripturation of these oracles was the idea that Israel could no longer be saved by deeds, that now and in distant generations the service of YHWH had to find acceptance by word and reasoned persuasion.[1] Prophets began to write because they wished to address people other than those who could hear them.

f. There is a difference between the received word and the spoken or written word. It would not have been humiliating for the prophets had they recorded the received word as literally as possible. But even in the moment of divine inspiration, revelation continued, modifying and completing the earlier revelation, and hence the latter was reproduced freely. The prophets therefore demanded the same authority for their written word as for the spoken word. This even applies to the prophet's discourses in between the actual words of YHWH (e.g., in Isa. 6; 10:24–12:6; 31:1–3; 32) or the prophet's elaboration of a word from YHWH (52:7–12; 63:15–64:12). The passage of a statement from YHWH to a statement of the prophet is frequently so abrupt and the two are so closely intertwined (cf. Jer. 13:18f.) that no separation is possible. They have the same authority (Jer. 36:10, 11; 25:3). In 34:16 Isaiah calls [the volume of] his own recorded prophecies the Book of YHWH.

g. The prophets did not infer their revelation from the law. Although the scope of the Torah cannot be determined from their writings, prophecy does presuppose a Torah. All the prophets stand on the foundation of a body of law and put themselves along with their opponents on a common basis. They all assume a covenant made by God with Israel, a gracious election of Israel (Hos. 1:1–3; 6:7; 8:3; Jer. 11:6f.; 14:21; 22:9; 31:31f.; Ezek. 16:8f.; Isa. 54:10; 56:4, 6; 59:21). The prophets were not the founders of a new religion, a religion of ethical monotheism. YHWH's relation to Israel was never like that of Chemosh to Moab. The prophets never mention such opposition between their religion and that of the people. They recognize that throughout almost all the centuries of their existence the people committed idolatry; but they always and unanimously view it as unfaithfulness and apostasy on the assumption that the people knew better. With the people

---

1. A. Kuenen, *The Prophets and Prophecy in Israel*, trans. Adam Milroy (Amsterdam: Philo, 1969; reprinted, London, 1877) (ed. note: pagination in the Dutch edition, *De Profeten*, I, 74; II, 345f.).

they fasten themselves onto the same revelation and the same history. They speak from the conviction that they and the people have in common the same service of God, that YHWH elected and called them to his service. From this conviction they draw their strength and therefore test the people by the legally-existing relation between them and YHWH (Hos. 12:14; Mic. 6:4, 8; Isa. 63:11; Jer. 7:25; etc.).[2]

The torah does not just refer to a divine instruction in general but is often also the name of an already-existing objective revelation of YHWH (Isa. 2:3; Mic. 4:2; Amos 2:4; Hos. 8:1; 4:6; Jer. 18:18; Ezek. 7:26; Zeph. 3:4). God's covenant with Israel, on the foundation of which the prophets stand with all the people, naturally also contains an assortment of statutes and ordinances, and the prophets therefore repeatedly speak of commandments (Isa. 48:18), statutes (Isa. 24:5; Jer. 44:10, 23; Ezek. 5:6, 7; 11:12, 20; 18:9, 17; 20:11f.; 36:27; 37:24; Amos 2:4; Zech. 1:6; Mal. 3:7; 4:4), and ordinances (Ezek. 5:7; 11:12; etc.). This torah must have contained the teaching of the oneness of YHWH, his creation and government over all things, the prohibition of idolatry, and other religious and moral commandments, as well as a range of ceremonial (sabbath, sacrifice, purity, etc.) and historical (creation, exodus from Egypt, covenant-making) components. About the scope of the torah before prophetism there may be disagreement, but the relation between the law and the prophets cannot be reversed without violating the whole history of Israel and the essence of prophetism. The prophet in Israel was as it were "the living voice of the law" and "the mediator of its fulfillment" (Staudenmaier). The most negative criticism still finds itself compelled to accept as historical the personality of Moses and his monotheism, the sojourn in Egypt, the exodus, the conquest of Canaan, etc., although, given their critique of the Pentateuch, all ground for that acceptance is lacking.

h. It is a priori likely that in the case of a people long familiar with the art of writing, the law had already long existed in written form as well. This fact seems to be made explicit in Hosea 8:12.[3] This torah had authority in Israel from the beginning. We hear nothing about doubt or opposition. Moses' place among the prophets was unique (Exod. 33:11; Num. 12:6–8; Deut. 18:18; Ps. 103:7; 106:23; Isa. 63:11; Jer. 15:1; etc.). His relation to YHWH was special: the Lord spoke to him as a friend. He was the mediator of the Old Testament. The law everywhere ascribes to itself a divine origin. It is YHWH who by Moses gave the torah to Israel. Not only the ten words (Exod. 20) and the book of the covenant (Exod. 21–23) but all other laws as well are derived from God's speaking to Moses. Over and over, in the laws of the Pentateuch, we encounter the formula: "The Lord said," or "the Lord

---

2. Eduard König, *Die Hauptprobleme der altisraelitischen Religionsgeschichte* (Leipzig: J. C. Hinrichs, 1884), 15ff., 38ff.

3. C. J. Bredenkamp, *Gesetz und Propheten: Ein Beitrag zur alttestamentlichen Kritik* (Erlangen: Deichert, 1881), 21ff.; Eduard König, *Der Offenbarungsbegriff des Alten Testamentes*, 2 vols. (Leipzig: J. C. Hinrichs, 1882), II, 333.

spoke to Moses." Almost every chapter begins with it (Exod. 25:1; 30:11, 17, 22; 31:1; 32:7, 33; Lev. 1:1; 4:1; 6:1, 8, 19, 24; Num. 1:1; 2:1; 3:44; 4:1; etc.). And Deuteronomy gives nothing but what Moses spoke to the children of Israel (Deut. 1:6; 2:1, 2, 17; 3:2; 5:2; 6:1; etc.).

i. All the historical books of the OT were written by the prophets and in a prophetic spirit (1 Chron. 29:29; 2 Chron. 9:29; 20:34; etc.). In their speeches and writings the prophets not only refer repeatedly to Israel's history, but they are also the people who preserved, edited, and handed it down. But their purpose is by no means to furnish us with an accurate, connected story of the fortunes of the Israelitish people, as other historiographers aim to do. Also in the historical books of the OT, the prophets base themselves on the torah and from its viewpoint regard and describe the history of Israel (Judg. 2:6–3:6; 2 Kings 17:7–23, 34–41). The historical books are commentary on the facts of God's covenant with Israel. They are not history in our sense of the word but prophecy; they are meant to be judged by another standard than the history books of other peoples. It is not their aim that we should acquire accurate knowledge of Israel's history but that *in* the history of Israel we should gain understanding of the revelation of God, his thought and his counsel. The prophets, both when they look back upon history and when they look forward into the future, are always messengers of the word of YHWH.

j. Finally, as it pertains to the strictly poetic books that have been included in the canon, they, like the other OT writings, bear a religious-ethical character. They presuppose the revelation of God as their objective basis and display the detailed development and application of that revelation in the various states and relations of human life. Ecclesiastes sketches the vanity of the world without, and in opposition to, the fear of the Lord. Job is preoccupied with the problem of the justice of God vis-à-vis the sufferings of the pious. Proverbs depicts to us true wisdom in its application to the many aspects of human life. The Song of Solomon celebrates the intimacy and power of love. And, in the mirror of the experiences of God's devout people, the Psalms display the manifold grace of God. Both lyrical and didactic poetry in Israel are deployed in the service of divine revelation. David, the sweet psalmist of Israel, spoke by the Spirit of the Lord, whose word was on his tongue (2 Sam. 23:1–3).

k. As the various writings of the OT originated and became known, they were also recognized as authoritative. The laws of YHWH were deposited in the sanctuary (Exod. 25:22; 38:21; 40:20; Deut. 31:9, 26; Josh. 24:25f.; 1 Sam. 10:25). The poetic products were preserved (Deut. 31:19; Josh. 10:13; 2 Sam. 1:18); at an early stage the Psalms were collected for use in the cult (Ps. 72:20); the men of Hezekiah made a second collection of the Proverbs (Prov. 25:1). The prophecies were widely read: Ezekiel knows Isaiah and Jeremiah; later prophets based themselves on earlier ones. Daniel (9:2) is already familiar with a collection of prophetic writings including Jeremiah. In the postexilic community the authority of the law and the prophets is certain and fixed, as is clear from Ezra, Haggai, and Zechariah. Jesus Sirach has a very high view of the law and the prophets (15:1–8; 24:23; 39:1f.; 44–49). In the preface his grandson mentions the three parts in which Scripture is divided. The LXX contains several apocryphal writings, but these themselves witness to the authority of the canonical books (1 Macc. 2:50; 2 Macc. 6:23; Wisdom 11:1; 18:4; Baruch 2:28; Tob. 1:6; 14:7; Sir. 1:5 [marg.]; 17:12; 24:23; 39:1; 46:15; etc.). Philo cites only the canonical books. The fourth book of Ezra ([= 2 Esdras] 14:18–47) knows of the division into 24 books. Josephus counts 22 books divided into three parts. In the opinion of all concerned, the OT canon of Philo and Josephus was identical with ours.[4]

The Witness of the New Testament

[107] For Jesus and the apostles, as for their contemporaries, this canon had divine authority. This is clearly evident from the following facts:

a. The formula with which the OT is cited in the NT varies, but it always shows that to the writers of the NT the OT is of divine origin and bears divine authority. Jesus sometimes cites a verse from the OT by the name of the author, e.g., Moses (Matt. 8:4; 19:8; Mark 7:10; John 5:45; 7:22), Isaiah (Matt. 15:7; Mark 7:6); David (Matt. 22:43, 45), and Daniel (Matt. 24:15), but he also frequently uses the formula "it is written" (Matt. 4:4ff.; 11:10; Luke 10:26; John 6:45; 8:47) or "Scripture says" (Matt. 21:42; Luke 4:21; John 7:38; 10:35) or the name of the primary author, i.e., God or the Holy Spirit (Matt. 15:4; 22:43; Mark 12:26, 36). The evangelists often use the expression "that which was spoken of by the prophet" (cf. Matt. 1:22; 2:15, 17, 23; 3:3; etc.) or "by the Lord" or "by the Holy Spirit" (Matt. 1:22; 2:15; Luke 1:70; Acts 1:16; 3:18; 4:25; 28:25). John usually cites material by the name of the secondary author (1:23, 45; 12:38). Paul always speaks of Scripture (Rom. 4:3; 9:17; 10:11; 11:2; Gal. 4:30; 1 Tim. 5:18; etc.), which is sometimes even portrayed as entirely personal (Gal. 3:8, 22; 4:30; Rom. 9:17). The Letter to the Hebrews most often mentions God or the Holy Spirit as the primary author (1:5f.; 3:7; 4:3, 5; 5:6, 7; 7:21; 8:5, 8; 10:16, 30; 12:26; 13:5). This manner of citation clearly and distinctly teaches us that to Jesus and the apostles the Scripture of the old covenant, though composed of various parts and traceable to different authors, actually formed one organic whole whose author was God himself.

b. Several times Jesus and the apostles also definitely affirmed and taught the divine authority of OT Scripture (Matt. 5:17; Luke 16:17, 29; John 10:35; Rom. 15:4; 1 Pet. 1:10–12; 2 Pet. 1:19, 21; 2 Tim. 3:16). Scripture

---

4. G. Wildeboer, *Het ontstaan van den kanon des Oude Verbond* (Groningen: Wolters, 1891), 126ff., 134; in English: *The Origin of the Canon of the Old Testament*, trans. Benjamin Wisner Bacon (London: Luzac, 1895); H. L. Strack, "Kanon des Alten Testaments," *PRE³*, IX, 741–68; Gustav Hölscher, *Kanonisch und Apokryph: Ein Kapitel aus der Geschichte des alttestamentlichen Kanons* (Leipzig: A. Deichert, 1905).

is a unified whole, which can neither be broken up and destroyed as a totality or in its parts. In the last-cited text [2 Tim. 3:16], the translation "every scripture inspired by God is also profitable" suffers from the fact that after ὠφέλιμος the predicate ἐστιν would have had to be present. The translation "every scripture (in general) is inspired by God and profitable" is self-evidently excluded. What remains, therefore, is a choice between only two translations: "all Scripture" or "every Scripture," included, that is, in the sacred writings (v. 15), "is inspired by God" (cf. "whatever was written in former days," Rom. 15:4). Materially this does not yield any difference and, in light of verses like Matthew 2:3; Acts 2:36; 2 Corinthians 12:12; Ephesians 1:8; 2:21; 3:15; Colossians 4:12; 1 Peter 1:15; James 1:2, πας can apparently also mean "all."

c. Jesus and the apostles never take a critical position toward the content of the OT but accept it totally and without reservation. They unconditionally accept the Scripture of the OT as true and divine in all its parts, not only in its religious-ethical pronouncements or in the passages in which God himself speaks, but also in its historical components. Jesus, for example, attributes Isaiah 6 to Isaiah (Matt. 13:14), Psalm 110 to David (Matt. 22:43), the prophecy cited in Matthew 24:15 to Daniel, and the law to Moses (John 5:46). The historical narratives of the OT are repeatedly cited and unconditionally believed, including the creation of human beings (Matt. 19:4, 5), Abel's murder (Matt. 23:35), the flood (Matt. 24:37–39), the history of the patriarchs (Matt. 22:32; John 8:56), the destruction of Sodom (Matt. 11:23; Luke 17:28–33), the burning bush (Luke 20:37), the serpent in the wilderness (John 3:14), the manna (John 6:32), the histories of Elijah and Naaman (Luke 4:25–27), Jonah (Matt. 12:39–41), etc.

d. Dogmatically, to Jesus and the apostles the OT is the foundation of doctrine, the source of solutions, the end of all argument. The OT is fulfilled in the New. Events are frequently presented as though everything happened for the purpose of fulfilling Scripture, "all this took place to fulfill what was said . . ." (Matt. 1:22 [and passim]; Mark 14:49; 15:28; Luke 4:21; 24:44; John 13:18; 17:12; 19:24, 36; Acts 1:16; James 2:23; etc.). That fulfillment is noted even in minor details (Matt. 21:16; Luke 4:21; 22:37; John 15:25; 17:12; 19:28; etc.); everything that happened to Jesus was described in advance in the OT (Luke 18:31–33). Over and over Jesus and the apostles justify their conduct and prove their teaching by an appeal to the OT (Matt. 12:3; 22:32; John 10:34; Rom. 4; Gal. 3; 1 Cor. 15; etc.). And, to their mind, this divine authority of Scripture is extended so far that a single word, even an iota or a dot, is covered by it (Matt. 5:18; 22:45; Luke 16:17; John 10:35; Gal. 3:16).

e. Notwithstanding all this, the OT is consistently quoted in the NT in the Greek translation of the LXX. The writers of the NT, writing in Greek and for Greek readers, commonly used the translation that was known and accessible to them. The citations can be divided, in terms of their relation to the Hebrew text and Greek translation, into three groups. In some texts there is deviation from the LXX and agreement with the Hebrew text (e.g., Matt. 2:15, 18; 8:17; 12:18–21; 27:46; John 19:37; Rom. 10:15, 16; 11:9; 1 Cor. 3:19; 15:54). Conversely, in other texts there is agreement with the LXX and deviation from the Hebrew (e.g., Matt. 15:8, 9; Acts 7:14; 15:16, 17; Eph. 4:8; Heb. 10:5; 11:21; 12:6). In a third group of citations there is more or less significant deviation both from the LXX and Hebrew text (e.g., Matt. 2:6; 3:3; 26:31; John 12:15; 13:18; Rom. 10:6–9; 1 Cor. 2:9). Furthermore, it is noteworthy that some books of the OT, viz., Ezra, Nehemiah, Obadiah, Zephaniah, Esther, Ecclesiastes, and Song of Solomon, are never cited in the NT. Also, although no apocryphal books are cited, in 2 Timothy 3:8, Hebrews 11:34f., Jude 9f., 14f. names and facts are mentioned that do not occur in the OT. Finally, on a few occasions even Greek classics are referred to (Acts 17:18; 1 Cor. 15:33; Titus 1:12).

f. Finally, as for the material use of the OT in the NT, there is great diversity in that as well. Sometimes the citations serve as proof and confirmation of a given truth (e.g., Matt. 4:4, 7, 10; 9:13; 19:5; 22:32; John 10:34; Acts 15:16; 23:5; Rom. 1:17; 3:10f.; 4:3, 7; 9:7, 12, 13, 15, 17; 10:5; Gal. 3:10; 4:30; 1 Cor. 9:9; 10:26; 2 Cor. 6:17). Very often the OT is cited to prove that it *had to* be fulfilled and was fulfilled in the NT, either in a literal sense (Matt. 1:23; 3:3; 4:15, 16; 8:17; 12:18; 13:14, 15; 21:42; 27:46; Mark 15:28; Luke 4:17f.; John 12:38; Acts 2:17; 3:22; 7:37; 8:32; etc.) or typologically (Matt. 11:14; 12:39f.; 17:11; Luke 1:17; John 3:14; 19:36; 1 Cor. 5:7; 10:4; 2 Cor. 6:16; Gal. 3:13; 4:21; Heb. 2:6–8; 7:1–10; etc.). Citations from the OT repeatedly serve simply to clarify, inform, admonish, console, etc. (e.g., Luke 2:23; John 7:38; Acts 7:3, 42; Rom. 8:36; 1 Cor. 2:16; 10:7; 2 Cor. 4:13; 8:15; 13:1; Heb. 12:5; 13:15; 1 Pet. 1:16, 24, 25; 2:9). In that connection we are often surprised by the meaning that the NT authors find in the text of the OT (esp. in Matt. 2:15, 18, 23; 21:5; 22:32; 26:31; 27:9, 10, 35; John 19:37; Acts 1:20; 2:31; 1 Cor. 9:9; Gal. 3:16; 4:22f.; Eph. 4:8f.; Heb. 2:6–8; 10:5). In the case of Jesus and the apostles, this exegesis of the OT in the NT assumes the understanding that a word or sentence can have a much deeper meaning and a much farther reaching thrust than the original author suspected or put into it. This is often the case in classical authors as well. No one will think that Goethe, in writing down his classical poetry, consciously had before his mind the things that are now found in it. "Surely that person has not gotten far in poetry / In whose verses there is nothing more than what he had [consciously] written into them."[5] In Scrip-

---

5. Cf. Robert Hamerling, "Epilog an die Kritiker," *Hamerlings Werke in vier Bänden* (Leipzig: M. Hesse, 1900), I, 142ff. For the meaning of Scripture, see J. J. P. Valeton, "Eenige Opmerkingen over Hermeneutiek met het Oog op de Schriften des Ouden Verbonds," *Theologische Studiën* 3 (1887): 509–25; Franz Theremin, *Die Beredsamkeit eine Tugend* (Berlin: Duncker und Humblot, 1837), 236; in English: *Eloquence a Virtue; or, Outlines of a Systematic Rhetoric*, trans. William G. T. Shedd (Boston: Draper and Halliday, 1867).

ture this is even much more strongly the case since, in the conviction of Jesus and the apostles, it has the Holy Spirit as its primary author and bears a teleological character. Not only in the few verses cited above but in its entire view and interpretation of the OT, the NT is undergirded by the thought that the Israelitish dispensation has its fulfillment in the Christian. The whole economy of the old covenant, with all its statutes and ordinances and throughout its history, points forward to the dispensation of the new covenant. Not Talmudism but Christianity is the rightful heir of the treasures of salvation promised to Abraham and his seed.[6]

[108] In the writings of the apostles, we find the following data for the inspiration of the NT:

a. Throughout the NT Jesus' witness is considered divine, true, infallible. He is the Logos who makes known the Father (John 1:18; 17:6), the faithful and true witness (Rev. 1:5; 3:14; cf. Isa. 55:4), the Amen in whom all the promises of God are "yes" and "amen" (Rev. 3:14; 2 Cor. 1:20). There was no guile (δολος) on his lips (1 Pet. 2:22). He is the apostle and high priest of

---

6. For the literature about the Old Testament in the New Testament, see Glassius, *Philologia Sacra,* 6th ed. (1691); Surenhuis, "Biblos Katallagés," in *Quo sec. vet. theol. hebr. formulas allegandi et modes interpretandi conciliantur loca V.T. in N.T. allegata* (Amsterdam, 1713); Immanuel Hoffmann, *Demostratio evangelica per ipsum scripturarum concensum in oraculis ex Vet. testamento in novo allegatis declarata,* 3 vols. (Tübingen: Georgii Henrici Reisil, 1773–81); Thomas Randolph, *The Prophecies and Other Texts Cited in the New Testament Compared with the Hebrew Original and with the Septuagint Version* (Oxford: Printed for J. and J. Fletcher, 1782); Henry Owen, *The Modes of Quotation Used by the Evangelical Writers Explained and Vindicated* (London: J. Nichols, 1789); Thomas H. Horne, *An Introduction to the Critical Study and Knowledge of the Holy Scriptures,* 4 vols. (London: Printed for T. Cadell, 1821), II, 356–463; C. Sepp, *De Leer des Nieuwe Testament over de Heilige Schrift des Oude Verbond* (Te Amsterdam: J. C. Sepp & Zoon, 1849); August Tholuck, *Das Alte Testament im Neuen Testament,* 6th ed. (Gotha: F. A. Perthes, 1877); Richard Rothe, *Zur Dogmatik* (Gotha: F. A. Perthes, 1863), 184ff.; J. C. K. Hofmann, *Weissagung und Erfüllung im alte und neuen Testamente* (Nördlingen: C. H. Beck, 1841); Erich Haupt, *Die alttestamentlichen Citate in den vier Evangelien* (Colberg: Carl Jancke; London: Williams & Norgate, 1871); E. Kautzsch, *De Veteris Testamenti locis a Paulo Apostolo allegatis* (Leipzig: Metzger & Wittig, 1869); Eduard Böhl, *Forschungen nach einer Volkshibel zur Zeit Jesu* (Wien: Wilhelm Braumüller, 1873); idem, *Die alttestamentlichen Citate im Neuen Testament* (Wien: Wilhelm Braumüller, 1878); K. Walz, *Die Lehre der Kirche von der Schrift nach der Schrift selbst geprüft* (Leiden: E. J. Brill, 1884); Kuenen, *De Profeten,* II, 199ff. (English: *The Prophets and Prophecy*); William Caven, "The Testimony of Jesus to the Old Testament," *Presbyterian and Reformed Review* 3 (July 1892): 401–20; August Clemen, *Der Gebrauch des Alten Testamentes in den neutestamentlichen Schriften* (Gütersloh: C. Bertelsmann, 1895); A. Kuyper, *Encyclopaedie der Heilige Godgeleerdheid,* 3 vols. (Kampen: J. H. Kok, 1894), II, 378ff.; in English: *Principles of Sacred Theology,* trans. J. Hendrik De Vries (1898; reprinted, Grand Rapids: Eerdmans, 1968), 428ff.; Hans Vollmer, *Die alttestamentlichen Citate bei Paulus textkritisch und biblisch-theologisch gewürdigt* (Freiburg i.B.: J. C. B. Mohr [Paul Siebeck], 1895); J. J. P. Valeton, *Christus en het Oude Testament* (Nijmegen: Ten Hoet, 1895); J. Meinhold, *Jesus und das Alte Testament* (Freiburg i.B. and Leipzig: Mohr [Siebeck], 1896); Martin Kähler, *Jesus und das Alte Testament* (Leipzig: A. Deichert, 1896); Wilhelm Volck, *Christi und der Apostel Stellung zum Alten Testament* (Leipzig: A. Deichert [Georg Böhme], 1900); Theodor Walker, *Jesus und das Alte Testament in ihrer gegenseitigen Bezeugung* (Gütersloh: C. Bertelsmann, 1899); W. Dittmar, *Vetus Testamentum in Novo: die alttestamentlichen Parallelen des Neuen Testaments im Wortlaut der Urtexte und der Septuaginta* (Göttingen: Vandenhoeck & Ruprecht, 1899–1903); Erich Klosterman, *Jesu Stellung zum Alte Testament* (Kiel: Robert Cordes, 1904).

our confession (Heb. 3:1; 1 Tim. 6:13). He does not speak ἐκ τῶν ἰδίων, like Satan who is a liar (John 8:44), but God speaks through him (Heb. 1:2). Jesus was sent by God (John 8:42) and bears witness only to what he has seen and heard (John 3:32). He speaks the words of God (John 3:34; 17:8) and only bears witness to the truth (5:33; 18:37). For that reason his witness is true (John 8:14; 14:6), confirmed by the witness of God himself (5:32, 37; 8:18).

Not only is Jesus holy and without sin in an ethical sense (John 8:46) but also intellectually he is without error, lies, or deception. It is absolutely true that Jesus was not active in the field of science in a restricted sense. He came to earth to make known the Father and to accomplish his work. The inspiration of Scripture on which Jesus makes pronouncements is not a scientific problem but a religious truth. If he erred in this respect, he was wrong at a point that is most closely tied in with the religious life and can no longer be recognized as our highest prophet in religion and theology either. The doctrine of the divine authority of Holy Scripture constitutes an important component in the words of God that Jesus preached. In the case of Jesus, however, this infallibility was not an extraordinary supernatural gift—no gift of grace or passing act—but *habitus,* nature. If Jesus had written anything, he would not have needed special assistance from the Holy Spirit to do it. He did not need inspiration as an extraordinary gift inasmuch as he did "not receive the Spirit by measure" (cf. John 3:34), was himself the Logos (John 1:1), and the fullness of God dwelt in him bodily (Col. 1:19; 2:9).

b. Jesus has not left to us anything in writing, however, and he himself is gone away. He therefore had to ensure that his true witness was passed on pure and unalloyed to humankind. To that end he chose the apostles. The apostolate is an extraordinary office and an utterly unique ministry in Jesus' church. The apostles were specifically given him by the Father (John 17:6), chosen by himself (John 6:70; 13:18; 15:16, 19), and in various ways prepared and equipped by him for their future task. That task was to serve publicly as Jesus' *witnesses* after his departure (Luke 24:48; John 15:27). They had been the ear- and eyewitnesses of Jesus' words and works. They had seen the Word of life with their eyes and touched him with their hands (1 John 1:1) and were now called to bring this witness concerning Jesus to Israel and to the whole world (Matt. 28:19; John 15:27; 17:20; Acts 1:8). But all human beings are false, and God alone is true (Rom. 3:4). Even the apostles were unfit for the task of witnessing and, accordingly, were not the actual witnesses. Jesus only employs them as his instruments. The actual witness who is faithful and true as he himself is, is the Holy Spirit. He is the Spirit of truth and will bear witness to Jesus (John 15:26); the apostles can only serve as witnesses after and through him (John 15:27). That Spirit, accordingly, is uniquely promised and granted to the apostles (Matt. 10:20; John 14:26; 15:26; 16:7; 20:22). Especially John 14:26 teaches this: he "will bring to your remembrance all that I have said to you." He will take the disciples into his service *with* their personalities and gifts, their memory and judgment (etc.). He will not add to the revelation anything that is materially new, that was not already present in Christ's person, word, and work, for he takes everything from Christ and only to that extent brings everything to the apostles' remembrance, thus guiding them into all truth (John 14:26; 16:13, 14). And this witness of the Holy Spirit by the mouth of the apostles is the glorification of Jesus (John 16:14), just as Jesus' witness was a glorification of the Father (17:4).

c. After the day of Pentecost, equipped with that Spirit in a special sense (John 20:22; Acts 1:8; Eph. 3:5), the apostles now also openly act as witnesses (Acts 1:8, 21, 22; 2:14, 32; 3:15; 4:8, 20, 33; 5:32; 10:39, 41; 13:31). The significance of the apostolate lies in bearing witness to what they have seen and heard. To that end they have been called and equipped. From this task they derive their authority. In the face of opposition and challenge, they appeal to this. God, in turn, seals this witness by signs and wonders and spiritual blessing (Matt. 10:1, 8; Mark 16:15f.; Acts 2:43; 3:2ff.; 5:12, 16; 6:8; 8:6f.; 10:44; 11:21; 14:3; 15:8; etc.). From the beginning and in their own right the apostles are the leaders of the Jerusalem church, exercise supervision over the believers in Samaria (Acts 8:14), visit the churches (Acts 9:32; 11:22), make decisions in the Holy Spirit (Acts 15:22, 28), and enjoy generally recognized authority. They speak and act in virtue of the authority of Christ. And although Jesus nowhere left an express command also to record his words and deeds (only in Revelation is there a repeated command to write, 1:11, 19, etc.), the apostles in their writing speak with the same authority, writing being a special form of witness. Also in writing they are witnesses of Christ (Luke 1:2; John 1:14; 19:35; 20:31; 21:24; 1 John 1:1–4; 1 Pet. 1:12; 5:1; 2 Pet. 1:16; Heb. 2:3; Rev. 1:3; 22:18, 19). Their witness is faithful and true (John 19:35; 3 John 12).

d. Among the apostles, Paul again stands by himself. He sees himself called to defend his apostolate against the Judaizers (Gal. 1–2; 1 Cor. 1:10–4:21; 2 Cor. 10:13). Over against this opposition he maintains that he was set apart before he was born (Gal. 1:15), called to be an apostle by Jesus himself (Gal. 1:1), had personally seen Jesus himself (1 Cor. 9:1; 15:8), was granted revelations and visions (2 Cor. 12; Acts 26:16), had received his gospel from Jesus himself (Gal. 1:12; 1 Tim. 1:12; Eph. 3:2–8), and hence is as much an independent and trustworthy witness as the other apostles, especially among the Gentiles (Acts 26:16). Also, his apostolate was confirmed by miracles and signs (1 Cor. 12:10, 28; Rom. 12:4–8; 15:18, 19; 2 Cor. 11:23f.; Gal. 3:5; Heb. 2:4) and by spiritual blessings (1 Cor. 15:10; 2 Cor. 11:5; etc.). He is therefore convinced that there is no other gospel than the one he preaches (Gal. 1:7), that he is trustworthy (1 Cor. 7:25), that he has the Spirit of God (1 Cor. 7:40), that Christ speaks through him (2 Cor. 13:3; 1 Cor. 2:10, 16; 2 Cor. 2:17; 5:20), that he preaches the word of God (2 Cor. 2:17; 1 Thess. 2:13), right down to the phraseology and words

(1 Cor. 2:4, 10–13), not only when he speaks but also when he writes (1 Thess. 5:27; Col. 4:16; 2 Thess. 2:15; 3:14). Like the other apostles, Paul repeatedly acts with full apostolic power (1 Cor. 5; 2 Cor. 2:9), and issues binding commands (1 Cor. 7:40; 1 Thess. 4:2, 11; 2 Thess. 3:6–14). And though he occasionally appeals to the judgment of the church (1 Cor. 10:15), it is not to subject his statement to their approval or disapproval but, on the contrary, to be vindicated by the conscience and judgment of the church, which, after all, also has the Spirit of God and the anointing of the Holy Spirit (1 John 2:20). Paul is so far from making himself dependent on the judgment of the church that he says (1 Cor. 14:37) that if anyone thinks he is a prophet or spiritual, this will come out in the acknowledgment that what Paul is writing is a command of the Lord.

e. From the very beginning these apostolic writings had authority in the churches where they were known. They were soon circulated and as a result gained ever more extensive authority (Acts 15:22f.; Col. 4:16). The Synoptic Gospels show so much kinship between them that the one must have been known either totally or in part to the others. Jude was known to Peter, and 2 Peter 3:16 already implies familiarity with many letters of Paul and puts them on the same level with the other Scriptures. Gradually translations of NT writings appeared for the purpose of being read in the church. These translations must already have existed in the first half of the second century.[7] A dogmatic use was already made of them by Athenagoras who proves his argumentation by reference to 1 Corinthians 15:33 and 2 Corinthians 5:10. Theophilus also cites texts from Paul with the formula "he teaches," "the word of God orders."[8] Irenaeus, Tertullian and others, the Peshitta and the fragment of Muratori, all establish beyond doubt that in the second half of the second century most NT writings had canonical authority and enjoyed equal status with the books of the Old Testament. Differences continued to exist about some books: James, Jude, 2 Peter, 2 and 3 John, but in the third century the objections against these disputed works (ἀντιλεγομενα) increasingly diminished. And the Synod of Laodicea (366), Hippo Regius (393) and Carthage (397) were able to include them and to close the canon.

These decisions of the church were not self-willed, authoritarian acts but merely the codification and registration of the precedents that had long been operating in the churches with respect to these writings. The canon was not formed by any decree of councils: "The Canon has not been produced, as some say, by a single act of human beings, but little by little by God, the director of minds and times."[9] In the important debate between Harnack and Zahn about the history of the NT canon, Harnack undoubtedly too one-

---

7. Papias, according to Eusebius, *Ecclesiastical History,* III, 39; Justin Martyr, *Apology,* I, 66, 67.

8. Athenagoras, *Resurrection of the Flesh,* chap. 16; Theophilus, *To Autolychus,* III, 4.

9. Ed. note: Bavinck's note reads simply "Loescher cited in *PRE²* VII, 424." The reference is to Valentin Loescher, *De Causa Linguae Ebraeae* (1706) and appears in the article "Kanon des alten Testaments," by Herman L. Strack, *PRE²,* VII, 412–51.

sidedly emphasized the terms "divinity," "infallibility," "inspiration," and "canon," i.e., the formal establishment of the dogma of NT Scripture. Long before this occurred, in the second half of the second century the NT writings had achieved generally recognized authority as a result of the authority of the apostles and public reading in the churches. Zahn very correctly called attention to this internal process.[10]

f. The principles that both under the Old and the New Testament guided the church in this recognition of the canonicity of the OT and NT writings cannot be determined with certainty. Apostolic origin cannot have been the deciding factor, for Mark, Luke, and the Letter to the Hebrews were also included. Neither is the recognition of canonicity grounded in the fact that no other writings concerning Christ existed, for Luke 1:1 makes mention of many others and, according to Irenaeus,[11] there was this "immense mass of apocryphal and spurious writings." Nor can the principle of canon formation lie in size or importance, for 2 and 3 John are very small; or in the authors' familiarity with the apostles, for the Letters of Clement and Barnabas were not included; or in originality, for Matthew, Mark, and Luke, the Letters to the Ephesians and Colossians, Jude, and 2 Peter are interdependent. All that can be said is that the recognition of these writings in the churches occurred automatically, without any formal agreement. With only a few exceptions, the OT and NT writings were immediately, from the time of their origin and in toto, accepted without doubt or protest as holy, divine writings. The place and time at which they were first recognized as authoritative cannot be indicated. The canonicity of the Bible books is rooted in their existence. They have authority of themselves, by their own right, because they exist. It is the Spirit of the Lord who guided the authors in writing them and the church in acknowledging them.[12]

The outcome of this investigation into the doctrine of Scripture concerning itself can be summed up by saying that it considers itself, and makes itself known as, the Word of God. The expression "word of God" or "word of the Lord" has various meanings in Scripture. Often it denotes the power of God by which he creates and upholds all things (Gen. 1:3; Ps. 33:6; 147:17, 18; 148:8; Rom. 4:17; Heb. 1:3; 11:3). The term further describes the special revelation by which God makes something known to the prophets. In the OT the expression occurs in this sense on almost every page; over and

10. On this debate, cf. W. Koeppel, "Die Zahn-Harnacksche Streit über die Geschichte des neutestamentlichen Kanons," *Theologische Studien und Kritiken* 64 (1891): 102–57; Barth, "Die Streit zwischen Zahn und Harnack über der Ursprung des N. T. Kanons," *Neue Jahrbuch für deutsche Theologie* (1893): 56–80.

11. Irenaeus, *Against Heresies*, I, 20.

12. A. von Harnack, *History of Dogma*, II, 38ff.; Wildeboer, *Het Ontstaan van de Kanon des Oude Verbond*, 107ff.; Eduard Reuss, *Die Geschichte der heiligen Schriften, Neuen Testaments* (Braunschweig: C. A. Schwetschke, 1874), §298f.; William Lee, *The Inspiration of Holy Scripture*, 3d ed. (Dublin: Hodges, Smith and Co., 1864), 43; Theodor Zahn, "Kanon des Neue Testament," *PRE³*, IX, 768–96; idem, *Grundriss der Geschichte des neutestamentlichen Kanons* (Leipzig: Deichert, 1901).

over we read: "the word of the Lord came." In the NT we find it in this sense only in John 10:35; now the word does not "come" anymore; it does not come now and then from above and without to the prophets but has come in Christ and remains. The "word of God" further denotes the content of revelation. In that use the reference is to a word or words of God, alongside of ordinances, laws, commandments, statutes, which have been given to Israel (Exod. 9:20, 21; Judg. 3:20; Ps. 33:4; 119:9, 16, 17, etc.; Isa. 40:8; Rom. 3:2; etc.). In the NT it is the name for the gospel, which has been disclosed by God in Christ and proclaimed by the apostles (Luke 5:1; John 3:34; 5:24; 6:63; 17:8, 14, 17; Acts 8:25; 13:7; 1 Thess. 2:13; etc.). It is not unlikely that the term "word of God" is sometimes used in Scripture also to designate the written law, hence a part of Scripture (Ps. 119:105). In the NT such a use cannot be shown to exist. Also in Hebrews 4:12 the "word of God" is not identical with Scripture. Nevertheless the NT in fact regards the books of the OT as nothing other than "the word of God." God, or the Holy Spirit is the primary author who spoke in Scripture through (διά w. gen.) the prophets (Acts 1:16; 28:25). In that case Scripture is so called both on account of its origin and on account of its content. The formal and the material meaning of the expression are most intimately bound up with each other in Scripture.

Finally the designation "word of God" is used for Christ himself. He is the Logos in an utterly unique sense: Revealer and revelation at the same time. All the revelations and words of God, in nature and history, in creation and re-creation, both in the Old and the New Testament, have their ground, unity, and center in him. He is the sun; the individual words of God are his rays. The word of God in nature, in Israel, in the NT, in Scripture may never even for a moment be separated and abstracted from him. God's revelation exists only because he is the Logos. He is the first principle of cognition, in a general sense of all knowledge, in a special sense, as the Logos incarnate, of all knowledge of God, of religion, and theology (Matt. 11:27).

THE TESTIMONY OF THE CHURCH

[109] From the beginning Holy Scripture was recognized as the Word of God by all Christian churches. There is no dogma about which there is more unity than that of Holy Scripture. The genesis of that belief can no longer be traced; it exists as far back in history as we can go. In the OT, from the most ancient times on, the authority of YHWH's commandments and statutes, i.e., of the torah and of the prophets, is established. In Israel, Moses and the prophets have always been men of divine authority, and their writings were immediately recognized as authoritative. In this connection the Torah [the Pentateuch] is primary. In later times the Jews identified it with divine wisdom and called it the "image of God," "the daughter of God," "the all-sufficient revelation meant for all peoples," "the highest good," "the way to life."

If Israel had not sinned, it would have been sufficient. But the prophetic writings were added for the purpose of explaining it. All those writings are divine and holy, the standard of doctrine and life, and have an unbounded content. Nothing in it is superfluous; everything has meaning—every letter, every sign, right down to the very form and shape of the word—for everything comes from God. According to Philo and Josephus, when inspiration struck, the prophets were in a state of ecstasy and unconsciousness, which these authors compared to pagan divination and also occasionally extended to people other than the prophets. But for all that, the divine authority of Holy Scripture was unshakably firm in their thinking. Factually, however, that authority was undermined by the gradually emerging doctrine of tradition. Scripture as such was again judged insufficient after all and was augmented by an oral tradition. This oral tradition too [so it was believed] came from God and was passed on to the scribes by Moses, Aaron, the elders, the prophets, and the men of the great synagogue. It was finally laid down in the Mishna and Gemara, which, as the subordinate norm, was added to the primary norm and harmonized with Scripture with the aid, especially, of thirteen hermeneutical rules.[13]

The Early Church

Although the Christian church, with Jesus and the apostles, rejected the entire Jewish tradition, it did from the beginning recognize the divine authority of OT Scripture.[14] The church was never without a Bible. It immediately accepted the OT, with its divine authority, from the hands of the apostles. From the beginning, the Christian faith included belief in the divine authority of the OT. Clement of Rome taught the inspiration of the OT with utter clarity.[15] He calls the OT writings "the oracles of God" (1 Cor. 53), "the Holy Scriptures which are true and inspired by the Holy Spirit" (ch. 45), cites texts from the OT with the formula: "the Holy Spirit says" (ch. 13) and says of the prophets ("the ministers of God's grace preached . . . with the help of the Holy Spirit" (ch. 8). Extending inspiration also to the apostles, he says that they went forth to preach "with full assurance of the Holy Spirit" (ch. 42) and that Paul had written to the Corinthians "under inspiration of the Spirit" (ch. 47). For the rest, the Apostolic Fathers furnish little material on the dogma of Scripture. Though there is agreement on inspiration as such, there is some disagreement on its scope and boundaries. Little is said about the NT Scriptures; and apocryphal writings are sometimes cited as though they were

---

13. Leopold Zunz, *Die gottesdienstlichen Vorträge der Juden* (Berlin: A. Asher, 1832), 37ff.; F. W. Weber, *System der altsynagogalen palästinischen Theologie* (Leipzig: Dörffling & Franke, 1880), 14ff., 78ff.; Emil Schürer, *Geschichte des juden Volkes,* II,3 305ff.; in English: *A History of the Jewish People in the Time of Jesus Christ,* 5 vols. (1890; reprinted, Peabody, Mass.: Hendrickson, 1994), III, 306ff.

14. A. von Harnack, *History of Dogma,* I, 41ff., 175ff., 287ff.; idem, *The Mission and Expansion of Christianity in the First Three Centuries,* trans. James Moffatt (New York: Harper & Brothers, 1961), 242.

15. The numbered references that follow in the text are to the chapters in Clement's *First Epistle to the Corinthians.*

canonical. The apologists of the second century compare the authors of Scripture to a cither, lyre, or flute that the divine musician employed as his instrument.[16] The doctrine of the apostles is on the same level as that of the prophets. As Abraham did, so we also have believed "the voice of God which was spoken again through the apostles of Christ and had been declared through the prophets."[17] The gospels share in the same inspiration as the prophets "because all of them as Spirit-bearers have spoken by the one Spirit of God."[18] In Irenaeus there is already present a full recognition of the inspiration of both Testaments: "The Scriptures are perfect for they have been spoken by God and his Spirit." They have a single author and a single purpose.[19] The church fathers further cite the Holy Scriptures as "divine writing," "the Lord's writings," "God-breathed writings," "heavenly literature," "divine voices," "a holy library," "the handwriting of God." The authors are called "ministers of the grace of God," "organs of the divine voice," "the mouth of God," "Spirit-bearers," "Christ-bearers," "inspirited ones," "those borne by God," "those flooded by," or "full of, the divine Spirit," etc.

The event of inspiration is thus presented as an act of driving or leading but especially as an act of dictation by the Holy Spirit. The writers [of Scripture] are not authors but only scribes. God is the author of Holy Scripture and its [human] writers were simply the hands of the Holy Spirit. The Scripture is "a letter of an omnipotent God to his creature."[20] There is nothing in Scripture that is indifferent and superfluous, but everything is full of divine wisdom; "for nothing is without meaning or without the seal that belongs to God."[21] Origen in particular beat this drum and stated that not a jot or tittle was in vain in Scripture, that there was nothing in Scripture "which did not come down from the fullness of the divine majesty." Similarly Jerome said: "Each and every speech, all syllables, marks and periods in the divine scriptures are full of meanings and breathe heavenly sacraments." Hence Holy Scripture was without any defect or error, even in chronological, historical matters.[22] What the apostles have written must be accepted as though Christ himself had written it, for they were his hands, as it were. Augustine, in his letter to Jerome, writes that he firmly believed that none of the canonical writers "erred in anything they wrote." Hence when there is mistake, "one is not allowed to say: the author of this book did not hold to the truth but either the copy of a book is faulty, or the interpreter erred, or you do not understand it."[23] At the same time, over against Montanism, the self-consciousness of the writers in the

---

16. Justin Martyr, *Discourse to the Greeks,* chap. 8; Athenagorus, *Heg. pro Christo,* chap. 7.

17. Justin Martyr, *Dialogue with Trypho,* 119.

18. Theophilus, *To Autolychus,* III, 12.

19. Irenaeus, *Against Heresies,* II, 28, IV, 9.

20. Cf. Irenaeus, Augustine, Isidore, etc. in P. Dausch, *Die Schriftinspiration: Eine biblisch-geschichtliche Studie* (Freiburg im Breisgau: Herder, 1891), 87.

21. Irenaeus, *Against Heresies,* IV, 21, 3.

22. Theophilus, *To Autolychus,* 21; Irenaeus, *Against Heresies,* III, 5.

23. Augustine, *Against Faustus,* XI, 5.

event of inspiration was stressed as strongly as possible. Irenaeus, Origen, Eusebius, Augustine, Jerome, et al. fully recognized the presence of prior investigation, differences in intellectual development, the use of sources and of memory, differences in language and style. Some even assumed a difference in the manner of inspiration between Old and New Testament times, or even a difference in the degree of inspiration depending on the moral state of the author.[24] But nothing of all this detracted from [their] belief in the divine origin and authority of Holy Scripture. This conviction was universally accepted. This is even more powerfully evident from the practical use of Scripture in preaching, in argumentation, in the exegetical treatment of Scripture, etc. than from isolated statements these men made. In this first period the church was preoccupied more with the establishment of the canon than with the concept of inspiration but understood by canonical writings the "divine scriptures" and ascribed authority to them alone.[25]

The Medieval Church

The theology of the Middle Ages did not go beyond the church fathers nor further develop the doctrine of inspiration. John of Damascus mentions Scripture only in passing and says that the law and the prophets, evangelists and apostles, pastors and teachers spoke by the Holy Spirit and therefore Scripture is "God-breathed."[26] Erigena states that one must follow the authority of Holy Scripture in all parts, for "true authority does not only not resist right reason" but "all authority which is not approved by right reason is seen to be unsound."[27] Thomas does not treat the doctrine of Holy Scripture

24. Novatian, *On The Trinity*, 4; Origin, *Against Celsus*, VII, 4.

25. H. Denzinger, *Enchiridion symbolorum et definitionum* (Wirceburgi: sumptibus Stahelianis, 1865), n. 49, 125; K. R. Hagenbach, *Lehrbuch der Dogmengeschichte*, 3 vols. in 2 (Leipzig: Weidmann, 1840–41), I, §31ff.; English translation: *A Textbook of the History of Doctrines*, trans. C. W. Buch and rev. Henry B. Smith, 2 vols. (New York: Sheldon, 1867); A. Zöllig, *Die inspirationslehre des Origenes* (Freiburg im Breisgau and St. Louis, Mo.: Herder, 1902); *Rudelbach, *Zeitschrift für die Geschichte Luthersche Theologie und Kirche* (1840); W. Rohnert, *Die Inspiration der Heiligen Schrift und ihre Bestreiter* (Leipzig: Georg Böhme [E. Ungleich], 1889), 85ff; Wilhelm Kölling, *Die Lehre von der Theopneustie* (Breslau: C. Dülfer, 1891), 84ff.; *Cramer, *Godgeleerde Bijdrage*, IV, 49–121; W. Sanday, *Inspiration: Eight Lectures on the Early History and Origin of the Doctrine of Biblical Inspiration; being the Bampton lectures for 1893* (London and New York: Longmans, Green, and Co., 1893).

Ed. note: In addition, see the following references for which the full publication data is given in the bibliography. These are works Bavinck refers to in this footnote, works that are given at the beginning of this portion of the *Gereformeerde Dogmatiek* (par. 13, "Theopneustie," and par. 11, "Bijzondere Openbaring").

Fritzche (1828); König (1882); the Old Testament theologies of Oehler, Schultz, Smend, Marti, A. B. Davidson; W. Lotz (1892); Kahler (*PRE*³); Nitzch (*Lehrbuch*), W. Schmidt (*Dogmatik*), von Oettingen (*Dogmatik*); Voigt (*Fundamentadogmatik*); A. Kuyper, *Encylopaedie*, II, (347ff., 429ff.); Riemens (1905); K. Walz (1884); J. Delitzsch (1872); P. Dausch (1891); K. Holzhey (1895); C. Resch (1906); Kropatschek (1903); Bellarmine (*Verbi Dei*); Franzelin (1882); C. Pesch (*Inspir.*); J. Gerhard (*Loc Theol.* I); Quenstedt (*Theologia*, I. chap. 3, 4); J. Calvin (*Institutes*, I. VIff.); B. De Moor (*Comm.* I, 114–446); C. Vitringa (*Doct. Christ* I, 36–123); Schleiermacher (*Christian Faith*, §128ff.); Rothe (*Zur. Dogm.*, 121ff.); Phillippi (*Kirch. Glaub.*, 3, I, 125ff.).

26. John of Damascus, *The Orthodox Faith*, IV, 17.

27. J. S. Erigena, *The Division of Nature*, I, 66ff.

any more than Lombard but in his doctrine of prophecy offers his thoughts on inspiration.[28] Prophecy is definitely a gift of the intellect and consists, first, in inspiration, i.e., an "elevation of the mind toward the perception of divine things," which occurs "by a movement of the Holy Spirit." Second, it occurs in revelation, by which divine things can be known, darkness and ignorance are removed, and the prophecy itself is completed. Prophecy further consists in prophetic light by which divine things become visible, as natural things do by the natural light of reason. But that revelation varies; sometimes it occurs by the mediation of the senses, sometimes by the power of the imagination, sometimes also in a purely spiritual manner as in the case of Solomon and the apostles. Prophecy "by intellective vision," speaking generally, is superior to that which occurs "by the vision of the imagination." However, if "intellective light" does not reveal supernatural things but also makes known to us and enables us to discern naturally knowable things in a divine manner, then such an "intellective prophecy" is inferior to the "imaginative vision," which reveals supernatural truth. The writers of hagiographa often wrote about matters that are knowable by nature, speaking in that case "not as if from the person of God but from their own person with the help of divine light." Hence Thomas recognizes various modes and degrees of inspiration. He also writes that the apostles received the gift of languages in order to be able to preach the gospel to all nations, "but so far as it concerns the things which are added by human art and ornate and elegant speech the apostle was instructed in his own language, not in foreign languages"; similarly, the apostles were sufficiently equipped for their office with knowledge but did not know everything there is to be known, e.g., arithmetic, etc. But no error or untruth can occur in Scripture.[29]

Scripture is most extensively treated by Bonaventure in the prologue to his *Breviloquium*. Holy Scripture, he writes, originates, not in human research, but in divine revelation from the Father, through the Son, in the Holy Spirit. No one can know it apart from faith, for Christ is its content. It is the heart of God, the mouth of God (the Father), the tongue of God (the Son), the pen of God (the Holy Spirit). Worthy of consideration are four aspects of Scripture: (1) its *breadth:* it contains many parts, Old and New Testament, and various kinds of books, legal, historical, and prophetic, etc.; (2) its *length:* it describes all times and periods from the beginning of the world to the day of judgment in three phases, under the law of nature, the written law, and the law of grace, or in seven specific periods; (3) its *height:* it describes the different hierarchies, the ecclesiastical, angelical, and divine; (4) its *depth:* it has several figurative meanings. Although Holy Scripture employs various ways of speaking, it is always genuine. There is no falsehood in it. For the all-perfect author, the Holy Spirit, could inspire nothing untrue,

28. Thomas Aquinas, *Summa Theol.,* II, 2, qu. 171ff.
29. Ibid., I, qu. 32, art. 4; II, 2 qu. 110, art. 4 ad. 3.

trivial, or degraded. Reading and studying Scripture is therefore an urgent necessity; and to this end Bonaventure wrote his precious *Breviloquium.*

While Duns Scotus, in the prologue to his *Sententiae,* does advance various grounds on which belief in Holy Scripture rests (such as prophecy, the internal harmony, the authenticity, the miracles, etc.), he does not deal with the doctrine of Scripture. Elsewhere, too, we find little material for the dogma of Scripture in scholasticism. No need was felt for a special treatment of the locus of sacred Scripture, because its authority was well-established and uncontested. Yet, continued research always finds more than was expected at the outset. Kropatscheck, in his opus,[30] first treats the practical use of Scripture in the Middle Ages and then proceeds to examine the doctrine of Scripture in various theologians such as Grosseste, Occam, Biel, etc. The most remarkable and extensive treatment of the doctrine of Scripture comes from Wycliffe, a most rigorous proponent of the sole and divine authority of Holy Scripture, who says that it is God's holy Word, never lies, has Christ as its content, and is given to all Christians to read and to explore.[31] The so-called formal principle of the Reformation was not first articulated by Luther and Zwingli but existed long before them, both in theory and in practice. At least formally, Scripture enjoyed undisputed sway in the Middle Ages. It was symbolically represented as the water of life, glorified in panegyrics, venerated and adored like the image of Christ, copied, illustrated, bound, and displayed in the most luxurious manner. It occupied a place of honor at the councils, was preserved as a relic, worn around the neck as an amulet, buried along with the dead, and used as basis for taking an oath. It was also read, studied, explained, and translated—much more than Protestants later thought.[32] Opposition to Scripture simply did not exist. Even Abelard does not say that the prophets and apostles erred in writing, only that they sometimes erred as persons.[33] In this connection Abelard appealed to Gregory, who also acknowledged that point in the case of Peter. Sometimes, so he argued, they were deprived of the "grace of prophecy" that they might remain humble and acknowledge that they received and possessed the Spirit of God ("who can neither lie nor deceive") only as gift. Neither is Agobard of Lyon an opponent of inspiration. He only advocated, against Fredegis of Tours, a more organic view, which offers a better explanation of the Bible's language, style, grammatical irregulari-

30. Friedrich Kropatscheck, *Das Schriftprinzip der lutherischen Kirche* (Leipzig: A. Deichert, 1904).

31. John Wiclif, *De Veritate Sacrae Scripturae,* critical edition of Rud Buddensieg, 3 vols. (Leipzig: Dieterich, 1904).

32. F. Vigouroux, *Les Livres Saints et la critique rationaliste,* 5 vols. (Paris: A. Roger et F. Chernoviz, 1890–1902), I, 226ff.; J. Janssen, *Geschichte des deutschen Volkes seit dem Ausgang des Mittelalters,* 8 vols. (Freiburg im Breisgau: Herder, 1881–94), I, 48ff.; Kropatscheck, *Das Schriftprinzip*; G. Rietschel, "Bibellesen und Bibelverbot," *PRE³,* II, 700–713; Franz Falk, *Die Bibel am Ausgange des Mittelalters* (Köln: J. P. Bachem, 1905).

33. P. Abelard, *Sic et Non,* ed. E. L. T. Henke and G. S. Lindenkohl (Marburgi Cattorum: Sumtibus et typis Librariae academ. Elwertianae, 1851), 10–11.

ties, etc.[34] Ecclesiastically, the inspiration and authority of Holy Scripture was repeatedly declared and acknowledged.[35]

Tridentine Roman Catholicism

[110] The Council of Trent, in its Fourth Session, declared that the truth is "contained in the written books and in the unwritten traditions which, received by the apostles from the mouth of Christ himself, or from the Apostles themselves, the Holy Ghost dictating. [They] have come down to us, transmitted as it were from hand to hand. Following, then, the example of the Fathers, [the church] receives and venerates with a feeling of piety, and reverence all the books both of the Old and New Testaments, since one God is the author of both. The traditions [are also accepted] whether they relate to faith or to morals, as having been dictated either orally by Christ or by the Holy Ghost. . . ." While inspiration is here extended to the tradition, still it is clearly attributed to Holy Scripture as well. Among Roman Catholic theologians, however, there soon arose disagreement about the nature and scope of inspiration. Both the expression "the author of both [Testaments]," and the word "dictated" were variously interpreted.

In general, the theologians of the sixteenth century were still committed to the more rigorous outlook of the church fathers and scholastics. They were mostly adherents of Augustine in the doctrine of grace, Jansenists, Augustinians, and Dominicans. The most prominent members of this "school" are Melchior Canus, Bannez, Baius and Jansen, Billuart, Rabaudy, Fernandez, but also a number of Jesuits, like Testatus, Costerus, Turrianus, Salmeron, Gregory de Valencia, *et al.* All these men maintained that the Spirit of God exerted a positive influence upon the authors, an influence that extended even to the individual words. But soon there arose a less rigorous school of thought among the Jesuits. In 1586 Lessius and Hamelius started giving lectures at the Jesuit college in Louvain and there defended (*inter alia*) the propositions (1) "that in order for something to be Holy Scripture it is not necessary that its individual words be inspired by the Holy Spirit; (2) nor is it necessary that individual truths and sentences be immediately inspired by the Holy Spirit himself as author; (3) that some book, on the level, say, of 2 Maccabees, though written by human effort without the assistance of the Holy Spirit, yields Holy Scripture if the Holy Spirit later testifies that there is nothing false in it." Verbal inspiration is rejected here; the immediate inspiration of many things—historical times with which the authors were familiar—deemed unnecessary; and for some books a later inspiration (called a "subsequent or a posteriori approbation of the Holy Spirit" by Bon-

34. W. Münscher, *Dr. Wilhelm Münschers Lehrbuch der christlichen Dogmengeschichte*, ed. D. von Coelln, 3d ed. (Cassel: J. C. Krieger, 1832–38), II, 1, 105; P. A. Klap, "Agobard van Lyon," *Theologische Tijdschrift* 29 (March 1895): 146ff.

35. Heinrich J. D. Denzinger, *Enchiridion symbolorum definitionum et declarationum de rebus fidei et morum* (Wirceburgi: Sumptibus Stahelianis, 1865), nos. 296, 386, 367, 600.

frère) was considered sufficient. The faculties of Louvain and Douai condemned the propositions, but others disapproved of this censorship, and the pope took no decision. The first two propositions were widely accepted, but the third occasioned a difference of opinion on inspiration, which persisted among Catholic theologians even into recent times.

It was the infallible doctrine of the church that God was the primary author of Scripture, and this doctrine was therefore binding upon all and beyond all doubt. But there remained room nevertheless for the question of what kind of activity on the part of God was needed for him to be the author of a Bible book and to confer divine authority on it. In general, the answer was still that the divine activity had to be present and in fact was present in inspiration, but the nature of inspiration itself was in turn very differently interpreted. Some believed it always included revelation, not only of what was unknown to the authors but also of what was known to them. Others were of the opinion that in the latter case inspiration did not have to include revelation but needed only to consist of a divine impulse and divine guidance in writing the book. Still others leaned toward the idea that a negative kind of assistance, one that kept the authors from error, was sufficient, or that in any case a special and positive guidance in the process of writing was limited to matters of faith and conduct. Thus Bonfrère, in his *Praeloquia in Scripturam Sacram* (ch. 8), distinguished three ways in which the Holy Spirit could guide the authors of Bible books: antecedently, concomitantly, and subsequently. The first was real, concrete inspiration and occurred primarily in prophecy when it concerned matters that the authors could not know of themselves. The second consisted in a negative form of assistance, which protected the authors from error and was mainly given in the process of recording history that the authors could know as a result of their investigation. The third, consisting in subsequent approbation of a book by the Holy Spirit, could in the abstract be sufficient as well for the purpose of conferring divine authority on a given book, but Bonfrère said that this was a matter of judgment, not of fact. In fact, according to him, not a single book in Scripture had been made a canonical book solely by a subsequent approbation of God. This theory of inspiration, though in principle it should not be condemned, could therefore in practice be applied, as Mariana said, only to a few sayings of profane authors that were cited in Holy Scripture and so acquired divine authority, such as Acts 17:28 and Titus 1:12. Only a few theologians, such as Daniel Haneberg,[36] went further and asserted that there was also a group of books in the Bible that had secured canonical authority solely by a subsequent approbation.

Much more prevalent, however, was the view that the guidance of the Spirit—at least where it concerned matters that the authors could know of

---

36. In his *Versuch einer Geschichte der biblischen Offenbarung als Einleitung ins alte und neue Testament* (Regensburg: G. Joseph Manz, 1850).

themselves by their own investigation—consisted solely in a passive or negative assistance that preserved the authors from error. This was the view of inspiration held (*inter alis*) by Philipp Neri Chrismann in his *Regula fidei catholicae* (1854) and Richard Simon in his *Histoire critique du Vieux Testament* (1689). A modification of this view was introduced by Holden, a doctor of the Sorbonne, who in his *Divinae fidei analysis* (1770), assumed a real inspiration in the case of truths of faith and morality but with respect to the remaining content of Scripture taught only the kind of assistance that every believer enjoys. Inspiration was thereby limited to the religious-ethical part of Holy Scripture and a greater or lesser degree of fallibility was allowed for the rest of its content. This had earlier already been Erasmus's view and in the nineteenth century found acceptance with a variety of Roman Catholic theologians. Under Schleiermacher's influence, the representatives of the Catholic school of Tübingen, Drey, Kuhn, and Schanz related inspiration to the organism of Scripture and taught, accordingly, that it extended to the different parts of Scripture in varying degrees.[37] Although inspiration was therefore a property of Holy Scripture as a whole, it is linked with infallibility only in the parts that contain truths of faith and morality. In the case of other, incidental, and secondary matters, one may admit that Scripture contains smaller or greater errors. Also later, even after the Vatican Council [I], we encounter this view in the works of various Roman Catholic theologians, among them Bartolo, Cardinal Newman, Abbé Le Noir, Fr. Lenormant, the archbishop of Hulst, de Broglie, Langen, Rohling.

Modern Roman Catholicism

Still, this view of inspiration is far from being the generally accepted one. After the Reformation and even today, the majority of Roman Catholic theologians walk a middle course. On the one hand, they reject the broad kind of inspiration that is assumed to have consisted only in negative assistance or subsequent approbation, for in that case all the decisions of councils, all truth wherever it occurs, could be called inspired. On the other hand, they also reject strict verbal, textual, and "punctual" inspiration according to which not only all matters but even all individual words, consonants, and vowels were dictated and inspired, believing that many matters and words were known to the authors and therefore did not have to be inspired. The differences in language and style, the use of sources, etc. also proves this verbal and literal inspiration is incorrect. Sufficient, therefore, is a "real inspiration," which sometimes consists in specific revelation and

37. J. S. von Drey, *Die Apologetik als wissenschaftliche Nachweisung der Göttlichkeit des Christenthums in seiner Erscheinung*, 2 vols. (Mainz: Florian Kupferberg: 1838–43), I, 204ff.; J. von Kuhn, *Einleitung in die Katholische Dogmatik* (Tübingen: Laupp and Siebeck, 1859), 9ff.; Paul Schanz, *Apologie des Christenthums*, 3 vols. (Freiburg im Breisgau: Herder, 1895), II, 318ff.; in English: *A Christian Apology*, 2d ed., 3 vols., trans. Michael F. Glancey and Victor J. Schobel (Dublin: M. H. Gill; New York: F. Pustet, 1897–1902).

sometimes solely in assistance. We find this theory in Bellarmine, C. a Lapide, the Wirceburg theology, Marchini, and numerous theologians in recent times.[38]

It seems also that Vatican Council [I] and the papal pronouncements have taken decisions that favor this trend. Although Vatican Council [I] did not advance any specific theory, it did single out for condemnation the theory of subsequent inspiration and of mere assistance and, after repeating the decree of the Council of Trent, declared that the church regards the books of Holy Scripture "holy and canonical not because they were composed by human industry alone and later approved by [the church's] authority; nor because they contain revelation without error; but because, written under the inspiration of the Holy Spirit, they have God as their author; and because they have been entrusted as such to the Church." In chapter 2.4 the Council once more calls the books of Holy Scripture "divinely inspired," and in chapter 3, "On Faith," declares that "the divine and catholic faith believes all those matters that are contained in the word of God, whether in Scripture or tradition. . . ." This decree is perfectly clear in that it views inspiration as a positive activity of God, on the one hand, and on the other regards the infallibility of Scripture as a consequence of that inspiration. Leo XIII adopted the same position in his encyclical *On the Study of Holy Scripture,* November 18, 1893; in his letter of September 8, 1899, to the French clergy; and in his letter of November 25, 1899, to the Order of the Friars Minor (Franciscan). In the encyclical, inspiration is defined as follows:

> For, by supernatural power, He [the Holy Spirit] so moved and impelled them [the sacred authors] to write—He was so present to them—that the things which He ordered, and those only, they, first, rightly understood, then willed faithfully to write down, and finally expressed in apt words and with infallible truth. Otherwise, it could not be said that He was the Author of the entire Scripture.[39]

38. J. B. Franzelin, *Tractatus de divina traditione et scriptura,* 3d ed. (Romae: Typographia Polyglotta, 1882); G. Perrone, *Praelectiones theologicae,* 9 vols. (Lovanii: Vanlinthout et Vandenzande, 1838–43), IX, 66ff.; Joseph Kleutgen, *Die Theologie der Vorzeit,* 5 vols. (Münster: Theissing, 1867–74), I, 50ff.; Franz L. B. Liebermann, *Institutiones theologicae,* 2 vols. (Moguntiae: Sumptibus Francisci Kirchhemii, 1857), I, 385; Heinrich Denzinger, *Vier Bücher von der religiösen Erkenntniss,* 2 vols. (Würzburg: Verlag der Stahel'schen Buch-und-Kunst-handlung, 1856–57), II, 108; M. J. Scheeben, *Handbuch der katholischen Dogmatik,* 4 vols. (Freiburg i. B.: Herder, 1873–1903), I, 109ff.; in English selected translations, see *A Manual of Catholic Theology Based on Scheeben's Dogmatik,* 2d ed., trans. and ed. Joseph Wilhelm and Thomas B. Scannell, 2 vols. (London: Kegan Paul, Trench, Trübner; New York: Catholic Publication Society, 1899–1901); J. B. Heinrich, *Dogmatische Theologie,* 2d ed., 10 vols. (Mainz: F. Kirchheim, 1881–1904), I, 709ff.; Franz Schmid, *De inspirationis bibliorum vi et ratione* (Brixinae: Typis et sumptibus bibliopolei Wegeriani, 1885); G. J. Crets, *De divina bibliorum inspiratione* (Lovanii: Excudebant Vanlinthout Fratres, 1886); C. Pesch, *De inspiratione sacrae scripturae* (Friburgi Brisgoviae: Herder, 1906), 402ff.; G. M. Jansen, *Praelectiones Theologiae Fundamentalis* (Utrecht, 1875–77), I, 767ff.; Paulus Mannens, *Theologiae Dogmaticae Institutiones,* 3 vols. (Roermond: J. J. Romen, 1901–3), I, 190ff.

39. *The Papal Encyclicals,* 1878–1903, Claudia Carlen IHM, 1981.

Among Roman Catholic theologians, however, all these pronouncements are far from having brought unity in their views on inspiration. They have admittedly had indirect influence. Whereas in the past the proponents of a looser view were inclined to restrict inspiration to the religious-ethical content of Scripture, and in other matters to grant its fallibility, they now look for the solution to the difficulties in another direction. For them the dogma of inspiration, they say, is certain: all of Scripture is inspired and therefore infallible in its entirety and in all of its parts. Thus the difference is not about the dogma itself, they claim, but about that which flows from it for the criticism and exegesis of Scripture. When some theologians deduce from this dogma that Scripture is absolutely infallible in all the matters it contains, this is just as one-sided as the position of others who assume the presence of errors and mistakes in Scripture. Scripture is most certainly true but true in the sense in which Scripture itself intends to be and not in the sense we with our exact natural and historical science would impose on it. Hence before everything else, as we consider every narrative and report in Scripture, we are obligated to examine what the author, and what God through the author, intended to say by it. In general we can already say at this point—and in the abstract this is conceded by everyone—that the Bible is not a handbook for geology, physics, astronomy, geography, or history. That does not mean that Scripture does not contain various statements about them, but in each case we have to examine what the author intended to say by it, whether he really wanted to give us information pertaining to those sciences or whether he included and recorded these statements for another purpose. If in a handbook on logic a sentence is quoted (say: "Gaius is a criminal"), it is not the purpose of the author to communicate a historical fact but only to make known the logical content of that sentence. This is frequently the case in Scripture also. Psalm 14 contains the words "there is no God"; this is not the opinion of the author, however, but a pronouncement cited by him to convey to us the sentiments of a godless person. Paul often uses *ad hominem* arguments, but this is not to give us a lesson in logic, nor to bind us to his argumentation but only to the matter he wants to prove.

This truth must now be expanded and applied to the whole of Scripture. Readers must distinguish between absolute and relative (or economic) truth, between formal and material errors, between what the authors say and what they mean by it, between strictly (natural), scientific or historical truth and literary or poetic truth in general, between the manner in which we write history and the way the ancient Semites did it. If we carefully keep this distinction in mind [so it is said] and apply it in our criticism and exegesis of Scripture, it may very well happen that many parts of Scripture, which up until now we had viewed as history, prove upon study not to be history in our sense at all and were not so intended by the author, hence by the Holy Spirit, either. Materially, therefore, these parts may be fables, myths, sagas, legends, allegories, or poetic representations, which the author, under the guidance of the Holy Spirit, took from other sources or from popular oral traditions, not to tell us that everything literally happened in this way, but to teach us some religious or moral truth by such an illustration. This is, so they argue, probably the case with the creation story, with the story of Adam and Eve in paradise, with many narratives in the first eleven chapters of Genesis and in patriarchal history, etc. Even the authenticity of the books of the Bible may be freely examined. Even if the Pentateuch is not from Moses, and many Psalms attributed to David are not from David, and the second part of Isaiah is from another author than the first part, this does not detract from the divine inspiration and authority of Scripture. The inspiration is certain, but the authenticity is an open question. As a divine book the Bible is above all criticism, but as a human book it may, like all literature, be examined by historical-critical methods and standards. Roman Catholic theologians were mistaken, it is now said, when some time earlier, under the influence of the strict verbal-inspiration theory of Protestants, they turned against their fellow Roman Catholic Richard Simon [1638–1712]. Protestants have no choice but to hold a strict theory of inspiration, for if it should collapse, everything else would collapse for them as well. But Roman Catholics can in all sorts of ways accommodate present-day modern scholarship, inasmuch as for them the dogma remains firm on the basis of the church's authority.[40]

This trend of "concessionism," as it is called in France, has pitched the Roman Catholic doctrine of Scripture into a serious crisis, the further course and outcome of which deserves to be followed with interest. Although many people contradict and oppose it,[41] its influence is spreading, not only in exegetical circles but in the circles of historians and dogmaticians as well, and not just among Jesuits but also among members of other orders. In the case of some scholars, it is also clearly linked with the movement of Americanism or Reform Catholicism. In January 1902, Leo XIII appointed an interna-

40. Marie-Joseph Lagrange, articles in *Revue biblique internationale,* 1896 and 1897 (ed. note: the following pages in *Revue biblique* 5 [1896] contain items written by Lagrange: 5, 78, 127, 199, 281, 381, 440, 452, 485, 618, 644); idem, *La méthode historique surtout à propos de l'Ancien Testament* (Paris: Lecoffre, 1903); F. Prat, "Le nom divin est-il intensif en hébreu?" *Revue biblique internationale* 10 (1901): 497ff.; idem, *La Bible et l'histoire* (Paris: Librairie Bloud et Cie, 1905); A. F. Loisy, *Etudes bibliques* (Paris: A. Picard et Fils, 1901); A. Houtin, *La question biblique chez les catholiques de France au XIXe siècle* (Paris: A. Picard, 1902); F. von Hummelauer, *Exegetisches zur Inspirationsfrage* (Freiburg im Breisgau and St. Louis, Mo.: Herder, 1904); *A. Poels, *Katholiek* (December 1898); *Rieber, *Der moderne Kampf um die Bibel* (1905); N. Peters, *Die grundsätzliche Stellung der katholische Kirche zur Bibelforschung* (Paderborn: F. Schöningh, 1905); H. Höpfl, *Die höhere Bibelkritik,* 2d ed. (Paderborn: Ferdinand Schöningh, 1905); C. Holzhey, *Schöpfung, Bibel und Inspiration* (Mergentheim: Carl Ohlinger, 1902). In addition also see the works of Cornely, Knabenhauer, Zapetal, Engelkemper, Schell, Zanecchia, etc.

41. A. J. Delattre, *Autour de la question biblique* (Liége: H. Dessain, 1904); L. Fonck, *Der Kampf um die Wahrheit der h. Schrift seit 25 Jahren* (Innsbrück: F. Rauch, 1905); *G. Pletl, *Wie steht's mit der menschliche Autorität der heilige Schrift* (Fulda, 1905); Pesch, *De Inspiratione Sacrae Scripturae,* 511–52; idem, "Zur Inspirationslehre," *Stimmen aus Maria Laach* (January–March 1906); R. Peeters, "Onze heilige boeken," *De Katholiek* (March–April 1906); L. Billot, *De Inspiratione sacrae Scripturae* (Rome: ex Typographia Polyglotta S. C. de Propaganda Fide, 1903).

tional commission of fourteen members whose mandate was to study all the Scripture-related issues. Pius X, in his letter of March 27, 1906, insisted on the study of Scripture, calling for scholars not to deviate from the teaching of the church but nevertheless take serious account of recent scholarship. But only the future can tell whether this whole development will end in a papal decision.

THE RISE OF CRITICAL PROTESTANTISM

[111] The Reformers accepted Scripture and its God-breathed and God-breathing character as it had been handed down to them by the church. Luther now and then, from his soteriological position, expressed an unfavorable opinion about some books of the Bible (Esther, Ezra, Nehemiah, James, Jude, Revelation) and admitted some minor discrepancies, but on the other hand he clung to the inspiration of Scripture in the strictest sense, even extending it to the very letters.[42] Although the Lutheran confessions have no separate article on Scripture, its divine origin and authority is everywhere assumed.[43] The Lutheran dogmaticians, Melanchthon in his preface to his *Loci,* Chemnitz, Gerhard, etc., all have the same view. Quenstedt and Calovius were not the first to use such language, but Gerhard already calls the authors the "amanuenses of God," the "hands of Christ," and the "notaries public" and "stenographers of the Holy Spirit."[44] Later theologians only further developed and applied this notion.[45] Among Reformed scholars we en-

42. K. G. Bretschneider, *Luther an Unsere Zeit* (Erfurt: G. A. Keysers, 1817); D. Schenkel, *Das Wesen des Protestantismus,* 3 vols. (Schaffhausen: Brodtmann, 1846–51), II, 56ff.; J. Köstlin, *The Theology of Luther,* trans. Charles E. Hay, 2 vols. (Philadelphia: Lutheran Publication Society, 1897), II, 521ff.; W. Rohnert, *Was lehrt Luther von der inspiration der Heiligen Schrift* (Leipzig: Ungleich, 1890); Fr. Pieper, "Luther's Doctrine of Inspiration," *Presbyterian and Reformed Review* 4 (April 1893): 249–66; Thimm, "Luther's Lehre von dem Heilige Schrift," *Neue Kirchliche Zeitschrift* (1896): 644–75; Undritz, "Die Entwicklung des Schriftprinzips bei Luther in den Anfangjahren der Reformatie," *Neue Kirchliche Zeitschrift* (1897): 521–42; J. Kunze, *Glaugensregel, Heilige Schrift, und Taufbekenntnis* (Leipzig: Dörffling & Franke, 1899), 496–529; Johannes Preuss, *Die Entwicklung des Schriftprinzips bei Luther bis zur Leipziger Disputation* (Leipzig: Chr. Herm, Tauchnitz, 1901); K. Thieme, *Luthers testament wider Rom in seinen schmalkaldischen Artikeln* (Leipzig: A. Deichert'sche Verlagsbuchh. nachf. [Georg Böhme], 1900); Otto Scheel, *Luthers Stellung zur heiligen Schrift* (Tübingen: J. C. B. Mohr [Paul Siebeck], 1902); J. C. S. Locher, *De leer van Luther over Gods woord* (Amsterdam: Scheffer, 1903).

43. *Augsburg Confession,* preface 8, art. 7; *Smalcald Articles,* II, art. 2, 15; *Formula of Concord,* I, Epit. de comp. regula atque norma, 1; cf. Nösgen, "Die Lehre der Lutherschen Symbole von der heilige Schrift," *Neue Kirchliche Zeitschrift* (1895): 887–921.

44. I. Gerhard, *Loci Theol.,* 1, chap. 2, §18.

45. Heinrich Heppe, *Dogmatik des deutschen Protestantismus im sechzehnten Jahrhundert,* 3 vols. (Gotha: F. A. Perthes, 1857), I, 207–57; K. A. von Hase, *Hutterus redivivus: Oder, Dogmatik der Evangelisch-Lutherischen Kirche* (Leipzig: Breitkopf und Härtel, 1883), §38ff.; H. F. F. Schmid, *Die Dogmatik der evangelisch-lutherischen Kirche* (Erlangen: C. Heyder, 1843), chap. 4.; in English: *The Doctrinal Theology of the Evangelical Lutheran Church,* trans. and rev. H. E. Jacobs and C. E. Hay, 5th ed. (Philadelphia: United Lutheran Publication House, 1899); W. Rohnert, *Die Inspiration der heiligen Schrift und ihre Bestreiter* (Leipzig: Georg Böhme [E. Ungleich], 1889), 169ff.; Wilhelm Kölling *Die Lehre von der Theopneustie* (Breslau: C. Dülfer, 1891), 212ff.

counter the same doctrine of Scripture. Zwingli frequently gives priority to the internal over the external word, points out historical and chronological inaccuracies, and sometimes extends inspiration also to pagan authors.[46] But Calvin regards Scripture in the full and literal sense as the Word of God.[47] While he does not recognize the Letter to the Hebrews as Pauline, he does consider it canonical, and he assumes the presence of error in Matthew 22:9 and 23:25 but not in the autographa.[48] The Reformed confessions almost all have an article on Scripture and clearly express its divine authority;[49] and all the Reformed theologians without exception take the same position.[50] Occasionally one can discern a feeble attempt at developing a more organic view of Scripture. Inspiration did not always consist in [new] revelation but, when it concerned familiar matters, it consisted in assistance and direction. The authors were not always passive but also at times active. They used their own intellect, memory, judgment, and style but always in such a way that they were guided and kept from error by the Holy Spirit.[51] Also in that way there was not the least tendency to detract from the divinity and infallibility of Scripture. The writers were not authors but scribes, amanuenses, notaries, the hands and pens of God. Inspiration was not negative but always positive, an "impulse to write" and "the suggestion of matters and words." It not only communicated unfamiliar but also familiar matters and words, for certainly the writers had to know them precisely thus and precisely so, not only materially but also formally, not only humanly but also divinely.[52] Inspiration extended to all chronological, historical, and geographic matters, indeed to the words, even the vowels and the diacritical marks.[53] Barbarisms and solecisms were not accepted in Holy Scripture. Differences in style were explained in terms of the will of the Holy Spirit, who wanted to write now in one way

---

46. Eduard Zeller, *Das theologische System Zwinglis* (Tübingen: L. F. Fues, 1853), 137ff.; C. Sigwart, *Ulrich Zwingli* (Stuttgart and Hamburg: Rudolf Besser, 1855), 45ff.

47. J. Calvin, *Institutes,* I. VII–VIII; *Commentary,* on 2 Tim. 3:16 and 2 Peter 1:20.

48. Cramer, "De Schrift beschouwing van Calvijn [and Other Older Reformed Writers]," *De Heraut* 26 (Juni 1878)–33 (Juli 1878); H. C. G. Moore, "Calvin's Doctrine of Holy Scripture," *Presbyterian and Reformed Review* 4 (January 1893): 49–77.

49. First Helvetic Confession, 1–3; Second Helvetic Confession, 1, 2, 13, 18; Gallican Confession, 5; Belgic Confession, 3; Ang., 6; Scots Confession, 18, etc.

50. Z. Ursinus, *Tract. Theol.* (1584), 1–33; J. Zanchi, *Op. Theol.,* VIII, col. 319–451; F. Junius, *Theses Theol.,* chap. 2; Polanus, *Syn. Theol.,* I, 15; *Synopsis Purioris Theologiae,* disp. 2; G. Voetius, *Select. Disp.,* I, 30ff.; Cramer, "De Roomsch-Katholieke en oudprotestanse Schriftbeschouwing," *De Heraut* 26ff. (Juni 1878); H. Heppe, *Die Dogmatik der evangelisch-reformirten Kirche* (Elberfeld: R. L. Friderichs, 1861), 9ff.

51. *Synopsis Purioris theologiae,* 3:7; A. Rivetus, *Isagoge, seu introductio generalis ad Scripturam Sacram* (1627), chap. 2; J. H. Heidegger, *Corpus Theologiae,* loc. 2, §§33, 34.

52. Schmid, *Dogmatik der evangelische-Lutersche Kirche,* 23, 24; in English: *Doctrinal Theology of the Evangelical Churches,* trans. Charles A. Hay and Henry E. Jacobs (Philadelphia: United Lutheran Publication House, 1899); G. Voetius, *Select. Disp.,* I, 30.

53. J. Buxtorf, *Tractatus de punctorum origine, antiquitate et auctoritate* (1648); idem, *Anticritica* (1653); Alsted, *Praecognitio Theol.,* 276; Polanus, *Syn. Theol.,* I, 75; G. Voetius, *Select. Disp.,* I, 34; *Corsensus Helvetica,* art. 2.

and now in another.[54] Materially, as it concerns letters, syllables, and words, Scripture is "considered from the human perspective" but formally as it pertains to the inspired sense, since it is the mind, the counsel, the wisdom of God, "this is a poor perspective from which to view it."[55] In 1714, according to Tholuck,[56] Nitzsche in Gotha wrote a dissertation on the question of whether Holy Scripture itself was God.

But when the theory of inspiration had drawn its most extreme conclusions, just as it did in the case of the Jews and the Muslims, opposition arose on every side. Even in earlier times there was no lack of criticism vis-à-vis Scripture. Jehoiakim had burned the scroll of Baruch (Jer. 36). Apion summed up all the accusations made by Gentiles against the Jews with reference to circumcision, the prohibition against eating pork, the exodus from Egypt, the sojourn in the wilderness, etc.[57] Gnostics, Manichees, and related medieval sects tore the New Testament apart from the Old and ascribed the Old to a lower deity, a demiurge. Especially Marcion in his *Antitheses,* and his disciples Apelles and Tatian, proceeding from the Pauline opposition of righteousness to grace, law to gospel, works to faith, and flesh to spirit, aimed their attack at the anthropomorphisms, the contradictions, and the immorality of the OT. They asserted that a God who is angry, repents, avenges himself, is jealous, orders theft and lies, descends to earth, issues a strict law, etc., cannot be the true God. They also loved to point to the big difference between Christ, the true Messiah, and the Messiah as the prophets pictured and expected him to be. Marcion rejected all NT writings except those of Luke and Paul and spoiled the latter by abbreviation and interpolation.[58]

Celsus shrewdly continued this battle and sharply criticized the first chapters of Genesis, the creation days, the creation of human beings, the temptation, the fall, the flood, the ark, the building of the tower of Babel, and the destruction of Sodom and Gomorrah. Further, he criticized the books of Jonah, Daniel, the supernatural birth of Jesus, his death, his resurrection, the miracles, and he accused Jesus and the apostles, for lack of a better explanation, of deception. Porphyry made a start with the historical criticism of the Bible books. He opposed the allegorical exegesis of the OT, attributed the Pentateuch to Ezra, considered Daniel a product from the time of Antiochus, and also subjected many narratives in the Gospels to sharp criticism. Later, in his *Speeches against Christians,* Julian [the Apostate] again renewed all these assaults against Scripture. But with that work the criticism of the

54. J. Quenstedt and Hollaz, according to Rohnert, *Inspiratione,* 205, 208; G. B. Winer, *Grammatik des neutestamentlichen Sprachidioms,* 6th ed. (Leipzig: F. C. W. Vogel, 1855), 11ff.; G. Voetius, *Select. Disp.,* I, 34; Gomarus, *Opera omnia theologica,* 601.

55. D. Hollaz, *Examen Theologicum Acroamaticum* (Rastock and Leipzig: Russworm, 1750), 992.

56. A. Tholuck, *Vermischte Schriften grösstentheils apologetischen Inhalts,* 2 vols. (Hamburg: F. Perthes, 1862), II, 86.

57. J. G. Muller, ed., *Des Flavius Josephus schrift gegen den Apion* (Basel: Barnmaier, 1877).

58. Tertullian, *Against Marcion*; Epiphanius, *Haeresis* 42; Irenaeus, *Against Heresies,* passim; Von Harnack, *History of Dogma,* I, 267ff.; G. Krüger, "Marcion," *PRE³,* XII, 266–77.

time ended. Scripture achieved universal and undisputed dominance, and criticism was forgotten. It revived at the time of the Renaissance but was then for a long time held in check by the Reformation and the Roman Catholic Counter-Reformation. Next it surfaced again in rationalism, deism, and French philosophy. First, in the rationalist eighteenth century, it tended to be directed against the content of Scripture. Then, in the historically-minded nineteenth century, it called in question the authenticity of the biblical writings. Porphyry replaced Celsus, Renan followed Voltaire, Paul of Heidelberg made way for Strauss and Baur. But the result consistently remained the same: Scripture is considered a book full of error and lies.

As a result of this criticism, many theologians modified the doctrine of inspiration. First, inspiration was still generally retained as a supernatural operation of the Holy Spirit in the writing process but restricted to the religious-ethical dimension. With respect to chronological, historical, and such matters, it was weakened or denied so that on this level larger or smaller errors could occur. The Word of God was to be distinguished from Holy Scripture, as the Socinians already asserted. The authors of the OT and NT admittedly wrote "under the impulse and dictation of the Holy Spirit," but the OT has merely historical value. Only doctrine is immediately inspired; in the rest error was easily possible.[59] The Remonstrants took the same position. In their confession they recognized inspiration but conceded that the authors sometimes expressed themselves "less precisely,"[60] or sometimes erred in "circumstantial aspects of the faith,"[61] or—more strongly—neither needed nor received inspiration in producing the historical books.[62] We then find the same theory of inspiration in S. J. Baumgarten, J. G. Töllner, Sember, Michaelis, Reinhard, Vinke, Egeling,[63] and others.

Still, this theory encountered numerous objections. The split between "that which is needed for salvation" and "the incidentally historical" is impossible, since in Scripture doctrine and history are completely intertwined. The distinction fails to do justice to the consciousness of the authors, who certainly did not limit their authority to the religious-ethical dimension but extended it to the whole content of their writings. It is at variance with the way Jesus, the apostles, and the whole Christian church used Scripture. Consequently, this dualistic view made way for another, the dynamic conception of Schleiermacher.[64] Here divine inspiration is transferred from the intellectual to the ethical domain. Inspiration is not primarily a quality or

---

59. Otto Fock, *Der Socinianismus* (Kiel: C. Schröder, 1847), 326ff.

60. Episcopius, *Inst. Theol.*, IV, chap. 4.

61. P. Van Limborch, *Theol. Christ.*, I, chap. 4, §10.

62. H. Grotius, *Votum pro pace ecclesiae*; Clericus, according to Cramer, *De Geschiedenis van het Leerstuk der Inspiratie in de laatste Twee Eeuwen* (1887), 24.

63. Cf., e.g., Reinhard, *Dogmatik*, §19; Vinke, *Theol. Christ.* (1853), 53–57; *Egeling, *De Weg der Zaligheid*, 3d ed., II, 612.

64. F. Schleiermacher, *The Christian Faith*, §128–32.

property of Scripture but of the authors. These were born-again holy men; they lived in the proximity of Jesus, underwent his influence, found themselves in the sacred circle of revelation, and were thus renewed also in their thinking and speech. Inspiration is a habitual property of the authors, and their writings share in it, bearing as they do a new and holy character. This inspiration of the authors, therefore, is not essentially different but only different in degree from that of all believers, inasmuch as all believers are led by the Holy Spirit. Nor may it be viewed mechanically, as though it were the experience of the authors only now and then, and then only in connection with some subjects. God's Word is not mechanically contained in Scripture, like a painting in a frame, but penetrates and animates all parts of Scripture, as the soul animates all the organs of the body. Not all parts of Scripture, however, share in this inspiration, this word of God, to the same degree. Rather, the closer a thing is to the center of revelation, the more it breathes the Spirit of God. Scripture, accordingly, is simultaneously a divine and a human book containing the highest truth on the one hand and being at the same time weak, fallible, and imperfect. Scripture is not the revelation itself but only the record of revelation; not the word of God itself but only an account of that word.

While Scripture is in many respects defective, yet it is also an instrument that is sufficient for us to arrive at a fallible knowledge of revelation. Finally it is not Scripture but the person of Christ or revelation in general that is the first principle of theology. This theory of inspiration admits of course of a great many modifications. Divine inspiration can be understood in a more or a less intimate connection with revelation; the operation of the Holy Spirit can be more or less concretely conceived; the possibility of error can be more or less generously conceded. But the fundamental ideas remain the same. Inspiration is in the first place a property of the authors and secondarily of their writings; it is not a momentary act or special gift of the Holy Spirit but a habitual quality. It functions so dynamically that the possibility of error is not excluded in all parts.

This theory has almost completely replaced the old doctrine of inspiration. Only a few theologians are left who have not substantially adopted it. Even men like Franz Delitzsch, A. Köhler, W. Velck, A. J. Baumgartner (*et al.*), who first took the old position, later switched to the critical school of thought and abandoned the infallibility of Scripture. Everywhere, in scientific theology, the inspiration and authority of Scripture is in discussion.[65]

65. The literature is immense: Rothe, *Zur Dogmatik,* 121ff.; Twesten, *Vorlesungen,* I, 401ff.; Dorner, *Glaubenslehre,* I, 620ff.; in English: *System of Christian Doctrine,* II, 184ff.; Lange, *Dogmatik,* I, §76; A. Tholuk, "Inspiration," *PRE¹* (in the English Schaff-Herzog the article "Inspiration" is co-authored by several scholars); Hermann Cremer, "Inspiration," *PRE³,* 183–203; idem, *Glaube, Schrift und heilige Geschichte* (Gütersloh: C. Bertelsmann, 1896); Wilhelm Volck, *Christi und der Apostel Stellung zum Alte Testament* (Leipzig: A. Deichert [Georg Böhme], 1900); J. Chr. K. von Hofmann, *Weissagung und Erfüllung im Alten und Neuen Testamente,* 2 vols. (Nördlingen: C. H. Beck, 1841), I, 25ff.; idem, *Der Schriftbeweis,* 2d

Although in the last several decades a great deal of attention and effort has been devoted to the doctrine of Scripture, no one will claim that a satisfactory solution has been found. While on the one hand the self-testimony of Scripture remains unimpaired, on the other the contemporary investigation of Scripture brings to light phenomena and facts that are hard to reconcile with that self-testimony. One does not do justice to that dilemma by saying that neither the prophets and apostles nor even Christ but only the

ed., 2 vols. in 3 (Nördlingen: C. H. Beck, 1857–60), I, 670ff.; III, 98ff.; J. T. Beck, *Vorlesungen über christliche Glaubenslehre*, 2 vols. (Gütersloh: C. Bertelsmann, 1886–87), I, 424–530; idem, *Einleitung in das System der christlichen Lehre*, 2d ed. (Stuttgart: J. F. Steinkopf, 1870), §82ff.; F. A. Kahnis, *Die Luthersche Dogmatik*, 3 vols. (Leipzig: Dörffling und Francke, 1861–68), I, 254–301; F. H. R. Frank, *System der Christliche Gewissheit*, 2 vols. (Erlangen: A. Deichert, 1884), II, 57ff.; idem, *System der Christlichen Wahrheit*, 2d ed., 2 vols. (Erlangen: A. Deichert, 1878–80), II, 409ff.; W. F. Gess, *Die Inspiration der Helden der Bibel und der Schriften der Bibel* (Basel: Reich, 1892); W. Volck, *Zur Lehre von der Heilige Schrift* (Dorpat: E. J. Karow, 1885); R. Grau, "Über des Grund des Glaubens," *Beweis des Glaubens* 26 (1890): 225ff.; Otto Zöckler, "Zur Inspirationsfrage," *Beweis der Glaubens* 28 (1892): 150ff.; Martin Köhler, *Die Wissenschaft der christlichen Lehre* (Erlangen: A. Deichert, 1883), 388ff.; R. B. Kübel, *Über den Unterschied zwischen der positiven und der liberalen Richtung in der modernen Theologie*, 2d ed. (München: C. H. Beck, 1893), 216ff.; F. Delitzsch, *A New Commentary on Genesis*, trans. Sophia Taylor (Edinburgh: T. & T. Clark, 1899); A. W. Dieckhoff, *Inspiration und Irrthumslosigkeit der heiligen Schrift* (Leipzig: Justus Naumann, 1891); A. Köhler, *Über Berechtigung der Kritik des Alten Testaments* (Erlangen: Deichert, 1895); Bruno Baentsch, *Die moderne Bibel Kritik und die Autorität des Gotteswortes* (Erfurt: H. Güther, 1892); Karl Haug, *Die Autorität der heilige Schrift und die Kritik* (Strassburg: Strabburger Druckerei und Verlagsanstalt, 1891); *Eichhorn, *Unsere Stellung zur heilige Schrift* (Stuttgart, 1905); *C. Dahle, *Der Ursprung der heilige Schrift aus d. Dän. von H. Hansen* (Leipzig, 1905); August Klostermann, J. Lepsius, D. Haussleiter, K. Müller, D. Lutgert, *Die Bibelfrage in der Gegenwart: Fünf Vorträge* (Berlin: Fr. Zillesen, 1905); L. G. Pareau and H. de Groot, *Lineamenta theologiae Christianae universae: Ut disquisitionis de religione una verissima et praestantissima, sive brevis conspectus dogmatices et apologetices Christianae* (Groningen: C. M. van Bolhuis Hoitsema, 1848), 200ff.; H. de Groot, *De Groninger Godgeleerden* (Groningen: A. L. Scholtens, 1855), 59ff.; H. Bavinck, *De Theologie van Daniel Chantepie de la Saussaye* (Leiden: Donner, 1884); *Roozemeyer, in *Stemmen voor Waarheid en Vrede* (July 1891) and (February 1897); Isaäk van Dijk, *Verkeerd bijbelgebruik* (Groningen: Wolters, 1891); François E. Daubanton, *De theopneustie der Heilige Schrift* (Utrecht: Kemink & Zoon, 1892); J. J. Van Oosterzee, *Christian Dogmatics*, trans. J. Watson and M. Evans, 2 vols. (New York: Scribner, Armstrong, 1874), §35ff.; idem, *Theopneustie* (Utrecht: Kemink, 1882); J. I. Doedes, *De leer der zaligheid* (Utrecht: Kemink en Zoon, 1868), §§1–9; idem, *De Nederlandsche Geloofsbelijdenis en de Heidelbergsche Catechismus*, 2 vols. (Utrecht: Kemink & Zoon, 1880–81), I, 11–36; J. J. P. Valeton, *Christus en het Oude Testament* (Nijmegen: Ten Hoet, 1895); H. Zeydner, "De houding van het Evangelie dienaars ten opzichte van het Oude Testament," *Theologische Studiën* 14 (1896): 291ff.; Otto Schrieke, *Christus en de Schrift* (Utrecht: C. H. E. Breijer, 1897); A. H. de Hartog, *De historische critiek en het geloof der gemeente* (Groningen: J. B. Wolters, 1905); R. F. Horton, *Inspiration and the Bible*, 8th ed. (London: T. Fisher Unwin, 1906); Matthew Arnold, *Literature and Dogma* (New York: Thomas Nelson, 1873); Charles Gore, *Lux Mundi*, 13th ed. (London: Murray, 1892), 247; F. W. Farrar et al., *Inspiration: A Clerical Symposium*, 2d ed. (London: J. Nisbet & Co., 1886); W. Gladden, *Who Wrote the Bible?* (Boston: Houghton, Mifflin, 1891); C. A. Briggs, *Inspiration and Inerrancy* (London: J. Clarke, 1891); W. Sanday, *Inspiration: Eight Lectures on the Early History and Origin of the Doctrine of Biblical Inspiration*, 4th ed. (London; New York: Longmans, Green and Co., 1901); J. Clifford, *The Inspiration and Authority of the Bible*, 2d ed. (London: James Clarke & Co., 1895); Marcus Dods, *The Bible, Its Origin and Nature* (Edinburgh: T. & T. Clark, 1905); A. Sabatier, *Les religions d'autorité et la religion de l'espirit* (Paris: Librairie Fischbacher, 1904), in English: *Religions of Authority and the Religion of the Spirit*, trans. L. S. Houghton (New York: McClure, Phillips, 1904); *A. J. Baumgartner, *Traditionalisme et Critique Biblique* (Geneva, 1905); *A. Berthoud, *La parole de Dieu* (Lausanne, 1906).

Jewish tradition has taught the dogma of the inspiration and absolute authority of Scripture. Nor does one resolve the dilemma in all its sharpness by closing one's eyes to the serious objections that careful Bible research derives from the facts it discovers and can advance against the self-testimony of Scripture. This dilemma assumes an even more serious character because throughout all the centuries of its existence and still today in all countries, the church of Christ unconditionally accepts the authority of Scripture and lives by it from day to day. Furthermore, it is clear, on the other hand, that the objections to Scripture definitely do not concern merely a few subordinate points but touch the central truth of Scripture itself. They are not aimed at the periphery but at the center of revelation and are integrally linked with the person of Christ. Others, accordingly, have gone much further and denied all of inspiration as a supernatural and special operation of God's Spirit. To many scholars the Bible has become an accidental collection of human documents, though written by men of a deeply religious temperament and originated among a people who may be called the people of religion par excellence. One can speak of revelation and inspiration only in a metaphorical sense. At best, one can observe a special leading of God's general providence in the origination and collection of those documents. Inspiration differs only in degree from the religious enthusiasm that all devout people share.[66]

To the left of these stand the radicals who have completely finished with Scripture, shed all feelings of reverence toward it, and frequently have nothing left but mockery and contempt for it. In the first centuries Celsus and Lucian were the interpreters of this attitude. Toward the end of the Middle Ages, the blasphemy of "the three impostors" found acceptance. In the eighteenth century this hatred against Christianity was expressed by Voltaire, who from 1760 on had no other name for Christianity (which coincided for him with the Roman Catholic Church) than "the disgrace" ("l'infame") and from 1764 on usually signed his letters off with the phrase: "Crush the beast!" ("ecrasez l'infâme"). In the nineteenth century this apostasy from and hostility toward Christ and his word still gradually increased. Straus voiced the thoughts of many when, to the question of whether we are still Christians, he gave a negative reply and wanted to replace Christianity with a religion of humanity and morality, for which Lessing's [dramatic poem] Nathan the Wise constituted "the basic holy book."

66. B. Spinoza, *Tractatus Theologico-Politicus*, chap. 12; J. Wegschneider, *Institutiones Theologiae Christianae dogmatical* (Halle: Gebauer, 1819); Strauss, *Die Christliche Glaubenslehre*, 2 vols. (Tübingen: C. F. Osiander, 1840–41), I, 136ff.; Alexander Schweizer, *Die Glaubenslehre der evangelisch-reformirten Kirche* (Zurich: Orel Fussli, [1847]), I, 43ff.; A. E. Biederman, *Christliche Dogmatik* (Zurich: Orell Fussli, 1869), §§179–208; O. Pfleiderer, *Grundriss de Christlichen Glaubens- und Sittenlehre* (Berlin: G. Reimer, 1888), §39ff.; R. A. Lipsius, *Lehrbuch der evangelisch-protestantischen Dogmatik* (Braunschweig: C. A. Schwetsche, 1893); J. H. Scholten, *De Leer der Hervormde Kerk*, 2d ed., 2 vols. (Leiden: P. Engels, 1850–51), I, 78ff.; S. Hoekstra, *Bronnen en Grondslagen van het Godsdienstelijke Geloof* (Amsterdam: P. N. van Kampen, 1864), 188ff.

Still, for the majority of people this goes too far. There is nobody who does not sometimes receive a deep impression of the majesty of Holy Scripture. Even Ernst Haeckel acknowledged that [to him] the Bible was a mixture of some of the worst but also of some of the best components. Modern theologians, for all their criticism, continue to acknowledge the religious value of Holy Scripture, and not only regard it as a source for knowledge of Israel and early Christianity but continue to maintain it as a means for nurturing the religious-ethical life.[67] Among the proponents of a more relaxed view of inspiration, there are a great many people who, though attesting to their agreement with modern criticism, still strive seriously to cause Scripture to be for the church what it was for centuries: the completely reliable Word of God.

Furthermore, Ritschl and his school have contributed to a greater appreciation for Scripture insofar as over against "consciousness-theology" it again powerfully stressed the objective revelation of God in Christ.[68] This comes out clearly, especially in the work of Julius Kaftan. Rejecting the experiential, the speculative, as well as the history-of-religions method, he insisted that dogmatics should again become dogmatics and begin to speak "dogmatically." Straightforwardly he states that authority is indispensable to dogmatics and something totally natural: the "authority principle is the natural first principle of dogmatics." However, dogmatics can only speak in such absolute tones and believe in such an authority principle if it proceeds from belief in a divine revelation and derives its own authority from it. But the latter is inseparable from the former: ". . . the absolute tone goes hand in hand with the authority-principle of divine authority and vice versa." According to the Christian faith, revelation is not first of all to be found in human beings but lies outside them in history. Hence the external historical revelation of God is the cognitive source of the Christian faith and consequently the authority principle, the natural and necessary first principle of dogmatics.[69]

Now Kaftan himself, in various ways, weakens this position, which he so stoutly assumes. He one-sidedly reduces revelation to manifestation, viewing Scripture solely as a record of revelation and denying inspiration, and especially by letting himself be guided in his use of Scripture by the two practical ideas of "the kingdom of God" and of "reconciliation," which he had established in advance as the essential content of the Christian religion. Hence he rejects everything, even in Scripture, that does not agree with those two

---

67. S. Hoekstra, *Bronnen en Grondslagen*, 323ff.; Bruining, "De Moderne Richting en de Dogmatiek," *Theologische Tijdschrift* 28 (November 1894): 578ff.

68. A. Ritschl, *Rechfertigung und Versohnung*, 4th ed., 3 vols. (Bonn: A. Marcus, 1895–1903), II, 9ff.; W. Herrmann, *Die Bedeutung der inspirationslehre für die evangelische kirche* (Halle: Niemeyer, 1882); J. Kaftan, *Wesen der christelichen Religion* (Basel: Bahnmaier's Verlag, 1881), 307ff.; C. I. Nitzsch, *System of Christian Doctrine* (Edinburgh: T. & T. Clark), 212–52; E. Haupt, *Die Bedeutung der Heiligen Schrift für den evangelischen Christen* (Bielefeld and Leipzig: Velhagen & Klasing, 1891).

69. J. Kaftan, *Zur Dogmatik* (Tübingen: J. C. B. Mohr [Paul Siebeck], 1904), 21ff., 109ff.

ideas.[70] In reality, in Kaftan's case, his dogmatics still ends up being under the influence of an a priori neo-Kantian, voluntaristic view of Christianity. He is completely correct, nevertheless, in asserting that the authority of revelation is the indispensable foundation of dogmatics and that Scripture and the confessions are *the* authorities that decide what is Christian and reformational. Just as authority is the condition for all culture,[71] so also in the religious and moral life of humanity it is an essential factor and only comes fully into its own in free and unconditional submission to the supreme, divine authority.[72] It is not surprising, therefore, that the God-breathed character and authority of Scripture not only remains firm in the consciousness of the church but up until most recently still has any number of defenders among scientific theologians as well.[73]

THE CHALLENGE TO INSPIRATION DOCTRINE

[112] Holy Scripture nowhere offers a clearly formulated dogma on inspiration but confronts us with the witness of its God-breathed character and in addition furnishes us all the components needed for the construction of the

70. J. Kaftan, *Dogmatik* (Freiburg i.B.: J. C. B. Mohr, 1897), §§1–5; idem, *Zur Dogmatik*, 47ff., 117ff.

71. Ludwig Stein, *Die soziale Frage im Lichte der Philosophie*, 2d ed. (Stuttgart: F. Enke, 1903), 535.

72. Kaftan, *Zur Dogmatik*, III; cf. L. Ihmels, *Die Bedeutung des Autoritätsglaubens* (Leipzig: Diechert, 1902), 13ff.

73. I. De Costa, *Over de goddelijke Ingeving der Heilige Schrift*, prepared for publication by Rev. Egglestein (Rotterdam: Bredée, 1884); Kuyper, *De Schrift het Woord Gods* (Tiel: H. C. A. Campagne, 1870); idem, *De Hedendaagsche Schriftkritiek* (Amsterdam: J. H. Kruyt, 1881); idem, *Encyclopaedie*, II, 492ff.; J. J. van Toorenenbergen, *Bijdragen tot de verklaring, toetsing, en ontwikkeling van de leer der hervormde kerk* (Utrecht: Kemink, 1865), 9ff.; L. Gaussen, *Théopneustie ou, pleine inspiration des Saintes Écritures* (Paris: L.-R. Delay, 1840); idem, *Le canon des Saintes Écritures au double point de vue de la science et de la foi* (Lausanne: George Bridel, 1860); J. H. Merle d'Aubigné, *L'autorité des Écritures inspirées de Dieu* (Tolouse: Librairie protestante, 1850); A. de Gasparin, *Les écoles du doute et l'école de la Foi* (Genève: E. Beroud, 1853); F. A. Philippi, *Kirchliche Glaubenslehre*, 6 vols. (Gütersloh: Bertelsmann, 1902), I, 125ff.; F. C. Vilmar, *Dogmatik*, 2 vols. (Gütersloh: Bertelsmann, 1874), I, 91ff.; W. Rohnert, *Die Inspiration der heiligen Schrift und ihre Bestreiter* (Leipzig: Georg Böhme [E. Ungleich], 1889); Wilhelm Kölling, *Die Lehre von der Theopneustie* (Breslau: C. Dülfer, 1891); *E. Haack, *Die Autorität der Heilige Schrift, ihr wesen und ihre Begründung* (Schwerin, 1899); W. Walther, *Das Erbe der Reformation im Kampfe der Gegenwart*, 4 vols.: vol. I, *Der Glaube an das Wort Gottes* (Leipzig: A. Deichert, 1903–17); J. H. Ziese, *Die Inspiration der Heilige Schrift* (Schleswig: I. Johannsens, 1894); K. F. Nösgen, *Die aussagen des Neuen Testaments über den Pentateuch* (Berlin, 1898); F. Bettex, *Die Bibel Gottes wort* (Stuttgart: Steinkopf, 1903); E. Henderson, *Divine Inspiration* (London: Jackson and Walford, 1836); Robert Haldane, *The Verbal Inspiration of the Old and New Testaments* (Edinburgh: T. & T. Clark, 1830); Th. H. Horne, *An Introduction to the Critical Study and Knowledge of the Holy Scriptures*, 2d ed., 4 vols. (London: Printed for T. Cadell, 1821), vol. I; Eleazer Lord, *The Plenary Inspiration of the Holy Scriptures* (New York: A. D. F. Randolph, 1858); W. Lee, *The Inspiration of Holy Scripture, Its Nature and Proof*, 3d ed. (Dublin: Hodges, Smith and Co., 1864); Charles Hodge, *Systematic Theology*, 3 vols. (New York: Charles Scribner's Sons, 1888), I, 151; W. T. Shedd, *Dogmatic Theology*, I, 61; B. B. Warfield, "The Real Problem of Inspiration," *Presbyterian and Reformed Review* 4 (April 1893): 177–221; idem, "God-Inspired Scripture," *Presbyterian and Reformed Review* 11 (January 1900): 89–130; idem, "The Oracles of God," *Presbyterian and Reformed Review* 11 (April 1900): 217–60; John Urquhart, *The Inspiration and Accuracy of the Holy Scriptures* (London: Marshall Brothers, 1895); W. E. Gladstone, *The Impregnable Rock of Holy Scripture*, 2d ed. (London: Isbister, 1892).

dogma. It contains and teaches the God-breathed character of Scripture in the same sense and in the same way—just as firmly and clearly but just as little formulated in abstract concepts—as the dogma of the Trinity, the incarnation, vicarious atonement, etc. This has repeatedly been denied. Every sectarian and heretical school of thought initially begins with an appeal to Scripture against the confession and would have us believe that its deviation from the doctrine of the church is required by Scripture. But in most cases further investigation leads to the admission that the confession of the church has the witness of Scripture on its side. Modernists today generally concede that Jesus and the apostles accepted OT Scripture as the Word of God.[74] Others like Rothe,[75] though they grant this point with respect to the apostles, believe that church dogmatics cannot appeal to Jesus for its doctrine of inspiration. But Jesus' positive pronouncements about the Old Testament (Matt. 5:18; Luke 16:17; John 10:35) and his citations from and repeated use of OT Scripture leave no doubt whatever that for him, as much as for the apostles, Moses and the prophets were the bearers of divine authority. The contrast that Rothe construes between the teaching of Jesus and that of the apostles does not elevate but in fact undermines the authority of Jesus himself. For we know nothing about Jesus other than what the apostles tell us. Hence those who discredit the apostles and portray them as unreliable witnesses to the truth prevent themselves from finding out what Jesus himself has taught us and immediately also contradict Jesus himself. For he appointed his apostles as totally trustworthy witnesses who by his Spirit would guide them into all truth. Surely this also includes the truth concerning Holy Scripture. In the case of this dogma, as in the case of all other doctrines, the slogan "Back to Christ" is misleading and false if it is opposed to the witness of the apostles.

There is also another very common contrast, one that is created by those who want to be freed from the witness of Scripture concerning itself. Scripture, so we are told, may teach inspiration here and there, but really to do justice to and fully to understand the teaching of Scripture concerning itself, one must also consult the data that Scripture reveals to us as we investigate its genesis and history, its content and form. Only such a doctrine of inspiration, accordingly, is true and good which is consistent with the phenomena of Scripture and deduced from them. In this connection people very often make it appear as if the opposing party forces its own a priori opinion on Scripture and presses it into the straitjacket of scholasticism. These people use the argument that, over against all those theories and systems, they above all want to let Scripture speak for itself and bear witness of itself. Orthodoxy, they say, above all lacks respect for Scripture. It does violence to the text, to the facts of Scripture.[76]

74. Lipsius, *Dogmatik*, §185; Strauss, *Dogmatik*, I, 79; Otto Pfleiderer, *Der Paulinismus*, 2d ed. (Leipzig: O. R. Reisland, 1890), 87ff.

75. R. Rothe, *Zur Dogmatik*, 178ff.

76. G. Wildeboer, *De Letterkunde des Ouden Verbonds* (Groningen: Wolters, 1893), V.

This idea, when first introduced, sounds attractive and acceptable, but upon further reflection proves untenable. In the first place, it is incorrect to say that the teaching of inspiration, as it is maintained by the Christian church, forms a contrast to what Scripture says about itself. For inspiration is a fact taught by that very Holy Scripture. Jesus and the apostles have given us their witness concerning Scripture. Scripture contains teaching also about itself. Aside from all the dogmatic or scholastic development of this teaching, the question is simply whether or not Scripture deserves credence at the point of this self-testimony. There may be disagreement about whether Scripture teaches this divine inspiration of itself; but if it does, then it must also be believed at this point just as much as in its pronouncements about God, Christ, salvation, etc. The so-called phenomena of Scripture cannot undo this self-testimony of Scripture and may not be summoned against it as a party in the discussion. For those who make their doctrine of Scripture dependent on historical research into its origination and structure have already begun to reject Scripture's self-testimony and therefore no longer believe that Scripture. They think it is better to build up the doctrine of Scripture on the foundation of their own research than by believingly deriving it from Scripture itself. In this way, they substitute their own thoughts for, or elevate them above, those of Scripture.

Furthermore, the witness of Scripture is plain and clear and even recognized as such by its opponents, but the views about the phenomena of Scripture arise from prolonged historical-critical research and change in varying ways depending on the differing positions of the critics. Theologians who want to arrive at a doctrine of Scripture based on such investigations in fact oppose their scientific insight to the teaching of Scripture about itself. But by that method one never really arrives at a doctrine of Scripture. Historical-critical study may yield a clear insight into the origination, history, and structure of Scripture but never leads to a doctrine, a dogma of Holy Scripture. This can, in the nature of the case, be built only on Scripture's own witness concerning itself. No one would dream of calling a history of the origin and components of the Iliad a doctrine. Therefore, it is not just some inspiration theory that [stands or] falls with this method but inspiration itself as a fact and testimony of Scripture. Inspiration in that case—even if the word is still retained—becomes no more than a short summary of what the Bible *is*,[77] or rather of what people *think* the Bible is, and may be diametrically opposed to what the Bible itself says it is, claims to be, and presents itself as being. The method used in that case is at bottom none other than that by which the doctrine of creation, of humanity, of sin, etc. is constructed, not from the witness of Scripture concerning these things, but from one's independent study of those facts. In both cases it is a method of correcting the doctrine of Scripture in light of one's own scientific investigation, making

77. Thus, for example, Horton, *Inspiration and the Bible,* 10.

the witness of Scripture dependent on human judgment. The facts and phenomena of Scripture, the results of scientific investigation, may serve to explain and illumine the doctrine of Scripture concerning itself but can never undo the fact of inspiration to which it witnesses. Hence, while on the one side there are those who assert that only such an inspiration is acceptable which agrees with the phenomena of Scripture, on the other side the principle is that the phenomena of Scripture are, not as the critics see them, but as they are in themselves, consistent with its self-witness.

As a rule the term "divine inspiration" serves as a summary of what Scripture teaches concerning itself. The word θεοπνευστος, which in Scripture occurs only in 2 Timothy 3:16, can be taken both actively and passively and can mean both "God-breathing" and "God-breathed." But the latter meaning (contra Cremer's NT Lexicon) undoubtedly deserves preference, for (1) objective verbals compounded with θεος most frequently—though not always—have a passive meaning as in the case of θεογνωστος, θεοδοτος, θεοδιδακτος, θεοκινητος, θεοπεμπτος, etc.; (2) the passive meaning is supported by 2 Peter 1:21, where it is said that holy men spoke "borne by the Holy Spirit" (φερομενοι); (3) where the word occurs outside the NT it always has a passive meaning; and (4) it is unanimously understood in that sense by all the Greek and Latin church fathers and authors.[78] In the Vulgate it is accordingly translated by "divinitus inspirata" as well.

Originally the word "inspiration" had a much broader meaning. Greeks and Romans attributed to all people who accomplished something great and good a divine afflatus or instinct. "No one ever became a great man without divine inspiration" [Cicero]. "God is within us; we grow warm by him stirring us up" [Ovid]. Now, the inspiration of poets, artists, seers, and others can indeed serve to illumine the inspiration of which Holy Scripture speaks. Almost all great men have stated that their most beautiful ideas arose in their mind suddenly and involuntarily and were a surprise to themselves. One such testimony may suffice here. Goethe once wrote to Ekkermann: "All productivity of the highest sort, every significant perception, discovery, great idea which bears fruit and has consequences is elevated above all earthly power and under no one's control. Human beings have to consider such [things] as unhoped-for gifts from above, as pure offspring of God, which they must receive and honor with joyful thanksgiving. In such cases human beings are to be viewed as vessels found worthy to receive a divine influence."[79] Carlyle for that reason points to heroes and geniuses as the core of the history of humankind. These geniuses, each in his own field, in turn inspired the masses. Luther, Bacon, Napoleon, Hegel, and others have trans-

---

78. Cf. the thorough argumentation of Prof. B. B. Warfield, "God-Inspired Scripture," *Presbyterian and Reformed Review* 11 (January 1900): 89–130.

79. Other such testimonies by Schopenhauer, Grillparzer, Jean Paul Haydn, can be found in *Wynaend's Francken, *Psychologische Omtrekken* (Amsterdam, 1900); cf. H. Bavinck, *Bilderdijk als Denker en Dichter* (Kampen: Kok, 1906), 159.

formed the thinking of millions and changed the human mind. This fact as such teaches us that the action and impact of one mind upon another is a possibility. The manner of it varies when one person speaks to another, such as when an orator electrifies a crowd by his message or a hypnotizer transfers his ideas to the person being hypnotized, but there is always a process of suggesting thoughts: inspiration in a broad sense.

Now Scripture teaches us that the world is not independent, does not exist and live by itself, but that the Spirit of God is immanent in everything that has been created. The immanence of God is the basis of all inspiration, including divine inspiration (Ps. 104:30; 139:7; Job 33:4). Existence and life is conferred upon every creature from moment to moment by the inspiration of the Spirit. More particularly, that Spirit of the Lord is the principle of all intelligence and wisdom (Job 32:8; Isa. 11:2); all knowledge and skill, all talent and genius proceeds from him. In the church he is the Spirit of rebirth and renewal (Ps. 51:13; Ezek. 36:26, 27; John 3:3), the distributor of gifts (1 Cor. 12:4–6). In the prophets he is the Spirit of prediction (Num. 11:25; 24:2, 3; Isa. 11:4; 42:1; Mic. 3:8; etc.). So also in the composition of Scripture he is the Spirit of inspiration. This last activity of the Holy Spirit, accordingly, is not an isolated event; it is linked with all his immanent activity in the world and the church. It is the crown and zenith of it all. The inspiration of the authors in writing the books of the Bible is based on all those other activities of the Holy Spirit. It assumes a work of the *Father,* by which the organs of revelation were prepared—long before, from their birth on, indeed even before they were born, in their families of origin, by their environment, upbringing, education, etc.—for the task to which they would later be called with a special vocation (Exod. 3–4; Jer. 1:5; Acts 7:22; Gal. 1:15; etc.). Hence we may not, as modernists do, equate their inspiration with heroic, poetic, or religious inspiration. It is not a work of the general providence of God, not an effect of God's Spirit in the same measure and manner as occurs in the lives of heroes and artists, though it is true that this internal impact of God's Spirit is frequently assumed in the lives of prophets and biblical authors. The Spirit in creation precedes and prepares the way for the Spirit in re-creation. In addition, the actual inspiration [of Scripture] also assumes an antecedent work of the *Son.* The gift of divine inbreathing is granted only within the circle of revelation. Theophany, prophecy, and miracle all precede the actual inspiration. Revelation and inspiration are distinct; the former is rather a work of the Son, the Logos, the latter a work of the Holy Spirit. There is therefore truth in Schleiermacher's idea that the holy authors were subject to the influence of the holy circle in which they lived. Revelation and inspiration have to be distinguished.

If those authors could know or find out the things they had to write from what they had seen or from their personal investigation and consultation of sources, they would not have needed to receive any revelation on those topics. Jesus himself says that his apostles, whose calling was to act in the world as his witnesses, would be reminded by the Holy Spirit of what they themselves had seen and heard (John 14:26). He clearly distinguishes this activity of the Spirit from the activity by which he would reveal to them the things which, though they were included in the appearance of Christ (whence the Holy Spirit would take them), the disciples could not bear to know before the resurrection and ascension of Christ (John 16:12–14). But though there is a clear distinction between revelation and inspiration, this distinction may not be misused to separate inspiration completely from the revelation, to place it outside of the sphere of revelation, and thus in fact totally to deny it.

For, in the first place, while revelation often precedes inspiration, this is not always so. When the Holy Spirit also had the task to make known the things to come, he could collapse this revelation with inspiration. The apostles then received the thoughts of the Holy Spirit as they were writing them down, and inspiration was at the same time revelation. Second, also in matters that the apostles could know from having seen them and from their own inquiries, a special revelation of the Holy Spirit was needed of the kind that Jesus himself describes as a process of learning and remembering things he had said (John 14:26). Third, we need to remember that, while the prophets and apostles could know much of revelation because they had witnessed it, the whole of revelation becomes known to us only from and through their written witness. Hence for the church of all ages, Scripture is *the* revelation, i.e., the only instrument by which the revelation of God in Christ can be known. Accordingly, in inspiration the revelation is concluded, gets its permanent form, and reaches its end point. On the one hand, it is true that "inspiration is not revelation." On the other hand, it is equally true that "all matters inspired are matters revealed."[80] Finally, inspiration usually—but not always—also assumes a work of the Holy Spirit in regeneration, faith, and repentance. Most of the prophets and apostles were holy men, children of God. Hence also this idea of "ethical" theology contains elements of truth.[81] Yet inspiration is not identical with regeneration. Regeneration encompasses the whole person, while inspiration is an operation in the conscious mind. The former sanctifies and renews a person; the latter illumines and instructs the person. The former does not automatically include inspiration, and inspiration is possible without regeneration (Num. 23:5; John 11:51; cf. Num. 22:28; 1 Sam. 19:24; Heb. 6:4). Regeneration is a permanent way of being; inspiration a transient act. Inspiration, accordingly, is closely connected with all the aforementioned activities of God. It may not be isolated from them. It is incorporated in all those influences of God in

80. C. Pesch, *De Inspiratione Sacrae Scripturae*, 414.

81. Ed. note: Bavinck is referring here to a distinct nineteenth-century Dutch Reformed school of theology for whom the living Christ was clearly distinguished from doctrine and propositional truth (see H. Bavinck, *De Theologie van Daniel Chantepie de la Saussaye* [Leiden: Donner, 1885]). The word "ethical," a literal translation of the Dutch "ethische," is misleading. The heart of this theology was not a *moral* Christianity but an *existential,* living faith.

the created world. But here too we have to oppose the evolutionary theory that the higher can only proceed from the lower by an immanent development. The operations of God's Spirit in nature, in humankind, in the church, in the prophets, and in the biblical authors, though related and analogous, are not identical. There is harmony but no uniformity here.

DIFFERING VIEWS OF INSPIRATION

[113] In what, then, does inspiration consist? Scripture sheds light on that question when it repeatedly states that the Lord speaks through the prophets or through the mouth of the prophets; we read in Scripture "that which was spoken by the Lord through the prophet saying . . ." [cf. Gr. Matt. 1:22]. Of God the preposition ὑπο is used; he is the one speaking, the actual subject. The prophets, however—speaking or writing—are God's instruments; in reference to them the preposition διά with genitive is used, never ὑπο (Matt. 1:22; 2:15, 17, 23; 3:3, 4:14, etc.; Luke 1:70; Acts 1:16; 3:18; 4:25; 28:25). God, or the Holy Spirit, is the actual speaker, the informant, the primary author, and the writers are the instruments by whom God speaks, the secondary authors, the scribes. Additional light is shed by 2 Peter 1:19–21, where the origin of prophecy is not found in the will of humankind but in the impulse of God's Spirit. Being driven (φερεσθαι, cf. Acts 27:15, 17, where the ship is driven by the wind) is essentially distinct from being led (ἀγεσθαι, used of the children of God, Rom. 8:14). The prophets were borne, impelled by the Holy Spirit, and thus spoke. Similarly the preaching of the apostles is called speaking "in the Holy Spirit" (cf. Matt. 10:20; John 14:26; 15:26; 16:7; 1 Cor. 2:10–13, 16; 7:40; 2 Cor. 2:17; 5:20; 13:3). Prophets, and apostles, accordingly, are people "borne by God": it is God who speaks in and through them. The correct view of inspiration apparently depends therefore on putting the primary author and the secondary authors in the right relationship to each other. Pantheism and deism cannot describe that relationship correctly and fail to do justice either (in the case of pantheism) to the activity of human beings or (in the case of deism) to the activity of God. Only the theism of Scripture preserves us from error, both to the right and to the left.

The activity of God in inspiration does not come into its own when it is described as "subsequent approbation," as "mere preservation from error," or even as "dynamic," as the inspiration of persons. It is true that Lessius and Bonfrere did not assert that in fact a given book in Scripture was raised to the rank of an inspired and canonical book by a subsequent divine declaration that there was nothing false in it. However, they did entertain this idea as a possibility, appealing for this position to the citations of profane authors that occur in Scripture (Acts 17:28; Titus 1:12) and that consequently achieved canonical authority. This appeal fails to prove their position, however, because the two cases are not the same. In the biblical references cited, two profane authors are quoted by Paul, confronting us thereby by the fact of a *subsequent approbation on the part of God.* But in the cases assumed by Lessius and Bonfrere such later approbation is missing, unless one wants to find it in the church's formation of the canon. The church, however, did not cause the canon or any single book to be inspired but only recognized and confessed that which had long been established and held authority as an inspired and canonical writing in the church. If the church had raised to the rank of an inspired book any writing that was in fact not inspired, it would have been guilty of deception. Therefore, it is impossible even for God himself, by a simple declaration at a later date, to put a document that had been written without the special leading of the Holy Spirit in a group of writings that had originated with such leading. The Vatican Council [I], session 3, chapter 2, accordingly, rightly rejected Lessius's sentiments and declared that the church does not regard the books of the Bible holy and canonical "because they were composed by human industry alone and later approved by her authority." At the same time and for the same reasons, the council also rejected the sentiments of Chrismann, Jahn, and others, according to which inspiration consists only in "preservation from error." Here too "that which was spoken by God" (ῥηθεν ὑπο θεου) does not fully come into its own. The Christian church, both the Roman Catholic and the Protestant, do not regard the books of the Bible holy and canonical "because they contain revelation without error, but because, written under the inspiration of the Holy Spirit, they have God as their author, and because they have been entrusted as such to the church."

Also opposed to this confession, which is undoubtedly grounded in Scripture, is the view of inspiration according to which it consists only in arousing religious affections in the heart of prophets and apostles, affections that were then expressed in their writings. For this position not only confuses inspiration with regeneration and puts Scripture on a par with devotional literature, but also denies in principle that God revealed himself to human beings by speaking, by thoughts, and by words. All of revelation in Scripture is one continuous proof, however, that God not only speaks to human beings metaphorically, by nature and history, facts and events, but also repeatedly comes down to them to convey his thoughts in human words and language. Divine inspiration is above all God speaking to us by the mouth of prophets and apostles, so that their word is the word of God. What has been written is "that which has been spoken by God"; the Holy Spirit will speak (λαλησει) whatever he hears and will declare (ἀναγγελει) the things that are to come (John 16:13). The words of God (λογια θεου, Acts 7:38; Rom. 3:2; Heb. 5:12; 1 Pet. 4:11) are always "oracular utterances, divinely authoritative communications."[82] The word of the apostles is the word of God (1 Thess. 2:13). In 2 Timothy 3:16 Scripture is called "God-breathed," not

---

82. B. Warfield, "The Oracles of God," *Presbyterian and Reformed Review* 11 (April 1900): 217–60.

primarily with a view to its content but in virtue of its origin. It is not "inspirited because and insofar as it inspires" but, conversely, "it breathes God and inspires because it has been inspired by God."[83]

Erring in the other direction are those who favor a *mechanical* inspiration, thereby failing to do justice to the activity of the secondary authors. What we must understand by mechanical inspiration, however, is far from certain. Some writers use this term when they reject all special guidance of the Holy Spirit in the writings of the biblical books. According to them, any kind of miracle, all prophecy, all supernatural influence of God in the world and in human beings is contrary to the nature of things. So no revelation can exist other than that which comes to human beings in the ordinary course of nature and is historically as well as psychologically mediated. The inspiration that the biblical authors enjoyed is then on a par with, or at least only different in degree from, the heroic, poetic, or religious inspiration that other people experienced as well.

After everything we said earlier about revelation, however, it needs no further argument that this view is diametrically opposed to Scripture. Scripture everywhere asserts that God can and actually does reveal himself to human beings, not only by nature and history, by the heart and conscience, but also directly and in the way of extraordinary means. God reveals himself not only *in* human beings but also—by special words and deeds—*to* human beings. Even aside from this, however, on a theistic view it is not at all clear why such a special revelation to humanity is mechanical and in violation of human nature. If it is not mechanical for children to believe their parents and teachers on authority and simply to learn from them, and if it is not unfitting for a hired man to receive orders from his boss—orders he sometimes does not even understand and only has to carry out—then neither is there anything unnatural for human beings to receive a word from God that they have to accept and obey in childlike faith. If someone objects that such a revelation of God, which comes to humanity from without and cannot be inferred and explained from the things that occurred beforehand outside of and within them, always remains outside and above them and cannot be assimilated by them, we have to distinguish two things. To a child who is being brought up; to a student who is being educated; to a scholar, progress and development consists in large part in the reception and acquisition of new knowledge that cannot be derived by reflection and reasoning from what these people knew before. In logic and mathematics this may in the abstract be somewhat possible, but in history and in the natural sciences new knowledge has to be imparted to human beings from without.

At the same time, it is the task of every teacher and every scholar to introduce order into his or her teaching and studies and to proceed step-by-step from one thing to another. Those who neglect the latter cause confusion in

83. Pesch, *De Inspiratione*, 412.

people's mind; but those who deny the former—the need for new knowledge—make progress in knowledge impossible. Both of these elements are observed and combined by God in his revelation. By his revelation he constantly introduces new knowledge and information; his revelation comes in the shape of a centuries-long history. But in this connection he follows a regular pedagogical order and proceeds from the lower to the higher, from the lesser to the greater. Those in our day who oppose the former—the need for new knowledge—on the ground that human beings cannot assimilate a special revelation, gradually go on to reject all revelation. They relapse into a mechanistic view of nature and lose the right to speak of development and progress in general and specifically in the area of religion. In the end they no longer even have a standard by which to distinguish between the true and the false in what they still consider to be revelation. Those, on the other hand, who neglect the pedagogical order that God follows in his revelation run the danger of adhering to a mechanical view of revelation that is contradicted by Scripture itself.

All this applies to inspiration as well. A mechanical notion of revelation one-sidedly emphasizes the new, the supernatural element that is present in inspiration, and disregards its connection with the old, the natural. This detaches the Bible writers from their personality, as it were, and lifts them out of the history of their time. In the end it allows them to function only as mindless, inanimate instruments in the hand of the Holy Spirit. To what extent theologians in the past held to such a mechanical view cannot be said in a single sweeping statement and would have to be explored separately in each individual case. It is true that the church fathers already started comparing the prophets and apostles, in the process of writing, with a cither, a lyre, a flute, or a pen in the hand of the Holy Spirit. But we dare not draw too many conclusions from these comparisons. In using these similes they only wanted to indicate that the Bible writers were the secondary authors and that God was the primary author. This is evident from the fact that, on the other hand, they firmly and unanimously rejected the error of the Montanists, who claimed that prophecy and inspiration rendered their mouthpieces unconscious, and often clearly recognized the self-activity of the biblical authors as well. Still, from time to time, one encounters expressions and ideas that betray a mechanical view. In general, it can be said without fear of contradiction that insight into the historical and psychological mediation of revelation—now taken in a favorable sense—only came to full clarity in modern times and that the mechanical view of inspiration, to the extent that it existed in the past, has increasingly made way for the organic.

[114] This organic view, far from weakening the doctrine of Scripture at this point, enables it more fully to come into its own. It is Scripture itself that requires us to conceive inspiration—like prophecy—organically, not mechanically. Even what it teaches us in general about the relationship between God and his creature prompts us to suspect that also the leading of

God's Spirit in divine inspiration will confirm and strengthen, not destroy, the self-activity of human beings. For in creation God confers on the world a being of its own, which, though not independent, is distinct from his. In the preservation and government of all things, God maintains this distinct existence of his creatures, causes all of them to function in accordance with their own nature, and guarantees to human beings their own personality, rationality, and freedom. God never coerces anyone. He treats human beings, not as blocks of wood, but as intelligent and moral beings. The Logos, in becoming flesh, does not take some unsuspecting person by surprise, but he enters into human nature, prepares and shapes it by the Spirit into his own appropriate medium. In regeneration and conversion he does not suppress and destroy the powers and gifts of human persons but restores and strengthens them by cleansing them from sin. In short, the revelation between God and his [human] creation, according to Scripture, is not deistic or pantheistic—but theistic, and that is how it will therefore have to be in inspiration as well. Scripture itself teaches this directly and concretely. The Spirit of the Lord entered into the prophets and apostles themselves and so employed and led them that they themselves examined and reflected, spoke and wrote as they did. It is God who speaks through them; at the same time it is they themselves who speak and write. Driven by the Spirit, they themselves yet spoke (ἐλάλησαν, 2 Pet. 1:21). In the NT the OT Scriptures are frequently quoted by reference to the primary author (Luke 1:70; Acts 1:16; 3:18; 4:25; 28:25), and always in the Letter to the Hebrews (1:5ff.), but no less often by reference to the secondary authors. This demonstrates that Moses, David, Isaiah, and others, though led by the Spirit, were in fact in the full sense of the word the authors of their books (Matt. 13:14; 22:43; John 1:23, 45; 5:46; 12:38). All the various components that come under consideration in divine inspiration show that the Spirit of the Lord, so far from suppressing the personality of the prophets and apostles, instead heightens the level of their activity. This is evident first of all from the fact that they were set apart, prepared, and equipped from their youth on for the task to which God would later call them (Exod. 3, 4; Jer. 1:5; Acts 7:22; Gal. 1:15). Their native disposition and bent, their character and inclination, their intellect and development, their emotions and willpower are not undone by the calling that later comes to them but, as they themselves had been already shaped by the Holy Spirit in advance, so they are now summoned into service and used by that same Spirit. Their whole personality with all of their gifts and powers are made serviceable to the calling to which they are called.

Second, the so-called "impulsion to write" yields a tangible proof of this Spirit-led organic activity of the prophets and apostles, for in only a few texts is there any indication of a direct command to write; and these texts by no means cover the entire content of Scripture. But also the occasions that impelled the prophets and apostles to write belong to the leading of the Spirit; it was precisely through these occasions that he impelled them to write. The prophetic and apostolic calling automatically and naturally included the calling to speak and witness (Exod. 3; Ezek. 3; Amos 3:8; Acts 1:8; etc.) but not that of writing. Indeed, many prophets and apostles did not write. Nor can we infer a special injunction to write from Matthew 28:19. Writing is not mentioned as one of the charismata (1 Cor. 12).[84] But the Holy Spirit guided the history of the church in Israel and in the New Testament in such a way that deeds became words and words were set down in writing. Sellin observes on occasion that while the other prophets addressed the court, the later prophets, beginning with Amos, directed their messages more to the people.[85] To reach the people and to make known to them the thoughts of God, they simply had to utilize the means of writing. Similarly, when the apostles, after having founded the church by their preaching, wanted to impart to it the fullness of the revelation granted them in Christ, the epistolary form naturally presented itself to them as the obvious means to that end. In that respect the task of teaching all the nations, enjoined upon them in Matthew 28:19, gradually also began to take the form of witnessing by means of writing. From this guidance of the church, the calling or impulse to write was born in the life of the prophets and apostles. That activity of writing was the highest, most powerful and most universal witness that could proceed from them. By it the word of God was made permanent and became the possession of the whole human race. And precisely because the writings of the prophets and apostles did not arise outside of but in history, there is also a branch of theology that explores and makes known all the occasions and circumstances in which the books of the Bible originated. But while "unspiritual" persons stop with these secondary causes, the "spiritual" person [cf. 1 Cor. 2:14, 15] goes on to the primary cause and, in the light of Scripture, discovers in all this a special leading of the Holy Spirit.

Third, we observe that the prophets and apostles, as they proceed to write, completely remain themselves. They retain their powers of reflection and deliberation, their emotional states and freedom of the will. Research (Luke 1:1), reflection, and memory (John 14:26), the use of sources, and all the ordinary means that an author employs in the process of writing a book are used. So far from being spurned or excluded by divine inspiration, these means are incorporated into it and made to serve the goal that God has in mind. In several cases the personal experience and life history of the prophets and apostles even yielded the material they needed for their writing. In the Psalms it is the devout singer who alternately laments and shouts aloud in jubilation, sits down in sadness or loudly expresses his joy. In Romans 7 Paul describes his personal life experience; and throughout all of Scripture it is over and over again the persons of the authors themselves whose life and

84. Bellarmine, *De Verbo Dei,* IV, chap. 3, 4.
85. Ernst Sellin, *Beiträge zur Israelitischen und Jüdischen Religionsgeschichte,* 2 vols. (Leipzig: A. Deichert, 1896–97), I, 136 n. 1.

experience, hopes and fears, faith and trust, complaints and wretchedness, are depicted and portrayed. The deep and abundant life experience of the men of God (David, for example) is so shaped and led by the Spirit of the Lord that, incorporated in Scripture, it would serve to instruct later generations, "that by the steadfastness and by the encouragement of the scriptures we might have hope" (Rom. 15:4). It has all been written for our instruction (2 Tim. 3:16). Hence there is room in Scripture for every literary genre, for prose and poetry, ode and hymn, epic and drama, lyrical and didactic poems, psalms and letters, history and prophecy, vision and apocalyptic, parable and fable (Judg. 9:7f.); and every genre retains its own character and must be judged in terms of its own inherent logic.

If, then, the prophets and apostles so witness as they write, they also retain their own character, language, and style. At all times this stylistic variation in the books of the Bible has been recognized, but it has not always been satisfactorily explained. It is not to be explained by saying that the Holy Spirit out of sheer caprice decided to write one way today and another at some other time. Rather, entering these authors, he also entered into their style and language, their character and unique personality, which he himself had already prepared and shaped for this purpose. Integral to this purpose is also that in the OT he chose the Hebrew and in the NT Hellenistic Greek as the vehicle of divine thoughts. This choice was not an arbitrary one either. (Purism, let it be said in passing, in its own awkward way defended an important truth.) Judged by the Greek of Plato and Demosthenes, the NT is full of barbarisms and solecisms; but the marriage between pure Hebrew and pure Attic that resulted in Hellenistic Greek, between the mind of the East and the mind of the West, was the linguistic realization of the divine idea that salvation is from the Jews but intended for all humankind. From a grammatical and linguistic viewpoint, the language of the NT is not the most beautiful, but it is certainly the best suited for the communication of divine thoughts. In this respect, too, the word has become truly and universally human.

In view of all this, the theory of organic inspiration alone does justice to Scripture. In the doctrine of Scripture, it is the working out and application of the central fact of revelation: the incarnation of the Word. The Word (Λογος) has become flesh (σαρξ), and the word has become Scripture; these two facts do not only run parallel but are most intimately connected. Christ became flesh, a servant, without form or comeliness, the most despised of human beings; he descended to the nethermost parts of the earth and became obedient even to the death of the cross. So also the word, the revelation of God, entered the world of creatureliness, the life and history of humanity, in all the human forms of dream and vision, of investigation and reflection, right down into that which is humanly weak and despised and ignoble. The word became Scripture and as Scripture subjected itself to the fate of all Scripture. All this took place in order that the excellency of the power, also of the power of Scripture, may be God's and not ours. Just as every human thought and action is the fruit of the action of God in whom we live and have our being, and is at the same time the fruit of the activity of human beings, so also Scripture is totally the product of the Spirit of God, who speaks through the prophets and apostles, and at the same time totally the product of the activity of the authors. "Everything is divine and everything is human" (Θεια παντα και ανθρωπινα παντα).

ORGANIC INSPIRATION

[115] This organic view has been repeatedly used, however, to undermine the authorship of the Holy Spirit, the primary author. The incarnation of Christ demands that we trace it down into the depths of its humiliation, in all its weakness and contempt. The recording of the word, of revelation, invites us to recognize that dimension of weakness and lowliness, the servant form, also in Scripture. But just as Christ's human nature, however weak and lowly, remained free from sin, so also Scripture is "conceived without defect or stain"; totally human in all its parts but also divine in all its parts.

Yet, in many different ways, injustice has been done to that divine character of Scripture. The history of inspiration shows us that first, till deep into the seventeenth century, it was progressively expanded even to the vowels and the punctuation (*inspiratio punctualis*) and in the following phase progressively shrunk, from the punctuation to the words (verbal inspiration), from the individual words to the Word, the idea (Word in place of verbal inspiration).[86] Inspiration further shrunk from the word as idea to the subject matter of the word (*inspiratio realis*), then from the subject matter to the religious-ethical content, to that which has been revealed in the true sense, to the Word of God in the strict sense, to the special object of saving faith (*inspiratio fundamentalis, religiosa*), from these matters to the persons (*inspiratio personalis*), and finally from this to the denial of all inspiration as supernatural gift. Now it is a source of joy that even the most negative school of thought still wants to assign to Scripture a place and some value in the religious life and thought of Christianity.

The doctrine of Scripture is not an opinion of this or that school, not the dogma of a particular church or sect, but a fundamental article, an article of faith of the one holy universal Christian church. Its significance for the whole of Christianity is ever better understood; its unbreakable connection with Christian faith and life is ever more clearly recognized. For a certain period the doctrine of Holy Scripture was relegated, in dogmatics, to "the means of grace," but it has again reconquered with honor a place at the entrance of this discipline.[87] The entire Roman Catholic Church and the Eastern Orthodox churches are still standing firm in the confession of the divine

---

86. Cf. Philippi, *Kirchliche Glaubenslehre*, 3d ed., I, 252.
87. Nitzsch, *Lehrbuch*, 212.

inspiration of Holy Scripture. Many Protestant churches and schools of theology have up until now resisted every attempt to force them to give up that foundation. The church—by preaching and teaching, by reading and study—continues to live indirectly or directly out of the Scriptures and to feed itself with the Scriptures. Even those who deny Scripture's inspiration in theory often act and speak in practice as though they fully accept it.

According to many people, as it concerns the doctrine of Scripture, orthodoxy is caught up in the dualism of believing and knowing. However, this does not begin to compare with the ambivalent position of mediating theology (*Vermittelungstheologie*), which from university lecterns denies inspiration but actually confesses it from the pulpit.[88] Radicalism is increasingly coming to acknowledge that the inspiration of Scripture is taught by Scripture itself and has to be accepted or rejected along with it. All this shows that life is stronger than theory and that Scripture itself again and again reacts against every naturalistic explanation. Scripture itself claims that it proceeded from the Spirit of God and maintains this claim over against all criticism. Every attempt to divest it of the mysterious character of its origin, content, and power has up until now ended in defeat and in letting Scripture be Scripture. A [doctrine of] inspiration, therefore, is not an explanation of Scripture, nor actually a theory, but it is and ought to be a believing confession of what Scripture witnesses concerning itself, despite the appearance that is against it. Inspiration is a dogma, like the dogma of the Trinity, the incarnation, etc., which Christians accept, not because they understand the truth of it but because God so attests it. It is not a scientific pronouncement but a confession of faith. In the case of inspiration, as in the case of every other dogma, the question is not in the first place how much can I and may I confess without coming into conflict with science, but what is the witness of God and what, accordingly, is the pronouncement of the Christian faith? And then there is only one possible answer: Scripture presents itself as the word of God and in every century the church of God has recognized it as such. Inspiration is based on the authority of Scripture and has received the affirmation of the church of all the ages.

The so-called "personal" and "fundamental" approach to inspiration is in conflict with this dogmatic and religious character of the doctrine of the inspiration of Scripture. It must be granted that there is value also in these views. For it is certainly the inspired persons who were employed by the Holy Spirit, along with all their gifts and powers, and those persons were holy men, men of God, fully equipped for this work. When and as long as we think of this personal inspiration in our doctrine of inspiration, we discover there is even a difference in the measure and extent of it.[89] Just as, in virtue of God's providence, the authors of the books of the Bible were per-

---

88. Cf. G. Hulsman, *Moderne Wetenschap of Bijbelsche traditie?* (Utrecht: Kemink, 1897).
89. A. Kuyper, *Encyclopaedie*, II, 425.

sonally distinct from each other, so also the manner in which they were shaped and led by the Holy Spirit differed. There is a distinction here between the prophets and the apostles, and in each category there is diversity among them as well. Among the prophets Moses has primacy: God spoke with him as a friend. In the case of Isaiah, the impulse of the Spirit differs from that in the case of Ezekiel. Jeremiah's prophecies differ in their simplicity and naturalness from those in Zechariah and Daniel. In all the prophets of the OT, the impulse of the Holy Spirit is more or less transcendent; it comes upon them from above and from without, falls upon them, and then ceases. In the case of the apostles, on the other hand, the Holy Spirit dwells immanently in their hearts, leads and impels them, illumines and instructs them. There is therefore a vast amount of difference in the character of personal inspiration and hence also between the different parts of Scripture: not all the books of the Bible are of equal value.

But this difference in personal or so-called prophetic inspiration may not be misused to weaken or limit the so-called "graphic" inspiration, as the proponents of a "personal" and "fundamental" inspiration in fact do. Both of these conceptions, after all, are in conflict with Scripture's self-witness. The "all Scripture" (πασα γραφη) of 2 Timothy 3:16 is decisive here. Even if this expression could not be translated by "all Scripture" or "Scripture as a whole," it certainly does not, as the context shows, refer to some writing in general, which, if it were "God-breathed," would be profitable. Rather, it refers to the "sacred writings" of verse 15 and therefore has in view a certain Scripture, namely that of the Old Testament. Therefore the reference here corresponds in thrust to the phrase "whatever was written" in Romans 15:4. Furthermore, the theory of personal inspiration runs up against the objection(s) that it wipes out the distinction between inspiration and illumination (regeneration), between the intellectual and the ethical life, between the "being borne" of the prophets (2 Pet. 1:21) and the "being led" of the children of God (Rom. 8:14), between Holy Scripture and devotional literature. Moreover, along with Roman Catholicism, it turns the relation between Scripture and church into its opposite, robs the church of the certainty it needs, and makes it dependent on science, which has to decide what in Scripture is or is not the word of God.

Many proponents of this theory of inspiration indeed try to escape these objections by appealing to the person of Christ as the source and authority of dogmatics, but this does not benefit them because there is disagreement precisely on the question of who Christ is and what he taught and did. If the apostolic witness concerning Christ is not reliable, no knowledge of Christ is possible. Add to this that if Christ is authoritative he is authoritative also in the teaching concerning Scripture. In that case inspiration has to be accepted above all on his authority. The "personal" theory conflicts with the authority of Christ himself.

The theory of "fundamental" inspiration is distinguished from that of "personal" inspiration by the fact that while it still assumes a special activity of the Spirit in the writing process, it is limited to only certain parts of Scripture. This conception is so deistic and dualistic, however, that it is unacceptable for that reason alone. Furthermore, word and fact, the religious and the historical dimensions, that which was spoken by God and that which was spoken by human beings, is so tightly interwoven and intertwined that separation is impossible. The historical parts in Scripture are also a revelation of God. And, finally, these two theories still do not meet the objections advanced by science against Scripture and its inspiration. For these objections, far from pertaining to a few subordinate points on the periphery of revelation, touch the heart and center of it. The "personal" and "fundamental" theories of inspiration are absolutely not more scientific and rational than the most rigorous theories of verbal inspiration.

The other theories of inspiration ("punctual," "verbal," "real") and also the Word-inspiration of Philippi do not differ all that much from each other. With a more or less mechanical view of divine inspiration, disagreement about its extent can arise easily. Since clear insight into the close connectedness between thoughts (things), words, and letters was lacking, people in the past could often argue over whether inspiration extended only to the first or also to the last.[90] But if divine inspiration is understood more organically, i.e., more historically and psychologically, the importance of these questions vanishes. The activity of the Holy Spirit in the writing process, after all, consisted in the fact that, having prepared the human consciousness of the authors in various ways (by birth, upbringing, natural gifts, research, memory, reflection, experience of life, revelation, etc.), he now, in and through the writing process itself, made *those* thoughts and words, *that* language and style, rise to the surface of that consciousness, which could best interpret the divine ideas for persons of all sorts of rank and class, from every nation and age.

Included in the thoughts are the words; included in the words are the vowels. But from this it does not follow that the vowel signs in our Hebrew manuscripts derive from the authors themselves. Nor does it follow that every word is full of divine wisdom, that every jot and tittle is charged with infinite content. Certainly, everything has its meaning, provided it is seen in its place and in the context in which it occurs. Scripture may not be viewed atomistically as though every word and letter by itself is inspired by God as such and has its own meaning with its own infinite, divine content. This approach leads to the foolish hermeneutical rules of the Jewish scribes and, rather than honoring Scripture, dishonors it.

Inspiration has to be viewed *organically*, so that even the lowliest part has its place and meaning and at the same time is much farther removed from

90. For literature, see M. Vitringa *Doctr. Christ. Relig.*, I, 46; cf. also S. Pesch, *De Inspiratione Sacrae Scripturae*, 439–89.

the center than other parts. In the human organism nothing is accidental, neither its length, nor its breadth, nor its color or its tint. This is not, however, to say that everything is equally closely connected with its life center. The head and the heart occupy a much more important place in the body than the hand and the foot, and these again are greatly superior in value to the nails and the hair. In Scripture as well, not everything is equally close to the center. There is a periphery, which moves in a wide path around the center, yet also that periphery belongs to the circle of the divine thoughts. Accordingly, there are no kinds and degrees in "graphic" inspiration. The hair of one's head shares in the same life as the heart and the hand. There is one soul, which is totally present in the whole body and in all of its parts. It is one and the same Spirit from whom, through the consciousness of the authors, the whole of Scripture has come. But there is a difference in the manner in which the same life is present and active in the different parts of the body. There is diversity of gifts, also in Scripture, but it is the same Spirit.

A DEFENSE OF ORGANIC INSPIRATION

[116] Many and very serious objections are raised against this view of the inspiration of Scripture. They derive from the historical criticism that questions the authenticity and credibility of many biblical books. The challenge comes from the mutual contradictions that occur time after time in Scripture; from the manner in which OT texts are cited and interpreted in the NT; and it comes from secular history with which the narratives of Scripture can often not be harmonized. Nature also, which both in its origin and existence contradicts Scripture with its creation and its miracles, raises other issues, as do the areas of religion and morality, which often pass a negative judgment on the faith and life of persons in the Bible. Finally, we encounter objections from the present state of Scripture whose text, according to textual criticism, having been lost with the autographa, is corrupt in the apographa and defective in its translations. It is vain to ignore these objections and to act as if they don't exist. Still, we must first of all call attention to the ethical battle, which at all times has been carried on against Scripture. If Scripture is the word of God, that battle is not accidental but necessary and completely understandable. If Scripture is the account of the revelation of God in Christ, it is bound to arouse the same opposition as Christ himself who came into the world for judgment (κρισις) and is "set for the fall and rising of many" [Luke 2:34]. He brings separation between light and darkness and reveals the thoughts of many hearts. Similarly Scripture is a living and active word, a "discerner" of the thoughts and intentions of the heart [cf. Heb. 4:12]. It not only *was* inspired but is still "God-breathed" and "God-breathing." Just as there is much that precedes the act of inspiration (all the activity of the Holy Spirit in nature, history, revelation, regeneration), so there is much that follows it as well. Inspiration is not an isolated

event. The Holy Spirit does not, after the act of inspiration, withdraw from Holy Scripture and abandon it to its fate but sustains and animates it and in many ways brings its content to humanity, to its heart and conscience. By means of Scripture as the word of God, the Holy Spirit continually wars against the thoughts and intentions of the "unspiritual" person (ψυχικος ἀνθρωπος). By itself, therefore, it need not surprise us in the least that Scripture has at all times encountered contradiction and opposition. Christ bore a cross, and the servant [Scripture] is not greater than its master. Scripture is the handmaiden of Christ. It shares in his defamation and arouses the hostility of sinful humanity.

Of course not all opposition to Scripture can be explained in terms of this [spiritual hostility]. Still, the attacks to which Scripture is exposed in this century must not be viewed on their own. They are undoubtedly an integral part of the intellectual trend of this age. It is not for us to judge persons and intentions, but it would be superficial to say that the battle against the Bible in this century stands completely by itself and is controlled by very different and much purer motives than in earlier centuries. It is unlikely that today it is only the head that speaks and that the heart remains completely outside of it. All believers have the experience that in the best moments of their life they are also most firm in their belief in Scripture. The believer's confidence in Christ increases along with their confidence in Scripture and, conversely, ignorance of the Scriptures is automatically and proportionately ignorance of Christ (Jerome). The connection between sin and error often lies hidden deep below the surface of the conscious life. One can almost never demonstrate this link in others, but it is sometimes revealed to our own inner eye [with respect to ourselves]. The battle against the Bible is, in the first place, a revelation of the hostility of the human heart. But that hostility may express itself in various ways. It absolutely does not come to expression only—and perhaps not even most forcefully—in the criticism to which Scripture has been subjected in our time. Scripture as the word of God encounters opposition and unbelief in every "unspiritual" person. In the days of dead orthodoxy, an unbelieving attitude toward Scripture was in principle as powerful as in our historically-oriented and critical century. The forms change, but the essence remains the same. Whether hostility against Scripture is expressed in criticism like that of Celsus and Porphyry or whether it is manifest in a dead faith, that hostility in principle is the same. For not the hearers but the doers of the word [James 1:22] are pronounced blessed. "The servant who knew his master's will but did not make ready or act according to his will will receive a severe beating" [Luke 12:47].

It remains the duty of every person, therefore, first of all to put aside his or her hostility against the word of God and "to take every thought captive to obey Christ" [2 Cor. 10:5]. Scripture itself everywhere presses this demand. Only the pure of heart will see God. Rebirth will see the kingdom of God. Self-denial is the condition for being a disciple of Jesus. The wisdom of the world is folly to God. Over against all human beings, Scripture occupies a position so high that, instead of subjecting itself to their criticism, it judges them in all their thoughts and desires.

And this has been the Christian church's position toward Scripture at all times. According to Chrysostom, humility is the foundation of philosophy. Augustine [once] said: "When a certain rhetorician was asked what was the chief rule in eloquence, he replied, 'Delivery'; what was the second rule, 'Delivery'; what was the third rule, 'Delivery'; so if you ask me concerning the precepts of the Christian religion, first, second, third, and always I would answer, 'Humility.'" Calvin cites this statement with approval.[91] And Pascal cries out to humanity: "Humble yourself, powerless reason! Be silent, stupid nature! . . . Listen to God!"

This has been the attitude of the church toward Scripture down the centuries. And the Christian dogmatician may take no other position. For a dogma is not based on the results of any historical-critical research but only on the witness of God, on the self-testimony of Holy Scripture. A Christian believes, not because everything in life reveals the love of God, but rather despite everything that raises doubt. In Scripture too there is much that raises doubt. All believers know from experience that this is true. Those who engage in biblical criticism frequently talk as if simple church people know nothing about the objections that are advanced against Scripture and are insensitive to the difficulty of continuing to believe in Scripture. But that is a false picture. Certainly, simple Christians do not know all the obstacles that science raises to belief in Scripture. But they do to a greater or lesser degree know the hard struggle fought both in head and heart against Scripture. There is not a single Christian who has not in his or her own way learned to know the antithesis between the "wisdom of the world" and "the foolishness of God." It is one and the same battle, an ever-continuing battle, which has to be waged by all Christians, learned or unlearned, to "take every thought captive to the obedience of Christ" (2 Cor. 10:5).

Here on earth no one ever rises above that battle. Throughout the whole domain of faith, there remain "crosses" (cruces) that have to be overcome.[92] There is no faith without struggle. To believe is to struggle, to struggle against the appearance of things. As long as people still believe in anything, their belief is challenged from all directions. No modern believer is spared

---

91. J. Calvin, *Institutes*, II. 2, 11. Ed. note: According to John T. McNeill, editor of the Battles translation of Calvin's *Institutes* (Library of Christian Classics 20 and 21), the citation from Chrysostom is *De profectu evangelii* 2 (*MPG* 51, 312). This reference appears to be in error. *MPG* 51, 312 contains a homily on Phil. 1:18, but the reference is more likely to Homily 2 on Philippians 1:8–11, where Chrysostom does relate philosophy to the strength of humility. However this homily is found in *MPG* 62, 180 (*NPNF¹*, XIII, 191). The citation from Augustine, according to McNeill, is *Letters* cxiii, 3, 22 (*MPL* 33, 442; cf. *Fathers of the Church*, 18, 282). Bavinck also refers to Edwards, *Works* III, 139 without going into further detail.

92. Ed. note: Here and later the author uses the Latin for cross (*crux*) to emphasize difficult problems in the apparent conflict between modern science and the Bible.

from this either. Concessions weaken believers but do not liberate them. Thus for those who in childlike faith subject themselves to Scripture, there still remain more than enough objections. These need not be disguised. There are intellectual problems (cruces) in Scripture that cannot be ignored and that will probably never be resolved. But these difficulties, which Scripture itself presents against its own inspiration, are in large part not recent discoveries of our century. They have been known at all times. Nevertheless, Jesus and the apostles, Athanasius and Augustine, Thomas and Bonaventure, Luther and Calvin, and Christians of all churches have down the centuries confessed and recognized Scripture as the word of God. Those who want to delay belief in Scripture till all the objections have been cleared up and all the contradictions have been resolved will never arrive at faith. "For who hopes for what he sees?" [Rom. 8:24]. Jesus calls blessed those who have not seen and yet believe [John 20:29].

In any case, there are objections and conundrums in every science. Those who do not want to start in faith will never arrive at knowledge. Epistemology, the theory of knowledge, is the first principle of philosophy, but it is riddled with mystery from start to finish. Those who do not want to embark on scientific investigation until they see the road by which we arrive at knowledge fully cleared will never start. Those who do not want to eat before they understand the entire process by which food arrives at their table will starve to death. And those who do not want to believe the Word of God before they see all problems resolved will die of spiritual starvation. "By comprehension we won't make it; therefore lay hold of it uncomprehended" (N. Beets). Nature, history, and every science present as many "cruxes" as Holy Scripture. Nature contains so many enigmas that it can often make us doubt that there exists a wise and just God. There are any number of apparent contradictions on every page of the book of nature. There is an "inexplicable remnant" (Schelling) that defies all explanation. Who, for that reason, abandons belief in the providence of God, which covers all things? Islam, the life and destiny of primitive peoples, are "cruxes" in the history of humankind as big and as difficult as the composition of the Pentateuch and the Synoptic Gospels. Who for that reason questions whether God with his almighty hand also writes the book of nature and history? Of course, here and so also in the case of Scripture, we can throw ourselves into the arms of agnosticism and pessimism. But despair is a death leap also in the area of science. The mysteries of existence do not decrease but instead increase with the adoption of unbelief. And the unease of the heart grows larger.

[117] Nonetheless, the organic view of inspiration does furnish us with many means to meet the objections advanced against it. It implies the idea that the Holy Spirit, in the inscripturation of the word of God, did not spurn anything human to serve as an organ of the divine. The revelation of God is not abstractly supernatural but has entered into the human fabric, into persons and states of beings, into forms and usages, into history and life. It does

not fly high above us but descends into our situation; it has become flesh and blood, like us in all things except sin. Divine revelation is now an ineradicable constituent of this cosmos in which we live and, effecting renewal and restoration, continues its operation. The human has become an instrument of the divine; the natural has become a revelation of the supernatural; the visible has become a sign and seal of the invisible. In the process of inspiration, use has been made of all the gifts and forces resident in human nature.

Consequently, and in the first place, the difference in language and style, in character and individuality, that can be discerned in the books of the Bible has become perfectly explicable. In the past, when a deeper understanding was lacking, this difference was explained in terms of the will of the Holy Spirit. Given the organic view, however, this difference is perfectly natural. Similarly, the use of sources, the authors' familiarity with earlier writings, their own inquiries, memory, reflection, and life experience are all included, and not excluded, by the organic view. The Holy Spirit himself prepared his writers in that fashion. He did not suddenly descend on them from above but employed their whole personality as his instrument. Here too the saying "grace does not cancel out nature but perfects it" is applicable. The personality of the authors is not erased but maintained and sanctified. Inspiration, therefore, in no way demands that, literarily or aesthetically, we equate the style of Amos with that of Isaiah or that we deny all barbarisms and solecisms in the language of the NT.

Secondly, the organic view of revelation and inspiration brings with it the notion that ordinary human life and natural life, so far from being excluded, is also made serviceable to the thoughts of God. Scripture is the word of God; it not only contains but *is* the word of God. But the formal and material element in this expression may not be split up. Inspiration alone would not yet make a writing into the word of God in a Scriptural sense. Even if a book on geography, say, was inspired from cover to cover and was literally dictated word-for-word, it would still not be "God-breathed" and "God-breathing" in the sense of 2 Timothy 3:16. Scripture is the word of God because the Holy Spirit testifies in it concerning Christ, because it has the Word-made-flesh as its matter and content. Form and content interpenetrate each other and are inseparable. But in order to paint a full-length portrait of this image of Christ, human sin and satanic lies in all their horror would have to be pictured as well. Shadows are needed in this portrait in order to bring out the light more brilliantly. Sin, also when it occurs in the biblical saints, must be called sin, and error may not be excused even in them. And as the revelation of God in Christ incorporates unrighteousness within itself as antithesis, so also it does not spurn to include elements of human weakness and human nature. Christ counted nothing human as alien to himself; and Scripture does not overlook even the most minor concerns of daily life (2 Tim. 4:13). Christianity is not antithetically opposed to that which is human but is its restoration and renewal.

Thirdly, the intent and purpose of Scripture is integrally given with its content. "Whatever was written in former times was given for our instruction" [Rom. 15:4]. It is "useful for teaching, for reproof, for correction, and for training in righteousness, so that everyone who belongs to God may be proficient, equipped for every good work" (2 Tim. 3:16, 17 NRSV). It serves to make us wise unto salvation [2 Tim. 3:15]. Holy Scripture has a purpose that is religious-ethical through and through. It is not designed to be a manual for the various sciences. It is the first foundation (*principium*) only of theology and desires that we will read and study it *theologically.* In all the disciplines that are grouped around Scripture, our aim must be the saving knowledge of God. For *that* purpose Scripture offers us all the data needed. In *that* sense it is completely adequate and complete. But those who would infer from Scripture a history of Israel, a biography of Jesus, a history of Israel's or early-Christian literature, etc. will in each case end up disappointed. They will encounter lacunae that can be filled only with conjectures.

Historical criticism has utterly forgotten this purpose of Scripture. It tries to produce a history of the people, religion, and literature of Israel and a priori confronts Scripture with demands it cannot fulfill. It runs into contradictions that cannot be resolved, endlessly sorts out sources and books, rearranges and reorders them, with only hopeless confusion as the end result. No life of Jesus can be written from the four Gospels, nor can a history of Israel be construed from the OT. That was not what the Holy Spirit had in mind. Inspiration was evidently not a matter of drawing up material with notarial precision. "If indeed in the four gospels words are put in Jesus' mouth with reference to the same occasion but *dis*similar in the form of their expression, Jesus naturally could not have used four different forms; but the Holy Spirit only aimed to bring about for the church an impression which completely corresponds to what came forth from Jesus."[93]

Scripture does not satisfy the demand for exact knowledge in the way we demand it in mathematics, astronomy, chemistry, etc. This is a standard that may not be applied to it. For that reason, moreover, the autographa were lost; for that reason the text—to whatever small degree this is the case—is corrupt; for that reason the church, and truly not just the layman, has the Bible only in defective and fallible translations. These are undeniable facts. And these facts teach us that Scripture has a criterion of its own, requires an interpretation of its own, and has a purpose and intention of its own. That intention is no other than that it should make us "wise unto salvation." The Old Testament, while not a source for the history of Israel's people and religion, is such a source for the history of revelation. The Gospels, while not a source for a life of Jesus, are such a source for a theological (dogmatic) knowledge of his person and work. The Bible is the book for Christian reli-

---

93. A. Kuyper, *Encyclopaedie,* II, 499; cf. also Dieckhoff, *Die Inspiration und Irrthumslosigkeit der Heilige Schrift;* idem, *Noch einmal über die Inspiration und Irrthumslosigkeit der Heiligen Schrift* (Rostock: Stiller, 1893); Th. Zahn, "Evangelienharmonie," *PRE³,* V, 653–61.

gion and Christian theology. To that end it has been given, and for that purpose it is appropriate. And for that reason it is the word of God given us by the Holy Spirit.

Finally, from this perspective the relation in which Scripture stands to the other sciences becomes clear. Much misuse has been made of Baronius's saying: "Scripture does not tell us how the heavens move but how we move to heaven."[94] Precisely as the book of the knowledge of God, Scripture has much to say also to the other sciences. It is a light on our path and a lamp for our feet, also with respect to science and art. It claims authority in all areas of life. Christ has [been given] all power in heaven and on earth. Objectively, the restriction of inspiration to the religious-ethical part of Scripture is untenable; subjectively the separation between the religious life and the rest of human life cannot be maintained. Inspiration extends to all parts of Scripture, and religion is a matter of the whole person. A great deal of what is related in Scripture is of fundamental significance also for the other sciences. The creation and fall of humankind, the unity of the human race, the flood, the rise of peoples and languages, etc. are facts of the highest significance also for the other sciences. At every moment science and art come into contact with Scripture; the primary principles for all of life are given us in Scripture. This truth may in no way be discounted.

On the other hand, there is also a large truth in the saying of Cardinal Baronius. All those facts in Scripture are not communicated in isolation and for their own sake but with a theological aim, namely, that we should know God unto salvation. Scripture never intentionally concerns itself with science as such. Christ himself, though free from all error and sin, was never, strictly speaking, active in the field of science and art, commerce and industry, law and politics. His was another kind of greatness: the glory of the only begotten of the Father, full of grace and truth. But precisely for that reason he was a source of blessing for science and art, society and state. Jesus is Savior, only that but that totally. He came not only to restore the religious-ethical life of human beings and to leave all other things untouched as if they were not corrupted by sin and did not need to be restored. Indeed not, for as far as sin extends, so far also the grace of Christ extends.

The same is true for Scripture. It too is religious through and through, the word of God unto salvation, but for that very reason a word for family and society, for science and art. Scripture is a book for the whole of humankind in all its ranks and classes, in all its generations and peoples. But for that very reason too it is not a scientific book in the strict sense. Wisdom, not learning, speaks in it. It does not speak the exact language of science and the academy but the language of observation and daily life. It judges and describes things, not in terms of the results of scientific investigation, but in

94. Augustine already said, "We do not read in the gospel how our Lord said: 'I will send you the Paraclete who will teach you about the course of the sun and the moon.' For he wanted to make Christians, not mathematicians" (*Acts or Disputation against Fortunatus the Manichaean*, I, 10).

terms of intuition, the initial lively impression that the phenomena make on
people. For that reason it speaks of "land approaching," of the sun "rising"
and "standing still," of blood as the "soul" of an animal, of the kidneys as the
seat of sensations, of the heart as the source of thoughts, etc. and is not the
least bit worried about the scientifically exact language of astronomy, physiology, psychology, etc. It speaks of the earth as the center of God's creation
and does not take sides between the Ptolemaic and the Copernican worldview. It does not take a position on Neptunism versus Plutonism, on allopa-
thy versus homeopathy. It is probable that the authors of Scripture knew no
more than all their contemporaries about all these sciences, geology, zoology,
physiology, medicine, etc. Nor was it necessary. For Holy Scripture uses the
language of everyday experience, which is and remains always true. If, instead of this, Scripture had used the language of the academy and spoken
with scientific precision, it would have stood in the way of its own authority.
If it had decided in favor of the Ptolemaic worldview, it would not have been
credible in an age that supported the Copernican system. Nor could it have
been a book for life, for humanity. But now it speaks in ordinary human language, language that is intelligible to the most simple person, clear to the
learned and unlearned alike. It employs the language of observation, which
will always continue to exist alongside that of science and the academy.

In recent times a similar idea has been articulated by many Roman Catholic theologians with respect to the historiography found in Scripture. In order to reconcile the doctrine of divine inspiration with the results of modern
Bible criticism, they have made a distinction between absolute and relative
truth, between the truth of the thing cited and the truth of the citation, between a story that is true in terms of its content and a story that has simply
been taken over for some reason by the biblical authors from other sources
or from popular tradition without answering for, or wanting to answer for,
the objective truth of its content. According to these theologians, the authors of the biblical books frequently wrote—as they did in speaking about
natural phenomena, so also in narrating history—in accord with the subjective appearance of things and not in terms of objective reality.

But, in my judgment, this way of presenting the issue is inadmissible in
connection with historiography. For when the prophets and apostles speak
in the context of nature about the "sun rising" and the "land approaching,"
etc., they cannot give us a false impression since they are dealing with phenomena that we still see every day and about which we speak in the same
way they do. But if in the area of history they write "in accordance with appearance," that certainly has to mean not in accordance with what happened
objectively but in accordance with what many in their day believed subjectively. In that case they give us a false impression and are therefore being
compromised in their authority and reliability.

If theologians were to apply this principle consistently, then not only the
early chapters of Genesis could be dissolved into myths and legends—as is al-

ready happening at the hands of many Roman Catholic theologians today—but the entire history of Israel and original Christianity. If Scripture obviously intends to present a story as historical, the exegete has no right, at the discretion of historical criticism, to turn it into a myth. Yet it is true that the historiography of Holy Scripture has a character of its own. Its purpose is not to tell us precisely all that has happened in times past with the human race and with Israel but to relate to us the history of God's revelation. Scripture only tells us what is associated with that history and aims by it to reveal God to us in his search for and coming to humanity. Sacred history is religious history.

Considered from the viewpoint and by the standards of secular history, Scripture is often incomplete, full of gaps and certainly not written by the rules of contemporary historical criticism. From this it surely does not follow that the historiography of Scripture is untrue and unreliable. Just as a person with common sense can put up a good logical argument without ever having studied logic, so a reporter can very well offer a true account of what has happened without having first studied the rules of historical criticism. If historical criticism should deny this aspect of real life, it degenerates into hypercriticism and destroys the object it is designed to address. But all the historiography in Holy Scripture bears witness to the fact that it follows a direction of its own and aims at a goal of its own. In its determination of time and place, in the order of events, in the grouping of circumstances, it certainly does not give us the degree of exactness we might frequently wish for. The reports about the main events, say, the time of Jesus' birth, the duration of his public activity, the words he spoke at the institution of the Lord's Supper, his resurrection, etc., are far from homogeneous and leave room for a variety of views.

Furthermore, it is perfectly true that there is a distinction between "historical" and "normative" ["descriptive" and "prescriptive"] authority. Not everything that is incorporated and cited in Scripture is for that reason true in terms of content. The "truth of citation" is not identical with the "truth of the thing cited." In Scripture, after all, also the literal words of Satan, the false prophets, and the ungodly are cited. It is evident from the citation that these words have indeed been uttered by these persons, but they do not for that reason contain truth (Gen. 3:1; Ps. 14:1; Jer. 28:2f.). In some cases it is even hard to tell whether or not we are dealing with a citation, whether not just the accuracy of the citation but also its content is covered by the authority of Scripture, whether to a given section of Scripture only a descriptive or also prescriptive authority is due. On these points the dogma of Scripture is far from being fully developed and leaves room for many special studies.

Finally, we must add that, though Scripture is true in everything, this truth is certainly not homogeneous in all its components. Divine inspiration, as we remarked earlier, made all literary genres subservient to its aim. It included prose and poetry, history and prophecy, parable and fable. It is self-evident that the truth in all these scriptural components has a different character in each case. The truth of a parable and fable is different from that of a historical narrative, and the latter again differs from that in wisdom literature, prophecy, and psalmody. Whether the rich man and the poor Lazarus are fictitious characters or historical persons is an open question. Similarly, we can differ about whether and in how far we must regard the book of Job, Ecclesiastes, and the Song of Solomon as history or as historical fiction. This is especially clear in the case of prophecy. The Old Testament prophets picture the future in colors derived from their own environment and thereby in each case confront us with the question of whether what they write is intended realistically or symbolically. Even in the case of historical reports, there is sometimes a distinction between the fact that has occurred and the form in which it is presented. In connection with Genesis 1:3 the Authorized Version [Dutch] comments in the margin that God's speech is his will, his command, his act, and in connection with Genesis 11:5 that this is said of the infinite and all-knowing God in a human way. This last comment, however, really applies to the whole Bible. It always speaks of the highest and holiest things, of eternal and invisible matters, in a human way. Like Christ, it does not consider anything human alien to itself. But for that reason it is a book for humanity and lasts till the end of time. It is old without ever becoming obsolete. It always remains young and fresh; it is the word of life. The word of God endures forever.

14

THE ATTRIBUTES OF SCRIPTURE

A doctrine concerning Scripture's attributes developed in the Reformation churches as a counter to Roman Catholicism on the one hand and Anabaptism on the other. The key issue was the nature and extent of scriptural authority. Rome honors church and tradition above Scripture, while Anabaptism respects the inner word at the expense of the external word of Scripture. In Roman Catholicism the precedence of the church over Scripture eventually led to the dogma of papal infallibility—Ubi papa, ibi ecclesia. Here, materially, Scripture is unnecessary. Over against this position, the Reformers posited their polemical doctrine of Scripture's attributes: authority, necessity, sufficiency, and perspicuity.

The issue between Rome and the Reformation has to do with the ground of **authority.** *For the Reformers Scripture was self-authenticating; the church was founded on the truth of Scripture. For Rome, the church is temporally and logically prior to Scripture, which needs the church's acceptance and recognition. Thus a Roman Catholic Church Council (Trent) established the canon of Scripture including the Apocrypha. The believer accepts Scripture "because, written under the inspiration of the Holy Spirit, they have God as their author; and because they have been entrusted as such to the church."*

While Protestants agree that the church's testimony is a motive for faith, they do not believe it can be the ground of faith. Instead, the Reformation insisted that Scriptures are self-authenticating; the Holy Spirit who inspired the biblical writers confirms the inner testimony within the believer. Protestants did disagree among themselves about such issues as whether scriptural authority is only descriptive (historical) or normative (prescriptive). A balanced view acknowledges that while not all historical accounts in Scripture set prescriptive rules for believers, nonetheless the descriptions are true and also the Word of God to his people.

Modern theology has significantly devalued the coin of biblical authority. It picks and chooses for itself what parts of Scripture are normative (the "religious-ethical dimension") even if they are fallible and encrusted with error. Others describe the nature of biblical authority as "moral"; items are included in Scripture only because they are true. Belief based on Scripture alone turns the Bible into a paper pope. However, the authority issue does not go away. All religion rests on authority as does every area of life, notably in such academic spheres as history. So, too, true religion rests on divine authority. However, contrary to the conviction of modern people, to believe in God and accept the authority of his word in

449

no way diminishes human beings or robs them of their dignity. God's authority is unique and ennobles us.

*The Reformation also parts with Rome on the **necessity** of Scripture. In Roman Catholicism the church, living by the Holy Spirit, is self-sufficient. The Bible, strictly speaking is not necessary; Scripture does need the church for its authority and interpretation. The tradition of spiritualist mysticism, too, does not really need Scripture. Communion through ascetic practice and contemplation was able to buy the believer into union with God. The same phenomenon—internal word above external word—led to rationalist critique of scriptural authority and necessity. Even if the Scriptures were lost, the religious-ethical truth of Christianity would survive. The "church" survives the vanishing of Scripture because it produced Scripture. The church lives by the "Spirit," in whatever form.*

*Protestants acknowledge that the external word alone is insufficient; it needs the internal testimony of the Holy Spirit. For the conscious life of the church, however, Scripture is essential, indispensable for grounding the truth of the Christian gospel. The church, so believed the Reformers, needs Scripture to survive. Admittedly, there was a significantly long time in salvation history when God's people did not yet have written Scriptures. Though the necessity of Scripture is not absolute, it has been God's good pleasure to keep the church in truth by it. In our era of salvation history, Scripture is our only sure guide to apostolic teaching and preserves it for the generations. Unlike Rome, the Reformation believes that the apostolic period ended with the Pentecostal reality of the Holy Spirit's being given to the church in accord with Jesus' promise. There is no knowledge of or fellowship with Christ apart from Scripture. Scripture does have a provisional character, but until our Lord returns it is **necessary**. Scripture's necessity thus provides a guard against all premature attempts to achieve the full glory of union with God in this dispensation.*

*The Bible, according to Reformation conviction is also **clear** or **perspicuous**. This does not mean that the Bible is so transparent as to need no interpretation. Protestants too live in the history of biblical interpretation. Perspicuity does not mean that there are no mysteries or difficult passages in Scripture. What perspicuity means is that the path of salvation is clearly taught and explained. The mediation of church or priest is not essential for this mediation, and the Bible should therefore be the common possession of every believer. This teaching of scriptural perspicuity is one of the strongest bulwarks of the Reformation, though it does have a shadow side in the tragic divisions that are commonplace in Protestantism. Yet this shadow does not turn out the light of freedom set on fire by the common access to God's Word for Reformation-era believers. While the divisions of the Protestant world contributed to the rise of secular rationalism, Rome's hierarchical authority structure also failed to reign it in. Arbitrariness in Protestant Scripture interpretation must be acknowledged; the only antidote is a conscious application of the "analogy of faith."*

*Convictions about necessity and perspicuity lead quite naturally to the doctrine of Scripture's **sufficiency**. Unlike Rome, the Reformation tradition does not* consider the Bible as in some sense inadequate and therefore needing to be augmented by ecclesiastical tradition. Rome argues that a number of doctrines and practices, going back to the apostles and our Lord himself, have been entrusted to the magisterial church through an oral tradition. Based on the criteria of Vincent Lerins for determining what is genuinely apostolic—that which is believed everywhere, always, and by all—the Roman Church claims that it has safeguarded the apostolic tradition in the person of the pope, who is infallible when he speaks **ex cathedra.** These criteria are distributive rather than copulative. **Either** universality or antiquity is sufficient to make it a dogma of the church. Distinguishing the listening church from the teaching church, Rome considers the former only passively infallible, while the location of active infallibility resides in the teaching church. Rome, however, has not defined the one and only proper means for determining what is a genuinely apostolic tradition or teaching. It is not clear whether the pope, for example, is infallible on his own authority or together with the other bishops and councils. Does a majority vote get full approbation, or must it be unanimous for it to be infallible? How these questions are answered is less important than the strong conviction that the pope is the "Vicar of Christ"; he is the voice of God to the world. From this it is little surprise to see the First Vatican Council (1871) declare papal infallibility.

When the Reformation affirmed the perfection of Scripture, it did not deny that there were times when God's people had little or no written word and lived by the revelation of oral tradition. However, with the completion of the canon, it denies that there exists another Word of God alongside it in unwritten form. It is also true that some of the church's dogmas are legitimate inferences from Scripture. Furthermore, while acknowledging that the Bible does not contain all the divine revelation given to apostles, prophets, and our Lord himself, it does not believe that written forms of some dogmas were lost while only the oral tradition remained. The result is that the truly universal dogmas of the church are derived from Scripture, while Rome's tradition produces only distinctively Roman doctrine such as papal infallibility and the bodily assumption of Mary.

There is an important reality of salvation history at stake here. The canon of the OT and NT was not closed until all new initiatives of salvation history were present. The work of Christ is complete. In this dispensation the Holy Spirit's task is not to provide further new revelation but to apply the work of Christ. That work and word requires no supplement. At the same time there is value in tradition understood in its broad sense as the thought and action of a religious community in its customs, practices, mores, confessions, and liturgies. No intergenerational community can continue to exist without tradition.

For religions of the Book, the need for tradition as an interpretive guide is essential. The distance of time between the writing of the book and our times means that the community's tradition is its necessary connection to the past. Radical groups that deliberately set aside all intervening tradition to return, in a primitivist way, to the letter of the Bible alone doom themselves to extinction unless they adapt to a new age. The Reformation did not reject all tradition; it

wanted only to reform tradition and purge it from its errors. What the Reforma-
tion rejected was an ecclesiastical tradition alongside Scripture. The only tradi-
tion that may be accepted is the one that is founded on and flows from Scripture.
Our dependence on Scripture and Scripture alone will last until the time when
Scripture and temple are no longer needed and we are all taught by the Lord
himself and filled with the Holy Spirit.

ATTRIBUTES IN GENERAL

[118] The doctrine of the attributes of Scripture has developed completely as a result of the [Reformation's] struggle with Roman Catholicism
and Anabaptism. In the confession of the inspiration and authority of Scripture, there was agreement between Rome and the Reformation, but for the
rest, as it pertains to the locus of Holy Scripture, there was much disagreement. The way in which Rome had related Scripture and church was fundamentally changed in the Reformation. In the church fathers and the scholastics, Scripture, at least in theory, was on a level far above the church and
tradition; it rested in itself, was trustworthy in and of itself (αὐτόπιστος), and
the primary norm for church and theology. Augustine said "canonical scripture is contained by its own fixed boundaries"[1] and reasons (*Conf.* 6, 5; 11,
3) as if the truth of Scripture depends only on itself. Bonaventure writes:
"For the church is founded upon the pronouncements of the Holy Scriptures; if they are deficient, so is the [church's] understanding. . . . For since
the church is founded upon Holy Scripture, those who do not know Scripture do not know how to guide the church."[2] Similar statements are cited by
Gerhard[3] from the works of Salvian, Biel, Cajetan, Hosius, Valentia, et al. In
his *Summa doctrinae christianae* Canisius writes: "Consequently, just as we
believe Scripture and attach and attribute great authority [to it], on account
of the testimony of the Spirit of God speaking in it, so we also owe loyalty,
reverence, and obedience to the church."[4] Also Bellarmine states: "Nothing
is more widely known and certain than the Scriptures contained in the prophetic and apostolic writings. Accordingly, anyone who denies that we ought
to have faith in them has to be extremely stupid."[5] All of these theologians
believed that Scripture could be sufficiently demonstrated to be true from
and by [Scripture] itself. It does not depend on the church; on the contrary,
the church depends on it. The church with its tradition may be the rule of

---

1. A. von Harnack, *History of Dogma,* trans. N. Buchanan, J. Miller, E. B. Speirs, and W. McGilchrist
and ed. A. B. Bruce, 7 vols. (London: Williams & Norgate, 1896–99), III, 208. Ed. note: The reference is
to Augustine's *On Baptism, against the Donatists,* II. 3, 4.

2. Bonaventure, "De Sept. don.," nn. 37–43; cited in the 1881 edition of the *Breviloquium*
(Freiburg: Herder, 1881), 370.

3. J. Gerhard, *Loci Theol.,* I, 3 §45, §46.

4. Canisius, *Summa doctrinae Christianae,* "De praeceptis ecclesia," §16.

5. Bellarmine, "De Verbo dei," *Controversiis,* I, 2.

faith (*regula fidei*); it is not its foundation (*fundamentum fidei*). That distinction belongs to Scripture alone.

In Roman Catholicism, however, the church with its offices and tradition began increasingly to assume an independent position and to acquire authority alongside of Holy Scripture. At first the relation between the two was not precisely defined but soon required further regulation. And when the church continued to increase in power and self-sufficiency, authority was increasingly shifted from Scripture to the church. A series of different moments in history indicate the process by which the church, instead of being subject to Scripture, elevated itself to a place alongside of Scripture and finally to a place above Scripture. The question of which of the two, Scripture or the church, had precedence was first stated clearly and deliberately in the time of the reform councils. Despite the opposition of Gerson, d'Ailly, and especially of Nicolas of Clemange,[6] it was settled in favor of the church. Trent sanctioned this position over against the Reformation. In the struggle against Gallicanism the issue was defined in greater detail and resolved by the Vatican Council (1870) by declaring the church infallible.

The subject of this infallibility, however, was not the listening church, nor the teaching church, nor the bishops gathered collectively in council, but specifically the pope. And the pope was the subject of infallibility, not as a private person, nor as bishop of Rome or patriarch of the West, but as the chief shepherd of the entire church. Granted, he possesses this authority as head of the church and not apart from it; still he possesses it, not through and along with the church, but above and in distinction from it. Even bishops and councils participate in this infallibility, not apart from, but only in union with and submission to the pope. He stands above all and alone makes the church, tradition, councils, and canons infallible. Councils without a pope can err and have erred.[7] The church as a whole, both the teaching and the listening church, is infallible only with and under the Roman pontiff. As a result of this process, the relation between church and Scripture has been reversed. The church, more concretely the pope, has precedence over and stands above Scripture. Where the pope is, there the church is (*Ubi papa, ibi ecclesia*).[8] The infallibility of the pope renders that of the church, the bishops and councils, as well as that of Scripture, unnecessary.

From this Roman Catholic view of the Scripture-church relation flow all the differences that exist between Rome and the Reformation in the doctrine of Scripture. They concern above all the necessity of Scripture, the Apocrypha of the OT, the Vulgate edition, the proscription of Bible reading, the exposition of Scripture, and tradition. Formally, the reversal in the Scripture-church relation is most clearly demonstrated in the fact that modern Catholic theologians treat the doctrine of the church in the "formal part" of

6. Cf. C. Schmidt, "Clémanges," *PRE²*, III, 247.

7. Bellarmine, "De Conc. et. Eccl.," *Controversiis*, II, 10–11.

8. G. M. Jansen, *Prael. Theol. Dogm.*, I, 506, 511.

dogmatics. The church belongs to "the first principles of the faith." Like Scripture in the Reformation, so the church, the magisterium, or really the pope, is the formal principle, the foundation of faith, in Roman Catholicism.[9]

Over against this development, the Reformers posited the doctrine of the attributes of Scripture. It bore a polemical character through and through and was consequently fixed, in the main, from the beginning.[10] Gradually it was also included in dogmatics in a more or less systematic and methodical form, not yet in Zwingli, Calvin, Melancthon, et al., to be sure, but certainly already in Musculus, Zanchius, Polanus, Junius, and others[11] and, among the Lutherans, in Gerhard, Quenstedt, Calovius, Hollaz, et al. But they differed among themselves in the manner of treatment. Sometimes a variety of historical and critical matters were discussed. Dogmatics included virtually the whole "Introduction," the theory of "general and special canonics." Also the number and arrangement of the attributes were variously described. The authority, utility, necessity, truth, perspicuity, sufficiency, origin, division, content, apocrypha, council, church, tradition, authentic edition, translations, exposition, the testimony of the Holy Spirit—all this and much more were dealt with in the doctrine of Scripture and its attributes. Gradually the material was more strictly defined. Calovius and Quenstedt distinguished between the primary and secondary attributes. Belonging to the former category were the authority, truth, perfection, perspicuity, the "capacity to interpret its very self," its power to judge, and its efficacy. Counted among the latter were the necessity, the integrity, purity, the authenticity, and "the permission granted to all to read [Scripture]."

Even more simple was the popular order: authority, necessity, perfection or sufficiency, perspicuity, the capacity to interpret its very self, and its efficacy.[12] But even this arrangement can be made more simple. The historical, critical, archeological material, and so forth does not belong in dogmatics but in the bibliological branches of theology. The authenticity, integrity, purity, and so forth, accordingly, cannot be fully treated in dogmatics; there they come up only to the extent that the doctrine of Scripture also provides certain data for its composition. After "inspiration" and "authority," the "truth" [of Scripture] no longer needs separate treatment and would more likely be weakened than strengthened by it. "Efficacy" has its place in the doctrine of the means of grace. Thus only the authority, necessity, suffi-

9. Ibid., I, 829.

10. H. Heppe, *Dogmatik des deutschen Protestantismus,* 3 vols. (Gotha: F. A. Perthes, 1857), I, 207–25.

11. Musculus, *Loci Comm.* (1567), 374ff.; J. Zanchi, "De Sacra Scriptura," *Op. Theol.,* VIII, 319ff.; A. Polanus, *Synt. Theol.,* 17ff.; F. Junius, "Theses Theol.," *Op Theol. Select,* I, 1594ff.

12. K. A. von Hase, *Hutterus Redivus* (Helsingfors: A. W. Gröndahl, 1846), §43ff.; H. Schmid, *Doctrinal Theology of the Evangelical Churches,* trans. Charles A. Hoy and Henry E. Jacobs (Philadelphia: United Lutheran Publication House, 1899), 27ff.; H. Heppe, *Dogmatik der evangelische reformirten Kirche* (Elberseld: R. L. Feriedrich, 1861), 9ff.; Voigt, *Fundamentaldogmatik* (Gotha: F. A. Perthes, 1874), 644ff.; M. Kähler, "Bibel," *PRE³,* II, 686–91.

ciency, and perspicuity remain. Among these there is still the distinction that the "authority" of Scripture is not coordinate with the other attributes, for it is given with inspiration itself. On the one hand, the necessity, perspicuity, and sufficiency do not all flow from inspiration in the same sense. It is conceivable in fact that an infallible Bible had to be augmented and explained by an infallible tradition. Rome, while recognizing the authority of Scripture, denies its other attributes.

THE AUTHORITY OF SCRIPTURE

Rome and the Reformation

[119] The authority of Scripture has always been recognized in the Christian church. Jesus and the apostles believed in the OT as the Word of God and attributed divine authority to it. The Christian church was born and raised under [the influence of] the authority of Scripture. What the apostles wrote must be accepted as though Christ himself had written it, said Augustine.[13] And in Calvin's commentary on 2 Timothy 3:16, he states that we owe Scripture the same reverence we owe to God. Up until the eighteenth century, that authority of Scripture was firmly established in all the churches and among all Christians. On the other hand, between Rome and the Reformation there arose a serious difference about the ground on which this authority is based. The church fathers and the scholastics still frequently taught the self-attested trustworthiness (αὐτοπιστια) of Scripture, but the dynamic drive of the Roman Catholic principle increasingly gave precedence to the church over Scripture. The church, according to what is today the universally accepted Catholic doctrine, is temporally and logically prior to Scripture. It existed prior to Scripture and does not owe its origin, existence, and authority to Scripture but exists in and of itself, i.e., in virtue of Christ or the Holy Spirit who dwells within it. Scripture, on the other hand, proceeded from the church and is now recognized, confirmed, preserved, explained, defended, and so forth by the church. Scripture, accordingly, needs the church, but the reverse is not true. Without the church there is no Scripture, but without Scripture the church still exists. The church joined to an infallible tradition is the original and sufficient means of preserving and communicating revelation. Holy Scripture was added later, is insufficient of itself, but is useful and good as support and confirmation of the tradition. In fact, in the thinking of Rome, Scripture is totally dependent on the church. The authenticity, integrity, inspiration, canonicity, and authority of Scripture are all established as certain by the church.

In this connection, however, Rome does make the distinction that Scripture is totally dependent on the church, not with reference to itself, but with reference to *us*. The church, by its recognition, does not make Scripture in-

13. Augustine, *The Harmony of the Gospels*, I, 35.

spired, canonical, authentic, and so forth; yet it is the only agency that can infallibly know these attributes of Scripture. Certainly the self-testimony of Scripture does not decide that precisely these books of the Old and New Testament—no other and no fewer—are inspired. Scripture nowhere offers a list of the books that belong to it. The texts that teach the inspiration of Scripture never cover the whole Bible; 2 Timothy 3:16 applies only to the OT. Furthermore, an argument for the inspiration of Scripture that appeals to Scripture itself is unavoidably merely circular. Protestants, accordingly, are divided among themselves about the books that belong to the Bible. Luther's opinion on James differs from that of Calvin, and so forth. The proofs for Scripture derived from the church fathers (etc.) are not sufficiently strong and firm. As "motivations toward belief" (*motiva credibilitatis*) they have great value, yet they offer no more than probability: human and therefore fallible certainty. Only the church furnishes divine, infallible certainty. As Augustine said, "I indeed would not have believed the gospel had not the authority of the Catholic church moved me."[14] Similarly Protestants were able to accept and recognize Scripture as the word of God only because they received it from the hand of the church.[15] The Vatican Council recognized the books of the Old and New Testaments as canonical, "because, written under the inspiration of the Holy Spirit, they have God as their author; and because they have been entrusted as such to the church."[16] Guided by these thoughts, Rome, at the Council of Trent (session 4) and the Vatican council (session 3, chap. 2), established the canon. Following the example of the Septuagint and the practice of the church fathers, it included also the apocryphal books of the OT and in addition declared the Vulgate version to be the authentic text, so that it has final authority both in the church and in theology.

Over against this Roman Catholic doctrine, the Reformation posited the self-attested trustworthiness (αὐτοπιστια) of Scripture.[17] In this controversy the question was not whether the church had to fulfill a responsibility with respect to Scripture, for on both sides it was agreed that the church is of great significance for the Bible. The church's witness is most important and a motivation toward belief (*motivum credibilitatis*). In its testimonies the church of the early centuries possesses strong support for Scripture. For every person, the church is the guide that leads one to Scripture. In this sense, Augustine's saying is and remains true that he was moved by the church to believe the

14. Augustine, *On Two Souls, against the Manichaeans,* 5; idem, *Reply to Faustus the Manichaean,* I, 28; 2, 4, 6.

15. Bellarmine, "De Verbo Dei," *Controversiis,* IV, 4; Perrone, *Praelect. Theol.,* IX, 71ff.; J. B. Heinrich and C. Guiberlet, *Dogmatische Theologie,* 2d ed., 10 vols. (Mainz: Kirchheim, 1881–1900), I, 764; Jansen, *Prael. Theol.,* I, 766ff.

16. *Documents of Vatican Council I, 1869–70,* selected and trans. by John F. Broderick (Collegeville, Minn.: Liturgical Press, 1971), session 3, chap. 2.

17. J. Calvin, *Institutes,* I, vii; Ursinus, *Tract. Theol.* (1584), p. 8ff.; A. Polanus, *Syn. Theol.,* I, 23–30; J. Zanchi, "De Sacra Scriptura," *Op. Theol.,* VIII, 332–53; F. Junius, *Theses Theol.,* 3–5; *Synopsis Purioris Theologiae,* disp. 2 §29ff.; J. Gerhard, *Loci Theol.,* I. 3.

Scriptures. Protestant theologians[18] have weakened this saying of Augustine by applying it only to the past, to the origin of faith. But Augustine's reasoning in the previously cited text is clear when he confronts his Manichean opponent with a dilemma. Either, he says, you must say to me: believe the Catholics, but they emphatically warn me not[19] to believe you; *or* do not believe the Catholics, but in that case you cannot appeal to the gospel against me either, "because I have believed by the very gospel the Catholics preach."

For Augustine the church is indeed a motive for faith, a motive he here utilizes against the Manicheans. But there is a difference between a motive for believing and the final ground of faith. Elsewhere he himself clears up the way he sees a motive for believing in the church when he says: "Why not rather submit to the authority of the gospel, which is so well founded, so confirmed, so generally acknowledged and admired, and which has an unbroken series of testimonies from the apostles down to our own day."[20] The church with its dignity, power, hierarchy, and so forth always made a profound impression on Augustine. It continually moved him toward faith, supported and strengthened him in times of doubt and struggle; it was the church's firm hand that always again guided him to Scripture. But Augustine does not thereby mean to say that the authority of Scripture depends on the church, that the church is the final and most basic ground of his faith. Elsewhere he clearly states that Scripture has authority of itself and must be believed for its own sake.[21]

The Church's Authority

The church has and continues to have a many-sided and profound pedagogical significance for all believers till the day they die. The cloud of witnesses that surrounds us can strengthen and encourage us in our struggle. But this is something very different from saying that the authority of Scripture depends on the church. Even Rome does not yet dare to say this openly. The Vatican Council (1870), after all, recognized the books of the Old and the New Testament as canonical precisely "because, *written under the inspiration of the Holy Spirit, they have God as their author* and as such have been entrusted to the church." And Roman Catholic theologians distinguish between the authority of Scripture with respect to itself (*quoad se*) and with respect to us (*quoad nos*). But this distinction cannot be applied here. For if the church is the final and most basic reason why I believe Scripture, then the church, and not Scripture, is trustworthy in and of itself (αὐτόπιστος).

---

18. Calvin, *Institutes*, I, VII, 3; A. Polanus, *Syn. Theol.*, 30; F. Turretin, *Institutes of Elenctic Theology*, II, 6. Ed. note: Bavinck erroneously cites III, 13; J. Gerhard, *Loci Theol.*, I, 3 §51.

19. Ed. note: The Dutch text lacks the negative here, but it seems essential to the argument.

20. Augustine, *Reply to Faustus the Manichaean*, I, 32, 19; cf. *On the Profit of Believing*, 14.

21. Clausen, *Augustinus S. Sa. interpres* (1827), 125; A. J. Dorner, *Augustinus* (Berlin: W. Hertz, 1873), 237ff.; Reuter, *Augustinische Studien* (Gotha: F. A. Perthes, 1887), 348ff.; *Schmidt, *Jahrbücher für deutsche Theologie* 6 (1863): 235ff.; Hase, *Protestantische Polemik*, 5th ed. (Leipzig: Breitkopf und Hartel, 1891), 81; A. von Harnack, *History of Dogma*, V, 78–79; A. Kuyper, *Encyclopaedie her Heilige Godgeleerdheid* (Amsterdam: J. A. Wormser, 1894), II, 503.

We have to make a choice: either Scripture contains a witness, a teaching about itself, its inspiration and authority, and in that case the church simply accepts and confirms this witness; or Scripture itself does not teach such an inspiration and authority, and in that case the church's dogma about Scripture stands condemned for a Protestant. Roman Catholic theologians, accordingly, face a powerful contradiction. On the one hand, in the doctrine of Scripture they attempt to prove its inspiration and authority from Scripture itself. On the other, having come to the doctrine of the church, they attempt to weaken those proofs and to demonstrate that only the witness of the church offers conclusive certainty.

But if Scripture's authority with respect to itself depends on Scripture, then it is authoritative also for us and the final ground of our faith. The church can only recognize that which is; it cannot create something that is not. The charge that in this way one is guilty of circular reasoning and Scripture is proven by Scripture itself can be thrown back at Rome itself, for it proves the church by means of Scripture and Scripture by means of the church. If in response Rome should say that in the first case it uses Scripture not as the word of God but as a human witness, which is credible and trustworthy, the Protestant theologian can adopt this approach as well: inspiration is first derived from Scripture as reliable witness; with this witness Scripture is then proved to be God's word. Much more important, however, is that in every scientific discipline, hence also in theology, first principles are certain of themselves. The truth of a fundamental principle (*principium*) cannot be proved; it can only be recognized. "A first principle is believed on its own account, not on account of something else. Fundamental principles cannot have a first principle, neither ought they to be sought."[22]

Scripture itself clearly teaches, accordingly, that not the church but the word of God, written or unwritten, is trustworthy in and of itself (αὐτόπιστος). The church has at all times been bound to the word of God insofar as it existed and in the form in which it existed. Israel received the law on Mount Horeb; Jesus and the apostles submitted to OT Scripture. From the very beginning the Christian church was bound to the spoken and written word of the apostles. The word of God is the foundation of the church (Deut. 4:1; Isa. 8:20; Ezek. 20:19; Luke 16:29; John 5:39; Eph. 2:20; 2 Tim. 3:14; 2 Pet. 1:19; etc.). The church can indeed witness to the word, but the word is above the church. It cannot confer on anyone a heart-based belief in the word of God. That is something only the word of God can do by itself and the power of the Holy Spirit (Jer. 23:29; Mark 4:28; Luke 8:11; Rom. 1:16; Heb. 4:12; 1 Pet. 1:23). And for that reason alone the church appears to stand on a level below Scripture. Consequently, the church and believers in general can learn to know the inspiration, authority, and canonicity of Scripture from Scripture itself, but they can never announce and

22. J. Gerhard, *Loci. Theol.*, I, chap. 3; J. Zanchi, *Op. Theol.*, VIII, 339ff.; A. Polanus, *Syn Theol.*, I, 23ff.; F. Turretin, *Institutes of Elenctic Theology*, II, 6; Trelcatius, *Schol. et. method. loc. comm. S. Theol. Institutio* (1651), 26.

determine these attributes on their own authority. The Reformation preferred a measure of uncertainty to a certainty that can be obtained only by an arbitrary decision of the church. For, in fact, Scripture never offers a list of the books it contains. In the most ancient Christian church, and later as well, there was disagreement about some books. Nor does the text of Scripture have the integrity that also Lutheran and Reformed theologians yearned for. The Reformation, nevertheless, maintained the self-attested trustworthiness (αὐτοπιστια) of Scripture over against the claims of Rome, declared the church to be subordinate to the word of God, and so rescued the freedom of Christians.

Descriptive and Prescriptive Authority

[120] In addition to this dispute between Rome and the Reformation about the basis of the authority of Scripture, in the Protestant churches themselves there arose in the seventeenth century a further significant disagreement about the nature of that authority. They were agreed on the premise that Scripture, having God as its author, had divine authority. This authority was further defined by saying that Scripture had to be believed and obeyed by everyone and was the only rule of faith and conduct. This definition, however, automatically led to a distinction between historical (descriptive) and normative (prescriptive) authority. Divine revelation, after all, was given in the form of a history; it has passed through a succession of periods. Far from everything recorded in Scripture has normative authority for our faith and conduct. Much of what was commanded and instituted by God, or prescribed and enjoined by prophets and apostles, no longer applies to us directly and pertained to persons living in an earlier age. The command to Abraham to offer up his son, the command to Israel to kill all the Canaanites, the ceremonial and civil laws in force in the days of the OT, the decrees of the synod of Jerusalem, and many more things, while indeed useful for instruction and correction as history, cannot and may not any longer be obeyed by us. Furthermore, the record of revelation not only includes the good works of the saints but also the evil deeds of the ungodly. Frequently words and actions are recorded in Scripture, therefore, that, while they are represented as historically true, are not presented as normative. It is far from being the case that these words and actions can be regulatory for our faith and conduct, for in fact they must more often be rejected and censured. Also the sins of the saints, of Abraham, Moses, Job, Jeremiah, Peter, etc., are given as a warning, not as models for our conduct. Finally, with respect to many persons—the patriarchs, Deborah, the judges, the kings, the friends of Job, Hannah, Agur, the mother of Lemuel, the composers of some of the psalms, like the imprecatory psalms (Ps. 73:13, 14; 77:7–9; 116:11), and further with respect to Zechariah, Simeon, Mary, Stephen, and others—one may raise the question whether their words are only formally inspired, i.e., as it concerns their being recorded with accuracy, or also materially, as it concerns their content.

Voetius judged that many of these persons, like Job and his friends, cannot be counted as prophets, maintaining this sentiment against Maresius.[23] Granted, this issue had no further consequences but was still in many respects significant. For the first time it clearly brought out that there is a distinction between the word of God in a formal sense and the word of God in a material sense and compelled people to reflect on the relation between them. Now that relation was certainly conceived far too dualistically by the majority of the above-mentioned theologians. The authority of history and the history of a norm cannot be so abstractly separated in Scripture. The formal and the material meaning of the term "word of God" are much too tightly intertwined. Even in the deceptive words of Satan and the evil deeds of the ungodly, God still has something to say to us. Scripture is not only useful for teaching but also for warning and reproof. It teaches and corrects us, both by deterrence and by exhortation, both by shaming and by consoling us. But the above distinction does make clear that Scripture cannot and may not be understood as a fully articulated code of law. Appeal to a text apart from its context is not sufficient for a dogma. The revelation recorded in Scripture is a historical and organic whole. That is how it has to be read and interpreted. A dogma that comes to us with authority and intends to be a rule for our life and conduct must be rooted in and inferred from the entire organism of Scripture. The authority of Scripture is different from the authority of an act of parliament or congress.

Now the nature and basis of the authority of Scripture have been brought up for discussion especially in modern theology. In earlier times the authority of Scripture was based on its inspiration and was implied in it. But when inspiration was abandoned, the authority of Scripture could no longer be maintained. Although this was still attempted in various ways, theologians saw themselves compelled to construe both the grounds and the character of Scripture very differently. The authority of Scripture, to the degree it was still recognized, was based on the premise that it is the authentic record of revelation, expresses the Christian idea in its purest form—just as water is purest at its source. It was based on the conviction that it is the fulfillment of the OT idea of redemption and contains within it, be it germinally, the complete doctrine of the Christian faith and serves as the source of the beginning and ongoing renewal of the Christian spirit in the church. These and similar considerations for the support of the authority of Scripture can be found in theologians of widely diverging schools.[24]

---

23. G. Voetius, *Select. Disp.*, I, 31, 40–44; V, 634–40; Maresius, *Theologus paradoxus*, 83–87; Maccovius, *Loci. Com.*, 31–32; Cloppenberg, *De canone theol. desp.*, 3, op. II, 18–23; H. Witsius, *Misc. Sacia*, I, 316–18; B. De Moor, *Comm. In Marckii Comp.*, I, 131–34; Carpzovius, *Critica S. Vet. Test*, I, 2, §3.

24. J. H. Scholten, *Leer der Hervormde Kerk*, I, 78ff.; H. Bavinck, *De theologie van Daniel Chantepie de la Saussaye* (Leiden: Donner, 1884), 53ff.; F. Schleiermacher, *The Christian Faith*, ed. H. R. MacIntosh and J. S. Steward (Edinburgh: T. & T. Clark, 1928), §129ff.; R. Rothe, *Zur Dogmatik* (Gotha: F. A. Perthes, 1863), 166ff.; Lipsius, *Lehrbuch der evangelisch-protestantische Dogmatik* (Braunschweig: C. A. Schwetschke, 1983), §193ff.; A. E. Biedermann, *Christliche Dogmatik* (Zürich: Orrel, Füssli, 1869); A. Schweizer, *Christliche Glaubenslehre* (Leipzig: S. Hirzel, 1863–72), I, 178ff.; J. Chr. K. Hofmann, *Weissagung und Erfüllung* (Nördlingen, C. H. Beck, 1841); A. Ritschl, *Rechtfertigung und Versöhnung* (Bonn: A. Marcus, 1882–83), II, 5ff., 9ff.

Nonetheless, all these grounds are not strong enough to support the authority that religion requires. They may be considered useful as motivations toward belief, but as grounds they are untenable. For, in the first place, by the distinction between revelation and its documentation, between the word of God and Scripture, they in fact render the authority of Scripture completely illusory. For if Scripture does not have authority in its entirety but only "the word of God in Scripture," the "religious-ethical dimension," the "revelation," or whatever people want to call it, then people have to decide for themselves what that word of God in Scripture is and do this at their own discretion. The point of gravity is then shifted from the object to the subject. Scripture does not criticize human beings, but they judge Scripture. The authority of Scripture is then dependent on human discretion. It exists only to the degree that people want to acknowledge it and is therefore totally nullified.

Now, even if these grounds could warrant some degree of authority for Scripture, it would still be no other than a purely historical authority. And in religion this is not enough; here a historical, i.e., a human and fallible authority, is not sufficient. Because religion pertains to our salvation and is related to our eternal interests, we can be satisfied with nothing less than divine authority. We must not only know that Scripture is the historical record of our knowledge of Christianity and that it most accurately contains and reproduces the original Christian ideas, but in religion we must know that Scripture is the word and truth of God. Without this certainty there is [for us] no comfort either in life or death. And not only does every Christian need this assurance, but the church itself as institution cannot dispense with this certainty either. For if a minister is not convinced of the divine truth of the word he preaches, his preaching loses all authority, influence, and power. If he is not able to bring a message from God, who then gives him the right to act on behalf of people of like nature with himself? Who gives him the freedom to put himself on a pulpit [a few feet] above them, to speak to them about the highest interests of their soul and life and even to proclaim to them their eternal weal or woe? Who would dare, who would be able to do this, unless he has a word of God to proclaim? Both the Christian faith and Christian preaching require divine authority as their foundation. "Faith will totter if the authority of the divine Scriptures begins to waver."[25]

Moral Authority Only?

It is therefore an error to describe the nature of scriptural authority as "moral." Lessing already began this trend when he said that a thing is not true because it is in the Bible, but it is in the Bible because it is true. Since the time of his audible groaning to be rescued from the authority of the letter and the paper pope, believing on authority has in various ways been made to look absurd. Christian theologians, letting themselves be influenced by this, have

25. Augustine, *On Christian Doctrine*, I, 37.

modified or challenged belief in authority. Doedes, for example, wants nothing to do with believing on authority and confines himself to speaking about moral authority in religion. Saussaye states that there is no other than moral authority and the moral is all the authority there is. There is no intellectual authority; moral authority equals morality, religion itself. People do not believe the truth on authority, but truth has authority, i.e., the right to exact obedience.[26] This way of putting it, however, suffers from conceptual confusion. Certainly, truth has authority; no one denies it. But the question is: what is truth in the area of religion, and where can it be found? To that question there are only two possible answers. Either the apostles, i.e., the Scriptures, tell us what truth is, or, if you will, who Christ is; or this is determined by one's own judgment, by the intellect or by each person's conscience. In the latter case, there is no longer any (scriptural) authority; it is totally subject to the criticism of the subject. In that case, it no longer helps in any way to say with Rothe that the Bible is the perfectly adequate instrument for arriving at a pure knowledge of God's revelation.[27] For any objective criterion by which to judge and to find that revelation in Scripture is lacking.

There is in fact only one ground on which the authority of Scripture can be based, and that is its inspiration. When that goes, also the authority of Scripture is gone and done with. In that case, it is merely a body of human writings, which as such cannot rightfully assert any claim to be a norm for our faith and conduct. And along with Scripture—for the Protestant—all authority in religion collapses. All subsequent attempts to recover some kind of authority—say, in the person of Christ, in the church, in religious experience, in the intellect or conscience—end in disappointment.[28] They only prove that no religion can exist without authority. Religion is essentially different from science. It has a certainty of its own, not one that is based on insight but one that consists in faith and trust. And this religious faith and trust can rest only in God and in his word. In religion a human witness and human trust is insufficient; here we need a witness from God to which we can abandon ourselves in life and in death. "Our heart is restless until it rests in Thee, O Lord!" Accordingly, Harnack is right when he says: "There has never existed a strong religious faith in the world which did not at some decisive point base itself upon an external au-

26. Doedes, *Inleiding tot de Leer van God* (Utrecht: Kemink, 1880), 29–40; Saussaye in H. Bavinck, *Theologie van Chantepie de la Saussaye*, 53ff.

27. Rothe, *Zur Dogmatik*, 287.

28. Cf. Stanton, *The Place of Authority in Matters of Religious Belief* (London: Longmans, 1891); James Martineau, *The Seat of Authority in Religion* (London: Longmans, 1891); C. A. Briggs, *The Authority of Holy Scriptures* (inaugural address), 4th ed. (New York: Scribner, 1892); L. Monod, *Le problème de l'autorité* (Paris: Fischbacher, 1892); E. Doumerge, *L'autorité en matière de foi* (Lausanne: Payot, 1892); E. Ménégoz, *L'autorité de Dieu, réflexions sur l'authorité en matière* (Paris: Fischbacher, 1892). G. Godet, "Vinet et l'autorité en natière de foi," *Revue de théologie et de philosophie* 26, no. 2 (March 1893): 173–91; Sabatier, *Les religions de l'autorité et la religion de l'esprit* (Paris: Fischbacher, 1904); cf. further, Lobstein, *Einleitung* (Freiburg i.B.: J. C. B. Mohr, 1897), 94ff.; Riemens, *Het Symbol Fideisme* (Rotterdam: Van Sijn & Zoon, 1900), 81ff.

thority. Only in the abstract discussions of philosophers of religion or in the polemical projects of Protestant theologians was a faith construed which derived its certainty solely from its own inner components."[29] The validity and value of authority in religion is gradually being recognized again.

The Universality of Authority

[121] Though religion can be satisfied only with a divine authority, the nature of that authority still needs to be further examined. Generally speaking, authority is the power of a person who has something to say, the right to have a voice in some matter.[30] Now one can speak of authority only between nonequals: it always expresses a relation between a superior to his inferior. Because there is no equality among human beings but all sorts of distinctions, there can be authority-relations among them. And since that nonequality is so extensive and diverse, authority plays a very large role among people. It is even the foundation of the entire structure of human society. Those who undermine it are engaged in the destruction of society. It is therefore foolish and dangerous to make believing on [the basis of] authority look ridiculous. Augustine already raised the question: "For I ask, if what is not known must not be believed, in what way may children do service to their parents, and love with mutual affection those whom they believe not to be their parents? . . . Many things may be alleged to show that nothing at all of human society remains safe if we shall determine to believe nothing, which we cannot grasp by full apprehension."[31]

We live by authority in every area of life. In the family, in society, and in the state, we are born and nurtured under authority. Parents have authority over their children, teachers over their pupils, the government over its citizens. In each of these cases the authority relation is clear. It gives expression to a power that legally belongs to one person over another. It therefore openly acts by means of commands and laws, demands obedience and submission, and, in case of rebellion, even has the right to employ coercion and to inflict punishment.

But, extending the concept of authority further, we also apply it in science and art. Here, too, there is diversity of gifts, and a relation between "superiors" and "inferiors," between teachers and pupils, arises. There are people who, by their genius and unremitting labor, have achieved mastery in a given field and who can therefore speak with authority in this field. From the discoveries of these masters, those with less mastery, the laypeople, live and learn. Indeed, as a result of the tremendous expansion of knowledge, even the most eminent person can be a master only in a very small area; in all else

---

29. A. von Harnack, *History of Dogma*, V, 82; *cf. also P. D. Chantepie de la Saussaye, *Zekerheid en Twijfel* (1893), 138ff.

30. Ed. note: Bavinck here adds the etymological information that the Dutch word for authority—*gezag*—originally signified force *(geweld)* or power *(macht)*. He refers the reader to *Woordenboek der Nederlandsche Taal* (W.d.N.T.), s.v. "gezag."

31. Augustine, *On the Profit of Believing*, 12.

he or she is a learner and must depend on the research of others. This authority in science and art, however, bears a very different character from that of parents, teachers, and government; it is not juridical in nature but ethical. It cannot and may not use coercion; it does not have the power to punish. However prominent and important these people who act with authority are, their witness counts only to the extent that they can advance grounds for it. Hence their authority finally rests, not in the persons (so that the statement: "he himself said it" would suffice), but in the arguments on which their assertions are based. And since all people have a measure of understanding and judgment, blind faith is impermissible here, and the striving for independent insight, insofar as it is necessary and possible, a duty. Also in the field of history this is the case. In fact, knowledge of history is totally based on authority, on the testimonies of others. These testimonies, however, need not be blindly believed but may and must be rigorously examined so that the historian's own insight comes into its own as much as possible. In short, in the sciences human authority is as strong as its reasons are.

We find this notion of authority, finally, also in religion and theology. Here authority is needed, not less but much more than in the family, society, science, and art. Here it is a necessity of life. Without authority and faith, religion and theology cannot exist for a moment. But the authority in question here bears an utterly unique character. In the very nature of the case, it has to be a divine authority. And by this fact alone it is different from authority in society and state, science and art. From the latter it differs mainly in that in science and art personal insight *may* judge and decide. But in the case of divine authority, this is out of order. When God has spoken, all doubt has to stop. Divine authority, therefore, cannot be called "moral," at least not in the sense in which we speak when referring to the moral superiority of a person, for religion is not a relation of an inferior to his superior but of a creature to his Creator, of a subject to his Sovereign, of a child to his or her Father. God has the right, when issuing commands to human beings, to demand unconditional obedience. His authority is rooted in his being, not in "reasons." In that respect the authority of God and of his word is like that of the government in the state and of a father in the family. There is nothing humiliating, nor anything that in any way detracts from a person's freedom, in listening to the word of God like a child and in obeying it. Believing God at his word, i.e., on his authority, is in no way inconsistent with human dignity, anymore than that it dishonors a child to rely with unlimited trust on the word of her or his father. So far from gradually outgrowing this authority,[32] Christian believers rather progressively learn to believe God at his word and to renounce all their own wisdom. On earth believers never move beyond the viewpoint of faith and authority. To the degree that they increase in faith, they cling all the more firmly to the authority of God in his word.

32. A. Schweizer, *Christliche Glaubenslehre*, I, 186ff.

On the other hand, there is also a huge difference between the authority of God in religion and that of a father in his family and of a government in the state. A father, if need be, will force his child to conform and by punishing the child make that child submit to his authority; neither does the government bear the sword in vain. Coercion is inseparable from the authority of earthly governments. But God does not coerce people. His revelation is a revelation of grace. And in that revelation he does not come to people with commands and demands, with coercion and punishment, but with an invitation, with the admonition and plea to be reconciled to him. God could act toward people as a sovereign. Someday he will sentence as a judge all those who have disobeyed the gospel of his Son. But in Christ he comes down to us, becomes like us in all things, and deals with us as rational and moral beings in order then, as he encounters hostility and unbelief, to resume his sovereignty, to carry out his counsel, and to prepare glory for himself from every creature. The authority with which God acts in religion, accordingly, is completely in a class of its own. It is not human but divine. It is sovereign but still operates in a moral manner. It does not resort to coercion, yet manages to maintain itself. It is absolute, yet resistible. It invites and pleads yet is invincible.

So also it is with the authority of Scripture. As the word of God it stands on a level high above all human authority in state and society, science and art. Before it, all else must yield. For people must obey God rather than other people. All other [human] authority is restricted to its own circle and applies only to its own area. But the authority of Scripture extends to the whole person and over all humankind. It is above the intellect and the will, the heart and the conscience, and cannot be compared with any other authority. Its authority, being divine, is absolute. It is entitled to be believed and obeyed by everyone at all times. In majesty it far transcends all other powers. But, in order to gain recognition and dominion, it asks for no one's assistance. It does not need the strong arm of the government. It does not need the support of the church and does not conscript anyone's sword and inquisition. It does not desire to rule by coercion and violence but seeks free and willing recognition. For that reason it brings about its own recognition by the working of the Holy Spirit. Scripture guards its own authority. In earlier times, therefore, people occasionally also spoke of the "causative authority" (*auctoritas causativa*) by which Scripture "generates and confirms assent to the things to be believed in the human intellect."[33]

THE NECESSITY OF SCRIPTURE

Against Rome

[122] There is substantial agreement among Christian churches on the authority of Scripture. However, on the three following attributes, there is significant disagreement. Based on the relation it assumes between Scripture

---

33. H. Schmid, *Doctrinal Theology*, §8.

and the church, Rome can neither understand nor recognize the necessity of Holy Scripture. In Roman Catholicism the church, living from and by the Holy Spirit, is *trustworthy in and of itself* (αὐτόπιστος), self-sufficient. It possesses the truth, faithfully and purely, and preserves it by means of the infallible teaching office of the pope. Scripture, on the other hand, having proceeded from the church, may be useful and good as norm, but it is not the "first principle" of the truth. It is not necessary for the "being" of the church. The church does not really need Scripture, but Scripture—for its authority, augmentation, exposition, etc.—does need the church. The grounds for this position are derived from the fact that before the time of Moses and the early Christian church the church had no Scripture and that many believers, living under the old and still also under the new covenant, never possessed and read Scripture but lived solely from the tradition.[34]

Against Mysticism

However, not only does Rome oppose the necessity of Holy Scripture, but also many mystical movements have weakened and denied the significance of Scripture for the church and theology. Gnosticism did not just reject the OT but applied the allegorical method to the NT, attempting thereby to harmonize its system with Scripture. Here the perceptible forms and historical facts only have symbolic meaning. Biblical data are the outward shells that are necessary for people on a lower level but that can be omitted for the spiritually enlightened, the πνευματικοι. The Bible is not a source of truth but only the means by which the elite can elevate themselves to the higher level of *gnosis*.[35] In Montanism there appeared a new revelation, which augmented and improved that of the NT. Montanism, especially in its moderate form in Tertullian, on the one hand sought to be nothing new and fully to maintain the authority of Scripture; yet in Montanus it embraced a prophet in whom the Paraclete promised by Jesus, the final and highest revelation, had appeared. In that way Scripture simply had to yield to the new prophecy proclaimed by Montanus.[36]

The church indeed condemned these movements, and the church fathers fought this spiritualism. Augustine, in the prologue to his book on Christian doctrine, wrote against it. Still, Augustine also assumed that the devout, especially monks, are endowed with such a great measure of faith, hope, and love that they could dispense with Scripture for themselves and live in solitude without it.[37] Spiritualism repeatedly reemerged, reacting against the crushing

---

34. Bellarmine, "De Verbo Dei," *Controversiis,* IV, 4; Heinrich, *Dogmatik,* I, 708ff.; Liebermann, *Inst. Theol.* (1851), I, 449ff.; F. X. Dieringer, *Lehrbuch der Katholischen Dogmatik,* 4th ed. (Mainz: Kirchheim, 1858), 633; Gutberlet, *Lehrbuch der Apologetik,* 3 vols. (Munster: Theissing'schen, 1888–94), III, 21; Jansen, *Prael. Theol.,* I, 786.

35. Krüger, "Gnosis," *PRE³,* VI, 728–38; A. von Harnack, *History of Dogma,* I, 252–53.

36. Bonwetsch, "Montanismus," *PRE³,* XIII, 417–26; A. von Harnack, *History of Dogma,* II, 95.

37. Augustine, *On Christian Doctrine,* I, 39.

powers of church and tradition. Various sects, the Cathars, Amabric of Bena, Joachim of Floris, the Brothers and Sisters of the Free Spirit, and later the Libertines in Geneva believed that after the era of the Father and the Son that of the Holy Spirit had dawned, an era in which everyone lived by the Spirit and no longer needed the external means of Scripture and church.[38] Mysticism, which flourished during the Middle Ages in France and Germany, sought, by means of ascesis, meditation, and contemplation, to attain a communion with God that could dispense with Scripture. Indeed, Scripture was needed as a ladder to ascend to this high level but became superfluous when union with God, or the vision of God, had been reached.[39] Especially the Anabaptists exalted the internal at the expense of the external Word. As early as 1521, a contrast between Scripture and Spirit was forged, a dichotomy that became a permanent characteristic of Anabaptism.[40] Holy Scripture is not seen as the true word of God but only a witness and a record of it; the true word is that which is spoken in our hearts by the Holy Spirit. The Bible is merely a book containing letters; the Bible is a Babel [of tongues] full of confusion, which cannot generate faith in human hearts. Only the Spirit teaches us the true word. And when the Spirit teaches us, we can do without Scripture as well, since it is a temporary aid and not necessary to the spiritual person.[41] Hans Denck already equated that internal word with natural reason and pointed out numerous contradictions in Scripture. Ludwig Hetzer deemed Scripture totally unnecessary. Knipperdolling demanded at Münster that Holy Scripture be abolished and that people should live by nature and Spirit alone.[42]

Against Rationalism

Mysticism turned into rationalism. Later we see the same phenomenon in the Anabaptist and independentist sects of England at the time of Cromwell, among the Quakers, and in Pietism. The elevation of the internal over the external word always led to the identification of the teaching of the Spirit with the natural light of reason and conscience and thus to complete rejection of revelation and Scripture. No one opposed the necessity of Scripture more fiercely than Lessing in his *Axiomata* against Goeze. He too creates a split between letter and spirit, Bible

---

38. Zöckler, "Spiritismus," *PRE³*, XVIII, 654–66; Kurtz, *Lehrbuch der Kirchengeschichte* (Leipzig: Augus Neumanns Berlag [Fr. Lucas], 1906), §108, §116; Reuter, *Geschichte der religiöser Aufklärung im Mittelalter,* 2 vols. (Berliin: W. Hertz, 1875–77), II, 198ff.; Hahn, *Geschichte der Ketzer im Mittelalter,* 3 vols. (Stuttgart: J. F. Steinkopf, 1845–50), II, 420ff.; III, 72ff.; *Geiseler, *Kirchengeschichte* (1826), II, 2, 437ff.; Hagenbach, *Kirchengeschichte in Vortesungen,* 3d ed. (Leipzig: S. Hirzel, 1886), II, 480ff.

39. A. von Harnack, *History of Dogma,* VI, 97–117; Herzog, "Quietismus," *PRE¹*, XII, 427ff.

40. Sepp, *Kerkhistorische Studiën* (Leiden: E. J. Brill, 1885), 12.

41. A. Hegler, *Geist und Schrift bei Sebastian Franck* (Freiburg i.B.: J. C. B. Mohr, 1892); J. H. Maronier, *Het Inwendige Woord* (Amsterdam: T. J. van Holkema, 1890); Vigouroux, *Les Livres saints et la critique rationaliste,* 2d ed., 4 vols. (Paris: A. Roger & F. Chernoviz, 1886, 1890), I, 435–53; C. Hodge, *Systematic Theology,* 3 vols. (New York: Scribners, 1906), I, 61–104; R. H. Grützmacher, *Wort und Geist* (Leipzig: A. Deichert, 1902); also cf. the articles in *PRE³* on Denck, Frank, Münzer, David Joris, Münster.

42. D. Thelemann, "Münster (Widertaufer)," *PRE²*, X, 362.

and religion, theology and religion, the Christian religion and the religion of Jesus, and asserts that the latter did and can exist independently of the former. Religion, after all, existed before there was a Bible. Christianity existed before the evangelists and apostles wrote a word. Thus, the religion they taught can continue to exist even if all their writings were lost. Religion is not true because the evangelists and apostles taught it, but they taught it because it is true. Their writings, accordingly, may and must be interpreted in accordance with the internal truth of religion. An attack on the Bible is not yet an attack on religion. Luther has delivered us from the yoke of tradition; who will now deliver us from the much more intolerable yoke of the letter?

These ideas on the non-necessity of Scripture were, in principle, taken over by Schleiermacher. In his *Christian Faith* he writes that faith in Christ is not based on the authority of Scripture but precedes belief in Scripture and causes us to give special status to Scripture. Among the early Christians, faith in Christ did not arise from Holy Scripture, he says, nor can it arise from it in our case. In both cases faith must have the same ground. Scripture, accordingly, though it is not the source of religion, is its norm. It is the first of a series of Christian writings. It is closest to the source, i.e., the revelation in Christ, and so ran but little risk of absorbing impure constituents. But all these writings of the evangelists and apostles, like all subsequent Christian writings, proceeded from the same Spirit, the "common Spirit" of the Christian church. The church is not built on Scripture; instead, Scripture proceeded from the church.[43] Through Schleiermacher these ideas have become the common property of modern theology. They seem to be so obviously true that no doubt or criticism even arises with respect to them. In virtually all theologians today, one can now find the idea that the church existed before Scripture and can therefore also exist independently of Scripture. The church rests in itself, lives from itself, i.e., from the Spirit, who dwells in it. Holy Scripture, which proceeded from the church at its beginning in the freshness and vitality of its youth, though its norm, is not its source. The source is the personal living Christ who indwells the church. Dogmatics is the description of the life, the explication of religious consciousness, of the church. In that process, as its guideline, dogmatics has Scripture, which interpreted the life of the church first and most clearly. Hence the church is actually the author of the Bible, and the Bible is the reflection of the church.[44]

In Orthodox Protestantism, all these ideas, those of Rome, Anabaptism, mysticism, rationalism, Lessing, Schleiermacher, etc., are mutually and inti-

---

43. F. Schleiermacher, *Christian Faith*, §128, §129.

44. J. P. Lange, *Philosophische Dogmatik* (Heidelberg: K. Winter, 1849), §77; Rothe, *Zur Dogmatik*, 333ff.; Frank, *System der Christlichen Gewissheit*, 2d ed., 2 vols. (Erlangen: Deichert, 1884), II, 57ff.; F. A. Philippi, *Kirchliche Glaubenslehre*, 6 vols. (Gütersloh: Bertelsmann, 1902), I, 190ff.; Hofstede de Groot, *De Groninger Godgeleerden* (Groningen: A. L. Scholtens, 1855), 71ff., 97ff.; H. Bavinck, *De Theologie van Daniel Chantepie de la Saussaye* (Groningen: A. L. Scholtens, 1855), 49ff.; J. H. Gunning and de la Saussaye Jr., *Het Ethisch Beginsel der Theologie* (Groningen, 1877), 34ff.

mately connected. Especially Schleiermacher, by his reversal of the Scripture-church relation, has offered strong support to Rome. All of these groups and persons agree that Scripture is not necessary but at most useful and that the church can also exist from and by itself. The difference is only that, whereas Rome finds the ground and possibility for the continued existence of the Christian religion in the institutional church, i.e., the infallible pope, Schleiermacher and his kind find it in the church as organism, i.e., in the religious community, while mysticism and rationalism find it in religious individuals. All of them explain the continued existence of the church in terms of the leading of the Holy Spirit, the indwelling of Christ, but this has its organ, the pope in the case of Rome, the organism of the church in the case of Schleiermacher, and for Anabaptism, in every believer individually.

It is not hard to see that in this lineup Rome occupies the strongest position. For certainly, there *is* a leading of the Holy Spirit in the church, Christ *did* rise from the dead, *does* live in heaven, and dwells and works in his church on earth. There *is* a mystical union between Christ and his body. The Word alone *is* insufficient: the external principle also requires an internal principle. Protestantism knew all this very well and confessed it heartily. But the question was whether or not the church was bound to the Word, to Scripture, for the *conscious* life of religion. Religion, surely, is not only a matter of the heart, the emotions, the will, but also of the head. God must also be served and loved with the mind. For the *conscious* life, accordingly, the church must have a source from which it draws the truth.

Now Rome, with its infallible pope, can assert that Scripture is not necessary; the infallibility of the church indeed renders Scripture superfluous. But Protestantism has no such infallible organ, neither in the institution, nor in the organism, nor in the individual members of the church. If Protestantism should deny the necessity of Scripture, it would weaken itself, strengthen Rome, and lose the truth, which is an indispensable element of religion. For that reason the Reformation insisted so firmly on the necessity of Holy Scripture. Scripture was the place for the Reformation to stand (δος μοι που στω). It succeeded because, against the authority of church councils and the pope, it could pose the authority of God's Holy Word. One who abandons this position of the Reformation unintentionally works for the upbuilding of Rome. For if not Scripture but the church is necessary to the knowledge of religious truth, then the church becomes the indispensable means of grace. The Word loses its central place and only retains a preparatory or pedagogical role. While Scripture may be useful and good, it is not necessary, neither for the church as a whole, nor for believers individually.

SCRIPTURE AND THE CHURCH

[123] Thus, although against Rome the Reformation found its strength in Scripture and maintained its necessity, yet it did not thereby deny that before

Moses the church had long existed without Scripture. It is also true that the church of the NT was founded by the preaching of the apostles and existed for a long time without a NT canon. Furthermore, the church today is still always fed and planted in the non-Christian world by the proclamation of the gospel. The books of the Old and New Testament, further, only originated gradually; before the invention of the art of printing, they were distributed in small numbers. Many believers in earlier and later years died without ever having read and examined Scripture, and even now the religious life seeks to satisfy its needs not just in Scripture but at least as much in a wide assortment of devotional literature. All this can be frankly acknowledged without thereby in any way detracting from the necessity of Scripture. And if it had so pleased God, he could most certainly have kept the church in the truth in some way other than the written word. The necessity of Scripture is not absolute but "based on the premise of the good pleasure of God."

Thus understood, this necessity is beyond all doubt. The word of God has been the seed of the church from the beginning. Certainly before Moses the church existed without Scripture. Yet there was an unwritten (ἄγραφον) word before it was recorded (ἔγγραφον). The church never lived from itself or rested upon itself but always lived by and in the word of God. (Rome, to be sure, does not teach that it lived from itself, but assumes a tradition that infallibly preserves the word of God.) Yet this needs to be asserted over against those who reduce revelation to "life," the infusion of divine powers, the arousal of religious emotions. The church, therefore, may be older than the written word, but it is definitely younger than the spoken word.[45] The common assertion that for a long time the NT church existed without Scripture must be carefully understood as well. It is true that the canon of NT books was not generally recognized until the second half of the second century. But from the beginning the Christian churches had the Old Testament. They were founded by the spoken word of the apostles. At a very early stage many churches came into possession of apostolic writings, which were also shared with other churches, were read publicly in the churches, and were widely distributed. Naturally, as long as the apostles were alive and visited the churches, no distinction was made between their spoken and their written word. Tradition and Scripture were still united. But when the first period was past and the time-distance from the apostles grew greater, their writings became more important, and the necessity of these writings gradually intensified. The necessity of Holy Scripture, in fact, is not a stable but an ever-increasing attribute. Scripture in its totality was not always necessary for the whole church. Scripture came into being and was completed step-by-step. To the extent that revelation progressed, Scripture increased in scope. Whatever part of Scripture existed in a given period was sufficient for that period.

45. J. Zanchi, *Op. Theol.*, VIII, 343ff.; A. Polanus, *Syn. Theol.*, I, 15; *Synopsis Purions Theologiae*, disp. 2; J. Gerhard, *Loci Theol.*, I, 1, §5ff.

Similarly, the revelation that had occurred up until a given time was sufficient for that time. Scripture, like revelation, is an organic whole that has
gradually come into being; the mature plant was already enclosed in the
seed, the fruit was present in the germ. Revelation and Scripture both kept
pace with the state of the church, and vice versa. For that reason one can
never draw conclusions for the present based on conditions prevailing in the
church in the past. Granted, the church before Moses was without Scripture,
and before the completion of revelation the church was never in possession
of the whole Bible. But this does not prove anything for the dispensation of
the church in which we now live, one in which revelation has ceased and
Scripture is complete. For this dispensation Scripture is not only useful and
good but also decidedly necessary for the being (*esse*) of the church.

Scripture is the only adequate means of guarding against the corruption
of the spoken word and of making it the possession of all human beings.
The sound of a voice passes away, but the written letter remains. The brevity
of life, the unreliability of memory, the craftiness of the human heart, and a
host of other dangers that threaten the purity of transmission all make the
inscripturation of the spoken word absolutely necessary if it is to be preserved and propagated. In the case of the revealed word, this applies even to
a higher degree. For the gospel is not flattering to human beings; it is directly opposed to their thoughts and wishes, and, as divine truth, gives the
lie to their falsehood. Revelation, furthermore, is not intended for one generation and one time only but for all peoples and ages. It must complete its
course throughout all humankind and to the end of the ages. There is one
truth, and Christianity is the universal religion. How else will this intention
of the revealed word be reached except by its being recorded and written?
The church cannot perform this ministry of the word. It is nowhere promised infallibility. Always in Scripture the church is referred to the objective
word, "to the teaching and to the testimony" [cf. Isa. 8:20]. Actually even
Rome does not deny this. The church, i.e., the gathering of believers, is not
infallible in the understanding of Rome, neither is the gathering of bishops,
but only the pope. The declaration of papal infallibility is proof of the Reformation's thesis of the unreliability of tradition, the fallibility of the church,
and even of the necessity of Scripture. For this declaration of infallibility implies that the truth of the revealed word is not or can not be preserved by the
church as the gathering of believers, inasmuch as the church is still liable to
error. The truth of the revealed word can be explained only in the light of
the special assistance of the Holy Spirit of which, says Rome, the pope is the
beneficiary. Rome and the Reformation agree, accordingly, that the revealed
word can be preserved in its purity only by the institution of the apostolate,
i.e., by inspiration. And the controversy between them pertains only to
whether that apostolate has ceased or is continued in the person of the pope.

On the other hand, the assertion of mediating theology (*Vermittelungsthe-*
ologie) that Scripture proceeded from the church and that the church is

therefore the actual author of Scripture is completely untenable. One can make this assertion only if one denies the true office of prophets and apostles, equates inspiration with regeneration, and completely divorces Scripture from revelation. According to the teaching of Scripture, however, inspiration is a unique activity of the Holy Spirit, a special gift to prophets and apostles, enabling them to transmit the word of God in pure and unalloyed form to the church of all ages. Scripture, therefore, did not proceed from the church but was given to the church by a special operation of the Holy Spirit in the prophets and apostles. Scripture is part of the revelation that God has given to his people. On this point Rome and the Reformation are agreed. But, against Rome, the Reformation maintains that this special activity of the Holy Spirit has now stopped; in other words, that the apostolate no longer exists and is not continued in the person of the pope. The apostles completely and accurately recorded their witness concerning Christ in the Holy Scriptures. By these Scriptures they have made the revelation of God the possession of humankind.

Scripture is the word of God that has completely entered into the world. It makes that word universal and everlasting, and rescues it from error and lies, from oblivion and transience. To the degree that humankind becomes larger, life becomes shorter, the memory weaker, science more extensive, error more serious, and deception more brazen, the necessity of Holy Scripture increases. Print and the press are gaining in significance in every area of life. The invention of printing was a giant step to heaven and to hell. Scripture also shares in this development. Its necessity becomes ever more clearly evident. It is being distributed and made universally available as never before. As it is translated into hundreds of languages, it comes within the purview of everyone. Increasingly it proves to be the ideal means by which the truth can be brought to the attention of all people. It is true that religious literature remains for many people the primary nourishment for their spiritual life. Still, this proves nothing against the necessity of Holy Scripture. Since directly or indirectly, all Christian truth is drawn from it. The diverted stream also gets its water from the source. It is untenable to say that today we continue to receive Christian truth apart from Holy Scripture. In the first century something like that was possible, but the streams of tradition and Scripture have long since converged, and the former has long been incorporated into the latter. Rome can maintain its position only by its doctrine of the continuation of the apostolate and the infallibility of the pope. But this is impossible for a Protestant. The Christian character of truth can be asserted solely because it is rooted with all its fibers in Holy Scripture. There is no knowledge of Christ apart from Scripture, no fellowship with him except by fellowship in the word of the apostles.[46]

46. Z. Ursinus, *Tract. Theol.*, 1ff.; J. Zanchius, *Op. Theol.*, VIII, 343ff.; A. Polanus, *Syn. Theol.*, I, 15; *Synopsis Purioris Theologiae*, disp. 2; G. Turretin, *Institutes of Elenctic Theology*, loc. 2, qu. 1–3; H. Heppe, *Dogmatik der evangelischen reformierten Kirche* (Elberseld: R. L. Friedrich, 1861), 25, 26.

BEYOND SCRIPTURE?

[124] Even when the necessity of Scripture is recognized, there can still be disagreement about the duration of that necessity. Even those who believe that Scripture has had its day often readily agree that in its time it was immensely important for the education of individuals and peoples. But in various ways the duration of that necessity has been curtailed. Gnosticism recognized its necessity for the "unspiritual" (ψυχικοι) but denied it for the "spiritual" (πνευματικοι). Mysticism indeed deemed Scripture necessary on the level of thought and meditation, but no longer on the level of the contemplation and vision of God. The rationalism of Lessing and Kant reserved a pedagogical role for revelation, Scripture, and statutory religion in order thus to prepare for the rule of the religion of reason. Hegel similarly judged that in religion the form of visual representation was necessary for the common people but that the philosopher with his conceptual apparatus no longer needed this. And one often hears it said that, while religion is good for the controlling masses, educated and civilized folk are far beyond it.

Now in this depiction of things there is an undeniable and wonderful truth. Revelation, Scripture, the church, the whole Christian religion, indeed bears a provisional, preparatory and pedagogical character. Just as the OT economy of the covenant of grace was left behind, so also this dispensation of the covenant of grace in which we live will one day belong to the past. When Christ has gathered his church and presented it to his Father as a chaste bride, he will deliver the kingdom to God. Moreover, the duality of grace and nature, revelation and reason, authority and freedom, theology and philosophy, cannot last forever. Certainly the supreme goal in religion is that we shall serve God without coercion and fear, motivated only by love, in accordance with our natural inclination. In revelation it is God's own purpose to mold people in whom his image is again fully restored. He gave us not only his Son but also the Holy Spirit in order that the Spirit should regenerate us, write his law in our heart, and equip us for every good work. Regeneration, adoption, sanctification, glorification—are all proofs that God educates his children for freedom, for a ministry of love we will never regret. To that extent the above notions [of mysticism and rationalism] can be considered an anticipation of an ideal that will be realized in the future.

Nevertheless, they indicate a very dangerous line of thought. They all proceed from a confusion between the present dispensation and that of the hereafter. While the New Jerusalem will no longer need a sun or moon, these two heavenly bodies nevertheless remain necessary here on earth. The fact that we will one day walk by sight does not cancel out the necessity of walking by faith in this dispensation. Although the church militant and the church triumphant are fundamentally one, there is nevertheless a difference between them in position and life in the present. The boundary line cannot and may not be erased. We will never achieve a heavenly life while we are here on earth. We walk by faith, not by sight. Now we see in a mirror dimly; in the hereafter, and not before, we will see face to face and will know as we are known. The vision of God has been reserved for heaven. On earth we will never be self-reliant and independent. We remain bound to the cosmos that surrounds us. Authority and its implications can never be surmounted here on earth.

The doctrine of a temporary necessity of Scripture, moreover, creates a huge gap between the "unspiritual" and the "spiritual," between the civilized and the masses, between philosophers and the common people. Yet such a gap is by no means warranted. If religion consisted in knowledge, the erudite would have an advantage over the uneducated. But religiously all people are equal; they have the same needs. In Christ there is no distinction between the Greek and the barbarian. Religion is the same for all people, however much they may differ in class, rank, education, and so forth, for to religion, i.e., before the face of God, all these distinctions of rank and privilege by which people stand out above others are worthless. The division between these two kinds of people, accordingly, is evidence of spiritual pride, which is radically opposed to the essence of the Christian religion, to the humility and lowliness that it requires. In the kingdom of heaven, publicans have precedence over Pharisees and the least over the greatest.

Furthermore, some ground for this division could still be claimed if rationalism were right and revelation consisted in nothing but "the truths of reason." Then these truths, though known provisionally from revelation, could later by reflection be derived from reason itself. But revelation has a totally different content from that of a rational theory. It is history; its content is grace, its center the person of Christ, its purpose the re-creation of humankind. None of this can be discovered by reflection or derived from reason. For human beings to know such a revelation, Scripture remains a necessity at all times. Even a divine revelation to every person individually could not provide what the revelation in Christ now offers through Scripture to all people. The historical character of revelation, the fact and idea of the incarnation, and the organic view of the human race all demand Scripture in which the revelation of God has been laid down for all humankind. Just as one sun illumines the whole earth by its rays, so Christ is the "daybreak" from on high, which appears to those who sit in darkness and the shadow of death [cf. Luke 1:78–79]. So also one Scripture is the light upon everyone's path and the lamp for everyone's feet. It is the word of God to all humankind. History itself bears strong witness to this necessity of Scripture. The most highly spiritual mysticism has over and over turned into the most vulgar rationalism; and "enthusiastic" spiritualism has often ended in the crudest materialism.

Negatively, the necessity of Holy Scripture is as strongly demonstrated from within the schools that oppose it as positively from within the churches that affirm it.

THE CLARITY OF SCRIPTURE

[125] Another important attribute that the Reformation ascribed to Scripture in opposition to Rome was perspicuity, or clarity. According to Rome, Scripture is unclear (Ps. 119:34, 68; Luke 24:27; Acts 8:30; 2 Pet. 3:16). Also, in the things that pertain to faith and life, it is not so clear that it can dispense with interpretation. It deals, after all, with the deepest mysteries, with God, the Trinity, the incarnation, predestination, and other truths. Even in its moral precepts (e.g., Matt. 5:34, 40; 10:27; Luke 12:33; 14:33), it is often so obscure that misunderstandings and misconceptions have always abounded in the Christian church. Essential to a correct understanding of Scripture, after all, is a many-sided knowledge of history, geography, chronology, archeology, languages, etc., knowledge that is simply not attainable by laypeople. Protestants themselves, accordingly, write numerous commentaries, and in the case of even the most important texts they differ in the exegesis. Holy Scripture necessarily has to be interpreted. Such interpretation cannot be provided by Scripture itself; Scripture cannot be its own interpreter.

Plato already wrote that the letter is abused and cannot protect itself and therefore needs the help of its father.[47] It is mute and cannot settle disagreements. It is like a law in terms of which the judge issues his verdicts, but it is not simultaneously law *and* judge. The learned Jesuit, Jacob Gretser, a participant in the conference on religion held in Regensburg (1601), made a deep impression when he exclaimed: "We are in the presence of Holy Scripture and the Holy Spirit. Let him pronounce sentence. And if he should say: you, Gretser, are mistaken, your case has collapsed; you, Jacob Heilbrunner, have won; then I will immediately cross over to your seat. Let him come; again, let him come, let him come and condemn me!" Hence there has to be an interpreter and a judge who gives a decision according to Scripture.

In the absence of such a judge [i.e., The Roman Catholic Church], every interpretation becomes completely subjective; everyone judges at his pleasure and considers his own individual opinion infallible. Every heretic (Dutch: *ketter*) has his own favorite text (*letter*).[48] Everyone, as Werenfels's well-known couplet has it, finds precisely his own dogmas in Scripture. [Apart from the Roman Church, so it is claimed] Scripture is at the mercy of all sorts of arbitrariness: individualism, "enthusiasm," rationalism. In the end endless division prevails. Worst of all, in the absence of an infallible interpretation, there is no absolute certainty of faith either. The foundation on which a Christian's hope then rests is pious opinion, scientific insight, but not a divine and infallible witness. It is so far from being the case that a person can shape his own conviction or teaching on the basis of Scripture that even Protestants, actually no less than Roman Catholics, live by tradition

47. Plato, *Phaedrus*, 274–75.
48. Ed. note: The complete Dutch saying is: "Ieder ketter heeft zijn letter."

and trust in the authority of the church, of synods, fathers, authors, and so forth, to guide them.

But [so Roman Catholics claim], such an infallible divine interpretation of Scripture, however, has been granted by God in his church. Not the dead, uncomprehended, obscure, and bare Bible, but the church, the vital, always present church, which ever renews itself by the power of the Spirit, is the mediatrix of truth and the infallible interpreter of Holy Scripture. Everyone, after all, is the best interpreter of his or her own words. The true interpreter of Scripture, therefore, is the Holy Spirit, its author. And the Spirit possesses his own infallible organ of interpretation, the church; better still, the pope. By tradition, the church is in possession of the truth. It is led by the same Spirit who originated Scripture. The church is akin to Scripture; she alone can understand its meaning. She is the "pillar and bulwark of the truth" (1 Tim. 3:15).

In practice [so it is said] this is how it has always been. Moses, the priests of the OT, Christ, and the apostles explained and decided things on behalf of the church (Exod. 18; Deut. 17:9f.; 2 Chron. 19:9f.; Eccles. 12:12; Hag. 2:2; Mal. 2:7; Matt. 16:19; 18:17; 23:2; Luke 22:32; John 21:15f.; Acts 15:28; Gal. 2:2; 1 Cor. 12:8f.; 2 Pet. 1:19; 1 John 4:1). Popes as well as councils have simply followed their example. For that reason the Council of Trent decided (session 4) that no one may interpret Holy Scripture "contrary to the sense which Holy Mother Church held or holds, since it is her task to judge the true sense and interpretation of Holy Scripture. Similarly, it is not permitted [to interpret Scripture] contrary to the unanimous opinion of the Fathers." Trent thereby restricted exegesis not only negatively—as some Roman Catholics attempted to view the decision—but very definitely also positively. No one may give any exegesis other than that which the church has given through its "fathers," it councils, or its popes.

The "declaration of faith"[49] of Pius IV and the Vatican Council[50] leave no doubt on that score. Not only does this doctrine of the obscurity of Scripture subject scientific exegesis to the authority of the pope; even more dependent and restricted is the layperson. On account of its obscurity, Scripture is not fit reading for laypersons. Without interpretation it is unintelligible to the common people. For that reason Rome increasingly restricted the translation of Scripture into the vernacular and Bible reading by the common people because of the misuse that was made of this privilege in the Middle Ages and later. The reading of Scripture is not allowed to laypeople except by permission of the church authorities. Protestant Bible Societies have been repeatedly condemned by the popes and, in the encyclical dated December 8, 1864, were placed on a par with socialistic and communistic

49. H. Denzinger, *Sources of Catholic Dogma*, n. 1566.

50. *Vatican Council I*, session 3, chap. 2. Ed. note: see Denzinger, *Enchiridion*, 33d ed., #3007; also found in Karl Rahner and H. Roos, *The Teaching of the Catholic Church* (Staten Island, N.Y.: Alba House, [1966]), 62.

societies.[51] And though Pope Leo XIII in his encyclical *Providentissimus Deus* on the study of Holy Scripture (November 18, 1893) recommended the study of Scripture, this did not apply to laypersons.[52]

The doctrine of the perspicuity of Holy Scripture has frequently been misunderstood and misrepresented, both by Protestants and Catholics. It does not mean that the matters and subjects with which Scripture deals are not mysteries that far exceed the reach of the human intellect. Nor does it assert that Scripture is clear in all its parts, so that no scientific exegesis is needed, or that, also in its doctrine of salvation, Scripture is plain and clear to every person without distinction. It means only that the truth, the knowledge of which is necessary to everyone for salvation, though not spelled out with equal clarity on every page of Scripture, is nevertheless presented throughout all of Scripture in such a simple and intelligible form that a person concerned about the salvation of his or her soul can easily, by personal reading and study, learn to know that truth from Scripture without the assistance and guidance of the church and the priest. The way of salvation, not as it concerns the matter itself but as it concerns the mode of transmission, has been clearly set down there for the reader desirous of salvation. While that reader may not understand the "how" (πως) of it, the "that" (ὁτι) is clear.[53]

Thus understood, perspicuity is an attribute Holy Scripture repeatedly predicates of itself. The torah has been given by God to all of Israel, and Moses conveys all the words of the Lord to all the people. The law and the word of the Lord is not far from any of them but a light on their path and a lamp for their feet (Deut. 30:11; Ps. 19:8, 9; 119:105, 130; Prov. 6:23). The prophets, whether by speech or in writing, address themselves to all the people (Isa. 1:10f.; 5:3f.; 9:1; 40:1f.; Jer. 2:4; 4:1; 10:1; Ezek. 3:1). Jesus speaks freely and frankly to all the crowds (Matt. 5:1; 13:1, 2; 26:55; etc.), and the apostles wrote to all those called to be saints (Rom. 1:7; 1 Cor. 1:2; 2 Cor. 1:1; etc.) and they themselves took responsibility for the circulation of their letters (Col. 4:16). The written word is recommended to the scrutiny of all (John 5:39; Acts 17:11) and is written for the express purpose of communicating faith, endurance, hope, consolation, teaching, etc. (John 20:31; Rom. 15:4; 2 Tim. 3:16; 1 John 1:1f.). There is nowhere any indication of with-

51. Denzinger, *Sources of Catholic Dogma*, n. 1566.

52. Vincent of Lerins, *Commonitorium*, chap. 3; Bellarmine, "De Verbo Dei," *Controversiis*, bk. III; M. Canus, *Loci Theol.*, II, 6ff.; Perrone, *Praelect. Theol.*, IX, 98ff.; Heinrich, *Dogmatik*, 2d ed., 764ff.; Möhler, *Symbolik*, §38ff.; Jansen, *Prael. Theol.*, I, 771ff.; Rietschl, "Bibellesen," *PRE³*, II, 700–713; C. Pesch, *Die Inspiratione Sacra Scriptura*, 573ff.

53. U. Zwingli, *De Claritate et certitudine Verbi Dei Opera*, ed. Schuler and Schulthess (Turici: Officina Schulthessiana, 1842), I, 65ff.; Luther, in J. Köstlin, *Theology of Luther*, trans. Charles E. Hay, 2 vols. (Philadelphia: Lutheran Publication Society, 1897), I, 281; J. Zanchi, "De Scriptura Sacra," *Op. Theol.*, VIII, 407ff.; Charmier, *Panstratia Catholica* (1626), loc. I, bk. I, chap. 13–32; W. Ames, *Bellarminus enervatus* (Amsterdam, 1630), bk. 1, chaps. 4 and 5; F. Turretin, *Institutes of Elenctic Theology*, loc. 2, qu. 17; Trigland, *Antapologia*, chap. 3; *Synopsis Purious Theologiae*, disp. 5; J. Gerhard, *Loci. Theol.*, loc. 1, chap. 20ff.; Glassius, *Philogra Sacra* (1691), 186ff.

holding Scripture from laypersons. The believers are themselves of age and able to judge (1 Cor. 2:15; 10:15; 1 John 2:20; 1 Pet. 2:9). To them are entrusted the oracles of God (Rom. 3:2).

The church fathers, accordingly, know nothing of the obscurity of Scripture in the later Roman Catholic sense. They do indeed speak often about the depths and mysteries of Holy Scripture,[54] but with equal frequency they praise its clarity and simplicity. Thus Chrysostom, comparing the writings of the prophets and apostles with those of the philosophers, writes: "The prophets and the apostles did the complete opposite; for they established for all the things that are sure and clear, inasmuch as they are the common teachers of the whole world so that each person by himself or herself might be able to understand what was said from the reading alone." And elsewhere he says: "All things are clear and open that are in the divine Scriptures; the necessary things are all plain."[55] Similarly in Augustine we read: "Hardly anything may be found in these obscure places which is not found plainly said elsewhere"; and "Among those things which are said openly in Scripture are to be found all those teachings which involve faith and the mores of living."[56]

Familiar also is the saying of Gregory I, in which he compares Scripture "to a smooth and deep river in which a lamb could walk and an elephant could swim." Even today Roman Catholic theologians still have to admit that much material in Scripture is so plain that not only can the believer understand it, but even the unbeliever, who rejects the plain sense of it, is inexcusable.[57] The church fathers, accordingly, did not dream of forbidding the reading of Scripture to laypeople. On the contrary, over and over they insist on the study of Scripture and tell of the blessing they themselves received from reading it.[58] Gregory I still recommended the reading of Scripture to all laypersons. The restriction of Bible reading did not come up until the twelfth century, when a number of sects began to appeal to Scripture against the church. At that point the idea that the practice of Bible reading by laypersons was the prime source of heresy began to prevail. In self-defense Rome then increasingly taught the obscurity of Scripture and tied the reading of it to consent from the church authorities.

[126] Over against Rome, the churches of the Reformation indeed have no more powerful weapon than Scripture. It delivers the deadliest blows to the ecclesiastical tradition and hierarchy. The teaching of the perspicuity of Scripture is one of the strongest bulwarks of the Reformation. It also most certainly brings with it its own serious perils. Protestantism has been hopelessly divided by it, and individualism has developed at the expense of the

---

54. Cf. places in Bellarmine, "De Verbo Dei," *Controversiis,* III, I; C. Pesch, *De Inspiratione Sancta Scriptura,* 577.

55. J. Chrysostom, "Homily on Lazarus," homily 3 in 2 Thess.

56. Augustine, *On Christian Doctrine,* II, 6 and 9.

57. Heinrich, *Dogmatik²,* 788.

58. Vigouroux, *Les livres Saints³,* I, 280ff.

people's sense of community. The freedom to read and to examine Scripture has been and is being grossly abused by all sorts of groups and schools of thought. On balance, however, the disadvantages do not outweigh the advantages. For the denial of the clarity of Scripture carries with it the subjection of the layperson to the priest, of a person's conscience to the church. The freedom of religion and the human conscience, of the church and theology, stands and falls with the perspicuity of Scripture. It alone is able to maintain the freedom of the Christian; it is the origin and guarantee of religious liberty as well as of our political freedoms.[59]

Even a freedom that cannot be obtained and enjoyed aside from the danger of licentiousness and caprice is still always to be preferred over a tyranny that suppresses liberty. In the creation of humanity, God himself chose this way of freedom, which carried with it the danger and actually the fact of sin as well, in preference to forced subjection. Even now, in ruling the world and governing the church, God still follows this royal road of liberty. It is precisely his honor that through freedom he nevertheless reaches his goal, creating order out of disorder, light from darkness, a cosmos out of chaos. Rome and the Reformation both share the conviction that the Holy Spirit alone is the true interpreter of the word (Matt. 7:15; 16:17; John 6:44; 10:3; 1 Cor. 2:12, 15; 10:15; Phil. 1:10; 3:13; Heb. 5:14; 1 John 4:1). But Rome believes that the Holy Spirit teaches infallibly only through the agency of the pope. The Reformation, however, believes that the Holy Spirit indwells the heart of every believer, that every child of God shares in the anointing of the Holy One. It therefore puts the Bible in the hands of everyone, translates and distributes it, and in church uses no other language than the vernacular.

Rome boasts of its unity, but this unity seems greater than it really is. The split of the Reformation between the Lutheran and the Reformed church has its parallel in the split between the Greek [Orthodox] and the Latin church. In Rome, hidden under the semblance of external unity, there is an almost equally extensive inner dividedness. In Roman Catholic countries the number of unbelievers and indifferent people is not less than in Protestant countries. Rome has no more succeeded in turning the tide of unbelief than the churches of the Reformation have. Even before the Reformation, in Italy for example, unbelief had spread over large areas. The Reformation did not bring it about but rather arrested it and awakened Rome itself into vigilance and resistance. Descartes, the father of rationalism, was Roman Catholic. German rationalists have their counterparts in materialists; Rousseau has his counterpart in Voltaire, Strauss in Renan. Revolution has sunk its deepest roots and borne its most bitter fruits in Roman Catholic countries. It remains to be seen, moreover, whether the number of parties, schools, and

59. Stahl, *Der Protestantismus als Politiek Princip,* 2d ed. (Berlin: W. Schultz, 1853); D. Chantepie de la Saussaye, *Het Protestantism als Politiek Beginsel* (Rotterdam, 1871); A. Kuyper, "Calvinism: Source and Stronghold of Our Constitutional Liberties," in *Abraham Kuyper: A Centennial Reader,* ed. J. D. Bratt (Grand Rapids: Eerdmans, 1998), 279–322.

sects that keep surfacing would not be as numerous in Rome as in Protestantism if Rome did not have the power and the courage to suppress every deviant group by means of censorship, excommunication, interdict, and, if need be, even by the sword. It is truly not owing to Rome that so many flourishing Christian churches have appeared alongside of it. Whatever the dark side of the dividedness of Protestantism may be, it does prove that the religious life here is a power that keeps engendering new forms and, for all its diversity, also manifests a deeper unity. In any case, Protestantism with its division is preferable to the frightful superstition in which the people are increasingly becoming entangled in the Greek Orthodox and Roman Catholic Church. Mariolatry, the veneration of relics, image worship, and adoration of the saints increasingly crowd out the worship of the one true God.[60]

On account of this perspicuity, Scripture also possesses the "power of interpreting itself" and is the "supreme judge of all controversies."[61] Scripture interprets itself; the obscure texts are explained by the plain ones, and the fundamental ideas of Scripture as a whole serve to clarify the parts. This was the "interpretation according to the analogy of faith," which was also advocated by the Reformers. They too did not come to Scripture without presuppositions. They adopted the teaching of Scripture, the Apostles' Creed, the decisions of the early councils, virtually without criticism. They were not revolutionary and did not want to begin all over again but only protested against the errors that had crept in. The Reformation was not the liberation of the "natural man" but of the Christian person. From the start, therefore, the Reformers had "an analogy of faith" in which they themselves took position and by which they interpreted Scripture. By that analogy of faith they originally understood the sense derived from the clear texts of Scripture itself, which then was later laid down in the confessions.[62] In connection with that, the church also had a responsibility with respect to the interpretation of Scripture.

In virtue of the power of teaching (*potestas doctrinae*) conferred on it by Christ and the gift of interpretation given to it by the Holy Spirit (1 Cor. 14:3, 29; Rom. 12:6; Eph. 4:11f.), the church has the obligation not only to preserve the Scriptures but also to interpret and defend them, to formulate the truth in its confession, to unmask errors, and to oppose them. Within its

---

60. Trede, *Das Heidenthum in der Römischen Kirche*, 4 vols. (Gotha: Perthes, 1889–92); Kolde, *Die Kirchliche Bruderschaften und das religiose Leben im Moderne Katholismus* (Erlangen: F. Junge, 1895); idem, "Herz-Jesu-Kultus," *PRE³*, VII, 777; R. Andree, *Votive und Weihegaben des Katholischen Volks in Süddeutschland* (Braunnschweig: F. Vieweg und Sohn, 1904).

61. *Synopsis Purious Theologiae*, disp. 5, §20ff.; A. Polaniss, *Syn. Theol.*, bk. I, 45; F. Turretin, *Institutes of Elenctic Theology*, loc. II, qu. 20; W. Ames, *Bellarminus enervatus*, bk. I, 5; J. Cloppenburg, "De Canone Theol.," disp. 11–15; *Op. Theol.*, II, 64ff.; A. De Moor, *Comm. In Marcki*, I, 429ff.; J. Gerhard, *Loci Theol.*, loc. I, 21, 22; H. Schmid, *Doctrinal Theology of the Evangelical Churches*, 69ff.

62. G. Voetius, *Select Disp.*, V, 9ff.; A. De Moor, *Comm. In Marki Comp.*, I, 436; VI, praefatio; F. Turretin, *Institutes of Elenctic Theology*, I, qu. 19; Philippi, *Kirchliche Glaubenslehre*, I, 217ff.; O. Zöckler, *Handbuch* (München: C. H. Beck, 1890), I, 663ff.; Lutz, *Hermeneutik*, 154–76.

own circle and jurisdiction, therefore, the church also is the judge of controversies and has to test all opinions and to judge them in the light of Holy
Scripture. It need not, for that purpose, be infallible, for also the judiciary in
the state, though bound by the law, is fallible in its pronouncements. The
situation in the church is the same. Scripture is the norm, the church the
judge. Here too one can appeal to a higher court. Rome, denying this, states
that the pronouncements of the church are supreme and final. From them
an appeal to God's judgment is no longer even possible. The Roman Church
binds the human conscience.

By contrast, the Reformation asserted that a church, however venerable,
can still err. Its interpretation is not "magisterial" but "ministerial." It can
bind a person in conscience only to the degree that a person recognizes it as
divine and infallible. Whether it indeed agrees with God's Word no earthly
power can decide, but it is for everyone to judge solely for himself or herself.[63] The church can then cast someone out as a heretic, but ultimately that
person stands or falls before his or her own master [Rom. 14:4]. Even the
most simple believer can and may if necessary, Bible in hand, stand up to an
entire church, as Luther did to Rome. Only thus the freedom of the Christian, and simultaneously the sovereignty of God, is maintained. There is no
higher appeal from Scripture. It is the supreme court of appeal. No power or
pronouncement stands above it. It is Scripture, finally, which decides matters
in the conscience of everyone personally. And for that reason *it* is the supreme arbiter of controversies.

THE SUFFICIENCY OF SCRIPTURE

[127] Finally, the Reformation also confessed the perfection or sufficiency
of Holy Scripture. The Roman Catholic Church believes that in some parts
Scripture is incomplete and has to be augmented by tradition. It declared at
Trent (session 4) "that it receives and venerates with an equal affection of piety and reverence the said traditions as well as those pertaining to faith and
morals as having been dictated either by Christ's own word of mouth or by
the Holy Spirit and preserved in the Catholic church by a continuous succession." The Vatican Council (session 3, chap. 2) declared that this supernatural revelation is contained "in written books and in the unwritten traditions
that were received from the mouth of Christ Himself by the apostles or from
the apostles themselves under the dictation of the Holy Spirit, and that have
come down to us, transmitted, as it were, from hand to hand."

The grounds that Rome cites for this doctrine of tradition are various. It
is first pointed out that before Moses the church was totally without Scripture and that after that time up until the present many believers lived and
died without ever reading or examining Scripture. By far the majority of
God's children live by tradition and know little or nothing of Scripture. It

---

63. *Synopsis Purioris Theologiae*, V, 25ff.

would also be strange if in the area of religion and the church this were different from any other area. After all, in law and morals, in art and science, in the family and society, tradition is the bearer and nurturer of human life. Tradition connects us with our ancestors; by it we receive their treasures and again bequeath them to our children. This analogy requires that there should be a tradition also in the church; but here the tradition must be so much more glorious and certain than elsewhere, inasmuch as Christ has given the Holy Spirit to his church and by the Spirit infallibly leads his church into all truth (Matt. 16:18; 28:20; John 14:16). Add to this the many statements of Scripture that recognize the validity and value of tradition (John 16:12; 20:30; 21:25; Acts 1:3; 1 Cor. 11:2, 23; 2 Thess. 2:15; 1 Tim. 6:20; 2 John 12; 3 John 13, 14). Both orally and by his Spirit, Jesus taught his disciples many more things, which, though not recorded, were passed down from mouth to mouth. Church fathers, councils, and popes have also from the very beginning recognized such an apostolic tradition.

Actually, the church always lives from and by this vital oral tradition. Scripture by itself is insufficient. Aside from the fact that by far not everything has been recorded, various writings by prophets and apostles have been lost as well. Though the apostles were instructed to witness, they were not told to do this in writing. They resorted to writing only in response to circumstances, "compelled by a kind of necessity." Their writings, accordingly, are mostly occasional writings and fall far short of what is necessary for the teaching and life of the church. For example, we find little or nothing in Scripture about the baptism of women, observance of the Lord's Day, the episcopacy, the seven sacraments, purgatory, the immaculate conception of Mary, the salvation of many Gentiles in the days of the OT, the inspiration and canonicity of several Bible books, and so forth. According to Rome even dogmas like the Trinity, the eternal generation [of the Son], the procession of the Holy Spirit, infant baptism, and so forth cannot be found literally and explicitly in Scripture. In short: while Scripture is useful, tradition is necessary.[64]

The Conflict with Rome

Over against this Roman Catholic doctrine of tradition, the Reformation posited that of the perfection and sufficiency of Holy Scripture. The validity of this polemic against Rome has been highlighted over time by the evolution of the very concept of tradition. The first Christian churches, like the churches in the non-Christian world today, were founded by the preaching of the gospel. The doctrine and practices that they received from the apostles or

---

64. Bellarmine, "De Verbo Dei," *Controversiis*, bk. IV; M. Canus, *Loci Theol.*, bk. 3; Peronne, *Praelect Theol.*, IX, 228ff.; Klee, *Dogmatik* I, 277; Heinrich, *Dogmatische Theologie*, II, 3ff.; Jansen, *Praelect Theol. Dogm.*, I, 788ff.; Möhler, *Symbolik*, §38ff.; J. Kleutgen, *Philosophie der Vorzeit*, 2d ed., 5 vols. (Münster: Theissing, 1867–74), I, 72ff.; Dieringer, *Dogmatik*, §126; Liebermann, *Inst. Theol.*, I, 448ff.; C. Pesch, *De Inspiratione Sacra Scripturae*, 578ff. For the Greek Church, cf. Kattenbusch, *Confessionskunde* (Freiburg i.B.: J. C. B. Mohr, 1892), I, 292.

their associates were for a considerable time passed down from mouth to mouth and from generation to generation. This concept of tradition was clear; it referred to the doctrine and practices that had been received from the apostles and were preserved and reproduced in the churches. But as the distance from the apostolic age became greater, it became progressively more difficult to tell whether a given thing really was of apostolic origin. For that reason the African church protested against the exaggerated value attached in the second half of the second century to this tradition, especially against Gnosticism. Tertullian said: "Our Lord called himself the 'truth,' not 'custom.'"[65] Similarly, Cyprian cited against the tradition (to which the bishop of Rome appealed) the texts Isaiah 29:13; Matthew 15:9; 1 Timothy 6:3–5; and stated: "Custom without truth is the antiquity of error."[66] Christ did not call himself the "custom" but the "truth." The former must yield to the latter.

It therefore became necessary to further define the tradition and to indicate its features. Vincent of Lerin, in his *Commonitory*, chap. 2, defined the criteria of an apostolic tradition by the fact that something "had been believed everywhere, always, and by everyone. And indeed, this is truly and characteristically catholic." First, the mark of tradition was apostolic origin. Now there was added that something may be deemed to be of apostolic origin if it is truly universal, or catholic. Apostolicity can be known from the universality, antiquity, and consensus concerning a doctrine or practice. The Council of Trent, the Vatican Council, and also the theologians adopted these criteria of Vincent. But materially there was divergence; the logical implications did not stop there. It could not be maintained that something was apostolic only if it had really been believed always, everywhere, and by all. Of what doctrine or custom could such absolute catholicity be demonstrated? The three criteria, accordingly, gradually weakened. The church may indeed not pronounce something new to be a dogma and must adhere to the tradition, but the preservation of that tradition must not be understood mechanically as a treasure in a field but organically, the way Mary kept the shepherds' words and pondered them in her heart.[67] A given truth may therefore very well not have been believed in the past, at least not universally; it is nevertheless an infallible apostolic tradition if only it is now believed universally.

These two criteria, antiquity and universality, therefore, are not copulative but distributive marks of the tradition. They do not have to occur together and at the same time since either one of the two is sufficient. Factually antiquity has thereby been sacrificed to universality. But also the latter is again qualified. People raised the question of who or what would be the organ for the preservation and recognition of the tradition. This could not be the church in general. It is true that Möhler still identified the tradition with

---

65. Tertullian, *On the Veiling of Virgins*, chap. 1.
66. Cyprian, *Epistle* 74.
67. Heinrich, *Dogmatik*, II, 11, 12.

"the Word which lives perpetually in the hearts of believers,"[68] but this answer was much more a Protestant than a Roman Catholic construal. According to Rome, the task of preserving and defining the teachings of the church could not and should not be laid on the shoulders of the church in general, i.e., on laypeople. In the church one must distinguish between the listening church (*ecclesia audiens*) and the teaching church (*ecclesia docens*). The two indeed belong together and are imperishable, but the former possesses only a passive infallibility, i.e., it is infallible in believing only because and for as long as it remains linked with the teaching church.

But it is questionable whether even the latter is the real organ of doctrinal transmission. Gallicanism, the old Episcopal clergy, and the old Catholics stopped here and attribute infallibility to the body of bishops. But this position is untenable. When are these bishops infallible—outside of or only when gathered in council? If the latter, are they infallible only when they are unanimous or is only the majority infallible? How large must this majority be? Is fifty percent of the votes plus one sufficient? Is the council infallible without or even against the pope or only when in agreement with the pope? All of these questions seriously troubled Gallicanism. The papal system therefore took a further step and ascribed infallibility to the pope. This primacy of the pope is the product of a centuries-long development, the consequence of a trend that was already present in the church from early times. Gradually the pope began to be regarded as the infallible organ of divine truth and therefore also of tradition. Bellarmine [d. 1621] included among the marks of tradition the following rule: "that is to be believed without doubt to have descended from the apostolic tradition which is held to be such by those churches where there is an unbroken succession from apostolic times."[69] Now in antiquity, he continues, there were many such churches aside from Rome. Today [1590s?], however, only Rome is left. Therefore "from the testimony of this church alone a sure argument can be derived for the purpose of proving the apostolic traditions."

The church of Rome thus decides what the apostolic tradition is. Later theologians, especially among the Jesuits, have further developed this doctrine. And on July 18, 1870, during the fourth session of the Vatican Council, papal infallibility was publicly proclaimed as dogma. Now it is certainly the case that with respect to this infallibility the pope cannot be viewed in isolation from the church, especially not from the "teaching church." In addition, the symbols, decrees, liturgies, fathers, doctors, and the entire history of the [Catholic] church constitute so many monuments of tradition with which the pope links up and which he has to take into account in establishing a dogma. Still, the tradition is not formally identical with the content of all these monuments. The tradition is infallible; but, in the final analysis,

---

68. Möhler, *Symbolik*, 357.
69. Bellarmine, "De Verbo Dei," *Controversiis*, IV, 9.

what tradition is is decided by the pope with, without, or, if need be, against the church and the councils. The judgment of whether and in how far something has been believed always, everywhere, and by all cannot be up to the church, neither the listening nor the teaching church, but is naturally and exclusively the responsibility of the infallible pope. For Rome, when the pope proclaims a dogma, it is by that very fact apostolic tradition. The criterion of tradition has therefore been successively found in apostolicity, in episcopal succession, and in papal decision. With that the process has reached its conclusion. The infallible pope is the formal principle of Romanism. When Rome has spoken, the matter is settled (*Roma locuta, res finita*). Where the pope is, there the church is, there the Christian religion is, there the Spirit is (*Ubi Papa, ibi ecclesia, ibi religio Christiana, ibi Spiritua*). One cannot appeal from the pope to a higher authority, not even to God. Through the pope God himself speaks to humanity.[70]

Tradition and Papal Infallibility

[128] This result, the outcome of the course of the development of tradition, demonstrates the falseness of the principle operative in it from the beginning. Papal infallibility can be treated at length only later, in the doctrine of the church. But at this point it is already clear that the sound and true element at stake in the maintenance of tradition in the early centuries has been completely lost. At that time the goal was the preservation of that which, in virtue of apostolic institution, had been believed and was practiced in the churches. It goes without saying that people then attached great importance to the tradition and did not yet understand the indispensability and necessity of the apostolic writings. But the mark of apostolicity, which was then an integral part of the tradition, was bound to disappear when people were further removed from the time of the apostles. The relative independence of tradition alongside of Scripture also disappeared. The streams of Scripture and tradition flowed into a single channel. And soon after the death of the apostles and their contemporaries, it became impossible to prove a thing to be of apostolic origin except by an appeal to the apostolic writings. Apostolic origin cannot be proven of a single dogma the Catholic Church confesses outside of and apart from Scripture. Rome's doctrine of tradition serves only to justify Rome's deviations from Scripture and the apostles. Mariolatry, the seven sacraments, papal infallibility, etc. are the dogmas that cannot survive without tradition. At an evil hour the apostolic tradition was equated with ecclesiastical customs and papal decisions. Tradition, in the case of Rome, says Harnack, is "common superstition, paganism."[71]

70. Perrone, *Prael. Theol.*, I, 229; IX, 279; Jansen, *Praelect Theol.*, I, 804, 822ff., 829; Heinrich, *Dogmatik*, I, 699 note; II, 157ff.; de Maistre, *Du Pape, Oeuvres Choisies de Joseph de Maistre* (Paris: Hachette, 1890), III, 71.

71. Harnack, *History of Dogma*, III, 559 note.

Actually, by this doctrine of tradition Scripture is totally robbed of its authority and power. Roman Catholics predicate infallibility of both Scripture and tradition (the pope) but also recognize that there is a big difference between the two. Infallibility in both cases is traced to a special supernatural operation of the Holy Spirit, for Rome understands very well that the infallibility of the tradition cannot be derived from believers as such, from the power and spirit of the Christianity that resides and works in believers. In the church and among believers, after all, many errors occur, errors that often prevail for a long time and lead many people astray. Accordingly, the infallibility of the pope, like that of Scripture, is explained, on the basis of Matthew 16:18; 28:20; John 14:16f.; 15:26; 16:12f., in terms of a special operation of the Holy Spirit. Yet there is a difference. The activity of the Holy Spirit in the apostles consisted in revelation and inspiration; in the case of the pope it consists in assistance. The Vatican Council (ch. 4) says: "For the Holy Spirit has promised the successors of Peter, not that they may disclose new doctrine by his revelation, but that they may, with his assistance, preserve conscientiously and expound faithfully the revelation transmitted through the Apostles, the deposit of faith."[72]

Scripture, therefore, is the word of God in the true sense, inspired, at least according to many theologians, right down to the individual words. The decrees of councils and popes, on the other hand, are the words of the church, which faithfully reproduce the truth of God. Scripture *is* the word of God; tradition *contains* the word of God. For Rome, Scripture preserves the words of the apostles in their original form; tradition only reproduces the substance of their teaching. The books of the prophets and apostles were often written without investigation, by revelation alone. However, in the case of the divine assistance promised to the church, the persons themselves are always active, investigating, pondering, judging, and deciding. According to Rome, in inspiration the activity of the Spirit was, strictly speaking, supernatural, but in the case of assistance it frequently consists in a complex of providential provisions by which the church is kept from error. Finally, inspiration in Scripture extends to all matters, also those of history, chronology, and so forth; but thanks to the assistance of the Holy Spirit, the pope is infallible only when he speaks *ex cathedra,* i.e., "when in the discharge of his office as shepherd and teacher of all Christians . . . he defines that a doctrine concerning faith and morals must be held by the whole church." In Rome, accordingly, Scripture still has a few prerogatives over tradition.[73]

But in fact tradition inflicts great damage on Scripture. In the first place, Trent decrees that Scripture and tradition must be venerated "with an equal affection of piety and reverence." Second, the inspiration of Holy Scripture is conceived by most Catholic theologians as "material" inspiration (*inspira-*

---

72. *Documents of Vatican Council I, 1869–1870* (Collegeville, Minn.: Liturgical Press, 1971), session 4.

73. Bellarmine, "De Conc. et Eccl.," *Controversiis,* II, 12; Heinrich, *Dogmatik,* I, 699ff.; II, 212ff.; Jansen, *Prael. Theol.,* I, 616; Mannens, *Theol. Dogm. Institutiones,* I, 174.

tio realis): not the individual words, but the subject matter is inspired. Further, in the doctrine of infallibility, form and substance are so tightly bound up with each other that no boundary can be drawn between the two. Also, while the pope is, strictly speaking, infallible only in matters of faith and morals, in order for him to be able to be this he also has to be infallible in his judgment concerning the sources of faith and in interpreting them. This includes the determination of what Scripture and tradition is, what is the authority of the church fathers, of councils, and so forth. It also applies to the assessment of errors and heresies and even basic doctrinal truths (*facta dogmatica*), in the prohibition of books, in matters of discipline, in the endorsement of orders, in the canonization of saints, and so forth.[74] And although in all other things the pope is not, strictly speaking, infallible, his power and authority nevertheless extends over all matters "pertaining to the discipline and governments of the church throughout the world," and this power is "full and supreme" and extends to "all shepherds and all the faithful."[75]

Many Roman Catholics even demand that the pope, in order to exercise this spiritual sovereignty, has to be a secular ruler as well. The claim is, if not directly then indirectly, the Pope has "the supreme power to settle the temporal affairs of all Christians."[76] The power and authority of the pope far exceeds that of Scripture. He is above Scripture, determines its content and meaning, and by his authority establishes the dogmas of the [church's] teaching and conduct. Scripture may be the primary means of proving the harmony of present-day doctrine and tradition with the teaching of the apostles. It may also contain a great deal that would not be well known otherwise and be a divine instruction in the teaching that surpasses all others. Nonetheless, to Rome Scripture is never more than a means that, while useful, is not necessary. The church existed before Scripture, and the church contains the full truth and not just a part, while Scripture contains only a part of the doctrine. Whereas Scripture needs tradition, the confirmation of the pope, tradition does not need Scripture. The tradition is not a supplement to Scripture; Scripture is a supplement to tradition. While Scripture alone is not sufficient, tradition alone is. While Scripture is based on the church, the church is based on itself.[77]

From Tradition to Sufficiency

The development of tradition into papal infallibility and the degradation of Scripture, which necessarily results from it, already implies that the Reformation had good warrant for opposing Rome's tradition. It did not confine itself to attack, however, but over against Rome's doctrine asserted that of

74. Heinrich, *Dogmatisch Theologie*, II, 536ff.

75. *Documents of Vatican I*, session 4, chap. 3.

76. Bellarmine, "De Romano Pontifice," *Controversiis* I, V; de Maistre, *Du Pape*, I, 2; Jansen, *Prael. Theol.*, I, 651.

77. Heinrich, *Dogmatische Theologie*, I, 702ff.; Mannens, *Theol. Dogm. Institutiones*, I, 171.

the perfection or sufficiency of Scripture.[78] This attribute of Holy Scripture also must be correctly understood. It does not mean that all that has been said or written by the prophets, by Christ, and the apostles is included in Scripture. Many prophetic and apostolic writings have been lost (Num. 21:14; Josh. 10:13; 1 Kings 4:33; 1 Chron. 29:29; 2 Chron. 9:29; 12:15; 1 Cor. 5:9; Col. 4:16; Phil. 3:1), and Jesus as well as the apostles have spoken many more words and performed many more signs than are recorded (John 20:30; 1 Cor. 11:2, 23; 2 Thess. 2:5, 15; 3:6, 10; 2 John 12; 3 John 14; and so forth). Nor does this attribute imply that Scripture contains all the practices, ceremonies, rules, and regulations that the church needs for its organization but only that it completely contains "the articles of faith" (*articuli fidei*), "the matters necessary to salvation." Neither does this attribute of Scripture mean that these articles of faith are literally and in so many words contained in it. Rather, it only [claims that], either explicitly or implicitly, they are so included that they can be derived from it solely by comparative study and reflection, without the help of another source.

And, finally, this perfection of Holy Scripture must not be interpreted to mean that Scripture was always the same in degree of its perfection (*quoad gradum*) with respect to length. In the different periods of the church, Scripture was unequal in scope right up to its completion, but in every period that word of God, which existed in unwritten or written form, was sufficient for that time. The Reformation also made a distinction between an unwritten and a written word.[79] But Rome assumes their existence side by side, considering them species of a single genus, while the Reformation views this distinction as referring to the same word of God that first existed for a time in unwritten form and was subsequently recorded. The dispute between Rome and the Reformation, accordingly, concerns only the question of whether now, after Scripture has been completed, there still exists another word of God alongside it in unwritten form. In other words, the question is whether the written word of God explicitly or implicitly contains everything we need to know for our salvation and therefore is "the total and sufficient rule of faith and morals" or whether, in addition, we must assume the existence of still another principle of knowledge (*principium cognoscendi*).

78. Luther, in J. Köstlin, *Luther's Theology*, II, 279ff., 501ff.; J. Gerhard, *Loci Theol.*, loc. 1, 18, 19; Schmid, *Doctrine of Evangelical Churches*, §9; J. Calvin, *Institutes*, IV, X; Polanus, *Syn. Theol.*, I, 46; J. Zanchi, *Op. Theol.*, VIII, col. 369ff.; Ursinus, *Tract Theol.* (1584), 8ff., 22ff.; Chamier, *Panstratia Catholica*, loc. I, bks. 8 and 9; W. Ames, *Bellarminos enervatus*, bk. I, 6; Holtzmann, *Kanon und Tradition* (Ludwigsberg, 1859); E. W. Dieckhoff, *Schrift und Tradition* (Rostock: Stiller, 1870); J. L. Jacobi, *Die Kirchliche Lehre von der Tradition und heiligen Schrift* (Berlin: Luderitz, 1847); P. Tschackert, *Evangelische Polemik gegen die romischen Kirche* (Gotha: F. A. Perthes, 1885); idem, "Tradition," *PRE²*, XV, 727–32; Hase, *Protestantische Polemik*, 5th ed. (Leipzig: Breitkopf und Hartel, 1891), 77ff.; Harnack, *History of Dogma*, III, 593ff., 623ff.; C. Hodge, *Systematic Theology*, I, 104; Daubanton, *De Algenoezaamheid der Heilige Schrift* (Utrecht: Kemink & Zoon, 1882).

79. Belgic Confession, art. 3.

Framed in this manner, however, the question hardly allows for a two-fold answer. The Roman Catholic Church also acknowledges that Scripture is complete, constitutes an organic whole, and that the canon is closed. However highly it esteemed tradition, in theory it never ventured to put the decisions of the church on a par with Scripture. It still makes a distinction between the word of God and the word of the church. But how, as long as the church still takes the word of God seriously, can it ever teach the insufficiency of Scripture? This never occurred to the church fathers who clearly voice the complete sufficiency of Holy Scripture. Irenaeus says that we know the truth from the apostles, "through whom the gospel came to us which at that time they proclaimed and afterwards by the will of God handed down to us in the Scriptures as the future foundation and pillar of our faith."[80] Tertullian marvels at the "plenitude" of Scripture and rejects everything that is "extra-Scriptural."[81] Augustine testifies: "Whatever you have heard in it, know that it is good for you; whatever is outside of it, refuse."[82] And numerous others strike the same note.[83]

However, they also most certainly acknowledge the tradition they include in it, an element that undermines their conviction that Scripture is sufficient. This element ends in the later Roman Catholic doctrine of the insufficiency of Holy Scripture and the sufficiency of tradition. Scripture and tradition, in the case of Rome, cannot be maintained side by side; that which is withheld from the one is [bound to be] granted to the other. The tradition can increase only if and to the extent that Scripture decreases. It is very strange, accordingly, that Rome, on the one hand, regards Scripture as completed and considers the canon closed, indeed even recognizes Scripture as the word of God; and, on the other, views Scripture as insufficient and augments it with tradition. Nowadays many Roman Catholic theologians correctly assert that Scripture is—not the necessary but—at most a useful complement of tradition.[84]

A Scriptural View of Tradition

[129] But this theory is diametrically opposed to Scripture itself. At no time is the church in the OT and the NT ever directed to anything other than the always available Word of God, either written or unwritten. By it alone human beings can have a spiritual life. The church finds all it needs in the Scripture available to it at a given time. Subsequent Scriptures presuppose, link up with, and build upon, preceding Scripture. The prophets and psalmists assume the Torah. Isaiah (8:20) calls everyone to the law and to the testimony. The NT considers itself the fulfillment of the OT and refers back

---

80. Irenaeus, *Against Heresies,* III, preface, chap. 1.
81. Tertullian, *Against Hermogenes,* chap. 22; idem, *On the Body of Christ,* chap. 8.
82. Augustine, *Sermon on Pastorals,* chap. 11.
83. Cf. the references gathered by Chamier, *Panstratia Catholica,* loc. 1, bk. 8, chap. 10.
84. H. Höpfl, *Die Höhere Bibelkritik* (Paderborn: Schöningh, 1902).

to nothing other than the existing Scripture. Even more telling is the fact that all that lies outside of Scripture is as firmly as possible ruled out. Traditions are rejected as the institutions of human beings (Isa. 29:13; Matt. 15:3, 9; 1 Cor. 4:6). The tradition that developed in the days of the OT prompted the Jews to reject the Christ. Over against it Jesus posited his "but I say to you" (Matt. 5:27, 32, 34, 38, 44), and against Pharisees and scribes he again aligned himself with the Law and the Prophets. The apostles appeal only to the OT Scriptures and never refer the churches to anything other than the word of God proclaimed by them. Inasmuch as in the early period tradition sought to be nothing other than the preservation of the things personally taught and instituted by the apostles, it was not yet dangerous. But the Roman Catholic tradition has utterly deteriorated from that level. It cannot be demonstrated that any doctrine or practice is of apostolic origin except insofar as this can be shown from their writings. The Roman Catholic tradition, which gave rise to the mass, to Mariolatry, to papal infallibility, and other Roman distinctives, is nothing but a sanctioning of the actual state of affairs of the Roman Catholic Church, a justification of the superstition that has crept into it.

Furthermore, the sufficiency of Holy Scripture results from the nature of the NT dispensation. Christ became flesh and completed all his work. He is the last and supreme revelation of God, who declared to us the Father (John 1:18; 17:4, 6). By him God has spoken to us in the last days (Heb. 1:1–2). He is the supreme and only prophet. Even the Vatican Council [I] acknowledges that the divine assistance given to the pope does not consist in revelation and the disclosure of a new doctrine. And Rome still tries as much as possible to urge the necessity of its dogmas, however new they are, from Scripture and to represent them as a development and explication of what is germinally present already in Scripture.[85] But in the process it entangles itself in grave difficulty. For either the dogmas are all in the same sense the explication of elements contained in Scripture (as, e.g., the dogmas of the Trinity and the two natures of Christ), or they are in fact new dogmas, which have no support in Scripture. In the former case tradition is not necessary and Scripture is sufficient, and in the latter case the so-called "divine assistance" to the pope is actually a revelation of new doctrine. The latter may still be denied in theory; in practice it is nevertheless accepted.

Post-Reformation Roman Catholic theologians, accordingly, have as a rule been more generous than their pre-Reformation counterparts in acknowledging that some dogmas are based only on tradition. And so arguments are advanced in support of the tradition today that were not used, at least not in the same sense or to the same degree, in earlier periods. Today the insufficiency of Scripture and the validity of tradition are argued on the

---

85. P. Lombard, *III Sent.*, dist. 25; Thomas Aquinas, *Summa Theol.*, II, 2 qu. 1, art. 7; qu. 174, art. 6; Schwane, *Dogmengeschichte*, 2d ed. (Freiburg i.B.: Herder, 1892), I, 7; Heinrich, *Dogmatische Theologie*, II, 22ff.

grounds that some prophetic and apostolic writings have been lost, that Christ did not teach his apostles everything, and that the apostles recommended many things to the church orally. But the idea that some writings were lost and the issue of whether they were inspired[86] or not[87] are not at all to the point. The question is only whether the present Bible contains everything we need to know for our salvation and not whether it contains everything the prophets and apostles ever wrote and Christ himself said or did. Even if still other prophetic and apostolic writings were found, they could no longer serve as Holy Scripture. The same is true of the instruction given by Jesus and the apostles. They have said and done more than has been written down for our benefit. Though acquaintance with such writings would be historically important, it is religiously unnecessary. For our salvation Scripture is sufficient; we do not need any more documents, even if they came from Jesus himself. That was the teaching of the Reformation. Quantitatively revelation was much richer and more comprehensive than Scripture has preserved for us; but qualitatively and in terms of substance, Holy Scripture is perfectly adequate for our salvation.

Rome, accordingly, can list no other dogmas than those of Mariolatry, the infallibility of the pope, and the like that have developed apart from Scripture out of tradition. All those that pertain to God, humanity, Christ, salvation, and other basic doctrines can also be found in Scripture itself, as Rome admits. Then, what further need of witnesses have we? The Roman Catholic tradition serves only to prove specifically Roman Catholic dogmas, but the Christian dogmas, the truly catholic dogmas, are all, according to Rome itself, grounded in Scripture. This also shows that Scripture is sufficient and that the nature of the NT dispensation logically brings with it and demands this sufficiency of Holy Scripture. Christ has fully—personally and orally, or by his Spirit—revealed everything to the apostles. Upon this word we believe in Christ and have fellowship with God (John 17:20; 1 John 1:3). The Holy Spirit no longer reveals any new doctrines but takes everything from Christ (John 16:14). In Christ God's revelation has been completed. In the same way the message of salvation is completely contained in Scripture. It constitutes a single whole; it itself conveys the impression of an organism that has reached its full growth. It ends where it begins. It is a circle that returns into itself. It begins with the creation of heaven and earth and ends with the re-creation of heaven and earth.

The canon of the OT and NT was not closed until all new initiatives of redemptive history were present.[88] In this dispensation the Holy Spirit has no other task than to apply the work of Christ and similarly to explain the word of Christ. To neither does he add anything new. The work of Christ does not need to be supplemented by the good works of believers, and the

---

86. Bellarmine, "De Verbo Dei," IV, 4.
87. Augustine, *City of God,* XVIII, 38.
88. Hofmann, *Weissagung und Erfüllung,* I, 47.

word of Christ does not need to be supplemented by the tradition of the church. Christ himself does not need to be succeeded and replaced by the pope. The Roman Catholic doctrine of tradition is the denial of the complete incarnation of God in Christ, of the all-sufficiency of his sacrifice, of the completeness of his Word. The history of the Roman Catholic Church shows us the gradual process of how a false principle creeps in. It first subordinates itself to Christ and his Word, then puts itself on a par with him, later elevates itself above him, to end in the complete replacement of Scripture by tradition, of Christ by the pope, of the church community by the church institution. Certainly this process has not yet reached its conclusion. It seems an anomaly that the pope, who gradually assumed a position above Scripture, the church, council, and tradition, is still appointed by fallible people, even though they are cardinals. Who is in a better position than he who is himself infallible to designate his successor? It is therefore very well possible that in the future papal sovereignty will prove to be incompatible with the power of cardinals. In any case Rome has not yet walked the road of the deification of humanity to its conclusion.

Still, for all this, our purpose is not to deny the good and the true component inherent in the theory of tradition. The word *tradition* also has a broader meaning than that which Rome has given it. Rome understands by it a doctrine that has been handed down by the apostles, preserved by the bishops, specifically the pope, and defined and proclaimed by him, a view shown to be untenable. Tradition can also be understood, however, in its reference to the entire scope of religious life, thought, feeling, action, which is found in every religious communion and which comes to expression in a wide assortment of forms, mores, customs, practices, religious language and literature, confessions and liturgies. In this sense there is tradition in every religion. The term can even be further expanded to include all those rich and multifarious bonds that link succeeding generations to preceding ones. In this sense, no family, no generation, no society, no people, no art, and no science can exist without tradition. Tradition is the means by which all the treasures and possessions of our ancestors are transmitted to the present and the future. Over against the individualism and atomism of a previous century, de Bonald, Lamennais (et al.) and Bilderdijk (in our own country) have again brilliantly highlighted the significance of community, authority, language, and tradition.

Such a tradition most certainly exists also in religion and in the church. Its very universality demonstrates that we are not dealing here with an accidental phenomenon. We find tradition not only in the Roman Catholic Church but also among Jews, Muslims, Buddhists, and other religions. In the more advanced religions, there is an additional reason for the necessity of tradition. They are all bound to a holy book that originated in a certain period and in that sense becomes ever farther removed from the generation now living. Also the Bible is a book that was written in ancient times and under all sorts of historical circumstances. The various books of the Bible all bear the stamp of the time in which they originated. Hence, however clear the Bible may be in its doctrine of salvation, and however certainly it is and remains the living voice of God, for a correct understanding it still often requires a wide range of historical, archeological, and geographical skills and information. The times have changed, and with the times people, their life, thought, and feelings, have changed. Therefore, a tradition is needed that preserves the connectedness between Scripture and the religious life of our time. Tradition in its proper sense is the interpretation and application of the eternal truth in the vernacular and life of the present generation. Scripture without such a tradition is impossible. Numerous sects in earlier and later times have attempted to live that way. They wanted nothing to do with anything other than the words and letters of Scripture, rejected all dogmatic terminology not used in Scripture, disapproved of all theological training and scholarship, and sometimes got to the point of demanding the literal application of the civil legislation of ancient Israel and the precepts of the Sermon on the Mount. But all these movements thereby doomed themselves to certain destruction or at least to a life that could not flourish. They place themselves outside of society and forego all influence on their people and their age. Scripture does not exist to be memorized and parroted but to enter into the fullness and richness of the entire range of human life, to shape and guide it, and to bring it to independent activity in all areas.

The Reformation, however, adopted another position. It did not reject all tradition as such; it was *reformation,* not *revolution.* It did not attempt to create everything anew from the bottom up, but it did try to cleanse everything from error and abuse according to the rule of God's Word. For that reason it continued to stand on the broad Christian foundation of the Apostles' Creed and the early councils. For that reason it favored a theological science, which thought through the truth of Scripture and interpreted it in the language of the present.

The difference between Rome and the Reformation in their respective views of tradition consists in this: Rome wanted a tradition that ran on an independent parallel track alongside of Scripture, or rather, Scripture alongside of tradition. The Reformation recognizes only a tradition that is founded on and flows from Scripture.[89] To the mind of the Reformation, Scripture was an organic principle from which the entire tradition, living on in preaching, confession, liturgy, worship, theology, devotional literature, etc., arises and is nurtured. It is a pure spring of living water from which all the currents and channels of the religious life are fed and maintained. Such a tradition is grounded in Scripture itself. After Jesus completed his work, he sent forth the Holy Spirit who, while adding nothing new to the revelation, still guides the church into the truth (John 16:12–15) until it passes through

---

89. B. De Moor, *Comm. In Marcke Comp.,* I, 351.

all its diversity and arrives at the unity of faith and the knowledge of the Son of God (Eph. 3:18, 19; 4:13). In this sense there is a good, true, and glorious tradition. It is the method by which the Holy Spirit causes the truth of Scripture to pass into the consciousness and life of the church. Scripture, after all, is only a means, not the goal. The goal is that, instructed by Scripture, the church will freely and independently make known "the wonderful deeds of him who called it out of darkness into his marvelous light" (1 Pet. 2:9). The external word is the instrument, the internal word the aim. Scripture will have reached its destination when all have been taught by the Lord and are filled with the Holy Spirit.

PART **V**

FAITH
(*PRINCIPIUM*
INTERNUM)

15

FAITH AND THEOLOGICAL METHOD

Revelation must be received as well as given. In the same way that human beings are connected to their external world by many relationships, so too they have a faculty for perceiving the divine. This religious capacity always occurs in the concrete and is instilled in us by our parents and religious caretakers in community. Faith does not arise from reflection; we live first, then we philosophize.

Critical reflection on faith does have a positive side, though it cannot compensate for lost faith. The nature of religion requires of theology its own epistemology. While the mystery of faith and the variety of grounds for faith must be respected, we can explore the means by which faith comes to fruition. The organ by which we obtain religious knowledge—intellect, heart, conscience—receives content from the outside. Religion presupposes and demands the existence, self-revelation, and knowability of God.

Though human beings are by nature religious, this capacity is always expressed concretely, awakened by and accommodated to a historical religion. This capacity is also corrupted by sin and itself needs redemption. It is the confession of the Christian church that God's redemption and revelation in Christ is subjectively applied to believers by the Holy Spirit. God's objective revelation in Christ, recorded in Scripture, is the prior external source of religious knowledge (principium cognoscendi externum); the Holy Spirit is the internal source of knowledge (principium cognoscendi internum). While Rome teaches that the institutional church is the dwelling place of the Spirit, according to the Reformation this temple is the church as organism, the community of the faithful.

The first theological activity in the church arose from apologetic need to defend the gospel against Jews and Greeks. Christian apologists compared their faith with the intellectual and practical content of paganism and judged the former to be vastly superior. Christianity was seen to be a blessing to the state, conducive to the prosperity of the empire and a benefaction to all humanity.

Medieval scholastic theology turned this apologetic method into a division between natural and supernatural truth, between scientific reason and faith. In response to the Reformation, Roman Catholic thought turned to the church itself as the most compelling ground for belief in Scripture and revelation. Though Vatican I affirmed the internal help of the Holy Spirit, it also anathematized those who reject the church as a necessary external sign. External proofs are, for

497

Rome, "preambles of faith," the necessary foundation for supernatural infused grace. Human beings proceed upwards to the vision in degrees as on a ladder.

The Reformation, in principle, opposed this hierarchical system of Rome and affirmed faith's sole dependence on divine authority and the work of the Holy Spirit. Yet Protestant theologians too returned to notions of natural theology and sought historical proofs for the truth of revelation. Rationalism, in the form of Socinianism, Arminianism, and Cartesianism, infiltrated Protestant theology, resulting in significant movements such as deism and the history-of-religions method. By this historical-apologetic approach, scientific theology was divorced from faith and the church and became an objective, neutral, historical-critical method of research. The response of supernaturalism affirmed the divine authority of revelation but yielded to the radical divorce between piety and reason.

While subjected to serious critique by such thinkers as Kant and Schleiermacher, the truth inherent in the historical-apologetic stance must not be lost. All believers have a duty, with gentleness and fear, to give an account of the hope that is in them and to confute those who contradict the gospel. A valid apologetic, however, follows faith and does not attempt to argue the truth of revelation in an a priori fashion. Christians need not hide from their opponents in embarrassed silence; the Christian faith is the only worldview that fits the reality of life. Apologetic intellectual labor should not lead to exaggerated expectations or deny the genuine subjectivity of Christian truth. Submitting to the validation of revelation by an intellectual priesthood provides feeble certainty. Finally, faith rests on the testimony of the Holy Spirit, which provides a sure certainty.

In reaction and response to this divorce of revelation and reason, European intellectual thought of the nineteenth century yielded to romanticism, to the dominance and autonomy of the subject. Idealism sought objectivity from within the subject; the world (non-ego) was seen as the product of the human subjects' mind (ego). The philosophic prophet of this restoration of idealism was Hegel, for whom the universe itself became a process of becoming, the evolution of the logical idea. From the theological rationalism of God, virtue, and morality, Hegel turned classic Christian dogma such as the Trinity and incarnation into speculative philosophic truths. Dogmas must be stripped of their historic symbolic forms to uncover their underlying idea. In this way theology and philosophy were reconciled, but the historic Christian faith was radically transformed. A personal God is exchanged for the absolute idea.

While Schleiermacher shared Hegel's subjective starting point, he took his position in experience, in feeling, rather than reason. Dogmatics was the fruit of the Christian community, a description of pious states of mind (consciousness) or the faith of the church. Here philosophy and theology are again separated, but a priority is given to philosophy. Following Schleiermacher, so-called mediating theology, took its departure in the consciousness of the church and linked it with Hegel's speculative method in order to elevate faith to the level of knowledge.

Whereas rationalism falsified the whole Christian religion, Hegel and Schleiermacher are to be commended for their courage in returning to the church *and its dogma. Both rose above the vulgar rationalism of their day and pointed to the harmony of subject and object, thinking and being. Their error was the basic flaw of all speculative philosophy or idealism (from Plato to Fichte). They equate the two, believing that ideas are the real world. Created reality is an emanation of thought. The Christian teaching, by contrast, affirms that the essence of all things is due to the thought of God but the existence is due to his will, to his exercise of creating power. This speculative theology was therefore not innocent. Theology became anthropology, "pisteology," or ecclesiology rather than the knowledge of God, a new form of Gnosticism. As a result the speculative method also led to the rejection of the Christian religion in toto. Christianity is history, a history of grace, and this can never be the conclusion of a mere logical system. Concrete religions do not flow from intellectual proof but from revelation and the religious nature of human beings. As an abstraction it is sterile; no one can live by it.*

When historical and speculative argumentation failed to bear fruit, many theologians turned to religious experience to derive grounds for the certain truth of Christianity. The influence of Schleiermacher is crucial for this development. With a waning faith in biblical authority, thanks to historical criticism, the Christian experience became the ground of certainty and opened the door to a scientific, religious-empirical approach to theology. Here too Christian certainty is not sought in external historical or rational proofs but in believing consciousness. The most thorough systematic formulation of a dogmatic theology in this vein was produced by the Erlangen dogmatician F. H. R. Frank.

According to Frank neither external proofs nor the authority of Scripture, church, and tradition are able to provide religious certainty, only the experience of rebirth. From the new life in Christ, believers are able to immediately posit the entire content of the truths of the Christian faith. Frank's system contains an important truth: rebirth is necessary to see the kingdom of God. Had he restricted his insight to the epistemological issue—how does a believer arrive at certainty?— no objection would be raised. However, to infer content from experience and epistemology confuses being and knowing, objective truth and subjective certainty. This confusion is typical of modern thought in both its empiricist and idealist form. The major objection to this approach is its indifference to the reality of objective, historical facts on which Christianity stands or falls. The organization of dogmatics into a twofold system of certainty and a system of truth cannot be maintained, since the Christian certainty cannot be described apart from the truth to which it pertains. The charge of subjectivism against Frank stands.

Other efforts to ground theological certainty in experience by modifying Frank's standpoint have not succeeded either. Certainty with respect to the truth of Christianity is not grounded in the Christian person but in the Word of God attested by the Holy Spirit. Part of the problem is the ambiguity of the word "experience." Experience is crucial to all religion, but in Christianity it must be prompted by the Word of God, accompany and follow faith, not precede it, and always be subject to correction by Scripture. Scripture, not experience, is the norm for our faith. In the articles of the Apostles' Creed, for example, we cannot simply exchange "I experience" for "I believe." The effect of belief must not be confused with its content and ground. The truth of historic Christianity cannot rest on experience as its ultimate ground.

Closely linked to the religious-empirical method associated with Schleiermacher and Frank is the ethical-psychological method, which is closer to Kant and accents ethical self-assertion rather than emotional experience. Here, Christianity is not a feeling, or a doctrine, or historical fact but a religious-ethical power addressed to the human conscience. This posture, which argues for the agreement or superiority of the Christian faith for human morality, goes back to the apologists and comes to strong expression in the work of Blaise Pascal (1623–62) and A. R. Vinet (1797–1847). It is possible, in this view, by practical reason to rationally infer the existence of God, freedom, and immortality (Kant).

Kant's divide between the world of pure (senses and facts of science) and practical (supersensible values) reason had a profound influence on theology. If the supersensible (noumenal) world is unknowable, theology as knowledge of God is impossible and becomes an examination of human moral conduct, a form of religious moral idealism. This understanding of religion and theology came to a highpoint in the cultural Protestantism (theological liberalism) of Albrecht Ritschl. For Ritschl religion and theology are not part of the world of nature and law but of the spirit and freedom. Christianity is an ethical religion, an ellipse with two foci: Redemption and the kingdom of God, the absolutely spiritual and the absolutely moral religion.

This ethical-practical method of vindicating religion and Christianity has much to commend it. Here religion is judged by its ability to satisfy the human heart, to provide consolation and comfort for guilty consciences and troubled souls. To be true a religion must provide consolation, but, conversely, this provision does not prove a religion's truth. Religious-ethical experience and appraisal cannot guarantee the truth of their object. It is not enough to seek and to meet people's perceived needs. Efforts to postulate the reality of God, freedom, and immortality from practical, moral reason (Kant) demonstrate nothing more than the "good" within us. In the end what is produced was contained in the point of departure itself.

Apart from these meager results, the very premise of efforts to postulate religion from practical moral experience is flawed since it turns the order of our experience upside down. Religion does not follow but is prior to morality; there is no morality without metaphysics, no sense of duty apart from an absolute power that binds the conscience.

The most serious objection here is that this approach always proceeds from and ends in a radical dualism between faith and knowledge. This is intolerable and unnecessary. In its domain the heart is as good an organ for the perception of truth as the head. Faith with its grounds has as much validity as science with its proofs. The unity of the human spirit rebels against such a separation, and the variety of forms such separation takes demonstrates its arbitrariness. In particular the historical content of the Christian has an objectivity that is not reducible to religious experience. Redemption includes liberation from falsehood and discovery of the truth. Objective religion is not the product of subjective religion but is given in divine revelation; dogma is not a symbolic interpretation of spiritual experience but an expression of truth given by God in his Word.

INTERNAL RECEPTION OF REVELATION

[130] Corresponding to the external principle [revelation] discussed in the previous chapter, there has to be an internal principle in human beings themselves [to receive revelation]. Herbert Spenser describes life as "the continuous adjustment of internal relations to external relations";[1] and indeed in the case of human beings all of life is based on the reciprocal correspondence between subject and object. Human beings are in every respect dependent on the world outside of them. In no area are we autonomous; we live by what is given, i.e., by grace. But, reciprocally, we are made and designed for that whole world outside of us and connected to it by a whole spectrum of relations. A human body has been taken from the dust of the earth, is composed of the same basic elements as other bodies, and is therefore akin to the physical world. Its vegetative life is nourished from the earth. Food, shelter, and clothing are given to human beings by means of nature. People need light, air, plus the alternation of day and night, for their physical life. They are microcosms, earthy, from the earth. As sentient souls, they have received organs by which they can perceive and picture the eternal world in its various relationships. By the *logos* (reason) inherent in them, they address the world of intelligible things and trace the *logos* (design) embodied in the visible realm. Religiously and ethically as well, human beings are connected with a genuine world of ideal and spiritual goods and have received a faculty to perceive and know this world. Earlier in this volume our investigation of the essence of religion already led us to a certain religious disposition in human beings, to a natural human capacity for perceiving the divine. As Scripture puts it, human beings are created in God's image; they are his offspring and in the mind (νοῦς) they possess an organ enabling them to observe God's revelation in his creation. Religion presupposes that human beings are akin to God.

Religion Is Always Concrete

But although this religious capacity may be an integral part of human nature, in reality it never occurs in a pure form and without content. However rich a talent for science and art may be hidden in a baby, it is nevertheless born in a state of helplessness. It depends on the "grace" of its environment. We receive food and drink, shelter and clothing, ideas and concepts, percep-

---

1. Herbert Spencer, *Principles of Psychology* (London: Longman, Brown, Green and Longmans, 1855), §120.

tions and wants from the circle in which we are born and reared. Religion also is instilled in us by our parents and caretakers. As with language, so it is with religion. The faculty of speech is something we possess at birth, but the language in which we will later express our thoughts is given us by our environment. Schopenhauer correctly remarks, therefore, that religions have a great advantage over philosophical systems since they are instilled in children from their earliest youth on.[2] Religion develops from childhood on in conjunction with the most intimate and tender parts of life and is in part for that reason ineradicable. The [general] rule is that people die in the religion in which they were born. As a rule Muslims, Christians, Roman Catholic or Protestant, remain faithful to the religion of their youth and parents until they die. Except for times of religious crisis, such as the rise of Christianity, Islam, or the Reformation, conversions are rare. A change of religion is the exception, not the rule. Most people even live and die without ever being shaken in their religious beliefs by serious doubt. The question of why they believe in the truth of the religious ideas in which they were brought up does not occur to them. They believe, find more or less satisfaction in their faith, and do not think about the grounds on which their conviction is based. If their faith is vigorous, there is no room for such an inquiry into the grounds of their religious beliefs. A hungry man does not first examine the way the bread that is put before him has been prepared. We live first, then we philosophize, since there is a great difference between life and reflection. It is evidence, not of the richness, but rather of the poverty of their religious life when people devote most of their attention to such formal questions. When their power to philosophize has been exhausted, people cast themselves upon the history of philosophy. When people are no longer vitally connected with the confession of the church, they examine its origin and history. And when their faith has lost its vitality and confidence, they explore the grounds on which it rests.

Still, such inquiry has a good and useful side. Kant transformed all of philosophy into the critique of reason, the faculty of knowledge. And no one will scorn the inquiries, which have been devoted, since Kant, to the nature and certainty of our knowledge. Nonetheless, in this area overcharged expectations are always followed by disappointment. The problems here are so complex that solutions seem unattainable. All the attempts made to achieve a satisfactory resolution to this question run into serious objections. Sometimes voices are raised calling us to abstain from further investigation since it is totally futile. In any case, these formal questions have no effect on the pursuit of science itself. Whether one is an idealist or an empiricist, a realist or a

---

2. A. Schopenhauer, *Die Welt als Wille und Vorstellung*, 6th ed., 2 vols. (Leipzig: Brockhaus, 1887), II, 181 (in *Sammtliche Werke*, vols. 2 and 3 [Leipzig: F. M. Brodhaus, 1919]). Ed. note: English translation: *The World as Will and Idea*, trans. R. B. Haldane and J. Kemp, 3d ed., 3 vols. (London: Kegan Paul, Trench, Trübner, 1891).

nominalist, one can only achieve scientific knowledge in the way of observation and reflection.

Theology's Distinct Method

Also in theology and religion there is reason for us to caution against inordinate expectations. Epistemology, or the theory of knowledge, cannot compensate for the loss of faith; the formal part of dogmatics cannot replace the material part. The investigation of the grounds of belief is even much more difficult than that of the grounds of knowledge. In the first place, for believers in general it is unfeasible to give a scientific account of the reasons why they believe. To them their faith-driven life is proof enough of the truth and value of that faith. A person who is hungry and eats experiences automatically the nourishing power of the food consumed and has no need to study its chemical components. Second, even for scientific theologians the demand that they must demonstrate the scientific validity of the epistemological theory they follow before undertaking their theological work is exaggerated.[3] A theologian, after all, is not a philosopher. Although philosophical training is indispensable to a theologian, he or she need not first have examined all philosophical theories of cognition before embarking on his or her work as a theologian. Theology has its own epistemology and, though dependent on philosophy, it is not dependent on any particular philosophical system. Finally, the object of investigation is so deeply hidden in the life of the soul and so closely interwoven with the finest and most tender fibers of the human heart that it almost completely eludes our own perception and even more that of others.

Religion is more deeply rooted in human nature than any other power. For a person's religion he or she is prepared to sacrifice everything: money, possessions, spouse and children, name, honor, even life itself. Only religion breeds martyrs. Retaining it, a person can lose everything and still retain his or her own identity. But denying it, he or she is lost. Who then will trace to its source the root of this life that is integrally one with a person's life itself? Who will be able to lay bare the grounds on which believing rests? Faith itself is already a most marvelous and mysterious power. We describe it with terms like knowing, consenting, trusting, etc. but immediately sense the weakness of the description and in the end, after long argumentation, have still said very little or nothing. The question, how and why do I know? is so difficult that all our philosophical powers have not yet succeeded in answering it. Even more difficult, however, is the question, how and why do I believe? It is a riddle to us, inasmuch as we cannot plumb the depths of our own heart or penetrate with our eyes the darkness that lies behind our consciousness. And to others it is an even greater mystery. Valid to ourselves as grounds for believing are all sorts of moods and emotions, considerations

---

3. A. Ritschl, *Theologie und Metaphysik* (Bonn: A. Marcus, 1881), 38.

and attitudes that accompany our faith and inseparably fasten to the object of our faith. But we cannot communicate them to others; they are not meant for disclosure and cannot be communicated. If we sometimes try to communicate them, they lose their power and value in the process, and we ourselves feel satisfied least of all. The end, frequently, is that what we put forward as a ground cannot stand the test and proves not to be a ground. Nevertheless, despite all the argumentation, faith maintains itself and says, "I cannot do otherwise, so help me, God."

[131] It is therefore not at all surprising that the grounds for religious and hence also for the Christian faith are cited in very different ways. To the question of how persons came to believe and why they believe, the answers are most divergent. Some think that people possess sufficient data within themselves and their own nature to recognize, assess, and accept a given religious view, revelation, or Scripture. The faculty for the evaluation and acceptance of revelation is variously identified. One of them is the intellect. In that case faith is based on historical apologetic grounds. Another is reason; in that case faith is constructed on the basis of speculative argumentation. In addition, conscience, the mind, or the heart can be considered the faculty for the perception or evaluation of the divine. In that case faith is based on religious experience or on practical ethical grounds. Whatever important element of truth these methods may contain and defend, they do not describe the deepest ground of faith and hence the true internal principle of theology. The following investigation will show that the grounds mentioned by each of these schools of belief are inadequate. But the inadequacy of the above methods can even be demonstrated a priori. In the first place, in the view that the intellect, the reason, the heart or the conscience must yield religious knowledge and certainty, people very easily overlook the distinction between the *source* and the *organ* of knowledge. All these functions of the human mind, which people describe with the terms "intellect" and "reason," "heart" and "conscience," are nowhere the sources but very specifically the *organs* of knowledge (except in those cases where these functions themselves are the object of study). They do not contribute content from within themselves but receive it from without, i.e., from perception (contemplation or observation), and concepts without observations are empty. Only after a given content has been obtained and accepted from without can these faculties or organs—each according to its own nature—proceed to work with it, derive concepts, opinions, and decisions from it or react to it by feelings and passions. People therefore evince a lack of psychological and epistemological sophistication when they claim to have arrived at religious knowledge and certainty simply by intellect, reason, heart, and conscience. Before these organs can appropriate the religious content in question, the question needs to be answered where this religious content comes from and by what organ a person has come into contact with it. In the second place, religion is a unique phenomenon, one that is essentially distinct from science, art, and morality.

And our earlier investigation of the essence of religion brought out that it can have, and in fact has, its source only in revelation. Religion presupposes and demands the existence, self-revelation, and knowability of God.

Inner Testimony of the Spirit

But if that is the case, if in virtue of its nature religion has its own external principle of knowledge (*principium cognoscendi externum*), then there also has to correspond to it a unique internal principle of knowledge (*principium cognoscendi internum*). Just as the eye answers to light, the ear to sound, the logos (reason) within us to the logos (rationality) outside of us, so there has to be in human beings a subjective organ that answers to the objective revelation of God. Eventually, all philosophers of religion are finally and willy-nilly brought to the recognition that human beings are by nature religious beings, that they are akin to God, and his image.

But we cannot stop here. We cannot stop at the position of this religious susceptibility of human beings in general. For in the first place, it never and nowhere occurs in a completely pure state and without content; always, from its initial awakening, it is rooted in a historical religion and is accommodated to it. And, second, revelation in Scripture assumes that humanity is also corrupted in its religious disposition and needs re-creation. It would therefore deny itself if it recognized the "unspiritual" person as its rightful judge. If Christianity is a religion of redemption in the full and true sense of the word and hence seeks to redeem human beings from all sin, from the errors of the mind as well as the impurity of the heart, as much from the death of the soul as from that of the body, it in the nature of the case cannot subject itself to the criticism of human beings but must subject them to its criticism. The revelation that comes to us in Christ through Scripture in fact takes that position toward us. It does not put itself on a level below us to ask for our approving or disapproving judgment on it but takes a position high above us and insists that we shall believe and obey. Scripture even expressly states that the unspiritual cannot understand the things of the Spirit, that they are folly to them, that they reject and deny them in a spirit of hostility [1 Cor. 2:14]. The revelation of God in Christ does not ask for the support or approval of human beings. It posits and maintains itself in sublime majesty. Its authority is normative as well as causative. It fights for its own victory. It itself conquers human hearts and makes itself irresistible.

Revelation, accordingly, now divides itself in two grand dispensations. When the economy of the Son, of objective revelation, is completed, that of the Spirit begins. God is the author also of this subjective revelation, in other words, of this illumination and regeneration. The action proceeds from him. He is the first and the last. People do not [of their own accord] come to revelation to seek God; God searches for them. He seeks them in the Son; he seeks them also in the Spirit. In the last days, after God spoke to us by the Son, the Holy Spirit came to take up the defense of Christ in the world, plead his cause, defend his Word, and incline the hearts of human beings to obedience. The Holy Spirit is the great and powerful witness to Christ, objectively in Scripture, subjectively in the very hearts of human beings. By that Spirit we receive a fitting organ for the reception of external revelation. God can be known only by God; the light can be seen only in his light. No one knows the Father except the Son and anyone to whom the Son chooses to reveal him [Matt. 11:27], and no one can say "Jesus is Lord" except by the Holy Spirit [1 Cor. 12:3]. God himself, therefore, is the principle of existence (*principium essendi*) of religion and theology. Objective revelation in Christ, recorded in Scripture, is its external source of knowledge (*principium cognoscendi externum*). And the Holy Spirit, who has been poured out in the church, regenerates and leads it into the truth, is the internal source of knowledge (*principia cognoscendi internum*). By this witness of the Holy Spirit, revelation is realized in humanity and reaches its goal. For it is God's good pleasure to re-create humankind in his likeness and after his image. Objective revelation, accordingly, is not enough; it must, as it were, prolong and complete itself in subjective revelation. Indeed, the former is the means; the latter the goal. The external principle is instrumental; the internal principle is the formal and primary principle.

For that reason the Christian church has at all times made confession of the testimony of the Holy Spirit. God is the author of external revelation, but it is also he who chooses the believing community, founds the church, and witnesses to Christ in it. Scripture is his word; the church community is his temple. To that extent there is agreement in the confession of all churches with respect to the testimony of the Holy Spirit. Not the "natural" (unspiritual) but the spiritual person knows the things given him or her by God (1 Cor. 2:12f.). But otherwise there is nevertheless a great deal of difference with respect to this testimony of the Holy Spirit, especially between the Roman Catholic Church and the churches of the Reformation. Indeed, according to Rome, Scripture has been given to the church, specifically to the church as institution and only through it to the believers. The church receives, preserves, authorizes, and interprets Holy Scripture. All God's revelation is mediated to believers through the institution of the church. The church always stands in between God and believers. The church is mediatrix, a means of grace, the external principle. *It* is the temple of the Holy Spirit. In Roman Catholicism the testimony of the Holy Spirit expresses itself solely through the church as institution, through the teaching church, the magisterium, the pope. According to the Reformation, revelation, Scripture, is indeed given to the church also, but to the church as organism, to the community of the faithful, to believers. *They* are the temple of the Holy Spirit. The testimony of the Holy Spirit is the property of all believers. Where two or three are gathered in Jesus' name, there he is in the midst. According to Rome, the institution is the essence of the church; according to the Reformation, it is a temporary means, but the essence of the church consists in the gathering of believers. *It* is the dwelling of God, the body of Christ, the temple of the Holy Spirit.

THE HISTORICAL-APOLOGETIC METHOD

[132] Inasmuch as the revelation of God in Christ is not naturally palatable to humanity, it has, from its earliest beginning, had to endure all sorts of attack and so continually saw itself called to self-defense. Apologetic is nothing new but as old as revelation itself. Israel as the people of God had to assert itself against all the enemies surrounding it. The pious had to resist the attacks of the ungodly. The prophets were frequently compelled to prove by word and deed the truth of their mission and message. When Christ came on earth, though not accepted by his own and not recognized by the world, he remained true to the good confession and appealed to the OT Scriptures, the witness of the Father, the words he spoke, and the works he performed. All his teaching and life were one ongoing witness and at the same time one powerful apologetic. After his departure, the apostles appeared on the scene to act as his witnesses and to prove his messiahship, his divine sonship, his death, and his resurrection. The Gospel of Matthew is an apologetic tract, which demonstrates over against the Jews that everything has been fulfilled in Christ. And all believers are admonished to give to any one an account of the hope that is in them and to confute those who contradict [the gospel] (1 Pet. 3:15; 2 Tim. 4:2; Titus 1:9). Paul writes that he has been put on earth for the defense of the gospel (Phil. 1:7, 16). Initially this defense bore a largely practical character (Luke 12:11; 21:14; Acts 22:1; 25:16; 1 Cor. 9:3; 2 Tim. 4:16), but gradually and imperceptibly it changed—in the NT already, e.g., 1 Cor. 15—into a more theoretical and scientific defense of Christianity or of a specific Christian doctrine. This transition occurred especially in the second century when, despite all persecution, Christianity expanded and began to attract the attention of the science of the day. The apologists, consequently, saw themselves obligated to reflect on the grounds on which the truth of Christianity rested and to give an account of it to its opponents. They wrote against the Jews[4] and against the Gentiles[5] and in their writings already advanced all the arguments that later, in a more elaborate and systematic form, were to serve consistently as a defense of Christianity.

True Philosophy; Practical Blessing

In the defense of Christian truth, the apologists do not start from a base of doubt or neutrality but from a position of firm belief and unshakable con-

4. Justin Martyr, *Dialogue with Trypho*; Tertullian, *Against the Jews*; Eusebius, *Demonstration of the Gospel*.

5. Justin Martyr, *Apology* (major and minor); Tatian, *Oration against the Greeks*; Athenagoras, Theophilus, *To Autolycus*; Origen, *Contra Celsus*; Tertullian, *Apology* and *To the Nations*; Arnobius, *Dispute against the Nations*; Minucius Felix, *Octavius*; Eusebius, *Preparation for the Gospel*; Athanasius, *Oration against the Nations*; Cyril, *The Arguments of the Emperor Julian against the Christians*; Augustine, *The City of God*.

viction. They face the enemy, not in dread and fear, but with a strong sense of spiritual superiority. Harnack has highlighted the high-minded and spirited self-consciousness, which in that early period sustained Christians in their struggle against Jewish and pagan science.

"We have been rescued from darkness and lifted into the light"—such was the chant that rose from a chorus of Christians during those early centuries. It was *intellectual truth and lucidity* in which they revelled and gloried. Polytheism seemed to them an oppressive night; now that it was lifted off them, the sun shone clearly in the sky! Wherever they looked, everything became clear and sure in the light of spiritual monotheism, owing to the living God. . . . They gaze at Nature, only to rejoice in the order and unity of its movement; heaven and earth are a witness to them of God's omnipotence and unity. They ponder the capacities and endowments of human nature, and trace in them the Creator. In human reason and liberty they extol his boundless goodness; they compare the revelations and the will of God with this reason and freedom, and lo, there is entire harmony between them! Nothing is laid on man which does not already lie within him, nothing is revealed which is not already presupposed in his inward being. The long-buried religion of nature, religion μετὰ λόγου, has been rediscovered. They look at Christ, and scales fall, as it were, from their eyes! What wrought in him was the Logos, the very Logos by which the world had been created and with which the spiritual essence of man was bound up inextricably, the Logos which had wrought throughout human history in all that was noble and good, and which was finally obliged to reveal its power completely in order to dissipate the obstacles and disorders by which man was beset—so weak was he, for all the glory of his creation. Lastly, they contemplate the course of history, its beginning, middle, and end, only to find a common purpose everywhere, which is in harmony with a glorious origin and with a still more glorious conclusion. The freedom of the creature, overcome by the allurements of demons, has occasioned disorders, but the disorders are to be gradually removed by the power of the Christ-Logos. At the commencement of history humanity was like a child, full of good and divine instincts, but as yet untried and liable to temptation; at the close, a perfected humanity will stand forth, fitted to enter immortality. Reason, freedom, immortality—these are to carry the day against error, failure, and decay.

Such was the Christianity of many people, a bright and glad affair, the doctrine of pure reason. The new doctrine proved a deliverance, not an encumbrance, to the understanding. Instead of imposing foreign matter on the understanding, it threw light upon its own darkened contents. *Christianity is a divine revelation, but it is at the same time pure reason; it is the true philosophy.*[6]

And just as they knew that in Christ they possessed the true philosophy, so they were also convinced that the church of Christ was the true humanity,

6. A. von Harnack, *The Mission and Expansion of Christianity in the First Three Centuries,* trans. James Moffat (London: Williams and Northgate, 1908; reprinted, New York: Harper Torchbooks, 1961), 225–26.

the true Israel, the original people and at the same time the people of the future for whom the world was created and destined.

In this mind-set the apologists dealt with the attackers of Christianity. The odd time we encounter "the argument from the safer to the less safe" (*argumentum a tutiori*), which presents it as safer, of two uncertain things, to believe that "which would bring certain hope rather than that which would bring no hopes at all."[7] But they had much better arguments at their disposal. These arose, first of all, from the comparison of Christianity with the religious and philosophical systems in paganism. This religion-historical comparison, on the one hand, brought to light the agreement and, on the other, the difference between them. Also in the pagan world there was much that is true and good and beautiful. The "seeds of truth" present there, however, are traceable to the Logos, who created the world, enlightens every human being coming into the world, and in Christ became flesh. Or they originate in the special revelation that from ancient times on was given by God to humankind and later to the people of Israel, and filtered through to or has been preserved to some degree also among other peoples. All that still exists in the way of true religion, true doctrine, or pure morality among pagans, specifically in Greek philosophy, is derived from revelation and therefore actually belongs to Christianity. Christianity, accordingly, does not first begin in the days of the apostles but was germinally present from the beginning in [divine] revelation. It is as old as the world and therefore receives testimony from all the true and the good that is found in the religions and philosophical systems of paganism, in fact even from every human soul. "The soul is naturally Christian."

Yet this agreement does not cancel out the enormous difference in substance that exists between Christianity and the other religions. Comparative research reveals a series of differences, which demonstrate the superior excellence of Christianity over all [other] religions and can therefore serve as so many proofs for its truth. Belonging to these internal criteria are the knowledge of the one true God who has been revealed only in Christianity, the complete redemption from sin and death, which has been won and is given by Christ, and the hope of eternal life, which has been brought to light by the resurrection of Christ. Also included are the holy character and life of the prophets and apostles and above all of Christ himself. Finally, it includes the antiquity and unity, the sublimity and simplicity, the riches and many-sidedness of Holy Scripture, which as a second book has been added by God to the first book (nature) and is in complete harmony with it, the predictions along with their fulfillment and the miracles, which lift the truth of Christian doctrine above all doubt.

Added to these internal criteria, finally, came the external ones: the witness of the church in its rule of faith, and tradition; the miracles, especially

7. Arnobius, *Dispute against the Nations*, II, 4.

the miracles of healing, which still regularly occur; the tenacity and perseverance of the martyrs; the holiness of Christian ascetics; and above all else the countless rich blessings conferred through Christianity upon the family, society, and the state. Christianity, moreover, warred against the horrible sins of idolatry, the deification of human beings, superstition, magic, astrology, lies, dishonesty, greed, fornication, adultery, abortion, etc. In place of these vices, Christianity fostered the virtues of brotherly love, hospitality, generosity, the care of widows and orphans, the poor and the sick, prisoners and slaves, the persecuted and the dead. Christianity was a blessing to the state, conducive to the prosperity of the empire, a benefaction to all humanity. These, in the main, were the arguments the apologists advanced in support of the truth of the Christian religion. These arguments were not without cogency, because they arose from the full assurance of faith and found support in the practice of the Christian life.

Roman Catholic Apologetics

[133] All these arguments were later taken over in Christian theology but in the process frequently changed in position and character. Scholasticism, though based on faith, in its attempt to turn the truth of faith into the content of reason, in time created a division between natural and supernatural truths, a division that had a detrimental effect on both. For the former could be established by reason, but the latter could only be accepted on authority. In the former, therefore, real science was possible; in the latter there was room only for faith. So the process became as follows: first, the validity of "natural truths" was asserted on scientific grounds; second, the possibility, necessity, and reality of special revelation to reason was brought out; finally, since the rationality of believing had been established, on the basis of the external fact of revelation, an urgent appeal was now made to reason to blindly accept revelation's content in faith. Hence from the forecourt of strictly demonstrable truths, people proceeded through the holy place of rational proofs for a special revelation, into the inner sanctum of absolute supernatural mysteries. The motives that could be adduced for belief in a special revelation were summarized under the term "inductive reasons" or "motivations toward belief" (*motiva credibilitatis*).[8]

After the Reformation, mainly the argument derived from the church was further developed. In Catholic doctrine, the church increasingly became the foundation and rule of faith. Augustine had already said that it was the church that moved him to believe in Scripture. After the Reformation, Catholics made the church the most compelling ground for belief in Scripture or revelation.[9] The "motivations toward belief" were often split up into

8. Thomas Aquinas, *Summa Theol.*, II, 2, qu. 2, art. 9, ad 3; art. 10; Duns Scotus, *Prol. Sentent.*, qu. 2; Ludovices Vives, *De Veritate fidei Christi* (1543); Cf. Frohschammer, *Die Philosophie des Thomas von Aquino* (Leipzig: F. A. Brockhaus, 1889), 130ff.

9. Becanus, *Theol. Schol. Tom.*, II, part II, tract. 1, chap. 6 (Mogunt, 1623), 93.

three categories: those which apply to Jews and pagans; those which were especially meaningful to Catholics themselves; and those which are valid in the controversy with heretics. Now to this last group belongs especially the church with its fifteen marks, as Bellarmine listed them.[10] What the Reformers said of the Bible was now applied to the church. The church is like the sun, which emits its rays and can easily be known by its own light. Among the proofs for revelation, the church now occupies the primary position; of all the motivations for believing the church is the most compelling. The Vatican Council [I] session III, chap. 3, "On Faith," declared: "For the Catholic Church alone possesses all those numerous and wonderful signs that are divinely arranged to make clear the credibility of the Christian faith. Indeed, the Church by herself is a great and perpetual motive of credibility, and an irrefutable witness of her divine mission, because of her astonishing expansion, her extraordinary holiness, her unexhausted fruitfulness in all that is good, her Catholic unity, and her unconquered stability." The value of all these proofs, also that of the church, consists in the fact that they can demonstrate the credibility of revelation. They are able to bring about a "human faith" (*humana fides*) and prove the rationality of believing. They clarify the truth of revelation to such a degree and to such a high level that all rational doubt is excluded.

[Thus, according to Rome,] if on the part of human beings no sinful selfishness and no inner hostility came into play, these motives would be compelling enough to move them to belief in revelation. While they do not make revelation manifestly true (for, if that were the case, faith would no longer be necessary and would lack all merit), they *are* manifestly credible.[11] Catholic theologians, accordingly, usually incorporate all these apologetic arguments in their dogmatics and treat them at great length.[12] Some even went so far as to say that they considered all these proofs sufficient also for the unbeliever.[13] But the majority acknowledged that all these proofs were only motives and did not constitute the final and deepest ground of faith. That could only be the authority of God.[14] And that belief in revelation on the basis of divine authority is not affected by these proofs but by a form of divine assistance, an interior drive, which moves the will toward believing.[15] The Vatican Council

10. Bellarmine, "De Conciliis et Ecclesia," *Controversiis*, I, IV.

11. Aquinas, *Summa Theol.*, II, 2, qu. 1, art. 4, ad 2, 4; art. 5, ad 2, qu. 2, art. 1, ad 1. Bellarmine, "De Conciliis et Ecclesia," IV, 3. Billuart, *Summa Sanctae Thomae hodiernis acad. moribus accommodata*, VIII, 25ff. P. Dens, *Theologia ad usum. seminariorum*, 7 vols. (Mechlinae: P. J Hanicq, 1819) II, 275ff.

12. Perrone, *Prael. Theol.*, I; Jansen, *Prael. Theol.*, I, 117ff.; Hake, *Handbuch der allgemeine Religionswissenschaft* (Freiburg i.B.: Herder, 1875–87), II, 1ff.; H. Heinrich, *Dogmatik*, I, 279ff.; Liebermann, *Dogmatik*, I, 33ff.

13. Billuart, *Summa Sanctae Thomae*, I, 28, 29; P. Dens, *Theologia*, II, 292.

14. Aquinas, *Summa Theol.*, II, 2, qu. 2, art. 1, ad 3; art. 10; idem, *Summa contra Gentiles*, I, 9; Billuart, *Summa Santae Thomae*, VIII, 1ff.; Becanus, *Theol. Schol. Thom.*, II, II, tract. 1, chap. 6, 1–37; P. Dens, *Theologia*, II, 280ff.; Jansen, *Prael. Theol.*, I, 701–6.

15. Aquinas, *Summa Theol.*, II, 1, qu. 109 art. 6; qu. 112, art. 2 and 3; qu. 113, art. 4.

[I] session III, chap. 3, "On Faith," similarly recognized, on the one hand, that faith was a "supernatural virtue by which, with the inspiration and help of God's grace, we believe that what He has revealed is true, not because its intrinsic truth is perceived by the natural light of reason, but because of the authority of God who reveals." On the other hand, attaching great value to the apologetic arguments, it immediately added: "Nevertheless, in order that the submission of our faith be conformed to reason, God willed that, joined to internal helps of the Holy Spirit, there be external proofs of His revelation, which . . . are most reliable signs of revelation, and adapted to the intelligence of all men." In canon III, 3 it even anathematized the person who says "that divine revelation cannot be made credible by external signs; and that, as a result, men should be moved to faith only by the internal experience of each individual, or by private inspiration."

This appreciation for apologetics, in the theology of Rome, is integral to the system. Supernatural revelation is erected on the basis of natural revelation. The former is only attained successively and by degrees. In the things that are purely natural a person first, by means of proofs, arrives at natural theology. This is the "preamble of faith." Here science is even possible. The proofs are compelling. At this point we are not yet speaking of faith. Now a person who has come this far and stands on the foundation of natural theology can, by the "motivations toward belief," especially by the signs and marks of the church, perceive the credibility of revelation and acknowledge the rationality of believing. And when thus a *fides humana* ("the natural human capacity to hold convictions concerning things")[16] has been obtained and this person has prepared himself or herself by "preparatory actions," he or she is incorporated in the supernatural order by "infused grace" itself and again prepares himself or herself by good works for heaven, i.e., for the vision of God. From the state of nature, a person proceeds upward by degrees. Each time he or she rises higher by one degree. The "purely natural things," "natural theology," "motivations toward belief," "preparatory acts," "infused grace," "good works," and "the vision of God" form the different steps of the ladder, which, while it stands on earth, reaches into heaven.

Protestant Rationalism

Now, in principle, the Reformation opposed this hierarchy of Rome and took a different stance. It took its position, not in natural reason in order by successive steps to lead it to the level of faith, but in the Christian faith. And it affirmed as decisively as possible (as we will show later) that that faith depended only on divine authority and was effected only by the Holy Spirit. But Protestant theologians, it must be admitted, have not always rigorously adhered to this principle and have repeatedly returned to the theory of natural theology and of the historical proofs for the truth of revelation. Calvin says that he would find it easy to

16. Richard A. Muller, *Dictionary of Latin and Greek Theological Terms* (Grand Rapids: Baker, 1985), 116.

prove the divinity of Holy Scripture and cites various grounds for it.[17] So also many other theologians speak and act.[18] The conviction that these proofs are sufficient to bring about at least a "human faith" has involuntarily contributed to the emancipation of reason from faith and to placing the dogmas of natural theology and of Holy Scripture outside of saving faith.

With that tendency, accordingly, rationalism achieved a foothold in Protestant churches. Socinianism rejected the testimony of the Holy Spirit and based the truth of Christianity on historical proofs.[19] Remonstrantism pursued the same path.[20] Through Descartes rationalism also penetrated the Reformed churches. Natural theology gradually assumed a place of independence alongside of revealed theology. And, within the latter, reason was granted the right to examine and explain the credentials of revelation. Leibnitz voiced a prevailing sentiment when he positioned revelation before reason, as an envoy extraordinary stands before a qualified audience. The latter examines the envoy's credentials and, when they have been found in order, begins respectfully to listen to him.[21] Deism in England and rationalism in Germany soon drew the conclusion that natural theology was completely adequate. And the supernaturalism that conceded the emancipation of reason in natural theology and in the inquiry into the truth of revelation could appear before that reason with nothing other than historical and natural proofs. Christianity was defended and dogmatics was practiced in that fashion by a number of men in England, Germany, the Netherlands. Examples: Butler, Paley, Chalmers;[22] Reinhard, Morus, Doederlein, Knapp, Storr (et al.); van Nuys Klinkenberg, Muntinghe, Heringa, Vinke (etc.), and by the authors of the works of the Hague Society. Later we still find this position adopted by Pareau and Hofstede de Groot;[23] by Van Oosterzee, who first

17. J. Calvin, *Institutes*, I.vii.4, 8.

18. Z. Ursinus, *Tract. Theol.*, 1–33; J. Zanchi, *Op. Theol.*, col. 335ff.; A. Polanus, *Syn. Theol.* I, 17ff., 27, 28. *Synopsis Purioris Theologiae*, disp. 2, 10ff.; Du Plessis-Mornay, *Traité de la vérité de la religion Chrétienne contre les Athees* (Anvers: C. Plantin 1581); J. Abbadie, *Traité de la vérité de la religion Chrétienne* (1684); cf. Heppe, *Dogmatik der evangelisch-reformierte Kirche* (Elberseld: R. L. Friedrich, 1861), 20–22; Ed. note: English translation: *Reformed Dogmatics*, trans. Ernst Bizer (London: Allen & Unwin, 1950). Hase, *Hutt. Rediv.* §37; H. Schmid, *Doctrinal Theology of the Evangelical Lutheran Church*, trans. Charles A. Hay and Henry E. Jacobs (Philadelphia: United Lutheran Publication House, 1899), 57ff.

19. *Racovian Catechism*, qu. 530, O. Fock, *Der Socinianismus* (Kiel: C. Schröder, 1847), 338ff.

20. S. Episcopius, *Instit. Theol.*, IV, 2; P. van Limborch, *Theol. Christ.*, I, 4; idem, *De Veritate relig. Christ. collatio cum erudito Judaeo* (Govdae: J. ab Hoeve, 1687); Hugo Grotius, *De Veritate religio Christ.* (1627); Wijnmalen, *Hugo de Groot als Verdediger van beet Christendom* (Utrecht: W. F. Dannenfelser, 1869).

21. *Leibniz, *Discourse sur la conformité de la foi avec raison*, §29.

22. Butler, *The Analogy of Religion, Natural and Revealed*, 2d ed. (London: Knapton, 1736); W. Paley, *View of the Evidences of Christianity* (London: Religious Tract Society, 1794); idem, *Natural Theology* (Philadelphia: H. Maxwell, 1802); Chalmers, *The Evidence and Authority of the Christian Revelation* (Philadelphia: Anthony Finley, 1817); idem, *Natural Theology* (London: Printed for T. and J. Allman, 1823); Cf. Tholuck, *Vermischte Schriften*, 2 vols. (Hamburg: F. Perthes, 1839), I, 163–224.

23. *Compendium Dogmatique et Apologetique Chretiénne* (1848), 179ff.

followed Schleiermacher but later sought refuge in an apologetics that preceded dogmatics;[24] by Doedes, who wanted to acquaint himself with Christianity by way of unbiased, purely historical investigation;[25] in countries abroad, by Voigt, König, A. B. Bruce, Pheeters, Gretillat,[26] and numerous apologetic authors.[27] To be counted as members of this school of thought in very recent times are the advocates of the history-of-religions method, such as Troeltsch, and the defenders of a complete split between a believing-ecclesiastical theology and an exact-scientific study of religion, such as Lagarde, Overbeck, and others.[28] For they too emancipate theology, in whole or in part, from faith and attempt to gain knowledge of Christianity by way of objective, historical-critical research.

[134] This historical-apologetic method has been proven untenable by the history of supernaturalism itself and further also by the sharp criticism of Rousseau and Lessing, Kant and Schleiermacher. In this connection, however, we must clearly distinguish between the error, which—in that method—collapsed under the impact of criticism, and the truth, which inheres in it and which must be preserved even now. Apologetics at all times had a right to exist and still has that right today. In fact, today its task is more important than ever before. It must maintain and defend the truth of God in the face of all—internal as well as external—opposition. Prophets and apostles and Christ himself modeled this approach, ever and again defending themselves against their accusers. Furthermore, Scripture imposes on all believers the duty, with gentleness and fear but also with willing hearts, to give to anyone an account of the essence and ground of the hope that is in them and to confute all those who contradict the gospel (1 Pet. 3:15; Titus 1:9). The apologists of the second century, the church fathers, the scholastics, the Reformers (etc.), all held the firm belief that the truth of God had to be defended against the opposition to which they were exposed on all sides. They did not leave the attacks unanswered nor did they proceed to the defense with reluctance and hesitation. Rather, they were profoundly convinced that the truth was on their side and that it was capable of defense;

24. J. J. van Oosterzee, *Jaarboeken van Wetenschappelijke Theologie* (1845): 174; (1851): 406; J. J. van Oosterzee, *De Leer der Hervormde Kerk van J. H. Scholten Beschouwd* (1851), 51, 53; idem, *Christian Dogmatics*, trans. J. Watson and M. Evans, 2 vols. (New York: Scribner, Armstrong, 1874), §30, §34, §38.

25. Doedes, *Het Regt des Christendoms tegenouer de Wijsbegeerte Gehandhaafd* (Utrecht: Kemink en Zoon, 1847); idem, *Modern of Apostolisch Christendom* (Utrecht: Kemink, 1860); idem, *De Zoogenaamde Moderne Theologie Eenigszins Toegelicht* (Utrecht: Kemink, 1861). Ed. note: Bavinck cites the publication date as 1862.

26. Voigt, *Fundamentaldogmatik* (Gotha: F. A. Perthes, 1874), 184ff., 232ff.; König, *Der Glaubensact des Christen* (Erlangen & Leipzig: Georg Böhme, 1891), 143ff.; Bruce, *Apologetics* (Edinburgh: T. & T. Clark, 1892), 42; W. M. McPheeters, "Test of Canonicity, Apostolic Authorship and Sanction," *Presbyterian and Reformed Review* 6 (January 1895): 26; Grétillat, *Exposé de théol. System*, 4 vols. (Paris: Librairie Fischbacher, 1885–92), II, 176ff.

27. Cf. L. Lemme, "Apologetik, Apologie," *PRE³*, I, 679–98.

28. See above, pp. 49, 70–76, 170–74.

they attached great value to the arguments they put forward and therefore sought out the enemy, not resting until they had vanquished him. That belief itself was a great strength and practically half the victory. Doubt and distrust in the cause we champion renders us powerless in the battle.

A Valid Apologetic

In saying this, however, we have already indicated the position from which alone a sound defense of the truth can be undertaken. Apologetics cannot precede faith and does not attempt a priori to argue the truth of revelation. It assumes the truth and belief in the truth. It does not, as the introductory part or as the foundational science, precede theology and dogmatics. It is itself a theological science through and through, which presupposes the faith and dogmatics and now maintains and defends the dogma against the opposition to which it is exposed. Thus understood, apologetics is not only perfectly justified but a science that at all times, but especially in this century, deserves to be seriously practiced and can spread rich blessing all around. First of all, it has the immediate advantage of forcing Christian theology to take deliberate account of the grounds on which it is based, of the principles on which it is constructed, and of the content it has within itself. It brings Christian theology out of the shadows of the mysticism of the human heart into the full light of day. Apologetics, after all, was the first Christian science. Secondly, it teaches that Christians, even though they cannot confer faith on anyone, need not hide from their opponents in embarrassed silence. With their faith they do not stand as isolated aliens in the midst of the world but find support for it in nature and history, in science and art, in society and state, in the heart and conscience of every human being. The Christian worldview alone is one that fits the reality of the world and of life. And finally, if it seriously and scrupulously performs its task, it will very definitely succeed in impressing opponents with the truth of Christian revelation, refuting and silencing them. It cannot truly convert people to God. Not even the preaching of the gospel is able to do that; only God, by his Spirit, can accomplish that. But subject to this working of God and as a means in his hand, apologetics, like the ministry of the Word, can be a source of consummate blessing. For this fact the early centuries of Christianity offer abundant evidence.

Apologetics as it has often been practiced was mistaken, however, in that (1) it detached itself from the Christian faith and thus put itself outside of, above, and before theology; (2) it so separated believing from knowing that religious truth came to rest in part (in natural theology, in exegetical and historical theology, etc.) or in toto, on purely intellectual proofs; and (3) that, as a result, it began to foster exaggerated expectations from its scientific labor as though by the intellect it could change the human heart and by reasoning engender piety.

Against this mistaken direction in apologetics, the criticism of Kant and Schleiermacher was appropriate. For, in the first place, inherent in this approach was a denial of the essence of religion, objectively of the character and content of religious truth, subjectively of religious faith. Religion is something other than the acceptance, on rational grounds, of a merely theoretical doctrine. Just as religious truth is essentially different from some scientific theorem or other, so there is an essential distinction between an intellectual insight into a scientific result and the faith with which I embrace religious truth. Second, this mistaken apologetic trend proceeded from a denial of Christianity. If Christian revelation, which presupposes the darkness and error of unspiritual humanity, submitted in advance to the judgments of reason, it would by that token contradict itself. It would thereby place itself before a tribunal whose jurisdiction it had first denied. And having once recognized the authority of reason on the level of first principles, it could no longer oppose that authority in the articles of faith. Dualistic supernaturalism always has to lead to rationalism, inasmuch it is rationalistic in principle. In the third place, regardless of this principal objection, historical-apologetic argumentation in the sense described above also fails to lead to the desired and expected result. It could still travel some distance at a time when the authenticity of the books of the Bible and the historical truth of their content were quite generally accepted. But today the miracles and predictions of Scripture are themselves so much in need of defense that they could hardly any longer serve as arguments. In order to prove anything, apologetics would first have to treat the entire field of introductory Bible science and incorporate into itself any number of other disciplines before it could make a start with the exposition of truth. In that way it would never get to the faith, to dogmatics proper, and the formal part would expand to such an extent that neither time or space would be left for the material part.

Now, such a long road would perhaps still be traversable by someone who had enough time and energy and talent to undertake an investigation into the truth of the Christian faith. But it would be totally inaccessible to the simple person who—certainly as much as the scholar and not just tomorrow but now at this very moment—needs the peace and consolation of the faith and who for that reason would become dependent for the salvation of his or her soul on an intellectual—and hence all the more intolerable—clericalism. Even if this were not an insurmountable objection and that for all people historical study were the only road to the knowledge of the truth, then the result that could be achieved even under the most favorable circumstances would still be no more than a human faith (*fides humana*), which could be shaken and overthrown the next day by other and better studies. Certainly, eternity cannot hang from a spider web. In religion no human being and no creature can stand between God and my soul. To live and die in the comfort and blessing of salvation is not possible so long as I must rest on fallible human testimony. In religion we need not less but much stronger and firmer certainty than in science. Peace can be found only in the witness of God.

In addition, the witness of the church is also insufficient. Certainly it is of great value at the origin and also for the continuation of Christian faith. It remains a support to the very end of life and is indeed a permanent motivation toward belief. Throughout our life we are bound to a community and that community upholds us each time we threaten to stumble and fall. The cloud of witnesses that surrounds us cheers us on in the struggle. It takes exceptional courage and spiritual vitality to remain absolutely firm when everyone else abandons and opposes us. Still, for all this, the witness of the church cannot be the ultimate ground of faith. As we will see later, also Catholic theologians recognize this truth. Even with their infallible church, in studying the grounds for believing, they are absolutely in no better position than Protestants. For they too have to pose the question: on what grounds does faith in the church rest? If it rests on apologetic grounds, they face the same objections we advanced a moment ago. If it rests on the testimony of the Holy Spirit, then, also for them, this teaching is the cornerstone of the Christian faith.

THE SPECULATIVE METHOD

Triumph of Reason: Hegel

[135] Supernaturalism succumbed under the blows of Rousseau and Kant, Lessing and Schleiermacher, and a mighty reversal followed. In every area classicism yielded to romanticism, the dominance and autonomy of the subject. In its early period, in connection with the sense of freedom, this reaction was so extreme that it obliterated the objective [world] and considered the subject sufficient to itself. The subject produces, if not the matter (Fichte), then certainly the form (Kant) of the world. The non-ego is a product of the ego; the moral world order comes into being by the agency of human beings themselves; and the moral law is freely and royally set aside by genius. Schleiermacher, too, initially adopted this position. But this absolute idealism led to various appalling results. The French Revolution demonstrated the dangerous potential of this human autonomy. Certainly something had to be objective, something that was firm and had authority. Thus arose the Restoration, i.e., the attempt, while preserving the same starting point, still to arrive at objectivity from within the subject. The philosophical interpreter of that restoration was Hegel. He raised the subjective ethical idealism of Fichte to the level of an objective logical idealism and replaced the idea of being by that of becoming. The universe became a process, a development of the logical idea. In this evolution religion also had its place.

In this view religion cloaks itself in forms and symbols, which in their deep significance can only be understood by speculative reason. Rationalism did not grasp this at all and simply set aside the dogmas of the church, not knowing what to do with them. But, [so it is argued] those dogmas are full of profound philosophical meaning. Hegel's intellect threw itself upon these dogmas, stripped them of their historic symbolic forms, and tracked down the idea underlying them. History is but the shell, the wrapping; the core itself is deep and true philosophy. Not the rationalistic doctrines of God, virtue, and morality, but the most sublime and profound Christian dogmas, such as the Trinity, the incarnation, vicarious atonement, now became the object of bold philosophical speculation. Quite aside from Scripture and any other authority, these dogmas were deduced from reason as reason's own necessary implications and proven to be utterly rational. Ostensibly theology and philosophy were reconciled; faith was transformed by speculative reason into absolute knowledge. A number of men, adopting this speculative method, applied it to dogmatics, though with very different results. Included among them were Daub, Marheineke, Strausz, Feuerbach, Vatke, Weisse, and last of all Biedermann. Biedermann at important points diverges from Hegel and does not accept his aprioristic method. Proceeding from the Christian dogmas, he nevertheless still attempts, in the Hegelian manner, to dissect them into the religious principle underlying them and the historic form they have assumed, and then to speculatively and practically develop them further. In this process he was guided by the idea that metaphysics is a possibility (viz., knowledge of the final grounds of being and knowing) and achievable by strictly logical reasoning from experience. By that method he arrives at abstract logical determinations concerning the fundamental reality of the world and believes that in them he possesses genuine knowledge of the absolute, which constitutes the core of religious truth. The difference is only that the believer possesses that truth in visual representations, whereas the dogmatician and philosopher have converted it into concepts and ideas.[29]

In a similar way, in our own country, Scholten separated the fundamental principles from the doctrines of Reformed theology, criticized the latter to death by means of the former, and was finally left with nothing but a monistic deterministic system. This intellectualistic trend is continued among modernist theologians by Dr. Bruining.[30] Bruining rejects the method of experience in its various forms on the following grounds: (1) Religion presupposes the idea of God; (2) it implies a relation to God; and (3) consists in a complex of emotions (etc.), which develops in human beings under the influence of a certain kind of belief. He believes, however, that

---

29. On Biedermann, see R. A. Lipsius, "Neue Beiträge zur wissenschaftliche Grundlegung der Dogmatik," *Jahrbuch für Protestantische Theologie* 11 (1885): 177ff.; Kaftan, *Zur Dogmatik*, 139ff.; Max Henning, *A. E. Biedermanns Theorie der religiöse erkenntnis* (Leipzig: Druck von J. B. Hirschfeld, 1902); Urban Fleisch, *Die erkenntniss theoretische und metaphysische Grundlagen der dogmatische Systeme von A. E. Biedermann und R. A. Lipsius* (Berlin: Schwetske & Sohn, 1901); E. Böhl, *Dogmatik* (Amsterdam: Scheffer, 1887), L.

30. Bruining, "Over de Methode van Onze Dogmatiek," *Teylers Theologische Tijdschrift* (1903): 153ff., 306ff., 426ff.; idem, "Pantheisme of Theïsme," *Teylers Theologische Tijdschrift* (1904): 433ff.

the only path a dogmatician can pursue is one in which, by reasoning from the phenomena with which experience acquaints him, he attempts to ascend to the supersensible ground behind those phenomena. Accordingly, he tries to restore to a position of honor the proofs for the existence of God and the immortality of the soul, for, although these arguments are not strictly compelling, they can definitely serve as a reliable basis for our religious convictions. This is all the more so because also in the other sciences only a very slim part of our knowledge is based on exact proofs. Along with Biederman and Scholten, therefore, Bruining is committed to the speculative method, but differs from them in two respects. In the first place, he does not base that speculation on an aprioristic principle but on experience, meaning, not on a few isolated phenomena, nor only on inner experience, but on consideration of the world in its totality. In that way he believes he can do more justice, for example, to the theistic concept of God and to the fact of sin. In the second place, he would rather no longer link up with the earlier dogmatics in order to then subject it to continual criticism, but prefers a constructive approach, viz., to build a dogmatics on a faith position of his own.

Religious Experience and Mediating Theology

This speculative method also found acceptance in the school of Schleiermacher. Schleiermacher shared the subjective starting point with Hegel but took his position, not in reason, but in feeling. Religion to him is a peculiar configuration of feeling and immediate self-consciousness. He further conceived that feeling, not individually but historically, as it exists in a religious community and has been specifically formed by Jesus as Savior in the Christian church. Finally, he regarded dogmatics, not as a speculative development, but solely as a description of pious states of mind or of the faith of the church. In theory Schleiermacher opposed all forms of mingling theology and philosophy. On the other hand, Schleiermacher's doctrine of faith (*Glaubenslehre*) shows that his own religious experience very markedly diverged from that of the Christian church and had certainly been formed in part under Spinoza's influence. And in his *Brief Outline* he gave a position of priority to philosophical theology, which was assigned the task of determining the essence of Christianity. Actually, in Schleiermacher, theology became totally dependent on philosophy.[31]

Mediating theology[32] (*Vermittelungstheologie*), with Schleiermacher, took its stance in the consciousness, the faith, the confession of the church, but linked with it the speculative method of Hegel in order thus to elevate faith to the level of knowledge and to force authority to yield to independent rational insight. It is Twesten's aim, by means of reasoning from the pious con-

---

31. F. Schleiermacher, *Brief Outline on the Study of Theology*, trans. Terrence N. Tice (Richmond, Va.: John Knox Press, 1966), §24, §32; cf. idem, *Christian Faith*, §2ff.; see also above, pp. 47–49.

32. Ed. note: see above, p. 49 n. 49.

sciousness, to deduce an orthodox Lutheran dogmatics.[33] Müller—by a regressive method of reflecting on his own experience—seeks to move from the certainty of faith to an objective knowledge of God.[34] Martensen assigns to the regenerate consciousness the task of scientifically reproducing, from within its own depths, the doctrine of Scripture and the church.[35] In Dorner the doctrine of faith (*Glaubenslehre*) is not merely descriptive but also constructive and progressive; it carries out the systematic grounding and development of religious knowledge. Dorner attempts to show that the Christian idea of God is logically necessary by demonstrating that it is the augmentation and completion of the concept of God in general.[36] Especially in Rothe the speculative method of mediation theology stands out sharply: God-consciousness is the idea from which, by means of the Hegelian dialectic, he infers all of creation, nature, history, sin, and redemption.[37] There is great diversity in the mediating theology movement, but its theologians all have a starting point and method in common. They do not base themselves on some sort of authority but on the Christian consciousness of the church and seek proof for the truth of faith, not in an appeal to one authority or another, but in its self-evident inner nature, in its cognitive necessity.

Critique of the Speculative Method

[136] This speculative method has certain important advantages over the apologetic method of the rationalistic era. The lucidity that was held to be the criterion of truth in the eighteenth century had transformed revelation into "doctrine," the church into a school, regeneration into moral amendment, the crucified Christ into the sage of Nazareth. Rationalism falsified the whole Christian religion. People of culture turned away from revelation and religion, from church and faith, with contempt. It took real courage to go back to the church and its dogmas, as Schleiermacher and Hegel did, and to discover there, be it only in a certain sense, deep religious truth. It was a manifestation of moral strength to break with the rationalistic demand for lucidity, to take up the cudgels for the despised religion of the church and again to assert the validity and value of the Christian faith. Even more, inherent in He-

33. Twesten, *Vorlesungen über die Dogmatik,* 2d ed., 2 vols. (Hamburg: F. Perth, 1829–37), I, 21ff.

34. Müller, *Dogmatische Abhandlungen* (Bremen: C. E. Müller, 1870), 142; J. Köstlin, "Dogmatik," *PRE¹*, IV, 733–52.

35. H. L. Martensen, *Christian Dogmatics: A Compendium of the Doctrines of Christianity,* trans. William Urwick (Edinburgh: T. & T. Clark, 1871), §31ff.

36. I. A. Dorner, *A System of Christian Doctrine,* trans. Alfred Cave and J. S. Banks, 4 vols. (Edinburgh: T. & T. Clark, 1888), I, 168.

37. R. Rothe, *Theologische Ethik,* 2d rev. ed., 5 vols. (Wittenberg: Zimmerman, 1869–71), §7; cf. Hauck, "Rothe," *PRE²*, XVII, 653–62; and Sieffert, "Richard Rothe," *PRE²*, XVII, 169–78; as well as the abundant literature that appeared in 1899 in honor of his birthday, January 28, 1899. Inter alia: H. J. Holtzmann, *Rothe's Speculatives System* (Freiburg i.B.: J. C. B. Mohr, 1899) (ed. note: Bavinck cites the publication date as 1898); O. Flügel, *R. Rothe als speculativer Theologe* (Langensalza, 1898); W. Flade, *Die philosophischen Grundlagen der Theologie R. Rothe's* (Leipzig: Reudnitz, August Hoffman, 1901).

gel's and Schleiermacher's starting point, there was a splendid truth. Thinking and being are most intimately related and correspond to each other. Rationalism attempts to justify religion before the unqualified court of common sense. But Hegel and Schleiermacher both understood that religion occupies a place of its own in human life, that it is a unique phenomenon and therefore also requires a uniquely appropriate organ in human nature. Hegel and Schleiermacher differed in their designation of that organ, one locating it in reason, the other in feeling. But both rose above the vulgar rationalism of the day, and both pointed to the harmony between subject and object. If that was all they intended, with their subjective starting point, their victory over rationalism would have deserved only agreement. The objective [world], after all, exists for us only to the extent that it comes to our consciousness. It can be approached in no other way than through our consciousness. Similarly, religion is not a reality for me except insofar as I have absorbed it in feeling or reason, or whatever its organ may be.

But Hegel and Schleiermacher were not content with the thesis that thinking and being correspond to each other; they equated the two. This equation of thinking and being is the basic error of speculative philosophy. Plato already proceeded from this philosophy when he held ideas to be the real world. Descartes took it over in his "I think, therefore I am" philosophy. Spinoza, thinking along the same lines, spoke of "a rational principle of its own whose essence involves existence," a view that Fichte brought to dominance in modern philosophy. The crucial question in this connection is this: Do we think a thing because it exists or does a thing exist because we necessarily and logically have to think it? Speculative philosophy affirmed the latter. But however much resemblance there may be between thought and existence, the difference between them is no less real. From thought one cannot conclude to existence because the existence of all creatures is not an emanation of thought but arises from an act of power. The essence of things is due to the thought of God; only their existence is due to his will. Human thought, accordingly, presupposes existence. It arises only upon the basis of the created world. We can only reflect (re-flect) on that which has been pre-conceived and comes to our consciousness through the world. But if with modern philosophy one rejects all matter that has come to us from without and adopts as one's starting point pure reason or abstract feeling, one retains nothing, or at most a principle so general, so devoid of content and vague that nothing—let alone the entire universe or all of Christian revelation and religion—can be deduced from it.

Hegel's philosophy was therefore not as harmless as it originally seemed to be. It was the working out and application of Fichte's thesis that the ego posits the non-ego, that the subject creates the object. Schleiermacher, in theology, returned to this principle, since all authority in religion had ceased to function for him, the rational and historical proofs for Christianity failed to satisfy him, and God, in his view, was unknowable to reason. Just as Kant sought to restore by practical reason what he had lost by the critique of pure reason, so Schleiermacher saw no way he could save religion except by proceeding from the religious subject, from feeling, from the [pious] consciousness. From this position it followed that dogmatics could be nothing other than the description of states of mind and therefore really belonged in historical theology. Theology became anthropology, "pisteology," ecclesiology and ceased to be what it had always claimed to be: knowledge of God.

But Schleiermacher could not really stop at that point. In religion, too, he said, we are not concerned with reality but with truth. The justification of Christianity was therefore assigned—in the first part of the encyclopedia of theology—to philosophy. Since there is no longer any other ground on which faith rests, philosophy is given the task of maintaining the validity and value of religion. Meditating theology, adopting Schleiermacher's starting point, followed the path he had marked for the defense of religious truth and so came naturally to ally itself with the dialectical and speculative method of Hegel. It could not be satisfied with the empirical knowledge of the content of the Christian consciousness. Such a knowledge, after all, was not science. Not just the fact of faith had to be ascertained, also the validity and truth of the faith had to be established. And since they had no other proof, theologians resorted to speculation. The speculative theology that arose after Schleiermacher strove for a knowledge of Christianity that was higher than that which was based on authority and obtained by faith. It was a new version of ancient Gnosticism. Christian dogmas, such as the Trinity, the incarnation, vicarious atonement, were not confessed merely as articles of faith but seen and understood also in their necessity. The "that" is not sufficient; also the "how" and "why" must be understood. Speculative mediating theology therefore sought to escape the inferior stance of authority in order to ground Christianity in itself as absolute truth. Though it started out from faith, its goal was knowledge. For mediating theology, cognitive necessity was proof of truth.

It could be foreseen and has been strikingly proven by history that this method would not produce the desired result either in philosophy or in theology. Refutation is virtually superfluous. Speculation had already long had its day. The philosophy of Hegel, in the work of Feuerbach and Strauss, led to the rejection of the Christian faith *in toto*. The philosophical treatment of orthodox dogmatics by Schweizer, Scholten, and Biedermann only for a short while concealed the dogmatic poverty of modern theology. The more orthodox wing of mediating theology can with reason boast of the works of Rothe, Dorner, Lange, Martensen, Müller (etc.), which are full of deep and beautiful thoughts. But it has certainly not met the expectations it aroused. It did not succeed in changing the folly of the cross into worldly wisdom, nor did it succeed, by its sagacious insights, in winning back the children of this age for Christ. On the contrary, the mediation project ended with an even more radical split between believing and knowing, between theology and philosophy, between the church and the world. The speculation pursued by a segment of meditating theology proceeded as well from the incorrect assumption that Christianity was a logical system of ideas, by which all doctrines could be deduced by thinking and reasoning from a basic idea. But if even the existence of things in general is based not on thought but on volition; if history, however much it may be the outworking of the counsel of God, is nevertheless something essentially different from a mathematical model; then the Christian religion is even more markedly distinct from a logical system of thought. For Christianity is history, a history of [divine] grace, and grace is something other and more than a logical conclusion. In the Christian religion, accordingly, even the most profound thinker can never rise above a childlike position of authority and faith.

The speculative method changes character when, as in the case of Dr. Bruining, people ground it on experience, on the consideration of the universe, and then, by thinking and reasoning, attempt to ascend to the supersensible ground of things. The peculiar nature of the speculative method, as it is described and applied in modern philosophy, has then been abandoned, and people have returned to the usual method of argumentation practiced in rational theology. Immediately rising up against this position are all the objections that were advanced earlier in this chapter against the historical-apologetic method.

In brief, they come down to the following: (1) By this method one does not get beyond a poor set of abstract ideas, as they were reformulated, for example, by Shaftesbury, or the well-known rationalistic trilogy of God, virtue, and immortality. Such a set of ideas never occurs in reality as such as the content of religion, can never be maintained in that abstract form, and is utterly unsuited for fostering a religious life and the formation of a religious community. (2) Everything we know of the origin and essence of religion is one powerful protest against the assertion that religion rests on, and is dependent on, intellectual proofs. Religion is something very different from science. It never arose from the force of causality and never, as it pertains to its essence, consisted in a primitive worldview, however true it is that every religion implies a specific world-and-life view. The idea of God, i.e., the revelation of God, is undoubtedly logically antecedent to religion; all religion assumes the existence and revelation of God. That God concept never arose as a conclusion from a line of reasoning but was well established prior to all reasoning and proof in virtue of God's revelation and the corresponding religious nature of human beings. The study of religion always leads to a "seed of religion," the presence of the divine image, in human beings. If this were not the case and religion, like the many results of science, were based on intellectual proofs, the extraordinarily strong subjective assurance that all religion brings with it would simply be inexplicable and impossible. No one is prepared to sacrifice his life for a truth of natural science or mathematics. (3) Finally, this rationalistic method, though claiming to be based on experience, on the empirical consideration of the universe, slaps in the face the most powerful empirical evidence available to it. Perhaps it takes account of the empirical evidence that nature supplies, but it forgets that which greets it in history and in life. It draws its abstractions from the religious environment, from the family, society, the church, Christianity, and Scripture, then acts as if these phenomena do not exist and have contributed absolutely nothing to the fostering and formation of the religious life. Religious rationalism moves in a tiny circle of intellectual arguments and abstract ideas no one cares about and no soul can live by. But by that token it also dooms itself to sterility. The currents of life flow past it undisturbed.

THE RELIGIOUS-EMPIRICAL METHOD

Triumph of Feeling: Schleiermacher

[137] When historical and speculative argumentation failed to bear fruit, many theologians took their stance in the experience of believers, seeking to derive from it grounds for the certainty of faith as well as for the truth of Christianity. Perhaps the influence of Schleiermacher on modern theology nowhere comes out more clearly than in its acceptance of this subjective starting point. The reasons for this influence are not hard to find.

In the first place, Schleiermacher himself had taught [his students] that religion was not a matter of knowing or doing but of a certain state of feeling and, in keeping with this, that dogmatics is a description of pious states of mind. In this connection people frequently forget that Schleiermacher had antecedently assigned the task of arguing the truth of Christianity to apologetics and could therefore consider himself free from this obligation in dogmatics. They nevertheless adopted his dogmatic position and sought proof for the truth of Christianity in the certainty of the Christian.

In the second place, to the degree that Bible criticism made progress, an appeal to the Bible no longer seemed to yield sufficient warrant for the truth of what they confessed. Not even all the external historical or rational proofs people could scrape together in support of Christianity any longer made any impression in a time that, as a result of Kant's and Schleiermacher's own teaching, had learned to see the limitations of our cognitive powers and had consigned all invisible things, scientifically speaking, to an unknowable world.

Thirdly, people entertained the conviction that, by taking its position in religious experience, Christian theology would regain its honorable status in the eyes of secular science. For gradually in the course of the nineteenth century the latter had turned its back on all speculation and metaphysics and, with an appeal to Kant's criticism and Comte's positivism, positioned itself on the basis of pure facts. Theology would all at once seem to regain its scientific position if it became empirical through and through and located the basis for its scientific construction in the facts of religious experience.

These reasons persuaded a large number of theologians to apply the religious-empirical method in dogmatics. Actually all theology after Schleiermacher already took its position in the believing consciousness, not only mediating theologians in a narrow sense, but also those who adopted an independent position vis-à-vis Hegel and Schleiermacher nevertheless proceeded in dogmatics from the starting point of the believing subject. Hofmann, for example, though he does not interpret dogmatics as the description of states of mind, nor as the reproduction of the teaching of Scripture or the church, nor as the development of Christian doctrine from a general principle, like Schleiermacher nevertheless proceeds from Christian piety. Dogmatics, to him, is the unfolding of that which makes a Christian Christian, of the Christ-mediated communion of God with human beings. "The knowledge and message of Christianity is above all the self-knowledge and self-expression of the Christian."[38] Philippi and Kahnis have this very same subjective starting point, and Ebrard attempts in his dogmatics to demonstrate the truth and necessity of all the facts of redemption by comparing them at all points with the scientifically developed need for redemption.[39]

F. H. R. Frank and the Erlangen School[40]

But especially Fr. H. R. Frank, professor at Erlangen (1827–94), took this position with utter seriousness, thought it through, and based a system on it. J. Chr. K. von Hofmann took his position in the fact of God's communion with human beings. This fact is self-existent and bears certainty within itself and is supported by the witness of Scripture. Here, there was therefore no room for a system of Christian certainty. The Christian is conscious of himself or herself, and that says it all. But Frank does not stop here; he attempts to explain why Christians accept as truth everything their faith implies. In place of the so-called prolegomena of dogmatics, which he vigorously opposes, he constructs a *System of Christian Certainty*.[41] This title is not partic-

38. J. C. K. von Hofmann, *Der Schriftbeweis*, 3 vols. (Nördlingen: Beck, 1857–60), I, 516.

39. F. A. Philippi, *Kirchliche Glaubenslehre*, 6 vols. (Gütersloh: Bertelsmann, 1902), I, 52ff.; F. A. Kahnis, *Die Luthersche Dogmatik, historisch-genetisch dargestellt*, 3 vols. (Dörffling & Francke, 1861–68), I, 7, 8. J. H. A. Ebrard, *Christliche Dogmatik*, 2d ed., 2 vols. (Königsberg: A. W. Unzer, 1862–63), §52.

40. Ed. note: The Erlangen School refers to a group of Lutheran theologians who, since ca. 1840, taught in the theology faculty at the University of Erlangen (Bavaria). Among its influential members are the biblical theologian J. Chr. K. von Hofmann (1810–77), New Testament scholar Theodor Zahn (1838–1933), and dogmaticians G. Thomasius (1802–75) and Franz Herrmann Reinhold Frank (1827–94). Theologically, the experience of regeneration, in accord with biblical teaching concerning the history of salvation and with the Lutheran confessional tradition, provide the material for dogmatic theology. Though less bound to Lutheran confessional orthodoxy than many other Lutherans, the Erlangen School did contribute to a nineteenth-century revival of Lutheran confessional and theological interest.

41. F. H. R. Frank, *System der Christlichen Gewissheit*, 2 vols. (Erlangen: A. Deichert, 1870–73). Ed. note: To understand Bavinck's point here, it is necessary to know that Frank wrote two major works, *System der Christlichen Gewissheit* [*System of Christian Certainty*] and *System der Christlichen Wahrheit* [*System of Christian Truth*]. *System der Christlichen Wahrheit* was published as 2 volumes in 1878–80 by A. Deichert, Erlangen; 2d ed., 1885, 1886; 3d ed., 1894.

ularly clear and needs explanation. Certainty is a state of the soul and as such rules out system. But if Frank here takes certainty, not in a subjective but an objective sense, for the objects of faith of which a Christian is certain, then *A System of Christian Certainty* amounts to *A System of Christian Truth*. That cannot be Frank's intention, however, for the latter is precisely the title of his second major work. In his first-mentioned work, he explains himself in more detail,[42] saying that this system of his has as its object certainty insofar as it extends to the "truth-content" (*Wahrheitsgehalt*) to be established, i.e., certainty as a psychological state along with all that of which it gives assurance, to the extent it gives assurance. This system of Christian certainty, accordingly, comes down to a formal scheme of the various kinds and degrees of certainty that ensue from the Christian self-consciousness with respect to the objects of faith. Frank is not saying, however, that the objects of the Christian faith do not exist and are not known prior to their appropriation. In fact, he expressly states the opposite.[43] Neither does he deny that Christian certainty is produced by the Word,[44] and he does not want to derive objective truths from the born-again subject.[45] Further, when he has derived from Christian self-consciousness all that follows from it and developed and completed the system of Christian certainty, he clearly states that now a reversal occurs and that the last becomes the first. From and through their own certainty, Christians derive the objective ground on which their faith-life rests, viz., the grace of God in Christ, and from that they now construct the system of Christian truth.[46] It is solely Frank's intent therefore, to answer the question: how do people get to the point of surrendering themselves to those objective factors of salvation (God, Christ, Holy Scripture, etc.), to unconditionally accept Scripture as the Word of God?[47] In his *System of Christian Certainty* Frank, therefore, does not so much unfold the grounds of truth as the ways by which a person arrives at certainty with respect to the Christian truths of faith.

[138] The question Frank asks himself is therefore most important; it is also necessary and good, for Christian certainty is not self-evident and often subject to doubt. But everything depends on the answer. Generally speaking, Frank now says that a person gains certainty concerning the Christian truths of faith, not by means of historical or rational proofs, nor by the authority of Scripture, church, or tradition, but only through the experience of rebirth.[48] Theology, in distinction from philosophy, must not position itself outside

42. Frank, *Gewissheit*, I, 48.

43. Ibid., I, 313.

44. Frank, *Dogmatische Studien* (Erlangen: A. Deichert, 1892), 56.

45. Ibid., 68, 69. Ed. note: References to Frank's works in the long series of notes that follow will be given by title only.

46. *Gewissheit*, II, 281ff.

47. *Gewissheit*, II, 285ff.; *Dogmatische Studien*, 56.

48. *Gewissheit*, I, 314.

but at the center of Christian consciousness and from there survey and assess everything, also the natural.[49] For Christian certainty has its basis not in all kinds of external proofs, nor even in an external authority, but in Christians themselves, in their moral experience and self-definition, i.e., in their rebirth and conversion.[50] Christians know that a change has occurred and still continually occurs in them, so that now a twofold directedness, a twofold self lives in them.[51] Of this they are as certain as a patient who has recovered is conscious of her earlier illness and present health.[52] From within the experience of rebirth, Christians now spontaneously and immediately posit the entire content of the truths of the Christian faith. They do this by virtue of the nature of the new life granted them and can no more divest themselves of this truth than of themselves.[53]

This Christian truth groups itself around the experience of rebirth in three circles. First, by virtue of their new life, Christians posit those truths of faith, which are directly and immediately given with the fact of rebirth, viz., the reality of sin, righteousness, and future perfection. This is the area of the immanent core truths, which still completely belong to the *self*-consciousness of a Christian. Surrounding this core there is a second circle of truths. Believers can explain this new state in which they live only by reference to the reality of a personal God, the existence of God as the triune being, and the atonement secured by the God-man. These three truths jointly form the group of transcendent truths and indicate the factors that have brought about this moral change of rebirth in Christ. Finally, surrounding the former there is a third group of truths, viz., the transient, which indicate the means by which the above-mentioned transcendent factors effect the redemptive experience in the life of the Christian. They are the church, the word of God, Scripture, the sacrament, miracles, revelation, and inspiration. In conclusion, Christian certainty also entails a certain relation of the born-again person to the natural life, to the world, and to humanity.[54]

Implied in this answer is an important truth. Just as the eye is necessary to see light, so in fact rebirth is necessary to see the kingdom of heaven. But one can legitimately question whether Frank's *System of Christian Certainty* correctly applies and develops this truth. For if Frank had wanted only to describe how the believer arrives at certainty, he would have clarified the origin and nature of that certainty and stopped there. Just as epistemology only unfolds the grounds on which belief in the external world rests but does not deduce every object in that world from that certainty, so Frank's system of Christian certainty should have confined itself to stating the grounds for that

49. *Gewissheit,* I, 26ff., 31, 119, 137.
50. *Gewissheit,* I, 113.
51. *Gewissheit,* I, 120.
52. *Gewissheit,* I, 129.
53. *Gewissheit,* I, 193.
54. *Gewissheit,* I, 191.

certainty but not have gone on to discuss its content. In that case, however, no system (strictly speaking) of the objects to which the certainty is related would have been possible. But Frank does much more: he produces a system. He successively deduces all the truths of faith—not in a temporal but in a logical, causal sense[55]—from the experience of rebirth. He lets Christians gradually get from the experience of rebirth to all the Christian dogmas "as though" earlier and by another way they knew nothing about them. Frank does this with all the dogmas, the dogmas of sin, guilt, God, Trinity, incarnation, resurrection, etc. We get the impression that all these truths can be inferred by Christians from their experience of rebirth apart from Scripture and the church. Frank incessantly confuses the "cause of existence" with the "cause of knowing" and vice versa, the objective ground of the truths of faith and the subjective process by which a person arrives at certainty concerning those truths. He interchanges and equates objective truth and subjective certainty. He frequently speaks as if the born-again person posits the objective truths of faith as realities simply in virtue of his or her spiritual experience.[56] He refers to "the autonomy of the Christian subject as guarantor of truth."[57]

All this stems in Frank from a peculiar epistemology. A good stretch he travels along with the idealism of modern philosophy.[58] The object as object, i.e., to the subject, is only present as a result of being posited by the subject.[59] Frank admittedly recognizes the reality of the objective world, although not in an empiricist and sensualistic sense.[60] But our knowledge never concerns a thing as such and for itself but always as being "for us." That we attribute independent existence to an object arises from the fact that we find ourselves compelled to posit the object thus and not otherwise. Both schools, both empiricism and idealism, do this; they differ only in the manner in which they do it.[61] Certainty therefore is always certainty with respect to an object. It exists precisely "in being cognizant of the object as truth."[62] We make no progress in this argument except by realizing that our mind is so designed that it has to accept the objective reality of the objects of which it is certain. Whether the human mind is right in doing this and is not hallucinating is not a question to Frank. The necessity of postulation is to him the final ground of objective reality. To him certainty is not essentially but epistemologically the warrant of truth. Reality indeed is the ontological ground of certainty, but the latter is the cognitive ground of reality. Frank also applies this cognitive theory to the Christian faith. Essentially and causally the objective

---

55. *Gewissheit*, I, 47; II, 290.
56. *Gewissheit*, I, 94, 193.
57. *Gewissheit*, I, 151.
58. *Gewissheit*, I, 58.
59. *Gewissheit*, I, 61.
60. *Gewissheit*, I, 59, 60.
61. *Gewissheit*, I, 61.
62. *Gewissheit*, I, 63.

truths and facts of Christianity are anterior to faith, but epistemologically they follow it. Just as in philosophy he takes the self-consciousness of a person as his starting point, so in theology he takes the self-consciousness of the Christian, the experience of rebirth, as his starting point.

Against this starting point and against this method, however, there are many objections.

a. This rebirth of Christians, and similarly also their other spiritual experiences, including even their certainty, did not arise spontaneously but were from the beginning and are still continually connected with the objective factors of Scripture, church, etc. Frank repeatedly recognizes this fact himself.[63] But he then mistakenly and a priori detaches the spiritual experience from those objective factors and posits it by itself and makes it self-existent. Frank's starting point, the certainty of a Christian, is a pure abstraction; that certainty is grounded from the start and continually in the objective factors of salvation, which come to the believer from without.

b. By recognizing—as we noted earlier—that he now reverses the order, Frank himself admits that rebirth does not offer sufficient warrant for the objective truth of the Christian faith. For if the objective causal order is in fact as Frank describes it in his *System of Christian Truth*, viz., as being antecedent, then this has to be the order of the entire system. The system must bear the impress of the ontological order, not of the manner in which a person arrives at knowledge and certainty concerning objective truth. For this manner is so diverse that it is not amenable to systematic description.

c. The method Frank uses in constructing the objective dogmas from the certainty of a Christian is one that does not fit the Christian religion and Christian theology. It is derived from speculative philosophy. Just as the latter took its starting point in a general, totally abstract, and vague principle, so also the totally detached self-consciousness of Christians, their certainty as such, is the I-think-therefore-I-am, the Archimedean starting point of Frank. From it he first of all deduces the immanent truths of faith. Next, he seeks the assistance of the method of the natural sciences, retrogressively moves from the result to the cause, and wants to explain the new life of the Christian entirely along the lines of the empirical method.[64] Just as a physicist attempts by spectral analysis to discover the chemical components of the sun, so Frank attempts by dissection to trace the reborn life to its objective originating factors.[65] Christians, by reflecting on their spiritual life, cannot explain it except by assuming that God is triune, that Christ became human, and made satisfaction, etc.

d. This method is also contrary to all Christian experience. No Christian ever achieved certainty concerning the objective truth in that way. It totally misses reality. In addition it is impractical, for in doubt and disbelief Chris-

---

63. *Gewissheit,* I, 123, 124, 191, and so forth.
64. *Gewissheit,* I, 39.
65. *Gewissheit,* I, 315.

tians lack precisely the certainty that alone, according to Frank, can guarantee the truth of their faith. At such times what they need is an objective word, or an objective deed, which upholds them, to which they can cling and by which they can again raise themselves up from the depths of doubt and inner conflict.

e. Finally, several more objections can be leveled at Frank's system. In his thinking the transition from natural to spiritual knowledge and, similarly, the connection between the two is murky. The distinction of a twofold self in the reborn person is wide open to misunderstanding: no new self is created in a person by rebirth, but the "I" of the unspiritual person is renewed. The organization of dogmatics into a system of certainty and a system of truth cannot be maintained, since the certainty of a Christian cannot be described apart from the truth to which it pertains. The preceding comments are enough, however, to show that the charge of subjectivism, though vague, has not entirely been leveled against Frank's theology without warrant as it has not against that of Ritschl either.[66]

Experience, Certainty, and Theology

[139] The objections raised from various quarters against Frank's subjectivism are so serious that almost no one has adopted his method unmodified. Also, those who, like G. Daxer,[67] have stuck to his position show, by the effort they exert to defend Frank's purpose against the misconstrual of his opponents, that they feel the weight of those objections. Generally speaking, among the theologians who still assign to experience a place among the *principia* of dogmatics, there is a discernible attempt not to isolate it, as Frank did, from the objective factors under whose influence it came into being but from the beginning to relate it to the revelation that comes to us in the Word of God. The result is to portray experience, not as an independent source of knowledge alongside of or over against Scripture but rather as a cognitive faculty adapted to the truth of Scripture. Kähler, for example, though he says

66. Further on Frank, see Georg Daxer, *Der Subjektivismus in Franks "System der christlichen Gewissheit"* (Gütersloh: C. Bertelsmann, 1900); Henri Bois, *De la Certitude Chrétienne: Essai sur la theologie de Frank* (Paris: Fischbacher, 1887); F. K. E. Weber, *Franks Gotteslehre und de ren erkenntniss theoretische Voraussetzungen* (Leipzig: Deichert, 1901) (ed. note: Bavinck cites the publication date as 1900); R. Seeberg, "Frank," in *PRE³*, VI, 158–63.

Ed. note: Bavinck also makes reference to a large number of general works on religious certainty. Rather than provide the full bibliographic information here, reference is given simply to author and date of the publication so that the bibliographic data can be obtained from the bibliography at the back of the volume. Most of the references are simply to the volume; in select cases where Bavinck cites specific pages they will be indicated. Flugel (1888: 188ff.); Carlblom (1874); Dorner (1879: 1, 50ff.) Pfleiderer (1891: 406ff.); Postorff (1893); Gottschick (1890: 110ff.); Ihmels (1901: 88); J. Köstlin (1895; 1893); Steude (1899); Sogemeier (1902); E. Petran (1898); Haack (1894); G. Heine (1900); Bachmann (1899); H. Cremer (1896); Lobstein (1897: 72–93); Kähler (1905: 1, 12ff.); P. Paulsen (1900); Ihmels (1901); Karl Wolf (1906); A. Reymond (1900); B. Warfield (March 1895); F. H. Foster (1901).

67. Daxer, *Der Subjektivismus in Franks System;* also his critique of Ihmels, "Zur Lehre von der Christliche Gewissheit," *Theologische Studien und Kritiken* 77 (1904): 82–123.

that Christianity requires a science of its own, "since its comprehension is conditioned by its possession" and faith therefore is the condition for theological knowledge, first of all prefers to speak of faith rather than of experience and further stresses that faith is not the source, not even an instrument, but merely the presupposition and confirmation, of such knowledge.[68] Von Oettingen, to be sure, does not want to proceed from an external authority in Scripture or confession, but neither does he want to start from a purely personal feeling or value judgment and therefore takes his position in the assurance of salvation as a Christian, as a child of God and a member of the church, possesses it by the power of the gospel.[69]

The same drive is discernible in Köstlin, H. Cremer, Schlatter, and others, but it emerges most vigorously in Ihmels who, though a pupil of Frank, still at important points distances himself from him. Ihmels has great appreciation for Frank's endeavor, charging that his opponents have often misunderstood him and therefore done him less than justice. Still Ihmels recognizes that in Frank's thinking Scripture does not get its due and demonstrates that certainty of Christians concerning their rebirth cannot be the starting point and foundation of their certainty concerning the truth of Christianity. For that reason he himself does not start from the experience of rebirth but from the fact of the communion that a Christian has with God. A Christian, however, receives this communion by means of the word of God and therefore includes from the start all those objective factors that Frank, proceeding from the experience of rebirth, could find only after lengthy analysis. Ihmels, accordingly, seeks to demonstrate how certainty with respect to the truth of Christianity, though it comes into being in the way of experience and hence is "the certainty of experience," nevertheless proceeds from and is effected by the self-attestation of God by his word and is from the beginning, therefore, the certainty of faith. Certainty with respect to the truth of Christianity as such is not a certainty grounded in the Christian himself or herself, i.e., in their rebirth, but in the word of God, which by the agency of the Holy Spirit attests itself in the way of experience as being true and which on our part is recognized and accepted in faith.[70]

So, while Ihmels definitely considers experience indispensable to the formation of certainty concerning truth, he attaches another meaning to it than Frank. The latter understands by it the experience that Christians live through and continue to live through in the transformation of rebirth; but Ihmels identifies it solely with the impressions that God by his self-attestation brings about in our heart with respect to his revelation and which on our part are received in faith.[71] Of course he does not deny that faith also

---

68. Kähler, *Die Wissenschaft der Christliche Lehre,* 2d ed. (Leipzig: A. Deichert [Georg Böhme], 1893), 5, 15, 57.

69. A. von Oettingen, *Lutherische Dogmatik,* 2 vols. (München: C. H. Beck, 1897–1902), I, 35.

70. Ihmels, *Die Christliche Wahrheitsgewissheit* (Leipzig: A. Deichert, 1901), 168ff.

71. Ibid., 182ff.

works various other experiences (guilt, mortification, trust, and joy) in people, but these experiences are left out of consideration when the question concerns the ground of our certainty with respect to the truth of Christianity. In that case we are dealing only with faith, not as it actively produces many kinds of fruit, but as it passively accepts the revelation of God and accepts it as true.[72]

In this respect Ihmels distinguishes himself also from R. Seeberg, who again construes experience in a different sense. Proof for the truth of Christianity, according to this professor, is not furnished by an appeal to Scripture, for Scripture contains all kinds of errors and contradictions, and though it is a historic source of knowledge, it is absolutely not an inspired codebook. The Bible has authority only in a religious-ethical sense, in the knowledge of Jesus Christ, or, stated otherwise, in what it contains about the sovereignty and kingdom of God.[73] For these two elements capture the essence of Christianity. Human beings need two things for the life of their soul: they need a powerful spiritual authority who is nearby and a final goal that is distant. These two needs are absolutely fulfilled by Christianity. It gives people spirit and power, peace and action, the sovereignty of God and the kingdom of God, which together have become fully manifest in the person of Christ.[74]

It is because Christianity does this that it is the absolute religion, and this is established not by the authority of Scripture but only by the experience that it in fact meets our needs. The only fully satisfactory proof is the proof of discovery and experience, of spirit and power. Just as I know another person's love for me only by experiencing it, so I also get to know God only by the experience of his love. Now, corresponding to God's sovereignty, subjectively, is the faith of the believer, and corresponding to God's kingdom is love. "To be a Christian means to have faith and to love." Those who believe and love are thereby assured of God's love and the end he pursues in the history of the human race. But faith and love must be properly understood: faith is not a matter of "holding true" but a personal experience, and love is to devote oneself to the goal of God and to work with him at building his kingdom.[75] Seeberg, accordingly, does not, like Frank, proceed from a person's rebirth but with Ihmels from faith. But coupled with this agreement there are three differences: (1) alongside of faith Seeberg also postulates love as a starting point; (2) he here views faith not in terms of its passive but its active side and views it in conjunction with love as something to experience personally, to process practically, to feel immediately; and (3) while in Ihmels the objective factors, specifically God's revelation in Scripture, are im-

72. Ihmels, "Glaube und Erfahrung," *Neue Kirchliche Zeitschrift* 8 (1902): 971–73.

73. R. Seeberg, *The Fundamental Truths of the Christian Religion,* trans. Rev. George E. Thomson and Clara Wallentin (New York: G. P. Putnam Sons, 1908), 65ff., 109, 110.

74. Ibid., 17–54.

75. Ibid., 136–38, 171–72.

mediately given in the context of faith, Seeberg can arrive at it only in the way of reasoning from the effects to the cause: "These effects necessarily presuppose something effective. . . . The experience of my soul thus forces me to recognize a manifested, absolute authority and sovereignty above the world to trace back the goal of my love to them."[76]

[140] There is evidently all sorts of disagreement and misunderstanding about the essence of experience and its significance for the principles of dogmatics. In part the cause of this is the word itself, for Eucken is right when he says: "The term 'experience' has in the course of time become ever more ambiguous and in individual thinkers is subject to so many variations that it can hardly be considered a fixed term."[77] This in itself is already a serious objection to its use in the theory of dogmatic principles. But we must immediately add a second. Although the term *experience* is sometimes used in a more general sense—and is then more or less synonymous with perception and observation—it usually, in distinction from these terms, implies a subjective element. We mean by it that, as a result of the relation that has come into being between ourselves and some object, we have received an impression or a sum total of impressions, an insight, conviction, or information that we value highly precisely because it was not dreamed up by ourselves but was as it were produced in us from without. We need to note, further, that the term can denote both the act of experiencing (the reception of such an impression) and the result of that act (the impression itself). Already in Greek philosophy the word became a scientific term to indicate that the content of our knowing is acquired by way of external and internal observation (empiricism vs. rationalism). But in religion the word occurs neither in Holy Scripture,[78] nor in the older theology, and seems to have been used first by the Reformers. It achieved special status in pietism, which, in reaction to orthodoxy, stressed that divine truth not only had to be accepted by intellectual consent but experienced and lived through in the heart. Now such religious-ethical experiences most definitely exist, even too many to enumerate. They occur in all religions, in the domain of general revelation, and especially in Christianity: a sense of guilt, pangs of conscience, doubt, unbelief, the feeling of God-forsakenness, longing for God, communion with God, delight in God, desire for and a sense of the forgiveness of sin, a thirst for holiness, and many more. These experiences do not merely exist but have a

76. Ibid., 70. A similar view of experience can be found in R. Grützmacher, "Hauptproblem der Gegenwart: Dogmatik," *Neue Kirchliche Zeitschrift* 8 (1902): 859–92, 959–72; Th. Kaftan, *Moderne Theologie des alten Glaubens* (Schleswig: J. Bergas, 1905), 83ff.; Girgensohn, *Zwölf Reden über die Christliche Religion* (München: C. H. Beck, 1906), 127ff., 251ff.

77. Eucken, *Geistige Strömungen der Gegenwart* (Leipzig: Veit & Comp., 1904), 84; cf. R. Eisler, *Kant-Lexikon* (Berlin: Mittler & Sohn, 1930), s.v. "Erfahrung."

78. The Greek word δοκιμή (Rom. 5:4) does not mean religious experience but the "testedness" or soundness that a believer evinces when he or she suffers affliction with endurance. The word is translated elsewhere by "testing" (2 Cor. 2:9; 8:2; 9:13; Phil. 2:22) and "proof" (2 Cor. 13:3).

right to exist; they are inseparable from godliness, and therefore find their classic expression in the Bible as a whole, especially in the Psalms.

But these experiences—and that is the second objection referred to above—all bear the following character: (1) they are consistently religious-ethical in nature; (2) insofar as they are Christian, they are always prompted by the word of God, whether it comes directly through Scripture or indirectly through edifying discourse or devotional literature, etc.; (3) they do not precede faith but accompany and follow it, and therefore cannot be the ground of it; and (4) since they are subject to all sorts of pathology, they consistently need the corrective of the Word of God. Experience by itself is not sufficient. Scripture is the norm also for our emotional life and tells us what we ought to experience.

When we lose sight of these things and extend to experience the status of the foundation and cognitive source of Christian truth, theology as well as the practice of godliness run a threefold danger. In the first place, as long as theologians who follow the religious-empirical method still adhere to Scripture and accept the historical nature of Christianity, they will find themselves forced to turn religious experience into something it is not and cannot be. After all, what is there in a historical religion that can really be the content of experience and can therefore be inferred and known from that experience? We experience certain religious-ethical feelings of guilt, repentance, forgiveness, gratitude, joy, and the like, but all the other things that occur in a historical religion, strictly speaking, fall outside of experience. In none of the twelve articles of faith can "I believe" be replaced by "I experience." That God is the Creator of heaven and earth, that Christ is God's only begotten Son, conceived by the Holy Spirit and born of the Virgin Mary, are things that cannot, in the nature of the case, be experienced. Although there certainly are effects in the church that directly proceed from its glorified head in heaven, that Christ arose from the dead, ascended to heaven, and is now seated at the right hand of God are things we know only from Holy Scripture. Our heart can most certainly bear witness to all these facts and experience their power, but as facts they are firmly established to our mind only by the testimony of the apostles. If, denying this, people want to deduce and construct these facts from Christian experience, they do violence to that experience. They make of experience—as mystical philosophy did with respect to intellectual contemplation—an organ that is foreign to human nature and so turn Christians into a separate class of people, something like the "spirituals" (πνευματικοι) among the Gnostics, the born-again among Anabaptists, and those equipped with a superadded gift among Catholics.

On the other hand, everyone has to admit that these historic facts of Christianity are not as directly and immediately implicit in religious experience as, for example, the sense of God's existence, the consciousness of guilt, etc. are in every human heart. If those facts can be derived from religious experience, it can be done only by a long and sophisticated process of reasoning, such as Frank furnishes in his *System of Christian Certainty*. Theologians will have to employ keen analysis in the same way a physicist uses spectral analysis; they will have to work retrogressively from the effects to the effecting cause. But—if for once I may also appeal to experience—experience teaches us that no individual believer ever arrived at knowledge and acceptance of the historical facts and truths of Christianity by this method; on the contrary, he or she knows them only from Scripture and accepts them on its authority. And that is fortunate, for simple believers would never be able to follow that complicated and ever fallible (of course!) process of reasoning, and if they tried, they would become dependent on the human authority of theologians and daily have to revise their faith. Not even a single believing theologian accepts the truth of Christianity on the basis of reasonings constructed from his or her religious experience; for them, as for Frank, that truth was certain before they started. The *System of Christian Certainty* is only one attempt—though a most important one—to explain how a Christian arrives at certainty. Finally, if despite these serious objections to the religious-empirical method, people still stick with it, they run a serious risk of increasingly robbing historic Christianity of its significance for the religious life. Experience cannot bear the burden laid on it; the truth of historic Christianity cannot rest on experience as its ultimate ground. The obvious thing to do then is to relieve experience—which they do not wish to abandon as foundation—of this burden, to sever the content of faith and doctrine from all its historical connections, and to limit it to the so-called "religious-ethical" dimension. The theology of experience offers abundant proof of this. One theologian infers from his experience a complete Lutheran dogmatics, another constructs from it only the reality of the person of Christ as Redeemer or as a moral example; a third, following this procedure, winds up having no Christianity left. Religious experience is such a subjective and individualistic principle that it opens the door to all sorts of arbitrariness in religion and actually enthrones anarchism: religion as a private thing. But Scripture says: "to the teaching and to the testimony! Surely for this word which they speak there is no dawn" (Isa. 8:20).[79]

THE ETHICAL-PSYCHOLOGICAL METHOD

The Human Need for God and Morality

[141] The religious-empirical method agrees in many respects with the ethical-psychological, so much so that they frequently go together or blend into one another. The distinction between them consists primarily in the fact that the former is closer to Schleiermacher and the latter to Kant; and the former therefore tends to accentuate emotional experience, while the latter places

---

79. Kaftan, *Zur Dogmatik*, 153ff.; G. Wobbermin, *Theologie und Metaphysik* (Berlin: Alexander Duncker, 1901), 121–42; F. R. Lipsius, *Kritik der theologische Erkenntnis* (Berlin: C. A. Schwetschke, 1904); Bruining, "Methode der Dogmatiek," *Teylers Theologische Tijdschrift* (1903).

more stress on "ethical self-assertion." For those who follow the latter (Kantian) method, Christianity, generally speaking, is not a doctrine that can be demonstrated or a historical fact that can be proven but a religious-ethical power that addresses itself to the human heart and conscience. Thus, while it does not think that Christianity can be made plausible to all persons without distinction or under all circumstances, it does demand in people an antecedent moral state, a predisposition toward the good, a need for redemption, a feeling of dissatisfaction, etc. And when Christianity comes into contact with such persons, it commends itself without argument and proof to their conscience as divine truth. For it satisfies their religious-ethical needs, accords with their noble and higher aspirations, reconciles them to themselves, liberates them from the guilt and burden of sin, gives them peace, comfort, blessedness, and in all these things proves itself to be the power and wisdom of God.

Also, this line of argument for the truth of Christianity is very old. Tertullian already appealed to the witness that the soul involuntarily bears to Christ.[80] In many apologists we encounter the idea that pagan philosophy and mythology are powerless to give a satisfying answer to the questions concerning God, humanity, and the world, to satisfy religious needs, and to foster a genuinely moral life. Christianity, by contrast, contains all the good and true elements that are still also present, though scattered, in the pagan world. It furnishes material for thought, renews the heart, and fosters a wide range of virtues. Christianity is the true philosophy. "Whatever things are well spoken of by all are ours as Christians."[81] Duns Scotus, in the prologue to his *Sentences,* similarly points to the rationality of the content of revelation, to its moral influence, and to its sufficiency for human beings seeking to attain their destiny. The arguments advanced by Catholic and Protestant theologians for the truth of revelation were derived not only from the miracles and predictions, etc. Appeal was made also to the beauty and majesty of the style of Scripture, to the harmony among its parts, to the sublimity and divinity of its content, to the impact the Christian religion had on the intellectual, moral, aesthetic, social, and political life of individuals, of families and of peoples.[82] Even Rousseau in his *Emile* could not refrain from praising the life and teaching of Jesus: "Indeed, if the life and death of Socrates are those of a sage, the life and death of Jesus are those of a God." Supernatural-

80. Tertullian, *The Soul's Testimony,* 1. Cf. idem, *The Apology,* 17.

81. Justin Martyr, *Apology,* II, 13; cf. A. von Harnack, *History of Dogma,* trans. N. Buchanan, J. Miller, E. B. Speirs, and W. McGilchrist and ed. A. B. Bruce, 7 vols. (London: Williams & Norgate, 1896–99), II, 129ff., 144ff.

82. Bellarmine, *Controversiis,* "De Conc. et Eccl.," IV, 11ff.; Perrone, *Praelect. Theol.,* I, 129ff.; G. M. Jansen, *Praelectiones Theologiae Fundamentalis* (Utrecht, 1875–77), I, 158ff., 269ff.; Hake, *Handbuch der allgem. Religionswissenschaft* (Freiburg i.B.: Herder, 1875-87), II, 228ff.; J. Calvin, *Institutes,* I.viii.; S. Maresius, *Syst. Theol.,* I, §31; *Synopsis Purioris Theologiae,* disp. 2, §17ff., §25; C. Vitringa, *Doctr. Christ.,* 2, §26–29; Hoornbeek, *Theol. Pract.* (Frankfurt: Ernst Claudium Bailliar, 1680), I, 48; J. Quenstedt, *Theologia,* 10. I, 3, sect. 2, qu. 16; Glassius, *Philologiae Sacrae* (Jenae: Steinmann, 1668), I, tract. 3.

ism split the proofs for Christianity into two groups, the external and the internal, and meant by the latter precisely those that demonstrated Christianity's agreement with the rational and moral nature of human beings and applied especially to their heart and conscience. Also the theologians of this school understood that these proofs were not adequate for everyone without distinction, that they furnished moral, not mathematical, certainty, and therefore also presupposed a certain moral state in people.[83]

The ethical-psychological method came especially into vogue, however, by the work of Pascal and Vinet. In both cases there was as yet no opposition between this method and the historical arguments. The historical proofs even form a necessary element in Pascal's apologetic and were greatly valued by him personally.[84] Still, he gave to these historical proofs another place and meaning. His *apologia* is anthropological; it proceeds from humanity's misery and seeks to arouse in people a felt need for redemption. It then shows that those needs remain unmet in pagan religions and philosophical systems and find satisfaction only in the Christian religion as based on the faith of Israel. Though Vinet for his part did not spurn the historical proofs,[85] he attaches greater value to the internal evidence. He wants the apologist to take the ethical road, commending Christianity to the human conscience from the side of its ethics as embodying true humanity.[86] Since then this method has been taken over—with the neglect of and sometimes even disdain for the historical proofs—by Astié, Pressensé, Sécrétan, de la Saussaye,[87] and also by numerous Protestant[88] and Catholic apologists. Admittedly, the Catholic defenders of the Christian faith for the most part follow the old scholastic method. Yet there are many, especially in France, who under the influence of

83. Knapp, *Glaubenslehre*, 12 vols. (Halle: G. C. Knapp, 1840), I, 71ff.; K. G. Bretschneider, *Handbuch der Dogmatik* (Leipzig: J. A. Barth 1838), I, 281ff.; idem, *Systematische Entwicklung aller in de Dogmatik verkommende Begriffe*, 4th ed. (Leipzig: J. A. Barth, 1828), 219–30; Muntinghe, *Theol. Christ.* (Hardervici: I. van Kasteel, 1800), pars theor. §38; Vinke, *Theol. Christ. Dogm. Comp.*, 17ff.; Voigt, *Fundamentaldogmatik* (Gotha: F. A. Perthes, 1874), 269ff.; J. J Van Oosterzee, *Christian Dogmatics*, trans. J. Watson and M. Evans, 2 vols. (New York: Scribner, Armstrong: 1874), I, 137, 162ff., 175ff.; A. Grétillat, *Exposé de Theologie Systématique*, 4 vols. (Paris: Fischbacher, 1885–92), II, 163ff., 176ff.; A. B. Bruce, *Apologetics* (Edinburgh: T. & T. Clark, 1892), 42.

84. Wijnmalen, *Pascal als Bestrijder der Jesuïeten en verdediger des Christendoms* (Utrecht: W. F. Dannenfelser, 1865), 164–88.

85. Vinet, *Discours sur quelques sujets religieux*, 6th ed. (Paris: Ches Les Èditeurs, 1862), 29; idem, *Essais de philosophie, morale, et religion* (Paris: L. Hachette, 1837), 36ff.

86. Vinet, *L'Evangile compris par le coeur*, Discours, 6th ed. (Paris: Ches Les Èditeurs, 1862), 29–41; idem, "Le regard," *Etudes Evangéliques* (1847); J. Cramer, *Alex. Vinet* (Leiden: Brill, 1883), 99ff., 117ff.

87. Astié, *De Theologie des Verstands en de Theologie des Gewetens*, trans. D. Ch. de la Saussaye (Rotterdam: Wijt, 1866); Pressensé, *Les Origines* (Paris: Fischbacher, 1883), 114–28; Sécrétan, *La civilization et la croyance* (Paris: Alcan, 1887); further on de la Saussaye, see H. Bavinck, *De Theologie van Prof. Dr. Daniel Chantepie de la Saussaye*, 2d rev. ed. (Leiden: D. Donner, 1903), 55ff., 64ff.

88. F. Delitzsch, *System der christlichen Apologetik* (Leipzig: Dörffling und Franke, 1869), 30, 34ff.; Chr. E. Baumstark, *Christliche Apologetik auf antropologische Grundlage* (Frankfurt a.M: Heyder & Zimmer, 1872), I, 34–36; J. Köstlin, *Die Begründung unserer sittlich-religiose Überzeugung* (Berlin: Reuther & Reichard, 1893), 58ff.

Kant and Comte attach but little value to the old arguments for the existence of God, as much as possible avoid metaphysics, and in their defense follow a psychological procedure.[89]

Kant indeed has great significance for this ethical-psychological method. For according to his system of philosophy, there are two sources of human knowledge, the senses for the matter and the intellect for the form of our knowledge. Above them stands reason, pure reason, whose a priori synthetic principle is that it rises from the conditioned to the unconditioned.[90] In virtue of this characteristic, theoretical reason forms principles or ideas that are absolute, unconditioned, transcendent. These ideas are not arbitrarily produced by reason but in keeping with its very nature. These ideas, in the main, are the trio: God, freedom, and immortality. They cannot be exhibited in the form of objective truth, however, but can only be subjectively inferred from the nature of reason. The objects of these ideas are not perceptible and therefore not knowable. We arrive at them only by necessary rational inference.[91] All three of them are theoretically unprovable. They do not increase our knowledge but merely regulate and order it and prompt us to view and consider everything "as if" those ideas had reality.[92] Theoretical reason cannot teach us that these ideas have reality or what they are.

Reason, however, is not only theoretical but also practical. It carries within itself a moral law, a categorical imperative, and confronts us with our duty. It demands that we will perform that duty unconditionally, without ulterior motives, solely out of respect for that duty as such. It reveals, accordingly, that a human being still belongs to an order other than nature, viz., to a moral world order. We all strive after a supreme good, which far transcends the material goods of this world and consists in nothing other than the union of virtue and happiness. If this imperative of duty is not an illusion but realizable and the supreme good, the union of duty and happiness will actually be attained some day, in other words, if the moral world order within and outside of us will triumph over the order of nature—then freedom, and with it God and immortality, has to exist as well. These three, accordingly, are the postulates of practical reason; their reality is required by the moral law. Practical reason demands that they exist.[93]

89. Cf. Schanz, *Über neue Versuche der Apologetik* (Regensburg: Nationale Verlagsanstalt, 1897); English translation: *A Christian Apology,* trans. Michael F. Glancey and Voctor J. Schobel, 4th rev. ed. (Ratisbon: F. Pustet, 1891); C. Pesch, *Alte und neue Apologetik: Theologische Zeitfragen* (Freiburg i.B.: Herder, 1900), 69–114.

90. I. Kant, *Kritik Der Reinen Vernunft* (Berlin & Leipzig: Walter De Gruyter & Co., 1919), 300–347. Ed. note: Pp. 300–347 in the German edition cited are the equivalent of pp. 252–98 in I. Kant, *Critique of Pure Reason,* trans. F. Max Müller (New York: Macmillan Company, 1915).

91. I. Kant, *Reinen Vernunft,* 308–21. Ed. note: For English pagination see n. 90.

92. I. Kant, *Reinen Vernunft,* 425, 512, 530, 535, 537, 539ff. Ed. note: p. 425 corresponds to pp. 445–46 in the English version.

93. I. Kant, *Critique of Practical Reason,* trans. Mary Gregor (Cambridge: Cambridge University Press, 1997), 92–122.

That, in the main, is Kant's famous theory of postulation. But it is not above criticism. In the first place, it is not clear who infers these postulates from practical reason. Kant seems to think that practical reason itself does. But then come two practical reasons, one antecedent, the other consequent; one that holds up the duty and another that by reasoning infers from it the existence of the ideas. Practical reason itself then again becomes theoretical.[94] Of greater weight even is another objection: what could be the ground on the basis of which the theoretical or practical reason infers the existence of these ideas? What is the urgent motive for these postulates? If that ground or motive lies in practical reason by itself, in the categorical imperative, in the command of duty as such, then even the most immoral person can deduce from the phenomenon of that practical reason the reality of these three ideas. Now it sometimes seems as if Kant really thinks this. He repeatedly gives the impression that practical reason by itself as such, to be able to realize itself, has to pose these postulates. He does not only say that every morally mature person is competent to produce these postulates but that it is unavoidable for every rational being to draw these conclusions. In other words, the assumptions of the existence of freedom, God, and immortality are equally as necessary as the moral law itself,[95] and Kant argues above all that the moral law, to be realizable, has to assume these three ideas as existent. But, if this is Kant's opinion, we are dealing not with psychologically mediated but with objectively logical postulates; and the question arises: why then is such a logical postulate not a matter of knowledge, not an element of theoretical reason? Why does Kant call this knowing only practical? There is more reason to think, therefore, that the ground and motive for these postulates does not lie in practical reason by itself but in the moral disposition, the moral will, of the person who seriously, be it also in weakness, seeks to obey the duty prescribed to him or her by practical reason. Elsewhere,[96] therefore, he declares that moral faith is held to be true on the basis of psychological-moral grounds. This moral faith, therefore, does not say, "It is certain" but "I am morally certain." It therefore rests on the presupposition of moral convictions.[97]

In line with this view, he writes in his *Critique of Practical Reason:* "The person of integrity may say: 'I will that there be a God; I will let no one deprive me of this faith. My moral interest demands the existence of God. Moral faith is not a commandment; a faith that is commanded is an absurdity. The sense of duty is objective; so also is the capacity to act morally and to be happy.' But whether that connection between virtue and happiness is forged by a personal God or by the nexus of nature is something we do not know. Moral interest is decisive here. It is within our power of choice, but

94. L. W. E. Rauwenhoff, *Wijsbegeerte van den Godsdienst* (Leiden: Brill & Van Doesburgh, 1887), 325, 328.

95. Kant, *Practical Reason*, trans. Gregor, 119 note.

96. Ibid., 92–122.

97. Kant, *Pure Reason*, 640–66.

practical reason decides in favor of belief in a wise creator of the world."[98] In Kant, in fact, one discerns a double aim: on the one hand he aims to maintain the rationality, on the other, the freedom of faith. Belief in freedom, God, and immortality is objective insofar as it is postulated by the practical reason that belongs to all; yet it nevertheless also depends on the moral disposition of the individual person.[99]

The Legacy of Immanuel Kant

[142] Kant's significance for theology consisted primarily in the fact that he created a split between "phenomenon" and "noumenon," between the reality that can be explained and the reality that can be experienced, between the world of existence and the world of values, between knowing and believing, between science and religion, between theoretical and practical reason. Religion was given a position alongside and outside of science, and had its own foundation: the moral nature of humanity.

The influence of Kant's philosophy on theology became immediately noticeable. In view of "the unknowability of the supersensible," supernaturalism asserted the necessity of revelation. Rationalism, by contrast, adopted the rational morality and moralistic religion of Kant. Schleiermacher took over Kant's theory of the unknowability of the supernatural and his dichotomy of religion and science but sought for religion a safe refuge in feeling. Especially after the inadequacy of the historical-apologetic and the speculative lines of reasoning had become evident, however, many theologians returned to Kant. In our country this already occurred in the case of Hoekstra. Dissatisfied with the intellectualism and determinism of Scholten, he located the basis for religious faith, with Kant, in practical reason and its postulates. According to Hoekstra, believing is a moral act of the will, a postulate of our internal spiritual self in the face of the experiences of life. It rests on faith in the truth of our own inner being. Only that worldview is true that corresponds to our inner being, our moral needs.[100] In an article in *Theologisch Tijdschrift*, Hoekstra later explained himself in greater detail, basing religious faith, not on our needs, ideals, and aspirations in general, but specifically on an unconditional sense of duty.[101]

98. Kant, *Practical Reason*, 119–21.

99. On the practical reason as a theoretical postulate of Kant, see, *inter alia*, Schopenhauer, *Die Welt als Wille und Vorstellung*, 6th ed., 2 vols. (Leipzig: Brockhaus, 1887), I, 610–25 (ed. note: English translation available: *The World as Will and Representation*, 2 vols. [New York: Dover Pub., 1969]); Gottschick, *Kants Beweis für das Dasein Gottes* (Torgau: Lebinsky, 1878); E. Katzer, "Der Moralische Gottesbeweis nach Kant und Herbart," *Jahrbuch für Protestantische Theologie* 4 (1878): 482–532; B. Punjer, *Geschichte der Christlichen Religionsphilosophie*, 2 vols. (Braunschweig: C. A. Schwetske, 1880), II, 19–30; Fr. Paulsen, "Was uns Kant sein Kann," *Separat-Abdruck aus der Vierteljahrsschrift für wissenschaftliche Philosophie*, vol. 5 (Leipzig, 1881), 57ff.; Rauwenhoff, *Wijsbegeerte van de Godsdienst*, 321ff.; P. Leendertz, *Het Ethisch-evangelisch Standpunt en het Christlijke-godsdienst Geloof* (1864), 23ff., 45ff.

100. S. Hoekstra, *Bronnen en Geslagen van het Godsdient Geloof* (Amsterdam: P. N. van Kampen, 1864), 23ff., 45ff.

101. S. Hoekstra, *Theologische Tijdschrift* 5 (1872): 1–44; cf. Rauwenhoff, *Wijsbegeerte*, I, 220.

Others, such as Ph. R. Hugenholz, Rauwenhoff, and Leendertz, aligning themselves with Hoekstra, base religious belief on moral self-awareness.[102] Ethical modernists went a step further. Abstaining from attempts at fashioning a philosophical system, they separated faith and science as sharply as possible, and restricted religion to the realm of morality. Religion here is moral idealism, devotion to a moral ideal, belief in the power of goodness, a power that, according to the majority, does have objective existence but in some is nothing more than a conception of the human mind.[103] In recent times some among the moderns again tend to locate the foundation and cognitive source in feeling, the emotional life, in religious experience, and are thereby returning to Schleiermacher.[104] We find a similar dualism between believing and knowing also outside the circle of the moderns, in Gunning and Doedes. The latter makes a distinction between faith, which rests on grounds, and science, which is based on proofs.[105]

Albrecht Ritschl and Moral Religion

In Germany, the return to Kant dates from the beginning of the second half of the nineteenth century. In 1855, Helmholtz, giving a lecture at Königsberg, concluded by saying that Kant's ideas are still alive and unfolding in ever-increasing richness. In 1860 Kuno Fischer's work on the philosophy of Kant made its appearance, and in 1865 and 1866 Liebmann and F. A. Lange coined the slogan: "Back to Kant." In theology Kantianism was renewed by Ritschl and Lipsius. The *principia* of the theology of Ritschl and his school, to the degree they need to be discussed here, can be summed up as follows:[106]

102. Hugenholtz, *Studiën op Godsdienstlijk en Zedekundig Gebied,* 3 vols. (Amsterdam: 1884), II, 192; Rauwenhoff, *Wijsbegeerte,* 335ff.; Leendertz, *Het Ethisch-Evangelisch Standpunt,* I, 7, 10, 57ff.

103. Rauwenhoff, *Wijsbegeerte,* 116ff., 366ff.; also see the literature cited on p. 116; *also: J. W. v.d. Linden, *De Gids* (December 1883); idem, *Bijblad van de Hervorming,* September 9, 1887; A. Bruining, "Verschillende Schakeeringen van Modernen," *Bijblad van de Hervorming,* February 10, 1885; De Bussy, *Ethische Idealisme* (Amsterdam: J. H. de Bussy, 1875); idem, *Over de Waarde en den Inhoud van Godsdienst Voorstellingen* (Amsterdam: J. H. de Bussy, 1880); idem, *De Maatstaf van het Zedelijke Oordell* (Amsterdam: J. H. de Bussy, 1889); idem, *Theologisch Tijdschrift* 29, no. 1 (January 1895): 1–14, 101.

104. F. C. Fleischer, *Bijvoegsel van de Hervorming* (May 17, 1902); *Groenewegen, *De Theologie en hare Wijsbegeerte* (1904); T. Cannegieter, "De Godsdienst in den Mensch en de Mensch in den Godsdienst," *Teylers Theologische Tijdschrift* II/2 (1904): 178–211.

105. J. H. Gunning, *Overlevering en Wetenschap* (Gravenhage: W. A. Beschoor, 1879); J. W. Gunning, Introduction to *Christus en Natuurwet: Acht Voordrachten van Fred. Temple* (Haarlem, 1887); Doedes, "Introduction," in *De Leer Van God,* p. 7.

106. On the abundant literature see above (p. 172 n. 16) and the following: Pfleiderer, "Die Ritschlsche Theologie," *Jahrbuch für Protestantische Theologie* (1889): 162ff.; On Hermann, Kaftan, and Bender, see idem, *Jahrbuch für Protestantische Theologie* (1891): 321–83; idem, *Die Entwicklung der Protestantische Theologie* (1891), 228ff.; Flügel, *Die Spekulative Theologie der Gegenwart* (Göthen: Otto Schulze, 1888), 230ff.; idem, *Ritschl's philosophische und theologische Ansichten,* 2d ed. (Langensalza: Beyer, 1892); Frank, *Die Theologie Albrecht Ritschl's,* 3d ed. (Erlangen: A. Deichert, 1891); G. Mielke, *Das System Albrecht Ritschl's dargestellt, nicht Kritisirt* (Bonn: A. Marcus, 1894); Ecke, *Die theologische Schule Albrecht Ritschl's und die evangelishe kirche der Gegenwart,* 2 vols. (Berlin: Reuther & Reichard,

1. Ritschl makes a sharp distinction between religion and science and, further, between theology and metaphysics. Initially he followed Hegel and Bauer but in their conceptual framework missed the proper appreciation for historical personalities, whose significance he increasingly began to understand as a result of his historical studies. Consequently he bade the Hegelian school farewell. It became his ambition, against Hegel and also against Schleiermacher (with "his feeling of absolute dependence"), in and by means of religion to reassert the independence of personality, freedom, and spirit. But to that end it was necessary sharply to distinguish religion from science and to assign to the former a place of its own in the life of the mind. That difference does not so much arise in the object, for both religion and science function in the same area of world and life, or in the subject for the subject has a voice not only in religion but also in science. But it arises from the different interests people pursue in each of these areas.

Science seeks to discover the laws that govern knowledge and existence but does not rise to the universal perspective from which all things can be understood as a single whole. Religion, by contrast, is not a kind of knowledge of the world, not a preliminary stage of science, but the blueprint of a worldview (*Weltanschauung*). Religion takes in the whole picture, determines the value of the human spirit over against nature, and elevates humanity, along with God, above the world. It has its origin in the contrasting position in which human beings find themselves. On the one hand, humanity is a part of the world, on the other it is essentially distinct from nature and elevated above it by being "spirit." In that conflict humanity seeks refuge in a being who is above nature and hence himself has to be "spirit" and "person," who accepts them into his fellowship and so liberates them from the world. The essence of religion, accordingly, consists in two elements: in dependence on (communion with) God and in independence vis-à-vis the world. While this essence is common to all religion, it occurs in its purest form in Christianity. For in Christianity the entire world is understood as a single whole, made subordinate to the final goal, the kingdom of God, while human beings are nevertheless regarded as being of such high value that, by comparison, the world as a whole cannot match them. Christianity interprets the two elements of religion—worldview and self-appraisal—most soundly and is, accordingly, not a circle with one center, not just a logical or ethical religion à la Schleiermacher, but an ellipse with two foci: redemption

1897–1904), I; Traub, "Ritschl's Erkenntnisstheorie," *ZThK* 4 (1894): 91–130; James Orr, *Ritschlianism, Expository and Critical Essay* (New York: A. C. Armstrong, 1903); A. E. Gervie, *The Ritschlian Theology, Critical and Constructive* (Edinburgh: T. & T. Clark, 1899); P. D. Chantepie de la Saussaye, "De Theologie van Ritschl," *Theologische Studiën* 2 (1884): 259–93; H. Bavinck, "De Theologie van Albrecht Ritschl," *Theologische Studiën* 6 (1888): 369ff.

On Hermann, see the following: Peters, "Zur Frage nach dem Glauben," *Neue Kirchliche Zeitschrift* 9 (1903); Kaftan, *Zur Dogmatik*, 161ff.; Ihmels, *Die Christliche Wahrheit*, 124ff.; Maurice Goguel, *Wilhelm Heirman et le problème religieux actual* (Paris: Fischbacher, 1905).

and kingdom of God. It is both religion and morality: the absolutely spiritual and the absolutely moral religion.

2. Although religion and science are thus totally distinct and separate, Ritschl nevertheless tries to forge a link between the two, and that by the moral argument or proof. The other proofs for the existence of God are inadequate and do not lead us beyond the world. Although philosophy frequently speaks of a final cause and purpose of things, of the absolute, of God, this God is not the God of religious faith but merely an entity in the world, nothing but the idea of the world itself. But with moral proof things are otherwise. Whereas the other proofs take no account of the distinction between nature and spirit, moral proof is characterized by the fact that it is based on "the inescapable data of the spiritual life of humanity," on the independence and self-appraisal of "spirit." For if the spirit assumes a position high above nature, views nature as a means and itself as end, then this appraisal is either mere illusion or correct. In the latter case, the basis for it can only lie in God and his will. The spirit who recognizes and asserts himself therefore has to accept the existence of God, i.e., of a spiritual and moral leader of the world, not just, as Kant said, by a practical faith, but also by an act of theoretical knowledge. The idea of God, which the moral proof supplies, actually coincides with the Christian idea of God. And thus this proof in principle demonstrates the rationality of the Christian worldview and the scientific character of theology. Faith and science, so far from being in conflict, complement and need each other.

3. If Ritschl had held onto and developed this idea of the connection between faith and knowledge, his theology would have assumed another form. Despite this view of the moral proof, however, Ritschl continued to work along the lines of separation and so arrived at the demand that all metaphysics be removed from theology. His notion about the moral proof therefore impresses us as being an alien element in his theology that is incompatible with his principles and has, accordingly, been totally abandoned by others as well. When he then further wants to banish all metaphysics from theology, he defines metaphysics as ontology: the theory of the universal grounds of existence. This discipline, in his opinion, abstracts the unique characteristics from things, wipes out the distinction between nature and spirit, only seeks the universal, and therefore always ends in materialism and pantheism. What Ritschl objects to in metaphysics is its inevitable (in his view) indifference to the distinctiveness and independence of the spirit over against nature. Since this is the basic idea and foundation of religion and theology, metaphysics is incompatible with both. But he rejects metaphysics for still another reason: its connection with a false epistemology. It proceeds, after all, from the distinction between "things in themselves" and "things for us," considers the latter to be merely deceptive appearance, and hypostatized the former into neutral Platonic essences lying behind the changes. According to Ritschl, this is completely mistaken. He does reject Kant's theory insofar as

Kant contrasted "things in themselves" and "things for us" and even left the existence of the former in doubt, for an appearance apart from a thing that appears is a mere illusion. But he opposes with equal vigor the opinion of Plato that the essence of things can be known apart from their appearance. So, approaching the position of Lotze, he says that there is nothing other than that which manifests itself to us in its appearance. The "things in themselves behind and prior to their appearance" are unknowable and do not exist. We only know a thing in its appearance, the subject in its predicates, the cause in its effects, the final end in changes that occur. We know things only inasmuch and insofar as they impact us, stand in relation to us, are things "for us."

[143] 4. This theory of knowledge (epistemology), which Ritschl substitutes for the Platonic or metaphysical view, is of the greatest significance for his theology. It would be rather harmless if it only meant that we could never learn to know things apart from perception, solely by speculative thinking and reasoning. But it becomes much more serious if it implies the idea that a thing completely coincides with and is exhaustively present in its appearance. Anyone familiar with Ritschl's theology knows that he does not—to put it mildly—strictly observe the distinction between the two views and repeatedly leaves the impression that the latter view was his real opinion. If this is true—something we cannot and need not further examine here—if, according to Ritschl, no substance or bearer exists behind the phenomena, if there really exist only effects, not things, if the existence of things are no more than "subsistence in relationships," then all objects would depend, in their "being" and their "being thus," on the observing subject and all science would run aground on the reef of illusionism and solipsism. However this be, Ritschl in any case inferred from his principles, as we have so far explained them, that to get to know religion a person must himself or herself take a position in religion. It is therefore wrong to first construct a natural theology apart from the Christian faith and to make it the preamble to one's theology. Religion is in a class of its own and never the fruit of a scientific study of nature. It is always positive [concrete], has its own source, and is the product of revelation. It can only be known, therefore, if one takes one's position within its circle, the circle of revelation.

In earlier times scholars did in fact first consider God, humanity, sin, redemption, etc. prior to and apart from Christ; but this position is fundamentally false. All dogmas must be understood from the perspective of the church. Orthodoxy likewise sometimes treated "historical faith" and "intellectual faith" prior to "saving faith" (*fiducia*), but that was inconsistent with the original doctrine of the Reformation as we find it in the work of Luther, Melanchthon, and Calvin. In that way faith would again depend on science, on external proofs, and be essentially sold short; for then it would consist essentially in knowledge (*notitia*) and not in trust (*fiducia*) and thus be deprived of its freedom, independence, and certainty. These are completely maintained, however, if one takes one's position, not outside but in the faith of the church. Revelation and religion belong together, just as grace and faith do. For dogmatics this means that, on the one hand, it cannot have the confessions or religious experience as its source and content, nor, on the other hand, derive its material from Scripture apart from the faith of the church. For to capture the significance of Jesus, one must be incorporated in the church he founded, the church that is conscious of having received the forgiveness of sins by his action. To attempt to describe Jesus' teaching and life apart from his church is to fail to do justice to his religious significance. A "Life of Jesus" is contrary to the religious importance of his person. Therefore the cognitive source for dogmatics, according to Ritschl, is the New Testament, or rather the revelation disclosed in the person of Christ, but then that revelation understood as it comes to us, not only in Jesus' own words, but also through the consciousness of the original church, i.e., through the witness of the apostles.

5. If the Christian religion is bound to the person of Christ, and faith (in the sense of trust) has him as its object, there is again implied some prior knowledge of that object, and the question arises: how do we recognize the revelation of God in the person of Christ or in Holy Scripture, and how does certainty concerning its reality come into being? Ritschlians tend to respond to that question with a great many different answers. Ritschl himself actually refrains from answering it. He refers the individual person to the church, which has the experience of the forgiveness of sins and of the "sonship" of God, but does not say what should prompt a person to join the church. For Ritschl the transition between a person and being a Christian is scientifically grounded in the moral argument that the Christian worldview is moral since it maintains the self-appraisal of the spirit. But this mediation could hardly be taken over by the followers of Ritschl, at least if they wished to remain faithful to his principle of separation between believing and knowing. As a rule they therefore pursue other paths, ground the truth of revelation in inward experience, and thereby accept a foundation that was certainly not laid by Ritschl, the opponent of all mysticism and pietism.

Especially Herrmann in Marburg adopted this position. He—even more forcefully than Ritschl—separates metaphysics and religion, the reality that can be explained and the reality that can be experienced, the natural and the moral world. Even if knowledge (*notitia*) is a precondition for faith,[107] it is itself nothing other than trust (*fiducia*) and practical through and through. Knowledge does not consist in the acceptance of a doctrine but in reliance on a person. It can therefore come about only by an experience, by the personal experience that, in Christ as his self-revelation, God visits us in our life and incorporates us in his fellowship. No Bible, no doctrine of inspiration,

---

107. Hermann himself recognizes that knowledge (*notitia*) is a precondition for faith (*Vorbedingung des Glaubens*); see his essay, "Verkehr des Christen mit Gott," *ZThK* 4 (1894): 273.

no apologetic proofs, not even rebirth (as in Frank), but only the person of Christ can be the ground of our faith. In that connection, however, Herrmann makes a sharp distinction between the ground and the content of faith; the latter can be and usually is much richer than the former. The ground of faith is only that which motivates a "not yet" believer, the unspiritual person, toward faith in God's love; its content, on the other hand, is all that the believer gradually learns to believe and confess via his or her religious-moral experiences of God, Christ, church, the means of grace, etc. By means of this distinction Herrmann makes a concession to the unbelievers of this age. These people may be subject to all sorts of doubt and accept all the true or supposed results of historical criticism—it does not matter. If they on their part meet the condition essential to the origination of faith, if they still have a moral consciousness and feel a moral need, if they thirst for the moral ideal and seek after God, they cannot resist the powerful impression that the image of Jesus in the Gospels exerts on them. Such people as yet have no interest in Christ as the Son of God, the Redeemer, the miracle worker, the risen and glorified Savior. If necessary, this will come later. But even if all these things were to vanish, one thing remains certain, viz., the "historical Jesus," his "inner life," i.e., the fact that Jesus saw, spoke, did, and suffered for "the good," and is goodness himself.

Of course this "historical Jesus" is known to us only from Scripture and is to that extent also again an object of historical criticism, a criticism that has to be completely free, but Herrmann thinks that this is not really an objection. He says that this historical Jesus, as he understands him and has as it were detached from the notions concerning the Christ of faith in Scripture, is an "undisputed fact." He believes that the basic features of the image of Jesus do not admit of any doubt concerning the historical reality of his person and accepts this objective truth, not on the basis of proofs, but because he has felt and experienced the power of the life of Jesus in his own life. This historical Jesus cannot be the product of invention. Also in this sense, therefore, he is the ever-certain, never-faltering ground of faith. Even if we divest the image of Jesus of all the things with which the church has rightly or wrongly adorned him, his moral greatness still remains. In his person and life he manifests the reality and power of the good; his "inner life" continues to create the impression that God was present in him and revealed himself to us in him. Those who have received this impression have begun to be believers and will make progress. This progress comes not by science, by speculation, by belief in authority, but by personal experiences through which believers gradually achieve a fuller grasp of the content of faith.

This is as far as the school of Ritschl went in providing us with an analysis of the truth and certainty of faith. The impression that the person of Christ makes on us, the power that flows from the gospel in our heart, the moral experience of mortification and joy, the correspondence between the idea of the kingdom of God and our needs and demands, appear to be the final grounds for the truth of revelation in the person and life of Christ. In this connection, however, we also observe a twofold disagreement in the school of Ritschl: (1) about what truly belongs, or does not belong, to the image of the historical Jesus; and (2) about the manner in which this historical Jesus works faith in our heart. Herrmann thought that the "inner life" of Jesus includes only his moral greatness, his moral knowledge, and his moral energy. Others, however, are of the opinion that a number of facts from the life of Jesus also necessarily belong to his historical image and hence constitute a part of the ground for our faith. The line of demarcation between the historical Jesus and the Christ of faith is variously drawn. And as it concerns the other point of dispute, Herrmann believes that the image of Jesus has to impact a person directly to arouse faith in him, whereas others, such as Otto Ritschl, Johann Weiss, Gottschick, etc., prefer to think that the image of Jesus can also come to us indirectly through our upbringing, through sermons, public addresses, and the like. In the latter case faith can better be called a fruit of the work of the Holy Spirit in the church than an effect proceeding from the historical Jesus himself.

6. What finally follows from all the above is that in the school of Ritschl the content of faith is restricted to the religious-ethical dimension. Ritschl himself said: "All forms of religious knowledge are direct value judgments." Philosophy also makes its judgments, but its value judgments are incidental and concomitant. Religion, however, consists in independent value judgments, which bear on people's relationship to the world in its totality, furnish feelings of pleasure or displeasure to the degree they enjoy dominion over that world or have to do without it, and are completely independent of science. Accordingly, if science confines itself to its own domain and does not attempt to construct a worldview, there is no possibility of conflict between it and religion. Herrmann, taking a further step, even declared that to science the reality of faith was an illusion. In connection with his distinction between the ground and content of faith, he came to the position that the content of faith can be different in different Christians. In any case, since this content is acquired, not by the study of Scripture or by reflection but only by personal experience, and this experience is most diverse among Christians, the content of faith will be correspondingly diverse. That which is valid to us need not be valid to others or to people who live in a later period, and it is the task of theology to distinguish the essential from the nonessential. Thus Herrmann builds a bridge to the left, to the proponents of the religion-historical method who completely detach religion from history and equate it with "mood."

Still, we would be unfair to Ritschl and his school if we interpreted their theory of value judgments in this sense. For they all attempt to some extent to hold onto the historical revelation of God in Christ as the foundation and source of religious faith and to that extent see religion as consisting not only in value judgments but also in factual judgments. It is patently clear as well that religious knowledge includes a conviction of the reality of its object as much as science does. Value judgments either depend on factual judgments or are illusory. Kaftan, accordingly, admits that value judgments presuppose objective truth, even though in an epistemological sense he views that truth as dependent on the former.[108] And Häring, though he says that it is practical moral grounds that motivate us toward faith, adds that Christian faith does not carry within itself any warrant for the truth of that which is believed, since wishing for a thing is no proof of the fulfillment of that wish, but that it finds that warrant in the historical fact of the revelation of God in Christ.[109] Others, for that reason, point out that, however much of Scripture succumbs to criticism, enough of it remains certain. Certainly, the entire appearance of Christ cannot be unhistorical. Faith does not depend on the supernatural birth of Christ, on the resurrection, or on the miracles.[110] In his *Essence of Christianity* Harnack—in distinction from Ritschl—even conceived religion solely as a relation between God and the soul and asserted that only the Father and not the Son belonged in the gospel as Jesus proclaimed it. But, in saying that, he absolutely did not wish to deny that the person of Jesus remains important for the religious life. On the contrary, the experience that God is our Father arises in us as a result of the influence of the image of Jesus in our soul, for only life begets life. Jesus was the Son of God and remains the Son of God for us, because he knew the Father in a manner completely peculiar to himself. For that reason Ritschlians still have a—be it impoverished—Christology and virtually all of them still insist that should historical-critical research deprive us of the lordship of Christ, the Christian faith would rise up in protest.

The Search for the Unity of Believing and Knowing

[144] In religion and theology R. A. Lipsius, like Ritschl, returned to Kant, confining science to the domain of internal and external experience.[111]

108. Kaftan, *Das Wesen der Christliche Religion* (Basel: Bahnmaier's Verlag, 1881), 35ff., 41ff., 55ff.

109. Th. Häring, "Zur Lehre von der heilige Schrift," *Theologische Studien und Kritiken* 66 (1893): 177–212, esp. p. 199; idem, *The Christian Faith*, trans. John Dickie and George Ferries, 2 vols. (London: Hodder & Stoughton, 1913), 159ff., 191ff.

110. A. von Harnack, *Das Apostolische Glaubenskenntnis* (Berlin: A. Haack, 1892); idem, *History of Dogma*, I, 74; Gottschick, *Die Kirchlichkeit* (Freiburg i.B.: J. C. B. Mohr, 1890), 90.

111. R. A. Lipsius, *Lehrbuch* (Braunschweig: C. A. Schwetschke, 1893); idem, *Philosophie und Religion* (Leipzig: Johann Ambrose Barth, 1885); idem, *Die Hauptpunkte der Christliche Glaubenslehre* (Braunschweig: C. A. Schwetschke, 1889). On the theology of Lipsius, see Friedrich Reinhard Lipsius, "Richard Adelbert Lipsius," *PRE*³, XI, 520; Ed. von Hartmann, *Die Krisis in der moderne Theologie* (Berlin: C. Duncker, 1880), 69ff.; Biedermann, *Christliche Dogmatik*, 2d ed., 2 vols. (Berlin: G. Reimer, 1884–85), I, 58ff., 160ff.; Flügel, *Spekulative Theologie* (Cöthen: O. Schulze, 1881), 95ff.; O. Pfleiderer, *Development of Dogmatic Theology*, trans. J. Frederick Smith, 3d ed. (London: George Allen & Unwin, L&D, 1909), 195ff.; A. Bruining, "De Moderne Richting en de Dogmatiek," *Theologische Tijdschrift* 28 (1894): 563ff.; Traub, *Theologische Studiën und Kritiken* 68 (1895): 471–529; Fleisch, *Die erkenntniss theoretische und metaphysische Grundlagen der dogmatische Systeme von A. E. Bierdermann und R. A. Lipsius* (Berlin: Schwetschke, 1901); Pfennigsdorf, *Vergleich der dogmatische Systeme von R. A. Lipsius und A. Ritschl* (Gotha: F. A. Perthes, 1896).

But unlike Ritschl and Herrmann, to some extent he still acknowledges the validity of metaphysics. Our reason feels a need and compulsion to rise above the world of experience to an "unconditioned ground," and forming concepts of the absolute, of the soul, etc., our mind strives toward unity. But this metaphysical or philosophic type of thinking is no longer real science. It does not produce any positive (concrete) content. It does not, as Biedermann believes, increase our stock of truth. It only yields "formal determinations," "basic concepts," "regulative principles." If we nevertheless insist on putting some content into it and want to achieve transcendent knowledge by it, we are projecting sensible forms into it and entangle ourselves in an antinomy. The logical and the symbolic view of the metaphysical come into conflict. This, therefore is not the way to achieve knowledge of the supersensible. But there is still another way, that of practical-moral "compulsions." We are not only thinking but also willing and acting beings, and we feel a compulsion to assert ourselves as such over against the world. Religion is born in us from this contradiction between the human spirit and nature. This is a practical matter of the spirit and does not arise first of all from theoretical but from practical needs. This practical-ethical compulsion to maintain oneself in one's existence pushes a person toward faith in God, to postulating a supersensible world. Faith therefore begins where science ends.

This faith carries with it a certainty of its own, not a scientific but a moral certainty, the certainty of experience, based on the "experienced certainty" of one's own person. To another person this certainty is perhaps no more than an illusion, but to the subject himself or herself it is certain. Such experience is also the sole criterion for the truth of the Christian religion, the revelation in Christ. A personal appropriation of the historical revelation is the only direct proof for the truth of the Christian religion. The personal experience of believers confirms the historical revelation, just as the latter arouses and reinforces the former. And the Christian, believing thus, then confesses supersensible realities. In the dogmas he or she does not merely furnish a description of "states of mind" and "value judgments," but "factual judgments" concerning the relation between humanity and God as well as between God, humanity, and the world. These religious assertions are true if they stand in a logically compelling relation to the realization of our highest destiny. Not incidental but necessary value judgments prove the objective truth of religious statements. To believers themselves these proofs are sufficient; and for nonbelievers there is an indirect apologetic proof in the fact that practical compulsions force people toward religion. Religion is not coercive. It is not a natural power, but it is practically and psychologically necessary and to that extent grounded in human nature.

Dogmatically, furthermore, believers have the obligation to combine the content of their faith into a single whole with all their knowledge of the world. Herrmann kept "believing" and "knowing" as rigorously as possible and to the very end in separate compartments. Lipsius, on the other hand, though he derives the content of each from its own source, finally wants to gather up those contents into a single unified worldview. Dogmatics, he writes, though it cannot prove the content of faith and lift faith to the level of knowledge, can and must somehow link the Christian teleological world-view with the causal worldview, the knowledge of the world obtained else-where. It must also attempt to demonstrate that there is no conflict between these two worldviews, that the conflict is only apparent, and unity indeed exists. Even though the dogmas [of the church] do not contain scientific truth or any theoretical forms of knowledge, and are pictorial and anthropo-logical, they may not be inconsistent with the firm results of science. The unity of our spirit forbids the acceptance of a double truth. The religious idea of God and the concept of the absolute, freedom, and necessity, the tel-eological and the causal worldview must be compatible.

We encounter the same ideas we found in Ritschl and Lipsius, be it in a slightly different form and less sharply defined, in Sabatier and the Parisian school.[112] Kant, by his limitation of the cognitive capacity of human beings, again secured a place for mystery and religion. Though in our search for univer-sal regularity we seek knowledge by means of the intellect, we are also volitional, free, moral agents, subject to the law of the categorical imperative. Hence there is in us a conflict between intellect and will, theoretical and practical reason, deter-minism and freedom, science and morality, knowledge and value judgment. That conflict is necessary and good; it is the condition for all progress and the origin of religion. "The solution of the conflict is religion." In religion the hu-man spirit affirms and asserts its superiority over nature, saving itself by faith in a divine power. "The human spirit cannot believe in itself without believing in God; on the other hand, it cannot believe in God without finding him in itself." Religion, accordingly, is essentially not a doctrine, not an intellectual insight, but a new life, a "moral act which carries its own legitimization and its sufficient war-rant within itself." It is the fruit of an interior revelation of God, which is never the communication of a doctrine, but the enrichment of life, "an elevation and enrichment of the interior life of the subject."

Though that essence of religion underlies all religion, it nevertheless devel-oped gradually, just as, for that matter, human beings themselves gradually be-came "spirits." It is fully revealed in the person of Christ, who was the first to experience a perfect relation between God and his soul, who reproduces this religious experience in the hearts of his disciples, and therefore retains a place of permanent significance in Christianity. He is the author, prophet, initiator, and master of the religion he founded. This religion is not a doctrine, but spirit, the religion of the spirit, of love, freedom, and holiness. Jesus did not demand the acceptance of any doctrine or belief but only faith, trust in God,

---

112. On symbolo-fideism in France, see Joh. Steinbeck, *Das Verhältnis von Theologie und Erkennt-nisstheorie . . . A. Ritschl und A. Sabatier* (Leipzig: Dörffling & Franke, 1898); Wobbermin, *Theologie und Metaphysik* (Berlin: Alexander Duncker, 1901), 100ff.; *E. Doumergue, *Les étapes du fidéisme* (Toulouse, 1906). Also see the references above, p. 196 n. 40.

and subordinately, in himself. Though Christianity is a historical religion, which remains bound to the person of Christ, it is therefore, nevertheless, the perfect, the absolute, and definitive religion. But this is not how the church has understood it. The history of dogma has been a corruption of original Christianity. "The history of a dogma is its true criticism." In the pagan and Jewish eras of the past, nothing else was possible. But now the religion of the priest and the book is yielding to the religion of the spirit. "The authentically Christian era is now beginning." In earlier times people did not understand that religion was not a doctrine. They simply equated religion with orthodoxy, and faith with accepting as true some doctrine or another, and revelation with the communication of ideas. It was all intellectualism in either the orthodox or the rationalistic form. But now after Kant and Schleiermacher, we have much better insight into all these things. Religion is life: subjective religion is primary and central and constitutes the heart of objective religion.

In dogma, therefore, there are two components, a religious and a theoretical one, which relate to each other as soul and body, as core and shell. Hence the form or expression of a dogma is variable, inasmuch as it is determined by the level of civilization achieved by the given religious community, which interprets its religious life in dogma. Even more important is the vast difference between religious and scientific knowledge. In the latter one can obtain objective, adequate knowledge, but in religion, in the moral sciences in general, knowledge is and always remains *subjective* and *symbolic*. It is the task of theology (dogmatics), therefore, to study the religious life. This is its true object and the basis of its independence as a science. This must be done scientifically, i.e., by the psychological and historical method. Then theology must seek new forms in which the religious life can express itself as authentically as possible, and so to aim for the realization of a religious worldview in tune with the present day. If theology understands this unique calling, it will bring peace between the two groups of sciences, which in our day are so often at each other's throat. The natural and the human (moral) sciences are not identical; one cannot be traced to the other; morality cannot be reduced to physics, nor physics to morality. Still, though both groups have to be maintained side by side, they are not incompatible, any more than mechanicism and teleology. They go together, develop in response to each other's influence, need each other, and correspond to each other. Although theoretical and practical reason, human receptivity and activity, are distinct, human beings are all of a piece and continue to look for a synthesis. In God there is unity, for humanity and the world both owe their existence to him. Thus there is hope for a definitive solution in the future.

Critique

[145] This ethical-practical method of vindicating religion and Christianity, which proves to be closely related to the religious-empirical method, certainly deserves preference over the historical and speculative methods. It

does not just view religion as doctrine, which has to be justified to the human intellect, nor as a state of the subject, which has to be intellectually analyzed. Instead it views religion as an objective historical power corresponding to the moral needs of human beings and finds its proof and justification in those needs.

Yet this method too is open to serious objections. In the first place, we have to grant that the correspondence between a religion and the moral needs of human beings are of great significance. The satisfaction of the human heart and conscience are the seal and crown of religion. A religion that has no consolation to offer in time of mourning and sorrow, in life and in death, cannot be the true religion. From other sciences, from logic, mathematics, physics, etc., we do not expect comfort for the guilty conscience and the saddened heart. But a religion that has nothing to say at sickbeds and deathbeds, that cannot fortify the doubting ones, nor raise up those who are bowed down, is not worthy of the name.[113] The contrast often made between truth and consolation does not belong in religion. A truth that contains no comfort, which does not connect with the religious-ethical life of human beings, ceases by that token to be a religious truth. Just as medical science in all its specialties is oriented to the healing of the sick, so in religion people have a right to look for peace and salvation.

Yet, however highly we may esteem this element of comfort in religion, and however much it may be considered, along with other proofs, as a powerful motivation toward belief, as proof solely in and by itself it is insufficient. After all, some comfort and satisfaction can be found in all religions. The experiences of misery and guilt, of doubt and confidence, of endurance and hope, are present not only among Christians but also in varying degrees among Muslims and Buddhists. A religion that fails to furnish comfort and satisfaction to the moral needs of people is certainly false. Conversely, not every religion in which people look for comfort or satisfaction is true. Moreover, the needs of heart and conscience that some religion relieves or satisfies are either aroused by the influence of that religion itself—in that case their satisfaction is rather natural and not a strong proof—or they may have originated apart from that religion under other influences and under the impact of another religion, and then the peculiar need that presupposes this religion is not present and satisfaction is totally lacking.

In the real world one finds almost no sign of an unconscious aspiration of the soul toward Christianity. The history of missions teaches us almost nothing about a ripeness of people for the gospel. The gospel is not to the liking of human nature, not a ready match for the needs of people as they themselves picture those needs. Outside of revelation human beings do not even know themselves. The often-repeated claim that Christianity corresponds to

113. Gottschick, *Die Kirchlichkeit der sogenannte Kirchliche Theologie* (Freiburg i.B.: J. C. B. Mohr, 1890), 4.

human needs brings with it the very real danger that the truth is tailored to suit human nature. The thesis that the truth is authentically human because it is so intensely divine so easily turns into its opposite, viz., that it is only divine because it is human. The preaching that, rather than speaking to the heart of Jerusalem, flatters it is not uncommon even on Christian pulpits. In that setting we need no longer speak of religious experience. However important it may be, it cannot serve as adequate proof for the truth of Christianity. And those who elevate it to the status of a source or standard of the truth of the Christian faith gradually rob the latter of its historical character and permit it to be reduced to a number of vague religious-ethical propositions. This, however, is nothing but a new form of the frequently but futilely attempted split between "idea" and "fact" in Christianity. Cut down the tree, and its fruit can no longer be picked. Stop up the spring, and fresh clear water will no longer flow from it.

Others have sought the content and proof of the Christian religion in so-called "value judgments" instead of in the satisfaction of the human heart and conscience. If all this meant was that a dogma must always contain a religious-ethical value, no one could raise any objections against these "value judgments." Indeed, in every dogma one must be able to hear the heartbeat of religion. One could also settle for "value judgments" if Ritschl had only meant by them that with respect to the truths of faith one cannot arrive at complete certainty by means of philosophical reasoning or intellectual proofs but only "by the experience of the values expressed in the ideas of faith."[114] For in that case the subjective appreciation would presuppose the objective reality of Christian truth and serve only as a means to give us subjective assurance of that reality. The value of a thing in that case would not be the ground of its existence but only prompt us to acknowledge its existence subjectively. But even Ritschl's followers admit that he did not express himself clearly on this point, thus giving occasion for misunderstanding, and that the expression "value judgments" can easily be misunderstood.

It is in any case certain that when value judgments are detached from all metaphysics, they cannot be the foundation and content of dogmatics. Religion implies the conviction of the reality of its object. Religious and ethical appraisal assumes the truth of the person or matter to which it relates. Value judgments, accordingly, depend on factual judgments; they stand or fall together. If the assessment of an object is not grounded in its reality, it is nothing but illusion, a creation of the imagination, or the formation of an ideal in the sense of Lange and Pierson. Therefore it will not do to say,[115] "Let the facts be what they may, the appraisal decides," since the appraisal changes along with the facts. If the people and religion of Israel developed as modern

114. This is how Ritschl is interpreted by Traub, "Ritschl's Erkenntnisstheorie," *ZThK* 4 (1894): 91–114; cf. author, "Die Beurteilung der Ritschlschen Theologie," *ZThK* 12 (1902): 497–548.

115. As, for example, O. Ritschl does in his "Theologische Wissenschaft und religiöse Spekulation," *ZThK* 12 (1902): 202–48, 255–315.

criticism pictures that development, the assessment of the OT has to be fundamentally rewritten. A modern view of history and an orthodox appraisal of its content do not fit together. If Christ is not truly God, he cannot for the Christian have the value of God. And that is true of all the dogmas. Religious evaluation is integrally bound up with objective truth. Much of the nebulous character of modern theology would disappear if Biedermann's wish came true and the fashionable term "value judgments" were banished.[116] There is a growing conviction that religious-ethical experience and appraisal, however important, cannot guarantee the truth of their object, nor can they be the criterion for the content of dogmatics. Also psychologically this notion cannot be justified. For the decision about the reality of things cannot be made in the domain of the will or of feeling, in the heart or the conscience, but only in the domain of consciousness. Only if the reality of a thing is established for the mind can the other faculties of the soul work with it. Wishing, feeling, experiencing, imagining in no way imply the reality of their objects. The way to the heart runs through the head.

Nevertheless, though seeing the weakness of experience-and-appraisal-based proof, many thinkers still attempt to rescue some of it by means of Kant's theory of postulation. They do indeed grant that the moral nature of human beings may not be the ground from which the reality of all sorts of religious ideas or even the truth of the Christian religion is inferred. Nonetheless, they derive from it the right to postulate the actual existence of everything that is necessarily bound up with that moral nature without which it is undermined and destroyed. But just in what this "everything" consists no one can tell. Opinions vary radically. After all, who can determine in the abstract what things are directly and immediately tied in with the moral nature of human beings? In each person that moral nature differs, depending on the environment in which it was shaped. People tend to postulate precisely as much as is needed to satisfy their own religion. Kant derived from practical reason that which formed the content of his moral religion of reason: the existence of freedom, God, and immortality. For Fichte the moral world order was enough. And Rauwenhoff claims that faith in ourselves necessarily postulates faith in a state of the world such that the logic of a sense of duty can prevail.[117] Just in what that state consists he does not say. The

116. Biedermann, *Christliche Dogmatik,* I, 54. In addition to the literature cited above on pp. 172 n. 16 and 541 n. 106, see Scheibe, *Die Bedeutung der Werthurtheile für das religiöse Erkenntniss* (Halle a.s.: Buchdruckerei des Waisenhauses, 1893); O. Ritschl, *Über Werthurtheile* (Freiburg: Mohr, 1895), as cited by Kaftan, *Theologische Literaturzeitung* (1894): col. 194; Traub, *Theologische Studiën und Kritiken* (1895): 489ff.; Max Reischle, *Werturteile und Glaubensurteile* (Halle a.s.: Max Niemeyer, 1900); Wobbermin, *Theologie und Metaphysik,* 95ff.; Girgensohn, *Die Religion* (Leipzig: A. Deichert, 1903), 105ff.; M. Kähler, *Beweis des Glaubens* (1903): 309–26.

117. Rauwenhoff, *Wijsbegeerte van de Godsdienst,* 343. Literature on Rauwenhoff's *Wijsbegeerte* is cited by A. Kuenen in his biographical article on Rauwenhoff, *Maatschappij voor Nederlands Letterkunde* (1889): 126; cf. de Bussy in *De Gids* (October 1889); T. Cannegieter, *De Godsdienst uit Plichtbesef* (Leiden, 1890).

moral world order he postulates is nothing other than the "good" within us.[118] But this does not help one bit. For this power of the good is already present in us now and totally coincides with that moral nature on which the postulate was constructed. Whether that postulate includes anything else— e.g., that the good will triumph, that some day all people will be able and willing to accomplish it—on that question Rauwenhoff remains silent. He does expect this triumph of the good, but on what ground he does not say. If, however, the present state of the world is consistent with the rule of the moral law in us, why should it not be so in the future as well? What right does the moral nature of human beings give us to demand the complete, final triumph of the good, the harmony of virtue and happiness, the correspondence between the natural and the moral world order? In Rauwenhoff the theory of postulation ends by returning to its point of departure. In the end it did not produce anything that was not contained in it at the start.

But apart from its meager results, the question arises whether we can trust the basis on which the postulate is constructed. For the modern philosopher of religion, this basis is not beyond all possibility of objection. In religion this philosopher wants nothing to do with a human nature that is religious in origin. That would be at variance with a scientific explanation. Religion has to be deduced from factors each of which as such is as yet non-religious. But when he comes to the moral nature of humanity, he seems completely to forget this demand of his scientific interpretation. Without being at all concerned about the objections raised from the side of materialistic science, he then proceeds from the moral nature of humanity as from a permanent, invariable, original attribute and builds upon it the reality of a moral world order or even of a totally metaphysical world. The right to do this should at the very least have been demonstrated. If this investigation had been undertaken beforehand, it could perhaps have become clear that the moral nature of humanity itself already presupposes religion. In an epistemological sense one may, as with the moral proof for existence of God, move upward from the moral to the religious; logically and realistically, nevertheless, religion is prior to the ethical. There is no morality without metaphysics. The idea of duty involves that of an absolute power that binds the conscience.[119]

[146] A more serious objection to the above school of thought is that it always proceeds from and therefore always has to end as well with a certain dualism between faith and knowledge. Some have expressed this in very black-and-white terms. Scholasticism in the Middle Ages ended, in the case of some theologians, with the proposition that a given thesis could be true in theology but false in philosophy. Jacobi confessed he was a pagan in his intellect but a Christian at heart. Herrmann called the reality of faith an illusion to science. The ethical moderns demanded a complete separation be-

118. Rauwenhoff, *Wijsbegeerte*, 536ff.
119. On Rauwenhoff's philosophy of religion, see the lit. cited by Kuenen in his biographical sketch, *Maatschappij voor Nederlands Letterkunde*, 126.

tween philosophy and the religious life. The majority, however, did not dare to go that far and understood the impossibility of saying no as philosophers and yes as religious people. They recognize that in the end there has to be harmony between the pronouncements of faith and the results of science.

While philosophy may not be able to legitimate religious ways of putting things, it certainly cannot demonstrate their falseness either. The outcomes of scientific research and the assertions of religious belief must be capable of being united into a single whole or at least exist side-by-side without conflict and hostility. Scholars then try to achieve this agreement in the end, in the results, on the one hand by making science agnostic in relation to the super-sensible and supernatural and, on the other, by limiting the assertions of religious belief to the religious-ethical dimension. But even though in that way they seek to avoid dualism in the result, they in fact continue to perpetuate it in the faculty and the method by which they arrive at the knowledge of truth. In its domain the heart is as good an organ for the perception of truth as the head. Religious-moral experience guarantees the reality of invisible things as certainly as sense perception does that of the visible world. Faith with its grounds has as much validity as science with its proofs. But it is hard to see how in the end and in the result one can escape the dualism one has accepted in principle in the beginning. If both head and heart have a life of their own in the sense that each is an independent organ for acquiring knowledge of the truth, then also the unity of truth, of the world, indeed of God himself can no longer be maintained. Just as, subjectively speaking, a human falls apart in two pieces and is on the one hand an a-religious being enclosed within the world of nature and on the other a religious-ethical being, the citizen of a moral world order, so speaking objectively, science and religion, the reality that can be explained and the reality that can be experienced, the world of existence and the world of appraisal, the visible things and the invisible things, the absolute power of nature and the religious concept of God, exist side-by-side and before long face each other from opposing hostile camps.

Now, wrapped up in this dualism there is undoubtedly also a truth that must not be denied. Beside a logical certainty there is also a certainty of faith. But this distinction—as will become evident later—is very different from the split presented in the dualism described above. For this twofold certainty does not divide either human beings or the world into two halves. What it does is to make a distinction within the sphere of science itself between that which is added to our stock of knowledge immediately and that which is added by means of proofs. But the dualism that has come to prevail in modern philosophy permits the entire created world to fall apart in two totally separate sections and is consequently in conflict with the unity of the human spirit, the unity of science and of truth, the unity of the world, the unity of the divine Being himself. For that reason it is also unable to reconcile believing and knowing with each other; in fact, it rather intensifies the conflict. The history of recent decades has clearly shown up this process. From the side of science people have increasingly started to acknowledge that empiricism is not enough. To the degree that with the progress of research in chemistry, biology, etc., the mysteries increased and the so-called exact sciences failed to produce solutions, the need arose more urgently than ever to fill up with reflection the gaps left behind by experience. Natural science itself strives to become philosophy of nature. Men such as Von Hartmann, Paulsen, Wundt, Haeckel, etc. absolutely do not respect the boundaries that neo-Kantians have drawn around science but try, on an empirical basis, to build a world system. In the thought of Ziegler, Schmidt, and Drews, the dualistic theology of Ritschl has a very hard time justifying itself. Similarly on the side of religion and theology, there is an increasing number of people who consider the proposed divorce impossible. Wobbermin, himself a product of the school of Ritschl, has argued for the restoration of metaphysics in theology. The proponents of the history-of-religions method also consider themselves dissatisfied on account of the isolation into which Ritschl had pressed Christianity and theology. The theology of separation has had its day.

Neo-Kantian theologians, for that matter, themselves do not consistently follow the lines of separation and diverge a great deal from each other when they point out the direction where the boundary between religion and science has to be drawn. Does it run between factual judgments and value judgments (Ritschl), or between empiricism and speculation (Lipsius), or between natural science and human science (the physical and the moral sciences—Sabatier)? Must it be drawn in theology itself between theological science and religious speculation (O. Ritschl), or between scientific and ecclesiastical theology (Lagarde), or between exegetical historical and dogmatic practical theology (Bernoulli), or between faith and beliefs (Sabatier)? Everyone senses that the boundary is completely arbitrary here or rather that every theologian draws it just on the other side of what he considers the essence of religion so as to safeguard it from science. One division is as untenable as another. Sabatier, for example, influenced as he is by the importance of French science, believes that the boundary between the natural and the moral sciences is continuous and considers the latter, specifically the science of religion, subjective, inasmuch as in the case of the former the object of knowledge lies outside of humanity and in the case of the latter in humanity. But that is definitely wrong. Aside from the question of whether the objects of the moral sciences can be known by the subjects solely internally from within themselves, in any case God, the soul, immortality, the moral law, etc., definitely belong to the objective world of existence and certainly do not exist as ideas in their own mind. Indeed, if this were the case, all the moral sciences would be based, not on reality, but on illusion.

The arbitrariness of separation becomes even more obvious when we turn our attention to a specific point. All the scholars who belong to this neo-

Kantian school of thought, while they intend to ascribe to the person of Christ ongoing importance for the religious life, offer very differing answers to the question of what in the person of Christ is of passing and what is of permanent significance. Herrmann, who makes a distinction between the ground and the content of faith, believes that the "inner life" of Jesus alone is absolutely certain both for the unbeliever and for the believer and can therefore alone be the ground of faith. Others, rejecting that distinction, count that which belongs to the content of faith also as its ground but then again describe that content in very different ways. Häring, for example, maintains against Reischle that also the resurrection of Christ belongs to the content of faith. Kirn distinguishes the elements in Jesus' life that are certain to history from those that are certain to faith. History can and does teach that Jesus really existed and was a benefactor to humankind, and faith augments this with the conviction that in him God's revelation was given. Traub consoles himself with the idea that historical science in any case can never prove that Jesus did not exist. That is sufficient for faith, for it tells us that which is possible to science is necessary to me.[120] Others again draw the boundary between judgments of knowledge and judgments of faith.[121] But for as long as they want to maintain that Christianity is the perfect, absolute, definitive, and simultaneously a historical religion that remains bound to the person of Christ, so long also they will not be able to make faith absolutely independent of "beliefs," nor rob it of all intellectual knowledge and assent. Nor can they reduce it to trust (*fiducia*) or, better still, to a vague and indefinite mood, and thus they will suffer in principle from the same defect they so strenuously oppose in orthodoxy. For we have to choose: faith is either bound to the historical revelation in Christ, includes some knowledge, however little, of that revelation and thereby binds free inquiry, or it is entirely separate from the person of Christ but is then no longer Christian faith. The historical Jesus then has to yield his place, as in the philosophy of Hegel, to the ideal Christ. One retains nothing of the former, and the latter is the product of the imagination.

Given the proposed separation, therefore, science, but also the Christian religion, falls short. The latter is evident from the fact that the content of the Christian faith is ever-increasingly restricted, e.g., to the religious experience—which Jesus first experienced to perfection—that God was his Father and he was his Son. Furthermore, by the standard of this principle, the entire history of dogma was one enormous aberration. And finally the essence of all religions is then identical, consisting as it does in the immanence of God, be it that, depending on the state of culture, this immanence is interpreted and represented more or less correctly. The core of all religions, then,

---

120. Th. Häring, "Gehört die Auferstehung Jesu zum Glaubensgrund?" *ZThK* 7 (1897): 330–51; Kirn, *Glaube und Geschichte* (1901); Traub, "Die religionsgeschictliche Methode und die systematische Theologie," *ZThK* 11 (1901): 323ff.

121. E.g., Th. Kaftan, *Modern Theologie des alten Glaubens* (Schleswig: J. Bergas, 1905).

is faith (*foi*) independent of beliefs (*croyances*). Stated more clearly, this core is the self-assertion of the human spirit with the aid of the idea of God over against nature as a force that oppresses it, one of the many expressions of the instinct of self-preservation. We have demonstrated earlier that religion cannot have originated in that fashion and that its essence cannot be located there either. In any case, the Christian religion is misconstrued here, for it is based, not on the contrast between nature and spirit, between theoretical and practical reasons, but on the opposition between sin and grace. Christianity does not consist in the revolution of the conflict between subject and object but in reconciliation between God and humanity; it is defined, not by three but by two points, as Harnack and Kaftan have recognized contrary to Ritschl.

If this is so, if Christianity is indeed a religion of redemption, then the revelation from which it has sprung also includes the communication of truth, the discovery and liberation from falsehood. Then word and fact, prophecy and miracle, illumination and regeneration also combine to support that truth. Also, subjectively, cognition and trust (*fiducia*) are always united in that faith. Objective religion, then, is not the product of subjective religion but given in divine revelation that we should walk in it. And dogma is not merely a symbolic interpretation of the spiritual life but an expression, be it a human one, of the truth God has given in his Word. All our religious knowledge is certainly nonexhaustive, anthropomorphic, analogical. By confusing this reality with the "symbolical," Sabatier is thereby doing an injustice to the history of dogma. For that matter, when he himself again calls certain symbolic representations—such as that of the unity of God, the kingdom of God—permanent symbols, it is clear that he considers symbolic only the dogmas with which he himself no longer agrees. And that indeed is how the issue stands: dogma is either a pure expression of our faith or that is no longer so. In the latter case, we must abandon or revise it, but it can no longer be rescued by means of the term "symbolic."

16

FAITH AND ITS GROUND

In the previous chapter we considered the possibility that the human will or intellect of the "natural" person could be the means by which divine revelation is appropriated. Though we rejected this possibility, nonetheless it is true that Christian theology as an area of scientific inquiry must begin with the human subject. It is here that one finds the internal principle corresponding to divine revelation. Christian theology has always taken its position in the believing subject, in faith, in the believing community. The slogan that guides and controls Christian theology is per fidem ad intellectum ("through faith to understanding").

Scripture itself directs us to this, to the inner illumination of the Holy Spirit. The truth of God can be known only in faith. Though terms such as "rebirth," "purity of heart," "the Spirit of God," among others, are used in Scripture for the internal principle, the means by which revelation is appropriated, the preferred term is "faith." Since all knowledge is mediated through human consciousness, revelation too is known as an act of human consciousness, namely faith. Both objectively and subjectively revelation connects with nature, re-creation with creation. In all areas of life we start by believing. The universality of faith points to the importance of immediate, intuitive grasp of truth; our sure knowledge of reality is not limited to that which we obtain through our senses. It is immediate certainty rather than demonstrable certainty that makes life in community, in society, possible.

Nonetheless, general immediate certainty is not identical to religious faith. Saving faith has as its object, not simply God's words and deeds as such, but the grace of God in Jesus Christ. Faith is also a matter of knowledge and truth, but above all it is trust and surrender to God. Knowledge of saving faith comes to us through the testimony of others (e.g., the apostles). The road to the human heart taken by the Spirit of God runs through the human head and human consciousness. This knowledge of saving faith is bound to Scripture, to the apostolic witness.

When faith is understood primarily as intellectual assent, as it is in Roman Catholicism, it becomes objectified as "historical faith." Understandably, this faith was considered insufficient for salvation and had to be augmented. Still, in this way the Reformation's sola fide was denied in favor of the meritoriousness of intellectual assent as preparation for the infused grace of justification. While this idea of faith as intellectual assent played only a preparatory role in Roman Catholic thinking, in Reformation thought faith was an act of the newly regenerated person who had been made new by the special grace of the Holy Spirit. Faith was religious through and through and had its own kind of certainty.

Faith's certainty rests on the testimony and promises of God himself and has the power victoriously "to overcome the world" (1 John 5:4). It is here, in the matter of certainty, that we see the real difference between Rome and the Reformation. The moral certainty that Kant argued for as the foundation of practical reason divorces practical and theoretical reason and thus cannot sustain the truth of Christian revelation. Whereas, on Kant's terms, believing is a weaker form of knowing, in the Christian religion believing is certainty itself. The certainty of faith is as firm as that of knowledge, though it is more intense, unshakable, and ineradicable. Scientific theories do not produce martyrs; religion does.

For this reason intellectual and historical proof cannot provide the final ground of faith. While revelation may be made credible by proofs, it is and remains a truth of faith, a gift of grace. Only the Spirit of God can make a person inwardly certain of the truth of divine revelation. God's revelation can be believed only in a religious sense, on God's own authority. The ground for faith is the internal testimony of the Holy Spirit. This position, however, seems circular: We believe Scripture is God's revelation because the Bible tells us so. Such circularity can be broken only by the inner conviction that God has spoken. This witness of God is the final ground of faith; our will to believe is, by God's grace, the final cause of our faith.

While the church as the community of believers is the context within which the Spirit's testimony is confirmed, Scripture's authority is not granted by the church's decision. The opposite is true: Scripture founded the church. Through the gracious work of the Holy Spirit, Scripture is self-authenticating. Under pressure from the rationalism of the Socinians, Remonstrants, and Roman Catholics, even some Reformed theologians such as Amyrald weakened this inner testimony by identifying it with the illumination of the intellect.

In modern theology of the nineteenth century, the rationalism of Kant and Lessing and the romanticism of Schleiermacher contributed to a return of the conviction that the truth of faith is different and cannot be validated finally by proofs of reason. Though modern theologians are still far from Calvin's doctrine of the testimony of the Holy Spirit, the turn away from external proofs to the religious subject as the final ground of faith is a salutary development.

At the same time the uniqueness of faith's ground and thus of theology as a science must not lead us to overlook the fact that all truth, all science, has a subjective starting point. All that is objective can be approached only from the vantage point of the subject; the thing in itself is unknowable and does not exist for us. All knowledge is based on a kind of agreement between subject and object, an agreement that originates from the divine mind of the Creator. It is the one selfsame Logos who made all things in and outside of human beings. And it is the Spirit of God who is the source and agent of all life in humanity and in the world. All cognition of truth is a witness of the Spirit of God to the Word, by whom all things are made.

Nonetheless, the external source of the Christian religion is not God's general revelation in nature but his special revelation in Scripture and in Christ. And it is the internal testimony of the Spirit that must correspond to that external source. This inner testimony is not a new revelation but recognition of a truth that exists independent of our subjective awareness. The parallel is with the moral law whose authority as God's will is also self-authenticating. Christians believe the truth of Scripture because "God said it."

This does not mean, however, that believers have nothing but their subjectivity as a response to opponents of the faith. Unbelief too, it must be said, is also rooted in the human heart. In addition, the inner testimony of the Spirit is not private but universal. The church of all ages bears witness to Scripture as the Word of God. Nurtured in community, faith does not come into being by the insight of our intellect or a decision of our will but by the gracious and overpowering illumination of God's Spirit. Because our wills are transformed and renewed, our believing is a free act of self-denial. True knowledge of God is compelling but never coerced.

Opposition to faith also comes from within. Sins of the heart and errors of the mind gang up on faith as believers continue to experience the conflict within between "spirit" and "flesh." God himself is the final ground of our faith and the testimony of the Holy Sprit is, in the first place, assurance that we are God's children. The illumination of the Holy Spirit is not the cognitive source of Christian truth; it only seals in our hearts the truth of Scripture and salvation history. Faith is concentrated on the historic realities of redemption and results in trust that these historic acts are God's saving acts for us. It is the same Spirit that inspired the apostolic witness that now seals the truth of that witness in believers' hearts. Christians submit to Scripture because they believe it is a divine word, a word from God.

This testimony of the Holy Spirit is not nullified by the variable responses to it among believers. Still, when it comes to convictions concerning Scripture itself, there is remarkable unity among different church groups. Scripture has been given to the whole church, and the Spirit's testimony concerning Scripture is a cornerstone of the church's very existence. The authority of Scripture, accepted in Spirit-inspired faith, is a powerful self-asserted authority. We believe it because God said it, and God's speaking is the final ground of our faith. There is no power in the world comparable to that of Scripture.

APPROPRIATING REVELATION BY FAITH

[147] The preceding chapter has shown that the "internal principle" of the Christian religion and theology cannot be located in the intellect or reason, in the heart or the will of the "natural" [unspiritual] person. No proofs and arguments, no religious experience or ethical satisfaction, after all, constitute the deepest ground of faith; they all presuppose a sturdier foundation on which they are built and from which they themselves derive their value.

All the schools of thought described earlier to some extent realized this as well. Even those who sought to prove the truth of the Christian religion intellectually were still of the opinion that what was needed on the human side was a moral disposition to sense the power of those proofs. Pascal, in the first part of his apology, attempted to arouse in people an awareness of their misery and need for redemption and peace. And through and after Schleiermacher most theologians have arrived at the insight that religion is unique and can be known only in a manner corresponding to that uniqueness. While epistemology is always the same, it is nevertheless adapted to the object that is being considered in every science, and so in religion as well. By making this statement Christian theology indeed takes its starting point in the human subject. The accusation of subjectivism immediately launched against this position, however, is unwarranted and in any case premature. For, in the first place, in no area of knowledge and science is there any other starting point. Light presupposes the eye, and sound is perceptible only by the ear. All that is objective exists for us only by means of a subjective consciousness; without consciousness the whole world is dead for us. Always in human beings an internal principle has to correspond to the external principle [revelation] if there is to be a relation between object and subject.

Second, from the very beginning Christian theology has taken its position in the believing subject. It was born out of faith, was at all times intimately bound up with the church, and continually guided and controlled by the slogan: "through faith to understanding" (*per fidem ad intellectum*). Whenever apologetics for a time abandoned this position, it returned to it. Specifically the Reformation and, following the rationalism and supernaturalism of the eighteenth century, modern theology again took its stance in the believing consciousness. All of theology has become ethical in the sense that it takes seriously the thesis that only the regenerate "see the kingdom of God" and that only "those who are resolved to do the will of God will recognize Jesus' teaching as coming from God" [cf. John 3:3; 7:17].

And finally, as is evident from these last quotations, this is also the teaching of Scripture. It speaks not only of a revelation of God in Christ outside of us but also of an illumination of the Holy Spirit within us. After God spoke to us by the Son, the Holy Spirit came to lead us into the truth. God not only gave us the Scriptures but also founded and maintains a church, which by faith accepts and confesses the Word of God.[1] The charge of subjectivism has no force, therefore, against the thesis that the truth of God can be known only in faith by the illumination of the Holy Spirit. If that charge were true, it would apply, *mutatis mutandis,* to all science, to all theology, to Holy Scripture itself. It would be valid only if the subjective condition by which alone the object can be known were made the "first principle" of knowledge. For though the eye may be the indispensable organ for the per-

1. See above, pp. 504–7.

ception of light, it is not its source. It is precisely the error of idealistic rationalism that it equates the organ of knowledge with the source of knowledge.
Thinking is not the source of the idea; the intellectual representation is not
the cause of the thing; the "I" is not the creator of the "non-I"; similarly
faith, regeneration, or experience cannot be the source of our religious
knowledge, nor the first principle of our theology. Hence, however correct
modern theology is in taking its stance in the subject, it errs when, under the
influence of idealistic philosophy, it converts theology into anthropology, ecclesiology, and the science of religion. To that extent Ritschl was correct in
calling the theology of consciousness, which had universally made its debut
after Schleiermacher, back to the objective, historic revelation in Christ.

Believing God's Promises

In Scripture, at least in the New Testament, this internal principle is
most frequently denominated by the term *faith*. Indeed, also "rebirth," "purity of heart," "love for the will of God," the "spirit of God" are presented
in Scripture as the internal principle (Matt. 5:8; John 3:3, 5; 7:17; 1 Cor.
2:12; etc.). Yet the term *faith* deserves preference as the designation of this
principle. This is not only because faith is most prominently featured as
such in Scripture but especially because the term *faith* situates us in the area
of consciousness and so preserves the link with the way we gain knowledge
in other areas as well. Earlier we saw that human reason is never and nowhere the source of knowledge; innate ideas do not exist. Both physically
and intellectually human beings are completely dependent on the world
outside of them. All knowledge comes from without. But on the human
side all that knowledge is mediated by their consciousness. Not feeling or
the heart but the mind, consciousness as a whole (perception, awareness,
observation, intellect, reason, conscience) is the subjective organ of truth.
Now when Scripture calls "faith" the internal principle, then by that token
it has the same view and recognizes that also the revelation of God can become knowledge only through the conscious mind. Not that in that connection rebirth, love, and purity of heart are not of the greatest importance.
Later on the contrary will be shown to be true. But the real means by which
the revelation of God is known is an act of the human consciousness, viz.,
faith. The revelation of God is a system of words and deeds of God, which
exist outside and independently of us. How could they ever become our
knowledge apart from our consciousness? The revelation of God is gospel,
promise, the promise of forgiveness and salvation; but on our part nothing
can match a promise except believing it: faith. Only by faith does a promise
become our possession. Faith, accordingly, is the internal principle of
knowledge (*principium internum cognoscendi*) of revelation and thus of religion and theology.[2]

2. E. von Hartmann, *Religionsphilosophie*, 7 vols. (Leipzig: Friedrich, 1885), II, 65ff.

All Knowledge Grounded in Faith

But there is still another reason for denominating the internal principle by the term *faith:* by it the nexus between religious knowledge and all other forms of human knowledge is preserved. Certainly there is distinction between them, but we must first of all note the agreement. In religion and theology we arrive at knowledge in no other way than in other sciences. Faith is not a new organ implanted in human beings, not a sixth sense, or "superadded gift." However much it disagrees with the "natural" [unspiritual] human, it is nevertheless completely natural, normal, and human. Both objectively and subjectively revelation connects with nature, re-creation with creation. Believing in general is a very common way in which people gain knowledge and certainty. In all areas of life we start by believing. Our natural inclination is to believe. It is only acquired knowledge and experience that teach us skepticism.[3] Faith is the foundation of society and the basis of science. Ultimately all certainty is rooted in faith.

Granted, the word *believe* is also used in a weaker sense when we are not sure about something but still consider it likely on grounds that to ourselves are sufficient. In that case "believing" forms a contrast with "knowing" and is related to "thinking." It occurs in the expression: "I do not know this, but I believe it is so." But the use of the word *believe* is not exhausted by this meaning. The very etymology of the word already indicates that there is another and deeper meaning concealed in the word *belief.* It derives from the same stem [*leubh*] as to care, desire, love, permission, furlough, leave, trust. It is related to "loving" and expresses total confidence in, as well as loving surrender and devotion to someone.[4] In other languages as well, the word *faith* or *belief* has this original meaning of devotion, trust, certainty: הֶאֱמִין, אֱמוּנָה; πειθω, πιστις; fido, fides; foi; "faith" and "belief."[5] Believing, accordingly, is frequently used for all forms of certain knowledge that are based, not on proofs, but on immediate and direct insight. Plato distinguished between ἐπιστημη, διανοια, πιστις, and εἰκασια and meant by πιστις certainty concerning the sensible world on the basis of perception.[6] For that reason he says: "Truth is to belief what being is to becoming." Aristotle made a distinction between knowledge acquired by demonstration and knowledge of "first principles," which was inferred from the mind (νους) itself. Now, while he

3. S. Hoekstra, *Bronnen en Grondslagen van het Godsdienstlijke Geloof* (Amsterdam: P. N. Van Kampen, 1864), 383.

4. F. A. Kahnis, *Die Luthersche Dogmatik,* 3 vols. (Leipzig: Dörffling & Francke, 1861–68), I, 106; S. Hoekstra, *Wijsgerige Godsdienstleer,* 2 vols. (Amsterdam: Van Kampen, 1894), I, 95; *Woordenboek der Nederlandsche Taal,* s.v. "geloof."

5. On the meaning of the Hebrew and Greek words, see Schlatter, *Der Glaube im Neuen Testament,* 3d ed. (Stuttgart: Verlag der Vereinsbuchhandlung, 1905), 555ff.

6. Zeller, *Philosophie der Griechen,* 4th ed., 3 vols. (Leipzig: Fues's Verlag, 1875–81), II, 591, 593 (ed. note: English translation available: E. Zeller, *Outlines of the History of Greek Philosophy,* trans. L. R. Palmer [New York: Humanities Press, 1969]). Siebeck, *Geschichte der Psychologie,* 2 vols. (Gotha: F. A. Perthes, 1880–84), 209.

does not call the latter knowledge by the name of *belief* he does say: "Whenever he somehow believes and the principles are known to him, he understands." When subsequently the word *belief* acquired such a deep religious meaning in Christianity, many church fathers pointed with fondness to the important place that believing has in life and science. Clement of Alexandria in many places uses πιστις to denote all immediate knowledge and certainty and then says that there is no science without belief, that the first principles, including, for example, the existence of God, are believed, not proven.[7] Especially Augustine highlighted the significance of belief for society and science. Those who do not believe, he says, never arrive at knowledge: "Unless you have believed you will not understand."[8] Belief is the foundation and bond uniting the whole of human society. If people accepted the proposition "I ought not to believe what I do not see," all the ties of family, friendship, and love would be ruptured. "If, then, it is the case that, when we do not believe what we cannot see, human society, itself, suffering the collapse of concord, will not stand, how much more should faith be applied to divine things, although they cannot be seen."[9] Since then, these same ideas keep recurring among Christian theologians, also in modern times.[10] The term *faith* is then applied to immediate knowledge of the first principles: to reliance on self, our perception and our thinking; to the recognition of the objective existence of the external world; to the mutual trust on which all of human society is built; to all that is known and done by intuition. In such a faith Schiller saw the guarantee of the existence of the new world that Columbus sought: "If it didn't yet exist, it would now rise up from the waves."

Upon further reflection no one would deny this deep significance of πιστις for life, art, and science. Over against those who think that nothing can be considered true that cannot be perceived by the senses or mathematically proven, it is a towering certainty that by far the most and the most important things we know are based, not on proofs, but on immediate certainty. The area covered by the latter is far bigger than that of demonstrable certainty. And the latter is always based again on the former and stands or falls

7. Denzinger, *Vier Bücher von der religiösen Erkenntnis,* 2 vols. (Würtzburg: Verlag der Stahel'schen Buch-und-Kunsthandlung, 1856–57), II, 470; Kleutgen, *Philosophie der Vorzeit,* 4 vols. (Münster: Theissing, 1863), I, 749; J. Schwane, *Dogmengeschichte,* 4 vols. (Freiburg i.B.: Herder, 1882–95), I, 110; Strauss, *Christliche Glaubenslehre,* 2 vols. (Leipzig: Hirzel, 1872), I, 301.

8. Augustine, *On the Trinity,* XV, 2, and passim.

9. Augustine, *Concerning Faith of Things Not Seen,* chap. 3; idem, *On the Profit of Believing,* chap. 10ff.; idem, *Confessions,* VI, 5; cf. Ritter, *Geschichte des Christlichen Philosophie,* 4 vols. (Hamburg: F. Perthes, 1841), II, 252ff.; Gangauf, *Metaphysische Psychologie des Augustinus* (Augsburg: K. Kollmann, 1852), 52ff.

10. I. Dorner, *A System of Christian Doctrine,* trans. Alfred Cave and J. S. Banks, rev. ed., 4 vols (Edinburgh: T. & T. Clark, 1888), I, 3, 33–168. J. P. Lange, *Christliche Dogmatik,* 3 vols. (Heidelberg: K. Winter, 1852), I, 342ff.; J. J. van Oosterzee, *Voor Kerk en Theologie* (Utrecht: Kemink, 1875–79), I, 94; A. Kuyper, *Encyclopaedie der Heilige Godgeleerdheid,* 3 vols. (Amsterdam: J. A. Wormser, 1894), II, 71ff.

with it. The way of arriving at knowledge and certainty by a method other than mathematical and logical proofs, therefore, is not at all foreign to human nature. Belief in a broad sense is an indispensable element in society and the normal road to science. It did not just become necessary as a result of sin; in fact, apart from sin intuitive knowledge and immediate certainty would have cut an even more generous swath in human life. Even now human originality is greater to the degree that human beings live by intuition rather than reflection. All the above examples, accordingly, can do eminent service as analogies of religious faith. They have in common with religious faith that knowledge is acquired immediately, not by reflection, and that in degree of certainty they are in no way inferior to that which is based on proofs. In addition they retain the connection existing between the usual way people arrive at knowledge and the way of faith that leads to certainty in the domain of religion. They show that believing as such is so far from being inimical to human nature and the demands of science that without it there cannot be normal people and a normal science.

TWO KINDS OF FAITH

[148] Still, for all the similarity, we may not ignore the difference that exists between faith as immediate certainty and faith in a religious sense. In religion, specifically in the Christian religion, πιστις acquires a value of its own. Also the ancient Greeks used the word in a religious sense, of faith in the gods,[11] but even then the word as such still has no religious content, any more than when we speak of belief in God, the soul, and its immortality, etc. Belief, here, is still the ordinary belief we practice every day but now applied to religious ideas. In the New Testament, however, πιστις is totally defined religiously—in its object, basis, and origin; it denotes a religious relationship between a human being and God. In Hebrews 11:1 "the things hoped for, the things not seen" are called the general object of Christian faith. By this fact alone faith in a religious sense is distinct from the knowledge we possess by immediate certainty. Belief in the external world, the senses, the laws of logic, etc. is based on one's own internal perception. Of all these things we have an immediate sense. But the object of Christian faith is invisible and not susceptible to observation. If a thing can be immediately observed by us, faith is superfluous; faith is opposed to sight (Rom. 8:24; 2 Cor. 5:7). This does not conflict with the fact that revelation certainly took place in space and time and that the person of Christ could be seen and touched. For as the object of faith this revelation as a whole was not observable. Many people saw Jesus and still did not believe in him; only his disciples saw in him "a glory as of the only begotten of the Father"

---

11. Cremer, *Biblio-Theological Lexicon of New Testament Greek*, trans. D. W. Simon and William Urwick (Edinburgh: T. & T. Clark, 1872), s.v. πιστις (*pistis*); cf. on the word πιστις as used by Polybius, the LXX, and Philo; also see Schlatter, *Der Glaube*, 565ff.

(John 1:14). Word and deeds are the object of faith only when considered from the divine perspective. But in Scripture, πιστις, as saving faith, acquires an even more pregnant meaning; its object is not all sorts of words and deeds of God as such but the grace of God in Christ (Mark 1:15; John 3:16; 17:3; Rom. 3:22; Gal. 2:20; 3:26; etc.). To [Christian] faith this special object is considered under still another heading than that of truth versus falsehood. The universal nature of faith is not exhausted by being characterized as a firm and sure knowledge, an objective holding for truth, since it also includes a heartfelt trust in a total surrender to God, who has revealed himself in Christ, and a personal appropriation of the promises extended in the gospel.

Faith in the religious sense, moreover, is distinguished from immediate certainty by the fact that the latter is based on one's own insight whereas the former is rooted in the insight of others. It is already remarkable that the word *faith* is not generally current in all the cases in which knowledge is based on immediate perception or observation. Belief in an external world, in the senses, the laws of logic, and the first principles is usually described as immediate knowledge. And indeed this immediate knowledge, like demonstrable knowledge, is based on one's own observation and insight. To that extent it can therefore also be called "knowing" in distinction from "believing."

But in the case of saving faith (*fides salvifica*), things are different. It most certainly has as its object the grace of God in Christ. But of that grace of God we would not have the slightest knowledge if it had not come to us through the witness of others, if it had not been assured to us in Holy Scripture. Between the person of Christ and our faith, therefore, stands the witness of the apostles. The word of God is a means of grace. Faith, to be sure, considers Scripture only under the aspect of its being the word of God (1 Thess. 2:13). For religious faith can rest only in a divine witness (John 3:33; Rom. 10:14f.; 1 John 5:9–11). Still faith is bound to Scripture. It has as its object the grace of God as it is attested in Scripture; or as Calvin puts it, its object is Christ "clothed with his gospel."[12] Faith, consequently, reaches out in a single act to the person of Christ as well as to Scripture. It embraces Christ as Savior and Scripture as the word of God. Therefore both approaches are true: by Christ to Scripture and by Scripture to Christ; Scripture leads us to Christ and directs the thought and affections of human beings to him who now dwells in heaven. Even those who want to remove all intellectual knowledge (*notitia*) and assent from saving faith and to reduce it completely to trust (*fiducia*) cannot avoid tracing this trust to an impression imprinted on the soul by the image of Christ; and fideism dare not say that "faith is independent of beliefs" but confines itself to the assertion (one which, for that matter, is also untenable) that "we are saved by faith inde-

12. J. Calvin, *Institutes,* III.ii.6; cf. Luther in J. Köstlin, *Theology of Luther,* trans. Charles E. Hay, 2 vols. (Philadelphia: Lutheran Publication Society, 1897), II, 434ff.

pendently of beliefs."[13] Also pietism is bound to external means. It may limit these means and want nothing to do with a catechism or dogmatics; yet, it tries to lead children to conversion by speaking to them of the dear Jesus.[14] There is in fact no road to the human heart other than that which runs through the head and consciousness. Only the Spirit of God can work immediately in the heart; we, by contrast, are bound to means. Scripture is and remains a "means of grace." Conversely, faith in Christ in turn affects our belief in Scripture. It binds and fastens us securely to Scripture and causes us to trust it in times of distress and death. Our soul, accordingly, may be inseparably bound to Christ, the living Lord in the heavens, by the mystical union forged by the Holy Spirit; still, to our consciousness, Christ, in fact the whole realm of "things hoped for," exists only through the witness of God in his Word. And, for that reason, saving faith always includes a cognitive component as well. Granted, this knowledge of saving faith is essentially distinct from the knowledge of historical faith. Even if the latter precedes the former, it is later grafted anew upon saving faith and changes in character. It is no mere "holding as true" but a firm and certain knowledge in the sense of Holy Scripture; the biblical idea of "knowing" is quite different and much deeper than that implied in ordinary usage. Nevertheless, the knowledge that believers possess is not immediate and not acquired by their insight. It is bound to Holy Scripture; it rests upon the witness of the apostles and prophets as the word of God.

Finally, Christian faith is also distinguished from immediate certainty by the fact that it does not automatically arise from human nature. All people believe in the external world, in the first principles, in observation, in the laws of logic, etc. automatically, without any command to that effect, on the basis of their own insight. But this is not the case with Christian faith. Not all have faith (2 Thess. 3:2). Although it is perfectly human, not a "superadded gift" but the restoration of a human being, still the "natural" [unspiritual] person is hostile in his or her attitude to believing. For faith in the Christian sense presupposes self-denial, the crucifixion of one's own ideas and will, distrust of self, and confidence in the grace of God in Christ instead. Therefore, just as saving faith has God himself as its object and grounds itself on his testimony, so it has him as its author as well. It is he himself who, by the Holy Spirit, moves human beings to faith and takes every thought captive to the obedi-

---

13. Cf. A. Ritschl, *Fides Implicita* (Bonn: Adolphus Marcus, 1890), 69; Gottshick, *Die Kirchlichkeit*, 2 vols. (Freiburg i.B.: J. C. B. Mohr, 1890), 11–53, 69ff.; Traub, "Glaube und Theologie," *Theologische Studiën und Kritiken* 65 (1893): 568–88; Hermann, *Die Gewissheit des Glaubens*, 2d ed. (Freiburg: J. C. B. Mohr, 1899), 83ff., 92ff.; idem, *Faith and Morals,* trans. Donald Matheson and Robert W. Stewart (New York: G. P. Putnam's Sons, 1904); idem, "Grund und Inhalt des Glaubens," *Beweis des Glaubens* 26 (1890): 89–109; Kaftan, *Brauchen wir ein neues Dogma* (Bielefeld: Velhagen & Klasing, 1890), 37; idem, "Glaube und Dogma," *ZThK* 1 (1891): 478ff.; idem, *ZThK* 3 (1893): 93; Kattenbusch, *Über religiöse Glauben im Sinne des Christenthum* (Giessen: C.v. Münchow, 1887); Ménégoz, *Publication diverses sur le Fidéisme* (Paris: Fischbacher, 1900), 15, 17, 33, 119, 244, 250.

14. A. Pierson, *Eene Levensbeschouwing* (Haarlem: Kruseman & Tjeenk Willink, 1875), 13.

ence of Christ (Matt. 16:17; John 6:44; 1 Cor. 12:3; 2 Cor. 10:5; 1 Thess.
2:13; 2 Thess. 3:2; Eph. 1:15, 16; Col. 1:13; Phil. 1:29). As a result, Christian faith is religiously qualified through and through. Its object, ground, and
origin are exclusively located in God. In consequence of this religious character, saving faith is essentially distinct from the immediate certainty that is
sometimes labeled "faith," as well as from the πιστις of which the Greeks
sometimes spoke in a religious sense. The Christian faith is sheer religion,
subjective religion. Those persons are truly religious who believe thus: they
are the image, the children, and heirs of God.

FAITH AS INTELLECTUAL ASSENT

In the Christian church, however, the view that saw faith as intellectual
assent to revealed truth soon became dominant. Very common is the definition of faith as the "voluntary assent of the soul," or as "drawing the soul toward agreement past the methods of logic."[15] Augustine offers the same definition: "believing is knowledge with assent," "what is believing unless it is to
agree to that which is said is true," and "faith is the virtue by which the
things that are unseen are believed."[16] Scholastic theology usually began its
study of the nature of faith with the description of Hebrews 11:1 and the
last mentioned definition of Augustine.[17] Thomas says that the object of
faith is God and other things "except insofar as they have some other order
toward God." The ground of faith consists solely in the fact that "something
has been revealed by God," and its author is God alone.[18] The Vatican
Council [I] described faith as "a supernatural virtue by which, with the inspiration and help of God's grace, we believe that what he has revealed is
true, not because its intrinsic truth is perceived by the natural light of reason, but because of the authority of God himself who reveals, and who can
neither deceive nor be deceived."[19] Faith, in Roman Catholic thought, is a
firm and certain assent to the truths of revelation on the basis of the authority of God in Scripture and the church.[20]

In practice, this view of faith had very harmful consequences. In the first
place, faith actually became mere intellectual assent to a mysterious doctrine

15. J. C. Suicerus, *Thesaurus ecclesiasticus*, 2 vols. (Amsterdam: J. H. Wetstein, 1682), s.v. πιστις (*pistis*); Denzinger, *Vier Bücher von der religiöse Erkenntnis*, II, 467. Kleutgen, *Theologie der Vorzeit*, IV, 246ff.

16. Augustine, *On the Predestination of the Saints*, chap. 2; idem, *On the Spirit and the Letter*, chap. 31; idem, *Enchiridion*, chap. 8; idem, *On the Trinity*, 13, 1; idem, *Homily on the Gospel of John*, 40, 9.

17. P. Lombard, *III Sent.*, 23.

18. Thomas Aquinas, *Summa Theol.*, II, 2, qu. 1ff.

19. *Documents of Vatican Council I, 1869–1870*, sel. and trans. John F. Broderick (Collegeville, Minn.: Liturgical Press, 1971), session III, "On Faith," chap. 3.

20. Aquinas, *Summa Theol.*, II, 2, qu. 2, art. 1, qu. 4, art. 2; Bellarmine, "De Justific," *Controversiis*, I, 5, 6; Becanus, *Theol. Schol.* tom. II, 2, tract. 1, chap. 1ff.; Perrone, *Praelect. Theol.* (1840), V, 251ff.; Jansen, *Praelect. Theol.*, I, 684; Kleutgen, *Theologie der Vorzeit*, IV, 205ff.; Denzinger, *Vier Bücher*, II, 426ff.

far surpassing reason, either explicitly to all its different dogmas or implicitly to certain necessary dogmas. Given this view, the distinction between this faith and the "historical faith" assumed by Protestants is not possible and was, accordingly, decisively rejected by Roman Catholic theology. Rome does not have anything other than "historical faith." From this it then followed that this faith, if it was no more than intellectual assent, could not possibly be sufficient for salvation. It had to be augmented by another virtue in the will, namely love, and so becomes a "formed faith" (*fides formata*). As a result, faith loses its central place in the Christian life. It is degraded to one of the seven "preparations" for the "infused grace" of "justification"; and the point of gravity then shifts to love, i.e., good works. Finally, it could scarcely be maintained that faith in the above sense was a fruit of "internal grace" as Augustine understood it. The confession that faith is a gift of God was weakened. The "assistance" and "inspiration" mentioned by the Vatican Council [I] is frequently restricted in Catholic theology to the gift of common grace or even to the gift of natural powers. Believing was all the more meritorious to the degree that it was a free personal act of a human being and consisted more in the acceptance of the incomprehensible "mysteries of faith," in a "sacrifice of the intellect."

The Reformation modified this Roman Catholic view of faith in all respects. It restored the religious nature of πιστις. In the first place, it made a fundamental distinction between "historical faith" and "saving faith." In some cases historical faith might indeed precede saving faith and be of great value as such; but it was and remained essentially different from saving faith. All the Reformers were of the opinion that saving faith consisted if not exclusively then certainly also in knowledge. Not one of them allowed faith to be reduced to an unconscious feeling or mental state. But the knowledge that was an element in saving faith was certainly very different in kind from that of historical faith. The latter might later on be of benefit to saving faith; but it changed thereby in character and began to live by a new principle. Faith, in the thinking of the Reformers, therefore again acquired a spiritual-religious nature of its own, distinguished not in degree but in essence from every other faith in life and in science, indeed even from historical faith. Such a faith could not, of course, stem from the same principle from which all other belief arises among human beings. The Reformation was unanimous in confessing that saving faith is a gift of God. It was not the product of natural human powers, nor of common grace, but of the special grace of the Holy Spirit; it was an activity of the new born-again person and therefore also sufficient for salvation. In Roman Catholicism faith plays a merely preparatory role, and correctly so, because basically it is nothing more than historical faith. But in Reformation theology it regained the central place it occupies in the New Testament; it does not have to be augmented by love; it is sufficient to obtain a share in all the benefits of salvation. Those who believe in that way are not in the vestibule but in the very sanctuary of Christian truth. They are incorporated into Christ, participants in all his benefits, heirs of eternal life. It was hard, however, given this deep view of saving faith, correctly to describe its nature and to reproduce it in clear language. The theology of the Reformation at all times struggled with this issue. With respect to the question in what the real nature of faith consists, the answers have been radically divergent. It has been defined as "knowing," "agreeing," "trusting," "taking refuge in," etc. by just one of these terms or by all of them together. Later, in the doctrine of faith, we will examine all this in greater detail. This much is certain: faith in Reformation theology was not a matter of knowing a number of doctrinal truths but consisted in the soul's union with the person of Christ according to the Scriptures and with Scripture as the word of Christ. Saving faith was again religious through and through. Its object was the grace of God in Christ; its foundation the witness of God in his Word; its author the Holy Spirit. In every respect it was religiously determined.

THE CERTAINTY OF FAITH

[149] According to Scripture, this faith brings its own certainty with it. It is the assurance (ὑποστασις) of things hoped for and the conviction (ἐλεγχος) of things not seen (Heb. 11:1), not because it is inherently so solid and firm but because it is grounded in God's testimony and promise, as the sequel of Hebrews 11 clearly teaches. It makes the invisible goods of salvation utterly certain for us; indeed, even much more certain than one's own insight or a given scientific proof could ever make it. For that reason Scripture speaks of the confidence (παρρησια, Heb. 4:16), the confidence of access (πεποιθησις, Eph. 3:12), the full assurance (πληροφορια, Heb. 6:11, 12; 10:22) of faith; attributed to it are such qualities as courage (θαρσος, Matt. 9:2), rejoicing (καυχησις, Rom. 5:11), and joy (χαρα, 1 Pet. 1:8, etc.). It contrasts with doubt, anxiety, fear, distrust (Matt. 6:31; 8:26; 10:31; 14:31; 21:21; Mark 4:40; Luke 8:25; John 14:1; Rom. 4:20; James 1:6). Certainty is a characteristic of faith throughout Scripture. Even in the midst of the most severe trials, when everything is opposed to them, hoping against hope, believers stand firm as seeing the Invisible (Job 19:25; Ps. 23; 32; 51; Rom. 4:20, 21; 5:1; 8:38; Heb. 11; etc.). Believers will sooner give up everything than renounce their faith. Nothing is more precious to them than faith, not their money, their goods, their honor, or even their lives. Faith is "the victory that overcomes the world" (1 John 5:4).

This certainty of faith was unknown to science. It made its entry into the world with the coming of Christianity.[21] Greek philosophy recognized two kinds of certainty, one obtained by sense perception, another acquired by reflection. Usually the former was ranked far below the latter; sense perception only yielded opinion (δοξα), but reflection led to knowledge (ἐπιστημη). In the latter, Aristotle again made a distinction between the knowledge that is

21. Janet and Séailles, *Histoire de la Philosophie* (Paris: Ch. Delagrave, 1887), 668.

based on proofs and that which rests on evidence. So in science there were three ways to obtain certainty: perception, argumentation, and evidence. These three kinds of certainty were adopted in philosophy on the understanding that empiricists primarily located certainty in perception and rationalists in reflection. Alongside of this philosophical certainty, Christianity posited the certainty of faith. Concretely and practically this certainty was displayed to a skeptical world in the believing community, especially in its martyrs. Theoretically it was asserted and unfolded in Christian theology.

Rome and the Reformation

In the doctrine of certainty there exists an important difference between Rome and the Reformation with respect to the question of whether the certainty of faith also includes the assurance of salvation, absolute certainty of one's own salvation. From Augustine on, this assurance of salvation has been denied and combated by the Roman Catholic Church and Catholic theology. Rome claims that absolute assurance of salvation accrues only to a handful of believers who have received it by a special revelation, but it is not something that is integral to the nature of faith itself. With respect to their salvation, ordinary believers only have a kind of moral or conjectural certainty, no certainty of faith. In the Roman Catholic system there is really no room for this certainty, since (1) it is consistent only with the confession of God's electing love and (2) it would make the laity independent of the church and the priesthood.[22] Roman Catholic theologians do, however, recognize the certainty of faith with respect to the objective truths of revelation. "I would more easily doubt that I lived," wrote Augustine, "than doubt that there truth existed, which is 'clearly seen, being understood by the things that are made' (Rom. 1:20)."[23] Albert the Great made a distinction between "faith" in philosophy and "faith" in theology. In the former "faith" is nothing more than "trustfulness" (*credulitas*) and not a way to knowledge; but in theological matters "faith is a light making adhesion and assent very certain . . . and therefore a way and means toward knowledge of the truth of divine things."[24] And with that opinion Protestant theologians generally concur. No one has articulated this certainty of faith more sharply and vigorously than Calvin. In his thinking faith is "certain," "firm," "full and fixed," more "certainty" than "apprehension," "heartfelt confidence and assurance."[25] In

22. Cf. Augustine, *On the Gift of Perseverance*, 8, 13, 22; idem, *The City of God*, XII; idem, *Letters*, 107; G. J. Vossius, *Historia Pelagiana* (1652), 578ff.; Commentary on *Sentences*, I, dist. 17; Aquinas, *Summa Theol.*, II, 1, qu. 112, art. 5; Bellarmine, "De Justific," *Controversiis*, I, 10; IV, 2ff.; Council of Trent, session 6, chap. 9, canon 13, 4, and later in the doctrine of faith.

23. Augustine, *Confessions*, VII, 10.

24. In A. Stöckl, *Philosophie des Mittelalters*, 3 vols. (Mainz: Kirchheim, 1864–66), II, 365; cf. further Aquinas, *Summa Theol.*, II, 2, qu. 4, art. 8; Bellarmine, "De Justific," *Controversiis*, III, 2; Billuart, *Summa Sanctae Thomae*, VIII, 86ff.; P. Dens, *Theologia Moralis et Dogmatica*, 8 vols. (Dublin: Richard Coyne, 1832), II, 241; Daelman, *Theologie*, 9 vols. (Louvaine: Martinum van Overbeke, 1759), I, 12ff.

25. J. Calvin, *Institutes*, I.vii.5; II.ii.8; III.ii.14ff.; III.xiv.8; III.xiv.24.

the thinking of Lutheran as well as Reformed theologians, faith is "firm assent," a "certain knowledge," which excludes all doubt and uncertainty.[26]

Little attention, generally speaking, has been paid to this certainty of faith by science, specifically philosophy. Not until Kant's debut was it incorporated and recognized in a modified sense. Kant for the most part accepted three kinds of certainty. The first is the problematic empirical certainty, which is based on perceptions, one's own or someone else's, and consists in opinion, a theoretical or practical faith. Next there is a logical, scientific, and apodictic certainty. This certainty comes in two versions, being intuitive as in mathematics, or discursive as in philosophy. There are the kinds of certainty assumed already also in Greek philosophy. But, in addition, Kant now makes room also for a moral, assertively sure certainty. The supersensible and supernatural, according to Kant, is unknowable. God has deliberately withheld that knowledge from us so that we would not posit knowing as the purpose of humanity, but action, the fulfillment of our moral calling. Now with a view to this ethical destiny, human beings assume the truth of certain theses without which they cannot fulfill this ethical task. So, on practical and psychological grounds, human beings believe in the existence of God, the soul, and immortality. This is moral faith. The certainty secured by this faith is not theoretical in nature but practical and moral. It prompts people to say not "I am certain," nor "It is morally certain," but "I am morally certain." Hence there are three kinds of certainty: an empirical, a logical, and a moral one, expressed and conveyed by the terms "thinking," "knowing," and "believing."[27] Philosophy after Kant, though it has in part adopted this theory of certainty from him, has added nothing essentially new to it.[28]

Kant and Moral Certainty

Kant's theory of moral certainty, on the other hand, *has* exerted great influence on theology. After the authority of Scripture and the church had been undermined, people sought the foundation of religion and theology in moral certainty. The familiar text John 7:17, already cited by Kant himself,[29] became the starting point of this school of thought. There is indeed profound truth in this moral certainty, and we may gratefully recognize that Kant has made room for it in his philosophy. Concerning invisible things we have a very different certainty than concerning the things we can perceive with our senses or prove with our logical faculties. Faith in the things we

26. H. Schmid, *Doctrinal Theology of the Evangelical Churches*, trans. Charles A. Hay and Henry E. Jacobs (Philadelphia: United Lutheran Publication House, 1899), 412ff.; Hase, *Hutt. Rediv.*, §108; *Heidelberg Catechism*, Q. & A. 21; Heppe, *Dogmatik der evangelischen Reformierte Kirche* (Eberfeld: R. L. Friderichs, 1861), 384ff.

27. I. Kant, *Critique of Pure Reason*, trans. J. M. D. Meiklejohn (New York: Colonial Press, 1899), Methodology, II, 3.

28. Cf. Franz Grung, *Das Problem der Gewissheit* (Heidelberg: Weis, 1886).

29. I. Kant, *Religion within the Limits of Reason Alone*, trans. Theodore M. Greene and Hoyt H. Hudson (New York: Harper & Row Publishers, 1934), 104.

hope for and do not see, moreover, does not function apart from our will, our moral disposition, and spiritual experience. Still, it is not advisable for us to exchange the religious certainty of Holy Scripture, the church, and Christian theology for Kant's brand of moral certainty.

In the first place, it needs saying that certainty is always a state of mind. The human mind can relate to a given question or proposition in a variety of mental states. It can relate to it in a state of uncertainty, doubt, suspicion, impression, etc. but also in a state of complete certainty. Certainty is the peace of mind one experiences in finding and recognizing truth. The intellect pursues knowledge, truth. That is the nature of the intellect; truth is its "good," its wealth, the fulfillment of its hunger. When it finds truth, it is satisfied; it rests in it; it feels safe and secure. Certainty is rest, peace, joy, bliss; there is rest and relaxation in truth (*in veritate requies*). Certainty is the normal state of the human mind, just as health is of the body. Doubt, uncertainty, by contrast, is unrest, unease, wretchedness. Strictly speaking, certainty itself is not moral; it is so called only because the grounds on which "moral truth" rests are of a moral nature. Furthermore, the grounds on which scientific and moral truth rest cannot thus be split apart and set over against each other as being "theoretical" and "practical." In reality no such dualism exists, as Kant, with his two kinds of certainty, assumes. The head and the heart, subjectively speaking, and objectively speaking, visible and invisible things, cannot be split in two in that way. The heart also has its say in our scientific exploration. Πιστις, in its broad sense, also plays a large role there. Much of what passes for "established" and "certain" in the sciences is based on moral or immoral grounds. Conversely, it is the mind, after all, that in the case of moral certainty weighs and assesses the moral grounds on which a given proposition is recognized and accepted as true. While the will may prompt the intellect to accept a given truth, that acceptance itself is an act of the intellect; and the intellect can do this only because it itself to some extent recognizes and understands the truth. The certainty of faith does not come by way of theoretical proofs, but even less through a decision of the will.

Finally, while earlier in this volume we already advanced a number of objections to Kant's theory of postulation, these can be augmented by the following questions. Does it agree with the nature of true morality—which after all consists also in humility and lowliness, etc.—to postulate the existence of God and of immortality on the basis of our moral nature and destiny? Does moral certainty retain its validity when a moral person falls into sin, is caught up in temptation and inner conflict, and is swung back and forth by doubt? Are moral grounds strong enough for us to build on them belief in God's existence, the consciousness of forgiveness, and the hope of salvation, in the face of scientific opposition? But even if moral certainty is enough for the philosopher, it is useless for the Christian. For although Kant's "religion of reason" could rest on it as on a sure foundation, it cannot sustain the truth of the Christian religion.

Believing Is Certainty

For all these reasons, the moral certainty of Kant cannot replace the Christian's assurance of faith. This is also proven—if further proof is needed—by the distinctions Kant makes between "thinking," "believing," and "knowing." According to him, "thinking" [in the sense of entertaining opinions] was to hold a thing to be true on insufficient grounds, "believing" on subjectively sufficient grounds, and "knowing" on objectively sufficient grounds.[30] Now this distinction is correct with reference to "believing" in ordinary daily life and in relation to things that can be known. Then "believing" is in fact a weaker form of knowing. But in religion believing is certainty itself. The distinction was more correctly defined already by Augustine. Says he: "There are also three things, as it were bordering upon one another, in the minds of men well worth distinguishing: understanding, belief, opinion. And, if these be considered by themselves, the first is always without fault, the second sometimes with fault, the third never without fault."[31] "Now between believing and opining there is this difference, that sometimes he who believes feels that he does not know that which he believes (although he may know himself to be ignorant of a thing, and yet have no doubt at all concerning it, if he most firmly believes it) whereas he who opines, thinks he knows that which he does not know."[32]

Thomas defines the difference as follows: "For it is essential to opinion that we assent to one of two opposite assertions with fear of the other, so that our adhesion is not firm; to science it is essential to have firm adhesion with intellectual vision, for science possesses certitude which results from the understanding of principles; while faith holds a middle place, for it surpasses opinion insofar as its adhesion is firm, but falls short of science in this because it lacks sight."[33] Zanchius, thinking along similar lines, gave this definition: "Opinion is knowledge that is neither certain nor evident; faith is certain knowledge but not evident; science is knowledge that is both certain and evident."[34] Believing and knowing are not distinct in the matter of certainty. The certainty of faith is as firm as that of knowledge. Indeed, the certainty of faith is the more intense of the two: it is virtually unshakable and ineradicable. For their faith people are prepared to sacrifice everything, including their life. Galileo three times retracted his agreement with the Copernican system.[35] Kepler, against his conviction, occupied himself at Graz with astrology to maintain his livelihood; the needy mother (astronomy) had to live from her foolish daughter (astrology). Who would give his or her life

30. I. Kant, *Reinen Vernunft*, 632ff.

31. Augustine, *On the Profit of Believing*, 11.

32. Augustine, *On Lying*, 3.

33. Aquinas, *Summa Theol.*, II, 1, qu. 67, art. 3.

34. J. Zanchius, *Op. Theol.*, II, 196.

35. O. Zöckler, *Geschichte der Beziehungen Zwischen Theologie und Natuurwissenschaft*, 2 vols. (Gütersloh: C. Bertelsman, 1877–79), I, 534ff.

for a scientific thesis, for example, that the earth rotates around the sun? But religion produces martyrs. In terms of sheer power the assurance of faith far exceeds scientific certainty. In this connection, however, Bonaventure rightly distinguishes between "the certainty of assent" (*certitudo adhaesionis*) and "the certainty of speculation" (*certitudo specutationis*).[36] The former is greater in the assurance of faith than in scientific certainty, for in many cases no arguments, flatteries, or torments can cause people to waver in their faith. With all their soul they cling to the object of faith. Yet the certainty of speculation can sometimes—not always—be stronger in science than in the faith. It is the same idea as that expressed by Augustine: understanding is always "without fault" but believing sometimes occurs "with fault." Believing itself is no proof for the truth of that which is believed. There is a huge difference between subjective certainty and objective truth. In the case of faith or belief, everything depends on the grounds on which it rests.

THE GROUND OF FAITH

Inadequacy of Proofs

[150] As soon as Christian theology started to reflect seriously on the final and deepest ground of faith, it came to the conclusion that no single intellectual or historical proof advanced for the truth of revelation can ultimately serve as such. The apologists of the second century attached great value to those proofs and, against pagan naturalism, stressed that faith is a free rational act.[37] Still, even among them one already finds the realization that all those proofs are powerless to effectually move a person to faith. Something different and something more is needed, viz., divine grace.[38] Irenaeus compares it to the dew and the rain, which make the fields fruitful.[39] But Augustine was the first to clearly understand and confess the necessity of internal grace. Elsewhere he ascribes great value to the church as a motive for believing; but his doctrine of internal grace proves that this motive was not for him the final and deepest cause of his faith. That cause was God alone. "God works our faith, acting in a marvelous way in our heart in order that we may believe."[40] Believing, after all, is always voluntary: "no one believes except willingly." To that end God by his grace bends the will and prompts us to believe with the intellect.[41] Later theologians as well ascribed great

---

36. P. Lombard, *III Sentences*, dist. 23, art. 1, qu. 4; cf. Stöckl, *Philosophie des Mittelalters*, II, 883.

37. Justin Martyr, *Dialogue with Trypho*, 88, 102, 131; Theophilus, *To Autolychus*, II, 27; Irenaeus, *Against Heresies*, IV, 37, 5.

38. Justin Martyr, *Dialogue*, 119; idem, *Apology*, I, 10; II, 12; Irenaeus, *Against Heresies*, IV, 39; Origen, *On First Principles*, I, 10, 14, 19.

39. Irenaeus, *Against Heresies*, III, 17, 2, 3.

40. Augustine, *On the Predestination of the Saints*, 2, 6.

41. Augustine, *Confessions*, XIII, 1; idem, *To Simplician—On Various Questions* (de div. quaest.), 1, qu. 2, n. 21; available in J. H. S. Burleigh, *Augustine: Earlier Writings* (Philadelphia: Westminster Press, 1953), 404–5; idem, *On the Predestination of the Saints*, 19; idem, *On the Gift of Perserverance*, 16.

power to the "preamble of faith" and the motivations toward belief (*motiva credibilitatis*); and among them the church increasingly assumed a more prominent place. But all these theologians admit that these motives do not make revelation "evidently true" but only "evidently credible." They rule out rational doubt and demonstrate that it is not unreasonable to believe while it is unreasonable to assume the contrary.[42] But they are not sufficient. Indeed, when dealing with the philosophical proofs for the Trinity, Thomas expressly states: "Whoever tries to prove the Trinity of persons by natural reason detracts from faith."[43] Such proofs are of little value against opponents "because the very insufficiency of the reasons confirms them in their error inasmuch as they judge that we consent to the truth of faith on the basis of such weak reasons."[44] Revelation may ever so much be made credible by the proofs, yet it is and remains a truth of faith.[45] In Roman Catholic theology too it must remain that, for otherwise the voluntary nature and the meritoriousness of faith would be lost.[46] Faith, therefore, accepts the truth, not on the basis of one's own insight, but on that of divine authority. "For faith does not assent to anything except on the ground that it has been revealed by God."[47] And in order for human beings to acknowledge that authority of God, an antecedent change of will has to occur. Believing is indeed an act of the intellect,[48] but it presupposes a bending of the will by grace; the intellect must be disposed toward faith by the will.[49] The assent of faith, accordingly, occurs only by an act of God "moving inwardly through grace."[50] Gregory XVI, in a letter dated September 26, 1835, condemned the opinion of Hermes that the motivations toward belief (*motiva credibilitatis*) were the true ground of faith in revelation. And the Vatican Council decreed that though these motives could make divine revelation credible, still "no one can consent to the gospel preaching, as he must to obtain salvation, without the illumination and inspiration of the Holy Spirit."[51]

Spiritual Illumination Is Necessary

By taking this position, Rome in fact adopts the same subjective standpoint as the churches of the Reformation. The motives, however strong, cannot in fact move a person toward faith. It is the Spirit of God alone who can

42. Aquinas, *Summa Theol.*, II, 2, qu. 1, art. 5, ad 2; idem, *Summa contra Gentiles*, I, 9.

43. Aquinas, *Summa Theol.*, I, qu. 32, art. 1.

44. Aquinas, *Summa contra Gentiles*, I, 9.

45. Bellarmine, "De Conc. et. Eccl.," *Controversiis*, IV, 3.

46. Aquinas, *Summa Theol.*, II, qu. 2, art. 9 and 10.

47. Aquinas, *Summa Theol.*, II, 2, qu. 1, art. 1; *Summa contra Gentiles*, 1, 9; Becanus, *Summa Theologiae*, II, 2, 3–17; Billuart, "De fide," *Theol. Sanctae Thom.*, II, 2, tom. 1, 1ff.; P. Dens, *Theologia*, II, 280ff.; Jansen, *Praelect. Theol.*, I, 701–11.

48. Aquinas, *Summa Theol.*, II, qu. 4, art. 2.

49. Ibid., II, qu. 2, art. 1, ad 3.

50. Ibid., I, qu. 62, art. 2, ad 3; II, 1, qu. 109, art. 6; qu. 112, art. 2; II, 2, qu. 6, art. 1.

51. *Documents of Vatican Council I*, session 3, "De fide," chap. 3.

make a person inwardly certain of the truth of divine revelation. Hence, also in Rome, not Scripture or the church but the interior light is the deepest ground for believing, as several theologians have acknowledged. For the sake of clarity, let us for a moment dissect the act of believing in the form of a syllogism. The major premise, then, is: God is true; if he reveals himself, his revelation must be accepted in faith. The minor premise is: these facts (the church, say, or Scripture) are revelations of God. The conclusion follows: therefore these facts must be believed. About the major premise there is no quarrel. In virtue of the idea of God, it is unquestionable and is therefore accepted by all. No one denies that, if God reveals himself, he that is faithful and true deserves to be believed. Everything therefore depends on the minor premise. The disagreement concerns whether and where God has revealed himself. The believing Christian says "in Scripture" or "in the church." But how and why are these entities recognized as the revelation of God? If on the ground of proofs, the motives for believing, then that ground is human, fallible, and faith is not purely religious and certain. The revelation of God can be believed only in a religious sense on the basis of God's authority. But the voice of that divine authority can only be heard either *outside of* myself in Scripture or the church, whose final ground of faith it is I am now examining; or *within* myself, in the grace that moves me to believe, in the interior light, the testimony of the Holy Spirit. Those who want to maintain the authority of God as the ultimate ground of faith and so faith in its religious character, must adopt one or the other of these positions. Now it was Canus who said outright that this final ground lay in the grace that internally moved him to faith. "I believe," he said, "that God is triune, since God has revealed it"; to this he then adds: "God has revealed it; I believe it immediately, being moved by God through a special prompting."[52] Hence for Canus the final ground for his faith lay objectively in the testimony of God; but that he recognized this testimony as divine was due to the grace that moved his will and intellect to believing. Canus's sentiment was indeed accepted by a few other Roman Catholic theologians such as Arragon, Gonet, et al., and Professor Hayd even spoke of an immediate witness of God within us, which assures us of the divinity of Jesus' person and teaching.[53] Many theologians, however, objected that Canus actually gives no answer to the question on what ground he accepts the witness of God in Scripture and the church as divine. He only says that God thus internally, by his grace, persuades him to believe this but gives no further account of his reasons. Another reason why this sentiment of Canus did not commend itself was that, as Suarez already pointed out, it bore such a strong resemblance to, and could so easily lead to, Calvin's doctrine concerning the testimony of the Holy Spirit. For that reason Roman Catholic theologians were intent on looking elsewhere than in

52. Canus, *Loc. Theol.*, I, 2, chap. 8, ad. 4.
53. *Philosophisch Jahrbuch* of C. Gutberlet (1890), 27.

the "interior light" for the final ground of faith. Suarez held the view that not only the object but also the ground of faith itself was a matter of faith. We do not only believe that Scripture is true *since* God has revealed himself there, but we also believe *that* God revealed himself there because God himself witnesses to that fact in Scripture. Revelation is simultaneously the "by which" (*quo*) it is believed and the what (*quod*) that is believed. "For it is one and the same act that believes God and believes by God." Just as the eye perceives the colors as well as the light by which those colors become visible, and as reason knows the derivative truths as well as the first principles by which the secondary truths become knowable, so faith knows both the revealed truths and the witness on which they rest, as divine.

Breaking the Circle: God Speaks!

A great many theologians, also in recent times, have expressed their agreement with Suarez, but not all were satisfied. The circular reasoning was evident: Scripture is believed because it is revealed and that it has been revealed is believed because Scripture says it is. It also leads to an infinite regression: I believe a given revelation because another revelation says I should, etc. Suarez does reply to this objection by saying that revelation should be believed for its own sake, that God, in revealing himself, at the same time reveals that it is he who reveals himself. Still the question of why we believe the witness by which God declares that it is *he* who revealed himself remains open. Lugo, accordingly, taught that acceptance of the fact that God has revealed himself in Scripture, though this acceptance could be called supernatural, could not be called faith in the true sense of the word. Believing something, after all, is always an act of holding something to be true on the basis of a testimony. If the acceptance of the fact that God has revealed himself were faith in the true sense, this would again presuppose a divine witness and so on *ad infinitum*. Lugo therefore assumed that the recognition of the fact of revelation did not rest on a testimony from God but on the ground that the believer immediately recognized revelation itself, with its miracles, prophecies, etc., as revelation, just as reason immediately recognizes the truth of first principles. Revelation announces itself as divine by its content, just as in Thomas's image[54] an ambassador authenticates himself by the content of his message, e.g., by secrets that only the one who commissioned him can know. But this idea again has to face the objection that this recognition of revelation is *either* really immediate, in which case it becomes a new revelation in the subject, a vision of the divine, which, since we walk by faith, we do not receive here on earth, *or* that it is in fact mediate but then arises from the indices and criteria of revelation and thus again rests on "the proofs" for revelation, the motives for believing. Hence this solution too is unsatisfactory.

54. Aquinas, *Summa Theol.*, III, qu. 43, art. 1.

Others, therefore, again said the witness of God is the final ground of faith. To the question "Why do you believe?" Christians reply, "Because God has spoken" (*Deus dixit*). They cannot indicate another, deeper ground. If you then ask them, "But why do you believe that God has spoken, say, in Scripture?" they can only answer that God so transformed them internally that they recognize Scripture as the word of God. But having said that, they said it all. The witness of God is the ground, but God's grace, the will, is the cause of faith.[55] The proofs may be motives for believing [*motiva credibilitatis*]; the will [itself bent by grace] finally is the mover of faith [*motivum credendi*]. This position, too, is vulnerable to criticism. For one can ask—and people *have* asked—what ground does the *intellect* have for accepting Scripture as the word of God? The reply that the will, or God's grace,[56] moves the intellect to that end is insufficient. Certainly, the will cannot persuade the intellect to accept something as true without [external] reasons or grounds, and the will on its own cannot determine whether something is believable or true.[57] The intellect itself, after all, has to acknowledge that something is divine and therefore deserves to be believed. Otherwise faith is unreasonable and the believer brushes aside this difficulty by saying: "This is what I wish; this is what I command; my will takes the place of my reason." Roman Catholic theologians, accordingly, also fail to answer the question concerning the ultimate ground of faith in a way that satisfies everyone. A great many of them simply abstain from making a decision and leave the choice among the above-described sentiments open. This account is sufficient, however, to show that Rome, with its infallible church and its infallible pope, has no advantage over the churches of the Reformation. Faith's deepest ground, in Rome as in Protestantism, is located in the subject.[58]

55. Ed. note: To avoid confusion in the argument that immediately follows, it is necessary to note that Bavinck does not *identify* grace and the will as the grammar suggests here and in the original Dutch. Earlier in this chapter, Bavinck declares faith to involve the intellect (*notitia*) as it is disposed by the will (*assensus*) leading to trust (*fiducia*). In *logical* order, the will must be bent by divine grace, by the power of the Holy Spirit (see above, pp. 568–78).

56. Ed. note: Once again, will and grace are not to be regarded as identical; the *or* is not appositive. Expanded, the meaning is "The reply that the will, or God's grace [which bends the will], moves the intellect to that end is insufficient."

57. Ed. note: In Bavinck's epistemology, the intellect does have final priority over the will. The resolution of the circularity discussed in the preceding paragraphs is found in Bavinck's doctrine of the Logos. Certainty about the truth of divine revelation occurs when the Holy Spirit creates a holy confluence between the Eternal Logos by whom all things were made and the human logos. The true *principium cognoscendi internum* of theology, therefore, is not faith as such but believing thinking, the *ratio christiana* (see below, p. 616). For a helpful discussion of Bavinck's understanding of this foundational doctrine of revelation and faith (*principium cognoscendi internum*), see R. H. Bremer, *Herman Bavinck als Dogmaticus* (Kampen: Kok, 1961), 176–81.

58. M. J. Scheeben, *Handbuch der Katholische Dogmatik*, 4 vols. (Freiburg i.B.: Herder, 1933 [orig. pub. 1874–98]), I, 287 (ed. note: English translation: *A Manual of Catholic Theology: Based on Scheeben's "Dogmatik,"* trans. Joseph Wilhelm and Thomas Bartholomew Scannell, 4th ed., 2 vols. [London: Kegan Paul, Trench, Trübner and Co.; New York: Benziger Brothers, 1909]); J. B. Heinrich and C. Guthberlet,

SCRIPTURE IS SELF-AUTHENTICATING

[151] The Reformation—deliberately and freely—took its position in the religious subject, in the faith of the Christian, in the testimony of the Holy Spirit. Admittedly, only a few statements about the Holy Spirit occur in the works of Luther, Zwingli, and Melanchthon.[59] But Calvin developed this doctrine at length and related the subject matter to the content as well as to the form and authority of Scripture. That Scripture is the word of God, says Calvin, was not established by the church but was certain prior to the church's decision, for the church is built on the foundation of apostles and prophets. Scripture brings with it its own authority; it is self-based and self-attested as trustworthy (αὐτόπιστος). Just as light is distinguished from darkness, white from black, sweet from bitter, so Scripture is recognized by its own truth. But Scripture acquires certainty as God's own Word with us by the testimony of the Holy Spirit. Though proofs and reasonings are of great value, this testimony surpasses them by far; it is more excellent than all reason. Just as God can only witness concerning himself in his Word, so his Word does not find belief in the hearts of human beings before it is sealed by the internal testimony of the Holy Spirit. The same Spirit who spoke through the mouths of the prophets must work in our hearts to persuade us that they faithfully proclaimed what had been commanded by God. The Holy Spirit, accordingly, is the "seal" and "guarantee" for confirming the faith of the godly. If we have that testimony within us, we do not rest in any human judgment but observe without any doubt as if we were gazing upon God himself in it—that Scripture came from the mouth of God through the ministry of human beings. We subject our judgment to it "as to a thing far beyond any guesswork!"

But that must not be understood as if we blindly submit to a thing that is unknown to us. No; we are conscious that in Scripture we possess unassailable truth and feel that "the undoubted power of his divine majesty lives and breathes there," a power by which we are drawn, knowingly and willingly, yet vitally and effectively, to obey him.[60] Calvin knew that in this doctrine of the testimony of the Holy Spirit he was not describing some private revela-

---

Dogmatische Theologie, 2d ed., 10 vols. (Mainz: Kirchheim, 1881–1900), I, 606ff.; C. Pesch, *Praelect. Theol.*, VIII, 78ff.; Jansen, *Praelect. Theol.*, I, 711ff.; Mannens, *Theol. Dogm. Institutiones*, I, 424ff.

Ed. note: In the original Dutch edition of the *Gereformeerde Dogmatiek* (par. 21, "De Grond des Geloofs"), Bavinck cites additional literature. Rather than cite the full bibliographic information, only author and publication date (or title key word) are given below for references not already included in this note 58. Full bibliographic data can be found in the bibliography at the end of this volume. Denzinger (*Vier Bücher*, II, 486–500); Kleutgen (*Vorzeit*, IV, 473–532); Von Schäzler; Al. Schmid; Klaiber; G. Martius; Aug. Benezeh; Pannier (*Le témoignage*); Leliêuvre.

59. J. Köstlin, *Luther's Theology*, I, 369ff.; II, 536ff.; J. H. Scholten, *De Leer der Hervormde Kerk*, 2d ed., 2 vols. (Leyden: P. Engels, 1850–51), I, 186ff.; Locher, *De Leer van Luther over Gods Woord* (Amsterdam: Scheffer, 1903), 230, 320.

60. J. Calvin, *Institutes*, I.vii; *Commentary* on 2 Tim. 3:16. Ed. note: Bavinck again refers to the literature he cites in par. 21 in *Gereformeerde Dogmatiek*, which is given above in n. 58.

tion but the experience of all believers.[61] Nor was this testimony of the Holy Spirit isolated from the totality of the work of the Holy Spirit in the hearts of believers but integrally united with it. By it alone the entire church originates and exists. The entire application of salvation is a work of the Holy Spirit; and the witness to Scripture is but one of many of his activities in the community of believers. The testimony of the Holy Spirit is not a source of new revelations but establishes believers in relation to the truth of God, which is completely contained in Scripture. It is he who makes faith a sure knowledge that excludes all doubt. It finds its analogy, finally, in the testimony our conscience offers to the law of God and in the assurance we have concerning God's existence. This doctrine of the testimony of the Holy Spirit, incorporated in the French, the Belgic, and Westminster Confessions, was developed in the spirit of Calvin by Ursinus, Zanchius, Polanus, and numerous others.[62] It found acceptance also outside of Reformed theology, among the Lutherans, not as yet in the work of Chemnitz, Heerbrand, et al. but in Hutter, Hunnius, Gerhard, Quenstedt, and Hollaz.[63]

This doctrine was opposed, however, from the side of Socinianism, Remonstrantism, and Romanism.[64] And gradually the doctrine of the internal testimony began to lose its place of honor even in Reformed theology. Already in Turretin, Amyrald, Molina, et al., it was weakened and identified with the so-called illumination of the Holy Spirit by which the intellect is enabled to note the marks and criteria of the divinity of Holy Scripture.[65] Faith no longer connects directly and immediately with Scripture but is the product of insight into the marks of truth and divinity it bears. Inserted between Scripture and faith, then, are the marks of the truth of Scripture. This occurred first in the sense that the recognition of those criteria was attributed to an illumination of the intellect by the Holy Spirit. But rationalism soon also considered this illumination unnecessary, assigned the study of the truth of revelation to reason, and based the authority of Scripture on

61. Ibid., I.vii.5. Erasmus also affirms that it is especially the Spirit of Christ who, by his secret working, communicates unwavering certainty to the human mind." Cf. Martin Schulze, *Calvins Jenseitschristemtum in seinem Verhältnisse zu den religiösen Schriften des Erasmus* (Görlitz: Rudolf Dulfer, 1902), 54.

62. Z. Ursinus, *Tract. Theol.*, pp. 12, 13; J. Zanchius, *Op. Theol.*, VIII, 332ff.; Polanus, *Synt. Theol.*, I, 16; Trigland, *Antapologia*, 42ff.; Maccovius, *Loci Comm.*, 28; Alsted, *Theol. Schol. Did.* (1618), 10ff., 29ff.; S. Maresius, *Syst. Theol.*, I, 33; J. Edwards, *Works of President Edwards* (New York: Burt Franklin, 1968), IV, 132ff. (ed. note: Bavinck cites this as *Works* III, 132 in the *Gereformerde Dogmatiek*).

63. Hase, *Hutterus Rediv.*, §37, §45; *Schmidt, *Dogmatik der Ev. Luth. Kirche*, 31; I. Dorner, *Geschichte der protestantischen Theologie* (München: J. G. Coth, 1867), 539–49 (ed. note: English translation available: *History of Protestant Theology Particularly in Germany*, trans. George Robson and Sophia Taylor [Edinburgh: T. & T. Clark, 1871]); *Klaiber, "Die Lehre der altprotestantische Dogmatik von dem Testimonium Spiritus Sancti," *Jahrbuch für Deutsche Theologie* (1857): 1–54.

64. O. Fock, *Der Socinianismus* (Kiel: C. Schröder, 1847), 336ff.; Episcopius, *Instit. Theol.*, IV, sect. 1, chap. 5, §2; P. van Limborch, *Theol. Christ.*, I, 4, §17; Bellarmine, "De verbo Dei," *Controversiis*, IV, 4; cf. J. Pannier, *Le témoignage du St. Esprit.* (Paris: Librairie Fischbacher, 1893), 140ff.

65. F. Turretin, *Institutes of Elenctic Theology*, II, qu. 6 §11ff.; idem, *Decas disp. Miscell.*, 30–70; M. Amyrald, *Synt. Thesium theol. In acad. Dalmur* (1665), 117–43; Molina, *Le juge des controverses*, 16, 17.

historical proofs. Even orthodox theologians scarcely dared any longer to speak of the "internal testimony."[66] Even when the testimony of the Holy Spirit is brought up to confirm Scriptural authority, it comes limping behind and is transformed into a proof of experience.[67] Michaelis declared he had never perceived such a witness of the Holy Spirit in his heart or found it in Scripture; and Strauss asserted that the testimony of the Holy Spirit led to fanaticism or rationalism and was the Achilles' heel of the Protestant system.[68]

Various factors have contributed, however, to a partial rehabilitation of this doctrine. Kant's critique of rationalism, "the proof of the spirit and of power" to which Lessing appealed, the romanticism of Jacobi and Schleiermacher, plus the sterility of apologetics, generated the conviction that the validation of the Christian religion must be grounded in the faith of the church. Religious truth must be proven in a way that differs from proving a proposition in mathematics. To revelation as the external principle of religion there must be a corresponding organ in human beings themselves. Admittedly, this is still miles away from the doctrine of the testimony of the Holy Spirit as Calvin developed it. Frequently this witness is stripped of its whole supernatural character by modern theologians. As a rule it is linked not with the form but only with the content, sometimes only with the religious-ethical content of Scripture. But like the Roman Catholic theologians, so also Protestant theologians have to admit that the final and deepest ground of faith cannot lie outside of us in proofs and arguments, in church and tradition, but can be found only in human beings themselves, in the religious subject. And that conviction is helpful for the doctrine of the testimony of the Holy Spirit. A few may still champion the historical proofs and oppose the testimony of the Holy Spirit,[69] but most theologians again include it in dogmatics and reserve more or less space for it.[70]

66. W. Brakel, *The Christian's Reasonable Service*, trans. Bartel Elshout, 4 vols. (Ligonier, Pa.: Soli Deo Gloria, 1992–), II, 209ff.; Marck, *Merch Godgeleeerdheid*, II, 6.

67. F. V. Reinhard, *Grundriss der Dogmatik*, 5th ed. (Munich: Seidel, 1824), 69; K. G. Bretschneider, *Handbuch der Dogmatik* (Leipzig: J. A. Barth, 1838), I, 283; Hase, *Hutter Rediv.*, §37, n. 4; Vinke, *Theol. Christ. Dogm.* (Trajecti ad Rhenum: Kemink, 1853–54), 21, 22.

68. Michaelis, *Dogmatik*, 2d ed. (1784), 92; D. Strauss, *Die Christliche Glaubenslehre*, 2 vols. (Tübingen: C. F. Osiander, 1840–41), I, 136.

69. König, *Der Glaubensakt des Christen* (Erlangen und Leipzig: G. Böhme, 1891), 92–99; idem, *Die letzte Instanz des biblischen Glaubens* (1892).

70. Weisenger, *Neue Kirchliche Zeitschrift* 12 (1898): 763–87; *Karl Müller, *Ref. Kirchenz*; Kaftan, *Zur Dogmatik*, 49–56; W. Schmidt, *Dogmatik*, I, 393; J. J. Van Oosterzee, *Jaarboek van wetenschappelijke Theologie* (1845); idem, *Christian Dogmatics*, I, 172ff.; J. H. Scholten, *De Leer der Hervormde Kerk*, I, 115–233; Twesten, *Vorlesungen über die Dogmatik* I, 433–37; J. P. Lange, *Christliche Dogmatik*, 3 vols. (Heidelberg: K. Winter, 1853), I §84; Kahnis, *Luth. Dogm.*, I, 291; Philippi, *Kirchliche Dogmatik* (3d. ed.), I, 135ff.; Cremer, "Inspiration," *PRE²*, VI, 746; Frank, *System der christlichen Gewissheit*, 2 vols. (Erlangen: A. Deichert, 1818–80), I, 139; idem, *Dogmatische Studien*, 38–57; Thomasius, *Christi Person und Werk*, 3d ed. (Erlangen: A. Deichert, 1886–88), II, 268ff.; R. A. Lipsius, *Jahrbuch für Protestantische Theologie* 11 (1885): 614; C. Hodge, *Systematic Theology*, 3 vols. (New York: Charles Scribner's, 1888), III, 69; Pannier,

DIVINE AND HUMAN LOGOS

[152] Both Roman Catholic and Protestant theology, in investigating the deepest ground of faith, have ended up with the religious subject and have to take their stance in the faith of the church. Every other path taken toward proving religious truth has dead-ended. This is seemingly disappointing and is so experienced by every theologian who misconstrues the real nature of revelation and religion and changes it into an intellectually demonstrable doctrine. But actually this result is to the advantage of theology. For it proves that theology has arrived at the insight that though religion is unique it is in the same position as all other sciences. Certainly the subjective starting point is not peculiar to theology. All that is objective can be approached only from the vantage point of the subject: the "thing in itself" is unknowable and does not exist for us. The world of sounds has reality only to those who hear; the world of ideas is real only to the thinking mind. It is futile to attempt to prove the objective existence of colors to the blind. All life and all knowledge is based on a kind of agreement between subject and object. Human beings are so richly endowed because they are linked with the objective world by a great many extremely diverse connections. They are related to the whole world. Physically, vegetatively, sensorily, intellectually, ethically, and religiously there is correspondence between them and the world; they are microcosms.

Now Scripture leads us to view all these human connections with the world religiously and to explain them theistically. Human beings have not put themselves in this relation to the world. They were adapted to the world from the beginning, and this world was reciprocally adapted to them. Since they are the image bearers of God, they are also masters of the earth. God not only forged these connections between human beings and the world; from moment to moment he also consistently maintains them and causes them to function. It is the one selfsame Logos who made all things in and outside of human beings. He is before all things, and they still continue jointly to exist through him (John 1:3; Col. 1:15–17). In addition, Scripture makes known to us the Spirit of God as the source and agent of all life in humanity and the world (Gen. 1:2; Ps. 33:6; 104:30; 139:7; Job 26:13; 33:4), especially of the intellectual, ethical, and religious life (Job 32:8; Isa. 11:2). Naturally the operations of that Spirit differ in keeping with the relations in which people stand to the world. Physically that operation consists only in the impulse that drives them and animals to seek their food from God (Ps. 104:20–30). At that level it is like an instinct, which unconsciously guides the action. But this operation of the Spirit of God assumes a higher form in the intellectual, ethical, and religious life of people. It then takes the form of reason, conscience, and the sense of divinity, which are not inactive

---

Le témoignage du S. Esprit, 193ff.; Kuyper, *Encyclopaedie*, II, 305–17, 336, 501–11; John de Witt, "The Testimony of the Holy Spirit to the Bible," *Presbyterian and Reformed Review* 6 (1895): 69–85.

abilities but capacities that, as a result of stimuli from related phenomena in the outside world, leap into action.

Now this action can be called a witness of the human spirit to the corresponding phenomena outside itself. Our spirit does nothing but continually bear witness to the truth that comes to us from without. That spirit does not, by thinking and reasoning, bring forth that truth from within itself; it does not create or produce it; it only re-produces it and re-flects on it. The truth is antecedent to and independent of the human spirit; it rests within itself, in the Logos, in which all things have their existence. On the human side it is only required that we grasp the truth and absorb it, that we bear personal witness to it, and by cognitive activity confirm it. Thus Jesus witnessed to what he had seen and heard (John 3:32). He bore witness to the truth (John 18:37); similarly the apostles were witnesses of the word of life they had seen and touched in Christ (John 15:27; 1 John 1:3). For the human spirit to bear such witness to the truth is rest, joy, blessedness. In such situations the distance between us and the truth has vanished. The truth has found us, and we have found it. There is immediate contact. The truth by itself makes us witnesses to it. All truth turns those who know it into witnesses, proclaimers, prophets. Entering into our spirits, it brings its own witness along with it; it engenders that witness in us by itself. Construed religiously, it is the Logos himself who through our spirit bears witness to the Logos in the world. It is the one selfsame Spirit who objectively displays the truth to us and subjectively elevates it into certainty in our spirit. It is his witness given in our consciousness to the thoughts God embodied in the creatures around us. This witness of the Holy Spirit to the truth is especially clear in religion. God has not left us without a witness. He reveals his power and deity in creation and by his Spirit bears witness to their reality in our mind (νοῦς). All cognition of truth is essentially a witness that the human spirit bears to it and at bottom a witness of the Spirit of God to the Word, by whom all things are made.

This witness of the human spirit to truth is the presupposition and foundation, as well as an analogy, of the testimony of the Holy Spirit. Calvin and others already pointed out this similarity.[71] But analogy is not identity. The external foundation (*principium externum*) of the Christian religion is not the general revelation of God in nature but a special revelation of God in Christ. The internal principle (*principium internum*) must correspond to that external principle. The mind (νοῦς) of the "natural" [unspiritual] person is not equipped to discern the things of the Spirit of God. God can be known only through God. Those who are of God hear the words of God (John 8:47; 3:21; 7:17; 10:3f.; 18:37). No one can speak about God except those who speak from and through God. For that reason alone the same

---

71. Calvin, *Institutes,* II.viii.1; Maresius, *Syst. Theol.,* I, 33; Alsted, *Theol. Schol. Did.,* 31; cf. Rabus, "Vom Wirken und Wohnen des göttlichen Geistes in der Menschenseele," *Neue Kirchliche Zeitschrift* 10 (1904): 768ff., 825ff.

Spirit who spoke through the prophets and apostles can bear witness in our hearts to the truth and thereby lift it beyond all doubt to the level of absolute certainty. Such a witness of the Holy Spirit in the hearts of believers is most clearly taught in Scripture. Included in objective revelation, i.e., in the person of Christ and in Scripture as his word, is everything human beings need to know God and to serve him. The revelation of God was completed in Christ and recorded with complete adequacy in Scripture. But this revelation in Christ and in his Word is a means, not an end. The end is the creation of a new humanity, which will fully unfold the image of God. Therefore the whole revelation must be transmitted from Christ to the church, from Scripture to the [believer's] consciousness. God seeks a dwelling place in humanity.

This enormous, divine work of the application of salvation, of leading [the church] into all truth, has been mandated to the Holy Spirit. Already in the days of the old covenant, he was the author of all religious-ethical knowledge and life (Ps. 51:13; 143:10; Isa. 63:10). But Israel was not yet of age and therefore under the guardianship of the law (Gal. 4:1f.). As yet the Holy Spirit had not been given because Jesus was not yet glorified (John 7:39). For that reason the prophets eagerly looked forward to the days of the new covenant, in which everyone would know the Lord and be guided by the Holy Spirit (Jer. 31:34; Ezek. 36:25f.; Joel 2:28f.). In keeping with this promise, the Spirit was poured out on the day of Pentecost. Jesus describes all of the Spirit's activity as witnessing to and glorifying him (John 15:26; 16:14). The Holy Spirit is the true and all-powerful witness to Christ. The whole world is hostile to Christ; no one stands by him. But in the face of that world, the Holy Spirit acts as *paraclete,* as Christ's public defender. He does this, in the first place, in Scripture; Scripture is the witness, the defender's public address on behalf of Christ, which he voices and maintains throughout all the ages. This testimony of the Holy Spirit in Holy Scripture precedes and is foundational to the witness the Spirit bears in the hearts of believers. Just as the thoughts of God are objectively embodied in the world and derived from there by the human spirit, so also the word of revelation was first fully described in Holy Scripture in order subsequently to be sealed in our hearts by the witness of the Holy Spirit. Here too the activity of the human spirit consists in nothing else than in bearing witness to the truth, in thinking God's thoughts after him. The testimony of the Holy Spirit in the hearts of believers is found not to be a new revelation or communication of unknown truths. It is essentially distinct from prophecy and inspiration; it only causes us to understand the truth that exists outside and independently of us as truth and therefore confirms and seals it in the human consciousness. The relation of the Holy Spirit's witness in the hearts of believers to the truth of revelation in Holy Scripture is, *mutatis mutandis,* no other than that of the human spirit to the object of its knowledge. The subject does not create the truth; the subject only recognizes and affirms it.

But the analogy extends even further. The objects of human knowledge are all self-attested (αὐτόπιστα); they rest in themselves. Their existence can be recognized but not proven. Proofs in the strict sense are possible only with respect to derivative propositions and consist in reducing them to general propositions. To prove a thing is to trace the unknown to the known, the uncertain to the certain. Perhaps it is more correct to say that to prove a thing consists in resolving uncertain and problematic propositions into propositions such as are generally accepted as certain. For the first principles, on which all proofs ultimately rest, are not themselves susceptible of being proven: they are certain only by and to faith. Proofs, therefore, are compelling only to those who agree with us in accepting those principles. "There is no point in arguing against a person who rejects the first principles" (*Contra principia negantem non est disputandum*). So, in morality, stealing can be proven to be wrong to those who recognize the authority of the moral law, but no proof is compelling for those who deny this authority. The moral law is trustworthy in itself (αυτοπιστις): it rests in itself. It is like the sun, which can only be seen by its own rays. It does not depend on any proof or argument. It is powerful because it exists, posits, and maintains itself. Its power consists in its authority, in the divine majesty with which it brings its "thou shalt" home to our conscience. The moral law would weaken itself if it reasoned with us and subjected itself to our judgment. It speaks and acts categorically and does not want to listen to exceptions and excuses. To the question "Why do you submit to the moral law?" there is only one possible answer: "Because it reveals God's will to me." But if someone further asks you, "Why do you believe that this moral law is an expression of the will of God?" you can no longer give a decisive and effective answer. Those who nevertheless want to respond will take a side path and appeal to various marks and criteria that convince them of the divinity of the moral law. But such "proofs" are not compelling. And this is how it is with all "first principles." They are self-based and certain only to those who believe them.

The same situation prevails in theology. Proofs here are possible only with respect to inferred propositions. The deity of Christ can be proven to the person who recognizes the authority of Scripture. But the authority of Scripture rests in itself and cannot be proven. Holy Scripture is self-attested (αὐτόπιστος) and therefore the final ground of faith. No deeper ground can be advanced. To the question "Why do you believe Scripture?" the only answer is: "Because it is the word of God." But if the next question is "Why do you believe that Holy Scripture is the word of God?" a Christian cannot answer. That Christian will admittedly appeal to the marks and criteria of Scripture, to the majesty of its style, the sublimity of its content, the depth of its ideas, the abundant fruit it has borne, etc. But these are not the grounds of his or her faith; they are merely the attributes and characteristics that the believing mind later discovers in Scripture, just as the proofs for God's existence do not precede and undergird faith but flow from it and are constructed by it.

All the proofs for belief in Scripture derived from its marks and criteria show with utter clarity that no deeper ground can be indicated. *"God said it"* (*Deus dixit*) is the foundational principle (*primum principium*) to which all dogmas, including the dogma of Scripture, can be traced. The soul's bond to Scripture as the word of God lies behind the [believer's] consciousness and underneath the proofs. It is mystical in nature—like the belief in the first principles of the various sciences.

DEMONSTRATING THE TRUTH OF FAITH

[153] From a number of sides objections are raised against this view to the effect that faith thereby becomes totally arbitrary. Instead of giving reasons why people believe Scripture to be the word of God, they answer that God has so given it to us to believe. By such an answer a Muslim can "prove" his faith in the Koran and every superstitious person his or her private superstition. The statement: "This is what I want, therefore this is what I command" takes the place of reasoning and proof.[72] Let me grant, in the first place, that the believer cannot cite a deeper ground for revelation than its divine authority, which he or she recognizes by faith. But this is not to say that believers have nothing to say to the opponents of that revelation. True: they have no airtight proofs; they cannot move the opponent toward faith; but they have at least as much to say in defending as the opponent has in attacking scriptural authority.[73] Unbelief, too, is rooted, not in proofs and arguments, but in the heart. In this respect believers and unbelievers are in exactly the same position. Their convictions are integrally bound up with their whole personality and are only a posteriori supported by proofs and arguments. And now, when the two parties oppose each other with these a posteriori proofs and arguments, the position of believers is not less favorable than that of unbelievers. God is sufficiently knowable to those who seek him and also sufficiently hidden to those who run away from him. "There is enough light for those who only desire to see and enough darkness for those of a contrary disposition. There is enough clarity to illumine the elect and enough darkness to humble them. There is enough darkness to render the reprobate sightless and enough clarity to condemn them and to render them inexcusable."[74] The state of religion, theism, revelation, and Scripture is not as hopeless as science has for years wanted us to believe. Theodor von Lerber was not altogether wrong when he wrote about science: "As dilettante I have too often sat next to her and looked into her cards and upon her hands to

---

72. Cf. J. H. Scholten, vs. Sausaye, *De Leer der Hervormde Kerk*, foreword.

73. Ed. note: Bavinck here anticipates developments in twentieth-century Christian philosophy, namely the notion of "basic beliefs" in the Reformed epistemology of Alvin Plantinga, Nicholas Wolterstorff, and others. For an introduction to this philosophy, see Alvin Plantinga and Nicholas Wolterstorff, eds., *Faith and Rationality: Reason and Belief in God* (Notre Dame and London: University of Notre Dame Press, 1983).

74. B. Pascal, *Oeuvres*, 3 vols. (Paris: Hachette, 1869), I, 345.

still be overly enchanted with the old lady. She will have to inscribe on my gravestone: 'he thought little of me and died.'"[75] Historical and rational proofs will not convert anybody. Still, for the defense of the faith they are as strong as the arguments advanced by opponents for the justification of their unbelief.

Also, the witness given by believers to divine revelation, to Scripture that is, though not universally human *is* universally Christian. In making this confession, all of Christianity speaks with a single voice. The testimony of the Holy Spirit is not the witness of a private spirit but of one and the same Spirit who dwells in all believers. Calvin, in discussing this witness, stated he was describing nothing but the experience of all believers. It is a mighty witness that the church of all the ages has borne to Scripture as the word of God. On no other dogma is there so much unanimity. This is a fact that may not be put on a par with hallucination or arbitrariness and needs to be explained. While believers most certainly cannot point to a deeper ground for their faith than the divine authority of Scripture, they *can* explain in greater detail how they arrived at this faith. As a rule people are born and nurtured in the faith. Later they discover they are bound to Scripture with all the fibers of their soul, and then, in reflecting on it, they try to explain this mystical bond. But it frequently happens that someone is converted and comes to believe in Scripture at a later age. And also those who from their youth on have lived by that faith are often shocked and swayed by criticism. Only gradually do they arrive at the firm assurance of faith. Now what is the experience by which faith in revelation is first aroused and invigorated? It naturally differs in different believers, but it is always of a religious-ethical, a spiritual nature. What really causes us to believe is not the insight of our intellect, nor a decision of our will, but a power that is superior to us, bends our will, illumines our mind, and without compulsion still effectively takes our thoughts and reflections captive to the obedience of Christ [2 Cor. 10:5]. This is what Augustine confessed when he attributed faith to "internal grace"; what Thomas recognized when he said that "the assent of faith" came from God, "inwardly moving us through grace"; what the Vatican Council stated when it testified that faith does not arise "apart from the illumination and inspiration of the Holy Spirit." This was the conviction of the entire Reformation movement: faith is a gift of God, an effect of the Holy Spirit's working. Believing is an act of the intellect, an immediate (= unmediated by proofs) linkage of the human consciousness to divine revelation.

But that faith presupposes a change in the relation of the whole person to God: it presupposes the new birth, the transformation of the will. "No one believes except willingly" (*Nemo credit nisi volens*). Knowledge is compelling; no one can deny a mathematical proposition. But believing is free; it is an

75. A. Zahn, *Social demokratie und Theologie* (Gütersloh, 1895), 34 (ed. note: This may be a reference to Th. von Lerber, *Professoren, Studenten, und Studentenleben vor 1500 Jahren* [Bern: Mann, 1867]).

act of supreme freedom inasmuch as it is an act of the deepest self-denial.
When God links salvation, not to knowing but to believing, that is proof
that he does not coerce nor wishes to coerce anyone. The Letter to Diognetus states beautifully: "It is not like God to use compulsion."[76] Precisely because faith is not the fruit of scientific proofs, it does not arise outside of the
human heart and will. That is the truth implicit in the doctrine of Kant and
the neo-Kantians concerning moral faith. Faith is not the conclusion of a
syllogism. Nor, on the other hand, is it a decision of the will, a postulate.
The prodigal son, upon his return to his father's house, did not postulate.
Neither is faith an imperative of the will. People cannot believe when they
please; the will cannot order the consciousness to accept something as truth
when that consciousness itself does not in any way grasp that truth. Believing is not arbitrary, but neither is it blind. It presupposes a change of will:
function follows being. It is itself a free, spontaneous, intellectual recognition of the word of God. Just as the human eye, seeing the sun, is immediately convinced of its reality, so the regenerate person "sees" the truth of
God's revelation. For the regenerate person faith in revelation is as natural as
the recognition of the moral law is for the moral person. It is increated in the
nature of the spiritual life; it is rooted in the mysterious depths of the regenerate heart. Believers cannot relinquish this faith anymore than they can relinquish themselves. Indeed, they *can* deny themselves, sacrifice their lives,
but they *cannot* relinquish their faith. In the life of Christians, faith in revelation is inseparable from faith in themselves.[77] Christians would have to
abandon faith in themselves, in their adoption as children of God, in the
forgiveness of their sins, in the trustworthiness and faithfulness of God, if
they ceased to understand revelation as the word of God. Faith in revelation
is inseparable from the best that is in them. In their best moments they are
most firmly established in that faith. Whatever may arise to challenge it,
they cannot and may not act otherwise.

Finally, opposition to and resistance against this faith of theirs is rife, not
just from without, but even much more from within. However much their
will has been bent and their intellect enlightened, there remains much in believers that resists the obedience of faith. Faith, since it is the conviction of
things not seen, is a continual struggle. The sins of the heart and the errors
of the mind gang up on faith and often have appearance in their favor. As
long as believers are on earth, there remains in them a dualism, a dualism
not of the head and the heart, but of the flesh (σαρξ) and the spirit (πνευμα),
of the "old" (παλαιος) and the "new" (καινος) person (ἀνθρωπος). Faith more
or less retains a supernatural character insofar as it transcends the nature of

76. *Epistle to Diognetus*, chap. 7.
77. S. Hoekstra, *Wijsgerige Godsdienstwetenschap*, I, 222; A. Kuyper, *Encyclopaedie*, II, 77. This element of truth is also present in the earlier explanation of the rise of religion from the conflict we experience between the sense of distress and self-esteem. In God, we maintain and affirm our own spiritual
identity.

unspiritual persons. It is not yet fully natural; the moment it becomes natural it ceases and becomes sight. Faith is above all faith because it sees something that the unspiritual do not perceive. On the other hand, this dualism, however painful, serves to confirm faith. For if faith does not arise from the natural habits of human beings and is not the conclusion of a syllogism nor a decision of the will, its presence is simultaneously a proof of its truth. Our own spirit does not by nature impel us to call God our Father and to count ourselves among his children. There is an essential and easily recognizable difference between the witness of the Holy Spirit, when he says to our soul, "I am your salvation," and the temptation of Satan, when he whispers, "Peace, peace, and no danger." "Can a person, impelled by the devil, possibly call God Abba! Father! in faith?"[78] Christian faith points back to the testimony of the Holy Spirit. "Though theology scoffs and philosophy scorns, God himself is the final ground of my faith in God" (Beets).

THE TESTIMONY OF THE SPIRIT

[154] This witness of the Holy Spirit has been all too one-sidedly applied, by Calvin and later Reformed theologians, to the authority of Holy Scripture. It seemed that it had no other import than the subjective assurance that Scripture is the word of God. As a result this testimony came to stand by itself. It was separated from the life of faith and seemed to refer to an extraordinary revelation of which Michaelis was honest enough to admit that he had never experienced it. Scripture, however, teaches very differently.

Generally speaking, the Holy Spirit was promised by Jesus as the Comforter, the Spirit of truth, who leads first the apostles, then, by their word, also all other believers, into the truth. He witnesses of Christ to them and glorifies him (John 14:17; 15:26; 16:14). To that end he convicts people of sin (John 16:8–11), regenerates them (John 3:3), and prompts them to confess Christ as Lord (1 Cor. 12:3). He further assures them of their adoption as children of God and of their heavenly inheritance (Rom. 8:14f.; 2 Cor. 1:22; 5:5; Eph. 1:13; 4:30), makes known all the things believers have received from God (1 Cor. 2:12; 1 John 2:20; 3:24; 4:6–13), and in the church is the author of all Christian virtues and all spiritual gifts (Gal. 5:22; 1 Cor. 12:8–11). It is evident from all these passages that the testimony of the Holy Spirit is of a religious-ethical kind and intimately bound up with people's own faith life. It does not bypass people's faith; it is not a voice from heaven, a dream or a vision. It is a witness that the Holy Spirit communicates *in, with,* and *through* our own spirit in faith. It is not given to unbelievers but is the portion only of the children of God. Episcopius therefore raised the objection[79] that the testimony of the Holy Spirit cannot be a ground of faith because it is something that only comes later (John 7:38;

---

78. Heidegger, *Corpus Theol.,* XXIV, 78.
79. Episcopius, *Inst. Theol.,* IV, sect. 1, c. 5, §2.

14:17; Acts 5:32; Gal. 3:2; 4:6). But from the very beginning faith itself is the work of the Holy Spirit (1 Cor. 12:3) and receives its seal and confirmation in the Spirit of adoption. Believing itself is a witness of the Holy Spirit in our hearts and through our spirit.

Assurance

There exists a distinction between the Spirit of God and our spirit in this witness only insofar as our spirit still continually fights it and must constantly be guided toward obedience. The witness of the Holy Spirit, accordingly, gives no assurance of the objective truths of salvation aside from the state of the religious subject. The Spirit guarantees those truths because they are inseparable from regeneration and conversion, forgiveness and the adoption of the believer as a child of God. The testimony of the Holy Spirit is first of all the assurance that we are children of God. That is the central truth, the core and focus of this witness. And in that connection this witness also seals the objective truths of salvation, the transcendent and surpassing truths, as Frank called them. This is stated with this further proviso, however, that the testimony of the Holy Spirit does not reveal to us any of these truths, nor even enables us by reflection to infer them from the nature of our spiritual life. The illumination of the Holy Spirit is *not* the cognitive *source* of Christian truth. It does not disclose to us any material truths that are hidden from the "natural" [unspiritual] person. It only gives us a spiritual understanding of these same things, one that is different and deeper. Paul expressly states that the Spirit makes known to us the things objectively granted us by God in Christ (1 Cor. 2).[80] The Spirit whom believers receive is the Spirit of Christ, who takes everything from Christ and is received from the preaching of the gospel (John 14:17; Acts 5:32; Gal. 3:2; 4:6; 1 John 2:20, 24, 27). But the truths themselves are known to us from other parts of Scripture; they are only subjectively sealed by the witness of the Holy Spirit.

From this it follows that the actual object to which the Holy Spirit bears witness in the hearts of believers is nothing other than the *divinity* of the truth granted us in Christ. Historical, chronological, or geographical data as such, by themselves, are never the object of the witness of the Holy Spirit. Even the facts of salvation as brute facts (*nuda facta*) are not the content of that witness. Not a single believer is assured, in a scientific sense, of the supernatural conception and resurrection of Christ by the witness of the Holy Spirit. The only thing to which the witness of the Holy Spirit relates is the *divinity* of these truths, that is, the divinity of all those truths that are revealed in Scripture and have been granted us by God in Christ. It is wrong to apply the testimony of the Holy Spirit only to that which is religious-ethical in a narrow sense. That divinity indeed is the only direct object of that witness, but it is not just an attribute of a few religious and moral pro-

---

80. S. Hoekstra, *Grondslag, Wezen, en Openbaring van het Godsdienstlige Geloof* (Rotterdam: Altman & Roosenburg, 1861), 165, 184.

nouncements but also of facts and deeds. Christ himself is a historic person; redemption was brought about by historic deeds, and the witness of the Holy Spirit also puts the stamp of divinity on this history. In Christianity ideas and facts can absolutely not be separated. However often this has been attempted by rationalism, various philosophical systems, and in recent years to some extent by the school of Ritschl and Sabatier, the outcome invariably shows us that in making that attempt people lose Christianity itself. We have to choose between converting Christianity into a religion of reason and maintaining it, as in fact it is, a religion of redemption, but also to have the courage to express "the superiority and general validity of the 'faith-view' in cases of conflict with science."[81]

History is not a matter of indifference in a single religion,[82] but Christianity itself *is* and *creates* a history. Precisely because it is the perfect, absolute, and definitive religion, it is and has to be a historical religion. The reason is that Christianity regards sin not as ignorance, which can easily be overcome by some enlightenment, but as an appalling power, which produces its effects throughout the cosmos; and over against this power it brings reconciliation and redemption in the deepest and broadest sense of those terms. It brings redemption from the guilt and the stain, from all the consequences of sin, from the errors of the intellect and the impurity of the heart, from the death of soul and body. It brings that redemption not only to the individual but also, organically, to the family and generations of families, to people and society, to humanity and the world. For that reason Christianity has to be a history, rooted in facts, producing facts. The facts are the skeletal system of Christianity; specifically, the cross and the resurrection of Christ are the two mainstays on which the Christian faith rests. When that gospel is preached purely, it always includes those facts; and when the preaching of that gospel is blessed and effects faith and conversion, then, in the religious experience of sin and grace, the divinity of this history is sealed. For if Christ did not die and was not raised from the dead, our faith is vain. Those facts, accordingly, are not events that took place at some time in the past and have now lost their significance. They do not stand between us and God, keeping us separate from him. "To the New Testament writers this concentration of faith upon the historic realities of redemption does not in the least interfere with its personal character as a direct act of trust in God and in Christ. The Person is immanent in the facts, and the facts are the revelation of the Person."[83] And because those facts, along with the words, are the revelation of God, they are integrally connected with the Christian faith and can, in this connection, also be confirmed and sealed to our hearts by the Holy Spirit.

81. *Peters, *Neue Kirchliche Zeitschrift* 9 (1903): 349.

82. Karl Bauer, "Die Bedeutung geschichtlicher Thatsacher für den religiöse Glauben," *Theologische Studien and Kritiken* 77 (1904): 221–73.

83. Geerhardus Vos, "Christian Faith and the Truthfulness of Bible History," *Princeton Theological Review* 4 (July 1906): 289–305.

Scripture as Word of God

For that reason Calvin also rightly linked the testimony of the Holy Spirit to Scripture as the word of God. This testimony has a "material object" in the content but also a "formal object" in the witness of Scripture, and the two are inseparable. When the Holy Spirit guarantees to us the divine character of the gospel, he also indirectly guarantees the trustworthiness of the apostolic witnesses who first, in Jesus' name, proclaimed that gospel and thereby bound all humankind to their witness.[84] But he also offers direct assurance of it. For the Holy Spirit does not reveal to the believer any previously unknown truth, neither in respect of Christ nor in respect of Scripture. He takes everything from Christ, and so the believer can only confess what Christ has given him or her. Scripture, however, contains a doctrine about itself, as much as about Christ. And the testimony of the Holy Spirit with respect to Scripture as Scripture consists in the fact—not that believers receive an immediate heavenly vision of the divinity of Scripture, nor that they mediately infer its divinity from the marks and criteria of Scripture, or, even less, that on the basis of the experience of the power that is unleashed by it they conclude that it is divine, but—that they freely and spontaneously recognize the authority with which Scripture everywhere asserts itself and which it repeatedly expressly claims for itself.

In this connection it is not the authenticity, nor the canonicity, nor even the inspiration, but the *divinity* of Scripture, its divine authority, which is the true object of the testimony of the Holy Spirit. He causes believers to submit to Scripture and binds them to it in the same measure and intensity as to the person of Christ himself. He assures them that in life and death and all the crises of life, they can bank on the Word of God and even fearlessly appear with it before the Judge of heaven and earth. Historical criticism, accordingly, encounters resistance from the believing community only to the degree that it detracts from this divinity of Holy Scripture and thus undermines its witness concerning the adoption as children, the hope of glory, and the assurance of salvation. Hence the doctrine of Scripture entails a profound religious interest. Its God-breathed and God-breathing character and authority is not an indifferent matter, which the Christian community has taken over from Jewish scribes or pagan fortune-tellers, but is confessed by that community on the basis of God's Word and is integrally connected with its own existence. For that reason faith in Scripture cannot and does not rest on intellectual arguments but has its deepest ground in the witness of the Holy Spirit. Proofs and arguments can recommend it and hence, as subordinate means, undeniably have value. But we are only fully persuaded of the truth of Christianity

---

84. Cf. Ihmels, *Die christliche Wahrheitsgewissheit* (Leipzig: A. Deichert [Georg Böhme], 1908), 191ff., 225ff.

and the authority of Scripture by the testimony of the Holy Spirit, who illumines our intellect, opens our hearts, and assures us that "the Spirit is the truth" (1 John 5:6).

Finally, if we look at the testimony of the Holy Spirit in its totality and briefly sum it up, it proves to be threefold. Included in it, in the first place, is the witness the Holy Spirit offers in Scripture concerning Scripture itself. This witness comes to us indirectly in all the divine characteristics (criteria, marks), which are imprinted on the content and form of Scripture. It also comes to us directly in all those positive pronouncements Scripture contains with respect to its divine origin. Secondly, subsumed under this heading of the testimony of the Holy Spirit is the witness the Spirit has borne to Scripture in the church throughout the centuries; and this witness is indirectly embodied in all the blessings that accrued to the church as church from Scripture (in the existence and continuing existence of the church as church) and directly in the united confession of the believing community throughout the centuries that Scripture is the word of God. Finally, the testimony of the Holy Spirit also includes the witness the Holy Spirit bears in the heart of every believer concerning the divine authority of Scripture. This witness is implied in the bond by which believers are bound in their spiritual life to Scripture with its self-witness and to the believing community with its confession, and comes to expression in the personal conviction that the Word of God is the truth.

This threefold testimony is one and from the same Spirit. From Scripture, through the church, it penetrates the heart of the individual believer. Still, in each of these three forms, it has a meaning of its own. The testimony of the Holy Spirit in Scripture is "the primary motive toward faith or the principle by which, or the argument on account of which, Scripture becomes regulative (κανονικον) and non-apodictic (ἀναποδεικτον)." The testimony of the Holy Spirit in the church is "the other motive or instrument through which we believe. It is introductory (εἰσαγωγικον) and supportive (ὑπουργικον)." The witness of the Holy Spirit in the heart of the believer is the "efficient cause of faith, the principle by which or through which we believe. It is originating (ἀρχηγικον) and effecting (ἐνεργητικον)."[85]

Given these distinctions, also the charge of circular reasoning usually advanced against the testimony of the Holy Spirit is invalidated. For, strictly speaking, the testimony of the Holy Spirit is not the final ground but the means of faith. The ground of faith is, and can only be, Scripture, or rather, the authority of God, which comes upon the believer materially in the content as well as formally in the witness of Scripture. Hence the ground of faith is identical with its content and cannot, as Herrmann believes, be detached from it. Scripture as the word of God is simultaneously the material and the formal object of faith. But the testimony of the Holy

85. Spanheim, *Opera*, III, 1202.

Spirit is "the efficient cause," "the principle by which," of faith. We believe Scripture, not because of, but by means of the testimony of the Holy Spirit. Scripture and the testimony of the Holy Spirit relate to each other as objective truth and subjective assurance, as the first principles and their self-evidence, as the light and the human eye. Once it is has been recognized in its divinity, Scripture is incontrovertibly certain to the faith of the believing community, so that it is both the principle and the norm of faith and life.

Variable Testimony in the Church

[155] This testimony of the Holy Spirit is not nullified by the fact that it is seemingly so variable among believers. Bellarmine already raised the objection that, despite this testimony of the Holy Spirit, Luther and Calvin judged very differently about the Letter of James. But the Holy Spirit testifies in the heart of believers not only with respect to Scripture but also with respect to all other redemptive truths. There is not a church that does not, in this sense, accept a testimony or illumination of the Spirit. Yet this fact does not rule out differences in the confession of various truths. We believe in one holy catholic Christian church, a communion of saints. All believers confess one Lord, one faith, one baptism, and are baptized into one Spirit. Still there is division and conflict among the churches and with respect to the fundamental articles of faith. The unity of the Christian church with respect to Scripture is much greater than in any other dogma, not even excepting that of the Trinity and the deity of Christ. Still all these differences do not make us doubt the unity of faith and knowledge, the catholicity of the church, the Spirit's leading into all truth, for differences will remain as long as the church is imperfect, the human heart is corrupt, our insight is limited, our faith small and weak. The testimony of the Holy Spirit is not always equally strong and clear in the heart of the individual believer. Since it is intimately tied in with a person's faith and life of faith, it fluctuates and is subject to doubt and opposition. When sin gains the upper hand in a believer, the consciousness of his or her forgiveness is blurred and the witness of the Holy Spirit loses its force. Our faith in Scripture increases and decreases along with our trust in Christ. The confession of the testimony of the Holy Spirit is so sublime and ideal that the reality of the Christian life often remains starkly inferior by comparison.

Add to this that Scripture, though certainly also a book for the individual believer, has in the context of the church of all ages been given to the whole church, to believers of all times and places. The individual believer always tends to feed on a small part of Scripture. There are whole sections of Scripture that, to individual believers and even to entire churches and times, remain a closed book. But the confession of Scripture as the word of God is a confession of the whole church to which the individual believer consents and which he or she supports and upholds personally and in the measure of his or her faith.[86] The testimony of the Holy Spirit is not a private opinion but the witness of the church of all ages, of Christianity as a whole, of reborn humankind in its entirety. At one time the church in all of its members, like the world, was hostile to the word of God. But the Holy Spirit, working in it and with it, took up the defense of the truth of Christ. He has broken its enmity, illumined its intellect, bent its will, and keeps it in touch with the truth from century to century and from day to day. The whole testimony of the believing community is a testimony of the Holy Spirit. It is the "yes!" and "Amen!" which that community utters in response to the truth of God. It is the "Abba! Father! Your word of truth" that rises up from the hearts of all believers. The testimony of the Holy Spirit is so far from being the Achilles' heel of Protestantism that it should rather be called the cornerstone of our Christian confession, the crown and seal of all Christian truth, the triumph of the Holy Spirit in the world. Take away the testimony of the Holy Spirit, not only in relation to Scripture, but to all the truths of redemption, and there is no more church. For the witness the Holy Spirit bears to Scripture as the word of God is but a single tone in the song he has put on the lips of the believing community. It is but a small part of that splendid divine work assigned to the Holy Spirit: to cause the fullness of Christ to dwell in his community.

But considered in this light, this witness of the Holy Spirit is also not devoid of all value even over against the [church's] opponents. Certainly, when it is separated from its whole environment and abstracted from the life of faith in which it is rooted, from the communion of saints in which it flourishes, from the entire matrix of Christian truth to which it belongs, then, over against its opponents, it loses all its power, and the "yes" of one person is no stronger than the "no" of another. But conceived as the witness rendered by the Holy Spirit in the hearts of all the children of God concerning the truth as it is in Christ Jesus our Lord, it does not fail to impress even the most stubborn adversary. Even then it is not on a par with a logical argument or mathematical proof. It retains a power of its own. But science would be in bad straits if it could only reckon with that which is demonstrable. Is the human conscience powerless because immoral people oppose its witness every moment of the day? Do the first-order principles of science deserve no credence because skeptics refuse to recognize them? Is Scripture ineffectual because its truth falls on deaf ears in unspiritual people? The power of all these moral forces lies precisely in the fact that they do not offer rational proof for themselves but with sublime majesty confront the consciousness of every human being. They are powerful as a result of the authority with which they assert themselves. A father does not "prove" his authority to his children but maintains it by "divine right." So

---

86. J. C. K. Hofmann, *Weissagung und Erfüllung im Alten und Neuen Testamente,* 2 vols. (Nördlingen: C. H. Beck, 1841), I, 45ff.; A. Kuyper, *Encyclopaedie,* II, 315.

also Scripture. It has maintained its authority in the church of Christ to this day. It has prompted all believers—including the greatest minds and noblest spirits—to yield to its authority. What power in the world is comparable to that of Scripture? The testimony of the Holy Spirit is the triumph of the foolishness of the cross over the wisdom of the world, the victory of the thoughts of God over the deliberations of human beings. In this sense the apologetic value of the testimony of the Holy Spirit is second to none. Surely this is the victory that overcomes the world: our faith! (1 John 5:4).

17

FAITH AND THEOLOGY

The certainty of faith rests in the Word of God and does not require theological science. Some Christians even deny the validity and value of theology, favoring a simple, practical Christianity. Following Renaissance humanism's repudiation of scholasticism, Reformation thinkers initially also concentrated on the practical benefits of faith. Over time antipathy to dogmatics became more general. Theology became regarded as the offspring of an ill-starred marriage between original Christian and Greek philosophy in which the pure, simple gospel of Jesus had been falsified. The life of Christian love was said to have been turned into cold and arid orthodoxy, a "knowledge" that conflicts with modern science.

Some of these complaints against theology are valid. It has sometimes lacked appropriate humility and degenerated into hairsplitting. However, abuse does not cancel out use, and ignoring theology reduces the Christian religion to feeling. Not only is theology important for the sake of clarity; it is also important to avoid the one-sided interpretations of the gospel that arise from a split between faith and metaphysics. Efforts to locate a "pure" gospel behind the dogmas of the Christian church lead to a canon within the canon and break fellowship with the universal church of all ages. Invalidating the history of dogma also forfeits the opportunity to influence the culture and science of our own day. The Christian life slips into the pathologies of mysticism and separatism, and scientific thought is not freed from error by the truth of Christ.

The validity of theology arises from the essence of the Christian faith itself as divine revelation addresses humanity in its totality and in all its life relationships. From the beginning Christian theology has used the insights of the philosophic tradition to understand and explain the faith. Christian theology did not simply adopt one philosophic system wholesale but borrowed from many, though always testing philosophies by revelation. Theology thus arises from the church as believers think through the precepts of the faith.

Though theology moves "from faith to understanding" (Augustine), it is nevertheless distinct from faith and is a fruit of the church as organism rather than institute. The distinction between faith and theology is clear from efforts in the church to distinguish the basic truths that must be affirmed to be a Christian from the larger body of truths discussed by theologians. The Roman Catholic notion of "implicit faith," as well as the Protestant distinction be-

tween "infused theology" (all believers) and "acquired theology" (scientific theologians only), or later between "fundamental" and "non-fundamental" articles of faith, all reflect the distinction between faith and theology both in content and scope. Sadly, these discussions led in some quarters to divisions among believers along the lines of head and heart, doctrine and life, and rationalism versus pietism.

Though the distinction between essential and non-essential articles of faith was important for ecumenical relations between different Protestant groups, it had the potential for reducing the faith to quantitative measurement. Such an arithmetic of belief obscured the qualitative gracious, personal, organic relation to Christ so important in the Reformation protest against Roman Catholic sacramentalism and its doctrine of implicit faith. For the Reformers all believers, in principle, share the same knowledge and trust in the grace of God. Theology deepens and broadens this faith-knowledge but remains inextricably connected to it. Theology is a source of faith; its "object" is accessible only through faith, it reflects on the content of faith, and it is to be done in faith. They both need each other. Faith preserves theology from secularization; theology preserves faith from separatism. Thus the church and theological schools ought to be in solidarity with each other.

Since theology is believing reflection on faith, we must also consider the role of reason in theology. Reason and faith must not be dualistically separated. Faith is, after all, not an organ or faculty next to or above reason but a disposition or habit of reason itself. Faith is a voluntary act of the human consciousness and as a habit becomes the natural breath of the children of God. Faith does not relieve Christians of the desire and need to study and reflect on faith, it spurs them on to that end. Theology requires disciplined preparation in the arts more broadly. This equips one for the task of building a theological system organically from the whole of Scripture in its literary diversity. Then follows the task of intellectually mining the material gathered from Scripture and recapitulating it into a meaningful system of thought in the language of the day.

The theological task also calls for humility. Full comprehension is impossible; wonder and mystery always remain. This must not be identified with the New Testament notion of mystery, which refers to that which was unknown but has now been revealed in the history of salvation culminating in Christ. Neither is it a secret gnosis available only to an elite, nor is it unknown because of the great divide between the natural and the supernatural. The divide is not so much metaphysical as it is spiritual—sin is the barrier. The wonder of God's love may not be fully comprehended by believers in this age, but what is known in part and seen in part is known and seen. In faithful wonder the believer is not conscious of living in the face of mystery that surpasses reason and thus it is not an intellectual burden. Rather, in the joy of God's grace there is intellectual liberation. Faith turns to wonder; knowledge terminates in adoration; and confession becomes a song of praise and thanksgiving. Faith is the knowledge which is life, "eternal life" (John 17:3).

AVERSION TO THEOLOGY

[156] The Christian church, not content to limit itself to faith, almost from the beginning pursued knowledge of religious truth and gave birth to a special branch of science: theology. Yet it cannot be said that this drive toward a scientific understanding is inherent in faith as such. For faith is certainty and excludes all doubt. It rests in the Word of God and is satisfied with it. "As far as we are concerned, there is no need for curiosity after Jesus Christ, nor for inquiry after the gospel. When we believe, we desire nothing beyond believing."[1] "Godliness has immediate certainty within itself."[2] For that reason the validity and value of theological science have frequently been contested in the Christian church. At the time of the monophysite and monotheletic disputes, there was already a party called "Gnosimachi," who considered all science unnecessary for Christians. They taught that God does not desire anything from Christians other than good works and that it is better "with a simple unfettered mind-set to pursue one's own course than to devote a lot of care to the study of decrees and learned opinions."[3] Toward the end of the Middle Ages, aversion to theology was universal. Scholasticism had lost all public trust. In all circles and among all sects, there was a deep longing for a simpler and more practical form of Christianity.[4] Humanism looked down its nose at scholasticism. And resistance to scholasticism in the Catholic Church has hardly ever been silent since. Baius, Jansen, Launoy, numerous theologians in the eighteenth and nineteenth centuries, like Günther for example, lodged all sorts of serious objections against scholastic theology.[5]

Initially the Reformation took the same position. Luther's assessment of Aristotle, scholasticism, and reason is well known. Melanchthon, in the first edition of his *Loci,* wrote: "This is what it is to know Christ: to know his benefits, not what you (scholastics) teach, to gaze upon his natures and the modes of this incarnation." Zwingli said that being a Christian "did not consist in prattling about Christ but to walk as he walked." Calvin puts an equally strong emphasis on this practical side of the faith.[6] But many people went farther than the Reformers and rejected all theology. Carlstadt, appeal-

1. Tertullian, *The Prescription against Heretics,* 8.

2. R. Rothe, *Theologische Ethik,* 2d rev. ed., 5 vols. (Wittenberg: Zimmerman, 1867–71), §7; cf. A. Kuyper, *Encyclopaedie der Heilige Godgeleerdherd,* 2d ed., 3 vols. (Kampen: Kok, 1908–9), II, 278, 541.

3. John of Damascus, "De haeresibus," *Opera Omnia* (Basel, 1575), 585.

4. A. von Harnack, *History of Dogma,* trans. N. Buchanan, J. Millar, E. B. Speirs, and W. McGilchrist and ed. A. B. Bruce, 7 vols. (London: Williams & Norgate, 1896–99), VII, 13.

5. J. Kleutgen, *Philosophie der Vorzeit,* 2d ed., 5 vols. (Münster: Theissing, 1867–74), IV, 133ff.; H. Denzinger, *Vier Bücher von der religiöse Erkenntnis* (Würzburg: Stahleschen Buch und Kunst, 1856–57), II, 566ff.

6. J. Köstlin, *Theology of Luther,* trans. Charles E. Hay, 2 vols. (Philadelphia: Lutheran Publication Society, 1897), I, 137ff.; P. Melanchthon, *Loci Comm.,* ed. Augusti (1821), p. 9; H. Bavinck, *De Ethiek. van Ulrich Zwingli* (Kampen: Zalsman, 1880), 119; J. Calvin, *Institutes,* I.ii.2; I.v.9; I.xii.1; *Commentary,* on Rom. 1:19.

ing to Matthew 23:8, rejected all titles and assumed the lifestyle of a farmer living among farmers. The Anabaptists and Mennonites wanted nothing to do with an academic training for the ministry of the Word and accorded the right to "exhort" to all believers. Menno Simons frequently leveled a scathing judgment at the church and its ministers concerning study and erudition.[7] Only later did Mennonite teachers get academic training.[8] And in the seventeenth century when in Protestant churches the scholastic treatment of theology began to make headway, there was reaction on all sides. Calixtus and Cocceius, Spener and Zinzendorf, Fox and Wesley, etc., were all driven by a desire for more simplicity and truth in the doctrine of faith. To that end people had to go back from doctrine to life, from the creeds to Scripture, from theology to religion. Even deism and rationalism showed kinship with this trend; seeing the universal and common features that underlie all religions and creeds, they appealed from the Christian religion to the religion of Christ, from statutory religion to the religion of reason. As a result of agnostic trends in philosophy, Schleiermacher's theology of feeling, the historical criticism of Scripture, and other influences, this endeavor grew even stronger. Nowadays aversion to dogmatics is universal. Many look forward eagerly to a new word, a new dogma, wanting a religion without theology, life without doctrine, and therefore devote themselves to a practical, undogmatic Christianity (Dreyer, Egidy, Drummond, Tolstoy, etc.). To some degree this striving has found its scientific defense in the school of Ritschl. It demanded that theology must be completely liberated from the influence of metaphysics and return to the revelation implicit in the person of Christ. Harnack and E. Hatch applied this principle to the history of dogma and attempted to show that theology was the offspring of an ill-starred marriage between original Christianity and Greek philosophy.[9] The indictments lodged by all these schools against theology, specifically against dogmatics, basically boiled down to saying that it falsifies the purity and simplicity of the Christian religion, changes religion into a doctrine that has to be proven and accepted intellectually, kills the religious life, promotes a cold and arid orthodoxy and makes "implicit faith" a necessity; and finally that it brings religion as doctrine into conflict with science and alienates the educated classes from the Christian faith.[10]

No one will deny that there is seriousness and truth in these complaints against theology. It has often overshot its goal and degenerated into repeat-

---

7. M. Simons, *Alle de Godgeleerde Wercken* (Amsterdam, 1681), 34ff., 59, 260, 270.

8. De Hoop Scheffer, "Mennoniten," *PRE²*, IX, 575; C. Sepp, *Kerkhistorische Studiën* (Leiden, 1885), 84, 85.

9. Harnack, *History of Dogma*, I, 17; E. Hatch, *The Influence of Greek Ideas and Usages upon the Christian Church* (London, 1890); cf. also J. Kaftan, *The Truth of the Christian Religion,* trans. George Ferries, 2 vols. (Edinburgh: T. & T. Clark, 1894); and the works by Loofs and by Seeberg on the history of dogma.

10. Cf., e.g., J. Kaftan, *Glaube und Dogma,* 3d ed. (Bielefeld: Velhagen & Klasing, 1889).

ing the same empty phrases (βαττολογια, cf. Matt. 6:7 [Gr.]). All too often it has forgotten that our knowing on earth is a knowing in part and looking into a mirror dimly. Sometimes it seemed to proceed from the idea that it could answer all questions and resolve all issues. It has often been lacking in modesty, tenderness, and simplicity. This was all the worse inasmuch as theology has to do with the deepest problems and comes into contact with the most delicate stirrings of the human heart. More than any other science, it has to take to heart the admonition "not to think of itself more highly than it ought to think" (cf. Rom. 12:3). It is better to honestly admit that a thing is not clear than to make a wild guess. "To be willing not to know what the best Teacher does not wish to teach—that is learned ignorance." But this is not to condemn theology in principle.

FAITH'S KNOWLEDGE

After all, if revelation consisted only in the communication of life and religion, only in emotional states, there would be no room for real theology. But revelation is systematic disclosure of the words and deeds of God; it encompasses a world of thoughts and has its center in the incarnation of the Logos. And religion is not feeling and sensation alone but also belief, living for and serving of God with both heart and head. And that revelation of God can therefore be intellectually penetrated in order that it may all the better enter into the human consciousness. In that connection one cannot even take it ill of theology if it aims at clarity in thought, at making lucid distinctions and at precision in articulation. Such precision is pursued and valued in all the sciences; it is equally appropriate in theology. The danger of its degenerating into hairsplitting exists equally in other sciences, say, in jurisprudence and the study of literature. But no one would for that reason deny to these other sciences the right to exist. Also theology has its periods of florescence and decay. But it is misguided to condemn theology itself on account of the bad use that has been made of it. The abuse of it does not cancel out the use of it (*Abusus non tollit usum*).

Furthermore as we found earlier, the split between the Christian religion on the one hand and metaphysics (etc.) on the other can neither be cleanly conceived nor practically executed. History has repeatedly demonstrated this fact in the past and again shows it today. For to make such a split somewhat possible, all the above schools are compelled to form a one-sided and incomplete picture of the gospel of Christ. Almost never do they go back to the whole Bible but only to a part of it: to the New Testament alone, or to the Gospels, or to the Sermon on the Mount, or even to a single text. Francis of Assisi, for example, based his entire life on Matthew 10:9, 10.[11] Tolstoy finds

11. On Francis of Assisi, see Reuter, *Geschichte der religiössen Aufklärung im Mittelatter,* 2 vols. (Berlin, 1875–77), II, 184, 186; Paul Sabatier, *Leben des heiligen Franz von Assisi,* trans. Margarete Liso (Berlin: G. Reimer, 1895), 53.

the core of the gospel in Matthew 5:38, 39. Drummond locates the supreme good in the love of 1 Corinthians 13. Ritschl transmutes the dogmas into religious-ethical value judgments. Harnack, in his construal of the original gospel, agrees with Ritschl and discovers the essence of Christianity in the message of the fatherhood of God and the nobility of the human soul. And today many people ask why the Christian church is not content with the Sermon on the Mount. What the essence of Christianity is, in what things the revelation or word of God consists, who the person of Christ is, is not decided by the apostles; everyone settles these matters in accordance with his or her own insights. The result is that all these schools not only have to oppose the church, the confession, and theology but even the apostles to Jesus and the original gospel. Harnack, for example, acknowledges that even the apostolic-catholic doctrine of the NT no longer reproduces the gospel of Jesus accurately.[12] Perceptible in it at this early stage already is the influence of Judaism, Hellenism, and Graeco-Roman philosophy of religion. The apostles, particularly Paul and John, already falsified the gospel. As early as 1893 Ernst von Bunsen already asserted that Paul changed the gospel of Jesus into a speculative theology, and many people concur with him.[13] And if a fact like the resurrection of Christ, after all, cannot be excised from the original gospel, people try to rob it of its religious value.[14]

A further consequence of this view is that the history of dogma cannot come into its own. It becomes one enormous aberration of the human, i.e., of the Christian, spirit. The promise of the Spirit who would lead God's people into all truth proves to have been empty. The church is deprived of the possibility even to know the truth, since the apostles already enter into the world on the wrong track. The doctrines of the Logos, the Trinity, the first and second Adam (etc.), all of them dogmas that are said to prove the admixture of Greek philosophy, are found, perhaps not in so many words but certainly in substance, already in Scripture. In a word: the history of dogmas is (as in Strauss) the history of their criticism.[15] The church has not overcome the world; the reverse is true. Finally, in the case of this one-sided view of the original gospel, there is a danger that one loses fellowship with the church of all ages and therefore with one's own time. That has been the nemesis of all sects. Cut off from the churches and despising theology, they forfeited the chance to influence their own age and lost contact with the culture of their own time. The believing community and the world, church and school, religion and science, fall dualistically apart. By contrast, theology has the marvelous calling to keep each of these sets in touch with each other, the

---

12. Harnack, *History of Dogma*, V, 57ff.

13. Ernst Bunsen, *Die Reconstruction der Kirchlichen Autorität* (Leipzig: Brockhaus, 1893); see also above, pp. 117–18.

14. Harnack, *History of Dogma*, V, 83ff.

15. Even Sabatier says: "The history of a dogma is its true criticism" (*Les religions d'autorité et la religion de l'esprit* [Paris: Librairie Fischbacher, 1904], xi); cf. idem, *Esquisse* (Paris: Fischbacher, 1898), 208ff.

purpose being, on the one hand, to secure the Christian life against the pathologies of mysticism and separatism and, on the other, to free scientific thought from error and lies by means of the truth of Christ.

The justification of theology is grounded in the essence of the Christian religion. Revelation addresses itself to human beings in their totality and has the whole world as its object. In all areas of life it joins the battle against deception. It offers material for the profoundest thought processes and in the field of science plants the knowledge of God alongside of and in organic connection with that of humanity and the world.[16]

DOGMA AND GREEK PHILOSOPHY

[157] Though Christian dogma cannot be explained in terms of Greek philosophy, it also did not come into being apart from it. There is as yet no dogma and theology, strictly speaking, in Scripture. As long as revelation itself was still in progress, it could not become the object of scientific reflection. Inspiration had to be complete before reflection could begin. To speak of "Mosaic," "Pauline," or the "Bible's" theology and dogmatics, therefore, is not advisable; the word *theology*, for that matter, does not occur in Scripture and has only gradually acquired its present meaning. Theology first arose in the Christian community after the naiveté of childhood lay behind it and the adult thinking mind had awakened. Gradually a need arose to think through the ideas of revelation, to link it with other knowledge and to defend it against various forms of attack. For this purpose people needed philosophy. Scientific theology was born with its help. This did not, however, happen accidentally. The church was not the victim of deception. In the formation and development of the dogmas, the church fathers made generous use of philosophy. They did that, however, in the full awareness of and with clear insight into the dangers connected with that enterprise; they were conscious of the grounds on which they did it, and they did it with express recognition of the word of the apostles as the only rule of faith and conduct. For that reason also they did not utilize the whole of Greek philosophy but made a choice; they only utilized the philosophy that was most suited to help them think through and defend the truth of God. They went to work eclectically and did not take over any single philosophical system, be it either from Plato or from Aristotle, but with the aid of Greek philosophy produced

16. On the views of Harnack and Hatch concerning the history of dogma, the following can be consulted: Pfleiderer, *Entwicklung der Protestantischen Theologie* (Freiberg: J. C. B. Mohr, 1891), 369ff.; A. Kuenen, "Dogmengeschiedenis," *Theologische Tijdschrift* 25 (1891): 491; C. H. van Rhijn, "Bijdragen ter Waardeering van de Christelijke Dogmengeschiedenis," *Theologische Studiën* 9 (1891): 365ff.; W. Schmidt, *Der alte Glaube und die Wahrheit des Christenthums* (Berlin: Wigant, 1894); Henry Bois, *Le dogme grec.* (Paris: Fischbacher, 1892); Loofs, "Dogmengeschichte," *PRE³*, IV, 752–64; Bousset, "Die Religionsgeschichte und das Neue Testament," *Theologische Rundschau* 7 (1904): 266ff.; I. Dorner, "Die Hellenisierung des altkirchlichen Dogmas," *Die Studierstube* (April 1906): 198–208; see also above, pp. 117–18.

a Christian philosophy of their own. Furthermore, they only used that philosophy as a means. Just as Hagar was the servant of Sarah, as the treasures of Egypt were employed by the Israelites for the adornment of the tabernacle, as the wise men from the East placed their gifts at the feet of the child in Bethlehem, so, in the opinion of the church fathers, philosophy was the servant of theology. From everything it is clearly evident that the use of philosophy in theology was based, not on a mistake, but on firm and clear conviction. The church fathers knew what they were doing. Mind you, this does not rule out the possibility that at some points the influence of philosophy was too strong. But in that connection we must make a distinction, nevertheless, between the theology of the fathers and the dogmas of the church. The church was at all times alert against the misuse of philosophy; it not only rejected Gnosticism but also condemned Origenism. And up until now no one has succeeded in explaining the dogmas materially in terms of philosophy; however often this has been attempted, in the end the scriptural character of orthodoxy has always been vindicated.[17]

Initially the Reformation assumed a hostile posture toward scholasticism and philosophy. But it soon changed its mind. Because it was not, nor wanted to be, a sect, it could not do without theology. Even Luther and Melanchthon, therefore, already resumed the use of philosophy and recognized its usefulness.[18] Calvin assumed this high position from the start, saw in philosophy an "outstanding gift of God," and was followed in this assessment by all Reformed theologians.[19] The question here is not whether theology should make use of a specific philosophical system. Christian theology has never taken over any philosophical system without criticism and given it the stamp of approval. Neither Plato's nor Aristotle's philosophy has been held to be the true one by any theologian. That theologians nevertheless preferred these two philosophical systems was due to the fact that these systems best lent themselves to the development and defense of the truth. Present also was the idea that the Greeks and Romans had been accorded a special calling and gift for the life of culture. Still to this day, in fact, our whole civilization is built upon that of Greece and Rome. And Christianity has not de-

---

17. J. Kleutgen, *Theologie der Vorzeit*, IV, 143ff.; Denzinger, *Vier Bücher*, II, 572; J. Schwane, *Dogmengeschichte*, 4 vols. (Freiburg i.B.: Herder, 1882–95), I, 67; Mausbach, *Christenthum und Weltmoral*, 2d ed. (Münster i.W.: Aschendorff, 1905).

18. Cf. Ritter, *Geschichte der neuern Philosophie*, vols. 9–12 (Hamburg: F. Perthes, 1829–53), I, 495ff.; Ueberweg-Heinze, *Geschichte der Philosophie*, 9th ed., 5 vols. (Berlin: E. S. Mittler & Sohn, 1923–28), III, 23ff.; Hase, *Hutterus Redivus*, §30; H. Schmid, *Doctrinal Theology of the Evangelical Churches*, trans. Charles A. Hay and Henry E. Jacobs (Philadelphia: United Lutheran Publication House, 1899), §5.

19. J. Calvin, *Institutes*, II.ii.12ff.; idem, *Opera Amst.*, IX, B, 50; Hyperius, *De theologo seu de ratione studii theologia* (1566), bk. 1; J. Zanchi, *Op. Theol.*, III, 223ff.; VIII, 653ff.; J. Alsted, *Praecognita Theol.*, 174ff.; G. Voetius, *Select. Disp.*, III, 741ff., 751ff.; Owen, *Theologumena*, 509ff. (ed. note: English translation available: *Biblical Theology*, trans. Stephen P. Westcott [Pittsburgh: Soli Deo Publications, 1994]); B. de Moor, *Comm. in Marcki Comp.*, I, 71ff.

stroyed but Christianized and thus consecrated those cultures. Still, theology is not in need of a specific philosophy. It is not per se hostile to any philosophical system and does not, a priori and without criticism, give priority to the philosophy of Plato or of Kant, or vice versa.[20] But it brings along its own criteria, tests all philosophy by them, and takes over what it deems true and useful. What it needs is philosophy in general. In other words, it arrives at scientific theology only by thinking. The only internal principle of knowledge, therefore, is not faith as such, but believing thought, Christian rationality. Faith is self-conscious and sure. It rests in revelation. It includes cognition, but that cognition is completely practical in nature, a knowing (γιγνωσκειν) in the sense of Holy Scripture. Theology, accordingly, does not arise from believers as such; it is not a product of the church as institution; it does not have its origin in the official ministry Christ has given his church. But believers have still another, fuller life than that which comes to expression in the church as institution. They also live as Christians in the family, the state, and society, and pursue the practice of science and art. Many more gifts than are operative in the offices are granted them, gifts of knowledge and wisdom and prophecy. Among them, too, there are those who feel a strong impulse toward study and knowledge, who have received gifts for apprehending and systematizing the truth of God. Thus theology arises in the church of Christ; its subject is not the institutional church but the church as organism, the body of Christ. It is a product of Christian thinking.

[158] Faith and theology, therefore, are distinct. People were at all times more or less aware of this distinction. The sharp contrast made by Gnosticism between faith (πιστις) and knowledge (γνωσις) was rejected, and also the relation assumed by the Alexandrian school between the two was not in all respects endorsed and approved. Still, while the distinction was firmly maintained, the close connectedness between the two was retained and recognized at the same time. Augustine made the saying "through faith to understanding" the first principle of theology. He assumed that between them there was a relation like that between conception and birth, labor and wages. "The fruit of faith is understanding," he wrote, "Understanding is the reward of faith." Augustine therefore urges "that the things which you already hold in the firmness of faith, you may also see by the light of reason." God does not despise reason. "Let it never be [said] that God hates in us that by which he created us more excellent than other living beings."[21] And this was the first principle and basic idea of all scholasticism. Faith and theology were distinguished as "basic disposition" (*habitus*) and "act" (*actus*); as "infused" theology and "acquired" theology. Faith is assent to, theology is the knowledge of, revealed truths. Faith, to be sure, includes some knowledge of God and divine things, but this knowledge pertains more to the "existence" of

20. As Theod. Kaftan does, for example, *Moderne Theologie des Alten Glaubens* (Schleswig: Julius Bergas, 1906), 76, 102; and all neo-Kantians with him.

21. Augustine, *Tractates on John,* 22, 2; ibid., 29, 6; Epistle 120 to Consent.

than to the "reasons" for those truths. The theologian, however, working his way intellectually down to the idea, tracks down the connections between truths and by thinking infers others from them.[22] Awareness of the distinction between religion and theology is evident also from the theory of "implicit faith." If faith, as Rome believed, consisted in assent to revealed truths, then sooner or later the question had to arise as to which and how many of these truths one at least had to know and accept to be sure of salvation. That question made sense with respect to Gentiles, to OT believers, as well as to ignorant and uneducated believers in the days of the NT. Augustine had already said: "While the liveliness of understanding does not create confusion, the simplicity of believing renders things very safe." But Lombard was the first to clearly raise this question in his *Sentences*.[23] Since then the issue was treated at length in theology. Even in France, in the seventeenth century, it gave rise to a serious controversy, which was not resolved, though terminated, by Innocent XI.

How Much Knowledge?

As a rule the theory of "implicit faith" is presented in Roman Catholic theology as follows. A "charcoal-burner's faith," a rudimentary homespun faith, was expressly rejected. All Catholic theologians maintain that some, however rudimentary, knowledge is required for saving faith. Faith, accordingly, may and can never be totally implicit. But that knowledge varies in the different dispensations of grace. In the days of the OT, from Adam to the fall of Jerusalem, before the true mysteries of Christianity—such as the Trinity and the incarnation—were promulgated, it was necessary (by necessity of the mean) only to believe that "God exists and is a rewarder of those who seek him" (Heb. 11:6). This is not to say that many OT believers did not have a broader and deeper knowledge of the truth. Adam, for example, also knew the Trinity and the incarnation (Gen. 1:26; 2:23; 3:15). But for simple believers the two articles [God exists and rewards] were sufficient, since implicitly they certainly believed in the true mysteries of Christianity, the Trinity and the incarnation. Implicit in the existence and oneness of God is the Trinity; and implicit in the fact that he is the "rewarder" (remunerator) is the incarnation. Now others, like Wiggers, Daelman, etc., unable to "see" clearly this latter point, said that OT believers had to accept four articles; in addition to the first two, also that of the immortality of the soul and the pollution of sin (*infectio animarum*), which implicitly contained the two principal dogmas of Christianity. The more common view, however, was that the two articles mentioned above were sufficient for OT believers. But after the fall of Jerusalem, these two principal truths [Trinity and incarnation] of Christianity had been clearly revealed and made known; hence now, by necessity of the mean,

22. Liebermann, *Instit. Theol.*, 8th ed. (Moguntiae, 1857), chap. 1, §1.
23. Augustine, *C. Epist. fundamenti*, chap. 4; P. Lombard, *III Sent.*, dist. 25.

it is necessary for those who want to be saved to accept the following four articles: God, God as the rewarder, the holy Trinity, the mediator. Others added
still more, such as God the Creator, the grace of God necessary to salvation,
immortality, and some even mentioned the acceptance, in substance, of the
twelve articles of the Apostles' Creed as being necessary. But the proponents
of the four articles express what is the most common sentiment. This entire
theory of implicit faith was then supported with an appeal to Job 1:14: the
oxen (i.e., educated believers) were plowing, and the donkeys (i.e., simple laypeople) were feeding beside them. This exegesis, which already occurs in
Gregory the Great, was taken over by Lombard, Thomas, Bellarmine, etc.[24]
The question that underlies this theory of implicit faith is itself serious and
important enough. It pertains after all to nothing less than the essence of
Christianity itself, the significance of Israel, the compatibility of progressive
revelation with the absoluteness of truth. But an intellectualistic view of faith
gave rise to the practice of solving this issue quantitatively. The acceptance of
four articles of faith is what makes a Christian. In practice the legend of the
"charcoal burner's faith" turned out to contain all too much truth.[25] In any
case, the theory of implicit faith is clear evidence that Catholic theologians
make a distinction between faith and theology both in content and scope.

Also the Reformation remained aware of this distinction. Lutheran and
Reformed theologians took over the distinction between the basic disposition (*habitus*) and the act (*actus*) of theology, between "infused" and "acquired" theology. The former is the property of all believers. In principle
they knew "the whole of theology," having a true and accurate knowledge of
God. But as "acquired" theology it belongs only to those who study the
knowledge of God scientifically. For in their case it is "the knowledge of conclusions derived from theological principles by theological discussion of the
traditions collected and arranged in a certain order and impressed on the
mind by prolonged labor and training."[26] Admittedly the terms *religion* and
theology were frequently used interchangeably,[27] something that could hap-

24. Gregory the Great, *Moralia in Iobum*, II, 25; cf. P. Lombard, *III Sent.*, dist. 25; Thomas Aquinas,
Summa Theol., II, 2, qu. 2, art. 5–8; Bellarmine, "De justificatio," *Controversiis*, I, 7; Billuart, *Summa
Sanctae Thomae sive cursus Theol.*, 19 vols. (Maastricht: Jacobi Lekens, 1769–70), VII, 46ff. Daelman,
Theologia seu Observ. Theologia in Summam D. Thomae, 9 vols. (Louvaine: Martinum van Overbeke,
1759), IV, 44. Dens, *Theologia in usum Seminarium*, 7 vols. (Mechliniae: P. J. Hanica, Typographum Il-
lust. ac Celsiss Principis-Archiep. Mechlin., 1819), II, 278ff.; M. Becanus, *Theologia Scholastica*, bk. II,
part II, tract. 1, pp. 22ff.; Jansen, *Praelect. Theol.*, 4 vols. (Utrecht: J. R. van Rossum, 1875–79), I, 699ff.;
A. Ritschl, *Fides Implicita* (Bonn: Adolph Marcus, 1890); Georg Hoffmann, *Die Lehre von der Fides Implicita* (Leipzig: Hinrichs, 1903–9), I (1903), II (1904).

25. This legend occurs for the first time in the last years of the life of Biel. Albrecht Pighius, born
around 1490, remembers he heard it as a boy. G. Hoffmann, *Die Lehre von der Fides Implicita*, II, 217.

26. Alsted, *Methodus sacrosanctae theologiae* (1623), 117, 126, 175; J. Owen, *Theologoumena* (New
York: Robertus Carter, 1854), 465ff. (ed. note: Modern English translation available: *Biblical Theology*,
trans. Stephen P. Westcott [Pittsburgh: Soli Deo Publications, 1994]). Calovius, *Isagoge ad summa theologia* (Wittenberg: A. Hartmanni, typis J. W. Fincelli, 1652), 17, 18.

27. For example, in J. Cloppenburg, *Op. Theol.*, I, 699; P. van Mastricht, *Theologia*, I, 2, §3.

pen all the more easily because theology and dogmatics were approximately the same. But even in the heyday of orthodoxy, the distinction between faith and theology was not completely lost, as is demonstrable from the theory of "fundamental" and "non-fundamental" articles of faith. The Reformation firmly rejected the Catholic doctrine of "implicit faith."[28] It had to do this because it did not define saving faith as a "holding for true" of a number of uncomprehended articles but as personal trust in the grace of God in Christ. But in the place of it there soon came the distinction between "fundamental" and "non-fundamental" articles. Calvin already said that people should not separate from the church over less essential points. "For not all the articles of true doctrine are of the same sort. Some are so necessary to know that they should be certain and unquestioned by all men as the proper principles of religion. Such are: God is one; Christ is God and the Son of God; our salvation rests in God's mercy; and the like. Among the churches there are other articles of doctrine disputed, which still do not break the unity of faith."[29] The juxtaposition—employed in the description of faith—of a certain knowledge "by which I hold as true all that God has revealed in his Word" and the "confidence that all my sins have been forgiven me for Christ's sake" could give rise to locating the point of gravity either in the "general" faith or in the "special" faith. The large number of churches that successively came out of the Reformation and differed from each other in various articles favored the distinction between essential and non-essential elements in revelation. A gradually emerging syncretism and indifferentism, which went back from the particular to the common, made it necessary to indicate clearly what belonged to the foundations of the Christian religion. Thus the theory of the "fundamental articles" originated. It seems that Nic. Hunnius was the first to use it in his Διασκεψις *de fundamentali dissensu doctrinae Lutheranae et Calvinianae, 1626.* Quenstedt spoke of "primary" and "secondary" articles. Others followed him, both in Lutheran and Reformed churches.[30] Orthodoxy, naturally, was not inclined to reduce the fundamental articles to a small number; still one can detect an effort to grasp these articles from a central perspective and to group them around the person of Christ. Roman Catholic theologians, however, rejected this distinction, however much resemblance it showed to their own theory of implicit faith. They caused no little embarrassment to Reformed and Lutheran theologians. They asked them where in his Word God had made a distinction be-

---

28. J. Calvin, *Institutes*, III.ii.2–6; D. Chamier, *Panstratiae Catholicae*, 4 vols. (Geneva: Rouer, 1626), III, 12, 5; A. Polanus, *Syn. Theol.*, 592; S. Maresius, *Syst. Theol.*, II, §29.

29. J. Calvin, *Institutes*, IV.i.12; IV.2.1.

30. Cf. G. Runze, *Katechismus der Dogmatik* (Leipzig: J. J. Weber, 1898), §7; G. Voetius, *Select. Disp.*, II, 511–38; H. Alting, *Theol. probl. nova*, I, 9; F. Spanheim (younger), *Opera*, III, col. 1289. J. H. Heidegger, *Corpus Theologiae*, I, §51ff.; F. Turretin, *Institutes of Elenctic Theology*, I, qu. 14; B. De Moor, *Comm. Theol.*, I, 481; H. Witsius, *Excercitat. Sacrae in Symbolism*, II, §2; J. A. Turretin, *Opera*, III, 1–88. Bretschneider, *Systematischer Entwicklung aller in der Dogmatik* (Leipzig: J. A. Barth, 1841), 103; A. Tholuck, *Der Geist der Lutherschen Theologie Wittenberg* (Hamburg: F. & A. Perthes, 1852), 252ff.

tween essential and secondary truths, where they got the right to distinguish
in divine revelation between the fundamental and the non-fundamental.
Which truths, then, had to be counted in the category of fundamental
truths? Who had to decide? And how, in such a position, can one avoid rationalism and indifferentism? The object of faith, as they asserted, certainly
was not restricted to divine mercy[31] but included everything revealed by
God.[32] According to the Jesuits at the Regensburg conference on religion
(1601), it was also an article of faith "that the dog of Tobias wagged his
tail."[33] Against all these objections Protestant theologians indeed appealed to
Scripture (Matt. 16:16; 1 Cor. 2:2; 3:11f.; Eph. 2:20; Gal. 6:14; 1 Pet. 2:6;
etc.) and indeed made an assortment of distinctions.[34] But they did not pretend there were no difficulties. They were afraid to err either by saying too
much or too little and ended by saying that they could not determine the
minimum of knowledge necessary to a sincere faith.[35] Orthodoxy ended up
in rationalism on the one hand and pietism on the other. Doctrine and life
increasingly distanced themselves from each other. Head and heart vied for
priority. Theology and religion became polar opposites. Even now we have
not yet overcome this polarity. For years people cried: "Religion is not a matter of doctrine but of life"; "it does not matter what you believe but only
how you live." Gradually, however, people's eyes are being opened to the
one-sidedness of this view, and they are increasingly beginning to recognize
the value of religious conceptions for the religious life.[36]

THE GRACE OF FAITH

[159] In studying the relation between faith and theology, we need to frame
the question properly. It should not be: what is the minimum of truths a person must know and hold as true to be saved? Leave that question to Rome,
and let Catholic theology decide whether to that end two or four articles are
needed. Admittedly, Protestant theology, in the theory of "fundamental articles," has given the impression of wanting to take that road. But it ended with
the acknowledgment that it did not know the magnitude of God's mercy and
therefore could not measure the amount of knowledge that is necessarily in-

31. *Council of Trent,* session VI, canon 12.

32. Bellarmine, "De justif.," *Controversiis,* I, 8.

33. Cf. Denzinger, *Vier Bücher,* II, 277ff.; Heinrich, *Dogmatik,* II, 658; Jansen, *Prael. Theol.,* I,
449ff.; Lammenais, *Essai sur l'indifférence,* I, 6, 7; 34.

34. F. Spanheim, *Opera,* III, 1308ff.

35. G. Voetius, *Select. Disp.,* II, 537, 781; F. Spanheim, *Opera,* III, 1291; H. Witsius, *Exercitat. Sacrae in Symb.,* II, §2 and §15; Hoornbeek, *Conf. Socin.,* I, 209.

36. Cf., e.g., Bruining in various publications: "De Theologie in den Kring der Wetenschapper," *De
Gids* (June 1884); idem, *Moderne Mystiek* (Leiden: Van Doesburgh, 1885); idem, *Het Bestaan van God*
(Leiden: S. C. van Doesburgh, 1892); idem, "De Moderne Richting en de Dogmatiek," *Theologische
Tijdschrift* 28 (November 1894). C. P. Tiele, *Elements of The Science of Religion,* 2 vols. (Edinburgh &
London: William Blackwood and Sons, 1897), I, 152, 156–57; II, 21–22, 25ff.

herent in a sincere faith. In addition, between the theory of "implicit faith" and that of the "fundamental articles" there is, for all their seeming similarity, an important difference. On the Catholic side, that theory was developed with a view to the simple laity, the "donkey" of Job 1:14. But in the theology of the Reformation, it sprang from the fact that a number of different churches emerged side by side with confessions that diverged from each other on many points. For that theology, therefore, the focus was the question concerning the essence of Christianity. Faith, on the part of Rome, is assent to an assortment of revealed truths, which can be counted, article by article, and which in the course of time increased in number. Faith on the side of the Reformation, however, is special (*fides specialis*) with a particular central object: the grace of God in Christ. Here an arithmetic addition of articles, the knowledge of which and the assent to which is necessary for salvation, was no longer an option. Faith is a personal relation to Christ; it is organic and has put aside quantitative addition. Rome, therefore, had to determine a minimum without which there could not be salvation. On the side of the Reformation, faith is trust in the grace of God and hence no longer calculable. Every believer, both in the OT and the NT, in principle possesses the same knowledge, which in theology is developed both in breadth and in depth. From this vantage point also the relation between faith and theology can be further elucidated.

First of all, there is strong resemblance between the two. They have in common the principle, the Word of God; the object, the knowledge of God; the goal, the glory of God. Also theology as a science functions on the basis of faith. The role assigned in the other sciences to observation is here assumed by faith. Faith supplies to theology the "stuff" of thought. In secular science the watchword is: sense perception precedes understanding; there is nothing in understanding that was not first in the senses; in theology the slogan is: faith precedes understanding; there is nothing in understanding that was not first present in faith.[37] Leibnitz therefore compared faith to experience.[38] Concepts without visual content are empty, said Kant; similarly, theology has no content apart from and through faith. The moment it abandons faith, it ceases to exist as theology. Nor does it ever by thinking leave behind the viewpoint of faith. Though in all sorts of ways this has been attempted, it has been in vain. Faith is the beginning as well as the end of theology; it never becomes knowing in the strict sense, i.e., knowing on the basis of personal observation and insight. But this is not to deprive theology of its freedom. Faith simply posits and maintains the relation that ought to exist in this area between subject and object. It situates the theologian under and in the truth that he or she has to examine, not outside and over against and above that truth. It only binds theology to its own object in no other way than every other science is and remains bound to observation and by it exists in relation to its object. Theology is just

37. R. Rothe, *Theologische Ethik*, 2d rev. ed., 5 vols. (Wittenberg: Zimmerman, 1867–71), §267, II, 180.

38. *Leibnitz, *Discourse on the Conformity of Faith with Reason*, chap. I.

as free and just as dependent as every other science. It is free from all bonds that militate against its nature but is totally defined by the object it seeks to understand and has this characteristic in common with all the sciences. The more rigorously it binds itself to its object, the less it runs the risk of degenerating into arid scholasticism and empty rhetoric. By faith theology remains a science of religion, a "theology of facts," which does not think about concepts but about things and does not lose itself in ethereal abstractions but has both feet firmly planted in that world of realities that Scripture reveals to us.[39]

On the other hand, however, there is a notable difference between faith and theology, not in essence but in degree. Theology remains a science of faith, not only because it lives from the same principle from which faith draws its contents, but also because as a science it retains the same religious character that belongs to the knowledge of faith. "A theology of the unregenerate" is possible in the same sense as a "historical faith," but it corresponds equally as little or as much to true theology as "historical faith" does to "saving faith." But since saving faith includes true knowledge, theology can deepen and expand the latter by ongoing intentional investigation.[40] In an earlier age the two of them could be easily interchanged, because theology and dogmatics plus ethics were virtually synonymous. But today theology has become the name for a whole cycle of disciplines. The distinction therefore now leaps out at anyone considering the topic. Nowadays theology encompasses a multitude of sciences, which a simple believer does not even know by name. Still, even if theology were understood in the old sense, the distinction would remain substantial. In every area there is a difference between ordinary, everyday, empirical knowing and true, advanced, scientific knowledge. Every human has some empirical knowledge of the sun, moon, and stars, but this knowledge is a million miles removed from the scientific knowledge of the astronomer. The former only knows the facts (*facta*); the latter the reasons (*rationes*). The scientist does not spurn ordinary empirical knowledge; he or she does not overthrow natural certainty; yet he or she has the calling to clarify, to expand, and if necessary to correct and improve that ordinary knowledge. Nor is this different in theology. Faith pauses to consider the facts; theology, on the other hand, attempts to get down to the idea. Faith is content with the *that;* theology inquires into the *why* and the *how.* Faith is always personal; it always relates the object to persons themselves and is directly interested in the religious content of the dogmas. Theology, on the other hand, in a sense "objectivizes" the object; it attempts to

39. Vilmar, *Die Theologie der Thatsachen wider die Theologie der Rhetorik,* 4th ed. (Gütersloh: C. Bertelsmann, 1876).

40. This fundamentally answers the question that Dr. Riemens raises concerning the distinction and connection between religious and theoretical knowing: "Principia in de Dogmatiek," *Theologische Studiën* 21 (1903): 383ff.; idem, "Intellectueele en Intuitieve Kennis," *Theologische Studiën* 22 (1904): 137–61; see also above, 40–43; *W. Brandt, "Kenvermogen, Goddelijke Geesten Kennis in het N.T.," *Teylers Theologische Tijdschrift,* I, 377ff.

see the truth as it objectively exists in itself. It explores its unity and inner coherence and seeks to arrive at a system. Faith focuses directly on the central object; theology expands its horizon to the entire circumference. But, however diverse the two may be, they cannot do without each other. Faith preserves theology from secularization; theology preserves faith from separatism. For that reason the church and the school (seminary, department of theology and religion), though two entities, ought to be in solidarity with each other. This arrangement, it must be said, in no way detracts from the freedom and independence of theology. Every college or university department does scientific work, not only for its own sake, but also for the purpose of training students for various positions in society. Every science, actually, has to take account of the demands of life. Similarly, theology does not occupy a position high above real life but is situated in its midst, in the life of the Christian community. The distorted relation that everywhere exists today between the church and theology is a disaster for both.

REASON SERVING FAITH

If theology thus has its internal principle not in faith as such but in believing reflection, the task of reason in theological science calls for further definition. In this context we must first of all and fundamentally reject the notion that regards faith and reason as two independent powers engaging in a life-and-death struggle with each other. In that way one creates a dualism that does not belong in the Christian domain. In that case faith is always above (*supra*) or even opposed (*contra*) to reason. Threatening on the one hand is rationalism and on the other supernaturalism. Faith, the faith by which we believe, is not an organ or faculty next to or above reason but a disposition or habit of reason itself. Reason, or if people prefer, thinking, is certainly not a source of theology, not a principle by which or through which or from which or on account of which we believe.[41] Reason is a source, not the source of any science; at most it is only for the formal sciences such as logic or mathematics. Still reason is the recipient subject of faith, capable of faith; faith is an act of the human consciousness; an animal is not capable of believing. Furthermore, faith is not an involuntary but a free act. Christians do not believe on command, out of fear, or in response to violence. Believing has become the natural habit of their mind, not in the sense that there is often not considerable resistance in their soul to that believing, but still in such a way that, though often doing what they do not want to do, they still take delight in God's law in their inmost self [cf. Rom. 7:22]. Believing is the natural breath of the children of God. Their submission to the Word of God is not slavery but freedom. In that sense faith is not a sacrifice of the intellect but mental health (*sanitas mentis*). Faith, therefore,

41. G. Voetius, *Select. Disp.*, I, 3.

does not relieve Christians of the desire to study and reflect; rather it spurs them on to the end. Nature is not destroyed by regeneration but restored.

Believers who want to devote themselves to the study of theology, accordingly, must prepare their minds for the task awaiting them. There is no admission to the temple of theology except by way of the study of the arts. Indispensable to the practitioner of the science of theology is philosophical, historical, and linguistic preparatory training. Philosophy, said Clement of Alexandria, "prepares the way for the most royal teaching." Emperor Julian knew what he was doing when he deprived Christians of pagan learning; he feared he would be defeated by his own weapons. This thinking, thus prepared and trained, has, in the main, a threefold task in theology. First, it offers its services in finding the material. Scripture is the principle of theology. But the Bible is not a book of laws; it is an organic whole. The material for theology, specifically for dogmatics, is distributed throughout Scripture. Like gold from a mine, so the truth of faith has to be extracted from Scripture by the exertion of all available mental powers. Nothing can be done with a handful of proof texts. Dogma has to be built, not on a few isolated texts, but on Scripture in its entirety. It must arise organically from the principles that are everywhere present for that purpose in Scripture. The doctrines of God, of humanity, of sin, of Christ, etc., after all, are not to be found in a few pronouncements but are spread throughout Scripture and are contained, not only in a few proof texts, but also in a wide range of images and parables, ceremonies and histories. No part of Scripture may be neglected. The whole of Scripture must prove the whole system.[42] Also in theology we must avoid separation. It is a mark of many sects that they base themselves on a small part of Scripture and neglect everything else. The worst and most widespread error is the rejection or neglect of the Old Testament. Marcionism repeatedly reemerged in the Christian church and plays a large role in modern theology as well.[43] All this arbitrary use of Holy Scripture leads to one-sidedness and error in theology and to pathology in the religious life. In that setting the full and rich configuration of truth does not come to light. Either the person and work of the Father or of the Son or of the Holy Spirit is then sold short. Injustice is done to Christ either in his prophetic, or his priestly, or his royal office. The Christian religion loses its catholicity. The Christian head, heart, and hand are not harmoniously molded and guided by the truth. Only the whole Bible in its fullness preserves us from all these one-sidednesses. For that very reason, however, the thinking mind has an important role in tracking down the theological material.

Next, the theologian must intellectually process the material thus acquired. The dogmas are not spelled out in Scripture in so many words; they are there

42. J. C. C. von Hofmann, *Der Schriftbeweis*, 3 vols. (Nördlingen: Beck, 1857–60), I, 1–32.
43. Cf. Diestel, *Geschichte des Alten Testament in der Christliche Kirche* (Jena: Mauke, 1869); H. Schmidt, "Der Marcionitismus in der neueren Theologie," *Neue Jahrbuch für deutsche Theologie* (1893); and later the doctrine of the covenants.

in the thought, not in the letter. They are the conclusions of faith. The doctrines of the Trinity, the two natures of Christ, of vicarious atonement, the sacraments, etc., are not based on a single scriptural utterance but are constructed from many givens distributed throughout the Bible. Dogmas are concise summaries in our own language of everything Scripture teaches about the subject in question. Against all sorts of schools that wanted to stick with the literal phraseology of Scripture, accordingly, Catholic as well as Protestant theologians defended the right to use dogmatic terminology. They did this, not because they wanted to be less but more scriptural than these others. To their mind, Scripture above all came into its own in all its splendor—not when a single text was literally cited but—when the whole truth contained in many texts was condensed and reproduced in a dogma. Theology, therefore, is not only a noetic but also a dianoetic science; not an apprehensive but a discursive branch of knowledge. It reflects, compares, evaluates, sums up, infers other truths from the truth acquired, etc. Also Jesus and the apostles followed this procedure (Matt. 22:32, 44f.; John 10:34f.; Acts 15:9f.; 18:28; 1 Cor. 15; etc.); and church fathers, scholastics, Catholic and Protestant theologians followed that example. God has not called us to literally repeat but to *re*-flect on, what he has antecedently thought and laid out in his revelation.

Finally, it is the task of the thinking theological mind to gather up and recapitulate all truth in one system.[44] System is the supreme desideratum in all science. Also theology does not rest until it has discovered the unity underlying revelation. It may not impose that system from without, nor press the truth into a philosophical system that is foreign to its nature. But it keeps searching until the system that is present in the object itself has been reproduced in the human mind. In all this theology operates like other sciences. Like these other sciences, it is bound to its object. In the process of thinking, it is subject to the laws that apply to this process. It too cannot violate the laws of logic with impunity.[45] For theology, too, the supreme desideratum is the unity of truth, the system of the knowledge of God. Accordingly, however much theology may differ from the other sciences in principle, object, and goal, formally it agrees with them and may rightly claim the name of science. And since revelation does not *per se* clash with human reason but only "on account of the accident of corruption and a depraved disposition," theology may even in a sense be called "natural" and "rational."[46] The Christian religion is a "reasonable form of worship" (λογικη λατρεια, Rom. 12:1).

44. See above, pp. 38–46.

45. J. Alsted, *Praecognita,* 186.

46. Voetius, *Select. Disp.,* disp. I, 3. The literature on the use of reason and philosophy in theology is astonishingly abundant. For the church fathers, cf. J. Kleutgen, *Theologie der Vorzeit,* 2d ed., 5 vols. (Münster: Theissing, 1867–74), IV, 143ff.; Denzinger, *Vier Bücher,* II, 574ff.; and in addition, G. Voetius, *Select. Disp.,* I, 1–11; F. Turretin, *Institutes of Elenctic Theology,* loc. I, qu. 8–13; H. Witsius, *Misc. Sacra,* II, 584ff.; and further literature in M. Vitringa's edition of C. Vitringa, *Docr. Christ.,* I, 32–34. Cf. also A. Kuyper Jr., *Openbaring en Rede* (Kampen: Kok, 1902).

[160] Although knowledge is attainable in theology, this is not true of comprehension. There is substantial difference between "being acquainted with," "knowing," and "comprehending." True, these words are often used interchangeably. But there are demonstrable differences among them. "Being acquainted with" pertains to a thing's existence, the *that;* "knowing" concerns a thing's quality, the *what;* comprehending relates to its inner possibility, the *how* of a thing. There are few things we comprehend; actually we comprehend only the things that are totally in our power, the things we can make or break. I comprehend a machine when I see how it is put together and how it works, and when there is nothing left in it I still think strange. Comprehension excludes amazement and admiration. I comprehend or think I comprehend the things that are self-evident and perfectly natural. Often comprehension ceases to the degree a person digs deeper into a subject. That which seemed self-evident proves to be absolutely extraordinary and amazing. The farther a science penetrates its object, the more it approaches mystery. Even if on its journey it encountered no other object it would still always be faced with the mystery of being. Where comprehension ceases, however, there remains room for knowledge and wonder. And so things stand in theology. Disclosed to us in revelation is "the mystery of our religion": the mystery of God's grace [1 Tim. 3:16]. We see it; it comes out to meet us as a reality in history and in our own life. But we do not fathom it. In that sense Christian theology always has to do with mysteries that it knows and marvels at but does not comprehend and fathom.

Very often, however, mystery in Christian theology has been construed very differently. The word μυστηριον (derived from μυστης, μυω, i.e., to close, be shut, of eyes, lips, or wounds) in ordinary Greek is the name for the secret religious-political doctrine that in some fellowships of Eleusis, Samothrace, etc., was communicated only to initiates and concealed from all others.[47] In the NT the word consistently has a religious meaning and refers to a matter belonging to the kingdom of God, which, either on account of the obscure and enigmatic form in which it was presented (Matt. 13:11; Mark 4:11; Luke 8:10; Rev. 1:20; 17:5, 7), or on account of its content, is hidden. This, above all, is the word for the universal (including also the Gentiles) decree of God concerning redemption in Christ (Rom. 16:25; Eph. 1:9; 3:3; 6:19; Col. 1:26, 27; 2:2; 4:3), as well as the manner in which it is carried out (Rom. 11:25; 1 Cor. 15:51; 2 Thess. 2:7; Rev. 10:7). But this mystery is so called, not because it is still hidden in the present, but because it had been unknown in the past. Now—of all things—it has been made public by the gospel of Christ, is proclaimed by the apostles as the stewards of the mystery

47. E. Hatch, "The Influence of Greek Ideas and Usages upon the Christian Church," *The Hibbert Lectures, 1888,* trans. A. M. Fairbairn, 7th ed. (London: Williams and Norgate, 1898), 296. Gustav Anrich, *Das antike Mysteriewesen in Seinim Einfluss auf das Christenthum* (Göttingen: Vandenhoeck und Ruprecht, 1894); Wobbermin, *Religionsgeschichtliche Studien zur Frage nach der Beeinflussung des Urchristenthum durch das antike Mysterienwesen* (Berlin: E. Ebering, 1896).

of God (Rom. 16:25, 26; Col. 1:26; 1 Cor. 4:1; Matt. 13:11; 1 Cor. 4:1), and from now on will be increasingly manifest in history (1 Cor. 15:51, 52; 2 Thess. 2:7). The NT term μυστηριον, accordingly, does not denote an intellectually uncomprehended and incomprehensible truth of faith but a matter that was formerly hidden in God, was then made known in the gospel, and is now understood by believers.[48]

In church usage, however, the word soon began to mean something that was incomprehensible, something far surpassing even the intellect of believers, such as the incarnation, the mystical union, the sacraments, etc., and later all the "pure articles" (*articuli puri*), which could not be proven by reason.[49] Even at that there remained a stark distinction between the pagan and the Christian use of the word. For in the former it denoted a secret doctrine, which had to be kept hidden from the uninitiated; but in the Christian church there had never been a truly "arcane discipline," even though a certain order was observed in the communication of the truth.[50] Still the dogmas were the uncomprehended and incomprehensible truths of faith, admittedly not contrary to reason, but certainly far above it.[51] In the church's condemnation of Erigena, Raymond Lull, Hermes, Günther, and Frohschammer, it pronounced its disapproval of every attempt to prove the mysteries of faith from reason. And the Vatican Council [I] confessed: "For by their nature divine mysteries so far surpass the created intellect that, even when transmitted by revelation and received by faith, they remain covered with the veil of faith itself, and shrouded in a certain obscurity as long as, in this mortal life, we are exiled from the Lord: for we walk by faith and not by sight!"[52]

The Reformation admittedly recognized the supernatural character of revelation but nevertheless in fact brought about a great change. In the case of Rome, the mysteries are incomprehensible, primarily because they belong to another, higher, supernatural order, which surpasses the human intellect as such. It therefore has to put a heavy accent on the incomprehensibility of the mysteries, as well as protect and maintain it. The dimension of incomprehensibility seems by itself to be a proof of validity and truth. "It is believable because it is absurd. . . . Certain, because it is impossible."[53] But the Reformation replaced this contrast between the natural and the supernatural order by that of sin and grace. It located the essence of mystery, not in the fact that it is incomprehensible to human beings as such but to the intellect

48. Cremer, *Biblico-Theological Lexicon of New Testament Greek,* trans. D. W. Simon and William Urwick (Edinburgh: T. & T. Clark, 1872), s.v. "pronoia."

49. Suicerus, *Thesaurus Eccl.,* s.v. "μυστηριον."

50. G. N. Bonwetsch, "Arkandisziplin," *PRE³,* II, 51–55.

51. Aquinas, *Summa Theol.,* I, qu. 32, art. 1; idem, *Summa contra Gentiles,* I, 3; IV, 1; Bellarmine, "De Christo," *Controversiis,* I, 2; II, 6; J. B. Heinrich and C. Gutberlet, *Dogmatische Theologie,* 2d ed., 10 vols. (Mainz: Kirchheim, 1881–1900), II, 772ff.; Denzinger, *Vier Bücher,* II, 80–150; J. Kleutgen, *Theologie der Vorzeit,* V, 164ff.

52. *Vatican Council I,* session III, "De fide," chap. 4.

53. Tertullian, *On the Flesh of Christ,* 5.

of the "natural" (i.e., unspiritual) person.[54] This view is undoubtedly much more consonant with NT usage. Nowhere in the NT is the abstract supernatural and scientifically incomprehensible character of mystery in the foreground. But while it is folly in the eyes of the "natural" person, however wise he or she may be, it is revealed to believers who see in it the wisdom and grace of God (Matt. 11:25; 13:11; 16:17; Rom. 11:33; 1 Cor. 1:30). Naturally it is also not the intent of Scripture to say that the believer grasps those mysteries in a scientific sense. We walk by faith, after all; we know in part and now see in a mirror dimly (Rom. 11:34; 1 Cor. 13:12; 2 Cor. 5:7). But believers *do* know those mysteries; they are no longer a folly and an offense to them; they do marvel at God's wisdom and love manifest in them. "The secret of God ought to produce earnest people, not hostile ones" (Augustine). It does not even occur to them, therefore, that the mysteries surpass their reason, that they are above reason; they do not experience them as an oppressive burden but rather as intellectual liberation. Their faith turns into wonder; knowledge terminates in adoration; and their confession becomes a song of praise and thanksgiving. Of this kind, too, is the knowledge of God theology aims for. It is not just a knowing, much less a comprehending; it is better and more glorious than that: it is the knowledge which is life, "eternal life" (John 17:3).[55]

---

54. J. Calvin, *Institutes,* II.ii.20; G. Voetius, *Select. Disp.,* I, 3.

55. On μυστηρια, in addition to the literature cited above (pp. 619–20 nn. 47–49), also see Bretschneider, *Systematische Entwicklung aller in de Dogmatiek* (Leipzig: J. A. Barth, 1841), I, 168. J. Boeles, *De mysteriis in relig. Christ.* (Gronigen: C. M. van B. Hoitsema, 1843). J. H. Scholten, *De Leer der Hervormde Kerk,* 2d ed., 2 vols. (Leyden: P. Engels, 1850–51), I, 223. J. J. van Oosterzee, *Christian Dogmatics,* trans. J. Watson and M. Evans, 2 vols. (New York: Scribner, Armstrong, 1874), I, 116. Philippi, *Commentary on St. Paul's Epistle to the Romans,* trans. John S. Banks (Edinburgh: T. & T. Clark, 1878–79). Grétillat, *Exposé de théol. syst.,* 6 vols. (Paris: Neuchatel: J. Attinger, Librairie Fischbacher, 1885–99), I, 182ff.; II, 183; S. Cheetham, *The Mysteries: Pagan and Christian* (London: MacMillan, 1897); R. H. Grützmacher, *Modern-positive Vorträge* (Leipzig: A. Deichert, 1906), 27ff., 32ff.

BIBLIOGRAPHY

This bibliography includes the items Bavinck listed at the heads of paragraphs throughout volume 1 of the *Gereformeerde Dogmatiek,* as well as any additional works cited in his footnotes. It does not include the numerous references Bavinck cites in the body of the historical chapters (part II), except where they are cited elsewhere in this volume. Particularly with respect to the footnote references, where Bavinck's own citations were quite incomplete by contemporary standards, with titles often significantly abbreviated, this bibliography provides fuller information. In some cases full bibliographic information was available only for an edition other than the one Bavinck cited. Where English translations of Dutch or German works are available, they have been cited rather than the original. In a few instances where Bavinck cited Dutch translations of English originals, the original work is listed. In cases where multiple versions or editions are available in English (e.g., Calvin's *Institutes*) the most recent, most frequently cited, or most accessible edition was chosen. In spite of the best efforts to track down each reference to confirm or complete bibliographic information, some of Bavinck's abbreviated and cryptic notations remain unconfirmed or incomplete. Where information is unconfirmed, incomplete, and/or titles have been reconstructed, the work is marked with an asterisk.

ABBREVIATIONS

ANF   *The Ante-Nicene Fathers.* Edited by Alexander Roberts and James Donaldson. 10 vols. New York: Christian Literature Co., 1885–96. Reprinted, Grand Rapids: Eerdmans, 1950–51.

The improvement of this bibliography over Bavinck's own citations in the *Gereformeerde Dogmatiek* is largely thanks to a valuable tool he did not have available to him—the Internet—and its diligent perusal by a number of Calvin Theological Seminary students who labored as the editor's student assistants. Graduate students Raymond Blacketer and Claudette Grinnell worked on the eschatology unit in *GD IV,* which was published separately as *The Last Things* (Baker, 1996). Colin Vander Ploeg, Steven Baarda, and Marcia De Haan-Van Drunen worked on the creation unit of *GD II,* which was published as *In the Beginning* (Baker, 1999). Ph.D. students Steven J. Grabill and Rev. J. Mark Beach worked on the present volume, and Courtney Hoekstra worked full-time during the summer of 2002 to complete the bibliography. Dr. Roger Nicole carefully checked the eschatology and creation bibliographies and helped reduce the errors and asterisks. The assistance of all is gratefully acknowledged here.

NPNF (1)   *A Select Library of Nicene and Post-Nicene Fathers of the Christian Church.* Edited by Philip Schaff. 1st series. 14 vols. New York: Christian Literature Co., 1887–1900. Reprinted, Grand Rapids: Eerdmans, 1956.

NPNF (2)   *A Select Library of Nicene and Post-Nicene Fathers of the Christian Church.* Edited by Philip Schaff and Henry Wace. 2d series. 14 vols. New York: Christian Literature Co., 1890–1900. Reprinted, Grand Rapids: Eerdmans, 1952.

PG   Migne, J. P. *Patrologia Graeca.*

PL   Migne, J. P. *Patrologia Latina.*

PRE[1]   *Realencyklopädie für protestantische Theologie und Kirche.* Edited by J. J. Herzog. 1st ed. 22 vols. Hamburg: R. Besser, 1854–68.

PRE[2]   *Realencyklopädie für protestantische Theologie und Kirche.* Edited by J. J. Herzog and G. L. Plitt. 2d rev. ed. 18 vols. Leipzig: J. C. Hinrichs, 1877–88.

PRE[3]   *Realencyklopädie für protestantische Theologie und Kirche.* Edited by Albert Hauck. 3d rev. ed. 24 vols. Leipzig: J. C. Hinrichs, 1896–1913.

BOOKS

Abbadie, Jacques. *Traité de la vérité de la religion Chrétienne.* Rotterdam: Renier Leers; London: Jean de Beaulieu, 1684.

Abelard, Peter. *Introductio ad Theologiam,* in *PL* 178.

———. *Sic et Non.* Edited by E. L. T. Henke and G. S. Lindenkohl. Marburgi Cattorum: Sumtibus et typis Librariae academ. Elwertianae, 1851.

Achelis, Thomas. *Die Ekstase in ihrer kulturellen Bedeutung.* Berlin: J. Räde, 1902.

Acta et decreta Sacrorum Conciliorum recentorium. Collectio Lacensis. 7 vols. Freiburg: Herder, 1870–92.

Adler, F. *Die ethischen Geselschaften.* Berlin: Ferd. Dümmlers Verlagsbuchhandlung, 1892.

Alaux, J. E. *La religion progressive.* 2d ed. Paris: B. Baillère, 1872.

Albert the Great. *Super IV sententiarum.* Vols. 25–30 of *Opera.*

Alexander of Hales. *Summa Theologica.* 4 vols. Quarracchi: Collegium S. Bonaventurae, 1924–58.

Alsted, Johann Heinrich. *Johannis Henrici Alstedii Encyclopaedia septem tomis distincta.* Herborn: G. Corvini, 1630.

———. *Praecognita theologiae, I–II.* Books I and II of *Methodus sacrosanctae theologiae octo libris tradita.* Hanover: C. Eifrid, 1619.

———. *Theologia catechectica.* 1616.

———. *Theologia scholastica didactica exhibens locos communes theologicos.* Hanover: C. Eifrid, 1618.

Alting, Heinrich. *Loci communes, cum didacticos, tum elencticos,* in *Scripta theologia Heidelbergensia.* Amsterdam: J. Jansson, 1646.

———. *Oratio inauguralis de methodo loci communes.* Heidelberg, 1613.

———. *Theologia Elenctica Nova.* Amsterdam: J. Jansson, 1654.

Alting, Jacob. *Opera Omnia Theologica.* 5 vols. Amsterdam: Borst, 1687.

Ambrose. *Hexameron, Paradise, and Cain and Abel.* Book VI of *The Fathers of the Church.*

———. *On the Mysteries.* NPNF (2), X, 315–26.

Ames, W. *Bellarminus enervatus.* Amsterdam, 1630.

———. *Guiliel Amesii Medulla theologica.* 12 vols. Amsterdam: Loannem Lanssonium, 1628.

———. *The Marrow of Theology.* Edited by John D. Eusden. Grand Rapids: Baker, 1997 [1968].

Ammon, C. F. von. *Die Geschichte des Lebens Jesu.* Leipzig: Vogel, 1847.

Amyrald, M. *Synt. Thesium theol. In acad. Salmur.* 1665.

Anastasius of Sinai. *Anagogicae contemplations in hexaemeron.* Book XII.

Andree, R. *Votive und Weihegaben des Katholischen Volks in Süddeutschland.* Braunnschweig: F. Vieweg und Sohn, 1904.

Anrich, Gustav. *Das antike Mysteriewesen in Seinem Einfluss auf das Christenthum.* Göttingen: Vandenhoeck und Ruprecht, 1894.

Anselm. *Basic Writings.* LaSalle, Ill.: Open Court, 1962.

———. *Why God Became Man, and The Virgin Conception, and Original Sin.* Translated by Joseph M. Colleran. Albany: Magi Books, 1969.

Aquinas, Thomas. *The Disputed Questions on Truth.* Translated by Robert W. Mulligan, James V. McGlynn, and Robert W. Schmidt. Chicago: H. Regnery, 1952–54.

———. *On the Power of God.* Translated by Lawrence Shapcote. Westminster, Md.: Newman Press, 1952.

———. *Summa Contra Gentiles.* Translated by the English Dominican Fathers. London: Burns, Oates and Washbourne, 1924.

———. *Summa Theologiae.* Translated by Thomas Gilby et. al. 61 vols. New York: McGraw-Hill, 1964–81.

Aristotle, *Nicomachean Ethics.* Translated by Terence Irwin. Indianapolis: Hackett, 1985.

———. *De Somniis.* In *The Basic Works of Aristotle,* edited by Richard Peter McKeon. New York: Random House, 1941.

Arminius, Jacobus. *Opera Theologica.* Frankfurt: Anglum, 1631.

Arnobius. *Against the Heathen. ANF,* VI, 413–540.

Arnold, Matthew. *Literature and Dogma.* New York: Thomas Nelson, 1873.

Astié, d. F. *De Theologie des Verstands en de Theologie des Gewetens.* Translated by D. Ch. de la Saussaye. Rotterdam: Wijt, 1866.

Athanasius, *Against the Arians. NPNF (2),* IV, 303–447.

———. *Against the Heathen. NPNF (2),* IV, 1–31.

———. *On the Incarnation. NPNF (2),* IV, 31–67.

Athenagoras. *A Plea for the Christians. ANF,* II, 129–48.

———. *The Resurection of the Dead. ANF,* II, 149–62.

Auberlen, Carl August. *The Divine Revelation: An Essay in Defence of the Faith.* Translated by A. B. Paton. Edinburgh: T. & T. Clark, 1867.

Augsburg Confession. In vol. 3 of *The Creeds of Christendom,* edited by Philip Schaff and revised by David S. Schaff. 6th ed. 1919. Reprinted, Grand Rapids: Baker, 1983.

Augustine, Aurelius. *Acts or Disputation against Fortunatus the Manichaean. NPNF (1),* IV.

———. *Against the Academics.* Translated by John J. O'Meara. Vol. 12 of *Ancient Christian Writers.* Westminster: Newman Press, 1950.

———. *Against the Epistle of the Manichaeans called Fundamental. NPNF (1),* IV.

———. *The City of God. NPNF (1),* II, 1–511.

———. *Concerning Faith of Things Not Seen. NPNF (1),* III, 337–43.

———. *Confessions. NPNF (1),* I, 27–207.

———. *Enchiridion. NPNF (1),* III, 229–76.

———. *De Genesi contra Manichaeos.* I, II. *PL,* 34, 173–220.

———. *The Harmony of the Gospels. NPNF (1),* VI, 65–236.

———. *Homilies on the Gospel of John. NPNF (1),* VII, 7–42.

———. *The Literal Meaning of Genesis.* Translated by John Hammond Taylor. Vols. 41–42 of *Ancient Christian Writers.* New York: Newman Press, 1982.

———. *Of True Religion.* Pp. 218–83 of *Augustine: Earlier Writings,* edited by J. H. S. Burleigh. Philadelphia: Westminster, 1953.

———. *On Christian Doctrine. NPNF (1),* II, 519–97.

———. *On the Gift of Perserverance. NPNF (1),* V, 521–52.

———. *On the Manichaean Heresy. PL* 42, 173.

————. *On the Predestination of the Saints.* *NPNF (1)*, V, 493–515.

————. *On the Profit of Believing. NPNF (1)*, III, 347–66.

————. *On the Spirit and the Letter. NPNF (1)*, V, 80–114.

————. *On the Trinity. NPNF (1)*, III, 1–228.

————. *Reply to Faustus the Manichaean. NPNF (1)*, IV, 155–345.

————. *The Retractations.* Translated by Mary Inez Bogan. Washington, Catholic University of America Press, 1968.

————. *Sancti Aurelii Augustini Hipponensis episcopi Operum tomus primus.* Edited by François Delfau et. al. 12 vols. Antwerp: Societatis, 1700–1703.

————. *Soliloquies. NFPF (1)*, VII, 537–60.

————. *To Simplician—On Various Questions. Book I.* Pp. 370–406 of *Augustine: Earlier Writings,* edited by J. H. S. Burleigh. Philadelphia: Westminster, 1953.

————. *Two Souls, Against the Manichaeans. NPNF (1)*, IV, 95–107.

Bach. *Dogmengeschichte des Mittelalter.* 2 vols. Wien, 1873–75.

Bachmann, Philipp. *Die Persönliche Heilserfahrung des Christen und ihre Bedeutung für den Glauben nach dem Zeugnisse der Apostel ein Beitrag zur neutestamentlichen Theologie.* Leipzig: A. Deichert, 1899.

Baentsch, Bruno. *Die moderne Bibelkritik und die autorität des Gotteswortes.* Erfurt: H. Güther, 1892.

Baier, Johann Wilhelm. *Compendium Theologiae Positivae.* 3 vols. in 4. St. Louis: Concordia, 1879.

Balfour, A. J. B. *The Foundations of Belief: Being Notes Introductory to the Study of Religion.* London: Longmans, Green, & Co., 1895.

Bardenhewer, Otto. *Geschichte der altkirchlichen Litteratur.* 5 vols. Freiburg i.B.: Herder, 1902.

————. *Patrologie.* Freiburg i.B.: Herder, 1894.

————. *Patrology: The Lives and Works of the Fathers of the Church.* Translated by T. J. Shahan. St. Louis: Herder, 1908.

Basil. *Books against Eunomius. Adversus Eunomium, PG* 29, 497–669.

————. *Hexaemoron. NPNF (2)*, VIII, 101–7.

————. *On the Holy Spirit. NPNF (2)*, VIII, 1–49.

Bauch, Bruno, and Kuno Fischer. *Die Philosophie im beginn des zwanzigsten jahrhunderts: Festschrift für Kuno Fischer.* Heidelberg: Carl Winter, 1904–5.

Bauer, G. L. *Biblische Theologie des Neuen Testaments.* Leipzig: Weyand, 1800.

Baumgarten, A. J., with A. D. C. Twesten. *Vorlesungen über die Dogmatik der Evangelisch-Lutherischen Kirche.* 2 vols. Hamburg: F. Perth, 1837, 1838.

Baumgartner, A. J. *Traditionalisme et Critique Biblique.* Geneva, 1905.

Baumstark, Chr. E. *Christliche Apologetik auf anthropologischen Grundlage.* Frankfurt a/M., 1872.

Baur, Ferdinand Christian. *Kirchengeschichte der drei ersten Jahrhunderte.* Tübingen: L. F. Fues, 1863.

Bavinck, Herman. *De Algemeene Genade.* Kampen: G. Ph. Zalsman, 1894.

————. *Beginselen der Psychologie.* Kampen: Kok, 1897.

————. *Bilderdijk als Denker en Dichter.* Kampen: Kok, 1906.

————. *The Certainty of Faith.* Translated by H. der Nederlanden. Jordan Station, Ont.: Paideia, 1980.

————. *Christelijke Wereldbeschouwing.* Kampen: J. H. Bos, 1904.

————. *Christelijke Wetenschap.* Kampen: Kok, 1904.

————. *De Ethiek van Ulrich Zwingli.* Kampen: G. P. Zalsman, 1880.

————. *Gereformeerde Dogmatiek.* 4th ed. 4 vols. Kampen: Kok, 1928.

————. *Godsdienst en Godgeleerdheid.* Wageningen: Vada, 1902.

————. Ed. *Synopsis Purioris Theologiae.* Leiden: D. Donner, 1881.

————. *De Theologie van Prof. Dr. Daniel Chantepie de la Saussaye.* 2d rev. ed. Leiden: D. Donner, 1903.

————. *Verzamelde Opstellen.* Kampen: Kok, 1921.

————. *De Zekerheid des Geloofs.* 1901.

Becanus, Martin. *Summa Theologiae Scholasticae.* Rothmagi: I. Behovrt, 1651.

Beck, J. T. *Die Christlich Lehrwissenshaft nach den biblischen Urkunden.* Stuttgart: J. F. Steinkopf, 1875.

———. *Einleitung in das System der christlichen Lehre.* 2d ed. Stuttgart: J. F. Steinkopf, 1870.

———. *Vorlesungen über christliche Glaubenslehre.* Gütersloh: C. Bertelsmann, 1886–87.

Belgic Confession. In vol. 3 of *The Creeds of Christendom,* edited by Philip Schaff and revised by David S. Schaff. 6th ed. 1919. Reprinted, Grand Rapids: Baker, 1983.

Bellarmine, Robert. *De Controversiis Christianae fidei adversus huius temporis haereticos.* Cologne: Gualtheri, 1617–20.

———. *Disputationum ven servi Dei.* 4 vols. Roma: Typographia Bonarum Artium, 1840.

———. *Opera Omnia.* Edited by J. Fèvre. 12 vols. Paris: Vivès, 1870–74.

———. *De Scriptoribus ecclesiasticis.* Rome, 1673.

Bender, Willhelm. *Das Wesen der Religion und die Grundgesetze der Kirchenbildung.* Bonn: M. Cohen, 1886.

———. *Der Wunderbegriff des Neuen Testaments.* Frankfurt: Verlag von Heyder & Zimmer, 1871.

Bénézeh, Auguste. *Théorie de Calvin sur l'Ecriture Saint.* Paris, 1890.

Bengel, John Albert. *Gnomon of the New Testament.* Edinburgh: T. & T. Clark, 1877.

Berguer, Georges. *L'application de la Méthode Scientifique á la Théologie.* Genèva: Romct, 1903.

Berlage, H. P. *Over de Waarschijnlijke Ontwikkeling der Architecture.* Delft: J. Waltman Jr., 1905.

Bernoulli, Carl Albrecht. *Die wissenschaftliche und die Kirchliche Methode in der Theologie: Ein encyklopädischer Versuch.* Freiburg i.B.: J. C. B. Mohr (Paul Siebeck), 1897.

Berthoud, A. *La parole de Dieu.* Lausanne, 1906.

Beth, Karl. *Das Wesen des Christentums und die moderne historische Denkweise.* Leipzig: Deichert, 1904.

Bettex, Frédéric. *Die Bibel Gottes wort.* Stuttgart: Steinkopf, 1903.

Beza, Theodore. *Tractationum Theologicarum.* Volumen I. Geneva: Jean Crispin, 1570.

Bibliotheca fratrum Polonarum. 6 vols. Irenopoli, 1656.

Bibliothek der Kirchenvätter. 80 vols. Kempten: Kösel, 1869–88.

Biedermann, Alois Emanuel. *Christliche Dogmatik.* Zurich: Füssli, 1869.

Biesterveld, P. *De jongste methode voor de verklaring van het Nieuwe Testament.* Kampen: Bos, 1905.

Bilderdijk, W. Willem. *Brieven.* 5 vols. Amsterdam: W. Messchert, 1836, 1837.

———. *Taal- en dichtkundige verscheidenheden.* 4 vols. Rotterdam: J. Immerzeel Jr., 1820–23.

———. Verhandelingen, Ziel- Sede- en Rechtsleer Betreffende. 1821.

Billot, L. *De Inspiratione sacrae Scripturae: theologica disquisitio.* Rome: Typographia Polyglotta S. C. de Propaganda Fide, 1903.

Billuart, Charles Rene. *Summa Sanctae Thomae hodiernis academiarum moribus accommodata.* 10 vols. Paris: Lecoffre, 1878.

———. *Summa Sanctae Thomae sive Cursus Theol.* 19 vols. Maastricht: Jacobi Lekens, 1769–70.

Bigg, Charles. *The Christian Platonists of Alexandria.* Oxford: Clarendon Press; New York: Macmillan, 1886.

Boeles, J. *De mysteriis in relig. Christ.* Gronigen: C. M. van B. Hoitsema, 1843.

Böhl, Eduard. *Die Alttestamentlichen Citate im Neuen Testament.* Wien: Wilhelm Braumüller, 1878.

———. *Dogmatik.* Amsterdam: Scheffer, 1887.

———. *Forschungen nach einer Volksbibel zur Zeit Jesu.* Wien: Wilhelm Braumüller, 1873.

Bois, Henri. *De la Certitude Chrétienne. Essai sur la theologie de Frank.* Paris: Fischbacher, 1887.

———. *Le dogme grec.* Paris: Fischbacher, 1892.

Bonaventure. *The Breviloquium.* Vol. 2 of *The Works of Bonaventure.* Translated by Jose De Vinck. Paterson, N.J.: St. Anthony Guild Press, 1963.

Bonet-Maury, Gaston. *Etudes de théologie et d'histoire publiées.* Paris: Fischbacher, 1901.

Bornhaüser, K. B. *Die Vergottungslehre des Athanasius und Johannes Damasenus.* Gütersloh: C. Bertelsmann, 1903.

Bouché-Leclercq, Auguste. *Histoire de la divination dans l'antiquité.* 4 vols. Paris: E. Leroux, 1879–82.

Bousset, Wilhelm. *Das Wesen der Religion.* Halle a. S.: Gebauer-Schwetschek, 1903.

———. *What Is Religion?* Translated by F. B. Low. New York: G. P. Putnam, 1907.

Bovon, Jules *Dogmatique Chrétienne.* 2 vols. Lausanne: Georges Bridel, 1895–96.

Bowie, W. Copeland, ed. *Liberal Thought at the Beginning of the 20th Century.* London: P. Green, 1901.

Bradlaugh, Charles, A. Besant, and Ch. Watts. *The Freethinker's Textbook.* London: Charles Watts, 1876.

*Brahe, J. J. *Aanmerkingen Over de Vijf Walchersche Artikelen.*

Brakel, Wilhelmus. *The Christian's Reasonable Service.* 4 vols. Translated by Bartel Elshout. Ligonier, Pa.: Soli Deo Gloria Publications, 1992–96.

Braun, Carl. *Amerikanismus.* Würzburg: Göbel & Scherer, 1904.

Braun, Johannes. *Doctrina Foederum, Sive Systema Theologiae Didacticae et Elenchticae.* Amsterdam: A. Van Sommeren, 1668.

Bräunlich, P. *Der neueste Teufelsschwindel in der römisch-katholischen Kirche.* Leipzig: Braun, 1897.

Bredenkamp, C. J. *Gesetz und Propheten: ein Beitrag zur alttestamentlichen Kritik.* Erlangen: Deichert, 1881.

Bretschneider, Karl Gottlieb. *Handbuch der Dogmatik der Evangelischlutherischen Kirche, oder Versuch einer beurtheilenden Darstellung der Grundstze, welche diese Kirche in ihren symbolischen Schriften bei die Christliche Glaubenslehre ausgesprochen hat, mit vergleichung der Glaubenslehre in der Bekenntnisschriften der reformirten Kirche.* Leipzig: J. A. Barth, 1838.

———. *Luther an Unsere Zeit.* Erfurt: G. A. Keysers, 1817.

———. *Systematische Entwicklung aller in der Dogmatik verkommenden Begriffe nach den symbolischen Schriften der evangelisch-*
lutherischen und reformirten Kirche und den wichtigsten dogmatischen Lehrbüchern ihrer Theologen. Leipzig: J. A. Barth, 1841.

Briggs, C. A. *The Authority of Holy Scriptures* (Inaugural address). 4th ed. New York: Scribner, 1892.

———. *The Bible, the Church, and the Reason: The Three Great Fountains of Divine Authority.* New York: Scribner's, 1892.

———. *Inspiration and Inerrancy.* London: J. Clarke, 1891.

———. *Messianic Prophecy.* 2d ed. New York: Charles Scribner's Sons, 1893.

Brown, John. *The Stundists: The Story of a Great Religious Revolt.* London: James Clarke, 1893.

Bruce, A. B. *Apologetics or Christianity Defensively Stated.* Edinburgh: T. & T. Clark, 1892.

Brühl, J. A. Moriz. *Geschichte der Katholischen literatur Deutschlands vom 17. jahrhundert bis zur gegenwart.* Wien: Wagner, 1861.

Bruining, A. *Het Bestaan van God.* Leiden: S. C. van Doesburgh, 1891.

———. *Moderne Mystiek.* Leiden: van Doesburgh, 1885.

Bucanus, Guillaume. *Institutiones Theologicae, Seu Locorum Communium Christianae Religionis, ex Dei Verbo, et Praestantissimorum Theologorum Orthodoxo Consensu Expositorum.* Bernae Helvetiorum: Johannes & Isaias Le Preux, 1605.

Buchanan, James. *The Doctrine of Justification.* Edinburgh: T. & T. Clark, 1867.

Büchner, L. *Force and Matter: Or Principles of the Natural Order of the Universe.* 4th ed. New York: P. Eckler, 1891.

Buckle, Henry T. *History of Civilization in England.* 2 vols. New York: D. Appleton & Co., 1861, 1862.

Buddeus, Joannes Franciscus. *Elementa Philosophiae Instrumentalis.* 5th ed. 2 vols. Halae Saxonum: Orphanotrophii glavcha-halensis, 1714–15.

Buddeus, Johann Franz. *Institutiones Theologiae Dogmaticae.* 1724.

———. *Institutiones Theologiae Moralis.* Leipzig: T. Fritsch, 1715.

Bunsen, Ernest de. *Die Reconstruction der kirchliche Autorität.* Leipzig: F. A. Brockhaus, 1892.

Burmann, Frans. *Synopsis Theologiae & Speciatim Oeconomiae Foederum Dei: Ab Initio Saeculorum Usque ad Consummationem Eorum.* 2 vols. in 1. Amsterdam: Joannem Wolters, 1699.

Burmeister, Hermann. *Geschichte der Schöpfung: eine Darstellung des Entwickelungsganges der Erde und ihrer Bewöhner.* 7th ed. Leipzig: C. G. Giebel, 1872.

Büsching, Anton Friderich. *Dissertatio theologica inauguralis exhibens epitomen theologiae e solis sacris litteris eoncinnatae et ab omnibus rebus et verbis scholasticis purgatae.* Göttingen: Eliam Luzac, 1756.

———. *Epitome Theologiae e solis sacris literis concinnatae.* Lemgo, 1755.

Butler, Joseph. *The Analogy of Religion, Natural and Revealed.* 2d ed. London: Knapton, 1736.

Buxtorf, Johannes. *Anticritica seu viniciae veritas hebraica.* Basel, 1653.

———. *Tractatus de punctorum origine, antiquitate et auctoritate.* 1648.

———. *Tractatus de punctorum vocalium, et accentum, in libris veteris Testamenti hebraicis.* Basileae: L. König, 1648.

Byington, E. H. *The Puritan in England and New England.* London: Sampson Low, Marston, 1896.

Calovius, Abraham. *Isagoge ad summa theologia.* Wittenberg: A. Hartmann, typis J. S. Fincelli, 1652.

Calvin, John. *Commentary on The Epistle to the Hebrews and the First and Second Epistles of Saint Peter.* Translated by William B. Johnston and edited by David W. Torrance and Thomas F. Torrance. Grand Rapids: Eerdmans, 1963.

———. *Commentary on The Second Epistle of Paul the Apostle to the Corinthians and the Epistles to Timothy, Titus, Philemon.* Translated by T. A. Smail and edited by David W. Torrance and Thomas F. Torrance. Grand Rapids: Eerdmans, 1964.

———. *Institutes of the Christian Religion* (1559). Edited by John T. McNeill and translated by F. L. Battles. 2 vols. Philadelphia: Westminster, 1960.

Canisius, Petrus. *Summa doctrinae Christianae.* Antwerp: J. Withagus, 1558.

Cannegieter, T. *De Godsdienst uit Plichtbesef.* Leiden: 1890.

Cano, Melchior. *De Locis theologicae* (1564). In vol. 1 of *PL, Theologiae cursus completus.*

Carlblom, A. *Zur Lehre von der Christlichen Gewissheit.* Leipzig: E. Bidder, 1874.

Carpzovius, Johann Gottlieb. *Critica sacra Veteris Testamenti.* 2d ed. Leipzig: J. Chr. Martin, 1748.

Casini, Antonio. *Controv. de statu purae naturae.* Appendix to librum II de opificio. sex dierum. Vol. 4, pp. 512–96 of *De Theologicus dogmatibus,* edited by D. Petavius. Paris: Vivès, 1866.

The Catechism of the Council of Trent. Translated by J. Donovan. New York: Catholic Publ. Society, 1829.

Cave, W. *Scriptorum ecclesiasticorum historia literaria.* 2 vols. London: 1689, Basel: 1741.

Chalmers, T. *The Evidence and Authority of the Christian Revelation.* Philadelphia: Anthony Finley, 1817.

———. *Natural Theology.* London: Printed for T. & J. Allman, 1823.

Chamberlain, H. S. *Foundations of the Nineteenth Century.* Translated by John Lees. 2 vols. [1911]. Reprinted, New Orleans: Flander Hall, 1988.

———. *Die Grundlagen des neunzehnten Jahrhundert.* 4th ed. 2 vols. München: F. Bruckmann, 1903.

Chamier, Daniel. *Panstratiae Catholicae, sive Controversiarum de Religione Adversus Pontificios Corpus.* 4 vols. Geneva: Rouer, 1626.

Chantepie de la Saussaye, Daniel. *Leven en Rigting.* Rotterdam, 1865.

———. *Het Protestantism als Politiek Beginsel.* Rotterdam, 1871.

———. *Zekerheid en Twijfel.* 1893.

Chantepie de la Saussaye, Pierre Daniel. *De godsdienstige bewegingen van dezen tijd in haren oorsprong geschetst.* Rotterdam: E. H. Tassemeijer, 1863.

———. *Lehrbuch der Religionsgeschichte.* 2 vols. Tübingen: J. C. B. Mohr (Paul Siebeck), 1905.

Cheetham, S. *The Mysteries: Pagan and Christian.* London and New York: MacMillan, 1897.

Chemniz, M. *Loci Theologici.* 3 vols. Frankfurt and Wittenberg: T. Merius and E. Schumacher, 1653.

Christliche Glaubenslehren im Lichte der liberalen Theologie. Hamburg, 1903.

Chrysostom, John. *The Homilies.* Oxford: J. H. Parker, 1843.

———. *On Providence.* Translation and theological interpretation by Christopher Alan Hall. Ph.D. diss., Drew University, 1991.

———. *On the Incomprehensible Nature of God.* Translated by Paul W. Harkins. Washington, D.C.: Catholic University Press, 1984.

Chrysostom, John; Bernard de Montfaucon. *Tou en hagiois patros hemon Ioannou archiep. Konstantinoupoleos* 13 vols. Paris: Ludovici Guerin, 1718–38.

Cicero, Marcus Tullius. *Academica.* Translated by James S. Reid. London: Macmillan and Company, 1880.

———. *Brutus. On the nature of the gods. On divination. On duties.* Translated by Hubert M. Poteat. Chicago: University of Chicago Press, 1950.

———. *De Divinatione.* Translated by W. A. Falconer. Loeb Classical Library. Cambridge: Harvard University Press, 1923.

———. *De finibus bonarum et malorum.* Edited by Johan Nikolai Madvig. Hildesheim: G. Olms, 1963 (reprint of 1876 edition).

———. *De Inventione.* 4 vols. Translated by H. M. Hubbell. Loeb Classical Library. Cambridge: Harvard University Press, 1949.

Clarisse, Johannes. *Encyclopediae theologicae epitome.* Leiden: J. Luchtman, 1852.

Clausen, H. N. *Aurelius Augustinus hipponensis sacrae Scripturae interpres.* Hauniae: Schultz, 1827.

Clemen, August. *Der Gebrauch des Alten Testamentes in den neuestamentlichen Schriften.* Gütersloh: C. Bertelsmann, 1895.

Clemen, Carl. *Die religionsgeschichtliche Methode in der Theologie.* Giessen: J. Ricker, 1904.

Clement of Alexandria. *Exhortation to the Heathen. ANF,* II, 171–206.

———. *Stromateis.* Translated by John Ferguson. Vol. 85 of *The Fathers of the Church.* Washington, D.C.: Catholic University of America Press, 1991.

Clement of Alexandria; Otto Stählin. *Clemens Alexandrinus.* 4 vols. Leipzig: J. C. Hinrichs, 1905–36.

Clifford, J. *The Inspiration and Authority of the Bible.* 2d ed. London: James Clarke & Co., 1895.

Cloppenburg, Johannes. *Disputatio de Foedere Dei.* 1643.

———. *Exercitationes Super Locos Communes Theologicos.* Franeker: Black, 1653.

———. *Theologica Opera Omnia.* 2 vols. Amsterdam: Borstius, 1684.

Coccejus, Johannes. *Summa Doctrinae de Foedere et Testamento Dei.* 2d ed. Leiden: Elsevier, 1654.

———. *Summa Theologiae ex Scripturis Repetita.* Amsterdam: J. Ravenstein, 1665.

Coignet, C. *La morale indépendante, dans son principe et dans son objet.* Paris: G. Baillière, 1863.

Coit, Stanton. *Die ethische Bewegung in der Religie.* Translated by Georg von Gizychi. Leipzig: Reisland, 1890.

Collatio Hagensis. 1611.

Collet, Pierre. *Institutiones theologiae moralis.* 4 vols. Lyon: J. M. Bruyset, 1768.

Comrie, Alexander, and Nicolaus Holtius. *Examen van het Ontwerp van Tolerantie.* 10 vols. Amsterdam: Nicolaas Byl, 1753.

Comte, Auguste. *Cours de philosophie positive.* 6 vols. Paris: Bachelier, 1830–42.

———. *The Essential Comte: Selected from Cours de philosophie positive.* Translated by Margaret Clarke and edited by Stanislav Andreski. London: Croom Helm; New York: Barnes & Noble, 1974.

———. *La Philosophie Positive.* 2 vols. Edited by Jules Rig. Paris: J. B. Baillére et fils, 1880–81.

Cornill, Carl H. *Der Israelitische Prophetismus.* Strausburg: Trübner, 1894.

Costa, Isaac da. *Over de goddelijke ingeving (theopneustie) der Heilige Schriften.* Rotterdam: J. M. Bredée, 1884.

Cramer. De Geschiedenis van het Leerstuk der Inspiratie in de laatste Twee Eeuwen. 1887.

Cramer, Jacob. *Alexandre Vinet als Christelijk Moralist en Apologeet Geteekend en Gewaardeerd.* Leiden: Brill, 1883.

———. *De Roomsch-Katholieke en Oudprotestantische Schriftbeschouwing.* Amsterdam, W. H. Kirberger, 1883.

————. *De Schriftbeshouwing van Calvijn.* Amsterdam: W. H. Kirberger, 1881.

Cramer, S. *De Godsvrucht Voorwerp van Christliche historische Onderzoek.* Amsterdam: s.n., 1900.

Cramp, J. M. *Baptist History: from the Foundation of the Christian Church to the Close of the Eighteenth Century.* London: Elliot Stock, 1868.

Crell, Johann. *Liber de deo euisque attributis.* In vol. 4 of *Opera Omnia.* Amsterdam: Irenicus Philalethes, 1656.

Cremer, Hermann. *Biblico-Theological Lexicon of New Testament Greek. S.v. προνοια.* Translated by D. W. Simon and William Urwick. Edinburgh: T. & T. Clark, 1872.

————. *Biblisch-theologisches Wörterbuch der neutestamentlichen Gräcität.* Gotha: F. A. Perthes, 1880.

————. *Christi und der Apostelstellung zum Alten Testament.* Leipzig, 1900.

————. *Glaube, Schrift und Heilige Geschichte: Drei Vorträge.* Gütersloh, C. Bertelsmann, 1896.

————. *Die Grundwahrheiten der christlichen Religion nach Dr. R. Seeberg.* Gütersloh: Bertelsmann, 1903.

Crets, G. J. *De divina bibliorum inspiratione.* Lovanii: Excudebant Vanlinthout Fratres, 1886.

Cumont, Franz. *Die Mysterien des Mithra: ein Beitrag zur Religionsgeschichte der römischen Kaiserzeit.* Leipzig: Teubner, 1903.

Curcellaeus, Stephanus. *Opera theologicae.* Amsterdam: Elsevir, 1675.

Cyprian. *Sancti Cypriani Episcopi Opera.* Turnholt: Brepols, 1972.

Cyril. *The Arguments of the Emperor Julian against the Christians.*

Daelman, Carolus Gislenus. *Theologia seu Observationes Theologia in Summam D. Thomae.* 9 vols. Louvaine: Martinum van Overbeke, 1759.

*Dahle, C. *Der Ursprung der heilige Schrift aus d. Dän von H. Hansen.* Leipzig, 1905.

Dahle, Lars Nilsen. *Der Ursprung der heiligen Schrift.* Leipzig: E. Ungleich, 1904.

Dalton, Hermann von. *Evangelische Strömungen in der russischen Kirche der Gegenwart.* 3 vols. Heilbronn: Henninger, 1881.

————. *Die russische Kirche.* Leipzig: Duncker & Humbolt, 1892.

Danaeus, P. *Ethices Christianae.* 1577.

Darwin, Charles. *The Descent of Man.* Rev. ed. New York: D. Appleton, 1896.

Daubanton, François Elbertus. *De Algenoezaamheid der Heilige Schrift.* Utrecht: Kemink & Zoon, 1882.

————. *Confessie en Dogmatiek.* Utrecht: Kemink & Zoon, 1886.

————. *De theopneustie der Heilige Schrift.* Utrecht: Kemink & Zoon, 1882.

D'Aubigné, J. H. Merle. *L'autorité des Écritures inspirées de Dieu.* Tolouse: Librairie protestante, 1850.

————. *Duitschland, Engeland en Schotland.* Rotterdam: Van der Meer & Verbruggen, 1849.

Dausch, P. *Die Schriftinspiration: eine biblisch-geschichtliche Studie.* Freiburg i.B.: Herder, 1891.

Davidson, A. B. *Old Testament Prophecy.* Edited by J. A. Paterson. Edinburgh: T. & T. Clark, 1903.

————. *The Theology of the Old Testament.* Edited by S. D. F. Salmond. Edinburgh: T. & T. Clark, 1904.

Daxer, Georg. *Der Subjektivismus in Franks "System der christlichen Gewissheit."* Gütersloh: C. Bertelsmann, 1900.

De Bussy, Isaak Jan le Cosquinode. *Ethische Idealisme.* Amsterdam: J. H. de Bussy, 1875.

————. *De Maatstaf van het Zedelijke Oordell.* Amsterdam: J. H. de Bussy, 1889.

————. *Over de Waarde en den Inhoud van Godsdienst Voorstellingen.* Amsterdam: J. H. de Bussy, 1880.

De Costa, I. *Over de goddelijke Ingeving der Heilige Schrift.* Rotterdam: Bredée, 1884.

De Gasparin, A. *Les écoles du doute et l'école de la Foi.* Genève: E. Beroud, 1853.

De Groot, Hofstede. *De Groninger Godgeleerden.* Groningen: A. L. Scholtens, 1855.

————. *Institutio Theologia Natura.* 4th ed. Groningen: W. Zuidema, 1861.

Deharbe, Joseph. *Verklaring der Katholieke Geloofs- en Zedeleer.* Edited by B. Dankelman. 3d ed. 4 vols. Utrecht: J. R. Van Rossum, 1880–88.

Delattre, A. J. *Autour de la question biblique une nouvelle école d'exégèse et les autorités qu'elle invoque.* Liége: H. Dessain, 1904.

Delitzsch, Franz. *System der Christlichen Apologetik.* Leipzig: Dörffling und Franke, 1869.

———. *A System of Biblical Psychology.* Translated by Robert E. Wallis. Edinburgh: T. & T. Clark, 1899.

Delitzsch, Friedrich. *Babel and Bible.* Translated by W. H. Corruth. Chicago: Open Court, 1903.

———. *A New Commentary on Genesis.* Translated by Sopia Taylor. 2 vols. Edinburgh: T. & T. Clark, 1899.

Delitzsch, Johannes. *De inspiratione Scripturae Sacrae quid Statverint Patres Apostolici et apologetae secundi saeculi.* Leipzig: A. Lorentz Bibliopolam, 1872.

Demetrius Cydones. *The Contempt of Death.* Leipzig: Kühnol, 1786.

Dens, Pierre. *A Synopsis of the Moral Theory of Peter Dens; as Prepared for the Use of Romish Seminaries and Students of Theology* [*Theologia ad usum seminarium et sacrae theologiae alumnorum*]. 4th ed. Translated by Joseph F. Berg. 1790. Reprinted, Philadelphia: Lippincott, Grambo, 1855.

———. *Theologia ad usum Seminarium.* 7 vols. Mechlinrae: P. J. Hanica, 1819.

———. *Theologia Moralis et Dogmatica.* 8 vols. Dublin: Richard Coyne, 1832.

Denzinger, Heinrich. *Enchiridion symbolorum et definitionum, quae de rebus fidei et morum a conciliis oecumenicis et summis pontificibus emanarunt.* Edited by Ignatius Stahl. Wirceburgi: Benzinger fratres, 1888.

———. *The Sources of Catholic Dogma (Enchiridion Symbolorum).* Translated from the 30th ed. by Roy J. Deferrari. London and St. Louis: Herder, 1955.

———. *Vier Bücher von der religiösen Erkentniss.* 2 vols. 1856. Reprinted, Frankfurt/M.: Minerva-Verlag; Würzburg: Stahel, 1967.

De Wette, W. M. L., and Julius Räbiger. *Lehrbuch der hebräisch-jüdischen Archäologiei.* Leipzig: F. C. W. Vogel, 1864.

*De Wijs, G. E. W. *De droomen in en buiten de Bijbel.* 1858.

Dieckhoff, A. W. *Inspiration und Irrthumslosigkeit der Heiligen Schrift.* Leipzig: Justus Naumann, 1891.

———. *Noch einmal über die Inspiration und Irrthumslosigkeit der Heiligen Schrift.* Rostock: Stiller, 1893.

———. *Schrift und Tradition.* Rostock: Stiller, 1870.

Dieringer, Franz. *Lehrbuch der Katholischen Dogmatik.* 4th ed. Mainz: Kirchheim, 1858.

Diestel, Ludwig. *Geschichte des Alten Testament in der christlichen Kirche.* Jena, 1869.

Dieterich, Konrad. *Philosophie und Naturwissenschaft: ihr neustes Bündniss und die monistische Weltanschauung.* Tübingen: H. Laupp'schen Buchhandlung, 1875; 2d ed. Freiburg, 1885.

Dillmann, August. *Genesis.* Edinburgh: T. & T. Clark, 1897.

Dilthey, Wilhelm. *Einleitung in die Geisteswissenschaften.* Leipzig: Duncker & Humbolt, 1883.

———. *Introduction to the Human Sciences.* Princeton, N. J., and Oxford: Princeton University Press, 1991.

Dittmar, W. *Vetus Testamentum in Novo: die alttestamentlichen Parallelen des Neuen Testaments im Wortlaut der Urtexte und der Septuaginta.* Göttingen: Vandenhoeck & Ruprecht, 1899–1903.

Dobschütz, Ernst von. *The Apostolic Age.* Translated by F. L. Pogson. London: P. Green, 1909.

———. *Probleme des apostolische Zeitalters.* Leipzig: J. C. Hinrichs, 1904.

Documents of Vatican Council I, 1869–1870. Selected and translated by John F. Broderick. Collegeville, Minn.: Liturgical Press, 1971.

Dods, Marcus. *The Bible, Its Origin and Nature.* New York: Scribner, 1905.

Doedes, Jacobus Izaak. *Encyclopedie der Christelijke Theologie.* Utrecht: Kemink, 1876.

———. *De Heidelbergsche Catechismus.* Utrecht: Kemink & Zoon, 1881.

———. *Inleiding tot de leer van God.* Utrecht: Kemink, 1870.

———. *De Leer der Zaligheid Volgens het Evangelie in de Schriften des Nieuwen Ver-

bonds Voorgesteld. Utrecht: Kemink, 1876.

—. *Modern of Apostolisch Christendom?* Utrecht: Kemink, 1860.

—. *De Nederlandsche Geloofsbelijdenis en de Heidelbergsche Catechismus.* Utrecht: Kemink & Zoon, 1880–81.

—. *Het Regt des Christendoms tegenover de Wijsbegeerte Gehandhaafd.* Utrecht: Kemink en Zoon, 1847.

—. *De Zoogenaamde Moderne Theologie Eenigszins Toegelicht.* Utrecht: Kemink, 1861.

Döllinger, J. J. I. *Beiträge zur Sektengeschichte des Mittelalters.* 2 vols. München: Beck, 1890.

Dorner, A. J. *Augustinus.* Berlin: W. Hertz, 1873.

—. *Grundriss der Encyklopädie der Theologie.* Berlin: Georg Reimer, 1901.

Dorner, Isaak August. *Gesammelte Schriften aus dem Gebiet der systematische Theologie* Berlin: W. Hertz, 1883.

—. *History of Protestant Theology Particularly in Germany.* Translated by G. Robson and S. Taylor. Edinburgh: T. & T. Clark, 1871.

—. *A System of Christian Doctrine.* Translated by Rev. Alfred Cave and Rev. J. S. Banks. Rev. ed. 4 vols. Edinburgh: T. & T. Clark, 1888.

Doumerge, E. *Jean Calvin.* 7 vols. Lausanne: G. Bridel & C., 1899–1927.

—. *L'autorité en matière de foi.* Lausanne: Payot, 1892.

—. *Les étapes du fidéisme.* Toulouse, 1906.

Drews, Arthur. *Die deutsche Spekulation seit Kant.* 2 vols. Berlin: P. Maeter, 1893.

—. *Die Religion als Selbst-bewusstsein Gottes.* Jena und Leipzig: E. Diederichs, 1906.

Drey, J. S. von. *Die Apologetik als wissenschaftliche Nachweisung der Göttlichkeit des Christenthums in seiner Erscheinung.* 2 vols. Mainz: Florian Kupferberg: 1838–43.

Dreyer, Otto. *Undogmatisches Christentum.* 3d ed. Braunschweig: C. A. Schwetschke und Sohn, 1890.

—. *Zur undogmatischen Glaubenslehre Vorträge und Abhandlungen.* Berlin: C. A. Schwetschke, 1901.

Drummond, Henry, *The Greatest Thing in the World.* New York: J. Pott & Co., 1897.

—. *The Natural Law in the Spiritual World.* London: Hodder and Stoughton, 1905.

Druskowitz, Helene von. *Moderne Versuche eines Religionsersatzes.* Heidelberg: G. Weiss, 1886.

Du Fresne Du Cange, C. *Glossarium ad scriptores mediae et infimae graecitatis.* 3 vols. Paris, 1678.

Duhm, Bernhard. *Das Geheimnis in der Religion.* Tübingen: Mohr, 1899.

Duker, A. C. and W. C. van Manen. *Oud Christelijke Letterkunde: De Geschriften der Apostolische Vaders.* 2 vols. Amsterdam: C. L. Brinkman, 1869–71.

Du Moulin, Pierre. *Du juge des controversies.* Geneva: Pierre Aubert, 1631.

Dunlop, William. *A Collection of Confessions of Faith, Catechism, Directories, Books of Disciplinne, etc. of Publick Authority in the Church of Scotland.* 2 vols. Edinburgh: James Watson, 1719.

Duns Scotus, Johannes. *Opera Omnia.* 26 vols. Paris: Vives, 1891–95.

Du Pin, Louis Ellies. *Nouvelle bibliothèque des auteurs ecclèsiastiques.* 47 vols. Paris: Chez André Pralard, 1686–1714.

Du Plessis-Mornay, Philippe. *Traité de la vérité de la religion Chrétienne contre les Athéens, Epicuriens, payens, Juifs, Mahumedistes, et autres infidels.* Anvers: C. Plantin, 1581.

Du Toit, J. D. *Het Methodisme.* Amsterdam: Höveker & Wormser, 1903.

Ebrard, Johannes Heinrich August. *Apologetics: The Scientific Vindication of Christianity.* Translated by William Stuart and John Macpherson. 2d ed. 3 vols. Edinburgh: T. & T. Clark, 1886–87.

—. *Christliche Dogmatik.* 2d ed. 2 vols. Königsberg: A. W. Unzer, 1862–63.

Eck, John. *Enchiridion of the Commonplaces against Luther and Other Enemies of the Church.* Translated by Ford Lewis Battles. Grand Rapids: Baker, 1979.

Ecke, Gustav. *Die evangelische Kirchen Landeskirchen Deutschlands im neunzehnten Jahrhundert.* Berlin: Reuther & Reichard, 1904.

————. *Die theologische Schule Albrecht Ritschls und die evangelische Kirche der Gegenwart.* 2 vols. Berlin: Reuther & Reichard, 1897–1904.

Edwards, Jonathan. *Dissertation concerning the End for Which God Created the World.* In *The Works of Jonathan Edwards,* vol. 8, *Ethical Writings.* Edited by Paul Ramsey. New Haven: Yale University Press, 1989.

————. *Works of President Edwards.* New York: Burt Franklin, 1968.

Egidy, C. M. von. *Ernste Gedanker.* Leipzig: 1890.

Ehrenfeuchter, F. *Christenthum und moderne Weltanschauung.* Göttingen: Vandenhoeck und Ruprecht, 1876.

Eichhorn, N. *Jesus von Nazaret: Ein tragisches Festspiel.* Berlin: B. Bemmster, 1880.

————. *Unsere Stellung zur heilige Schrift.* Stuttgart, 1905.

Eicken, Heinrich von. *Geschichte und System der mittelalterlichen Weltanschauung.* Stuttgart: J. G. Cotta, 1887.

Einig, P. *Katholischer "Reformer."* Trier: Paulinusdruckerei, 1902.

Eisler, Rudolf. *Kritische Einführung in die Philosophie.* Berlin: E. S. Mittler, 1905.

————. *Wörterbuch der philosophische Begriffe.* 2 vols. Berlin: E. S. Mittler, 1904.

Elliot, G. *Bilder aus dem kirchlichen Leben Englands.* Leipzig: Akademische Buchhandlung, 1896.

Ennemoser, Joseph. *The History of Magic.* Translated by William Howitt. London and New York: George Bell & Sons, 1893.

Epiphanius. *Contra Octoaginta haereses opus.* Basle: Hervagius, E. Episcopius, 1578.

Episcopius, Simon. *Apologia pro Confessione Sive Declaratione Sententiae Eorum, qui in Foederato Belgio Vocantur Remonstrantes, Super Praecipuis Articulis Religionis Christianae contra Censuram Quatuor Professorum Leidensium.* In vol. 2, pp. 95–283 of *Opera.* 1629.

————. *Confessio.* In vol. 2, pp. 69ff. of *Opera.*

————. *Institutiones theologicae.* In vol. 1 of *Opera.* Amsterdam: Johan Blaeu, 1650.

————. *Opera theologica.* 2 vols. Amsterdam: Johan Blaeu, 1650–65.

Erdmann, Johann Eduard. *Grundriss der Geschichte der Philosophie von Johann Eduard Erdmann.* 4th ed. Berlin: W. Hertz, 1896.

Erhard, Albert. *Der Katholizismus und das Jahrhundred im Lichte der kirchliche Entwicklung der Neuzeit.* Stuttgart and Vienna: J. Roth, 1902.

Erigena, Johannes Scotus. *The Division of Nature* (1681). Translated by Myra L. Uhlfelder. Indianapolis: Bobbs-Merrill, 1976.

Esser, T. *Die Lehre des heiligen Thomas von Aquino über die Möglichkeit einer anfanglosen Schöpfung.* Münster: Aschendorff, 1895.

Eucken, Rudolph. *Geistige Strömungen der Gegenwert.* Leipzig: Veit & Co., 1904.

————. *Der Wahrheitsgehalt der Religion.* 2d ed. Leipzig: Veit & Co., 1905.

Eusebius of Caesaria. *Ecclesiastical History. NPNF (2),* I.

————. *Historiae ecclessiasticae libri decem.* Oxonii: E. Typographeo Academico, 1842.

————. *Praeparatio Evangelica. PG,* 21.

————. *The Proof of the Gospel.* Translated by W. J. Ferrar. Grand Rapids: Baker, 1981.

Evans, Thomas. *An Exposition of the Faith of the Religious Society of Friends.* Philadelphia: Kimber & Sharpless, 1828.

Fabri, Friedrich. *Die Entstehung des Heidenthums und die Aufgabe der Heidenmission.* Barmen: W. Langewiesche, 1859.

Fairbairn, A. M. *Philosophy of Christian Religion.* New York: Macmillan, 1902.

————. *The Place of Christ in Modern Theology.* New York: Scribner, 1893.

Falk, Franz. *Der Bibel am Ausgange des Mittelalters.* Köln: J. P. Bachem, 1905.

Farrar, Frederic William, James Hogg, and Thomas De Quincey. *The Wider Hope.* London: T. Fisher Unwin, 1890.

Farrar, F. W., et. al. *Inspiration: A Clerical Symposium.* 2d ed. London: J. Nisbet & Co., 1886.

Feine, Paul. *Das Wunder im Neuen Testament.* Eisenach: M. Wilkens, 1894.

Fichte, Immanuel Hermann von. *Anthropologie.* Leipzig: Brockhaus, 1860.

Fichte, Johann Gottlieb. *Attempt at a Critique of All Revelation.* Translated by Garrett Green. Cambridge: New York: Cambridge University Press, 1978.

————. *Werke.* 6 vols. Leipzig: F. Meiner, 1922.

Fischer, Engelbert L. *Die Grundfragen der Erkenntnisstheorie.* Mainz: F. Kirchheim, 1887.

————. *Heidenthum und offenbarung.* Mainz: F. Kirchheim, 1878.

————. *Die modernen Ersatzversuche für die aufgegebene Christentum.* Regensburg, 1902.

Fischer, Kuno. *Francis Bacon und seine Nachfolger.* 2d ed. Leipzig: F. A. Brockhaus, 1875.

Flacius Illyricus, Matthias. *Clavis scripturae sacrae.* Frankfurt: Impersis Hieronymi Christiani Pauli, 1719.

Flade, W. *Die philosophischen Grundlagen der Theologie R. Rothe's.* Leipzig: Reudnitz: August Hoffmann, 1901.

Flathe, L. *Geschichte der Ketzer im Mittelalters.* 3 vols. Stuttgart, 1845.

Fleisch, Urban. *Die erkenntniss theoretische und metaphysische Grundlagen der dogmatische systeme von A. E. Biedermann und R. A. Lipsius.* Berlin: Schwetske & Sohn, 1901.

Fleischer, F. C. *Bijvoegsel van de Hervorming.* 1902.

Fletcher, Joseph. *The History of the Revival and Progress of Independency in England.* London: John Snow, 1847–48.

Flournoy, Théodore. *Les principes de la psychologie religieuse.* Genève: H. Kündig, 1903.

Flügel, Otto. *Die Probleme der Philosophie und ihre Lösungen.* Cöthen: O. Schulze, 1888.

————. *Ritschl's philosophische und theologische Ansichten.* 2d ed. Langensalza: Beyer, 1892.

————. *Die spekulative theologie der Gegenwart.* Cöthen: O. Schutze, 1888.

Fock, Otto. *Der Socinianismus nach seiner Stellung in der Gesammtentwicklung des christlichen Geistes, nach seinem historischen Verlauf und nach seinem Lehrbegriff.* Kiel: C. Schröder, 1847.

Fonck, Leopold. *Der Kampf um die Wahrheit der h. Schrift seit 25 Jahren.* Innsbrück: F. Rauch, 1905.

Forcellini, E. *Totius latinitatis lexicon.* 4 vols. Padua: J. Manfie, 1771.

Formby, Henry and Cornelius Krieg. *Der Monotheismus der Offenbarung und das Heidenthum.* Mainz: F. Kirchheim, 1880.

Formula of Concord. In vol. 3 of *Creeds of Christendom,* edited by Philip Schaff and revised by David S. Schaff. 6th ed. 1919. Reprinted, Grand Rapids: Baker, 1983.

Foster, F. H. *Christian Life and Theology; or, the Contribution of Christian Experience to the System of Evangelical Doctrine.* New York: Revell, 1900.

Frank, Franz Hermann Reinhold. *Dogmatische Studien.* Erlangen: A. Deichert, 1892.

————. *Geschichte und Kritik der neueren Theologie.* Erlangen: A. Deichert, 1894.

————. *System der Christlichen Gewissheit.* 2 vols. Erlangen: A. Deichert, 1870–73.

————. *System der Christlichen Wahrheit.* 2 vols. Erlangen: A. Deichert, 1878–80.

————. *Die Theologie der Conkordienformel.* 4 vols. Erlangen: T. Blaesing, 1858–65.

————. *Über die Kirchliche Bedeutung der Theologie Albrecht Ritschls.* 3d ed. Erlangen: A. Deichert, 1891.

Frank, Viktor. *Russisches Selbstzeugnisse.* Vol. I, *Russisches Christenthum.* Paderborn: Russ. Christ., 1889.

Franzelin, J. B. *Tractatus de divina traditione et scriptura.* 3d ed. Romae: Typeographia Polyglotta, 1882.

Fraser, Alexander Campbell. *Philosophy of Theism.* New York: Scribner's, 1899.

Fritzche, Christian Frider. *De Revelationis notione Biblica commentatio.* Leipzig: Hartmann, 1828.

Frohschammer, Jakob. *Die Philosophie des Thomas von Aquino.* Leipzig: F. A. Brockhaus, 1889.

Fulliquet, G. *Le Miracle dans la Bible.* Paris: Fischbacher, 1904.

Funk, F. X. *Die apostolischen Väter.* Tübingen: J. C. B. Mohr, 1901.

Gabler, G. A. *Lehrbuch der philosophischen Propädeutik: als Einleitung zur Wissenschaft.* Erlangen: Palm, 1827.

————. *System der theoretischen Philosophie.* Erlangen: Palm, 1827.

Gallandi, Andreas. *Biblotheca veterum patrum antiquorumque scriptorum ecclesiasticorum, postrema Lugdunesi longe locupletior atque accuratior.* Venetiis: J. B. Hieron fil., 1765–81.

Gallican Confession. In vol. 3 of *The Creeds of Christendom,* edited by Philip Schaff and revised by David S. Schaff. 6th ed. 1919. Reprinted, Grand Rapids: Baker, 1983.

Gangauf, Theodor. *Metaphysische Psychologie des Augustinus.* Augsburg: K Kollmann, 1852.

Garvie, Alfred Ernest. *The Ritschlian Theology, Critical and Constructive.* Edinburgh: T. & T. Clark, 1899.

Gasparin, Agénor, comte de. *Les écoles du doute et l'école de la Foi.* Genève: E. Beroud, 1853.

Gass, Wilhelm. *Beitrage zur kirchliche Literature und Dogmengeschichte des grossen Mittelalters.* 2 vols. Breslau, 1844–47.

———. *Geschichte der christlichen Ethik.* Berlin: Reimer, 1881–86.

———. *Geschichte der protestantischen Dogmatik.* 4 vols. Berlin: G. Reimer, 1854–67.

———. *Symbolik der Griechischen Kirche.* Berlin: Georg Reimer, 1872.

Gaussen, L. *Le canon des Saintes Écritures au double point de vue de la science et de la foi.* Lausanne: George Bridel, 1860.

———. *Théopneustie ou, pleine inspiration des Saintes Écritures.* Paris: L. R. Delay, 1840.

Gebhart, O., et.al., eds. *Patrum apostolicorum opera.* 3 vols. Leipzig: J. C. Hinrichs, 1876–78.

Gebhart, O. and A. Harnack. *Texte und Untersuchungen zur Geschichte der altchristliche Literatur.* Leipzig: Hinrichs, 1882.

*Gedanken von der Beschaffenheit und dem Vorzüge der biblischen dogmatischen Theologie vor der scholastischen. 1755.

Geesink, Wilhelm. *De Ethiek in de Gereformeerde Theologie.* Amsterdam: Kirchner, 1897.

———. *Van 's Heeren Ordinantiën.* 1st ed. 3 vols. Amsterdam: W. Kirchener, 1907.

Gehring, J. *Die Sekten der russischen Kirche (1003–1897): Nach Ursprunge und inneren Zusammenhange.* Leipzig: F. Richter, 1898.

Gellius. *Noctes atticae.*

Gerbel-Embach, Nicolaus von. *Russische Sectirer.* 2 vols. Heilbronn: Henninger, 1833. Vols. VI and VIII of *Aeitfragen des Christlichen Volkslebens.* 20 vols. Stuttgart: C. Belser, 1876.

Gerhard, Johann. *Loci Theologici.* Edited by E. Preuss. 9 vols. Berlin: G. Schlawitz, 1863–75.

Gersdorf, Ephraim G., ed. *Bibliotheca patrum ecclesiasticorum latinorum selecta.* 13 vols. Leipzig: sumptibus B. Tauchnitz jun., 1838–47.

Gess, Wolfgang. F. *Die Inspiration der Helden der Bibel und der Schriften der Bibel.* Basel: Reich, 1892.

Giesebrecht, Friedrich. *Die Berufsbeganbung der Alttestamentliche Propheten.* Göttingen: Vandenhoeck & Ruprecht, 1897.

Gieseler, Johann Karl Ludwig. *Lehrbuch der Kirchengeschichte.* Edited by C. R. Redepenning. 7 vols. Bonn: Adolph Marcus, 1828–57.

Giesswein, Alexander. *Deterministiche und metaphysische Schichtsauffassung.* Wien: Mayer, 1905.

Girgensohn, Karl. *Die moderne historische Denkweise und die christliche Theologie.* Leipzig: A. Deichert, 1904.

———. *Die Religion.* Leipzig: A. Deichert, 1903.

———. *Zwölf Reden über die christliche Religion.* München: C. H. Beck, 1906.

Gladden, Washington. *Who Wrote the Bible?* Boston: Houghton, Mifflin and Company, 1891.

Gladstone, W. E. *The Impregnable Rock of Holy Scripture.* 2d ed. London: Isbister, 1892.

Glassius, Salmo. *Philologiae Sacrae.* Jenae: Steinmann, 1668.

Glossarium ad scriptores mediae et infimae latinitatis. 3 vols. Paris, 1678.

Glossner, Michael. *Der moderne idealismus.* Münster: Theissing, 1880.

Goblet d'Alviella, Eugène. *L'évolution religieuse contemporaine chez les anglais, les américains et les hindous.* Bruxelles, Lausanne: C. Muguardt, B. Bende, 1884.

Goebel, Max. *Geschichte des christlichen Lebens in der rheinisch-westphälischen Evangelischen Kirche.* 3 vols. Coblenz: K. Bädeker, 1849–60.

———. *Die religiöse Eigenthümlichkeit der lutherischen und der reformirten Kirche.* Bonn: Adoph Marcus, 1837.

Goguel, Maurice. *Wilhelm Herrmann et le problème religieux actual.* Paris: Fischbacher, 1905.

Goltz, Hermann, Freiherr von der. *Die Christlichen Grundwahrheiten.* Gotha: Freidrech Andreas Perthes, 1873.
———. *Die Reformirte Kirche Genf's im neunzehnten Jahrhundert.* Basel: H. Georg, 1862.

Gomarus, F. *Disputationum theologicarum quarto repetitarum quadragesima-tertia de paedobaptismo.* Lugduni Batauorum: Ex officina Ioannis Patii, 1606.
———. *Opera omnia theologica.*

Gore, Charles. *Lux Mundi.* 13th ed. London: Murray, 1892.

Gottschick, Johannes. *Kants Beweis für das Dasein Gottes.* Torgau: Lebinsky, 1878.
———. *Die Kirchlichkeit der sogenannte Kirchliche Theologie.* Frieburg i.B.: J. C. B. Mohr, 1890.

Goyau, Georges. *L'Allemagne religieuse.* Vol. 1, *le Protestantisme;* vol. 2, *le Catholicisme.* Paris: Perrin & Cie, 1898–1901.

Graesse, J. G. Th., ed. *Orbis Latinus: Oder, Verzeichniss der lateinischen benennungen der bekanntesten städe, mere, seen, berge und flüsse in allen theilen der erde, nebst einem deutsch-lateinischen register derselben.* Dresden: G. Schonfeld, 1861.

Grass, K. K. *Geschichte der Dogmatik in russischer Darstellung.* Gütersloh: C. Bertelsmann, 1902.

Gregory, J. *Puritanism in the Old World and in the New.* London: J. Clarke, 1895.

Gregory of Nyssa. *Explicatio apologetica in hexaemoron en hominis opificio* [*On the Making of Man*]. NPNF (2), 387–427.

Gregory the Great. *Moralia in Iobum.* In *Corpus Christianorum,* Series Latina CXLIII. A Turnholti: Typographi Brepols Editores Pontifici, 1979.

Greijdanus, S. *Menschwording en vernedering.* Wageningen: Vada, 1903.

Grétillat, Augustin. *Exposé de Théologie Systématique.* 4 vols. Paris: Fischbacher, 1885–92.

Grill, Julius. *Die persische Mysterienreligion im römischen Reiche und das Christentum.* Tübingen: Mohr, 1903.

Groenewegen, Herman. *De Metaphysica in de Wijsbegeerte van de Godsdienst.* Amsterdam, 1903.
———. *De Theologie en hare Wijsbegeerte.* Amsterdam, 1904.

Gross, G. *Die Bedeutung des Ästhetischen in der evangelischen Religion.* Gütersloh: C. Bertelsmann, 1905.
———. *Glaube, Theologie, und Kirche.* Tübingen, 1902.

Grotius, Hugo. *De veritate religionis christianae.* Amsterdam: Elzeviriana, 1662.
———. *Votum pro pace ecclesiae.* Paris, 1642.

Gruber, Hermann. *Auguste Comte: Der Begründer des Positivismus.* Freiburg i.B.: Herder, 1889.

Grundlehner, *Johannes Damascenus.* Utrecht: Kemink & Zoon, 1876.

Grung, Franz. *Das Problem der Gewissheit.* Heidelberg: Weisee, 1886.

Grützmacher, Richard. H. *Modern-Positive Vorträge.* Leipzig: A. Deichert, 1906.
———. *Die Religionsgeschichte eine Zeugin für die Wahrheit des Christentums.* Hamburg: G. Schlössman, 1902.
———. *Studien zur systematische Theologie.* 3 vols. Leipzig: A. Deichert, 1905–9.
———. *Wort und Geist.* Leipzig: A. Deichert, 1902.

Guinness-Rogers, J. *Present-Day Religion and Theology.* London, 1888.

Gunkel, Hermann. *Das Alte Testament im Licht der modernen Forschung.* München: J. F. Lehmanns Verlag, 1905.
———. *Zum religionsgeschichtlichen Verständnis des Neuen Testaments.* Göttingen: Vandenhoeck & Ruprecht, 1903.

Gunning, Johannes. H. *Blikken in de Openbaring.* Amsterdam: Höveker, 1866–69.
———. Introduction to *Christus en Natuurwet: Acht Voordrachten van Fred. Temple.* Haarlem, 1887.
———. *Overlevering en Wetenschap.* Gravenhage: W. A. Beschoor, 1879.

Gunning, J. H., and Chantepie de la Saussaye. *Het Ethische Beginsel der Theologie.* Groningen, 1877.

Gutberlet, C. *Lehrbuch der Apologetik.* 3 vols. Munster: Theissing'schen, 1888–94.
———. *Der Mensch: Sein Ursprung und seine Entwicklung.* Paderhorn: Schöningh, 1903.

Haack, Ernst. *Die Autorität der Heilige Schrift, ihr wesen und ihre Begründung.* Schwerin, 1899.
———. *Die Modernen Bemühungen um eine Zukunftreligion.* Leipzig, 1903.

———. *Über Wesen und Bedeutung der christliche Erfahrung.* Schwerin: Fr. Bahn, 1894.

Haeckel, Ernst Heinrich Philipp August. *Der Monismus als Band zwischen Religion und Wissenschaft.* 6th ed. Bonn: Verlag von Emil Strauss, 1893.

———. *The Riddle of the Universe.* Revised by E. R. Lankester. 2 vols. New York: Appleton, 1883.

———. *The Wonders of Life.* New York: Harper, 1904.

Hagenbach, Karl Rudolf. *Encyclopaedie und methodologie der theologischen Wissenschaften.* Leipzig: Weidmann'sche Buchhandlung, 1833.

———. *Kirchengeschichte in Vortesungen.* 3d ed. Leipzig: S. Hirzel, 1886.

———. *A Text-Book of the History of Doctrines.* Translated by C. W. Buch. Rev. ed. 2 vols. New York: Sheldon, 1867.

———. *Über die sogenannte Vermittelungstheologie.* Zürich: Meyer & Zeller, 1858.

Hahn, C. U. *Geschichte der Ketzer im Mittelalter.* Stuttgart: J. F. Steinkopf, 1845.

Hahn, W. *Die Entstehung der Weltkörper.* Regensburg: Pustet, 1895.

Hake, P. *Handbuch der allgemeine Religionswissenschaft.* Freiburg i.B.: Herder, 1875–87.

Haldane, Robert. *The Books of the Old and New Testaments Proved to Be Canonical.* Edinburgh; London: W. Whyte, T. Hamilton & Co., 1830.

———. *The Verbal Inspiration of the Old and New Testaments.* Edinburgh: T. & T. Clark, 1830.

Hall, Christopher Alan. "John Chrysostom's On Providence," Translation and theological interpretation. Ph.D. diss., Drew University, 1991.

Hamerling, Robert. *Ahasver in Rome: Eine Dichtung in sechs Gesängen; mit einen Epilog an die Kritiker.* Hamburg: J. F. Richter, 1890–99.

Hampden, R. D. *The Scholastic Philosophy Considered in Its Relation to Christian Theology.* London: Simpkin, Marshall, 1832.

Haneberg, Daniel. *Versuch einer Geschichte der biblischen Offenbarung als Einleitung in's alte und neue Testament.* Regensburg: G. Joseph Manz, 1850.

Hardeland, Theodor. *Die Heilsarmee nach Geschichte, Wesen und Wert.* Stuttgart: Belser, 1898.

Hardouin, Jean, ed. *Acta conciliorum et epistolae decretales.* 12 vols. Paris, 1714–15.

———. *Conciliorum cellectio regia maxima.* Paris, 1714.

Häring, Theodor. *The Christian Faith.* 2 vols. Translated by John Dickie and George Ferries. London: Hodder and Stoughton, 1913.

Harnack, Adolf von. *Das Apostolische Glaubenskenntnis.* Berlin: A. Haack, 1892.

———. *Die Aufgabe der theologischen Facultäten und die Allgemeine Religionsgeschichte.* Berlin: G. Schade, 1901.

———. *Geschichte der altchristlichen Literatur bis Eusebius.* Leipzig: J. C. Hinrichs, 1897–1904.

———. *History of Dogma.* Translated by N. Buchanan, J. Millar, E. B. Speirs, and W. McGilchrist and edited by A. B. Bruce. 7 vols. London: Williams & Norgate, 1896–99.

———. *Lehrbuch der dogmengeschichte.* Frieburg i. B. und Leipzig: Mohr, 1894.

———. *The Mission and Expansion of Christianity in the First Three Centuries.* Translated by James Moffat. London: Williams and Northgate, 1908. Reprinted, New York: Harper Torchbooks, 1961.

———. *What Is Christianity?* Translated by Thomas Bailey Saunders. New York: Harper & Brothers, 1957.

———. *Zur gegenwärtigen Lage des Protestantismus.* Leipzig: Fr. Wilh. Grunow, 1896.

Harnack, Th. *Luthers Theologie.* 2 vols. Erlangen: T. Blaesing, 1862–66. Reprinted, Amsterdam: Editions Rodopi, 1969.

Hartmann, Eduard von. *Eduard von Hartmann's ausgewählte Werke.* 3d ed. 13 vols. Bad Sachsa im Harz: H. Haacke, 1907.

———. *Gesammelte Studien und Aufsätze.* Leipzig: Friedrich, 1891.

———. *Die Krisis des Christenthums in der modernen Theologie.* Berlin: C. Duncker, 1880.

———. *Kristische Grundlegung des transcendentalen Realismus.* Leipzig: Hermann Haacke, 1885.

————. *Neukanntianismus, Schopenhauerianismus, und Hegelianismus in ihrer Stellung zu den philosophischen Aufgaben der Gegenwart.* Berlin: C. Duncker, 1877.

————. *Die Religion des Geistes.* 2d ed. Leipzig: W. Friedrich, 1889.

————. *Religionsphilosophie.* 2d ed. 2 vols. Bad Sachsa im Harz: Hermann Haacke, 1907.

Hartog, A. H. de. *De Historische Critiek en het Geloof der Gemeente.* Groningen: J. B. Wolters, 1905.

Hase, Karl A. von. *Evangelische Dogmatik.* Leipzig: Breitkopf und Härtel, 1860.

————. *Hutterus Redivius.* Helsingfors: A. W. Gröndahl, 1846.

————. *Das Leben Jesu.* Leipzig: Breitkopf und Härtel, 1853.

————. *Life of Jesus.* Translated by James Freeman Clark. Boston: Walker, Wise, 1860.

————. *Protestantische Polemik.* 5th ed. Leipzig: Breitkopf und Härtel, 1891.

Hastie, William. *The Theology of the Reformed Church in Its Fundamental Principles.* Edinburgh: T. & T. Clark, 1904.

Hatch, Edwin. *The Influence of Greek Ideas and Usages upon the Christian Church.* Translated by A. M. Fairbairn. London: Williams and Norgate, 1898.

————. *The Organization of the Early Christian Churches.* London: Rivingtons, 1881.

Haug, Karl. *Die Autorität der heilige Schrift und die Kritik.* Strassburg: Strabburger Druckerei und Verlagsanstalt, 1891.

Haug, Ludwig von. *Darstellung und Beurtheilung der Ritschl'schen Theologie.* Stuttgart: D. G. Bundert, 1895.

Haupt, Erich. *Die alttestamentlichen Citate in den vier Evangelien.* Colberg; London: Carl Jancke; Williams & Norgate, 1871.

————. *Die Bedeutung der Heiligen Schrift für den evangelischen Christen.* Bielefeld, Leipzig: Velhagen & Klasing, 1891.

Hauréau, B. *De la philosophie scolastique.* 2 vols. Paris: Pagnerre, 1850.

Hävernick, Heinrich Andreas Christoph; Carl Friedrich Kiel. *Handbuch der historisch-kritischen Einleitung in das Alte Testament.* Frankfurt a. M.: Heyder und Zimmer, 1849.

Heard, J. B. *Alexandrian and Carthaginian Theology.* Edinburgh: T. & T. Clark, 1893.

Hecker, I. T. *The Church and the Age: An Exposition of the Catholic Church in View of the Needs and Aspirations of the Present Age.* New York: Catholic World, 1887.

Hefele, Karl Joseph von. *Conciliengeschichte.* 9 vols. Freiburg i.B.: Herder, 1855–90.

Hegel, Georg Wilhelm Friedrich. *The Encyclopaedia of Logic (with the Zusätze).* Translated by T. F. Geraets et al. Indianapolis and Cambridge: Hackett, 1991.

————. *Lectures on the Philosophy of Religion.* Translated by E. B. Spiers and J. Burdon Sanderson. 3 vols. London: Kegan Paul, Trench, Trübner & Co., 1895.

————. *Philosophy of Nature.* Translated by M. J. Petry. London and New York: Allen Unwin, Humanities Press, 1970.

————. *Sämtliche Werke.* 26 vols. Stuttgart: F. Frommann, 1949–59.

Hegler, A. *Geist und Schrift bei Sebastian Franck.* Freiburg i.B.: J. C. B. Mohr, 1892.

Heidegger, Johann Heinrich. *Corpus Theologiae Christianae.* 2 vols. Zurich: J. H. Bodmer, 1700.

————. *De Libertate Christianorum a lege cibaria veteri.* 2d ed. Zürich: Gessner, 1678.

Heijmans, G. *Schets eener Kritische Geschiedenis van het Causalititsbegrip in de Nieuwere Wysbegeerte.* Leiden: Brill, 1890.

Heine, Gerhard. *Das Wesen der religiösen Erfahrung.* Leipzig: E. Haberland, 1900.

Heinrich, Joann Baptist, and Constantin Gutberlet. *Dogmatische Theologie.* 10 vols. 2d ed. Mainz: Kirchheim, 1881–1900.

Heinrici, C. F. Georg. *Durfen wir noch christen bleiben?* Leipzig: Dürr, 1901.

————. *Theologie und Religionswissenschaft.* Leipzig: Dürr, 1902.

Hellwald, Friedrich von. *Kulturgeschichte in ihrer natürlichen Entwickelung bis zur Gegenwart.* 4 vols. Leipzig: Friesenhahn, 1896–98.

Helvetic Confessions (I and II). In vol. 3 of *The Creeds of Christendom,* edited by Philip Schaff and revised by David S.

Schaff. 6th ed. 1919. Reprinted, Grand
Rapids: Baker, 1983.

Heman, Karl F. *Über wissenschaftliche Versuche neuer Religionsbildungen.* Basel: C.
Detloff, 1884.

———. *Der Ursprung der Religion.* Basel: C.
Detloff's Buchhandlung, 1886.

Henderson, E. *Divine Inspiration.* London:
Jackson and Walford, 1836.

Hengstenberg, Ernst Wilhelm. *Christologie
des Alten Testamentes und Commentar über
die messianischen Weissagungen.* 2d ed. 3
vols. Berlin: L. Oehmigke, 1854–57.

Henning, Max. *A. E. Biedermanns Psychologie
der religiösen Erkenntnis.* Leipzig: J. B.
Hirschfeld, 1902.

Heppe, Heinrich. *Dogmatik der evangelischen
reformierten Kirche.* Elberseld: R. L.
Friedrich, 1861.

———. *Dogmatik des deutschen Protestantismus im sechzehnten Jahrhundert.* 3 vols.
Gotha: F. A. Perthes, 1857.

———. *Reformed Dogmatics: Set Out and Illustrated from the Sources.* Revised and edited by Ernst Bizer. Translated by G. T.
Thomson. Grand Rapids: Baker, 1978
[1950].

Heringa, Jodocus. *De twistzaak van den hoogleeraar Johannes Maccovius.* Leyden,
1831.

Herrmann, Wilhelm. *Die Bedeutung der inspirationslehre für die evangelischen kirche.*
Halle: Niemeyer, 1882.

———. *The Communion of the Christian
with God.* Translated by J. Sandys Stanyon. 2d ed. revised by R. Wallace Stewart. New York: G. P. Putnam's Sons,
1906.

———. *Der evangelische Glaube und die
Theologie Albrecht Ritschls Rektoratsrede*
Marburg: N. G. Elwert, 1890.

———. *Faith and Morals.* Translated by
Donald Matheson and Robert W. Stewart. New York: G. P. Putnam's Sons,
1904.

———. *Die Gewissheit des Glaubens.* 2d ed.
Freiburg: J. C. B. Mohr, 1899.

———. *Die Religion in Verhältniss zum Welterkennen und zur Sittlichkeit.* Halle: M.
Niemeyer, 1879.

———. *Römische-katholische und evangelische Sittlichleeit.* Marburg: N. G. Elwert,
1900.

———. *Die Verkehr das Christen mit Gott.*
4th ed. Stuttgart: Cotta, 1903.

Hertling, Georg. *Das Princip des Katholizismus und die Wissenschaft.* 4th ed. Freiburg
im B. and St. Louis: Herder, 1899.

Herzog, J. J., and Philip Schaff. *Encyclopedia
of Living Divines and Christian Denominations in Europe and America.* New York:
Funk & Wagnalls, 1887.

Heymans, Gerard. *Schets eener Kritische Geschiedenis van het Causaliteitsbegrip in de
Nieuwere Wijsbegeerte.* Leiden: Brill,
1890.

Hildebrand (N. Beets). *Dichtwerken.* Leiden:
A. W. Sijthoff, 1885.

Hilgenfeld, Adolf. *Novum Testamentum extra
canonem receptum.* Leipzig: T. O. Weigel,
1866.

———. *Oud Christelijke Letterkunde: De
Geschriften der Apostolische Vaders.* Translated by A. C. Duker and W. C. van
Manen. 2 vols. Amsterdam: C. L. Brinkman, 1869–71.

Hodge, A. A. *Evangelical Theology.* London:
T. Nelson, 1890.

———. *Outlines of Theology.* Edited by
W. H. Goold. London: T. Nelson &
Sons, 1867.

Hodge, Charles. *Systematic Theology.* 3 vols.
New York: Charles Scribner's Sons, 1888.

Hoekstra, Sytse. *Bronnen en Grondslagen van
het Godsdienstig Geloof.* Amsterdam: P. N.
van Kampen, 1864.

———. *Godgeleerde Bijdragen.* Amsterdam:
Van Kampen, 1864.

———. *Godsdienst en Kunst.* Amsterdam:
J. C. B. Mohr, 1859.

———. *Grondslag, Wezen en Openbaring
van het Godsdienstig Geloof.* Rotterdam:
Altmann & Roosenburg, 1861.

———. *Wijsgerige Godsdienstleer.* Amsterdam: Van Kampen, 1894–95.

Hoeven, Abraham des Amorie van der, Jr. *De
Godsdienst het wezen van den mensch.*
Leeuwarden: G. T. N. Suringar, 1857.

Hoffmann, Georg. *Die Lehre von der Fides
Implicita.* Leipzig: Hinrichs, 1903–9.

Hoffmann, Immanuel. *Demostratio evangelica per ipsum scripturarum concensum in
oraculis ex Vet. testamento in novo allegatis
declarata.* 3 vols. Tübingen: Georgii Henrici Reisil, 1773–81.

Hofmann, Johann Christian Konrad von. *Der Schriftbeweis.* 3 vols. Nördlingen: Beck, 1857–60.

———. *Weissagung und Erfüllung im alte und neue Testament.* 2 vols. Nördlinger: C. H. Beck, 1841.

———. *Weissagung und Versöhnung.* Bonn: A. Marcus, 1882–83.

Hofmann, Rudolf Hugo. *Symboliek of Stelselmatige Uiteenzetting van het Onderscheidene Christelijke Kerkgenootschappen en Voornaamste Sekten.* Utrecht: Kemink en Zoon, 1861.

Hollaz, David. *Examen Theologicum Acroamaticum.* Rostock and Leipzig: Russworm, 1718.

Hölscher, Gustav. *Kanonisch und Apokryph: Ein Kapitel aus der Geschichte des alttestamentlichen Kanons.* Leipzig: A. Deichert, 1905.

Holtzmann, H. J. *Kanon und Tradition.* Ludwigsberg, 1859.

———. *Rothe's Speculatives System.* Freiburg i.B.: J. C. B. Mohr, 1899.

Holzhey, Carl. *Die Inspiration der Heiligen Schrift in der Anschauung des Mittelalters.* München: J. J. Lentner, 1895.

———. *Schöpfung, Bibel und Inspiration.* Mergentheim: Carl Ohlinger, 1902.

Homer. *The Odyssey.* Translated by W. H. D. Rouse. New York: Thomas Nelson, 1937.

Hoornbeeck, Johannes. *Disputatio theologica practica.* 1659–61.

———. *Socianismi confutati.* Utrecht: Johannis á Waesberg, 1650–54.

———. *Summa controversiarum religionis, cum infidelibus, haereticis et schismaticis.* Utrecht: J. à Waesberge, 1658.

*Hooykaas, I. *God in de Geschiedenis.* 1870.

———. *Godsdienst Volgens de Beginselen der Ethische Richting Onder de Modernen.* 's Hertogenbosch: G. H. van der Schuyt, 1876.

Höpfi, H. *Die Höhere Bibelkritik.* Paderborn: Schöningh, 1902.

Horne, Thomas H. *An Introduction to the Critical Study and Knowledge of the Holy Scriptures.* 4 vols. London: Printed for T. Cadell, 1821.

Horton, Robert. F. *Inspiration and the Bible.* 8th ed. London: T. Fisher Unwin, 1906.

Houtin, Albert. *L'Americanisme.* Paris: E. Nourry, 1904.

———. *La question biblique chez les catholiques de France au XIXe siècle.* Paris: A. Picard, 1902.

Houtsma, M. Th. *De strijd over het dogma in den Islam tot op el-Ash'ari.* Leiden: S. C. van Doesburgh, 1875.

Höveler, P. *Professor A. Harnack und die katholische Ascese.* Düsseldorf: L. Schwann, 1902.

Hugenholtz, P. H. *Ethisch Pantheisme.* Amsterdam: Van Holkema & Warendorff, 1903.

———. *Studiën op Godsdienstlijk en Zedekundig Gebied.* 3 vols. Amsterdam, 1884.

———, ed. *Religion and Liberty.* Leiden: Brill, 1904.

Hugh of St. Victor. *De Sacramentis christianae fidei.* In *PL* 176, cols. 173–618.

———. *Summa sententiarum septem tractatibus distincta.* In *PL* 176, cols. 41–174.

Hugo Grotius. *De Veritate religio Christ.* 1627.

Hulsman, G. *Moderne Wetenschap of Bijbelsche Traditie?* Utrecht: Kemink, 1897.

Hummelauer, F. von. *Exegetisches zur Inspirationsfrage.* Freiburg i.B. and St. Louis, Mo.: Herder, 1904.

Hundeshagen, Karl Bernard. *Die Conflikte des Zwinglianismus, Lutherthums und Calvinismus in der bernischen Landeskirche von 1532–1558.* Bern: C. A. Jenni, 1842.

Hundeshagen, Karl Bernard, and M. Schneckenburger. *Vorlesungen über die Lehrbegriffe des kleineren Protestantischen Kirchenparteien.* Frankfurt a.M.: H. L. Brönner, 1863.

Hunt, John. *Religious Thought in England in the Nineteenth Century.* London: Gibbings & Co., 1896.

Hurter, Hugo. *Nomenclator literarius recentioris theologiae catholicae.* 4 vols. Innsbruck: Libraria Academica Wagneriana, 1871–86.

Hyperius, Andreas. *Methodi theologiae, sive praecipuorum Christianae religionis locurum communium libri tres jam demum diligenter recogniti.* Basel: Oporiniana, 1574.

Ihmels, L. *Die Bedeutung des Autoritätsglaubens.* Leipzig: Diechert, 1902.

———. *Die Christliche Wahrheitsgewissheit ihr letzter Grund und ihre Entsehung.* Leipzig: A. Deichert, 1901.

―――. *Die Selbständigkeit der Dogmatik gegenüber der Religionsphilosophie.* Erlangen: Deichert, 1901.

Irenaeus. *Against Heresies. ANF,* I, 309–567.

―――. *Sancti Irenaei episcopi lugdunensis Quae supersunt omnia.* Edited by Adolphus Stieren. Leipzig: T. O. Weigel, 1853–58.

Isidore of Seville. *Etymologies.* Edited by W. M. Lindsay. 2 vols. Oxford, 1911.

Jacobi, J. L. *Die Kirchliche Lehre von der Tradition und heiligen Schrift.* Berlin: Luderitz, 1847.

James, William. *The Varieties of Religious Experience.* London; New York: Longmans Green, 1904.

―――. *The Will to Believe and Other Essays in Popular Philosophy.* Cambridge, Mass.: Harvard University Press, 1979. German edition: *Der Wille zum Glauben: Und andere popularphilosophische Essays.* Translated by Th. Lorenz. Stuttgart: Fr. Frommanns Verlag (E. Hauff), 1899.

Janet, Paul. *La Morale.* Paris: C. Delagrave, 1874.

―――. *The Theory of Morals.* Translated by Mary Chapman. New York: Scribner, 1883.

―――. *Traité élémentaire de philosophie á l'usage des classes.* Paris: C. Delagrave, 1887.

Janet, Paul, and Gabriel Séailles. *Histoire de la philosophie.* Paris: Ch. Delagrave, 1887.

Jansen, G. M. *Praelectiones Theologiae Fundamentalis.* 4 vols. Utrecht: J. R. van Rossum 1875–77.

―――. *Theologia Dogmatica Specialis.* Utrecht, 1877–79.

Janssen, Johannes. *Geschichte des deutschen Volkes seit dem Ausgang des Mittelalters.* 8 vols. Freiburg i.B.: Herder, 1883–1901.

Jeremias, A. *Monotheistische Strömungen innergalp der babylonischen Religion.* Leipzig: J. C. Hinrichs, 1904.

Jessen, E. A. F. *Die Hauptströmungen des religiösen Lebens der Jetztzeit in Dänemark.* Gütersloh: Bertelsmann, 1895.

John of Damascus. *Exposition of the Orthodox Faith. NPNF (2),* IX, 259–360. In *Writings, The Fathers of the Church.* Washington, D.C.: Catholic University of America Press, 1958.

―――. *Three Apologies against Those Who Attack the Divine Images.* Crestwood, N.Y.: St. Vladimir's Seminary Press, 1980.

Jones, Spencer. *England and the Holy See.* London: Longmans, Green & Co. 1902.

Josephus, Flavius. *Des Flavius Josephus Schrift gegen den Aipon.* Edited by J. G. Müller. Basel: Bahnmaier, 1877.

―――. *The Works of Josephus.* Translated by William Whiston. New updated ed. Peabody, Mass.: Hendrickson, 1987.

Junius, Franciscus. *Opuscula Theologica Selecta.* Edited by Abraham Kuyper. Amsterdam: F. Muller, 1882.

―――. *Theses Theologicae.* In vol. 1 of *Opuscula.*

Justin Martyr. *Dialogue with Trypho. ANF,* I, 194–270.

―――. *Loci Aliquot Selecti.* Zürich: Schulthess, 1824.

―――. *Discourse to the Greeks. ANF,* I, 271–73.

―――. *The First and Second Apologies. ANF,* I, 163–93.

Kaftan, Julius. *Dogmatik.* Tübingen: Mohr, 1901.

―――. *Glaube und Dogma: Betrachtungen über Dreyers undogmatisches Christentum.* Bielefeld: Velhagen & Klasing, 1889.

―――. *The Truth of the Christian Religion.* 2 vols. Translated by George Ferries. Edinburgh: T. & T. Clark, 1894.

―――. *Zur Dogmatik: Sieben Abhandlungen aus der "Zeitschrift für Theologie und Kirche."* Tübingen: Mohr (Paul Siebeck), 1904.

Kaftan, Theodor. *Moderne Theologie des alten Glaubens.* Schleswig: Julias Bergas, 1906.

―――. *Vier Kapitel von der Landeskirche.* Schleswig: J. Bergas, 1907.

Kähler, Martin. *Jesus und das Alte Testament.* Leipzig: A. Deichert, 1896.

―――. *Die Wissenschaft der Christlichen Lehre von dem evangelischen Grundartikel aus.* Leipzig: A. Deichert, 1905.

Kahnis, Friedrich August. *Die Luthersche Dogmatik, historisch-genetisch dargestellt.* 3 vols. Leipzig: Dörffling & Francke, 1861–68.

Kahnis, K. F. *Internal History of German Protestantism.* Translated by T. Meyer. Edinburgh: T. & T. Clark; Philadelphia: Smith & English, 1856.

Kalb, Ernst. *Kirchen und Sekten der Gegenwart, unter Mitarbeit verschiedener evangelischer Theologen.* 2d ed. Stuttgart: Verlag für Buchhandlung der Evangelische Gesellschaft, 1907.

Kant, Immanuel. *Critique of Practical Reason.* Translated by Mary Gregor. Cambridge: University Press, 1997.

———. *Critique of Pure Reason.* Translated by Norman Kemp Smith. New York: St. Martin's Press, 1965 [1929].

———. *Religion within the Limits of Reason Alone.* Translated by Theodore M. Greene and Hoyt H. Hudson. New York: Harper and Brothers, 1934.

Kattenbusch, F. *Confessions Kunde.* Freiburg i.B.: J. C. B. Mohr, 1892.

———. *Lehrbuch der vergleichenden Confessionskunde.* Vol. 1. Freiburg i.B.: J. C. B. Mohr (Paul Siebeck), 1894.

———. *Über religiöse Glauben in Sinne des Christenthum.* Giessen: C. v. Münchow, 1887.

———. *Von Schleiermacher zu Ritschl.* Giessen: J. Ricker, 1892.

Kautzsch, E. *De Veteris Testamenti locis a Paulo Apostolo allegatis.* Leipzig: Metzger & Wittig, 1869.

Keckerman, B. *Systema sacrosanctae theologiae.* Heidelberg, 1602; Geneva, 1611.

Keerl, P. F. *Die Lehre des Neuen Testaments von der Herrlichkeit Gottes.* Basel: Bahnmaier, 1863.

Keil, Carl Friedrich. *Manual of Biblical Archaeology.* Translated by A. Cusin. 2 vols. Edinburgh: T. & T. Clark, 1887–88.

———. *Manual of Historical-Critical Introduction to the Canonical Scriptures of the Old Testament.* Translated by G. C. M. Douglas. 2 vols. Edinburgh: T. & T. Clark, 1869. Reprinted as, *Introduction to the Old Testament.* Peabody, Mass.: Hendrickson, 1988.

Keller, Ludwig. *Geschichte der Wiedertäufer und ihres Reichs zu Münster.* Münster: Coppenrath, 1880.

———. *Die Reformation und die älteren Reformparteien in ihrem Zusammenhange.* Leipzig: S. Hirzel, 1885.

Kellner, K. A. *Christianity and the Leaders of Modern Science.* Translated by T. M. Ket-

tle. Fraser, Mich.: Real-View Books, 1995 [1911].

———. *Hellenismus und Christenthum.* Köln: M. DuMont-Schauberg, 1866.

Kihn, H. *Encyklopädie und Methodologie der Theologie.* Freiburg im B.: Herder, 1892.

Kimmel, Ernst Julius. *Monumenta fidei ecclesiae Orientalis.* 2 vols. Jenae: F. Mauke, 1850.

Kirn, Otto. *Glaube und Geschichte.* Leipzig: A Edelmann, 1901.

Kittel, Rudolf. *Profetie und Weissagung.* Leipzig: J. C. Hinrichs, 1899.

Klee, Heinrich. *Katholische Dogmatik.* 2d ed. Mainz: Kirchheim, 1861.

Kleutgen, Joseph. *Beilagen zu den Werken über die Theologie und Philosophie der Vorzeit.* Münster: Theissing, 1868.

———. *Philosophie der Vorzeit.* 2 vols. Münster: Theissing, 1863.

———. *Die Theologie der Vorzeit.* 2d ed. 5 vols. Münster: Theissing, 1867–74.

Kleyn, H. G. *Jacobus Baradaeüs: de stichter Syrische Monophysietische Kerk.* Leiden: Brill, 1882.

Kling, Christian Friedrich. *Descriptio Summae theologicae Thomae Aquinatis Succincta.* Bonn: Litteris Georgianis, 1846.

Klosterman, Erich. *Jesu Stellung zum Alte Testament.* Kiel: Robert Cordes, 1904.

Klostermann, August, et. al. *Die Bebelfrage in der Gegenwart: fünf Vorträge.* Berlin: Fr. Zillesen, 1905.

Knapp, G. C. *Glaubenslehre.* 12 vols. Halle: G. C. Knapp, 1840.

Kneller, Karl Alois. *Christianity and the Leaders of Modern Science.* Translated by T. M. Kettle. London, St. Louis: B. Herder, 1911. Reprinted, Fraser, Mich.: Real-View Books, 1995.

Knie, F. *Die Russisch-schismatische Kirche: Ihr Lehre und ihr Cult.* Graz: Verlagsbuchhandlung Styria, 1894.

Knopf, Rudof. *Das nachapostolische Zeitalter: Geschichte der christlichen Gemeinden vom Beginn der Flavierdynastie bis zum Ende Hadrians.* Tübingen: J. C. B. Mohr (P. Siebeck), 1905.

Knuze, Johannes. *Glaubensregel, Heilige Schrift und Taufbekenntnis Untersuchungen über diedogmatische Autorität, ihr Werden und ihre Geschichte, vornehmlich in der alten Kirche.* Leipzig: Dörffling & Franke, 1899.

Köberle, Justus. *Natur und Geist nach der Auffassung des Alten Testaments.* München: C. H. Beck, 1901.

Koch, Anton. *Lehrbuch der Moraltheologie.* Freiburg i.B.: Herder, 1905.

Koch, Hugo. *Pseudodionysius Areopagita in seinen Beziehungen zum Neuplatonismus und Mysterienwesen eine litterarhistorische Untersuchung.* Maniz: F. Kirchheim, 1900.

———. *Die Theologie der Vorzeit vertheidigt.* 2d ed. 5 vols. Münster: Theissing, 1867–74.

Koenig, Edmund. *Die Entwicklung des Causalproblems.* 2 vols. Leipzig: Wigand, 1888–90.

Köhler, August. *Über Berechtigung der Kritik des alten Testaments.* Erlangen: A. Deichert, 1895.

Kolde, T. *Die Heilsarmee (The Salvation Army): Ihre Geschichte und ihr Wesen.* Erlangen: A. Deichert, 1899.

———. *Die Kirchliche Bruderschaften und das religiose Leben im Moderne Katholismus.* Erlangen: F. Junge, 1895.

———. *Der Methodismus und seine Bekämpfung.* Erlangen: A. Deichert, 1886.

Kölling, Wilhelm. *Die Lehre von der Theopneustie.* Breslau: C. Dülfer, 1891.

König, Eduard. *Das Berusungsbewusstsein der alttestamentlichen Propheten.* Barmen: Wupperthaler Traktat Gesellschaft, 1900.

———. *Der Glaubensact des Christen nach Begriff und Fundament.* Erlangen und Leipzig: G. Böhme, 1891.

———. *Die Hautprobleme der altisraelitischen Religionsgeschichte.* Leipzig: J. C. Hinrichs, 1884.

———. *Die letzte Instanz der biblischen Glaubens.* Leipzig: J. C. Hinrichs, 1892.

———. *Der Offenbarungsbegriff des Alten Testamentes.* 2 vols. Leipzig: J. C. Hinrichs, 1882.

Köstlin, Julius. *Die Begründung unserer sittlich-religiosen Überzeugung.* Berlin: Reuther & Reichard, 1893.

———. *Der Glaube und seine Bedeutung für Erkenntnis, Leben, und Kirche.* Berlin: Reuther & Reichard, 1895.

———. *Religion und Reich Gottes: Abhandlungen zur Dogmatik und Ethik.* Gotha: F. A. Perthes, 1894.

———. *Theology of Luther in Its Historical Development and Inner Harmony.* Translated by Charles E. Hay. 2 vols. Philadelphia: Lutheran Publication Society, 1897.

*Kranich. *Über die Empfänglichkeit der menschlichen Natur für die Güter der übernaturlichen Ordnung nach der Lehre des h. Augustijn und das h. Thomas.* Paderborn.

Krauss, Alfred Ed. *Die Lehre von der Offenbarung.* Gotha: F. A. Perthes, 1868.

Kreyher, J. *Die mystischen Erscheinungen des Seelenlebens und die biblischen Wunder: Ein apologetischer Versuch.* Stuttgart: J. F. Seinkopf, 1880.

Kropatscheck, Friedrich. *Das Schriftprinzip der lutherischen Kirche.* Leipzig: A. Deichert, 1904.

Krüger, Gustav. *Geschichte der altchristlichen Litteratur in den ersten drei Jahrhunderten.* Freiburg i.B.: Mohr, 1895.

Krumbacher, Karl. *Geschichte der byzantinischen Litteratur.* München: Beck, 1891.

Kübel, Robert Benjamin. *Das christlichen Lehrsystem nach der Heiligen Schrift.* Stuttgart: J. F. Steinkopf, 1873.

———. *Über den Unterschied zwischen der positiven und der liberalen Richtung in der modernen Theologie.* 2d ed. München: C. H. Beck, 1893.

Kuenen, Abraham. *Historisch-Critische Onderzoek naar het ontstaan en de verzameling van de boken des Ouden Verbonds.* 3 vols. Leiden: P. Engels en zoon, 1885, 1893.

———. *The Prophets and Prophecy in Israel.* Translated by Adam Milroy. London, 1877. Reprinted, Amsterdam: Philo, 1969.

———. *The Religion of Israel to the Fall of the Jewish State.* Translated by A. H. May. 3 vols. London: Williams and Norgate, 1874, 1875.

Kuhn, Johannes von. *Einleitung in die Katholische Dogmatik.* 9 vols. Tubingen: Laupp and Siebeck, 1859.

Külpe, Oswald. *Introduction to Philosophy: A Handbook for Students of Psychology, Logic, Ethics, Aesthetics, and General Philosophy.* London: S. Sonnenschein & Co.; New York: Macmillan Co., 1901.

Kunze, Johannes. *Glaubensregel, Heilige Schrift und Taufbekenntnis.* Leipzig: Dörffling & Franke, 1899.

Küper. *Das Prophetenthum des alten Bundes.* Leipzig: Dörffling und Franke, 1870.

Kurtz, J. H. *Lehrbuch der Kirchliche Geschichte.* 2 vols. Leipzig: F. A. Brockhaus, 1885.

————. *Text-Book of Church History.* 2 vols. Philadelphia: Lippincott, 1886–90.

Kuyper, Abraham. *Het Calvinisme en de Kunst.* Amsterdam: J. A. Wormser, 1888.

————. *Encyclopaedie der Heilige Godgeheerdherd.* 3 vols. 2d ed. Kampen: Kok, 1908–9.

————. *De Gemeene Gratie.* 3 vols. Amsterdam: Höveker & Wormser, 1902–4.

————. *De Hedendaagsche Schriftkritiek.* Amsterdam: J. H. Kruyt, 1881.

————. *Openbaring en Rede.* Kampen: Kok, 1902.

————. *Principles of Sacred Theology.* Translated by J. Hendrik De Vries, 1898. Reprinted, Grand Rapids: Eerdmans, 1968.

————. *De Schrift het Woord Gods.* Tiel: H. C. A. Campagne, 1870.

————. *Uit het Woord.* 6 vols. Amsterdam: J. A. Wormser, 1880–89.

Kuyper, Abraham, Jr. *Johannes Maccovius.* Leiden: D. Donner, 1899.

Laas, Ernst. *Idealismus und Positivismus.* Berlin: Weidmann, 1879–84.

Lactantius, Lucius C. *The Divine Institutes.* Translated by Sister Mary Francis McDonald. Washington, D.C.: Catholic University of America Press, 1964.

————. *De Ira Dei.* 1543. Reprinted, Darmstadt: Gentner, 1957.

Ladd, George T. *The Philosophy of Religion.* 2 vols. New York: Scribner, 1905.

Lagarde, Paul de. *Ueber das Verhaltniss des Deutschen Staates zu Theologischen Kirche und Religion.* Göttingen: Dietrich, 1891.

Lagrange, Marie-Joseph. *La méthode historique surtout à propos de l'Ancien Testament.* Paris: Lecoffre, 1903.

Lamennais, Félicité Robert de. *Essay on Indifference in Matters of Religion.* Translated by Lord Stanley of Alderley. London: John Macqueen, 1895.

Lamers, G. H. *Godsdienst en Zedelijkheid.* Amsterdam, 1882.

————. *De Godsdienst evenmin Moraal als Metaphysica.* Amsterdam, 1885.

————. *De Wetenschap van de Godsdienst.* Utrecht: C. H. E. Breijer, 1891–93.

Lämmer, Hugo. *Die vortridentinisch-katholische Theologie des Reformations-Zeitalters.* Berlin: Schlawitz, 1858.

Land, J. P. N. *Inleiding tot de wijsbegeerte.* s'Gravenhage, Nijhoff, 1900.

Lange, Friedrich. A. *Geschichte des Materialismus und Kritik seiner Bedeutung in den Gegenwart.* 8th ed. Leipzig: Gaedeker, 1908.

Lange, Johann Peter. *Christliche Dogmatik.* 3 vols. Heidelberg: K. Winter, 1852.

————. *Philosophische Dogmatik.* Heidelberg: K. Winter, 1849.

Langen, Joseph. *Johannes von Damaskus: eine patristische Monographie.* Gotha: F. A. Perthes, 1879.

Lasch, G. A. *Die Theologie der Pariser Schule: Charakteristik und Kritik des Symbolo-Fideismus.* Berlin: C. A. Schwetschke, 1901.

Lechler, Gotthard Victor. *Das apostolische und das nach apostolische Zeitalter.* Karlsrube und Leipzig: H. Reuther, 1885.

————. *Geschichte des Englischen Deismus.* Stuttgart: J. G. Cotta, 1841.

Lecky, W. E. H. *Entstehungsgeschichte und Charackteristik des Methodismus aus dem England.* Leipzig, Heidelberg: C. F. Winter, 1880.

Leder, Hermann. *Untersuchungen über Augustins Erkenntnistheorie.* Marburg: N. G. Eltwert, 1901.

Lee, William. *The Inspiration of Holy Scripture.* 3d ed. Dublin: Hodges, Smith, and Co., 1864.

Leendertz. *Het Ethisch-evangelisch Standpunt en het Christelijke Geloof.* 1891.

Lehmann, A. G. L. *Aberglaube und Zauberei von den ältesten Zeiten an bis in die Gegenwart.* Stuttgart: F. Enke, 1898.

Lehmann, Fritz. *Die Katechetenschule zu Alexandria.* Leipzig: A. Lorentz, 1896.

Lehmkuhl, Augustin. *Theologia moralis.* 2 vols. Freiburg i.B.: Herder, 1898.

Leibnitz, Gottfried Wilhelm. *Discourse on the Conformity of Faith with Reason.*

————. *Nouveaux essays sur l'entendement humain.* Paris: C. H. Delagrave, 1886.

———. *Theodicy.* Translated by E. M. Huggard. Lasalle, Ill.: Open Court, 1985.

Lelièvre, Matth. *La maitrise de l'Esprit, essai critique sur le principe fundamental de la théologie de Calvin.* Paris: Cahors, Coveslant, 1901.

Lemme, Ludwig. *Christliche Apologetik.* Berlin: E. Runge, 1922.

———. *Religionsgeschichtliche Entwicklung oder göttliche Offenbarung.* Karlsruhe, 1904.

———. *Die Vertreter der systematischen Theologie.* Heidelberg: C. Winter, 1903.

Lequien, Michel. *Oriens Christianus.* 3 vols. Paris: ex Typographia regia, 1740.

Leroy-Beaulieu, Anatole. *The Empire of the Tsars and the Russians.* Translated from the 3d ed. by Zénaïde A. Ragozin. New York, London: G. P. Putnam, 1893–96.

———. *Die Macht der Religion, Kirche, Geistlichkeit und Sektenwezen im Russland.* Vol. 3 of *Das Reich des Czaren und der Russen.* Translated and edited by L. Pezold and J. Müller. Sondershausen, 1844–90.

Lessing, Gotthold Ephraim. *Die Erziehung des Menschengeschlechts.* Berlin: C. F. Voss und Sohn, 1780.

Leverett, F. P., ed. *A New and Copious Lexicon of the Latin Language; compiled chiefly from the Magnum totius latinitatis lexicon of Facciolati and Forcellini, and the German works of Scheller and Luenemann.* 2 vols. Boston: Wilkins, Carter, and Co., 1845.

Leydekker, Melchior. *Fax Veritatis, seu Exercitationes ad nonnullas Controversias quae Hodie in Belgio Potissium Moventur, Multa ex Parte Theologico-philosophicae.* Leiden: Daniel Gaesbeeck & Felicem Lopez, 1677.

———. *De veritate fidei reformatae, eiusdem sanctitate, Libri III: Sive commentarius ad catechesis Palatinian.* Utrecht, 1694.

Lezius, Friedrich. *Zur Charakteristik des Religiösen Standpunktes des Erasmus.* Gütersloh: C. Bertelsmann, 1895.

Liberatore, Matteo. *Die Erkenntniss-theorie des heiligen Thomas von Aquino.* Mainz: F. Kirchheim, 1861.

———. *Institutiones Philosophicae.* 8th ed. 3 vols. Rome: n.p., 1855.

Lichtenberger, F. A. *Historie des idées religieuses en Allemagne depuis le milieu du XVIIIe sièle jus gu'a nos jours.* 3 vols. Paris: Sandoz & Fischbacher, 1873.

Liebermann, Franz B. *Institutiones Theologicae.* 8th ed. 2 vols. Moguntiae: Sumptibus Francisci Kirchhemii, 1857.

Liebmann, Otto. *Zur Analysis der Wirklichkeit: Eine Erörterung der Grundprobleme der Philosophie.* 3d ed. Strassburg: K. J. Trübner, 1900.

Liechtenhan, R. *Die Offenbarung im Gnosticismus.* Gottingen: Vandenhoeck & Ruprecht, 1901.

Lightfoot, J. B. *The Apostolic Fathers: A Revised Text with Introductions, Notes, Dissertations, and Translations.* 2d ed. London and New York: Macmillan, 1889–90.

Limborch, Phillip van. *Theologia Christiana ad praxin pietatis ac promotionem pacis christianae unice directa.* Amsterdam: Wetstein, 1735.

———. *De Veritate religionis Christianae amica collatio cum erudito Judaeo.* Goudae: J. ab Hoeve, 1687.

Linde, Ernst. *Religion und Kunst.* Tübingen: J. C. B. Mohr, 1905.

Lindsay, James. *The Progressiveness of Modern Christian Thought.* Edinburgh: Blackwood, 1892.

Lipsius, F. R. *Kritik der theologische Erkenntnis.* Berlin: C. A. Schwetschke, 1904.

Lipsius, Richard Adelbert. *Die Hauptpunkte der Christliche Glaubenslehre.* Braunschweig: C. A. Schwetschke, 1889.

———. *Lehrbuch der Evangelisch-Protestantischen Dogmatik.* Braunschweig: C. A. Schwetschke, 1893.

———. *Philosophie und Religion.* Leipzig: Johann Ambrose Barth, 1885.

Lobstein, Paul. *Einleitung in die Evangelische Dogmatik.* Freiburg i.B.: J. C. B. Mohr, 1897.

———. *Zum evangelische Lebensideal in seiner lutersche und reformirte Ausprägung Theologische Abhandlung.* Tübingen, 1902.

Locher, J. C. S. *De Leer van Luther ouer Gods Woord.* Amsterdam: Scheffer, 1903.

Loescher, Valentin. *De Causa Linguae Ebraeae.* 1706.

Loisy, A. *Autour d'un petit livre*. Paris: A. Picard, 1903.

———. *Études bibliques*. Paris: A. Picard et fils, 1901.

———. *Evangelium und Kirche*. München: Kirchheim, 1904.

Lombard, Peter. *Sententiae in IV Liberis Distinctae*. 3d ed. 2 vols. Grottaferrata: Colleggi S. Bonaventurae et Claras Aquas, 1971–81.

Lommatzsch, Siegfried. *Luthers Lehre von ethische-religiöse Standpunkt*. Berlin: L. Schleiermacher, 1879.

Loofs, Friedrich. *Handboek voor de beofening van de dogmengeschiedenis*. Gronigen: J. B. Wolters, 1902.

Lord, Eleazer. *The Plenary Inspiration of the Holy Scriptures*. New York: A. D. F. Randolph, 1858.

Lorenz, Th. *Essays Deutsch*. Stuttgart, 1899.

Loserth, Johann. *Hus and Wiclif*. Translated by M. J. Evans. London: Hodder and Stoughton, 1884. Reprinted as, *Wiclif and Hus*. New York: AMS Press, 1980.

Lotz, Wilhelm. *Geschichte und Offenbarung im Alten Testament*. Leipzig: J. C. Hinrichs Buchhandlung, 1892.

Lotze, Hermann. *Microcosmus: An Essay concerning Man and His Relation to the World*. 2 vols. New York: Scribner and Welford, 1885.

Love, Christoph. *Theologia Practica*. 4th ed. Amsterdam: J. H. Boom, 1669.

Lucian of Samosata. *The Passing of Peregrinus*. Translated by A. M. Harmon. Loeb Classical Library, Lucian vol. 5. London: William Heinemann; Cambridge, Mass.: Harvard University Press, 1936.

Ludovices Vives. *De Veritate fidei Christi*. 1543.

Lüken, Heinrich. *Die Einheit des Menschengeschlichts und dessen Ausbreitung über die ganze Erde*. Hannover: Hahn, 1845.

Luthardt, Christoph Ernst. *Apologetische Vorträge uber die Grundwahrheiten des Christenthums*. 8th ed. Leipzig: Dörffling und Franke, 1878.

———. *Die Ethik Luthers: In ihren Grundzügen*. 2d ed. Leipzig: Dörffling & Franke, 1875.

———. *Geschichte der Christlichen Ethik*. Leipzig: Dörffling & Franke, 1888–93.

Luther, Martin. *Luther's Works*. Vol. 1, *Lectures on Genesis 1–3*. St. Louis: Concordia, 1958.

Lutz, Johann Ludwig Samuel. *Biblische Hermeneutik*. Pflorzheim: Flammer und Hoffmann, 1849.

Maccovius, Johannes. *Loci Communes Theologici*. Amsterdam: n.p., 1658.

Maistre, Joseph Marie de. *Du Pape, Oeuvres Choisies de Joseph de Maistre*. Paris: Hachette, 1890.

———. *The Pope*. Translated by Aeneas McD. Dawson. New York: H. Fertig, 1975.

Makari. *Geschichte der Dogmatik in russischer Darstellung*. Gutersloh: C. Bertelsmann, 1902.

———. *Handleitung zum Erlernen der Christliche rechtglaübigedogmatische Gottesgelhrtheit*. Translated by Blumenthal. 1875.

———. *Rechtglaübige dogmatische Gottesgelehrtheit*. 5 vols. St. Petersburg, 1849–53.

Mannens, Paulus. *Theologiae Dogmaticae Institutiones*. 3 vols. Roermond: Romen, 1910–15.

Mansi, Giovan Domenico, ed. *Sacrorum conciliorum nova et amplissima collectio*. 31 vols. Flor, 1759–98.

———. *Sacrorum conciliorum nova et amplissima collectio*. 60 vols. Graz: Akademische Druck, 1901. Reprinted, 1960.

Marck, Johannes à. *Het merch der Christene Got-geleertheit*. Rotterdam: P. Topyn, 1758.

Marckius, Johannes. *Compendium theologiae christianae didactico-elencticum*. Groningen: Fossema, 1686.

———. *Historia Paradisi*. Amsterdam: Gerardus Borstius, 1705.

Maresius, Samuel. *Collegium Theologicum sive Systema Breve Universae Theologiae Comprehensium Octodecim Disputationibus*. Groningen: Francisci Bronchorstii, 1659.

———. *Theologus paradoxus retectus et refutatus*. 1649.

Maronier, J. H. *Het Inwendige Woord*. Amsterdam: T. J. van Holkema, 1890.

Marsden, J. B. *The History of the Early Puritans: From the Reformation to the Opening of the Civil War in 1642*. London: Hamilton, Adams & Co., 1853.

————. *The History of the Later Puritans: From the Opening of the Civil War in 1642, to the Ejection of the Non-conforming Clergy in 1662.* London: Hamilton, Adams, & Co., 1854.

Marshall, Newton H. *Die gegenwärtigen Richtungen der Religionsphilosophie in England und ihre erkenntnistheoretischen Grundlagen.* Berlin: Reuther & Reichard, 1902.

Martensen, Hans Lassen. *Christian Dogmatics: A Compendium of the Doctrines of Chrisitianity.* Translated by William Urwick. Edinburgh: T. & T. Clark, 1871.

————. *Die Christliche Ethik.* 3d ed. Gotha: Besser, 1878.

Martineau, James. *The Seat of Authority in Religion.* London: Longmans, 1891.

Martius, Guilelmus. *Locus dogmaticus. de testimonium Spiritus Sancti historice et systematice explicatur.* 1875.

Mastricht, Peter van. *Theoretico-practica theologia.* Utrecht: Appels, 1714.

Maury, Léon. *La réveil religieux dans l'église réformée a Genève et en France.* 2 vols. Paris: Fischbacher, 1892.

Mausbach, Joseph. *Christentum und Weltmoral.* 2d ed. Münster i. W.: Aschendorff, 1905.

Maximus Confessor. *Selected Writings.* Translated by George C. Berthold. Classics of Western Spirituality. New York: Paulist Press, 1985.

Mayer, E. W. *Christentum und Kultur.* Berlin: Trowitzch, 1905.

————. *Über die Aufgaben der Dogmatik.* Tübingen: Mohr, 1902.

Meinhold, Johannes. *Jesus und das Alte Testament.* Freiburg i.B. and Leipzig: Mohr [Siebeck], 1896.

Melanchton, Philipp. *Die Loci Communes.* Translated by G. L. Plitt & Th. Kolde. Leipzig: A. Diechert, 1900.

————. *Philippi Melancthonis Loci Theologici.* Edited by Johann Christian Wilhelm Augusti. Lipsiae: Biblio polio Dykiano, 1821.

Ménégoz, Eugene. *L'autorité de Dieu, reflexions sur l'autorité en matière.* Paris: Fischbacher, 1892.

————. *La notion biblique du miracle.* Paris: Fischbacher, 1894.

————. *Publications diverses sur le fidéisme et son applicatin à l'enseignement chrétien traditionnel.* Paris: Fischbacher, 1900.

Meyer, Ph. *Die theologische Litteratur der griechischen Kirche im sechzenten Jahrhundert.* Leipzig: Deichert, 1899.

Michaelis, J. D. *Dogmatik.* 2d ed. 1784.

Michalcescu, Jon. *Darlegung und Kritik der Religionsphilosophie Sabatiers.* Bern: Scheitlin, Spring & Cie., 1903.

Middleton, Conyers. *A Free Inquiry into the Miraculous Powers Which Are Supposed to Have Subsisted in the Christian Church.* 3d ed. London: R. Manby and H. S. Cox, 1749.

Mielke, G. *Das System Albrecht Ritschl's dargestellt, nicht Kritisirt.* Bonn: A. Marcus, 1894.

Migne, J. P., and A. G. Hamman. *Patrologiae cursus completes, sive biblioteca universalis, integra, uniformus. . . .* Paris: Migne, 1844–91.

Minucius Felix, Marcus. *The Octavius of Marcus Minucius Felix.* Translated by G. W. Clarke. Ancient Christian Writers, vol. 39. New York: New Press, 1974.

Möhler, Johann Adam. *Symbolik: Oder Darstellung der Dogmatischen Gegensätze der Katholiken und Protestanten nach Ihren öffentlichen Bekenntnisschriften.* Mainz: F. Kupferberg, 1838.

Monod, Léopold. *Le probléme de l'autorité.* 2d ed. Paris: Fischbacher, 1891.

Moor, Bernhard de. *Commentarius Perpetuus in Joh. Marckii Compendium Theologiae Christianae Didactico-elencticum.* 6 vols. Leiden: J. Hasebroek, 1761–71.

More, Henry. *Mysterium pietatis, An Explanation of the Grand Mystery.* 3 vols. London: J. Fletcher, 1660.

Morus, Samuel F. N. *Epitome theologiae christianae.* Lipsiae: E. B. Schwickerti, 1820.

Mücke, A. *Die Dogmatik des neunzehnten Jahrhunderts.* Gotha: F. A. Perthes, 1867.

Müller, Ernst Friedrich Kart. *Symbolik.* Erlangen: A. Deichert, 1896.

Müller, Eugen. *Natur und Wunder, ihr Gegensatz und ihre Harmonie.* Freiburg i.B: and St. Louis: Herder, 1892.

Müller, F. Max. *Das Denken im Lichte der Sprache.* Leipzig: W. Engelmann, 1888.

————. *Theosophy, or Psychological Religion.* London and New York: Longmans, Green and Co., 1893.

————. *Vorlesungen über den Ursprung und die Entwicklung der Religion.* Strassburg: K. J. Trübner, 1880.

————. *Vorlesungen über die Wissenschaft der Sprache.* 3d ed. Leipzig: Mayer, 1866.

Muller, J. G., ed. *Des Flavius Josephus schrift gegen den Apion.* Basel: Barnmaier, 1877.

Muller, Johann Wilhelm. *Lexicon manuale, geographiam antiquam et mediam cum Latine tum Germanice illustrans.* Leipzig: Impensis Hartmanni, 1831.

Müller, Joseph T. *Der Reformkatholizismus.* 2d ed. Zurich: C. Schmidt, 1899.

————. *Reformkatholizismus im Mittelalter und zur Zeit der Glaubensspaltung.* Strassburg i. E.: C. Bongard, 1901.

————. *Die Symbolischen Bücher der Evangelisch-Lutherischen Kirche.* 8th ed. Gütersloh: Bertelsmann, 1898.

Müller, Julius. *The Christian Doctrine of Sin.* Translated by Rev. Wm. Urwick. 5th ed. 2 vols. Edinburgh: T. & T. Clark, 1868.

————. *Dogmatische Abhendlungen.* Bremen: C. E. Müler, 1870.

Münscher, Wilhelm. *Dr. Wilhelm Münschers Lehrbuch der christlichen Dogmengeschichte.* Edited by Daniel von Coelln. Cassel: J. C. Krieger, 1832–38.

————. *Lehrbuch des Christlichen Dogmengeschichte.* Edited by Daniel von Coelln. 3d ed. Cassel: J. C. Krieger, 1832–38.

Muntinghe, Hermann. *Pars theologiae christianae theoretica.* Hardervici: I. van Kasteel, 1800.

Murisier, Ernest. *Les Maladres du sentiment religieux.* 2d ed. Paris: Félix Alcan, 1903.

Musculus, Wolfgang. *Common Places of Christian Religion.* Translated by John Man. London, 1563.

Nathusius, Martin von. *Die Mitarbeit der Kirche an der Lösung der sozialen Frage.* 2d ed. Leipzig: J. C. Hinrichs, 1897.

Neal, Daniel. *The History of the Puritans or Protestant Non-conformists.* London: J. Buckland, 1754.

Neale, J. M. *A History of the Holy Eastern Church.* 2 vols. London: J. Masters, 1850.

Neander, August. *Geschichte der Pflanzung und Leitung der christlichen Kirche durch die Apostel.* 5th ed. Gotha: Friedrich Andreas Perthes, 1862.

Newman, John Henry. *Two Essays on Biblical and on Ecclesiastical Miracles.* 8th ed. London: Longmans, Green, 1890.

Nicolas Cabasilas. *The Life in Christ.* Gass, 1849.

Niemeyer, H. A. *Collectio confessionum in ecclesiis reformatis publicatarum.* 2 vols. Leipzig: Sumptibis Iulii Klinkhardti, 1840.

Nietzsche, Friedrich W. *The Anti-Christ.* Translated by H. L. Menchen. Tucson: See Sharp Press, 1999.

Nippold, Friedrich. *Amerikanische Kirchengeschichte seit der Unabhängigkeitserklärung der Vereinigten Staaten.* Berlin: Wiegandt & Schotte, 1892.

————. *Die jesuitischen schriftsteller der gegenwart in Deutschland.* Leipzig: F. Jansa, 1895.

Nitzsch, Friedrich. *Augustinus' Lehre vom Wünder.* Berlin: E. S. Mittler, 1865.

————. *Lehrbuch der Evangelischen Dogmatik.* 3d ed. Prepared by Horst Stephan. Tübingen: J. C. B. Mohr, 1902.

Nitzsch, Karl Immanuel (Carl Emmanuel). *System of Christian Doctrines.* Edinburgh: T. & T. Clark, 1849.

Nösgen, K. F. *Die aussagen des Neuen Testaments über den Pentateuch.* Berlin, 1898.

Novatian. *Novatiani Romanae urbis presbyteri De Trinitate liber.* Cambridge: Cambridge University Press, 1909.

Oehler, G. F. *Theology of the Old Testament.* Translated by Ellen D. Smith and Sophia Taylor. Edinburgh: T. & T. Clark, 1892–93.

————. *Über Verhältniss der alttestamentische Prophetie zur Heiden.* Mantik, 1861.

Oetinger, F. C. *Die Theologie aus der Idee des Lebens abgeleitet und auf sechs Haupstücke zurückgeführt.* Translated by Julius Hamberger. Stuttgart: J. F. Steinkopf, 1852. Republished by Konrad von Ohly. 2 vols. Berlin and New York: W. De Gruyter, 1979.

————. *Theologia ex idea vitae deducta.* Berlin and New York: W. De Gruyter, 1979.

Oettingen, Alexander von. *Lutherische Dogmatik.* 2 vols. München: C. H. Beck, 1897–1902.

———. *Lutherische Dogmatik.* Vol. 1, *Principienlehre: Apologetische Grundlegung zur Dogmatik.* Munich: C. H. Beck, 1897.

Olevian, Caspar. *De Bediening van het Genade Verbond* [*De Substantia Foederis Gratiae* (1585)]. Rotterdam: Mazijk, 1939. Also in *Geschriften van Caspar Olevianus.* The Hague: Het Reformatorische Boekhandel, 1963.

Oosterwijk Bruyn, W. van. *Het Réveil in Nederland.* Utrecht: C. H. E. Breijer, 1890.

Oosterzee, J. J. van. *Christian Dogmatics.* Translated by J. Watson and M. Evans. 2 vols. New York: Scribner, Armstrong, 1874.

———. *Theopneustie.* Utrecht: Kemink, 1882.

———. *Voor Kerk en Theologie.* 2 vols. Utrecht: Kemink, 1872–75.

Opzoomer, C. W. *De Godsdienst Dogmatices Christianae initia.* 2d ed. Lyons: P. Engels, 1858.

———. *Het Wezen der Kennis.* Amsterdam: J. H. Gebhard, 1863.

———. *Wetenschap en Wijsbegeerte.* 1857.

Origen. *Against Celsus. ANF,* IV, 395–669.

———. *On First Principles. ANF,* IV, 239–384.

———. *Origenes opera omnia quae graece vel latine tantum exstant et eius nomine circumferunter.* 4 vols. Paris: Jacob Vincent, 1733–59.

Orr, James. *The Christian View of God and the World, As Centering in the Incarnation.* Edinburgh: Elliott, 1893. Reprinted, Grand Rapids: Kregel, 1989.

———. *Neglected Factors in the Study of the Progress of Christianity.* London: Holder and Stoughton, 1899.

———. *The Progress of Dogma.* London: Hodder and Stoughton, 1901.

———. *Ritschlianism, Expository and Critical Essay.* New York: A. C. Armstrong, 1903.

Otto, Rudolf. *Naturalism and Religion.* Translated by J. Arthur Thomson and Margaret R. Thomson and edited by W. D. Morrison. London: Williams & Norgate, 1907.

———. *The Philosophy of Religion.* London: Williams & Norgate, 1931.

Overbeck, Franz. *Über die Christlichkeit unserer heutigen Theologie.* Leipzig: C. G. Naumann, 1903.

Owen, Henry. *The Modes of Quotation Used by the Evangelical Writers Explained and Vindicated.* London: J. Nichols, 1789.

Owen, John. *Biblical Theology, or, The Nature, Origin, Development, and Study of Theological Truth, in Six Books.* Translated by Stephen P. Westcott. Morgan, Pa.: Soli Deo Publications, 1994.

———. *Theologoumena pantodapa, sive, De natura, ortu progressu, et studio verae theologiae, libri sex.* Oxford, 1661.

Paley, W. *Natural Theology.* Philadelphia: H. Maxwell, 1802.

———. *Views of the Evidences of Christianity.* London: Religious Tract Society, 1794.

Palmer, Christian. *Die Moral des Christenthums.* Stuttgart: Verlag von A. Liesching & Co., 1864.

Pannier, Jacques. *Le témoignange du Saint-Esprit.* Paris: Fischbacher, 1893.

Pareau, L. G., and H. de Groot. *Lineamenta theologiae Christianae universae: ut disquisitionis de religione una verissima et praestantissima, sive brevis conspectus dogmatices et apologetics Christianae.* Groningen: C. M. van Bolhuis Hoitsema, 1848.

Pascal, B. *Oeuveres.* 3 vols. Paris: Hachette, 1869.

Pastor of Hermas. ANF, II, 1–58.

Paulsen, Friedrich. *Einleitung in die Philosophie.* Berlin: Hertz, 1892.

———. *System der Ethik.* Berlin: W. Hertz, 1889.

Paulsen, P. *Die Gewissheit der christlichen Weltanschauung im modernen Geistesleben.* Stuttgart: C. Belser, 1900.

Paulus, H. E. G. *Exegetisches Handbuch über die drei ersten Evangelien.* 3 vols. Heidelberg: C. F. Winter, 1830–33.

———. *Das leben Jesu.* Heidelberg: C. F. Winter, 1828.

———. *Philogisch-kritischer und historischer commentar über das Neue Testament.* 4 vols. Lübeck: J. F. Bohn, 1800–1804.

Pautz, Otto. *Mohammends Lehre von der Offenbarung.* Leipzig: J. C. Hinrichs, 1898.

Pelt, Aton Friedrich Ludwig. *Theologische Encyklopädie als System.* Hamburg: F. & A. Perthes, 1843.

Perrone, Giovanni. *Praelectiones Theologicae.* 9 vols. Louvain: Vanlinthout & Vandezande, 1838–43.

Perty, Maximilian. *Der jetzige Spiritualismus und verwandte erfhrungen.* Leipzig: Winter, 1877.

Pesch, Christian. *Alte und neue Apologetik Theologische Zeitfragen.* Freiburg i.B.: Herder, 1900.

———. *Gott und götter.* Freiburg i.B.: Herder, 1890.

———. *Die Inspiratione Sacra Scriptura.* Friburgi Brisgoviae: Herder, 1906.

———. *Praelectiones Dogmaticae.* 9 vols. Freiburg: Herder, 1902–10.

Pesch, Tilmann. *Die grossen Welträthsel.* 2d ed. 2 vols. Freiburg i.B.: Herder, 1892.

Petavius, Dionysius. *De Theologicis Dogmatibus.* 8 vols. Paris: Vives, 1865–67.

Peters, Norbert. *Die grundsätzliche Stellung der katholische Kirche zur Bibelforschung.* Paderborn: F. Schöningh, 1905.

Petran, Ernst. *Beiträge zur Verständizung über Begriff und Wesen der sittlichreligiösen Erfahrung.* Gütersloh: Bertelsmann, 1898.

Pfaff, C. M. *Introductio in historiam theologiae literariam notis amplissinis. . . . 3* vols. Tubingen: Cottae, 1724–26.

Pfanner, Tobias. *Systema Theologiae Gentilis Purioris.* Basel: Joh. Hermann Widerhold, 1679.

Pfennigsdorf, E. *Vergleich der dogmatische Systeme von R. A. Lipsius und A. Ritschl.* Gotha: F. A. Perthes, 1896.

Pfleiderer, Otto. *The Development of Theology in Germany since Kant, and Its Progress in Great Britain since 1825.* Translated by J. F. Smith. London: S. Sonnenschein; New York: Macmillan, 1893.

———. *Grundriss der Christlichen Glaubens- und Sittenlehre.* Berlin: G. Reimer, 1888.

———. *Moral und Religion.* Haarlem: n.p., 1872.

———. *Der Paulinismus.* 2d ed. Leipzig: O. R. Reisland, 1890.

———. *Religionsphilosophie auf geschechtlicher Grundlage.* Berlin: G. Reimer, 1883–84.

———. *Religion und Religionen.* München: J. F. Lehmann, 1906.

*Philaret, Metropolitan of Moscow. *Orthodox Dogmatic Theology.* 1882.

Philippi, Adolph. *Commentary on St. Paul's Epistle to the Romans.* Translated by John S. Banks. Edinburgh: T. & T. Clark, 1878–79.

Philippi, Friedrich A. *Kirchliche Glaubenslehre.* 6 vols. Gütersloh: Bertelsmann, 1902.

Philo. *De Somniis.* In *The Works of Philo: Complete and Unabridged.* Translated by C. D. Yonge. Peabody, Mass.: Hendrickson, 1993.

Philoponus, Johannes. *De aeternitate mundi c. Proclum, en de mundi creatione. 1. VII.*

Photius. *Liber de Spiritus Sancti my stagogia.* Edited by Joseph Hergenröther. Ratisbonae: G. J. Manz, 1857.

Pictet, Benedict. *De christelyke god-geleertheid.* 's-Gravenhage: Pieter van Thol, 1728–30.

Pierson, A. *Bespiegeling, Gezag, en Ervaring.* Utrecht: Kemink, 1885.

———. *Disquisitio historico-dogmatica de realismo et nominalismo.* Trajecti ad Rhenum, 1854.

———. *Eene Levensbeschouwing.* 2 vols. Haarlem: Kruseman & Tjeenk Willink, 1875.

———. *Geestelijke voorouders: Studien over onze beschaving.* 5 vols. Haarlem: H. D. Tjeenk Willink, 1887.

———. *Geschiedenis van het Rommsch-katholicisme tot op het Concilie van Trente.* 4 vols. Haarlem, A. C. Kruseman, 1868–72.

———. *Gods Wondermacht en ons Geestelïjke Leven.* Haarlem: H. D. Tjeenk Willink, 1887.

———. *De Moderne Richting en de Kristelijke Kerk.* Arnhem: D. A. Thieme, 1866.

———. *Oudere Tijdgenooten.* Amsterdam: Kampen, 1888.

———. *Studien over Johannes Kalvijn.* Amsterdam: P. N. Van Kampen & Zoon, 1881.

———. *Ter Uitvaart.* 1876.

———. *Wijsgeerig Onderzoek.* Deventer, 1882.

Pillon. *L'evolution historique de l'idealisme, L'année philosophique.* Paris, 1902.

Plato. *The Laws.* Translated by E. B. England. 2 vols. New York: Longmans, Green & Co., 1921.

————. *Phaedrus.* Translated by C. J. Rowe. Warminster: Aris & Phillips, 1986.

————. *The Republic.* Translated by Benjamin Jowett. Oxford: Clarendon, 1888.

Platz, Bonifacius. *Der Mensch.* Würzburg & Leipzig: Woerls Rusenbucher-verlag, 1898.

*Pletl, G. *Wie steht's mit de menschliche Autorität der heilige Schrift.* Fulda, 1905.

Polanus, Amandus. *Syntagma Theologiae Christianae.* 5th ed. Hanover, Aubry, 1624.

Polstorff. *Der Subjecktivismus in der modernen Theologie und sein Anrecht in Randbemerkungen.* Gütersloh: C. Bertelsmann, 1893.

Portig, Gustav. *Religion und Kunst in ihrem gegeseitigen Verhältnis.* 2 vols. Iserlohn: J. Bädeker, 1879, 1880.

Prat, F. *La Bible et l'histoire.* Paris: Librairie Bloud et Cie, 1905.

Preger, Wilhelm. *Geschichte der deutschen mystik im mittelalter.* 3 vols. Leipzig: Dörffling und Franke, 1874–93.

Pressensé, Edmond de. *Les Origines.* Paris: Fischbacher, 1883.

Preuss, Johannes. *Die Entwicklung des Schriftprinzips bei Luther bis zur Leipziger Disputation.* Leipzig: Chr. Herm, Tauchnitz, 1901.

Pseudo-Dionysius the Areopagite. *The Divine Names and Mystical Theology.* Translated by John D. Jones. Milwaukee: Marquette University Press, 1980.

————. *Pseudo-Dionysius: The Complete Works.* Edited by Paul Rorem and translated by Colm Luibheid. New York: Paulist Press, 1987.

Punjer, B. *Geschichte der Christlichen Religionsphilosophie.* 2 vols. Braunschweig: C. A. Schwetske, 1880.

Quenstedt, Johann Andreas. *Theologia Didactico-polemica Sive Systema Theologicum.* 1685. English edition: chapters 1–3, *The Nature and Character of Theology.* Abridged, edited, and translated by Luther Poellot. St. Louis: Concordia, 1986.

Quirmback, Joseph. *Die Lehre des heiligen Paulus von der natüralichen Gotteserkenntnis und dem natürlichen sittengesetz.* Freiburg i.B.: Herder, 1906.

Räbiger, Julius Ferdinand. *Lehrbuch der hebräisch-jüdischen Archäologiei.* Leipzig: F. C. W. Vogel, 1864.

————. *Theologik; oder, Encyklopädie der Theologie.* Leipzig: R. Reisland, 1880.

Rabus, Leonherd. *Logik und System der Wissenschaften.* Erlangen: A. Deichert, 1895.

The Racovian Catechism. Translated by Thoman Rees. London: Longman, Hurst, Rees, Orme and Brown, 1818. Reprinted, Lexington, Ky.: American Theological Library Association, 1962.

Rademacher, Arnold. *Die Übernatürliche lebensordnung nach der Paulinischen und Johaneischen Theologie.* Freiburg i.B. and St. Louis: Herder, 1903.

Rademaker, C. S. M. *Life and Work of Gerardus Joannes Vossius (1577–1649).* Assen: Van Gorcum, 1981.

Randolph, Thomas. *The Prophecies and Other Texts Cited in the New Testament Compared with the Hebrew Original and with the Septuagint Version.* Oxford: Printed for J. and J. Fletcher, 1782.

Ranke, Leopold von and George Winter. *Weltgeschichte.* Edited by Alfred Wilhelm Dove and Theodor Wiedermann. 9 vols. Leipzig: Dunker & Humblot, 1886.

Rashdall, Hastings. *Christus in Ecclesia.* Edinburgh: T. & T. Clark, 1904.

Rausch, Erwin. *Kirche und Kirchen im Lichte grieschischer Forschung.* Leipzig: Deichert, 1903.

Rauschen, Gerhard. *Grundriss der Patrologie mit besonderer Berücksichtigung der Dogmengeschichte.* Freiburg i.B.: Herder, 1903.

Rauwenhoff, L. W. E. *Wijsbegeerte van den Godsdienst.* Leiden: Brill & van Doeburgh, 1887.

*————. *De Zelfstandigheid van den Christen.* 1857.

Raymond of Sabunde. *Theologia naturalis seu liber creaturarum.* Sulzbach: J. E. de Seidel, 1852. Reprinted, Stuttgart, Bad Cannstatt: Frommann, 1966.

Reiche, Armin. *Die künsterlichen Elemente in der Welt- und Lebensanschauung des Gregor von Nyssa.* Jena: A. Kámpte, 1897.

Reiff, Franz. *Die christliche Glaubenslehre.* Basel, 1884.

Reiff, Friederich. *Die Christliche Glaubens-lehre als Grundlage der Christlichen Weltanschauung.* Basel: Bahnmaier, 1872.

Reinhard, Franz Volkmar. *Grundriss der Dog-matik.* Munich: Seidel, 1802.

Reinholdt, Alexander von. *Geschichte der rus-sischen Litteratur von ihren aufänger bis auf die neueste zeit.* Leipzig: W. Friedrich, 1884–86.

Reinke, Johannes. *Die Entwicklung der Naturwissenschaften insbesondere der Bio-logie im neunzehnten Jahrhundert.* Kiel: Universitäts-Buchandlung (P. Toeche), 1900.

———. *Die Welt als Tat.* Berlin: Gebrüder Paetel, 1905.

Reischle, Max. *Der Streit über die Begründ-ung des Glaubens auf den geschichtlichen Jesus Christus.* Freiburg i.B.: J. C. B. Mohr, 1897.

———. *Theologie und Religionsgeschichte.* Tübingen: J. C. B. Mohr [Paul Siebeck], 1904.

———. *Werturteile und Glaubensurteile.* Halle a.S.: Max Niemeyer, 1900.

Remonstrance of 1610. In vol. 3 of *The Creeds of Christendom,* edited by Philip Schaff and revised by David S. Schaff. 6th ed. 1919. Reprinted, Grand Rapids: Baker, 1983.

Renan, Ernest. *The Life of Jesus.* Translated by William G. Hutchinson. New York: A. L. Burt, 1897.

Reuss, Eduard. *History of the Sacred Scrip-tures of the New Testament.* 2 vols. Trans-lated by Edward Lovell Houghton. Bos-ton: Houghton, Mifflin, 1884.

Reuter, H. *Augustinische Studien.* Gotha: F. A. Perthes, 1887.

———. *Geschichte der religiösen Aufklärung im Mittelalter.* 2 vols. Berlin: W. Hertz, 1875–77.

Reymond, A. *Essai sur le subjectivisme et le problème de la connaissance religieuse.* Laussanne, 1900.

*Rieber. *Der moderne Kampf um die Bibel.* 1905.

Riehm, Eduard. *Handwörterbuch des bibli-schen Altertums für gebildete Bibelleser.* Bielefeld, Leipzig: Velhagen & Hasing, 1893–94.

———. *Messianic Prophecy.* Translated by Lewis A. Muirhead. Edinburgh: T. & T. Clark, 1891.

Riemens, Johannes. *Het begrip der openbar-ing in het Christendom.* Utrecht: C. H. E. Breijer, 1905.

———. *Het Symbol Fideisme.* Rotterdam: Van Sijn & Zoon, 1900.

Ritschl, Albrecht. *Die Christliche Lehre von der Rechfertigung und Versöhnung.* 4th ed. 3 vols. Bonn: A. Marcus, 1895–1903.

———. *Fides Implicita.* Bonn: Adolphus Marcus, 1890.

———. *Geschichte des Pietismus.* 3 vols. Bonn: A. Marcus, 1880–86.

———. *Theologie und Metaphysik.* Bonn: A. Maucus, 1881.

———. *Über Werthustheile.* Freiburg: Mohr, 1895.

———. *Unterricht in der Christlichen Reli-gion.* 3d ed. Bonn: A. Marcus, 1886.

Ritschl, Otto. *Wissenschaftliche Ethik und moralische Gesetzgebung.* Tübingen: Mohr, 1903.

Ritter, Heinrich. *Geschichte des Christlichen Philosophie.* 4 vols. Hamburg: F. Perthes, 1841.

———. *Geschichte der Philosophie.* 12 vols. Hamburg: Perthes, 1829–53.

Ritter, Heinrich, and Ludwig Preller. *Histo-ria philosophiae Graecae.* Gothae: F. A. Perthes, 1888.

Rivetus, Andreas. *Isagoge, seu introductio gen-eralis ad Scripturam Sacram.* 1627.

———. *Operum theologicorum.* 3 vols. Rot-terdam: Leers, 1651–60.

Rogers, J. Guinness. *The Church Systems of England in the Nineteenth Century.* Lon-don: Congregational Union of England and Wales, 1891.

Rohnert, W. *Die dogmatik der evangelischen lutherischen Kirche.* Braunschweig: H. Wollermann, 1902.

———. *Die Inspiration der Heiligen Schrift und ihre Bestreiter.* Leipzig: Georg Böhme (E. Ungleich), 1889.

———. *Was lehrt Luther von der Inspiration der Heiligen Schrift?* Leipzig: Ungleich, 1890.

Rothe, Richard. *Theologische Ethik.* 2d rev. ed. 5 vols. Wittenberg: Zimmerman, 1867–71.

———. *Zur Dogmatik*. Gotha: F. A. Perthes, 1863.

Rousseau, Jean-Jacques. *Profession de foi du vicaire savoyard*. Paris: Persan et Cie, 1822.

Runze, Georg. *Katechismus der Dogmatik*. Leipzig: J. J. Weber, 1898.

Rutgers, F. L. *Calvijns Invloed op de Reformatie in de Nederlanden, voor zooveel die door hemzelven is uitgeoefend*. Leiden: D. Donner, 1899.

Ryssen, Leonardus. *Summa theologiae electicae completa, et didacticae quantum sufficit*. Edinburgh: G. Mosman, 1692.

Sabatier, Auguste. *De la vie intime des dogmes et de leur puissance d'évolution*. Paris: Librarie Fischbacher, 1890.

———. *Die Christlichen Dogmen, ihr Wesen und ihr Entwicklung*. Translated into German by M. Schwabb. Leipzig: Otto Wigand, 1890.

———. *The Doctrine of the Atonement and Its Historical Evolution*. Translated by V. Leuliette. New York: G. P. Putnam; London: Williams and Norgate, 1904.

———. *Outlines of a Philosophy of Religion Based on Psychology and History*. Translated by T. A. Seed. New York: James Pott, 1902.

———. *Religions of Authority and the Religion of the Spirit*. Translated by Louise Seymour Houghton. New York: McClure, Phillips, 1904.

———. *The Vitality of Christian Dogmas and Their Power of Evolution*. Translated by E. Christen. London: Adams & Charles Black, 1898.

Sabatier, Paul. *Leben des heiligen Franz von Assisi*. Translated by Margarete Liso. Berlin: G. Reimer, 1895.

Sack, Karl. *Christliche Apologetik*. Hamburg: Friedrich Perthes, 1841.

Salter, W. M. *Ethical Religion*. Boston: Roberts Brothers, 1889.

———. *De Godsdienst der Moraal*. Translated by Hugengoltz. 1889.

———. *Die Religion der Moral*. Translated by G. von Gizycki. Leipzig: W. Friedrich, 1885.

Sanday, W. *Inspiration: Eight Lectures on the Early History and Origin of the Doctrine of Biblical Inspiration; Being the Bampton Lectures for 1893*. London and New York: Longmans, Green, and Co., 1893.

Sanseverino, Gaetano. *Philosophia Christiana cum antiqua et nova comparata*. Neapoli: officinam Bibliothecae Catholicae Scriptorum, 1878.

Sartorius, Karl. *Die Leichenverbrennung innerhalb der christlichen Kirche*. Basel: C. Detloff, 1886.

Satha, Constantine. *Neo-Hellenic Philology*. Athens, 1868.

Schaepman, H. J. A. M. *Menschen en Boeken*. Utrecht: Wed. J. R. van Rossum, 1893–1903.

Schaff, P. *The Creeds of Christendom*. Revised by David S. Schaff. 6th ed. 3 vols. New York: Harper, 1931. Reprinted, Grand Rapids: Baker, 1983.

———. *The Person of Christ: The Miracle of History*. New York: C. Scribner, 1871.

———. *Theological Propaedentic*. New York: Scribner, 1893.

Schaff, P., and S. M. Jackson, eds. *Encyclopedia of Living Divines and Christian Workers of All Denominations in Europe and America*. New York: Funk & Wagnalls, 1887.

Schanz, Paul. *A Christian Apology*. Translated by Michael F. Glancey and Victor J. Schobel. 4th rev. ed. Ratisbon: F. Pustet, 1891.

———. *Ist die Theologie eine Wissenschaft?* Stuttgart: Wien, 1900.

———. *Über neue Versuche der Apologetik genenüber dem Naturalismus und Spiritualismus*. Regensberg: Nationale Verlagsanstalt, 1897.

Schäzler, Konstantin, Freiherr von. *Neue Untersuchungen über das Dogma von der Gnade und das Wesen des christlichen Glaubens*. Mainz: Franz Kirchheim, 1867.

Scheeben, Matthias Joseph. *Handbuch der katholischen Dogmatik*. 4 vols. Reprinted, Freiburg im Breisgau: Herder, 1933. Originally published 1874–98.

———. *A Manual of Catholic Theology Based on Scheeben's "Dogmatik."* Translated and edited by Joseph Wilhelm and Thomas B. Scannell. 4th ed. 2 vols. London: Kegan Paul, Trench, Trübner and Co.; New York: Benziger Brothers, 1909.

————. *Natur und Gnade.* Mainz: Kirch-heim, 1861.

Scheel, Otto. *Luthers Stellung zur Heiligen Schrift.* Tübingen: J. C. B. Mohr (Paul Siebeck), 1902.

Scheibe, Max. *Die Bedeutung der Werthur-theile für das religiöse Erkenntniss.* Halle a.s.: Max Niemeyer, 1893.

Schell, Herman. *Der Katholizismus als Prin-cip des Fortschritts.* Würzburg: A. Göbel, 1899.

————. *Die neue Zeit und der Alte Glaube.* Würzburg: A. Göbel, 1898.

————. *Theologie und Universität.* Würzburg: A. Göbel, 1896.

Schelling, F. W. J. von. *Ausgewählte Werke.* 4 vols. Darmstadt: Wissenschaftliche Buch-gesellschaft, 1968.

————. *Einleitung in die Philosophie der My-thologie.* 2 vols. Darmstadt: Wissen-schaftliche Buchgesellschaft, 1957 [1857].

————. *Philosophie der Mythologie.* 2 vols. Darmstadt: Wissenschaftliche Buchge-sellschaft, 1957 [1857].

————. *Philosophische Untersuchungen über das Wesen der menschlichen Freiheit.* Reut-lingen: J. N. Enklinschen, 1834.

Schenkel, Daniel. *Das Wesen des Protestantis-mus.* 3 vols. Schaffhausen: Brodtmann, 1846–51.

Schiere, Nicolaus. *Doctrina testamentorum et foederum divinorum omnium.* Leovar-diaw: M. Ingema, 1718.

Schlatter, Adolph von. *Der Glaube im Neuen Testament.* 3d ed. Stuttgart: Verlag der Vereinsbuchhandlung, 1905.

Schleiermacher, Friedrich. *Brief Outline on the Study of Theology.* Translated by Ter-rence N. Tice. Richmond, Va.: John Knox Press, 1966.

————. *The Christian Faith.* Edited by H. R. MacIntosh and J. S. Steward. Ed-inburgh: T. & T. Clark, 1928.

————. *Die Christliche Sitte nach dem Grundsazen der evangelischen Kirche dar-gestellt.* Berlin: G. Reimer, 1884

————. *Dialektik.* Hamburg: Meiner, 1986.

————. *Introduction to Christian Ethics.* Translated by John Shelley. Nashville: Abingdon, 1989.

————. *Über die Religion.* Edited by C. Schwarz. Leipzig: F. A. Brockhaus, 1868.

Schmid, Alois. *Erkenntnislehre.* 2 vols. Freiburg i.B.: Herder, 1890.

————. *Untersuchungen über den letzen Gewissheitsgrund des Offenbarungs-glaubens.* München: Ernst Stahl, 1879.

Schmid, H. F. F. *The Doctrinal Theology of the Evangelical Lutheran Church.* Trans-lated by Charles A. Hay and Henry Ja-cobs. 5th ed. Philadelphia: United Lu-theran Publication House, 1899.

————. *De inspirationis bibliorum vi et ra-tione.* Brixinae: Typis et sumptibus biblio-polei Wegeriani, 1885.

Schmid, Rudolf. *The Scientific Creed of a Theologian.* Translated by J. W. Stough-ton from the 2d ed. New York: A. C. Armstrong, 1906.

Schmidt, F. J. *Der Niedergang des Protestan-tismus.* Berlin, 1904.

Schmidt, Hermann. *Handbuch der Symbolik.* Berlin: H. Reuther, 1890.

Schmidt, Wilhelm. *Der alte Glaube und die Wahrheit des Christenthums.* Berlin: Wigand & Grieben, 1891.

————. *Christliche Dogmatik.* 4 vols. Bonn: E. Weber, 1895–98.

Schmitt, Gregor. *Die Apologie der drei ersten Jahrhunderte in historisch-systematischer Darstellung.* Mainz: Rupferberg, 1890.

Schneckenburger, Matthew. *Vorlesungen über die Lehrbegriffe der kleineren protestanti-schen Kirchenparteien.* Frankfurt: H. L. Brönner, 1863.

Schneckenburger, Matthew, and Eduard Gueeder. *Vergleichende Darstellung des Lutherischen und Reformirten Lehrbe-griffs.* 2 vols. Stuttgart: J. B. Metzler, 1855.

Schnedermann, Georg. *Der Christliche im Sinne der gegenwärtigen evangelischen lutherischen Kirche.* 3 vols. Leipzig: A. Deichert, 1899–1902.

————. *Von dem Bestande unserer Gemein-schaft mit Gott durch Jesum Christum.* Leipzig: F. C. Hinrichs, 1888.

Schöberlein, Ludwig. *Prinzip und System der Dogmatik.* Heidelberg: C. Winter, 1881.

Scholten, Johannes Henricus. *Dogmatices Christianae initia.* 2d ed. Lyons: P. En-gels, 1858.

————. *Het Evangelie naar Johannes.* Leiden: P. Engels, 1864.

———. *De Leer der Hervormde Kerk in hare Grondbeginselen.* 2d ed. 2 vols. Leiden: P. Engels, 1850–51.

———. *Supranaturalisme in Verband met Bijbel Christendom en Protestantisme.* Leiden, 1867.

Schopenhauer. A. *Sammtliche Werke.* Vols. 2 and 3. Leipzig: F. M. Brodhaus, 1919.

———. *The World as Will and Idea.* Translated by R. B. Haldane and J. Kemp. 3d ed. 3 vols. London: Kegan, Paul Trench, Trüber, 1891.

Schrieke, Otto. *Christus en de Schrift.* Utrecht: C. H. E. Breijer, 1897.

Schroeder, Leopold von. *Wesen und Ursprung der Religion.* München: J. F. Lehmanns Verlag, 1905.

Schuler, J. M.; Zwingli, U. *Opera.* 8 vols. Edited by Johannes Schulthess. Turici: F. Schulthess, 1842.

Schultz, Hermann. *Alttestamentliche Theologie.* 2d ed. Göttingen: Vandenhoeck & Ruprecht, 1889.

Schultze, Martin. *Calvins Jenseits Christentum in seinem Verhältnisse zu den religiösen Schriften des Erasmus.* Görlitz: Rudolph Dulfer, 1902.

Schürer, Emil. *A History of the Jewish People in the Time of Jesus Christ.* 5 vols. 1890. Reprinted, Peabody, Mass.: Hendrickson, 1994.

Schwane, Joseph. *Dogmengeschichte.* 4 vols. Freiburg im Breisgau: Herder, 1882–95.

Schwarz, Carl. *Zur geschichte der neuesten Theologie.* Leipzig: F. A. Brockhaus, 1864.

Schwarzlose, Karl. *Der Bilderstreit, ein Kampf der Griechische Kirche um ihre eigenart und um ihre Freiheit.* Gotha: Perthes, 1890.

Schweizer, Alexander. *Christliche Glaubenslehre.* Leipzig: S. Hirzel, 1863–72.

———. *Die Christliche Glaubenslehre nach protestantischen Grundsätzen.* Leipzig: G. Hirzel, 1877.

———. *Die Glaubenslehre der evangelischreformirten Kirche.* Zurich: Orell, Füssli., 1844–47.

———. *Die protestantischen Centraldogmen in ihrer Entwicklung inerhalb der reformirten Kirche.* 2 vols. Zürich: Orell, Fuessli, 1854, 1856.

Schwetz, Johannes. *Theologia Dogmatic Catholica.* Vienna: Congregatio Mechitharistica, n.d.

Scots Confession. In vol. 3 of *The Creeds of Christendom,* edited by Philip Schaff and revised by David S. Schaff. 6th ed. 1919. Reprinted, Grand Rapids: Baker, 1983.

Sécrétan, Charles. *La civilization et la croyance.* Paris: Alcan, 1887.

Seeberg, Alfred. *Das Evangelium Christi.* Leipzig, 1905.

———. *Der Katechismus der Urchristenheit.* München: Kaiser, 1966.

Seeberg, Paul. *Vorstudien zur Dogmatik.* Leipzig: Richard Wöpke, 1902.

Seeberg, Reinhold. *The Fundamental Truths of the Christian Religion.* Translated by Rev. George E. Thomson and Clara Wallentin. New York: G. P. Putnam's Sons, 1908.

———. *Die Kirche Deutschlands im neunzehnten Jahrhundert.* Leipzig: Deichert, 1903.

———. *Textbook of the History of Doctrine.* Translated by Charles A. Hay. 2 vols. Philadelphia: Lutheran Publication Society, 1905.

Sellin, Ernst. *Beiträge zur Israelitischen und Jüdischen Religionsgeschichte.* 2 vols. Leipzig: A. Deichert, 1896–97.

Semisch, J. G. *Justin Martyr: His Life, Writings, and Opinions.* Translated by J. E. Ryland. 2 vols. Edinburgh: Thomas Clark, 1843.

Seneca, Lucius Annaeus. *De Beneficiis.* Translated by John W. Basore. Loeb Classical Library. Cambridge, Mass.: Harvard University Press, 1928.

———. *Naturales Quaestiones.* Translated by Thomas Corcoran. 2 vols. Loeb Classical Library. Cambridge: Harvard University Press, 1971–72.

———. *De Providentia.* In vol. 1 of *Moral Essays.* Translated by John W. Basore. Loeb Classical Library. New York: G. P. Putnam's Sons, 1928.

———. *17 Letters.* Translation and commentary by C. D. N. Costa. Warminster: Aris and Phillips, 1988.

Sepp, Christian. *Geschiedkundige Nasporingen.* Leiden: De Breuk & Smits, 1872–75.

————. *De Leer des Nieuwe Testament over de Heilige Schrift des Oude Verbonds.* Te Amsterdam: J. C. Sepp & Zoon, 1849.

————.

————. *Het Godgeleerd Onderwijs in Nederland, Gedurende de 16e en 17e Eeuw.* 2 vols. Leiden: De Breuk en Smits, 1873–74.

————. *Kerkhistorische Studiën.* Leiden: E. J. Brill, 1885.

Sepp, J. R. *Das Heidenthum und dessen Bedeutung für Christenthum.* Regensburg: G. Joseph Manz, 1853.

Sewel, William. *History of the Rise, Increase, and Progress of the Christian People Called Quakers.* London: J. Sowle, 1725.

Shedd, William Greenough Thayer. *Dogmatic Theology.* 3d ed. 3 vols. New York: Scribner, 1891–94.

Siebeck, Hermann. *Geschichte der Psychologie.* 2 vols. Gotha: F. A. Perthes, 1880–84.

————. *Lehrbuch der Religionsphilosophie.* Freiburg i.B. und Leipzig: Mohr, 1893.

————. *Religionsphilosophie.* Tübingen: J. C. B. Mohr, 1893.

Sigwart, Christoph. *Ulrich Zwingli.* Stuttgart and Hamburg: Rudolf Besser, 1855.

Silbernagl, Isidor. *Verfassung und gegenwärtiger Bestand sämtlicher kirchen des Orients.* Edited by Joseph Schnitzer. 2d ed. Regensburg: Q. J. Manz, 1904.

Simar, H. Th. *Lehrbuch der Dogmatik.* 2 vols. Freiburg i.B.: Herder, 1879–80.

Smalcald Articles. In vol. 3 of *The Creeds of Christendom,* edited by Philip Schaff and revised by David S. Schaff. 6th ed. 1919. Reprinted, Grand Rapids: Baker, 1983.

Smend, Rudolf. *Lehrbuch der Altestamentlichen Religionsgeschichte.* Freiburg i.B.; Leipzig: J. C. B. Mohr, 1893.

Smith, Henry Boynton. *System of Christian Theology.* Edited by William S. Karr. 4th ed. rev. New York: A. C. Armstrong, 1890, 1892.

Sogemeier, Heinrich. *Der Begriff der christlichen Erfahrung hinsichtlich seiner Verwendbarkeit in der Dogmatik untersucht.* Gütersloh: C. Bertelsmann, 1902.

Sohm, R. *Kirchenrecht.* Leipzig: Duncker & Humbolt, 1892.

Sohn, Georg. *Opera Sacrae Theologiae.* 2 vols. Herborn: C. Corvin, 1598.

Southey, Robert. *The Life of John Wesley.* London: Hutchinson, 1903.

Spanheim, Friedrich. *Opera.* 3 vols. Leiden: Cornelius Boutestein et al., 1701–3.

Specht, Karl A. *Theologie und Wissenschaft.* 3d ed. Gotha: Stollberg, 1878.

Spencer, Herbert. *Principles of Psychology.* London: Longman, Brown, Green and Longmans, 1855.

Spinoza, Baruch. *Ethics.* Translated by G. H. R. Parkinson. Oxford and New York: Oxford University Press, 2000.

————. *Tractatus Theologico-Politicus.* Translated by Samuel Shirley. Leiden: Brill, 1991.

————. *Works of Spinoza: A Theologico-Political Treatise and a Political Treatise.* Translated by R. H. M. Elwes. New York: Dover Publications, 1951.

Spitzer, Hugo. *Nominalismus und Realismus in der neuesten deutschen Philosophie, mit Berücksichtigung ihres Verhältnisses zur modernen Naturwissenschaft.* Leipzig: 1876.

Splittgerber, Franz. *Schlaf und Tod.* 2d ed. 2 vols. Halle: Julius Fricke, 1881.

Sprinzl, J. Die *Theologie der apostolischen Väter: Eine dogmengeschichtliche Monographie.* Wien: W. Braumüller, 1880.

Spruyt, Cornelius B. *Proeve van eene Geschiedenus van de Leer der Aangeboren Begrippen.* Leiden: Brill, 1879.

Stahl, F. J. *Der Protestantismus als Politiek Princip.* 2d ed. Berlin: W. Schultze, 1853.

Stahl, Ignaz. *Die natürliche Gotteserkenntniss aus der Lehre der Väter dargestellt.* Regensburg and New York: Friedrich Pustet, 1869.

Stählin, Leonhard. *Kant, Lotze, Albrecht Ritschl.* Leipzig: Dörffling & Franke, 1884.

————. *Kant, Lotze, and Ritschl: A Critical Examination.* Edinburgh: T. & T. Clarke, 1889.

————. *Über den Ursprung der Religion.* München: C. H. Beck, 1905.

Stange, Carl. *Das Dogma und Seine Beurteilung in der neueren Dogmengeschichte.* Berlin, Reuther & Reichard, 1898.

Stanton, V. H. *The Place of Authority in Matters of Religious Belief.* London: Longmans, 1891.

Staudenmaier, F. A. *Encyklopädie der theologischen Wissenschaften als System der gesammten Theologie.* 2d ed. Vol. 1. Mainz: Florian Kupferberg, 1840.

Stead, W. T. *The Wider Hope.* London: Fisher Unwin, 1890.

Stein, Ludwig. *Die Soziale Frage im Lichte der Philosophie.* 2d ed. Stuttgart: F. Enke, 1903.

Steinbeck, John. *Das Verhältnis von Theologie und Erkenntnisstheorie . . . A. Ritschl und A. Sabatier.* Leipzig: Dörffling & Franke, 1898.

Steude, E. Gustav. *Der Beweis für die Wahrheit des Christentums ein Beitrag zur Apologetik.* Gütersloh: C. Bertelsmann, 1899.

———. *Entwicklung und Offenbarung.* Stuttgart, 1905.

Stirner, Max. *The Ego and His Own.* Translated by Steven T. Byington. New York: B. R. Tucker, 1907.

Stöckl, Albert. *Lehrbuch der Philosophie.* 2 vols. Mainz: Kirchheim & Co., 1905, 1912.

———. *Philosophie des Mittelalters.* 3 vols. Mainz: Kirchheim, 1864–66.

Stosch, G. *Das Heidenthum als religiöses Problem.* Gütersloh, 1903.

Stoughton, John. *History of Religion in England from the Opening of the Long Parliament to 1850.* 8 vols. London: Hodder and Stoughton, 1881–84.

Strauss, David Friedrich. *Die Christliche Glaubenslehre in ihrer Geschichtlichen Entwicklung und im Kampf mit der Moderne Wissenschaft.* 2 vols. Tübingen: C. F. Osiander, 1840–41.

———. *Das Leben Jesu.* 2 vols. Tübingen: C. F. Osiander, 1835–36.

———. *The Old Faith and the New.* Translated by Mathilde Blind. New York: Hold, 1873.

Strong, Augustus Hopkins. *Systematic Theology.* 3 vols. Philadelphia: Griffith & Rowland Press, 1907–9.

Strümpell, Ludwig. *Die Einleitung in die Philosophie vom Standpunkte der Geschichte der Philosophie.* Leipzig: G. Böhme, 1886.

Suicerus, J. C. *Thesaurus ecclesiasticus.* 2 vols. Amsterdam: J. H. Wetstein, 1682.

Sylvester [Silwestr]. *Versuch der rechtgläubigendogmatischen Gottesgelehrtheit.* 5 vols. Kiev, 1884.

Tatian. *Oratio ad Graecos.* Edited by Eduard Schwarz. Leipzig: J. C. Hinrichs, 1888.

Temple, Fred. *Dictation from Fred Temple.* Radersburgh, 1884–85.

Tertullian. *Against Hermogenes.* In *Ancient Christian Writers,* vol. 24. Westminster, Md.: Newman Press, 1956.

———. *Against Marcion. ANF,* III, 269–475.

———. *Against Praxeas. ANF,* III, 597–632.

———. *An Answer to the Jews. ANF,* III, 151–73.

———. *The Apology. ANF,* III, 17–60.

———. *On the Resurrection of the Flesh. ANF,* III, 545–95.

———. *On the Veiling of Virgins. ANF,* IV, 27–38.

———. *The Prescription against Heretics. ANF,* III, 243–67.

———. *Quae supersunt omnia.* Edited by Franz Oehler. Lipsiae: T. O. Weigel, 1853.

———. *Quinti Septimii Florentis Tertulliani quae supersunt Omnia.* 2 vols. Edited by Franz Oehler. Leipzig: T. O. Wiegel, 1853.

———. *To the Nations. ANF,* III, 109–48.

———. *A Treatise on the Soul. ANF,* II, 181–235.

Theodoret, Bishop of Cyrrhus. *Divine Providence.* Translated by Thomas Halton. New York: Newman, 1988.

Theologia Wirceburgensi (Theologia Dogmatica: Polemica, Scholastica et Moralis). 5 vols. Wirceburgensi, 1852–53.

Theophilus. *To Autolycus. ANF,* II, 89–121.

Theremin, Franz. *Die Beredsamkeit eine Tugend.* Berlin: Duncker und Humblot, 1837.

———. *Eloquence a Virtue; or, Outlines of a Systematic Rhetoric.* Translated by William G. T. Shedd. Boston: Draper and Halliday, 1867.

Thieme, Karl. *Luthers Testament wider Rom in seinen schmalkaldischen Artikeln.* Leipzig: A. Deichert'sche Verlagsbuchhandlung (Georg Böhme), 1900.

Thilo, C. A. *Die Wissenschaftlichkeit der modernen speculativen Theologie in ihren Principien.* Leipzig: F. Fleischer, 1851.

Tholuck, August. *Das Alte Testament im Neuen Testament.* 6th ed. Gotha: F. A. Perthes, 1877.

———. *Der Geist der lutherischen Theologen Wittenbergs im Verlaufe des 17. Jahrhunderts.* Hamburg: F. und A. Perthes, 1852.

———. *Geschichte des Rationalismus.* Berlin: Wiegandt & Grieben, 1865.

———. *Die Propheten und ihre Weissagungen.* Gotha: F. A. Perthes, 1860.

———. *Der sittliche Character des Heidenthums.* Gotha: F. A. Perthes, 1867.

———. *Vermischte Schriften.* 2 vols. Hamburg: F. Perthes, 1839.

———. *Vorgeschichte des Rationalismus.* 4 vols. in 2: vol. 1—*Das akademische Leben des siebzehnten Jahrhunderts*; vol. 2—*Das kirchliche Leben des siebzehnten Jahrhunderts.* Halle: E. Anton, 1853, 1862.

Thomasius, Gottfried. *Christi Person und Werk.* 3d ed. Erlangen: A. Deichert, 1886–88.

———. *Die Christliche Dogmengeschichte als Entwicklung-geschichte Kirchlichen Lehrbegriffs.* 2 vols. Erlangen: A. Deichert, 1886–89.

Tiele, Cornelis Petrus. *Elements of the Science of Religion.* 2 vols. Edinburgh & London: William Blackwood & Sons, 1897–99.

———. *Verslag en Mededeelen van de Koninglijke Akademie van Wetenschappelijke Letterkunde.* 1895.

Toorenenbergen, J. J. van. *Bijdragen tot de verklaring, toetsing, en ontwikkeling van de leer der hervormde kerk.* Utrecht: Kemink, 1865.

Totius. *Het Methodisme.* Amsterdam. Höveker & Wormser, 1903.

Trechsel, F. *Die protestantischen Antitrinitarier vor Faustus Socin.* 2 vols. Heidelberg, K. Winter, 1839–44.

Trede, Th. B. *Das Heidenthum in der Römischen Kirche.* Gotha: Perthes, 1889–92.

Trelcatius, Lucas, Jr. *Scholastica et methodica locorum communium institutio.* London, 1604.

Trench, Richard Chenevix. *Notes on the Miracles of Our Lord.* New York: Appleton, 1870.

Trigland. *Antapologia, sive examen atque refutatio totius Apologiae remonstrantium.* Amsterdam: Joannem Janssonium et al., 1664.

Trip, C. J. *Die Theophanien in den Geschichtesbuechern des Alten Testaments.* Leiden: D. Noothoven van Goor, 1858.

Troeltsch, Ernst. *The Absoluteness of Christianity and the History of Religions.* Translated by David Reid. 1902. Reprinted, Richmond, Va.: John Knox, 1971.

———. *Geschichte und Metaphysik.* Freiburg: Mohr, 1888.

———. *Psychologie und Erkenntnistheorie in der Religionswissenschaft.* Tübingen: J. C. B. Mohr, 1905.

———. *Vernunft und Offenbarung bei Johann Gerhard und Melanchthon.* Göttingen: Vandenhoeck & Ruprecht, 1891.

———. *Die Wissenschaftliche Lage und ihre Anforderungen an die Theologie.* Tübingen: Mohr, 1900.

Tschackert, P. *Evangelische Polemik gegen die römischen Kirche.* Gotha: F. A. Perthes, 1885.

Tulloch, John. *Rational Theology and Christian Philosophy in England in the Seventeenth Century.* 2 vols. Edinburgh: W. Blackwood, 1872.

Turretin, Francis. *Institutes of Elenctic Theology.* Translated by George Musgrove Giger and edited by James T. Dennison. 3 vols. Phillipsburg, N.J.: Presbyterian and Reformed, 1992.

Tuuk, H. Edema van der. *Johannes Bogerman.* Gronigen: Wolters, 1868.

Twesten, August. *Vorlesungen über die Dogmatik.* 2d ed. 2 vols. Hamburg: F. Perthes, 1829–37.

Ueberweg-Heinze, Friedrich. *Geschichte der Philosophie.* 9th ed. 5 vols. Berlin: E. S. Mittler & Sohn, 1923–28.

Uhlhorn, Gerhard. *Der Kampf des Christenthums mit dem Heidenthum.* Stuttgart: Gundert, 1899.

Urquhart, John. *The Inspiration and Accuracy of the Holy Scriptures.* London: Marshall Brothers, 1895.

Ursinus, Zacharias. *Catechismus Major.* In *Opera Theologica.* Heidelberg: John Lancellot, 1612.

———. *The Commentary of Dr. Zacharius Ursinus on the Heidelberg Catechism.* Translated by G. W. Williard. Grand Rapids: Eerdmans, 1954.

———. *Volumen Tractationum Theologicarum*. Neustadii Palatinorum: Mathes Harnisch, 1584.

Usher. *Corpus theologiae*. Dublin, 1638.

———. *'t Lichaam der Goddelyke Leer*. Translated by Ruytingius. Amsterdam, 1656.

Uytenbogaert, Joh. *Onderwijzing in de Christlijke Religie*. Amsterdam: Ian Fred. Stam, 1640.

Vacherot, E. *La religion*. Paris: Chamerot et Lauwereyns, 1869.

Valeton, J. J. P. *Christus en het Oude Testament*. Nijmegen: Ten Hoet, 1895.

Van Bell, F. G. B. *Disputatio academica de patefactionis Christianiae indole e vocabulis "φανερόω et ἀποκρύπτω" in libris N. T. efficienda*. Lugduni-Batavorum: P. Engels, 1849.

Van der Tuuk, H. E. *Johannes Bogerman*. Groningen: Wolters, 1868.

Van Dijk, Isaac. *Aesthetische en Ethische Godsdienst*. In vol. I of *Gesammelte Geschriften*. 1895.

———. *Verkeerd bijbelgebruik*. Groningen: Wolters, 1891.

Van Leeuwen, E. H. *Prolegomena van Bijbelsche Godgeleerdheid*. Utrecht: C. H. E. Breijer, 1890.

Van Til, S. *Theologiae utriusque compendium cum naturalis tum revelatae*. Leiden, 1704.

Veil, Heinrich. *Justinus des Philosophen und Märtyrers Rechtfertigung des Christentums: Apologie I. u. II*. Strassburg: Heitz, 1894.

Verbrodt, G. *Beiträge zur religiosische Psychologie*. Leipzig, 1904.

———. *Psychologie des Glaubens*. Göttingen, 1895.

———. *Psychologie in Theologie und Kirche*. Leipzig, 1893.

Vetter, Benjamin. *Die moderne Weltanschauung und der Mensch*. 5th ed. Jena: G. Fischer, 1906.

Vigouroux, F. *Les Livres saints et la critique rationaliste*. 2d ed. Paris: A. Roger and F. Chernoviz, 1886, 1890.

Vilmar, August Friedrick Christian. *Dogmatik*. 2 vols. Gütersloh: C. Bertelsmann, 1874.

———. *Die Theologie der Thatsachen wider die Theologie der Rhetorik*. 4th ed. Gütersloh: C. Bertelsmann, 1876.

Vincent of Lerins. *Commonitorium pro catholicae fidei antiquitate et universitate adversus profanes omnium haereticorum novitiates*. Frankfurt: Minerva, 1925.

———. *A Commonitory. NPNF (2)*, XI, 131–56.

Vinet, Alexandre. *Discours sur quelques sujets religieux*. 6th ed. Paris: Ches Les Editeurs, 1862.

———. *Essais de philosophie, morale, et religion*. Paris: L. Hachette, 1837.

Vinke. *Theologae Christianae Dogmaticae*. Trajecti ad Rhenum: Kemink, 1853–54.

Visscher, H. *Guilielmus Amesius: zijn leven en werken*. Haarlem: J. M. Stap, 1894.

———. *De Oorsprong der Religie*. Utrecht: Kemink, 1904.

———. *De religie en de gemeenschap*. Utrecht: G. J. A. Ruys, 1907.

———. *Religie en Zedelijke Leven*. Utrecht, 1904.

Vitringa, Campegius. *Doctrina Christianae Religionis*. 8 vols. Leiden: Joannis le Mair, 1761–86.

Voetius, Gisbert. *Selectae disputationes theologicae*. 5 vols. Utrecht, 1648–69.

Vogrinec, Anton. *Nostra maxima culpa*. Vienna: C. Fromme, 1904.

Vogt, Karl C. *Köhlerglaube und Wissenschaft*. 3d ed. Giessen: J. Ricker, 1855.

Voigt, Heinrich. *Fundamentaldogmatik*. Gotha: F. A. Perthes, 1874.

Volck, Wilhelm. *Christi und der Apostel Stellung zum Alten Testament*. Leipzig: A. Deichert (Georg Böhme), 1900.

———. *Zur Lehre von der Heilige Schrift*. Dorpat: E. J. Karow, 1885.

Volkel, Johann. *De Vera Religione Libri Quinque*. Racoviae, 1630.

Vollmer, Hans. *Die alttestamentlichen Citate bei Paulus textkritisch und biblisch-theologisch gewürdigt*. Freiburg i.B.: J. C. B. Mohr (Paul Siebeck), 1895.

Von der Goltz, H. *Die christlichen Grundwahrheiten*. Gotha: Perthes, 1873.

Vorbrodt, Gustav. *Beitrage zur religiösen Psychologie*. Leipzig: A. Deichert, 1904.

———. *Psychologie des Glaubens*. Göttingen: Vandenhoeck und Ruprecht, 1895.

———. *Psychologie in Theologie und Kirche?* Dessau and Leipzig: Anhaltische Verlagsanstalt, 1893.

Vos, Geerhardus. *The Idea of Biblical Theology as a Science and a Theological Discipline.* New York: A. D. F. Randolph, 1894. Reprinted in *Redemptive History and Biblical Interpretation: The Shorter Writings of Geerhardus Vos.* Edited by Richard B. Gaffin Jr. Phillipsburg, N.J.: Presbyterian and Reformed, 1980.

Voss, Gerhard Johannes. *Historiae de controversies.* 2d ed. Amsterdam: L. & D. Elzevirios, 1655.

———. *Historiae Pelagius.* 1655.

———. *De Origine et Progressu Idololatriae.* Amsterdam: Blaeu, 1641.

Wagenaar, L. H. *Het Réveil en de Afscheiding.* Heerenveen: J. Hepkema, 1880.

Walch, Johann George. *Bibliotheca Theologica selecta, litterariis adnotationibus instructa.* 4 vols. Ienae: vid. Croeckerianal, 1757–65.

Walker, James. *The Theology and Theologians of Scotland: Chiefly of the Seventeenth and Eighteenth Centuries.* Edinburgh: Clark, 1872.

Walker, Theodor. *Jesus und das Alte Testament in ihrer gegenseitigen Bezeugung.* Gütersloh: C. Bertelsmann, 1899.

Walther, Wilhelm. *Das Erbe der Reformation im Kamfpe der Gegenwart.* 4 vols. Leipzig: A. Deichert, 1903–17.

Walz, K. *Die Lehre der Kirche von der Schrift nach der Schrift selbst geprüft.* Leiden: E. J. Brill, 1884.

Warfield, B. B. *The Confession of Faith as Revised in 1903.* Richmond, Va.: Whittet & Shepperson, 1904.

Weber, E. E. J. *Satan franc-maçon la mystification de Léo Taxil.* Paris: René Julliard, 1964.

Weber, Eduard. *Der moderne Spiritismus.* Heitbronn: Henninger, 1883.

Weber, Ferdinand Wilhelm. *System der altsynagogalen palästinischen Theologie: Aus Targum, Midrasch und Talmud.* Leipzig: Dörffling & Franke, 1880.

Weber, Friedrich K. E. *Franks Gotteslehre und de ren erkenntniss theoretische Voraussetzungen.* Leipzig: Deichert, 1901.

Wedgwood, Julia. *John Wesley and the Evangelical Reaction of the Eighteenth Century.* London: Macmillan, 1870.

Wegscheider, Julius August Ludwig. *Institutiones Theologiae Christianae Dogmaticae.* Halle: Gebauer, 1819.

Weingarten, Hermann. *Die Revolutionskirchen Englands.* Leipzig: Breitkopf und Härtel, 1868.

Weiss, Albert. M. *Apologie des Christenthums.* 3d ed. 5 vols. Freiburg i.B.: Herder, 1896.

———. *Die religiöse Gefahr.* Freiburg i. B.: Herder, 1904.

Weiss, Johannes. *Die Nachfolge Christi und die Predigt der Gegenwart.* Göttingen: Vandenhoeck & Ruprecht, 1895.

Weisse, Christian Herman. *Philosophische Dogmatik oder Philosophie des Christentums.* 3 vols. Leipzig: Hirzel, 1855–62.

Wellhausen, Julius. *Die Christliche Religion.* Berlin and Leipzig: B. G. Teubner, 1905.

Wendt, Hans Heinrich. *Die Aufgabe der Systematische Theologie.* Göttingen: Vandenhoeck und Ruprecht, 1894.

———. *Der Erfahrungsbeweis für die Wahrheit des Christenthums.* Göttingen: Vandenhoeck & Ruprecht, 1897.

Werner, J. *Hegels Offenbarungsbegriff.* Leipzig: Breitkopf & Härtel, 1887.

Werner, Karl. *Franz Suarez und die Scholastik der letzten Jahrhunderte.* Regensburg: G. J. Manz, 1861–62.

———. *Geschichte der apologetischen und polemischen literatur der christlichen Theologie.* 5 vols. Schaffhausen: Hurter'sche Buchhandlung, 1861–88.

———. *Geschichte der Katholischen Theologie: seit dem Trienter Konzil bis zur Gegenwart.* München: Cotta, 1866.

———. *Der Heilige Thomas von Aquino.* Regensburg: G. J. Manz, 1858–59.

———. *Die Scholastik des späteren Mittelalters.* Wien: W. Braumüler, 1881–87.

Wernle, Paul. *Die Anfänge unserer Religion.* 2d ed. Tubingen: J. C. B. Mohr (Paul Siebeck), 1904.

———. *The Beginnings of Christianity.* New York: G. P. Putnam, 1903.

Wiclif, John. *De Veritate Sacrae Scripturae.* 3 vols. Leipzig: Dieterich, 1904.

Wiedeman, Alfred. *Magie und Zauberei im alten Ägypten.* Leipzig: J. C. Hinrichs, 1905.

Wijnmalen, T. C. L. *Hugo de Groot als Verdediger van beet Christendom.* Utrecht: W. F. Dannenfelser, 1869.

———. *Pascal als Bestrijder der Jesuïeten en verdediger des Christendoms.* Utrecht: W. F. Dannenfelser, 1865.

Wildeboer, G. *De letterkunde des Ouden Verbonds.* Groningen: Wolters, 1893.

———. *Het Ontstaan van den Kanon des Oude Verbond.* Groningen: Wolters, 1891.

———. *The Origin of the Canon of the Old Testament.* Translated by Benjamin Wisner Bacon. London: Luzac, 1895.

Willmann, Otto. *Geschichte des Idealismus.* 3 vols. Braunschweig: F. Vieweg, 1894.

Winckler, H. *Die Weltanschauung des Alten Orients.* Leipzig: E. Pfeiffer, 1904.

Windelband, W. *Lehrbuch der geschichte der philosophie.* Tübingen and Leipzig: J. C. B. Mohr, 1903.

Winer, Georg Benedikt. *Biblisches Realwörterbuch zum Handgebrauch.* Leipzig: C. H. Reclam, 1847.

———. *Grammatik des neutestamentliche Sprachidioms.* 6th ed. Leipzig: F. C. W. Vogel, 1855.

———. *A Greek Grammar of the New Testament.* Translated by Moses Stuart and Edward Robinson. Andover: Flagg & Gould, 1825.

Witsius, Herman. *Hermanni Witsii excercitationes sacrae in symbolum quod Apostolorum dicitur.* Amsterdam: Johannem Wolters, 1697.

———. *Miscellaneorum sacrorum.* 3d ed. 2 vol. Herborn, Germany: Iohannis Nicolai Andreae, 1712.

———. *The Oeconomy of the Covenants between God and Man: Comprehending a Complete Body of Divinity.* 3 vols. New York: Lee & Stokes, 1798.

———. *Twist des Heeren met zijn Wijngaart.* Utrecht: Balthasar Lobe, 1692.

Wittewrongel, Petrus. *Oeconomia Christiana ofte Christelicke Huys-houdinghe.* Amsterdam: Brant and A. van den Burgh, 1661.

Witz, Harmannus. *Twist des heeren met sijn wyngaert.* Utrecht: Balthasar Lobe, 1692.

Wobbermin, Georg. *Grundprobleme der Systematisch Theologie.* Berlin, 1899.

———. *Religionsgeschichtliche Studien zur Frage nach der Beeinflussung des Urchristenthum durch das antike Mysterienwesen.* Berlin: E. Ebering, 1896.

———. *Theologie und Metaphysik.* Berlin: Alexander Duncker, 1901.

———. *Zwei akademische Vorlesungen über Grundprobleme der Systemischen Theologie.* Berlin: Alexander Duncker, 1899.

Wolf, Karl. *Ursprung und Verwendung des religiösen Erfahrungsbegriffes in der Theologie des 19. Jahrhunderts ein Beitrag zur Geschichte der theologischen Erkanntnistheorie.* Gütersloh: Bertelsmann, 1906.

Wollebius, Johannes. *Compendium theologiae christianae.* Basel, 1626; Oxford, 1657.

———. *Reformed Dogmatics.* Edited and translated by John W. Beardslee III. New York: Oxford University Press, 1965. Originally published 1657.

Woltjer, J. *Ideëel en reëel.* Amsterdam: Höveker, 1896.

Woolston, Thomas. *Six Discourses on the Miracles of Our Saviour and Defences of His Discourses.* 1727. Reprinted, New York: Garland Pub., 1979.

Wundt, Wilhelm. *Psychologische Studien.* 10 vols. Leipzig: W. Englemann, 1905–18.

Wuttke, A. *Christian Ethics.* Translated by John P. Lacroix. New York: Nelson & Phillips, 1873.

Wycliffe, John. *Johann Wiclif's De veritate Sacrae Scripturae.* Edited by Rudolph Buddensieg. 3 vols. Leipzig: Dieterich, 1904.

Wynaend, Francken. *Psychologische Omtrekken.* Amsterdam, 1900.

Xenophon. *Memorabilia.* Translated by Amy L. Bonnette. Ithaca: Cornell University Press, 1994.

Ypey, Annaeus. *Beknopte letterk gesch der syst Godgeleerdheid.* 1793–98.

———. *Geschiedenis van de Kristlijke kerk in de achtiende eeuw.* Utrecht: W. van Ijzerworst, 1797–1811.

Zahn, A. *Abriss einer Geschichte der evangelische Kirche in Amerika im neunzehnten Jahrhundert.* Stuttgart: Steinkopf, 1889.

———. *Abriss einer Geschichte der evangelischen Kirche auf dem europäischen Fest-*

lande im neunzehnten Jahrhundert. 3d ed. Stuttgart: J. B. Metzler, 1893.

———. *Social demokratie und Theologie.* Gütersloh, 1895.

———. *Die Ursachen des Niederganges der reformirten Kirche in Deutschland.* Barmen: H. Klein, 1881.

Zahn, Theodor. *Grundriss der Geschichte des neutestamentlichen Kanons.* Leipzig: Deichert, 1901.

Zanchi[us], Jerome. *Operum Theologicorum.* 8 vols. [Geneva]: Sumptibus Samuelis Crispini, 1617.

———. *De sacra scriptura tractatus integer.* Neustadii in Palatinatu: Viduam Wilhelm Harnisii, 1598.

Zeller, Eduard. *Outlines of the History of Greek Philosophy.* Translated by L. R. Palmer. 13th ed. New York: Humanities Press, 1969.

———. *Die Philosophie der Griechen.* 4th ed. 3 vols. Leipzig: O. R. Reisland, 1879, 1919.

———. *Das Theologische System Zwingli's.* Tübingen: L. F. Fues, 1853.

———. *Vorträge und abhandlungen geschichtlichen inhalts.* 3 vols. Leipzig: Fues's Verlag (L. W. Reisland), 1865–84.

Ziegler, Theobald. *Die geistigen und socialen Strömungen des neunzehnten Jahrhunderts.* Berlin: G. Bondi, 1901.

Ziese, J. H. *Die Gesetz- und Ordnungsgemätzheit der biblischen Wunder.* Schleswig: Johs. Ibbeken, 1903.

———. *Die Inspiration der Heilige Schrift.* Schleswig: I. Johannsens, 1894.

Zimmer, Patritius Benedict. *Philosophische Untersuchung über den allgemeinen Verfall des menschlichen Geschlechtes.* Landshut: Weberschen Buchhandlung, 1809.

Zöckler, Otto. *Geschichte der Beziehungen Zwischen Theologie und Natuurwissenschaft.* 2 vols. Gütersloh: C. Bertelsman, 1877–79.

———. *Gottes Zeugen im Reich der Natur.* 2 vols. Gütersloh: C. Bertelsmann, 1881.

———. *Handbuch der theologischen Wissenschaften.* 3d ed. 5 vols. Nördlingen and Münich: C. H. Beck, 1889–90.

———. *Lehre vom Urstand des Menschen.* Gütersloh: C. Bertelsmann, 1879.

———. *Theologia naturalis: Entwurf einer systematischen Naturtheologie vom offen-*

barungsgläubigen Standpunkte aus. Frankfurt a.M.: Heyder & Zimmer, 1860.

Zöllig, August. *Die Inspirationslehre des Origenes.* Freiburg i.B. and St. Louis: Herder, 1902.

Zunz, Leopold. *Die gottesdienstlichen Vorträge der Juden.* Berlin: A. Asher, 1832.

Zwingli, Ulrich. *Commentary on True and False Religion.* Edited by Samuel Macauley Jackson and Clarence Nevin Heller. Durham, N.C.: Labyrinth Press, 1981.

———. *De Claritate et certitudine Verbi Dei.* In *Opera.* Edited by Schuler and Schulthess. Turici: Officina Schulthessiana, 1842.

———. *On Providence and Other Essays.* Translated by Samuel Macauley Jackson and edited by William John Hinks. Durham, N.C.: Labyrinth Press, 1983.

———. *A Short Pathway to the Right and True Understanding of the Holy and Sacred Scriptures.* Translated by John Veron. Worcester: John Oswen, 1550.

ARTICLES

Bachmann, Ph. "Natur und Gnade." *Neue Kirchliche Zeitschrift* (November 1905).

Barth, Fritz. "Die Streit zwischen Zahn und Harnack über der Ursprung des N. T. Kanons." *Neue Jahrbuch für deutsche Theologie* (1893): 56–80.

Bauch, Bruno. "Ethik." In vol. 1, pp. 54–103 of *Die Philosophie im Begin des Zwanzigsten Jahrhunderts: Festschrift für Kuno Fischer.* Edited by W. Windelband. Heidelberg: C. Winter, 1901.

Bauer, Karl. "Die Bedeutung geschichtlicher Thatsacher für den religiöse Glauben." *Studien und Kritiken* 77 (1904): 221–73.

Bavinck, H. "Calvinistisch en Gereformeerd." *Vrije Kerk* 19 (February 1893): 49–71.

———. "Confessie en Dogmatiek." *Theologische Studiën* 9 (1891): 258–75.

———. "Eene Belangrijke Apologie van het Christelijke Wereldbeschouwing." *Theologische Studiën* 12 (1894): 142–52.

———. "The Future of Calvinism." *Presbyterian and Reformed Review* 5 (January 1894): 1–24.

———. "Recent Dogmatic Thought in the Nederlands." *Presbyterian and Reformed Review* 3 (April 1892): 209–28.

———. "De Theologie van Albrecht Ritschl." *Theologische Studiën* 6 (1888): 369–403.

———. "Theologische Richtingen in Nederland." *Tijdschrift voor Gereformeerde Theologie* 1 (June–July 1894): 161–88.

Bender, W. "Zur Geschichte der Emancipation der natüralichen Theologie." *Jahrbuch für Protestantischen Theologie* (1883): 529–92.

Benzinger, Immanuel. "Los bei den Hebräern." *PRE³*, XI, 642–47.

Bjerring, Nicholas. "Religious Thought in the Russian Empire." *Presbyterian and Reformed Review* 3 (January 1892): 103–22.

Blötzen. "Der Anglikanismus auf dem Wegen nach Rome." *Stimmen aus Maria Laach* (1904): 125ff.

Bonet-Maury, Gaston. "Jean Cameron." In *Etudes de théologie et d'histoire*. Paris: Fischbacher, 1901.

Bonwetsch, G. N. "Arkandisziplin." *PRE³*, II, 51–55.

———. "Bilderverehrung und Bilderstreitigkeiten." *PRE³*, III, 221–26.

———. "Dionysius Areopagita." *PRE³*, IV, 687–96.

———. "Justin der Märtyrer." *PRE³*, IX, 641–50.

———. "Montanismus." *PRE³*, XIII, 417–26.

Borchert, P. "Die Visionen der Propheten." *Theologische Studien und Kritiken* 68 (1895): 217–51.

———. "Die Wunder der Propheten." *Beweis des Glaubens* 33 (1897): 177–89.

Bousset, Julius. "Die Religionsgeschichte und das Neue Testament." *Theologische Rundschau* 7 (July 1904): 265–77, 311–18, 353–65.

Brehm. "Das Christl. Gesetzthum der apost Väter." *Zeitschrift für Kirchliche Wissenschaft und Kirchliches Leben* 7 (1886).

Brendel, L., and Pannebecker. "Nordamerika." *PRE³*, XVI, 165–74, 784–801.

Bronsveld, A. W. "Die englische Kirchenarmee." *Neue Kirchlichen Zeitschrift* 13 (February 1899).

Bructiére. "L'oevre literairre de Calvin." *Revue de deux Mondes* (October 15, 1900).

Bruining, A. "De Moderne Richting en de Dogmatiek." *Theologische Tijdschrift* 28 (1894): 563ff., 598ff.

———. "Over de Methode van Onze Dogmatiek." *Teylers Theologische Tijdschrift* 1 (1903): 153–85.

———. "Pantheisme of Theisme." *Teylers Theologische Tijdschrift* 2, no. 4 (1904).

——— "De Roomsche leer van het donum superadditum." *Teylers Theologische Tijdschrift* 5 (1907): 564–97.

———. "De Theologie in den Kring der Wetenschappen." *De Gids* 47 (June 1884): 449–501.

———. "Verschillende Schakeeringen van Modernen." *Bijblad van de Hervorming* (February 10, 1885).

———. "Wijsbegeerte van de Godsdienst." *Theologische Tijdschrift* 15 (1881): 365–428.

Buddensieg, Rudolph. "Quäker." *PRE³*, XVI, 356–80.

———. "Tractarianismus." *PRE³*, XX, 18–53.

Burckhardt, Abel. "Aus der modernen systematischen Theologie Grossbritanniens." *Zeitschrift für Theologie und Kirche* 9 (1899).

Bussy, I. J. de. "Mortuos Plango." *Theologische Tijdschrift* 29, no. 1 (January 1895): 1–14.

———. "De Ontwikkelingsgang der Moderne Richting." *De Gids* 7, no. 3 (October 1889): 91–135.

Cannegieter, Tjeerd. "De Godsdienst in den Mensch en de Mensch in den Godsdienst." *Teylers Theologische Tijdschrift* II/2 (1904): 178–211.

Caven, William. "The Testimony of Jesus to the Old Testament." *Presbyterian and Reformed Review* 3 (July 1892): 401–20.

Chantepie de la Saussaye, P. D. "De Theologie van Ritschl." *Theologische Studiën* 2 (1884): 259ff.

Cramer, Samuel. "De Roomsch-Katholieke en oudprotestanse Schriftbeschouwing." *De Heraut* 26 (June 1878).

———. "De Schrift beschouwing van Calvijn [and Other Older Reformed Writers]." *De Heraut* 26 (June 1878)–33 (July 1878).

Cramer, S. "Mennoniteten." *PRE³*, XII, 594–616.

———. "Menno Simons." *PRE³*, XII, 586–94.

Cremer, Hermann. "Ebenbild Gottes." *PRE³*, V, 113–18.

———. "Engel." *PRE³*, V, 364–72.

———. "Geist." *PRE³*, VI, 444–50.

———. "Gerechtigkeit." *PRE³*, VI, 546–53.

———. "Herz." *PRE³*, VII, 773–76.

———. "Himmel." *PRE³*, VIII, 80–84.

———. "Inspiration." *PRE³*, 183–203.

Dalmann, Gustaf. "Bath Kol." *PRE³*, II, 443–44.

Daxer, Georg. "Zur Lehre von der Christliche Gewissheit." *Studien und Kritiken* 77 (1904): 82–123.

De Hoop, Scheffer. "Mennoniten." *PRE²*, IX, 566–77.

De Witt, John. "The Testimony of the Holy Spirit to the Bible." *Presbyterian and Reformed Review* 6 (1895): 69–85.

Diestel, Ludwig. "Der Monoth. des Heidenthums." *Jahrbuch für deutsche Theologie* (1860).

———. "Studien zur Foederal Theologie." *Jahrbuch für deutsche Theologie* (1865).

Dorner, A. "Über das Verhältnis der Dogmatiek und Ethik." *Theologische Jahrbuch für Protestantische Theologie* (October 1889).

———. "Über das Wesen der Religion." *Theologische Studien und Kritiken* 56 (1883): 217–77.

Dorner, I. "Die Hellenisierung des altkirchlichen Dogmas." *Die Studiestube* (April 1906): 198–208

Dosker, Henry E. "Urim and Thummim." *Presbyterian and Reformed Review* 3 (October 1892): 717–30.

Edgar, Robert McCheyne. "Christianity and the Experimental Method." *Presbyterian and Reformed Review* 6, no. 22 (April 1895): 201–23.

Ehni, J. "Ursprung und Entwicklung der Religion." *Theologische Studien und Kritiken* 71 (1898): 581–648.

Eisler, Rudolf. "Zufall." *Wörterbuch der Philosophischen Begriffe*. 3 vols. Berlin: E. S. Mittler, 1910.

Eucken, Rudolf. "Wissenschaft und Religion." In *Beiträge zur Weiterentwicklung der christlichen Religion,* edited by Gustav

Adolf Deissmann. München: J. F. Lehmann, 1905.

Gass, Wilhelm. "Griechische und griechisch-russische Kirche." *PRE³*, V, 409–30.

———. "Konstantinopel." *PRE²*, VIII, 207–12.

Gloatz, P. "Wunder und Naturgesetz." *Theologische Studien und Kritiken* 59 (1886): 403–548.

Godet, G. "Vinet et l'autorité en natière de foi." *Revue de théologie et de philosophie* 26, no. 2 (March 1893): 173–91.

Gooszen, M. "Nog eens een Tertium Genus." *Geloof en Vrijheid* 28, no. 6 (December 1894).

Gottschick, Johannes. "Die Entstehung der Losung der Unkirchlichkeit der Theologie." *Zeitschrift für Theologie und Kirche* 13 (1903): 77–94.

———. "Das Verhältnis von Diesseits und Jenseits im Christ." *Zeitschrift für Theologie und Kirche* 9 (February 1899).

Grau, R. "Über des Grund des Glaubens." *Beweis des Glaubens* 26 (1890): 225ff.

Grétillat, A. "Movements of Theological Thought among French-Speaking Protestants from the Revival of 1820 to the End of 1891." *Presbyterian and Reformed Review* 3 (July 1892): 421–47.

———. "Theological Thought among the French Protestants in 1892." *Presbyterian and Reformed Review* 4 (July 1893): 390–417.

Groenewegen, H. I. "De Theologie aan de Universiteit." *Theologische Tijdschrift* (May 1905): 193–224.

Grützmacher, R. "Hauptprobleme der Gegenwärt: Dogmatik." *Neue Kirchliche Zeitschrift* 8 (1902): 859–92; 959–70.

Gunkel, H. "Das Alte Testament im Licht der modernen Forschung." In *Beiträge zur Weiterentwicklung der christlichen Religion,* edited by Gustav Adolf Deissmann. Munchen: J. F. Lehmann, 1905.

Hamerling, Robert. "Epilog an die Kritiker." Pp. 142ff. of *Hamerlings Werke in vier Bänden.* Leipzig: M. Hesse, 1900.

Häring, Th. "Gehört die Auferstehung jesu zum Glaubensgrund?" *Zeitschrift für Theologie und Kirche* 7 (1897): 332.

———. "Zur Lehre von der heilige Schrift." *Studien und Kritiken* 66 (1893).

————. "Zur Verständigung in der systematischen Theologie." *Zeitschrift für Theologie und Kirche* 9 (1899): 97–135.

Harnack, A. "Alexandrinische Katechetenschule und Schule." *PRE³*, I, 356–59.

————. "Apostolisches Symbolum." *PRE³*, I, 741–55.

————. "Beiträge zur Förderung christlicher Theologie VII." *Theologische Literaturzeitung* 28 (1903): 476.

Hauck, Albert. "Rothe." *PRE²*, XVIII, 653–62.

————. "Theophanie und Schechina." *PRE²*, XV, 537–44.

Hegler, Alfred. "Hans Denck." *PRE³*, IV, 576–80.

————. "Johann David Joris." *PRE³*, IX, 349–52.

————. "Kirchengeschichte oder christliche Religionsgeschichte?" *Zeitschrift für Theologie und Kirche* 13 (1903): 1–38.

————. "Sebastian Franck." *PRE³*, VI, 142–50.

Heinze, M. "Naturgesetz." *PRE³*, XIII, 657–59.

Heinze, W. "Religionsphilosophie." *PRE³*, XVI, 597–630.

Heringa, J. "De twistzaak van Johannes Maccovius." *Archief voor Kerkelijke Geschiedenis* 3 (1831).

Hermann, W. Review of E. Troeltsch, *Die Absolutheit des Christenthums und die Religionsgeschichte*. *Theologische Literaturzeitung* 27 (1902): 330.

————. "Grund und Inhalt des Glaubens." *Beweis des Glaubens* 26 (1890).

————. "Verkehr des Christen mit Gott." *Zeitschrift für Theologie und Kirche* 4 (1894).

Herrlinger, A. "Philippus Melanchton." *PRE²*, IX, 471–525.

Herzog, J. J. "Quietismus." *PRE¹*, XII, 427ff.

Herzog, J. J., and O. Zöckler. "Socin und der Socinianismus." *PRE²*, XIV, 376–401.

Hesseling, D. C. "Een Protestantsche patriarch." *Theologische Tijdschrift* 36 (May 1902): 218–54.

Hoekstra, S. "Godsdienst en Zedelijkheid." *Theologische Tijdschrift* 2 (1868): 117–55.

Hoffmann, Heinrich. "Die Frömmigkeit der deutschen Aufklärung." *Zeitschrift für Theologie und Kirche* 16 (1906): 234–50.

Hofmann, Rudolph. "Baptisten." *PRE¹*, II, 385–93.

Hollenberg, W. A. "Bonaventura als Dogmaticus." *Theologische Studien und Kritiken* 41 (1868): 95–132.

Honert, Johan van den. "Voorrede." In *Schatboek der Vaerlkaringen over den Nederlandschen Catechismus* by Z. Ursinus. Gorinchem: Nic. Goetze, 1736.

Hurgronje, Snouck. "De Islam." *De Gids* 50 (1886): 239–73, 454–98.

Hylkema, C. "S. Cramer, De Godsvrucht Voorwerp van Christelijke historische Onderzoek." *Theologische Tijdschrift* 34 (1900): 385–98.

Ihmels, L. "Die Aufgabe der Dogmatik im Lichte ihrer Geschichte." *Neue Kirchliche Zeitschrift* (1902).

————. "Blicke in die neue dogmatische Arbeit II: Die Dogmatik von Kaftan." *Neue Kirchliche Zeitschrift* 11 (1905): 273–311.

————. "Blicke in die neue dogmatische Arbeit III." *Neue Kirchliche Zeitschrift* 11 (1905): 495–522.

————. "Glaube und Erfahrung." *Neue Kirchliche Zeitschrift* 8 (1902): 971–73.

Kaftan, Julius. "Glaube und Dogmatik." *Zeitschrift für Theologie und Kirche* 1 (1891): 479.

————. "Was ist Schriftgemäss?" *Zeitschrift für Theologie und Kirche* 3 (1893): 93.

————. "Zur Dogmatik, Sieben Abhandlungen." *Zeitschrift für Theologie und Kirche* 13 (1903): 96–149, 214–66, 457–519; 14 (1904): 148–92, 273–357.

Kähler, M. "Bibel." *PRE³*, II, 686–91.

————. "Offenbarung." *PRE³*, XIV, 339–47.

Kattenbusch, F. "Anglikanische Kirche." *PRE³*, I, 525–47.

————. "Grass, Geschichte der Dogmatik in russischer Darstellung." *Theologische Literaturzeitung* 28 (1903): 183–86.

————. "Johannes von Damaskus." *PRE³*, IX, 286–300.

————. "Die Lage der Systematische Theologie in der Gegenwart." *Zeitschrift für Theologie und Kirche* 15 (March 1905): 103–46.

———. "Orientalische Kirche." *PRE³*, XIV, 436–67.

———. "Photius." *PRE³*, XV, 374–93.

———. "Protestantenverein." *PRE³*, XVI, 156.

———. "Protestantismus." *PRE³*, XVI, 135–82.

———. "Puritaner." *PRE³*, XVI, 323–48.

Katzer, E. "Der Moralische Gottesbeweis nach Kant und Herbart." *Jahrbuch für Protestantische Theologie*. Leipzig: Brockhaus, 1877.

Kautzsch, E. "Theophanie." *PRE²*, XV, 537–42.

———. "Urim & Thummim." *PRE²*, XVI, 226–33.

Keizer, G. "De Parijsche School." *Tijdschrift voor Gereformeerde Theologie* 6 (1899): 19–42.

Klaiber, Karl Hermann. "Die Lehre altprot. Dogma von dem testimonium Spiritus Sancti." *Jahrbuch für deutsche Theologie* (1857): 1–54.

Klap, P. A. "Agobard van Lyon." *Theologische Tijdschrift* 29 (March 1895): 146ff.

Kleinert, P. "Naturanschauung des Alten Testaments." *Theologische Studien und Kritiken* 64 (1891): 1ff.

Koeppel, W. "Die Zahn-Harnacksche Streit über die Geschichte des neutestamentlichen Kanons." *Theologische Studien und Kritiken* 64 (1891): 102–57.

Kohler, Walther. "Münster (Wiedertäufer)." *PRE³*, XIII, 538–53.

Kolde, Theodore. "Die Engelsche Kirchenarmee." *Neue Kirchliche Zeitschrift* (February 1899): 101–38.

———. "Heilsarmee." *PRE³*, VII, 578–93.

———. "Herz-Jesu-Kultus," *PRE³*, VII, 777.

———. "Thomas Müntzer." *PRE³*, XIII, 556–66.

Köstlin, J. "Calvin's Institutio nach Form und Inhalt in ihrer geschichtliche Entwicklung." *Theologische Studien und Kritiken* 34 (1861): 7–62, 410–86.

———. "Luther." *PRE³*, XI, 720–56.

———. "Religion nach dem Neuen Testament, mit bessonder Beziehung aus das Verhaeltnis des Sittlichen und Religioesen und Mystischen in der Religion." *Theologische Studien und Kritiken* 61 (1888).

———. "Religion und Sittlichkeit." *Theologische Studien und Kritiken* 43 (1870): 50–122.

———. "Der Ursprung der Religion." *Theologische Studien und Kritiken* 63 (1890): 213–94.

———. "Wunder." *PRE²*, XVII, 358–70.

Krüger, G. "Gnosis." *PRE³*, VI, 728–38.

———. "Marcion." *PRE³*, XII, 266–77.

Kübel, Robert. "Rationalismus und Supernaturalismus." *PRE²*, XII, 507–35.

Kuenen, A. "Dogmengeschiedenis." *Theologische Tijdschrift* 25 (1891): 491ff.

Kunze, Johannes. "Loci Theologici." *PRE³*, XI, 570–72.

Kuyper, A. "Calvinism: Source and Stronghold of our Constitutional Liberties." In *Abraham Kuyper: A Centennial Reader*, edited by J. D. Bratt. Grand Rapids: Eerdmans, 1998.

———. "Vruchten der Naturlijke Godskennis." *Uit het Woord III*. Amsterdam: Höveker & Wormser.

Lagrange, Marie-Joseph. "Chronique de Jérusalem. Ain Kedeis." *Revue Biblique Internationale* 5 (1896): 440.

———. "Chronique de Jérusalem. Voyage de l'école biblique de Suez au Sinaï." *Revue Biblique Internationale* 5 (1896): 618.

———. "Comment elle se concilie avec la liberté de l'exégèse." *Revue Biblique Internationale* 5 (1896): 485.

———. "Difficultés soulevées contre l'opinion théologique traditionnelle. Lettre de M. Dick." *Revue Biblique Internationale* 5 (1896): 485.

———. "Du Sinaï à Jérusalem." *Revue Biblique Internationale* 6 (1897): 605.

———. "Épigraphie sémitique." *Revue Biblique Internationale* 6 (1897): 83.

———. "Hexaméron. Traduction, commentaire, origine du récit de la creation." *Revue Biblique Internationale* 5 (1896): 381.

———. "Jérusalem d'après la mosaïque de Mâdaba." *Revue Biblique Internationale* 6 (1897): 423.

———. "La Mosaique Géographique de Madaba." *Revue Biblique Internationale* 6 (1897): 165.

———. "Les Sources du Troisième Évangile." *Revue Biblique Internationale* 5 (1896): 5.

—————. "L'Innocence et le Péché." *Revue Biblique Internationale* 6 (1897): 341.

—————. "L'Inspiration des Livres Saints." *Revue Biblique Internationale* 5 (1896): 199.

—————. "Notre Exploration de Pétra." *Revue Biblique Internationale* 6 (1897): 208.

—————. "Origène, la critiqu textuelle et la tradition topographique." *Revue Biblique Internationale* 5 (1896): 78.

Lagrange, Marie-Joseph and Séjourne. "Dernières Découvertes." *Revue Biblique Internationale* 6 (1897): 643.

—————. "Le Sinaï." *Revue Biblique Internationale* 6 (1897): 107.

—————. "Nouvelles de Jérusalem." *Revue Biblique Internationale* 6 (1897): 107.

Lemme, L. "Apologetik." *PRE³*, I, 679–98.

Lindberg, Conrad Emil. "Recent Dogmatic Thought in Scandinavia." *Presbyterian and Reformed Review* 4 (October 1893).

Linden, J. W. van der. "De Geschiedenis en de Beteekenis der Ethische Richting onder de Modernen." *De Gids* (December 1883).

Lipsius, F. A. "Lipsius," *PRE³*, XI, 520–24.

Lipsius, R. A. "Neue Beiträge zur wissenschaftliche Grundlegung der Dogmatik, I II III." *Jahrbuch für Protestantische Theologie* (1885): 177–288, 369–453.

Lobstein, Paul. "Zum evangelischen Lebensideal in seiner lutherischen und reformierten Ausprägung." In *Collected Works: A Corpus of the Monographic Publications of Paul Lobstein (1850–1922).* 2 reels. Chicago: University of Chicago, 1977.

Loman, A. D. "Symbool en Werkelijkheid in de Evangelische Geschiedenis." *De Gids* 48 (Feb. 1884): 265–304.

Loofs, Friedrich. "Dogmengeschichte." *PRE³*, IV, 752–64.

—————. "Methodismus." *PRE³*, XII, 747–801.

*Lübkert. "Die Theologische der apost Väter." *Niedners Zeitschrift für historische Theologie* (1854).

Mallet, Herm. "Schechina." *PRE²*, XIII, 458–59.

McPheeters, W. M. "Test of Canonicity, Apostolic Authorship and Sanction." *Presbyterian and Reformed Review* 6 (January 1895).

Meyer, Ph. "Joseph Bryennios als Theolog. Ein Betrag zur Kenntnis der griech. Theologie im 15 Jahrh." *Theologische Studien und Kritiken* 69 (1896): 282–319.

—————. "Lukaris." *PRE³*, XI, 682–90.

Moore, H. C. G. "Calvin's Doctrine of Holy Scripture." *Presbyterian and Reformed Review* 4 (January 1893): 49–77.

Müller, J. "Dogmatik." *PRE¹*, III, 433–50.

Müller, M. "Lukaris." *PRE³*, XI, 682–90.

—————. "Vorlesungen Uber Ursprung und Entwicklung der Religion." *Deutsche Rundschau* (September 1898).

Nestle, E. "Jacobiten." *PRE³*, VIII, 565–71.

Niermeijer, A. "Het Wezen der Christelijke Openbaring." *De Gids* 14 (1850): 109–49.

Nösgen, D. F. "Die Lehre der Lutherschen Symbole von der heilige Schrift." *Neue Kirchliche Zeitschrift* (1895): 887–921.

—————. "Die Religiongeschichte und das Neue Testament." *Neue Kirchliche Zeitschrift* (1904): 923–55.

—————. "Wezen und Umfang du Offenbarung nach dem Neuen Testament." *Beweis des Glaubens* 26 (1890): 416–17.

Orelli, B. "Feuer und Wolkensäule." *PRE³*, VI, 60–62.

—————. "Träume," *PRE²*, XVI, 734.

—————. "Weissagung." *PRE²*, XVI, 724.

Pannebecker. "Nordamerika, Vereinigte Staaten." *PRE³*, XIV, 784–801.

Paulsen, Fr. "Was uns Kant Sein Kann." *Separat-Abdruck aus der Vierteljahrsschrift für wissenschaftliche Philosophie.* Vol. 5. Leipzig, 1881.

Peeters, R. "Onze heilige boeken." *De Katholiek* (March–April 1906).

Pesch. "Zur Inspirationslehre." *Stimmen aus Maria Laach* (January–March 1906).

Peters, M. "Zur Frage nach dem Glauben." *Neue Kirchliche Zeitschrift* (1903).

Pfleiderer, O. "Die Aufgabe der wissenschaftlichen Theologie für die Kirche der Gegenwart." *Protestantische Kirchzeitung* 50 (1891): 97–110.

—————. "Die Entwicklung der protestantischen Theologie seit Kant. Populäire Vortrag." *Protestantische Kirchzeitung* 49 (1891): 1101–10; 50 (1891): 1117–27.

—————. "Die Theologie der Ritschl'schen Schule, nach ihrer religionsphilosophischen Grundlage kritisch beleuchtet."

Jahrbuch für Protestantische Theologie 17, no. 3 (1891): 321–83.

———. "Die Theologie Ritschl's nach ihrer biblischen Grundlage kritisch beleuchtet." *Jahrbuch für Protestantische Theologie* 16, no. 1 (1889): 42–83.

Pieper, Fr. "Luther's Doctrine of Inspiration." *Presbyterian and Reformed Review* 4 (April 1893): 249–66.

Pierson, A. "Een Keerpunt in Wijsgeerige Ontwikkeling." *De Gids* 9 (June 1871): 455–87.

Poels, H. "De Oorsprong van de Pentateuch. De Stand van het Vraagstuk. Het God Recht der Kritik." *De Katholiek* (December 1898).

Prat, F. "Le nom divin est-il intensif en hébreu?" *Revue biblique internationale* 10 (1901): 497ff.

Rabus, Leonhard. "Vom Wirken und Wohnen des göttlichen Geistes in der Menschenseele." *Neue Kirchliche Zeitschrift* (1904).

Rade, Martin. "Zum Streit um die rechte Methode der christlichen Glaubenslehre." *Zeitschrift für Theologie und Kirche* 11 (1901): 429–34.

Reischle, Max Wilhelm Theodor. "Historische und dogmatische Methode der Theologie." *Theologische Rundschau* 4 (1901): 261–75.

———. "Kirchliche Lehre und theologische Wissenschaft." *Theologische Rundschau* 1 (1868): 619–29.

———. "Der Streit über die Begründung des Glaubens auf den geschichtlichen Jesus Christus." *Zeitschrift für Theologie und Kirche* 7 (1897): 171–264.

Riemens, Johannes. "Intellectueele en Intuitieue Kennis." *Theologische Studien* 22 (1904): 137–61.

———. "Principia in de Dogmatiek." *Theologische Studien* (1903): 379–97.

Rietschel, G. "Bibellesen und Bibelverbot." *PRE³*, II, 700–713.

Ritschl, O. "Die Ethik der Gegenwart in der Deutschen Theologie." *Theologische Rundschau* (1903): 399–414, 445–61, 491–505.

———. "Der geschichtliche Christus, der christliche Glaube und die theologische Wisssenschaft." *Zeitschrift für Theologie und Kirche* 3 (1893): 371.

———. "Studien zur Geschichte der Protestantischen Theologie im 19. Jahrhundert." *Zeitschrift für Theologie und Kirche* 5 (1895): 486–529.

———. "Theologische Wissenschaft und religiöse Spekulation." *Zeitschrift für Theologie und Kirche* 12 (1902): 202–48.

Rödiger, E. "Jakobiten." *PRE²*, VI, 455–60.

Rütschi, R. "Die Lehre von der natürlichen Religion und von Naturrecht." *Jahrbuch für Protestantischen Theologie* (1884): 1–48.

Schian, Martin. "Der Einfluss der Individualität auf Glaubensgewinnung und Glaubenstellung." *Zeitschrift für Theologie und Kirche* 7 (1897): 513.

———. "Glaube und Individualität." *Zeitschrift für Theologie und Kirche* 8 (1898): 170–94.

Schinz, A. "Le récent mouvement moral en Amérique et en Europe." *Revue de Theologie* (September 1896): 419–46.

Schmidt, C. "Clémanges." *PRE²*, III, 247.

Schmidt, H. "Der Marcionitismus in der neueren Theologie." *Neue Jahrbuch für deutsche Theologie* (1893).

Schoell, C. "Methodismus." *PRE²*, IX, 681–719.

———. "Traktarianismus." *PRE³*, XV, 738–91.

Schultz, Hermann. "Religion und Sittlichkeit in ihrem Verhältniss zu einander, religionsgeschichtlich untersucht." *Theologische Studien und Kritiken* 56 (1883): 60–130.

Schweizer, A. "Die Entweckung des Moralsystems in Reformirte Kirche." *Studien und Kritiken* 23 (1850): 1ff.

Seeberg, R. "Frank." *PRE³*, VI, 158–63.

Sieffert, Fr. "Ethik." *PRE³*, V, 532–58.

———. "Rothe." *PRE³*, XVII.

Späth, Adolph. "Nordamerika, Vereinigte Staaten." *PRE³*, XIV, 165–213.

Steffens, N. M. "Calvinism and the Theological Crisis." *Presbyterian and Reformed Review* 12 (April 1901): 211–25.

Steude, E. Gustav. "Die apologetische Bedeutung der allgemeine Religionsgeschichte." *Beweis des Glaubens* (1896): 457–84.

Strack, Herman L. "Kanon des alten Testaments." *PRE²*, VII, 412–51.

———. "Kanon des alten Testaments." *PRE³*, IX, 741–68.

Strauss und Torney, Victor Friedrich von. "Das unbewust Weissagende im vorchristliche Heidenthum." *Zeitschrift des Christliche Volkslebens* VIII.

Stowe. "J. Edwards." *PRE³*, V, 171–75.

Surenhuis. "Biblios Katallagés." *Quo sec. vet. theol. hebr. formulas allegandi et modes interpretandi conciliantur loca V.T. in N. T. allegata.* Amsterdam, 1713.

Thelemann, D. "Münster (Widertäufer)." *PRE²*, X, 360–63.

Thimm, Rudolf. "Luther's Lehre von dem Heilige Schrift." *Neue Kirchliche Zeitschrift* (1896): 644–75.

Tholuck, A. "Gefühl." *PRE¹*, IV, 704–9.

———. "Inspiration." *PRE¹*, VI, 692–99.

———. "Über die Wunder der Katholischen Kirche." *Vermischte Schriften* I, 22–48.

Traub, F. "Die Beurteilung der Ritschlschen Theologie." *Zeitschrift für Theologie und Kirche* 12 (1902): 497.

———. "Glaube und Theologie." *Studien und Kritiken* 66 (1893).

———. "Kirchliche und unkirchliche Theologie." *Zeitschrift für Theologie und Kirche* 13 (1903): 39–76.

———. "Die religionsgeschichtliche Methode und die Systematische Theologie." *Zeitschrift für Theologie und Kirche* 11 (1901): 301–40.

———. "Ritschl's Erkenntnisstheorie." *Zeitschrift für Theologie und Kirche* 4 (1894): 91.

———. "Zur dogmatischen Methodenlehre." *Theologische Studien und Kritiken* 78 (1905): 425–52.

Troeltsch, E. "Aufklärung." *PRE³*, II, 225–41.

———. "Deismus." *PRE³*, IV, 532–59.

———. "Geschichte und Metaphysik." *Zeitschrift für Theologie und Kirche* 8 (1898): 1.

———. "Idealismus, deutscher." *PRE³*, VIII, 612–37.

———. "Die Selbständigkeit der Religion." *Zeitschrift für Theologie und Kirche* 6 (1896): 167.

———. "Ueber historische und dogmatische Methode in der Theologie." In *Gesammelte Schriften von Ernst Troeltsch.*

Tübingen: J. C. B. Mohr (Paul Siebeck), 1913.

Tschackert, P. "Tradition." *PRE²*, XV, 727–32.

Tschadert, Paul. "Trienter Konzil." *PRE²*, XVI, 4.

Ullman, C. "Über die dogmatische Entwickelung der griechischen Kirchen im zwölften Jahrhundert." *Theologische Studien und Kritiken* 6 (1833): 647–743.

Undritz. "Die Entwicklung des Schriftprinzigs bei Luther in den Anfangjahren der Reformatie." *Neue Kirchliche Zeitschrift* (1897): 521–42.

Valeton, J. J. P. "Eenige Opmerkingen over Hermeneutiek met het Oog op de Schriften des Ouden Verbonds." *Theologische Studiën* 3 (1887): 509–25.

———. "Het Theologisch Hooger Onderwijs." *Onze Eeuw* (1905).

Van Rhyn, C. H. "Bijdragen ter Waardeering van de Christelijke Dogmengeschiedenis." *Theologische Studiën* 9 (1891): 365ff.

Vos, Geerhardus. "Christian Faith and the Truthfulness of Bible History." *Princeton Theological Review* (July 1906).

Wagenmann, R. "Thomas von Aquino." *PRE²*, XV, 570–94.

Walker, Norman L. "Present Theological Drifts in Scotland." *Presbyterian and Reformed Review* 4 (1893).

Warfield, B. B. "God-Inspired Scripture." *Presbyterian and Reformed Review* 11 (January 1900): 89–130.

———. "The Latest Phase of Historical Rationalism." *Presbyterian Quarterly* 9 (1895): 36–67, 185–210.

———. "The Literary History of Calvin's Institutio." *Presbyterian and Reformed Review* 10 (April 1899): 193–200.

———. "The Oracles of God." *Presbyterian and Reformed Review* 11 (April 1900): 217–60.

———. "The Real Problem of Inspiration." *Presbyterian and Reformed Review* 4 (April 1893): 177–221.

———. "St. Paul's use of the Argument from Experience." *The Expositor* (March 1895).

Wegener, R. "Kurze Darstellung und Kritik der philosophischen Grudlage der Ritschl-Hermann'schen Theologie." *Jahr-*

buch für protestantische Theologie 11/2 (1884): 193–227.

Weiss, J. "Heitmüller, 'Im Namen Jesu.'" *Theologische Rundschau* 7 (May 1904): 186ff.

Weiszäcker, Ferdinand Christian Baur. "Die Theologie des Justin Märtyrer." *Jahrbuch für die Theologie* (1867).

Wiesinger, D. "Die Predigt des Apostels Paulus als Vorbild all Predigt nach I Kor. 2." *Neue Kirchliche Zeitschrift* 9 (1898): 763–87.

Wildeboer, G. "Urim en Thummim in de Priester wet." *Theologische Studiën* 23 (1905): 195–204.

Winer, G. B. "Urim & Thummim." *Biblisches Realwörterbuch*. 2 vols. Leipzig: C. H. Reclam, 1847–48.

———. "Wolken und Feuersäule." *Biblisches Realwörterbuch*. 2 vols. Leipzig: C. H. Reclam, 1847–48.

Zahn, Theodor. "Evangelienharmonie." *PRE³*, V, 653–61.

———. "Glaubensregel." *PRE³*, VI, 682–88.

———. "Kanon des Neue Testament." *PRE³*, IX, 768–96.

———. "Natur und Kunst im Neuen Testament." *Neue Kirchliche Zeitschrift* 5 (April 1899).

Zeller, E. "Über Ursprung und Wesen der Religion." In *Vorträge und Abhandlungen* II. Leipzig: Fues, 1877.

Zenos, A. C. "Symbolo-Fideisme." *Presbyterian and Reformed Review* 11 (1900): 397.

Zeydner, H. "De houding des Evangelie dienaars ten opzichte van het Oude Testament." *Theologische Studiën* 14 (1896): 291ff.

Zöckler, Otto. "Magier, Magie." *PRE³*, XII, 55–70.

———. "Polytheïsmus." *PRE³*, XV, 538–49.

———. "Positivismus." *PRE³*, XV, 569–74.

———. "Socinianismus." *PRE²*, XIV, 376–401.

———. "Spiritismus." *PRE³*, XVIII, 654–66.

———. "Zur Inspirationsfrage." *Beweis des Glaubens* 28 (1892): 150ff.

Select Scripture Index

Ed. note: The Scripture index follows the pattern of the Dutch original, indicating only those passages that receive more or less detailed attention. The key Scripture texts for all four volumes of the *Gereformeerde Dogmatiek* appear at the conclusion of volume 4.

Name Index

Ed. note: This index is based on Bavinck's own name index for all four volumes, found in *Gereformeerde Dogmatiek*, 4:719–30. Minor modifications have been made by the editor.

SUBJECT INDEX

Ed. note: This index is based on Bavinck's own subject index for all four volumes, found in *Gereformeerde
Dogmatiek,* 4:731–57. Minor modifications have been made by the editor.